GERARD CHRISPIN

THE BIBLE PANORAMA

Enjoying the whole Bible with a chapter-by-chapter guide

DayOne

© Day One Publications 2005
First printed 2005

ISBN 1 903087 98-8

9 781903 087985

British Library Cataloguing in Publication Data available

Published by Day One Publications
Ryelands Road, Leominster, HR6 8NZ
☎ 01568 613 740   FAX 01568 611 473
email—sales@dayone.co.uk
web site—www.dayone.co.uk
North American—email—sales@dayonebookstore.com
North American—web site—www.dayonebookstore.com

Designed by Steve Devane

Printed in Canada

GERARD CHRISPIN

THE BIBLE PANORAMA

Enjoying the whole Bible with a
chapter-by-chapter guide

PART ONE

Surveying the scenery of Scripture

Each chapter of each book of the Bible plainly
summarised and explained

PART TWO

Enjoying the unhindered view with confidence

Practical topics about the Bible to help you
trust and read it

Dedication

This is lovingly dedicated to Georgia, Anastasia, Clara and Harriet (and to any brothers, sisters or cousins who may yet join them!). These four lovely little girls have made a late but amazingly profound impact in my life. I may be in glory before they read and understand this book for themselves. My prayer is that God will give them His grace to enable them and their generation to take the Bible and the Saviour far more seriously than I and my generation have.

CONTENTS

THE BIBLE PANORAMA

Enjoying the whole Bible with a chapter-by-chapter guide

PART ONE

THE BIBLE PANORAMA

Enjoying the whole
Bible with a chapter-by-
chapter guide

PART TWO

THE BIBLE PANORAMA

COMMENTS ON PART ONE AND PART TWO

Foreword by Lord Mackay of Clashfern,
former Lord Chancellor of the United Kingdom

The Bible is the fundamental book of the Christian faith. It is a very substantial collection of books written by many different people over a considerable tract of time which ended almost 2,000 years ago. Written originally principally in Hebrew and New Testament Greek, rather than classical Greek, it has been translated into English in a number of versions and into very many of the other languages of the world and has attained an unrivalled readership.

If one wishes to consider the Christian faith, it is important to read and understand at least to a degree what is written in the Bible. For the Christian, the Bible is the revelation by God of His will and purposes for the human race and, indeed, for the world.

I was brought up in a home where the Bible was read as part of an act of family worship morning and evening, and I have heard over the years many expositions of different parts of it. But there is always more to learn from it than one has learnt, even after a long life in which its reading has played an important role.

For those who have no acquaintance with the Bible, it is not easy to read without some guidance. This very substantial volume is written as an attempt to provide comprehensive guidance to anyone who wishes to read the Bible with appreciation and a degree of understanding in particular of its relevance to our lives today.

If one wishes to become familiar with a landscape, it is often useful to seek a hill or other high ground from which to view the layout and to put into relative position the various parts that one encounters at lower levels.

It would be easy for a person who took up the Bible and started to read it to become immersed in detail which might have the effect of mystifying the reader and discouraging further progress. Gerard Chrispin has sought to prevent this obstacle to appreciation of the Bible by proceeding by way of overview so that the broad outlines of the various books that make up the Bible form an introduction to each book, which in no sense replaces the teaching of the Bible itself, but helps the reader to approach it with understanding. The underlining of the principal emphases that one encounters on entering the books, chapters and verses is complementary to this technique.

In addition, in Part Two, readers are helped to deal with the various challenges that they may encounter in reading the Scriptures, as, for example, the suggestion of contradictions or inaccuracies or the like occurring within the Bible, and other suggestions that might be made by those wishing to undermine the authority of the Scriptures as the ground of Christian faith.

Finally, I would mention the flexible reading scheme suggested to enable a person interested in the Scriptures to find his or her way through the Bible as a whole in a manner which would contribute to an overall understanding and appreciation of this precious book which has been the foundation of the faith of Christians down through the generations. Many generations of devout readers of the Scriptures have found in them the words of eternal life and I commend this volume, whose purpose is to lead people of our day to a like precious faith, to all who are prepared to give the Bible an opportunity to speak to them.

Appreciation by Prof. Michael A G Haykin
Principal, Toronto Baptist Seminary, Toronto, Canada, and writer

Ours is a curious day. On one hand, we are awash with Bible translations. Never before have there been so many available to so many English-speaking readers. And yet, ours is a day in which biblical illiteracy is rampant. This illiteracy is not simply limited, as one might expect, to the homes of unbelief, but is increasingly apparent in Evangelical contexts, both families and congregations. Having had the privilege to teach in various Bible college and seminary contexts over the past twenty-three years, I have been regularly shocked to find young men and women, raised in Christian homes, ignorant of some of the basic facts and the storyline of Scripture.

There are probably a variety of reasons for this state of biblical illiteracy in English-speaking Evangelicalism. The theological unravelling of Evangelicalism that is transpiring on both sides of the Atlantic and other parts of the English-speaking world is certainly a key factor. Stiff competition from other forms of media would be another. The transition from modernity to post-modernity, which also entails a shift from the word to the image, is also central. But whatever the reasons, we need tools to help God's people mine the riches of His Word.

Gerard Chrispin has given us such a tool in this panoramic study of Scripture. Actually, it would be more correct to say 'tools', for in this book there are several Bible helps that, if faithfully used, will get the reader into the Scriptures and learning their content, overarching structure, and central message. I was thrilled to see the emphasis on Christ as the heart of the Scriptures. He is the One, in the plan of God, who joins the Testaments together. Then, Gerard Chrispin's plain and succinct overviews of each of the books of the Bible will give the reader a solid grasp of what the Bible is saying in each of its various parts. And the advice regarding how to read God's Word is extremely helpful for not only novices in the Scriptures but also for those who have been on the Way awhile. I sincerely hope this excellent work gets a wide readership.

Appreciation by Richard Cunningham
Director of Universities and Colleges Christian Fellowship (UCCF), UK

The church in the UK has reached a very significant moment in history. For the first time in 250 years, the secularists are within touching distance of being able to destroy what is left of our Judeo-Christian heritage. The student radicals of the 1960s, who ushered us into our post-Christian era, are now in power. And these poachers-turned-gamekeepers now shape the political and cultural landscape with instincts that are actively hostile both to the Christian worldview and to those who love the gospel of our Lord Jesus Christ. But it is not enough simply to lament our predicament. The real issue is how will God's people respond? The church has developed a relatively recent tendency to compromise or to withdraw in the face of such opposition. To compromise the foundational truths, which have become so odious to our society (such as the Bible's teaching on sexuality, the uniqueness of Christ, and the realities of heaven and hell) is clearly not an option. But neither is withdrawal from our lost world which so desperately needs the salt and light of Christian witness.

We must equip the next generation of Christians to know and to love the Scriptures so deeply and thoroughly that they will be able to shun the twin temptations of withdrawal or compromise. Romans 12:1–2 tells us that we will only be able to discern God's will for how we should live in this world if we can both resist worldly conformity and actively renew our minds. Only then will we display the transforming, non-conforming living which Paul describes as acceptable spiritual worship.

This timely and impressive tome by Gerard Chrispin is a valuable tool to get us all into the Bible and all the Bible into us. Gerard once said to me, 'Read the Bible to get blessing, Richard, but read the whole Bible to get balance.' He said this in the context of encouraging me to read the whole Bible through in a year. How grateful I am for such a lead then and, through his book, such a practical help now to continue reading through the whole Bible.

We all need constant help to know what we believe and why we believe it. And the two sections of *The Bible Panorama* combine to achieve these twin goals of reading the Bible with understanding, and developing confidence in the truth of its contents. This is surely the right formula for avoiding compromise and withdrawal. May the Lord use this work to get His people back to daily, disciplined and thoughtful study of Scripture.

Appreciation by David Harding
Pastor of Milnrow Evangelical Church, Milnrow, Rochdale, UK, and writer

There are two views of the Bible that are crucial to master before ever taking out the microscope: first, the overview, and second, the sense of progress in each book (largely related to the chapters). Gerard Chrispin has wonderfully brought us both in this work. This devotional-discipleship commentary on each chapter is therefore complemented by the appendices which give that larger view and sense of unity and cohesion of the Scriptures as a single volume with a single main theme of salvation through faith in Christ.

COMMENTS FROM CHRISTIAN LEADERS FROM AROUND THE WORLD

GENESIS—PROF. ANDY MCINTOSH
Professor of Thermodynamics and Combustion Theory, University of Leeds, England, and writer

In this most instructive overview of Genesis, and of the whole Bible, Gerard Chrispin brings out nuggets of truth which not only warm the heart of the young diligent reader, but also instruct the mind of the careful student. Summarising each chapter with major themes and headings, he leads us to an overall view of the unfolding drama of God's redemptive dealings with mankind. I am delighted to recommend this book as a companion to the new convert who wishes to understand the major themes in each book of the Bible, and also to the older believer seeking to gain a helpful breakdown for leading studies in the Scripture. This book should be on the shelf of every pastor and student of God's Word.

EXODUS—REV. MARTIN HOLDT
Pastor of Constantia Park Baptist Church, Pretoria, South Africa

I was very pleased recently to read Exodus in *The Bible Panorama*. More than once, Jesus asked his hearers whether they understood what was read. Reading the Scriptures is important but understanding what you are reading is better, and that is what we are marvellously helped to do in this clear and most helpful overview of the Bible. I will personally commend this book over and over again. It will definitely awaken a fresh love for the Word of God.

LEVITICUS—REV. ANDY PATERSON
Senior Pastor, Kensington Baptist Church, Bristol, England and Past President of the Fellowship of Independent Evangelical Churches, UK

Leviticus jars with the modern mind. And so many believers quickly give the book a skim-reading with superficial attention. They fail to appreciate its riches or clear pointers to Christ. But here Gerard Chrispin provides an ideal introduction to its big teaching which will stimulate a deeper and more detailed examination. Preachers also will value the clear and memorable subject divisions.

NUMBERS—REV. DR D. ERYL DAVIES
Principal of Evangelical Theological College of Wales, Bryntirion, Wales, and writer

I found *The Bible Panorama* on the book of Numbers an interesting, stimulating and helpful aid to understanding this part of God's inerrant Word. I enjoyed reading it and benefited from it.

DEUTERONOMY—REV. DAVID CHANSKI
Pastor of Providence Reformed Baptist Church, Minneapolis, Minnesota, USA
Gerard Chrispin has produced a summary that will help to familiarise less experienced readers with the Bible's general contents and enable readers to navigate lengthy and more difficult portions of the Scriptures with greater ease. It will also serve to suggest useful outlines and lessons for Bible study leaders. I found the section on the chapters of Deuteronomy particularly helpful.

JOSHUA—REV. DR NIGEL SCOTLAND
Lecturer in Church History, University of Gloucestershire, England, and writer
A valuable, practical and condensed overview of each chapter in the Bible. I found Joshua clear and easy to follow. It will be a useful, quick and handy guide to the contents.

JUDGES—REV. DR TROY L. PRITT
Associate Reformed Presbyterian Minister, Arkansas, USA
I reviewed comments from *The Bible Panorama* on Judges in some detail. This book will be particularly valuable as a companion book to the Bible for the young Christian and for those who are reading through the whole Bible for the first time. It is reminiscent of the Geneva Bible Notes which are still much loved and much used several centuries later.

RUTH—BRYAN STONEHOUSE
Former Executive Director, Scripture Gift Mission, London, England
The Bible Panorama includes amazing detail as you journey through Ruth— extremely helpful and engaging. It will give you an appetite to journey through the Bible itself.

1 & 2 SAMUEL—REV. DR JOHN SCOTT
Minister of Chelmsford Evangelical Presbyterian Church, England, and writer
Gerard Chrispin's panorama of 1 and 2 Samuel serves as a road map through this narrative section of the Old Testament. This will be a helpful aid to lead the new reader into meaningful Bible study.

1 & 2 KINGS—DR PETER J. WILLIAMS
Deputy Head of Divinity, History and Philosophy, University of Aberdeen, Scotland, and Executive Member of Missions Vacances, France and Belgium.
We can be very grateful for Gerard Chrispin's clear, vivid, accurate and memorable overview of 1 and 2 Kings specifically and of the Bible as a whole. What makes this different from other attempts to make the Bible memorable is that the mnemonics carefully follow the text, without getting in its way. The book contains enough detail to be useful, but does not lose sight of the overall message of each passage. I warmly commend this book to readers.

1 & 2 CHRONICLES—REV. SIMON J. ROBINSON
Senior Pastor Walton Evangelical Church, Chesterfield, England, and writer.

1 and 2 Chronicles are two of the more difficult books of the Bible to read. Gerard Chrispin provides us with helpful overviews which get to the heart of the message of each book. This will be an invaluable tool for people who have just come to Christ and for those who have been Christians for some years.

EZRA—BISHOP FRANK RETIEF
Presiding Bishop of the Church of England in South Africa, Cape Town, South Africa, and writer

Ezra and Nehemiah are so important to understanding the biblical flow of God's promise to Israel. At the end of Israel's exile, the people of God return to the promised land. But they are still slaves. They are conscious that another greater exodus awaits them and so they renew their covenant with God. This overview of Ezra is excellent. It divides up the book simply and logically, and enables the reader to follow the sequence of events the author describes. There is much material here for personal reflection or for preachers and teachers. Gerard Chrispin has done Christians everywhere a great service.

NEHEMIAH—MAJOR IAIN A. MACDONALD
Soldiers' and Airmen's Scripture Reading Association Representative for Scotland, Isle of Man and English Border.

It is a privilege to commend such a clear, simple and fruitful overview of the Book of Nehemiah, laced with helpful practical application for our own day.

ESTHER—REV. DR ANDREW YOUNG
Principal, Grace Theological College, Auckland, New Zealand

Having set the scene for each Bible book with a series of brief, insightful 'images', Gerard Chrispin guides readers through the text using carefully worded and colourful section headings. These bring into focus the content and significance of each section and at the same time provide a bridge to their application to life today. *The Bible Panorama* will not only help readers understand the message and relevance of the Bible, but will also provide expositors and Bible teachers with a wealth of suggestive outlines. I particularly enjoyed reading his overview of Esther.

JOB—REV. DOUG MCMASTERS
Senior Pastor of Calvary Bible Church, Grass Valley, California, USA, and USA Board Member of the Dr Martyn Lloyd-Jones Trust

A veritable 'Lonely Planet travel guide' to the book of Job, this helpful resource brings clarity to this oft-misunderstood book. It skilfully unravels the tangled conversation between Job and his 'friends', allowing the forceful concepts of suffering and God's sovereignty to emerge unfettered.

PSALMS—REV. DR ACHILLE BLAIZE
Pastor of Leyton Evangelical Church, London, England

For those who need a terse pithy summary of each Psalm, Gerard Chrispin's basic outline will be an immediate help as well as a springboard to further and more in-depth study.

PROVERBS—REV. CHRIS RICKETTS
Pastor of Sholing Independent Baptist Church, Southampton, England

Like Gerard Chrispin, I have never been able to find a convincing schematic arrangement of the content of Proverbs—often great nuggets of truth seem to stand alone, unrelated to the surrounding verses. In view of this, he gives a useful brief summary of each chapter—a bit like a contents list. Somewhere in each chapter you will find these treasures. He then focuses on one theme, drawing out its salient points, encouraging us to dig deeper and examine the rest.

ECCLESIASTES—RUDY DE VRIES
Executive Director of Cornerstone Bible Institute's Prison Ministry, Canada

This work is an excellent resource as a Bible-reading companion and as a beginning point in the study of Ecclesiastes. Chrispin's brief, but pregnant, summary style, together with his alliterations, will help any student of the Word grasp and remember this book's important message, which is aptly summarised by 'The book of Ecclesiastes pleads for a Saviour.'

SONG OF SOLOMON—PASTEUR TOM FOHNER
Pastor, Église Évangelique, Houlgate, France

The allure of sexual promiscuity has produced a lot of discarded people. The Bible has much to say about real sexual pleasure. This study underscores the power of fidelity and sexual intimacy in marriage. Read it out loud if necessary. God desires this one thing for you and that is to guard your heart.

ISAIAH—REV. PHILIP HACKING
Former vicar of Christ Church, Fulwood, Sheffield, England, and Chairman of Keswick Convention

In a biblically-illiterate age we need stimulation. Good preaching should send people back to the Scriptures. Written summaries provide extra ammunition. To change the metaphor, the meal is more exciting than the menu, but a well-presented menu, such as *The Bible Panorama*, will encourage a good appetite.

JEREMIAH—GEORGE VERWER
Founder of Operation Mobilisation, and writer

The book of Jeremiah is a neglected and misunderstood book. *The Bible Panorama* is going to really open eyes and hearts about the powerful message of this book. Let's all make a commitment to spend more time in God's Word.

LAMENTATIONS—DR JAMES M. RENIHAN
Dean and Associate Professor of Historical Theology, Institute of Reformed Baptist Studies at Westminster Seminary, Escondido, California, USA

Reading some books of the Bible can be difficult—even for experienced Christians. Gerard Chrispin has provided a simple and very helpful outline of one of the more obscure and perhaps difficult prophetic books, Lamentations. After using this aid, the reader will understand the terrible nature of the destruction of Jerusalem, its root cause, and Jeremiah's response. Every Bible reader will benefit from this helpful tool.

EZEKIEL—REV. JOSEPH FELL
Minister of Ebrington Presbyterian Church, Londonderry, Northern Ireland, and Clerk of the Derry and Strabane Presbytery of the Presbyterian Church in Ireland

Gerard Chrispin is a Bible teacher and Prison evangelist who spends his life telling the Bible story in an easy-to-understand way. His summary of Ezekiel is first class, very useful for all readers, and both readable and interesting for the beginner. The Bible is an ancient book written originally in languages unfamiliar to most people today. *The Bible Panorama* is an overview of the Bible to help the reader grasp its essential message. This book is a useful tool to help us unlock the revealed and saving truths contained in the Bible. I am sure that it will bless Christians seeking to understand the whole Bible better. I wish such a book had been available to me as a younger Christian.

DANIEL—REV. NICO VAN DER WALT
Antipas Reformed Baptist Church, Pretoria, South Africa

I suppose every pastor has a forty-inch shelf within arm's length of his desk. On my shelf I have two dozen books I use again and again. Among them are two Dutch books (The book of Snoek, 'Leerboek voor de Heilige Geschiedenis', and G.J. Vrijmoeth's 'Ken uw Bijbel'), which are similar to this book by Gerard Chrispin. I have just read the very useful comments on Daniel in *The Bible Panorama*. For a busy preacher, books like these, which can help you get a quick overview of a portion of Scripture within seconds or minutes, are worth their weight in gold. My shelf is full, so one of the old books will have to be demoted in order to make space for Chrispin.

HOSEA—REV. ALUN MCNAB
Former Pastor of Dudley Baptist Church, England

An ideal help, but without taking away the need for readers to think for themselves. It opens up the chapters of Hosea well, in a particularly helpful compact form. A real encouragement to read the Bible right through with a straightforward guide at hand.

JOEL—ARCHBISHOP GREG VENABLES
Primate of the Southern Cone of the Church of England—Argentina, Ecuador, Peru, Paraguay and Bolivia

Such clear and helpful writing on Joel and on the Bible is an encouragement at a time when many have abandoned the Bible and many others remain tragically ignorant of its message.

AMOS—REV. DR LARRY SAUNDERS
Associate Pastor of The Toronto Free Presbyterian Church, and Administrator of The Whitefield Christian Schools, Toronto, Canada

This overview of Amos is interesting, insightful and succinct. It is a valuable tool for the Bible student.

OBADIAH—JOHN ROBERTS
Director of Day One Christian Ministries, and Director of The Lord's Day Observance Society, Leominster, England

The Minor Prophets are probably the most neglected books of the Bible, yet they have so much to convey to this generation. Obadiah contains one chapter dealing with God's coming judgement upon Edom and looking towards Israel's triumph. Gerard Chrispin, as he also does with the other sixty-five books, makes Obadiah relevant for any person who wishes to delve into and understand the precious truths of Scripture. *The Bible Panorama* will be a valuable asset to both the young Christian and mature believer. A most useful tool to use alongside the Bible.

JONAH—PHIL JOHNSON
Executive Director of Grace to You, California, USA, writer and editor

Here's a wonderfully rich handbook for anyone seeking to understand what Jonah or any other book or chapter of the Bible means. Gerard Chrispin has assembled helpful overviews of every passage of Scripture, with clear outlines, that will give you a better grasp of Scripture, no matter where you are in your spiritual journey.

MICAH—REV. MALCOLM MACLEOD
Minister of Shawbost Free Church, Isle of Lewis, Scotland, and Clerk of the Western Isles Presbytery, Scotland

Gerard Chrispin has provided us with a succinct and encapsulating overview of Micah's message. The 'court of law' scene into which he places his message sets God's controversy with His people in its covenantal context with its triadic theme of reproach, doom and hope. The theme of hope reaches to 'Bethlehem's Christ' and the 'last days'. An illustrative summary that provides an accessible point of entry to Micah's message. I commend it to new readers and serious readers of the Bible alike.

NAHUM—STUART SHEPHERD
Crisis Management Consultant with SIL International and Crisis Consulting International, Waxhaw, North Carolina, USA
I found the summary of the book of Nahum from *The Bible Panorama* very helpful and I look forward eagerly to using *The Bible Panorama* as an aid to Bible study in the future.

HABAKKUK—MICHAEL PATON
Retired pastor and missionary, formerly in France and North Africa
This summary of Habakkuk helps us in understanding the truth that God is always in control, even when evil seems to be winning. The prophet stresses God's care for His people. If they were to lose everything, His love for them would outweigh their loss. Gerard Chrispin brings these points out clearly, and I recommend this study.

ZEPHANIAH—REV. RICO TICE
Curate at All Souls, Langham Place, London, UK, and course producer
The great reality of life lies in the fact that sinful people live their lives before a holy God. This is a truth which we long to deny even in our churches and it is a reason that we must keep hearing the message of Zephaniah. I am delighted to recommend a resource which draws us back so clearly to reality.

HAGGAI—MARK MULLINS
Barrister at Law, executive of the Lawyers' Christian Fellowship, London, England, and editor of *The Christian Lawyer*
Gerard Chrispin clearly brings out the lessons from this little jewel. The challenge for the twenty-first century Christian is easily discerned: are we more interested in building our own houses than helping rebuild the Lord's House? Are we too complacent to care? This little commentary will stir you to sit up and take note when you are next about to pass by this minor prophet!

ZECHARIAH—REV. JOHN LITTLE
Chaplain at Her Majesty's Prison, Frankland, Durham, England
Here we have a clear, concise, helpful and balanced guide to this neglected book. Zechariah's call to repentance and holiness is shown to be a vital message for today. We see Jesus as the Branch, Priest, King and Shepherd. When I found myself differing from the author on minor points, I found that I needed to go back and look at the Scriptures afresh. For that I am thankful.

MALACHI—REV. VAL ENGLISH
Minister of Portstewart Baptist Church, Portstewart, Northern Ireland
This provides an excellent insight into the last Old Testament book. Before the silence of what is to be some four hundred years, the voice of Malachi rings out

loud and clear. In it we capture something of the blessings of the past and move across the bridge to the future. Savour the message!

MATTHEW—DR STEVE TAYLOR
Reader in Electrical Engineering and Electronics, University of Liverpool, England, and Chairman of United Beach Missions, UK and Europe

This is an excellent and very helpful summary of Matthew's Gospel, which rightly divides the Word of Truth and presents helpful comments to explain the main themes of each chapter. The biblical text is broken down into headed sections—which I do find genuinely useful—with a brief expository comment on each. This makes *The Bible Panorama* ideal for preachers and for those who want an overview of a particular passage.

MARK—BISHOP WALLACE BENN
Bishop of Lewes, England

Gerard Chrispin has produced a very useful tool. It is in essence a concise summary of all the action in Mark's Gospel that also offers occasional little nuggets of helpful insight. In particular, its beauty is in its brevity. In just thirty minutes you have engaged with all of the events of Mark's Gospel. Reading it is undoubtedly half an hour well spent.

LUKE—DR CARL VENN
General medical practitioner, Christian leader and preacher, Brynmawr, Wales

I found the comments on Luke's Gospel extremely easy to read and I appreciated the alliterative signposts. I'm sure it will be helpful for preachers and students of the Bible alike.

JOHN—REV. LARRY MAIB
Senior Pastor of First Baptist Church of Canoga Park, Los Angeles, USA

The essence of good teaching is to take something complex and make it simple; to take something lengthy and state it precisely. This was the beauty of Jesus' teaching, and, in this work by Gerard Chrispin, the length and depth of the Gospel of John are crystallised in short headings and sentences for immediate understanding. I highly recommend this study guide for those who want the highest level of comprehension with a small amount of personal investment.

ACTS—RAYMOND J. JONES
Chairman, New Tribes Mission of Canada

In a clear, easily readable style, with helpful headings, Gerard Chrispin has reflected the soul-winning heart and eternal love of our Lord Jesus Christ shown in the lives and acts of His apostles.

ROMANS—DR JOHN BLANCHARD
International evangelist, Bible teacher, writer and broadcaster

If we think of the Bible as a range of mountains, Romans is the Himalayan range. In this excellent summary of its powerful message, Gerard Chrispin proves to be a sure-footed guide, leading us up the rugged pathways of truth to the places from which we get such glorious views of God's plan for his people.

1 & 2 CORINTHIANS—REV. CONRAD MBEWE
Pastor of Kabwata Baptist Church, Lusaka, Zambia, and associate editor of
Reformation Zambia

The breadth of subjects handled in 1 and 2 Corinthians is simply breathtaking! Where would the church of Christ be today were it not for these epistles? Like Atlas, they carry a world on their shoulders. Coming to grips with the contents of these two epistles has been made easier by Gerard Chrispin's excellent use of mnemonics in *The Bible Panorama*. New converts especially will love it!

GALATIANS—REV. DR JACK SIN
Pastor of Maranatha Bible Presbyterian Church, Singapore, and Lecturer in Church History,
Far Eastern Bible College, Singapore

If one is looking for an efficient and readable summary of the Bible, here it is. The author has some insightful and enlightening comments and an accurate basic exposition of the books of the Bible that should enthuse and saturate the hearts and minds of redeemed men. A quick and meaningful survey of the books of the Bible in simple and practical terms for all preachers and lay people today. I found the comments on Galatians very helpful.

EPHESIANS—REV. GEOFF THOMAS
Pastor of Alfred Place Baptist Church, Aberystwyth, Wales, and writer

I read the summary of Ephesians and appreciated it very much. If you are someone new to the Bible, and 'all thumbs' or just intimidated as to how to begin to access a mini-library of sixty-six books—because that is what God has given us in the Scriptures—this panoramic vista by Gerard Chrispin will lead you with certainty through the whole Bible from Genesis to Revelation, and lay a sound foundation for a life of growing understanding of the wonderful Word of God.

PHILIPPIANS—REV. PHILIP CAMPBELL
Minister, Coleraine Congregational Church, Northern Ireland

If the books of the Bible are like pictures in an art gallery, then Gerard Chrispin's *The Bible Panorama* allows the visitor to pause, stand in front of each masterpiece, and grasp the essence of what the 'Divine Artist' is saying. In his survey of Philippians, the purpose and key themes of the letter are accurately identified, and each chapter summary leaves the reader with a clear understanding of its teaching, and the preacher with some useful alliterated headings to 'borrow'! It is the kind of book I would like to have had as a young believer, and will use as a preacher!

COLOSSIANS—REV. DR JOHN S. ROSS
Minister of Greyfriars Free Church of Scotland, Inverness, Scotland
Colossians in *The Bible Panorama* enables readers to see the big picture of a book whose themes are hugely relevant today: the supremacy of Jesus Christ and the life-affirming liberty He brings, contrasted with the confusion of sentimental mysticism and depressing legalism. Gerard Chrispin's approach is refreshing, stimulating and sound.

1 & 2 THESSALONIANS—REV. DR STUART OLYOTT
Pastoral Director of the Evangelical Movement of Wales, and writer
I am enthusiastic about this book. If you want to read through the whole Bible, or to look into just a part of it, as here in 1 and 2 Thessalonians, it is always useful to have the big picture first. This is what Gerard Chrispin gives us, succinctly, attractively, accurately, and in a way that is easy to remember. Many will now study the Scriptures with new zest.

1 & 2 TIMOTHY—TONY RUSTON
Director of the Martyn Lloyd-Jones Recording Trust and European Director of Grace to You
What an excellent little summary this is, offering a secure and sound introduction to Paul's letters to Timothy. With a light touch, which misses none of the important teaching in these epistles, Gerard Chrispin has produced a commentary which gives the reader a good grasp of its subject. I'm sure all who read it will be encouraged to go on to further and deeper Bible study which, in this day and age, can only be a good thing.

TITUS—STEVE WRIGHT
Barrister at Law, Director of Young Life, Northern Ireland and United Beach Missions, Ireland
The Bible Panorama combines the need for an instantly helpful, thorough but concise guide to each chapter of the Bible with a spiritual and devotional summary of all its verses, clustered under relevant and striking headings. Greatly helpful for anyone reading through the Bible for the first time, it also provides a valuable resource for those who, in teaching others, look for a ready reminder of each chapter's contents. I found the summary on Titus spiritually refreshing and practical. *The Bible Panorama* frame displays the biblical picture well, rather than competing with it for one's attention.

PHILEMON—ROBIN GRIFFITHS
Missionary in translation team in the New Tribes Mission Pwo Karen tribe, Thailand
This overview of Philemon gives a refreshing and challenging summary of this oft-neglected book. It brings home the grace and graciousness of the gospel and

the need for us as believers to see both, especially in our relationships with one another. The summary challenges us believers to accept one another as Christ accepts us, to have that godly love and concern for one another.

HEBREWS—TREVOR KNIGHT
Bible teacher, writer and former Director of Young Life, UK

For anyone wanting an overview of any Bible book, helpful alliterated headings (as the author gives here in Hebrews in abundance) are like mountain peaks, which help us to get a better perspective of the whole landscape.

JAMES—REV. DAVID JACKMAN
President of Proclamation Trust, London, England, Bible teacher and writer

In this comprehensive, but focused, outline you will find: *Clarity* about the theme tunes of the letter of James, which bind it all together; *Certainty* that faith and works are not opposed; *Challenge* that our own faith proves itself to be alive by love and good works.

1 & 2 PETER—REV. WES MCNAB
Pastor of Slade Evangelical Church, London, England

In days of moral laxity and doctrinal confusion and decay, an understanding of Peter's letters has never seemed more vital. This concise overview is an extremely helpful tool for unravelling Peter's message as we read it for ourselves. The vital themes of God's grace and our living hope through a knowledge of the truth are clearly revealed. They lead us on in plain terms how to live effective godly and transformed lives in the midst of assaults from outside and at times within the church. I wholeheartedly recommend these notes to get all Christians enthused about 1 & 2 Peter.

1, 2 & 3 JOHN—REV. IAN DENSHAM
Minister of Alexandra Road Congregational Church, Hemel Hempstead, England

These outlines will be helpful to encourage those who are making their first attempts to study the Bible. Anything that can be used to encourage people to 'give attention to reading' that they might learn more of the truth of God's grace is to be commended. May the Lord bless the publication of these outlines as His Word is spread.

JUDE—REV. BOB AKROYD
Chaplain at Her Majesty's Prison Edinburgh, Scotland

We live in an age when many people do not read the Bible or know much about the message of Jesus. The church needs resources which explain, expound and apply the Word of God for this generation. I commend both this summary of the short but important letter of Jude and *The Bible Panorama* as it reaches out with the Word of God.

REVELATION—DR JOHN MACARTHUR
Pastor of Grace Community Church, Los Angeles, USA, writer and broadcaster
No student of Scripture should ever expect to truly understand the depth of a biblical book until he has understood the breadth of it. This overview sets in place the sweeping essential drama of the apocalypse and is, thus, the essential starting place for the believer who seeks to understand the rich treasure buried in the details.

COMMENTS ON PART TWO OF THE BIBLE PANORAMA

PROF. EDGAR ANDREWS
Scientist, writer and co-editor of Evangelical Times, Darlington, England
Writing in a relaxed and readable style, Gerard Chrispin provides a 'beginner's guide' to the Bible that deserves to be read by more than beginners! Of particular importance in Part Two is the chapter on 'The central message of the Bible' which demonstrates convincingly that the whole Bible points us to the glorious Person and saving work of the Lord Jesus Christ.

REV. JONATHAN STEPHEN
Director of Affinity, UK, Past President of the Fellowship of Independent Evangelical Churches, UK, Senior pastor of Carey Baptist Church, Reading, England, and writer.
Single-author Bible handbooks inevitably convey the personality and background of their writers. No wonder Gerard Chrispin's *The Bible Panorama* is such a fascinating read! Part Two, in particular, is a box of delights—a veritable cornucopia of reasons why the Bible can be trusted. Here are simple and convincing apologetics for ordinary people.

I am neither academic nor intellectual. Sometimes I wish it were otherwise. I do struggle on occasions. But I am encouraged by recalling a 'brilliant' man who lectured me in law but who left me wondering what I had been listening to for the previous ninety minutes. I would have preferred to watch paint dry! By contrast another law lecturer—just a 'plain man'—taught me far more about the subject at a crucial time when I needed to pass to qualify! When the brilliant 'egg head' had left me cold and confused, the man who helped me was ordinary enough to understand how another very ordinary person thought. That is why he communicated so well.

My only qualification—apart from knowing the Lord Jesus Christ as my Saviour and being objectively and passionately convinced that the Bible is God's infallible, inspired and complete Word—is that I am just an 'ordinary' Christian. (Perhaps that is why my own ministry has developed in prison rather than in a seminary.) I hope my ordinariness helps me communicate with others who sometimes struggle with understanding some difficult things in the Bible.

How glad I am that, as a wayward and backsliding law student, God introduced me to Leeds Branch of Young Life ('YL') and soon after to United Beach Missions ('UBM'). I saw in those young adults a commitment to Christ and to spreading His gospel which I had never encountered before. More important still, I learned to respect, love, believe, read through and consider the Bible. I was also urged to *apply* it practically and personally and, although that has changed my life, I confess that many years later I am still struggling to do that as I ought to. What a gracious God of mercy and help we have!

If *The Bible Panorama* helps anyone to come to a settled confidence in and wonder at God's Word, and a desire to follow its teachings by God's grace, I shall be far happier than I can describe here.

This book started because YL and UBM taught me not only the urgency of having a daily quiet time (which I had heard recommended before elsewhere), but also *how* to read the Bible and pray. I started making the simplest of notes as I read through the Bible each year. I built up my own extremely fallible partial commentary—fallible because of my almost illegible writing as well as my own deficiency in understanding God's Word! But I persevered and God helped and blessed me until, about three years ago, I started putting my quiet time thoughts on tape which were then transcribed. *The Bible Panorama* was coming to birth.

The main emphasis of the book in Part One is to seek to teach (I hope clearly yet concisely) what each chapter of the Bible is about. This is not a verse-by-verse commentary, but all the verses are covered under linked headings. The vast majority of those headings are alliterated. One or two people, whom I respect greatly, have questioned the wisdom of that, but many more critics have told me they think it is beneficial and helpful. All I can say is that this is my style and I find it comes naturally to me. I have tried not to force the alliteration, though inevitably there have been a few times (remarkably few in fact) when I have had to stop and think again, or rework the headings. If you do not like 'what it says on the tin', I hope you will, nevertheless, enjoy the contents!

The emphasis of the book in Part Two is to encourage the reader to have full confidence in the Bible as God's inerrant Word, and to provide some alternative schemes to help to read it through at a pace appropriate to the reader. I hope I have included subjects that the 'ordinary Christian' encounters and has to address. I would have liked to have added a brief Christology of each book but I felt it was outside the immediate scope of *The Bible Panorama* and there is a chapter in Part Two which provides a summary. Also, as each chapter of the Bible is opened, I hope that the pre-eminence of the Lord Jesus Christ, who is the key to and the message of the Bible, will be readily apparent.

This is the right place to thank so many people who have encouraged, criticised (usually constructively!) and helped me. Anthea Fryatt has cheerfully and meticulously helped to bring some order out of the chaos of the many tapes I sent to her, after first Amy Wilcox and then Becky Boxhall started me on that road. David Harding—whom I should call 'Faithful are the wounds of a friend' Harding—has always put his faithfulness to God's Word first and thereby proved yet again to be a great and dear pal to me. Jim Holmes of Day One has been tireless and efficient in so many ways of encouragement and assistance. Steve Devane has applied his usual flair to the question of presentation, and I am grateful. He has that special touch, whether designing an evangelistic booklet or a large tome. I have had four red-pen-wielding school teachers, and one wife of a school teacher who is just as thorough, who trawled and crawled their way through each chapter of my book (and therefore also through each chapter of the Bible) to seek to minimise my inevitable mistakes. Thank you, therefore, to Sarah Cooper, Sue Hawley, Judy Kitching, Tim Moore and Bill Scully—all of whom also learned much about Bible reading through the same fellowships that taught me before them. Special thanks, too, to Alison Graham and Suzanne Mitchell for their work in proof-reading and editing.

I am truly humbled by the kindness of an army of men of God to whom I look up and respect greatly and who have written 'sound bites' either about each chapter-by-chapter commentary of individual books of the Bible in Part One, or about my attempt to increase the ordinary person's trust in the Bible in the much shorter Part Two. I feel like a minnow supported by a shoal of surrounding whales. I know how busy some of these world-prominent Christian leaders are, and to think they have taken time to recommend this book—and at times to shape, amend and even edit it—leaves me, for once, speechless. I am so grateful. I hope that the endorsement of such sane and committed Bible believers will encourage Christians to engage with the aims of this book—that is, to read the Bible through and to keep reading it through.

Especially do I thank four of the busiest of them, who each read the *whole* book through before giving their written comments. Lord Mackay is not only a giant in terms of legal brilliance, spotless track record of integrity, and earnest endeavour both in the 'direct' kingdom of God and his salt-like influence on our septic society, but he is a gracious man who willingly gave his precious time to support this effort to help ordinary people read the whole Bible. Prof. Michael

Haykin, a prolific author and writer who is responsible for the oversight of one of the West's leading Bible-believing seminaries (in Toronto), could easily have said, 'Sorry, Gerard—I am too busy.' I am very grateful to him that he did not say that. Richard Cunningham is overloaded in his onerous privilege of seeking to encourage students at university and in the colleges also to be students of Christ and His word, a far more important task. Dave Harding amazes me. He is always so busy yet always makes time to help and encourage others. Many thanks to all four of them for their comments on the whole book.

Phillippa, my wife, best friend, most objective critic, and handmaid of the Lord, could also have said, with complete justification, that she was too busy to help. As well as tirelessly arranging our ongoing prison itinerary and coming with me all over the UK to support the preaching of the gospel in prisons and the teaching of the Bible in many other places, she has spent hours and hours of what we used to call 'free time', checking my work and checking the checkers' work too! I once got into trouble, when replying to a public question, 'Do you believe in the "second blessing"?' I replied that I had married her! I then vigorously refuted the criticism that I was being flippant. I have rarely said anything more serious. Thank you, Phillippa—my 'second blessing'.

The Bible Panorama is intended to help people to *read through* the whole Bible at a pace they select, by all means taking time to dwell at a particularly attractive 'picnic' spot en route, from time to time. The desire to help folks to read through is why there is the emphasis on the Bible reading schemes, for much of which I am grateful to the now glorified Robert Murray McCheyne, to IFES and to YL/UBM. Their schemes feature in the Appendices to this book.

I want Christians to *enjoy* reading through the Bible. The length taken to do so is for each person to decide individually: that is why I have suggested, in the Appendices, some alternative reading-through schemes with in-built flexibility. But there is no reason why a long time could not be taken on one book and a quicker pace adopted for another one.

However, no scheme, no human teacher, and no help in *how* to read the Bible can ever replace or rival the place of God's guidance through His Holy Spirit to make God's spiritual truth, encapsulated in the Bible, real to the reader. Hence my plea to you—and my reminder to myself—is to read the Bible with a repentant and cleansed heart and mind. Remember that God's Spirit who will lead us into all truth is the *Holy* Spirit. A desire for holiness is the best aid we can offer to understanding and being blessed by reading and studying the Bible. God's light of biblical illumination will be most evident in our minds where the curtains of our sin are drawn as widely open as they possibly can be. Submission to Christ is more important by far than intellectual ability, academic achievement or even evangelical tradition.

Gerard A. Chrispin
Farnham, Surrey

THE BIBLE
PANORAMA

Surveying the scenery of Scripture
Each chapter of each book of the Bible plainly
summarised and explained

OLD TESTAMENT

GENESIS

OVERVIEW

PEOPLE AND PRELIMINARIES

✳Genesis (fifty chapters) is the first of five books of the law (the 'Pentateuch') written by Moses. He wrote it at some time between 1491 and 1405 BC during the children of Israel's desert wanderings and before entering the promised land. An estimate of the period covered by this book is 2,315 years.

PLAN AND PURPOSE

ⓘ Written for Jews, Christians and all mankind, Genesis ('beginnings' or 'origins') contains timeless principles. God's existence is eternal in the past, present and future. His character is unchanging. Recorded are the origins of the creation of the universe, the earth, animal and plant life, human life, the Sabbath, work, marriage, sin, death, suffering, conflict, sacrifice, judgement, salvation by faith, prayer, different languages, farming, and people groups. All principles of modern life are here.

PROFILE AND PROGRESSION

Creation (1:1–2:25); fact and results of sin and redemption foretold (3:1–24); children born and early civilisation (4:1–7:24); from judgement by the worldwide flood, to God's confusion of languages at Babel (8:1–11:9); forefathers of God's earthly people from Abraham to Joseph (11:10–50:26).

PRINCIPLES AND PARTICULARS

☛ God's character and power are manifested in His creation of the universe and the world, and everything in them, from nothing. We see here the origin of sin and man's spreading sinfulness. God's judgement and man's consequent need of redemption are revealed. God's concern for people is manifest, as is His provision for their salvation by faith in Him. Prophecies and types of Jesus Christ, as Saviour, are introduced. We learn how God can take and use people who trust and obey Him. Genesis is the seedbed of all God's revelation in the Bible and through the Lord Jesus Christ.

GENESIS

CHAPTER ONE

V 1: START Genesis and the Bible begin with God who created everything. **V 2: SPIRIT** God's Holy Spirit is there in the beginning, bringing order from chaos and light from darkness. **V 3–31: SEQUENCE** The order of God's six-day creation is as follows: Day one—light; Day two—sky; Day three—land and sea; Day four—sun, moon and stars; Day five—sea-life and birds; Day six—animals and finally man as a special creation.

CHAPTER TWO

V 1–3: SABBATH After the completion of the first six days of creation God makes the Sabbath, one day in seven, as a holy day of rest and blessing. **V 4–6: SUPPLY** A mist supplies the earth with water. **V 7: SPECIAL** God gives the details of the special creation of man, whom He creates from dust and breathes into his nostrils the breath of life. **V 8–9: SIGNIFICANT** It is significant that in the middle of the garden are the tree of life and the tree of the knowledge of good and evil. **V 10–14: SITUATION** The geographical situation of the garden is given. **V 15–17: STIPULATION** God tells Adam to work to keep the garden, to eat what he likes, provided it is not from the tree of the knowledge of good and evil because, if he does so, he will die. **V 18–25: SPOUSE** Adam gives names to all the living creatures. Then God gives Adam a spouse as a helper from one of his ribs.

CHAPTER THREE

V 1–3: DOUBT Doubt is sown by the serpent about what God has said, first of all in Eve. The serpent is later identified as the Devil. **V 4–5: DENIAL** This leads to Satan's denying the truth of God's word and maligning God's character and motives. **V 6: DISOBEDIENCE** Eve and then Adam disobey when they see all the wrong reasons why they want to eat the fruit. **V 7–13a: DISASTER** Disaster follows; shame, guilt, hiding from God, and discord between human beings come in the chain of disobedience. **V 13b–15: DECEIVER** The serpent is also condemned and his final judgement foretold when he will be defeated by the woman's offspring, later revealed as the Lord Jesus Christ. **V 16–19: DESERVED** Both the woman and the man will suffer as a result; she will suffer in childbirth and be under the rule of her husband, and he will find work onerous. The ground is cursed. Thorns spring up. Man's physical body will return to dust. **V 20–21: DEATH** After the woman is given a name, Eve, God reveals that an animal must die in order to cover the nakedness and shame of Adam and Eve by animal skin. This is an early picture of covering for our sin through a God-given sacrifice and shed blood. **V 22–24: DRIVEN** Finally, Adam and Eve are driven out from the Garden of Eden and permanently excluded. Sin excludes us from God's best blessings.

CHAPTER FOUR

V 1–2: SONS The first two sons of Adam and Eve are Cain (who becomes a worker on the land) and Abel (who becomes a shepherd). **V 3–7: SACRIFICE** As an offering, Abel sacrifices his best sheep, which pleases God, but Cain's bloodless offering does not please Him. **V 8–12: SIN** Sin begins to spread through anger, jealousy, and murder and leads Cain to lie to God. God sees Cain's sin in murdering Abel, curses him, and makes him homeless. **V 13–15: SIGN** God puts a sign on Cain, by way of a mark, to protect him and prevent him being killed. **V 16–24: SETTLING** Cain and his descendants settle in the land of Nod on the east of Eden. **V 25–26a: SETH** Adam and Eve's third son is called Seth who later has a son called Enosh. He begins a godly line leading to Abraham, David and eventually Christ. **V 26b: START** This is the beginning of people calling on the name of the LORD.

CHAPTER FIVE

V 1–2: LIKENESS God's creation of mankind in His spiritual likeness is stated. **V 3–5: LIFE** Adam's new and long life (though shorter than some who follow him soon) produces none of the degenerative factors evident in interbreeding that have caused human life to shorten since creation. He has other sons and daughters besides Cain, Abel and Seth, and they are the 'founding members' of the human race. **V 6–32: LIST** Adam's early descendants are detailed.

This brings us to Noah, about whom we read in the next few chapters.

CHAPTER SIX

V 1–4: GREAT GROWTH The population grows, and godly men err in marrying ungodly women. **V 5–7: GOD'S GRIEF** God's grief at man's sinfulness causes Him to decide to destroy the whole earth (later revealed to be by flood). **V 8–22: GOD'S GRACE** God's grace is on Noah and his family. Noah walks with God. Provision is made for him and his family to escape the coming flood by constructing an ark, which will also preserve the animal kingdom. Noah will be sustained in the ark, and benefit from God's covenant. The same grace enables him to obey God.

CHAPTER SEVEN

V 1: COME God tells Noah to enter the ark because his right standing and obedience (through his believing what God had said) have made him acceptable to God. **V 2–9: COMMAND** God then commands Noah to take the designated animals, clean and unclean, into the ark and Noah obeys. Later he will sacrifice the clean animals to God. **V 10–12: COMMENCEMENT** After entering the ark with his family and the animals, Noah waits for seven days until the flood commences. The rain lasts for forty days and forty nights. **V 13–16: CLOSED** God shuts the door of the ark behind Noah, his family and the animals. **V 17–24: CONSUMED** All life on the whole earth outside the ark is consumed, whereas those who trusted and obeyed God, by going into the ark, are saved.

CHAPTER EIGHT

V 1–14: PATIENCE God remembers Noah, his family, and animals in the ark, and stops the rain and the flood. As the waters recede, Noah exercises diligence in seeing when it is safe to go out, yet patience in waiting for God. **V 15–19: PROMPTNESS** As soon as God tells Noah and his party to disembark with the animals, he does so. **V 20–21a: PLEASED** God is pleased with Noah's sacrifice of clean animals. **V 21b–22: PROMISE** This leads to His promise never to curse the earth again, never to destroy all living creatures again and to continue to give earth its harvests.

CHAPTER NINE

V 1–7: CLEAR COMMANDS God gives Noah two instructions—to be fruitful and multiply, and not to murder because man is made in God's image. God decrees that any such murderer should have his blood shed by man. **V 8–17: COLOURFUL COVENANT** God vows never again to cut off all flesh by a flood and never to destroy the earth by flood. The sign of this is to be the rainbow in the sky. **V 18–27: CARELESS COMPROMISE** Noah gets drunk and lies naked in his tent and is seen by Ham. Because of Ham's disrespect for his father, and irresponsibility in broadcasting this to his brothers, God is displeased with him, and curses Canaan, who is Ham's son. This curse is fulfilled in the later conquest by Joshua. Shem and Japheth are blessed for their right action in discreetly covering Noah. **V 28–29: COURSE COMPLETED** Noah lives for another three hundred and fifty years after the flood—nine hundred and fifty in total.

CHAPTER TEN

V 1: FACT That the global flood is factual is shown by the historical records of the genealogies which follow. **V 2–31:**

FAMILIES Right from the start of creation and early history, God decrees that civilisation will be best served by family units. **V 32: FOUNDATION** The foundation of the population of today's entire human race dates back to this chapter.

CHAPTER ELEVEN

V 1–2: COMMUNICATION Initially the human race communicates in one language. **V 3–4: CONSPIRACY** Mankind conspires to get to heaven by its own efforts, via the Tower of Babel, for fear of being scattered around the earth. **V 5–9: CONFUSION** God comes down to confuse their rebellious efforts and scatters them around the earth with different languages. **V 10–26: CONTINUATION** The continuation of the human race is traced to Abram, through the descendants of Shem. **V 27–32: CHALDEA** Terah's genealogy continues and includes Abram, and his wife Sarai, moving to Ur of the Chaldeans.

CHAPTER TWELVE

V 1–9: ABRAM'S BLESSING God tells Abram to leave his country, that He will bless him by making him into a great nation, and that all peoples on earth will be blessed through him. Abram obeys God and gets as far as Negev in the south. **V 10–20: ABRAM'S BLAME** Even Abram hides behind a half-truth in order to avoid trouble, instead of trusting God. Sarai is, in fact, his half-sister as well as his wife. Abram pretends that she is only his sister. God overrules and protects Abram, who is sent out of the country by Pharaoh.

CHAPTER THIRTEEN

V 1–4: DEVOTION Note that material prosperity has not stopped Abram in his prayer-life as he journeys with Lot. **V 5–7: DISPUTE** Lot also has great possessions and livestock, and there is not enough room for them both. Their servants quarrel. **V 8–9: DEFERENCE** Abram generously offers Lot his choice of the land before them. **V 10–18a: DECISIONS** Despite the wickedness of Sodom, Lot chooses that lush valley area because it appeals to his desire for material prosperity, but God promises Abram great blessing in the less attractive hill country, and that his descendants will be impossible to number. **V 18b: DEVOTION** Abram builds an altar at Hebron showing his praise and worship.

CHAPTER FOURTEEN

V 1–12: CAPTIVITY The king of Sodom, in coalition with other kings, is defeated by another coalition. Lot is taken captive. **V 13–14: CRISIS** An escapee brings news of Lot's captivity to Abram who, in turn, takes his trained men to rescue Lot. **V 15–17: CONQUEST** Abram defeats Lot's captors and rescues him, his people and his possessions. **V 18–20: CHRIST** Melchizedek is a type of the Lord Jesus Christ, and arguably an Old Testament appearance of Jesus Christ, known as a 'theophany'. Abram gives him a tithe of everything he has. **V 21–24: CONSECRATION** Abram refuses to accept any gift from the king of Sodom for his rescue act.

CHAPTER FIFTEEN

V 1: COMMUNICATION God reassures Abram in a vision. **V 2–3: CONCERN** Abram is concerned that he and Sarai are childless. **V 4–5: COMFORT** God comforts Abram by showing him the stars and telling him that, just as he cannot count the stars because they are so numerous, neither will he be able to count his descendants, for exactly the same reason. **V 6: COUNTED** Because Abram believes God's promise, he is counted as righteous by and before God. The whole gospel principle of justification by faith is confirmed here. **V 7–21: CONFIRMATION** God confirms His promise by sacrifice and a covenant made with Abram.

CHAPTER SIXTEEN

V 1–4: UNBELIEF Despite God's promise, Sarai and Abram proceed as if the promise will not be fulfilled. By agreement between them, Abram has a child through Hagar, Sarai's maid. **V 5: UNSATISFACTORY** This leads to friction between Sarai and Hagar. **V 6: UNFAIR** With Abram's permission, Sarai deals harshly with Hagar, who flees from her. **V 7–14: UNCONDITIONAL** God shows His unconditional love for Hagar. He takes the initiative and sends the Angel of the LORD to find Hagar, speak to her and comfort her. He confirms that her son, to be called Ishmael, will survive and also father a great nation. **V 15–16: UNFOLDING** Watch the whole middle-eastern situation unfold, with the birth of Ishmael, the father of the Arab nations. Abram is eighty-six at this time.

CHAPTER SEVENTEEN

V 1–8: PROMISE OF COVENANT Abram, now ninety-nine years old, is promised a covenant and a worldwide family for generations to come. He will become the father of many nations. God marks this by changing his name from Abram to Abraham. The land of Canaan is promised to Abraham as his possession. **V 9–14: PRACTICE OF CIRCUMCISION** The covenant will be confirmed by the circumcision of all male persons in the Israelite community, and will include Israelite baby boys when they are eight days old. Circumcision will become the sign of the covenant. **V 15–16: PROPHECY OF CHILDBEARING** Abraham will change the name of Sarai to Sarah to mark God's telling him that she will not only be a mother, but a mother of nations and the ancestor of many kings. **V 17–22: PRECISENESS OF CONFIRMATION** Abraham, unable to believe this, thinks it must be through Ishmael that God's promises will come true, so he asks that Ishmael might live. God confirms Ishmael will be a great nation, but Sarah's son to be, Isaac, will be the beneficiary of His covenant with Abraham. **V 23–27: PRIORITY OF COMMAND** Abraham trusts God and obeys His command, despite his fears, by circumcising all the males, including Ishmael and himself.

CHAPTER EIGHTEEN

V 1–8: HOSPITALITY AND HURRY Abraham gives hospitality to three men, who mysteriously are a manifestation of the LORD. Abraham and Sarah hurry to provide them with food. **V 9–15: LAUGHING AND LYING** Sarah laughs when she overhears Abraham being told that they will have a son in their old age. When asked 'Is anything too hard for the LORD?' she lies about the fact that she had laughed. **V 16–21: JUSTICE AND JUDGEMENT** God shares with Abraham the fact that the great wickedness of Sodom and Gomorrah means the men are going to investigate first-hand with a view to judging Sodom and Gomorrah. God expects Abraham and his descendants to do what is right and just. **V 22–33: PLEADING FOR PEOPLE** After the three men leave, in a series of petitions Abraham pleads with God personally not to destroy Sodom. God's first response is that He will not destroy Sodom if fifty righteous men are found there. Abraham continues interceding and asks if there are fewer than fifty men—going in stages from forty-five to forty to thirty to twenty—will God spare Sodom? His intercession ceases when God confirms that He will not destroy Sodom if only ten righteous men can be found there.

CHAPTER NINETEEN

V 1–3: ANGELS' VISIT God sends two angels to visit wicked Sodom and to see Lot and his family. Lot offers them hospitality. **V 4–11: AWFUL VILENESS** The sexually perverted Sodomites demand to have sexual relations with the visiting men (not recognising them as angels). Lot rightly resists, but is no less vile in suggesting they abuse his two daughters instead. As the Sodomites attack Lot at the door of his house, the two angel guests strike the attackers with blindness. **V 12–14: ANGRY VENGEANCE** The guests then tell Lot that God will destroy Sodom, but when he seeks to tell his sons-in-law, they think he is joking. **V 15–17: ANGUISHED VACILLATION** While Lot lingers, he and his family are taken by the hand, through the LORD's mercy, and delivered from Sodom. They are told to escape up to the mountains to avoid destruction. **V 18–26: ABSENT VISION** Even then, Lot objects to escaping to the mountains, having no vision of God's holiness, separation from sin, or the need for a complete escape. He chooses the inferior option of going to Zoar, while God destroys Sodom and Gomorrah and the rest of the plain with brimstone and fire. His wife also hankers after Sodom, looks back, and is turned into a pillar of salt. **V 27–29: ABRAHAM'S VICTORY** Lot's escape from Sodom and Gomorrah

is attributed to the victory Abraham had in his early morning prayer before God. **V 30–38: APPALLING VICE** From Zoar, Lot and his two daughters go to live in a cave in the mountains. His daughters conspire to get him drunk in order to have sexual relationships with him. They succeed, and the children resulting from this immorality and incest become the fathers of the Moabite and the Ammonite nations. In the future, they will be a constant thorn in the flesh of the children of Israel because of their wicked practices. Sin breeds sin.

CHAPTER TWENTY

V 1–2: COMPROMISE Through fear of death, Abraham compromises again by telling the half-truth that Sarah is his sister. In fact she is his half-sister but, far more important, she is his wife. Abimelech sends to take Sarah, not knowing this. **V 3–7: CONSCIENCE** God warns Abimelech that He will slay him because he is about to take Abraham's wife. Abimelech protests that his conscience is clear and his hands are clean. God tells him that provided he restores Sarah and asks Abraham to pray for him, he will be spared. **V 8–16: CONFRONTATION** Abimelech confronts Abraham with this situation and Abraham explains why he told the half-truth. Abimelech gives gifts to Abraham and restores Sarah to her husband. **V 17–18: CONCLUSION** Abraham prays to God for Abimelech. God heals Abimelech, his wife, and his female servants who before had been made barren because Abimelech had taken Sarah, Abraham's wife.

CHAPTER TWENTY-ONE

V 1–8: SON As God has promised, Sarah

bears Isaac to Abraham, who is one hundred years old. Abraham circumcises Isaac at eight days old as God has commanded him. On the day that Isaac is weaned, Abraham gives a feast. **V 9: SCOFFING** Ishmael, Hagar's son, scoffs at either Isaac, or Sarah, or both. **V 10–13: SOVEREIGNTY** Sarah reacts by wishing to cast out Hagar and Ishmael. Abraham is not pleased with this, but God tells him to go ahead because it is part of His plan to make Ishmael a nation, though not the nation that He has promised Abraham through Isaac. **V 14–16: SADNESS** Hagar and Ishmael are sent into the Wilderness of Beersheba and the water supply in the skin bottle is exhausted. Hagar weeps because she thinks Ishmael is going to die. **V 17–21: SUSTAINED** But God hears Ishmael's voice, speaks to Hagar confirming that Ishmael will father a great nation, opens her eyes, and provides a well of water which sustains and saves them both. Ishmael dwells in the Wilderness of Paran, and Hagar finds a wife for him from Egypt. **V 22–32: SWEAR** Abimelech gets Abraham to swear to deal well with him in the future. This is tested in a dispute over a well of water, resulting in them making a covenant together. **V 33–34: SUPPLICATION** Abraham plants a tamarisk tree to mark the covenant. He stays in the land of the Philistines a long time. He begins to call on the name of 'the LORD, the Everlasting God'.

CHAPTER TWENTY-TWO

V 1–7a: PROVING God is to prove Abraham's faithfulness and obedience by telling him to take Isaac and sacrifice him. Abraham takes steps to obey Him. **V 7b–8: POINTER** Abraham's reply to Isaac, about where the lamb for the burnt offering will come from, is a pointer to Jesus Christ, the 'Lamb of God', who

later will be given for sinners. **V 9–12: PICTURE** Abraham's building an altar, putting wood on it, placing his son on that wood, and willingness to slay his beloved son pictures what will happen at Calvary to the Son of God Himself. The big difference is that the execution will not be stayed for Jesus. **V 13–14: PROVISION** God provides the ram, whose head is surrounded by thorns of a thicket. The ram will be the sacrifice. One day, Jesus will become a thorn-crowned sacrifice. **V 15–19: PROMISE** God renews His promise of blessing to Abraham, which is based on his obedience to God's word, which springs from faith in God's word. **V 20–23: PEOPLE** Abraham's family begins to grow.

CHAPTER TWENTY-THREE

V 1–2: BEREAVEMENT Sarah dies at the age of 127 years, and is mourned by Abraham. **V 3–18: BUSINESS** Abraham's grief does not prevent him proceeding with the business he has to do, that of negotiating for a burial place for Sarah. This he does with great dignity, honour, and success. **V 19–20: BURIAL** Sarah is buried by Abraham in the cave of the field of Machpelah near Mamre, at Hebron in Canaan.

CHAPTER TWENTY-FOUR

V 1–9: WISE SERVANT Abraham sends his faithful servant to find a suitable wife from his own people for his son, Isaac. **V 10–60: WIFE SEARCH** Most of the chapter deals with the way that his servant honourably and diligently performs this difficult task, blending prayer, obedience, initiative, singleness of purpose, patience and gratitude with a real trust in God and awareness of His presence. It is successful! Bethuel's highly eligible daughter,

Rebekah, is ready to go with Abraham's servant to marry Isaac. **V 61–67: WEDDING SERVICE** Isaac and Rebekah meet and get married.

CHAPTER TWENTY-FIVE

V 1–26: FAMILY Important family matters reveal Abraham's taking another wife, Keturah, and traces the descendants of Abraham through her. Abraham dies at 175 years of age, having left everything to Isaac, but having given gifts to the sons of his concubines during his life. Isaac and Ishmael bury Abraham alongside Sarah. Ishmael dies at 137 years old, and his descendants are noted. Isaac's wife, Rebekah, bears twins, Jacob and Esau, when Isaac is sixty years old. God reveals they shall be the fathers of two nations and that the older, Esau, will serve the younger, Jacob. **V 27–34: FOOLED** Esau, the outdoor son, is manipulated by Jacob, the schemer. He is fooled into exchanging his birthright for food when he is hungry. He thus sells his birthright, as the first-born, to Jacob.

CHAPTER TWENTY-SIX

V 1–6: FAMINE Despite famine in the land, Isaac obeys God's command to stay in Gerar after God has confirmed that He will fulfil His oath to Abraham for the blessing of Isaac. **V 7–11: FAILURE** Isaac fails, in much the same way as Abraham failed before, in claiming that Rebekah, his wife, was his sister. Abimelech (probably a dynastic title rather than the same man whom Abraham had encountered) realises from Isaac's familiar conduct with Rebekah that he is married to her. Abimelech accordingly forbids anyone to molest either Isaac or Rebekah. **V 12–22: FRUITFULNESS** God blesses Isaac so much materially that Abimelech asks him to move away. His fruitfulness continues as he causes a well to be dug. Previously, he has reopened wells used in Abraham's time, and this has caused conflict with surrounding herdsmen. **V 23–25: FAITH** After God appears to Isaac to confirm His promise to Abraham, Isaac builds an altar, calls on God, pitches his tent, and digs a well. **V 26–31: FEAR** Abimelech reappears. He has noted God's presence with Isaac and the prosperity that has followed. Fearful of what Isaac may do, as he grows stronger, he asks for a peace treaty. Isaac makes a feast for them and they swear oaths to each other. **V 32–33: FOUND** Isaac's servants dig another well and find water, so essential to life and growth. **V 34–35: FOREIGNER** Esau takes a foreign wife, much to the grief of Isaac and Rebekah.

CHAPTER TWENTY-SEVEN

V 1–4: BLINDNESS Aged Isaac is blind and getting nearer to death. He calls Esau, his older son, to ask him to prepare the savoury meal expected, prior to giving his son his blessing. **V 5–10: BIAS** Rebekah hears Isaac speaking to Esau. Jacob is her favourite son, whom she loves more than Esau. She schemes to send Jacob in to his blind father with the required savoury meal she has prepared, before Esau arrives back, so that Jacob can receive his father's blessing. **V 11–17: BLATANT** Rebekah not only devises this evil scheme and prepares food that Isaac will like, but she also gives Jacob goatskins and Esau's clothes so that he will smell and feel like his hairy outdoor brother. **V 18–29: BETRAYAL** Jacob (which means 'deceiver') deceives his father, even though his father is suspicious at one stage. **V 30–40: BLESSING** Esau then comes in with the food for his father, as requested. Isaac trembles as he realises that God has overruled in fulfilling His promise to bless Jacob. Esau learns that he has been cheated, and asks whether his father has only one blessing to give. Isaac gives Esau a lesser blessing than the one he has mistakenly just given to Jacob. Esau is grieved. **V 41–46: BITTERNESS** This leads to bitterness from Esau who plans to kill Jacob when their father is dead. Rebekah tells Jacob to flee from that land and to go to Laban, her brother, in Haran. To justify Jacob's moving away, she tells Isaac that she does not want Jacob to take a wife from the local Hittite women who have settled nearby.

CHAPTER TWENTY-EIGHT

V 1–9: SUITABLE SPOUSE Isaac charges his son, Jacob, to find a wife from his own people and sends him to Laban. Perhaps to curry favour with Isaac, and maybe to seek to try to get things reversed, Esau takes a wife from Abraham's family in addition to the wives he already has. **V 10–17: SIGNIFICANT SLEEP** En route to Laban, Jacob sleeps. In a dream, he is given a vision of angels ascending and descending a ladder. God's covenant with Abraham is renewed and Jacob, on awaking, knows that God has been present. **V 18–22: SPIRITUAL START** This leads to Jacob rising early and marking the place, Bethel, with an anointed pillar. He makes a vow of commitment to God. He also undertakes to give a tenth of all that he has to God in the future.

CHAPTER TWENTY-NINE

V 1–14: GOD'S GUIDANCE God guides Jacob by circumstances in his journey. He meets Rachel who is a relative of his father. Rachel informs her father, Laban. Jacob stays with Laban, initially for a

month. **V 15–27: DECEIVER DECEIVED** Jacob arranges with Laban to marry Rachel, but Laban substitutes Leah by trickery. Jacob, having worked for Rachel and having been given Leah, undertakes to work for Rachel, too. In total, he will work fourteen years as payment for being able to marry Rachel. **V 28–30: LOVE'S LABOURS** Jacob fulfils the second seven-year period because of his love for Rachel, whom he loves more than Leah. **V 31–35: FAMOUS FAMILY** These verses mark the entry into history of the children of Jacob, later known as the children of Israel.

CHAPTER THIRTY

V 1–2: SISTERS Being the husband of two sisters is not the recipe for a happy family life. Leah has borne sons (Reuben, Simeon, Levi and Judah). Rachel, Jacob's favourite wife, has no children and is jealous of her sister, Leah. She demands children from Jacob, who protests that this is outside his control. **V 3–13: SERVANTS** To make her a surrogate mother, Rachel prevails upon Jacob to have sexual relationships with Bilhah, her maidservant. Bilhah conceives twice and gives birth to Dan and Naphtali. Leah has borne no children since Judah. Copying Rachel, she sends her maidservant, Zilpah, in to Jacob. Two sons are born, Gad and Asher. **V 14–24: SCHEMING** Leah then schemes to resume sexual relationships with Jacob, by giving some of her son's mandrakes to Rachel in exchange for that opportunity. Three times more, Leah conceives and bears two sons, Issachar and Zebulun, and one daughter, Dinah. Finally, Rachel herself conceives and bears her first son, Joseph. **V 25–43: SUCCESS** Jacob has been successful in serving Laban, who recognises God's hand in all this. Jacob expresses his desire to leave Laban and return home. Laban offers to pay him the wages he stipulates, but, instead of taking wages from Laban, Jacob asks for all the sheep and goats that are speckled or spotted, and all the lambs that are brown. Laban concurs. God provides Jacob with the strongest animals as he sees an increase in his flocks. Perhaps this occurs by God's overruling and adopting Jacob's fanciful plan to encourage his marked animals to mate, or perhaps God has already devised this plan for Jacob to use and has revealed it to him to encourage him. Either way, Jacob is successful, and becomes exceedingly prosperous and influential.

CHAPTER THIRTY-ONE

V 1–21: FLEEING Jacob is concerned about Laban's changed attitude towards him, and about Laban's sons, who eye Jacob's growing wealth suspiciously. After conferring with his wives, Leah and Rachel, he flees from Laban toward Gilead. **V 22–23: FINDING** Laban pursues and finds Jacob. **V 24: FAITHFULNESS** God is faithful to both Laban and Jacob. He warns Laban, in a dream, not to oppose Jacob. **V 25–30: FAMILY** Laban and his relatives encompass Jacob and ask for an explanation. They also claim that their family gods have been stolen. **V 31–35: FURTIVENESS** Jacob responds and says that he knows of no stolen family gods. In fact, Rachel has stolen them and is furtively hiding them inside the saddle of her camel. When her tent is searched, she sits on them, excusing herself for not rising because she says that she is having a period. They considerately leave her alone. **V 36–54: FINALE** A frank discussion ensues. A covenant is made and witnessed by both a stone pillar and a heap of stones, called 'Mizpah'. Jacob

takes an oath, offers a sacrifice, and invites the relatives to a meal. **V 55: FAREWELL** After dining and spending the night together, early the next morning Laban kisses his grandchildren and daughters farewell, blesses them, and returns home.

CHAPTER THIRTY-TWO

V 1–8: PERTURBED Jacob meets God's angels, but is very frightened and distressed at the thought of again meeting Esau, the brother whom he tricked. Accordingly, he divides the people who are with him into two groups in order that one group might escape if Esau attacks the other one. **V 9–12: PRAYER** Jacob asks God for his protection and reminds God of his promise to him. **V 13–23: PLANNING** Jacob plans gifts to pacify Esau, puts his servants in the first party, and then divides into two parties in the hope that by the time Esau and Jacob meet, Esau will be pacified by his gifts. **V 24–32: PENIEL** While the parties go west towards Esau, Jacob is left alone and wrestles all night with a Man, who elsewhere is revealed as the Angel of God. Many hold this to be another theophany, or Old Testament appearance of Christ. Jacob prevails in this prayer and overcomes, calling the place Peniel. The mark of prevailing in his struggle is that he will limp for the rest of his life because the socket of his hip had been touched near the tendon while he was wrestling. Prayer still changes the way that people walk with God.

CHAPTER THIRTY-THREE

V 1–3: SUSPICIOUS DEFENSIVENESS As Jacob sees Esau, with his 400 men, he meets them first with his maidservants and their children, then with Leah and her children. When, finally, he and Rachel meet Esau, he prostrates himself seven times before his brother. **V 4–5a: SURPRISE DRAMA** However, Esau enthusiastically greets Jacob and asks him about his children. This response is something that Jacob is not expecting! **V 5b–11: SUBMISSIVE DEMEANOUR** After the introductions, Jacob insists on giving his gift to Esau, and tells him how gracious God has been to him. Esau himself does not need to receive the gift because he, too, has been blessed materially, but he accepts the gift nevertheless. **V 12–20: STILL DEVIOUS!** After Esau offers to accompany Jacob, Jacob makes a false excuse why he cannot do this. He arranges to meet Esau again in Seir, but goes in another direction, first Soccoth and then to Shechem. He buys a plot of ground, sets up an altar, and calls it El Elohe Israel, which means 'God, the God of Israel'.

CHAPTER THIRTY-FOUR

V 1–2: DEFILEMENT Dinah, the daughter of Jacob and Leah, is sexually violated by Shechem, the son of Hamor, the Hivite ruler of that area. **V 3–7: DISGRACE** Shechem now feels tenderly towards Dinah and asks his father to arrange the marriage. Jacob keeps silent, but his sons are filled with grief and anger because of the disgrace done to Israel by Shechem. **V 8–12: DIRECTNESS** After a shameful beginning, Hamor and Shechem are direct in their approach to Jacob to ask for Dinah's hand in marriage and to propose future intermarriage. They express their desire to pay the price for the bride, which is required in that culture at that time. **V 13–24: DECEITFULNESS** Dinah's brothers deceitfully pretend to accede to their request and lay down a condition, which is readily accepted by Hamor and

Shechem. That condition is that all of their men must be circumcised if there is to be a marriage between the Israelites and the Hamorites. The brothers know that circumcision will leave a short period of time until the Hamorites are healed, when they will be too sore to do combat. **V 25–29: DISASTER** Dinah's brothers, Simeon and Levi, then attack the city and kill all the incapacitated males including Hamor and Shechem. They plunder all the wealth and livestock, and carry off all the women and children. **V 30–31: DESPERATION** Jacob remonstrates with Simeon and Levi about the trouble they have caused. He fears it will attract the opposition of the Canaanites and the Perizzites, as well as those living around them, and that Israel will be destroyed. Their reply is that Dinah should not have been treated as a prostitute.

CHAPTER THIRTY-FIVE

V 1–15: BETHEL God tells Jacob to go to Bethel and build an altar. Jacob does so, and insists that idolatry must cease. Bethel means much to Jacob. It is where God first communed with him directly and where the covenant promises to Abraham were confirmed. Deborah, Rebekah's nurse, dies here and is buried. God renews the covenant with Jacob, calling him 'Israel', who marks that renewal with a stone pillar. **V 16–20: BENJAMIN** Rachel, Jacob's favourite wife, bears her second and final son, called Benjamin, who later becomes Jacob's favourite son when Joseph is believed to have died. Rachel dies in childbirth and is buried. **V 21–22a: BILHAH** Israel moves on beyond the tower of Eder. He hears that Reuben, his son, lay with his concubine, Bilhah. **V 22b–26: BIRTH** The birth of the Israelite nation comes from Jacob's twelve sons by Leah (Reuben, Simeon,

Levi, Judah, Issachar and Zebulun), Rachel (Joseph and Benjamin), Bilhah (Dan and Naphtali), and Zilpah (Gad and Asher). (They are not listed in the order of birth.) **V 27–29: BURIAL** Jacob comes home for the death of Isaac, who is 180 years old. Accompanied by Esau, Jacob buries his father.

CHAPTER THIRTY-SIX

V 1–8: ESAU A brief summary of the genealogy and life of Esau is given. **V 9–30: EDOMITES** Details of the Edomites, the descendants of Esau, are given. **V 31–43: EDOM** Before any king is appointed in Israel, kings reign in Edom. Their details are given, as are the chiefs descended from Esau by name according to their clans and regions.

CHAPTER THIRTY-SEVEN

V 1–10: JOSEPH AND JACOB Joseph, the first son of Rachel, is Jacob's favourite son. The significance of Joseph's dreams is not lost on his father, who realises that they indicate that the day will come when all the Israelites will be submissive before Joseph. **V 11: JOSEPH AND JEALOUSY** While his father remembers the dreams, they simply make his brothers very jealous of him. **V 12–24: JOSEPH AND JEOPARDY** When Joseph goes to see his brothers, they plot to take his life. At Reuben's intervention, they throw him into a dried out cistern (an underground pit where any available water would normally be stored). Reuben intends to rescue him later and take him back to his father. Joseph is stripped of his coat of many colours given to him as his father's favourite son. **V 25–30: JOSEPH AND JUDAH** Judah is instrumental in averting the murder of Joseph, who is sold on to travelling Ishmaelites who are Midianite merchants. They pay twenty shekels of silver for him. Reuben is absent at the time, and returns too late to rescue Joseph. **V 31–36: JOSEPH AND JACOB** Jacob's sons return home and present their father with Joseph's coat, which they have dipped in the blood of a slaughtered animal. He assumes his son has been killed by a wild beast, and weeps in mourning for him. The deceiver of Isaac and Esau is now deceived by his own sons. Meanwhile, Joseph is sold in Egypt to one of Pharaoh's officers, Potiphar, who is the captain of the guard.

CHAPTER THIRTY-EIGHT

V 1–6: WIFE In an interlude in the Joseph saga, the focus is on Judah. He fathers three sons, Er, Onan and Shelah, and obtains a wife for Er, called Tamar. **V 7: WICKEDNESS** Er is so wicked in God's sight that God puts him to death. **V 8–10: WILFULNESS** Judah's second son, Onan, in accordance with the law at that time, is expected to marry his widowed sister-in-law to ensure that the family line will continue. By using a crude form of contraception, he wickedly refuses to prolong the line of his brother and he, too, is put to death by God. **V 11–14: WIDOWHOOD** Judah tells Tamar to live as a widow until his son Shelah grows up, when she will be able to prolong the family line through his marriage to her. However, Shelah is not given to her when he becomes an adult. Tamar disguises herself at the entrance to Enaim on the road to Timnah, where Judah is about to go. **V 15–19: WAYWARDNESS** Judah fails to recognise veiled Tamar. Thinking she is a prostitute, he goes in to her for immoral purposes. He is temporarily unable to pay for her immoral services, and so gives her a pledge of his seal, his cord, and his staff, against his promise to send her a young goat in payment. Having conceived, she then leaves and resumes the dress of a widow. **V 20–23: WONDERING** Judah is able neither to pay the 'prostitute' the promised young goat, nor to get his pledge back, because his messenger cannot find this woman. He has no option but to abandon his pledge to the unknown woman whom he cannot find. **V 24–26: WAIT** After waiting three months, Judah learns of Tamar's prostitution and resulting pregnancy. Not knowing that he is the father of the illegitimate offspring to be born, Judah orders Tamar to be killed. He then sees and recognises his pledge. He confesses that she is more righteous than he is since he has not kept his word in giving her his son, Shelah, in marriage to her. He never has sexual relations with her again. **V 27–30: WISH** Tamar's wish to have children is realised. She bears twins, Perez and Zerah (who appears first but is born second). God's grace is seen in that, despite the immoral background to the pregnancy, Perez becomes part of the Messianic line, which will go through Boaz and Ruth to David, the king.

CHAPTER THIRTY-NINE

V 1–2: GOD'S PRESENCE Returning to Joseph, we find him working for Potiphar, an officer of Pharaoh and captain of the guard. God is with Joseph and gives him success there. **V 3–6: GOD'S PROSPERING** God prospers Joseph so much that he is given total responsibility under Potiphar. Also, he is handsome. **V 7–18: GOD'S PRINCIPLES** Joseph honours God in rejecting immoral advances from his master's wife. Potiphar's wife, grieved by Joseph's godly refusal of her overtures, frames Joseph and falsely accuses him of seeking to assault her. **V 19–20: GOD'S PRISONER** Accordingly, Potiphar has

God's young servant thrown into prison, completely unjustly. **V 21–23: GOD'S PRESENCE** This chapter finishes where it started: God is with Joseph in the prison and he is so trusted by the keeper of the prison that he runs the prison for him. In such adverse circumstances, the LORD prospers him.

CHAPTER FORTY

V 1–5: FURY Pharaoh is angry with two of his officers, the chief butler and chief baker, and has them thrown into the same prison as Joseph. There they have dreams that they cannot understand. **V 6–7: FRIENDLINESS** Joseph shows an interest in their sadness, despite his own unwarranted problems. **V 8: FAITH** When they tell him about their unsolved dreams, Joseph says that God can help him to interpret them. **V 9–19: FAITHFULNESS** In interpreting their dreams, Joseph gives the good news of impending release to the chief butler and the bad news of impending death to the chief baker. He tells the truth faithfully, rather than seeking popularity. He also takes the opportunity to ask the chief butler on his release to mention the injustice of his own case to Pharoah. **V 20–22: FULFILMENT** On Pharaoh's birthday, the butler is restored and the baker is hanged, just as Joseph had said. **V 23: FORGETFULNESS** Despite the chief butler's earlier promise to the contrary, on his restoration to office he forgets Joseph.

CHAPTER FORTY-ONE

V 1–8: RESTLESS Pharaoh has two dreams, which none of his magicians or wise men can interpret. **V 9–14: REMEMBERING** This jogs the memory of the chief butler, who tells Pharaoh about Joseph's ability to understand and interpret dreams. Pharaoh calls for Joseph. Joseph shaves and changes before he goes in to Pharaoh. **V 15–16: RELIANCE** Right from the start, Joseph makes it quite clear to Pharaoh that he can do nothing without God's help, and that only God can give him an answer. **V 17–32: REVEALED** Pharaoh tells Joseph of the dreams of the seven thin cows eating the seven fat cows and the seven thin heads of grain eating the seven fat heads of grain. Joseph reveals to Pharaoh the unified message of the two dreams that seven years of plenty will be followed by seven years of famine. **V 32–36: RESPONSE** Joseph goes further and urges Pharaoh to respond by managing the situation and by putting officers over the land to collect and store one fifth of the produce of the land during the seven plentiful years. That will cover the seven years of famine. **V 37–49: RECRUIT!** Pharaoh takes Joseph's advice. Joseph is the best man for the task. Pharoah emulates Potiphar and the keeper of the prison earlier in investing his total authority and responsibility in Joseph. Thirty-year-old Joseph then begins to put his plan into action! **V 50–52: RECOGNITION** Joseph marries and has two sons. Even in the names of his sons, he recognises God's goodness to him throughout all afflictions. (Manasseh means 'making forgetful' and Ephraim means 'fruitfulness'.) **V 53–57: RESULT** Not only is Egypt saved through God's using Joseph in this way, but many surrounding countries come to Joseph to buy grain because of the severity of the famine.

CHAPTER FORTY-TWO

V 1–2: FOOD In famine conditions, Jacob tells his sons to go to Egypt to find grain. **V 3–7: FULFILMENT** Joseph's ten older brothers come to Egypt and appear before him. They do not recognise him and bow to him, unknowingly fulfilling his earlier dreams. **V 8–9a: FLASHBACK** Joseph, however, recognises them, recalls his earlier dreams and accuses them of being spies in Egypt. **V 9b–24: FORCEFUL** Joseph's accusation of espionage forces his brothers to leave Simeon as a surety against their bringing Benjamin to him in Egypt, to prove their honesty. In justifying themselves before Joseph, they bring Joseph up to date with the family news. They are conscience-stricken as they recall and discuss their wicked treatment of Joseph. They do not know he understands them. **V 25–28: FEAR** The brothers, apart from Simeon, set off for home with bags full of grain. They do not know that Joseph has restored the purchase price of the grain in their sacks. When one of them finds the money, they are all filled with fear because they do not know why or how it got there. **V 29–38: FATHER** The brothers report the whole situation to Jacob and tell him that the 'Egyptian' insists on seeing Benjamin. Despite Reuben's pressure, Jacob refuses to let Benjamin go to Egypt. He fears his youngest son will suffer a similar fate to that which he believes has claimed the life of Joseph.

CHAPTER FORTY-THREE

V 1–5: DELAY As famine hits the family, Judah tells Jacob that they must go back to Egypt. They have already delayed. **V 6–10: DEBATE** The brothers, spearheaded by Judah, continue to debate with Jacob. They need to go back to Egypt to get the grain, even though it will mean taking Benjamin with them. **V 11–14: DECISION** With great reluctance, Jacob agrees, makes sure that they will take gifts and double the money for Joseph, and commits the matter to

God for the release of Simeon and the safe return of Benjamin. He has no alternative as he sees it. **V 15–23: DOUBTS** The brothers go back to Egypt. Joseph sees Benjamin and arranges to dine with them all the next day. They approach Joseph's steward to explain that they do not know how the money got in their sacks and are worried about it. The steward reassures them, telling them that God has given them the money. He brings Simeon to them. **V 24–34: DRAMA** Joseph, still unrecognised by his submissive brothers, appears and receives their present. He asks them about Jacob, and sees his brother, Benjamin. He greets him, but has to go out to weep. Coming back, he allocates a separate dining area for the brothers and gives Benjamin five times more food than the others. The relieved brothers drink and are merry with him.

CHAPTER FORTY-FOUR

V 1–15: JOSEPH'S PLAN Joseph tells his steward to put food in the sacks of his brothers but to replace the money that they had paid in the mouth of the sack, and also to put his own silver cup in Benjamin's sack. The steward is sent to overtake the brothers, accuse them of stealing, and bring them back to Joseph. The steward does all this and, to the surprise of the men, the money and the cup are duly found. **V 16–17: JUDAH'S PANIC** Judah panics and does not know what to say. Joseph tells the brothers that all of them, except Benjamin, will be able to go in peace. Joseph will keep Benjamin as a slave. This is exactly what they did not want to hear. **V 18–34: JUDAH'S PLEA** Judah then pleads with Joseph, arguing that if Benjamin is left behind in Egypt, Jacob will die of grief. Judah offers to remain as a slave in Benjamin's place. His

part in masterminding Joseph's kidnap now comes full circle.

CHAPTER FORTY-FIVE

V 1–2: LOUD WEEPING After Judah's plea Joseph, unable to contain his emotions any longer, sends everyone from him. He makes himself known to his brothers and weeps loudly. **V 3–15: LOVING WELCOME** He then bids his brothers come near to him and tells them the whole of his story, in which he recognises God's sovereignty at work. He promises them that if they come to Egypt, he will provide and look after them all. They are to go and tell Jacob all this good news and bring him back with them. He greets, kisses, and weeps over all the brothers, especially his own full brother, Benjamin. **V 16–28: LOADED WAGONS** With Pharaoh's enthusiastic support, Joseph sends his brothers back to get Jacob. He offers them the best of the land. He is generous to each of the brothers but he gives extra gifts to Benjamin. He sends them to the land of Canaan with carts and donkeys loaded with gifts and provisions for the return journey. He assures them that, although they mistreated him so cruelly, God had His purpose in it all to preserve life in the coming years of famine. Jacob is stunned into silence and disbelief by what his sons tell him. But when they pass on to him the words of Joseph and show him so many provisions and generous gifts, his spirit revives. Overwhelmed that Joseph is alive, he promises to go and see him before he dies.

CHAPTER FORTY-SIX

V 1–4: COMMUNION Israel (Jacob) journeys to Beersheba and offers sacrifices. God communes with him and reassures him that he must not fear. He will make him into a great nation, accompany him, and bring him back to the land of Canaan again. Joseph will be with him when he dies. **V 5–30: CHILDREN** All the children of Israel, including his sons, Dinah his daughter, and their families, respond with Jacob to God's assurance. They travel with their livestock to Egypt. They are named in the passage. Thus there are seventy children of Israel in Egypt at this time: sixty-six come with Jacob, and the other four are Joseph, his wife, and their two sons. Judah goes to bring Joseph to Goshen, where Joseph at last meets his father. He falls on him and weeps for a long time. Israel is now ready to die since he has seen Joseph, remembering God's promise that Joseph will be present when he dies. **V 31–34: CARE** Joseph assures his brothers that they will be cared for in Egypt but tells them to emphasise to Pharaoh that their occupation is to look after livestock. Such an occupation is an abomination to the Egyptians and therefore they will be left to live separately and to get on with their job.

CHAPTER FORTY-SEVEN

V 1–10: PRESENTATION Five of Joseph's brothers are presented to Pharaoh and confirm that they wish to look after flocks. Pharaoh grants them to dwell in the land of Goshen. Then Jacob is introduced to Pharaoh, and he blesses Pharaoh. Jacob, by now, is 130 years old. **V 11–12: PROVISION** God provides the best of the land in Rameses, and food for all the children of Israel. **V 13–25: PRUDENCE** Joseph is in charge of the famine management in Egypt. In payment for the plenty that has been stored, Joseph receives money payment, then livestock, then lands and the service of the people, for Pharaoh. He does not buy the land of

the priests because Pharaoh has already granted them rations. Joseph then gives all the people seed to sow and authorises them to keep four-fifths of the resultant crops, passing the fifth to Pharaoh. The people recognise that Joseph has saved their lives and are happy with this arrangement. **V 26: PAYMENT** Thus the payment of one fifth of the crop to Pharaoh is made a law in Egypt as payment to be made for this life-saving policy. By it, Pharaoh and Egypt are enriched. **V 27–28: PROSPERITY** Meanwhile Israel grows and multiplies greatly in Goshen in the seventeen years which follow Jacob's coming down to Egypt. He is now 147 years old. **V 29–31: PROMISE** Jacob is about to die and he makes Joseph promise that he will be carried to Israel to be buried. Joseph swears that he will do this when his father dies.

CHAPTER FORTY-EIGHT

V 1–7: GOD'S PROMISE Jacob is sick and Joseph takes his sons, Manasseh and Ephraim, to see him. Jacob reminds Joseph of God's great promise to him, of making him fruitful and multiplying him, and giving the land to his people as an everlasting possession. Jacob confirms that Joseph's sons, Ephraim and Manasseh, will take their place in that inheritance and the promise will include them. **V 8–11: GOD'S PERMITTING** Joseph identifies his sons to his father, who kisses and embraces them. He tells Joseph that he never thought that he would see Joseph again, but now God has permitted him to see not only Joseph, but his two sons. **V 12–20: GOD'S PLAN** Despite Jacob's failing sight, he knowingly blesses Joseph's sons, clearly putting his right hand on Ephraim and his left hand on

Manasseh, thus signifying that the biggest blessing and inheritance will be with Ephraim, the younger son. Joseph remonstrates with him, telling him that it should be the other way round, but Jacob confirms that God will make the younger brother more powerful and influential than the older one, though He will bless them both. Joseph learns that God's plan does not always go according to human hopes, thoughts and expectations. **V 21–22: GOD'S PRESENCE** Israel confirms to Joseph that, although he is dying, God will continue with him and bring him back into the land of Israel. He also tells him that he has given him an extra inheritance, which he took from the Amorites. Joseph is still his favourite son!

CHAPTER FORTY-NINE

V 1–27: FAMILY BRIEFED Jacob is now very near to death, and calls all his sons together to tell them what will happen to them and their offspring in the future. The third in line of Israel's great forefathers, Abraham, Isaac and Jacob (often referred to as Israel because of his position as father of the nation) is about to pass away, but God's people will remain on earth through his children. **V 28: FUTURE BLESSING** Thus Israel speaks to his wider family and children, and blesses them 'according to his own blessing'. Their future blessing will depend on their relationship to God, and that is still true for the Christian today. **V 29–32: FATHER'S BURIAL** Israel tells his sons that he is to be buried in the field of Ephron, the Hittite, in the cave which Abraham bought and where Abraham, Isaac, Sarah, Rebekah and Leah are buried. **V 33: FINAL BREATH** Jacob's task is finished and so is his life. He breathes his last and is 'gathered to his people', a phrase indicating that Old Testament saints are saved through faith in God and by the future work of Christ.

CHAPTER FIFTY

V 1–11: MOURNING Joseph kisses his recently dead father and has him embalmed by the Egyptian physicians for forty days. There is great mourning in the land, not only by Joseph and his brothers, but by the Egyptians, as the Canaanites noted. **V 12–14: MACHPELAH** Jacob's sons bury him in the cave in the field of Machpelah, as he requested. **V 15–18: MISGIVINGS** Now Joseph's brothers have great misgivings about how they will be treated, after their father's death, by the brother they wronged so badly. They send messengers to him to ask for his forgiveness for the way that they treated him. Joseph weeps. They bow down before him and declare themselves to be his servants. The earlier dream is again fulfilled. **V 19–21: MEANT** Joseph reveals his belief in God's sovereign plan. They 'meant evil' against Joseph, but 'God meant it for good', in order to save many people alive. They must not fear because he will provide for them. He comforts them and speaks kindly to them. **V 22–26: MASTER PLAN** The chapter telescopes to the death of Joseph. Before dying at the age of 110 years, Joseph has seen successive generations from his own children, and speaks to his brothers who survive him. He tells them that God will bring them back to their own land just as He swore to Abraham, Isaac and Jacob. They take an oath to carry Joseph's bones to Israel, which will be fulfilled at the exodus of God's people years later.

EXODUS

OVERVIEW

PEOPLE AND PRELIMINARIES

✳ Exodus (forty chapters) is the second of five books of the law (the 'Pentateuch') written by Moses. He wrote it between 1445 and 1405 BC during the desert wanderings of the children of Israel and before they entered the promised land. An estimate of the period covered is 216 years.

PLAN AND PURPOSE

ⓘ Exodus demonstrates God's saving power. His unchanging moral principles and His righteous standards are exemplified by His moral law detailed in the Ten Commandments. This book teaches how to approach God in worship, This is illustrated in the purpose for and the making of the tabernacle and its furnishings. The importance of redemption through blood sacrifice is underlined. Exodus reveals God's requirements for His people and for their spiritual leader, Moses. It catalogues how He continually supports and helps those who are faithful to Him.

PROFILE AND PROGRESSION

🐚 After Joseph's death Israelites' cruel bondage in Egypt, plagues, 🐚 redemption by shedding Passover blood, exodus from Egypt under Moses, miraculous passage through the Red Sea (1:1–15:22); from the Red Sea, journey in wilderness up to desert before Mount Sinai (15:23–18:27); God's revelation to Israel, at Sinai, includes His changeless and universal moral law (the Ten Commandments) and His national laws for Israel, requirements for worship, including the plans and construction of tabernacle, God's assured continued presence (19:1–40:38).

PRINCIPLES AND PARTICULARS

☞ Teaching on redemption is given through the Passover, the Red Sea deliverance, the blood sacrifices, priesthood and the requirements for worship in the tabernacle. Moses exemplifies how a godly leader should walk with God when in conflict with God's enemies, led by Pharaoh. He also leads uncompromisingly when the Israelites fail to follow God wholly. The importance of a basic moral law and reasonable and righteous national laws is demonstrated. The journey through life is pictured here. The Christian's spiritual life is often foreshadowed by Israel's communal life in this book.

EXODUS

CHAPTER ONE

V 1–6: RECAP The book of Exodus begins by listing the children of Israel who came to Egypt to join Joseph. There were seventy persons in all. But now, Joseph and all his brothers from that generation have died. **V 7–10: RISK** The Israelites multiply in number and fill the land. The new king of Egypt sees that there is a risk of Israel siding with Egypt's enemies in any future war. **V 11–16: RUTHLESSNESS** To control the Israelites, taskmasters are set over them. The Israelites are given heavy burdens. They build supply cities for Pharaoh but, as they are afflicted, they grow even more. Their bondage increases and they are put to hard labour. Pharaoh tells the midwives to kill the baby sons of the Hebrews. **V 17–19: RESCUE** Because the midwives fear God, they disobey Pharaoh and save the male babies. They tell Pharaoh that the Hebrew women give birth too quickly for them. **V 20–21: REWARD** God rewards their faithfulness to Him, in saving the babies, by giving them households. Still the people multiply and grow 'very mighty'. **V 22: REACTION** Pharaoh reacts by commanding all his people to throw baby Hebrew boys into the river, while preserving baby girls.

CHAPTER TWO

V 1–2: BABY A baby son is born to a man of Levi and his wife. She hides him for three months. **V 3–4: BASKET** When she can no longer hide him, she provides a watertight basket (an ark) and places it in the reeds by the riverbank. The baby's sister watches from afar to see what will happen. **V 5–6: BATHING** One of Pharaoh's daughters finds the baby when she comes to bathe in the river. The baby cries and she has compassion on him and recognises him as a Hebrew. **V 7–10: BOLDNESS** The baby's sister approaches Pharaoh's daughter and arranges for the baby's mother to nurse the child on behalf of Pharaoh's daughter and to be paid for doing it! The child grows and is given the name 'Moses' which means 'drawn from water'. Moses is brought up by Pharaoh's daughter in Pharaoh's house. **V 11–15: BANISHED** One day, Moses intervenes to prevent an Egyptian beating a Hebrew. He kills the Egyptian and buries him. The next day, as he seeks to stop two Hebrews fighting, they tell him they know he has killed an Egyptian. Pharaoh hears of this and Moses flees for his life to the land of Midian where he sits down by a well. **V 16–17: BULLIES** Bullying shepherds

drive seven daughters of the priests of Midian away from the well so that they can have water first. Moses confronts them, helps the daughters, and waters their flock. **V 18–21a: BEFRIENDED** Their father, Reuel (also called Jethro) tells them to invite Moses to eat at their house. Moses is befriended and takes Jethro's daughter, Zipporah, as his wife. **V 21b–22: BASE** Moses continues to live in Midian as his family base and has a son by Zipporah, called Gershon. **V 23–25: BONDAGE** Meanwhile Pharaoh dies in Egypt, and the Israelites continue to groan because of their bondage. They call out to God who hears their cries and remembers His covenant with Abraham, Isaac, and Jacob. God looks on the Israelites and acknowledges them. He has plans for them that will involve unsuspecting Moses.

CHAPTER THREE

V 1: FLOCK Moses acts as a shepherd for Jethro and leads the flock to the back of the desert near Horeb, the mountain of God. **V 2–3: FIRE** The Angel of the LORD appears to him from a burning bush that is not consumed by the fire. Moses investigates the bush. **V 4–6: FEAR** God speaks to Moses by name from the bush and tells him to remove his sandals because here is holy ground. He reminds him that He is the God of his fathers, Abraham, Isaac and Jacob. Fear grips Moses who hides his face because he cannot look upon God. **V 7–10: FAITHFULNESS** God's faithfulness to His people is revealed as He tells Moses that He knows of His people's oppression by the Egyptians and that He wishes to take them to the land of Canaan, which He has promised to them. He tells Moses that, to deliver Israel from Egypt's oppression, He will send him to Pharaoh and liberate the children of Israel from Egypt. **V 11–14:**

FEEBLE Moses feebly questions whether he is qualified and able to do all this. God assures him that He will be present with him and that, after leaving Egypt, Moses will serve God on that very mountain of Horeb. God tells Moses that his name is 'I AM WHO I AM' and that he must tell anyone who asks him that 'I AM' has sent him. **V 15–22: FORETOLD** Before Moses starts his task, God foretells what will happen. He is to remind the Israelites of the promise of God to their forefathers Abraham, Isaac, and Jacob that they will enter the promised land 'flowing with milk and honey'. He tells him that Pharaoh will resist his request to go for three days into the wilderness to worship God. Ultimately, God will smite Pharoah to force him to let the people go, after they have found such favour with the Egyptians, that they will give them possessions and riches. It will be as if they will have plundered the Egyptians. God always knows what He is doing!

CHAPTER FOUR

V 1: DOUBTS Moses begins to doubt, and asks what will happen if he is not believed or listened to, or if they say that God has not appeared to him. **V 2–9: DEMONSTRATION** God demonstrates His miraculous power to Moses by turning his rod into a serpent in Moses' hand and then back again into a rod. He also makes Moses put his hand in his bosom and when it comes out, it is leprous. On putting it back, it is restored. He also tells him that a third sign will be to take water from the river which, when poured out, will become blood on the land. All these miracle gifts for Moses are signs so that people can believe in God as the God of Abraham, Isaac and Jacob, and also that He has appeared to Moses. **V 10–12: DISQUALIFIED?** Moses still protests that,

because he is not a good speaker, he is not qualified for the task. God tells him that He has made his mouth and that He will be with him and tell him what to say. **V 13–17: DISBELIEF** Still Moses does not believe God and asks Him to send someone else. God is angry but concedes to let Aaron go with him because he is a good speaker. Aaron, a Levite and Moses' brother, will be pleased to see Moses. He will take the message from Moses to relay to others. With the rod, the signs, and the support of Aaron, God commissions an uncertain Moses to the task of delivering the Israelites from Egypt. **V 18–20: DEPARTURE** Moses bids Jethro farewell. God directs him to Egypt where those who sought his life are dead. He takes his wife and sons, and has the rod of God in his hand. **V 21–23: DESIGN** God tells Moses of His grand plan. Pharaoh's heart will be hardened and he will not let the Israelites go into the desert to sacrifice to God, despite having seen the signs. Finally, his firstborn will be killed, because he will refuse to let the Israelites go until that point is reached. **V 24–26: DEFENDED** Moses has failed to have his son circumcised as a sign of the covenant with Abraham, Isaac, and Jacob. Moses is in fear of losing his life when Zipporah acts to circumcise her son. The need to trust and obey God is thus laid on them all, right at the start of the mission. **V 27–30: DEBRIEFING** Aaron meets up with Moses who debriefs him about what God has said. He shows him the signs as well. Together they gather the children of Israel, and Aaron tells them what God has said to Moses and performs the signs in the presence of the people. **V 31: DEVOTION** The people believe and bow their heads to worship God who has visited His children after all this time. It is good to begin any great work of God by devotion to Him.

CHAPTER FIVE

V 1–3: TASK Moses and Aaron begin their God-given task by telling Pharaoh of God's command that they should go into the wilderness and worship God. When Pharaoh asks who God is, they explain in more detail and tell Pharaoh that pestilence or sword could come in judgement if there is disobedience. **V 4–5: TERSENESS** Pharaoh tells them to get back to work and that Moses and Aaron are stopping the Israelites from doing their labour. **V 6–16: TALLY** Pharaoh reacts further by insisting that the Israelites gather their own straw or stubble without any reduction in their tally of bricks to be made. They are beaten and interrogated as to why they have not met their targets, and the officers of the children of Israel complain to Pharaoh. **V 17–21: TROUBLE** Pharaoh accuses them of idleness and says that this is the real reason why they want to go to sacrifice to God. He insists that they meet their quota of bricks without straw. Moses and Aaron then get the backlash from their people because of what Pharaoh is doing to them. **V 22–23: TALK** Moses talks to the LORD in prayer and asks why this is. Trouble has increased and there is no deliverance for God's people. He wonders what is really happening.

CHAPTER SIX

V 1: PROMISE God renews His promise to Moses that Pharaoh will ultimately drive out Israel from the land. **V 2–7: PERSON** God reveals to Moses that He is the LORD (or 'Jehovah') who appeared to Israel's forefathers as God Almighty. He will keep His covenant and has heard the groaning of His people. He will rescue and redeem them. They will know that He is their God who takes them from under the Egyptian burdens. **V 8: POSSESSION** He will give them the promised land. **V 9: PRESSURE** But the children of Israel are so anguished because of the bondage that they do not heed Moses. Further pressure is thus on the man who never sought leadership of this people in this 'impossible' situation. **V 10–13: PERPLEXED** When God tells Moses to go to Pharaoh again, to tell him to let the Israelites go, Moses is perplexed. Why will Pharaoh listen to him if the children of Israel will not? The LORD answers Moses and Aaron and gives them a command for both Moses and the children of Israel. **V 14–27: PEOPLE** A catalogue of the people who are with Moses and Aaron is given. **V 28–30: PATHETIC** We are reminded of Moses' pathetic response when commanded by God to repeat to Pharaoh, king of Egypt, all that God says to him. Moses cannot conceive how Pharaoh will hear him.

CHAPTER SEVEN

V 1–7: MASTER PLAN The summary of God's master plan is given. Although Pharaoh's heart will be hardened, God will multiply His signs and wonders through Moses, with Aaron as his prophet being able to give verbal support. God will bring judgements on the Egyptians and bring out the children of Israel. Moses and Aaron, aged eighty and eighty-three respectively, obey God's command. **V 8–13: MIGHTY POWER** As God commands Moses and Aaron, Aaron's rod becomes a serpent before Pharaoh. His sorcerers and magicians (through whatever method, be it magic or sleight of hand), produce rods that turn into serpents. But God's mighty power is shown in that Aaron's serpent swallows theirs. Nevertheless, Pharaoh's heart is hardened and he will not listen to God's word through His servants. **V 14–25: MIRACULOUS PLAGUES: PLAGUE ONE— BLOOD** God then begins to smite Egypt with miraculous plagues in order to demonstrate both His power, and that Moses and Aaron serve Him and have His authority. After due warning is given by Moses and Aaron to Pharaoh, the first plague is demonstrated to him. All the water in the River Nile, which is sacred to the Egyptians and is their highway to commercial success, is turned into blood so that the fish die and the Egyptians cannot drink the river water. Pharaoh's magicians perform a similar feat (again, we are not told by what means) and Pharaoh's heart once more grows hard. He will not listen to God's message through Aaron and Moses. The Egyptians have to dig round the river for water and drink from other sources.

CHAPTER EIGHT

V 1–15: MIRACULOUS PLAGUES: PLAGUE TWO—FROGS The Egyptians regard frogs as sacred. Pharaoh is now warned that his territory and all the households will be overrun by frogs if he does not let the Israelites go. Aaron then carries out the threat, and the frogs cover the land of Egypt, but the magicians duplicate this by producing frogs. (However, they seem to lack the power to get rid of them!) Pharaoh promises Moses that the Israelites can go and worship if he gets rid of the frogs. Moses agrees to do it on the next day. Moses and Aaron cry out to God and the frogs go back into the river. But Pharaoh, on seeing this relief, hardens his heart and breaks his word. **V 16–19: MIRACULOUS PLAGUES: PLAGUE THREE—LICE** Moses and Aaron then bring lice over the land, this time without warning his magicians. They are unable

to replicate this. (Could it be that the lack of notice meant that they are unable to plan their trickery?) With lice everywhere, the magicians tell Pharaoh, 'This is the finger of God.' Hardened Pharaoh does not even heed his own men. **V 20–32: MIRACULOUS PLAGUES: PLAGUE FOUR—FLIES** This time with pre-warning, the Lord sends thick swarms of flies over all Egypt, including Pharaoh's house, but not a fly lands in Goshen, where the Israelites are. Pharaoh tells Moses and Aaron that they can sacrifice to God in Egypt. Moses replies that it must be in the wilderness or there will be violent opposition (to their sacrifices) from the Egyptians. Pharaoh concurs as long as they do not go too far into the wilderness. Moses keeps his word in entreating God to remove the flies, which He does so that not one remains. Pharaoh's heart is hardened even further after the flies are taken away, and he refuses to let the people go.

CHAPTER NINE

V 1–7: MIRACULOUS PLAGUES: PLAGUE FIVE—LIVESTOCK The next plague involves all the livestock of Egypt being smitten with pestilence and dying, whereas not one of the Israelites' animals died. Despite the warning and the accomplishment by God, Pharaoh's heart is so hard that he will not let the people go. **V 8–12: MIRACULOUS PLAGUES: PLAGUE SIX—BOILS** Next, in the sight of Pharaoh, Moses and Aaron scatter handfuls of ash from a furnace and the fine dust becomes boils that break out in sores on men and animals throughout the land of Egypt. The magicians, who now seem to have given up the task of replicating these miraculous plagues (possibly because they were too hard to stage-manage), cannot stand before Pharaoh because they are smitten by boils. Pharaoh still will not listen to what Moses has said, and his heart is hardened further. **V 13–35: MIRACULOUS PLAGUES: PLAGUE SEVEN—HAIL** Moses and Aaron go before Pharaoh again and remind him that God is working all these plagues to show His power and that His name should be declared in all the earth. God has noted Pharaoh's self-exaltation against his people and that he will not let them go. He will now unleash hail upon the replacement livestock that Egypt has acquired since the fifth plague. God gives a warning so that any Egyptians wise enough to believe Him can remove their livestock from the fields and put them in safe quarters to avoid their being killed by the hail. However, Israel's livestock will not be touched. Moses stretches out God's rod and hail and fire strike everything in the fields of Egypt—man, beast, herbs and trees. No problem is caused by the hail in the land of Goshen where the Israelites are situated. Because the wheat and spelt are late crops, they are not struck and therefore, through God's graciousness, Egypt will not be smitten by a total famine. This time Pharaoh declares that he knows that God is righteous and his people and he are wicked. He asks Moses to stop the thunder and hail. He promises to let them all go and that they will stay no longer. As Moses calls out to God, the thunder and hail cease. Incredibly Pharaoh hardens his heart even more, reneges on what he has promised, and will not let the people go.

CHAPTER TEN

V 1–20: MIRACULOUS PLAGUES: PLAGUE EIGHT—LOCUSTS Moses is reminded that he must relate God's dealings with Egypt on behalf of the Israelites to future generations. Moses and Aaron tell Pharaoh of the plague of locusts that will eat everything, and fill the houses of all Egyptians. Pharaoh's servants plead with Pharaoh to let the Israelites go before Egypt is destroyed. Pharaoh has another audience with them and tells them to go, provided that only the men go. Moses and Aaron have made it quite clear that all the Israelites, including children, are to go. Pharaoh drives them out. Moses obeys God's command to stretch out his rod over Egypt and an enormous number of locusts produce great devastation in the land and cloud the sky. This time, Pharaoh calls Moses and Aaron in haste, confesses that he has sinned against God and against them, asks for forgiveness, and asks that God may take this plague and death away. As Moses entreats God, a very strong west wind takes the locusts away into the Red Sea, and not one locust remains. But Pharaoh's already hardened heart is hardened even further and he will not let the children of Israel go. **V 21–29: MIRACULOUS PLAGUES: PLAGUE NINE— DARKNESS** Without warning to Pharaoh, God instructs Moses to stretch out his hand, and great darkness extends over the whole land of Egypt for three days. The children of Israel, however, are never without light. Pharaoh seeks to negotiate the Israelites' going into the wilderness by stating that their flocks and herds must be kept back, even though their children may go. Moses insists that not a hoof shall be left behind. Hardened Pharaoh refuses to let them go and ejects them from his presence, claiming that if they see him again, they shall die. Moses impetuously says it is true that he will never see his face again. (In fact he will see his face again but only when Pharaoh finally concedes defeat.)

CHAPTER ELEVEN

V 1–10: MIRACULOUS PLAGUES: PLAGUE TEN—FIRSTBORN God tells Moses that after the final plague to come, Pharaoh will drive the Israelites out of Egypt. The Israelites are to talk to the Egyptians, with whom God will give them favour, so that they will receive silver and gold to take with them. Moses' God-given profile is very great among the Egyptians. Moses tells Pharaoh that all the firstborn in Egypt shall die, including servants and animals, and that there will be a horrendous and unprecedented cry throughout Egypt. Israel will not even hear a dog barking against them. The Egyptians will plead with Moses to leave, and after that they will go out. This time Moses, in great anger, leaves Pharaoh. The LORD confirms to Moses that Pharaoh will not heed him. In fact, after all these wonders, the LORD has hardened Pharaoh's unrepentant and arrogant heart so that he will not let the Israelites go. (The sending of the tenth miraculous plague on the firstborn is recorded in the next chapter.)

CHAPTER TWELVE

V 1–11: PASSOVER God gives to Moses and Aaron His instructions for the Passover. Each household (or combined households) must take a male lamb without blemish and keep it from the tenth to the fourteenth day of the month, and then kill it at twilight. The blood of the lamb is to be applied to the two doorposts and the lintel of the house where it is eaten. The roasted flesh is to be eaten with unleavened bread and bitter herbs, and any left is to be burned in the fire the following morning. It is to be eaten in haste with readiness for the journey. The Israelites are to wear belts

and have a staff in their hand. This is the LORD's Passover. **V 12–13: PROTECTED** God confirms that He will smite the firstborn of the Egyptians, man or beast, thus executing judgement against them and their gods. However, when He sees the lamb's blood on each house of the Israelites, God will pass over and the plague will not strike them. As with the other plagues that He has performed, His protected people shall not suffer in them. **V 14–20: PROHIBITIONS** In telling the Israelites to keep a memorial of this feast throughout future generations, He makes prohibitions for them. Leaven must neither be found in the house nor eaten. There must be no work done on the seventh day upon which the Passover will take place. **V 21–23: PROVISION** The elders have to pick out for the families the lambs that qualify as Passover lambs. They have to take a bunch of hyssop, a plant, dip it in the blood, and paint the lintels and the doorpost with the blood. Everyone must stay indoors until morning. God promises that when He goes to strike the Egyptians, He will pass over every house that is protected by the blood on the lintel and the doorpost. **V 24–28: POSTERITY** God commands that a memorial of Passover must be kept in future generations as a remembrance of how He delivered His people from Egypt. The people bow their heads, worship, go away, and do what Moses and Aaron have commanded. **V 29–30: PLAGUE** The tenth miraculous plague, the death of the firstborn, is fulfilled at midnight exactly as God said. Pharaoh and his servants and all the Egyptians rise in the night to hear 'a great cry in Egypt'. No Egyptian household escapes. **V 31–32: PERMISSION** Pharaoh calls for Moses and Aaron and tells them to leave as they have requested, with no reservations or compromises this time. He asks them to bless him, too.

V 33–42: PLUNDER The Egyptians want the Israelites to leave quickly, and favour the Israelites by giving them silver, gold and clothing. The Israelites not only plunder the Egyptians, but also take unleavened bread and kneading bowls along with their belongings. A huge crowd of Israelites leave, including 600,000 men on foot, probably their fighting men. They bake unleavened bread and are driven out by the Egyptians after 430 years in Egypt. The people are to observe this event solemnly in the future throughout their generations. **V 43–51: PARTICULARS** The particulars of how the Passover is to be kept are given. Basically, only circumcised Israelites, and those staying with them who are prepared to be circumcised, can keep it. None of the meat must be carried outside the house, and the bones must not be broken. Israel does what God commands and the LORD brings the children of Israel out of the land of Egypt.

CHAPTER THIRTEEN

V 1–2: CONSECRATED God tells Moses that every firstborn of man and animal is His and should be consecrated to Him. **V 3–10: COMMEMORATED** Israel's deliverance from Egypt is to be commemorated annually by the Feast of Unleavened Bread. Unleavened bread is to be eaten for seven days. Children are to be told the significance of this to remember God who delivered Israel from Egypt. **V 11–16: CANAAN** When Israel arrives in the land of Canaan, all the firstborn male animals are to be given to the LORD in sacrifice, apart from the firstborn of the donkeys, which will not be offered, but be redeemed with a lamb. Similarly, every firstborn boy will be redeemed by sacrifice. **V 17–18: COWARDLINESS** The people's cowardliness would make them

shrink from conflict with nations en route for the promised land. God therefore plans their long detour through the wilderness to avoid the conflict and temptations which their cowardliness would cause. **V 19: CARRYING** Moses meets the obligation that Joseph put upon the Israelites to carry his bones with them. They, too, will ultimately reach the promised land. **V 20–22: CARE** God's care for His people is shown in that He leads them in a pillar of cloud by day and in a pillar of fire by night. Thus they are always assured of His presence, protection and guidance.

CHAPTER FOURTEEN

V 1–4: FOLLOWING The children of Israel are following God's plan and God's servant Moses. God reveals that Pharaoh will pursue them, believing that they are lost and discouraged in the wilderness. This is God's plan to overthrow Pharaoh and his army, and teach the Egyptians that He is the LORD. **V 5–9: FICKLE** Pharaoh continues to break his word. He mobilises all Egypt's chariots to pursue the Israelites. They catch up with the Israelites as they camp beside the Red Sea. **V 10–12: FEAR** Faced with the sight of the Egyptians coming after them, the Israelites fear and tell Moses that they should have carried on serving the Egyptians rather than coming to die in the wilderness. Like Pharaoh, they are also fickle, but for a different reason. They are fearful because of their lack of trust in God. **V 13–14: FIRM** Moses is rock solid in his trust in God. He tells them to stand still and see God's salvation, which He will accomplish. The Egyptian army will be overthrown because God will fight for His people and give them peace. **V 15–18: FORWARD** God tells Moses this is not a time for praying, but for action. He tells

Moses to lift up his rod over the sea, which will divide. Israel will go through on dry ground to the other side. God will be victorious over Pharaoh's army. **V 19–20: FAITHFULNESS** God's faithfulness is seen as His Angel puts a pillar of cloud between the Israelites and the Egyptians. It is a cloud of darkness to the Egyptians and of light to the Israelites, and they are kept apart. God is merciful and gracious to those who trust Him, but those who rebel against Him face judgement. This is a principle throughout time and eternity. **V 21–23: FORCE** Moses stretches out the rod over the sea, and the force of God causes a strong east wind all night to dry the land and divide the waters. With the waters as walls on both sides, the Israelites walk through the midst of the Red Sea on dry ground and are pursued by Pharaoh's chariots and horsemen. **V 24–25: FRUSTRATED** God frustrates the Egyptians as they follow the Israelites. He troubles the Egyptian army and takes off their chariot wheels so that they cannot drive their chariots. The Egyptians want to flee from Israel as they recognise that God is fighting against them and against their efforts to pursue His people. **V 26–29: FLOW** God commands Moses to stretch out his hand over the sea. As he does so, the sea returns and swamps Pharaoh's army. What was formerly dry ground with walls of water to help Israel, now becomes a watery grave for their pursuers. **V 30–31: FEAR** God's saving work in delivering Israel and destroying the Egyptians produces reverential fear from His people and faith in the LORD and in 'His servant Moses'.

CHAPTER FIFTEEN

V 1–19: GRATITUDE Moses and the children of Israel sing a song of praise to God. This is a testimony of the people as a whole and also of each individual whose personal trust is in God. They affirm their personal trust in God. Those among them who are not yet personally trusting in God are taught great lessons about God and His salvation and His power through this song of praise they sing together and reflect on His mighty acts. **V 20–21: GLORIOUS!** Miriam, the prophetess and sister of Aaron, re-echoes the theme in timbrels and dancing as she sings of the glorious triumph that the LORD has performed for His people against their enemies. **V 22–24: GRUMBLING** How sad and how true to human nature that, in a time of hardship soon after this time of praise, the children of Israel complain against Moses. Having found no water to drink, they then find that the waters of Marah are bitter. They complain against their leader, asking what they will drink. **V 25–27: GRACE** God's grace is shown to His fickle people as He answers Moses' prayer by showing him a tree. The waters are made sweet as Moses casts the tree into them. God reminds His people that they must diligently hear His voice and obey Him. Then they will not suffer the diseases which the Egyptians have suffered. God brings them to Elim which has twelve wells of water and seventy palm trees. They camp there.

CHAPTER SIXTEEN

V 1–3: MOANING Soon after, in journeying from Elim, the Israelites murmur against Moses and Aaron in the wilderness. They look back to the food they had eaten in Egypt and again grumble that they have been brought out to die in the wilderness. **V 4–5: MIRACULOUS** God provides bread from heaven. They must gather it for six days, collecting double on the sixth day so that they can rest on the seventh day. God's

Sabbath principle is being applied to His people. **V 6–18: MEALS** God hears their complaints. He promises and provides bread in the morning and 'meat' (quails) in the evening. He tells them to gather according to their needs, which are met exactly. **V 19–20: MAGGOTS** Moses tells them to leave none of the bread until morning. They need to be neither greedy nor unbelieving in God's provision. Some disobey, and maggots infest the bread. Moses is angry with the people. **V 21: MELTING** Every morning they gather, according to their needs, the special bread that God provides. When the sun becomes hot, it melts. **V 22–30: MEMORIAL** The principle of keeping God's Sabbath, later given in the moral law of the Ten Commandments, is urged upon the people. As they gather double helpings of the bread on the sixth day, it is preserved in a perfect and consumable state for the seventh day, when no work must be done. **V 31–36: MANNA** The Israelites call this divinely given bread 'Manna' (which means 'What is it?'). It appears like coriander seed and tastes like wafers made with honey. God reminds the Israelites that this is the bread that God promised. As a memorial to God's faithfulness, a pot of manna must be kept for future generations. At God's command to Moses, Aaron keeps it before the Testimony and it will be later put within the ark of the covenant. The children of Israel eat manna for forty years until they come to the promised land.

CHAPTER SEVENTEEN

V 1–3: INSUBORDINATION In the Wilderness of Sin, when again there is no water, the people of Israel contend with Moses and complain that he has brought them from Egypt only to die of thirst in the wilderness. **V 4–7: INSTRUCTION** Moses takes their cry to the LORD to ask Him what to do because they are ready to stone him. God tells him to strike the rock with his rod before the elders and the people, and water will come so that the people may drink. Moses does so and calls the place 'Massah' and 'Meribah', which mean, 'testing' and 'contending'. **V 8–15: INTERCESSION** Amalek comes out to fight against Israel. Joshua leads the army. Moses, Aaron and Hur go to the hilltop to pray. As Moses prays, he raises his hands. When his hands are lifted, Israel prevails, and when they fall, Amalek prevails. Aaron and Hur support his hands until sundown. This is an object lesson in prayer and underlines the importance of constant prayer support for those in the battle of Christian service. God promises to blot out Amalek. Moses builds an altar called 'The-Lord-Is-My-Banner'.

CHAPTER EIGHTEEN

V 1–8: DEALINGS Jethro, Moses' father-in-law, comes to visit him with Moses' wife, Zipporah, and his two sons Gershom and Eliezer. Moses takes the time to welcome and show affection for his father-in-law and tells him of all God's dealings for Israel against the Egyptians and how God has delivered them. **V 9–12: DELIGHT** Jethro is delighted in the news and rejoices in what God has done. He blesses and thanks God, acknowledging that He is greater than all the gods of the nations. He takes burnt offerings and other sacrifices to present to God, and Aaron and the other elders come to meet with him along with Moses. In Old Testament terms, Jethro is converted as he sees God's faithfulness, power and dealings. It is a wonderful thing when a godly leader has an impact on his own unconverted family. **V 13–16: DISPUTES** Jethro observes Moses, as God's representative, acting as a judge from morning till evening, when the people have disputes or difficulties. **V 17–26: DELEGATION** Jethro advises that Moses should delegate routine matters to other God-fearing men and reserve more difficult cases for himself. Moses humbly learns from his more experienced father-in-law. **V 27: DEPARTURE** After a most blessed and profitable visit, Jethro departs. He has come to know God and has contributed towards the fashioning of a legal system, which remains in principle throughout the world today.

CHAPTER NINETEEN

V 1–6: COMMUNION Israel camps in the Wilderness of Sinai before Mount Sinai. There God communes with Moses and tells him that, just as He has brought out Israel from Egypt, so He will bless and keep His people as 'a special treasure'. He will make the people 'a kingdom of priests and a holy nation'. God will do this if Israel will obey Him and keep His covenant. **V 7–9: COMMUNICATION** Moses relays God's message to the elders. All the people concur that they will do what God has said. Moses tells the LORD what the people have said, and he is told that the LORD will come to him in a thick cloud, so that the people will hear when God speaks to Moses and accept Moses' leadership. Moses acts as a mediator between God and the children of Israel. **V 10–15: CONSECRATION** Moses descends from communicating with God on the mountain and sanctifies the people for two days for what is to follow. On the third day, God promises to come down at Sinai before all the people, but both they and the beasts must not even touch the mountain. They must approach when the trumpet sounds. Moses commands sexual abstinence in order to concentrate for a short time on something far more important. **V 16–20: COVERED** Thunder, lightnings, and a covering thick cloud on the mountain accompany the very loud sound of the trumpet that God promised. The people in the camp tremble. As Moses assembles the people at the foot of the mountain, God covers the mountain in smoke and the whole mountain quakes. The trumpet blasts more loudly, and Moses communes with God who speaks at the top of Mount Sinai. If anyone in Israel ever doubted God's holiness and power, or Moses' God-given authority, this should settle it. **V 21–25: CAUTION** God commands Moses to descend from the mountain to warn the people not to break through the smoke and cloud lest they gaze on the LORD and perish. The priests also must consecrate themselves to avoid being struck down by Him. Moses complies. The utter holiness of God is evident to Moses and to the people and priests.

CHAPTER TWENTY

V 1–17: TEN COMMANDMENTS God speaks to Moses and gives him the Ten Commandments, which are His moral law for all people for all time. The first four commandments concentrate on man's relationship with God. The second six commandments treat man's relationship with man, as commanded by God. Jesus later summarised the first four as loving God and putting Him first, and the last six as loving one's neighbour as oneself. **V 18–21: TESTING CIRCUMSTANCES** Thunder, lightnings, trumpet sound and smoke make the people tremble as they stand afar off. They beg that Moses should speak with them because they fear that they will die if God speaks to them. Moses tells them to demonstrate their fear of God by not sinning. The people stand afar off and Moses draws near to the thick darkness where God is. **V 22–26: TEACHING CONSECRATION** God reiterates that no gods of silver or gold must ever be made. An altar made of earth must be made for Him on which burnt offerings and peace offerings, sheep and oxen, must be sacrificed. He promises that He will come and bless His people. No altar of stone should ever be made of hewn stone, because the tools used by human beings would effectively profane it. Also, absolute purity must be observed by not going up to the altar by steps so that nakedness may never be visible to those below.

CHAPTER TWENTY-ONE

V 1–11: LAWS TO LIVE BY: PRINCIPLE OF INTEGRITY We now move from God's timeless moral law to all people, given in the Ten Commandments, to laws concerning Israel as a nation. This is their combined civil and criminal code applicable to them as a people and as a nation. Some laws regulate an existing state of affairs rather than justify that state of affairs. The first eleven verses concern integrity, which is the basis of any credible legal code. **V 12–36: LAWS TO LIVE BY: PROTECTION OF INDIVIDUALS** The second half of the chapter deals mainly with the protection of the individuals' rights and person. This is divided into two main categories: verses 12 to 27 **PROTECTION OF INDIVIDUALS AGAINST AGGRESSION** and verses 28 to 36 **PROTECTION OF INDIVIDUALS AGAINST ANIMALS.** People have a right to be protected by the law from violent lawbreakers, and also from carelessness involving them in personal hurt and damage, in this case

from the animals in a mobile farming community.

CHAPTER TWENTY-TWO

V 1–15: LAWS TO LIVE BY: PROTECTION OF PROPERTY The first half of this chapter deals with the fact that a person's property should be protected by law and that he should be compensated for any loss. **V 16–31: LAWS TO LIVE BY: PROTECTION OF PURITY** The main thrust of the second half of the chapter is to protect the purity of the people: sexually, spiritually, doctrinally, in dealing with the weaker members of society such as widows and orphans or the poor, in giving to God, and in eating habits. The key thought is 'and you shall be holy men to Me'.

CHAPTER TWENTY-THREE

V 1–9: FAIRNESS The principles covering all justice and dealings with one another must be those of fairness. **V 10–13: FAITHFULNESS** Faithfulness to all God's commandments is required. The land is to enjoy a Sabbath every seven years so that it can lie fallow. Emphasis is placed on the need to keep the weekly Sabbath, thus refreshing workers and strangers among God's people. Also stressed is the requirement not to make mention of other gods, so that God alone is to be worshipped. God requires faithfulness, especially in these matters. He knows that if the Sabbaths fail and the Israelites start loosely talking about other gods, their worship, trust and obedience will fail. **V 14–19: FESTIVALS** There are three festivals that must be kept in the year. These are the Feast of Unleavened Bread, the Feast of Harvest, and the Feast of Ingathering. Reminders of how to keep Passover and the bringing of first fruits are also given. **V 20–26: FOLLOW** God will send a protecting and guiding angel to go before them. They must regard him as the holy agent of God and, in following his leading, they must be very careful not to follow the gods of the ungodly nations in any way, but to obey him because God's name is in him. Faithful service, freedom from sickness, and safe and fruitful childbirth will be among the blessings that God guarantees if they will trust and obey Him. **V 27–30: FEAR** God will send His fear before the Israelites, so that they can drive out and conquer the people in the promised land. This driving out will be little by little, so that they can consolidate their entry, rather than having to deal with invading beasts in a desolate and empty land. They will increase, inherit and inhabit the land gradually, as they obey God. **V 31: FUTURE** God indicates the boundaries of their future land. He will deliver to them its inhabitants and drive them out, provided that His people trust and obey Him. **V 32–33: FORBIDDEN** They are forbidden to make covenants with the people they must drive out. If they do that, they will start worshipping and serving the gods of the pagan nations which will ensnare them. Consecration can have no compromise.

CHAPTER TWENTY-FOUR

V 1–2: REVERENCE God commands Moses to bring up Aaron, Nadab and Abihu (the priests), and seventy of Israel's elders to worship from afar. Moses alone shall come near God and the people must be kept away. God requires reverent fear. **V 3–4a: RECORDED** Moses tells the people what God has said and they promise that they will obey. Moses records all the words that God has given him. **V 4b–8: REPRESENTED** Moses builds an altar at the foot of the mountain with twelve pillars, representing the twelve tribes of Israel. Burnt offerings and peace offerings are sacrificed to God, and Moses takes the blood and sprinkles half on the altar and half on the people, having taken the Book of the Covenant (God's laws) and having read it to the people. He emphasises both the blood of the covenant when he sprinkles the people, and the fact that God has spoken and these are His words. Shed blood and God's Word are always at the centre of true worship of God. **V 9–12: REVELATION** God reveals Himself to Aaron, Nadab and Abihu and the seventy elders, as well as to Moses. He then tells them that on two tablets of stone He will give them the Ten Commandments, which He has written. **V 13–14: RESPONSIBLE** While Moses takes Joshua, his assistant and eventual successor, up the mountain, he leaves the elders to deal with any difficulties the people have, knowing that Aaron and Hur are there. He is responsible in making sure that things are dealt with properly while Joshua and he are away. **V 15–18: REMAINING** Moses goes up into the mountain cloud and the glory of the LORD rests on Mount Sinai for six days and His cloud covers it. On the seventh day, He calls to Moses out of the midst of the cloud and His glory is like a consuming fire visible to the Israelites below. Moses goes into the cloud and into the mountain, remaining there forty days and forty nights.

CHAPTER TWENTY-FIVE

V 1–7: GIVING PEOPLE Through Moses, the LORD asks the people to offer willingly, and from their hearts, materials with which he will construct the sanctuary. The materials are listed. **V 8–9: GOD'S PLAN** The sanctuary is to be God's dwelling place, or tabernacle. God will tell them exactly what the pattern will be for the tabernacle and for its furnishings. **V 10–39: GOLD PROMINENT** Gold in the Bible often speaks of deity and of God's glory, and it is fitting that gold is prominent in the furnishings for the tabernacle. This will include: The ark of the covenant, (verses 10 to 16), the atonement cover (verses 17 to 22), the acacia table (verses 23 to 30), and the lamp stand (verses 31 to 39). **V 40: GIVEN PATTERN** God had already given the pattern for these furnishings to Moses on the mountain, and He instructs that the furnishings should be according to that pattern.

CHAPTER TWENTY-SIX

V 1–13: THE CURTAINS Details are given about the curtains for the tabernacle. As with all the furnishings of the tabernacle, they have great spiritual significance in many aspects, including the colours. (See also comment on verse 31.) **V 14: THE COVERING** The tabernacle is to be covered by two layers of skins: first, red dyed ram skins (reminding us of the shed blood of Christ over our lives) and badger skins above that. **V 15–29: THE CONSTRUCTION** Next comes the construction of the frame, which would support the curtains and the covering of skins. It is sturdy and precise, but portable, as is necessary for a mobile tabernacle. (Later it will be replaced by Solomon's temple.) The materials also have spiritual significance. **V 30: THE COMMAND** Again, we read that the pattern for the tabernacle was given earlier to Moses on the mountain and it must be followed. True worship must always follow God's Word. **V 31–35: THE CLIMAX** The climax to the construction of the tabernacle is the Most Holy Place, in which the sacred furniture will be centred on the ark of the Testimony. A veil will be hung to separate the holy place from the Most Holy Place. All the furniture and the furnishings are spiritually significant for us. The cover of the veil between the holy place and the Most Holy Place is to be blue (speaking of heaven), purple (speaking of royalty), scarlet (speaking of shed blood), and fine woven linen (the whiteness speaking of God's holiness and righteousness). These colours reflect God's character, the person of the Lord Jesus Christ, and life-changing truths for those who trust in Christ today. **V 36–37: THE CONTEXT** The screen will cover the entrance into the tabernacle and set the context of worship as the worshippers enter. It is to be held with pillars overlaid with gold, which emphasise God's splendour and glory to those who come to worship there. Those worshipping God should always approach Him mindful of who He is and what He has done to enable them to know and worship Him.

CHAPTER TWENTY-SEVEN

V 1–8: ACACIA ALTAR The altar of burnt offering, overlaid with bronze and provided with a grate and with poles to make it portable, is to be made of acacia wood. The measurement of the square altar is given. **V 9–19: CURTAINED COURT** The court of the tabernacle is described. It will be surrounded with the curtains on all sides and the screen which forms the gate. **V 20–21: OLIVE OIL** Pure pressed olive oil is to be used for the light. The priests must tend it to make sure that it never goes out. That light is in the tabernacle, outside the veil, before the ark of Testimony.

CHAPTER TWENTY-EIGHT

V 1: CALLING OF PRIESTS Moses is told to take Aaron and his sons to minister before

God as priests. His sons are Nadab, Abihu, Eleazar and Ithamar. **V 2–43: CLOTHING OF PRIESTS** The priest is someone who represents the people before God and represents God before the people. As such, they are a picture of the great High Priest, the Lord Jesus Christ, who is to come, though His priesthood is an eternal and far superior one. The ephod, breastplate and other garments are all highly significant spiritually, and reflect the key thought in worship which is 'HOLINESS TO THE LORD'. Much important teaching about the character of God and the way to approach Him is contained in these glorious visual aids.

CHAPTER TWENTY-NINE

V 1–41: CONSECRATION In the consecration of the priests, the importance of sacrifice, cleansing, direct approach to God, shed blood, anointing oil, and daily observance are all underlined. **V 42–43: CONTINUATION** The burnt offerings are to be continual and point to the continual efficacy of Christ's work on the cross, and our need to trust and worship Him continually. **V 44–46: CONFIDENCE** God's consecration of Aaron and his sons as priests underlines the confidence that the children of Israel can have in knowing that God dwells among them and that He is their LORD and God who brought them out of Egypt. He emphasises again that He wishes to dwell among them and that He is 'the LORD their God'.

CHAPTER THIRTY

V 1–10: ALTAR Another altar, this time for the burning of incense perpetually before the LORD, is to be made of acacia wood and overlaid with pure gold. Its design is given. Aaron is to burn sweet incense on it every morning when he tends the lamps. He is to repeat this every evening. Once a year, an atonement sacrifice is to be made upon it. This will be the last piece of furniture that he passes before going into the Holy of holies (the Most Holy Place) once a year. **V 11–16: ATONEMENT** Atonement money from the children of Israel for the service of the tabernacle shall be given as a ransom whenever a census is taken of the children of Israel. **V 17–21: ABLUTIONS** A bronze laver is to be provided so that Aaron and the priests can wash their hands and feet in water before bringing an offering to the LORD. If they do not wash, they will die. This pictures our need to be cleansed in order to approach God. **V 22–33: ANOINTING** Special holy anointing oil is to be made, according to the specification and quantities given, to anoint all the furniture in the tabernacle, and to anoint Aaron and the priests. This is to consecrate everything anointed as holy to God. The oil must not be used in any other way or imitated or put on outsiders. Transgression of this command will mean being cut off from God's people. We, too, need the daily anointing of the Holy Spirit on our lives. **V 34–38: AROMA** God tells Moses the specification for making very special, holy incense with the 'art of the perfumer'. It is to be placed before the ark of the Testimony and is to be most holy. It is not to be imitated for personal use, or copied, upon pain of being cut off from God's people. Our Christian life should be an aroma reflecting our relationship with God.

CHAPTER THIRTY-ONE

V 1–11: SPIRIT-FILLED God provides Bezalel to Moses for accomplishing the manufacture of all these holy items for the tabernacle. For this task, God has 'filled him with the Spirit of God in wisdom, in understanding, in knowledge, and in all manner of workmanship'. He has provided a team for him as well. **V 12–17: SABBATH FAITHFULNESS** God emphasises that the fourth commandment, to remember the Sabbath day, is to form an essential part of the life and worship of His people. It is a sign that He is 'the LORD who sanctifies you'. Today, keeping the Lord's day also announces to the world that we love and serve our Lord, and is fundamental in the proper worship of Him on His holy day. A nation or society is blessed that, like the Israelites, adopts this timeless moral law as its own. **V 18: STATUTES FOREVER** The two tablets containing the Ten Commandments are then given to Moses by God, written with His own finger in tablets of stone. These commandments describe the character of God and are His unchangeable moral law for all people at all times. No other laws were written by God's finger in stone. Later, God's Ten Commandments will be placed in the ark of the covenant to signify their special, ongoing holiness.

CHAPTER THIRTY-TWO

V 1: WAITING The Israelites, with Aaron, are impatient at the delayed arrival of Moses from the mountain top and doubt whether he will return. They desire to make their own gods to go before them, despite all that the LORD God has done for them and commanded them! **V 2–4: WEAKNESS** Aaron shows that, in the absence of Moses, he is a very weak leader. He takes the people's golden earrings to fashion into a golden calf. They then proclaim it as the god which brought them out of Egypt! If Aaron had been faithful to God, Israel's history could have been very different. **V 5–6:**

WORLDLINESS As with all idolatry in the Bible, immorality soon follows it. A feast, declared to be 'to the LORD' and including burnt offerings and peace offerings, results in an orgy. Worldliness and immorality follow disobedience and idolatry. **V 7–10: WATCHING** The omniscient God is watching, and tells Moses to go down the mountain and deal with his stiff-necked people. He tells Moses that His intention is to consume them in His wrath so that He can re-make a great nation from faithful Moses. **V 11–14: WHY?** Moses asks why God's wrath should burn hot against the Israelites, and why the Egyptians should say that God had led them from Egypt to consume them. He asks God to remember His covenant with Abraham, Isaac and Israel, and His promise to them to multiply their descendants for ever. God responds to Moses' words, and, for the glory of His name, His covenant, and His promise, agrees not to harm His people. **V 15–16: WORK** Moses knows that he has serious work to do for God among the Israelites as he descends the mountain carrying the two stone tablets containing the Ten Commandments. Those tablets are God's work, containing God's writing, about God's law. **V 17–18: WAR?** Joshua, who is with Moses, mistakenly reports 'the sound of war in the camp'. Moses, having been informed by God, knows that it is not war he hears, but singing at an orgy. **V 19–20: WRATH** Moses' wrath reflects the wrath of his Master when he sees the idol calf and the dancing. He breaks the tablets at the foot of the mountain. He takes and burns the calf, grinds it to powder, and scatters it on the water, making the Israelites drink it. **V 21–24: WAYWARDNESS** Moses immediately holds Aaron accountable for such a great sin. Aaron tries to hide behind the people's sinfulness and tells

Moses of their unrest at Moses' delayed return. He weakly says that he cast the gold he gathered from them into the fire and that 'the calf came out'. Aaron is a negative example of how to own up to, confess, and forsake sin. **V 25–29: WILL** With an uncompromising and God-given will of iron, Moses challenges the unrestrained rebels with the words, 'Whoever is on the LORD's side—come to me!' The sons of Levi come to him. Moses sends them to slaughter those who will not consecrate themselves to God. Three thousand men die that day. Moses commands the people who remain to consecrate themselves to God. **V 30–33: WILLINGNESS** Moses now pleads with God to see if atonement can be made for their sin. He confesses the great sin of the people in their idolatry (which encompasses all the consequent sin and immorality) and even offers to be blotted out himself by God, if He will save Israel. God replies that there will be individual accountability for sin. He does not blot Moses from His book! **V 34–35: WITH** God confirms that His Angel will go before Moses, who is to lead the Israelites to the promised land. However, they will be punished for their idolatry. Plagues from the LORD follow. Significantly, this tragic chapter ends with the words 'the calf which Aaron made'.

obeyed God's command to strip them off to avoid being consumed by Him. Without ornaments, they will be less able to provide the material to make an idol. Penitence involves not only feeling, but also doing and forsaking. **V 7–16: PRESENCE** The people realise that the presence of the LORD is with Moses through the pillar of cloud, as God talks to Moses at the tabernacle door. At their tent doors, each of the Israelites worships God. God speaks with Moses 'face to face, as a man speaks with his friend'. When Moses returns to the camp, Joshua stays in the tabernacle. God renews His promise of His ongoing Presence with Moses, giving him rest, and Moses asks not to go forward unless God's Presence is with them. This will be His sign of authority to the Israelites, and demonstrates the Israelites' separation from the earth's other inhabitants. **V 17–23: PROCLAMATION** God promises to separate His people and to honour Moses. Moses then asks to see God's glory. God promises to make all His glory pass before him and proclaim His name to him. His graciousness and compassion will be evident. He will hide Moses in a rock as He passes by, and cover him with His hand so that he cannot see the fullness of His glory. No man can do that and live. He promises that Moses will see His back.

CHAPTER THIRTY-THREE

V 1–3: PROMISE God renews His promise of the land to the Israelites in line with His covenant with Abraham, Isaac and Jacob. His Angel will lead them and force out the inhabitants, but God will not go with them in their midst, lest He should consume them for being stiff-necked. **V 4–6: PENITENCE** The people mourn the fact that God will not be in the midst of them. They wear no ornaments, having

CHAPTER THIRTY-FOUR

V 1–4: BROKEN Because earlier Moses broke the two tablets of stone, on which God wrote the Ten Commandments, God tells Moses to meet Him again at the top of the mountain. He will replace the Ten Commandments there. **V 5–9: BOWED** The LORD descends in the cloud and proclaims His name to Moses. God emphasises His mercy, grace, goodness, truth, forgiveness, justice and judgement.

Moses hastily bows towards the earth and worships and asks God's grace to forgive this 'stiff-necked people', to pardon them, and take them as God's inheritance. **V 10–16: BEHOLD** God tells Moses to behold the covenant that God is making. If God's people will obey Him, He will drive out the inhabitants of the land. They must keep themselves from making covenants with them and must not engage in any kind of idolatry or in any religion or immorality associated with that idolatry. **V 17–26: BEHAVIOUR** The children of Israel are to be different in their behaviour. They must follow God's commands which will lead them to worship Him in the manner and at the times He has appointed. Their sacrifices must be in accordance with God's instructions and not be tainted by leaven, idolatry or sin. **V 27–28: BIDDEN** At God's bidding, Moses writes all the words that God gives him. He lives without bread and water, fasting for forty days and forty nights. God Himself writes on the two stone tablets the words of the Ten Commandments. **V 29–35: BRIGHTNESS** Moses descends from the mountain, and Aaron and the children of Israel see his face shining to the extent that they are afraid to approach him. Moses relays to them what God has said, and then puts a veil on his face. When Moses speaks to God, the veil is taken off. When he speaks to the Israelites, he puts the veil on. What is glorious before man cannot compare with the glory of God Himself.

CHAPTER THIRTY-FIVE

V 1–3: SABBATH Again Moses reminds the children of Israel that the fourth commandment is to be included in their civil life and that they must observe it in practice. **V 4–9: SPECIFIC** Moses reminds the children of Israel of God's specific request for a freewill offering for the materials that will be used to build the tabernacle and its furniture and to conduct the worship. **V 10–19: SKILLS** Skilled and gifted artisans are told to present themselves to manufacture the tabernacle and its furnishings and the holy garments of the priests. **V 20–29: SUPPORT** The support of the people, in terms of giving and working, shows that God has stirred their hearts, and that they are only too ready to make the freewill offerings. Willingness is translated into service as God's commands are enthusiastically followed. **V 30–35: SPIRIT** God's Spirit is filling Bezalel in all his design work and creative activity to produce a beautiful temple for God with the precious materials provided. The same Spirit gives him the ability to teach others on his team who also work for God.

CHAPTER THIRTY-SIX

V 1–2: TEAM SKILLS All the gifted craftsmen, led by Bezalel and Aholiab, heartily put together their individual skills to work together in a team for the LORD and His glory. **V 3–7: TREMENDOUS SUPPORT** Such is the support of the people who bring materials to the craftsmen, that Moses has to restrain them from bringing further offerings. When grace is present, generosity follows. **V 8–37: TASK STARTED** The task of building the tabernacle and its furnishings is started, as God has commanded. The tabernacle itself, its curtains, its frames, its crossbars, its veil and its screen for the door are all made from the provision of precious and specified materials by men who are obeying God's will.

CHAPTER THIRTY-SEVEN

V 1–39: GOLD FOR GLORY—THE OVERVIEW All the furniture in this chapter is overlaid with pure gold to speak of the glory of God. Everything here will be found in the holy place, except the ark of the covenant and the mercy seat upon it, which will be in the Most Holy Place. God emphasises this by overlaying everything with gold. **V 1–5: GOLD FOR GLORY—THE ARK** The ark of the Testimony or the 'ark of the covenant' is also to be inlaid with pure gold, as well as overlaid, providing a picture of the nature of the Lord Jesus Christ, who is God through and through. Its details are given. **V 6–9: GOLD FOR GLORY—THE MERCY SEAT** Details of the mercy seat, which was put as a covering over the ark, are given. Two cherubim of beaten gold overspread the mercy seat with their wings. **V 10–16: GOLD FOR GLORY—THE SHOWBREAD TABLE** Next, the table to be used for the showbread is to be made. Like the ark before it, it is made portable. All the utensils to be placed on the table are also overlaid with gold. **V 17–24: GOLD FOR GLORY—THE BRANCHING LAMPSTAND** A lamp stand is made from hammered gold with seven lamps, three branching from each side and one in the centre. The wick trimmers and trays are made of pure gold. **V 25–29: GOLD FOR GLORY—THE INCENSE BURNERS** The square altar of incense, also portable, is made. Holy anointing oil and pure incense of sweet spices are also made for it.

CHAPTER THIRTY-EIGHT

V 1–7: MATERIALS FOR MANUFACTURE—BRONZE FOR ALTAR A portable altar for burnt offerings, including all its utensils and grates, is made of bronze. **V 8: MATERIALS FOR MANUFACTURE—BRONZE FOR LAVER** The laver is made from the bronze mirrors of the serving women who assembled at the door of the tabernacle meeting. **V 9–20: MATERIALS FOR MANUFACTURE—BRONZE AND SILVER FOR SUPPORTS** The curtains are to hang from bronze sockets by silver hooks. The pillars, bands and capitols are overlaid with silver. The pegs for the tabernacle and for the courtyard are all made of bronze. **V 21–30: MATERIALS FOR MANUFACTURE— INVENTORY** The inventory of the bronze, silver and gold is given.

CHAPTER THIRTY-NINE

V 1–31: CLOTHING The items of the priests' clothing are described in detail. Each detail is spiritually significant for the priesthood of Christ, for the Christian individually, and for the priesthood of all believers. The ephod (verses 2 to 7), the breastplate (verses 8 to 21), the robe (verses 22 to 25), the tunics, turbans, short trousers and sashes are made. On the pure gold crown for the priest is written 'HOLINESS TO THE LORD', which is a summary of the whole of the tabernacle, its furniture, its furnishings and its priesthood. All worship of God should always reflect that theme. **V 32–41: COMPLETION** All the work is completed and brought to Moses. It is God-designed, God-commanded, God-aided, and God-honouring. **V 42–43: COMMAND** Moses approves all the work, which he inspects and recognises that it is done exactly in accordance with God's command. Moses pronounced a blessing upon his people.

CHAPTER FORTY

V 1–8: ACTION God tells Moses to put the parts together in the order He directs and to erect the tabernacle **V 9–16: ANOINTING** God tells Moses to anoint the tabernacle and everything in it, and to do the same to Aaron and his sons. They are to be washed with water before the holy garments are placed upon them. Moses obeys. **V 17–33: ARRANGEMENT** The tabernacle and its furnishings and furniture are arranged exactly as God commands Moses. Then we read, 'So Moses finished the work.' The Christian rejoices even more in the finished work of Christ, who tabernacled among us, and bore our sin and its punishment upon the cross. **V 34–38: AWESOME!** God's response is awesome. The cloud covers the tabernacle of the meeting which is filled with 'the glory of the LORD'. Even Moses, who alone has spoken to God on the mountain, cannot enter the tabernacle when the glory of the LORD fills it. Guidance for the Israelites now depends on where the cloud of the LORD is situated. This cloud, which turns to fire by night, dwells over the tabernacle when they are to remain in the same place and lifts when the children of Israel are to follow it.

LEVITICUS

OVERVIEW

PEOPLE AND PRELIMINARIES

Leviticus (twenty-three chapters) is the third of five books of the law (the 'Pentateuch'). It was written by Moses between 1445 and 1405 BC during the desert wanderings of the children of Israel before they entered the promised land.

PLAN AND PURPOSE

Leviticus teaches how to approach God through sacrifice, how to worship Him, and how to walk with Him as His people. It also teaches His people that God is always present with them. The emphasis of Leviticus is that, having been made right with God, we must walk with Him in full dedication, obedience and worship. In Exodus, God speaks from Mount Sinai to give His law. Now, in Leviticus, He speaks from the tabernacle, underlining His presence with His people, to teach them to be holy and to worship Him.

PROFILE AND PROGRESSION

Sacrifices to be made and the laws relating to them (1:1–7:38); consecration of the priesthood and the death of disobedient priests (8:1–10:20); God's attitude to and provision for uncleanness (11:1–15:33); atonement and sacrifice (16:1–17:16); practical and holy living for God's people (18:1–22:33); Jewish religious feasts (23:1–44); miscellaneous warnings and directions (24:1–27:34).

PRINCIPLES AND PARTICULARS

The significance of each of the five separate sacrifices and seven feasts. Contrast the awful simplicity of the sacrifice of Christ on the cross, which fulfilled all the requirements of the Old Testament sacrifices in one offering of Himself. The New Testament book of Hebrews is a commentary on much of the teaching in Leviticus on sacrifices and priesthood. God shows His strict requirement is for the holiness of His people. He demands that those worshipping and walking with Him must be clean. 'Holiness', or a word conveying the thought of being holy, occurs nearly eighty times. Tithing is also featured in Leviticus, as a reminder that the use of wealth should be consistent with the object of our worship, the glory of God.

LEVITICUS

Note: *Please see the chart on pages 68–69 headed 'Summary of Leviticus chapters 1 to 7: The five Old Testament offerings and the laws concerning them.' The first seven chapters of Leviticus will be understood better by referring to that chart.*

CHAPTER ONE

V 1–17: BRINGING THE OFFERINGS: THE BURNT OFFERING The worshipper is to bring a bull, ram or, if poor, a dove or pigeon, all without blemish, to be offered and fully consumed by the fire. For the offering's significance and fulfilment in Christ, see the chart on pages 68–69.

CHAPTER TWO

V 1–16: BRINGING THE OFFERINGS: THE GRAIN OFFERING Grain, flour (which could be made into cake or wafers), oil, frankincense and salt are to feature in the grain offering. No leaven or honey is to feature. It is offered along with the burnt offering or peace offering and a drink offering. For the offering's significance and fulfilment in Christ, see the chart.

CHAPTER THREE

V 1–17: BRINGING THE OFFERINGS: A PEACE OR FELLOWSHIP: OFFERING An unblemished lamb or goat must be brought. Unleavened cakes or wafers, which are anointed with oil, are offered alongside the lamb. For the offering's significance and fulfilment in Christ, see the chart.

CHAPTER FOUR

V 1–35: BRINGING THE OFFERINGS: THE SIN OFFERING The sin offering is dealt with in chapters 4 to 5:13. The offering to be made varies according to the person for whom the offering is to be made. Thus the offering is: a young bull for the priest and congregation, a male kid goat for a ruler, a female kid goat for the common people, two doves or two pigeons for the poor people, and a tenth of an ephah of fine flour for very poor people. For the offering's significance and fulfilment in Christ, see the chart.

CHAPTER FIVE

V 1–13: BRINGING THE OFFERINGS: THE SIN OFFERING Details of the sin offering dealt with are given in chapters 4 to 5:13. **V 14–19: BRINGING THE OFFERINGS: THE TRESPASS OR GUILT OFFERING** The details of the trespass (or guilt) offerings are found in chapters 5:14 to 6:7. A ram, without blemish, is to be offered, and restitution to the agreed person is to be made, plus the equivalent of a fine to one fifth of the value which is to accompany the sacrifice. For the offering's significance and fulfilment in Christ, see the chart.

CHAPTER SIX

V 1–7: BRINGING THE OFFERINGS: THE TRESPASS OR GUILT OFFERING Details of the trespass (or guilt) offering are dealt with in chapter 5:1–7. **V 8–30: BRINGING THE OFFERINGS: THE LAWS GOVERNING**

SUMMARY OF LEVITICUS CHAPTERS 1 TO 7: THE FIVE OLD TESTAMENT OFFERINGS

REFERENCE	OFFERING	COMPONENTS OF OFFERING
Leviticus 1, 6:8–13	Burnt	Bull, ram or (if poor) dove or pigeon. No blemishes. Fully consumed by fire.
Leviticus 2, 6:14–23	Grain	Grain, flour (cakes or wafers), oil, frankincense, salt; no honey or leaven. With Burnt, Peace and Drink Offerings.
Leviticus 3, 7:11–34	Peace (or Fellowship)	Lamb or goat. No blemishes. Oil-anointed unleavened cakes or wafers.
Leviticus 4:1–5:13; 6:24–30	Sin	Differs according to person sinning. Young bull (priest and congregation); male kid goat (ruler); female kid goat (common people); two doves or two pigeons (poor people); tenth of ephah of fine flour (very poor people).
Leviticus 5:14–6:7; 7:1–6	Trespass (or Guilt)	Ram without blemish. Restitution and effectively a fine of one fifth to accompany sacrifice.

NOTES

1. All the details of the sacrifices, and how they are to be observed, are significant and important and point to Christ and the gospel.

2. There is overlap between some of the sacrifices, but all are combined and fulfilled in Christ's sacrifice on the cross for us.

AND THE LAWS CONCERNING THEM

SIGNIFICANCE OF OFFERING	FULFILMENT IN CHRIST
Voluntary worship. Atoned for unintended sin. Devotion and surrender to God.	Sinless Saviour. Atonement. Jesus gave Himself fully.
Sweet aroma. Voluntary worship. Marks God's goodness. Total dedication. No pride. Salt speaks of God's covenant.	Fragrance of Jesus' life. Total doing of will of God. New covenant in Christ.
Peace, fellowship and reconciliation. Voluntary. Thankfulness. Communal worship with others.	Reconciled by Him. Peace with God. Peace of God. Fellowship with God/others.
Propitiation. Atonement commanded for unintended sin. Confession of sins. Pardon. Purification from sin's defiling effects.	Christ died as our substitute. When confession and faith, even our 'unintended' sins covered by His propitiatory death. All may approach Him for forgiveness.
Repentance—needing sacrifice and shown by restitution and payment of fine to person wronged.	Repentance and faith through Christ. He paid our 'fines' and changes our lives.

3. Recurring principles demonstrated are: our sinfulness, need to approach God and be accepted, need for holiness, perfection of the sacrifice, acceptance of sacrifice in our place, repentance, faith, obedience, thankfulness and consecration.

4. Chapters 1–6:7 cover the five Old Testament offerings. Chapters 6:8–7 cover the laws about their observance.

THE OFFERINGS The laws governing the offerings are given in chapter 6. Verses 8 to 13 cover the burnt offering, verses 14 to 23 cover the grain offering, and verses 24 to 30 cover the sin offering.

CHAPTER SEVEN

V 1–10: BRINGING THE OFFERINGS: THE LAWS GOVERNING THE TRESPASS OFFERINGS The laws are detailed about the 'most holy' trespass offering. **V 11–21: BRINGING THE OFFERINGS: THE LAWS COVERING THE PEACE OFFERINGS** The laws are detailed about the peace offering. **V 22–27: BRINGING THE OFFERINGS: THE FAT AND THE BLOOD** Neither the fat nor the blood (which speaks of the life of the animal or bird) must be eaten. Anyone transgressing those rules will be cut off. **V 28–36: BRINGING THE OFFERINGS: AARON AND THE PRIESTS** A summary follows of the portions of the sacrifices that are to be given to Aaron and his sons, the priests. **V 37–38: BRINGING THE OFFERINGS: A SUMMARY** Here is a very brief summary of what has gone before in the previous seven chapters.

CHAPTER EIGHT

V 1–5: CONGREGATION God commands Moses to take Aaron and his sons, with appropriate garments, oils and offerings, to meet the congregation at the door of the tabernacle. Moses tells the congregation about God's command. **V 6: CLEANSING** The priests are then washed with water. Cleansing must precede both communion with God and service for Him. **V 7–9: CLOTHING** The priests are then clothed with the special clothing and accessories that have been made for this purpose. **V 10–30: CONSECRATION** Both the altar and the priests are consecrated by the sprinkling of oil and of blood of the sacrifice. After the burnt offering is made, the ram of consecration is killed. The blood is then applied to the right ear, the thumb of the right hand, and the big toe of the right foot of Aaron and of each of the priests. This signifies cleansing for all they have heard and sensed, all they have done, and for everywhere that their feet have taken them. A wave offering follows. Then the priests are anointed again with the blood and oil by sprinkling. All this signifies the consecration of the priests. **V 31–32: CONSUMPTION** The priests then consume their food from the allocation taken from the bread and the flesh which has been used in the sacrifices. **V 33–36: CONFINEMENT** The priests are to remain consecrated in the tabernacle for seven days, and not to move from there. If they leave the tabernacle, they will die. Aaron and his sons obey God's command.

CHAPTER NINE

V 1–7: PRACTICE The priests under Aaron are now commanded by Moses to put into practice the offering system according to the laws of the offerings which have been recorded in Leviticus chapters 1 to 7. **V 8–14: PRIESTS** The priests lead the way, being the first to partake in the offerings, and thus show obedience to God and an example to the people. **V 15–22: PEOPLE** Aaron then offers the sacrifices on behalf of the people and concludes by blessing them after he has offered the sin offering, burnt offering, and peace offerings. **V 23–24: PRESENCE** After this first celebration of the sacrifices, Moses and Aaron leave the tabernacle and bless the people. God's glory appears to all the people, and fire comes from the LORD to consume the burnt offering and the fat on the altar. The people shout and fall on their faces.

CHAPTER TEN

V 1: CONTRAVENTION Despite all the clear instruction about how the sacrifices should be given and the need to keep holy and obedient to the LORD, Nadab and Abihu, Aaron's sons and priests, put fire in their censers, and place the holy incense on it to offer profane fire before the LORD. God had not commanded this. **V 2–5: CONSUMED** They are consumed by fire from the LORD, which kills them. Moses reminds Aaron of the need to be holy, and Aaron keeps silent. The remains are removed under Moses' supervision. **V 6–7: CAREFUL** Moses tells Aaron and his two remaining sons who are priests, Eleazar and Ithamar, not to show any signs of mourning, lest God's wrath comes upon all the people as well as killing them. Israel must bewail God's judgement and they must stay in the tabernacle because the anointing oil of the LORD is upon them. They obey what Moses says. **V 8–11: CONDUCT** Moses underlines the need for holiness in the priesthood, in this case specifying that neither wine nor intoxicating drink must be taken when going into the tabernacle. There must be a clear distinction between holy and unholy, clean and unclean, and this must be taught to the Israelites. **V 12–15: CARE** Moses gives instruction to the three priests about the care to be taken in dealing with the remains of the offerings, and eating that which has been allocated to them. He is taking the solemn occasion of the death of the eldest two sons of Aaron, to emphasise the importance of holiness and consecration for those who lead the people, so that their example will be followed. **V 16–18: CONFRONTATION** Moses confronts Eleazar and Ithamar and carefully enquires why they have not followed the instructions regarding the goat sin offering. It had been burnt up rather than used to sprinkle its blood in the holy place. It should have been eaten in the holy place. **V 19–20: CONSIDERATION** Aaron takes responsibility and tells Moses, in effect, that he did not think he would be accepted in eating the sin offering because of how he felt after the death of his two sons. Although individual feelings should not prevent obedience, Moses shows consideration for the reason given, and is content.

CHAPTER ELEVEN

V 1–2: STIPULATION God stipulates to Moses and Aaron which animals are regarded as clean and therefore may be safely eaten. **V 3–44: SUBSTANCE** Having stipulated that the clean animals are those that are easily observable as having cloven hooves and are seen to be chewing the cud, the substance of the unclean animals and birds is given. This includes animals not included in the clean animal description, water creatures other than fish with fins and scales, various birds (mainly those which feed on carrion or are hawk-like), bats, most winged insects, carcasses, and various reptiles, snakes and 'creepy crawlies'. All these will defile. Instruction is also given about washing clothes and being unclean until evening. **V 45–47: SUMMARY** God summarises the situation by reminding them He is the holy God who brought His people from captivity in Egypt. These laws are given to remind them of the distinction between the clean and the unclean and the animals which may and may not be eaten. The spin-off will be better health and diet than if they indulge in eating the unclean animals, birds, water creatures, reptiles and insects.

CHAPTER TWELVE

V 1–5: PURIFICATION SATISFIED After the birth of a child, the woman is to be regarded as unclean until the days of her purification. That purification is thirty-three days after giving birth to a boy, and sixty-six days after giving birth to a girl. No reason is given for the difference, but it could reflect Eve's part in the fall, which is now redressed by faith in Christ where there is neither 'male nor female'. **V 6–7: PRESCRIBED SACRIFICE** The sacrifices that the priests are to bring as the burnt and sin offerings are stipulated, so that atonement might be made for the woman. She shall be regarded as clean from the flow of blood. **V 8: POOR STATUS** A woman who is too poor to bring a lamb must bring two turtle doves or two pigeons as a burnt offering and sin offering respectively. She will be regarded as atoned for and clean. Lack of material prosperity is never a reason for someone to stay away from God's atonement and cleansing.

CHAPTER THIRTEEN

V 1–2: COMMUNICATION God speaks to Moses and Aaron in order that they may determine what constitutes cleanness or uncleanness ceremonially, and when skin disease is regarded as infectious and serious. **V 3–44: CONTAMINATION** Great detail on medical examination is given in order to determine what is unclean and what is clean, and also whether something previously unclean is cured or not cured. The priest is to perform the examination, and so it is important that Moses passes on to him the detailed criteria for examination that we find in this passage. **V 45–46: CRY** The leper is regarded as unclean and so must cry, 'Unclean! Unclean!' All the time that he is unclean,

he must dwell alone outside the camp. In the Bible, leprosy is sometimes used as a picture of sin, and it is good to know that Jesus, who touched and healed the lepers, can cleanse us from the leprosy of our sin so that we are not 'outside the camp' but rather, 'within His fold'. **V 47–59: CLOTHING** The law concerning clothing which is contaminated by leprosy is given, along with the procedure whereby it may be regarded as clean.

CHAPTER FOURTEEN

V 1–32: LEPROSY: CLEANSING OF PEOPLE This passage deals with lepers who are brought to the priest on the day of their cleansing. It explains the cleansing ceremonies to confirm that people are healed, and deals with sacrifices and ceremonial washings. It also deals with the consecration of the cleansed person's body. The extremities of the right ear, the right thumb, and the right big toe, respectively, symbolise their senses, their actions and where they go. These extremities and the head are to be anointed first with blood and then with oil. This symbolises cleansing through the shed blood of Christ and the renewing anointing of the Holy Spirit, both of which touch every area of our life and activity, and the very thoughts we think. **V 33–53: LEPROSY: CLEANSING OF PROPERTY** Property that has been rendered unclean by the leprosy of infectious growths, such as fungus or mould, also has to be cleansed ceremonially after decontamination, by the priest. Sacrifices and the ceremony required after the priest's examination are specified. **V 54–57: LEPROSY: CONFIRMATION OF POSITION** The previous chapter is summarised as dealing with the leprosy issues, the main principle being the teaching of what is clean and unclean. There are spiritual lessons and principles for us today.

CHAPTER FIFTEEN

V 1–30: BODILY DISCHARGES Bodily discharges render contact with people or objects ceremonially unclean. The chapter deals with how that uncleanness is to be ceremonially purged. It deals with men (in verses 1 to 18) and with women (in verses 19 to 30). **V 31–33: BANISH DEFILEMENT** The summary of the chapter again points out the need to distinguish cleanness from uncleanness. Defilement must be banished from God's tabernacle. Those who refuse to be cleansed will die. We should be cleansed not ceremonially, but from all our sin, when we seek to worship God and live for Him day by day.

CHAPTER SIXTEEN

V 1–2: AUTHORISED ACCESS God tells Moses to tell Aaron that, on pain of death, he cannot come just whenever he pleases to the Most Holy Place. God will appear in the cloud above the mercy seat. God's execution of Aaron's two profane sons has provided the occasion for Moses and Aaron to be reminded. **V 3–25: AARON'S APPROACH** The Day of Atonement is covered by the regulations declaring how Aaron, the high priest, is to approach God in the Holy of holies. Meticulous cleansing and obedience to the detail of the sacrifice is required, as is Aaron's personal cleansing and clothing, for this annual atonement for Israel as a nation and for each of its people individually. This atonement will cover all sins that other sacrifices could not have covered. Only the high priest may enter the Most Holy Place, with the shedding of blood. The sin offering is to be made on this occasion, and the scapegoat to be released, signifying the liberty that comes for those who confess their sins and come through the shed blood of Christ, in repentance and faith, to God. **V 26–28: ACCEPTANCE AFTER** After the sin offerings have been completely burnt in the fire outside the camp, the one burning them will wash his clothes and bathe his body in water so that he can be accepted and come back inside the camp. The same principle applies to the person who releases the scapegoat. Any contamination by sin should be dealt with immediately by seeking God's cleansing. This is available to us now through Christ crucified, our sin offering, and the risen Christ, our divine scapegoat. **V 29–34: ANNUAL ATONEMENT** The annual atonement is to be on the tenth day of the seventh month of the year, which Hebrew month was Tishri, corresponding to September/October in our calendar. This is to be taken very seriously and reverently with affliction of souls, meaning soul-searching and true repentance. Aaron obeys God's command through Moses to institute this most important of all occasions in Israel's calendar.

CHAPTER SEVENTEEN

V 1–5: PLACE The only place where God will accept sacrifice is in the tabernacle, on pain of the offender being cut off from His people. **V 6–7: PRIEST** The priest alone must present the sacrifice to prevent sacrifices to demons associated with the pagan nations. **V 8–9: PUNISHMENT** Anyone, Israelite or stranger, not following God's commands on this matter, will be cut off. **V 10–14: PROHIBITIONS** Because the life of the flesh is in the blood, and because it is the blood of the sacrifice that makes atonement, no one must consume the blood, again on pain of being cut off. **V 15–16: PURIFICATION** Anyone who eats flesh from an animal that dies naturally, or that is torn by other animals, needs to wash his clothes and bathe in water and be unclean until evening.

CHAPTER EIGHTEEN

V 1–5: SEPARATION PRINCIPLE God tells Moses to tell the Israelites to remember that 'I am the LORD your God.' They have to be separate from all the doings of the Egyptians and the Canaanites. Instead, they must obey God and walk with Him. **V 6–20: SEXUAL PURITY** The separate life and walk of God's people includes high morality and absolute integrity in sexual behaviour. **V 21: SACRIFICE PROHIBITED** Child-sacrifice, which is practised by the pagan nations and profanes God's name, is specifically forbidden. **V 22–23: SEXUAL PERVERSIONS** Sexual perversions are forbidden because they are abominations to God. This includes homosexuality and bestiality. The only sexual relationship having God's blessing and sanction is between a man and his wife. **V 24–25: SINFULNESS PUNISHED** God is punishing and driving out the pagan nations because of their defiling and sinful practices. He is giving their land to the Israelites, who must not fall into the same wicked ways. **V 26–30: STATUTES PRESCRIBED** God has given His laws to keep His people from the abominable customs of the surrounding pagan nations so that they are not defiled. He reminds them again that 'I am the LORD your God'; this is always a reason for living a holy life which is separate and different from those who do not know Him.

CHAPTER NINETEEN

V 1–2: MOTIVATION All the congregation of the Israelites are to be motivated by holiness, because God is holy. That is what He requires. **V 3–36: MISCELLANEOUS** God's holiness is not only the basis of the moral law of the Ten Commandments, but is also the reason why the principles of righteousness are embodied in the laws of the civil and criminal codes of His earthly people, the Israelites. Some of those individual laws are a repeat of some of the Ten Commandments. Accordingly, there follows a collection of miscellaneous laws covering a number of subjects, including honouring parents, Sabbath-keeping, idolatry, keeping sacrifices, generosity to the poor, false dealings or words, swearing, dealing with disadvantaged people, justice, hatred, vengeance, obedience, separation, sexual faithfulness, pagan practices, prostitution, showing reverence, rejecting spiritism, honouring the aged and strangers, and commercial integrity. In keeping these laws, the people are to remember that they belong to the LORD their God who brought them out of Egypt. They have left one pagan nation and must not repeat or copy paganism in their lifestyles now. **V 37: MANDATORY** Again God insists that they must 'observe all His statutes and judgements' and do them because He is the LORD.

CHAPTER TWENTY

V 1–21: DEATH PENALTIES The Israelite law, commanded by God for His people and strangers dwelling with them, carries death penalties for a number of offences, including: child sacrifice (Molech was an Ammonite god connected with that), spiritist practices, cursing parents, adultery, incest of all kinds, homosexual relations, and bestiality. Whether this practice is as a deterrent, or simply the putting away of something that will cause others to stumble, or both, is open to discussion; whatever it is, God commands the death penalty for these offences from His people, Israel, in their national legal system. **V 22–24: DIFFERENT PEOPLE** The Israelites are to be a different people, obeying God rather than following the wickedness of the surrounding nations, and remaining conscious that they belong to the LORD who has separated them to himself. Great blessings are in store for them. **V 25–27: DISTINCTIVE PRACTICES** Their separation is to be shown by distinctive practices, centring on being clean for God and avoiding all kinds of abomination, in order to be His separated people. Again, God emphasises the need to deal severely with those who practice spiritism.

CHAPTER TWENTY-ONE

V 1–4: DEFILEMENT FOR DEAD Apart from necessarily needing to deal with close relatives who have died, the priests must not defile themselves by touching dead people. **V 5–9: SANCTIFICATION FOR SOVEREIGN** The priests are to be sanctified for the Sovereign God whom they serve. This is to be reflected in the way they wear their beards and do not cut their flesh, in distinct difference from the pagan nations. Similarly, they are to be known for the holy way in which they offer sacrifices, for their choice of wives, and for the effect of holiness in their children. God is holy and they are to be holy. **V 10–15: CONSECRATION FOR CONDUCT** A priest, who is consecrated by anointing oil and is wearing priestly garments, must reflect that consecration in his conduct. He must not touch the dead, leave the sanctuary while the anointing oil in upon him, take a wife who is not a virgin, or allow his posterity to be

profaned. **V 16–23: DEFECTS FOR DISQUALIFICATIONS** The priest, in serving the altar of God, must be a man without physical defects. This reminds us that Jesus Christ was completely without moral and spiritual defect as our Holy Priest. **V 24: EXPLANATION FOR EVERYONE** As God has commanded all this to Moses, so he tells it to Aaron and his sons, the priests, and to all the Israelites. Here is an explanation that everyone must understand.

CHAPTER TWENTY-TWO

V 1–2: REVERENCE Aaron and his sons must be very reverent as priests. Moses is told to tell Aaron and his sons to reverently respect the holy things of the children of Israel, in order not to profane God's holy name by what is dedicated to Him. The centre of that reverence is that 'I am the LORD'. **V 3: RETRIBUTION** God will cut off anyone throughout their generations who approaches His holy things while unclean. **V 4–8: REFUSAL** Any descendant of Aaron who is a leper, or who has a discharge, or who is made unclean, must refuse to approach the holy offerings to eat them, unless and until he has been washed in water and declared clean. Cleansing is needed for contamination from contact with animals which have died naturally or which have been killed by other animals. **V 9: REQUIREMENT** God, who is holy and who hates profanity, sanctifies them and requires them to keep His ordinances. **V 10–13: RESTRICTION** Only the priest's family, or those treated as such if bought as slaves, can eat the holy offering with the priest. **V 14–16: RESTITUTION** If a man eats the holy offerings unintentionally, he must make generous restitution for it to the priest. **V 17–25: REJECTION** Any offering which is not perfect and spotless and following God's requirements is to be rejected. This again reminds us of the perfect offering of the Lord Jesus Christ when He gave himself on the cross for us. **V 26–30: REGULATIONS** Regulations are given about the age of an animal to be sacrificed, the need to sacrifice willingly, and the requirement to eat it on the same day and leave none of it until the next day. **V 31–32: REMINDERS** The chapter ends by God's reminder to His people to keep and do His commandments, that He is the LORD, that His holy name must be hallowed and not profaned, that He sanctifies His people, and that He brought them from Egypt to be their God.

CHAPTER TWENTY-THREE

V 1–2: SPEECH COMMANDED God commands Moses to speak to the Israelites about the feasts of the LORD which are to be holy convocations (a gathering together of the people) and God's feasts. **V 3: SABBATH CONSECRATED** Yet again, the moral principle of working for six days and resting from work on the seventh day in order to worship God is emphasised first, as one of the Ten Commandments. It comes with a reminder that it is 'the Sabbath of the LORD in all your dwellings'. **V 4–44: SPECIAL CONVOCATIONS** After dealing with the rest given by the Sabbath in verse 3, the remaining convocations and feasts deal with other aspects that God would bring to the mind and attention of His people: **V 4–8: REMINDER** of Passover and Feast of Unleavened Bread; **V 9–14: RECOGNITION** of God's goodness in the Firstfruits; **V 15–21: REJOICING** at God's blessing in Pentecost, also known as the Feast of Weeks, or Feast of Harvest; **V 22: REAPING** in such a way that some provision is generously left for other people; **V 23–25: REFRAIN** from customary work to make offerings to the LORD at the Feast of Trumpets; **V 26–32: RECONCILIATION** by Christ's atoning sacrifice foreshadowed in the Day of Atonement; **V 33–43: REMEMBER** how God brought His people out of Egypt in the Feast of Tabernacles; **V 44: RELAYING** by Moses of all these instructions for the Israelites to follow.

CHAPTER TWENTY-FOUR

V 1–4: BURNING Pure pressed olive oil for the light must be brought so that the lamps can burn continually for the tabernacle. This is to be outside the veil dividing the holy place from the Most Holy Place and has to be tended by Aaron continually. **V 5–9: BREAD** Requirements regarding the bread of the tabernacle are given. This has to be set in order every Sabbath, and is to be regarded as holy. **V 10–23: BLASPHEMY** Penalties are laid down for various sins, starting with death for blasphemy. At God's command, a blasphemer is stoned by the congregation. This sin, taken so lightly today, is regarded as very grave by God. Other sins dealt with include murder, killing an animal, and wounding causing disfigurement to the victim. The law has to be equitably applied to both strangers and Israelites.

CHAPTER TWENTY-FIVE

V 1–7: SPECIAL SABBATH Every seventh year is to be a special sabbath year. The land shall be at rest, and neither sowing nor reaping must occur and nor should any attention be given to what is grown. Any produce that comes from that year, however, shall be for the people, the strangers with them, and their animals. **V 8–22: JUBILEE JOY** Every fiftieth year (after seven lots of seven sabbath years), the year of Jubilee shall be proclaimed. It will start on the Day of Atonement, and liberty will be proclaimed to all inhabitants. It will be conducted in the same way as the seventh year sabbath, from the point of view of work on the land. Each person will return to his possession. There will be no oppression, prices will be regulated with fairness, and God is to be remembered. God promises that if His Jubilee year will be kept, He will produce enough in the preceding years to last for three years, so sowing can take place in the eighth year while produce is devoured from previous years until the ninth year. In other words, God will provide for those who honour His command by keeping the Jubilee year. **V 23–34: PROPERTY PROVISIONS** Provisions for the redemption of property are given. Again, there is a just regulation of prices based on the year of Jubilee. **V 35–38: COMPASSIONATE CARE** Poor people are to receive loans without any usury or interest applied to them. No one must profit from the poverty of others, and God reminds them that He is the one who brought the Israelites from Egypt to Canaan to be their God. **V 39–55: SLAVERY SOFTENED** Israelites must not compel slavery of their own brethren, but they may only serve one another as hired servants who will be released on the year of Jubilee. The buying of slaves from other nations was permitted at this time and regulated, but Israelites could not have their brethren as slaves. Provision is given as to how the children of Israel may redeem their own countrymen. All this is done with the reminder that they were in a terrible position in Egypt when God brought them out to be His servants.

CHAPTER TWENTY-SIX

V 1–13: PEACE, PROSPERITY AND POWER God's promise of blessing is preceded by the reminder that His people must not be idolaters, make images, or bow down to them, because He is their LORD and God. He reminds them that they must keep His Sabbaths and reverence His sanctuary. He then outlines all the blessings that He has for His people who walk with Him. Peace, prosperity and power are theirs through a faithful and obedient trust in and walk with God, who has delivered and liberated His people. **V 14–39: PUNISHMENT, POVERTY AND PERISHING** If they disobey God and repeatedly refuse to repent, God will act in punishment towards them, bringing them poverty and causing them to perish as a nation. **V 40–45: PENITENCE, PARDON AND PROMISE** These verses tell the Israelites how they can come back to God when they have strayed from Him. This involves confession, humility, honesty and a desire to come back to Him on the basis of His faithfulness and covenant. **V 46: PRINCIPLES, PRIORITIES AND PRACTICES** These principles, priorities and practices are all from God and are in 'His statutes and judgements and laws' which He makes for His people through Moses.

CHAPTER TWENTY-SEVEN

V 1–8: PROMISED PEOPLE This chapter deals with a situation where Israelites have made a vow to God which, without diminishing their love for Him, they now want to reverse. It tells how they can redeem what they have offered, and starts with the price to buy back people offered for the service of God. **V 9–25: PROMISED PROPERTY** The same principle applies to property that has been offered, be it animals (verses 9 to 13), houses (verses 14 to 15), family land (verses 16 to 21), or fields (verses 22 to 25). **V 26–29: PARTICULAR PROHIBITIONS** There are prohibitions which cover things that cannot be bought back. This includes the firstborn of animals (which have already been offered), devoted offerings or persons, or animals which are to be put to death for judicial reasons. Unclean animals may be redeemed by adding a surcharge of twenty per cent to the valuation. **V 30–33: PERTINENT**

PRINCIPLE There is a principle that man must pay God his tithes. Thus if a tithe is to be redeemed, it is to carry a surcharge of twenty per cent, and the herd or the flock is to be tithed to the extent that one animal in ten is to be given to God. **V 34: POINTED PRIORITY** The priority of what has gone before in the book of Leviticus is underlined by the final reminder that they are 'the commandments which the LORD commanded Moses for the children of Israel on Mount Sinai'.

NUMBERS

OVERVIEW

PEOPLE AND PRELIMINARIES

✱Numbers (thirty-six chapters) is the fourth of five books of the law (the 'Pentateuch'). It was written by Moses between 1445 and 1405 BC during the Israelites' desert wanderings and before they entered the promised land.

PLAN AND PURPOSE

(i) Numbers is so called because it records the numbering of the children of Israel and their organisation and tasks by tribes. Carrying on from Exodus, it relates the Israelites' wanderings in the desert after they fail to enter the promised land through unbelief. It deals with their daily walk with God, teaching the need to obey and serve Him. Sinfulness, failures, murmurings, jealousy and unbelief characterise God's wandering people in the wilderness. It has spiritual parallels for Christians today. Nevertheless, God's holy and enduring presence and guiding help are always at

hand. Numbers is an excellent encouragement and challenge for anyone today who is conscious of failure and the need for God in his or her life.

PROFILE AND PROGRESSION

Israel's first census and organisation by tribes around the tabernacle (1:1–10:10); Complaining en route from Sinai to Kadesh Barnea (10:11–12:16); Rebellions and their results and continued complaining (13:1–22:1); Balaam's unwilling blessings of Israel (22:2–24:25); Further rebellion (25:1–18); Israel's second census, revived obedience and preparing to conquer the promised land (26:1–32:42); Retrospect on the desert wanderings (33:1–49); The promise of the promised land (33:50–36:13).

PRINCIPLES AND PARTICULARS

☛ We see here how Israel is organised in its service for God, and how the work of God is carefully and appropriately shared. The murmurings and rebellions of the people against their leadership and against God result in sad and far-reaching consequences. Renewed obedience of God's people lead to their being prepared for the promised land. The review of the wilderness journey is instructive.

NUMBERS

CHAPTER ONE

V 1: DESERT Israel's thirty-nine year pilgrimage to the border of Canaan, the promised land, begins in the Sinai desert. Numbers begins with God speaking to Moses with instructions about how he should lead the Israelites. **V 2–19: DETAILS** The details of all the males of over twenty years, and able to go to war, are to be taken. They are to be numbered by their armies in the presence of the leader of each tribe. **V 20–46: DESCENDANTS** The numbers of the descendants of the sons of Israel who are fighting men are given. The total number is 603,550. These are composed of the descendants of the following named tribes: Reuben—46,500; Simeon—59,300; Gad—46,650; Judah—74,600; Issachar—54,400; Zebulun—57,400; Ephraim—40,500; Manasseh—32,200; Benjamin—35,400; Dan—62,700; Asher—41,500; Naphtali—53,400. Estimates are that the total population of Israel, including the 603,550 fighting men detailed above, is around two-and-a-half million people. **V 47–53: DIFFERENT** The Levites are not numbered because of their special duties in the tabernacle and in leading the worship of the people. They are to keep charge of the tabernacle and of the ark of Testimony. **V 54: DOING** At this early stage in Israel's history, the people do all that God commanded Moses.

CHAPTER TWO

V 1–2: THE TABERNACLE God tells Moses and Aaron that the tribes of Israel must camp some distance from the tabernacle, which is central in the placement. Each tribe is to be by its own standard (the insignia of the tribe on the flag) beside the emblems of their fathers' houses. **V 3–34: THE TRIBES** The tribes are to camp in four groups of three on the north, south, east, and west of the tabernacle, with Levi being in the centre with the tabernacle. It is also to be their marching order. The numbers of available soldiers involved, with Levites excluded, are: 186,400 from Judah, Issachar and Zebulun are to be on the east; 151,450 from Reuben, Simeon and Gad are to be on the south; 108,100 from Ephraim, Manasseh and Benjamin are to be on the west; and 157,600 troops from Dan, Asher and Naphtali are to be on the north.

CHAPTER THREE

V 1: RECORDS The records in chapter 3 are those of Aaron and Moses and show the Levites involved in worship. **V 2–4: REQUIREMENT** Holiness is God's requirement, and the solemn reminder is given that Nadab and Abihu were smitten because they offered profane fire before God. The current priests are Aaron and his sons Eleazar and Ithamar. **V 5–10: RESPONSIBILITIES** The Levites are solely and solemnly responsible for all aspects of the tabernacle worship. **V 11–13: RIGHT** God has taken the Levites to Himself as His specific right of ownership. They are substituted for the firstborn of the children of Israel whom He sanctified for Himself when He struck all the firstborn in Egypt. Thus, by substitution, the Levites belong specifically and specially to God. **V 13–38: REPRESENTATIVES** Levi is represented by his three sons and their descendants, namely, Gershon, Kohath and Merari, who report to Eleazar. Their details and numbers are given and their tasks are designated. Gershon, numbering 7,500 males, looks after the coverings of the tabernacle and camps on the west. Kohath numbers 8,600 males and is responsible for the holy things in the tabernacle and for carrying the ark. Their camp is on the south of the tabernacle. Merari numbers 6,200 males and has responsibility for the wooden framework of the tabernacle. They are to camp on the north of the tabernacle. Moses, Aaoron, Eleazar and Ithamar control the activities from their camp on the east of the tabernacle. **V 40–51: REDEMPTION** The 22,273 firstborn are redeemed because God chooses the Levites as His firstborn. This leaves a shortfall of 273 Levites for which five shekels per person is to be paid as further redemption. The redemption money is given to Aaron and his sons.

CHAPTER FOUR

V 1–20: CARE IN CARRYING The Kohathites are part of the tribe of Levi. A census is to be taken of their males between thirty and fifty years old who work in the tabernacle. Their main task is to show great care in carrying the holy things and tabernacle furnishings. First, Aaron and his sons must ensure that these sanctified items are adequately covered, in accordance with God's given instructions. The Kohathites are not to touch these things in case they die. God is a holy God and any work done for Him in His name has to be done with holiness in mind. **V 21–28: CARRYING THE CURTAINS** Another family of the tribe of Levi, the Gershonites, also are to have a census. Their task, under Ithamar's supervision,

is to carry the curtains and the coverings used in the tabernacle. **V 29–33: CARRYING THE CONSTRUCTION** Also undergoing a census is the third family in the tribe of Levi, the Merarites. Their task, again under Ithamar, is to carry the construction of crossbars and frames for the tabernacle. **V 34–49: COUNTING THE CONSECRATED** The consecrated families in Levi's tribe, dedicated to the service of the tabernacle, are counted as a result of each census taken. The total of thirty to fifty year olds in the LORD's service is 8,580 comprised of the Kohathites (2,750), the Gershonites (2,630), and the Merarites (3,200).

CHAPTER FIVE

V 1–4: SEPARATION Persons declared unclean, in accordance with the laws given, are to be put outside the camp. The children of Israel obey God's command. **V 5–10: REPARATION** Anyone committing a sin that harms other people must make reparation in full, plus one fifth of its value. Where the sin has resulted in the death of the person harmed, and there is no surviving relative of that person, the restitution must go to the LORD for the priest, with an atonement offering of a ram. Holy things offered are to be for the priest. **V 11–31: PREPARATION** The sanctity of marriage is underlined here as well as the importance of marital faithfulness. In this portion, a procedure is given for establishing the guilt or innocence of a wife suspected of adultery, where neither witnesses nor evidence is available. To protect marriage, and because there are no witnesses, God instigates a miraculous and unique procedure, outside the normal legal process, to establish guilt or innocence of those secret sins. He underlines at the beginning of Israel's history the importance of marital faithfulness. The nature of the test itself will be a deterrent to much of this kind of sin.

CHAPTER SIX

V 1–4: AVOIDANCE OF ALCOHOL A Nazirite is a person separated to God and His service by taking a vow for a period of time. For the duration of the vow, the Nazirite must have nothing to do with anything associated with the vine. This not only excludes any contact with wine itself, but also grapes, raisins and grape juice. In effect, God gives him a safety margin so that there is no possibility of wine being drunk by him. While the issue of drinking of alcohol is a personal matter, some Christians mark their service to the Lord by abstinence, giving them that safety margin to safeguard their holiness. This may be very wise individually, but it does not constitute a law for others to obey. **V 5–8: HAIR AND HOLINESS** The Nazirite was not to shave his head all the days of the vow of his separation. Neither must he touch a dead body during this set period in which he is regarded as holy to the LORD. **V 9–12: DEFILEMENT BY DEATH** If a sudden death causes a Nazarite to be in contact with a dead body, his head is to be shaved, and sacrifices must be made. His head is to be re-sanctified and he is to be re-consecrated from that day on. This is a wonderful picture of a Christian who should not sin but who, having sinned, confesses and forsakes it, knowing that God has cleansed him. He can move on again from there as one newly set apart for God. **V 13–21: SEPARATION AND SACRIFICE** When the days of the Nazirite's separation are ended, he is to shave his head and burn his hair on the fire under the sacrifice of a peace offering. A wave offering is to be made by the priest.

Only after that is the Nazirite free to drink wine, if he so chooses. **V 22–27: PRONOUNCEMENT OF PEACE** The LORD tells Moses to instruct Aaron and the priesthood how to pray for blessing for the children of Israel:

'The Lord bless you and keep you;
The Lord make His face shine upon you
And be gracious to you;
The Lord lift up His countenance
　　upon you
And give you peace.'

This is a wonderful prayer for anyone to pray for others! God promises in answer to this prayer that He will identify Himself with, and bless, His people.

CHAPTER SEVEN

V 1: INSTIGATION The instigation of worship in the finished tabernacle is marked by anointing and consecrating the tabernacle, its furnishings, its altar and its utensils. **V 2–9: INDICATION** Covered carts are given to the Gershonites and the Merarites to perform their duties of carrying tabernacle items. However the Kohathites are not given a cart because they must carry the holy things committed to them—including the ark of the covenant—on their shoulders. This early inherent emphasis that the ark must not be put on a cart will become highly significant in the later history of the Israelites. **V 10–11: INSTRUCTION** The leaders are also instructed to bring offerings of dedication. They obey. **V 12–88: IDENTIFICATION** The children of Israel are identified with God through the combined offering which He has commanded. They are identified with one another in that, on successive days, each of the twelve tribes brings exactly the same offering of various specified items on behalf of the tribe concerned. To emphasise the importance of each tribe's individual participation, the narrative is repeated twelve times with the only variant being the name of the tribe concerned. The order of offering by the four sets of three tribes is the same order as when Israel will move out from the camp. Judah's group on the east side of the tabernacle is followed by the groups led by Reuben, Ephraim and Dan, respectively on the south, west and north of the tabernacle. **V 89: INSPIRATION** God's voice speaks to Moses as he goes into the tabernacle of meeting. The voice comes from above the mercy seat on the ark of the Testimony and from between the two cherubim. God Himself speaks to Moses. We are not told, however, that Moses went into the Most Holy Place, but only that he went into the tabernacle, and that God spoke from the Most Holy Place.

CHAPTER EIGHT

V 1–4: SEVEN LAMPS The seven lamps of the hammered gold lampstand are now lit as part of the dedication. **V 5–14: SANCTIFIED LEVITES** God tells Moses how to sanctify the Levites. They are ceremonially cleansed by the sprinkling of water of purification, shaving their bodies, and washing their clothes. Then appropriate offerings are made and they are to be brought into the tabernacle before the congregation. The children of Israel are to identify with the Levites by the laying on of their hands, and Aaron is then to offer them as a wave offering before the LORD. Sin offerings are to be made like a wave offering to the LORD, by Aaron and his sons. The Levites are to be God's special possession. **V 15–19: SUBSTITUTED LEVITES** God has already substituted the Levites for the firstborn among the children of Israel. God gives the Levites as His special possession to

Aaron and the priests for the work of the tabernacle to make sure that that work is maintained clean, holy and pure, thereby avoiding a plague. **V 20–22: SEPARATED LEVITES** The Levites are separated from the congregation to do the work of God in the tabernacle before Aaron and his sons, the priests. God's commands are carried out. **V 23–26: SERVING LEVITES** Levites are to be between the ages of twenty-five and fifty, to serve the LORD. At the age of fifty, they are to stop doing the work prescribed, but they are still free to serve their brethren in the tabernacle to attend to their needs. No servant of God is ever permanently retired!

CHAPTER NINE

V 1–14: PASSOVER PRINCIPLES AND PRACTICE The principles and practice of Passover are reinstated. Some people are defiled by touching a corpse and want to know why they cannot keep the Passover. They are told by God, through Moses, to keep the Passover one month later, just as a man away on a journey must do. However, anyone who is ceremonially clean, and fails to keep the Passover, must be cut off. A stranger in the land who chooses to keep the Passover must do so in exactly the same way as if he were an Israelite. **V 15–23: COVERING CLOUD AND COMMANDMENT** When the tabernacle is erected, God covers it during the day by a cloud and during the night by the appearance of fire. When God commands the children of Israel to move, they move, and when He commands them to camp, they camp. When the cloud moves, the children of Israel move also, after taking down the tabernacle which will be re-assembled at the next camp. This procedure is to be followed as God commands, irrespective of the length of the stay.

CHAPTER TEN

V 1–10: SILVER TRUMPETS Two silver trumpets are to be made and blown by Aaron and the priests when more detailed instruction is to be given to the Israelites. When the two trumpets are blown, the whole congregation has to gather at the door of the tabernacle. When one only is blown, the leaders are to gather to Moses. The same trumpets sound the advance for the journeys and also are to mark an alarm when attacked by enemies. They are similarly to be used in days of gladness for appointed feasts and also to remind the children of Israel that the LORD is their God. Like prayer itself, the trumpets have many uses under God's gracious command. **V 11–13: SINAI'S TRAVELS** The travels from Sinai begin thirteen months after leaving Egypt and eleven months after arriving at Sinai. Canaan is in view! **V 14–28: STANDARDS TAKEN** The eastern section of the tribes led by Judah (including Issachar and Zebulun) follow the standard as the march to the promised land commences. Gershon and Merari follow, carrying the tabernacle. Next comes Reuben from the southern section (accompanied by Simeon and Gad), also following their standard. The Kohathites follow Reuben, carrying the holy things. The rearguard is taken by Ephraim from the west (accompanied by Mannaseh and Benjamin) and then by Dan from the north (accompanied by Asher and Naphtali). This is the marching order for Israel en route to the promised land. **V 29–32: SHARING THINGS** Moses persuades Hobab, his Midianite brother-in-law, to come with him to the promised land, and promises he will treat him well and share good things with him. He obviously values this man as a member of the wider family, and as someone who will help him. **V 33–36: SUPPLICATION**

THROUGHOUT The first journey is three days' unbroken march before stopping where the LORD indicates. This rigorous start to their journeyings demonstrates that the Israelites are now in a different mode. Whenever the ark sets out, Moses prays for victory over God's enemies. Whenever the ark returns, he prays for the presence of God. It is good, in working for and walking with the LORD, consciously to lift prayers to Him throughout the day.

CHAPTER ELEVEN

V 1–3: FIRE At a place later called Taberah (meaning 'Burning'), some people complain in the outskirts of the camp. God is displeased, His anger is aroused, and fire breaks out to consume them. Moses prays and the fire is quenched. **V 4–9: FOOD** Despite that, the 'mixed multitude' (including non-Israelites) crave intensely for the food that they ate in Egypt. The Israelites also weep and demand this food, being critical of the manna which God miraculously provides for them each day. **V 10: FICKLENESS** Moses hears the fickle people weeping throughout their families each at the door of his tent. God is angry with His people and Moses is displeased with them. **V 11–15: FRUSTRATION** In abject frustration, Moses tells God that he can cope no further with such a disobedient and demanding people. He even asks God to kill him so that God can see his wretchedness no more. Even leaders like Moses can go through times of depression and great discouragement, though that is never necessary through God's grace. **V 16–17: FELLOWSHIP** God's response is not to kill him. He tells him to gather seventy elders and enter the tabernacle. God will come and talk with them and give them His Spirit so that they can share the burden with Moses and he will not be alone. God's answer to this particular problem is fellowship in leadership. **V 18–20: FLESH** God tells Moses that He will send so much meat to eat for the 600,000 people during a month that they will be literally 'fed up' with it. **V 21–22: FAITHLESSNESS** Moses is so discouraged that his faith suffers and he asks God how he can find enough meat to feed 600,000 men in the wilderness. **V 23: FAITHFULNESS** God asks Moses whether His arm has ever been shortened. He tells him that he will see what happens. **V 24–32: FULFILMENT** God gives Moses the fellowship of seventy elders upon whom he places His Spirit, plus two others, Eldad and Medad, whom Joshua observes prophesying in the camp. Moses corrects inexperienced Joshua who feels that they should be forbidden rather than encouraged. Then God sends birds (quail) in huge quantities all around the camp for the people to eat. They are gathered by the Israelites. **V 33–34: FURY** While the meat is still being eaten, God's wrath is aroused against the people. They are struck with a great plague at Kibroth Hattavah, which means 'Graves of Craving'. God is angry that His grace and provision have been abused and belittled. These events emphasise again to the Israelites that He is a holy God who must not only be trusted, but must also be obeyed. **V 35: FORWARD** The Israelites move forward from Kibbroth Hattavah to Hazeroth and camp there.

CHAPTER TWELVE

V 1–2: MURMURING It seems that Zipporah must have died, for Moses has taken a wife from Ethiopia (a descendant of Cush, Noah's grandson). Miriam and Aaron speak against Moses because of his marriage to this woman. **V 3: MEEKNESS** Moses' humility is such that he is meeker than any man living. **V 4–9: MEETING** God instigates a meeting with Moses, Aaron and Miriam, and meets them in the pillar of cloud. He emphasises directly to Aaron and Miriam that Moses is His special servant with whom He speaks face to face. God is angry with them. **V 10–12: MIRACLE** When the cloud lifts, Miriam, who as the first named person and probably the instigator of the opposition, is made into a leper. (Aaron is not made into a leper, as that would affect his ability to perform as a holy priest.) Aaron pleads with Moses for her. **V 13: MEDIATOR** Moses again takes on his mediatorial and intercessory role and humbly and wholeheartedly prays to God for this woman who has opposed him personally. **V 14–15: MIRIAM** God insists that Miriam should be shut outside the camp for seven days, as would be the case if she had been spat at in her face. The camp does not move forward until Miriam is brought in again. God makes His point very personally and powerfully to Aaron, Miriam, and everyone else! **V 16: MOVING** After the seven day delay, the people move from Hazeroth and camp in the Wilderness of Paran.

CHAPTER THIRTEEN

V 1–2: CANAAN God commands Moses to send a spy from each tribe, twelve in total, into the land of Canaan. This is the promised land which He is going to give to Israel. **V 3–16: COMMAND** Moses obeys the command of God and sends out twelve named people. This includes Caleb, son of Jephunneh, from the tribe of Judah, and Joshua (whose name is changed from Hoshea), the son of Nun, from the tribe of Ephraim. Hoshea means 'desire for salvation' whereas Joshua means 'The Lord is salvation' or 'God saves', and is the same name as 'Jesus' in the Greek. **V 17–25: CONSIDER** Moses tells them to consider every aspect of the land and its people and return with some of the fruit of the land. They return accordingly after forty days of espionage. **V 26–29: CAUTIOUS** The cautious consensus from the spies is that this is a land of plenty in every way, but that the people are strong, the cities are fortified and very large, and the feared descendants of Anak are there. They report back the location of the inhabitants of the land—the Amelakites, Hittites, Jebusites, Amorites and Canaanites. **V 30: CALEB** Caleb encourages the people and urges immediate advance to take possession knowing that 'we are well able to overcome it'. **V 31–33: COWARDLY** The cowardly response from the other spies (except Joshua, as we learn later) is that the land cannot be taken because the people are too strong and that there are giants in the land (Anak's descendants). They feel like grasshoppers in comparison to the physical appearance of the descendants of Anak.

CHAPTER FOURTEEN

V 1–4: REBELLION Rebellion breaks out yet again against Moses and Aaron. They talk of choosing another leader to take them back to Egypt. It is sad, but still true, that people who have been so blessed and spoken to directly by God can respond so sinfully in times of testing. **V 5: REACTION** Moses and Aaron fall on their faces before the congregation. Prayer is needed! **V 6–9: RESOLUTION** But two of the spies, Joshua and Caleb, are resolute. They tell the children of Israel that the land 'flows with milk and honey' and that God will bring them into that land. They urge their brothers not to rebel against God, nor to fear the people of the land, because God is

on their side. **V 10a: REJECTION** Such is the groundswell of wicked opposition to God that the congregation are minded to stone Joshua and Caleb, and probably Moses and Aaron as well. **V 10b–12: REVELATION** At this very point, God's glory appears in the tabernacle before all the children of Israel. He is angry with the people's rejection and unbelief. He declares that He will strike them with pestilence, disinherit them, and make of Moses a greater and mightier nation instead of them. **V 13–19: REASONING** Not for the first time, Moses reasons with God in intercessory prayer. He argues that God's character will be misunderstood and maligned by the Egyptians, who will say that God cannot keep His people in the wilderness. **V 20–35: RESPONSE** God's response is immediate. They are pardoned, but the rebels will not enter into the promised land. They will die in the wilderness. Only Caleb, who has a 'different spirit in him', and Joshua will enter the promised land. God repeats His message twice for emphasis! He directs His people to continue their journey the next day by the wilderness to avoid conflict with the Amalekites and the Canaanites. **V 36–38: RESPONSIBILITY** The responsibility for the unbelief engendered by the bad report falls on the ten spies, whom God smites with a plague. Of the twelve spies, only Joshua and Caleb survive. **V 39: REPORT** Moses relates all these words to the children of Israel who mourn greatly. **V 40–44: RECKLESS** They recklessly tell Moses that they will attack the enemy armies of the Amalekites and the Canaanites in mountain terrain. They choose reckless action when first they should be exercising repentance and faith. Moses warns them of the certain failure of such a venture, and that defeat and death are inevitable. Nevertheless, they go up the mountain despite the fact that the ark and Moses remain in the camp. **V 45: ROUTED** They do not even get to the top of the mountain, because the Amalekites and the Canaanites descend the mountain, attack them, and drive them back to Hormah.

CHAPTER FIFTEEN

V 1–16: FULFILMENT OF PROMISE ASSUMED Despite what has gone before, God tells Moses to instruct the children of Israel about the sacrifices they must keep when they come into the promised land He is giving them. As they cannot sacrifice in the land unless they are there, this is a wonderful assurance that God will keep His promise to get them there. Despite their sins, forgiveness and walking with God is still open to them. Also, provision will be made for strangers who dwell with them so that they, too, may have fellowship with Israel's God. **V 17–21: FIRSTFRUITS OF PRODUCE ACKNOWLEDGED** When they enter the promised land, the Israelites must offer to God, as heave offerings, the first fruits of any produce. This is a reminder that everything comes from Him. **V 22–29: FAILURE OF PEOPLE ATONED** God's mercy not only covers sin, which is a result of rebellion and pride, but unintentional sin is covered. Now, God forgives all who come to Him through Christ, who has atoned for all our sins. **V 30–36: FLOUTING OF PRESUMPTUOUSNESS ADDRESSED** For presumptuous sin, manifested by deliberate flouting of God's commandments, the offender is to be cut off from the Israelites. God orders the stoning of a man who breaks the Sabbath. Today, we often regard the fourth commandment lightly, but God does not. That is why its principle found such vigorous enforcement in the civil code of Israel. **V 37–40: FORGETFULNESS OF POSITION ANTICIPATED** The children of Israel are to wear tassels on the corners of their garments, as a reminder to keep His commandments. **V 41: FAITHFULNESS OF PRESENCE ASSURED** God reminds them that He is the faithful God who kept His promise to them to bring them out of the land of Egypt. He is still the LORD their God.

CHAPTER SIXTEEN

V 1–11: PROTESTORS Headed by Korah the Kohathite, protestors rise up against Moses, including 250 renowned leaders of the congregation. They accuse Moses and Aaron of taking on too much authority, and state that everyone in the congregation is holy, and that there is nothing special about Moses and Aaron. Again, Moses humbly falls on his face. He tells Korah and all his supporters to come before the LORD the next day with censers containing fire and incense. God will choose between them. He accuses them of seeking the priesthood, and points out their existing privilege of serving in the temple as one of the three Levite families. **V 12–15: PRESUMPTION** Moses confronts Dathan and Abihu, the sons of Elab, Korah's main supporters in this rebellion. They refuse to come up and accuse Moses of not delivering on the promise of bringing the people to a land 'flowing with milk and honey'. They unfairly claim that Moses acts as a prince over them. Moses angrily asks the LORD to reject their offering, and reminds God that he has always treated them with integrity. **V 16–18: PRESENTATION** At Moses' suggestion, Korah and the 250 rebel leaders present themselves at the door of the tabernacle with their censers. **V 19–21: PRESENCE** God's glory appears to the entire congregation. Instantly, He tells Moses and Aaron to separate themselves from the congregation so that He can consume them in a moment. **V 22–27: PASSION** Moses and Aaron passionately pray to God not to judge the whole nation because of one man's sin. Through Moses, God tells the people to move away from the tents of Korah, Dathan and Abihu and touch nothing belonging to them, or they will be consumed also. God will not judge those who will repent and move away from His wrath. The congregation move away while Korah, Dathan and Abihu stand rebelliously with their wives, their sons, and children at the entrance to their tents. **V 28–30: PROPHECY** Moses prophesies that, if he is their chosen leader, God will cause the earth to swallow up the offenders, their families and belongings as evidence that they have rejected the LORD. **V 31–35: PROOF** The proof is given as God opens the earth around the rebels. Korah, his rebel leaders, their families, and their effects are swallowed up. Israel flees at their cry, in case they are swallowed up too. God's fire consumes the 250 leaders who are offering incense. **V 36–40: PRIEST** At God's instruction through Moses, Eleazar, the priest and the son of Aaron, collects the censers. Because they have been offered to the LORD, they are made into hammered plates as a covering for the altar and as a reminder that only God's priests must approach Him on behalf of the people. **V 41: PEOPLE** Amazingly, the people murmur again against Moses and Aaron, accusing them of having killed God's people. They still have not learned their lesson. **V 42–46: PLAGUE** God's glory covers the tabernacle. He tells Moses and Aaron to move away from the people so He can consume them. Moses and Aaron again fall on their faces, and Moses tells Aaron to take to the congregation a censer containing fire from the altar to make atonement for them, because God is wrathful and the plague has begun. **V 47–50: PLEA** Aaron runs into the midst of the people to make atonement for them. He stands between the dead and the living, the plague is stopped, and the rebellion is over. Nevertheless, in addition to the three rebel leaders and their families who were swallowed up earlier, 14,700 people die in the plague. Sin and rebellion are serious matters.

CHAPTER SEVENTEEN

V 1–7: SIGN God tells Moses to have each of the twelve tribes of Israel present a rod in the tabernacle before the ark of Testimony. The rod that buds will signify the person whom God has chosen. God intends to rid Himself of the complaints of the children of Israel. Aaron is to write his name on the rod of the children of Levi. Each tribe's staff, including that of Aaron, is then placed before the LORD in the tabernacle. **V 8–9: SPROUTED** The next day, Aaron's rod of the house of Levi is found to have sprouted and budded, produced blossoms and yielded ripe almonds—all in one day! No other rod does that. **V 10–11: SACRED** Aaron's rod is to be treated as sacred and kept before the Testimony. We learn elsewhere that it is placed in the ark of the covenant. This reminder is to stop complaints against God and His leaders, lest people should die. Moses obeys God's command. **V 12–13: SCARED** The children of Israel now know that if they approach God in their own strength, they will die. They even fear that anyone approaching the tabernacle of God shall die. They are frightened people

CHAPTER EIGHTEEN

V 1: PRIESTHOOD God solemnly speaks to Aaron directly in connection with the priesthood. The priests will be responsible for any sin which pollutes or defiles the sanctuary. They alone are the priests who perform the office of priesthood. **V 2–7: PARTICIPATION** Aaron and his sons are to attend to everything behind the veil, namely in the Most Holy Place. The Levites are to help them in all the work of the tabernacle but participation as priests is only open to Aaron and his sons. **V 8–20: PORTIONS** Because the priests have no inheritance in the land, God legislates for their support. Included in that support is the fact that they are to eat the meat from offerings made, as prescribed by God. **V 21–24: PEOPLE** The people are to support the Levites by tithing their income and possessions. Like the priests, the Levites have no inheritance given to them and thus will be supported by the people's tithes. **V 25–32: PRINCIPLE** The principle of tithing is also to be practised by the Levites. Just as they receive the tithes from the people, so they must tithe to the LORD a tenth of what they receive. This is to be offered by them as a heave offering to God.

CHAPTER NINETEEN

V 1–2: THE COW A red heifer, without blemish or defect, which has never been yoked, is to be brought by the Israelites. **V 3: THE CAMP** Eleazar, the priest, must take the heifer outside the camp to slaughter it. **V 4–10: THE CLEANSING** Eleazar must sprinkle the blood of the heifer seven times in front of the tabernacle of meeting. (The death of the heifer outside the camp reminds us of Jesus Christ who went 'outside the camp'

to bear our sin.) The priest and his clothing are then to be cleansed in water. The water of purification is to be sprinkled for ceremonial cleansing from sin. It is to be made up of the ashes of the heifer, cedar wood, hyssop and scarlet, all of which are to be totally consumed by the fire. **V 11–22: THE CONDUCT** Detail is given about how the water of purification is to be applied to unclean persons to make them ceremonially clean. Although God makes provision for unclean people to be counted clean through His mercy, grace and sacrifice, those who refuse to be cleansed will be cut off.

CHAPTER TWENTY

V 1: DESERT The children are at Kadesh, where Miriam dies and is buried. This is in the desert known as the Wilderness of Zin. **V 2a: DROUGHT** The congregation have no water. **V 2b–6: DISSENTION** Yet again they rebel against Moses and Aaron and claim that they have been brought from Egypt to die in the wilderness. They suggest that Egypt is a better place for provision of their preferred food and drink. Moses and Aaron fall on their faces before God, who appears to them in His glory. **V 7–9: DRINK** God tells Moses to take Aaron and his rod, and to speak to the rock before the congregation. He promises that the rock will yield water. **V 10–11: DISOBEDIENCE** Accompanied by Aaron, even Moses, whose humility and meekness have been shown on so many occasions, reaches the limits of his patience with these sinful people. Instead of speaking to the rock as God has commanded him, he disobeys God by turning on the rebels in anger and striking the rock twice with his rod. God graciously still provides the water promised, but Moses' disobedience will have severe consequences for him.

V 12–13: DISBELIEF God regards Moses' disobedience as disbelief. In effect Moses did not really believe that God was in control of this situation, and thus reacted in a way that diminished the holiness of God in the eyes of the children of Israel. God tells Moses and Aaron that they will not take Israel into the promised land, as a result of that disbelief. The water taken is called 'Meribah' (meaning 'contention' or 'quarrelling'). **V 14–21: DENIAL** The king of Edom denies Israel passage through Edom, and produces military force to underline that refusal. Israel turns away, having been instructed by God earlier not to make war with Edom. **V 22–29: DEATH** God tells Moses and Aaron of Aaron's impending death in the wilderness, because of the rebellion of Moses and Aaron against God's word at Meribah. Aaron and his son, Eleazar, who will be his successor as priest, ascend Mount Hor with Moses as the congregation look on. Moses strips Aaron of his priestly garments and puts them on Eleazar. Aaron dies on the top of the mountain, leaving Moses and Eleazar to descend it. Israel mourns for Aaron for thirty days.

CHAPTER TWENTY-ONE

V 1–3: ARAD Arad, in the south of Canaan, falls to the Israelites, who carry out their promise to God to destroy the cities. The name of the battle is called Hormah, which means 'destruction'. **V 4–9: BRONZE** This passage forms the background to the most famous Bible text of all, John 3:16. The people become discouraged and again complain against God and His servant, Moses, about the food, the drink and their wanderings in the desert. In judgement, God sends fiery serpents among them, and many die. They cry to God for forgiveness. Moses is told by God to make a bronze serpent and put it on a pole. Any Israelite, obviously repentant at heart and responding in faith to God's word by looking at the bronze serpent, is saved and lives. This is a picture of Christ's death on the cross. All who will turn from their sin and look to Him will be saved. **V 10–20: CONTINUE** The journey continues to Moab. En route, God provides them with water, and Israel sings a grateful song of thanks. **V 21–35: DEFEATS** Enabled by God and walking with Him, Israel defeats Sihon, king of the Amorites, and Og, king of Bashan.

CHAPTER TWENTY-TWO

V 1–4: COWERING! The Moabites are very frightened that they will lose everything to Israel, not knowing that earlier God had forbidden them to touch anything belonging to Moab. Balak is Moab's king. **V 5–7: CURSE** Balak sends for Balaam, who lives in an area where many false cult prophets are to be found. He asks Balaam to curse the Israelites so that he will be able to defeat them. With the fee for Balaam in his hand, Balak's representatives approach him. **V 8–12: COMMAND** While Balaam thinks about the offer overnight, God appears to him and tells him not to curse the Israelites, because they are blessed. **V 13–19: COMPENSATION** Balak offers more money, and sends more distinguished negotiators to Balaam. Balaam dare not do anything other than what God has told him. Nevertheless, he holds out a hope that he might be able to gain through cursing Israel, and asks them to stay the night so that he can know if God changes His mind! **V 20–22: COMPROMISE** God tells Balaam that if the men come to call him, then he must rise up and go with them, but he must obey God. There is no record of the men calling him, but Balaam goes with them in the morning anyhow. God's anger is aroused and His Angel stands in the way to stop him going. Balaam rides on a donkey and two servants are with him. **V 23–34: COMMUNICATION** The Angel, with sword drawn, is seen by the donkey but not by Balaam. He blocks the donkey's path. Balaam tries to continue, despite the donkey's reluctance. He becomes very angry and hits the donkey three times. God speaks to him through the donkey. The Angel tells him that, but for the donkey, Balaam would have been struck dead because his way is perverse before God. Balaam makes a show of repentance in offering to turn back. **V 35–41: COMPULSION** God's sovereignty and overruling will determine that He will use this false prophet to glorify Him. Therefore, He tells him to go with the men, but he must only speak what God tells him. Balaam, fearful and sensing his powerlessness, promises to do what God says. For Balaam, this falls far short of real conversion. The next day Balak takes Balaam to a high place of Baal so that Balaam may observe the Israelites.

CHAPTER TWENTY-THREE

V 1–12: ORACLE ONE: SORCERY STOPPED Despite the preparation that Balaam uses as his *modus operandi* (seven altars for sacrificing seven bulls and seven rams), God stops Balaam's sorcery and causes him to bless Israel, much to Balak's displeasure. Balaam is too frightened to disobey God. **V 13–26: ORACLE TWO: DIVINATION DENIED** Balak takes Balaam to another vantage point for him to curse Israel. The altars are set up. Again God intervenes and this divination is denied as well, resulting in Balaam's blessing of Israel. Balak objects, but God makes Balaam unable to disobey Him in cursing

Israel. **V 27–30: ORACLE THREE: ANOTHER ATTEMPT** Balak persists and once more Balaam attempts his sorcery. He sets up his seven altars at Peor to curse Israel from another place.

CHAPTER TWENTY-FOUR

V 1–14: ORACLE THREE: SOVEREIGN SPIRIT The Spirit of God comes upon Balaam and compels this false prophet to pronounce current and future blessings on Israel and defeat upon Israel's enemies. Balak is furious and refuses to pay Balaam. Balaam knows that God is sovereign and, regardless of bribery, that he can do nothing else! **V 15–19: ORACLE FOUR: BALAAM BEHOLDS** Balaam now seems unable to control the utterances that God is giving through him. Prophecies of Israel's blessing and the arrival of the Messiah who is the King are miraculously included. He can do no other as God overrules to control him. **V 20–25: ORACLES FIVE, SIX AND SEVEN: MISCELLANEOUS MATTERS** As God controls Balaam's mouth, Israel's blessing and victory is foretold and defeat to its enemies. Balak and Balaam part company. Much as Balaam wanted pecuniary gain, he finds himself unable to disobey almighty God in cursing Israel.

CHAPTER TWENTY-FIVE

V 1–3: IDOLATRY AND IMMORALITY How often in the Bible is idolatry linked with immorality as a cause or as an effect. Here the Israelite men take Moabite women in harlotry. They start to sacrifice to their gods, bowing down to them, as Israel is being joined to Baal of Peor. God is angry. **V 4–5: EXPOSURE AND EXECUTION** God tells Moses that the leaders must hang the offenders in order to turn away His fierce anger. Moses instructs the judges of Israel to kill the men who have been engaged in this immorality and idolatry. **V 6–9: EVIDENCE AND EXECUTION** An Israelite arrogantly brings a Midianite woman into the camp in the sight of Moses and all Israel. At that time they are weeping at the door of the tabernacle because of the sins of idolatry and immorality and God's judgement on those sins. Phinehas, the son of Eleazar the priest, takes a javelin and follows the couple into the tent and thrusts both of them through with the javelin. God stops the plague, but 24,000 people die. **V 10–15: COMMENDATION AND COVENANT** God commends Phinehas for his godly zeal and says that He will give him His covenant of peace and bless his descendants. The slain couple are identified. Both are from influential families; perhaps that is the cause of their sinful arrogance. **V 16–18: ENMITY AND EXECUTION** God tells Moses to harass and attack the Midianites because of their seductive harassment of the Israelites in seeking to pervert their worship and morality.

CHAPTER TWENTY-SIX

V 1–4: CRITERIA The criteria for the second census is given. All men of twenty years of age and over are to be counted. To conquer the promised land, soldiers are needed. **V 5–51: COUNT** The number of people in each tribe varies of course, but the final total counted is 601,730—very similar to the 603,550 counted in the census thirty-eight years earlier. **V 52–56: CALCULATION** Moses is told by God to calculate how much land to allocate to the tribes according to their size. The situation of each plot is to be decided by lot. **V 57–62: CONSECRATION** The consecration of the Levites is underlined again, by mention of the fact that Nadab

and Abihu died as a result of offering profane fire before God. No inheritance is given to the Levites and 23,000 males of a month or older are counted. **V 63–65: CALEB** Caleb and his colleague Joshua are the only two Israelites from their peers not to die in the wilderness, being the only two men to remain from the earlier census taken by Moses and Aaron. They will enter the promised land. Moses will not enter it because of his unbelief at Meribah.

CHAPTER TWENTY-SEVEN

V 1–11: INHERITANCE God confirms to Moses that the inheritance of Zelophehad should pass to his daughters following their approach to Moses, Eleazar, the leaders and the congregation at the door of the tabernacle. Their father died without sons and thus they have no brothers who can inherit. A new statute is passed to cover similar situations in the future. **V 12–17: INEVITABLE** It is inevitable that Moses will die soon, and God reminds him that he will not enter the promised land because he failed to honour and obey God at Meribah. Moses' prayer is that God will set a leader over the people who will care for them as a shepherd. **V 18–23: INAUGURATION** God tells Moses to take Joshua the son of Nun, identified as a man in whom is God's Spirit, and lay hands on him before Eleazar and the congregation. Some of Moses' authority is to be given to Joshua now, and Eleazar will enquire of the LORD for him. The inauguration of Joshua takes place as God commands before the congregation. Joshua has benefited from great training, from the encouraging example of Caleb, and especially from the role model Moses has been, despite his failure at Meribah.

CHAPTER TWENTY-EIGHT

V 1–2: SPECIFIC REMINDER With the death of Moses in view, God commands him to remind the people to make offerings by fire as a sweet aroma to Him at the appointed time. **V 3–31: SACRIFICES RE-EMPHASISED** Detail of the actual sacrifices is re-emphasised by God through Moses as follows: Daily (verses 1 to 8); Weekly on the Sabbath (verses 9 and 10); Monthly (verses 11 to 15); Annually, both at Passover (verses 16 to 25) and at Pentecost or 'Feast of Weeks' (verses 26 to 31).

CHAPTER TWENTY-NINE

V 1–6: HOLY CONVOCATION 1—FEAST OF TRUMPETS The first of three holy convocations—which means 'called together'—is for the Feast of Trumpets. The renewed emphasis on the sacrifices to be made continues with this convocation. **V 7–11: HOLY CONVOCATION 2—FOCUS ON ATONEMENT** The sacrifices to be made at the second holy convocation— the Day of Atonement—are detailed. **V 12–40: HOLY CONVOCATION 3—FEAST OF TABERNACLES** The sacrifices for each of the eight days of the Feast of Tabernacles (which title is not used here in the text) are detailed. Young bulls are to be offered each day, starting with thirteen and decreasing by one each day until seven are sacrificed on the seventh day. On each of the first seven days the offering also comprises two rams, fourteen lambs without blemish which are less than a year old, associated grain and drink offerings, one goat's kid and associated grain and drink offerings. The solemn assembly on the eighth day (obviously the first day of the week) is to be marked by no customary work being done and by a sacrifice of reduced volume but equal

significance. Some see this assembly as foreshadowing the Christian Lord's day, the first day resurrection Sabbath. Moses passes on all of God's word and instructions to the children of Israel to ensure that the sacrificial system is properly maintained.

CHAPTER THIRTY

V 1–2: INTEGRITY Moses tells the leaders of the tribes that integrity must prevail in the keeping of vows they make. **V 3–15: AUTHORITY** However, a vow made by someone under authority is not binding without that person's consent. If the person in authority keeps silent when he should annul the vow, the vow is binding. This applies to fathers and to husbands. Widows or divorced women are not under that authority. **V 16: SUMMARY** A one verse summary of the chapter is given.

CHAPTER THIRTY-ONE

V 1–11: GOD'S PUNISHMENT The last great task that Moses is given by God is to take vengeance on the Midianites because of their corrupting influence on His people. Balaam is among those killed. Women captives are taken. **V 12–24: GREAT PURITY** Among the women taken captive only virgins, including girls, are spared. Everything has to be cleansed by fire or by water. Great purity is the issue here, in taking in captives. Earlier the soldiers had brought back both captives and booty indiscriminately. God, through Moses, wants to avoid the Israelites being defiled by either. **V 25–47: GIVING PLUNDER** The plunder taken is divided equally between the men who fought the Midianites and the people who stayed behind. Provision is also made for the Levites and for the priests. All are in God's people, all have their part to play, and all are rewarded. **V 48–54: GRATEFUL PRESENTATION** The army officers are so grateful for God's protection in battle for the Israelite soldiers that they present gold from the plunder. It is put in the tabernacle as a memorial of God's faithfulness.

CHAPTER THIRTY-TWO

V 1–5: REQUEST The Reubenites and the Gadites own much livestock and ask Moses if they may settle in the land conquered on the east side of the Jordan, rather than on the west side. **V 6–15: RESERVATION** Moses shares his reservation that their brethren will need support when they go to war and that Reuben and Gad will not be able to give that support, thereby discouraging them. He is especially mindful of the disastrous consequences of the failure of the ten spies at Kadesh Barnea to follow the LORD, as Caleb and Joshua had done. **V 16–33: REPLY** The two tribes propose to build sheepfolds and cities now and promise to cross the Jordan to fight for the promised land alongside their Israelite brothers. They will then return afterwards to establish their families and base on the east side of the Jordan. Moses agrees after underlining the need for them to fight. He instructs Eleazar and Joshua to remember them in the later allocation of the promised land only if they fight for Israel. **V 34–42: RESPONSE** The building work starts and the half tribe of Manasseh, along with the Reubenites and Gadites, start to possess the new land.

CHAPTER THIRTY-THREE

V 1–2: REVIEW The review of the journeys of the Israelites since leaving Egypt is given, with Moses recording the details. **V 3–49: ROUTE** The children of Israel's route, from the wilderness to the River Jordan, is traced. It is good sometimes to look back to see God's faithfulness, and our mistakes and sins from which we should learn to walk more closely with God in the future. **V 50–55: REQUIREMENT** The '3D' requirement that God gives Moses to pass on to the children of Israel is to drive out the inhabitants of the land and live in it, to destroy idolatry and to divide the land among the twelve tribes of Israel.

CHAPTER THIRTY-FOUR

V 1–12: TERRITORIES ALLOCATED The territories of Canaan are allocated to the children of Israel and the boundaries are set. **V 13–15: TAKING ACTION** Moses takes action on his previous promise, to Reuben, Gad and half Manasseh, and records that they have received their inheritance on the other side of Jordan, whereas the west side of Jordan is allocated to the nine and a half tribes. **V 16–18: TEAM ASSIGNED** Moses obeys God's earlier command to give some of his authority to Joshua and assigns him and Eleazar as the team to oversee the division of the land between the tribes. They are to take a leader of every tribe into their 'advisory committee.' **V 19–29: TRIBES' APPOINTEES** The leaders from each tribe are appointed to the task of dividing the inheritance under the joint supervision of Eleazar and Joshua.

CHAPTER THIRTY-FIVE

V 1–15: COMMAND TO REMEMBER The children of Israel are told by Moses to give the Levites cities and lands as their inheritance. God's consecrated servants must not be forgotten in times of affluence and plenty any more than in times of need and poverty. Among the forty-eight cities to be given to the Levites, six are to be cities of refuge to which a person committing manslaughter, not murder, may flee for refuge. **V 16–34: CRITERIA FOR RESOLUTION** Details are given as criteria to establish the question of guilt, intention and protection. It is a serious thing to be charged with murder and important to establish who may take refuge in these cities of refuge. These criteria are to help in those kinds of judgements.

CHAPTER THIRTY-SIX

V 1–4: DIFFICULTY The early decision to include the daughters of Zelophehad in the inheritance, as he had left no sons, causes the problem of whether the land should go out of the tribe if the daughters marry someone from another tribe.

V 5–9: DECISION Moses makes a fair and clear decision and conveys it to them that daughters who inherit, as in the case of Zelophehad's daughters, should only marry within their tribes. **V 10–12: DEFERENCE** Zelophehad's daughters want to honour their fathers name. In willingly deferring to the authority of God through Moses, they provide an excellent example for everyone to follow, irrespective of gender. **V 13: DESCRIPTION** The summary of the chapter could well describe not only the book of Numbers, but also the Pentateuch, the Old Testament, and indeed the whole Bible: 'These are the commandments and judgements which the LORD commanded.' In the case of Numbers, the command was through Moses in the plains of Moab, by the Jordan, across from Jericho.

DEUTERONOMY

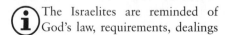

OVERVIEW

PEOPLE AND PRELIMINARIES

Deuteronomy (thirty-four chapters) is the fifth and last of the five books of the law (the 'Pentateuch') written by Moses. This book was probably completed in 1405 BC towards the end of Israel's desert wanderings and before the children of Israel entered the promised land. Joshua probably added the last short portion, under God's inspiration, soon after the death of Moses.

PLAN AND PURPOSE

The Israelites are reminded of God's law, requirements, dealings with them and love for them. Moses' final three speeches bring back to them the lessons learned from their wilderness wanderings and spell out how they must live in the promised land. The requirements of God's law are underlined, with an emphasis on God's past judgements. God's blessings are promised and curses are threatened depending on whether His people will trust and obey Him, or not. The change of leadership is dealt with. Moses teaches the Song of Moses, which is to be learned and sung to remind future Israel, even when backsliding, to obey God. Deuteronomy presents the great leader's final cry for holiness and wholeheartedness in following God. Despite the ups and downs of his people and himself, Moses has proved God's sovereignty, faithfulness, mercy, grace and help.

PROFILE AND PROGRESSION

Summary of God's dealings with Israel in Moses' first speech (1:1–3:29); obedience to God's law, and creation of cities of refuge (4:1–43); Moses' second speech about the Ten Commandments and observing them, surrender to God and holy distinctiveness from ungodly nations, lessons to be learned from the past leading to obeying and loving God now, how to live in the promised land, and the need to be holy to God (4:44–28:68); Moses' third speech anticipating the new covenant from the heart (29:1–30:20); leadership priorities regarding Joshua and the religious leaders, God's commissioning Joshua and instructing Moses to write his song (31:1–29); the Song of Moses and his last words (32:1–33:29); death of Moses and obituary (34:1–12).

PRINCIPLES AND PARTICULARS

God's sovereignty predominates. Moses' passionate concern is for his people to obey God. Whereas obedience is seen as the key to being blessed, disobedience triggers God's curse. Note the place of Scripture and good hymns about God's faithfulness to remind His people of their obligations to Him.

DEUTERONOMY

CHAPTER ONE

V 1–5: SUMMARY Moses is about to summarise the journey to the promised land from Horeb (which is Mount Sinai) and to review God's word to Israel. God has blessed them in their journey over nearly forty years since leaving Egypt. Their journey could have taken eleven days had Israel been faithful and trusted God. Unbelief and disobedience have robbed them of much blessing and effectiveness. On the verge of entering Canaan's promised land, Moses explains God's law and reminds the Israelites of important matters, before they advance. **V 6–8: START** The journey started at Horeb where God spoke to the Israelites and told them to go and possess the land which had been promised to Abraham, Isaac and Jacob and their descendants. **V 9–18: SELECTION** Leaders were selected to help Moses lead and judge the people, because there was too much for one man to do on his own. Moses passed on God's commands to them. **V 19–25: SPIES** From the wilderness, the twelve spies had been sent to Kadesh Barnea and reported on the good and fruitful promised land. **V 26–40: STUBBORNNESS** The stubbornness of the people, including the ten unfaithful spies, caused them to rebel against God, to doubt His purposes in bringing them out of Egypt, to fear the people they saw, and to refuse to go into the promised land. Their unbelief in not trusting God's faithfulness and guidance by the fire and the cloud made Him so angry that He determined that none of them would enter the promised land except Caleb, 'who wholly followed the LORD', and Joshua, who would later lead Israel into the promised land. These two faithful spies, their loved ones and their children would inherit the promised land, but the offenders would wander and die in the wilderness. **V 41–45: SIN** The people then regretted their rebellion and tried to enter the promised land through their own efforts and without God's blessing. They were routed by the Amorites. Their self-pity and weeping, which were not repentance, did not impress God. **V 46: SUSPENDED** So the Israelites' progress was suspended. They remained in Kadesh for a long time in order to learn the lessons that God would have them learn.

CHAPTER TWO

V 1: WANDERINGS Their wanderings started by journeying into the wilderness by the Red Sea, where, for many days, they journeyed around the area of Mount Seir. **V 2–12: WARY** The Israelites were told to be wary and not to meddle with the Edomites (Esau's descendants) nor fight with the Moabites (the descendants of Lot), because He had granted to both those peoples a possession. This meant that they did not have to fight the Emim, the 'terrible ones', who had occupied the land before Moab, and who were extremely large and powerful. In the middle of this review, Moses reminds them that God had been with them all the time, that He had blessed them, and that they had lacked nothing. **V 13–23: WAITING** The Israelites crossed over the Valley of Zered. The thirty-eight year wait from Kadesh to Zered was until the death of all the men of war who refused to follow the advice of the two faithful spies. The Israelites were told not to fight with the Ammonites, the descendants of Lot. God had given them the land as a possession and they had driven out the huge giants who had possessed their 'promised land'. **V 24–37: WAR** God told them to fight with Sihon, king of Heshbon, after he had refused to give Moses peaceful passage through the land. God said He would make all nations fear Israel, and gave Israel victory over Heshbon, which was completely destroyed. From there, God delivered all other cities into their hands. The people of Israel did not attack the Ammonites, however, because God had forbidden them.

CHAPTER THREE

V 1–11: DEFEAT Opposed by Og, king of Bashan, God promised victory to Israel at Edrei and delivered him into their hands. His sixty cities and many rural towns were taken. The people were put to the sword and the livestock and spoil was taken as booty. Og was the last of the giants in that region, with an iron bedstead almost fourteen feet by six feet! **V 12–20: DIVISION** The land on the east of the Jordan was divided as had been promised earlier to the two-and-a-half tribes. They would fight alongside the other tribes on the west side and return later to their territory on the east. **V 21–22: DISCIPLESHIP** Moses had taken the responsibility of discipling Joshua, his successor. He reminded him of what God has done and that God would complete the task. He also told him that he must not fear the enemy because God was the One who would fight for him. **V 23–27: DISAPPOINTMENT** Moses recalls that he pleaded with God, whom he had seen work such mighty things, to let him go into the promised land. God was angry with him and forbade him to speak of it any more. He told him to go to the top of Pisgah to survey the land, but that he would not cross into it. **V 28–29: DIRECTION** Instead, God had directed Moses to command, encourage and strengthen Joshua for his future task of leading the people into the promised land. So Moses and the people stayed out of the promised land at God's command and until God's timing. Later, Joshua would take them into it.

CHAPTER FOUR

V 1–14: COMMANDS Moses, having reviewed the history of Israel's wanderings, then urges the Israelites to keep the commands of God. He reminds them that God has acted in anger when they have refused to obey Him in the past and that they must carefully observe His laws now. Wisdom and understanding in the sight of all people will come from keeping them. God's provision of His statutes show God's nearness to Israel. His law must be taught to generations to come so that the descendants of the people will know and fear God. He reminds them that God gave His Ten Commandments on two tables of stone, and that they heard His voice but did not see Him. It has been Moses' task to teach those statutes and judgements so that they will be observed when the people cross over into the promised land. **V 15–20: CORRUPTION** Israel's worship of God is to be absolutely pure. All forms of idolatry corrupt that true worship of God and are to be rejected. **V 21–24: CAREFUL** Moses relates God's anger against him when he struck the rock. Moses himself is thus an object lesson to Israel in that he, too, must die in the wilderness because of his unbelief. They must be very careful to remember to obey God in every detail, especially with regard to rejecting idolatry. They must remember that God is 'a consuming fire, a jealous God'. **V 25–31: COVENANT** Moses predicts that they will, in fact, forsake God and consequently by scattered among the nations. He reminds them of God's mercy and that, if they seek Him wholeheartedly, they will find Him. God will never forget His covenant with the Israel's forefathers. **V 32–40: CALLING** God has called out Israel to be a special nation. He has revealed Himself to His people in miraculous, powerful and completely unique ways. He has delivered them and His purpose is to instruct them so that in driving out ungodly nations mightier than themselves, they may know

God, obey Him, and reflect Him to others as He blesses them in the land He is giving them. **V 41–43: COMPASSION** Moses then sets apart three cities of refuge, showing compassion for those who unintentionally kill someone, so that they can flee there and be safe. **V 44–49: CONFIRMATION** Before restating the Ten Commandments (in the next chapter) Moses confirms where and when God revealed His law. The land conquered is also confirmed, for the sake of record.

CHAPTER FIVE

V 1–5: REQUIREMENT The review of the Ten Commandments demonstrates God's changeless moral and spiritual character. Moses emphasises God's requirement that His law must be learned and observed. This revelation of God's law was given directly by God to him and witnessed by the people in an environment of absolute fear and holiness. **V 6–21: RESTATEMENT** Moses restates the Ten Commandments. The first four deal with man's relationship with God, and the second six deal with man's relationship with man. The fourth commandment regarding the Sabbath day links those two main divisions. No commandment is said to be more or less important than the others, though the second six obviously follow the first four. A correct relationship with God greatly affects man's relationship with man. **V 22–31: REMINDER** Moses reminds the people of the awesome circumstances surrounding the giving of those Ten Commandments, and that God requires a heart in His people to fear Him and 'always keep all my commandments'. Based on those Ten Commandments, which reveal God's moral law, Moses was told to instruct the Israelites on the statutes and judgements they would have as a nation. **V 32–33: RE-EMPHASIS** Moses therefore re-emphasises the need to be careful to do all that God has commanded, without any deviation, and to walk in His ways. Blessings will always follow such a walk with God.

CHAPTER SIX

V 1–3: SUMMARY Moses summarises the principle of keeping God's commands and of fearing God, with consequent future beneficial effects on the nation. He emphasises again the need to be careful to observe God's law and they will know God's blessing. **V 4–9: 'SHEMA'** These verses are called 'Shema'. The orthodox Jew uses them as a summary of what he believes and repeats them twice daily. They contain the summary of the greatest commandment which also summarises those first four commandments, namely, 'You shall love the LORD your God with all your heart, with all your soul, and with all your strength.' This is quoted by Jesus later as the greatest commandment. God's words are to govern His people in how they use their hands, how they see things, and how they live at home. **V 10–12: SINGLE-MINDEDNESS** The Israelites must not forget God's faithful provision and neither must they follow other gods. They are to be single-minded in following God. **V 13–19: SERVICE** Service for God must come from heartfelt obedience and acceptance of His perfect will. Conduct which reflects that will result in victory. **V 20–25: SONS** The Israelites are always to be ready to explain to their sons how God has blessed, helped, kept and cared for His people. The sons must learn that they, too, must observe His commandments and follow Him.

CHAPTER SEVEN

V 1–6: HOLY PEOPLE Moses again teaches that in the promised land, God's people must be holy and must not be defiled by liaisons with the pagan people. No marriages should be undertaken with them and their idolatry should be rejected by destruction of their altars and sacred places. They are to remember that they are holy people to God, who has chosen them as a 'special treasure over all the peoples on the face of the earth'. **V 7–11: HUMBLE PEOPLE** God's blessing on His people should make them humble, not proud. He did not choose Israel (or Christians today) because they were better or stronger than others, but because they were 'the least of all peoples'. It is only His love, power, redemption, faithfulness, and mercy that can ever accomplish this for His people. God will repay those who reject Him and His law. Obedience to His commandments is evidence of belonging to Him. **V 11–16: HONOURED PEOPLE** God has promised to give to Israel great physical blessings and to keep them well and supplied, provided they will keep His moral, spiritual and ceremonial laws. God keeps and blesses His trusting obedient people. They must not compromise with the gods of the peoples they are about to dispossess in the promised land. **V 17–26: HOPEFUL PEOPLE** The hope of the people is not in their own ability, but in God's promises, proven faithfulness, power, and willingness to deliver them and bless them. He is 'the great and awesome God' who is among them. This means that He will work for them in driving out the inhabitants of the land, but they must trust and obey Him. Again, the warning against idolatry and all manner of uncleanness is given.

CHAPTER EIGHT

V 1–5: PROVISION AND PROVING God reminds the Israelites that He has always provided for them, and that when He humbled them, it was in order to know what was in their hearts. His chastening them at times showed His father-like love for His children. **V 6–9: PRINCIPLE AND PLENTY** If the Israelites would fear and honour God, He would bless them in every way. **V 10–18: PRAISE AND PRIDE** God should be praised for His provision and generosity. The Israelites must never proudly think that they have achieved anything without God's gracious hand upon them. Praise, not pride, should characterise their relationship with God. **V 19–20: PROVOCATION AND PUNISHMENT** If the Israelites forget God and worship idols, He will punish them.

CHAPTER NINE

V 1–3: SUCCESS God promises success to the Israelites in driving out foreign nations. **V 4–6a: SINFULNESS** The sinfulness of ungodly nations is the reason why God will drive them out, not the righteousness of His people. **V 6b–12: STIFF-NECKED** Moses reminds the Israelites of their rebellion ever since leaving Egypt. This was so even while he was in the very act of receiving the Ten Commandments. **V 13–21: SALVATION** They were saved from God's wrath against their idolatry in answer to Moses' prayer and positive action. **V 22–24: STUBBORNNESS** Their obstinacy has been shown again and again by their repeated rebellion. **V 25–29: SUPPLICATION** Moses records his prostration before God for forty days and forty nights, in which he prayed for God's grace on this errant people. His plea was based on God's remembering His covenant with the nation's fathers, and on the importance of the Egyptians' recognition of His true nature and character.

CHAPTER TEN

V 1–5: DECALOGUE The Decalogue (another name for 'the Ten Commandments') was written again on stone by God and later put in the ark of the covenant by Moses. **V 6: DEATH** Aaron's demise and the succession of the priesthood by Eleazar is recorded. **V 7–9: DESIGNATION** The Levites were then designated to carry the ark. **V 10–11: DEDICATION** Moses' dedication was shown in praying again for forty days and forty nights on the mountain for God's people. Moses records that it was after he prayed that God told him to continue the journey to the promised land **V 12–14: DEMANDS** God's continuous demands of His people are summarised and repeated. **V 14–22: DESCRIPTION** Some of God's glorious attributes, and the response they should evoke, are detailed. Moses reminds his hearers that it is God alone who has made them into His people.

CHAPTER ELEVEN

V 1–7: CHILDREN The older Israelites must remember that their children have not seen God at work as they have themselves. **V 8–11: COMPARISON** Therefore, the greater responsibility to obey God is on the older Israelites. In some ways, the promised land will present a greater challenge to the Israelites than the slavery in Egypt. **V 12–15: CONFIRMATION** But God will watch over them. He cares for the land and will provide for His obedient children. **V 16–25: CAREFULNESS** The Israelites must take care to resist idolatry, and teach their children God's ways and to obey Him. There are conditions to fulfil in order to experience God's driving out the nations from the promised land. **V 26–32: CHOICE** God sets out the way of blessing (to be proclaimed from Mount Gerizim) and curses (to be proclaimed from Mount Ebal) and urges His people to obey Him to benefit from His blessings.

CHAPTER TWELVE

V 1–4: DESTRUCTION Pagan places devoted to idolatrous worship are to be destroyed by the Israelites in the promised land. **V 5–7: DIFFERENCE** A different place from the many pagan centres of worship is to be chosen by God, and His prescribed offerings and sacrifices are to be made there. **V 8–14: DWELLING PLACE** God will choose a special place for His people to worship, rejoice and rest in the promised land. **V 15–25: DIET** God permits the eating of meat, provided that the blood is not eaten. Offerings must be eaten before the LORD in the specified place of His choosing. **V 26–28: DILIGENCE** Diligence to observe and to obey God's directions is commanded. **V 29–32: DEVIATION** God forbids His people even to investigate false religions through curiosity, once they are in the promised land, even after they have driven out the nations.

CHAPTER THIRTEEN

V 1–5: REVELATION NOT EXPERIENCE God's revealed Word, His commandments, are to govern His people's conduct. If any prophet, dreamer or person claiming to have had a vision suggest otherwise, his opinion must be ignored and he must be put to death. **V 6–11: RELATIVES NOT EXEMPT** Even close relations who disobey God, to indulge in idolatry, must be punished. **V 12–18: REBELLION NOT EXCUSED** God will also deal harshly with those who rebel against Him in enticing others to follow false gods. God will destroy whole towns rather than allowing idolatry to linger there.

CHAPTER FOURTEEN

V 1–2: DIFFERENT The Israelites are to be different, in conduct and appearance, from the pagan people surrounding them. **V 3–21: DISTINCTION** God's people are to observe prohibitions in not eating unclean meat or blood. **V 22–29: DONATIONS** Donations of tithes of produce are required annually and dealt with in special ways at the end of the third and sixth years. The Levites are to be supported.

CHAPTER FIFTEEN

V 1–6: CANCELLATION All debts to fellow Israelites have to be cancelled at the end of the seventh year. God will bless those who honour Him in this. **V 7–11: COMPASSION** The Israelites are to lend open-handedly to their poor brothers, and this is not to diminish as the end of the seventh year and the release of all debts comes nearer. **V 12–18: CONSIDERATION** When a slave is released after six years, as God commands, the former owner must load him or her generously with as many goods and provisions as his prosperity allows. A slave wanting to stay in the family is to be welcomed back. **V 19–23: CARE** Care is to be taken both in the selection of first-born animals without defect, for sacrifice, and in where and when and how to eat these animals once they have been sacrificed.

CHAPTER SIXTEEN

V 1–17: REVIEW OF OBSERVATION The observance procedures are reviewed for the feasts of Passover (verses 1 to 8), Weeks (verses 9 to 12) and Tabernacles (verses 13 to 17). **V 18–20: REQUIREMENT OF ORDER** Honest judges and officials are to be appointed for each town possessed by each tribe. **V 21–22: REMINDER OF OFFENSIVENESS** The Israelites are reminded not to set up images on pillars and not to mix true worship with false. God hates it and will not tolerate it.

CHAPTER SEVENTEEN

V 1: REJECTING REJECTS Only the best must be given as a sacrifice to God. **V 2–7: INVESTIGATING IDOLATRY** Those who involve themselves in idolatry are to be investigated carefully. Idolaters are to be put to death. The goal in these verses is to eradicate idolatry. **V 8–13: PRIESTS' PRONOUNCEMENTS** The priests, the Levites and the judge are to decide upon the issue of guilt. Strict adherence to God's law is to be vigorously enforced by them. Anyone not heeding the judgement of the priest or judge will be cut off. **V 14–20: RULER'S REQUIREMENTS** Any future king is to be a true Israelite. He is warned against recruiting a personal army, and accumulating wives and wealth. He has to write out God's laws and remind himself of them regularly. This will help him to live a humble life and to obey God's commandments.

CHAPTER EIGHTEEN

V 1–8: PRIESTS The priests and Levites are to be provided for. **V 9–13: PRACTICES** Practices abominable to God—such as child sacrifice, divination, witchcraft or spiritism—are to carry the death penalty.

This is to keep God's people pure, and their worship of Him acceptable. **V 14–22: PROPHET** Unlike the false religious representatives of the nations around, God will raise a prophet for the nation of Israel who will honour Him and speak His word. If he is God's true prophet, the pronouncements he makes will take place. This is also a prediction of the Messiah to come, who will be the Prophet.

CHAPTER NINETEEN

V 1–13: PROVISION God reminds His people of the provision of cities of refuge, built to enable someone unintentionally killing another to escape death himself from 'the avenger of blood'. **V 14: PROPERTY** Stealing land by moving the boundary marker is forbidden. **V 15: PROOF** Proof of guilt requires more than one witness to testify against the accused. **V 16–21: PERJURY** Perjury is to be dealt with very severely. Those found guilty of it are to receive the penalty that the accused person would face if he were really guilty.

CHAPTER TWENTY

V 1–4: FIGHTING FAITH God's people must not fear when waging warfare. They must trust God. He will fight for them against their enemies. **V 5–9: PREOCCUPYING PRESSURES** Anyone whose heart will not be in the battle due to domestic considerations, work, new marital relationships, or faintheartedness is to leave the army. A smaller number of dedicated men will do better. **V 10–15: CONQUERING COMPASSION** Cities outside the promised land are to be offered peace terms on surrender and the inhabitants will then serve the Israelites. Only those resisting are to be destroyed— very different from the pagan result of a conquest. **V 16–18: ANNIHILATE ABOMINATION** Nations inside the promised land, however, are to be destroyed with no terms of peace being proposed. This is to maintain the purity of God's people, who may otherwise be contaminated by adopting pagan abominations. **V 19–20: SENSIBLE SIEGES** The Israelites are commanded not to use wood from fruit trees to build siege works, as the fruit is good to eat. There is no point in wasting food, especially in a siege situation.

CHAPTER TWENTY-ONE

V 1–9: CRIME The nearest city to an unsolved murder, and any other controversial matter or assault, shall take responsibility to deal with it and to provide atonement for it through its elders. However, the guilt for that crime does not attach to that city. **V 10–14: CAPTIVES** A captive woman taken as a wife must be properly honoured and protected. **V 15–17: CONSIDERATION** Where a man has complicated his life by having two wives and both have sons, the firstborn son must receive the property due to him, even if his mother was not the man's favourite wife. **V 18–21: CONDEMNATION** A seriously rebellious son must be condemned to death after his parents have presented the facts to the city elders. **V 22–23: CURSE** Any executed person, hanged on a tree, must be buried the same day, so as not to pollute the land. As anyone hanged is under God's curse, the removal of the body avoids the pollution of the land. Jesus will later be cursed on Calvary's tree when He will die for our sins.

CHAPTER TWENTY-TWO

V 1–12: MISCELLANEOUS POINTS Various points of law are detailed to control conduct and to protect individuals and society. **V 13–21: MARRIAGE PROTECTED** Laws concerning marriage are featured and penalties for breaking them are laid down. **V 22–30: MORAL PROVISIONS** Directives are stipulated which deal with moral laxity and sexual crime.

CHAPTER TWENTY-THREE

V 1–8: HOLY CONGREGATION The congregation of God's people is to be so holy to God that some people must be excluded from it. Contrast that with the grace of the gospel by which outcasts can come to know God! **V 9–14: HYGIENE CARE** Cleanliness is to be protected by careful sanitary laws. This outward and physical cleanliness pictures the need for inner and spiritual cleanliness before God. **V 15–24: HONOURABLE CONDUCT** Various other provisions covering a number of matters are given. Behaving honourably is a thread running through the provisions.

CHAPTER TWENTY-FOUR

V 1–4: DIVORCE While God hates divorce, it is necessary for Him to regulate it as a fact of life. This will also curtail the spread of rampant immorality. **V 5–18: DIVERSE** Laws follow on a number of varied subjects. **V 19–22: DELIBERATE** Remembering that they had been slaves in Egypt, the Israelites had to remember the poor. When they would harvest their fields and pick their olives and grapes, they must deliberately leave uncollected gleanings for the poor to gather.

CHAPTER TWENTY-FIVE

V 1–3: REGULATION Corporal

punishment is regulated and strict limitations set to prevent over-reaction. **V 4: REQUIREMENT** The principle given here, that a working animal must be looked after and fed, is later extended and applied in the New Testament to Christian workers. **V 5–10: REMARRIAGE** An unmarried brother is expected, but not compelled, to marry his brother's widow, in order to protect the family line. **V 11–12: RESTRAINT** Limits are placed on the level and type of force a woman can use if she comes to help her husband in a fight. **V 13–16: RIGHT** Righteous standards in commerce are to be adhered to. **V 17–19: REMEMBER** The Israelites are to remember the Amalekites' opposition and deal with them unsparingly.

CHAPTER TWENTY-SIX

V 1–11: GRATITUDE When entering the promised land, the Israelites are to express their gratitude to God for saving and keeping them by giving Him the first fruits of all the produce of the land. **V 12–15: GIVING** The Israelites are also commanded to give to the Levites, and specific classes of needy people, out of a holy tithe to be taken in the third year. **V 16–19: GODLINESS** As a nation of God's 'special people', the Israelites are to cultivate godliness by obeying God's commands and walking with Him. His promised blessings will follow.

CHAPTER TWENTY-SEVEN

V 1–10: COMMANDMENTS All the commandments of God are to be kept in the promised land and to be commemorated by writing on white washed stones. After crossing the Jordan, an altar of sacrifice is to be built and used. Moses, the priests and the Levites are to observe and obey God's commandments and statutes. **V 11–13: CONTRAST** The twelve tribes are then to be divided in two; six named tribes are to stand on Mount Gerizim to pronounce God's blessings, and the other six are to stand on Mount Ebal to pronounce His curses on disobedience. **V 14–26: CURSES** The Levites are to proclaim God's curses on certain specified representative sins (mainly ones which can be done in secret) and on the overarching sin of not confirming the whole law of God.

CHAPTER TWENTY-EIGHT

V 1–14: BLESSINGS AND BOUNTY What amazingly generous and widespread results of God's undeserved grace are there for those who diligently obey Him! **V 15–63: DISOBEDIENCE AND DISASTER** The consequences of the Israelites' disobedience, incurring God's curses on them for their sins, will be almost too terrible even to contemplate. Yet history has often confirmed the tragic experiences suffered by God's disobedient and wayward chosen people. **V 64–68: SCATTERED AND SCARED** Moses warns that the Israelites' rejection of God will cause them to be scattered, to suffer and to be in terror.

CHAPTER TWENTY-NINE

V 1: COVENANT God makes another covenant with the Israelites in Moab, through Moses, in addition to the previous one made at Horeb. **V 2–6: CONTINUATION** God's constant provision, even to the enduring clothes and footwear worn by the Israelites, testifies to His continuing faithfulness to them during their desert wanderings. They still lack spiritual perception to appreciate God's goodness to them. **V 7–8: CONQUEST** Moses records how the kings of Heshbon and Bashan were defeated and that their land was given to the two and half tribes on the other side of Jordan. **V 9–15: CAREFULNESS** Care in keeping the new covenant is commanded if God's blessings are to be experienced. **V 16–28: CONSEQUENCES** In urging obedience to God's covenant on the people, they are reminded of the disastrous consequences of disobeying God. Such consequences will be obvious to future generations. **V 29: CONFIDENCE** Some things are kept secret by God, but what He reveals to the Israelites and their children are theirs forever. God's revelation to them of both blessings and curses will help them to act according to God's law. Thus they have confidence in God's revelation and are encouraged to keep 'all the words of the law'.

CHAPTER THIRTY

V 1–10: RESTORATION AND RETURN When in captivity or exile, if Israel will remember and return to the law of God, He will restore them to a place of blessing. God will deal with their enemies and cause His people to return to the possession and bounty of their own land. **V 11–20: REALISE AND RESPOND** God's promise, in His Word, is always within reach of those willing to avail themselves of it. His people are urged to realise that it is never beyond them, but always near. They must trust it and obey it. Accordingly, God calls His people to respond to His Word positively, by choosing life and blessings. A sinful and negative response will lead to death and curses.

CHAPTER THIRTY-ONE

V 1–2a: CONCLUSION Moses, now aged 120, tells God's people that his life and leadership will soon be over. **V 2b–5: CROSSING** Moses cannot cross the Jordan with the Israelites. That will be Joshua's privilege and responsibility. But God will cross over before them, to help them and to drive out the nations. **V 6: COURAGE** With this encouragement, Moses commands them to have strength and courage to follow their ever-present LORD. **V 7–8: CONTINUITY** Moses commissions Joshua as his successor before all Israel. He urges him to be courageous, knowing God is with him. **V 9–13: COMMITMENT** Moses delivers the law of God to the Levites, who carry the ark of the covenant. The whole law is to be read every seven years at the Feast of Tabernacles. **V 14–23: COMMISSIONING** In the presence of Moses, God Himself commissions Joshua at the tabernacle. He warns of Israel's future corruption and rebellion, and encourages Joshua to be strong and courageous. He promises him that Israel will be taken to the promised land under his leadership. In future backslidings and rebellion, all Israel must sing the Song of Moses to remind them of how they ought to live before God. **V 24–29: COMMAND** Moses commands that the Book of the Law should be placed with the ark of the covenant as a witness against Israel. He commands that all the leaders must hear him read the law to them. This will remind them of the evil that God has said will follow in the train of corruption and disobedience. **V 30: COMMENCEMENT** For the first time, the Israelites hear the reading of the Song of Moses. This time it is Moses himself who reads it.

CHAPTER THIRTY-TWO

V 1–2: REFRESHING REMINDER Moses starts by asking God to bless his words and make them as refreshing as the dew to his hearers. That will not stop him saying some hard things to them. **V 3–4: GREAT GOD** In ascribing greatness to God, Moses praises His righteousness, perfect work, and Rock-like reliability. **V 5–6: CORRUPTED CHILDREN** He reminds the Israelites of their waywardness and of God's care and Fatherhood. **V 7–9: PAST PROVISION** God has divided the land between and for the twelve tribes of Israel. **V 10–14: WILDERNESS WANDERINGS** Even as Israel wandered in the desert, God supplied bountifully and miraculously for them. **V 15–18: FORGETFUL FOOLISHNESS** Nevertheless, self-seeking Israel forgot and forsook God, and went after false gods. **V 19–25: ANGRY AFFLICTION** God afflicted His people to cause them to see their sin and return to Him. **V 26–27: ENEMY'S ESTIMATION** God seriously considered destroying His people. Why did He not do that? Because He knew that His enemies, the pagan nations, would have dishonoured Him by claiming that it was their strength that beat the children of Israel, rather than God's chastisement. **V 28–33: UNENLIGHTENED UNDERSTANDING** The pagan nations lack wisdom, having neither counsel nor understanding. That is why they cannot consider their final future. **V 34–43: JUST JUDGEMENT** God will judge the people of Israel for their wickedness, but he will also judge the unrighteous nations who have afflicted His people. **V 44–47: OBEDIENT OBSERVATON** Moses urges great care in taking God's Word to heart. It must be observed and obeyed. All God's people, including children, must be instructed to keep it. **V 48–52: FACING FAILURE** God tells Moses to go up Mount Nebo. Just as Aaron died on Mount Hor, so Moses will die on Mount Nebo. From there, he will see the promised land, but not be able to cross into it, because he did not hallow God before the children of Israel at the waters of Meribah.

CHAPTER THIRTY-THREE

V 1: PERSONAL BLESSINGS Moses' final blessings are pronounced on God's people. **V 2–5: PRINCIPAL BLESSINGS** God has given His law through Moses. God's principal blessings are always to do with trusting, keeping, and obeying the words He gives. **V 6–25: PARTICULAR BLESSINGS** A blessing suited to each of the tribes of Israel, according to their individual need and situation, is given by their departing leader. Moses knows that only God can answer his prayers for Israel's blessing. **V 26–29: PARTING BLESSINGS** Here are Moses' last recorded words. He pronounces a blessing for Israel collectively, using the name 'Jeshurun'. That means 'the upright one', and is Moses' implied and final reminder to God's people that His blessings can only be fully realised when they walk uprightly with their God in obedience to His holy Word.

CHAPTER THIRTY-FOUR

V 1–3: THE PANORAMIC LOOK Moses' last climb up the mountain, Mount Nebo, allows God to show him the whole promised land. But what an encouragement, before dying, to know that God will see His people through. **V 4: THE PROMISED LAND** God reminds Moses he is looking at the land He promised to Abraham, Isaac and Jacob. God keeps His promises. Although Moses is reminded that he will not cross into it, he must be encouraged to know that his mission will be accomplished in God's purposes. God will ensure that His people will cross into the promised land. **V 5–8: THE POIGNANT LAMENT** No one knows where Moses' grave is, because we are told that God buried him. God's epitaph in Scripture is 'Moses, the servant of the LORD'. He does not die through physical illness or defect, because God kept him healthy and strong. Rather, at the age of 120 years, God's time has come for his work to be finished. For thirty days the Israelites weep over and mourn the loss of their leader. **V 9: THE PEOPLE LISTEN** Joshua, well trained by God through his mentor and example, is filled with the Spirit of wisdom. He takes over from Moses. The Israelites heed him and obey the commands that Moses has given. **V 10–12: THE POWERFUL LEADER** Moses and his ministry were unique. The LORD knew him 'face to face' and supported him with miraculous signs and wonders in order to liberate Israel from the tyranny of Pharaoh's Egypt. God brought terror to His people's enemy, in the sight of all Israel, through this meek and godly man.

JOSHUA

OVERVIEW

PEOPLE AND PRELIMINARIES

✱ Joshua (twenty-four chapters) is the first of the Old Testament's historical books. It follows on from the fifth and last book of Moses in the Pentateuch, namely Deuteronomy, and leads on to the book of Judges. The book covers God's dealings with His people in the promised land as they are led by Joshua. It was written by him probably between 1405 BC and 1385 BC. A 'postscript' is added after his death. An estimate of the period covered by this book is twenty-six years.

PLAN AND PURPOSE

ⓘ Joshua records God's faithfulness to His promises in bringing His people into the promised land and helping them in it. Their new God-given leader, Joshua, succeeds Moses, with the way ahead well prepared. God did not bring Israel out of Egypt and through the wilderness as an end in itself. His plan was to lead them into the promised land. The book of Joshua shows that Israel must trust and obey God to be victorious in warfare, and underlines the crucial value of God's Word. It also stresses the need to be organised in taking practical steps in holy living and fighting for God, while maintaining a clear personal faith and confidence in God alone. These principles are also priorities for Christians today.

PROFILE AND PROGRESSION

From Moses to Joshua, entering the promised land and conquering it in the centre, north and south of Canaan (1:1–2:24); apportioning the promised land on the west of Jordan to nine-and-a-half tribes, and confirming the apportionment in the east to two-and-a-half tribes after looming conflict had been averted, and designating Cities of Refuge and cities for the Levites (13:1–22:34); two speeches by Joshua on keeping the promised land, detail of his death, and burial of the bones of Joseph (23:1–24:33).

PRINCIPLES AND PARTICULARS

We see Joshua's leadership under God and the relationship between Israel's victory in warfare, on the one hand, and believing and following God, on the other. Achan's sin underlines that unconfessed sin brings defeat. The division of the promised land among the tribes of Israel reminds us of the duty to be responsible in spiritual battle, and yet not to misjudge others. Just as God led Israel out of Egypt into the promised land, so the Christian is to be brought out of a life of sin to enter into the promised new life in Christ. God's nearness and faithfulness means blessing is always at hand, but it is only appropriated by God's people when they engage faithfully in spiritual warfare.

JOSHUA

CHAPTER ONE

V 1–3: READY Joshua takes over leadership after the death of Moses, and God tells him to be ready to cross the Jordan and to take the promised land. **V 4–9: REMINDED** God reminds Joshua of the territory to be possessed and assures the new leader that as He was with Moses, so he is and always will be with Joshua. He also reminds him to be strong and courageous, to obey God's Word thoughtfully and wholeheartedly, and not to be frightened or discouraged. **V 10–11: RESOLUTE** Joshua's resolute leadership is shown in that he immediately orders the officers to prepare to cross the Jordan within three days. **V 12–15: REMEMBER!** The Reubenites, the Gadites, and half the tribe of Manasseh received their inheritance on the east of Jordan. Now they must travel with the rest of the

Israelites to fight for the promised land. Joshua charges them to remember that. Only then will they be free to return to their possessions which Moses conceded to them on the east of Jordan. **V 16–18: RESPONSE** The response to Joshua is obedient, immediate and encouraging. The people are conscious that they need God and that no rebellion can ever be tolerated. They repeat to Joshua what God has already told him: 'Be strong and of good courage.'

CHAPTER TWO

V 1: SPIES Joshua, himself a former spy with Caleb, sends two spies to look at the promised land and especially Jericho. They stay in the house of a prostitute called Rahab. **V 2–3: SEARCH** The king of Jericho is told that the spies are with Rahab and sends men to search them out. **V 4–7: SUPPORTED** Rahab protects the two spies by hiding them and sending their pursuers in another direction. **V 8–11: SCARED** Rahab then tells the spies that the whole of the country has heard of God's dealings for and through the Israelites and that they are in great fear of them, because God is on their side. **V 12–13: SALVATION** She then asks for them to save her and her family when the Israelites take the promised land. **V 14–21: SCARLET** On condition that she will keep their invasion plans secret and that she will put a scarlet cord in her window, the spies promise that she and her family will be saved when the Israelites invade. At once, she puts the scarlet cord in the window. It is an Old Testament picture looking forward to salvation from coming judgement through the blood that Christ would shed. **V 22–24: SAFE** The spies follow Rahab's advice and successfully evade their pursuers. They return to Joshua safely and debrief him.

Their encouraging message is that Israel is feared, and God's deeds for them are known by the inhabitants of the promised land.

CHAPTER THREE

V 1–4: WATCH Israel is to watch for the ark of the covenant as it is carried over Jordan by the priests and Levites. They must then follow at a distance and so cross over Jordan. **V 5–6: WONDERS** Joshua tells them to expect wonders from God and calls the priests to take up the ark. They do so and go out before the people. **V 7–8: WORD** God's word to Joshua is that he will be exalted because God is with him. Joshua is to tell the priests with the ark to stand in the Jordan. **V 9–17: WITNESSED** Joshua commands Israel to hear God's word. God will drive out the nations before them. They must choose a man from each tribe to witness God's piling up of the waters to allow them to cross Jordan. The priests then stay in the middle of the Jordan with the ark and all Israel crosses over on dry land.

CHAPTER FOUR

V 1–9: MEMORIAL At God's command through Joshua, a representative of each of the twelve tribes is to take a stone from the middle of the Jordan and reassemble them on the other side of the river as a memorial of what God has done in taking them across Jordan. Joshua places another unseen memorial on the riverbed where the priests stood with the ark. **V 10–18: MIRACLE** The ark of the covenant signifies the very presence of God. While it is in the middle of the Jordan, the waters are controlled to allow all the Israelites to cross. The two-and-a-half tribes with land on the east are mentioned specifically as being included.

As soon as the priests take the ark of the covenant to the other side of the river, the waters of the Jordan return. **V 19–24: MIGHTY** God's mighty power is known that day and is not to be forgotten in future generations. The twelve stones taken from the Jordan are assembled at Gilgal.

CHAPTER FIVE

V 1–9: CIRCUMCISION While the hearts of the terrified kings of the promised land melt after they hear of Israel's crossing the Jordan, the new generation of males in Israel are circumcised. This marks God's covenant with them and their new beginning with Him. The reproach of Egypt is past. **V 10–11: CELEBRATION** Israel celebrates the Passover in the promised land! They now eat the produce of Canaan. **V 12: CELEBRATION** God's provision of manna from above is no longer needed. It ceases. **V 13–15: CELESTIAL** The LORD sends the Commander of his heavenly armies to control Joshua's earthly battles. Joshua responds to the holiness of this Being with reverence and worship. Here is another theophany—an Old Testament pre-incarnation appearance of the Lord Jesus Christ.

CHAPTER SIX

V 1: SURROUNDED Jericho is besieged by the Israelites. **V 2–7: STRATEGY** God commands Israel to march around the walls of Jericho once a day for six days, making six circuits. This is to include all the people, armed men and priests with the ark. On the seventh day, they are to march around the walls again seven times. The people must shout when the priests sound their trumpets. The wall will then fall flat. Joshua tells the people to do so.

V 8–14: SIX For each of six successive days the priests, accompanied by the armed men, lead the Israelites once around the walls, as Joshua commanded. **V 15–21: SEVENTH** On the seventh day, the children of Israel march around the walls seven times. Joshua reminds them to save Rahab and her family. They must not take, as personal plunder, any 'accursed things'. Joshua specifies some valuable and useful metals that will be taken for the LORD's treasury only. The Israelites shout when the trumpets are sounded. The walls collapse. The inhabitants and livestock of Jericho are destroyed. **V 22–25: SPARED** As promised, Rahab and her family are removed and saved before the city is burned. **V 26: SOLEMN** Joshua solemnly announces that anyone seeking to rebuild Jericho will be cursed. **V 27: SPREADING** Because of God's presence with Joshua, the fame of the new leader spreads throughout the promised land.

CHAPTER SEVEN

V 1: COMPROMISE Unknown to the Israelites, one of their own people, Achan, has compromised their walk with God. He has taken accursed things from Jericho in blatant disobedience. God's anger burns against Israel. **V 2: COMMISSION** Meanwhile, unsuspecting Joshua commissions spies to assess the situation at Ai, his new target for attack. **V 3–4a: COMPLACENT** Following the spies' up-beat report, no more than 3,000 men—only a tenth of the best fighting men—are sent to conquer Ai. **V 4b–5: CRUSHED** The 'unexpected' happens. The men of Ai rout the Israelites and repel them. They lose heart. **V 6–9: CRY** Joshua cries in mourning to God and protests that He has not given Israel victory. His concern now is what the Canaanites and other nations will think of God's great name. **V 10–15: CONSECRATION** God highlights to Joshua the problem and the solution. Israel's problem is that there is sin in the camp. His covenant with Israel has been dishonoured and there has been stealing and lying in the matter of taking the accursed things. God tells Joshua to deal vigorously and harshly with that sin. The culprit must die and his body must be burned. Then Joshua must consecrate the people as holy to God. There can be no victory otherwise. **V 16–21: CONFESSION** After Joshua has interrogated the tribes, Achan is revealed to be the guilty party. Directly challenged by Joshua, he confesses his sin. He has disobediently stolen a beautiful Babylonian garment, silver and gold, which he coveted. It is the breaking of the tenth Commandment, not to covet, that is at the heart of Achan's sin. **V 22–26: CONDEMNATION** The spoils of Achan's sin are located. They are brought with Achan, his belongings and his family to the Valley of Achor. There Achan is executed with his family, which presumably knew of his sin and condoned it by silence. They are burned and a memorial mound of stones is raised over Achan.

CHAPTER EIGHT

V 1–2: PROMISE Sin having been dealt with, God promises the Israelites victory against Ai, and tells them how to achieve it by ambush. **V 3: PRUDENCE** No complacency now! Joshua mobilises by night 30,000 fighting men of the highest ability. **V 4–8: PLAN** Joshua explains God's strategy to take Ai by ambush. **V 9–14: PREPARATION** The ambushing party of 5,000 men take their place and the main force of 25,000 position themselves in the sight of the king of Ai. **V 15–17: PURSUED** All the men from Ai and nearby Bethel pursue the Israelite forces, who deliberately feign defeat and retreat to entice them out of Ai. The city is left open and unprotected. They are led beyond the point of Israel's hidden ambush. **V 18–23: POUNCE** The ambush party then capture Ai and set it on fire. Ai's soldiers are now surrounded by Israel and defeated. **V 24–29: PERISHED** All the inhabitants of Ai perish, their city is burned, and their king is executed and covered with a mound of stones, as a memorial in the city gate. **V 30–35: PRIORITIES** Faithful Joshua then demonstrates his spiritual priorities. Following Moses' earlier instructions, he builds an altar to make sacrifices to God, thereby also expressing his thankfulness to God. He writes a copy of the laws of Moses in stone. He underlines the importance of God's Word and God's law. He reads out to the people the blessings and curses, revealed to Moses by God, thus emphasising again the blessings of obedience and the disastrous consequences of disobedience.

CHAPTER NINE

V 1–14: DECEPTIVE PLAN Unlike other nations, which form a coalition to combat the threat from the Israelites, Gibeon decides to deceive Israel into sparing them by lying about where they have come from and how long their journey has been. The Israelites fail to pray to God to ask for His counsel, guidance or overruling. They are taken in by the Gibeonites' deceit. **V 15: DECLARED PEACE** Consequently a peace treaty is agreed between Israel and Gibeon. **V 16–21: DISGRUNTLED PEOPLE** When the people of Israel realise that the Gibeonites are neighbours and not from afar, they want to attack them. They complain against their leaders who, nevertheless, refuse to allow them to attack Gibeon. The promise to Gibeon

must be honoured. **V 22–27: DEMEANING POSITION** After remonstrating with the Gibeonites, Joshua tells them that their deception has caused them to be cursed. He keeps his word and his peace treaty, but tells them that from now on they will always have a lowly position in society as the servants of Israel, performing only menial tasks.

CHAPTER TEN

V 1–5: COALITION Gibeon is an important city, and five kings conspire to attack it, because of the Gibeonites' peace treaty with Israel. **V 6: COME!** The Gibeonites remind Joshua that they are the servants of Israel and ask for him to come and help against their attackers. **V 7–8: COMMITTED** Committed to his peace treaty with the Gibeonites, Joshua marches to fight for them. He is encouraged by God's reminder that He is with them and will give them victory. **V 9–28: COMPLETE** Having engaged the enemy, Joshua's victory is complete. God intervenes miraculously, sending hailstones and stopping the sun to enable Israel to have enough time to destroy the enemy. This intervention and Joshua's planning and action in attacking unexpectedly after an all-night march, and using his best troops again, combine to give Israel the victory. The five kings are captured and executed. Joshua uses the occasion to drive home to his people what God will do for Israel, if Israel follows Him. **V 29–43: CONQUESTS** God then gives victory after victory to His people.

CHAPTER ELEVEN

V 1–5: OPPOSITION A huge number of opposing troops, drawn from a variety of kings gathered by Jabin, king of Hazor, opposes Israel after news of Joshua's conquests circulates. **V 6–9: OBEDIENCE** Joshua leads Israel to a resounding victory against overwhelming numbers, because they believe God's promise of victory and obey His instructions. **V 10–15: ONGOING** Joshua then takes Hazor, the root of the latest source of opposition, and conquers all the cities set on mounds. He is successful because he continues to follow the directives Moses gave him from God. **V 16–22: OVERVIEW** An overview of all Joshua's conquests is given, and it is made clear that God is at work in all of this. **V 23: OUTCOME** The outcome of these God-given victories is possession of the land, partitioning of that land to the tribes of Israel, and peace.

CHAPTER TWELVE

V 1–6: CONQUESTS ON ONE SIDE The conquests over two kings, Sihon and Og, performed under Moses on the eastern side of Jordan, are summarised territorially. Moses already allocated this land between the Reubenites, Gadites and half tribe of Manasseh. **V 7–24: CONQUESTS ON OTHER SIDE** Joshua's conquests of thirty-one kings, on the western side of the Jordan, are summarised. This land is shared by Joshua among the remaining nine-and-a-half tribes. God is at work. His cause continues to prevail even after a significant and pivotal change of leadership.

CHAPTER THIRTEEN

V 1–13: EXHORTATION Joshua is now old and God tells him that there is still a lot of land to be possessed and exhorts him to allocate the land to the nine-and-a-half tribes of Israel. God says He will drive out the inhabitants if Joshua will divide the land between those tribes. Details of the allocation of the land on the east of Jordan are given, but it is noted that the two-and-a-half tribes have failed to drive out the Geshurites and Maachathites. **V 14: EXCEPTION** Only the Levites have no territorial allocation. Their inheritance is the making of sacrifices to God for the people. **V 15–31: EAST** The division of the land east of Jordan is detailed. In giving specific details of Reuben's eastern Jordan inheritance, it is reported that the false prophet, Balaam, son of Beor, is among those executed. In possessing God's possessions, it is always necessary to correct and deal with error. Gad's inheritance is described, with its boundaries including the edge of the Sea of Galilee ('Chinnereth'), with Jordan as its border. The half tribe of Manasseh has its boundaries laid down exactly, both because of its place in Israel as a whole, and so that the other half of the tribe on the west of Jordan is clear as to who owns what. **V 32–33: EMPHASIS** Again, it is emphasised that the Levites have no territorial allocation. They perform a special task for the LORD and He is their inheritance, by far the most important, lasting and life-changing inheritance that anyone could have!

CHAPTER FOURTEEN

V 1–5: COMMANDED ALLOCATION The allocation of land west of the Jordan between the two-and-a-half tribes is administered by Eleazar, the priest, and Joshua. This is done by lot, as God commanded Moses. Again, the exceptional position of the Levites is noted, as they only are given dwelling places in cities rather than territorial rights. Obedience to God's command to allocate is noted. **V 6–15a: CALEB ACKNOWLEDGED** Caleb and Joshua were the only two faithful spies at Kadesh

Barnea of the twelve sent to survey Canaan. Caleb is now honoured by being given Mount Hebron, occupied by the much-feared Anakim. At the age of eighty-five, this great servant warrior of God, who 'wholly followed the LORD God of Israel', is keen to do battle for God, trusting in His presence and help. Retirement does not appear to be an option for Caleb! **V 15b: CALM ACCOMPLISHED** The chapter ends with 'Then the land had rest from war'.

CHAPTER FIFTEEN

V 1–12: DEFINITION The land given to the tribe of Judah is defined by reference to its borders. **V 13–19: DEDICATION** Caleb's dedication to the LORD is shown by his driving out the Anakites. He also encourages Othniel to be positive in attacking the enemy, and rewards him with the hand of his daughter in marriage. Ruthless towards his ungodly enemy, this dedicated man is generous and kind to his daughter. **V 20–62: DWELLINGS** The land of Judah will accommodate the people in 111 cities. The cities are named here in their respective regions. **V 63: DIFFICULT** Inhabitants are not always easy to drive out, as the Jebusites demonstrate. They inhabit Jerusalem, the most significant city in the whole of the Bible.

CHAPTER SIXTEEN

V 1–4: DOUBLE Joseph's double allocation of land is for the western half of the tribe of Manasseh and for Ephraim, with a separate area for Ephraim. **V 5–9: DESCRIPTION** Ephraim's portion, north of Judah's, is described. Ephraim is also granted some cities in Manasseh's western territory. **V 10: DESTRUCTION** God commands that the

inhabitants, who are idolaters, must be driven out and destroyed. They will pollute God's people if they are allowed to stay. Ephraim fails to drive out the Canaanite dwellers in Gezer. Instead, they become forced labourers.

CHAPTER SEVENTEEN

V 1–11: MANASSEH'S LOT The land granted to the remaining half tribe of Manasseh on the west of Jordan is detailed. Manasseh's lot includes a grant to the daughters of Zelophehad by Eleazar, Joshua and the leaders, thus obeying God's command to Moses, which resulted in a change of the law to allow daughters to inherit when there were no sons. **V 12–13: MANASSEH'S LABOURERS** Just as Ephraim fails to drive out all the inhabitants of the land promised to it, so Manasseh also fails to drive out the determined Canaanite city dwellers. They are allowed to stay as forced labourers. **V 14–18: MORE LAND** Manasseh and Ephraim—'the children of Joseph'— complain that they do not have enough land. Joshua challenges them to drive out the warlike Canaanites, who use iron chariots and possess the wooded mountains. This will take courage and hard work, but Joshua reminds Joseph's sons that they are a 'great people' and have 'great power' available. They need to remember that this power comes from walking closely with their great God.

CHAPTER EIGHTEEN

V 1–2: SUBDUED TERRITORY The land is subdued and the tabernacle is set up for a meeting of the whole congregation of Israel. The purpose is to partition the land among the seven tribes who have not yet received an allocation. **V 3–8: SURVEY TAKEN** Joshua complains that the land given by the LORD has not yet been possessed. His command is obeyed that three men from each tribe conduct a survey of the unallocated land. He will divide it by lot among the seven remaining tribes. Joshua reminds them that Levi is not to be included in the allocation, because their inheritance is the priesthood. **V 9–10: SEVEN TRIBES** Accordingly, the land is divided into seven parts, by cities, and Joshua divides the territory by lot among the seven tribes. **V 11–20: SPECIFIED TERRITORY** Benjamin is the first tribe chosen by drawing the first lot, and its territory is specified. **V 21–28: SPECIFIC TOWNS** The fourteen towns included in Benjamin's apportioned allocation are detailed.

CHAPTER NINETEEN

V 1–9: SIX LOTS LEFT—SIMEON Simeon gets the second lot. The allocated land is taken from Judah, without discord, because Judah has too much to handle. **V 10–16: FIVE LOTS LEFT—ZEBULUN** The third lot falls to Zebulun. **V 17–23: FOUR LOTS LEFT—ISSACHAR** Issachar benefits from lot number four. **V 24–31: THREE LOTS LEFT—ASHER** Asher has lot five, which includes 'the fortified city of Tyre', now famous for specific fulfilled prophecies. **V 32–39: TWO LOTS LEFT—NAPHTALI** Lot six goes to Naphtali. The Jordan river provides one border. **V 40–48: ONE LOT LEFT—DAN** The last lot is Dan's, but their borders are extended by further conquests. **V 49–51: NO LOTS LEFT—JOSHUA** The lots are all allocated fairly and co-operatively under Joshua's leadership, which always involves others. God is central in this matter and the allocation takes place at the tabernacle, with the involvement of Eleazar, the priest. Joshua has the confidence of the people he leads, who

mark his inspired leadership by giving him the city he asked for, namely Timnath Serah in the mountains of Ephraim. Joshua builds the city and dwells there.

CHAPTER TWENTY

V 1–6: CITING OF RULES God tells Joshua to appoint cities of refuge, as He had indicated through Moses. The rules for their operation are laid out. They are to provide a safe haven for an unintentional killer of another person. The killer who flees there must present his case to the city elders. He will then be safe from the avenger of blood. He will later be free to return to normal life after his case is judged before the congregation, but not before the death of the high priest who was officiating at the time of the killing. **V 7–9: CITIES OF REFUGE** Six cities of refuge, spread out in the land, are named at this stage, and the reason for them is briefly restated. It is God's gracious provision to provide refuge at hand. The Christian has that close refuge constantly in the Lord Jesus Christ, not only for unintentional sins but also for wilful rebellion against God.

CHAPTER TWENTY-ONE

V 1–42: THE LEVITES' TOWNS As God commanded Moses, cities are given to the Levites from the territories of the twelve tribes. They are allocated between the Kohahthites, the Gershonites and the Merarites. The forty-eight cities, which include six cities of refuge, are spread around the territory of Israel, and benefit each branch of the Levites, who are to serve God. **V 43–45: THE LORD'S TRUSTWORTHINESS** God keeps His promise to give His people all the land. God gives the Israelites rest, victory, and deliverance. Every single word that God spoke is fulfilled. (Sadly, however, His privileged people have not driven out all the inhabitants.)

CHAPTER TWENTY-TWO

V 1–6: WARNING Joshua commends the tribes of Gad and Ephraim and the half-tribe of Manasseh. They have obeyed in helping Israel to conquer the promised land and thus establish the nine-and-a-half tribes on the west side of the Jordan. He sends them to their inheritance on the east side with his blessing. But first, he warns them wholeheartedly to obey and follow God. **V 7–9: WEALTH** Joshua ensures that the spoils, taken by Israel from the conquered and dispossessed nations in the promised land, are shared with the two-and-a-half tribes who will live in the east. Accordingly, they return with great wealth. **V 10–20: WAR?** The nine-and-a-half tribes hear that the two-and-a-half tribes have erected an altar. They fear idolatry and consequent judgement on the whole of Israel. They gather to go to war against them. But first they send Phinehas, the priest, with a party of leaders to remonstrate with the two-and-a-half tribes and warn them about their perceived idolatry. Phinehas tells the tribes in the east to come back to live with them if their land is so unclean. **V 21–34: WITNESS** The party of leaders from the west listens to and accepts the explanation from the two-and-a-half tribes. There is no idolatry involved. The altar was built, not for sacrifice, but as a memorial witness to God and His help in the past. They rejoice to hear of such loyalty to the LORD, abandon any plan to take military action, and acknowledge that the LORD is with them all. The altar is named 'witness' because it testifies that 'the LORD is God'.

CHAPTER TWENTY-THREE

V 1–3: LEADERS Joshua approaches the end of his life. He summons Israel's leaders. **V 4–5: LAND** He reminds them that God has allotted a land for their inheritance and that He will continue to help them to take it by driving out the inhabitants. **V 6–8: LAW** Joshua urges on them the need to keep God's law and obey it. They must always reject the idolatry of the surrounding nations. **V 9–11: LOVE** They are to love the LORD their God, who is all powerful and fights for them. **V 12–13: LIAISON** Liaison with foreign nations, including mixed marriages, is to be avoided. God will not fight for His people if they disobey Him. To allow ungodly nations to remain in the promised land will entrap, ensnare and scourge the children of Israel. Their vision will be spoiled as with thorns in their eyes, and they will perish. **V 14–16: LORD** Joshua points the people to the LORD. God keeps all His promises but will also carry out all His threats if His people are disobedient to Him.

CHAPTER TWENTY-FOUR

V 1–13: PRESENTATION Joshua gathers all the leaders of Israel to present themselves before God. Joshua reminds all the Israelites of God's wonderful dealings with them throughout their chequered history. It is God who has brought them thus far and given them the promised land. They have done nothing to merit it. **V 14–15: PERSONAL** God's faithfulness to His people demands a clear and definite response. They must choose to reject the surrounding gods. They must choose to serve the LORD. Joshua's personal response and choice is a challenging example to them, and to us today: 'As for me and my house, we will serve the LORD.' **V 16–27: PEOPLE** The people tell Joshua that they also will serve the LORD their God. Joshua impresses on them that He is holy and jealous and will treat gravely any disobedience and compromise with foreign gods. They repeat their commitment to serve the LORD. As a sign of that commitment and covenant, Joshua makes a statute at Shechem and records the things decreed in the Book of the Law of God. He places a large stone under an oak tree as witness to remind them not to disobey God. This is his last recorded act of service for his people and for His God. **V 28–35: PROMISE** Joshua dies. According to God's promise, he is buried in the land of his inheritance at Timnath Serah, in the promised land. Joseph's bones are brought up to the promised land and laid to rest. Eleazar, the son of Aaron dies and is buried.

JUDGES

OVERVIEW

PEOPLE AND PRELIMINARIES

Judges (twenty-one chapters) is the second historical book in the Old Testament. It was written in Israel, but views differ as to when it was written. Some think it was written between 1043 BC and 1004 BC. The human author is not clear either. Possibly it was Samuel, perhaps in an editorial role with input from others.

PLAN AND PURPOSE

Israel's slide and failure to conquer Canaan is noted, followed by the appointment of thirteen successive judges to rule parts of Israel after the death of Joshua. Israel's intermittent faithfulness and decline, even to anarchy, reflect the leadership that each judge gives, and the people's response to it. Israel's bondage to the surrounding hostile nations, or deliverance from them, and her final idolatry, immorality and internal fighting are all faithfully chronicled. How often the roller-coaster history of the church has mirrored a parallel sad state of spiritual affairs.

PROFILE AND PROGRESSION

Israel's disobedience, failure to conquer the promised land, backsliding and judgement (1:1–3:6); the appointment and influence of thirteen successive judges and Israel's intermittent deliverances during this period (3:7–16:31); the ongoing downward path through idolatry, immorality, cruelty, and war with the tribe of Benjamin (17:1–21:25).

PRINCIPLES AND PARTICULARS

The book of Judges deals with themes rather than chronology, and so not everything mentioned is in the order in which it happened. The backsliding of God's people from theocracy (God's rule) leads in time to the lawlessness of anarchy. The reminder is that humanity is unable to rule itself righteously without divine involvement. The different examples and leadership styles of the judges come and go. We see how idolatry leads to immorality, and godlessness leads to chaos. The book reminds us that, in the darkest hours, God can act where there is a turning to Him.

Even in times of rebellion and compromise, as with Samson in his own personal life, God is always at work and will achieve His sovereign purpose and will.

JUDGES

CHAPTER ONE

V 1–26: CONTINUING CONQUEST OF CANAAN The book starts with Judah and Simeon conquering the Canaanites and the Perizzites and then recaps Caleb's conquests. **V 27–36: COMPROMISED CONQUEST OF CANAAN** Judges tells of disobedience, compromise, idolatry and intermarriage with other nations. Defeat often comes and God often raises up judges to help restore Israel. In these verses, we see how the Israelites fail to obey God's command to drive out all the inhabitants, even though He is willing to enable them if they seek his help so to do. The children of Israel often prefer the compromise of allowing the inhabitants to remain as labourers, to obedience toGod and driving them out. Compromising God's command is never the way of blessing.

CHAPTER TWO

V 1–6: DISOBEDIENCE Through his Angel, God tells the Israelites that their disobedience means that He will not drive out the nations. They will be thorns in Israel's side. Their gods will ensnare the Israelites. The people weep, offer sacrifices, and return to their own possessions. **V 6–15: DEFEAT** After the death of Joshua, and those who followed God under his leadership and example, the people serve other gods, forsake God,

and suffer defeat from all their surrounding enemies. **V 16–19: DELIVERANCE** God raises up successive judges to lead the Israelites to repentance and victory. But after the death of each judge, the people return to their former sinful ways and are defeated again. They are stubborn and bent upon sin. **V 20–33: DEMONSTRATION** God says He will not drive out the nations but will allow them to remain. The Israelites' attitude to them will demonstrate whether they have passed the test of following God or not.

CHAPTER THREE

V 1–11: JUDGE ONE: OTHNIEL— IDOLATRY Israel's legacy of disobedience means that they now have to contend with the idolatrous nations specifically mentioned in this passage. God's people soon adopt the gods of their ungodly neighbours and intermarry with their people. This is despite all the warnings in the past. God judges them in His anger and allows them to be taken by the king of Mesopotamia. The people cry out to God. His response is to raise up the first of the judges to lead the Israelites. He is Othniel, of the tribe of Judah, the son of Kenaz and the younger brother of Caleb. He frees the Israelites from Chushan-Rishathaim, king of Mesopotamia. Forty years of rest follow eight years of bondage. **V 12–30: JUDGE TWO: EHUD— INITIATIVE** Ehud, of the tribe of Benjamin, is the son of Gera. He frees Israel from Eglon, king of Moab, the Ammonites, and the Amalekites. He takes the initiative in seeking a private meeting with Eglon. Being left-handed and having concealed his sword on his right side under his garments, he kills Eglon. He then leads Israel in triumph over the Moabites. Eighty years of rest follow eighteen years of forced service to

Eglon. **V 31: JUDGE THREE: SHAMGAR—INVOLVEMENT** Nothing is known of Shamgar's origin other than that he is the son of Anath. It is possible he is not even an Israelite. He is very involved personally in the deliverance of the Israelites from the Philistines, killing 600 of them himself with an ox-goad.

CHAPTER FOUR

V 1–23: JUDGE FOUR: DEBORAH—REST Deborah, a prophetess, is married to Lappidoth. She uses Barak, of the tribe of Naphtali and the son of Abinoam, as her agent and assistant when she is judging. She calls and encourages Barak to rise against King Jabin, king of Canaan, and Sisera, the commander of his army. The Canaanites are defeated and Sisera is killed by Jael when he takes refuge in her tent. Israel increases in strength until Jabin is destroyed.

CHAPTER FIVE

V 1–23: JUDGE FOUR: DEBORAH—RECORD Deborah and Barak record and celebrate their triumph in the Song of Deborah. They attribute this to God, to whom they commit their victory and their future. After twenty years of oppression, the Israelites have forty years of rest.

CHAPTER SIX

V 1–10: JUDGE FIVE: GIDEON—FAITHLESS God uses Midianite oppression against Israel after His people's evildoing and disobedience. Israel, cowering in fear and impoverished by the invaders, cries out to God. Through a prophet, He reminds them of His faithfulness to them and of their faithless disobedience. **V 11–27: JUDGE FIVE: GIDEON—FEAR** The Angel of the

LORD appears to Gideon and tells him that God is with him to overthrow the Midianites. Gideon is the weakest member of his family and is from the weakest tribe, namely Manasseh. He is hesitant and fearful. God endorses His Angel's appearance to him by consuming with fire the sacrifice that Gideon has prepared as homage. The Angel departs, but God tells Gideon to tear down the altar of Baal and offer a burnt sacrifice to God. Gideon is so frightened that he takes ten men and does it by night so that neither his father's household, nor the men of the city, might see him. **V 28–32: JUDGE FIVE: GIDEON—FATHER** Confrontation follows this act and Gideon's father, Joash, the Abiezrite, stands against the men of the city. They want to kill Gideon because he has destroyed Baal's altar. Joash tells them that Baal should plead for himself if he is concerned that his altar has been torn down. **V 33–35: JUDGE FIVE: GIDEON—FORTIFIED** Confronted by the Midianites and the Amalekites and the people of the east in the Valley of Jezreel, the Spirit of the LORD comes upon Gideon. He gathers his supporters from the Abiezrites and from Manasseh, Asher, Zebulon, and Naphtali. **V 36–40: JUDGE FIVE: GIDEON—FLEECE** Gideon is still unsure, even though he should trust the word that God has given him. God very graciously works a sign miracle for Gideon by making a fleece wet when the dew is not on the rest of the ground, and then reversing the miracle, just to assure him of God's presence with him.

CHAPTER SEVEN

V 1–8: JUDGE FIVE: GIDEON—REDUCED In two stages, God reduces the number of troops that Gideon will use from 32,000 down to 300. God intends to demonstrate that the coming victory over the Midianites will be His alone. **V 9–18: JUDGE FIVE: GIDEON—REASSURED** Gideon, who is obviously fearful, is led by God to go in secret to the extreme of the Midianite camp and hear a conversation which convinces him, as well as the Midianites, that God will deliver them into his hands. He worships God and goes back to spread the good news to his own troops. He prepares a plan of attack. **V 19–22: JUDGE FIVE: GIDEON—ROUTED** As Gideon's men put the plan into practice, breaking pitchers, holding torches, blowing trumpets, and shouting, 'The sword of the LORD and of Gideon,' the enemy is routed. In confusion, the Midianites fight among themselves and then flee from the camp. **V 23–25: JUDGE FIVE: GIDEON—REUNITED** Gideon encourages the Ephraimites to join the men from Naphtali, Asher and Manasseh. Oreb and Zeeb, princes of the Midianites, are killed.

CHAPTER EIGHT

V 1–3: JUDGE FIVE: GIDEON—DISSENSION Ephraim is annoyed that Gideon had not asked the tribe to join in the battle earlier. With wise and humble words, Gideon enables their anger to subside. **V 4–9: JUDGE FIVE: GIDEON—DISDAIN** The leaders at Succoth and Penuel treat Gideon with disdain. They refuse to give 300 men, who were 'exhausted but still in pursuit', any sustenance. This is because, at this stage, they have not yet gained the victory against Zebah and Zalmunna. Gideon threatens vengeance on them when his current task is finished. **V 10–21: JUDGE FIVE: GIDEON—DETERMINATION** Complete victory comes to Gideon's army as they pursue the very much larger forces of the enemy. Truly this is God's

victory through his faithful few. He takes vengeance on Succoth and Penuel and kills Zebah and Zalmunna himself. **V 22–28: JUDGE FIVE: GIDEON—DEVIATION** Gideon starts his era of peace well, by insisting that 'The LORD shall rule over you,' and by refusing to head up a dynasty himself. However, from his plunder, he makes an ephod which he sets up in his city, Ophrah. The correct use of an ephod is for the priesthood, but at other times it is abused as a pagan object of idolatry. Gideon may mean to show his civil authority by the ephod. Whatever the reason, it becomes an object of idolatry and a snare to Gideon and his house. Nevertheless, Midian is subdued and the country has peace for forty years. **V 29–32: JUDGE FIVE: GIDEON—DEATH** Gideon dies and is buried in his father's tomb in Ophrah. **V 33–35: JUDGE FIVE: GIDEON—DISOBEDIENCE** Immediately after his death, Israel reverts to Baal worship and forgetting God. No kindness is shown to Gideon's remaining family.

CHAPTER NINE

V 1–6: JUDGE SIX: ABIMELECH—MASSACRE Abimelech, Gideon's son by a concubine, persuades the men of Shechem to make him judge. He kills the seventy sons of Gideon, but Jotham escapes. **V 7–21: JUDGE SIX: ABIMELECH—MESSAGE** Speaking from Mount Gerizim, the mountain of blessing, Jotham curses Abimelech and those who have chosen him. The curse is also prophetic. **V 22–55: JUDGE SIX: ABIMELECH—MANIPULATION** Abimelech judges for three years. God sends a spirit of ill will between Abimelech and the men of Shechem. After battling with Gaal, Abimelech kills 1,000 people when he burns the town of Shechem. He himself is killed at Thebez.

**V 56–57: JUDGE SIX: ABIMELECH—
MEMORY** God does not forget the evil
done to the family of Gideon by the men
of Shechem and by Abimelech and fulfils
Jotham's justified prophetic curse over
them all.

CHAPTER TEN

**V 1–2: JUDGE SEVEN: TOLA—
CONTINUATION** Under judge Tola, God
continues to rule Israel. He does so for
twenty-three years. **V 3–5: JUDGE EIGHT:
JAIR—CONTROL** Judge Jair rules for
twenty-two years. He gives the control of
thirty towns to his thirty sons, who ride
donkeys. **V 6–14: JUDGE LACKING:
COMPROMISE—CAPTIVITY** Again,
wayward Israel takes on the gods of the
foreign nations around in idolatrous
rebellion. This leads to captivity by the
Philistines and Ammonites. In answer to
their cry to Him for help, God reminds the
Israelites of their fickleness that has led to
this oppression, and tells them to cry out
to the gods they have chosen. **V 15–16:
JUDGE LACKING: CONTRITION—
COMPASSION** Israel puts away foreign
gods, and shows the genuineness of their
new repentance. God cannot bear to hear
the cry of His people and moves to act.
**V 17–18: JUDGE LACKING:
CONFRONTATION—CALL** As the
Ammonites gather at Gilead to confront
Israel, God's people are ready to call their
new judge and to give him the highest
honour.

CHAPTER ELEVEN

**V 1–2: JUDGE NINE: JEPHTHAH—
REJECTED** Jephthah is of Gilead
(Manasseh) and is the son of a harlot by
Gilead. He is rejected out of hand by his
family. **V 3–11: JUDGE NINE: JEPHTHAH—
READY** After gaining experience by

leading a band of worthless men, he is
ready to lead the people who previously
rejected him, if they approach him. If they
will make him the head, he is prepared to
lead. Ammon attacks Israel who invite
Jephthah to lead them. He becomes their
next judge. **V 12–28: JUDGE NINE:
JEPHTHAH—REASONED** Jephthah's first
approach to Ammon is to reason with
him in order to avoid warfare. He traces
the facts of history and God's leading
Israel to show that the land is rightly
Israel's. Ammon takes no notice. The
conflict must be a military one. **V 29–40:
JUDGE NINE: JEPHTHAH—RASHNESS**
Jephthah vows to God that if victory
against the Ammonites is given, he will
sacrifice as a burnt offering whatever
comes out of his doors when he returns
home. God gives the victory. On his
return, his daughter is the first to leave his
doors. He keeps his rash vow, after a two
months' agreed stay of execution. Each
year, a custom is established to lament the
loss of his daughter.

CHAPTER TWELVE

**V 1–7: JUDGE NINE: JEPHTHAH—
DISASTROUS** Under Jephthah's
leadership, there is civil war with
Ephraim. In what seems like a petty
dispute, the Israelites are annoyed
because Jephthah conquered the
Ammonites without their involvement,
despite his explanation why. The
Gileadites kill 46,000 Ephraimites during
their ensuing disastrous civil war. After
six years in office, Jephthah dies. **V 8–10:
JUDGE TEN: IBZAN—DAUGHTERS** After
Jephthah dies, he is succeeded by Ibzan,
Elan and Abdon. Ibzan, from Judah or
Zebulun (he came from Bethlehem and
could have been from either tribe), judges
Israel for seven years. He majors on
marriage relationships within his family,

giving thirty daughters away in marriage and taking thirty in to marry his sons. **V 11–12: JUDGE ELEVEN: ELAN—DUTIFUL** Elan is from Zebulun and judges Israel for ten years. We read nothing else about this dutiful man. **V 13–15: JUDGE TWELVE: ABDON—DONKEYS** Abdon, the son of Hillel, is from Ephraim. He judges Israel for eight years. His forty sons and thirty grandsons ride on seventy young donkeys.

CHAPTER THIRTEEN

V 1–7: JUDGE THIRTEEN: SAMSON—SON Despite God's repeated dealings, the Israelites again do evil and find themselves in the hands of the Philistines for forty years. The Angel of the LORD tells the childless and barren wife of Manoah, a Danite, that she will bear a son who will deliver Israel from the Philistines. He is to be wholly given to God as a Nazirite. Among other things, he must abstain from alcoholic drink and food deemed to be unclean. She relays the Angel's message to her husband. **V 8–14: JUDGE THIRTEEN: SAMSON—SEPARATION** Manoah asks God to repeat the message to him. The Angel appears again to his wife, who tells Manoah. The Angel confirms his message and says that Manoah's wife must also separate herself from anything associated with the vine. **V 15–23: JUDGE THIRTEEN: SAMSON—SACRIFICE** The Angel of the LORD ascends in the flame of their burnt and grain offerings. They are afraid. Manoah thinks they will die, but his wife reassures him that God is on their side. God would neither have received the offering nor have communicated with them if His intention was to kill them. **V 24–25: JUDGE THIRTEEN: SAMSON—SPIRIT** Their son, named Samson, is born and grows, being blessed by God. God's Spirit begins to stir

Samson. In his up-and-down life to follow, it is the stirring of God's Spirit alone which enables him to make some remarkable achievements and to be a memorable deliverer of Israel.

CHAPTER FOURTEEN

V 1–4: JUDGE THIRTEEN: SAMSON—SPOUSE Samson rebels in seeking a Philistine wife. His parents protest, but God hides from them that He will overrule Samson's wrong intention, in order to lead to the overthrow of the Philistines who dominate Israel. **V 5–9: JUDGE THIRTEEN: SAMSON—SPIRIT** En route to Timnah, to see the woman whom Samson will marry, God's Spirit enables him to tear a young lion apart with his bare hands. Samson keeps this from his parents. Later he finds honey in the carcass, eats some, and gives some to his parents. **V 10–18: JUDGE THIRTEEN: SAMSON—SOLUTION** Samson makes up a riddle about the sweet honey he found in the strong lion. At his wedding feast, he asks thirty men to solve his riddle. He promises each of them a set of clothing if they can give him the solution to the riddle. If they are unable to do this, each of them must provide Samson with a set of clothing. Under physical threat from them, his new wife finally prevails on him to tell her the solution to the riddle. She passes it on to the thirty men, her compatriots, who then tell Samson. He knows that they have succeeded only through his wife's intervention. **V 19–20: JUDGE THIRTEEN: SAMSON—SOVEREIGNTY** In God's sovereign plan and by His Spirit's intervention, Samson kills thirty men of Ashkelon, and gives their clothes to the men who answered his riddle. He returns home in anger and later finds that his wife has been given to his best man. These apparently disconnected and bizarre happenings build up the animosity between the judge of Israel, Samson, and the ungodly inhabitants of the land. God will use this for His overruling purposes for Israel.

CHAPTER FIFTEEN

V 1–10: JUDGE THIRTEEN: SAMSON— REVENGE Annoyed at losing his new bride, Samson is responsible for burning the crops of the Philistines. They then murder his wife and father-in-law, by burning them. He responds by slaughtering many of them. The Philistines then gather to take further revenge on the men of Judah, whom they associate with Samson. **V 11–17: JUDGE THIRTEEN: SAMSON—RUSE** Samson allows the men of Judah to bind him with new ropes and hand him over to the Philistines. God's Spirit empowers him to break the ropes easily and he kills 1,000 of the Philistines with an ass's jawbone. **V 18–20: JUDGE THIRTEEN: SAMSON— REVIVED** Samson thinks that he is near to death through thirst and God intervenes to provide water for him. He leads Israel for twenty years.

CHAPTER SIXTEEN

V 1–3: JUDGE THIRTEEN: SAMSON— DEMONSTRATION At Gaza, Samson again demonstrates his great strength by moving a city gate and its surrounds to the top of a hill. **V 4–22: JUDGE THIRTEEN: SAMSON—DELILAH** Samson now has a relationship with Delilah. Bribed by the Philistines, she perseveres to discover the nature of his great strength, after he has deliberately misled her on three successive occasions. She reveals his secret to the Philistines so that they can overcome him. As a Nazirite, he is under a vow not to cut his hair. He knows that if he disobeys God by having his hair cut, his strength will disappear. While he is with Delilah, he falls asleep and she cuts his hair. The Philistines overpower Samson. On waking up, he does not realise that his strength has gone. They put out his eyes, put him in bronze fetters, and make him labour in prison. **V 23–31: JUDGE THIRTEEN: SAMSON—DEATH** The Philistines have a feast to their god, Dagon. Samson is brought into the temple to be an object of ridicule. The Philistines neglect to notice that his hair has grown and that his strength has returned. Samson prays that God will remember him, strengthen him and help him to avenge himself on the Philistines. He pushes down the two central temple pillars. He dies, but in his death, he kills more Philistines than in the whole of his life. He is buried in the tomb of his father. His twenty years of judging Israel is over.

CHAPTER SEVENTEEN

V 1–5: MICAH'S IDOLATRY Frightened by his mother's curse on the silver he has stolen, Micah gives it back to his mother. She reinvests it in his idolatrous setting up of a shrine. One of his sons will act as priest. **V 6: MASS INIQUITY** This key verse (repeated three times in Judges) describes Israel's sinfulness, which forms the background of anarchy against which God repeatedly intervenes by sending judges to lead the people. **V 7–13: MATERIALISTIC INFLUENCE** A wandering Levite is jobless, probably because of the apostasy. He is only too willing to prostitute his true religious calling to operate an idolatrous religious role for Micah, who will pay him well.

CHAPTER EIGHTEEN

V 1: BASIC PROBLEM Again, lack of

authority leads Israel into sin. The tribe of Dan, having failed to possess its allocated land because of its inability to drive out the inhabitants, disobediently seeks to solve its problem by taking allocated land elsewhere that is easier to conquer and possess. **V 2–27a: BAD PRIEST** The Danites, on a spying mission, come across the Levite when they stay at Micah's house. Having ignored God's will about their properly allocated land, they ask him if their journey will be successful. Keen to please, he answers affirmatively. They then return, with the Levite and Micah's gods, to take Laish. Micah is powerless to resist and the Levite prefers to work for a large clan than for a single family. **V 27b–31: BATTLE PLAN** At Laish, they attack the peaceful Sidonians, burn the city, and rebuild their own. The Levite leads their idolatry at that place and they establish a false priesthood.

CHAPTER NINETEEN

V 1a: DISGUSTING Anarchy continues in Israel. This chapter of increasingly disgusting incidents shows how low human nature can sink when God is ignored. Future chapters will show how the tremors arising from one vile sin will cause a tsunami of evil devastation on thousands of people. **V 1b–15: DEFLECTED** A very worldly and selfish priest takes a concubine. Concubinage, although socially acceptable, is never acceptable to God. After she regresses into harlotry, the priest seeks her at her father's house to restore the relationship. He is persuaded to stay on another four days simply to eat and drink with her father. Thus deflected from his purpose, he leaves late on the fifth day. Having decided not to stay in Jerusalem, he eventually arrives at the open square at Gibeah with nowhere to stay. **V 16–21:**

DISPOSITION An old man is disposed to press this stranger to accept his hospitality, as is the accepted custom. Although he cannot offer him protection against the wickedness to come, he is hospitable. **V 22–23: DISGRACEFUL** Perverted men wish to have sexual relationships with his guest and aggressively pursue that end. This sin triggers a vile catalogue of filth and iniquity in which no one emerges with any credit. **V 24–25: DEBAUCHERY** To appease the wicked desire of the perverted aggressors, the man shows that his debauchery is no less than theirs. Incredibly, he offers to substitute his daughter and his guest's concubine to gratify the lusts of these wicked men. They refuse. The guest then shows that he is as bad as all of them. He gives his concubine to them. They have sex with her and abuse her all night. **V 26–28: DEATH** By morning, his abused concubine is dead, murdered by the actions of these vile men. **V 29–30: DEFIANT** This hypocritical Levite is so annoyed, that having taken her corpse home, he cuts her up into twelve parts and sends her to all Israel. This is a call to rise against the tribe of Benjamin, in whose territory this whole uniquely vile episode took place.

CHAPTER TWENTY

V 1–3: RALLIED All the children of Israel are rallied together against the Benjaminites. Revenge is in the air. **V 4–7: REPORT** The Levite gives a highly selective report of what happened, carefully omitting the contributory sin and blame of himself and his host. **V 8–17: REFUSAL** A tenth of all Israel is mobilised against the Benjaminites, who are asked to hand over the offending wicked and perverted men of Gibeah. They refuse. Further and greater bloodshed will result from all this godlessness. **V 18–48: RETRIBUTION** Israel twice tries to defeat Benjamin, and is beaten off with great casualties. The third time, using an ambush plan reminiscent of that employed by Joshua at Ai, Israel succeeds with great slaughter leaving only six hundred Benjaminite men alive.

CHAPTER TWENTY-ONE

V 1–7: STOCKTAKING Israel comes to realise that soon Benjamin will be extinct as a tribe because all their women and children have been killed. Having vowed not to provide wives from the other tribes for the Benjaminites, Israel wonders how to help solve their problem. They recall that a vow was taken to kill any Israelites who refused to fight against Benjamin. **V 8–14: SOLUTION** It is reported that Jabesh Gilead did not fight against

Benjamin. A massacre of the inhabitants of Jabesh Gilead follows. The only survivors are 400 virgins taken to provide wives for the Benjaminites. 400 of the surviving Benjamite men are given the four hundred virgins to marry. **V 15–24: SHILOH** This leaves 200 men of Benjamin without wives. To meet that shortfall, 200 virgins are kidnapped when they dance at an annual feast in Shiloh. The cities of Benjamin are rebuilt and the other Israelites return home to their tribes and lands. **V 25: SUMMARY** The last four chapters, and indeed the whole book of Judges, show the horrific results of rampant anarchy, emphasised for the fourth time in verse 25. There is no hope or future for an individual or for a nation left to his, her or their own devices. There is no depth to which sinful human nature will not sink, unless God restrains or intervenes.

RUTH

OVERVIEW

PEOPLE AND PRELIMINARIES

✱ The book of Ruth (four chapters) is the third of the historical books of the Old Testament. It is not known for sure who the human author is, but it was written in Israel, very possibly by Samuel. Again, the exact time that it was written is unsure. Suggestions vary from around 1050 BC, to between 1030 BC and 1010 BC, or to 971 BC, or even to around 450 BC! One estimate of the period covering the events in Ruth that occur is ten years.

PLAN AND PURPOSE

(i) Ruth records a love-story during Israel's seesaw time of the judges. It shows the light of God's integrity shining through faithful individuals, against a very dark background. It is not only an historical account of how God honours those who honour Him, to reverse the sad circumstances of Naomi and Ruth, but also is an enacted picture of the blessed role of a redeemer (Boaz). As such, there is a 'sub-plot' of gospel truth. God's faithfulness and sovereignty, combining to bless the soul simply and obediently trusting Him, undergird this scene of human uncertainty to produce His perfect will. Matthew's genealogy of Jesus Christ includes Boaz, Ruth and Obed.

PROFILE AND PROGRESSION

Ruth's flight to Moab, and her sadness, loss and return with Naomi to Bethlehem (1:1–22); Ruth gleans in the field of protecting Boaz (2:1–23); Ruth's relationship with Boaz develops (3:1–18); Ruth, redeemed by Boaz, marries him and bears him Obed, a son (4:1–17); David is in the family line of Boaz, Ruth and Obed (4:18–22).

PRINCIPLES AND PARTICULARS

Customs of the time authenticate the book's historical accuracy, such as the right of the kinsman redeemer and the principle of levirate marriage. The fact that both David and Jesus Christ have ancestors found in this book again underlines the historicity and factuality of the Bible and the coming to earth of the Redeemer. The book of Ruth challenges us to be selflessly faithful to others, and that we need to cultivate godly integrity rather than exercise selfish opportunism. Its lessons include the need to trust God to bring about a solution which pleases him and blesses others, including oneself. Such trust encourages taking wise practical steps towards the fulfilment of the faith expressed. Real faith demands wise action consistent with its goals.

RUTH

CHAPTER ONE

V 1–5: CONTEXT Naomi, her husband and two sons leave Bethlehem in Judah to go to Moab to escape famine. First her husband, and then her two sons, now married, die in Moab. Naomi is left with Ruth and Orpah as widows of her two sons. **V 6–18: CONTRASTS** Now there is a shortage of food in Moab. Naomi hears that food is available in Judah, her homeland. She decides to return. She tells her daughters-in-law that they need not go with her. Orpah kisses her goodbye but Ruth decides to stay loyally with her and to remain with her, even though it means that the chance of remarriage is possibly very small. **V 19–22: CONCERN** On her return, the people of Bethlehem are so concerned at her deteriorated appearance that they hardly recognise Naomi. The barley harvest is beginning.

CHAPTER TWO

V 1–10: RELATIVE We need to bear in mind that if a man dies leaving a widow, the nearest relative can have the right of redemption of the land, by which he will buy the man's land and marry his widow, in order to ensure that the land passes to resultant children of that marriage. He is known as a 'kinsman-redeemer' and sometimes referred to as a 'near-relative' or 'close relative'. Boaz, a godly near relative of Naomi's husband, is in Bethlehem. He is kind and protective to Ruth as she seeks to survive by gleaning leftovers in the barley fields. **V 11–18: REPORT** Boaz has heard of Ruth's selfless loyalty to Naomi and is so impressed with the report that he makes sure that she is looked after, and that there are special gleanings left for her in the fields. **V 19–23: REVIEW** Ruth reviews her situation with Naomi, and learns from her that Boaz is a possible kinsman-redeemer. Naomi tells Ruth to stay close to the young women of Boaz as they glean in the fields.

CHAPTER THREE

V 1–11: READY We need to know that in a kinsman-redeemer situation, a woman who can qualify may approach the kinsman-redeemer to propose marriage, quite honourably and without any lack of morality or dignity. Ruth prepares as a bride and makes the approach to Boaz. It is quite clear that this is done on an honourable and open basis. She asks to be taken under his wing as a 'close relative'. He specifically remarks that she is virtuous. **V 12–15: REDEMPTION** Boaz promises that unless there is a nearer kinsman-redeemer who wishes to exercise his right of redemption, he will purchase the land as kinsman-redeemer. Meanwhile, he secretly gives her a generous supply of barley. **V 16–18: RETURN** Ruth returns and tells Naomi what has happened. Naomi wisely counsels patience.

CHAPTER FOUR

V 1–6: FAIRNESS Boaz' transparent integrity is shown in the open, friendly and fair way in which he approaches the man who has a prior right to redeem the land once owned by Elimelech, Naomi's dead husband. Initially, the man seems keen to redeem it. Then he learns that this will involve taking Ruth as his wife. To avoid ruining his own inheritance, he then declines. **V 7–12: FORCEFUL** Boaz observes the legal custom of witnessing the deal by giving a sandal to the other party. He makes it quite clear that he will redeem the land and take Ruth as his wife. He seems enthusiastic! **V 13–17: FATHERHOOD** Boaz marries Ruth and a child, Obed, is born to them. **V 18–22: FAMILY** Obed will become the grandfather of David, and thus be in the family line of the Messiah. What a wonderful ending to a very unpromising start! This parallels the gospel and is a principle that a Christian can rely on when times are difficult.

---

1 SAMUEL

OVERVIEW

PEOPLE AND PRELIMINARIES

1 Samuel (thirty-one chapters) and 2 Samuel (twenty-four chapters) were originally one book, as were the two books of Kings and the two books of Chronicles. They were divided simply because of length and practical considerations. Samuel and Kings—coming after Joshua, Judges and Ruth which are the first three historical books of the Old Testament—form the fourth, fifth, sixth and seventh historical books. They cover a period of nearly 550 years (1 and 2 Samuel from approximately 1105 BC to 971 BC, 1 and 2 Kings from approximately 971 BC to 561 BC). Chronicles form the eighth and ninth of the Bible's historical books and follow Samuel and Kings to provide a sweep of history from Adam until the return from Babylon in 538 BC. One estimate of the period covered by 1 Samuel is 115 years. The human author is not known, but it is thought that the combined books were written between 931 BC and 722 BC, possibly mainly in the central highlands of Israel, where the action was centred.

PLAN AND PURPOSE

1 Samuel records the transition from the last judge, Samuel, to the first king, Saul. It traces through the lives of Samuel, Saul and David the shift from Israel's theocracy (God as King) to the

monarchy of a united kingdom. It then records the anointing, training through service and fugitive years of David. It reveals Saul's sad decline and death.

PROFILE AND PROGRESSION

Samuel's birth, his dedication, his call as God's prophet, the capture of the ark by the Philistines, the death of the priest's (Eli's) wicked priest sons, and then the death of Eli (1:1–4:21); the ark in captivity and then returned to Israel, Israel's demand for a king, against Samuel's counsel (5:1–8:22); the rise and decline of Israel's first king, Saul (9:1–15:35); Samuel's anointing of David, Saul's seeking to kill David, Samuel's death, and the downfall and death of King Saul (16:1–31:13).

PRINCIPLES AND PARTICULARS

God answers a godly woman's prayer for a baby to be dedicated to God. Eli fails to discipline his sons and evil results. Samuel walks uprightly in a corrupt environment. He is faithful and insists on God's standards. Saul declines from his initial humble trust, to jealousy, moodiness, pride, disobedience and involvement with the occult. This is a warning to us to live close to Christ. David honourably follows God and twice refuses to act opportunistically to kill Saul and thus to succeed him as king. God's sovereignty is evident throughout.

1 SAMUEL

CHAPTER ONE

V 1–9: GRIEF Hannah, wife of Elkanah, is grieved because she is childless. She is provoked by her husband's other wife, Peninnah. Hannah goes to the temple each year and weeps before God. Elkanah finds it difficult to understand the depth of her grief. **V 10–18: GIVING** Outpouring her heart in prayer to God, she promises to give back to Him the baby boy she prays for. Eli, the priest, sees her lips move in prayer and thinks she is drunk. She explains her position to him that she is not drunk, but praying. Eli assures her that God will answer her prayer and she is no longer sad. **V 19–23: GOD** God answers her prayer, and Samuel (meaning 'Heard of God') is born. His parents agree that after he has been weaned, he will be given back to God. **V 24–28: GRATITUDE** In gratitude and faithfulness, Hannah has Samuel dedicated at the temple with sacrifices made to God. She reminds Eli of what has happened. She 'lends' Samuel to God and they worship God together.

CHAPTER TWO

V 1–11: PRAISE Hannah's prayer of praise and confidence in God is a model for all who believe that He is gracious in answering prayer. Elkanah then returns home and Samuel starts his ministry as a child, under Eli, in the temple. **V 12–17: PRIESTS** Ironically, Eli's natural sons, Hophni and Phinehas, are wicked and corrupt men, although they are serving priests in the temple. They sin greatly. They scorn, misuse and abhor God's sacrifices for their own pleasure. **V 18–21: PRAYER** During the yearly visits of Samuel's parents to their servant child, in which Hannah takes Samuel a little robe, Eli prays that God will honour them with children because of their 'loan' of Samuel to God. God answers that prayer abundantly with five children. Meanwhile, Samuel grows before the LORD. **V 22–36: PROPHECY** Eli's sons are also involved in sexual immorality in the temple itself where young Samuel is growing spiritually under Eli's care. They ignore Eli's protestations. A man of God comes to Eli and condemns both Eli's failure to discipline his sons and their wickedness. He prophesies their death, and the raising of a faithful priest in the future. This prophesied priest will reflect God's heart and mind: many see this fulfilled in our 'great High Priest', the Lord Jesus Christ.

CHAPTER THREE

V 1–10: CALL Against the dark background of a dearth of the word of God, God calls Samuel personally three times. On the first two occasions, Samuel mistakenly responds to Eli, not realising that it is God who is calling him. Samuel does not know the LORD yet and is a stranger to God revealing Himself through His word. Both of those will change now. Eli discerns the situation and tells Samuel how to respond to God. **V 11–14: CONDEMNATION** Having asked God to speak to him, Samuel hears that God will judge Eli's family for the sin of his sons. **V 15–17: CONSTERNATION** Samuel has all night to think about the fact that he has to tell Eli the vision, but is afraid to do so. Eli urges him to tell him the whole truth. **V 18: COURAGE** Samuel courageously passes on the grave message to Eli. Eli's response is an excellent example to the growing boy. **V 19–21: CONFIRMATION** God's presence is now with Samuel. He treasures God's word and is recognised by all Israel as a prophet of the LORD. God continues to speak to Samuel, revealing Himself through His word. God keeps, trains, and advances His young servant, despite the surrounding compromise and sin. This is good training for Samuel's future

ministry of bringing God's holy word to compromised Israel.

CHAPTER FOUR

V 1–2: DEFEAT The Philistines defeat Israel in battle, killing about 4,000 of them. **V 3–6: DECEIVED** The elders of Israel wrongly assume that if the ark is with them, they must prevail. They are looking at the externals and not at the need to trust and obey God. This is made evident by the fact that Eli's wicked sons are personally in charge of the ark of God. Nevertheless, the ark is brought back to the camp, and Israel shouts so loudly that the Philistines hear the shout and learn of the ark's return. **V 7–9: DETERMINATION** Although frightened, the Philistines decide that they will have to be strong and fight hard, otherwise they will be mastered by the Israelites. Their determination means that they do not give in. **V 10–11: DISASTER** This time, the defeat of Israel is disastrous. Thirty thousand soldiers are killed. Every Israelite flees from the battle, and Eli's two sons are killed, fulfilling the earlier prophecy of the man of God to Eli. Most important of all, the ark of God is captured. **V 12–18: DEATH** Eli hears all the bad news. On learning of the capture of the ark, he falls off his chair, breaks his neck, and dies. The ninety-eight-year-old priest has officiated for forty years. **V 19–22: 'DEPARTED'** The pregnant wife of Phinehas, daughter-in-law of Eli, gives birth to a boy. In despairing recognition of the complete defeat, loss of loved ones, and capture of the ark, she calls him 'Ichabod', which means 'The Glory has Departed'.

CHAPTER FIVE

V 1–5: SMASHED! The Philistines put the

ark of God by their god, Dagon. They find Dagon fallen face down before the ark. They place him upright again. They return to find that he has fallen on the ground again and is smashed. God can handle his own enemies! **V 6–8: STRUCK** The people of Ashdod, where the ark is now located, are devastated and afflicted with tumours. They insist that the ark must go! It is carried to Gath. **V 9–12: SPREADING** The panic spreads to Gath. In desperation, the men of Gath send the ark to Ekron. The Ekronites are even more frightened, presumably having heard what has happened before. The city is filled with death, God's hand is heavily upon them, the survivors are afflicted with tumours, and they are terrified. They want to send the ark anywhere. See what God can do when He is not hampered by disobedient servants!

CHAPTER SIX

V 1–12: RETURN The Philistines return the ark of the LORD to Beth Shemesh. They know how God dealt with the Egyptians for Israel's sake. They put the ark on a new cart and hitch two cows to the cart. They agree that if the cows go of their own accord towards the Levite city of Beth Shemesh, then they will know that it is the LORD who has judged them with tumours and with rats (which may have been the physical cause of that plague). Gold images of the tumours and the rats accompany the ark as their guilt offering. **V 13–18: REJOICING** At Beth Shemesh, the people look up from harvesting the wheat and rejoice as they see the ark coming towards them. Using the cart as wood and sacrificing the cows, they make a burnt offering to the LORD. The Levites take down the ark of the LORD, together with the chest of gold objects. The watching five rulers of the Philistines see

this and return to Ekron. Details of the Philistine guilt offering are also given. **V 19–20: REVERENCE** God puts many men of Beth Shemesh to death because they look into the ark of the LORD. Thus He reminds the Israelites of His holiness and of the need for reverence. **V 21: REQUEST** A request is sent to Kiriath Jearim, asking them to come and recover the ark.

CHAPTER SEVEN

V 1–2: INSTALLATION The ark is taken to Kiriath Jearim and installed in Abinadab's house. Eleazar, his son, is consecrated to guard it. It is there for twenty years and all Israel mourns and seeks the LORD. **V 3–4: INSISTENCE** Samuel insists that a returning to the LORD must include the putting away of foreign gods and idolatry, and involve a wholehearted commitment to serve Him. The Israelites do this and 'served the LORD only'. **V 5–9: INTERCESSION** In the context of fasting, confession, and sacrifice at Mizpah, Samuel intercedes for Israel to the LORD. As the Philistines approach to attack, that intercession is even more heartfelt. **V 10–11: INTERVENTION** As Samuel sacrifices, the Philistines draw near, but the LORD sends loud thunder and puts them into great panic. The men of Israel pursue and slaughter them. **V 12: INSIGHT** Samuel, knowing that the LORD alone has delivered them, wishes Israel to remember this and sets up a stone called Ebenezer. This means, 'Thus far has the LORD helped us.' **V 13–14: INEVITABLE** With a godly leader, renewed repentance, and wholehearted commitment of the people, it is inevitable that God's great grace and intervention change things. The Philistines are subdued so they do not invade Israel again, and their towns are recaptured. Israel also delivers the neighbouring territory from the Philistines and there is peace with the Amorites. **V 15–17: INFLUENCE** Samuel's godly ministry as judge over Israel is lifelong. He performs his task, both on a circuit and in his hometown of Ramah, where he builds an altar to the LORD.

CHAPTER EIGHT

V 1–3: SINFUL SONS Samuel's sons, Joel and Abijah, also are judges. Sadly, they do not follow God, but dishonestly accept bribes to pervert justice. **V 4–5: SEEKING SOVEREIGN** The people use the failure of Solomon's sons as an opportunity to request from him a king to lead them. The surrounding nations have kings. **V 6–18: SOLEMN STATEMENTS** Samuel is displeased and takes their request in prayer to God, who tells him to warn them of the downside of having a king. God says that their request is a rejection of Him, not just of Samuel. Samuel faithfully passes on God's words to the people. **V 19–20: SIMILAR STATUS** The real desire of the people is to be like the other nations, and they refuse to listen to Samuel. They insist that they want a king. **V 21–22: SAMUEL'S SUBMISSIVENESS** Samuel takes this back to God in prayer. God grants them their request, even though it will not be best for them. Samuel tells them this, and dismisses them. He has done his best, but accepts God's permissive will.

CHAPTER NINE

V 1–14: LOST DONKEYS Saul, of Benjamin, is the handsome man who is destined to be anointed as Israel's first king, by Samuel. His father asks him to seek his lost donkeys. A servant wisely counsels him to ask the nearby man of God which way to go. This puts him into contact with Samuel, who is that man of God. **V 15–16: LORD'S DOING** God has already revealed to Samuel that Saul will come to him, that he will anoint him as commander of Israel and that he will deliver Israel from the Philistines. God has heard the cry of His people. **V 17–27: LED DIVINELY** Although Saul cannot believe that he is important enough to become king, God clearly leads Samuel to him. Samuel even reserves a meal for Saul! After talking with Saul, Samuel asks him to send his servant on ahead while he announces God's word to him.

CHAPTER TEN

V 1: ANOINTED Samuel anoints Saul as king before God. This precedes Saul's appointment by men. **V 2–16: ASSURED** Samuel gives Saul a whole series of signs, which will confirm that God has called him to be king. All of these signs come to pass, though Saul keeps quiet about the whole situation. He only relates to his uncle that the donkeys are found. **V 17–24: APPOINTED** Already anointed by Samuel, Saul is then also chosen through the selection process involving all the tribes of Israel. God accomplishes His predetermined will, even though it is through the free choice of men. He is sovereign! **V 25: ADVISED** Samuel explains and writes down for the Israelites how a king must behave. This is kept as a record before the LORD. **V 26: ACCOMPANIED** Some valiant men, with hearts touched by God, accompany Saul to his home. **V 27: ANTAGONISTS** Saul is despised by an antagonistic rebel faction, but he keeps quiet.

CHAPTER ELEVEN

V 1–4: AMMONITES People weep in

Gibeah at the news that the Ammonites, under Nahash, have besieged Jabesh Gilead. They will accept a treaty with them only on condition that the right eye of each person must be gouged out. The elders of the city cry for help. **V 5–8: ANGER** Saul returns from work and hears of the predicament. God's Spirit comes upon him and he is justifiably angry. He demands forcibly from Israel, and backs his demand with a threat, that all Israelites must assemble to fight against the Ammonites. Saul leads 300,000 Israelites and 30,000 men of Judah. **V 9–11: ACCOMPLISHED** Saul sends messengers to Jabesh Gilead to tell them they will be liberated on the next day. The Ammonites are told that there will be a surrender the next day, to put them off guard. Saul uses three divisions to make a surprise attack in the early hours of the morning. The unprepared Ammonites are slaughtered and their survivors are completely scattered. **V 12–13: ADAMANT** The people ask Samuel to have the men killed who opposed Saul as king. Saul refuses to do so, because he wants to mark the day as a day of victory from the LORD. **V 14–15: ACCLAIM** Samuel leads the people to Gilgal to confirm Saul as king. Offerings to the LORD, and a great celebration, follow.

CHAPTER TWELVE

V 1–5: INTEGRITY In making his address at the coronation of Saul, Samuel starts by establishing, and having this confirmed by the people, that he has always acted with honesty and integrity. **V 6–15: HISTORY** Samuel briefly summarises the history of Israel, showing the intermittent obedience of the Israelites and the constant faithfulness of God, experienced when they repent and trust Him. God will remain faithful, but

future disobedience will set His hand against them. **V 16–17: REALITY** Samuel, who until now has not commented on God allowing them their choice of a king despite having warned them against it, now makes them face reality. He tells them directly that they are wicked to have asked for a king, even though God has allowed them their request and will still bless them if they trust and obey Him. To impress that this is not merely an opinion of one man who is out of touch, Samuel will call upon God to authenticate the authority of his servant by promptly and unusually sending thunder and rain during their current wheat harvest. **V 18: AUTHORITY** God sends the thunder and rain that day. The people greatly fear not only the LORD, but also His faithful servant, Samuel. **V 19: INIQUITY** At this point, the Israelites realise that they have sinned and ask Samuel to pray to the LORD, His God, for them so that they will not die because they have made this evil choice of requesting a king. **V 20–23: ACCOUNTABILITY** Samuel reassures them that if they will continue to repent, putting away idols and evil, and call upon the LORD and serve Him. God will not reject them. He promises to pray for them and to teach them God's way. He urges them to remember God's faithful dealings in the past. He gives them a grave warning of what will follow if they persist in doing evil.

CHAPTER THIRTEEN

V 1–8: PRESSURE Saul chooses 3,000 men (2,000 with Saul at Michmash and 1,000 with Jonathan at Gibeah) and Jonathan attacks the Philistine garrison. The Philistines later react to this attack with great numbers of soldiers and chariots. They so frighten the distressed Israelites that the men of Israel hide in caves, thickets, rocks, holes and pits. Saul leads his trembling troops as he remains at Gilgal for seven days, waiting for Samuel. Saul is about to make the worst decision of his life. **V 9–10: PROFANITY** Panicking, and impatient for Samuel, Saul profanely adopts the office of the priest to offer a burnt offering and peace offerings. Samuel arrives just as Saul has offered the burnt offering. **V 11–14: PRONOUNCEMENT** Unconvinced by Saul's self-justification, Samuel accuses him of foolishness and disobedience, and tells him that his kingdom cannot last, and that he will be replaced because he has broken God's command. God has already chosen someone after His own heart to succeed Saul as king. **V 15–23: PITIABLE** As Samuel leaves, Saul counts his troops and finds there are only 600 left with him. Only Saul and Jonathan, his son, possess a sword and spear, because the Philistines have monopolised the manufacture of iron, and there are no blacksmiths in Israel. Further, Israel is attacked by Philistine raiding parties, one of which has gone to Michmash.

CHAPTER FOURTEEN

V 1–14: TRUST As Jonathan and his armour-bearer trust the LORD, they make a brave attack on the Philistines which is successful. This sparks the turning point in the Israelites' battle against the Philistines, but not without some trouble. **V 15: TREMBLING** Not only do the Philistines tremble, but God sends a very great earthquake to add to their panic. **V 16–23: TUMULTUOUS** Saul's lookouts see what is happening. He calls for the priest to enquire for God's will at the ark of Israel. The noise of the tumultuous happenings in the Philistine camp causes him to tell the priest to cease his enquiry of the LORD. The Philistines are killing

one another and Israel comes out of hiding and chases them. God saves the Israelites. **V 24–30: TROUBLE** Jonathan, not having heard that Saul has put an oath against anybody eating anything until the enemy is completely vanquished, finds some honey and eats it to strengthen himself. When informed of the oath by one of the people, he rightly comments that, but for such an oath, the Israelites would have been stronger to slaughter the Philistines. But this trouble does not go away, as we see later. **V 31–35: TRANSGRESSION** The people are faint and perhaps hear of Jonathan's comments. They rush on the spoil, slaughtering and eating animals with the blood, which God has forbidden. Saul rightly corrects this. He builds an altar to God. **V 36–44: TEST** Saul then enquires, through the priest, whether he should pursue the Philistines, but gets no answer from God. Assuming that it is sin which is causing the silence, he causes lots to be taken to find the culprit. Jonathan confesses that, in ignorance of Saul's curse, he tasted some honey. Saul tells him he must die. **V 45–46: TURNING** The people, who know that their victory is due in the first place to Jonathan's bravery, will not allow this to happen. Saul ceases chasing the Philistines. **V 47–48: TRIUMPHANT** God is gracious to ambivalent Saul, and causes him to deliver Israel from the surrounding nations. **V 49–52: TROOPS** After giving details of Saul's family and army commander, the chapter concludes by telling us that Saul chooses valiant men from anywhere to fight with him. No doubt he remembers the earlier cowardice of the Israelites. This will provide the opening for him to enrol David in the future.

CHAPTER FIFTEEN

V 1–6: DESTROY! Samuel relays to Saul that the LORD says that Amalek must be utterly destroyed. Saul proceeds to attack, warning the friendly and helpful Kenites to escape first. **V 7–9: DEVIATION** Saul defeats the Amalekites, but, against instructions, spares King Agag and the best of his livestock. **V 10–11: DIALOGUE** God reveals this to Samuel and tells him that He greatly regrets that Saul is king because he has disobeyed Him. Samuel cries out to the LORD all night in response. **V 12–13: DECEPTION** Samuel arises early to confront Saul. Saul has raised a monument to himself on Mount Carmel and left for Gilgal. Samuel finds him. Saul dishonestly claims that he has performed the LORD's commands. **V 14–23: DENOUNCEMENT** Samuel shows Saul the falseness of his comments, and in answer to his supposed justification for breaking God's command—namely that he took the animals to sacrifice to God—emphasises that obedience to God from the heart and trust in Him is far better than external sacrifice. Saul's rebellion and stubbornness count as witchcraft and idolatry. God has rejected Saul, because he has rejected God's word. **V 24–25: DECLARATION** Saul confesses his sin to Samuel, stating he feared the people and obeyed what they said. He asks for pardon and that Samuel will go with him so that he may worship the LORD. **V 26–29: DOOMED** Samuel refuses to return with Saul and tells him that God has rejected him as king. Saul inadvertently tears Samuel's robe in an attempt to keep him there, and Samuel tells him that the kingdom of Israel will be torn from him by God in the same way, and will be given to a better neighbour. He tells him that God will not change His mind. **V 30–31: DEFERRED** When Saul again admits his sin and pleads with Samuel to go with him to the elders of Israel so they can worship Samuel's God, Samuel defers to Saul's request and goes back with him. **V 32–33: DUTY** Samuel does what Saul should have done. He kills Agag there and then. **V 34–35: DISTRESS** Samuel parts from Saul for the last time. Having performed his duty to denounce Saul's wickedness to his face, he is deeply distressed and mourns for Saul. Even more sadly, the LORD regrets that He had made Saul king of Israel, in answering the unworthy prayer of the Israelites. Sometimes God gives His people what they ask for when it would be better for them not to have asked but to have submitted to His will.

CHAPTER SIXTEEN

V 1: CONTINUE The LORD tells Samuel to stop mourning Saul and get on with anointing his successor from the family of Jesse in Bethlehem. **V 2–3: CONCERN** Samuel's concern is that if Saul hears that he is going to Jesse's family for that purpose, he will kill him. God tells him to go and make a sacrifice, thus justifying his visit, even apart from his personal mission from God to anoint the king elect. **V 4–5: COMPLIANCE** Samuel obeys God. He goes to Bethlehem, announces his intention to the elders, and consecrates Jesse and his sons, inviting them to come to the sacrifice. **V 6–10: CONSIDERATION** One by one, Jesse's sons are brought before Samuel. The obvious choice to human eyes is not God's choice, because God is looking at the heart. The first seven sons of Jesse pass before Samuel and none of them is to be anointed as the future king. **V 11–13: CONFIRMATION** Samuel asks if Jesse has any other sons. He is told that the youngest one, David, is absent from the sacrifice. He is a shepherd. Samuel sends for him. God immediately confirms to Samuel that he is to be the LORD's anointed. Samuel anoints him in the presence of his brothers, and the Spirit of the LORD comes upon him from then onwards. Samuel returns to Ramah. **V 14–17: COMFORTLESS** Saul's spiritual state gets worse. God's Spirit departs from him, and the LORD gives him a distressing spirit. He is advised to find someone who can play soothing music to him when this distressing spirit comes upon him. **V 18–22: CALL** One of the servants recommends David. He is a mighty man of valour, wise in speech and handsome in appearance. Also, he is a skilful player of the harp. More than that, he recognises that the LORD is with David. Saul sends for David, is pleased with him and appoints him as his armour-bearer. Saul asks David's father, Jesse, to let him stay with him. **V 23: COMFORTED** As Saul is distressed, David plays. Saul becomes refreshed and restored. This situation will deteriorate as Saul's spiritual life increasingly disintegrates, but God's hand is upon David.

CHAPTER SEVENTEEN

V 1–11: DISMAY Terrified Israel is pitched against the Philistine army. One huge giant, Goliath, the Philistine champion, terrorises them. No one will do battle with him as he openly defies them, apparently on a daily basis. **V 12–25: DAVID** David takes provisions to his older brothers, who are in the Israelite army. He notes what is going on and hears of the rewards for anyone who kills Goliath. **V 26–32: DEFIANT** David's curiosity turns to defiance and he perseveres in expressing his observations to others. However, they do not wish to hear what he has to say. Eventually, he is led to King Saul. David

wants to fight against Goliath. Saul tells him that Goliath is an experienced and capable soldier. **V 33–37: DELIVERED** David explains that God has delivered him from the paw of a lion and the paw of a bear, both of which he killed, as they were taking the sheep which he was protecting. He believes that God who delivered him from the wild animals will deliver him from Goliath. Saul agrees. It seems that the combination of Saul's desperation and David's confidence in God produces this decision. **V 38–39: DIFFERENT** Saul has David dressed in his own armour, but David takes it off because he is unable even to move properly in this strange battle gear. David's approach is very different! He takes his staff and sling and he selects five smooth stones. He bravely approaches Goliath. **V 41–47: DERIDED** Goliath belittles and completely underestimates David. He does not even notice the sling but comments on the staff that David is carrying. David declares his confidence in God, who will give him the victory. **V 48–54: DEFEATED** David needs to sling only one of the five stones. It hits Goliath on the head and the giant falls. David kills Goliath with his own sword and then beheads him. The Philistine army flees and is routed by Israel. David takes Goliath's weapons back to his own tent. **V 55–58: DOUBT** Saul appears to doubt (or possibly forget) what he already knew, namely that David is Jesse's son. Perhaps David's courageous attitudes and successful action, so different from his brothers who were cowering in fear, makes Saul wonder if he really could be from the same family.

CHAPTER EIGHTEEN

V 1–4: SOUL MATE After talking to David, Saul keeps him in his household and David becomes firm friends with Saul's son, Jonathan. This friendship will help David greatly in the future. **V 5: SUCCESSFUL MISSIONS** Everything that Saul gives David to do is accomplished with great success. Everyone is pleased. **V 6–9: SOURED MIND** However, jealousy takes over in Saul's mind when he hears people acclaiming David's achievements as greater than his. David becomes a marked man. **V 10–11: SAUL MURDEROUS** While David is playing his harp to calm Saul during oppression from his distressing spirit, Saul twice tries to kill David with a spear, but David escapes. **V 12–22: SINISTER MOTIVE** Fear of David leads Saul to send him away on military campaigns, hoping that he will be killed by the Philistines. Israel and Judah love David because he is such a good leader. David is offered the hand of one of the daughters of Saul, who promptly gives her to another man. Saul offers Michal, another daughter who is in love with David, on condition that David will fight in battles. Saul sees this as his chance to let the Philistines kill David. He has his servants tell David that Saul is pleased with him and that he should marry Michal. **V 23–27: STRATEGY MISFIRES** David responds, saying that to marry the king's daughter is no small matter for him. He is poor and lightly esteemed, and will not be able to afford the dowry. Saul tells David that he will accept as dowry 100 foreskins of Philistines he is to kill. He thinks that David will be killed in the attempt. David, aided by his men, provides 200 foreskins, and Saul has to let him marry Michal. **V 28–30: SUCCESS MOUNTING** Saul's fear of David grows as he realises that God is with him and that his daughter loves him. Meanwhile, David's continued success against the Philistines, greater than any other army officer, makes his reputation grow. He acts wisely.

CHAPTER NINETEEN

V 1–3: RUTHLESS Saul now tells his servants and Jonathan to kill David. Jonathan, however, tells David to be on his guard. He will speak with his father about David. **V 4–7: REPRIEVE** Saul, so often subject to swings of mood, is persuaded by Jonathan not to kill David. David resumes his former relationship with Saul. **V 8–10: RESURGENCE** David has renewed success in the war against the Philistines. This again leads to Saul's seeking to kill David, while he plays to calm Saul's troubled spirit. David escapes again. **V 11–17: RUSE** Saul's men go to David's house to kill him in the morning. Michal helps him to escape and, when challenged by Saul, claims that she helped him under threat of death. **V 18–22: REFUGE** David finds refuge with Samuel, the man of God. Saul's men, while pursuing David, meet a group of prophets and begin to prophesy themselves. They tell Saul that David is in Ramah. **V 23–24: RAMAH** Saul goes to Naioth, in Ramah. He, too, prophesies all day and all night. His mood swings continue to be unpredictable.

CHAPTER TWENTY

V 1–23: FRIENDSHIP COVENANT David flees from Ramah. He shares his concern and fear for his life with Jonathan. Jonathan undertakes to find out the position and let him know. By a covenant of oaths, Jonathan and David reaffirm their support for each other and for their families in the future. A plan is made as to how Jonathan can secretly contact David to inform him of whether or not he has to flee from Saul. **V 24–33: FURIOUS CRESCENDO** While David hides in the field, Jonathan tells Saul that David cannot be with him. Saul's anger is such that he reproves Jonathan, warns him that he can never be king if David is alive, and, in his illogical fury, then hurls a spear at Jonathan to kill him. **V 34–42: FLIGHT COMPELLED** Jonathan puts his plan into operation. By code words given to a young lad retrieving his arrows, David comes out of hiding to talk to Jonathan who informs him of his perilous position. The lad is unaware of this and thus can pose no threat to security. With great sadness, the two friends part, knowing that God is their witness between them and between their respective descendants for ever.

CHAPTER TWENTY-ONE

V 1–6: DECEIVED David goes to Nob. He deceives Ahimelech, the priest, into thinking he is on a mission from Saul. Ahimelech gives him the consecrated bread from the temple to eat. **V 7: DOEG** Doeg, an Edomite, is Saul's chief shepherd. He overhears what David says to Ahimelech. Perhaps that is why David openly deceives Ahimelech, in the hope that Ahimelech would not be punished by Saul for helping David. **V 8–9: DIFFERENT** David asks Ahimelech for a sword, and is given the sword of Goliath, which David himself took from Goliath when he killed him. That sword is unique. **V 10–15: DESPISED** David, now at Gath where Achish is king, is frightened because his fame has gone before him. So he makes himself despised by King Achish by behaving like a madman. His ruse is successful and Achish does not want him near his house.

CHAPTER TWENTY-TWO

V 1–2: CAVE At the cave of Adullam, David gathers 400 men who will follow him. Some are relatives and others are distressed, in debt, or discontented. **V 3–4:**

CONCERN Knowing that there is trouble ahead, David deposits his father and mother safely with the king of Moab. **V 5: COUNSEL** The prophet Gad tells David to leave and go to Judah, so he does. **V 6–19: CONSEQUENCES** Saul, furious over his own son's covenant with David, murders the priests of Nob when Doeg reveals that Ahimelech gave him bread and a sword. Doeg omits to say that David deceived Ahimelech. Saul does not listen to Ahimelech's truthful explanation. Doeg himself is elected as executioner, because others will not kill the priests. He expands the slaughter to Nob, the city of the priests. **V 20–23: CARE** Abiathar, one of Ahimelech's sons, escapes to David. David says he knew that Doeg would tell Saul, and insists that Abiathar stay under his care and protection.

CHAPTER TWENTY-THREE

V 1–5: DELIVERANCE David delivers the city of Keilah from the Philistines, having first enquired of the LORD twice. **V 6–13: DEPARTURE** David and his 600 men are forced to flee from Keilah after Abiathar, the priest, warns him that Saul will come there, and that the people of Keilah will deliver him to Saul. **V 14–18: DEFENCE** David's defence is to stay in strongholds in the wilderness, especially in the mountains. While he is there, Jonathan comes to strengthen him in God and to reassure him that he will be king. They ratify and renew their personal covenant before the LORD. **V 19–26: DETERMINED** Saul hounds David with great determination and gets information from the Ziphites about David's whereabouts. Finally, Saul has David encircled. **V 27: DEVIATED** With the net closing on David, Saul is deviated from his immediate aim of killing him. As a result of receiving a message, he moves away quickly to defend

Israel against the invading Philistines. David calls the place the 'Rock of Escape'. David flees from there to strongholds at En-Gedi.

CHAPTER TWENTY-FOUR

V 1–4: CHANCE As Saul pursues David in En-Gedi with 3,000 chosen men, David has a chance to kill Saul. David and his men are positioned in a cave when Saul enters the cave to relieve himself, unaware of their presence at the back of the cave. David's men urge him to kill Saul. Instead, David creeps up to cut a corner from Saul's robe. **V 5–7: CHOICE** David is even conscience stricken at having cut the corner from the cloak of the 'LORD's anointed'. He refuses to let his men attack Saul, who leaves the cave unaware either that his robe has been cut or that David is so near. **V 8–15: CHALLENGE** David follows Saul, but not with a sword. His humble challenge to Saul is moving. He bows and prostrates himself before the king and pleads with him to realise that he is not trying to kill him. **V 16–21: CHASTENED** Saul is chastened in his spirit by David's humility and weeps aloud. He admits that David has treated him well, but that he has treated David badly. He knows that David will be the king of Israel and asks David to swear that he will treat Saul's descendants well. David gives this oath to Saul and Saul returns home. **V 22: CHARY** Notwithstanding Saul's response at that time, David and his men go back to their stronghold, even though Saul goes home. David knows Saul well and is very aware of the possibility of his further mood swings. Saul will seek to kill David again before very long.

CHAPTER TWENTY-FIVE

V 1: DEATH Samuel dies and Israel gathers and laments him. He is buried at his home in Ramah. **V 2–13: DERIDED** Nabal, an evil descendant of righteous Caleb, is a rich and hard man with a beautiful wife, Abigail. Despite never having had problems caused by David or his men, he derides David as a runaway servant when David's men unsuccessfully and politely ask him for some provisions. David mobilises to take an armed force to deal with Nabal. **V 14–31: DECISIVENESS** One of Nabal's men tells Abigail, Nabal's wife, of David's goodness to them, calling Nabal a scoundrel. He tells her of the protection that David's men have given them and warns her that the whole household will fall to David because of his anger against Nabal. Abigail acts decisively. She prepares a present of provisions and goes before David, humbly putting her case and asking for his willingness not to avenge himself. **V 32–35: DECISION** David receives the gift from Abigail and agrees not to kill Nabal. **V 36–38: DEAD** When Nabal hears what Abigail has done, he has a heart attack and dies ten days later. **V 39–44: DELIGHT** David is so grateful to God that he has not wrongly killed Nabal, but that it is God who has taken Nabal's life. David wastes no time in proposing to Abigail, who then becomes his wife. At this time, David also takes Ahinoam of Jezreel as his wife. Michal, David's wife and Saul's daughter, has been given by Saul to Palti. (Note that at no time does the Bible ever command or commend having more than one wife. In fact, many problems are caused by this, even to otherwise godly people.)

CHAPTER TWENTY-SIX

V 1–9: AGAIN For the second time Saul, in pursuit of David, provides David with another opportunity to have him killed. David refuses to allow the eager Abishai to kill Saul. **V 10–12: ANOINTED** In refusing to harm the 'LORD's anointed', David knows that, as in the case of Nabal, God will take Saul's life when the time is right. The LORD gives Saul and his surrounding soldiers a deep sleep as David and Abishai enter their camp. They spare Saul but take away his spear and water jug. **V 13–16: ABNER** David now calls from the hilltop to Abner, Saul's son and the commander of Saul's army. He rebukes Abner for not having looked after Saul and tells him to look for the spear and the jug of water. **V 17–21: ACKNOWLEDGED** Saul acknowledges David's voice, calling him 'My son, David'. David again pleads with Saul not to pursue him as he means no harm to Saul. Saul, in another mood swing of contrition, admits that he has sinned, that he has played the fool. He says that he will harm David no more. **V 22–25: ANSWER** David answers by asking Saul to send a young man to collect the spear. He repeats that he will not harm Saul and prays that the LORD will also deliver him. Even though Saul blesses David, they go their separate ways. David cannot trust Saul and is wisely cautious.

CHAPTER TWENTY-SEVEN

V 1: FORESIGHT David realises that Saul intends to kill him and so he devises a plan to move right away from him by living with the Philistines, his sworn enemy. **V 2–7: FAVOUR** With 600 men, he approaches Achish, king of Gath, again. This time he does not feign madness to King Achish, as before, but presents himself as a credible opponent of Achish's enemy, King Saul. Achish allows him to live in Ziklag. This means that David is nearby to be able to support Achish in any battles against Israel. David lives there for sixteen months. **V 8–9:**

FERVOUR David does not use this as an opportunity to attack Israel and Judah, however, but to raid the Geshurites, the Girzites, and the Amalekites. He totally destroys every living person so that no report can be given to Achish of what he is really doing. However, the captured livestock and clothes are taken, and Achish sees this. **V 10–12: FOOLED** David tells Achish that he has been attacking the territory of Saul. Achish trusts David and believes that he has become so abhorrent to Israel that he will serve Achish for all his days. David has deceived him again.

CHAPTER TWENTY-EIGHT

V 1–2: DECEPTION Such is David's deception of Achish, that Achish tells David to accompany him in battle against Israel and protect him. David goes along with this suggestion at this time. Happily for David, Achish will soon be persuaded otherwise by his Philistine colleagues. **V 3–19: DEVIATION** Samuel is dead. Saul has rightly expelled the mediums and spiritists from the land. In face of the Philistine army, Saul enquires of the LORD. He is out of fellowship with God and gets no response from Him. He finds a woman who is a medium at Endor and goes to see her. Saul deceives her initially, but then she recognises Saul and calls on an evil spirit who imitates Samuel. God overrules this evil practice to tell Saul, saying to him that David will be king, that Saul will be rejected, that Israel will be delivered to the Philistines, and that he and his sons will die in the battle. **V 20–25: DEVASTATION** Devastated, Saul falls on the ground, is filled with fear and loses all strength. The woman and Saul's men persuade him to eat something, and then he leaves.

CHAPTER TWENTY-NINE

V 1–2: REVIEW David's deception leads him into a compromising position. He takes part in a Philistine military review with Achish, who enlists him to fight with him against Israel. Achish is convinced that Saul is David's enemy, not knowing of David's conviction that he must not harm 'the LORD's anointed'. **V 3–5: REJECTION** Happily for David, the leaders of the Philistines do not agree with Achish and insist that David is excluded from their forces. They fear that he can become reconciled to Saul by turning against them in the battle. **V 6–7: RELAYED** Achish relays this message to David, while confirming his personal confidence in him. Strangely, during this deception, Achish has learned to acknowledge the LORD. **V 8–10: REGRET** David carries on his deception and pretends that he is sorry that he cannot fight against Israel with Achish. Achish affirms his confidence in David again, but asks him to leave in the morning. **V 11: RETURN** David returns to his Philistine base while the Philistines go to fight Saul at Jezreel.

CHAPTER THIRTY

V 1–5: CRISIS David returns to Ziklag to find that the Amalekites have invaded the south. They have carried off all the wives, sons and daughters of himself and his men, and burned Ziklag. **V 6: COURAGE** Despite being distressed, and in danger of stoning from some who speak against him through grief of losing their loved ones, David strengthens himself 'in the LORD his God'. When discouraged, he finds courage in God. **V 7–8: COUNSEL** Before pursuing the Amalekites, David takes counsel from God through the priest, Abiathar. He is told to pursue the enemy and that he will succeed and recover

everything. **V 9–20: CONQUEST** David, with 600 men, goes in pursuit. They are guided there by an abandoned Egyptian who fought previously for the Amalekites. Four hundred young men of the Amalekites escape and all the rest are put to death. Great spoil is taken and complete recovery made of all the personnel and goods carried away earlier by the Philistines. Only 400 of David's men have been involved in this conquest, as 200 were too weary to make the journey in the night. **V 21–25: CONSIDERATE** On returning, some wicked men in David's force say that the 200 men should not have any of the spoil because they have not fought. David, knowing that this was not opposition but genuine exhaustion, insists that they get their fair share of the spoil as well. He is a considerate leader. **V 26–31: CREDIT** Returning to Ziklag, David sends some of the abundant spoil to some of the elders of Judah, who are his friends. Just as they now benefit from their friendship with exiled David, so he will benefit from his friendship with them in the days ahead when he needs Judah's support.

CHAPTER THIRTY-ONE

V 1–6: DEATHS In the ensuing battle with the Philistines, Saul and all his sons, including Jonathan, are killed. Saul is wounded and falls on his sword when his armour bearer (himself soon to commit suicide) cannot bring himself to accede to Saul's request to kill him. God's word is proved true again. **V 7: DEFEAT** The Israelite army flee along the valley and across the Jordan. The people of Israel abandon their towns and flee also. The Philistines occupy those towns. **V 8–10: DESECRATION** Saul's head is cut off and his armour is stripped from him. His armour is put in the temple of the

Ashtoreth and his body is fastened to the wall of Beth Shan, along with his sons' bodies. **V 11–13: DEDICATION** Valiant men from Jabesh Gilead, loyal to their king, journey all night to Beth Shan and take down the bodies of Saul and his sons. Their bodies are burnt in Jabesh and their bones are buried there, followed by a seven-day fast.

2 SAMUEL

OVERVIEW

PEOPLE AND PRELIMINARIES

✳See 1 Samuel—People and Preliminaries. The period of time covering the accounts in 2 Samuel is estimated as thirty-eight years.

PLAN AND PURPOSE

ⓘ We read about David's succession from Saul and his reign for forty years, firstly over Judah at Hebron and then over all Israel at Jerusalem. David is wayward in taking many wives. The book also reveals David's own great sins of adultery, murder by proxy, and suppressed conscience until confronted by Nathan, the faithful prophet. David also has family problems that he fails to grasp and deal with, especially Amnon's sin and Absalom's rebellion. Trouble results. He also faces troubles in ruling the nation.

PROFILE AND PROGRESSION

From the deaths of Saul and Jonathan to David's becoming king of Judah (1:1–27); David as king of Judah, including his anointing as king by the men of Judah, victories over Saul's descendants, and details of wives and sons of David (2:1–3:5); David as king of Israel, including deaths of Abner and Ishbosheth, his anointing as king by the elders of Israel, his victory over Jerusalem, and details of other wives and sons in Jerusalem (3:6–5:16); David's troubles, including his adultery and murder, grave family problems, and rebellions against him; (5:17–20:26); miscellaneous section covering David's dealings with the Gibeonites, heroic deeds done by his supporters, his songs of praise, his final words, his team of loyal and mighty men, and God's judgement on David's sin for numbering the people (21:1–24:25).

PRINCIPLES AND PARTICULARS

☜ David's strengths, weaknesses, sins and repentance act as both examples and warnings to us. The reminder is important that even forgiven sin brings ongoing consequences which cause suffering. David's mighty men show the value of a dedicated team for God's work. We see that yesterday's blessing does not make the man of God immune from today's or tomorrow's temptations or troubles. Especially do we learn the need to be careful and cautious in our attitudes and actions regarding the opposite sex. David's failures remind us to be firm, fair and decisive in dealing with family issues.

2 SAMUEL

CHAPTER ONE

V 1–12: SADNESS An Amalekite, possibly someone looking for plunder from dead bodies after the battle, tells David the bad news of the death of Saul and Jonathan. He dishonestly tells David that, at Saul's request, he killed Saul after Saul was wounded. Perhaps he hopes that David will be pleased that he killed someone who opposed him so vigorously. He presents Saul's crown and bracelet to David. David mourns, weeps and fasts because of the deaths of Saul and Jonathan. **V 13–16: SEVERITY** David orders the execution of the Amalekite for confessing to killing the 'LORD's anointed'. His lie, intended to ingratiate, costs him his life. **V 17–27: SONG** David sings a song of lament over Saul and Jonathan called 'The Song of the Bow'. The title may be based on verse 22 where the bow of Jonathan is referred to, recalling when Jonathan shot the arrows to warn David of Saul's wrath. We see here the principle that one can have tremendous affection for one's enemy as well as genuine grief at the loss of one's best friend. Jonathan was a real soul-mate to David. His loyalty and friendship surpassed the love of women. Some have slurred the reputation of David and Jonathan. However a deep, mutually supportive masculine relationship in no way implies homosexuality, especially when the underlying basis is godly fellowship. There really is such a blessed thing as true friendship.

CHAPTER TWO

V 1: CAREFUL David is careful to enquire of the LORD before approaching the cities of Judah. God tells him to go to Hebron.

V 2–4a: CROWNED The men of Judah are pleased to crown David as their king. **V 4b–7: CONFIRMATION** David confirms the bravery and loyalty of the men of Jabesh-Gilead, in burying Saul, by promising to repay their kindness. All Judah understands that David never wanted to oppose Saul. **V 8–11: CONTRARY** The old commander of Saul's army, Abner, has Ishbosheth, Saul's son, crowned as the king of Israel at Mahanaim. For seven years and six months, David will be the king over Judah alone. During that period, the other eleven tribes of Israel will not recognise him as their king. **V 12–17: CONFLICT** Inevitable conflict between Abner, leading Israel for Ishbosheth, and Joab, David's commander for Judah, leads to an almost Olympic-style contest in which all contestants are killed. A fierce battle ensues which is won by the servants of David. **V 18–32: COMMUNICATION** Joab, Abishai, and Asahel, all sons of Zeruiah, fight against Abner. Asahel chases Abner and, refusing to turn from pursuing him, is killed by Abner thrusting the blunt end of a spear through him while fleeing from him. Joab and Abishai continue the pursuit up to the point when the tribe of Benjamin is set for a further battle that would be very bloody. Abner and Joab shout to each other and agree to call off the battle at that stage. Abner and his fleeing troops return to Mahanaim, and Joab and his men to Hebron after Asahel is buried in Bethlehem. Nineteen of David's servants and 360 of Abner's men are killed.

CHAPTER THREE

V 1: STRENGTHENING In the ensuing war between the house of Saul and the house of David, David is increasingly strengthened, while the opposition is increasingly weakened. **V 2–5: SONS** David has six sons born to him in Hebron by different wives. **V 6–11: SPLIT** A split arises between Abner, the country's military commander, and Ishbosheth, his king. This starts because Abner goes into Saul's concubine, and objects strongly when Ishbosheth remonstrates with him. He threatens to take Israel over to David as king. Ishbosheth is frightened of Abner. **V 12–21: SWING** Abner approaches David, who accepts the approach and is willing to make a covenant with Abner, as long as he gets his wife, Michal, back. Abner delivers Michal, and promises David that he will lead Israel's swing back to him as king. **V 22–30: STEALTH** Joab, leading a strong faction, enters the drama. Although a commander of David's men, he has a private score to settle with Abner for the death of his brother, Asahel. On hearing that Abner has been sent away in peace by David, he entices him from Hebron, a city of refuge, and murders him just outside the city and thus away from its protection. David regrets this and states that this will be on the head of Joab and Zeruiah, his father. **V 31–39: SADNESS** David mourns and commands Joab to mourn for Abner. He laments that he died as a fool, because had he stayed in the city of refuge, he could not have been attacked. David is not yet strong enough to confront the sons of Zeruiah, much as he would like to.

CHAPTER FOUR

V 1–3: MORBID Saul's son, King Ishbosheth, at this stage appears not to have heard of Abner's approach to David. He loses heart, and Israel is troubled at the news of the death of Abner, who, in practice, led Israel for Ishbosheth. If he knew of the murderous intentions of Baanah and Rechab, the sons of Rimmon,

he would despair even more. **V 4: MEPHIBOSHETH** This account of the murder of Ishbosheth, along with what flows from it, reveals that Mephibosheth, one of Jonathan's sons, was injured and lamed when fleeing as a five-year-old with his nurse. He fled on hearing of the deaths of Saul and Jonathan. We will hear of Mephibosheth later. **V 5–7: MURDER** Rechab and Baanah murder and behead Ishbosheth while he is on his bed. **V 8–12: MISUNDERSTANDING** Thinking that David will commend them, they present the head of the son of Saul to David. David condemns them, reminds them that he executed the Amalekite who confessed to the killing of Saul, and reminds them of the wickedness of their act, in that Ishbosheth was a righteous man on his bed. He tells them that they will die for this. David has the two sons of Rimmon executed and Ishbosheth's head buried in the tomb of Abner in Hebron.

CHAPTER FIVE

V 1–5: CROWNED! All Israel comes to Hebron and David is crowned as king of united Israel and Judah. He reigns from the age of thirty to seventy, with seven years and six months of this being in Judah and thirty-three years over all Israel and Judah. Patience and faithfulness is rewarded. **V 6–10: CONQUEST** Jerusalem is regained from the Jebusites, and because God is with him, David becomes mightier. **V 11–12: COOPERATION** Hiram, king of Tyre, cooperates with David, sending him cedar trees, carpenters and masons to build him a house. David takes this as a sign of blessing on Israel from the LORD. **V 13–16: CONCUBINES** David takes more concubines as well as wives, and extends his family, despite knowing how a king should rule, based on Samuel's clear teaching. **V 17–19: CAREFUL** Nevertheless

David continues to be careful to seek the LORD before deciding whether to go and fight the perennial enemy, the Philistines. God tells him to go up and that He will deliver the Philistines into his hand. **V 20–25: CAUSE** In defeating the Philistines twice, at Baal Perrizim and in the Valley of Rephaim, it is clear that God intervenes to help David. He is only too ready both to follow God's commands and to acknowledge that God's hand in the battle gives him victory.

CHAPTER SIX

V 1–2: DESIRE David has a commendable desire to bring back the ark of God to its central position. **V 3–8: DOWNFALL** Sadly, he ignores the command of Scripture, that the ark must be borne by men carrying it on poles, to be located in the rings fixed on the ark for that purpose. Uzzah offends God's holiness, clearly taught before, by touching the ark when the oxen, which pull the cart, stumble. The ark was wrongfully carried on a cart. God slays Uzza. David, in his ignorance, negligence, or forgetfulness, is angry. **V 9–11: DREAD** David is also afraid of the LORD and will not take the ark into the city of David. The ark stays with the household of Obed-Edom, the Gittite, and God's blessing rests upon his household. **V 12–16a: DELIGHT** Hearing of the blessing of Obed-Edom, David has the ark brought to the City of David. Sacrifices, shouting, and the sound of a trumpet are augmented by David's vigorous leaping, whirling and dancing before the LORD. There is delight at the return of the ark. **V 16b: DESPISED** Michal, David's wife who was returned to him by Abner, despises David in her heart as she sees him dancing so enthusiastically. **V 17–19: DEVOTION** David continues with offerings, showing his devotion to the LORD, and distributes food to the people. **V 20–23: DOMESTIC** Returning to bless his own household, David has a serious domestic dispute with Michal. She accuses him of immodesty in his earlier gyrating. He protests that this was before the LORD, and that he will play music before the LORD also. He protests her opposition and states that he will be held in honour. Michal will never bear children to David. Whether the cause is David's possible abstention from sexual relations with her or simply because God prevented conception, we do not know. Also, opinions are divided as to who is right—David or Michal. Immodesty must never occur in worship, and in the Bible, dancing often accompanies sin. Worship should be conducted 'decently and in order'. But God-honouring, enthusiastic and spontaneous rejoicing should be encouraged.

CHAPTER SEVEN

V 1–2: CONCERN David is concerned that the ark of God does not have a permanent building, and he shares this concern with Nathan the prophet. **V 3: COUNSEL** Nathan tells David to go and do what is in his heart. **V 4–15: CORRECTION** God reveals to Nathan that David will not build a house for God, but his seed will. Moreover, God will build a house for David, meaning his dynasty. **V 16: COVENANT** God establishes the Davidic covenant in which he says 'your house and your kingdom shall be established forever before you. Your throne shall be established for ever.' This will find its fulfilment in great David's greater Son, the Lord Jesus Christ. **V 17–29: CONTINUATION** David humbly thanks and praises God, and is grateful that He has continued with David so far. He acknowledges God's faithful character and dealings with Israel and asks Him to continue to bless and keep 'the house of Your servant' so that it will 'be blessed for ever'.

CHAPTER EIGHT

V 1–12: ACQUIRE David defeats many enemies on many fronts and acquires towns, wealth, and people. **V 13–14a: ACCLAIM** David's reputation rises, and he is acclaimed as a mighty king through his conquests. **V 14b: ACKNOWLEDGEMENT** God's preserving hand on David is the reason why he has this success. **V 15–18: ADMINISTRATION** David's reign is characterised by wise administration of justice and judgement for his people. David attracts good men around him.

CHAPTER NINE

V 1: PROMISE REMEMBERED David, remembering his promise to Jonathan, looks for relatives of Saul and Jonathan to whom he can show kindness. **V 2–8: PRIVILEGED RELATIVE** Ziba, one of Saul's servants, tells him about the lame Mephibosheth, Jonathan's son. David summons Mephibosheth and reassures him that he wants to show kindness to him because of Jonathan. Despite his lameness, he will enjoy privilege and acceptance. Mephibosheth shows humility and dignity as well as gratitude. **V 9–13: PROVISIONS RESERVED** David decides that Mephibosheth will eat continually at the king's table, and that Ziba, his sons and his servants will serve Mephibosheth.

CHAPTER TEN

V 1–4: KINDNESS REJECTED David also wishes to show kindness to Hanun of Ammon, because of the way that his father Nahash had shown kindness to David. David sends his servants on a mission of peace. They are viewed with suspicion, ridiculed, abused, and sent away. **V 5–8: KING ROUSED** When David hears this, he tells them to wait until their beards have grown, half of which had been shaved off in their abuse by the Ammonites. David sends Joab with all the army and mighty men against the Ammonites and the Syrians who support them. **V 9–19: KINGS ROUTED** Joab and Abishai fight with courage and resolution against the enemy. They rout the enemy with great slaughter, and the other kings make peace with Israel when they see this. The Syrians do not support the Ammonites any more!

CHAPTER ELEVEN

V 1: INACTIVE David should be leading his army to battle but stays at home. **V 2–5: INIQUITY** David is tempted when he sees Bathsheba, the wife of Uriah, bathing. He sends for her, commits adultery with her, and she becomes pregnant. **V 6–8: INFERENCE** Uriah, Bathsheba's husband, is away fighting with the army. David recalls him to his palace under the pretext of asking how the battle is going. He releases Uriah to go home in the hope that the baby to be born will then be considered to be Uriah's. This plan cannot work unless Uriah goes home and sleeps with his wife. **V 9–11: INVOLVEMENT** Uriah is so involved and identified with Israel and its battles, and with the ark of God, that he refuses to go and sleep in his house, but sleeps alongside his master's servants. **V 12–13: INTOXICATION** David invites him to eat and drink with him, and gets him drunk. Even so, Uriah will not go home to his right and privilege of sleeping with his wife, but carries on in his identification with Israel by sleeping in the servants' quarters. **V 14–17: INSTRUCTION** David decides that he will murder Uriah by the hand of the enemy, and writes to instruct Joab to put Uriah in the front line of the battle and then retreat. The plan works and Uriah is killed, along with others of David's army. **V 18–25: INFORMATION** Joab sends a messenger to inform David of what has happened. David tells the messenger to encourage Joab, because this kind of thing happens in a war. **V 26–27: INDIGNATION** After a time of mourning, Bathsheba becomes David's wife and bears his child. But God is displeased with David's devious and sinful behaviour.

CHAPTER TWELVE

V 1–6: PROPHET Nathan the prophet tells David of a very rich man who killed the pet lamb of a very poor man, although he had many flocks and herds himself. Not recognising this as a parable, David is angry and says that this man must die. **V 7–10: POINTED** Nathan tells David that the parable refers to him. He has so much, yet he has stolen Uriah's wife and killed Uriah. **V 11–13a: PENITENT** Although one wonders why David took so long to recognise his sin and to repent from it, he is truly penitent when Nathan confronts him. He now admits his sin against the LORD. **V 13b: PARDON** As soon as David repents and confesses his sin, Nathan tells him that God has put away his sin. He will not die. **V 14: PUNISHMENT** David is told, however, that his sin has caused God's name to be blasphemed, and that God will punish him by not allowing his child by Bathsheba to live. **V 15–23: PURPOSE** The child dies despite David's intense prayer and fasting for a week. His servants are surprised when David's mood lightens after the death of the child. He gives the

reason that he prayed for his son while he was ill, but now it is too late. He must now get on with his life and accept God's purpose in all of this. **V 24–25: PREGNANT** Bathsheba becomes pregnant again, and Solomon is born to David and Bathsheba. **V 26–31: PRIZE** Meanwhile, David joins Joab to win the battle against the Ammonite royal city of Rabbah. The conquered Ammonites are made to labour. David and all the people return to Jerusalem.

CHAPTER THIRTEEN

V 1–14: RAPE David's son, Amnon, is infatuated with his half-sister, Tamar, the beautiful sister of Absalom. Taking cynical advice from cousin Jonadab, Amnon persuades his gullible father to send Tamar over to where he is pretending to be ill. She prepares food for him but he takes her and rapes her. **V 15–19: REJECTION** Amnon's wicked act is initially inspired by what he thinks is love for Tamar. Having gratified his lust, however, he now rejects her completely and throws her out unceremoniously. She mourns and weeps as she leaves. **V 20–22: RUINED** This young woman's life is ruined by her half-brother's sin. David is furious but does nothing. Absalom hears of it and refuses to speak to Amnon. He tries to comfort his sister. **V 23–29: REVENGE** Absalom, however, harbours hatred against his half-brother, Amnon, and conspires to have him killed by his men. Amnon is murdered. **V 30–33: REPORT** David receives a false report that all the king's sons have been killed, but is then assured that only Amnon has died. David learns from Jonadab, who gave the original wicked advice to Amnon that led to the rape, that Absalom intended to kill Amnon since the rape of Tamar. **V 34–39: REGRETS** Absalom flees. David's distressed sons come to him. David, his sons and his servants weep. David mourns every day for Absalom. For three years he longs to see Absalom, but cannot.

CHAPTER FOURTEEN

V 1–11: ANOTHER PARABLE Joab primes a wise woman from Tekoa to go to David and tell him an invented story about a conflict between her two sons. The story parallels the position between Absalom and Amnon. Joab must know that Nathan used the same tactic when confronting David with the murder of Uriah and adultery with Bathsheba. David's response is one that enables the woman to apply the parable to the king's situation. **V 12–17: APPLIED PERSONALLY** The woman applies the story personally to David and reminds the king that God Himself makes plans to enable a banished person to be reconciled to Him. **V 18–24: ACTION PROVOKED** David is provoked to act. Having discerned that Joab is behind this story, and having accepted his logic, David allows Absalom back to Jerusalem, but only to his own house. He will not allow himself to meet with Absalom face-to-face, probably because of the conclusions that people may draw. **V 25–32: ABSALOM PROACTIVE** Joab, possibly seeing the king's mood, refuses to respond to Absalom's communication, until Absalom burns his barley field and causes Joab to see him in person. In the ensuing discussion, Absalom persuades Joab to ask the king to accept Absalom completely. **V 33: ACCEPTED PERSON** Joab goes to the king, tells him what Absalom has said, and the king summons Absalom, who approaches him with great respect. David kisses Absalom.

CHAPTER FIFTEEN

V 1–6: COMING Absalom ingratiates himself with the people by thinly veiled offers of acquiring judicial satisfactions for them, and by personal contact with them. He steals their hearts. **V 7–12: CONSPIRACY** Absalom deceives David, goes to Hebron, and pursues his conspiracy to become king. Ahithophel joins him. So do many others. **V 13–18: COMPULSION** When David is told the hearts of Israel are with Absalom, he is counselled to flee Jerusalem with his household and people, except for ten concubines whom he leaves behind. He flees to avoid personal ruin and to save the city. **V 19–22: COMMITMENT** Ittai, the Gittite, refuses David's offer to go back to Jerusalem where he will be safe. Despite his very recent exile to Israel, he declares his obedience and loyalty to the king and marches with him. Such commitment and encouragement mean a lot at a time like this. **V 23: CRYING** As David proceeds by the Kidron valley to the desert, all the people weep as he passes by them. **V 24–37: CONSTRUCTIVE** Even in retreat and sadness, David thinks and acts constructively and strategically. Not only does he pray to God, but he plants key people, who go back to Jerusalem. Included among them are Zadok and Abiathar, the priests, and Hushai, his counsellor. As David's eyes, ears and mouthpiece, they will play an influential role in future events. David is not finished yet.

CHAPTER SIXTEEN

V 1–4: OPPORTUNISM Ziba, Mephibosheth's servant, maliciously tells David that Mephibosheth has defaulted to Jerusalem. David grants him everything belonging to Mephibosheth, not checking his false story. **V 5–14: OPPOSITION** Shimei curses and abuses David. David refuses to have him struck down and leaves the matter with the LORD. **V 15–19: OPPORTUNITY** Absalom has reached Jerusalem. Hushai, David's friend, joins him, pretending to be his servant. This will serve David well in the future. **V 20–23: ORACLE** Ahithophel persuades Absalom to lie with David's concubines as a sign of contempt. Ahithophel is regarded as the very oracle of God. Before long, Hushai will take over from him, to David's great benefit.

CHAPTER SEVENTEEN

V 1–4: GOOD COUNSEL Ahithophel tells Absalom to let him lead 12,000 men to attack David while he is weak. Absalom and the elders of Israel are about to follow that plan. **V 5–14: GOD'S CONFUSION** For confirmation, Absalom asks the advice of Hushai the Archite, David's 'plant'. He advises him to muster all Israel under Absalom's personal leadership , knowing that this will give David more time to escape. Hushai's advice is taken. God purposes to defeat Ahithophel's counsel by Hushai's advice. **V 15–22: GUIDED CROSSING** Hushai gets word to David through Jonathan and Ahimaaz, themselves informed by Zadok and Abiathar at Hushai's request, to cross quickly onto the other side of the Jordan to avoid any attack from Absalom. Jonathan and Ahimaaz narrowly escape capture. David and everyone with him cross over the Jordan before morning dawns. **V 23: GRIEVED COUNSELLOR** Ahithophel is so grieved by the rejection of his advice that he commits suicide. **V 24–26: GILEAD'S CAMP** Absalom, now with Amasa controlling his army, camps in the land of Gilead, on the other side of the Jordan to David. **V 27–29: GREATLY**

COMFORTED David and those with him in Mahanaim receive bedding, necessary articles, and much needed provision of food from those whose support must give great comfort.

CHAPTER EIGHTEEN

V 1–4: WAR David conducts a census and then appoints Joab, Abishai, and Ittai as his military commanders in the war against Israel. He takes their advice not to go out with them to the battle. **V 5: WARNING** David commands his leaders to deal gently with Absalom, his son, for his sake as his father. All the commanders of the army hear this. **V 6–18: WILFULNESS** David's troops win the battle in the woods of Ephraim, killing 20,000 of Saul's army. Absalom rides his mule into the bough of a tree and is suspended there by his head. Ignoring David's instructions, and the protest of one of his men who refuses to kill Absalom, Joab plunges three spears into the heart of defenceless Absalom who is also struck by Joab's men. Joab calls off the battle. Absalom is put in a pit and covered by a heap of rocks. This is a sad contrast to the monument he has already built for himself. **V 19–32: WONDERING** While King David wonders what has happened in the battle, a decision is taken to send two runners to him. Ahimaaz insists that he should go, but when he is the first runner to reach David, he only tells him of the victory, and lies about the fact that he does not know what has happened to Absalom. A Cushite runner, who started before Ahimaaz but took longer to reach David, arrives soon afterwards and tells David of Absalom's death. **V 33: WEEPING** The lament of David over Absalom is one of the saddest parts of Scripture. He weeps as he goes to a room over a gateway, and is totally consumed with grief for the death of his wayward, but beloved, son. How much more did God the Father feel the death of His completely righteous and totally loving Son, who died for our sins?

CHAPTER NINETEEN

V 1–7: DIRECTNESS David's intense and public mourning of Absalom causes Israel to treat the victory like a defeat. There are no celebrations of the triumph. Joab, possibly not appreciating that David knows that he slew Absalom, warns David that if he persists in this way, all his men will lose heart and he will be without followers. His army will desert him. Joab's direct approach works. **V 8: DUTY** Duly warned, David assumes the duties of kingship and takes his seat in the gateway of the city. The people come to him. **V 9–10: DEBATE** The Israelites who fled from the battle when Absalom was slain, now debate about bringing David back as king of Israel. His cause is growing. **V 11–15: DEMONSTRATION** Through his friends Zadok and Abiathar, the priests, and through offering to Amasa the leadership place of Joab, David asks and gets the support of Judah to bring him back as king over all Israel. To demonstrate this, Judah invites him back and goes up to meet him at Gilgal, to bring him back across the Jordan. **V 16–40: DEALINGS** The welcoming party includes Shimei, who cursed David before, 1,000 Benjamites, and Ziba, Saul's old steward and Jonathan's supposed servant. David now has dealings with different people. He graciously allows Shimei to live, despite pressure to the contrary from Abishai. He restores his relationship with Mephibosheth on hearing that Mephibosheth was cheated by Ziba. He offers to share out between Mephibosheth and Ziba that which he gave to Ziba. Mephibosheth is so pleased to see the king back that he says he wants nothing else. David rewards his ancient supporter, Barzillai the Gileadite, by promising to deal well with his nominee, Chimham. King David is in business in Israel! **V 41–43: DANGER** Dangerous tribal jealousies between Israel and Judah emerge. Both now want to claim David exclusively, who simply wants to rule over them all.

CHAPTER TWENTY

V 1–2: REBELLION Sheba leads Israel to rebel against David, while Judah remains faithful to him. **V 3: RETURN** On David's return to his house in Jerusalem, he cares for the concubines he left there, but has no sexual relations with them. **V 4–7: REGROUP** David's new commander, Amasa, is told to assemble the men of Judah to pursue Sheba. He does not do this within the three-day time limit set, so David appoints Abashai (not Joab) to lead his men. Joab and his men are included in the assembled army. **V 8–10: RUTHLESS** When Amasa, the new commander, arrives, Joab murders him with his sword. This is doubtless because Joab realises that David prefers Amasa to him as commander. Joab continues to pursue Sheba. **V 11–13: REMOVAL** The army, probably alarmed and confused at seeing their dead new commander by the roadside, hesitate as they come to his body. A supporter of Joab, who is urging them to follow Joab, removes Amasa's body from the roadside, and the army continues after Sheba. **V 14–15: RETREAT** Sheba and his forces retreat to Abel where David's men, under Joab, raise a siege mount against the ramparts of the city. They begin to batter the city. **V 16–21: REASON** A wise woman inside the city of Abel speaks with Joab. They agree that to kill Sheba and deliver him to Joab is better than the surrender and destruction of the whole city. **V 22: RESULT** Accordingly, Sheba is beheaded and his head is thrown to Joab, who withdraws and returns to the king at Jerusalem. Presumably Joab thinks that the king must be pleased with the result, irrespective of how he has achieved it. **V 23–26: RESTORED** In the appointment of David's officers to govern Israel, Joab resumes the command over all the army of Israel.

CHAPTER TWENTY-ONE

V 1: PARCHED David seeks God's face after three years of famine. God reveals that Saul's past sins, in breaking the covenant and killing the Gibeonites, must be addressed before there can be blessing. **V 2–9: PRINCIPLES** David responds to God. He speaks to the Gibeonites, and arranges to have seven of Saul's family executed, but keeps his promise to Jonathan to save Mephibosheth. He is carefully applying right principles in his rule. **V 10–14b: PROPRIETY** Hearing that Rizpah, Saul's concubine, acted to stop the birds eating the bodies of her two sons who were hanged, David realises that he too must act with propriety. He takes the bones of the men who were hanged, and those of Saul and Jonathan, which had been stolen from the Philistines by the men of Jabesh-Gilead, and buries them. **V 14c: PRAYER** When all this is done, God answers the prayer, and the famine is over. Sometimes there are things to put right before God blesses. **V 15–22: POWER** David has his life threatened by a Philistine who is killed by Abishai. Giants are in combat with David's men, but David's men prevail.

CHAPTER TWENTY-TWO

V 1: THE REASON FOR DAVID'S SONG Out of thankfulness to God for delivering him from his enemies and from Saul, David praises God in a song. It is good to thank God and to praise Him when we are conscious of His gracious help to us. **V 2–51: THE REMINDERS IN DAVID'S SONG** The rest of this chapter is also recorded as Psalm 18 and is dealt with in the comments on Psalm 18. There are many reasons why David is grateful to God and his song reflects them.

CHAPTER TWENTY-THREE

V 1–7: DAVID'S LAST WORDS The last words of David as literature (not the last words he spoke) are recorded here. Again, he is enthusiastic about what God has done for him in His everlasting covenant and in providing salvation. **V 8–39: DAVID'S LOYAL WARRIORS** Here are the 'mighty men' of David, who fought loyally for him, who loved him, who risked their lives even to get him a drink of water that he wanted from Bethlehem's well, and who did mighty exploits as God helped them. These men were in great need when they first gathered to David in the Cave of Adullam, when no one wanted them. What God did in grace for these men through David, He can do today spiritually for those who love and serve great David's Greater Son, the Lord Jesus Christ. However, David badly failed the last named mighty man, Uriah the Hittite. Jesus never fails anyone.

CHAPTER TWENTY-FOUR

V 1: DIVINE ANGER For some undisclosed reason, God is angry with Israel. In His sovereign will, He allows Satan (1 Chronicles 21:1) to move David to number his troops unnecessarily. Perhaps David acquired more troops than he needed, and consequently turned his trust away from God. We do not know. **V 2–4: DIVISION AROUSED** Joab, supported by the commanders of the army, is against this directive to number the troops, but King David insists that he does it. **V 5–9: DEED ACCOMPLISHED** At the end of the count, Joab tells David that there are 1,300,000 men, of whom 800,000 are from Israel and 500,000 are from Judah. **V 10–17: DAVID'S ACCOUNTABILITY** David is convicted of his sin and asks God to take away his iniquity. But God will chastise Israel, to accomplish His purpose, and gives David the choice of three different chastisements. David elects to fall into the hand of God and to suffer a plague for three days, rather than face a seven-year famine, or fall into the enemy's hands for three months. God stays the plague at Jerusalem, and David again confesses his sin and asks that the punishment should fall on him and his house. **V 18–25a: DEVOTIONAL ALTAR** Through the prophet Gad, David is told to build an altar on the threshing floor of Araunah, the Jebusite. David refuses to accept this property as a gift and pays fifty shekels of silver. The altar is built, and burnt offerings and peace offerings are offered to God. **V 25b: DEVASTATION AVOIDED** Although very serious, with 70,000 people having died in the plague, complete devastation is thus avoided in the three-day timescale that God gave. God heeds the prayers made to Him and stops His chastisement by plague on Israel.

1 KINGS

OVERVIEW

PEOPLE AND PRELIMINARIES

✳ 1 Kings (twenty-two chapters) and 2 Kings (twenty-five chapters) were originally one book, as were the two books of Samuel and the two books of Chronicles. They were divided simply because of length and for practical considerations. Together, they cover a period of nearly 550 years (1 and 2 Samuel from approximately 1105 BC to 971 BC, 1 and 2 Kings from approximately 971 BC to 561 BC, with 1 and 2 Chronicles summarising and adding to various events in the other books). 1 Kings and 2 Kings are thus the sixth and seventh historical books of the Old Testament, preceding 1 and 2 Chronicles and following 1 and 2 Samuel, to provide a sweep of history from Adam until the return from Babylon in 538 BC. An estimate of the period covered by 1 Kings is 118 years. Some suggest that Jeremiah wrote 1 and 2 Kings, but it is more likely that the author was relatively unknown. The books were written in Israel, probably between 561 BC and 538 BC.

PLAN AND PURPOSE

ⓘ The book covers Solomon's accession to the throne after his father, David. It deals with his wisdom, his building of the temple and the royal Palace, his wealth and acclaim, and his negligent and wilful backsliding and death. After his forty-year reign, the first eighty years of a divided kingdom are covered after wicked Rehoboam becomes king in Judah and Jeroboam becomes king in Israel. The book records Elijah's prophetic ministry to Israel against the background of idolatrous rebellion and sinful practices.

PROFILE AND PROGRESSION

From Adonijah's rebellion to the death of King David (1:1–2:11); King Solomon's rise, wisdom, wealth, building projects, including the temple, growth in wisdom and wealth, decline, including taking foreign wives and compromising with their gods, and death (2:12–11:43); the division of the kingdom into Israel and Judah, including spiralling idolatry, details of kings of Israel and Judah, King Omri's evil influence, the start of Baal worship and Elijah's stand against it (12:1–22:53).

PRINCIPLES AND PARTICULARS

Solomon fails to heed God's warnings. In this we see the danger of apathy tied up with material success and acclaim. The link is also clearly seen between idolatry and spreading sin in other areas. The book shows that it is difficult to stop a downward spiral, though that is always possible through God. Also wisdom, being a spiritual quality, suffers when sin is permitted and entertained. By comparison, we read of the uncompromising stand and example of Elijah, and how God keeps and uses him. Inevitable downfall comes to God's people who refuse to repent and who fail to seek and follow God consistently. We are reminded of the certainty that all that God foretells will actually come to pass, however unlikely it may seem at the time.

1 KINGS

CHAPTER ONE

V 1–4: SITUATION David is very old and cold. Strange to our thinking, a young Shunammite woman, Abishag, is found to act as a 'human hot water bottle' for the king. David has no sexual relationship with her. **V 5–10: SUBTERFUGE** Adonijah, one of David's sons by Haggith, exalts himself to assume the kingship. Adonijah, supported by Joab and Abiathar the priest, pursues this selfish and incorrect course of conduct. He invites his brothers and the officials of Judah to his sacrifice near En Rogel, where he is making himself king. Nathan, Benaiah, and Solomon are not invited. They are, respectively, God's prophet, one of the best of David's mighty men, and Adonijah's brother. Along with Zadok the priest, Shimei, Rei, and David's special guard, they are not part of the subterfuge. **V 11–27: SHREWDNESS** Nathan shrewdly orchestrates a dual presentation to David of the rebellion that is happening, to awaken his action. First Bathsheba, and then Nathan, advise David. Between them, they challenge him regarding his promise that Solomon will be the king. **V 28–40: SOLOMON** David is activated to take urgent steps to proclaim Solomon as king, and to have him anointed by Zadok. Supported by Nathan and Benaiah, this happens at Gihon. The great rejoicing from a huge crowd of people makes the ground shake! **V 41–51: SIDELINED** Adonijah, who with his guests and Joab is having a feast to celebrate his self-inauguration as king, hears of Solomon's coronation. All his guests disperse in fear and alarm, leaving Adonijah a very frightened man. He clings to the walls of the altar and asks that King Solomon will not put him to death. **V 52–53: STRENGTH** Solomon's strength of character is shown in that he tells his frightened brother that if he shows himself to be worthy, he will survive, but that if he acts wickedly, he will die. Adonijah leaves the altar and submits to Solomon who sends him home.

CHAPTER TWO

V 1–9: CHARGE David charges Solomon to be strong and to walk in the way that pleases God. He tells him to take revenge on Joab who killed Abner and Amasa, to show kindness to Barzillai, and to deal with Shimei who cursed David maliciously at the Jordan. **V 10–12: CHIEF** David dies, after reigning over Israel for forty years, and Solomon becomes king in his place. He is firmly established over the children of Israel. **V 13–25: CHALLENGE** Adonijah persuades Bathsheba to ask Solomon for Abishag as his wife. Abishag previously served David, but with no sexual relationship. Solomon sees this as the first step of a renewed challenge to take his throne, and has Adonijah executed by Benaiah. **V 26–46: CHANGES** Solomon exiles Abiathar, the priest, and has Joab executed by Benaiah. Zadok takes over as priest and Benaiah as military commander. Solomon instructs Benaiah to execute Shimei, who breaks the condition which Solomon imposed on him earlier, to limit his freedom, by negligently crossing the Brook Kidron.

CHAPTER THREE

V 1–9: WISDOM—ASKING Solomon is already married to the king of Egypt's daughter. Both king and people worship at high places, despite that being forbidden. Now Solomon asks God for wisdom. **V 10–15: WISDOM—ACCORDED** God is pleased that Solomon has not asked for long life, wealth, or death of his enemies, and promises to give him not only the wisdom and understanding for which he has asked, but riches and honour, too. Solomon returns to Jerusalem before the ark of the covenant and sacrifices there burnt offerings and fellowship offerings. **V 16–28: WISDOM—APPLIED** Solomon's first test of applying his wisdom comes when two women dispute which of their babies has died and therefore to whom the survivor belongs. Solomon makes as if to cut the baby in two to share between them, knowing that the real mother will be the one most grieved by such a suggestion. His wisdom begins to be recognised by all Israel.

CHAPTER FOUR

V 1–19: ADMINISTRATIVE WIDTH Solomon, ruling over all Israel, organises the whole nation through chief officials and geographical governors. He believes in good administration. **V 20–28: AMAZING WELLBEING** Receiving tribute from many kingdoms, Israel, under Solomon, lacks nothing. His provisions are amazing and Israel lives in safety and security. Solomon has great wealth and many horses. Provisions are continually arriving. **V 29–34: ACCLAIMED WISDOM** Because God gives Solomon wisdom, people from all nations come to hear it. He has an amazing and unrivalled breadth of understanding and knowledge.

CHAPTER FIVE

V 1–9: LIAISON Hiram, King of Tyre, a former friend of David, takes up contact with Solomon. Following liaison between them, the relationship deepens and Hiram responds eagerly to Solomon's request for him to supply raw materials for Solomon to use to build the temple. **V 10–12: LOGS** Cedar and pine logs and annual provisions of wheat and oil will be sent by Hiram to Solomon, year after year. With Solomon's God-given wisdom and a treaty between the two rulers, the supply chain to build the temple is off to a good start! **V 13–18: LABOUR** Thirty thousand

Israelite labourers, augmented by seventy thousand other labourers and eighty thousand quarry workers, are put under three thousand three hundred foremen, and put to work to build the temple.

CHAPTER SIX

V 1: TASK STARTED The Bible's accuracy and factual reliability is often shown by its pinpointing times and places. Starting to build the temple is no exception. **V 2–10: TEMPLE'S STAGES** Each stage of building the outside of the temple is covered. **V 11–14: TABERNACLE'S SUCCESSOR** In verse 13, God confirms His blessing and presence among those who trust and obey Him. God repeats His assurance of His presence with them (as in Exodus 29:45) when He spoke about what has preceded the temple—the tabernacle. God thereby confirms that the solid temple is His successor to the mobile tabernacle. **V 16–36: TEACHING SANCTIFICATION** The word 'holy' can be applied to all of the building of the temple, and especially to the inner sanctuary, where God will make Himself uniquely present. That is why it is called 'The Most Holy Place'. The ark of the covenant will be placed here. Israel is being taught that God not only demands their trust and obedience, but also requires them to be holy. **V 37–38: TIME SHORTER** It takes seven years to build the temple, which is six years less than Solomon takes to build his own house. (See 1 Kings 7:1.) We do not know if this is because he takes even more trouble over building his own house, or because his labour was so concentrated on the temple that he had less time to build his own house. God's work must always be the priority.

CHAPTER SEVEN

V 1–12: BUILDINGS INCLUDED Other buildings undertaken by Solomon are the House of the Forest of Lebanon, the Hall of Pillars, the Hall of Judgement, a lavish open court containing other buildings, and his own house of complicated structure, great size, and ornate decoration with costly stones. **V 13–47: BRONZE INVOLVED** Solomon uses a craftsman, Huram from Tyre. He is immensely wise, understanding, and skilful, to do all the bronze work for the temple. This includes the bronze pillars, the Sea supported by twelve oxen, the ten carts, the ten lavers, the pots, the shovels, and the bowls. There is so much bronze that it cannot be weighed or measured. **V 48–50: BIGGEST IMPACT** The furnishings which make the biggest impact are manufactured from gold. Each item has tremendous significance. Among the most important are the altar, the table carrying the showbread, the ten lamp stands of the inner sanctuary, the censers, and the hinges for the doors both of the temple and of the Most Holy Place. **V 51: BOUGHT IN** The silver and gold items, and the furnishings dedicated by his father, David, are placed in the treasuries of the temple, in addition to the articles commissioned by Solomon.

CHAPTER EIGHT

V 1–9: ARK'S WITNESS The elders of Israel and the priests bring the ark into the Most Holy Place of the temple. At this stage, the only items in the ark are the two tablets containing the Ten Commandments. They witness to the fact that God's Word is central in His worship and in His presence. (Later there will be two other significant placements within the ark.) **V 10–13: AWESOME WONDER**

The cloud of the glory of the LORD fills the temple so that the priests have to come out of the holy place. They cannot continue their ministry. Solomon reminds them that God has kept His word. **V 14–21: ACCOMPLISHED WORK** Solomon blesses the whole assembly of Israel and acknowledges God's faithfulness in the completion of building the temple. He rejoices that the ark is in God's temple. **V 22–53: APPEALING WORDS** Then, standing before the altar, Solomon prays a long prayer of worship and dedication based on the themes of God's faithfulness and His people's need. He appeals to God to deal with Israel's future needs and to answer His people's prayers where there is real repentance and faith. **V 54–61: APPROPRIATE WALK** When Solomon's prayer is finished, he blesses the people of Israel, reminds them of God's faithfulness and holiness, and admonishes them to have a loyal heart towards God. They must always walk with Him in obedience in the days ahead, just as they feel inclined to do now. **V 62–64: AMAZING WORSHIP** The scale of the worship that surrounds the dedication of the temple in making the peace offerings is amazing. The middle of the court in front of the house of the LORD has to be consecrated also, because the bronze altar is too small to receive all of the grain offerings and the fat and the peace offerings. **V 65–66: ACKNOWLEDGED WONDERS** Following a great feast for all Israel, the people go away, blessing Solomon and grateful that God has granted both David and them such good and wonderful blessings.

CHAPTER NINE

V 1–9: APPEARANCE God appears to Solomon a second time, encouraging him through His promises, and warning him of the need to walk constantly with God to avoid disaster. **V 10–14: AGREEMENT** The agreement between Solomon and Hiram blossoms, and after twenty years Solomon gives Hiram twenty cities in Galilee. Hiram responds by sending the king 120 talents of gold. **V 15–19: ACHIEVEMENTS** The conscripted labour force not only builds the house of the LORD, and Solomon's house, but other enterprises which Solomon undertakes. **V 20–23: ASSISTANCE** Solomon's forced labourers are not Israelites. They are survivors from the previous inhabitants of the land. The Israelites take the senior administrative positions, military responsibility, and leadership. **V 24: ABERRATION** Solomon's mental and spiritual aberration is shown in building a house for Pharaoh's daughter. Later, despite his wisdom, women will be one of his main downfalls. **V 25: ANNUALLY** Apparently, after the temple is completed, Solomon ceases to sacrifice at the high places and reverts to Israel's three annual Feasts of Unleavened Bread, Pentecost, and Tabernacles in the temple. **V 26: ACCORD** Hiram builds a fleet of ships. Solomon's accord with Hiram extends and results in great wealth coming to Solomon.

CHAPTER TEN

V 1–3: ANSWERS The Queen of Sheba visits Solomon with hard questions, all of which he answers. **V 4–9: AWE** She is awestruck, not only at Solomon's answers, but by the whole regime that he controls, and especially the entryway by which he went into the house of the LORD. **V 10–13: ABUNDANCE** This causes The Queen of Sheba to give a completely unique and abundant supply of spices which, with all that comes from Hiram, adds to Solomon's already abundant wealth. He is very generous to the Queen of Sheba, giving her whatever she asks for before she returns. **V 14–23: AFFLUENCE** Solomon not only surpasses all the kings of the earth in wisdom, but also in riches on every hand. **V 24–25: ACCLAIM** People come from all over the world wanting to see Solomon and to hear his wisdom. Each visitor brings other valuable gifts for the already affluent king. He is highly acclaimed. **V 26–29: ACCUMULATION** Thus Solomon accumulates chariots, horsemen, silver, and timber. He develops a very profitable export business to the Hittites and the kings of Syria.

CHAPTER ELEVEN

V 1–8: DIVERSION Possibly already turned in his mind by his might and his wealth, Solomon's wisdom gives way to a diverted heart. His sensual love of many women, combined with his adopting the idols of their pagan nations, causes his downfall. **V 9–13: DISPLEASURE** God is angry with Solomon because of this, and appears to him twice to seek to arrest his backsliding. Now God tells him that He will tear the kingdom from him and give it to another. However, to honour God's covenant with David, there will be one tribe that remains faithful to Him. **V 14–26: DANGER** God raises up various adversaries against Solomon from this time. These include Hadad the Edomite, Rezom the son of Eliada, and Jeroboam, who one day will become king. **V 27–40: DIVISION** The prophet Ahijah, the Shilonite, tells Jeroboam that God will tear the kingdom out of the hand of Solomon and give him ten of the tribes. When Solomon hears this, he seeks to kill Jeroboam, who flees to Egypt. **V 41–43: DEATH** Solomon dies. His spectacular forty-year reign over Israel comes to an end. After his death and burial, his son Rehoboam reigns.

CHAPTER TWELVE

V 1–15: INSENSITIVE REHOBOAM Israel, through Jeroboam, offers to serve Rehoboam as king if he would rule them with a lighter touch than his oppressive father had done. Rehoboam asks the elders who served his father well how he should respond. They tell him to adopt a servant-like attitude to the people in order to win them. Rehoboam rejects this advice and consults young men, who endorse his view that he should reign cruelly and with great harshness. God uses even this insensitivity to fulfil His will concerning Jeroboam becoming king of Israel. **V 16–24: ISRAEL'S REBELLION** There is rebellion by Israel and later by part of the tribe of Benjamin against Rehoboam. He is thus the king of Judah only, supported only by Judah and by some of the Benjamites. The kingdom is divided. **V 25–33: IDOLATROUS REASONING** Because Jerusalem and the house of David are situated in Judah, Jeroboam fears that if the true worship of God is continued that the Israelites may defect to Rehoboam by going to worship in Jerusalem. Accordingly, he introduces idolatry to Bethel and Dan. He builds shrines and makes offerings on the altars.

CHAPTER THIRTEEN

V 1–10: UNCOMPROMISING An unnamed man of God from Judah gives the word of the LORD to Jeroboam as he is about to make an offering. He tells him that his son to be born, Josiah, will sacrifice the priests of the high places on the altar. He says there will be a sign when the altar splits apart and the ashes pour down. As Jeroboam moves to seize the man, his hand withers, the altar splits, and the ashes pour out. Jeroboam changes his attitude! He asks for the man of God to intercede for his hand to be restored, and offers him food and a reward. Jeroboam's hand is restored, but the man of God refuses to go home with him to receive hospitality and the reward because God has told him to go back home immediately. At this stage, he is an uncompromising servant of God. **V 11–18: UNPRINCIPLED** However, an old prophet living in Bethel delays the man of God. The man of God tells the old man that God has told him to return home directly. Nevertheless, the old prophet claims that an angel has instructed him to invite the man of God to his house for food and water. The old prophet is lying. There are various theories why. **V 19: UNWISE** Even an uncompromising man of God can be unwise, and this one is. Instead of relying on what he knows is God's word, he listens to someone wrongly claiming to have special revelation. He goes home with him. This proves to be his downfall. **V 20–25: UNTOUCHED** Even through the lying old prophet, God confirms that the man of God is disobedient and will die. Accordingly, on his way home, he is killed by a lion. The lion does not touch his corpse or his donkey, but just stands there. **V 26–30: UNCONVINCING** The lying prophet goes to collect the body of the man. The lion is still standing there. The old man brings the corpse of the man of God back to his own city. He mourns for him and calls him his 'brother'. His grief is not very convincing, as his lying deceit caused the death of the man of God when he unwisely followed the false prophet's lying counsel. **V 31–32: UNDERSTANDING** Nevertheless, the lying prophet understands that the word the man of God spoke about the altar is true. He tells his sons that after his death they must bury him by the man of God. **V 33–34: UNREPENTANT** Even after this, Jeroboam

does not repent but appoints more priests for high places. Anyone wanting to be a priest can become one! God's strict requirements for priesthood and sacrifice are lost in this idolatrous sinfulness which will cause the destruction of Jeroboam and his house.

CHAPTER FOURTEEN

V 1–6: DETECTED DECEPTION The first part of the chapter carries on with Jeroboam in Israel. His son is sick and he sends his wife to see Ahijah, the prophet who is almost blind, to find out what will happen to his son. She disguises herself, but God reveals her identity to Ahijah, who tells her that he knows who she is, and that he has bad news for her. **V 7–16: DESTINED DECIMATION** But first Ahijah reveals God's message for Jeroboam. Because of his idolatrous rebellion against God, Israel will be decimated in the disaster that will come upon them. Jeroboam's son will die. Whereas the dogs and birds will eat the people killed in the disaster, Jeroboam's son will be buried, because he has an attitude to God that the others do not have. Israel will be scattered because of Jeroboam's sins. God will raise up a king who will cut off the house of Jeroboam and afflict and give up Israel for following Jeroboam's idolatry. **V 17–20: DEATH DETAILS** Jeroboam's son dies, is buried, and mourned. Jeroboam himself dies after a twenty-three year reign and his son Nadab succeeds him in Israel. **V 21–24: DETESTABLE DEVIATIONS** The chapter now switches to Judah and to Rehoboam, who starts his reign at the age of forty-one. Inevitably, immorality and perversion follow idolatry in this land. The spiritual and sexual abomination exceeds that of the nations which preceded Judah and which had been cast out by God. **V 25–28: DEVASTATING**

DEFEAT Shishak, king of Egypt, attacks Jerusalem in Rehoboam's fifth year and takes away the treasures from the temple, including Solomon's golden shields. Rehoboam replaces the golden shields with bronze shields. That is quite a spiritual picture of Israel—the gold of God's glory being replaced by the bronze of sinful compromise and evil. **V 29–31: DETERMINED DEADLOCK** Until the day of his death, when he is replaced by Abijah as king of Judah, Rehoboam is at war with Jeroboam, king of Israel.

CHAPTER FIFTEEN

V 1–8: ABIJAM'S REIGN Abijam becomes king of Judah in the eighteenth year of Jeroboam's reign in Israel. Although he follows all the wickedness of Rehoboam, God allows Judah to remain because of His promise to David. Abijam continues to fight against Jeroboam, king of Israel. After three years, he dies and his son, Asa, reigns in Judah. **V 9–15: ASA'S RIGHTEOUSNESS** During the twentieth year of Jeroboam's reign in Israel, Asa begins his forty-one year reign in Judah. He reverses much of the evil of his father, Abijam. He does what is right in the eyes of the LORD in expelling the 'perverted persons' and ridding the land of idols and its attendant immorality. His heart is right. He is not perfect, however, and leaves some of the high places of false worship. But he takes many steps in the right direction. **V 16–22: ASA'S RESCUE** Israel has effectively blockaded Judah by fortifying the city of Ramah. This prevents anyone from leaving or entering Asa's territory. Asa makes a treaty with Ben-Hadad, having sent the treasures of the temple to him. Ben-Hadad attacks key Israelite towns, causing the king of Israel, Baasha, to withdraw from his further building works in Ramah. Asa takes the building materials and timber to other towns. **V 23–24: ASA'S REST** Asa does much for Judah during his reign. After his death he is buried in the City of David and his son, Jehoshaphat, succeeds him as king of Judah. **V 25–34: AXED RULER** Meanwhile, in Israel, Nadab succeeds Jeroboam as king in the second year of Asa, king of Judah. His evil two-year reign in Israel is ended when Baasha has him killed and succeeds him. Baasha exterminates Jeroboam's family, in accordance with the earlier prophecy of Ahijah, and is constantly at war with King Asa of Judah. Ruling from the third year of Asa, king of Judah, Baasha reigns as king of Israel for twenty-four evil years following the rebellious ways of Jeroboam.

CHAPTER SIXTEEN

V 1–7: BAD BAASHA This chapter is devoted to the kings of Israel who reign during the reign of King Asa in Judah. God speaks through His prophet Jehu, the son of Hanani, predicting Baasha's downfall and the desecration of his house. God fulfils this because of His anger against Baasha for his evil ways. **V 8–14: ELAH EXECUTED** Elah, the son of Baasha, succeeds him as king of Israel for two years in Tirzah. He is executed by Zimri, who succeeds him. Zimri exterminates all of Baasha's household, according to God's word prophesied through Jehu. **V 15–20: SUPPLANTER'S SUICIDE** Zimri only reigns over Israel for seven days. The Israelites, hearing of his execution of Elah, make Omri the king. He is thus promoted from commander of the army. Under attack from Omri, Zimri commits suicide by burning the king's house in which he is dwelling. **V 21–28: OBNOXIOUS OMRI** After an initial struggle with Tibni, Omri succeeds as king of Israel. Six years of his twelve-year reign are in Tirzah. He builds Samaria and does evil in God's sight, worse than any who have gone before him. When he dies, Ahab, his son, takes his place as king of Israel. **V 29–33: APOSTATE AHAB** Throughout the period of the kings of Israel covered by this chapter, Asa is still ruling as a good king in Judah. In Asa's thirty-eighth year, Ahab takes over from his father Omri as king of Israel. His evil exceeds even the evil of his father, Omri, who was the most immoral and idolatrous king before his son began to reign. Ahab's vile influence on others enabled the spiritual and moral evil of Baal worship and child sacrifice to be added to the continuing evils inherited in the line of Jeroboam, king of Israel. Hiel of Bethel built Jericho during his reign and influence. Hiel wickedly set the foundations of Jericho on Abiram, his first born. He set up the gates on his slaughtered younger son, Segub. He thus fulfils the prophecy that Joshua made in Joshua 6:26.

CHAPTER SEVENTEEN

V 1–3: FAITHFUL God's prophet, Elijah the Tishbite, faithfully tells King Ahab of Israel that God will withhold dew and rain in the next few years. The drought will only be reversed in accordance with Elijah's word as the servant of God. God then tells Elijah to flee and hide at the brook Cherith. **V 4–6: FED** God promises that Elijah will drink water from the brook and that ravens will take him food. True to God's word, he drinks the brook's water, while bread and meat are brought to him morning and evening by ravens. It is all the more remarkable because ravens are carrion birds which normally eat any food that they find! **V 7–12: FAMINE** As the lack of rain in the land causes the brook to dry up, God tells Elijah to move to Zarephath and stay with a widow who will supply him with food. When Elijah gets there, he finds she has only a handful of flour and a small amount of oil remaining. **V 13–16: FOOD** Nevertheless, at Elijah's request, she makes a small cake of bread for him, and, as Elijah predicts to her, God gives her a plentiful supply of flour and of oil on a daily basis. The jar of flour and the jug of oil are never empty! **V 17–24: FAITH** The son of the hospitable widow dies. In despair she turns to Elijah. He takes the child, prays for him, and stretches out three times upon him. His prayer to God for the child is answered and he lives. The widow declares her confidence in Elijah as a man of God, and in God's word in his mouth as the truth.

CHAPTER EIGHTEEN

V 1: PROMISE After a long time, God's word comes to Elijah to tell him to go to present himself to Ahab. He promises Elijah that the time has come for Him to send rain on the earth. **V 2–15: PETRIFIED** On the way to present himself to Ahab and during a severe famine in Samaria, Elijah meets a faithful servant of the LORD, Obadiah. He instructs Obadiah to tell his master, King Ahab of Israel, that Elijah is ready to meet him. Obadiah is terrified. Knowing Ahab's unsuccessful attempts to find Elijah, and how God's Spirit can take him out of any situation to hide His servant, he fears that if he tells Ahab that Elijah is on hand, there is a strong possibility that Elijah will not be there when Ahab comes to meet him. Then he fears that he himself will be killed. Nevertheless, he fears the LORD, and has hidden a hundred of God's real prophets from the persecution under Jezebel. Elijah assures him that he will be there to meet his wicked adversary, King

Ahab. **V 16–17: PRESENTATION** The meeting happens as promised, with Ahab asking Elijah if he is the troubler of Israel. **V 18–19: POSITIVE** Elijah openly condemns Ahab for his idolatry, disobedience to God, and Baal worship. He demands that Ahab cause all Israel to witness who is the true God, with Ahab being represented on Mount Carmel by 450 prophets of Baal and 400 prophets of Asherah. These wicked prophets are all maintained by Jezebel, Ahab's wife. **V 20–29: PAGANISM** The difference between the real worship of God and man-made religion will soon be obvious. Elijah calls for a clear decision to be made to either follow the LORD or Baal. He alone represents his God in this contest. Sacrifices are to be prepared and the idolaters are to call on Baal. He will call on the LORD God. Whoever answers by consuming the sacrifice by fire will be recognised as the true God. All day long the prophets of Baal cry, cut themselves, and leap about the altar which they have made. But there is no answer from their false god. Elijah asks if Baal is asleep or otherwise engaged! **V 30–39: PREPARATION** Elijah repairs the broken altar of the LORD and uses twelve stones, representing the twelve tribes of Israel, to build another altar with a trench around it. He lays wood on the altar and prepares the sacrifice of a bull. He invites the opposition to douse it thoroughly three times with water. At the hour of evening sacrifice, God answers Elijah's prayer with fire, consuming the burnt sacrifice, the wood, the stones, the dust, and even the water. The Israelites fall down on their faces and confess that the LORD is God. **V 40: PROPHETS** Elijah has the prophets of Baal executed at the Brook Kishon. **V 41–45a: PRAYER** Elijah tells Ahab that the rain will come, and then prays to God seven times. God answers him after an unpromising start, in which there is no cloud in the sky. Elijah's God answers prayer thereby vindicating the truth of Elijah's message from God. The rebellious people, wicked King Ahab and his even more wicked wife, Jezebel, clearly know that the LORD is God and that He reveals His word through Elijah. **V 45b–46: POWER** Ahab rides away in his chariot and the LORD empowers Elijah to run before him to Jezreel. Runners ran before kings' chariots as a sign of loyalty and respect for the dignity of the office of the king. Elijah thus shows his high regard for the position of the king of Israel, even despite Ahab's abhorrent personal wickedness. He also demonstrates clearly that God's powerful hand is upon him, even in the physical realm.

CHAPTER NINETEEN

V 1–4: DEPRESSED STATE Elijah finds that the opposition does not die with the extermination of the prophets of Baal, nor with the arrival of the rain. Jezebel threatens to kill him. So soon after witnessing the triumph at Mount Carmel, Elijah flees and asks God to take his life. Depressed as he is, he does not consider suicide to be an option. **V 5–8: DERIVED STRENGTH** God provides for him shelter, rest, and—miraculously again—food and drink. In the strength of God's miraculous intervention, he goes forty days as far as Horeb. **V 9–12: DYNAMIC STILLNESS** Elijah laments his solitariness as God's prophet in a wicked and hostile environment. God speaks to Elijah again, showing him a great wind, earthquake, and fire, before speaking to him in a still small voice. The power of God's personal whisper is greater than these other phenomena. **V 13–18: DIVINE SOVEREIGNTY** God also reveals that He has His plan and tells Elijah of three men, whom He will ultimately use to destroy Baal worship. They are Hazael, Jehu and Elisha. Elijah is to make sure that these men are anointed and that Elisha is anointed as his successor. In the event, Elijah only anoints Elisha, who later anoints the other two. God reminds Elijah that there are 7,000 in Israel who are faithful to God and against Baal worship. **V 19–21: DEDICATED SUCCESSOR** Elijah throws his mantle on Elisha, who becomes Elijah's servant in preparation for the task which God will give him to do after Elijah's departure from the earth. Elisha breaks completely with his former legitimate lifestyle in order to follow God.

CHAPTER TWENTY

V 1–3: ENEMY King Ahab of Israel faces Ben-Hadad, king of Syria, who attacks Samaria and demands Ahab's wealth, loveliest wives and children. **V 4–6: EASY** Initially this looks like a very easy conquest for Ben-Hadad. Ahab says that he will do as Ben-Hadad asks. Ben-Hadad increases his demands to include plundering the palace and the houses of his servants. **V 7–9: ELDERS** Ahab consults with the elders of Israel. At one with all the people, they tell Ahab neither to listen to his enemy nor to agree to his demands. He repeats his willingness to accept the first conditions, but not the second. **V 10–12: EXCHANGE** After an exchange of messages, Ben-Hadad, under the influence of alcohol, orders preparations to be made to attack Samaria. **V 13–21: ENCOURAGEMENTS** God's unnamed prophet suddenly appears to tell Ahab that God will give him victory, so that Ahab will know that He is LORD. Ahab must gather his young leaders for the battle. True to God's word, the Israelites inflict heavy losses on the Syrians. **V 22–27: EXPLANATION** Ahab is advised by the prophet to be ready to repel another attack in the coming spring. Ben-Hadad's advisors tell him the reason for their defeat is because Israel's God is the God of the hills. They say that if they fight Israel in the plains, Israel will lose. **V 28–30: EMPOWERED** Through His servant, God tells Ahab that he will win against the army of the Syrians. This is to show the Syrians that God is not simply the God of the hill country and to show Ahab that He is the LORD. Sure enough, Israel completely overpowers the Syrians, killing one hundred thousand. Twenty seven thousand of the escapees die when a wall collapses on them. Ben-Hadad flees and hides. God's power achieves this victory. **V 31–34: ESCAPE** Ben-Hadad's servants appear dressed as repentant mourners. Ahab welcomes the representations of Ben-Hadad, whom he calls his 'brother'. In return for the previously taken cities being granted back to him, he makes a treaty to let Ben-Hadad go. **V 35–43: ENACTED** A prophet enacts a parallel situation to tell Ahab that he is wrong to let Ben-Hadad escape, and that this will cost him his life and his people's liberty. Ahab, angry and sulky, goes to his palace in Samaria.

CHAPTER TWENTY-ONE

V 1–4: GRASPING An insight into the wickedness of affluent Ahab is seen in his wanting selfishly to grasp the neighbouring vineyard of Naboth for his vegetable garden. Ahab is sullen and angry because Naboth is neither willing to sell him his inheritance nor to exchange it for another vineyard. **V 5–10: GOADED** Ahab's wicked wife, Jezebel, goads Ahab into embracing her criminal conspiracy to accuse Naboth falsely of blasphemy so that he can be stoned, and the vineyard become Ahab's. **V 11–14: GROUNDLESS**

Two false witnesses who will lie are found, and Naboth is put to death with no grounds at all to support this unjust and evil act. **V 15–16: GAIN** Again goaded on by Jezebel, Ahab takes possession of his ill-gotten gain. **V 17–24: GOD** Through God's prophet, Elijah, the downfall and death of both Ahab and Jezebel are prophesied to Ahab. **V 25–26: GODLESS** The unique vileness and idolatry of Ahab, encouraged by Jezebel, are recorded. **V 27–29: GRACE** Ahab humbles himself, putting on sackcloth and fasting. God is the God of grace and tells Elijah that he will delay the judgement on Ahab until a later generation because of this repentance.

CHAPTER TWENTY-TWO

V 1–5: TOGETHER Jehoshaphat, king of Judah, is at peace with Israel during his reign. He joins with Ahab, king of Israel, to fight against the Syrians. Jehoshaphat, a godly king, suggests that the LORD should be consulted first. **V 6–14: TEMPTING** Ahab obliges with 400 prophets, all encouraging him to go and fight against Syria. The prominent false prophet, Zedekiah, endorses and confirms this by an enacted prophecy. Jehoshaphat seems to discern that none of them are 'prophets of the LORD' and asks if there is one. Micaiah is brought forward with the tempting suggestion that he must agree with all the other prophets. He declares, to the man who suggests this to him, that he must give the LORD's message. The temptation for him to compromise must be strong. **V 15–25: TRUTHFUL** Micaiah then seems to 'parrot' the same advice given by the others, but in such a way that it is obvious to Ahab that he does not really believe what he is saying. Probably he is using heavy sarcasm. Ahab asks him for his

honest view, and Micaiah responds by predicting an overwhelming defeat for Ahab. Micaiah says that a lying spirit is guiding the other prophets. Zedekiah strikes him on the cheek. Micaiah predicts that Zedekiah will know that Micaiah is guided by God's Spirit when he seeks to hide himself in the inner chamber. **V 26–37: TRAGEDY** Sent to prison on minimum rations, Micaiah also predicts Ahab's death. This duly occurs as a result of the battle, despite an attempt to disguise himself. **V 38: TRUTH** Just as God said through His word, the dogs lick Ahab's blood as his chariot is washed in the pool where prostitutes bathe. God's word is true and accurate. **V 39–40: TRIVIAL** In describing the succession from Ahab to his son Ahaziah, as king of Israel, some of Ahab's building exploits are mentioned. How trivial they seem in this context. **V 41–50: TRANSFER** The crown of Judah was transferred from Asa to Jehoshaphat in the fourth year of Ahab, king of Israel, when Jehoshaphat was thirty-five years old. He reigns for thirty-five years in Jerusalem. He walks righteously, as Asa did, except that he does not remove the high places of sacrifice. A peacemaker with Israel, he banishes perverted persons from the land, and also unsuccessfully tries to operate merchant ships to trade with gold. When he dies, his throne transfers to his son, Jehoram, who succeeds him as king of Judah. **V 51–53: TAINTED** For two years, Ahaziah follows his father, Ahab, as king of Israel in Samaria. This is in the seventeenth year of Jehoshaphat, king of Judah. It is hardly surprising that he follows his father's sinful example of following on in the wicked ways of Jeroboam, in Baal-worship and in provoking God to anger. Ungodly parents often cause their children to fall.

2 KINGS

OVERVIEW

PEOPLE AND PRELIMINARIES

*See 1 Kings—People and Preliminaries. An estimate of the time covered by 2 Kings is 308 years.

PLAN AND PURPOSE

(i) The book records the ministry of Elijah and concentrates on that of Elisha, his successor. They faithfully convey God's message and stand against idolatry in the northern kingdom of Israel up to and including the death of Israel's tenth king, Jehu. Then it covers events and reigns of kings, in both Israel and in the southern kingdom of Judah, until Israel is taken captive by Assyria. It concludes with the happenings in Judah, until Judah is carried captive to Babylon.

PROFILE AND PROGRESSION

Elijah's continuing battle with the worship of Baal (1:1–1:18); Elisha's godly influence and the overthrow of Baal worship in Israel and in Judah, the evil influence of Ahab and Jezebel and their overthrow, the death of Elisha, more details of Israel's and Judah's kings and the conquest and captivity of Israel (but not Judah) by Assyria (1:19–17:41); Judah's kings, including the righteous reigns of Hezekiah and Josiah, with intervening wicked reigns by Manasseh and Amon (18:1–23:30); the conquest and captivity of Judah by Babylon (23:31–25:21); ongoing rebellion against God (25:22–30).

PRINCIPLES AND PARTICULARS

☛ Elisha takes over from Elijah, empowered and helped by God's Spirit. He shows the dual ministry of the prophet of God, to foretell and 'forth tell'. Sowing sin reaps its own harvest. Miracle signs authenticate God's prophets. Naaman's healing and conversion are recounted. The twin inevitability of God's word being accomplished, and biblical prophecy being fulfilled, is demonstrated. God's will allows His people to suffer because of their sins, and ultimately to be brought back to Himself. The chronology of the kings of Judah and of Israel is carefully logged by reference to which king was reigning in Judah when the next king of Israel came to the throne, and vice versa. In chapters 11 to 14, where the same name applies to both the king of Judah and the king of Israel, and is optional (as Joash or as Jehoash), this summary refers to the king of Judah to only as Joash and to the king of Israel only as Jehoash.

2 KINGS

CHAPTER ONE

V 1–2: AHAZIAH The immediate background is that Moab rebels against Israel. Ahaziah, king of Israel, sends messengers to consult Baal-Zebub, the idol god of Ekron, after he has injured himself by falling from an upper room. **V 3–4: ANGEL** An angel instructs Elijah to go and tell the messengers that, because Ahaziah is consulting an idol, he will certainly die. **V 5–8: ACKNOWLEDGED** The messengers return to the king and pass on the message. Ahaziah recognises that the message is from Elijah. **V 9–12: ARRESTS** Ahaziah makes two attempts to arrest Elijah by sending a captain with fifty men. On each occasion Elijah calls down fire from heaven and they are consumed. **V 13–15: APPROACHABLE** The third captain with his fifty men finds Elijah approachable as he begs for his life, rather than threatening to take Elijah by force. Elijah, assured by the angel of the LORD, accompanies the captain to King Ahaziah. **V 16–18: ACCOMPLISHED** Elijah repeats his message to Ahaziah and God's word is accomplished as Ahaziah dies. He has no son and so Jehoram takes over from him as king of Israel, in the second year of his namesake, Jehoram, who is the son of Jehoshaphat and the king of Judah.

CHAPTER TWO

V 1–6: STAYING CLOSE Elisha is soon to succeed Elijah as God's prophet. On three occasions, he demonstrates his determination to stay close to Elijah until that succession is accomplished. **V 7–8: SUPERNATURAL CROSSING** Fifty sons of the prophets watch Elijah and Elisha cross the Jordan as on dry land when Elijah's cloak is rolled up and used to strike the water. **V 9–10: SPIRIT CRAVED** Elijah asks Elisha what he can do for him before he is taken from him. Elisha asks to inherit a double portion of the Spirit that is upon Elijah. He is told that, providing he accompanies Elijah up to his point of departure, his desire will be granted. **V 11–12: SUDDEN CHARIOT** God intervenes and takes Elijah to heaven in a whirlwind, separating him from Elisha by a chariot of fire pulled by horses of fire. Elisha mourns the loss of Elijah by tearing his own clothes. **V 13–15: SOUND CONCLUSION** Elisha takes the cloak that has fallen from Elijah and smites the River Jordan with it, asking God to reveal Himself as He did for Elijah. Again, the

water divides and he walks over. The company of watching prophets rightly concludes that the Spirit of Elijah is resting on Elisha. They show their acceptance of his authority. **V 16–18: SURPRISING CONDUCT** The prophets wonder if God's Spirit has carried Elijah to some other mountain or valley. Elisha assures them this is not so but they persist in a three-day search using fifty men. They do not find him, and Elisha reminds them that he told them it would be so. **V 19–22: SALT CURE** Miraculously, God cures some bad water when Elisha puts some salt in it. This second sign shows that he is God's man with God's authority. **V 23–25: SOLEMN CURSE** Irreverent abuse is thrown at God's prophet, Elisha, by a mob of youths. Elisha curses them in God's name, and two female bears maul forty-two of them. God is establishing the seriousness of His word through His prophet at this time.

CHAPTER THREE

V 1–9a: JEHORAM AND JEHOSHAPHAT Jehoram, son of Ahab, succeeds Ahaziah as king of Israel. He is a wicked king, but not as wicked as some of his predecessors. Jehoshaphat is the God-fearing king of Judah. They join forces, aided by the king of Edom, against the rebellious king of Moab. **V 9b–20: PROPHET AND PROVISION** They run out of water and Jehoshaphat calls for Elisha, as the prophet of God, to aid them. Elisha makes it clear that he will only do this for a godly king like Jehoshaphat, but he prophesies that there will be ample water and that Moab will be defeated. The next morning the land is filled with water, as he said. **V 21–27: VICTORY AND VINDICATION** The Moabites see the red sun reflected in the water, and think that their enemy, the Israelites and Judaites, have slaughtered one another. Rushing to the plunder, they are routed by the joint forces. The wicked king of Moab sacrifices his son and returns to his land. God's man, Elisha, is vindicated.

CHAPTER FOUR

V 1–7: WIDOW'S WOE An impoverished widow of one of the prophets is about to lose her two sons to slavery, through their poverty. Through Elisha, God provides a jar of oil that never runs out. She is able to sell the oil to pay her debts, and save her sons. **V 8–37: SHUNAMMITE'S SON** A hospitable lady and her husband in Shunem provide a regular place for Elisha to stay. She is barren and her husband is old, but Elisha prophesies that she will bear a son. A year later, this occurs. Later the son dies and Elisha is miraculously used by God to restore the dead son, after his servant Gehazi has failed to do so. **V 38–41: SAVED STEW** Unwittingly, poisoned herbs are put into a stew which is being eaten by the sons of the prophets. They appeal to Elisha, who adds some flour to the stew, and it becomes safe to eat. **V 42–44: BARLEY BREAD** Fulfilling God's word, Elisha feeds a hundred people with a small amount of bread and some newly ripened grain.

CHAPTER FIVE

V 1: LEADER'S LEPROSY Naaman, a great and honourable Syrian commander, has leprosy. **V 2–7: CONFIDENCE CONTRASTED** A young Israelite captive girl tells Naaman's wife that he should go to Elisha to be healed. The Syrian writes to the king of Israel to arrange this. The king of Israel sees this approach as an attempt to seek a quarrel with him, as he clearly does not think that the healing is possible. He does not have the same confidence in God that the Israelite captive girl has. **V 8: ELISHA'S ENCOURAGEMENT** Elisha hears that the king of Israel is worried to the extent of tearing his clothes. He asks for Naaman to come to him so that Naaman will know that there is a prophet of God in Israel. **V 9–13: POINTLESS PRIDE** Having been received at Elisha's house by the messenger, rather than by Elisha himself, Naaman's pride stops him from going to the Jordan to dip seven times. He is offended because Elisha communicates to him through his messenger. Naaman prefers the rivers of Damascus. His wise servants persuade him to do what Elisha has told him to do. **V 14: READY RESTORATION** Naaman dips seven times in the Jordan, and his flesh is restored as that of a little child. He is clean. **V 15–16: TELLING TESTIMONIES** Naaman, with his aides, confesses his new-found faith in God, the God of Israel. He asks Elisha to take a gift, but Elisha refuses. Naaman's testimony to God's grace, and Elisha's testimony to not doing God's work for material gain, are indeed telling. **V 17–19: CONTRITE CONVERTS** Naaman, who earlier refused to bathe in Israel's River Jordan, now asks for two mule loads of earth from Israel, to take to Damascus. Many around him think that a god could only be worshipped on the soil of the nation concerned. These are early days for Naaman! He also asks forgiveness, in advance, for when he has to accompany his master to the temple of Rimmon. What a change of attitude! **V 20–24: GEHAZI'S GREED** Gehazi, the dishonest opportunist, seeks to get some wealth from Naaman. Unsuspecting Naaman willingly gives him twice as much as he is asked for. Gehazi puts it in his house. **V 25–27: LYING LEPER** Gehazi underestimates the God-given power of Elisha. Elisha knows what has happened, confronts Gehazi and his lies, and predicts that Naaman's leprosy shall be transferred to Gehazi and his descendants. Gehazi goes out a leper.

CHAPTER SIX

V 1–7: FLOATING IRON Elisha miraculously causes a sunken iron axe-head to be re-floated. **V 8–23: FREEING ISRAEL** The Israelite city of Dothan is surrounded by the Syrian army, who wish to take Elisha because his prophetic warnings to the king of Israel about the coming Syrian attacks act as an early warning system. Elisha asks God to open his frightened servant's eyes to see the horses and chariots of fire surrounding them. Then he asks God to strike the Syrians with blindness. When God does this, Elisha leads them into Samaria where they are captives of the king of Israel without any bloodshed. On Elisha's counsel, the king of Israel feeds them and sends them away. This gracious treatment means that the Syrian raiders do not come into the land of Israel again. **V 24–33: FAMINE'S IMPACT** However, Ben-Hadad, king of Syria, besieges Samaria later. Famine sets in and prices for food rocket. The king of Israel mourns when he hears about women eating their own children. He vows to kill Elisha. He sends his messenger to Elisha and makes it plain that he sees no prospect of the LORD reversing the terrible situation of siege and famine. God shows Elisha that a would-be executioner is coming for him from the king, and thus Elisha avoids death. His early warning system works for him, too!

CHAPTER SEVEN

V 1–2: FAITHLESS INDIVIDUAL Elisha states that in a very short time, food will be plentiful and cheap. An influential officer of the king expresses unbelief, and Elisha tells him that he will see it happen, but he will not eat the food. **V 3–16: FLEEING INTRUDERS** God causes the Syrian army to hear the noise of chariots and horses, as in a great army, and they flee from the siege. (Are these the same horses and chariots that Elisha's servant saw earlier?) Four lepers enter their camp and find great provisions, and come back to tell the king of Israel. Suspecting an ambush, the king checks out that the Syrian army really has fled. The road is strewn with their belongings. The Syrian camp is plundered, and food becomes plentiful and cheap, just as Elisha prophesied. **V 17–20: FORETELLING INSPIRED** The pinpoint accuracy of the inspired foretelling of Elisha, as God's prophet, is further demonstrated when the king's doubting officer, to whom Elisha spoke, sees the food, but is trampled to death at the gate during the people's stampede to take it.

CHAPTER EIGHT

V 1–6: GOD'S TIMING God's wonderful sense of timing for those trusting Him is seen in the case of the Shunammite woman, whose dead son was raised to life through Elisha. She was absent from the land for seven years, sheltering in the land of the Philistines because of famine. She approaches the king to ask for her land to be restored to her at the very time that Gehazi, the servant of Elisha, is telling the king about the incident of Elisha restoring her son to life. The king grants her land back to her. **V 7–15: GREAT TREACHERY** Hazael is sent by the king of Syria, Ben-Hadad, to ask if he will recover from his illness. Elisha knows that he will recover but that Hazael will kill Ben-Hadad and then inflict great damage on the children of Israel. Elisha tells Hazael to tell the king that he shall recover, but weeps over the great suffering which will be inflicted by Hazael's evil. Hazael denies that he will do this. Ben-Hadad recovers. The day after, he is murdered by treacherous Hazael. **V 16–24: GODLY TOLERANCE** Jehoram takes over as king of Judah from Jehoshaphat, a godly king, in the fifth year of Joram king of Israel. Although Jehoram is evil, God continues to spare Judah because of the promise he made to David. Jehoram's reign includes the rebellion of Edom and Libnah against Judah. Jehoram is succeeded by his son, Ahaziah, as king of Judah. **V 25–29: GODLESS TREND** Ahaziah's succession as king of Judah is in the twelfth year of Joram, king of Israel. His one-year reign is wicked. In it he is an ally with Joram, whom he goes to see after Joram is wounded in battle.

CHAPTER NINE

V 1–13: JEHU'S ANOINTING ACCLAIMED Elisha sends one of the prophets to Ramoth Gilead to anoint Jehu as king of Israel. The prophet does that and tells Jehu of his commission to exterminate the house of Ahab and Jezebel, his wife. Jehu's companions make him an impromptu throne of garments, and acclaim with trumpets that he is king. **V 14–29: JORAM AND AHAZIAH** Jehu rides to Jezreel where Ahaziah, king of Judah, is visiting the wounded Joram. Jehu kills Joram and Ahaziah is fatally wounded and flees to die at Megiddo. **V 30–37: JEZEBEL'S AWFUL APPOINTMENT** Jehu continues and, ignoring Jezebel's insult in calling him Zimri (a king who died seven days after he took the throne), he has Jezebel thrown down from an upstairs window. She is trampled by Jehu's horses and her corpse

is eaten by dogs. God's word is fulfilled again as she keeps her appointment with death.

CHAPTER TEN

V 1–11: AHAB Jehu fulfils Elijah's word in arranging for the death and beheading of the seventy sons of Ahab. Accordingly, no one remains of the house of Ahab. **V 12–14: AHAZIAH** Forty-two remaining relatives of Ahaziah, the slain wicked king of Judah, appear and are also put to death by Jehu. **V 15–17: ALLY** Jehonadab, the Rechabite, and thus a follower of the LORD and one who held to the importance of the law given by Moses, joins Jehu and sees his zeal in exterminating the house of Ahab, as prophesied by Elijah. **V 18–28: ACCOMPLISHED** Through pretending at first to be a Baal-worshipper, and encouraging all their worshippers to be present at the temple of Baal, Jehu has them all put to death. Thus he accomplished the destruction of Baal from Israel. **V 29–33: ADHERENCE** Although God acknowledges the good work done against the house of Ahab and against Baal, Jehu does not follow God's law with all his heart, and continues to promote idolatry with the golden calves of Bethel and Dan. Zeal for God to destroy negative influences does not necessarily imply a positive walk with Him. This may be a good reason why Israel loses ground to King Hazael. **V 34–36: ACHIEVEMENTS** Jehu's achievements are noteworthy. After reigning for twenty-eight years, he dies and is succeeded as king of Israel by his son, Jehoram.

CHAPTER ELEVEN

V 1: PERNICIOUS PLOT In Judah, Athaliah comes to reign as queen after the death of her son, Ahaziah. Like her evil grandfather, father and mother (Omri, Ahab and Jezebel), she is a wicked person, dedicated to destroying David's line (which is also Messiah's line) and restoring Baal-worship. That is her goal. **V 2–3: PROTECTED PRINCE** (See the note on Joash in 2 Kings Overview—Principles and Particulars.) One of the royal princes, Joash, escapes death and is hidden by Jehoshebah for six years in the temple, while Athaliah rules. David's line hangs on a very thin thread, humanly speaking. **V 4–11: PRIEST'S PART** Jehoiada, the priest, arranges for the protection of Joash during his investiture as king. **V 12: PUBLIC PROCLAMATION** Joash is crowned as king of Judah. **V 13–16: PLOTTER PERISHES** Queen Athaliah expresses publicly the depth of her outrage at the coronation of Joash. She is put to death at Jehoiada's command. **V 17–21: PEOPLE PURIFIED** Jehoiada makes a covenant of faithfulness to God between the LORD, Joash, and the people. All the Baal-worship which re-emerged during Athaliah's reign is destroyed. The priests of Baal are executed. The land rejoices and Joash starts his reign as a seven-year-old boy under the guidance of Jehoiada.

CHAPTER TWELVE

V 1–3: RIGHTEOUS Joash begins his forty-year reign in Jerusalem as king of Judah. Through the godly instruction of Jehoida, the priest, he is righteous but does not put away the high places of sacrifice and incense burning. However, he is a big improvement compared with his predecessors. **V 4–16: REPAIRS** Joash insists on the collection of money in the temple, under Jehoida's supervision, and appoints appropriate workmen to repair the temple. Those responsible for the collection and application of the money

are so honest that they are not required to give accounts. **V 17–18: RESCUE** When King Hazael of Syria threatens Jerusalem, Joash rescues the city by sending him sacred things from the treasury of the temple and the king's house. **V 19–20: REBELLION** Even righteous kings are not exempt from rebellion or murder. Joash is murdered by two of his own servants, and Amaziah, his son, takes his place as king of Judah.

CHAPTER THIRTEEN

V 1–8: RELIEF Jehoahaz, son of Jehu, becomes king of Israel in the twenty-third year of Joash, who is king of Judah. God is angry with him for his wickedness and allows Syrian oppression of Israel. Nevertheless, God has mercy upon Israel and relieves their suffering. Israel's blessing would have been far greater if they had turned to Him in repentance. Israel is reduced to a very weak military power. **V 9–13: RESUMPTION** In the thirty-seventh year of King Joash of Judah, the son of King Jehoahaz of Israel, Jehoash, succeeds his father as king of Israel. Jehoash reigns sixteen years and resumes the evil ways of the kings of Israel. Jehoash dies and Jeroboam succeeds him as king of Israel. **V 14–19: REMONSTRATION** An incident from King Jehoash's life is recorded. He travels to see Elisha, who is fatally ill. Elisha is very ill but is more concerned with God's people than his own health. He remonstrates with Jehoash, and tells him to strike the ground with arrows. Jehoash stops after striking the ground only three times. Elisha tells him that had he struck the ground five or six times, he would have completely destroyed Syria. Now he will only defeat them three times. **V 20–21: RESURRECTION** After the death and burial of Elisha, a dead man is revived when his body touches Elisha's bones. Here God takes the initiative to vindicate His man and His message. **V 22–23: REMEMBERED** During Jehoash's reign, Israel is sorely oppressed by King Hazael of Syria, but God has compassion on His people because of His covenant with Abraham, Isaac and Jacob. **V 24–25: RECOVERED** Hazael, king of Syria, dies. King Jehoash of Israel, true to Elisha's word, defeats the Syrians three times and recaptures the cities of Israel, before his death.

CHAPTER FOURTEEN

V 1–4: AMAZIAH Amaziah, son of Joash, takes over as king of Judah, when he is twenty-five years old. He reigns twenty-nine years in Jerusalem. He is righteous, as was his father Joash, but he does not remove the high places for sacrifice and burning incense. **V 5–7: ACCOMPLISHMENTS** His accomplishments include executing those who murdered his father (yet sparing their children), victory over the Edomites, and taking Sela, which he renames Joktheel. **V 8–14: ANTAGONISTS** King Amaziah of Judah challenges King Jehoash of Israel to war. He insists on conflict, despite Jehoash's telling him that Israel is far too strong for Judah. Amaziah suffers a heavy defeat and Jerusalem is ransacked and plundered. **V 15–16: ACCESSION** Jehoash, king of Israel, who accomplishes much militarily and politically for Israel despite his evil heart, dies and is replaced by his son, Jeroboam (the second King Jeroboam). **V 17–20: AMAZIAH** King Amaziah, king of Judah, is killed after a conspiracy against him and is buried in the City of David. He lives fifteen years after the death of Jehoash, king of Israel. **V 21–22: AZARIAH** At the age of sixteen, Azariah, son of Amaziah, succeeds his father as the king of Judah. **V 23–27: AFFLICTION** Jeroboam succeeds Jehoash as king of Israel in the fifteenth year of Amaziah, king of Judah, and reigns for forty-one years. Although he is evil, God sees the affliction of Israel, and, remembering the promise of His word, relieves that affliction through the conquests of Jeroboam. God, in his sovereignty, can work, even through evil men, to accomplish His purposes and His people's good. **V 28–29: ACTS** Jeroboam's acts and death are recorded. He is succeeded by his son, Zechariah, as king of Israel.

CHAPTER FIFTEEN

V 1–7: LENGTHY AND LEPROUS Azariah becomes king of Judah at the age of sixteen and reigns for fifty-two years. His reign begins in the twenty-seventh year of Jeroboam, king of Israel. His lengthy reign is marked by the fact that he becomes a leper and dwells in an isolated house. He acts in the same way as his father, King Amaziah, before him. He is righteous, but does not remove the high places of sacrifice. He dies and is buried in the City of David. His son, Jotham, judges the country. **V 8–12: EVIL AND EXECUTED** In the thirty-eighth year of Azariah, king of Judah, Zechariah becomes the king of Israel and reigns for six months. He is evil and is killed by Shallum, who takes over from him as king of Israel. Jehu's sons have reigned to the fourth generation, as God's word predicted. **V 13–16: MURDERING AND MURDERED** In the thirty-ninth year of King Azariah of Judah (here referred to as Uzziah), Shallum takes over as king of Israel from the man he murders. He only reigns for a month before Menahem murders him and takes his place as king of Israel. He is a cruel man. **V 17–22:**

MENAHEM AND MONEY Menahem reigns as king of Israel for ten years, beginning in the thirty-ninth year of Azariah, king of Judah. He continues in the same evil ways as Jeroboam, but averts invasion from the king of Assyria, Pul, by taking money from the wealthy and giving it to Pul. Pekahiah, his son, takes over from him as king of Israel at his death. **V 23–31: PEKAHIAH AND PEKAH** Pekahiah and Pekah are successive kings of Israel who reign for two years and twenty years respectively, during the ongoing reign of Azariah, king of Judah. Both continue in evil. Pekah conspires to kill Pekahiah and then succeeds him. Pekah himself is killed by Hoshea, who reigns as king of Israel in the twentieth year of Jotham, king of Judah. **V 32–38: JUDAH AND JOTHAM** Switching back to the kings of Judah, Jotham becomes king of Judah in Pekah's second year as king of Israel. Twenty-five years old at his accession, he reigns for sixteen years. He is righteous, but, again, does not remove the high places of sacrifice. Syria and Israel attack Judah during his reign. He dies and is buried in the City of David. His son, Ahaz, becomes king of Judah in his place.

CHAPTER SIXTEEN

V 1: AHAZ'S ACCESSION King Ahaz of Judah begins his reign in the seventeenth year of King Pekah of Israel. **V 2–4: AWFUL ABOMINATIONS** His evil ways include the worst abominations of the nations which the LORD had driven out from Israel, including burning his son and continued idolatry. **V 5–9: ASSYRIAN AID** Besieged by the kings of Syria and Israel, King Ahaz of Judah sends gold from the temple to buy the help of the king of Assyria. **V 10–16: ALTAR ADOPTED** Ahaz causes Urijah, the priest, to copy an Assyrian altar. He adds desecration and false sacrifices to his sins by ignoring God's holy instructions about the altar and sacrifices. **V 17–20: ADDED ALTERATIONS** Ahaz makes changes to other parts of the holy furniture of the temple. Personal taste predominates over obeying God's word. At his death, his son, Hezekiah, takes over as king of Judah.

CHAPTER SEVENTEEN

V 1–4: CONCLUSION King Hoshea, who comes to the throne in Samaria in the twelfth year of Ahaz, king of Judah, concludes the succession of the kings of Israel. He is evil and is imprisoned by the king of Assyria. **V 5–6: CAPTIVITY** In the ninth year of Hoshea's reign as king of Israel, Israel is carried away as captive to Assyria. **V 7–12: CAUSE** The cause for Israel's captivity is that God's people have rebelled against Him, fearing other gods, ignoring His statutes and commands, following the statutes of ungodly nations, pursuing idolatry, and practising wickedness. **V 13–18: COMMANDMENTS** Nevertheless, the LORD sends prophets to turn them from their sin and to keep His commandments. His commandments are rejected. In rebellion, their idol worship and evil become worse and worse. Child sacrifice, witchcraft and spiritism replace walking with God. Only Judah, out of the children of Israel, is left in the promised land. **V 19–23: CONTAGIOUS** But even Judah follows Israel's invented statutes, and neglects and rejects God's law. Israel is plundered and carried away captive to Assyria. **V 24–28: CALAMITY** As a reminder to the Assyrians, who resettle in the cities of Samaria where the children of Israel once lived, God sends lions among them because they do not fear Him. The king of Assyria, taking note of this, sends back an exiled Israelite priest to Bethel to teach them what he sees as 'the rituals of the God of the land'. This is so that they will fear the LORD. **V 29–41: COMPROMISE** The people resettled by the Assyrians thus mingle aspects of God's truth with their existing gross idolatry and abominable practices. They have a superficial fear of God, but they serve their own idols and images. Compromise is widespread and deep. There is no difference between those who claim to be God's people and those who are not. The fact that they disobey God's word and continue in idolatry makes it evident that they do not really 'fear the LORD'.

NOTE ON 2 KINGS 18:13 TO 2 KINGS 20:19

Isaiah chapters 36, 37, 38 and 39 are quoted in 2 Kings 18:13 to 2 Kings 20:19, almost verbatim. Isaiah chapter 38 includes the personal prayer of Hezekiah which is not included in 2 Kings. Either the compiler of 2 Kings used the same source as Isaiah or, more likely, quoted from Isaiah as the prophet of the day. Isaiah chapters 36 and 37 show how the predictions of Assyria's downfall, bringing the deliverance of Jerusalem, are fulfilled exactly. Isaiah chapters 38 and 39 set the scene for the rest of Isaiah, which deals with the Babylonian captivity. Because of the very close similarity of these chapters in Isaiah to those in 2 Kings, reference should be made back to the notes on the chapters in 2 Kings.

CHAPTER EIGHTEEN

V 1–3: NEW A new king reigns in Judah with a new inclination to do what is right in God's sight, in complete obedience to Him. His name is Hezekiah. At the age of twenty-five, he begins his twenty-nine year reign in Judah during the third year of Hoshea, king of Israel. **V 4:**

NEHUSHTAN Hezekiah removes the high places and gets rid of all the idols. He also breaks in pieces the bronze serpent that Moses lifted up in the wilderness to save the Israelites, bitten by serpents, who looked up to it in obedient trust. That serpent, called Nehushtan, has become an idol. **V 5–8: NO ONE** No other king of Judah, past or future, demonstrates a trust in God like Hezekiah. This causes him to follow the LORD and keep His word. God prospers him, and he rebels against the Assyrian domination and subdues the Philistines. **V 9–16: NEVERTHELESS** The Assyrians take the king of Israel, Hoshea, captive to Assyria, in the fourth year of King Hezekiah's reign in Judah. This is because of disobedience to God and His commandments. Hezekiah does trust God and obey His commandments but, nevertheless, Sennacherib, king of Assyria, invades and takes Judah's fortified cities. Hezekiah admits to Sennacherib that he is wrong in rebelling against him and pays him a ransom from the silver and gold, which is stripped from the temple. Even godliness does not always guarantee success. **V 17–35: NEGATIVES** Sennacherib, despite the ransom paid by King Hezekiah, then moves against Jerusalem and Hezekiah stands firm against him. A barrage of negative comments is made to the people of Jerusalem to discourage them and to point out the strength of Assyria and the weakness of Israel. Sennacherib seeks to persuade them that God can do nothing for them. **V 36–37: NOTHING** A gritty resolution prevails in Judah, and the people reply nothing to Sennacherib, just as King Hezekiah commands. In mourning, Hezekiah's officers repeat the words of Sennacherib's commander (the 'Rabshakeh') to godly Hezekiah.

CHAPTER NINETEEN

V 1–4: SEEKING In mourning and sackcloth, Hezekiah goes to the temple to seek God. He relays to Isaiah his concern for deliverance, and that God should hear and respond to the blasphemy from Sennacherib's command. He asks Isaiah to pray. **V 5–7: SURE** Isaiah assures him that God will work to cause the Assyrians to return, and that Sennacherib will be killed. **V 8–13: SENNACHERIB** Sennacherib returns to oppose the king of Ethiopia, who wars against him, but sends a letter to Hezekiah telling him that he will be back and that there is no hope for Judah. **V 14–19: SPREAD** Hezekiah receives, reads, and spreads the letter before the LORD in the temple. He prays for God to intervene to save Judah so all the nations may know that He really is the LORD God alone. **V 20–34: SPOKEN** Isaiah sends a message to Hezekiah to tell him that God Himself has spoken. He gives him assurance that the blasphemy of Sennacherib will be repaid, he predicts his downfall, and tells him that the future is good for God's people. There will be no attack on Jerusalem and the LORD will defend it for His own sake, and for David's sake. **V 35–37: STRUCK** God's angel intervenes to kill 185,000 Assyrians. Sennacherib returns home. In his idol temple, he is murdered by two of his own sons. Another of his sons takes his place as king.

CHAPTER TWENTY

V 1: SICK King Hezekiah is sick and Isaiah tells him that he will die. **V 2–11: SAVED** In answer to Hezekiah's prayer, God saves him and promises him another fifteen years. He confirms this to him by a sign. The sundial shadow goes backwards, rather than forwards, in degrees. **V 12–18:**

SAD How sad that such a godly king should then parade all his wealth to Babylon. Isaiah tells him that as a result of this, his people will be taken captive to Babylon in the future, and his sons will become eunuchs in the palace of the king of Babylon. **V 19: SELFISH** Surprisingly, Hezekiah's response is relief that this captivity will not come while he is alive. **V 20–21: SON** King Hezekiah is a mighty king and he even brought water into the city. However he dies and his son, Manasseh, succeeds him as king of Judah.

CHAPTER TWENTY-ONE

V 1–18: ABJECT EVIL Manasseh reigns as king of Judah for fifty-five years from the age of twelve. His reign is a catalogue of resolute evil, rebellion, idolatry, witchcraft and spiritism. God's holy displeasure with his wickedness will ultimately produce disaster on Jerusalem and Judah. Amon, his son, succeeds him as king of Judah. He has grown up observing that his father's rebellion against God has engendered a depth of evil conduct in Judah that is worse than that of the nations which were driven out initially. **V 19–22: ABOMINATIONS EXTENDED** Amon reigns in Judah from the age of twenty-two years to twenty-four years. He carries on the same abominable practices and lifestyle as his evil father. **V 23–26: AMON'S END** Amon is assassinated by officials, who are then killed by the people in the land. Josiah, Amon's son, succeeds him as king of Judah.

CHAPTER TWENTY-TWO

V 1–2: RIGHTEOUS Surprisingly, King Josiah is righteous. Coming to the throne at the age of eight, he reigns for thirty-one years in Jerusalem as king of Judah. He walks righteously and straightforwardly with the LORD. **V 3–7: REPAIRS** He orders the temple to be repaired. **V 8–11: READING** Hilkiah, the high priest, finds God's Book of the Law. Shaphan, the scribe, reads it to King Josiah, who immediately tears his clothes as a sign of mourning. **V 12–13: RESPONSIVE** So responsive is Josiah to the Word of God, that he commands that enquiry is made of the LORD about the book, recognising that God's wrath has been incurred by His people's disobedience. **V 14–20: REVELATION** A party of five men, including Hilkiah and Shaphan, go to Huldah the prophetess. She confirms God's anger against Israel and Judah, but that He has noted the tender-heartedness and humility of King Josiah. Accordingly, Josiah will not be judged for this with the rest of his people. God's revelation is relayed to Josiah.

CHAPTER TWENTY-THREE

V 1–3: READING AND RIGHTEOUSNESS King Josiah of Judah reads the Book of the Covenant before all the people, small and great. This includes the priests and the prophets. He makes a covenant on behalf of the people to follow the LORD wholly and wholeheartedly. All the people agree with this covenant, to practise righteousness according to God's Word. **V 4–16: REPENTANT AND RADICAL** In a sweeping, thorough and godly reformation, King Josiah removes anything used in worship which is tainted with idolatry, immorality, child-sacrifice or false worship. Idolatrous priests are also removed. Idols are ground to powder and cast in the brook Kidron. Even the bones of false prophets are burned. **V 17–18: REGARD AND REVERENCE** When Josiah realises that one of the tombs belongs to

the man who prophesied against idolatry and against the altar, and in fact had prophesied the very actions that Josiah was taking, the king highly esteems this prophet of God and reverently tells his men to leave his bones where they are. **V 19–25: REMOVAL AND REMEMBRANCE** All the shrines and the high places in Samaria are also removed, the priests executed, and mediums and spiritists put away. The remembrance of the Passover is reinstated in the eighteenth year of Josiah's reign. Just as Hezekiah's trust in God was unique among the kings of Judah, past or future, so is Josiah's wholehearted repentance. **V 26–27: RESOLUTE AND REJECTING** Even the righteousness of Josiah cannot turn away the wrath of God against all the wickedness that Judah has done through Manasseh and Ahab. Judah will still bear its judgement. **V 28–30: REIGN AND RESPECT** The reign of Josiah continues until he is killed in battle against Pharaoh Necho, king of Egypt. His respectful servants take him to Jerusalem to bury him. His son, Jehoahaz, succeeds him as king of Judah. **V 31–37: RULERS AND RETURN** King Jehoahaz of Judah only reigns for three months after succeeding Josiah, at the age of twenty-three. After such a godly father comes an evil son, who is taken captive by Pharaoh Necho of Egypt. He makes Eliakim, Josiah's son, king in the place of Jehoahaz, and changes his name to Jehoiakim. Jehoiakim is Necho's puppet, and gives him all the wealth of the country. He is twenty-five years old and reigns for eleven years in Jerusalem as king of Judah. He also is an evil king. After the reign of godly King Josiah, the kings return to evil.

CHAPTER TWENTY-FOUR

V 1–7: POWERLESS After Jehoiakim becomes the vassal of Nebuchadnezzar, king of Babylon, and later rebels against him, bands of raiding foreigners (Chaldeans, Syrians, Moabites, and Ammonites) come against Judah to destroy it. This is judgement from God for the sins of Manasseh. Judah is powerless to help itself. Jehoiakim dies and his son, Jehoiachin, reigns in his place as king of Judah. There is no more invasion from Egypt because the king of Egypt is occupied with the king of Babylon. **V 8–16: PRISONERS** After a three-month-long and evil reign, eighteen-year-old Jehoiachin, his mother, servants, princes and officers are taken captive by the king of Babylon. The treasures and gold of Jerusalem are removed to Babylon and only the poorest people in Jerusalem remain. All the fighting men and craftsmen are also taken. **V 17–20: PUPPET** The king of Babylon puts Mattaniah, Jehoiachin's uncle, as puppet king in his place, and changes his name to Zedekiah. He reigns from the age of twenty-one years for eleven years and continues the evil. But this puppet king finally rebels against the king of Babylon.

CHAPTER TWENTY-FIVE

V 1–21: CAPTIVITY During Zedekiah's ninth year, the king of Babylon invades and makes a siege of Jerusalem. Severe famine and oppression follow. The wall is broken through and Judah's army scattered. Zedekiah is blinded and taken captive to Babylon. The temple and the houses are burned and the walls of Jerusalem broken down. Only some of the poor of the land are left in Jerusalem to dress the vines and to farm the land. The remaining valuable materials from the temple are taken away as well. Men of influence and religious leaders are put to death. Judah is now taken captive to Babylon. **V 22–26: COMPLIANT** Gedaliah is appointed as governor over Judah and this compliant man takes an oath and tells his compatriots not to be afraid of the servants of the Chaldeans. If they dwell in the land of Babylon, he tells them that it will be well with them. Ishmael kills him and many people flee to Egypt through fear of the Chaldeans. **V 27–30: CONSIDERATION** King Evil-Merodach of Babylon takes pity on Jehoiachin and takes him out of prison and feeds him every day of his life.

1 CHRONICLES

OVERVIEW

PEOPLE AND PRELIMINARIES

✱As with the two preceding books of Samuel and the two preceding books of Kings, 1 Chronicles (twenty-nine chapters) and 2 Chronicles (twenty-six chapters) were originally one book, divided simply because of length and practical considerations. They are the eighth and ninth historical books of the Old Testament and were written in Israel probably between 450 BC and 430 BC and possibly by Ezra who might have drawn his material, under God, from different sources. They provide a sweep of history from Adam until the return from Babylon in 538 BC. An estimate of the events covered by 1 Chronicles, apart from the genealogies, is forty-one years.

PLAN AND PURPOSE

(i) I Chronicles provides a potted history from Adam to Zedekiah, and then gives the genealogies of the tribes and the allocations given to each tribe, prior to Israel's settlement after the exile. Then the reign of David is highlighted from his anointing, bringing the ark to Jerusalem, the establishing of the Davidic covenant, preparations for building the temple, and through to his death. Solomon is anointed king in place of his father. I Chronicles concentrates on Judah. Neither I nor 2 Chronicles is chronologically complete, and some of the events in Samuel and Kings are repeated and others omitted. Basically Chronicles majors on what makes a spiritual impact, as distinct from what makes a mere political impact.

PROFILE AND PROGRESSION

Selections from genealogies from Adam, then from David until the captivity, including the tribes of Israel and those living in Jerusalem (1:1–9:34); events from the death of Saul until the accession and anointing of David, the conquering of Jerusalem, and details of his loyal team of mighty men (9:35–12:40); David as king until his death, including the bringing back of the ark of the covenant, God's covenant with David, accounts of some conquests, David's sin in numbering Israel, his help in preparing to have the temple built by Solomon and his handing the baton of kingship on to him (13:1–29:30).

PRINCIPLES AND PARTICULARS

The emphasis on historical fact, as the basis for the book, is made evident by the family trees. Genealogies underline the historicity of the Bible.

They are inspired but not normally inspiring, but there are certain 'gems in the coal mine' of genealogies such as the Prayer of Jabez (to be understood in context, please!). Preparation is made for national life and for worship in the temple to be built. David's selfless loyalty in helping his son with this project, after God had forbidden him to do so himself, shows his heart for God's glory. The centrality of God's presence is pictured in the priority given to the ark of the covenant. The Davidic covenant, later fulfilled in Christ, is a key ingredient. It is interesting to make the comparison with the books of Samuel and Kings concerning material common to both, and what is excluded.

I CHRONICLES

CHAPTER ONE

V 1–4: ADAM TO NOAH AND SONS V 5–7: THE JAPHETHITES V 8–16: THE HAMITES V 17–27: THE SEMITES (The sons of Shem). **V 28–34a: ABRAHAM'S FAMILY V 34b–37: ISAAC'S FAMILY V 38–42: SEIR'S FAMILY V 43–50: KINGS OF EDOM**

CHAPTER TWO

V 1–2: ISRAEL'S SONS V 3–17: JUDAH TO DAVID AND HIS CLOSE FAMILY V 18–24: HEZRON'S FAMILY V 25–41: JEHRAMEEL'S FAMILY V 42–55: CALEB'S FAMILY

CHAPTER THREE

V 1–9: DAVID'S FAMILY The sons born to David both in Hebron and in Jerusalem are listed. **V 10–16: SOLOMON'S FAMILY** Remembering that I Chronicles concentrates on Judah, we see here the kings of Judah from Solomon onwards up to the captivity. **V 17–24: JECONIAH'S FAMILY** Jeconiah was also known as Jehoiachin. This dates from the captivity of Judah to Babylon.

CHAPTER FOUR

V 1–23: JUDAH'S FAMILY In verses 9 and 10, Jabez's prayer shines like a sparkling diamond in the coal mine of genealogies. The main concern of Jabez is not to get rich quick. In seeking blessing and legitimate expansion for himself, his priorities are to know God's hand upon him, to be kept from evil, and not to cause pain to God or to others. **V 24–43: SIMEON'S FAMILY**

CHAPTER FIVE

V 1–10: REUBEN'S FAMILY V 11–17: GAD'S FAMILY V 18–26: SEPARATED FAMILIES The Reubenites, Gadites, and the half tribe of Manasseh are on the east of the Jordan. They cry out in prayer to God in battle. God heeds and helps them to defeat the Hagrites because they trust in Him. However, the half tribe of Manasseh falls into unfaithfulness and spiritual harlotry. They, along with the other two tribes, are carried into captivity.

CHAPTER SIX

V 1–30: LEVI'S FAMILY V 31–48: MUSIC MAKERS Details are given for which of the Levites are responsible for the music for worship. **V 49–53: AARON'S FAMILY V 54–81: LEVITES' LOCATIONS** The towns which are allocated to the Levites and transferred to them from other tribes are detailed.

CHAPTER SEVEN

V 1–5: ISSACHAR'S FAMILY V 6–12: BENJAMIN'S FAMILY V 13: NAPHTALI'S FAMILY V 14–19: MANASSEH'S FAMILY Details of the other half tribe of Manasseh, in the west, are given. **V 20–29: EPHRAIM'S FAMILY V 30–40: ASHER'S FAMILY**

CHAPTER EIGHT

V 1–40: SAUL'S FAMILY The family tree of Benjamin is given. This is important because verse 33 shows that King Saul, Israel's first king, is included in it.

CHAPTER NINE

V 1: INSCRIPTION The record of Israel's genealogies is inscribed in the book of its kings. Sadly, Judah is carried away captive to Babylon because of unfaithfulness. **V 2–16: INHABITANTS** The dwellers in Jerusalem are listed in verses 1 to 9, the priests in verses 10 to 13, and the Levites in verses 14 to 16. **V 17–27: INCESSANT** Gatekeepers are on guard every day at stations in an incessant watch on the safety and life of Jerusalem. Lodging around the temple, they are responsible for opening it in the mornings. **V 28–34: INVOLVEMENT** The Levites are involved in other matters that enable the service of the sanctuary to take place and that provide music for the worship. **V 35–44: IMPORTANT** The line of King Saul is repeated again, leading in to the main theme of the book which focuses on King David, his successor.

CHAPTER TEN

V 1–6: DEATH In the battle against the Philistines, Saul is wounded and takes his own life. His armour bearer commits suicide. His three sons die in the battle. **V 7: DEFEAT** The Israelite army flees, and the abandoned towns are occupied by the Philistines. **V 8–10: DESECRATION** The bodies of Saul and his sons are stripped and desecrated. Saul's armour is displayed and his head is hung in the temple of Dagon, the Philistine idol god. **V 11–12: DEVOTION** The valiant men of King Saul retrieve the bodies of Saul and his sons and bury them in Jabesh, where they fast for seven days. Here is true devotion. **V 13–14a: DISASTROUS** Saul's unfaithfulness to God, breaking God's word, consulting a medium for guidance, and failure to enquire of the LORD, all proved disastrous. These are the reasons now stated why he is killed and why Israel is overcome. **V 14b: DAVID** David now becomes king of Israel.

CHAPTER ELEVEN

V 1–3: CONFIRMING COVENANT After Saul's death, all Israel come to Hebron to press David to become king, knowing that the LORD said this will happen. David agrees and a covenant is made. **V 4–9: CONQUEROR'S COMPENSATION** Jerusalem (or Jebus) now has to be conquered. David promises that whoever goes up first will be chief and captain, and Joab takes the honour. David lives there, Joab repairs the rest of the city, David becomes great, and it is known that the LORD is with him. **V 10–47: MIGHTY MEN** Under David is a pyramid leadership structure. Joab is the leader immediately under David, then three heads under him, then thirty chief mighty men under those three. This is the select band that will support David faithfully, and fight for him. Individually courageous, committed and men of initiative, they blend as a single team under his leadership. They are a model for all who work together for God.

CHAPTER TWELVE

V 1–37: FORCES Many other soldiers come to David from different quarters, from different tribes, and at different times. Each day, people join up until his army is great and numerous. Again, individuals and groups of individuals are noted for their achievements within the overall military team. **V 38: FERVENT** Not only are all the volunteer fighting men absolutely determined to make David king of Israel, but the rest of Israel is equally fervent and of one mind to see David rule. **V 39–40: FEAST** A great feast of celebration follows for three days. There is great joy in Israel in which the two-and-a-half tribes from the other side of the Jordan participate fully.

CHAPTER THIRTEEN

V 1–8: ARK ACCLAIMED With the support and enthusiasm of the whole of Israel, King David arranges for the ark to come back. However, it is to be carried on a new cart. (Remember that God decreed that the ark must be carried on poles on the shoulders of Levis. This command of God is forgotten, ignored or disobeyed.) **V 9–11: ACUTE ANGER** The oxen stumble and Uzza steadies the ark with his hand. He is struck dead by God. David, also, is angry: but his anger is wrongly directed at the LORD's outbreak against Uzza. **V 12–14: AWESOMELY AFRAID** David is also struck with awe and fear, so that he does not have the ark taken to the City of David, in Jerusalem. Instead it is kept at the house of Obed-Edom, who accordingly is greatly blessed, with all his house.

CHAPTER FOURTEEN

V 1–2: ESTABLISHED AND EXALTED God

is establishing David, who is exalted in the minds of his subjects. Hiram, king of Tyre, contacts David with a view to sending him provisions for building a palace. **V 3–9: FAMILY AND FOES** David takes more wives and becomes the father of more children. This is not commended, but simply reported. The Philistines oppose David and come for battle. **V 10–12: INQUIRY AND IDOLATRY** David inquires of God whether he should go up against the Philistines, and God tells him to do so. When he defeats them, he burns all their gods, demonstrating his determination to exclude idolatry. **V 13–17: FAITHFULNESS AND FAME** When the Philistines attack again, David follows his practice of praying to God, to ask whether he should fight at that time. God answers him, guides him and intervenes. The Philistines are defeated. David's fame spreads widely and all the nations begin to fear him.

CHAPTER FIFTEEN

V 1–24: READINESS AND RETURN David prepares for the return of the ark by making sure it is properly carried back on poles on the shoulders of the Levites, and that reverent preparation is made for the worship in the tabernacle. This involves the Levites, and those who assist in the worship. David has learned from Uzza's tragic mistake. **V 25–28: PRAISE AND PLAYING** The reverent preparation and waiting for the ark lead to great praise, observing the designated sacrifices, following the correct procedures, and playing the prescribed musical instruments to worship God. **V 29: DANCING AND DESPISING** David gets carried away in his enthusiastic gyrating dance and playing of music before the ark. His wife, Michal, sees him and despises him.

CHAPTER SIXTEEN

V 1–6: PLACE The ark is brought back to the tabernacle, offerings are made there in the correct place, provisions are distributed to all the Israelites, and those responsible for worship are also put in place by David. **V 7–36a: PRAISE** David's comprehensive praise follows. It records thanks to God for His involvement with the people of Israel throughout their history. (The major portions of his praise are found in Psalms 105:1–15 and 96:1–13.) **V 36b: PEOPLE** All the people join in. They praise the LORD, and say 'Amen'. **V 37–43: PARTICULARS** David ensures that every aspect of the worship is looked after by those with particular responsibilities. The people and David depart to their houses.

CHAPTER SEVENTEEN

V 1: CONCERN David is concerned that he has a magnificent cedar palace while the ark of the covenant is still in the tent of the tabernacle, and not in a permanent dedicated building. **V 2: CONFIRMATION** Nathan, a prophet of God, confirms David's intention to build a temple by telling him to do whatever is in his mind. **V 3–6: CORRECTION** Even men of God can get it wrong! God corrects Nathan and tells him that he must go and tell David that he is not the one who will build Him the temple. (God has other plans.) **V 7–14: COVENANT** God tells Nathan of the covenant He will make with David in which He promises to establish David's line. He says in the covenant that David's son will build the house for God and that his son's throne will be forever. (The prophecy within this covenant will have short-term fulfilment in Solomon's building of the temple, and eternal fulfilment because Jesus will come from

David's line, as the prophesied far greater eternal 'son' of David.) **V 15: CAREFUL** Nathan is careful to report to David everything that God says and shows to him in confirming that David will not build the temple but that his line will be established for ever. A godly man can be wrong, as Nathan shows, but his humility and faithful obedience are shown when he is corrected. **V 16–28: COMMITMENT** David humbly prays to the LORD, committing himself to Him again, and gives grateful thanks to Him for what He has promised to do. He accepts God's sovereign will and ruling. Here is real commitment from a man who is not going to do what his heart longs to do. He trusts God to do what is best.

CHAPTER EIGHTEEN

V 1–13a: COMBAT AND CONQUEST David defeats the Philistines, the Zohahites and the Syrians in battle. One king, Tou, King of Hamath, even comes to David to present articles of gold, silver and bronze to him. The Edomites become his servants. God is helping David. **V 13b: PRESENCE AND PRESERVATION** It is the LORD who preserves David, and this He does wherever David goes. God's presence is clearly with him. **V 14: JUDGEMENT AND JUSTICE** David administers justice and judgement to all the people of Israel. His success is not limited to the battlefield. **V 15–17: MEN AND METHOD** David has the right men in the positions of influence, in military, political, administrative, and religious spheres. His method is clearly to organise well, to trust God, and to seek to choose the right people.

CHAPTER NINETEEN

V 1–2: AMMONITES Nahash, king of the Ammonites, dies and is succeeded by his son Hanun. David sends a delegation to express sympathy because, in the past, Nahash had helped him. **V 3–6a: AFFRONT** Guided by others, Hanun rejects David's overture as a spying expedition. He seizes and shaves David's men. He cuts off their garments at the buttocks and sends them away. David tells his men to stay at Jericho till their beards have grown and then return. The Ammonites become obnoxious to David. **V 6b–7: ASSISTED** The Ammonites use much wealth to hire troops from elsewhere, including from Syria, to fight against David. **V 8–19: ARMY** David's army of mighty men is mustered and skilfully deployed by Joab and his brother Abishai. Both the Ammonites and the Syrians flee and are routed. Peace is made with David, and the Syrians are not willing to help the Ammonites any more.

CHAPTER TWENTY

V 1–3: CAPTURING RABBAH Joab again leads Israel out to battle on David's behalf, and captures Rabbah of which David becomes king, thus extending his kingdom. **V 4–8: COURAGEOUS RESULTS** Some courageous battles were fought and won by David's men against the Philistine opposition.

CHAPTER TWENTY-ONE

V 1–6: CAPRICIOUS COUNTING Despite the objections of Joab, who in any case did not include Levi and Benjamin among the census, Satan moves David to insist on a count being made of his fighting men. The sole reason is pride. **V 7–8: CONTRITE CONFESSION** God is so displeased that He strikes Israel. David immediately shows his contrite heart by confessing his foolishness to God and asks Him to take away his iniquity. **V 9–13: CRITICAL CHOICE** David faces God's judgement. Through Gad, the prophet, he is told that he can choose three years of famine, three months of defeat at the hands of his enemies, or three days' plague under God's destroying angel. David chooses to fall directly into his merciful God's hand, under the third alternative, rather than to commit his future to men. **V 14–27: CHASTENING CONCLUDED** Seventy thousand Israelites die. The destroying angel pauses at the threshing floor of Araunah the Jebusite. David pleads with God. The angel, through Gad, asks David to build an altar. David negotiates and insists on paying Araunah the full price for the property so that the altar can be built and offerings made. When the burnt offerings and peace offerings are made, and David calls on the LORD, God answers from heaven by fire consuming the burnt offering on the altar. At that point, the angel of the LORD sheathes his sword and ceases to afflict Israel. **V 28–30: CURTAILED COMMUNICATION** David continues to sacrifice, but personally cannot go before the altar to enquire of God, because he is afraid of the sword of the angel of the LORD. Even a man who loves God can get it very wrong when he sins.

CHAPTER TWENTY-TWO

V 1–5: PREPARATIONS Although David is not to build the temple himself, he has such a heart for it that he makes extensive preparations in order to help his young and inexperienced son, Solomon, to do this to the glory of God. David knows that his time is limited, and he wants his remaining days to count for God. Raw materials and workers are organised. **V 6–16: PRIORITIES** David's main priority is that God's will must be done, even

though it does not meet his personal preference. Accordingly, he encourages his son, Solomon, and explains the position to him. God has passed him by because, as a man of war, he has shed so much blood. He lists carefully what he has already arranged so that Solomon can have the temple built. Finally, he encourages him to start the work with the prayer that 'The LORD be with you'. **V 17–19: PRACTICAL** David orders all the leaders in Israel to support practically. They should help Solomon and devote their hearts to seeking God in the building of the temple. David does all he can to make sure that this work honours God and is done.

CHAPTER TWENTY-THREE

V 1: ACCESSION Solomon succeeds David as king of Israel. **V 2–27: ADMINISTRATION** Beginning here and going on to the end of chapter 27, David arranges the human resources and organises the administration of the work for the temple. More than raw materials are required to build the temple! In the chapters up to twenty-seven, this applies to priests, singers, gate-keepers, administrators, the military, and those in leadership. In this chapter, he deals with the Levites, sub-divided into the Gershonites (verses 7 to 11), the Kohathites (verses 12 to 20), and the Merarites (verses 21 to 23). The general comments about the Levites are in verses 24 to 27. **V 28–32: ACTIVITIES** The responsibilities which the Levites are to perform are then listed.

CHAPTER TWENTY-FOUR

V 1–19: LOTS The priests are divided into twenty-four sections. Eleazar has sixteen of these, and Ithamar eight. Their duties are sorted out by lot, which is often the way that God's will is discovered in practice at this time. Personal preference and pride play no part in this. **V 20–31: LEVITES** The rest of the Levites are listed and again their tasks are decided by lot.

CHAPTER TWENTY-FIVE

V 1–5: SONGS Those who will prophesy to music from the sons of Asaph, Jeduthun and Heman are set apart by David and the army commanders. Music is also used in thanksgiving and in worship. **V 6–31: SONS** The two hundred and eighty-eight musicians are subject to their respective twenty-four fathers. Thus each father has twelve sons involved in this way.

CHAPTER TWENTY-SIX

V 1–19: GUARDING THE GATES The gate-keepers are descendants of Korah and Merari, and get their assignments by lot. **V 20–28: TRUSTED WITH TREASURES** The oversight of the valuables fall to the Levites. **V 29–32: OFFICIALS AND OTHERS** Judges, magistrates, administrators, and other officials are appointed.

CHAPTER TWENTY-SEVEN

V 1–15: MILITARY MONTHS Two hundred and eighty-eight thousand men are put in divisions of twenty-four thousand under twelve captains. Each captain guards the nation and the temple for a designated month of the year. Naturally, the whole army is available in time of need. **V 16–22: TWELVE TRIBES** To perform these duties, each of the twelve tribes has an officer nominated whose task is to be responsible to lead that tribe. **V 23–24: LESSON LEARNED** David does not number those of twenty years old or under because of God's promise to multiply Israel like the stars of heaven. He learns the lesson from the plague that was released when he foolishly numbered the fighting men. **V 25–34: OFFICIALS ORGANISED** Different officials are detailed to take charge of specific important areas of supply, produce, inventory, livestock, counsel, and areas close to the king.

CHAPTER TWENTY-EIGHT

V 1: SUMMONS David summonses all the leaders, officers, captains, stewards, officials, valiant men and fighting men to hear his final instructions about the temple and his renewed commission to Solomon. **V 2–8: SUMMARY** David summarises why God refused to let him build the temple but how his son, Solomon, is instructed to do so. He tells them to be careful and to seek to obey God in the performance of this. In all of this, there is a flavour of gratitude, not regret, because of what God has done for David and promised for his house. **V 9–21: SOLOMON** David commissions Solomon, passes on all the plans and gold, and finally urges him to 'be strong and of good courage and do it'. He tells Solomon not to fear or be dismayed, because God is with him. He presents to him all the organisational structure and people considered in the immediately previous chapters. It is good for a father to encourage his son and it is even better for a father to encourage his son to work for God and to honour Him.

CHAPTER TWENTY-NINE

V 1–9: GOOD EXAMPLE David tells the assembly that he has given his personal wealth to the temple and asks who else is willing to consecrate himself to the LORD in the same way. Most generous giving follows from the leaders, and the people rejoice in this, as does King David. The best exhortation to do something good is to set a good example. **V 10–20: GRATITUDE EXPRESSED** David praises the LORD before the whole assembly, thanking Him for who He is and what He has done, with a humble recognition that his people are nothing in comparison. As they worship God, he asks for his son, Solomon, a wholehearted devotion to obey God and that he will be enabled to build the temple. **V 21–25: GOD'S EXALTING** Solomon is acknowledged as king for the second time, with great pomp and joy, in the presence of the LORD. He prospers and is obeyed by Israel, with all the officers and mighty men, and David's sons pledging allegiance to him. It is God who exalts Solomon and gives him splendour and majesty as never seen before. **V 26–30: GREATNESS ENDS** After a forty-year rule over Israel, David dies. The life of this great king is over, but not the promise to his line.

2 CHRONICLES

OVERVIEW

PEOPLE AND PRELIMINARIES

See 1 Chronicles overview—People and Preliminaries. An estimate of the period covered by the book of 2 Chronicles is 427 years.

PLAN AND PURPOSE

As stated in 1 Chronicles overview—Plan and Purpose, neither 1 Chronicles nor 2 Chronicles is chronologically complete, and some of the events in Samuel and Kings are repeated and others omitted. Basically, Chronicles majors on what made a spiritual, rather than a political, impact. 2 Chronicles covers the same time span as 1 and 2 Kings but focuses on the southern tribe of Judah, ignoring the idolatrous wickedness of the ten northern tribes. It covers Solomon's reign of forty years, including the building of the temple, and Solomon's power and influence up to his death. It then traces how the kingdom divides under Jeroboam and Rehoboam. Judah declines into apostasy, with occasional times of repentance and blessing under kings such as Asa, Jehoshaphat, Joash, Hezekiah and Josiah. After the reign of twenty kings, the deportation to Babylon takes place. Cyrus' decree about the rebuilding of the temple in Jerusalem ends with a dawning ray of hope.

PROFILE AND PROGRESSION

Solomon's coronation, kingship, building of the temple, fame, acclaim, and death (1:1–9:28); The reign of twenty kings in Judah (10:1–36:21); Cyrus' proclamation (36:22,23).

PRINCIPLES AND PARTICULARS

It is interesting to see which events are common, which are new, and which are omitted in comparing Chronicles with the previous books of Samuel and Kings. 2 Chronicles underlines the dangers associated with personal sin, idolatry, and a failure to trust in God. A man who is serious with God can reverse a trend, by God's grace, but past 'success' is no guarantee for tomorrow's victory. See the effect that a leader can have for bad, as well as for good, including the heritage a father gives his children.

2 CHRONICLES

CHAPTER ONE

V 1–6: STRENGTHENED AND SACRIFICING Solomon is strengthened by God, whose presence is obvious and who exalts Solomon exceedingly. Solomon leads the nation to the worship of God at the tabernacle and sacrifices 1,000 burnt offerings. **V 7–12: WISDOM AND WEALTH** When asked by God what he wants from Him, Solomon asks for wisdom and understanding. God gives him this, as well as great wealth and honour. God is pleased that his first request is for wisdom. **V 13–17: MIGHT AND MATERIALS** Nevertheless, Solomon ensures that he is strong militarily, with horses and chariots imported from abroad. He has an abundance of silver, gold, cedar, and sycamore wood. He trades internationally in horses and chariots.

CHAPTER TWO

V 1–2: COMMENCEMENT AND CONSCRIPTION Solomon begins to prepare for building the temple and appoints 153,600 men as carriers, quarriers and foremen. **V 3–10: AWARENESS AND APPROACH** An approach is made to Hiram, king of Tyre, with whom Solomon's father, David, enjoyed an excellent relationship. Solomon asks for his help in providing skilled labour and timber. He is,

nevertheless, aware that no man-made temple can be glorious enough to contain God Himself. **V 11–16: COMMUNICATION AND COOPERATION** Hiram replies very encouragingly, and is only too willing to send what Solomon asks for, plus wheat, barley, oil, and wine. **V 17–18: OUTSIDERS AND ORGANISATION** 153,600 alien men are numbered in the census. The hard labour and menial tasks are initially given to them by Solomon, who shows his organising ability right from the start.

CHAPTER THREE

V 1–2: START Solomon begins to build the temple at Mount Moriah. This is where the LORD appeared to David at the threshing floor of Ornan. It is also where Abraham was willing to sacrifice Isaac, and where God provided the sacrifice. Some think the same place is Mount Calvary. **V 3–7: SIZE** The size of the temple is given. **V 8–14: SANCTUARY** The Most Holy Place is overlaid with fine gold. It contains the carved cherubim, also overlaid with gold and which (as we read elsewhere) will be placed over the mercy seat, and the veil of significant colours, namely blue, purple, crimson, and fine linen. **V 15–17: SUPPORTS** Two ornate pillars are made for the front of the temple and given names which mean, 'He shall establish,' and, 'In it is strength.'

CHAPTER FOUR

V 1–18: HELP FROM HIRAM All the bronze items are prepared with great expertise and care by Hiram's specialists. These include the bronze altar, the Sea, twelve oxen, three thousand baths, ten lavers, ten lamp stands, ten tables, and all the utensils. **V 19–22: GOLD FOR GOD** Solomon takes responsibility for the gold furnishings in the temple which include the gold altar, the tables for the bread of the Presence, the lamp stands, and associated equipment. The entrance door, the inner doors to the Most Holy Place, and the doors of the temple's main hall are all made of gold.

CHAPTER FIVE

V1: DEDICATED BY DAVID When the temple is finished, Solomon first brings in the silver and gold and the furnishings which have been dedicated by David. They are placed in the treasuries. **V 2–10: ACCESS WITH ARK** There is much reverence on the part of the Israelites and their leaders and many sacrifices are offered according to God's word. The ark is carefully carried on the poles provided and placed in the inner sanctuary, the Most Holy Place. **V 11–14: GLORY OF GOD** Amidst amazing music, worship and praise that emphasise 'For He is good for His mercy endures forever', the temple is filled with the cloud of God's Presence. His glory is such that the priests have to stop ministering. God has revealed Himself again to His people.

CHAPTER SIX

V 1–2: ASSURANCE In the presence of the people, Solomon reminds them that the LORD said He would dwell in the dark cloud and that Solomon has built Him the temple that God sanctioned. **V 3: ASSEMBLY** Twice in verse 3 it is emphasised that all Israel is assembled at this crucial time, when the temple is dedicated and God has revealed Himself. **V 4–11: ADORATION** Before the prayer of dedication, Solomon rehearses the details of God's faithfulness to Israel in a spirit of adoration and praise. He records that God decreed that Solomon, as David's

son, should build the temple and that he has done it. He has put the ark of the covenant, a reminder of God's covenant promise to Israel, in the temple. **V 12–40: ALTAR** Standing before the altar, Solomon dedicates the temple. He starts with the uniqueness and splendour of God, remembers His faithfulness and word, and asks for grace to walk before Him properly. He asks that God will deal with him as He has dealt with his father, King David. He acknowledges that God is far greater than any man-made temple, but asks that God will graciously hear prayer made from that temple. He then lifts specific instances of great need or failure when forgiveness and God's help will be needed particularly, and pleads that God will hear and answer in those situations. **V 41: ARK** Solomon effectively asks God to be 'at home' in the temple as His 'resting place', where the ark is placed. He asks for saved priests and rejoicing saints. **V 42: ANOINTED** Because of the mercies that God has shown to David, he asks God not to turn His face away from him as the anointed king. His prayer of dedication is complete.

CHAPTER SEVEN

V 1–3: FIRE FALLS At the end of Solomon's prayer, fire falls from heaven and consumes the burnt offering and sacrifices. God's glory fills the temple, producing awe and worship and suspending the work of the priests. **V 4–6: PEOPLE PRAISE** All the people join Solomon in praising and approaching God. **V 7–11: SOLOMON'S SACRIFICES** There are so many sacrifices, that Solomon consecrates the middle part of the courtyard to take more. He keeps the feast for seven days. Then he carries on observing festivals and having assemblies until, on the twenty-third day of the seventh month, the people are sent home glad in heart for God's goodness to David and Solomon and to the nation of Israel. Solomon's task has been accomplished. **V 12: SOVEREIGN SPEAKS** After all this, the LORD appears to Solomon by night and says that He has heard his prayer. He confirms that He has chosen the temple for sacrifices to be made. **V 13–16: REPENTANCE REQUIRED** God then proceeds to reveal important truths to Solomon and the Israelites. He says that He will always be attentive and listening for prayer from His people and that, when calamity and troubles come, humility, prayer and repentance are required in order for Him to answer and bless. He hears and sees everything. **V 17–18: PERSONAL PROMISE** He renews to Solomon the promise made to David that he will be established and blessed if he walks with God. **V 19–22: DISASTROUS DEVIATION** He also warns Solomon and Israel that to turn away from Him and to forsake Him and seek other gods will be disastrous and bring about the downfall of the temple and of Israel. God has warned His people.

CHAPTER EIGHT

V 1–6: BUILDING BIG Solomon puts in a huge building programme and settles the children of Israel in the cities which Hiram gave to him. He engages in other building activities too. **V 7–8: FOREIGN FORCE** Solomon uses remaining foreign inhabitants as his labour force. **V 9–10: ISRAELITE INVOLVEMENT** His own people are involved in leading the army and the king's administration. **V 11: PAGAN PARTNER** Solomon brings up Pharaoh's daughter, his wife, who cannot dwell where the ark had been, because the ark is holy. The cracks of Solomon's eventual downfall are widening. Clearly,

he knows that his pagan wife adversely affects his walk with God. **V 12–15: OFFERINGS OFFERED** Solomon keeps God's law in offering the sacrifices and offerings ordained by God. **V 16: ORDERED ORGANISATION** Truly, Solomon does all things decently and in good order. **V 17–18: HIRAM'S HELP** As his father David did, Solomon gets the enthusiastic cooperation of Hiram, whose sailors help Solomon to run his ships to collect gold from Ophir.

CHAPTER NINE

V 1–12: SHEBA The Queen of Sheba brings great wealth to King Solomon because she wants to see his splendour and glory for herself. She is finally overcome when she sees how Solomon approaches God. She departs, having been given far more from Solomon than she brought to him. She expresses that not even half of the truth has been told to her. **V 13–28: SPLENDOUR** Solomon's material splendour, trading might, and military strength are listed. **V 29–31: SUCCEEDED** But even great kings have to die and Solomon does so, having reigned over Israel for forty years. Rehoboam succeeds him as king.

CHAPTER TEN

V 1–7: REHOBOAM Rehoboam becomes king of Israel. When Jeroboam returns from exile and goes with Israel to ask Rehoboam to lighten the load of harsh labour, the new king's response is that Jeroboam is to come back in three days, after he has consulted the elders who served King Solomon. Their advice is to listen to the people and to lighten their load. **V 8–11: REJECTION** King Rehoboam rejects their advice and then asks the younger element for their advice, which is to make things more oppressive still for the people. **V 12–15: RUTHLESS** When Jeroboam and the people come back to Rehoboam, his harsh answer to them reflects the advice of his younger counsellors. His refusal to listen to the people has degenerated into ruthlessness. God will use this to work out His sovereign purpose. **V 16–19: REBELLION** All Israel, except Judah, rebels against King Rehoboam, and stones to death Adoniram, who is in charge of the labour force. Israel is thus in open rebellion against the house of Judah and the line of David. King Rehoboam flees to Jerusalem and continues to reign over Judah.

CHAPTER ELEVEN

V 1–4: PREVENTED Benjamin sides with Judah. One hundred and eighty thousand fighting men are prepared to fight against Israel to make Rehoboam king again. But God speaks through Shemaiah, the man of God, to tell Rehoboam not to fight against Israel and Jeroboam. He obeys. **V 5–12: PREPARED** King Rehoboam fortifies the main towns of Judah and Benjamin, living in Jerusalem himself. **V 13–17: PRIESTS** The priests and Levites throughout Israel side with Rehoboam because Jeroboam and his sons refused to have them as priests. Many honest seekers of God follow them to Judah, but Jeroboam also appoints his high priests for high places and for idolatry. The influence of the honest seekers helps the kingdom of Judah to walk in the ways of the LORD. **V 18–21: PERSONAL** Rehoboam has eighteen wives, sixty concubines, twenty-eight sons, and sixty daughters. **V 22–23: PRUDENT** King Rehoboam appoints Abijah as chief prince among his brothers so that he can make him king later. He also prudently disperses his sons throughout Judah and Benjamin to the fortified cities, giving them abundant provisions. Many wives are taken for them.

CHAPTER TWELVE

V 1–5: ABANDONED Rehoboam becomes established and abandons God's law. God allows Shishak, king of Egypt, to take fortified cities and to attack Jerusalem. God tells Rehoboam that because he has abandoned God, he will be abandoned by God. **V 6–12: ACKNOWLEDGED** Rehoboam and his leaders humble themselves before God, acknowledging His justice. God spares Jerusalem because of this, but allows Shishak to take treasures from the temple, so that Rehoboam has to replace gold shields with bronze shields. They will be a reminder to him of the folly of his recent rejection of God. Things now go well with Judah. **V 13–16: ABIJAH** Rehoboam remains for seventeen years in Jerusalem. Because his heart is not set on seeking God, he does evil. He is succeeded by Abijah, his son. Abijah inherits a state of ongoing conflict between King Rehoboam's Judah and the rest of Israel under King Jeroboam.

CHAPTER THIRTEEN

V 1–3: OUTNUMBERED King Abijah of Judah will reign for three years. With 400,000 men, he faces 800,000 led by King Jeroboam of Israel, who is in the eighteenth year of his reign. **V 4–12: OUTSPOKEN** From Mount Zemaraiam, Abijah tells the opposing troops of Israel that God is with Judah because Israel has forsaken Him and even driven out the priests and Levites. He states that Judah is still faithful to God and pleads with Israel not to fight against the LORD, because they will not succeed. **V 13–22:**

OVERPOWERED Despite an ambush set by Israel, God answers the prayers of the men of Judah. The priests blow their trumpets, the men of Judah raise the battle cry, and Israel flees. Half a million casualties are recorded among Israel. Judah wins the battle because of reliance on God. Key villages and cities are regained, and Jeroboam is struck down dead by God. Abijah's strength grows, but he marries fourteen wives and has twenty-two sons and sixteen daughters.

CHAPTER FOURTEEN

V 1–6: ASA'S RIGHTEOUSNESS After King Abijah dies, his son, Asa, reigns for ten years, during which time the land enjoys quietness. His reign is summarised here. He does what is pleasing to God. Idolatry is purged away and he commands Judah to seek God and to obey Him. Even the high places are removed. **V 7: ASA'S REST** He rebuilds the cities and their walls and yet is conscious that the rest he has on every side is because of the LORD in whom he trusts. **V 8–15: ASA RESCUED** Asa has an army of 300,000 men from Judah and 280,000 from Benjamin. Nevertheless, he knows that it is God who will give the victory in battle against the Ethiopians, even though he is vastly outnumbered by them. He cries out to God and is delivered. The LORD strikes the Ethiopians. They are overthrown, and the men of Judah gain very much spoil and defeat all the cities around Gerar.

CHAPTER FIFTEEN

V 1–7: WORD As the Spirit of God speaks through Azariah to Asa, he heeds God's word to forsake all that is wrong and to follow and obey God. He knows the choice is to seek God and find Him, or forsake Him and be forsaken. His strength will be through his seeking God, who will reward him. **V 8: WAYS** Hearing God's word through Azariah changes the ways of Asa. All abominable idols in Judah and Benjamin are removed and the altar of the LORD is restored. **V 9–15: WORSHIP** Asa gathers all from Judah and Benjamin, and all Israelites with a faithful heart who have moved into Judah, to worship God with sacrifices and offerings. They enter into a covenant to seek God wholeheartedly. Those who refuse to covenant are to be put to death. The people rejoice in this oath and God blesses them with rest. **V 16–19: WILLINGNESS** Asa's willingness to put God first includes removing his mother, Maachah, as queen mother, because she made an obscene image of Asherah. Asa cuts this down, crushes it, and burns it by the Brook Kidron. He also brings into the house of God all the dedicated items of silver and gold. With God's help and rest, Asa enters into a war-free period.

CHAPTER SIXTEEN

V 1–6: UNGODLY RECOURSE King Asa, who has been so helped by God in battle, turns to Ben-Hadad, king of Syria, for help when he is attacked by the king of Israel. Ben-Hadad attacks the Israelites who, being preoccupied, cease to build the city of Ramah. The materials that they use are taken by Asa and all Judah to build Geba and Mizpah. **V 7–10: UNWELCOME REBUKE** Hanani, a prophet of God, rebukes Asa for his foolishness in relying on the king of Syria for help instead of trusting God. He tells him that, from now on, he will have wars. Asa is angry and has the seer put in prison and then begins to oppress some of the people. What a sad decline from such a close walk with God! **V 11–14: UNWILLING RESPONSE** When King Asa becomes diseased in his feet, possibly with gangrene, he does not respond by seeking God, but simply trusts the physicians. His forty-one year reign comes to an end after a most surprising and disappointing twilight for an otherwise godly king.

CHAPTER SEVENTEEN

V 1–2: STRENGHTHENED Jehoshaphat succeeds his father, Asa, in Judah. He strengthens himself and puts troops in all of Judah's fortified cities and in the towns in Ephraim, previously won by his father. **V 3–6: SPIRITUAL** God is with Jehoshaphat, who walks before Him as David did. He is honoured by the people of Judah, who give him presents. He becomes very rich. His spiritual approach involves not seeking Baal, but rather seeking and obeying God, delighting in God's ways, and removing high places and wooden images. **V 7–11: SCRIPTURES** He sends Levites with his leaders throughout the cities of Judah to teach the people God's law. The result is that the fear of the LORD falls on all the kingdoms around Judah, who therefore do not wage war against King Jehoshaphat. In fact, even Philistines bring him presents of silver as tribute and Arabians bring him large flocks. God is blessing his righteous stand. **V 12–19: SOLDIERS** King Jehoshaphat becomes increasingly powerful and not only builds fortresses and storage cities, but also has many mighty men of valour in Jerusalem. He has 1,160,000 soldiers at his disposal.

CHAPTER EIGHTEEN

V 1–3: COOPERATION After King Jehoshaphat aligns himself by marriage with King Ahab of Israel, he seeks to cooperate with him in a joint war effort against Ramoth Gilead. **V 4–27: CONSULTATION** King Jehoshaphat insists that, before going to war, God must be consulted for His counsel. King Ahab consults 400 of his prophets who tell him to go to war because God will give him victory. Jehoshaphat asks if there is a prophet of the LORD of whom he can enquire. Micaiah is brought who, refusing to take the majority view of the other false prophets, tells the kings that such an attack will result in them being defeated and in Ahab being killed. He incurs the hostile opposition of Zedekiah, the leading false prophet, and is imprisoned by King Ahab. He tells King Ahab that he will not come back from the battle. (His first, apparently compliant, prophecy with the false prophets is so obviously intentionally sarcastic or incorrect, that it emphasises the truth when he tells the kings what he knows will really happen. It is an obvious device he uses.) **V 28–34: CONFLICT** In the battle, King Jehoshaphat, although pursued, is delivered as he cries out to God to help him. His pursuers are diverted. Although disguised, King Ahab is killed by a random arrow. Micaiah's prophecy is thus confirmed.

CHAPTER NINETEEN

V 1–3: JEHU'S REBUKE When King Jehoshaphat returns to his palace, Jehu, the seer, rebukes him severely for his alliance with wicked King Ahab. However, he does commend Jehoshaphat for ridding the land of Asherah poles (idolatrous wooden images), and that his heart is set on seeking God. **V 4–7: JUDGES REMINDED** Jehoshaphat reminds his judges to judge justly in the fear of the LORD, without partiality or bribes. **V 8–11: JUSTICE REINFORCED** To reinforce his judicial system, he appoints some Levites, priests, and chief fathers of Israel to be involved in certain legal cases. He gives the authority to hear appeals to Amariah, the chief priest, and Zebadiah, the ruler of Judah for the king's matters. He appoints the Levites as officials and urges them all to behave courageously and to be assured of God's presence with them.

CHAPTER TWENTY

V 1–2: CONFRONTED Judah, under King Jehoshaphat, is confronted by a great coalition army led by Moab and Ammon. **V 3–13: COMPOSED** Although alarmed and fearful, Jehoshaphat responds by proclaiming a public fast and prayer. He encourages his people to look to God who has delivered and blessed in the past. He admits that he has no power of his own to win this victory, despite the forces that he has. Thus composed, all Judah stands before the LORD. **V 14–17: CONFIRMED** God confirms that victory will be theirs and that He will be with them. This He does through His Spirit coming upon Jahaziel, who declares God's word to Judah. God will fight this battle for them. All they have to do is to stand still and see Him do it! **V 18–22: CONSULTATION** This is immediately met by a worshipful obedience before the LORD and a consultation with the people who are encouraged to trust and praise the LORD for victory, by faith, even before the battle. This is not complacency, but, rather, confidence in God's promise. The people sing and praise the LORD. The LORD sets ambushes of His own against the men invading Judah from Moab, Ammon and Mount Seir. These men are defeated. **V 23–28: COMPLETED** Even as the people of Judah give thanks to God for His enduring love, the invaders turn on one another in confusion and destroy one another. This is without any intervention

from the forces of Judah. King Jehoshaphat arrives to find the dead bodies of his foes, and it takes three days to carry off the spoil. God has completed a victory without the need to be 'helped' by His people. **V 29–30: COUNTRIES** The surrounding countries are full of the fear of God when they hear this, and King Jehoshaphat has God-given peace as a result. **V 31–34: CONTINUATION** For twenty-five years, Jehoshaphat reigns as king of Judah. He walks with God as his father did, and seeks to do what is right in the sight of the LORD. The recurring problem of the high places for idolatry indicates that they are not completely removed and that there are some people who do not set their hearts faithfully on God alone. **V 35–37: COOPERATION** But Jehoshaphat has his weak spot. Just as earlier he had cooperated wrongly with King Ahab of Israel, so he makes an alliance with King Ahaziah, king of Israel, who is wicked. God causes the ships that he co-constructs with King Ahaziah to be wrecked, in accordance with the prophecy given against King Jehoshaphat by Eliezer. An otherwise good and righteous man fails by having unhelpful liaisons with the ungodly, and this resurfaces in older age. Here is a warning to established Christians.

CHAPTER TWENTY-ONE

V 1–7: SINFUL SON Jehoram succeeds Jehoshaphat as king of Judah. He kills his brothers who, like him, have received valuable gifts and fortified cities from their father. Commencing his reign at thirty-two years of age, he rules for eight years as a wicked king, marrying one of Ahab's daughters. But God remembers His covenant with David not to destroy his line. **V 8–11: RIGHTEOUS REBELLIONS** Edom rebels against Jehoram and is attacked by him. Libnah also rebels, because of Jehoram's godlessness. **V 12–15: ELIJAH'S EPISTLE** The prophet Elijah writes to Jehoram to tell him that, because of his wickedness and his murder of his brothers, his people and his family will be struck. After a lingering disease, he himself will die when his bowels come out. **V 16–17: ORCHESTRATED OPPOSITION** The LORD arouses the Philistines and the Arabs to attack Judah, invade it, and carry off all his goods and sons except one, Ahaziah. **V 18–20: DEADLY DISEASE** After an incurable disease, Jehoram dies as prophesied by Elijah. He is neither lamented nor mourned. He is not even buried in the tombs of the kings but elsewhere in the City of David.

CHAPTER TWENTY-TWO

V 1–6: SINFUL SUCCESSOR When King Ahaziah succeeds Jehoram as the king of Judah at the age of twenty-two, he reigns for one year and follows the wickedness of Ahab, encouraged by his mother. He allies with Joram, the wicked king of Israel, who is wounded in battle. Ahaziah goes to see King Joram of Israel in Jezreel where he is recovering from his wounds. **V 7–9: KING KILLED** While there, God arranges his execution by Jehu in his purge of the house of Ahab and those who are in wicked rebellion against God. **V 10–12: PROTECTED PRINCE** Ahaziah's wicked mother, Athaliah, proceeds to destroy all the royal family of Judah. But Prince Joash is hidden in the palace by the daughter of King Jehoram, and survives for six years during Athaliah's wicked rule. Jehoshabeath, the king's daughter, is also the wife of the priest Jehoiada and Ahaziah's sister. God is sovereign in His strategic placement of sympathetic people.

CHAPTER TWENTY-THREE

V 1–7: PRO-ACTIVE PRIEST Jehoiada, the priest, musters the military and religious heads of Judah to make a covenant with Joash, as king. He initiates intense security and detailed protection of Joash as the impending coronation draws nearer. **V 8–10: GODLY GUARD** The Levites take the lead, along with the men of Judah, to guard Joash, and are stationed strategically to ensure his safety. **V 11: CROWNING CLIMAX** Jehoiada has Joash crowned and gives him the Testimony, a copy of God's law, while the shout 'Long live the king!' goes up. **V 12–15: 'TREASON! TREASON!'** Queen Athaliah tears her clothes and shouts 'Treason! Treason!' as she hears the rejoicing, the trumpets and the music. She is taken and executed. **V 16–21: RIGHTEOUS REFORMER** The brave priest, Jehoiada, completes the reformation. He commences with a covenant that he, the people, and the king will honour God. The temple of Baal is torn down and its altars and idols are smashed. The priest of Baal is executed in front of them. Jehoiada then restores the Levites to their proper place in the temple, and ensures that the military commanders and administrative leaders support the king. Quietness reigns in the land because Athaliah has been killed.

CHAPTER TWENTY-FOUR

V 1–16: JEHOIADA'S JOASH Joash starts his forty-one year reign at the age of seven. During the life of Jehoiada, the faithful priest, Joash does right in the eyes of God. He even reminds Jehoiada to collect the necessary finance from the people to repair the temple. The people give abundantly. With Jehoida, he organises and facilitates the repairs.

Jehoiada dies at 130 years of age and is buried in the City of David to commemorate the good he has done. **V 17–22: PAGANS' PUPPET** But after Jehoiada dies, Joash feels the flattery of the officials and, won over by their mock homage, institutes idol worship once more, including Asherah poles. God's prophets who remonstrate against this wickedness are ignored. Joash refuses to listen to the stern rebuke of God's prophet, Zechariah, and has him stoned to death. Zechariah is the son of Jehoiada, who previously did so much for Joash and meant so much to him. When Zechariah dies, he says to Joash, 'The LORD look on it and repay.' **V 23–27: DEVIOUS DEATH** After a Syrian invasion decimates Judah, despite the fact that the Syrian army is far smaller than Joash's army, Joash lies wounded. He is then murdered by his own officials, who take revenge for the death of Zechariah. His son, Amaziah, succeeds him as king.

CHAPTER TWENTY-FIVE

V 1–4: HALF-HEARTED Amaziah reigns for twenty-nine years from the age of twenty-five. What he actually does is right in the eyes of the LORD, but his heart is not loyal to Him. He executes his father's murderers but he does not act vindictively against their children. **V 5–13: RAIDERS' REACTION** He gathers an army from Judah and augments it with hired Ephraimite troops from Israel. A man of God tells him not to do that. He complies and discharges the troops. The hired troops are furious and react by raiding Judean towns on the way. Amaziah wins the battle against 10,000 men of Seir (an alternative name for Edom). **V 14–16: ILLOGICAL IDOLATRY** With staggeringly poor logic, quite apart from the sin involved, Amaziah then adopts the gods

of his defeated foes, although those gods were useless to help them! God is angry with him for this and sends his prophet to tell the king to cease from his idolatry. The prophet is told to stop prophesying, under threat of death. He does so, but with a final warning to the king that he will be destroyed because he fails to listen to God's prophet. **V 17–24: DEVASTATING DEFEAT** Amaziah's pride against God is matched by his arrogance against Israel. He challenges the king of Israel to a battle. Despite being warned by Joash, king of Israel, not to fight, he insists on the battle and is routed. This is God's doing because of His anger at the king's idolatry. The defeat is devastating, and all the valuables in the temple are taken away. **V 25–28: SO SAD** Amaziah survives Joash, king of Israel, by fifteen years. Like his father, Joash, it is so sad that a man who begins well in many respects, ends in such spiritual rebellion and defeat. Here is a further warning for every person who loves and follows God.

CHAPTER TWENTY-SIX

V 1–15: HONOURING AND HONOURED Uzziah reigns as king of Judah for fifty-two years in Jerusalem, from the age of sixteen. In the first half of his reign, just like his father, Amaziah, he seeks God. He is helped in his battles against the Philistines and the Arabs. He builds towers in Jerusalem and in the desert. He gets people working in the fields, vineyards, and fertile lands. He irrigates the land and has much livestock. He has an army of nearly one third of a million men and designs machines to help in the siege of cities. He becomes famous and strong. **V 16–23: POWERFUL AND POWERLESS** After becoming strong, pride leads to his fall. His unfaithfulness to God means that he has usurped the priests' role, offering incense on the altar. Even as he is reprimanded by Azariah, the priest, with eighty courageous priests as his companions, he becomes furious. God smites him with leprosy and he quickly leaves the temple. He lives in isolation as a leper. In his absence through his disease, Jotham, his son, takes charge of the palace and governs the land and succeeds him after his death. Isaiah prophesies in Uzziah's reign.

CHAPTER TWENTY-SEVEN

V 1–2: RETURN Jotham, at twenty-five years of age, takes over as king of Jerusalem from Uzziah. He reigns for sixteen years and returns to righteousness. Although he does not usurp the priests' function in the temple, the people are corrupt. **V 3–4: REBUILDING** He undertakes the rebuilding of parts of the temple and of the wall. Towns, forts, and towers are built under his control. **V 5–9: RIGHTEOUS** He is successful in his war against the Ammonites and takes tribute from them during the following years. He grows more powerful as he walks in integrity before God. When he dies, Ahaz, his son, succeeds him as king of Judah.

CHAPTER TWENTY-EIGHT

V 1–4: ABOMINABLE AHAZ King Ahaz begins to reign in Judah when he is twenty years old and reigns for sixteen years. He is abominable, serving Baal, burning incense, burning children as sacrifices, and following the abominable things of the surrounding nations. Idolatry and high places abound throughout. **V 5–8: DREADFUL DEFEATS** Because of this, God gives him crushing defeats at the hands of both Syria and Israel. Many captives are taken by Syria. Israel takes 200,000 people

of Judah to be captives and slaves. **V 9–15: SLAVERY STOPPED** But Oded, one of God's prophets, speaks out against slavery, as well as against Israel's rage against Judah. God has decreed that His people (Israel and Judah) must not make one another slaves. Some of the heads of Israel also refuse to take the captives of Judah. Accordingly, the captives are given new clothes, provisions, and are dealt with compassionately and returned to their own country. **V 16–21: AHAZ ABANDONED** Because of Ahaz's wickedness, he is invaded by the Edomites and by the Philistines. Not only does the king of Assyria, Tiglath-Pilesar, refuse to help him, but he also distresses Ahaz and takes temple treasures from him. **V 22–27: AFFLICTED APOSTATE** Yet the more that Ahaz is afflicted, the more apostate he becomes. He sacrifices to his conqueror's gods and increasingly provokes God to anger. When he dies, he is not buried in the tombs of the kings of Israel. His son Hezekiah takes over as king after him.

CHAPTER TWENTY-NINE

V 1–2: RIGHTEOUS Hezekiah reigns as king of Judah from the age of twenty-five for twenty-nine years. He is righteous in the eyes of God, just as David was. **V 3: REPAIRS** In the very first month of his reign, he effects repairs to the temple doors and opens them again. **V 4–19: REFORMATION** He causes the priests and the Levites to remove all defilements from the sanctuary and re-consecrate the temple. He reminds them of God's anger against such abuses. Such reformations are dealt with zealously by the priests and Levites. **V 20–35: RESTORATION** Following this restoration of the temple, worship takes place. The Levites' diligence in sanctifying themselves is greater than that of the priests. Offerings and sacrifices are made and worship is restored. **V 36: REJOICING** After the re-establishment of the temple and worship, little wonder that all the people rejoice with Hezekiah at what God has done for them and at the speed with which things are put right.

CHAPTER THIRTY

V 1–5: PROCLAMATION Hezekiah decides to re-institute the Passover and writes to Ephraim and Manasseh to call them to celebrate with him. They can do this now that they have enough priests. All Israel is asked to come and celebrate the Passover. **V 6–14: PEOPLE** The people are approached through couriers throughout the land. The couriers take a letter from the king which urges repentance and consecration and reminds them that God will bless those who turn to Him. Some people scorn and ridicule, especially in Ephraim, Manasseh and Zebulun. Others take the call to repentance seriously, especially in Judah where there is a oneness of mind to comply with what God says through Hezekiah. **V 15–20: PASSOVER** The Passover lamb is slaughtered. Some of the strict regulations are not observed: some priests are not sanctified and some people from Ephraim, Manasseh and Zebulun have not been cleansed. Hezekiah pleads with God to look at the hearts of the people and accept them. God grants his request. **V 21–27: PRAISE** The celebration of worship continues, and Hezekiah encourages the Levites, who are teaching people to know God. After seven days, a further seven days is taken for this joyful occasion and sacrifices and offerings are made. The entire assembly of Judah rejoices along with the priests, Levites, those who have come from Israel, and those non-Israelites who are staying in the land. The people are blessed by the priests and the Levites, God being their witness.

CHAPTER THIRTY-ONE

V 1: DESTRUCTION The result of the blessing of coming back to God is that all things associated with idolatry are smashed in Judah and Benjamin, and also in Ephraim and Manasseh. The people then return to their own towns and to their own property. **V 2–19: DONATIONS** Hezekiah ensures that the priests and the Levites are supported in order to do their duties before God in the temple. The people are ordered to donate to support them, and a generous response follows, so much so that the excess has to be put into the temple store rooms. The donations are faithfully distributed to the priests and the Levites and those dependent upon them. **V 20–21: DOER** Hezekiah is not only right in his heart before God, but he also does what is good and right. He is wholehearted in his work for God, reflecting his relationship with God.

CHAPTER THIRTY-TWO

V 1–8: DETERMINATION Strengthened by the knowledge that God is there to help him fight his battles, Hezekiah strengthens the people against an attempt by Sennacherib, king of Assyria, to take the fortified cities. Hezekiah not only trusts God but also consults with his leaders as a team. His people work to stop the water supply available to Sennacherib from brooks and streams, to build up a wall, raise the towers, and set military captains over people and encourage them to be strong and courageous. The people's trust in God and the mutual trust between God's servants result in rugged determination in their work and battles for the LORD. Hezekiah reminds his people that the LORD God is with them, to help them fight their battles. **V 9–19: DISCOURAGEMENT** Sennacherib does all he can to discourage, threaten and frighten Hezekiah and the people. He says they will die by famine and thirst. He communicates with the people by words, letters and in their Hebrew language, to tell them how his army has conquered before and no one had been able to resist. He speaks against God and against Hezekiah, His servant. How can their God deliver them from his hand? **V 20–23: DEFEAT** But Sennacherib is defeated. This is because Hezekiah and the prophet Isaiah pray to God. God sends an angel to cut down all the Assyrian men of valour. Sennacherib returns in shame and is murdered in his own pagan temple. God's protection, victory and guidance are marked by His people's bringing their gifts to the LORD in Jerusalem. Presents are also given to Hezekiah so that he is exalted in the sight of the nations. That is dangerous! **V 24–26: DEVIATION** Pride sets in, as so easily can happen when God works through a man. Hezekiah prays when he is ill, requesting a sign, but his heart is proud. Then he humbles himself, along with the inhabitants of Jerusalem, and God's wrath does not come upon them during his life. We need to be more aware of impending downfall at times of victory than we are at times of defeat. **V 27–31: DOWNFALL** Hezekiah's downfall is tied up with his possessions and his achievements. God has blessed and helped him. But God withdraws from him to see how he will respond to the Babylonian ambassadors who come to enquire about the wonderful things done in the land. Prosperity can be harder to manage than adversity, because we so obviously need God's grace when times are hard. **V 32–33: DEATH** Hezekiah's death and burial in the kings' tombs in the

City of David are recorded. His son, Manasseh, now reigns in his place.

CHAPTER THIRTY-THREE

V 1–9: RETURN OF IDOLATRY The twelve-year-old Manasseh reigns for fifty-five years in Jerusalem and takes Judah back into idolatry. His sinful rebellion against God includes rebuilding the high places, building altars for Baal, making images, worshipping the stars, building his own altars in God's house, child sacrifice, soothsaying, witchcraft and sorcery, spiritism, and placing a carved image in the temple itself. His many and wicked ways provoke God to anger. Under his seduction, Judah and Jerusalem become more evil than the surrounding nations. **V 10–13: REPENTANCE OF IDOLATER** Yet God restores Manasseh to Himself through repentance. This painful path for him involves going into captivity in Babylon and being afflicted there, where he humbles himself and prays for forgiveness. God, who is always willing to forgive truly repentant people who turn to Him or who turn back to Him, forgives him, and brings him back to Jerusalem. **V 14–17: RESTORATION OF INTEGRITY** Manasseh's renewal of faith in God leads to a restoration in his integrity. Not only does he make necessary defence and military changes, but he also removes the gods, idols and altars he instigated. He repairs the altar of the LORD, sacrifices peace offerings and thank offerings, and commands Judah to serve 'the LORD God of Israel'. The high places are still used for sacrifice, however, but only to the LORD their God. **V 18–20: RECORD OF INTERVENTION** The record in Scripture of how God intervenes in answer to his repentant prayer is an encouragement to every sinner to turn to God. Manasseh dies, and his son, Amon, takes his place as king. **V 21–25: REIGN OF INFIDELITY** Amon comes to the throne at twenty-two years of age and only reigns two years. Those two years are evil, repeating the worst things that he learned from his father, but without his father's humble repentance. His sin increases more and more. Bloodshed sees out his reign. He himself is murdered by his servants and they are executed by the people. Josiah, his son, is now made king.

CHAPTER THIRTY-FOUR

V 1–7: PURGE Josiah begins to reign in Jerusalem at eight years of age and immediately starts to seek God at that very early stage of his life. He walks with God as David did. The result is that in his thirty-one year reign, he purges Judah and Jerusalem of the high places, the altars, the images of Baal, and all idolatry. He burns the bones of the idolatrous priests on their own altars and cleanses Judah and Jerusalem. This godly child becomes a godly man and purges his country openly from the defilement which greatly offends God. **V 8–13: POSITIVE** But his reforms are not merely the negative ones of getting rid of evil, but positive ones of building up the house of God as a place where He can be reverently worshipped. This he does by sending a high-powered delegation, and returning the money of the house of God to support the Levites so that they can do their work. Appropriate people, workmen and craftsmen are chosen, as well as skilful musicians, to establish this worship. They are under godly supervision and leadership. **V 14–28: PENITENCE** They bring out money found in the house of the LORD and give it to the Levites who oversee the work. Hilkiah, the priest, finds Moses' Book of the Law of the LORD. He gives it to Shaphan, the scribe. When Josiah hears

the law being read, he goes into mourning, tearing his clothes. He asks Hilkiah and others to enquire of the LORD for him because he realises that God's wrath is on His people because of their sin and idolatry. Huldah, the prophetess, is consulted. Through her, God confirms that wrath and indignation will be poured out on idolatrous rebellion, but because of Josiah's genuine repentance and seeking God, manifested by his attitude in seeking God's word, he will be pardoned and blessed. So will the people with him. This word is brought back to the king. God always accepts true penitence. **V 29–33: PEOPLE** Josiah's effect upon the people is immediate and remarkable. He restores true worship and presses this responsibility on all the elders, priests, Levites and people, so all the inhabitants of Jerusalem renew their covenant with God and turn from the abomination of idolatry to serve God.

CHAPTER THIRTY-FIVE

V 1–19: PASSOVER Josiah reinstates, keeps, and insists that all the people keep the Passover in Jerusalem. This is in accordance with the law of Moses. He also reinstates the ark in the temple. There has been no Passover on this scale since the days of Samuel the prophet. This is in his eighteenth year of reign. Those who worship and work for God make much of redemption through shed blood, and Josiah is no exception. **V 20–25: PATHOS** Despite his disguise, Josiah is killed in battle when he seeks to cut off an invasion by Necho, the Egyptian king, at Carchemish. He does not recognise God's voice when Necho warns him that he will be cut off if he meddles with Egypt. His attempt to prevent Egypt's growing threat to Israel is typical of his nettle-grasping approach in dealing with problems at their source. The pathos of the country is reflected in the mourning of all Judah and Jerusalem for him. Jeremiah laments for him. So deep is the pathos and the sense of loss of this spiritual leader, that his name is written into the laments of Israel's singers in the future. **V 26–27: PROSPERITY** Josiah's acts and God-given goodness are a biblical testimony to what great effects of blessing can come from the small beginning of an eight-year-old child seeking God and growing in grace. God influences a whole nation and many other people through him.

CHAPTER THIRTY-SIX

V 1–4: JEHOAHAZ Jehoahaz, Josiah's twenty-three-year-old son, reigns in Judah from Jerusalem. After only three months, he is replaced by Eliakim, his brother, whose name is changed to Jehoiakim, at the instigation of the king of Egypt. Jehoahaz is taken captive to Egypt by Necho. **V 5–8: JEHOIAKIM** Jehoiakim is a wicked king. He comes to Jerusalem to reign at twenty-five years of age. He reigns for eleven years. He does evil in God's sight and is carried off to Babylon by Nebuchadnezzar, along with articles from the temple. Jehoiachin, his son, reigns in his place. **V 9–10: JEHOIACHIN** Jehoiachin is made king in Jerusalem. His evil reign lasts for only three months and ten days before Nebuchadnezzar takes him captive to Babylon, along with articles from the temple. Zedekiah, his uncle, reigns in his place. **V 11–14: JUDAH** Judah's backsliding continues in the reign of Zedekiah, who reigns for eleven years

from the age of twenty-one. Not only does he do evil, but he also refuses to humble himself at the rebuke of Jeremiah. He rebels against King Nebuchadnezzar and becomes stiff-necked and hard-hearted against God. As a role model, he affects leaders, priests, and people alike, who follow the pagan abominations of the nations around, and defile God's house in Jerusalem. Downfall is inevitable. **V 15–21: JERUSALEM** God's concern for Jerusalem causes him to send messengers to warn the people. They are mocked, despised and scoffed at. God's wrath is poured out until there is no remedy. He causes the Chaldeans to attack, and they kill the young men in the temple, and have no compassion on the young, the virgins, the aged, or the weak. The temple is burned, the walls of Jerusalem broken, and the palaces and all precious possessions burned. Survivors from the sword are taken captive to Babylon where they serve King Nebuchadnezzar. Jeremiah's prophecy is fulfilled and Jerusalem will lie desolate to fulfil the seventy years' Sabbath. The Israelites evidently have not kept the Sabbath year every seventh year, as they should have done over the past 490 years. God therefore performs His will and honours the prophecy of His servant. **V 22–23: JEREMIAH** Light at the end of the tunnel appears in the last two verses. Jeremiah's prophecy of rebuilding and restoring Jerusalem and its temple will come to pass, under Cyrus, king of Persia. God is still sovereign. The successor to Nebuchadnezzar will be the person who instigates the rebuilding of the temple, as we now know.

EZRA

OVERVIEW

PEOPLE AND PRELIMINARIES

✳️ Ezra (ten chapters), probably written in Jerusalem by Ezra himself between 457 BC and 444 BC, might have originally formed one book with Nehemiah. Ezra is the first of six post-captivity books focusing on the small remnant of people seeking a close relationship with God, while most of the people were prospering in captivity and wished to stay there. With Nehemiah and Esther, it forms the last three historical books, which deal with the period after the Jews' return from exile in Babylon. The three non-historical books after the captivity are the prophetical books of Haggai, Zechariah and Malachi. It is estimated that the period covered by Ezra is eighty years.

PLAN AND PURPOSE

(i) The books of Ezra and Nehemiah cover the Jews' restoration to Israel. Two of the three stages (in chapters 1 to 6 under Zerubbabel and in chapters 7 to 10 under Ezra) are recorded in the book of Ezra. The return, thirteen years later under Nehemiah, is traced in the book of that name. The three returns focus on restoring the temple, the people and the walls respectively. Just as there had been three stages of deportation of God's people, so there shall be three stages of return. (The account in Esther recounts the saving of Israel nationally between the returns under Zerubbabel and Ezra.) The first six chapters of Ezra centre on temple restoration and the last four on restoring the people.

PROFILE AND PROGRESSION

🥚 The first return under the leadership of Zerubbabel, including the decree 🐚 of Cyrus, treasures provided for rebuilding the temple and identification of the returning remnant (1:1–2:70); the building of the second temple, including the start, the times of opposition, the pause and resumption of building, the completion of the restored temple and its dedication (3:1–6:22); Ezra's influence and ministry, including the second return under him and the revival he leads through God (7:1–10:44).

PRINCIPLES AND PARTICULARS

👉 God's sovereign overruling continues, even through the actions of ungodly rulers. The need is for godly leadership for His people to continue in the face of opposition. Ezra's spiritual leadership give evidence of how a godly man can influence a nation for and through God. The priority is shown to be worship and work for God. Humanly speaking, the dependence of the work of God was on a small nucleus of dedicated people, and the danger was affluent indifference. God worked in revival.

EZRA

CHAPTER ONE

V 1: CONTEXT DEFINED In fulfilment of Jeremiah's prophecy, Cyrus, king of Persia, makes a decree about the return of God's people to Jerusalem. (See **Plan and Purpose**, above, for the wider context.)

CHAPTER TWO

V 1–67: PEOPLE DETAILED All those

returning from captivity are detailed, with special mention of the priests, the Levites, and those involved in temple service. Any who cannot prove their origins are not allowed to be included in the priesthood. **V 68–69: PRECIOUS DONATIONS** Some leaders freely offer money, silver, and priestly garments, as they are able. The preciousness of their donations is not so much in their economic value, but in the fact of their willingness to offer as much as they can. **V 70: PRIESTLY DUTIES** Therefore the priests and the Levites, along with those supporting the work, dwell in the cities ready to perform their duties.

CHAPTER THREE

V 1–2: REBUILDING The worship of God in the Old Testament requires an altar. The spiritual leader, Joshua, and the civil leader, Zerubbabel, rebuild an altar to make offerings to God as commanded in His law through Moses. **V 3–6: RENEWAL** The renewal of the system of worship and offerings begins, along with the relevant feasts, and these are observed in advance of the rebuilding of the temple. **V 7–9: RECONSTRUCTION** Reconstruction of the temple begins. The needed workmen are provided for, and imports from Lebanon are arranged in accordance with the permission given by Cyrus, king of Persia. The rulers, spiritual leaders, and people begin to work to restore the temple. The Levites take a leading role. **V 10–13: REJOICING** Great rejoicing takes place when the builders lay the foundation of the temple. Songs of praise are raised to God by the Levites. His goodness and enduring mercy are gratefully acknowledged. The people shout, but many of the more experienced priests, the Levites, the heads, and the old men weep when they see what is happening. The

sound of shouting for joy and weeping is mixed in a heartfelt expression of gratitude to God who is so evidently working among them.

CHAPTER FOUR

V 1–3: OPPOSITION—CO-OPERATION When the enemies of Judah and Benjamin hear what is happening, they seek to undermine the work by asking to co-operate in the task and make it a joint venture. Zerubbabel stands firm and refuses to compromise. God's work cannot be done in a God-honouring way in co-operation with those who neither trust His word nor seek His glory. **V 4–5: OPPOSITION—COUNSELLORS** An attempt to discourage the people of Judah is manifest in people being troubled as they build, with hired counsellors seeking to frustrate their purposes. There is always worldly counsel that will prevent the children of God from building His work, if heeded and followed. **V 6–23: OPPOSITION—COMPARISON** Dealing with the theme of the opposition to this work of God, Ezra jumps ahead with the advantage of historical hindsight to note the later opposition which Israel faced. That opposition was under King Ahasuerus (also known as Xerxes) in Esther's time, and Artaxerxes, in Nehemiah's day. Their opposition, recorded in official letters, caused a great delay in the rebuilding. Having interposed those then future events into the current narrative, to demonstrate the opposition faced, Ezra is ready to return to the current position. **V 24: OPPOSITION—CONTINUATION** Ezra reverts to the continuation of the account of the opposition to Zerubbabel through the reign of Darius, who precedes both King Ahasuerus and King Artaxerxes.

CHAPTER FIVE

V 1–2: REBUILDING Under the prophetic work of Haggai and Zechariah, the Jews in Judah and Jerusalem are inspired to carry on the rebuilding. Zerubbabel and Joshua again take the responsibility but are helped by those two godly prophets of God. Spiritual input and earnest endeavour are always good partners in God's work. **V 3–10: REPORTED!** Tattenai, a Persian official, questions the Jews' authority to build a temple and finish the wall. Details are given to him and he intends to report this matter to Darius. Meanwhile, God enables the work to carry on. It is always wise to follow the principle of carrying on God's work in any time of uncertainty! Tattenai then writes to Darius, reporting the situation and asking him to review the position and give his instructions. **V 11–16: REVIEW** The letter carries a review of events in giving the testimony of the Jews, that they serve the God of heaven and are rebuilding His temple. **V 17: REQUEST** Tattenai asks the king to authorise a search to see whether Cyrus really did issue this decree to the Jews in the first place.

CHAPTER SIX

V 1–5: RESEARCH Darius issues a decree commanding that research be made into the archives. Sure enough, the decree of King Cyrus is found, including his authorising the payment of expenses from the king's treasury and the restoration to the temple of the articles taken before. Thus the permission to rebuild the temple is seen as a historical fact. **V 6–12: REAFFIRMATION** Darius tells Tattenai and his Persian companions to stay well away from the work, and to let the Jews build! He affirms that the cost must be paid at the king's expense, and that all that they need in terms of animals and items for sacrifice must be provided without fail. Anyone seeking to alter his edict shall be hanged and his house destroyed. He then asks God to destroy anyone who opposes this work in Jerusalem. In issuing the decree, he ends with the words, 'Let it be done diligently.' What sovereign overruling by God! **V 13–15: RESULT** The result is that King Darius' decree is observed, the building and the prophesying continue, and the temple is finished. **V 16–18: RESUMPTION** The resumption of worship, offerings, and the priesthood takes place, in accordance with God's law through Moses. **V 19–22: REJOICING** The priests and the Levites, after purification, slaughter the Passover lambs. The children of Israel, and those who have been cleansed before God, determine to keep the Feast of Unleavened Bread for seven days with joy. The LORD makes them joyful and turns the Assyrian king's heart towards them so that their hearts are strengthened in the work of the house of God.

CHAPTER SEVEN

V 1–9: EZRA'S COMING The second wave of returning Jews is documented, along with Ezra and leaders of Israel. Ezra is a descendant of Aaron and a skilled scribe in the law of Moses. Like Nehemiah after him, he knows 'the good hand of his God upon him'. **V 10: EZRA'S CONCERN** Ezra's personal concern is always to prepare his heart to seek God's law, then to do it, and then to teach it to others. Every Christian leader needs to follow that example carefully, today. **V 11–26: EZRA'S COMMUNICATION** King Artaxerxes sends a communication to Ezra, by way of a letter containing his decree. This goes into more detail to authorise, facilitate and encourage the work and worship of

God, through offerings and through teaching God's law. Ezra even gets tax concessions and is asked to appoint magistrates and judges. Those who disobey him will do so on pain of death! **V 27–28: EZRA'S CONFIDENCE** Ezra's confidence, and therefore his rejoicing, is wholeheartedly in the LORD God. He recognises that it is God who has worked this desire in the king's heart and extended mercy to him before the king and his followers. He is encouraged and freely acknowledges that 'the hand of the LORD my God' is upon him. He gathers the leaders of Israel to go up with him.

CHAPTER EIGHT

V 1–14: HEADING HOME The heads of the returning Israelites are detailed, as they head home to Jerusalem, with Ezra, during the reign of King Artaxerxes. **V 15–20: LEVITES LACKING** Ezra notes that there are no Levites, calls a council of understanding men, and tells them to request servants for the temple. God's hand is upon the venture and He sends him Levite servants, designated by name, to do this work for God. **V 21–23: PROTECTING PRAYER** Ezra calls a fast to pray, to humble themselves before God, and to seek His way for the returning party, their families and possessions. He dare not ask for human protection because he wants to witness to the outsiders that God can protect His own people. Knowing that God's good hand is upon them, and that His power and wrath are against His enemies, Ezra and his party fast and entreat God. They see Him answering their prayer. **V 24–30: GODLY GIFTS** Sherebiah, Hashebiah, and ten other leading priests are given gifts for God's service in the temple. The silver and gold are wholly for the LORD, and are to be taken by them to the temple in Jerusalem.

V 31–36: REMARKABLE RETURN With God's hand on the whole of the company, to deliver them and guide them, they arrive at Jerusalem and stay there for three days. On the fourth day, the silver and gold articles are weighed out and recorded. The returning captives offer burnt offerings. The king's orders are given to the local authorities so that support for the people in the house of God follows. What a remarkable return under the hand of the God of all grace!

CHAPTER NINE

V 1–2: MIXED MARRIAGES Leaders report to Ezra the mixed marriages of the people as well as of the priests and Levites, who should be holy people. They have compromised with pagan people and have disobeyed the LORD. **V 3–4: ABJECT ASTONISHMENT** Ezra is so aghast at such an affront to God's holiness and command that he goes into mourning, tears his garments, plucks out his hair and beard, and sits astonished until the evening sacrifice. Others come to him, who fear God's word, because of this transgression. He cannot comprehend how the people, and especially the Levites, can so gravely disobey and offend God, who has blessed them so abundantly. **V 5–15: INTERCESSORY INVOLVEMENT** At the evening sacrifice, he rises from his fasting, falls on his knees, and spreads out his hands to his God. He is ashamed and humiliated and intercedes for his people acknowledging God's gracious help and hand upon them. On behalf of his people, he identifies with their sin and admits their great guilt. He affirms that God will be correct and righteous if He decides to punish them. He asks for 'a measure of revival in our bondage'. Here is no cover up, or excuse, but a heartfelt prayer and confession of a man who earnestly desires

God's glory and holiness. What an example to us all!

CHAPTER TEN

V 1–2: CONTAGIOUS CONTRITION It seems that a spiritual wave of contrition comes over the people, starting with its leader Ezra. Before long, a very large assembly of the people are weeping with him bitterly, confessing their trespass and their sin in taking pagan wives from the land. Yet, in all of this, Shechaniah says to Ezra, 'Yet now there is hope in Israel in spite of this.' In their repentance for sin, they must do not lose sight of the fact that there is a God who can always step in to bless, irrespective of what needs to be put right as a result of that repentance. **V 3–4: COVENANT COMMITMENT** Shechaniah urges all the people to make a covenant with God to put away pagan wives and children, to obey God in a fearful way, to take their responsibility courageously, and to do it. The future of God's children is at stake and again the time has come for difficult choices and even more difficult action. **V 5–15: CORPORATE CONFESSION** Fasting, mourning, convocation, and corporate

and individual confession of sin all take place. The heavy rain seems to set the scene for their weeping over their sin. With one voice, the people acknowledge their sin and the need to put away pagan wives. The leaders stand to pray, and those with pagan wives will see them at appointed times to rectify the matter, until God's wrath is turned away. Only four named people oppose this overwhelming conviction from God in the hearts of His people. There are always some who will! **V 16–19: CAREFUL CONSIDERATION** Ezra, with the heads of households, spends three months in dealing with these matters. Repentance is not a mere momentary feeling or urge, but a continued and systematic yielding to God in the lives of those who turn in sorrow from their sin. **V 18–44: COMPREHENSIVE COMPLIANCE** Starting with the families of the spiritual leaders, the pagan wives and children are divorced from Israel. No doubt God makes adequate and gracious provision for those women and their children. Whatever their hardships, far greater hardships would have followed if there had been continued disobedience to God in these matters.

NEHEMIAH

OVERVIEW

PEOPLE AND PRELIMINARIES

✳Nehemiah (thirteen chapters), probably written in Jerusalem by Ezra between 424 BC and 400 BC, might have originally formed one book with Ezra. Nehemiah is the second of six post-captivity books covering the Jews'

restoration to Israel. With Ezra and Esther, it forms the last three of the twelve historical books. See comments in Ezra. The book of Nehemiah covers an estimated period of eleven years.

PLAN AND PURPOSE

(i) The books of Nehemiah and of Ezra cover rebuilding what is broken down in Jerusalem: in Nehemiah its walls, and in Ezra its temple. Both books also cover rebuilding God's people spiritually and in practical righteousness.

The Assyrians have scattered the ten northern tribes in captivity. The Babylonians have destroyed Jerusalem and carried away nearly all the people of Judah and Benjamin. During seventy years' Babylonian captivity, Cyrus of Persia takes over world domination from the Babylonians. Ezra returns with Zerubbabel and Jeshua to rebuild the temple. Ezra leads a second return (Ezra chapters 7 to 10). Nehemiah records the third return of the Jews around 445 BC to rebuild Jerusalem's walls. Ezra is present with Nehemiah to provide a strong united team giving spiritual and practical leadership to the people of Israel and their religious chiefs.

PROFILE AND PROGRESSION

Nehemiah's reconnaissance survey, representation to the king, organisation of the Israelites, rebuilding of the walls in the face of opposition outside and some discouragement within Israel, and discovery of the register made under Zerubbabel's earlier return (1:1–7:73); Ezra's influence and ministry in explaining God's law, leading Israel to turn to God in repentance and worship Him, and encouraging the renewal of the covenant (8:1–10:39); the resettlement of Jerusalem by a remnant, and the dedication of the walls by a praising people (11:1–12:47); Nehemiah's return and actions as governor (13:1–31).

PRINCIPLES AND PARTICULARS

We see how God equips and enables his leader to deal with crisis after crisis. Nehemiah leads by personal example, motivates others in a team, relies on God in prayer, confronts when he has to, and perseveres with the task, despite opposition and the threat of death. Great emphasis is placed on God's name, presence, work, Sabbath, word, worship, and thankfulness to Him. God's hand on Nehemiah, Ezra and their varied team achieves the outworking of His sovereign plan. Personal and communal thanksgiving to God permeate the book. Nehemiah's concern, willingness to risk his life for his people, blending of prayer with action, organisation of team participation, carefulness in assessing before acting, and decisiveness to 'grasp nettles' are all evidenced before the painstaking and mammoth job of rebuilding Jerusalem's walls is undertaken and achieved. These same qualities prevail as he leads the Jews in that task and deals with some very tricky situations and problems.

NEHEMIAH

CHAPTER ONE

V 1–4: INFORMATION AND INTERCESSION Nehemiah receives news from Hanani about the downtrodden state of the walls of Jerusalem and the distress of the Jews there, who have returned from captivity. This immediately causes him to weep, mourn, fast and pray. After two waves of captives have returned under Ezra, Jerusalem still has a long way to go! **V 5–11: PENITENCE AND PROMISE** Nehemiah pleads with God, acknowledging the sinfulness of his people. He reminds God of His promise of blessing, even though the people may be scattered, if they repent and come back to Him. He asks God to listen to his prayer and to answer it in a merciful way so that the king, for whom Nehemiah is an influential cupbearer, will be favourable towards him, and thus towards God's people.

CHAPTER TWO

V 1–3: SORROWFUL AND SCARED As the king's cupbearer, Nehemiah must take the wine to the king. This role thus developed into a position of counselling the king, and sharing confidences with him. Nehemiah looks miserable, which could have ended his career and life, and the king asks him why. Knowing that the king could summarily execute him for being miserable in the his presence, Nehemiah is 'dreadfully afraid'. He tells the king that his sadness is because of the state of Jerusalem, the place of his fathers. **V 4–8: SUPPLICATION AND SPECIFICS** The king asks him to share his request. Before answering the king, he quickly prays 'to the God of heaven' and gives the king the specifics of the request, in order that he may oversee the rebuilding of the walls of Jerusalem. So he asks for the king to authorise materials to be made available to him. The king grants his request, but only because the King of kings has already granted it! A common theme through Nehemiah (and through Ezra) is 'the good hand of my God upon me', which every Christian can know today. **V 9–10: DETERMINED AND DISTURBED** Nehemiah is determined, and with the letters from the king to authorise his visit and task, he goes to the governors beyond the river, protected by the king's military escort. The enemies of Israel, Sanballat the Horonite, and Tobiah an Ammonite official, are 'deeply disturbed' because Nehemiah comes to 'seek the well-being of the children of Israel'. **V 11–18: INSPECTION AND INSPIRATION** Nehemiah makes a clandestine and personal three-day inspection of Jerusalem, unknown to anyone except

God. Knowing God's good hand upon him, and encouraged by the words of the king spoken to him, Nehemiah urges the priests, nobles, officials, and others, to join him in rebuilding the wall, in order that the reproach will no longer be upon God's people and God's city. They are inspired by this and readily say, 'Let us rise up and build.' They start to work. **V 19–20: RIDICULE AND REPLY** Geshem, the Arab, joins Sanballat and Tobiah to make an opposing trinity of evil. They ridicule the efforts of Nehemiah and his people. The forthright governor of Jerusalem replies that God will prosper them and so they will get on with the job, but adds that his opponents have 'no heritage, or right or memorial in Jerusalem'. Here is a leader who is humble before God and bold before men on God's behalf—a good example to follow.

CHAPTER THREE

V 1–32: TEAM TIME A completely unique and amazing scene greets us in this chapter. Jews of all types, status, backgrounds, ages, abilities, gifts and experience are involved together in rebuilding the wall and gates of Jerusalem. When God is at work, under godly leadership, God's people work together as a team, with the sole aim to glorify Him. Some do far more than their call of duty, though, sadly, there are a few who fail to pull their weight. There always are. But the overwhelming response is encouraging as they work around the walls to repair them and the gates. The gates mentioned plot the course of the wall, and are the Sheep Gate, the Fish Gate, the Old Gate, the Valley Gate, the Refuse Gate, the Fountain Gate, the Water Gate, the Horse Gate, and the Mishkad (or Muster) Gate. The work is going well.

CHAPTER FOUR

V 1–3: MALICIOUS MOCKING Sanballat and Tobiah are furious that the work is carrying on well and they mock the Jews. Sanballat maligns them before his own brethren and the Samaritan army, and Tobiah comments that even a fox on the wall will knock it down. God's people have always been mocked by the unbelieving world and always will be. **V 4–6: PRAYERFUL PERSISTENCE** Nehemiah prays that God will deal with His enemies and they continue to build the wall, until the whole wall is built up to half its full height. The people have 'a mind to work'. **V 7–12: FEARFUL FRAILTY** The opposition increases, as Sanballat and Tobiah are joined by Arabs, Ammonites and Ashdodites who conspire to come and attack Nehemiah's men and cause confusion. Prayer is made and a watch is set day and night by Nehemiah. Judah, however, complains that the labourers' strength is failing and there is so much rubbish that they cannot build the wall. They discourage the Jews nearby. The counter-attack of enemies outside, and the fear and frailty of God's people within, give Nehemiah a challenging position to handle. **V 13–14: POSITIVE PROVISION** Nehemiah does two things: he reminds all the nobles, leaders and people that God is on their side and they should not be afraid; but he also positions armed guards at the gaps to protect the wall and its workers. Most biblical solutions involve a trust in God and a willingness to act wisely and boldly. **V 15–18: BATTLING BUILDERS** Nehemiah's response, under God, brings his enemies' plots to nothing. From then on, the team is both battling and building. Half do the building while the other half keeps an armed vigilance against possible attack. Every builder has a weapon with him and every soldier is prepared to build. They are encouraged by the presence with them of their leader, Nehemiah, and having a trumpet to sound an alarm if that is necessary. **V 19–20: ENCOURAGING EXHORTATION** Nehemiah encourages and exhorts them. God will fight for them and, if they are separated by an attack, the trumpet will sound and support will come from other members of God's team. If they hear the trumpet, they are to go and fight for their brethren under attack. **V 21–23: CONTINUAL COMMITMENT** From daybreak until the stars appear, the work is resolutely carried on without break except at night time when the wall is guarded. Personal hygiene is maintained. Their clothes only come off for washing!

CHAPTER FIVE

V 1–6: ABUSE Some nobles have abused their fellow Jews by charging them usury on the mortgage of their lands and vineyards. The poorer people need to mortgage these to buy food. Also, the poor people borrow money to pay the king's tax and are forced by these selfish nobles to sell their children into slavery in order to have the money to pay those taxes. They have insufficient money to redeem either their property or their children. Nehemiah, quite rightly, is angry when he hears of their terrible plight and the abuse of the poor by their rich countrymen. **V 7–11: ASSEMBLY** Nehemiah grasps the nettle and calls everyone to assemble together. He confronts and accuses the nobles and exposes the wicked system. He reminds them that they need to walk in the fear of God and be an example to the nations around. He also tells them that he and others are lending money and food to the afflicted Jews. He insists that they stop the usury and restore the mortgaged property to the exploited poor. They must also repay the money and goods paid by the exploited people as interest. **V 12–13: ACTION** The nobles confirm that they will restore it and require nothing from the people. They will do what Nehemiah says. Nehemiah cements this by demanding that the priests take an oath from them, and tells them that God will shake them out from their property if they do not keep their promise. The assembly say 'Amen' and they praise the Lord. The promise is made, the agreement is struck and the problem is solved. **V 14–18: ABUNDANCE** Nehemiah the governor has a right to huge provisions, mainly for giving hospitality but also to benefit his family and himself. However, he has not benefited from this personally for twelve years, unlike the former governors. He works on the wall and feeds many people, without demanding his governor's provisions, because his people are in heavy bondage. His abundance is not abused, but used to bless others. **V 19: ACKNOWLEDGEMENT** Nehemiah asks God to acknowledge his efforts for the people. This is not self-righteousness but the committing of everything he has and does to God.

CHAPTER SIX

V 1–4: CONTINUAL PRESSURE The unholy trio of Sanballat, Tobiah and Geshem, with the rest of Nehemiah's enemies, hear that there are now no breaks in the wall. The gates are not yet hung. They put pressure on Nehemiah by asking him to meet to discuss matters. He knows they mean harm and sends a reply saying he cannot come down from the great work he is doing. Four times they send him this message and four times he answers in the same way. The continual pressure is met by continual persistence in his work and in his confidence in God. **V 5–9: CONSPIRACY PLANNED** Sanballat then threatens to tell the king that Nehemiah is seeking to depose him as king, and has made arrangements to do so. Nehemiah simply replies saying that this is not true, and that he, Sanballat, is lying. Nehemiah knows that the opposition is trying to weaken the work, and so he prays that God will strengthen his hands. **V 10–14: COWARDLY PROPHECIES** There are those within Jerusalem who are working for the enemy. A secret informer and false prophet, Shemaiah, asks Nehemiah to meet him in the temple, behind closed doors because, he claims, the enemies of Nehemiah will come at night to kill him. God gives Nehemiah the perception that this false prophecy, intended to intimidate him, comes from Sanballat and Tobiah, Shemaiah's hirers. He refuses to go and commits his enemies and other false prophets into God's hands. This mixture of prayer and practice is an inspirational example to us all from this godly, devoted and lion-hearted leader. **V 15–16: COMPLETED PROJECT** The wall is finished in fifty-two days. The enemy is very disheartened. Even they perceive that this is work done by God for and through His people. True to human nature, this fact does not make them turn to God, but intensifies their useless opposition against Him. **V 17–19: COMMUNICATION PROBLEMS** Nehemiah notes that the compromised nobles, not willing to work, and going through marriage alliances with the opposition, were and are in communication with Tobiah. They seek to give Tobiah a 'good press' to Nehemiah, obviously thinking him to be more gullible than he is, and they report his words to Tobiah. Tobiah keeps sending letters to frighten Nehemiah. There is no chance of this happening!

CHAPTER SEVEN

V 1–2: RESPONSIBLE The wall is built and the doors are hung. The gatekeepers, singers and Levites are appointed. Nehemiah now delegates his responsibility for Jerusalem to two responsible people. They are his brother, Hanani, and the faithful leader of the citadel who 'feared God more than many', Hananiah. **V 3: REGULATED** There is still a security alert in Jerusalem. The times for opening the gates are regulated and armed guards are posted. **V 4–69: REGISTER** As Nehemiah plans to register all returning to this 'large and spacious' city with few houses in it, he finds a register of the genealogy of those who came before into Jerusalem. Minor discrepancies between this and Ezra's register may be either because those leaving with Ezra are not necessarily the same as those arriving at Jerusalem, or because the register that Nehemiah finds is inaccurate in some ways: some official documents are inaccurate. They are not infallibly inspired as the Bible is! This is a biblically correct record of the register found, even if it is not completely accurate itself. **V 70–72: RICHES** The riches given to the work are recorded. **V 73: RESIDENTS** The religious leaders and the people are recorded as resident in their cities.

CHAPTER EIGHT

V 1–6: GOD'S LAW—HEEDED All the people gather in the open square in front of the Water Gate. Ezra reads from God's law from morning until midday to all who can understand. His Word is heeded attentively, a sure sign of God's working. Blessing, worship, and commitment to God follow. **V 7–12: GOD'S LAW—HELPED** The people are helped by the priests and the Levites who read clearly from God's law, give its sense, and enable their hearers to comprehend the reading. Because the people weep through conviction on hearing the law, Nehemiah, Ezra and the religious people who are teaching temper that conviction with the joy that follows repentance and faith. They tell their hearers that they have wept enough. Now they must go and rejoice because the day is holy to God. They are told to go away and feast, remembering those who have nothing, and find that 'the joy of the LORD' is their strength. The Levites support this application of God's law by telling the people not to grieve. The people go away and rejoice greatly because they understand the words that the Levites declare to them. **V 13–18: GOD'S LAW—HISTORY** Observing the Feast of Tabernacles (or Booths) is now reinstated, as God's law becomes central again in the minds of His people. The children of Israel remember this feast with great gladness, by making booths to sit in. This reminds them of the history of God's faithfulness to the Israelites during their wanderings in the wilderness. They keep listening to God's Word and are blessed. Those who listen attentively to God's Word, with a heart for God, are always blessed.

CHAPTER NINE

V 1–3: CONFESSION The Israelites together mourn and fast, and separate themselves from foreigners in order to confess their sins and the sins of their forefathers, too. They spend quarter of the day in reading God's law, and quarter of it confessing and worshipping God. Confession of sin leads to true worship of God, and is blended with it. **V 4–5a: CRY** Godly leaders, including the Levites, cry with a loud voice to the LORD and lead the people in worshipping, confessing and praying to God. **V 5b–35: COMPASSIONATE** They start by praising God for who He is and then turning Israel's history into a prayer of confession and worship. God's compassionate grace is remembered in His dealing with the intermittent faith and the continual return to backsliding of His people. In all of this, they acknowledge their sins and the goodness and faithfulness of God. **V 36–38: COVENANT** Finally, they declare themselves to be His servants in His land and acknowledge that their distress is caused by their own sins. Because of all this, they commit themselves to a covenant which is sealed by their leaders, Levites and priests.

CHAPTER TEN

V 1–27: SEALED The names of those who seal the covenant headed by Nehemiah the governor are given. **V 28–30: SEPARATED** The people then join in with their religious and civil leaders to bind themselves by a curse and an oath to walk in God's law and to separate themselves from the pagan people to God. This will include committing themselves only to marry within God's children. **V 31: SABBATH** They covenant to keep the weekly Sabbath day and not to buy or sell on it, or any holy day specific to the Israelites. They will keep the seventh year Sabbath in order to forego the collection of outstanding debts. They are now seeking to address, at source, the earlier problem of abuse of the poor by the nobles. **V 32–38: SYSTEMATIC** They ensure that provision for the offerings, sacrifices and feasts of the LORD, and collection of tithes, will be systematically gathered in an orderly way. Good order and organisation is not negated when God works through His Spirit. Often it is

caused by such divine action. **V 39: SANCTUARY** The people covenant not to neglect the sanctuary of God. Offerings of grain, wine and oil are to be made to the storerooms in the temple, where the articles for use in the sanctuary are kept, and where the priests and temple servants are located.

CHAPTER ELEVEN

V 1–2: THE PLAN A plan is made to bring one tenth of the Jews from other cities into Jerusalem, where the leaders are. **V 3–24: THE PROPORTION** The small proportion of the people living in Jerusalem, namely the tenth who live with the leaders, is detailed. **V 25–36: THE POPULATION** The main population of the Jews is made up by the people living in the other cities, namely the other nine tenths. Details are given of those cities, inhabited by Judah and Benjamin.

CHAPTER TWELVE

V 1–26: PRIESTS AND LEVITES The priests and Levites coming to Jerusalem from the time of Zerubbabel and Jeshua are listed. **V 27–43: PRAISE AND LOUDNESS** It is time to dedicate the walls of Jerusalem! The Levites are to lead the dedication with gladness and enthusiasm, accompanied by music. Singers are gathered, and the priests and Levites purify themselves, the people, the gates, and the wall. Nehemiah himself brings the leaders of Jerusalem to the wall and appoints two large thanksgiving choirs. One goes to the right towards the Refuse Gate and the other goes to the left going past the Tower of the Ovens. The two thanksgiving choirs stand in the house of God after their procession, and the singers sing loudly under the director, Jezrahiah. How noisy, but joyfully ordered, is that day of rejoicing, accompanied by great sacrifices and the sense that God has done this for them. Everyone rejoices, including the women and children, and 'the joy of Jerusalem was heard afar off'. There is a time to be solemn and to confess sin, and there is a time to be enthusiastically loud in praising God! But all things are done 'decently and in order'! **V 44–47: PORTIONS AND LAW** Meticulous management of the store house and of the gathering of the first fruits, offerings and tithes is instigated in order to fulfil God's law. The priests and the Levites must be catered for, including the singers and the gatekeepers. All things are consecrated for the Levites, and the Levites consecrate them for the priests. When God's Spirit leads worship and revival, detailed and disciplined care is taken in giving and supporting God's workers and God's work. This is not haphazard or unplanned.

CHAPTER THIRTEEN

V 1–3: SCRIPTURAL SEPARATION Reading in the book of Moses, in the hearing of the people, the children of Israel realise that Ammonites and Moabites should not be in the assembly of God. Seeing the principle in Scripture, they apply this separation in practice to themselves and separate out the mixed multitude from Israel. They base their conduct on the principles of God's word. **V 4–9: RIGOROUS REFORMS** Earlier, Nehemiah promised to Artaxerxes that he would return to him. Now he keeps that promise. In his absence, some of Tobiah's allies, including Eliashib the priest, prepare a large room for Tobiah in the temple, where provisions for the offerings were stored previously. Gaining leave from the king to return, Nehemiah is grieved when he sees this rebellion. He throws all the household goods of Tobiah out of that room and commands that the room be cleansed. He commands that the articles of the temple and the provisions for the offerings be returned. He rebukes the rulers, because the Levites have not been receiving their designated portions. He makes the point strongly to them altogether in one place. All Judah brings back grain and wine to the storehouse, and Nehemiah appoints responsible representatives of the priests, Levites and scribes, who are faithful. They are to distribute these provisions to their brethren. Nehemiah is no coward and deals with problems as they arise, however unpopular this might make him. He appreciates the need for reform as well as revival. **V 14: CONTINUING CONCERN** Nehemiah prays to God, asking that the good things accomplished by God through him will be remembered and will continue. The effectiveness of God's work is only as good as it is at the present moment. It needs constant prayer, attention and application. **V 15–22: SABBATH STRENGTHENED** Nehemiah is appalled to see the Sabbath day broken in treading the wine presses and bringing in food. Men from Tyre are selling fish and all kinds of goods in Jerusalem, and to the Jews outside Jerusalem. Nehemiah deals with this evil profanity and points out that God has brought disaster on Israel in the past, because of their profaning of the Sabbath, God's special day. He commands the gates to be shut on the night before the Sabbath and he posts watchmen so that no burdens can be brought in on the day. Once or twice, the merchants and sellers wait outside Jerusalem, so Nehemiah reprimands them and tells them that if it happens again, he will lay hands on them. 'From that time on they came no more on the Sabbath.' The Levites are commanded to cleanse themselves and to guard the gates in order to sanctify the Sabbath. Nehemiah also asks God to remember him concerning this, and to spare him according to His mercy. **V 23–27: RIGHT RELATIONSHIPS** Nehemiah takes very strong action when mixed marriages with pagan people come to light again. His action is very strong because he knows that such mixed marriages are against God's command and will let in idolatry. He appeals to Scripture to urge them to turn from this sin against God. God's people should only marry God's people, a spiritual principle applying to people today. So many of the problems have come from the undercover activities of those who have affiliations with the enemies of Jerusalem. One of the sons of Joiada, the son of Eliashib, the high priest, is son-in-law of Sanballat! Nehemiah drives him away. **V 29–31: CONSECRATED CLEAN** Nehemiah looks for a consecrated priesthood and political order and so cleanses everything pagan. He assigns duties to the priests and Levites in connection with the offerings and first fruits. His final prayer again casts himself upon God: 'Remember me, O my God, for good!' We, too, should remember what good can come to a man who is wholeheartedly committed to God, His cause, His work, His special day and His people, even at personal cost and the risk of unpopularity. Nehemiah is an exemplary leader, by the grace of God.

ESTHER

OVERVIEW

PEOPLE AND PRELIMINARIES

Esther (ten chapters) is the twelfth and final book in the historical section of the Old Testament and the last of the three historical of the six post-exilic books. See comments in Ezra and Nehemiah. It is unclear who wrote it, but possibilities include Ezra, Nehemiah or Mordecai. It was probably written between 450 BC and 331 BC in the ungodly Persian court, during Israel's captivity. That may be why God is not mentioned by name. However, His presence and influence prevail throughout. It is estimated that this book covers events over a period of twelve years.

PLAN AND PURPOSE

(i) Sandwiched chronologically between the two returns under Zerubbabel and Ezra which are reported in the book of Ezra, this moving and factual story shows how the people of Israel are spared against overwhelming odds. For this to happen, it needs the intervention of a sovereign God, whose control of timing is a miraculous feature of this gripping little book. It also takes the personal sacrifice and commitment of an uncompromising Jew, Mordecai, and a brave young Jewess, Queen Esther. She was there for 'just a time as this'. See how, despite the fact that God is not mentioned by name in this book, He overrules time and again and teaches us that His presence can be detected not only by words spoken about Him, but through lives lived selflessly for Him, and through His answering heartfelt prayer.

PROFILE AND PROGRESSION

The background account of Queen Vashti's refusal to submit to an unreasonable king (1:1–22); Esther crowned as queen (2:1–18); the parts played by Mordecai and Haman, including Mordecai's loyal actions and Haman's hateful opposition to the Jews and his personal progression to authority, the sacrificial intervention of Esther, the downfall of Haman and deliverance for the Jews (2:19–7:10); the Jews' revenge and victory (8:1–9:19); the Feast of Purim (9:20–32); the honouring of faithful Mordecai (10:1–3).

PRINCIPLES AND PARTICULARS

King Ahasuerus's mistreatment of Queen Vashti, and Haman's consuming hatred for Mordecai show what trouble and suffering can be caused by knee-jerk reactions of proud people in authority and by fostering prejudice and hatred. Haman, the Agagite, so hates the Jewish people and especially Mordecai, the Benjamite, because of a history which started with the Jews being attacked by the Amalekites, and which included Samuel's killing of King Agag, an Amelikite. God's people must stand firm on principle, and honour God. Worldly opposition is the natural response to spirituality, and the need is for self-sacrifice and God-given bravery. God sovereignly overrules, even in the vilest plans of the most evil men. We see how relatively small things done for God and for good can lead to later unexpected blessing. Historically, God's preservation of the Jews is realised against seemingly overwhelming odds, and with it the preservation of the line from which the Lord Jesus Christ will come, as Messiah. He will finally bless both His physical people (Israel) and His spiritual people (Christians, be they Jews or Gentiles).

ESTHER

CHAPTER ONE

V 1–3: VAST CONTROL The book of Esther is set in the period between the first two returns of the captive Jews and is detailed in Ezra and Nehemiah. Ahasuerus (also known as Xerxes) is the king over 127 provinces from India to Ethiopia. He calls for a feast in the third year of his reign, with all his officials and servants there from Persia, Media, and from the nobles and the princes. He has vast control. **V 4–8: VANITY COMMUNICATED** The vanity of the king is communicated by his desire to show off his material splendour and affluence during 180 days. After that, he gives a seven-day banquet in his luxurious palace in the enclosed garden of his citadel. He makes wine abundantly available, but drinking is not compulsory and each man is free to drink as he likes. **V 9–12: VASHTI'S CONDUCT** Queen Vashti also makes a feast for the women in the royal palace. Vashti is a very beautiful woman and, on the seventh day of the feast, the intoxicated king commands that she appear in her crown, so that the equally intoxicated guests could feast their sensual eyes upon her. Queen Vashti refuses to come on that basis, and the king is furious and burning with anger. **V 13–20: VINDICTIVE COUNSEL** The proud king asks his wise men what to do. He is told by Memucan, one of the seven princes of Persia, that she has wronged the king and also all men in authority. He fears that women may treat the authority of their men with contempt and wrath.

He counsels that Vashti should be excluded from the royal presence and her position be given to another woman. This, he says, will make all women honour their husbands, whether great men or unknown. **V 21–22: VAIN CONSEQUENCES** The king and the princes are appraised of Memucan's unnecessary emphasis on male domination and the vain consequences of his counsel are that the king sends letters to all the provinces and to everyone in their own language, insisting that the man must be the master in his own house and speak in the language of his own people. All this is to rationalise the sensual behaviour of a self-seeking king and to vilify a woman who obviously has some principles of right and wrong in a company of people who have very few.

CHAPTER TWO

V 1–4: SEARCH The king accepts advice to look for beautiful young virgins and bring them to the citadel at Shushan under the custody of Hegai, the king's eunuch who looks after the king's women. Preparations are to be given and the young woman who pleases the king most will take over from Vashti as queen. The proud king is pleased with this idea. **V 5–9: SELECTION** The selection process begins. Esther, a very beautiful young Jewess, is taken to the palace to be considered. Esther is brought up by her older cousin Mordecai, a devout Jew, who raises her as his own daughter after her parents died. Hegai is very taken with the beauty of Esther and acts favourably towards her, giving her beauty preparations in addition to her allowance. She is given maidservants to help her, and Hegai moves her to the best place in the house of the women. **V 10–11: SECRET** At Mordecai's instruction, Esther has not yet revealed that she is a Jewess. Each day, Mordecai paces in front of the women's quarters to hear how Esther is doing. **V 12–16: SENSIBLE** The custom is that, after twelve months of preparation, every young woman candidate may ask for anything she wants to make her more beautiful and attractive, before she goes in to the king. Esther, however, is very sensible, and acts on the advice of Hegai as to what to have. Because of her undemanding and trusting disposition, she gains favour with all who see her. **V 17–18: SPECIAL** Esther finds special favour in the eyes of the king and he loves her more than all the other women. She so attracts his grace and favour over the others, that he gives her the royal crown and makes her queen instead of Vashti. The Feast of Esther, given for his officials and servants, marks this coronation and a holiday is proclaimed with generous gifts being given by the king. **V 19–20: SUPERVISED** Esther still remains under the authority of Mordecai, albeit secretly, and he sits within the king's gate. He tells her not to reveal her Jewish origin yet. **V 21–23: SAVED** An event occurs which will later play a key role in the history of the Jews. Mordecai learns the identity of two would-be assassins of King Ahasuerus. He tells Esther who relays the information, in his name, to the king. Enquiry confirms the truthfulness of the allegation, and the men are hanged on the gallows. No mention is made at this stage of any recognition of the crucial part played by Mordecai in the saving of the king's life, but it is noted in the court chronicles.

CHAPTER THREE

V 1–3: HAUGHTY HAMAN Haman an Agagite descendant, is promoted by the king. Everyone except Mordecai pays him homage and bows down to him. The king's servants within the king's gates ask Mordecai why he transgresses the king's command in not showing obeisance to Haman. Mordecai is a Benjamite and Haman an Agagite. Tension exists for historical reasons between these two groups of people. More important still, Mordecai is a faithful Jew who fears God and will not bow down to any mere man like haughty Haman. **V 4: MORDECAI'S MENTALITY** Eventually, this becomes a talking point, and Haman is told by the servants about Mordecai's persistent refusal to bow down, and that he is a Jew. **V 5–9: PERNICIOUS PLAN** All the stored opposition of the Agagite against the Jews is centred on Mordecai's refusal to bow down before him. The pernicious plan is to exterminate all the Jews, not just Mordecai. Haman then maliciously maligns the Jews to King Ahasuerus. He depicts them as lawbreakers scattered around the king's kingdom and, by implication, likely rebels. He urges the king to make a decree to destroy the Jews and gain great plunder from them. Ten thousand talents of silver will thus go into the king's treasuries. This is an interesting proposition for the worldly-minded king who loves his material wealth. **V 10–15: OUTRAGEOUS OPPOSITION** The king gives his signet ring to Haman to make his decree and promises to sign it. Haman invokes vicious opposition to the Jews to annihilate young and old, children and women. The date is set for the slaughter and for the plundering of their valuable possessions, soon to be transferred to the king. The decree is to be issued in every province and published to all the people so that they can be ready to exterminate these people of God. As the couriers leave with the message, Haman sits down to drink with the king, leaving the city of Shushan perplexed. The non-Jewish people are probably bewildered and appalled at such an outrageous and cruel opposition to exterminate innocent people.

CHAPTER FOUR

V 1–3: MORDECAI'S MOURNING Mordecai immediately identifies with the Jews and goes into mourning in torn clothes, sackcloth and ashes, in the midst of the city. He cries loudly and bitterly in front of the king's gate. No doubt, prayer to God plays a large part in this, and the Jews all over the province do the same. **V 4–5: ESTHER'S ENQUIRY** Esther hears of his plight, is deeply distressed, and sends garments to Mordecai. He will not replace his sackcloth with them and Esther sends a eunuch to ask him why. Serious enquiry is often the start of spiritual revival and life. **V 6–11: DANGEROUS DUTY** Mordecai relates to the eunuch what has happened, so he can pass on the information to Esther, including the amount of plunder to be paid to the king. He gives him a copy of the written decree covering the proposed annihilation of the Jews. He is to explain this to Esther so that she can go in to the king and make supplication to him and plead for the Jewish people. Hathach, the eunuch, returns and tells Esther this. Esther sends another message back by him to Mordecai, pointing out that if anyone enters the king's presence without his express calling, that person will be put to death, unless the king holds out his golden sceptre as a sign that the 'intruder' may live. Also, it seems at this time that Esther is not in favour. The king has not called for her for thirty days. **V 12–14: TELLING TIMING** Mordecai receives and replies to Esther's message. He tells Esther that she will not escape any coming persecution more than other Jews, and that she and her father's house will perish. He is confident that even if she stays silent, 'relief and deliverance will arrive for the Jews from another place', clearly referring to God, though not calling Him by name. Then he asks, 'Who knows whether you have come to the kingdom for such a time as this?' Mordecai sees Esther as God's person in God's place for God's purposes and God's people at God's time. **V 15–17: SERIOUS SUPPLICATION** Esther announces that she will go in to the king, in spite of it being illegal to do so, with the selfless resignation that 'If I perish, I perish!' But she uses her royal prerogative to urge Mordecai to gather all the Jews in Shushan to join in fasting for her. Fasting always includes prayer, and thus Esther goes to carry out her solemn commission in the knowledge that she is being supported in prayer.

CHAPTER FIVE

V 1–2: APPROACH ACCEPTED Esther goes in to the king in her royal robes, and the king stretches out his golden sceptre which Esther touches at the top. **V 3–8: PETITION POSTPONED** The king asks Esther what she wants and encouragingly promises to give her up to half the kingdom. Whatever this king's failings, lack of generosity is not one of them! Esther asks for the king and Haman to attend a banquet she has already prepared, and the king gives the order for Haman to come. At that banquet of wine, the king again asks the queen what her petition is. Esther asks if she may postpone the detail of her petition until a second banquet for Haman and the king, which she proposes to give the next day. **V 9–13: HAMAN'S HEART** Haman thinks that all is going well and goes out joyful and with a glad heart—that is, until he

sees his enemy Mordecai in the king's gate, again refusing to stand or tremble before him. Haman restrains himself, tells of his great riches to his friends and family, glories in his promotion above all the others, and boasts about the fact that Queen Esther has already invited him to a banquet with the king and that there is a second banquet the next day. But he says this is nothing to him as long as he is aggravated and annoyed by seeing the resolute Mordecai sitting at the king's gate and knowing that the faithful man will never bow to him. **V 14: WICKED WIFE** Zeresh, the wicked wife of Haman, supported by their shallow friends, suggests that a huge gallows be made. In the morning Haman should suggest to the king that Mordecai be hanged on it. Then they tell petulant Haman he can go merrily with the king to the banquet. Haman is very pleased and has the gallows made.

CHAPTER SIX

V 1–3: SLEEPLESS SOVEREIGN In an amazing sequence of timing that speaks of God's hand on the events of this book, the king cannot sleep. He decides that he will send for records of the chronicles to be read before him. It just so happens that the chronicle of Mordecai's reporting the would-be assassins is read. The king asks, 'What honour or dignity has been bestowed on Mordecai for this?' He is told that nothing has been done for Mordecai. **V 4–5: SINISTER SUGGESTION** Haman now arrives, about to make his sinister suggestion that Mordecai be hanged on the gallows that he has prepared. The king bids Haman come into the court. **V 6–9: SELF-SEEKING** Haman does not know that the king has just heard the chronicles read to him telling of his rescue from assassination through Mordecai's faithfulness. The king asks Haman directly, 'What should be done for the man the king delights to honour?' Haman, with an ego as large as the gallows he has had built, assumes the king is talking about him. He answers that such a person should be arrayed in the king's robes, be paraded around the city on the king's horse, and led by the king's most noble prince. **V 10–11: SUDDEN SURPRISE** This highly impressionable king instructs Haman to do for Mordecai exactly what Haman is now hoping will be done for himself by the king. Ironically, it is Haman who has to lead Mordecai on horseback through the city square, and proclaim that the king is delighting to honour Mordecai. What amazing timing God arranges to rescue Mordecai and, a little later, the whole of the Jewish people. **V 12–14: SORRY STATE** Now it is Haman's time to mourn. His story to his wife and friends is much sadder than the last one he related! They tell him that he cannot prevail now if Mordecai is of Jewish descent. At that very moment the king's eunuchs come to bring Haman to the banquet prepared by Esther, another evidence of God's timing in the whole matter.

CHAPTER SEVEN

V 1–2: PATIENCE Queen Esther does not immediately put her petition to the king but shows patience. It is the second day when the king asks her what the petition is and repeats his offer to grant to her up to half the kingdom. **V 3–4: PETITION** Now Queen Esther nails her colours to the mast, and, taking her life in her hands, tells of the proposed annihilation of her people. Slavery would be bad enough, but this is even worse, that she and her people are to be killed. **V 5–7: PLEADING** King Ahasuerus, who seems not to have realised the effect of Haman's scheming in his wanton delegation of power to that wicked man, asks who and where the person is who would dare to presume to do such an evil thing. Esther strikes. She names Haman. He is terrified before the king and queen. So desperate is Haman that after the angry king leaves in wrath to go into the palace garden, Haman now pleads with Queen Esther for his life because he sees that the king is determining evil against him. **V 8–9: PERIL** Again timing takes its place in this saga. The king returns and sees Haman fallen across the couch, where Esther is. He is livid and assumes that some kind of assault is in progress. Haman reaches his all-time low as one of the eunuchs points out the gallows, fifty cubits high, which Haman made for Mordecai, the man who 'spoke good on the king's behalf'. The king instantly says, 'Hang him on it!' **V 10: PERISH** So Haman is hanged on those gallows which he had himself made for Mordecai, the man whom he has had to honour before the people. As Haman is dead, the king's wrath subsides.

CHAPTER EIGHT

V 1–2: ROLE REVERSAL In a dramatic role reversal, the king gives Queen Esther the house of Haman, Mordecai comes before the king as Esther has now revealed her relationship to him, and the king places his own signet ring, previously given to Haman, on the finger of Mordecai. Esther appoints Mordecai over the house of Haman that she has been given. **V 3–10: ROYAL REVIEW** Esther puts herself in peril again by going in unannounced before the king, but again is welcomed with the golden sceptre. She pleads for the reversal of Haman's annihilation plans. King Ahasuerus tells Esther and Mordecai to write the decree themselves.

Mordecai must seal it with the king's signet ring. In this instance, his irresponsible delegation works in favour of God's people, and he probably knows that he can trust Mordecai to do the right thing. Mordecai dictates the terms of the decree and seals it accordingly. It is then sent by couriers on horseback to the far corners of King Ahasuerus' kingdom. **V 11–14: RETRIBUTIVE RIGHTS** Not only are the Jews permitted to gather together to save their lives, but they are also authorised to destroy and annihilate any forces or provinces that would seek to oppose them, including women and children, and to plunder their enemies' possessions. The decree is widely distributed. **V 15–17: REJOICING RESPECTED** The city of Shushan rejoices and is delighted that Mordecai appears in the robes of his new authority. The Jews experience 'light and gladness, joy and honour'. Joy, feasting and a holiday mark this happy outcome. God's influence is again seen in that many people become Jews because fear of the Jews comes upon them. That fear could only have been orchestrated by one person, God Himself.

CHAPTER NINE

V 1–17: ENEMIES EXECUTED But enemies of the Jews still exist. The Jews oppose them and have resounding victories, slaughtering their enemies who seek their harm. They make safe the people of God. The king asks Esther if she has any further petitions. She asks that Haman's ten sons, already slain, be hanged on the gallows and that the Jews be allowed to repeat the destruction of their enemies for the second time. This is done. The Jews do not touch the plunder of ungodly people, however. **V 18–32: PURIM PERPETUATED** The thirteenth, fourteenth and fifteenth days of the month Adar are called Purim, named after a word meaning 'the lot'. These days are for resting, feasting, gladness, a holiday, and sending presents to one another, especially to the poor. The Jews commemorate their rescue from the annihilation plans of wicked Haman and establish the keeping of Purim by their future generations. The memory is not to perish among their descendants. Queen Esther co-authors with Mordecai a decree to perpetuate Purim.

CHAPTER TEN

V 1–2: POWERFUL PEOPLE The Jews become a powerful people in the kingdom of a powerful king. The book of Esther starts with the folly of King Ahasuerus. It ends up, however, with his helping the Jews to escape and prosper. Again, this is evidence of God's influence, without the specific mention of God. **V 3: RESPECTED REPRESENTATIVE** Mordecai, the uncompromising Jew who lived wholeheartedly for his people, is now second only to King Ahasuerus, which may be one reason why Ahasuerus makes some good decisions. Mordecai is acclaimed among the Jews, well received by them, 'seeking the good of his people and speaking peace to all his countrymen'. The influence of this devoted godly man, through his faithful conduct and concern for others, encourages a beautiful, sacrificially compassionate, young queen to act for the good of God's people. His example stands for us all today, as does that of Queen Esther.

JOB

OVERVIEW

PEOPLE AND PRELIMINARIES

✳ Job (forty-two chapters) is the first of the five poetical books of the Old Testament. The others are Psalms, Proverbs, Ecclesiastes and Song of Solomon. Just like every other book in the Bible, the poetical books are completely accurate factually. We know neither the author nor the date of Job, but Moses or Solomon are possible candidates. Some think that Job is probably the oldest book in the Bible. Others think that it could have been written long after the main events recorded. It certainly deals with early history. It could have been written where the action was, in the land of Uz, east of Judah and towards the desert. The drama of Job unfolds probably within a single year.

PLAN AND PURPOSE

ⓘ The answer to why this book of Job was written could occupy another whole book! Job suffers at Satan's instigation, but under the permissive hand of God. He never knows why. He is sorely tested, not only by losing his loved ones, possessions and health, but also at the hands of his supposed 'comforters' who largely give the wrong answers to the wrong questions at the wrong time. This book is about how to face suffering and how God's grace can bring the sufferer through it. God's sovereignty and faithfulness shine through. So do affirmations of faith and amazing prophecies of the Redeemer to come, shining like searchlights in the dark night sky of Job's suffering and doubt.

PROFILE AND PROGRESSION

🐚 Job's character and circumstances, Satan's accusation and God's limited permission to test Job, the first wave of attack on Job, his resolute righteousness, Satan's further accusation and God's permission to afflict Job physically, and Job's testing through boils (1:1–2:8); Job's relationship with his suffering wife (2:9,10); Job's conversations with his three would-be comforting friends, Eliphaz, Bildad and Zophar (2:11–31:40); Job's conversations with Elihu (32:1–37:24); God's interrogation of, and answers to, Job (38:1–41:34); Job's submission to God (42:1–6); God's dealing with the three friends and Job's prayer for them (42:7–9); the greater blessing in the remainder of Job's life (42:10–17).

PRINCIPLES AND PARTICULARS

👉 Satanic opposition is limited, but powerful, within God's overall control and plan. The person suffering may never know why he suffers. The book of Job provides a case study of how and how not to comfort sufferers. God's perfect timing and ongoing faithfulness are underlined. We see glimpses of the coming Redeemer and of the real nature of personal faith in God, whose greatness is infinitely beyond human knowledge or comprehension. The principle is demonstrated of the final welfare of God's people, though not always on earth as for Job. Blessing often comes after praying for others.

JOB

In this long book, much of which consists of Job's supposed comforters speaking to him and his replying to them, there is certain repetition and convoluted argument. A change of speaker is shown below in parentheses containing the initials 'ss' followed by the name of the speaker—e.g. '(ss Eliphaz)'. Thus it should be simple, in these chapter summaries, to identify quickly who is speaking at any one time. Until the next parentheses containing 'ss' and followed by the name of the next speaker, the words belong to the last named speaker. The first speech of each speaker is denoted by (1) and the second speech by (2) and so on—e.g. '(ss Job) (2)' is Job's second speech.

CHAPTER ONE

V 1–3: BLAMELESS AND BLESSED Job is a godly, blameless, and upright man who hates evil. His blessings include a large family, a large household, and great possession of animals which signify his wealth and substance. He is the greatest man in the east. **V 4–5: FAITHFUL TO FAMILY** His children often meet together to feast and enjoy each other's company. Job is so concerned in case they have sinned or cursed God, that he regularly makes sacrifices for them, rising early in the morning to do so. He has a real concern for the spiritual welfare of his family. **V 6–12: SATAN TO SIFT** God's angels, called 'the sons of God', present themselves before God. His fallen angel, Satan, is also present, having returned from walking about in the earth. Job's holiness is noted by God, but Satan states that if he loses his possessions, he will curse God. God allows Satan to attack Job, with limitations that God puts on him. God sometimes allows attacks on Christians, both spiritual and otherwise, to demonstrate His grace to others and to bless Christians themselves, but, most of all, to glorify Himself. **V 13–19:**

CALAMITIES AND CRISES Huge calamities befall Job, each one being a major crisis. In separate but consecutive incidents, he loses his animals, his servants, and his children, who are killed when his eldest son's house falls in on them. He is deeply tested. **V 20–22: RIGHTEOUS IN RESPONSE** Job goes into mourning but worships God, acknowledging that everything that he has is from God, and that it is His prerogative to take it away. Job does not sin and he does not blame God for what has happened. Here is the correct attitude of a righteous man to his suffering, tragedies and difficulties. This is only possible because of God's grace in his heart.

CHAPTER TWO

V 1–8: SATAN'S NEXT STEP When God tells Satan that Job has not cursed Him, despite losing everything, Satan responds that if his body is touched, he will curse God. God gives Satan permission to afflict Job bodily, but his life must be spared. Satan responds by covering Job with painful boils from head to foot. While Job mourns in the midst of the ashes, he scrapes himself with a bit of broken pottery. **V 9–10: WISE TOWARDS WIFE** Job's wife tells Job to curse God, which is what Satan wants, and die, which is what God decreed must not happen. Job's response is spiritual and right. He accepts God's sovereignty in all that lies before him. He does not sin with his lips. **V 11–13: COMING OF COMFORTERS** Job's three friends, Eliphaz the Temanite, Bildad the Shuhite, and Zophar the Naamathite, hear what happened to Job and come to mourn with him and comfort him. For seven complete days, they sit speechless with him on the ground. He is unrecognisable through the boils and his grief is very great. Perhaps the best two things that the comforters do is to have compassion on Job, and then to keep quiet when they come to see him! Most of the rest is downhill from now on!

CHAPTER THREE

ss Job: 1:

V 1–19: SORRY TO SURVIVE Job laments the day of his conception, and the day of his birth. **V 20–24: DESIRING HIS DEATH** Job wishes to die, but death will not come. As a godly man, suicide is not an option, but he longs that God will take him. **V 25–26: RACKED WITH RESTLESSNESS** Because he has already suffered the worst of the fears that he ever had, he is uneasy, troubled, and restless. He does not know that God is at work behind the circumstances. Often we, too, fail to realise that when our circumstances are really hard.

CHAPTER FOUR

ss Eliphaz: 1:

V 1–6: SADNESS OF SITUATION Eliphaz summarises how Job has helped many in the past, but now is in great need himself. **V 7–11: MISUNDERSTANDING THE MYSTERY** Eliphaz cannot understand what is really happening. His argument is basically that the innocent and the upright do not suffer. Clearly, the Bible and experience prove him wrong. **V 12–16: VANITY AND VISIONS** Eliphaz bases his observation on his claim to have had a vision in the night. A frightening vision of an unknown spirit produces a voice that tells him what to say to Job. The visions of other people are never a good basis for sound counselling or for spiritual help. We must turn to biblical revelation and principles. **V 17–21: PURITY AND PERISHING** Here, Eliphaz

produces truth which, however, is unrelated to the situation. God is more pure than any man, including Job. We all fail; our lives are like clay houses that will crumble. None of this is relevant to Job's situation.

CHAPTER FIVE

V 1–7: HOPELESS AND HELPLESS Just as sparks fly upwards, man's natural life leads to trouble. He is hopeless and helpless to help himself. No one can help him, not even the angels ('the holy ones'). **V 8–16: APPEAL TO ALMIGHTY** Eliphaz tells Job that he will appeal to God who will save Job. Eliphaz does not know the background plot! God will save Job, but not yet. **V 17–18: DESPISING GOD'S DISCIPLINE** Eliphaz correctly states that a man is happy when corrected by God and that God's chastening must not be despised. This is true, but of no help to Job at present. **V 19–27: EXPERIENCE YOUR ESCAPE** Eliphaz tells Job that God will deliver him and that he will experience his escape at the hands of God. This is true, but, again, not yet. God has His timetable for each of His children. Eliphaz is looking for a 'quick fix' solution.

CHAPTER SIX

ss Job: 2:

V 1–7: I AM SUFFERING Job points out to Eliphaz that he has great cause for complaint. He is suffering very badly. **V 8–13: I AM STRENGTHLESS** Job again laments that God will not take his life from him, and declares himself to have no strength. **V 14–23: I AM SADDENED** In his sad state, Job lacks the kindness of a friend. His comforters have come to him and can bring him nothing. **V 24–30: I AM SINCERE** In sincerity, Job cannot confess to specific sin. He sincerely states that he is righteous, in that context.

CHAPTER SEVEN

V 1–6: TORMENTING TIMES At night, Job wishes for morning. His passing days seem hopeless to him, because of his great physical affliction. **V 7–10: PASSING PRESENCE** He realises that his life is like a breath, or a cloud, which vanishes away. **V 11–16: MEANINGLESS MESS** He cannot but speak of this and complain from his bitterness. Life is loathsome to him and seems to be a meaningless mess. **V 17–21: SIMPLE SOLUTION?** He finally replies to Eliphaz's first speech by suggesting there is a simple solution: if sin has caused his suffering, why does not God simply pardon it, and take away his iniquity? We know his sin did not cause his suffering.

CHAPTER EIGHT

ss Bildad: 1:
V 1–7: PLEADING AND PURITY Bildad now enters the discussion. He criticises Job, claiming that he is blaming God for not being just. Insensitively, he implies very directly that Job's sons were killed because they were sinners. He says if Job is pure and will plead, God will answer him. Helpful comfort indeed! **V 8–10: HELP FROM HISTORY** Bildad claims that those who lived before would endorse his words to Job. **V 11–18: NOTE FROM NATURE** He looks at illustrations from nature to show cause and effect. He regards Job's sin as a cause, and his suffering as the effect. Here are misapplied illustrations: this is a warning to any preacher! **V 19–22: BLAMELESS AND BLESSED** He maintains that blameless people will not be dealt with in the way Job suffers, but that they will be

blessed. He says that only the wicked have nowhere to dwell.

CHAPTER NINE

ss Job: 3:
V 1–13: GOD IS GREAT God is great. Job recites the righteousness, wisdom, power, creation, dealings and sovereignty of God. He knows that God is great. **V 14–20: POWER AND PERFECTION** God's strength and irresistible judgement give Job the sense of being completely overwhelmed and crushed by God. **V 21–24: INDIFFERENT TO INNOCENCE?** It seems to Job that God is not interested in whether people are innocent or guilty, from the point of view of making them suffer on earth. He cannot understand this. **V 25–31: DEPTHS OF DESPAIR** Thus Job is driven to the depths of despair. Life is passing quickly. Even if he can make himself as clean as possible, he will still be seen as filthy and guilty. **V 32–35: ASKING FOR ADVOCATE** The passage echoes the need of every sinner to have a mediator between God and man. The Man, Christ Jesus, is that mediator today for all who will repent and trust Him. Job longs for someone to plead his cause before a God whom he does not understand and to whom he feels he cannot relate. His feeling is wrong, as he will find out later!

CHAPTER TEN

V 1–7: ADVICE OF ACCUSATION Job complains. He is troubled that God is said to condemn him, but does not tell him on what charge. He asks for Him to advise the accusation against him. Job knows that although there is no unforgiven sin in his life, no one can deliver him from God, if God does not see it that way. He is confused. **V 8–12: CARE FROM CREATOR** Job argues that God, his Creator, has cared for him until his present afflictions. He cannot understand why that care seems to be withdrawn. **V 13–17: SIMILARITY OF SENTENCE** It seems to Job that the innocent are suffering the same way as the guilty, and he does not understand it. **V 18–22: LAMENT OVER LIVING** This leads Job again to cry out to God for death to come. Happily for him, God does not respond positively, nor heed his despairing plea of 'Leave me alone'.

CHAPTER ELEVEN

ss Zophar: 1:

V 1–9: ROUGH REBUKE Zophar takes over from Eliphaz, but on a far more critical note. He is very hard on Job and accuses him of empty talk and speaking against God. Job should have had it worse, according to him. **V 10–12: ABSOLUTE AUTHORITY** He reminds Job that God has absolute authority to act. He implies that Job is empty-headed. **V 13–15: REPENTANCE REQUIRED** More directly than Eliphaz, Zophar insists that Job must repent. **V 16–20: LOVELY LIFE!** Over-simplistically, he describes the trouble-free life which he says will follow if there is repentance. To him, everything is very simple; Job must repent and then he will automatically receive physical and material blessing. How shallow!

CHAPTER TWELVE

ss Job: 4:

V 1–3: INTELLIGENT INDIVIDUAL Job argues that his mind is as good as those who counsel him and he understands everything they say. **V 4–12: CURIOUS COMPARISONS** However he insists that he is, exceptionally, a laughing stock to his friends and under contempt because of his misfortune. He goes on to use curious comparisons to show that others who

have either sinned against God's will or have no relationship with Him do not suffer as he has suffered. His involved argument, presumably, is that if someone who has sinned, or who is without a relationship with God, does not suffer, how can suffering be said to be caused by sin? In this context, he deals with robbers, animals, birds, and fish. **V 13–25: SUPREME SOVEREIGN** Job goes on to show that God is the supreme Sovereign who raises up and puts down. He has complete final sway over everything and everyone, whatever their wisdom, intellect, political power, or strength.

CHAPTER THIRTEEN

V 1–12: COUNSEL OF CLAY Job reiterates that he knows as much as his friends, and accuses them of worthless and dishonest comments that are biased against him. He describes their defences as being 'of clay'. **V 13–15: DETERMINED TO DEFEND** He asks them to keep quiet because he is determined to defend his position before God. Here comes the wonderful verse, 'Though He slay me, yet will I trust Him', referring, in context, not only to Job's daring to defend his position before God, but also revealing a far broader and more important principle of complete trust in God. **V 16–19: FOUNDATION OF FAITH** Even in Job's despair, he knows that God will be his salvation. He has a basic foundation of faith. **V 20–27: STOP AND SHOW** Job asks two things from God: first, that He will stop his suffering—he feels abandoned, lonely and terrified and he wants that to stop; second, that He will show him his sins if he has committed them. He cannot see why God pursues him. He feels like a fallen leaf or stubble being blown by the wind. He does not understand why he is 'in the stocks'. Clearly, Job does not understand why he is suffering. This experience is shared by many who suffer. **V 28: DESTINED FOR DEATH** Job knows that man will decay and deteriorate.

CHAPTER FOURTEEN

V 1–6: FADING FLOWER Job's argument, again, is that his short life is fading as a flower or as a shadow and that man is born for trouble. **V 7–10: CONTINUOUS CYCLE** He compares mankind to a tree which, even if it is cut down, will sprout branches again and manifest new life. **V 11–12: DEPRESSING DRYNESS** He sees man as a dried-up river or as a sea that has been diverted, leaving only sand. **V 13–17: PLAINTIVE PRAYER** He asks God to hide him in the grave, conceal him from God's wrath, and ultimately to cover his sin. **V 18–22: PAINFUL PROCESS** He describes himself as an eroding mountain or as a stone worn away by water, or as soil washed away by the flow of torrents. His hope is eroded in that way and he has pain.

CHAPTER FIFTEEN

ss Eliphaz: 2:

V 1–6: FOOLISHNESS Eliphaz was formerly sympathetic, but now after hearing his colleagues' speeches, becomes far harder in his attitude towards Job. He accuses Job of being foolish. A wise man will not answer as Job answered, he says. **V 7–13: FORGETFULNESS** He says that Job does not agree with older and more experienced people. Thus he regards Job as rejecting God, rather than merely disagreeing with the opinions of the people to whom he refers. Job is accused of forgetting their wisdom. **V 14–16: FILTHINESS** Eliphaz's correct reference to man being abominable and filthy is, perhaps, more than a comment on human

nature, and, rather, a specific accusation against Job. This is why he is suffering so badly in the view of Eliphaz. **V 17–35: FALSENESS** After a long speech about how the wicked suffer, Eliphaz finally implies that Job is a hypocrite. He appears to be one thing when, in fact, he is another. He is false, in the eyes of Eliphaz.

CHAPTER SIXTEEN

ss Job: 5:

V 1–5: ASSESSMENT Job assesses his friends who are unsuccessful comforters to him. He says they are long-winded and miserable, and tell him nothing new. He reminds them that in a similar situation he would strengthen and comfort them. We can learn much about how to comfort others through our own sufferings. **V 6–14: AFFLICTION** Speaking or being silent does not take away Job's pain and affliction. He speaks to God and pours out his heart about his sufferings. He sees God as the primary cause and initiator of his sufferings, rather then the One who is allowing this to happen. **V 15–17: ADAMANT** After his personal mourning and suffering, he can claim that he has not acted violently and that his prayer is pure. He is adamant that his suffering is not a payment for any particular wickedness of his. **V 18–22: APPEAL** His appeal is that his case will be heard in heaven. His desire of verse 21, that 'one might plead for a man with God', underlines the Christian's privilege in having a Saviour, who is both Man and God and who intercedes for him.

CHAPTER SEVENTEEN

V 1–5: MEANINGLESS MOCKERY From the depth of his brokenness, Job is ready to die and sees his would-be comforters as mockers. Their lack of understanding has led to their ridicule of him. **V 6–10: OBNOXIOUS OPPOSITION** Job's pitiful state has led people even to spit in his face, and many speak disrespectfully against him. He is sorrowful and in the shadows. He encourages himself and other righteous people, nevertheless, to have clean hands morally and spiritually. Somehow, in his brokenness, he knows that a clear walk with God will make him stronger. He even asks them to come back to speak to him again, though he does not expect to hear any wisdom from them. **V 11–16: DARK DESTINY** Despite all this, all Job can see is death and destruction coming closer. Physically and humanly speaking, he can see no hope.

CHAPTER EIGHTEEN

ss Bildad: 2:
V 1–2: STOP SPEAKING Bildad tells Job, in effect, to 'shut up and wise up'. **V 3–4: SARCASTIC SCORN** He asks why Job should think himself to be more superior to them. He tells Job to look at his situation and ask himself whether he can change anything by it. This is a scornful reply from a would-be comforter. **V 5–20: SINNERS' SUFFERINGS** Bildad then gives a long speech about how the wicked suffer and how sin is manifest in suffering. **V 21: SAD STATE** He concludes that these things happen to those who are wicked and do not know God. He is on the verge of saying that Job does not know God. What comfort, indeed!

CHAPTER NINETEEN

ss Job: 6:
V 1–6: UNENVIABLE POSITION Job complains about the ongoing words of his friends that, in fact, torment him and break him. He says that if God sent them to say this, then God has wronged him,

too. **V 7–12: UNANSWERED PRAYER** Job complains that his prayers go unheard and that God continues to break him down and attack him as an invading army. That is how he feels, even though it is not the truth. **V 13–20: UNSYMPATHETIC PEOPLE** His sadness is deepened by the fact that those close to him find him repulsive or withdraw from him. Physically, he is so unattractive. He looks like a living skeleton. His breath is foul and he may also have lost his teeth. **V 21–22: UNWARRANTED PERSECUTION** He pleads for pity from his friends whom he sees as persecuting him by their attitude and persistence. **V 23–27: UNEXPECTED PROCLAMATION** Like a beam of light in all this darkness, Job declares what are, perhaps, the most famous words in the whole book. He wants these words to be indelibly recorded. He says, 'I know that my Redeemer lives, and He shall stand at last on the earth; And after my skin is destroyed, this I know, that in my flesh I shall see God, Whom I shall see for myself. And my eyes shall behold, and not another.' Sometimes in the depths of despair, God reminds his struggling people of the wonderful twin truths that there is a personal and risen Redeemer, and that there is a glorious future ahead because of Him! **V 28–29: UNDENIABLE PUNISHMENT** Job warns the comforters that they themselves are answerable to God and will be punished for their wrong.

CHAPTER TWENTY

ss Zophar: 2:
V 1–3: ANSWER FROM ANXIETY Zophar embarks on his second speech, saying that it is anxiety that makes him answer Job. He is disturbed by the rebuke he received. He claims that his spirit of understanding is behind his answer. **V 4–11: END OF EVIL**

He again concentrates on the fate of the wicked man, and starts by showing that his end is in the dust. Nothing that he has will last. **V 12–19: POINTLESSNESS OF PLANS** Zophar then lists things that the wicked man does, in the hope that he will benefit from them, but at the end there is no point because nothing succeeds. He seems never to have heard of wicked people who do prosper in this life! **V 20–29: DARKNESS AND DESTRUCTION** He develops the theme and is of the opinion that the wicked will suffer in this life, even before his wickedness will take him to destruction. He has grasped one truth, of course, that finally God will deal with the wicked.

CHAPTER TWENTY-ONE

ss Job: 7:
V 1–6: CAREFUL CONSIDERATION Job replies to Zophar by asking him to think carefully about what he is counselling. He has forgotten Job's position and complaint. **V 7–21: SINNERS SUCCEED** Job demonstrates that many wicked do prosper often in this life. Those bent on sin often do succeed on this side of the grave. **V 22–26: DIFFERENT DEMISES** Further, Job points out that some people die after a comfortable and secure life, while others suffer poverty, sickness and sorrow before death that claims all. **V 27–34: ILLOGICAL INPUTS** Job summarises his comments by stating that the so-called consolation is empty and false. His friends have not proved that suffering is caused immediately by specific sins, or that only the righteous prosper. Job tells them to talk to anyone who has travelled and seen the world, to establish that their conclusion is not correct.

CHAPTER TWENTY-TWO

ss Eliphaz: 3:
V 1–3: DISTANT DEITY Eliphaz suggests that Job's wisdom, righteousness and blamelessness are of no interest to a big God. **V 4–11: AWFUL ACCUSATIONS** Eliphaz, frustrated because his empty counsel is rejected by Job in all sincerity, gets nasty. He also lies. He accuses Job of things he has never done in order to make a point that should never be made. **V 12–20: TRUTH TURNED** Eliphaz uses undeniable truths about God to make a false accusation. He accuses Job of saying that God does not know what is going on. Job's actual point is that he does not know what God may be doing. Eliphaz's innuendo seems to be that Job is unrighteous and guilty, as evidenced by his lack of gladness and laughter. **V 21–30: SHAMEFUL SOLUTION** Eliphaz urges Job to repent from his sins and to turn to God so that everything will be all right for him. To urge someone to specific repentance over sins that he has committed is a shameful solution, and certainly not the way to seek that person's blessing.

CHAPTER TWENTY-THREE

ss Job: 8:
V 1–9: WHERE IS HE? Job answers that his problem is that he does not know how to find God. He does not know where He is. **V 10–12: WAY IS HOPEFUL** Despite the fact that Job does not know where to find God, he knows that God knows the way that he takes. Job is confident that after this testing, God will bring him forth as gold. In his darkness, Job still has his hope in God. This is why he has walked in God's ways, not deviated from His commandments, and treasured God's words. In trials, these things become more

precious to the believer. **V 13–17: WHO IS HE?** Job answers this question to himself. He sees God as unique, changeless, sovereign, and personal in arranging Job's life. Nevertheless, in these circumstances, Job is terrified. He fears that God has made his heart weak. He still wishes that he was cut off, rather than go through this darkness, even though he has an underlying faith in God. The experience of being pulled in opposite directions by conflicting inward desires is by no means new to the person who trusts in the Lord.

CHAPTER TWENTY-FOUR

V 1: WONDERING Job wants to know why it is, as God sees everything, that those who know Him do not always see blessing. **V 2–17: WICKEDNESS** Job then develops his earlier thought that the wicked do prosper, by tabling some of the sins of the wicked that do not necessarily take them into suffering or to an early grave. These sins include oppression, exploitation, murder, burglary and adultery. **V 18–21: WHY?** He raises the issues of why the wicked are not removed swiftly, why they are not cursed on the earth, why they are not made unsuccessful, and why they are not forgotten. **V 22–25: WHO?** Job concludes this speech by asking who, among his comforters, can say that this speech is empty, and that he is lying. He points out that God is in control, even over the mighty. Who can deny that God permits these things to happen?

CHAPTER TWENTY-FIVE

ss Bildad: 3:
V 1–3: GOD IS GREAT Bildad, in a speech which adds nothing to what has already been said, asserts God's greatness. This has never been challenged by Job. **V 4–6:**

GOD IS GOOD He then asserts God's goodness and righteousness, pointing out how much more righteous God is than man. Again, Job never contends that this is not so.

CHAPTER TWENTY-SIX

ss Job: 9:
V 1–4: UNHELPFUL UTTERANCES In his final speech replying to the three opening comforters, (Elihu, the fourth one, has not yet spoken), Job asks whether anything they have said has helped him, the sufferer, and where their words had come from. Is this really God's Spirit who is guiding them? **V 5–13: COMMON COMPREHENSION** Job shows again that he understands all they say about God's sovereignty and, in fact, it extends over death as well as over life and creation. By His Spirit, God created the world, put the stars in space and shows His control over everything. **V 14: WEAK WHISPER** But these things, which seem so huge to human beings, are but a mere token of the immense power and limitless greatness of God. They are only a weak 'whisper' from almighty God, in comparison with the volume He could use!

CHAPTER TWENTY-SEVEN

V 1–10: INSISTENCE ON INTEGRITY Job returns from commenting on God, again, to insist that, just as he has not harboured specific sins in the past, so now he intends to walk righteously. **V 11–12: NONSENSE ABOUT NOTHING** He then tells the comforters that what they have said is complete nonsense. Nothing they have said is relevant to his situation. He will not conceal anything from God. **V 13–23: SUFFERING FOR SINNERS** Job shows that he knows that sinners suffer and count for nothing at the end of their lives. That does not mean that his suffering is specifically caused by his sin.

CHAPTER TWENTY-EIGHT

V 1–11: FINDING TREASURES Job begins his talk on wisdom and points out that man goes to great lengths to find treasures by tunnelling in the earth and under mountains. **V 12–22: FRUITLESS TASK** But he has a fruitless task in seeking out wisdom. It is more precious than material treasure and cannot be found in the same way. **V 23–28: FINAL TRUTH** Only in God can wisdom be found, and only in fearing the Lord can one experience His wisdom. Understanding is the same as repentance from sin.

CHAPTER TWENTY-NINE

V 1–6: PAST Job has painful memories of his past when everything seemed good to him. This is before the events of chapters 1 and 2. **V 7–17: POSITION** Job enjoyed a position of great respect and influence, as one of the city's leaders. But he used that position to be a blessing to others who needed his help. He looks back with sadness to when he could help others because of what he was himself. **V 18–20: PEACE** He was at peace where he dwelt and his roots went deep and wide. He was strong and healthy. **V 21–25: POWER** He had power with men, so that after he gave his opinion, there was no more discussion. He was their chief and as a king in the army. Still, he comforted those who mourned.

CHAPTER THIRTY

V 1–8: RIDICULED Job complains, that by contrast, he is now mocked by younger men over whose fathers he once had authority. **V 9–15: REJECTED** With unrestrained contempt, they now reject him with the insults of spitting in the face and taunting songs. He also feels rejected by God, like a bow with the string removed. He cannot function properly. His honour and his prosperity have gone. **V 16–23: RACKED** He is racked with physical pain, mental torment, and anguish of soul. He says God does not answer his prayer and has become his cruel opposer. He knows that he is going to die. **V 24–31: RESTLESSNESS** He cannot understand why God seems still to afflict a heap of ruins, the phrase he uses for himself. He has sought to do good himself to those in need, and yet evil comes to him when he seeks good. He is mourning and brought low. He esteems himself no higher than wild animals and birds.

CHAPTER THIRTY-ONE

V 1–40a: WILLING EXAMINATIONS Job underlines his integrity in the details of his life. Job does not claim sinless perfection but merely shows that he is aware of no specific sins which cause specific suffering, as the supposed comforters say. He takes a tooth-comb through his life and shows that he is not aware of guilt, specifically regarding sexual purity, sin in general, telling the truth, dishonesty or covetousness, unfaithfulness to his wife, high-handedness against those under his authority, unwillingness to help those in need, pride over his possessions, erring from a true worship of the Creator rather than of created things, loving enemies and strangers, hiding his sin, or commercial matters. Because of all this, he asks God to let him know what he has done wrong. **V 40b: WORDS ENDED** This speech marks the end of his reply to the three original comforters.

CHAPTER THIRTY-TWO

ss Elihu: 1:

V 1–5: ENTRY OF ELIHU Elihu now enters into the discussion. He is younger than the other three comforters. He is angry with Job because he thinks Job is self-righteous and he is angry with the three counsellors because they found no answers. He will not comment on Job's plight, but only on what Job has said. In fact, he will misrepresent some of Job's words. Perhaps this intention to limit his observations is why, at the end, he is not condemned by God with the other three comforters. **V 6–9: RESPECT AND RELUCTANCE** Because he respects those older men, he waits until later to speak. He is reluctant to give his opinion if older people are giving the right opinion. He makes the good point that great men are not always wise, and that older people do not always understand justice. **V 10–22: WAITING FOR WORDS** Job waits for words from the comforters to provide reasons for his suffering but hears none. He commits himself not to use their words or arguments. Bursting with impatience for his turn to speak, he will now do so without flattering anyone.

CHAPTER THIRTY-THREE

V 1–7: SETTING SCENE Elihu sets the scene for his speech by saying how upright and sincere he is, that he is made by God, and has his Spirit. He then challenges Job to answer him. He tells Job he need not be frightened of him. **V8–11: INACCURATE INDICTMENT** He starts with the inaccurate accusation against Job that he has claimed sinless perfection, and that despite this, God has afflicted him. In fact, Job has not claimed that. He merely said that there is no specific sin that has caused this specific suffering. **V 12–30:**

REPENTANT RESTORATION Elihu makes a bold, well illustrated speech in which he misapplies truth. He makes the point that if there is real repentance, there will be real restoration. **V 31–33: CONFIDENT CLAIMS** Assuming a confidence which is far greater than his years and experience justify, he assures Job that he will learn wisdom if he will hold his peace and listen to Elihu. Job can speak to him so that Elihu can teach him.

CHAPTER THIRTY-FOUR

V 1–4: ELIHU EXHORTS Elihu calls the other comforters 'wise men' and urges them to witness what he says to Job. **V 5–9: FALLACIOUS 'FACTS'** He repeats the false accusation of Job's claim to sinless perfection. Job is accused of fraternising with sinful men because he is alleged to hold that it is profitless to delight in God. **V 10–20: ALMIGHTY'S ATTRIBUTES** He then gives a theologically correct commentary on the attributes and actions of God, which unfortunately does nothing to support his case. **V 21–30: JUST JUDGE** He rightly explains that God will judge sin. However, he fails to distinguish between calamities, which do not necessarily constitute judgement, and God's judgement on sin itself. **V 31–33: REPENTANCE REFUSED** He correctly says that if a man refuses to repent, but wants to change his conduct just to make life easier by escaping God's chastening, God will not deal with him. But this is not Job's case. **V 34–37: TESTING TIME** He contends that Job's words show his rebellion so Job ought to be tested further because of it.

CHAPTER THIRTY-FIVE

V 1–8: SINS' EFFECTS Elihu says that Job has said it does not matter whether he sins or not because he gains nothing by not sinning. He goes on to say that neither Job's sins nor his righteousness affect God at all because God is above Job. **V 9–13: SUPPLICATION'S EFFECTIVENESS** Elihu teaches that sin will stop God answering somebody. In this, he is right. But he is wrong in thinking that Job has sinned initially to cause the suffering described in the early chapters of the book. **V 14–16: SPEECH EMPTY** He criticises Job's intention to wait for God, stating that his speech is empty and his words are meaningless. God will not listen to Job, he says.

CHAPTER THIRTY-SIX

V 1–4: PERFECT GRASP! Elihu claims to have a perfect grasp of his subject. This is a proud claim for a young man to make. **V 5–12: PARDONING GRACE** He then describes how God will forgive those who have been arrogant and sinful against Him. Unlike the other three, however, Elihu concentrates on Job's words, even though he misrepresents them at times, rather than on his sufferings. **V 13–15: PAINFUL GODLESSNESS** Elihu speaks about hypocritical people. In their godlessness, they will not cry to God even though they are suffering and even though they may die young and face the wrath of God stored up against them. He introduces a new thought, however, that God speaks to the poor in their affliction and oppression. Here is a chink of light. God may speak to Job, who is impoverished in many ways through his sufferings, through those sufferings. **V 16–21: PRESUMPTUOUS GROUNDS** Elihu says that Job is under judgement and implies that he has presumed that his wealth and power will deliver him. He tells him that his prosperity will be restored if he turns back to God. **V 22–33:**

POWERFUL GOD Elihu tells Job how powerful and majestic God is. Job is already well aware of that wonderful fact.

CHAPTER THIRTY-SEVEN

V 1–13: WONDERFUL WORKS Elihu sums up some of the wonders of God's creation. He has observed thunder and lightning, snow, rain and cloud formation, and he sees God's planning behind it all. Job is told to remember all this. **V 14–18: STAND STILL** Elihu tells Job that, because his knowledge is so limited and God's is so great, he must stand still and just consider what God has done. He illustrates Job's ignorance of God's ways by pointing to cloud formation and the warming of the earth. This advice is better than what the other three have given. **V 19–24: AWESOME ALMIGHTY** Elihu then talks about the distance between man in his darkness and God in His awesome majesty and light. He underlines God's excellent power in judgement and justice and that He is unbiased in His dealings with men. All this is true, but it does not mean that Job had sinned specifically, or worse than others, against this almighty and holy God. Thus the scene is set for God Himself to intervene, which He does in the next chapter.

CHAPTER THIRTY-EIGHT

ss God speaks: 1:
V 1: DIRECT COMMUNICATION God now decides to speak directly to Job. He speaks to him out of a whirlwind. **V 2–3: DARK COUNSEL** God says that the counsel that Job has received is darkened, and now He will ask questions to Job himself. **V 4–7: DESIGNED CREATION** God underlines the fact that He is the Creator. He asks Job where he was when

creation was brought into being. **V 8–15: DIVINE CONTROL** By reference to the coming and going of the tides, and night and day, God demonstrates that He is in control of His creation. **V 16–18: DEEP CONSIDERATIONS** God tells Job how deep the sea is and asks him if he knows about it! He also cites death and the breadth of the earth as outside Job's understanding. **V 19–21: DARKNESS CONFINED** He points out to Job that He is the One who controls light and darkness. **V 22–30: DIVERSE CONDITIONS** God talks about snow, hail, the diffusion of light, the wind, water, thunderbolts, rain, dew, and ice. If Job cannot understand them, then he is not able to understand the God who controls them. **V 31–33: DAZZLING CONSTELLATONS** He turns His attention to the heavens and the stars, all of which are under His control. **V 34–38: DANGEROUS CLOUDS** He points out that even the clouds, from which we get our rain, can send out lightning and can send out floods on the earth. He controls that, too. **V 39–41: DEMONSTRATED CARE** He shows His uniqueness in how He cares and provides for lions and ravens. No doubt, Job is beginning to get the message, directly from God, that He is there and that He is in control. God is capable of doing whatever He desires that is consistent with His just, righteous and powerful character.

CHAPTER THIRTY-NINE

V 1–30: CREATOR'S CONTROL AND CARE FOR CREATURES God continues speaking to Job. He asks him questions about His animal creation and this makes Job realise that God is in sovereign control and has care for His creatures. The approach is that God knows all about this, causes it to come into being, upholds it, and directs it

through nature. Thus no human being must ever think that God has not got control of and care for him. The chapter deals with mountain goats (verses 1 to 4), wild donkeys (verses 5 to 8), wild oxen (verses 9 to 12), ostriches (verses 13 to 18), horses (verses 19 to 25), hawks (verse 26), and eagles (verses 27 to 30).

CHAPTER FORTY

V 1–2: CONTENTION AND CORRECTION God concludes His first direct revelation to Job by asking whether anyone who contends with God should seek to correct Him. Anyone seeking to rebuke God must answer to Him. **ss Job: 10: V 3–5: SINFUL AND SILENT** Job, having been spoken to directly by God and questioned by Him, sees himself as vile and completely unable to answer. He has no choice except to be silent and listen to God who loves him and knows all about him. **ss God: 2: V 6: WHIRLWIND AND WORDS** After Job's brief and humble reply, God continues His direct revelation to him. Again, He speaks to Job out of a whirlwind, emphasising His power, might, and difference from any created being. **V 7: READY TO REPLY** He tells Job to prepare himself to reply, remembering that he is a man. Now God will do the questioning and Job must do the replying. Perhaps this is the approach to all unanswered questions—to lay ourselves open to God's sovereignty in our own lives. **V 8: JUDGEMENT AND JUSTICE** God asks if Job would annul His judgement and condemn God in order that Job himself might be justified? This is clearly the wrong way round! **V 9–10: STRENGTH AND SPLENDOUR** God continues to speak out of the whirlwind. He asks Job if his arm is as strong as God's, and if he has a voice like the thunder of God. If so, perhaps Job can adorn himself with the same majesty, splendour, glory, and beauty that God displays inherently and, to some extent, through His many created beings. **V 11–14: WRATH AND WEAKNESS** If Job is able to display strength like God's, no doubt his wrath will be effective on those with whom he is angry. If that is so, God says that Job will also be able to save himself. Clearly Job can do neither, but God can do both. **V15–24: LOOK AND LEARN** God points out to Job the might and design of one of His created beings, Behemoth. This animal has certain characteristics of animals we know today, but seems different from them all. This seems to be a description of one of the now extinct dinosaurs.

CHAPTER FORTY-ONE

V 1–34: LOOK AT LEVIATHAN God then draws Job's attention to the most feared creature in creation, again which now appears to be extinct. The nearest we can get to him is a huge sea-going crocodile with fortified underbelly and added fearsome characteristics. He is more fearsome than Behemoth and, again, appears to be a sea-going dinosaur. He is so fearsome to the animal kingdom and humankind, but one of the small creations of a great God. God again impresses on Job that if God can make a creature like that, then God is well equipped to deal with Job and his problems, and He is in control.

CHAPTER FORTY-TWO

ss Job: 10:
V 1: REQUIRED REPLY Just as God has told Job he must reply, so Job does reply. All those from whom God requires an answer one day will be compelled to answer Him. **V 2: SUPREME SOVEREIGNTY** Job starts by acknowledging that God can do everything, and that His purpose is entirely sovereign. **V 3: CONTRITE CONFESSION** He confesses that he has spoken to God without understanding, and about things that are too wonderful for him to understand. **V 4–6: REVERENT REPENTANCE** Notwithstanding God's command to reply to Job, he humbly requests permission to speak to Him, reminding Him that God asked him to do this. Job tells God that now he has personal communications with Him, he repents in dust and ashes. His repentance is not for any specific sins that others may wrongly have thought caused his suffering. It is rather because, in the pressure of the suffering and in the frustration of the unhelpful contributions of the comforters, his attitude to God has sometimes been wrong. This is also because he has seen something of the splendour and majesty of God Himself. Even someone walking with the LORD closely has no alternative but to abhor himself and repent, when he realises how great and majestic his God really is. Job is no exception to that. **ss God speaks: 3: V 7–8: WRONG WORDS** God now speaks to Eliphaz about himself, Bildad, and Zophar. He tells them that His wrath is aroused against them because of the wrong words that they have used, reflecting wrong attitudes. Their guilt is increased further when God compares their wrong words with Job's right words. Elihu, the fourth comforter, is not included in the condemnation. Although he makes mistakes in his counsel, he has made no overt accusation that it was specific sin that actually caused Job's suffering. His criticism is more to do with Job's words than with Job's sufferings. There may be other reasons why God did not include him in the condemnation, of course. The three men are told to take

seven rams as sacrifices, and to go to Job, who will pray for them. God will accept his prayer, but not theirs, until sacrifice has been made and prayer has been made for them. **V 9: SACRIFICIAL SUPPLICATION** After Job's repentance and renewed trust in God have made him accepted by God, the three men obey God in making sacrifices to Him. **V 10–17: BOUNTIFUL BLESSINGS** After Job has prayed for his friends, God gives him bountiful blessings. He gets twice as much as before. His relatives and acquaintances come and eat with him again and console him. They bring him silver and gold. He has more livestock than before. He fathers another seven sons and three beautiful daughters, to whom he gives an

inheritance with the sons. He lives another 140 years and sees three generations of grandchildren following him. He dies 'old and full of days'. Here is a good principle for every Christian. Whatever our trials and tribulations are on earth, our final future with God is unmitigated and bountiful blessing. Note that at the end of the book, Job still does not know why he suffered. He simply learns to trust Almighty God who permitted it for His purposes, and for His servant's final good. His doubts and the arguments of others are dissipated when he listens to God as He speaks to him, and humbly repents and trusts Him. These are lessons we all still need to learn.

PSALMS OVERVIEW

PEOPLE AND PRELIMINARIES

The book of Psalms consists of one hundred and fifty chapters, the most in any book of the Bible. It is the second of the five poetical books of the Old Testament. See comments on Job. The book subdivides into five books, each ending with a doxology, but none of the five has any distinctive prevailing theme. God's character and every aspect of life are seen in each book. Under God, there were various authors of different Psalms. Nearly fifty Psalms have no named author. Of the others, David wrote at least half, Asaph wrote twelve, and the sons of Korah wrote ten. Other named authors are Solomon, Moses, Heman and Ethan. Through each and all of the human authors, God wrote the Book of Psalms, as He did the whole Bible. Obviously, many authors wrote in many places at different times between 1410 BC

and 450 BC. The time covered by Psalms is infinite, from before creation to 'for ever and ever'.

PLAN AND PURPOSE

The book of Psalms is by far the largest book in the Bible. Psalms 119 and 117 are the longest and shortest chapters in the Bible. This book mirrors human and spiritual experience at every level, and contains theological truth and inspired prophecy. It constantly points to God's glorious character and our need to approach Him humbly, honestly and reverently. It includes praise, thanksgiving, prayers, confessions, cries for help, laments, songs to be sung together (and alone!), Messianic prophecies, wisdom, poetry, prose, and proclamation. In fact, the book of Psalms echoes inspired biblical truth generally, mirrors real-life situations and struggles, and shows us our Lord. Many a person has found his own personal thoughts, moods, needs, problems, blessings and prayers already expressed in this unique section of God's Word and dealt with there by God's amazing grace.

PROFILE AND PROGRESSION

Book 1: Psalms 1–41; Book 2: Psalms 42–72; Book 3: Psalms 73–89; Book 4: Psalms 90–106; Book 5: Psalms 107–150.

PRINCIPLES AND PARTICULARS

Look for the 'Ps'—Praise, Prayer, Penitence, Persecution, Personal, Public, Prophecy, Principles, Preview of Christ. Some of the Psalms can be turned into immediate praise, penitence or prayer.

PSALMS

BOOK ONE—PSALM ONE TO PSALM FORTY-ONE

PSALM ONE

V 1–2: BLESSING God blesses the uncompromising and godly man who meditates on His Word. **V 3: BRINGING** This man will bring forth fruit, whatever the season. **V 4–6: BANISHED** Ungodly people are as blown chaff, neither able to stand in the judgement, nor to be found with those counted righteous. They will perish.

PSALM TWO

V 1–3: REBELLION Consider the stupidity of the nations in rebelling 'against the LORD and against His Anointed'. **V 4–5: REBUKE** God will rebuke them in His way

and in His time. Their position is laughable, though tragic. **V 6–9: RULE** The rule of God's Son is pictured. He shares sovereign power with the Father. **V 10–12: RESPONSE** In view of the truths expressed in these verses, even kings and judges must respond to God in wisdom, in heeding His instructions, in fearful service, in trembling rejoicing, and by trust in Him.

PSALM THREE

V 1–4: SHIELD Though opposed by many, David sees God as his shield, and much more! **V 4: SELAH** Used here, and elsewhere in the Psalms, the word 'Selah' literally tells us to stop and consider carefully what we have read. Here, it refers to God's hearing the psalmist's prayer. **V 5–6: SUSTAINED** In the midst of opposition from his son Absalom, David can sleep and then awaken, knowing that God sustains him despite his being surrounded by enemies. **V 7–8: SALVATION** 'Salvation belongs to the LORD', and, for this reason, David prays 'Save me, O my God!'

PSALM FOUR

V 1: SUPPLICATION David prays to be heard, and for God's mercy. **V 2–3: SEPARATE** He knows that God has set him apart from his enemies and will listen to his prayers. **V 4–5: SACRIFICE** David urges meditation and to offer God the sacrifice He treasures most, that of a righteous trust in Him. **V 6–8: SAFETY** Despite the despair of others, in the light of God's light, David knows that God can keep him safely.

PSALM FIVE

V 1–3: CRY David cries to God and

expects a response. Morning prayer is a part of David's life. **V 4–6: CONDEMNATION** Evil, arrogant, untruthful, bloodthirsty, and deceitful men are condemned by God. **V 7–8: CONSECRATION** By God's mercy and grace, David comes to God and commits himself to his merciful LORD. He asks to be clearly led by God in His righteousness. **V 9–10: CULPABLE** David's ungodly enemies sin greatly in their talk, as well as in a 'multitude of transgressions' that show their rebellion against God. **V 11–12: COMFORT** Gladness, singing, joy, and favour from God will surround and bless those who trust Him.

PSALM SIX

V 1–5: TROUBLE David is troubled both by physical and spiritual weakness. **V 6–7: TIRED** Sleeplessness and sorrow, in the face of his enemies, wear him down. **V 8–10: TRUSTING** Nevertheless, David knows that the LORD has heard him and will receive his prayer. He will be delivered from his enemies.

PSALM SEVEN

V 1–2: REFUGE In the face of cruel opposition, David turns to the LORD. **V 3–5: RIGHTEOUSNESS** David can tell the LORD that he is not a rebel against Him, nor unfair in his treatment of others. So sure is he of his honesty about this that he invites retribution against him if he is found to be lying. **V 6–10: RISE** David asks the LORD to rise up for him against his enemies. God is his defence. **V 11–16: RETRIBUTION** David knows that God, the 'just judge', will work appropriate retribution on his enemies who also oppose God. **V 17: RESULT** The result of all this is David's determination to praise the LORD.

PSALM EIGHT

V 1–2: LOFTINESS God's glory is 'above the heavens'. No wonder he can silence the enemy. **V 3–8: LOWLINESS** God's creation reminds man of his lowliness, and God reveals that man is made 'a little lower than the angels'. In fact, God has given man the task of overseeing the rest of His creation. **V 9: LORD** The Psalm finishes as it starts, by focusing on the LORD and by proclaiming the excellence of God's name throughout the earth.

PSALM NINE

V 1–2: PRAISE David's determination to praise God is wholehearted. He concentrates on God and on His 'marvellous works'. Gladness and rejoicing go hand-in-hand with praise. **V 3–6: PERISHING** God will judge nations and His enemies in the future, as He has in the past. **V 7–8: PERMANENCE** God, His justice and His righteous judgement are eternal. **V 9–10: PRESSURE** Those who trust in God find that they are not forsaken, but that He is a refuge for them when they are oppressed and in trouble. **V 11–12: PROCLAMATION** God's people are encouraged to praise God and declare what He has done. **V 13–14: PRAYER** David prays for mercy, asks for God to look after him, and states he will rejoice in God's salvation. **V 15–17: PIT** Again, David emphasises the eternal lostness of nations and people who reject God. **V 18: POOR** The poor and needy who trust in God will neither be forgotten nor shall they perish. **V 19–20: PREVAIL** David closes with a prayer for God to act so that man will not prevail, and that the nations will be judged and will realise that they are only men.

PSALM TEN

V 1: WHY? The psalmist asks why God seems a long way off and not to respond in his time of trouble. **V 2–11: WICKED** He then details some of the sins of the wicked, who think that God has forgotten and does not see what goes on. **V 12–15: WAITING** The psalmist goes on to wait on the Lord, now assured by God that He does see and can and will act. God helps him. **V 16–18: WORSHIP** Confidence in the eternal and kingly character of his God, and in the fact that He intervenes, ends this Psalm. God is in control and hears the psalmist's prayer.

PSALM ELEVEN

V 1–3: SETTLED David has settled his trust in the Lord. How then can he run away? If society's foundations crumble, where else can one's trust be safely placed? **V 4–6: SOVEREIGN** David's trust is fed as he considers the character of the Lord in whom He trusts. The Lord reigns in His temple and in His heaven. He tests His own people and will judge the wicked. God is in control! **V 7: SEEING** The Lord is righteous and loves righteousness. His face is set to look on His upright followers. He is looking at them.

PSALM TWELVE

V 1: WEAK David feels his own weakness and loneliness in the absence of godly men and faithful servants. **V 2–4: WANTON** The wicked show their disdain for God's standards by the wanton way they speak in idle conversation, flattery, hypocrisy, pride, and self-will. They reject God's lordship over them. **V 5: WILLING** God is always willing to help the poor and the needy who call to Him in any trouble, and keep them safe in Him during their pilgrimage on earth. **V 6–7: WORDS** God's words of purity, value, and eternal significance are contrasted with the vile conduct of the wicked. **V 8: WICKED** When vileness is exalted, the wicked prowl around everywhere.

PSALM THIRTEEN

V 1–2: PERSONAL PAIN David feels forgotten. He senses that God has hidden his face from him. He has daily sorrow as he sees his enemies apparently triumphing over him. **V 3–4: PRESSURE PRAYER** David asks God to consider and hear him and to enlighten him. Again he is conscious of pressure caused by the nearness and position of his enemies. **V 5–6: POSITIVE PURPOSE** David brings his song back to the bedrock of trusting in God's mercy, which he knows will enable him to rejoice in God's salvation and sing to God because of His bountiful dealings with him. Because he has trusted in God, rejoicing and singing to the Lord will follow in the train of that trust.

PSALM FOURTEEN

V 1: REBELLION The person who claims to be an atheist is a moral and spiritual rebel against God. He comes to that conclusion from a prejudiced heart, not from logical deduction of the mind. The basic reason is that he knows he is corrupted through sin, as his actions demonstrate. That is true for us all, but could it be that the atheist seeks to escape judgement for that sin by denying the existence of the Judge? **V 2–4: REGARDING** From heaven, God regards the conduct of sinners, and sees their rebellion against Him and their opposition to His people. David cannot understand their pointless opposition, persecution and refusal to call upon God. **V 5–6: REFUGE** The 'righteous' (those whose faith in God results in a holy lifestyle) have God with them as their refuge. They do not fear as the ungodly do. **V 7: REJOICING** The final rejoicing will be for those who love and know their saving and liberating God. This primarily applies to the Jews returning home from captivity, but is also true spiritually for any sinner turning from sin and coming home to God.

PSALM FIFTEEN

V 1: HOLY David asks who can be holy enough to approach God. **V 2-3: HEART** The answer is that God can be approached by an upright, truthful person whose conduct to others shows that his heart has been dealt with by God. In his cleansed heart, he will value truth because he knows the God of truth. His talk will reflect that. **V 4-6: HONOUR** Such a person will discern and oppose wickedness, and honour others who fear the LORD. He will keep his word and will not seek unfair financial gain. He will be unmoveable.

PSALM SIXTEEN

V 1-2: SUPPLICATION David prays for safety and refuge, acknowledging that every good thing comes from God. **V 3: SAINTS** God's set-apart people ('saints') are the object of David's delight, as well as God's, of course! **V 4: SORROWS** Idolatry will only bring sorrow upon people. **V 5-6: SUPPLY** David expresses his delight with God's supply and inheritance. **V 7-8: STABILITY** David praises God and His counsel, which he experiences even in the dark hours of the night. He sees God always before him and at his right hand, and knows that he will therefore not be shaken. **V 9-11: SECURITY** God's presence will be with David to the grave, through the grave, and beyond the grave. Eternally, he will be at the right hand of God.

PSALM SEVENTEEN

V 1-6: HEAR ME Again, David asks that God will hear him. He harbours no known sin. **V 7: SHOW ME** He asks to be made aware of his saving God's wonderful love. **V 8a: KEEP ME** He asks to be kept as the apple of God's eye. **V 8b-12: HIDE ME** He asks that, as a dangerous enemy stalks him, God will hide him under the shadow of His wings. **V 13-14: DELIVER ME** David asks for God's deliverance from his enemies. **V 15: BLESS ME** David will be satisfied with seeing the righteousness of God and being made like Him, when he awakes. Surely this reminds us, also, of the blessed satisfaction to be experienced by all who know God when they awaken from the sleep of death into God's welcoming and glorious presence.

PSALM EIGHTEEN

V 1-6: MY GOD 'I', 'me', and 'my' show the personal nature of David's relationship with God. **V 7-12: MAJESTIC GOD** Nature shows the majesty and power of God. **V 13-24: MIGHTY GOD** God, who is powerful in the thunderstorm, is the same God who has looked after David and kept him up till now. He has not only delivered him from an overwhelmingly strong enemy, but also enabled him to live righteously. **V 25-50: MERCIFUL GOD** The many blessings David has received include enlightenment, strength, stability, fighting ability, salvation, victory, deliverance, promotion, and the desire to thank and praise. All these blessings can be traced back to God's mercy to David. He summarises it as follows: 'Great deliverance He gives to His king, And shows mercy to His anointed, To David and his descendants forevermore.' God's mercy is the key to His rich treasure chest of grace.

PSALM NINETEEN

V 1–6: REVELATION IN HEAVENS' SPLENDOURS The reality and goodness of God is written in the heavens for all mankind to see. **V 7–11: REVELATION IN HOLY SCRIPTURE** But it is only through God using His Word that a soul can be converted and a heart can be changed. His Word is perfect, sure, right, pure, clean and true. It radically changes the lives of anyone who trusts in it. To such a person, God's Word is more valuable than gold, and sweeter than honey. **V 12–14: RESPONSE IN HEARTFELT SUBMISSION** The only appropriate response is for David to turn from sin, and to have his heart, mind and mouth controlled by submission to the LORD who alone is his 'strength' and 'Redeemer'.

PSALM TWENTY

V 1–5: COMFORT David knows that although God's people will have trouble and enemies, He saves, defends, helps, strengthens, and blesses them. **V 6: CONFIRMATION** David is confident that his God will answer his prayer and save him. He has been here before! **V 7–8: COMPARISON** David compares those with no knowledge of God who will fall, despite their confidence in chariots and horses, with those who will stand finally because 'they remember the name of the LORD our God'. **V 9: CRY** In two words, David prays the most important prayer of all: 'Save, LORD!' He asks his King to answer that prayer.

PSALM TWENTY-ONE

V 1–7: ENTHUSIASM David's enthusiasm in prayer is motivated by gratitude, and the realisation of who God is and what He has done. **V 8–12: ENEMIES** God's enemies have become David's enemies because he seeks to walk with God. He commits them into God's hand for Him to deal with them. **V 13: EXALTATION** David wants God to exalt Himself. He, with others, will sing and praise God's power.

PSALM TWENTY-TWO

V 1–2: HELPLESS This Psalm is set in the immediate context of David's position and sentiments. But it is also Messianic, depicting aspects of the death of Christ hundreds of years before death by crucifixion was known, as if it had already happened. The comments on this Psalm concentrate on the death of Jesus Christ as pictured here. It reflects the submission of the One who has put Himself in a place of helplessness, emptied Himself, and become forsaken on the cross by His Father. **V 3–5: HOLY** God's holiness is seen here as in His faithful dealings with Israel in the past. **V 6–8: HUMILITY** Beyond David's current feelings and predicament, we see the self-humbling of Jesus in these verses as a 'worm', and not as a man. See the reproach, lies and spite of those who ridicule Him and mock Him. **V 9–11: HISTORY** Jesus, the Son of Man, although conceived by the Holy Spirit through the virgin Mary, knows God as His Father in eternity, from eternity and for eternity. **V 12–13: HOSTILITY** Hostility abounds at the cross where men, like animals, encircle Jesus and threaten Him. **V 14–15: HEART** Not only does His body suffer, being out of joint on the cross, and His tongue dries up sticking to His jaws, but the heart of the Saviour is like melted wax on that cross as He bears our sin. **V 16–18: HORRIFIC** Christ is surrounded by wicked people baying for His death. His hands and feet are pierced and His bones can be seen, accentuated in His suspended and stretched body. Even His garments are the subject for division among the soldiers, who cast lots for some of them. This is a horrific way to treat any man, especially the sinless Son of God. (Remember that Psalm 22 was prophetically written before execution by crucifixion—a Roman, not Jewish form of death penalty—was practised.) **V 19–21a: HASTEN** Although abandoned on the cross, while bearing our sin, Jesus knows that His Father is not far away and that the resurrection will follow. He will be raised from the dead. He can pray for God the Father's hastening to help Him. **V 21b–24: HEARD** He knows that His prayer is heard. He will rise from the dead. **V 25–31: HOPE** As a result of the crucifixion of the Messiah, blessing will come on all sorts and conditions of people. Seekers will come to Him from all the ends of the world, from all nations, poor and prosperous, from dying and living, and from those yet to come. Only God can accomplish this. They rightly will say, 'He has done this.'

PSALM TWENTY-THREE

V 1–2: SHEPHERD David knows, as we can, that the LORD is his Shepherd. The meeting of his wants, rest and refreshment come through that wonderful relationship. **V 3: SOUL** With his soul restored, he is guided by his Shepherd in the paths of righteousness 'for His name's sake'. **V 4: SHADOW** Even when death casts its shadow in the valley, there is no fear of evil, because of the presence, protection and guidance of the LORD. **V 5–6: SURELY** The present experience of being fed and anointed by God encourages David to know 'surely' that goodness and mercy will be his during the rest of his life and throughout eternity.

PSALM TWENTY-FOUR

V 1–2: FULNESS AND FOUNDATION All the earth belongs to the LORD and everything in it. As the Creator God, He founded it and established it. **V 3–6: CLEANNESS AND CONSECRATION** Because God requires holiness, clean hands and a pure heart are required to approach Him. Such consecration will lead to a refusal of idolatry, to honest speaking, and to God's great blessing now and in the future. Those who seek Him will be blessed with His salvation and righteousness. **V 7–10: WORSHIP AND WONDER** In a Messianic portion dealing with Christ's coming in His kingdom, we sense the worship, the wonder, the strength and the might of the 'King of glory', 'the LORD of hosts'.

PSALM TWENTY-FIVE

V 1–3: TRUST David underlines his trust in God even though facing enemies and treacherous people. **V 4–5: TEACH** David asks for God to teach him His paths and His truth. His basis is that he knows the God of salvation and waits upon Him. **V 6–7: TENDERNESS** When asking for God's mercy over all his sins, he realises that they are 'tender mercies' and 'lovingkindnesses'. God is tender to those who repent and trust Him. **V 8–15: 'THEREFORE'** Because God is 'good' and 'upright', certain things follow, including His teaching, His guidance, His mercy and truth, His pardon, His spiritual and physical blessings, His covenant and His deliverance. He is delivered from his enemies' net as he looks to the LORD. **V 16–22: TROUBLES** David prays to God about His own desolation, afflictions, troubles, distresses and pain. He asks God to keep him in integrity and uprightness. He is also concerned for his people. He asks God to redeem Israel from 'all their troubles'.

PSALM TWENTY-SIX

V 1–5: PERSONAL David communes with God about himself. He asks God to vindicate him and he confesses his trust in the LORD, whom he asks to test him and try him to verify his walk with Him. He wants that walk to be separate from the influence of sinners who oppose him. **V 6–8: PROCLAMATION** Still in personal mode, David declares that he will proclaim aloud God's praise and tell of all His 'wondrous works'. He loves to worship God in the tabernacle. **V 9–10: PLEA** He asks to be spared from being dealt with in the same way as sinners and bloodthirsty men. They are wicked schemers and motivated by bribes. **V 11–12: PURPOSE** He purposes to walk in integrity through God's redemption and mercy. He wants to stand and bless God in the congregations.

PSALM TWENTY-SEVEN

V 1–8: TESTIMONY David's testimony is that the LORD is his light and his salvation. This drives away fear in the face of the enemy and gives him great confidence. He knows that, as he seeks God, He will keep him in the time of trouble and hide him. He will be enabled to praise God and to seek His face. **V 9–13: TRIALS** But trials do come through enemies, false witnesses, and violent men. In those trials, David prays for God to keep and care for him,

especially when he feels alone. He is encouraged to know that he will see the goodness of God 'in the land of the living'. **V 14: TRUST** In this confidence, he is determined to urge others also to 'wait on the LORD' in dependent trust. This will encourage God's people and strengthen them. He repeats it for emphasis: 'Wait, I say, on the LORD!' This is good advice for us all.

PSALM TWENTY-EIGHT

V 1–5: HEAR AND HELP David asks God to hear his prayer, knowing that the LORD is his Rock who answers. He requests God's continuing help with regard to those who oppose him. **V 6–7: HEARD AND HELPED!** He blesses God because he knows that his prayer has been heard and that he is being helped. God is his strength and shield. Accordingly, his heart greatly rejoices and is set to praise Him in song. **V 8–9: HAPPY AND HIS** David's rejoicing is that God is His people's 'strength' and the 'saving refuge of his anointed'. He asks God to bless His people, His inheritance. He wants God to shepherd them, and to 'bear them up for ever'. David's concern is wider than his own personal needs and extends to the people of God as well. They are all 'His'.

PSALM TWENTY-NINE

V 1–2: HEAVENLY HOLINESS The 'mighty ones' in heaven itself are told to 'worship the LORD in the beauty of holiness'. They are to realise His glory and strength, as well as the eternal value of His name. **V 3–10: WORLD'S WONDERS** The 'voice of the LORD' demonstrates the power of God in His wonderful creation, and speaks of His majestic character and strength. **V 11: PEACEFUL PEOPLE** This LORD is the one who blesses His people with peace and strengthens them to live for Him, to witness for Him, and to praise Him.

PSALM THIRTY

V 1–3: LIFTING LORD David praises God. Just as God has lifted him, he responds by gratefully praising God for His gracious works towards him. God has delivered him. **V 4–5: SINGING SAINTS** David exhorts the saints to praise God, to thank Him, to remember His holy name, and to remember that 'joy comes in the morning'. **V 6–7: FORTIFYING FAVOUR** David realises that it is not his prosperity which will make him unmoveable, as he had once wrongly said, but God's favour. Sometimes God hides His face in order that people might discover that lesson. **V 8–10: HEARING HELPER** David knows that without God's presence and help, all is vain, and he asks the LORD to hear him and to be his helper. **V 11–12: PURPOSEFUL PRAISE** Grateful that God has changed his heart and his circumstances, David is determined to glorify and praise God and to thank Him for ever.

PSALM THIRTY-ONE

V 1–5: ASKING David asks his Redeemer for deliverance and guidance. **V 6–8: AGAINST** David declares himself to be against idolatry, and confides in God, who has given him liberty, security and stability. **V 9–13: ANGUISH** The anguish of David's soul, aggravated by opposition from his enemies, is matched by his physical ailments. **V 14–18: AFFIRMATION** David affirms his trust in God and in God's timing. He asks God to deliver him from shame. **V 19–22: ASSURANCE** David reminds himself of who God is and how good He is. He

reflects on what He has done for him before in answer to his prayer. **V 23–24: ARRIVAL** David arrives at a place of personal confidence in God and encourages other saints of God to love the LORD. He is encouraged and knows that God will give strength.

PSALM THIRTY-TWO

V 1–2: SINS COVERED There is immense blessedness in having transgression forgiven, sins covered, and no iniquity imputed to the sinner. This removes deceit and guile from the spirit of the forgiven person. **V 3–4: SILENT COMPARISON** When David has not prayed but kept silent, he has been conscious of groaning and heaviness upon him. **V 5: SINCERE CONFESSION** God forgives his sin as soon as he confesses it to Him. David follows a good practice and a good principle in not trying to hide his sin from God. **V 6–7: SURE CAUSE** 'For this cause', all should seek God when He can be found, and find in Him a hiding place and preservation from trouble. Deliverance will be accompanied by songs of gratitude. **V 8–9: SPIRITUAL COUNSEL** The forgiven person begins to understand God's instructions and is assured of His guidance in walking with the LORD in the way he should go. **V 10–11: SORROWFUL CONTRAST** Although the wicked will be surrounded by many sorrows, those trusting in God are confident of His surrounding mercy. Joy and rejoicing accompany those who, by God's grace, are counted righteous and live uprightly.

PSALM THIRTY-THREE

V 1–3: RIGHTEOUS AND REJOICING God tells His righteous people to rejoice, praise, make melody, and sing a new song. Who said that knowing the LORD is miserable or boring? **V 4–5: WORD AND WORK** The earth, filled with God's goodness, is testimony to His word being right and His work being truthful. He, Himself, is righteous and just. **V 6–9: COMMAND AND CREATION** By the command of God's word, all of creation came into being and stands fast. The earth should fear God because of this, and should stand in awe of Him. **V 10–17: POWER AND PEOPLE** God is sovereign over all types and groupings of people, and even uses their plans to accomplish His sovereign will in an amazing way. People are blessed as He works in individual hearts. His ability to save is far beyond that of a strong army with military might. **V 18–19: INDIVIDUALITY AND INTEREST** Although God rules over everything in His sovereignty, He takes an individual interest in each person who fears Him and hopes in His mercy. He will deliver from death the souls of those who fear Him and He will keep them alive in famine. **V 20–22: COMMITMENT AND CONFIDENCE** The response from those who love Him is to wait upon Him, to recognise His help and defence, and to rejoice confidently. Mercy and help come from trusting in His name.

PSALM THIRTY-FOUR

V 1–3: PERSONAL PRAISE David, delivered from Abimelech, expresses his desire to praise the LORD at all times and continually. His boast is in the LORD, and he wishes others to join him in magnifying God who has blessed him. **V 4–7: GODLY GRATITUDE** He expresses his gratitude to God for delivering him, for answering his prayers, for saving him from troubles, and for encamping all round those who fear Him, through His angel. **V 8–10: TASTY TRUST** He encourages all to taste God's goodness and blessedness which come

from trusting in Him. Such a personal trust brings the assurance of God's complete and faithful support. **V 11–22: INSPIRED INSTRUCTION** David is inspired to instruct God's children in God's ways. Refusal to engage in evil speaking, in deceit, and in wrongdoing marks the man who fears the LORD in brokenness and contrition. God hears, sees, delivers, redeems, and saves those who trust Him. This Psalm reflects how the principles of God's word are experienced by one who trusts God. He will face afflictions, but he will be delivered, guided and redeemed by God.

PSALM THIRTY-FIVE

V 1–10: PERSONAL PLEA David asks God personally to plead his cause with and fight against those who are pursuing him. He asks for assurance from God that He is his salvation, and that his enemies will be confused, chased, and destroyed. He promises to rejoice in God's salvation when this happens. **V 11–18: WICKED WITNESSES** David raises with God the fierce opposition of false and wicked witnesses who have arisen against him. David feels this opposition even more because he had been good to them in the past and prayed for them earnestly as a brother. Now, he asks God to intervene in this, too, and to act for him promptly. Again, he promises to praise God and thank Him. **V 19–28: VICTORIOUS VINDICATION** David anticipates further opposition from those who have already opposed him. He asks God to intervene again and work against them. Once more, he undertakes to praise God vigorously and to magnify God in praise and in speaking about His righteousness. In each section of this Psalm, it is interesting that, at the darkest points, David anticipates both God's working to help him and his worship of God that will follow.

PSALM THIRTY-SIX

V 1–4: WICKED The transgression of wicked people occupies David's thoughts. The evil man does not fear God, flatters himself, and is deceitful, foolish, and scheming to pursue his wicked plans. **V 5–9: WONDER** David marvels at God's mercy, faithfulness, righteousness, judgements, lovingkindness, protection, fulfilment, life and light. He has a wonderful God. So have we! **V 10–12: WANTING** David's great desire is that God's lovingkindness and righteousness should continue to the upright in heart. He prays against straying from God because of pride within or because of external opposition. He does not want to be like workers of iniquity who are unable to rise, once cast down.

PSALM THIRTY-SEVEN

V 1–8: RESTFUL RELATIONSHIP David is troubled by what seems to be the success of the wicked. He passes on to others what God has shown him. God tells him not to fret because that 'only causes harm'. Rather, he must trust in the LORD, to dwell and feed on Him, to delight himself in God, to commit his way to God, to rest in and wait for Him, and to cease from anger and wrath. These responses enable a man of God to stand, regardless of the outward circumstances or inner pressures. **V 9–17: WAYS OF WICKEDNESS** Even though the wicked will vent their fury against the righteous, God will judge them and cut them off. All that they have will be nothing, compared with the blessings of the righteous man who is upheld by God. **V 18–26: SUPPORTED SAINTS** God knows, cares for, supports, upholds, and is merciful to those who trust Him. Saints of God must keep their eyes on the spiritual and eternal big picture, rather than on the passing scene of time. **V 27–38: PRACTICAL PROGRESSION** Knowing all this, David encourages God's people to depart from evil and do good, to treasure God's law, to believe in God's faithfulness, to wait on Him, to keep His way, and to follow godly examples of people who walk with God. God will keep them, bless them and give them His peace. They must remember the future of the wicked, who will be cut off, compared with the peace and eternal blessings of those who trust in God. **V 39–40: STRONG SALVATION** God provides believers with salvation, strength, and deliverance. He will 'save them, because they trust in Him'.

PSALM THIRTY-EIGHT

V 1–2: CHASTENED David is being chastened by conviction of his sin as well as by the opposition of others. God uses conviction and circumstances to bless and guide His people into a closer walk with Him. **V 3–10: CONVICTED** David's heart is in turmoil and his whole being afflicted by his guilt. This Psalm does not indicate what that sin may be, but this experience is by no means new to Christians. **V 11–14: CONFRONTED** While loved ones, friends, and relatives stand away from David, others deceitfully plan against him all day long and seek to kill him. He seems unable to respond. **V 15–20: CONFESSING** Tossed about both by his conscience and his circumstances, David's helplessness is accentuated and he turns to God. He asks Him to answer his prayer. He declares his iniquity and is in anguish over his sin. Even as he confesses his sin, he realises how much he depends on God to overthrow enemy opposition. A sense of weakness often helps heartfelt confession and speeds restoration. **V 21–22: CRY** The whole of the Psalm is summarised in the last two verses which are a cry from David not to be forsaken, to know God's presence, to be helped, and to be saved. He stresses that God is 'my God'. He can only pray to God for His salvation and nearness on the basis that his confession of sin leads him to surrender to Him.

PSALM THIRTY-NINE

V 1: MUZZLED MOUTH So aware is David that he may say the wrong thing in the presence of wicked people, that he vows to say nothing at all. **V 2–3: HOT HEART** In his silence and sorrow, David's heart is hot within him and, as the fire burns within, he has to speak. **V 4–6: LIMITED LIFESPAN** David asks God to help him realise how short his life is, and not to imitate the wicked in gathering passing treasures. **V 7–11: PRESSURE PRAYER** David asks God to deliver him from his transgressions and from being a reproach to the foolish. He knows that he is helpless without God. He asks for restoration. **V 12–13: LISTEN, LORD** David asks God to hear his prayer and his cry, and to answer him. He feels that he is a victim of God's distant gaze, but prays that God will deal with him again and strengthen him.

PSALM FORTY

V 1: PATIENCE David's patience in waiting for God is rewarded by the assurance that God has inclined to him and heard his cry. **V 2: PIT** He was morally and spiritually in a pit of clay before God answered him, lifted him out, and established him on solid rock. Now he walks with God. **V 3–5: PRAISE** His gratitude at his deliverance expands into a song of praise and an acknowledgement of how wonderful God is and how wonderful His works are. **V 6–8: PURPOSE** His purpose now is to please God, not in the superficial giving of sacrifices, but in a desire to do His will. There is an echo of this prayer later from Jesus in Gethsemane. **V 9–10: PROCLAMATION** David proclaims God's good news in the great assembly. He has hidden nothing from others of what he knows about God. He reveals the truths about God's righteousness, faithfulness, and salvation. **V 11–12: PRAYER** David still appreciates his essential dependence upon God, and asks Him not to withhold His tender mercies or lovingkindness. Without God's help, he cannot look up from the burden of his sins. **V 13–15: PROTECTION** He also asks for protection from his enemies who want to triumph over him in mocking scorn. **V 16–17: POOR** David balances the rejoicing in God's salvation and the matter of magnifying the LORD with his constant need to recognise his own poverty and need before God. It is as we humble ourselves before God that He lifts us spiritually. David asks God not to delay in helping him, knowing that God thinks about him, helps him and delivers him.

PSALM FORTY-ONE

V 1–3: DELIVERANCE A man whose heart is so trusting in the LORD (and pleasing Him that he considers the poor) can be sure that God will deliver him in his great hour of need. David finds this is so. **V 4–9: DEATH?** David's enemies ask when he is going to die, they devise his hurt, and reveal that the illness he is obviously suffering might lead to his death. Even his close friend turned on him in his hour of need. **V 10–13: DEFINITE** But David's response is definite. He prays to God for His mercy to raise him up. He thanks God that his enemy does not triumph over him. He ends with a note of definite praise to the Everlasting God and duplicates his 'Amen'.

BOOK TWO—PSALM FORTY-TWO TO PSALM SEVENTY-TWO

PSALM FORTY-TWO

V1–4: LONGING The psalmist longs and thirsts for God like a thirsty deer which has run to the water brook. His mockers cast doubt on his God, but he remembers the joy and spirit of praise enjoyed when he worshipped God, with God's people, in the past. **V 5–7: LAMENT** He laments that his soul is cast down within him. For that reason, he will remember God, as waves and billows of sorrow pass over him. **V 8: LOVE** However, his confidence is that God's lovingkindness will support him during the day and that he will have a song in the night and a prayer to God. **V 9–10: LOGIC** It is logical for him to pass on to God his concern that his enemies are oppressing him and that he feels forgotten and forsaken. Surely God can help him as they question His very existence. **V 11: LORD** Despite the fact that he repeats again his downcast state to God, he realises that he must hope in God, and that help will come from God. He will praise God again. The last two words are 'my God'. In times of distress, it is good to remember our personal relationship with the Lord.

PSALM FORTY-THREE

V 1: REPRESENTATION The psalmist asks God to vindicate him and plead his cause against an ungodly nation. Represented by God, he asks for deliverance from deceitful and unjust men. **V 2: REJECTION**

He senses that God has rejected him and cast him off because he experiences enemy oppression. This is not the case but this is what he feels. **V 3: RESTORATION** He pleads for God's light and truth to come to him, to lead him, and to take him in worship to the tabernacle. **V 4: REJOICING** When he is thus restored, he pledges himself to rejoice in God and praise Him. **V 5: REASON** As in Psalm 42, reason prevails after prayer, and he knows that God will bless him and help him.

PSALM FORTY-FOUR

V 1–3: HISTORY The psalmists, the sons of Korah, reflect that God has blessed, helped, fought for, and saved His people in times past. **V 4–8: HOPE** This leads them to a firm hope that, through God, they will continue to be victorious and boast in God's name, which they will keep on praising. **V 9–22: HUMBLED** But for now, they lament their state of defeat and dejection. They are doing badly against their enemies and turn this matter into prayer to God. They remind Him that their defeat is in spite of the fact that they have kept faithful to God. **V 23–26: HELP** Although God is not asleep, it seems to them as though He is and they ask Him to awaken and help and redeem them. Their basis for asking this is His 'mercies' sake'. The Psalm is a good pattern for how to pray when we are unaware of specific sin, and yet things seem to have gone wrong. There are times when we have no answer except to keep trusting Him.

PSALM FORTY-FIVE

V 1: MONARCH The psalmist writes about the king, possibly on the occasion of a wedding, picturing the King of kings, who comes for His bride, the church. **V 2–9: MAJESTY** The grace, glory and goodness of the King are proclaimed. Some of these Messianic verses are quoted in the New Testament, to give us reason to apply them to Christ. **V 10–15: MARVEL** The address to the bride shows how the King marvels at her. What a thought, that one day, purified and glorified, the King of kings will marvel at His redeemed church. **V 16–17: MEMORY** Through the church, many will be brought into new birth and new life spiritually. This will cause the King's name to be remembered in all generations, through all ages, for ever.

PSALM FORTY-SIX

V 1–3: REFUGE The psalmist is grateful for the strong refuge, strength and help in God which will endure both through time and eternity. **V 4–6: RIVER** Refreshment, as from a river, flows from God to His people. In the midst of opposition, His city will stand! God is powerful and He will help. **V 7: REASSURANCE** In that situation, the psalmist knows that the LORD of hosts is with them and that God is their refuge, as He was for Jacob. **V 8–10: REQUESTS** The psalmist bids his hearers to come and see God's works and power. God can stop wars at will, when His timetable so directs. God intervenes directly with a command which is also an invitation. He tells them to be still and to know Him. He will be exalted among the nations and in the earth. **V 11: REMINDER** The psalm ends with a reminder that God is with His people, and is a refuge to those who trust Him.

PSALM FORTY-SEVEN

V 1–4: ACCLAMATION The psalmist acclaims God as the 'Most High', as 'awesome', and the 'great King'. He will subdue nations and choose His people's inheritance. **V 5–7: ASCENSION** The ascension of the Lord Jesus Christ is foreseen in verses 5 and 7 after his resurrection. God is seen to be 'the King of all the earth'. **V 8–9: ASSEMBLY** God not only reigns over the nations, but also rules over the assembled princes of His people. He is greatly exalted.

PSALM FORTY-EIGHT

V 1–3: GOD'S PRESENCE God is present in Mount Zion, and is the refuge of His holy city of Jerusalem. **V 4–8: GOD'S PURPOSE** Jerusalem has always attracted the attention of kings. God's purpose is to establish Jerusalem for ever. The Christian knows that this will be realised eternally in the New Jerusalem, in the new heavens and the new earth wherein dwells righteousness. **V 9–13: GOD'S PRAISE** Based on His lovingkindness, name, and righteousness, God is to be proclaimed and praised to generations following. **V 14: GOD'S PERSEVERANCE** God is the God of His people for ever and will guide them until death. After that, no guidance will be needed because they will be at the perfect destination with Him eternally!

PSALM FORTY-NINE

V 1–4: WISDOM FOR ALL Here, wisdom is being spoken and sung about, and all people are asked to listen. **V 5: WHY FEAR ANYTHING?** With God's wisdom and perspective, there is no need to fear the 'days of evil'. **V 6–14: WEALTH'S FEEBLE ACCOMPLISHMENT** Those who trust in riches are not prepared for eternity. No soul can be ransomed eternally and no person can be saved from death by riches. Everyone will leave everything behind at death. **V 15: WONDERFUL FUTURE AWAITED** The psalmist knows that he will be redeemed from the power of the grave and be received by God in eternity. 'Selah' means 'Stop and think about that!' We should do that. **V 16–20: WHAT FALSE APPRECIATION** The person who dies trusting in riches, rather than in God, will never see light, but perish. His earthly glory will not accompany him beyond death. Animals have the same sort of limited earthly understanding as a rich man who trusts in what he has now.

PSALM FIFTY

V 1–3: THE WONDER OF GOD God's might, word, perfection, beauty and powerful holiness bring forth adoration from the psalmist. **V 4–15: THE WAYS OF GOD** God's dealings with men involve judgement, accepting His people by a covenant made with Him by sacrifice, obedience from the heart, and thanksgiving. He is not interested with mere externals, even though that results in sacrifices being made. He requires His people to call on Him sincerely. He will deliver them and they will glorify Him. **V 16–22: THE WRATH OF GOD** But God will judge the wicked who do not approach Him in the way He has prescribed. He hates their dishonesty, conspiracy to steal, adultery, deceit and slander. There will be no deliverance unless people come to Him on His terms. **V 23: THE WILL OF GOD** It is God's will that people should praise Him and honour Him in their conduct. They will see God's salvation.

PSALM FIFTY-ONE

V1–2: CRY David, has committed adultery with Bathsheba and has murdered, by proxy, her husband, Uriah. He has been confronted directly about his sin by Nathan, God's prophet. His response is to cry to God for mercy, for the blotting out of his transgressions, and for thorough cleansing. Psalm 51 records that response. **V 3–4: CONFESSION** He acknowledges and confesses his sin before God, who has seen everything. Although he has harmed others, his sin is primarily against God. **V 5–6: CONCEPTION** David acknowledges his sinful nature within, which he received at birth. This explains his wickedness but does not justify any individual act of sinfulness. His problem is his deep-rooted sinfulness. It is there where God needs to deal with him in His truth and wisdom. **V 7–9: CLEANSING** So, again, David pleads for cleansing, knowing that God can make him whiter than snow. Broken and joyless, he asks God to turn His back on his sins, to blot them out, and to restore God's joy and gladness to him. **V 10: CREATION** He asks God to create a clean heart within him and to renew a right spirit to him. **V 11: CONCERN** David is so experiencing conviction of sin that he is concerned lest God should cast him from His presence for ever and take His Holy Spirit from him. The very fact that he knows conviction of sin shows that God's Holy Spirit is working in him and that God will not abandon him. **V 12–16: CONSEQUENCES** David knows that the consequences of coming back to God are restoration and renewal. The joy of God's salvation will also be restored and he will be upheld by God. Only then can he teach transgressors God's ways and see sinners converted. So he asks to be delivered from his sin and for God to open his lips to praise Him. He knows that mere superficial giving of sacrifices means nothing without heartfelt repentance and returning to God. **V 17: CONTRITION** David demonstrates brokenness and contrition that he knows God will not despise. God welcomes sincere repentant sinners who return to Him. **V 18–19:**

CONSOLIDATION When restored himself, David can pray for the area of responsibility God has given him in Zion. He can then offer sacrifices because his heart is right with God.

PSALM FIFTY-TWO

V 1–4: CONCEIT David, thinking of Doeg who betrayed him to Saul, asks why he boasts. His enemy lives for destruction, deceit and evil. He lies. In contrast, David reminds himself that God's goodness endures continually. V 5–7: CATASTROPHE God will destroy this evil man. take him away and uproot him. The righteous will have the 'last laugh' at this man who trusts in riches and wickedness, rather than in God. V 8–9: COMPARISON David compares himself favourably with Doeg, even though he is being persecuted. Trusting in God's mercy, he is kept alive and as fresh as a green olive tree. This is by God's doing, not his. So he will praise God for ever with the other saints of God. He will wait on God's name.

PSALM FIFTY-THREE

V 1: PREJUDICE The atheist is a fool who is prejudiced against God. He is corrupt and sinful. Rather than using his mind to think objectively and fairly, he reacts from his prejudiced heart that there is 'no God'. This is not rational deduction but sinful bias coming from a heart at enmity with God. V 2: PRE-EMINENCE God is so far above man that He looks down from heaven to observe whether there are any who seek Him. He is pre-eminent. V 3–4: PRIDE Instead of seeking God, man's pride makes him turn away, and he becomes corrupt. No one does good by nature, and that is why there is persecution against God's people, and a refusal to call upon God. V 5: PETRIFIED

But the time will come when those who were formerly relatively at peace will be in great fear when circumstances change. In that day, those who despise God, by refusing even to admit that He exists, will be in greater fear still when they realise that God despises them because of their arrogance, pride and unbelief. V 6: PRAYER David completes the Psalm with a heartfelt prayer for God's salvation for His people which will produce liberty and rejoicing. Even those who deny Him today can know His blessing if they will turn in repentance to Him, and become a part of His spiritual people.

PSALM FIFTY-FOUR

V 1–3: SAVE! The Psalm begins by David's request to God to save him. Saul is persecuting him at the time of this prayer. David is also opposed by strangers. The title of the Psalm reveals that he is oppressed by the Ziphites. They are apostate Israelites who help Saul and reject David's God as well as David himself. V 4–5: SUPPORT David knows, however, that God is his helper, and that He will help those who support him. He will deal with His enemies. V 6–7: SACRIFICE David will sacrifice to God and praise Him. He is full of gratitude for God's deliverance, dealing with his enemies.

PSALM FIFTY-FIVE

V 1–3: TROUBLE David is troubled by those who oppress him. So he asks God to listen to his prayer, especially as his spirit is restless. V 4–8: TEMPEST David would like to fly away like a bird because he knows he is a target for murder. He sees that as escaping the coming tempest. V 9–11: THREATENING He asks God to intervene to destroy and confuse his enemies who seek for him in violence and strife. Trouble, iniquity, destruction, oppression and deceit lurk in the city where they practise their violence. **V 12–14: TIES** This is all the worse for David because he knows his enemy well. He was once very close to David and even went to worship God with him. Opposition is always more painful when it is the result of betrayal. **V 15–19: TURNING** David can see no alternative but to ask God to destroy his enemies. He cries to God to save him. Three times a day he will pray, knowing that God has rebuked him in the past and will hear him now. He is confident that God will deal with his enemies, even though they show no fear of God at this stage. **V 20–21: TREACHERY** He thinks, again, of his former close friend, and laments his treachery. The hypocrisy of his smooth words, when his heart seeks David's destruction, causes real anguish to David. Many think that he is referring to his son, Absalom. Others think he has Ahithophel in mind. Those who feel betrayed by close friends, even Christians, can imagine how David feels. **V 22–23: TRUST** David knows that he can trust God, cast his burden on Him, and know His sustaining power. God is well able to deal with the worst of his enemies. His determination is 'but I will trust in You'.

PSALM FIFTY-SIX

V 1–2: IN GOD—MERCY David, captured by the Philistines, uses the phrase 'in God' several times in this psalm. The thought permeates the whole of the psalm and is linked with David's determination to praise God's word. Although the first two verses do not use the actual phrase 'in God', they show that he knows that, in God, there is mercy to sustain him in his plight. **V 3–4: IN GOD—TRUST** Whenever

David fears, he will trust God in whom his faith has been placed. He knows that, because of that trust, he will live to praise God's word. **V 5–11: IN GOD—SUPPORT** David knows God's support and that 'God is for me'. He cries to the LORD as his enemies twist his words, devise evil against him, and threaten his life. God has numbered his wanderings and is aware of his tears as he cries to Him for help. Twice, David repeats with confidence that he will praise God's word because he is trusting in him. David will not be afraid because of what can man do to him, seeing as God is for him. **V 12–13: IN GOD—PRAISE** David recognises the vows he has made are binding on him and he will praise God who has delivered him from death before and kept his feet from falling. He will walk before Him in 'the light of the living'. Trusting in God's mercy and support brings forth grateful praise.

PSALM FIFTY-SEVEN

V 1: MY SOUL Hiding from Saul in a cave, David declares that his soul trusts in God and he hides in the shadow of His wings until the calamities have passed him. He seeks God's mercy. **V 2–3: MY SAVIOUR** He knows that the One to whom he cries shall send help from heaven and save him because of His mercy and truth. **V 4: MY SITUATION** David feels that his soul is in the lions' den! **V 5: MY SUPPLICATION** His prayer is in the context of God being exalted and glorified. **V 6: MY STEPS** Because his enemies have prepared a net and dug a pit for him, David has to place each step carefully. Because of this, his soul is bowed down. **V 7a: MY STEADFASTNESS** Nevertheless, David declares twice to God that his heart is steadfast. **V 7b–10: MY SONG** Because of his trust in God in adverse circumstances,

David declares that he will sing and give praise to God, and one day will sing to Him among the nations. The reason for his song is God's far-reaching mercy and truth. **V 11: MY SOVEREIGN** David asks that his sovereign God, who is above the heavens, will be seen to be exalted, and that His glory will be seen to be above all the earth. His desire is to glorify God.

PSALM FIFTY-EIGHT

V 1–2: INJUSTICE Violence, wickedness, and ungodly judgement surround David. **V 3–5: INIQUITY** The iniquity of human nature is described. From birth, the wicked go astray, lying, affecting people with their poison, proudly refusing to listen, and out of control. **V 6–8: INTERCESSION** David pleads with God to nullify their aggression and violence, and to deal with them. He asks for their teeth to be broken, for them to flow away like a river, for their arrows to be cut up, for them to melt away like a snail, and for them to be as lifeless as a stillborn child. **V 9–11: INEVITABLE** Confident that God will answer his prayer, David knows that God will judge the wicked, and that He will do it with whirlwind speed. Their blood will be shed. David is confident in the One 'who judges in the earth'.

PSALM FIFTY-NINE

V 1–2: SAVE David asks God to save, deliver and defend him from his pursuing enemies, Saul's men. **V 3–5: SEE** David asks God to observe that they are waiting to kill him, but not because of any sin that he has committed. He then asks God to help him and to punish the nations which are against God and against him. **V 6–8: SNARLING** He describes them as growling, snarling dogs with swords in their lips. But he knows that God, in His

might, can laugh at them in derision. **V 9–13: STRENGTH** David knows that God is his defence and shield, and that He reigns. He says that he will wait for God, his Strength, who will deal with his enemies. He asks for them to be scattered and then to be consumed. **V 14–17: SONG** Despite the dog-like growls and howls of his enemies, David will sing of God's power and mercy in the morning because he knows that God is his defence and refuge. He will praise God his Strength and defence. He thanks 'My God of mercy'.

PSALM SIXTY

V 1–5: RESTORATION FOR THE REJECTED God is always ready to restore and bless those who come to Him and rally under His banner of truth. David knows that God loves him and that he will be delivered and saved by God's right hand. God hears his prayer. **V 6–8: POSSESSIONS FOR THE PEOPLE** There will be a shout of triumph as God restores to His people their lost possessions and as He speaks in His holiness to them. **V 9–12: HELP FOR THE HELPLESS** David knows that man cannot help him but that God can. Through God, His people will do valiantly and know His victory.

PSALM SIXTY-ONE

V 1–2: HIGH ROCK David cries from his overwhelmed heart for God to hear him. He asks to be led to the rock that is higher than he is. We have that Rock in Christ. **V 3–4: HELPFUL REFUGE** Acknowledging that God has sheltered him as in a strong tower from the enemy, David now commits himself to abide with God and to trust in His sheltering wings. **V 5: HERITAGE RECEIVED** God, having heard David's vows, has already given him the heritage of those who fear Him. His long-term future is secure! **V 6–8: HEAVEN'S REST** Because of this, God will prolong his life and he will abide with God for ever. He will reap the benefits of mercy and truth. Performing his vows daily to God, he will sing praises to Him for ever.

PSALM SIXTY-TWO

V 1–8: WAITING Faced with intense opposition, David claims that God is his rock, salvation and defence. He instructs his soul to wait for God. He encourages others to trust in Him and pour out their hearts before God who is their refuge. **V 9: WEIGHING** God knows the true weight of ungodly men. They are lighter than vapour and have no righteousness that registers on the scales. **V 10: WORLDLINESS** Not only oppression and robbery must be rejected, but so must worldly and materialistic dependence upon increased riches. They can never meet man's spiritual needs. **V 11–12: WORD** Mercy, power, and justice are in David's mind after God has spoken to him. God's word is crucially important.

PSALM SIXTY-THREE

V 1: DAVID'S LONGING Everything about David underlines the fact that He longs to be with God. He is like a thirsty man in a parched wilderness looking for water. **V 2–5: LOVING DEVOTION** David's response of prayer and joyful praise are because he knows that the lovingkindness of the LORD satisfies and is better than life. **V 6–8: LYING DOWN** Even when he is lying on his bed at night, David will remember and meditate on God. Upheld by Him, he wants to follow Him closely. **V 9–10: LIVES DESTROYED** David knows that those who seek to destroy his life will, one day, reap destruction in their own

lives. **V 11: LIARS' DESTINY** Those who speak lies will one day be stopped, while those rejoicing in God will continue to praise and glorify Him. David knows that this eternal pleasure awaits him, too.

PSALM SIXTY-FOUR

V 1–4: PROTECTION David asks for protection from the wicked who oppress him. **V 5–6: PLOTTING** He knows that the evil plotters lay snares for his downfall. **V 7–9: PONDER** David is confident that God will deal with them, so that all men will fear when they see how God has worked, and will seriously ponder His actions. **V 10: PRAISE** Those in a right relationship with the LORD, trusting in Him, shall praise God and glorify Him.

PSALM SIXTY-FIVE

V 1–3: SALVATION PRAISE Praise is awaiting God in Zion because of the atonement to be provided for iniquities and transgressions. **V 4–8: SATISFIED PEOPLE** The mighty God of creation is the God of salvation who satisfies His people. He chooses them to approach Him in praise. Accordingly, they acknowledge His awesome deeds and salvation and praise Him. **V 9–13: SUCH PROVISION!** Not only has God created the earth and provided salvation, but also He abundantly provides physical needs and food. God's generosity is truly overwhelming!

PSALM SIXTY-SIX

V 1–5: AWESOME! God's works and power cause the psalmist to emphasise how awesome He is. **V 6–7: ACTION** God can act to turn sea into dry land, which He did both at the Red Sea and at the Jordan, to guide and help His people and glorify

His name. His people rejoice in Him. He rules over nations and has ultimate control even over the rebellious **V 8–12: AFFLICTED** Even though His people are sometimes afflicted and trodden underfoot, God goes through the afflictions with His people and brings them out to blessings at the other end. **V 13–15: ADORATION** This causes the psalmist to sacrifice to God and pay his vows in adoration. **V 16–20: ANSWER** The psalmist testifies to all who will come and hear, and all who fear God, that God has answered his prayer and not turned His mercy from him. Certainly, He has heard him. However, he knows that if he regards iniquity in his heart, God will not hear him. Repentance and faith are always necessary prerequisites for answered prayer.

PSALM SIXTY-SEVEN

V 1–2: PRAYER David's prayer is for God's mercy, blessing, and the knowledge of His face shining upon them so that His way might be known and nations might be saved. **V 3–5: PRAISE** David knows that if this happens, those who are saved will praise God, the righteous Judge, with the praise that is due to Him. His desire is to hear his God praised by all peoples. **V 6–7: PLENTY** David believes that if all the people of the earth will walk in fellowship with God and praise Him, then all will be blessed as God supplies their needs from His plentiful earth.

PSALM SIXTY-EIGHT

V 1–6: FAITHFUL FATHER Almighty God, who scatters the enemies of His people, is a Father of the fatherless and a defender of widows. He sets solitary people in families. He is a faithful Father to those who trust Him. **V 7–10: PERSONAL PROVIDER** Even in the wilderness, God personally provided for His people. He is a personal protector and provider. **V 11–14: SCATTERING SOVEREIGN** God scattered the kings who opposed His people. He provided for His own from the spoils of conquest. **V 15–18: GREAT GOD** God is a great and powerful God, towering over His creation. His ascension and leading 'captivity captive' are applied to the ascension of the Lord Jesus Christ in Paul's letter to the Ephesians. **V 19–23: DIVINE DELIVERER** God is sovereign over the enemies of His people and sovereign over His salvation. He loads His people with benefits each day. He brings salvation and delivers them by 'escapes from death'. He overcomes their enemies. **V 24–27: PRAISING PROCESSION** No wonder His people go in procession to the sanctuary, praising Him and praying to Him. **V 28–35: AWESOME ALMIGHTY** God's strength, power, kingdom, control over nature, strength, and excellence cause David to bless his God and say of Him that He is 'more awesome than [His] holy places'.

PSALM SIXTY-NINE

V 1–4: SAVE In distress over opposition from enemies who hate him, David calls for God to save him. He feels he is in the mire and is about to drown in the waters of sorrow and affliction. He seems to suffer from false accusation, since he must restore what he had not stolen. **V 5: SEEN** He knows that God sees him and knows his foolishness and his sins. **V 6: SEEKERS** He asks that those who seek God and those who wait for God will not be discouraged and put off by what happens to him. **V 7–12: SHAME** He has been shamed, isolated, reproached, maligned and ridiculed by those who are against him. He is reproached because of his zeal for God's house. Even drunkards sing against him. **V 13–29: SUPPLICATION** He pours out his heart in prayer and supplication to God. He asks for God speedily to show His mercy, deliverance, and salvation. He knows he is in trouble. He also asks God to deal with his enemies. It is always best for God's people to deal in prayer with those opposing them, rather than to take matters into their own hands. **V 30–36: SONG** David's faith in his God of salvation, who will answer his prayer, causes him to say that he will sing praises to Him in the future and 'magnify Him with thanksgiving'. He calls heaven and earth to praise God, who will save Zion and bless His servants in the future.

PSALM SEVENTY

V 1–3: HELP Again, David asks God to help him and to do it quickly. As others seek to harm him and kill him, he needs God's help urgently. **V 4: HAPPINESS** He asks for all who seek God to rejoice and to be glad in Him, and to magnify Him for His salvation. That obviously includes David himself. **V 5: HASTEN** Aware of his poor state and his great need, he urges God to 'make haste' to manifest His help and deliverance. He asks the LORD not to delay.

PSALM SEVENTY-ONE

V 1–8: REFUGE The psalmist's request for escape and deliverance is based on his refuge in the character of the God whom he has trusted and who has been his hope from his youth. He knows he has been upheld by Him since birth. Despite the attacks of others, he knows that God is his strong refuge and that he will be praising Him all day long. **V 9–13: REQUEST** He knows that when old age

comes and strength forsakes him, his weakness could easily make him a prey to the enemy, so he asks God to deliver him, and not to cast him off then or to forsake him. Right now, he asks for God's presence, help, and dealing with his enemies. **V 14–24: RESOLUTION** Meanwhile, he resolves to hope continually, to praise God, to tell of His righteousness, and to go in His strength. Now, in his old age, he is confident that God will not forsake him, but empower him, and that he will be revived and blessed by God. Thus he resolves to praise God and to witness to Him, knowing that his soul has been redeemed.

PSALM SEVENTY-TWO

V 1–4: THE SON'S RIGHTEOUSNESS The reign of the King's Son, surely foretelling the Messiah, will include righteous judgement, concern for the poor, peace and justice, saving of the needy, and the breaking of the oppressor. The psalm's immediate application is to Solomon, the son of King David. **V 5–11: THE SON'S REIGN** The Son will have an enduring, refreshing, righteous and complete reign over all territories and everything. All nations shall serve him, and all kings fall down before him. **V 12–14: THE SON'S RESCUE** The Son will rescue the helpless, the needy, the poor, and the oppressed. He will save and spare them when they cry. Their blood is precious in His sight. **V 15–16: THE SON'S RESOURCES** The resources of the earth belong to the Son to whom praise and prayer will continually be made. This will include all the valuables such as gold and all the produce such as grain. He can make the earth flourish either in city or on mountaintop, such is His power and greatness. **V 17–20: THE SON'S RENOWN** The whole context of this Psalm reveals the deity of the coming Son. The Lord Jesus Christ is the final focus. He only does wondrous things and His name will be blessed for ever. The whole earth will be filled with His glory.

BOOK THREE—PSALM SEVENTY-THREE TO PSALM EIGHTY-NINE

PSALM SEVENTY-THREE

V 1: PRINCIPLE God's goodness to His people who are 'pure in heart' is an unchanging principle. **V 2–16: PROSPERITY** The prosperity of wicked and ungodly people is a great problem to Asaph, the Psalm's writer. He nearly falls because of it. He catalogues their sinful lives and asks, in effect, 'Why do the wicked prosper?' **V 17: PIVOT** Verse 17 is pivotal. It reminds us to spend time with God in prayer and to look at the long-term future of those who reject God. We will then understand that their temporary gains in this life are useless. **V 18–20: PERISHING** Terrors will consume the wicked in the future. The description of their final and tragic hopelessness pinpoints their utter lostness. **V 21–28: PERSONAL** From his grief, vexed spirit, foolishness, and ignorant doubts over why the wicked prosper, Asaph turns back to his personal trust in God. He draws near to God, who has answered his problem and will guide him through life and then receive him in glory.

PSALM SEVENTY-FOUR

V 1: REJECTED Asaph asks why God has rejected His people. **V 2: REMEMBER** He asks God to remember His people, whom He had 'purchased of old'. **V 3–11: RAMPAGE** The destruction and desecration of the temple (by Nebuchadnezzar in 586 BC) and its

silencing effect on the prophetic ministry are described. Asaph asks why God does not strike back and destroy the wicked. **V 12–17: REFLECTION** Asaph's reflection on God's power and authority follows. **V 18–23: REQUEST** Asaph asks God to remember and rise up against those who oppose Him.

PSALM SEVENTY-FIVE

V 1: THANKFULNESS Asaph declares thanks to God for His works and nearness. **V 2–8: TIMING** God, the powerful Creator, will judge the earth and the wicked in His time and way. There is no room at all for human pride. **V 9–10: TESTIMONY** Asaph will continue to extol and praise God, who will judge the wicked and exalt the righteous.

PSALM SEVENTY-SIX

V 1–3: VICTORY God's great name is known in His victories. **V 4–10: VINDICATION** In all God's dealings with men, His power and position as Judge and Deliverer vindicate Him. **V 11–12: VOWS** Men should make and keep their vows to God, who is awesome and to be feared.

PSALM SEVENTY-SEVEN

V 1–2: MOURNING Asaph's soul has gone into mourning and he prays in anguish to God, even through the night. **V 3–6: MUSING** In his sleeplessness and groaning, he looks back nostalgically to better times in the past. **V 7–9: MISSING?** Asaph wonders if God has withdrawn His favour, love, and mercy from him for ever. Where is God with His missing mercies and blessings? **V 10–19: MEDITATING** He refocuses his meditations on the works and wonders that God has done in the past. He remembers God's moving among

His people and acting for them. He recalls His miracles, powerful deeds and sovereignty over nature. **V 20: MINDED** He concludes with the thought that God minded His people as a shepherd, through Moses and Aaron. The implication is that God has done this through good times and bad times for His people.

PSALM SEVENTY-EIGHT

V 1–8: POSTERITY HELPED Asaph writes this psalm so that its lessons can be shared with future generations of God's people. It is always wise to learn from history, especially when one has seen God so evidently at work. It is also wise to learn from the mistakes of others, and Israel's history has plenty to teach! **V 9–71: POTTED HISTORY** A broad sweep of God's dealings with the children of Israel follows, in which their repeated lack of faith and obedience is contrasted with God's continual mercy and help offered to them, although with chastisement. **V 72: POWERFUL HANDS** Underlining the lessons learned from Israel's intermittent walk with God, the Psalm concludes that God has shepherded His people and 'guided them by the skilfulness of His hands'. Those hands have never let His people go.

PSALM SEVENTY-NINE

V 1–4: DESTRUCTION Asaph recites the destruction of Jerusalem and the carnage of its inhabitants by the enemies of God (probably under Nebuchadnezzar). **V 5–12: DEMANDS** Asaph asks how long this will carry on and whether God will be angry for ever with His people, in the light of what has happened to Jerusalem. He asks God to hear the groanings of His imprisoned people, to save them, and to deal with their enemies. He requests this

for the sake of God's name, so that the nations will know that God is real. **V 13: DEVOTION** God's people, His sheep, will thank Him and declare His praise to future generations when God does act.

PSALM EIGHTY

V 1–3a: SHEPHERD Who better to ask for restoration than God the Shepherd of Israel, who has strength enough to save and revive His people, and who desires to lead them like a flock? **V 3b: SHINE** Asaph knows that if God's face shines on them in grace, they will be restored and saved. **V 4–11: SHADOW** The psalmist laments Israel's current downcast position and again prays for restoration. Such has been God's past blessing on His people that, like a spreading vine, they have covered the land with their shadow. **V 12–13: STATE** But Israel's current state is broken down, uprooted, and devoured after captivity. Asaph asks why this is. **V 14–18: SON** God's intervention is needed. The 'son of man' may refer to Israel itself, to David's line, or to Jesus Christ the Messiah, often referred to as 'the Son of Man' as well as 'the Son of God'. The sense is that a visitation from the 'Son of Man' is needed for restoration and revival of God's people. **V 19: SAVE** In a repeat of verses 3 and 7, the need to be saved by God is re-emphasised.

PSALM EIGHTY-ONE

V 1–5: INSTRUCTION The command to praise God is to be carried out with obvious enthusiasm! Although praise often involves our emotions, we should, in any case, praise God as an act of will because of who He is and what He has done. **V 6–7: INTERVENTION** God has intervened to unburden, rescue, and answer the prayers of the people He loves.

V 8–12: **INIQUITY** Israel's rebellion meant that they had missed God's best and that God had given them over to their proud and stubborn hearts. **V 13–16: IF** If only Israel will now trust God, they will receive the very best from God in being fed and satisfied by Him. He longs to bless them.

PSALM EIGHTY-TWO

V 1: JUDGING JUDGES Asaph pictures the corrupt judges, derisorily referred to here as 'gods', being judged by God, who alone is the ultimate and divine Judge. **V 2–4: DEVIOUS DEEDS** God reminds them of their failure to maintain justice responsibly, in the face of wickedness, for the poor, fatherless, afflicted and needy. **V 5: INIQUITOUS IGNORANCE** Because of their sin and prejudice, they neither know nor understand justice or God, and walk in darkness in an unstable world. **V 6–8: COMPELLING CONTRAST** With irony and sarcasm, God refers to their inflated status as 'gods', and their claim to be serving Him as His children. He reminds them that they must face death and judgement. Asaph prays for God to judge the earth. He will inherit all nations.

PSALM EIGHTY-THREE

V 1–4: ANNIHILATION Asaph is worried because the enemies of God want to annihilate Israel, God's people, as a nation. He pleads with God to act to oppose them. **V 5–8: ASSOCIATION** There is a very strong association of confederate enemies opposing God's people. **V 9–17: APPLICATION** Asaph applies himself in prayer by the encouragement of remembering how God has intervened to help Israel before. This strengthens his faith that God can still act in power to scatter His enemies and rescue His people. Even in this prayer, he asks that

his enemies will seek God. **V 18: AFFIRMATION** This prayer is not only to deliver and bless God's people, valid as that is, but to affirm to a hostile world the name, power, authority and position of God Himself. Every prayer asking for help and blessing should also seek God's glory and honour.

PSALM EIGHTY-FOUR

V 1–7: LONGING The writer is simply longing to worship God in Zion. He cannot wait to get there to praise his King and God, and even envies the sparrows that nest near to the altar of God in the temple. As a spiritual pilgrim, he seeks the blessing of communion with God. **V 8–9: LISTEN** He asks God to listen to his prayer and look upon him in view of his special relationship with Him as a child of Israel (Jacob). **V 10–12: LORD** One day invested in communing with God is better for Him than a thousand other days, or in time wasted pursuing the pleasures of sin. He concentrates on his LORD as a sun and shield. He rejoices in His grace and glory and in God's generous faithfulness. No wonder he concludes that 'Blessed is the man who trusts in You!' This psalm teaches us the right attitude to God and to worship.

PSALM EIGHTY-FIVE

V 1–3: REMEMBER The psalmist remembers what God has done for the people of Israel before. He has turned their captivity and forgiven them. **V 4–5: RESTORE** He asks God to turn from His anger at their sins and restore them again. **V 6–9: REVIVE** He pleads for physical and spiritual revival through God's mercy, producing salvation, rejoicing and peace. **V 10–13: RIGHTEOUSNESS** Because of God's mercy, truth, righteousness and peace, the supplicant is sure that God will lead them in fruitful righteousness and enable them to follow Him.

PSALM EIGHTY-SIX

V 1–7: HEAR The psalmist pleads that God will hear him. Feeling his own poverty and need, he rehearses aspects of God's character that assure him that God will answer his prayers. **V 8–10: HIGH** He has a very high view of God, as every child of God ought to have. He confesses God's uniqueness, sovereignty, greatness, and ability to work wonders. **V 11–13: HEART** The psalmist asks God to teach him, help him to walk in truth, and unite his heart. Like every sinful human being, he has a tendency to double-heartedness. He records that he then will praise God wholeheartedly. He acknowledges God's great mercy and deliverance in the past. **V 14–17: HELP** He asks for God's gracious and compassionate help against his enemies. Assured of His longsuffering and abundant mercy, he is confident that he will be able to say, 'You, Lord, have helped me and comforted me.'

PSALM EIGHTY-SEVEN

V 1–2: GATES The gates of Jerusalem, in Judah's hill country, speak of access to God in worship. **V 3–5a: GLORY** The glory of Jerusalem (or 'Zion') is such that other nations will come to worship God there one day. Those born there will be grateful for that privilege. **V 5b–7: GOD'S** In a real sense, Zion is God's city. This has been evident in history and it is around Zion that history will ultimately close. Revelation chapter 21 speaks of the New Jerusalem, for example. So much blessing has flowed from the springs of God's grace and goodness flowing from Jerusalem.

PSALM EIGHTY-EIGHT

V 1: PERSONAL The psalmist knows God as his personal Saviour. He continually communes with Him. **V 2: PRAYER** As he cries to God in prayer, he asks God to turn His ear towards him. **V 3–5: PROBLEMS** The worst of problems are a reason for praying, not a reason for not praying! **V 6–18: PIT** The psalmist feels truly abandoned and shut up in a pit. His dark feelings and forebodings do not stop him from praying, however, but rather the reverse. He pours out his soul and concerns to God. This is a good example to follow!

PSALM EIGHTY-NINE

V 1–2: MERCIES AND MERCY The psalmist is grateful, both for the mercies he receives to cover each of his individual sins, and for the mercy of his faithful God, upon which those mercies are built. **V 3–4: SWORN AND SEED** By a covenant, God has sworn to His servant, David, that He will establish his seed for ever and that he will have an eternal throne. This is a promise of the Messiah to come. **V 5–18: FAITHFUL AND FEARFUL** God is faithful and to be feared. He is almighty, righteous, creating, saving, merciful, truthful and glorious. **V 19–37: COVENANT AND CONSTANCY** God has made His covenant with David and with His people. He abounds in faithfulness, mercy, love, and lovingkindness. God will not change. He will uphold David and his posterity, from whom will come the Messiah, the Lord Jesus Christ. **V 38–45: 'BUT' AND BEWILDERMENT** The knowledge of God's character does not stop the psalmist wondering why things have not worked out the way he wants. Life is like that, sometimes, and we must accept God's overriding goodness and faithfulness, even when our preferences are not realised. **V 46–52: REMEMBRANCE AND REVERENCE** This drives the psalmist to ask God to remember that his time is limited and that His servants are being reproached. The psalm ends with a reverent note: 'Blessed be the LORD forevermore!' This third book of the Psalms ends by underlining this with 'Amen and amen'.

BOOK FOUR—PSALM NINETY TO PSALM ONE HUNDRED AND SIX

PSALM NINETY

V 1–6: IMMORTALITY Moses is the author of this Psalm. He recognises that God's everlasting nature is shown in His creation of the world and in His dealings with His very transient and temporary earthly people. **V 7–12: INIQUITY** Their sense of sin and wickedness underlines their realisation of the passing nature of their limited life spans. This leads them to the conclusion to number their days and ask for a heart of wisdom from God. **V 13–17: INTENSITY** The result is a prayer for God to manifest Himself among them, show His compassion, and work in them. Moses asks that they will rejoice and know satisfaction and gladness in Him, so that His glory and beauty is seen and their work is established.

PSALM NINETY-ONE

V 1–6: REFUGE The psalmist finds his refuge 'under the shadow of the Almighty'. He trusts in God and finds in Him his refuge, fortress, shield, buckler, and answer to fear when all around are suffering from it. No wonder that in World War 2 this psalm was known in Britain as the 'air raid psalm'. **V 7–13:**

REASSURANCE Despite fear and havoc on every side, the person who trusts in God knows that He is in charge. The LORD is well able to deliver him, if that is best for him. **V 14–16: RESPONSE** God promises to answer those who trust Him and call upon Him. His response includes deliverance and salvation, as well as satisfaction.

PSALM NINETY-TWO

V 1–4: SPIRITUAL REJOICING The title and first four verses remind us that each Lord's day specifically, (and every day in principle!) we can 'declare His lovingkindness in the morning', and His 'faithfulness every night'. It is good to sing about this together and to take it personally, too. It causes the psalmist to be glad. **V 5–9: SOVEREIGNTY REMEMBERED** God's sovereignty and ultimate triumph, as well as His great works, are contrasted with the foolishness of humanity and the scattering of His enemies. **V 10–15: SUSTAINING ROCK** The psalmist knows that God has anointed and blessed him, and that He will bless him in the future. In old age, God's people can still be fresh and flourishing spiritually and bring forth fruit. This comes from knowing the righteous LORD as their rock.

PSALM NINETY-THREE

V 1: MAJESTY God's reign and majesty is because 'He has girded Himself' with all the strength that He needs. He is the self-sufficient God who created the world and sustains it. **V 2: ETERNITY** Because He is from everlasting, so is His rule. **V 3–4: SUPREMACY** God is infinitely mightier than the most raging floods and the most mighty and angry sea. The most gigantic tsunami is but a ripple before Him. **V 5a:**

CERTAINTY 'Your testimonies are very sure' speaks for itself! **V 5b: HOLY** Everlasting holiness is the environment in which God dwells. That is why Christians must be holy.

PSALM NINETY-FOUR

V 1–3: AVENGING God is an avenging God. Vengeance belongs to Him. He will judge wicked men and women justly and severely. **V 4–7: ARROGANCE** The arrogant wicked speak, act, and boast as if God is blind and void of understanding. They say that His judgement will not come. **V 8–11: ACCOUNTABILITY** Nevertheless, God does hear, see, and know. Rebelling against Him is futile. **V 12–19: ASSURANCE** God blesses, teaches and accompanies those who trust Him. He helps them to stand against evil, holds them up when they slip, and, in the midst of anxieties, He comforts and delights the soul of the trusting person. **V 20–23: AFFIRMATION** In all of the opposition and chaos of the wicked, the psalmist knows God as his defence, as His refuge, and as the One who will finally deal with the iniquity of man.

PSALM NINETY-FIVE

V 1–5: WONDER A sense of wonder throbs through the first five verses in God the 'Rock of our salvation', the 'great King above all other gods' and the Creator. **V 6–7a: WORSHIP** An even greater cause for worship is that God's people are His personal possession and His own sheep. **V 7b–11: WARNING** But those who refuse to listen to His voice, those who rebel against Him, and those who go their own way will not enjoy the rest and blessing of knowing God.

PSALM NINETY-SIX

V 1–6: WONDER The wonder of the character of God—His name, salvation, glory, greatness, fear, creatorship, honour, majesty, strength and beauty—cause the psalmist to praise Him. **V 7–9: WORSHIP** Again, worship follows. Worship is giving the LORD the glory due to Him. This requires holiness and a due sense of reverence. **V 10: WITNESS** The nations have to be told the truths of God's sovereignty, power, judgement and righteousness. **V 11–13: WAIT** All creation will welcome the coming of the LORD to judge in righteousness. When this happens, men will be judged according to His truth.

PSALM NINETY-SEVEN

V 1: REIGN All can be glad that the LORD is in charge! **V 2–6: RIGHTEOUSNESS** Righteousness and justice are God's foundational qualities, and the heavens themselves declare both His righteousness and His glory. **V 7–9: REJOICING** Unlike the shame of those who worship other gods, rejoicing marks those people who respect His judgements and know He is exalted above all other gods. **V 10–12: REMEMBRANCE** Those who belong to Him, His 'saints', have light and gladness in Him, hate evil, and give thanks when they remember His holy name.

PSALM NINETY-EIGHT

V 1–3: SINGING The new song to be sung to the LORD is because of His marvellous deeds, victory, salvation, righteousness, revelation, mercy, and faithfulness. **V 4–6: SHOUTING** Joyful shouting and rejoicing, as well as singing and praises accompanied by music, are requested to mark the wonder of our Lord and King. **V 7–9: SUPPORTING** The supporting choir in this crescendo of praise consists of the sea, the world, all dwellers in the world, the rivers and the hills. The Judge is coming. He is righteous and equitable.

PSALM NINETY-NINE

V 1–5: AWESOME The awesomeness of God, His name, His doings and His holiness form the subject of this psalm. Twice we read that 'He is holy.' **V 6–8: ANSWERS** God has answered people in the past with His forgiveness. This gives us great confidence to ask today. **V 9: ADORATION** Because of this, we should exalt God and worship Him. In giving Him our adoration, we must remember that He is holy.

PSALM ONE HUNDRED

V 1–2: PRINCIPLES Some valuable principles for praising God are found in these two verses. All lands should be involved, joy is at the centre of worship, and this gladness should be expressed in songs. **V 3: PEOPLE** The foundation for our praise is that we belong to God and we are His sheep. **V 4–5a: PRAISE** We enter His gates with thanksgiving and should keep on praising Him. His goodness should be our focus of attention. **V 5b: PERPETUAL** The Lord's mercy and truth, like God Himself, last for ever.

PSALM ONE HUNDRED AND ONE

V 1: SINGING God's loving mercy and perfect justice cause David to sing His praises. **V 2: SINGLENESS** David intends to walk with a heart wholly set on God and in a wise way that wholly pleases God. **V 3–4: SEPARATION** The positive intent of the preceding verse involves a negative in these two verses. David refuses to look at anything wicked. He will dissociate with backsliding, and perverseness. He wants to exclude anything that displeases God or spoils his own walk with God. **V 5: SLANDER** Resulting from this, David will tolerate neither slander nor a proud heart. **V 6–8: STATEMENT** What David requires for himself, he will seek to enforce in the nation as king. He will support the godly, and deal with evil doing.

PSALM ONE HUNDRED AND TWO

V 1–2: PRAYING David asks God to hear him and to answer speedily. Troubles often increase the intensity of our prayers. **V 3–11: PROBLEMS** David feels physically tired and worn, lonely, rejected by men, opposed by enemies, and that his life is very transient. **V 12–17: PERMANENCE** Wisely, David takes his eyes off his own position and reflects on the character and eternal being of his merciful and faithful God. **V 18–22: POSTERITY** For generations to come, David knows that God will bless and establish His kingdom, despite the sinfulness of men. He hears even 'the groaning of the prisoner' and those under death sentence. **V 23–28: PERSONAL** David records his personal testimony and prayer. In so doing, he makes a messianic prophecy about Jesus, which we see later quoted in the letter to the Hebrews.

PSALM ONE HUNDRED AND THREE

V 1–5: SOUL David rehearses how God blesses his soul. Although his body may not always be well, by God's grace his soul always can be in good health. **V 6–18: SAME** The same gracious God, who has mercy on David, blessed Moses. His fatherly pity and blessing will everlastingly be on 'children's children' who fear and follow Him. **V 19–22: SOVEREIGNTY** God's eternal throne and the rule of His kingdom over all else causes David to conclude the psalm as he started it. He calls upon angels, ministers, and the whole of creation to praise God. He himself blesses and praises the LORD because of who He is and what He has done. 'Bless the LORD, O my soul!' starts and finishes this psalm. It is good to start and end our prayers in praise to God.

PSALM ONE HUNDRED AND FOUR

V 1–2: GOD'S CHARACTER God's self-emanating greatness, majesty, light and creatorhood occupy the thoughts and prayers of the psalmist. **V 3–26: GOD'S CREATORHOOD** As well as angels, God has created the world, animal life, vegetation, the water system, the seasons and the universe. He controls the sun, the moon, the sea and everything He has made. **V 27–30: GOD'S CONTROL** If God were to take away His control from his created beings, they would fail. It is by His Spirit that He has created everything. His glory and power are immense. **V 31–35: GOD'S CLOSENESS** The psalmist wants close communion with God. He wants to sing to the LORD for the rest of his life, to praise Him all his days, to meditate on Him and to be glad in Him. As he meditates on God, he wants his very thoughts to be sweet to God's taste. He sees how sinners violate God's holiness and plan, but dedicates himself to praise and bless the LORD.

PSALM ONE HUNDRED AND FIVE

V 1–3: SALUTE HIM God is to be saluted in thanksgiving, calling on Him, proclaiming His deeds, singing to Him, and talking of His works. His holy name is to be gloried in. This will enable the hearts of those who seek Him to rejoice. **V 4: SEEK HIM** His people must always seek the LORD, His strength and His face. **V 5–45: SEE HIM** His works throughout history for His people are to be remembered. It is here that we see God in His faithfulness, power and grace; these characteristics have been manifested abundantly in the past. The sweep of Israel's history up to the exodus from Egypt is rehearsed in the rest of this psalm. What God promised to Abraham, He confirmed to Isaac and Jacob, made possible through Joseph, and progressed towards through Moses and Aaron. (Psalm 106 will recapitulate and then take us further.) God is faithful and sovereign.

PSALM ONE HUNDRED AND SIX

V 1–5: REMEMBER Having first praised the LORD and given thanks to Him for His uniqueness and for His particular dealings, the psalmist asks God to remember him and to give him His salvation with all its attendant benefits. **V 6: RECOGNITION** Nevertheless, the psalmist identifies himself in confession with the sins of the people of Israel. He sees himself as no different in heart from them. **V 7–46: REVIEW** He then reviews the seesaw of Israel's repentance and rebelliousness against the ever-ready mercy and grace of God when God's people turn back to Him. He charts Israel through to Moses, by name. He then summarises the period from Joshua to Jeremiah, without naming them. Always in focus are God's goodness and His people's fickleness. **V 47–48: REQUEST** This reminder of human sinfulness and God's merciful grace causes him to ask God to save His people. Again, he ends on the same note of praise that opened the Psalm.

BOOK FIVE—PSALM ONE HUNDRED AND SEVEN TO PSALM ONE HUNDRED AND FIFTY

PSALM ONE HUNDRED AND SEVEN

V 1–3: DUE The psalmist recognises that thanks are due to the LORD for His mercy, redemption, and gathering in His captive people from far and wide from enemy hands. **V 4–32: DELIVERANCE** Time and again, God has delivered, blessed, helped and guided His people who have been in the worst of situations. Tossed about hopelessly on the sea of life, they have cried out to Him and been saved. Three times the psalmist yearns for people to thank God for His goodness and for His wonderful works. **V 33–42: DISTINCTION** Those are blessed whose poverty and low position cause them to rely on God. He sends barrenness as the result of wickedness. **V 43: DEDUCTION** The psalmist deduces that observant, wise people will understand God's lovingkindness.

PSALM ONE HUNDRED AND EIGHT

V 1: STEADFAST HEART David's heart is fixed on God, which causes him to praise God. **V 2–5: SINGING HEARTILY** He seeks God's exaltation and appreciates His mercy and His truth. So he praises God early and heartily, and sings His praises among the nations. **V 6–13: SAVING HAND** It is the right hand of God Himself that will bless Israel and Judah. He has withheld His blessing for their own good in past times of rebellion. God will give them help and victory as they look to Him.

PSALM ONE HUNDRED AND NINE

V 1–5: PRAYING MAN David, surrounded by opposition and discouragement, gives himself to prayer to God. **V 6–20: PUNISHMENT MATCHING** He asks God to deal with his enemies. They have been merciless, they have persecuted the poor and needy, they have cursed much and maligned others. David wants God's punishment to match the sins of those who oppose him. **V 21–29: PERSONAL MERCY** In his great need and weakness, he counts on God's mercy and asks for His help, knowing that he will rejoice in his God. **V 30–31: PRAISING MOUTH** Knowing God's faithfulness, he declares that he will praise God individually and with others. Only God can give long-term confidence to believers in a time of trouble.

PSALM ONE HUNDRED AND TEN

V 1–2: THE LORD'S PLACE The New Testament teaches that the resurrection from the dead, along with the ascension to heaven of the Lord Jesus Christ, is foreseen in the first verse. He will rule! **V 3: THE LORD'S POWER** A principle follows that when God's power controls a person's life, he or she is willing to live a holy and refreshed life that honours Him. **V 4: THE LORD'S PRIESTHOOD** Melchizedek was a priest who blessed Abraham. He had neither beginning nor end and had neither father nor mother. Many commentators see him as an Old Testament appearance of Jesus Christ. Here, we learn that the priesthood of Jesus is also eternal, and He pleads on our behalf. **V 5–7: THE LORD'S PROMISES** The LORD lifts up the head of His people in hope and blessing. This promise is fed by the fact that the Lord Jesus Christ is at the right hand of God the Father, and by the fact that He is also close to those who trust Him.

PSALM ONE HUNDRED AND ELEVEN

V 1: WHOLEHEARTED WORSHIP Willing praise, individually and with others who know God, is a mark of the psalmist's walk with God. **V 2–9: WONDERFUL WORKS** God's great and wonderful works in compassion, provision, covenant-keeping, justice, truth, redemption and holiness are heralded in this Psalm. **V 10: WHAT WISDOM!** God's wisdom gives a good understanding to all who trust and obey Him. This comes from a holy and reverential fear of God, and results in everlasting praise.

PSALM ONE HUNDRED AND TWELVE

V 1a: COMMENCEMENT It is always good to start by praising God. **V 1b: COMMANDMENTS** The blessings described in this Psalm come to people whose fear in the LORD is demonstrated in their attitude to keeping His commandments. **V 2–8: CONSEQUENCES** The consequences stemming from an obedient trust in God are blessing on children, riches (for us, these are not necessarily in physical terms), righteousness, light in darkness, gracious compassion, consideration for others, discretion, and confidence in God even when bad news and opposition surrounds him. **V 9: CONDUCT** Such a man is generous and gives widely both his substance and God's word. God counts him as righteous, honours him, and blesses him for ever. **V 10: CONTRAST** Not only is the life of a righteous man very different from the lives of those who do not keep God's commandments, his final state is also completely different.

PSALM ONE HUNDRED AND THIRTEEN

V 1–3: ENDURING PRAISE God is to be praised now and for ever by His servants everywhere. **V 4–6: ENTHRONED PRE-EMINENCE** God is exalted high over the nations and the heavens. He is the enthroned King. **V 7–9a: ELEVATED POOR** The poor, the needy, and the barren women who trust Him are raised up and blessed by Him. **V 9b: ENDING PRAISE** No wonder this Psalm also begins and ends with the same theme: 'Praise the LORD!'

PSALM ONE HUNDRED AND FOURTEEN

V 1–2: HISTORY God's deliverance of His people from Egypt, on condition that they were holy and under His dominion, sets the tone for this short psalm. **V 3–6: MAJESTY** God's majestic dealing is declared. Through an earthquake, the sea, mountains and land respond to His majesty. **V 7–8: SOVEREIGNTY** In response to God's presence, the earth itself should tremble. The God of Jacob sovereignly kept His people in the wilderness, even by turning the rock into a pool of water to keep them alive. He is sovereign over His people as well as over nature.

PSALM ONE HUNDRED AND FIFTEEN

V 1: GLORY It is God who must be glorified, because of His mercy and truth, and not His people. **V 2–8: GODS** Those who do not know God may ask where He is and worship their own idols which are useless and helpless. These false worshippers are just as unresponsive to the LORD as are their inanimate man-made gods. **V 9–11: GOD** By comparison, the LORD God is the One in whom His people can trust. 'He is their help and their shield' is repeated three times for emphasis. **V 12–15: GRACE** God's past gracious dealings cause confidence in His future blessings for all who fear Him, and cause prayer to be made to Him for blessing on His people and their children. **V 16–18: GRATITUDE** In ending on a note of praise, one can sense the psalmist's gratitude. God, who owns the heavens, has given the earth to men. Those who bless Him will praise Him in eternity as well as on earth.

PSALM ONE HUNDRED AND SIXTEEN

V 1–2: LOVE The LORD's answering of the psalmist's prayers has caused him to love God and to pray to Him for the rest of his life. **V 3–7: LIFTED** In the past, trouble, sorrow, fear of death, and generally being brought low were all dealt with by the gracious and righteous LORD. He saved the psalmist, gave him rest of soul, and dealt bountifully with him. **V 8–11: LIVING** Because of that, the psalmist knows that he has a spiritual life which enables him to come before God. He has been delivered from death, despair, and downfall. His impulsive reaction against men has given way to a trust in God. **V 12–14: LOYALTY** In gratitude to the LORD and because of His goodness to him, he loyally pledges to take the cup of salvation, pray to God, and immediately carry out publicly his vows made to God. **V 15–17: LIBERATED** Paradoxically, because he is God's servant, he is now out of bondage. He can thank and pray to God. He knows that when he dies, a precious homecoming awaits him. **V 18–19: LOGICAL** In view of all this, he repeats that he will pay his vows to God in the presence of God's people. He can do nothing else than end with the words 'Praise the LORD!'

PSALM ONE HUNDRED AND SEVENTEEN

V 1: PRAISE This very short Psalm starts, and later finishes, with praise to God. All peoples, including the Gentiles, are bidden to praise God. **V 2: PARTICULARS** The two subject matters for praise are, firstly, God's great merciful kindness toward us and, secondly, the eternally lasting nature of His truth. No wonder this Psalm ends in praise also!

PSALM ONE HUNDRED AND EIGHTEEN

V 1–4: MERCY God's enduring mercy and goodness are the reasons for thanking Him. **V 5–9: MAN** With God on his side, the psalmist can trust in Him against any opposition of man. **V 10–14: MIGHT** With the might of the nations arrayed against him, the psalmist looks to the LORD who has become his strength, song, and salvation. **V 15–18: MISSION** Rejoicing in God's salvation (accomplished by God's right hand) and recognising that God has chastened him but kept him from death, the psalmist has a mission. He wishes to use the remainder of his life to 'declare the works of the LORD'. **V 19–26: MESSIANIC** This Psalm refers to the Lord Jesus Christ and is quoted often in the New Testament. The day that the Lord Jesus Christ became the Chief Cornerstone, after being rejected by men, was a special day. Surely its fulfilment must have been on the first Lord's Day when Jesus rose victoriously from the tomb, having paid the price for our sins. **V 27–29: 'MY!'** In confirming his desire to praise and thank God and to be a willing living sacrifice for Him, the psalmist twice refers to the LORD as 'my God'. That is why he concludes in rejoicing in God's goodness and everlasting mercy.

PSALM ONE HUNDRED AND NINETEEN

Psalm 119 is the longest chapter in the Bible and by far the biggest Psalm. Someone has called this the 'Everest' among the psalms. To describe it briefly is like writing the inventory of a huge treasure chest on the back of a postcard! Nevertheless, some of the key thoughts in each section, headed up by the letter of the Hebrew alphabet which is used to introduce each new section of eight verses, are, hopefully, a useful guide. The Hebrew letter is spelled out below in italics placed in parenthesis. The most significant single theme is the wonder and effects of God's Word, referred to also as commandments, statutes, law, precepts, testimonies, judgements, and ordinances. **V 1–8: Aleph: UNDEFILED AND UNASHAMED** The blessing and results of keeping God's law. **V 9–16: Beth: SEEKING AND SINNING** Wholehearted seeking for God through His Word keeps us from sin. **V 17–24: Gimel: DESIRE AND DELIGHT** Enthusiasm for God's enlightening word delights the person who trusts in God. **V 25–32: Daleth: SORROW AND STRENGTHENING** Personal help is given from God's Word, for personal revival, teaching and strength, in the 'down times'. **V 33–40: He: TEACHING AND TURNING** The godly man or woman can avoid falling into covetousness and looking at worthless things by having a positive attitude to God's reviving Word. **V 41–48: Waw: TRUST AND TESTIMONY** God's Word is a basis for answering the sceptic and for witnessing even to kings. **V 49–56: Zayin: COMFORT AND COMMITMENT** The uncompromising keeping of God's law comforts the afflicted and the oppressed. **V 57–64: Heth: COMMANDMENTS AND COMPANIONS** Despite opposition, keeping God's words and commandments produces peace and oneness with other believers. **V 65–72: Teth: ASTRAY AND AFFLICTED** Affliction can deepen belief in and commitment to God's Word and help the believer not to stray from Him. **V 73–80: Yod: MERCY AND MEDITATION** The comfort of God's merciful kindness is very close to His servant who seeks to understand and learn God's commandments and who meditates on His precepts. **V 81–88: Kaph: PERSECUTION AND PRECEPTS** In times of intense opposition, God's reviving help comes to His people through His Word. **V 89–96: Lamed: EVERLASTING AND ENDURING** Everything about God is everlasting and enduring, including His Word and His faithfulness. **V 97–104: Mem: WISDOM AND WALK** Living for God's law gives supernatural wisdom, amazing understanding in a holy walk with Him, and brings honey-like sweetness to the soul. **V 105–112: Nun: LIGHT AND LIFE** Through God's enlightening and reviving Word, personal guidance, revival and rejoicing become realities to the person who inclines his heart to perform what God decrees. **V 113–120: Samek: SEPARATION AND SAFETY** The believer who rejects ungodly standards and loves God's law will be upheld spiritually through God's Word. **V 121–128: Ayin: PROTECTION AND PRECIOUSNESS** Protection from oppressors by God, through an understanding of His law, leads to a realization of how very precious are His commands. **V 129–136: Pe: LONGING AND LAW** A personal panting for God's illuminating and directing Word goes together with heartfelt sorrow over those who despise and break it. **V 137–144: Tsadde: RIGHTEOUS AND RIGHTEOUSNESS** God is righteous and upright, and this fact is reflected in His judgements, testimonies, words, precepts, law, commandments and everlasting righteousness. **V 145–152: Qoph: CRYING AND CLOSENESS** Crying out to God, mentioned here three times, underlines His nearness to the believer. **V 153–160: Resh: REVIVAL AND REVELATION** Spiritual personal revival comes through God's revealed Word, His judgements, and His lovingkindness. **V 161–168: Shin: AWE AND ABHOR** A heartfelt awe and rejoicing in God's Word produces not only abhorrence of lies and falseness, but continual praise to God, great personal peace, and a sense of God's omniscience. **V 169–176: Tau: SUPPLICATION AND SEEKING** Supplication from God's servant for understanding of God's Word, deliverance and help leads to another prayer that God will seek him as a shepherd seeks a straying sheep.

PSALM ONE HUNDRED AND TWENTY

V 1: DISTRESS The psalmist cries in his distress to the LORD and is confident that the LORD has heard him. **V 2–4: DELIVERANCE** He specifically asks to be delivered from lies and a deceitful tongue, which is as sharp as the arrows of the warrior. **V 5–7: DWELLING** He laments the fact that he has dwelt too long with those who are not peace-loving but who want war. Our lives will be greatly affected by how, where and with whom we spend our time.

PSALM ONE HUNDRED AND TWENTY-ONE

V 1–3: HIGHER HELP The help that comes to those who love God is higher than the hills. It comes from the LORD Himself. **V 4–6: SHIELDING SOVEREIGN** The LORD Himself is the ever awake and watchful keeper of His people. He never goes off duty at any time. **V 7–8: PERPETUAL PRESERVATION** Because of that, anyone

who trusts in Him knows that God preserves his soul perpetually from all evil. God knows all his comings and goings and has them under His plan and preservation.

PSALM ONE HUNDRED AND TWENTY-TWO

V 1–2: GLAD TO GO David is glad to go to the temple in Jerusalem to praise God. **V 3–5: TESTIMONY OF TRIBES** The tribes of Israel go there to thank the LORD, who Himself is the 'Testimony of Israel'. **V 6–9: PRAY FOR PEACE** David urges that prayer for the peace of Jerusalem be made.

PSALM ONE HUNDRED AND TWENTY-THREE

V 1–2: MASTER Just as an obedient servant looks to his good master for provision and for service, so the psalmist looks to the LORD for mercy. **V 3–4: MERCY** Twice more, he specifically asks God to 'have mercy on us' because of the scorn and contempt of God's people by the easy-living and proud faced.

PSALM ONE HUNDRED AND TWENTY-FOUR

V 1–5: CONJECTURE David considers what would have happened in the face of great enemy opposition against Israel if the LORD had not been on their side. He knows they would have been swamped. If we ask ourselves the same question, we will reach the same conclusion. **V 6–7: CONFIDENCE** David expresses grateful confidence in God who has provided escape both for His people and for David himself. **V 8: CONCLUSION** The encouraging and comforting lesson drawn from all this is that help comes from the LORD, the great Creator.

PSALM ONE HUNDRED AND TWENTY-FIVE

V 1–2: SURROUNDED As the mountains surround Jerusalem, the LORD surrounds His people for ever. That is why those who trust in Him cannot be moved. **V 3: SEPARATION** Those who seek to honour God in righteousness are to keep themselves separate from those who seek sin. **V 4: SUPPLICATION** The psalmist prays for God to do good to those who have upright hearts. **V 5a: SIN** Those who now turn to crooked ways will be led away by the LORD with other established workers of iniquity. **V5b: SERENITY** The psalmist prays for God's peace upon His people.

PSALM ONE HUNDRED AND TWENTY-SIX

V 1–3: SINGING The singing, laughter and joy of glad people returning from captivity are recalled, the psalmist knowing that God has done great things for them. **V 4: STREAMS** His prayer is that the completion of the return will be accomplished as streams flowing into the south. **V 5–6: SOWING** In that day, those who have sowed in tears shall reap in joy. This is true in history concerning the various returns of Israel from captivity. It is also a principle which applies to the sowing of gospel seed. When tears of compassion or affliction are in the eyes and heart of the sower of God's word, he or she can be assured that great joy will come in the future as sinners trust in Christ and are saved eternally.

PSALM ONE HUNDRED AND TWENTY-SEVEN

V 1–2: BUILDING OF A HOUSE Unless the LORD builds the house, the labour is in vain. Any work or task done for God needs His empowering blessing. Even in working for Him, He uses sleep as a source of strength and blessing. **V 3–5: BLESSING OF A HOUSEHOLD** It is a great and happy blessing to have children. The principle applies not only to our physical children, but also to those who come to know Christ through us. They are spiritual children for whom we take spiritual parental responsibility.

PSALM ONE HUNDRED AND TWENTY-EIGHT

V 1: FEAR Holy and reverential fear of the LORD brings blessing and causes people to walk in His ways. **V 2: FOOD** It is a good thing to labour to provide for oneself and one's family. **V 3–4: FAMILY** God's blessing is on family units consisting of a man, his wife and their children. To know God's blessing, the man must be God-fearing in his leadership of that family. **V 5–6: FUTURE** God's blessing is not only on Jerusalem. It is on the children of godly children. It includes His peace.

PSALM ONE HUNDRED AND TWENTY-NINE

V 1–4: OPPRESSION Although oppressed many times since God called His earthly people into existence, Israel has been preserved against wicked oppressors because of the righteous LORD's intervention and protection. **V 5–8: OPPOSITION** The psalmist asks God to shame, turn back, and deny fruitfulness and blessing to those who hatefully oppose His people.

PSALM ONE HUNDRED AND THIRTY

V 1–2: PLEA From the depths of human experience, the psalmist cries to God and asks him to listen to His voice. **V 3–4: PARDON** He knows that he can only approach and reverentially fear God through forgiveness for his sins. He has no righteousness of his own, but needs God's pardon. **V 5–6: PATIENCE** Hoping in God's word, he sets himself to wait upon the LORD. This calls for patience and trust. **V 7–8: PURPOSE** Based on hope in the mercy and abundant redemption of God, the psalmist knows that God will achieve His purpose of redeeming His people from all their iniquities. He urges Israel to 'hope in the LORD'.

PSALM ONE HUNDRED AND THIRTY-ONE

V 1: HUMILITY No haughty heart or lofty look thwarts David's relationship with God. He is neither preoccupied with 'great matters' nor with things 'too profound' for him. This is what he can claim openly before the LORD. **V 2: HAPPY** Consequently, he is as happy, calm, and quiet as a child who relies on its mother to provide its food. **V 3: HOPE** This gives David the motivation to encourage Israel to hope in the LORD for the rest of time and for eternity.

PSALM ONE HUNDRED AND THIRTY-TWO

V 1–5: DAVID With the ark of God in mind, David recalls his vow to prepare a place for the LORD. **V 6–9: DELIGHT** The delight of worship in the tabernacle is recalled with the ark in place, the priests officiating and the people joyful. **V 10–12: DEFINITE** God has sworn that for David's sake He will keep His covenant with David's descendants. David reminds God of this in his prayer. God requires that David's sons remain faithful to the covenant. **V 13–18: DWELLING** God has chosen Zion (Jerusalem) as His special resting place. He will bless its inhabitants and David's descendants.

PSALM ONE HUNDRED AND THIRTY-THREE

V 1: BRETHREN David records the great goodness and pleasantness of God's people dwelling together in unity as brethren. **V 2: BEARD** This is compared with the anointing oil running down the beard of Aaron, the high priest, to the edge of his garments. It spreads and soothes and shows God's hand upon His people. **V 3: BLESSING** This unity is like early morning dew descending down the mountains. It spreads to others the blessing of eternal life. Where God's people are united, God blesses with His eternal salvation.

PSALM ONE HUNDRED AND THIRTY-FOUR

V 1: SERVANTS God's servants, on night-shift, are praising God in His house, the tabernacle. **V 2: SANCTUARY** The lifting of hands in supplication is to be offered in the sanctuary. God is to be praised. **V 3: SOVEREIGN** The great Creator God, the LORD, blesses His worshipping people.

PSALM ONE HUNDRED AND THIRTY-FIVE

V 1–4: PRAISE God is to be praised for the wonder of His name, for His goodness, and the fact that His people are regarded as 'special treasure'. **V 5–7: PRE-EMINENCE** The LORD is above all gods. This is seen in the fact that He is free to do whatever He wants and that He is the LORD of His creation and nature. **V 8–12: POWER** In history, He has shown His power to bless His people. They have known deliverance and victory through His powerful intervention in Egypt and against the opposing kings in the promised land. **V 13–14: PERMANENCE** The name and the fame of God are everlasting and will work for both judgement and showing compassion on those who serve Him. **V 15–18: PATHETIC** Compare the mighty God of Scripture with the idols of men which are nothing more than useless inanimate objects that therefore can do absolutely nothing. It is pointless to trust in these pathetic man-made images. Those making and worshipping them are similarly powerless. **V 19–21: PEOPLE** Israel as a nation, Aaron and Levi as the priests, and everyone who fears the LORD should bless Him and praise Him.

PSALM ONE HUNDRED AND THIRTY-SIX

V 1–3: COMMAND TO THANK GOD Twenty-six times in this Psalm, we are reminded that 'His mercy endures for ever'. Originally, this was sung as a refrain in worship, but it is a constant reminder to us as well. Little wonder that the psalmist begins with a threefold command to thank God. **V 4–22: CAUSES TO THANK GOD** God is to be thanked for the miracle of His creation (verses 4 to 9), for His historical deliverance of His people (verses 10 to 15), and for His protecting influence in wilderness situations (verses 16 to 20), and for His promise to give the land to His people for all time (verses 21 to 22). **V 23–26: CONTINUING TO THANK GOD** As the Psalm ends, the psalmist continues to praise the God of heaven for His protection and mercy. We too rejoice that 'His mercy endures for ever'.

PSALM ONE HUNDRED AND THIRTY-SEVEN

V 1–4: SADNESS In captivity in Babylon, the psalmist sadly remembers Zion and laments that God's captive people cannot sing the songs of praise to God in captivity as if they were worshipping Him at liberty in their own land. **V 5–6: SILENCE** The psalmist asks for his tongue to be silent and his right hand to be

inactive if he ever forgets or fails to exalt Jerusalem. This unique city of God stands for God's historic dealings with and for His people and His promises made to them in that place. **V 7–9: SUPPLICATION** He asks God to remember the Edomites, who were confederate with the conquering Babylonians in their enthusiasm to raze Jerusalem to the ground. He muses on what will happen to those who dealt so harshly with God's people and their special city.

PSALM ONE HUNDRED AND THIRTY-EIGHT

V 1–3: COMMITMENT David commits himself to wholehearted praise. He acknowledges the boldness and strength that God has given in answer to his cries to God. **V 4–5: CONGREGATION** The congregation of praising people will include converted earthly kings. They will praise God as a result of hearing His word. God's glory is exalted. **V 6: CONDESCENSION** The LORD who is on high condescends to regard the lowly. He also knows where the proud are. **V 7–8: CONFIDENCE** In the midst of trouble and enemy opposition, David is confident that God will revive him, save him, perfect things for him, be merciful to him, and never forsake him.

PSALM ONE HUNDRED AND THIRTY-NINE

V 1–6: OMNISCIENT God not only knows everything about everything, but He knows everything about David. God is never surprised, but David is lost in amazement. **V 7–10: OMNIPRESENT** Wherever David goes and in whatever situation he finds himself, he finds that God is there. **V 11–12: OBSERVING** Day time and night time are the same to God. He observes David's actions at all times. **V 13–16: OBVIOUS** All the evidence of the wonder of God's creative and designing miracle of human conception and gestation is obvious. God's involvement in the life of a child does not begin at birth, but at conception. **V 17–18: OUTNUMBERED** God's gracious and precious thoughts towards David, and towards all His people, outnumber the very grains of sand. **V 19–22: OUTRAGED** David is so taken with the majesty and holiness of God that, by comparison, he hates the enemies of God. He is outraged by their rebellion. **V 23–24: OPEN** In perhaps the most open prayer in the Bible, David invites God to search him, know his heart, try him, deal with his anxieties, search out his wickedness, and lead him in His everlasting way. He wants to be as different as he can be from God's enemies who make him so angry. Only repentance and wholehearted faith can produce such a prayer in a child of God.

PSALM ONE HUNDRED AND FORTY

V 1–5: DELIVER David is surrounded and hunted by evil, violent and scheming men. He prays that God will deliver him. **V 6–8: DEVOTED** He reminds God that he is devoted to Him as his personal God, who has protected and delivered him in past battles. Accordingly, he asks for God to hear him, to stop the wickedness of his enemies, and to stop them being exalted. **V 9–11: DETAIL** Growing in confidence, David asks God to deal with his wicked enemies in specific detailed ways. **V 12–13: DEFINITE** There is no doubt in David's mind that God will act again to uphold the afflicted and the poor, and to encourage the upright and righteous to commune with God and thank Him.

PSALM ONE HUNDRED AND FORTY-ONE

V 1: CRY David cries to the LORD and asks Him to attend to him quickly and answer him. **V 2: COMPARISON** His prayer, signified by his uplifted hands, will be as the incense offered in the tabernacle and as the evening sacrifice. His prayer will rise to God. **V 3–4: CAREFUL** David asks God to guard his mouth and his heart. He wants to remain holy and separated from all evil things. **V 5–7: CONTRAST** David is prepared for the righteous to wound him with their words because he knows it will do him good. He compares this with the cruelty and injustice of the wicked. They throw their judges over the cliff just as they have done to righteous people, whose bones have been scattered. **V 8–10: CONSTANT** David takes refuge in the God to whom he always looks. He knows that this constant looking to God will be met by God's keeping him from snares and traps set for him. He will escape safely while the wicked fall.

PSALM ONE HUNDRED AND FORTY-TWO

V 1–2: OPEN David again cries to the LORD. He makes supplication to Him and tells Him of his complaint and his trouble. He is in a cave physically and feels that he is in a cave spiritually, too. This is how to pray when in trouble. **V 3–4: OVERWHELMED** Even though his spirit is overwhelmed, he knows that God knows his path and his way. Yet as he sees the snares set by the wicked, he knows also that there is no human being able to rescue him, give him refuge, or care for his soul. **V 5–7: OVERCOMING** David ends on a note of optimism, looking forward to a time when he will be with the righteous and will praise God for His bountiful dealings. For that to happen, he has to pray that his soul be brought out of prison so that he can praise God's name. But first, he cries from the depths of his persecution in fear of those who are stronger than he is. He calls to the LORD as his refuge and portion. In short, David prays it through with God, who will give him the victory.

PSALM ONE HUNDRED AND FORTY-THREE

V 1–2: PRAYER Again, David commences by praying. He asks God to answer because of His faithfulness and righteousness. David knows that he cannot stand in his own righteousness and faithfulness. **V 3–4: PERSECUTION** He tells God of his crushed spirit because he is overwhelmed and distressed by those who persecute him. **V 5–6: PAST** He recalls the past days and meditates on what God has done for him in those days. This causes him to thirst for God, and he thinks about that. **V 7–12: PETITIONS** He then brings petitions for God to answer his prayer 'speedily', as he senses his own failure and weakness. He seeks the sense of God's presence, realisation of God's lovingkindness, guidance, deliverance, His enabling him to obey, leading, revival, and victory over enemies. He reminds God and himself that he is God's servant. As such, he is right to make these petitions to the Master he serves.

PSALM ONE HUNDRED AND FORTY-FOUR

V 1–2: PERSONAL God is to David his Rock, lovingkindness, fortress, high tower, deliverer, shield, and place of refuge. This is all very personal: 'I', 'me', or 'my' appear eleven times in two verses. **V 3–4: PASSING** Man is like a breath or a shadow which will pass away. **V 5–8: POWER** God's power in nature is matched by the power with which He can rescue and deliver His people from those who would attack them with evil intent. **V 9–10: PRAISE** It is no wonder that David sings praises to God and salutes His great salvation. **V 11–15: PEOPLE** David prays

for God to rescue and deliver him from his wicked oppressors, and for God's resulting and plentiful blessing on the people of God, and specifically upon their sons and daughters. He concludes that people 'whose God is the LORD', are happy people.

PSALM ONE HUNDRED AND FORTY-FIVE

V 1–2: 'EVER AND EVER' 'For ever and ever' is the time frame in which David will extol, bless and praise his LORD and King. **V 3–6: GREATNESS AND GLORY** God's unsearchable greatness, glorious splendour, mighty acts, and wondrous works are to be praised. **V 7–13: GRACE AND GOODNESS** God's graciousness and goodness are themes upon which David's praise pivots. His glorious majesty and power are to be praised as a result. **V 14–16: UPHOLDING AND UNFAILING** All who fall are upheld by the LORD who never fails to give food, and who satisfies the desires of every living being through His gracious generosity. **V 17–20: RIGHTEOUS AND RESPONSIVE** In every way, the LORD is righteous. He responds to the cries of those who come to Him. He saves them and preserves them from their enemies. **V 21: PRAISE AND PERPETUITY** This Psalm ends again with the words 'For ever and ever'. David again ends the Psalm as he started it, by praising God.

PSALM ONE HUNDRED AND FORTY-SIX

V 1–2: DETERMINATION The psalmist is determined that while life is in him, he will praise the LORD. **V 3–4: DON'T!** All men's lives are passing. This includes princes, in whom trust cannot be placed for long-term solutions. The Psalm tells us: 'Do not put your trust' in them. **V 5–7: DELIGHT** We can sense the delight of the psalmist as he describes how happy someone is who finds his help and hope in God. He is the Creator, the keeper of truth and the executor of justice. He feeds the hungry and frees the prisoners. Spiritually, He still does that for every sinner who trusts in His saving grace. **V 8–9: DOINGS** Six things are then listed that the LORD does. All of them encourage the psalmist and should encourage us. He opens blind eyes, raises up the downcast, loves the righteous, watches over strangers, relieves the fatherless and widows, and overturns the wicked. **V 10: DOMINION** No wonder the psalmist concludes with praise to the LORD for His eternal reign for ever over all generations.

PSALM ONE HUNDRED AND FORTY-SEVEN

V 1–4: PLEASANT An excellent reason for singing praise to the LORD is because it is good, pleasant and beautiful to do so. Another reason for praising Him is His work of restoration in rebuilding Jerusalem and gathering in outcasts. **V 5–6: POWER** God's mighty power combines with His infinite understanding to deal with broken-hearted and cast-down people. He also casts down the wicked. **V 7–11: PLEASURE** Helpfully appropriate music and singing facilitate praise and thanksgiving to God, who meets all the earth's needs. Unlike man, God is not impressed by the physical display of strength in a horse or a man. God is pleased when people fear Him and hope in His mercy. **V 12–18: PRAISE** God's dealings with Jerusalem, His blessings on the children of those praising Him, His peace and provision, His word, and His power over nature are all further reasons for praising Him. **V 19–20: PEOPLE** His words, His statutes, and His judgements are unique to His own people. Israel is a very privileged people and so is every child of God. This Psalm, like a number of others, starts and ends by telling his people to 'Praise the LORD!'

PSALM ONE HUNDRED AND FORTY-EIGHT

V 1–6: PRAISE FROM ABOVE Everyone in heaven and everything above the earth is encouraged to praise God. The word 'praise' comes as a command nine times in six verses! **V 7–13: PRAISE FROM AROUND** As the scene shifts to the earth, all creation, nature, animal life and human inhabitants are bidden to praise Him, too. **V 14: PRAISE FROM ALL** All God's people get a special mention and have a special reason to praise Him. This is shown by the way they are addressed as 'His people', 'all His saints', and as 'a people near to Him'. God's children have excellent and special reasons to praise Him, of which the rest of creation knows nothing!

PSALM ONE HUNDRED AND FORTY-NINE

V 1: CONGREGATIONAL PRAISE Praise is encouraged in the congregation of God's people. **V 2–3: CREATION PRAISE** God is to be praised as Maker. **V 4–6a: CONVERSION PRAISE** Those humble people of God who enjoy His salvation, namely the 'saints', are to praise Him joyfully in song. **V 6b–9: CONCLUDING PRAISE** Judgement and punishment will fall on ungodly nations. This will happen in the end times. Again, this Psalm ends as it began with 'Praise the LORD!'

PSALM ONE HUNDRED AND FIFTY

V 1–2: MIGHT God is to be praised for 'His mighty acts' and for 'His excellent greatness'. **V 3–5: MUSIC** God has prescribed the use of music in praising Him. **V 6: MANDATORY** The command to 'praise the LORD' is for everything that breathes!

PROVERBS

OVERVIEW

PEOPLE AND PRELIMINARIES

✳Proverbs (thirty-one chapters) is the third of the five poetical books of the Old Testament. See comments on Job. Most of the Proverbs were written by Solomon or complied by him between 971 and 931 BC. This included a collection of wise sayings from others (chapter 22:17 to 23:34). Hezekiah compiled some proverbs (chapter 25:1 to 29:27) but they were written by Solomon. Other authors include Agur and Lemuel (possibly Solomon under another name). The book was probably written in Jerusalem.

PLAN AND PURPOSE

ⓘThe book of Proverbs deals with all aspects of life from many specific angles. It applies God's wisdom practically in and to each situation. It contains much logic, illustration, promise, warning, and exhortation—all from the point of view of God's wisdom. Strong on duty, living a righteous life, and the nearness and presence of God, the book has much to say about the prevailing sins and ungodliness of every age, including ours, and how to avoid them. Though some have attempted a schematic approach to this book, reading it is like dipping into a treasure chest of applied truths, many of which are intertwined with others. In God's sovereign planning of His Word, here is a book that gives variety and spontaneity to different subjects at different times, some of which are repeated in both similar and different ways. Various themes do emerge, however. These include: the priority of godly wisdom; the need to be pure and to resist sexual sin; the thoughtful and careful use of the tongue rather than in impulse and contention; hard work and resisting laziness; living on ill-gotten gains; and how having a little with peace and love is better than having much without them. At times, the apt and understated humour of some proverbs make us smile, if not laugh! At other times we should weep in shame and repentance. See the introductory note to Proverbs in the notes.

PROFILE AND PROGRESSION

Title, goal of the book, and relationship between fearing God and knowledge (1:1–7); counsel to sons (1:8–9:18); proverbs from Solomon (10:1–22:16); proverbs collected from others (22:17–24:34); proverbs in Hezekiah's selection from Solomon (25:1–29:27); Agur's words (30:1–33); and Lemuel's words, especially about the value of a godly wife (31:1–31).

PRINCIPLES AND PARTICULARS

👉The width of subject matter and depth of practical wisdom can only come from God. Here we see the competition between godly wisdom and immorality for 'clients'. There are many references to God. God is in every part of human life and He must be honoured there. Apt parabolic illustrations illuminate the truths here, as windows let light into a house. Solomon failed to apply to himself the good advice he gave to his son, and to everyone else, and this failure caused his own downfall. We are reminded that knowing truth does not save us—we must apply it in repentance and faith. The only possible way to apply this wisdom today is by beginning with a personal faith in Jesus Christ and in the Bible, and then applying its lessons in humble reliance on God's Word and God's Spirit. A constant theme is the battle between wisdom and sin, especially the sin of immorality. That battle can only be won by God's grace and with His help.

PROVERBS

Notes on Proverbs

It is difficult to outline many of the chapters. Precious truths lie intertwined, like necklaces, within each chapter. They need to be separated in order to be properly examined. Thus, under the title 'SUMMARY', these notes will highlight in single summary words or brief phrases the main subjects covered in each chapter of Proverbs. Then, taking a verse or a few consecutive verses, just one or two of the 'treasures' in that chapter will be looked at briefly in a little more detail and a brief analysis given. (See the section on 'Plan and Purpose' in 'Proverbs Overview' above.)

CHAPTER ONE

V 1–33: SUMMARY Wisdom, the fear of the LORD, refusing sinful relationships, illegal gain, wisdom's appeal, wisdom's rejection, unanswered prayer, wisdom's benefits. **V 7: SOURCE** It is the fear of God which produces true heart knowledge. Later we read that it also produces wisdom. The two are linked. **V 7: START** This reverential fear of God starts knowledge. It must be fed by daily searching God's word. **V 7 STUPIDITY** Fools stupidly despise wisdom and thus lack the discipline that follows from it.

CHAPTER TWO

V 1–22: SUMMARY Following God, the fear of the LORD, wisdom, wicked ways, resisting immorality, the future of the wise, the fate of the wicked. **V 6–7: WISDOM** Wisdom can only come from God. This wisdom comes to us through God's words. Scripture is essential to have real wisdom. God feeds His people from this store. **V 7: WALK** God shields those who walk uprightly with Him. **V 8–9: WAYS** God guards the paths of justice and preserves the way His own people ('saints') go. With such wisdom and protection from God, His people receive spiritual understanding from God.

CHAPTER THREE

V 1–35: SUMMARY God's law, mercy, truth, trust, obedience, guidance, humility, giving, discipline, wisdom, creation, fear, charity, integrity, attitude to the wicked, judgement, blessing, grace. **V 5: TOTAL TRUST** Our trust must be wholeheartedly in God and not limited to what we can understand. **V 5–6: DETAILED DISCIPLESHIP** God must be acknowledged in all our ways. Obedience always follows trust in God. **V 5–6: GOD'S GUIDANCE** Those who trust in the LORD and follow Him can be sure of God's guidance and direction. They stay close to the Guide.

CHAPTER FOUR

V 1–27: SUMMARY Parental guidance, doctrine, wisdom, separation from wicked people, guidance, healthy heart, talk, deviation. **V 23–24: GUARD** Keep your heart diligently in touch with God. Never practise deceit or perverseness in the words you use. Guard your heart and your lips. **V 25: GAZE** Look straight ahead to the LORD. **V 26–27: GO** By God's grace, you can then ponder your paths properly and go straight ahead, avoiding evil and honouring God.

CHAPTER FIVE

V 1–23: SUMMARY Wisdom, understanding, knowledge, immorality, marital faithfulness, God's omniscience, folly, sin's consequences.

V 21: SEEING The LORD sees our ways—nothing is hidden from Him. **V 22: SNARE** Sin snares the wicked man—he is the slave of sin without Christ. **V 23: STUPIDITY** Waywardness is folly. The folly of immorality and adultery is highlighted. If we go astray now, unless we repent and trust in Christ, we will die estranged from God.

CHAPTER SIX

V1–35: SUMMARY Folly of guarantees, laziness, wickedness, abominations, adultery.

V 6: EXAMPLE An example to follow is the ant. **V 7–8: ENTERPRISE** The enterprise shown by the ant. **V 9: EXHORTATION** The exhortation to wake up. **V 10: EXCUSES** The weak excuses we make to delay awaking to God's truth and working for Him. **V 11: END** The end of a lazy person is that poverty overtakes him.

CHAPTER SEVEN

V 1–27: SUMMARY God's word, obedience, application, wisdom, adultery, sexual temptation.

V 1: ACTION God's word is to be kept and treasured within. **V 2: APPLE** God's law is to be the 'apple of your eye', being as precious as our own eyesight. **V 3:**

APPLICATION What we do (our fingers) and why we do it (our heart) must reflect the influence of God's word. **V 4: ADOPT** Wisdom and understanding are to be adopted as our close relations. **V 5: ABSTAIN** Trusting God through His word will keep us from falling and help us to resist temptation, including sexual temptation.

CHAPTER EIGHT

V 1–36: SUMMARY Wisdom, understanding, creation, listening, application.

V 22–23a: ETERNALLY CONSTANT Wisdom has always been at the right hand of our eternal God. Without it, we understand none of His truth. **V 23b–29: EARTH'S CREATION** God applied His wisdom in His creation of the world and everything in it. (Unregenerate man does not have God's wisdom and thus cannot understand creation. So he poses his flawed theories.) **V 30–31: ETERNAL CRAFTSMAN** Although the quantity of what God made was immense, each part was individually crafted by the wisdom of this 'master craftsman', including the 'sons of men'.

CHAPTER NINE

V 1–18: SUMMARY Wisdom, correction of wrong-doers, rebuke, instruction, teaching, fear of the LORD, foolish women, immorality, sin's consequences.

V 9: INSTRUCTION Because wisdom is available for all who ask, teaching the wise will result in increased wisdom. The same principle applies to teaching a righteous man God's law. **V 10a: INTRODUCTION** Wisdom begins in fearing the LORD. **V 10b: INSIGHT** Wisdom enables one to know the Holy God.

CHAPTER TEN

V 1–32: SUMMARY Wisdom, family, wealth, righteousness, laziness, diligence, righteousness, wickedness, foolishness, integrity, speech, hatred, love, instruction, correction, blessing, fear of the LORD, laziness, destruction.

V 19: RESTRAINED WORDS Many words attract sin, but wisdom causes people to be careful what they say. **V 20–21: RIGHTEOUS WORDS** Compared with the worthlessness of wickedness, the use of the tongue by a righteous person is as 'choice silver'. Where people are dying through ignorance of God's wisdom, the righteous person feeds his hearers with spiritual food coming from his relationship with God and his knowledge of God's revealed wisdom.

CHAPTER ELEVEN

V 1–31: SUMMARY Dishonesty, pride, humility, wisdom, integrity, riches, wrath, righteousness, wickedness, death, hypocrisy, knowledge, rejoicing, understanding, gossip, faithfulness, counsel, surety, graciousness, mercy, punishment, deliverance, discretion, desire, generosity, seeking, vanity, soul-winning, recompense.

V 24: PLENTY The one who sows generously will get more. **V 24: POVERTY** The one who is mean in what he gives out will get less. **V 25: PRINCIPLE** Here we see, in different words, what Jesus said: 'It is more blessed to give than to receive.'

CHAPTER TWELVE

V 1–28: SUMMARY Instruction, favour, condemnation, stability, wife, thought, words, wisdom, self, honour, cruelty, industry, coveting, self-deceit, counsel, deceit, peace, righteousness, restraint,

diligence, friendships, laziness, life, death.

V 27a: LAZY We look at a man who is lazy. **V 27a: LAX** Having undertaken the difficult task of hunting an animal, he fails to prepare and roast it. He should have diligently finished what he had done with so much effort before. **V 27a: LACKING** By implication, this man will go hungry. **V 27a: LESSON** The lesson is obvious and practical. Finish what you start, as long as it is honourable before the LORD.

CHAPTER THIRTEEN

V 1–25: SUMMARY Wisdom, oneness, talk, violence, laziness, zeal, diligence, lying, righteousness, generosity, success, dishonesty, labour, hope, desire, word, commandment, law, understanding, fool, messenger, ambassador, corruption, reproof, accomplishment, companions, evil, good, inheritance, justice, discipline, satisfaction, want.

V 24: SPARING This verse deals with the father who refuses to discipline his son. **V 24: SON** A son who is truly loved by his father will be disciplined by him because of that love. **V 24: SPEED** To be effective, not only must discipline be balanced and loving, but also it must be applied promptly.

CHAPTER FOURTEEN

V 1–35: SUMMARY Wisdom, foolishness, uprightness, speech, balance, sufferings, knowledge, wicked, deception, death, laughter, grief, backsliding, satisfaction, simplicity, temper, prudence, poor, rich, despising, mercy, truth, labour, idleness, riches, witness, fear of the LORD, prosperity, kings' values, wrath, multitudes, impulse, envy, oppression, refuge, righteousness, nations, service.

V 34: RESULTS OF RIGHTEOUSNESS A nation is made truly great when it accepts, adheres to and applies God's righteousness. **V 34: REPROACH OF REBELLION** Conversely, sin, stumbling, and suffering abound where God's standards are ignored or rejected. It is not economic value but spiritual worth that makes a country great.

CHAPTER FIFTEEN

V 1–33: SUMMARY Speech, omniscience, instruction, correction, righteous rewards, abomination, delight, discipline, hell, merry, sorrow, understanding, foolishness, fear of the LORD, love, wrath, laziness, parents, counsel, thoughts, greed, bribes, consideration, pride, rejoicing, rebukes, humility.

V 1: SOFT ANSWER AND STIRRED ANGER Wrath is turned away by a soft answer, but harsh talk stirs up anger. **V 2: WISE TONGUE AND WANTON TALK** Knowledge is used correctly by those who speak wisely but fools can only produce foolishness.

CHAPTER SIXTEEN

V 1–33: SUMMARY Heart preparation, the LORD's answer, judgement, guidance, sovereignty, pride, atonement, fear of the LORD, pleasing God, direction, talk, honesty, righteousness, appeasement, kings, real values, uprightness, humility, trusting the LORD, wisdom, understanding, direction, fools, deception, death, labour, ungodliness, strife, whispering, violence, old age, anger, self-control, the LORD's overruling.

V 35: LOT CAST Some things that happen seem to be the result of chance. **LORD'S CONTROL** Even random things are under God's sovereign control. This is a great comfort to those who trust Him.

CHAPTER SEVENTEEN

V 1–28: SUMMARY Contentment, strife, wisdom, foolishness, prosperity, evil talk, mocking, poverty, punishment, grandchildren, arrogance, rulers, bribery, discernment, division, rebellion, officialdom, revenge, quarrelling, injustice, friendship, guarantees, deceit, cheerfulness, brokenness, restraint, understanding, self-control.

V 27a: CONSIDERED WORDS Knowledgeable people do not speak too much. **V 27b: CALM WAY** When we use our understanding, our spirit remains calm as we trust God. **V 28: CONSIDERED WISE** The best thing to do when we do not know what to say is to say nothing. Even someone who does not understand what is going on is considered wise when he does that!

CHAPTER EIGHTEEN

V 1–24: SUMMARY Isolation, selfishness, rebellion, fool, wicked, dishonoured, words, partiality, injustice, sloth, God's name, righteousness, security, wealth, self-esteem, destruction, haughtiness, honour, humility, pre-judging, spirit, knowledge, gifts, opportunity, examination, lots, offended brother, work, wife, favour, friendship.

V 24: FRIENDS To have friends one has to make the effort to befriend others. **V 24: FRIEND** There is one friend, above all others, who 'sticks closer than a brother'. He is the Lord Jesus Christ.

CHAPTER NINETEEN

V 1–29: SUMMARY Integrity, perverseness, knowledge, sin, twistedness, fretting, wealth, lying, insincerity, poor, lovelessness, wisdom, understanding, luxury, servanthood, discretion, anger, kindness, kings, sonship, contention, wife, inheritance, marriage, laziness, obedience, carelessness, pity, rewards, chastening, punishment, counsel, fear of the LORD, satisfaction, example, experience, honouring parents, straying, scorn, injustice.

V 16: COMMANDMENT The person who obeys God's commandment keeps his soul in good condition. **V 16: CARELESSNESS** Careless ways that ignore what God commands will lead to death.

CHAPTER TWENTY

V 1–30: SUMMARY Wine, strong drink, king's wrath, strife, laziness, counsel, foolishness, righteous, children, purity, dishonesty, deeds, creation, blessing, knowledge, pledges, deceit, planning, gossip, cursing parents, easy gain, waiting, guidance, rashness, judgement, spirit, mercy, strength, old age, chastisement.

V 1: ALCOHOL Note that wine produces mocking, and strong drink produces brawling. Mocking and brawling are to be avoided by God's people. **V 1: ASTRAY** Many are led astray by alcohol. **V 1: APPLICATION** Those who are 'not wise' are led astray in this way. A person with God's wisdom is not led astray. Christians need to apply these lessons and carefully consider, before God, their attitude to alcohol.

CHAPTER TWENTY-ONE

V 1–31: SUMMARY God's sovereignty, God's weighing hearts, righteousness, pride, diligence, dishonest gains, violence, perverseness, pure, intention, evil desire, scoffer, wise, poor, pacification, pleasure seeking, wisdom's strength, word control, laziness,

covetousness, wicked sacrifice, lying, God's counsel, God's universe.

V 1: GOD'S WILL The heart of even a mighty king is turned by God according to His sovereign will. **V 2: GOD'S WEIGHING** Irrespective of how a man feels about his own life, God weighs his heart. **V 3: GOD'S WISH** God wants to see righteousness and justice from the heart, and not just external compliance with ceremony or sacrifice.

CHAPTER TWENTY-TWO

Chapters 22:17 to 23:34 consist of Proverbs collected from others by Solomon.

V 1–29: SUMMARY Respect, God as man's maker, avoiding evil, humility and honour, perverse, child-training, rich, borrowing, sowing, generosity, scoffers, purity, gracious talk, knowledge, laziness, immorality, correction, poor. Collected wise sayings from others (22:17–23:34): listen, jest, assurance, trust, poor, associations, pledges, land-theft, work.

V 6a: DISCIPLINE A child should be trained up, just as a growing plant is trained. This involves the thought of caring guidance as well as obedient discipline. A child should be trained to know, love and follow God. This will affect everything else he does. **V 6b: DEPARTURE** A prayed-over, trained-up child, coming to a trust in God, will not depart from those good ways when he is old.

CHAPTER TWENTY-THREE

V 1–35: SUMMARY Restraint, riches, abstinence, careful words, exploitation, instruction, correction, heart wisdom, envy, hearing, excesses, respect for parents, truth, rejoicing parents, heart surrender, immorality, avoiding strong drink.

V 4a: **PROHIBITED** To work too much in order to be rich is wrong and is prohibited by God. **V 4b: PRUDENT** Base your life on your correct understanding of the teaching of God's word about riches. Our time should be occupied for God by something far more important than overworking and desiring to be rich. **V 5: PASSING** Why concentrate on things which have no lasting existence or value? Riches fly away like an eagle towards heaven. Even here on earth, they are very unpredictable and they certainly cannot be taken to heaven.

CHAPTER TWENTY-FOUR

V 1–34: SUMMARY Envy, wisdom, scheming, adversity, delivering others, righteous victory, loving enemies, fighting, fearing God, fearing the king, impartiality, answering, operations, deceit, laziness, poverty.

V 19a: FOOLISH FRETTING A person who trusts in his powerful God need never fret because of evildoers. **V 19b: ENVY EXCLUDED** Neither should he envy the wicked. **V 20a: PITIABLE PROSPECT** There is 'no prospect' for the evil man. **V 20b: DEATH DEFINITE** 'The lamp of the wicked will be put out' and then he will experience that darkness eternally. How different for those pardoned and saved by God! We are the ones to be envied!

CHAPTER TWENTY-FIVE

Chapters 25:1 to 29:27 are Solomon's Proverbs collected by Hezekiah.
V 1–28: SUMMARY Secrecy, searching, heart, refining, humility, hastiness, privacy, appropriate words, refreshing words, boasting, giving, forbearance, restraint, moderation, lying, unfaithfulness, insensitivity, loving enemies, back-biting, confrontation, good news, constancy, self-glorification, self-control.

V 19: TRUST Pain is avoided by placing confidence in someone trustworthy. God is the supreme example and there are friends in whom we can trust. **V 19: TROUBLE** However, to put or share a confidence with someone who is unfaithful will only bring trouble. Close friends should be faithful and God-fearing people. **V 19: TOOTHACHE** The pain from toothache pervades everything. It will persist until the problem causing the pain is dealt with. A foot out of joint produces the same type of problem. To trust an unfaithful person is worse than toothache and a bad foot, and it should be dealt with.

CHAPTER TWENTY-SIX

V 1–28: SUMMARY Honour, curse, dealing with a fool, repeated folly, conceit, laziness, meddling, deceit, gossip, contention, fervency, wickedness, consequences of evil, lying, flattery.

V 4: ANSWERING A FOOL—IDENTIFICATION The danger of answering a fool in like manner is that you may be identified with him. **V 5: ANSWERING A FOOL—INSTRUCTION** The value of answering a fool is that you can instruct him so that he ceases to be wise in his own eyes. In other words, there is both a right time to answer a fool and disagree with him, and also a right time to withhold an answer and let his words go over your head. Wisdom is needed in dealing with foolish people.

CHAPTER TWENTY-SEVEN

V 1–27: SUMMARY Presumption, humility, foolish wrath, jealousy, open rebuke, friendly faithfulness, hunger, wandering counsel, faithful support, wisdom, avoiding evil, surety, insensitivity, contention, constructive discussion, service, heart, satisfaction, valuation, foolishness, diligence, self-support.

V 23: DILIGENCE A farmer should always know the state of his flocks and herds and look after them. This is also a spiritual principle for Christians with pastoral care over others. **V 24: DECEITFULNESS** The Lord Jesus Christ spoke of 'the deceitfulness of riches'. Riches have wings. They 'are not forever'. Christians should focus their lives on enduring lasting treasures! **V 25–26: DEPENDENCE** The future of a farmer and his family depends upon his diligence. The future of God's flock, under His grace, depends to some extent on the diligent oversight given by other Christians.

CHAPTER TWENTY-EIGHT

V 1–28: SUMMARY Boldness, anarchy, law, justice, integrity, shame, usury, unanswered prayer, downfall, understanding, righteous, wicked, confession, reverence, wicked ruler, bloodshed, blamelessness, diligence, poverty, blessings, partiality, covetousness, rebuke, flattery, robbing parents, pride, trust, poor, wicked influence.

V 12: RIGHTEOUS REJOICING—GREAT GLORY When those who know God rejoice in Him and in His good, great glory is brought to God and great blessing to those around. **V 12: EVIL ELEVATED—PEOPLE PETRIFIED** The reverse is true when wicked persons rise to positions of influence and authority. God's standards are so undermined that people live in fear of what society becomes.

CHAPTER TWENTY-NINE

V 1–27: SUMMARY Hard-heartedness, righteous rulers, wisdom, wasting, justice, bribes, flattery, evil's snare, righteous rejoicing, poor, scoffers, wise, bloodthirsty, upright, free expression, evil rulers, truth, discipline, increased wickedness, correction, revelation, rashness, treating servants, anger, humility, evil association, fear of man, abomination.

V 1: REBUKE AND REFUSAL It is very dangerous to refuse to be rebuked from God's word. **V 1: RESULT AND REMEDY** This can result in the rebuked person becoming so hardhearted that he fails to respond in repentance to God. He will be cut off 'without remedy'. His refusal to listen humbly to the rebukes of others closes the path of repentance to him. Becoming hardened towards God is very dangerous.

CHAPTER THIRTY

These Proverbs are from Agar, of whom little is known.

V 1–27: SUMMARY Spiritual ignorance, God's greatness, God's word, sufficiency, careful criticism, wayward generation, satisfaction, honouring parents, pride, violence, greed, insatiability, wonderful ways, adultery, blindness to sinning, perturbed, industry, majesty, self-humbling, ceasing from evil.

V 5a: PURITY Every word of God is pure as well as being infallible and inspired. **V 5b: PROTECTION** Through His word, He protects spiritually those who trust Him. **V 6: PROHIBITION** God's word is complete, sufficient and unchangeable. It must undergo no additions or subtractions. The principle found here is endorsed throughout the Bible and finally restated in its last book, Revelation.

CHAPTER THIRTY-ONE

These are the words of King Lemuel which his mother had taught him. Lemuel may have been another name for Solomon.

V 1–31: SUMMARY Mother's concern, the moral king, the sober king, dangers of drink, representing the unrepresented, righteous judgement, poor, the virtuous wife, the value of a good wife, the qualities and character of a good wife, the effect on husband and children of a good wife.

V 10a: WIFE The need to find a wife who is virtuous (or noble) is a question that should be addressed by every Christian man seeking marriage. Spiritual and moral qualities are even more important than the other important and justified considerations. **V 10b: WORTH** The right wife really is a great treasure and far more valuable than jewellery or wealth. **V 11: WELL-BEING** Such is her marital fidelity and trustworthiness around the home and with money that her husband 'safely trusts her'. He knows that all is well at home. No wonder his children are blessed! **V 12–27: WILLING** Willingness to put herself out for her family is her key quality. This affects her work, her loving concern for her family, her wisdom, her kindness and her watchfulness over her loved ones.

ECCLESIASTES

OVERVIEW

PEOPLE AND PRELIMINARIES

Written by Solomon, probably in Jerusalem before 931 BC, Ecclesiastes (twelve chapters) is the fourth of the poetical books of the Old Testament. See comments on Job.

PLAN AND PURPOSE

This is a divinely inspired account of an ungodly man's search for reality without considering God's revelation and intervention. Solomon, like many others, believes that God exists and then reaches his opinions as if He did not exist. Solomon accurately observes life 'under the sun' (that phrase comes twenty-nine times), but reaches some vital conclusions erroneously. It is as if he looks at a very darkened and overcast sky, without God's revelation which comes from far above the sun! Now and then, the sun breaks through, and biblical truth is imparted. Thus 'vanity' is a recurring theme, even when it is not mentioned specifically, which it is thirty-seven times. Biblical revelation comes from a higher source than that, from God Himself! This book traces man's search for meaning and satisfaction in life, through concentrating on various philosophies and aspects of life and of living. It concludes that a person cannot be satisfied without God. It is unfruitful and vain to search for satisfaction through knowledge, pleasure, human wisdom, folly, hard work, achieving goals, materialism, resignation to fate, competition, power, or religion. Solomon's final advice sees him looking towards God. As with many of us, God was his last port of call rather than his first and only refuge.

ECCLESIASTES

Theme of vanity in human existence under the sun (1:1–11); Solomon's search for meaning through pleasure, wisdom, work, and wealth (1:12–6:9); Solomon's findings on the matters he investigates with regard to human ignorance, uncertainty, limitations, and mortality; the need to hear and value wisdom (6:10–9:18); Solomon shares some wise sayings; the sobering reminder of God's judgement; (10:1–11:10); the clouds disappear: remember, fear and obey God (12:1–14).

PRINCIPLES AND PARTICULARS

Solomon's wrong conclusions are taken up, erroneously and tragically, by some sects and false religions as tenets of their shaky and misleading faiths. This book is thus a favourite fishing spot for those cults who would seek to deny that man has an ever-living soul, and that the only alternatives after death are either eternal blessing or eternal punishment. Annihilation and its diluted derivatives furnish no option. Ecclesiastes demonstrates that lost man cannot be right in his conclusions, until he comes to God through the Saviour, the Lord Jesus Christ. Only then can God change the seeker's vain existence and thitherto meaningless search into a personal relationship with Himself, both now and eternally. It reminds us to reach no conclusions on vital matters of life by reasoning coming from 'under the sun'. We need God's Word, the Bible, and His new life in Christ.

CHAPTER ONE

V 1: SOURCE It is hard to reach any other conclusion than that King Solomon is the author of Ecclesiastes. He is the son of David, and is king in Jerusalem when he writes. **V 2: STATEMENT** Observing life through the eyes of man, his opening statement is that everything is vain or empty, or meaningless. **V 3–8: SO?** The underlying question he asks, humanly speaking, is 'So what?' Man labours and passes away, the year carries on as normal, yet man is never satisfied with what he sees or hears. So, what is the meaning of it all? **V 9–11: SUN** A key phrase in the book is the phrase 'under the sun'. Much of Ecclesiastes is man's observation of humanity, apart from God, in looking at 'everything under the sun'. This is punctuated with glimpses of truth through the eye of faith which puts all this in its context. The writer opens by commenting, 'There is nothing new under the sun.' Everything is as it was and as it will be. **V 12–15: SEARCHING** The Preacher, (the name Solomon gives himself), has set his heart to search out wisdom concerning everything under heaven. He has observed everything he can and concludes that it is vanity and nothing can really be changed. **V 16–18: SORROW** Wisdom and knowledge alone only produce sorrow because they produce more questions than answers. At this stage, he does not refer to godly wisdom which is a gift from the LORD.

CHAPTER TWO

V 1–3: PLEASURE Solomon decides to go on the pleasure trail as a means of giving him laughter and mirth. He fortifies his search with wine so that his wisdom can discern whether there is anything lasting in such an approach to life. **V 4–9: PROSPERITY** His search for pleasure includes heaping up things of great value and with even a little musical culture thrown in. He was greater in this than anyone else in all Jerusalem. **V 10: POWER** Whatever he wanted he took to test this theory to the full. **V 11: POINTLESS** His conclusion regarding all this is that 'there is no profit under the sun'. It is all pointless from the human point of view. **V 12–16: PRUDENCE** He then looks at wisdom, madness, and folly. He can see apparent benefits in wisdom, but comes to the conclusion that everybody dies, whether wise or foolish, and that this also is vanity. **V 17–26: PITIFUL** This experiment leads the Preacher to hate life itself because of its pointlessness and vanity. Even eating and drinking on a daily basis, to enjoy the pleasure of one's labours, becomes a pitiful emptiness when God is not central. This is a depressing conclusion at such an early stage of the book.

CHAPTER THREE

V1–8: TIME The Preacher observes that in life there is a time to do everything. **V 9–15: TOIL** Knowing this, he asks what the point of human toil is and answers that there is no point. However, he knows that what God does will endure forever. God is sovereign and to be revered. **V 16–17: TRAVESTY** He also sees that justice and judgement are turned to wickedness by man. This travesty of justice concerns him, but he perceives that God will judge things righteously in His time. Man has time to do what he wants, but God will judge him for what he does. **V 18–21: TEST** Viewed simply from an earthly perspective, man is no different from an animal. He is born, lives, and

dies. He suggests that God tests man so that he can see his animal existence has an end without a purpose in itself. Again, this leaves out the question of eternality and spirituality, which cannot be seen 'under the sun', without the help of God's Holy Spirit and the Scriptures. **V 22: TEMPORARY** Realising that man has only a temporary earthly existence, he concludes that all he can do is to rejoice in his works before giving way to the next generation.

CHAPTER FOUR

V 1–3: OPPRESSION OVERVIEW Oppression 'under the sun' leads the Preacher to conclude that it is better not to have existed than to be oppressed! **V 4–6: WHY WORK?** Although skills are envied by others, a foolish and unskilled person gets by with a quiet life without grasping for the wind. **V 7–12: LONELINESS LAMENTED** The Preacher sees the fact of being lonely as another vanity. Clearly, here on earth, it is better to have friends for support. **V 13–16: PASSING POPULARITY** A powerful king will pass away and it is better to be a poor and wise youth than a dead king. This further 'under the sun' observation pricks the inflated balloon of pomp and self-importance of many.

CHAPTER FIVE

V 1–7: GOD There is a temporary burst of sunlight through the clouds. The Preacher concentrates on God in the first half of this chapter. In contrast to his observations 'under the sun', he urges people to walk prudently when worshipping Him, to hear rather than make rash sacrifices, to watch careless speech, to remember that God is in heaven and sees things 'under the sun', to pay vows made to God, and, perhaps the most important thought in two words, to 'fear God'. Knowing that God is in sovereign control of affairs, and of the individual, sets a perspective for living. **V 8–10: GREED** Returning to the earth, he sees the vanity of greed which is so often accompanied by perversion of justice by those in high positions. **V 11–12: GAIN** Material gain is also vanity. It never brings satisfaction and the only point of having possessions is to show them to other people and say, 'I have got them.' Ironically, compare the sweet sleep of a man who is tired through labouring and the sleeplessness of a man who is concerned about the future of his riches. **V 13–17: GOODS** Everyone who is born must die. He will take nothing with him when he has to go. So what profit is there in piling up goods which, in any case, give him sorrow, sickness and anger? **V 18–22: GOOD** More sunshine breaks through for a while. When Solomon sees the things he has as gifts from God, it changes his picture of them. He knows it is good to enjoy them for a temporary period, before going to be with the God whom he trusts.

CHAPTER SIX

V 1–2: PASSING PROSPERITY The Preacher asks what the point is of having prosperity under the sun which then goes to someone else. **V 3–6: FINAL FUTILITY** He asks what the benefit of living a long life is and also what the benefit is of having plenty of children. Is not a stillborn child in a better position as he has avoided the vanity of it all? The false doctrine of annihilation after death feeds this depressing view. **V 7–9: SATISFIED SOULS** He sees that man's labour and possessions cannot satisfy the soul. The wise man is no better off than the fool. **V 10–11: NOTHING NEW** As life passes like a shadow, nothing new comes. We have seen it all before. **V 12: UNCERTAINTY UNDERLINED** Man does not really know what is best for him in the uncertainties of his transient life. Who knows what the future holds 'under the sun'?

CHAPTER SEVEN

V 1–12: PRUDENT PREFERENCES Solomon sees that there are several choices that are 'better' (a word which occurs several times) than more foolish choices. He can see practical advantages in applied wisdom. **V 13–14: SUPREME SOVEREIGNTY** More sunshine! Solomon now arrives at a point where he sees that God is supremely sovereign. This is the bedrock of the Christian's confidence. **V 15: LIVING LONG** God's sovereignty is set off against the observation that wicked men can live long, and relatively good men can live short lives. **V 16–22: ACTIVE APPLICATIONS** He then goes on to apply wisdom to the life we have, be it short or long. Legalistic over-righteousness and worldly wisdom should be avoided, as should wickedness and foolishness. Fearing God is the key and it leads to wisdom in evaluating the comments of others, in escaping immorality and in pleasing God. **V 27–29: COMPELLING CONCLUSION** Solomon's tentative conclusion at this point is that God made people upright but they invariably go astray .

CHAPTER EIGHT

V 1: COUNTENANCE Solomon observes that the wise man's face shines and is less stern! **V 2–9: COMMANDMENT** He urges his readers to keep the king's commandments because the king is in charge. He goes on to observe that no one is really in charge of his own spirit and that he or she will lose it at death. Also, a king can suffer because he is a ruler. **V 10–14: CONTRADICTION?** Observing the vanity of life, the Preacher says that he thinks it will be well with those who fear God and not well with those who do not. He goes on to observe that some righteous people are treated as though they were wicked and the wicked as though they were righteous and he sees it as vanity 'under the sun'. Much seems confused and contradictory! **V 15: COMMENDATION** He then says that this led him to commend enjoyment because in this life there seemed nothing better to do than 'eat, drink, and be merry'. **V 16–17: CLOSED** By wisdom, he then tries to find out what God has done and comes to the conclusion that this avenue is closed to him. Man cannot find God solely by his own efforts. He needs God's inspired revelation, which we have through the Bible and through the Lord Jesus Christ.

CHAPTER NINE

V 1–3: DESTINY From his purely human and worldly vantage point, the writer sees a common destiny for all. All must die. **V 4–6: DEAD** He then considers the fate of the dead and concludes that it nullifies everything for everyone. Thus, 'a living dog is better than a dead lion'. It is important to know that his vantage point is simply 'under the sun' and eternity is not under consideration here. **V 7–10: DETERMINATION** Seeing the futility of life, he then counsels a determination to enjoy life, to be well dressed, and to enjoy married life. Work hard now, because there will be no work afterwards! In other words, without taking eternity into view, live this life to the full. **V 11–12: DOOMED** But this leads him to the dead-end view

that all men are doomed, and one day will be caught in the snare or trap of death. Nobody knows when. This is how many people without Christ see life today. **V 13–17: DEMONSTRATION** Solomon notes a demonstration of wisdom that impressed him. A poor man saved a city by his wisdom. His wisdom is remembered but the poor man is forgotten. He feels this deeply and urges that wise words should be heard and valued.

CHAPTER TEN

V 1–20: PREFERRED PROVERBS Solomon now seeks to provide some of the wisdom he wants people to hear. Chapters ten to twelve provide this. Like the Book of Proverbs, there is no single theme in this chapter, which deals with fools and folly, relationships with rulers, care in conduct, sharpness and strength, wisdom with words, indolence and industry, money and might, and caution in cursing. Here is a collection of practical advice about how to live for those 'under the sun'.

CHAPTER ELEVEN

V 1–6: SOWING These verses tell us to sow generously and faithfully, irrespective of the weather conditions or of our expectation of fruitfulness. Just as we do not know how the bones of a child move in the womb, so we do not know how God works when a seed is sown. **V 7–8: SENSITIVITY** In enjoying the sunshine of life, we must remember that there is darkness, too. From a human point of view, this, too, seems to be vanity. **V 9–10: SEPARATION** There is a balance between knowing that God will bring us into judgement for our sins, a key thought in the whole of the Bible, and enjoying the good things which He has put on earth for us. It is right to rejoice in God's provision, but it is wrong to live in an evil way and forget that judgement is coming. A holy and biblical balance must govern our separation from what is wrong and our enjoyment of what is right, under God's hand.

CHAPTER TWELVE

V 1–5: CREATOR Now the clouds clear away, and God's truth shines clearly through. Bearing in mind the fact that life can become very difficult and more dangerous as one grows older, Solomon urges that before the difficult days come, one should 'remember [one's] Creator in the days of [one's] youth'. To those who have no youth left, now is a good time to start! **V 6–7: CLOSED** Especially, God should be remembered in personal faith, in the realisation that one day our lives will come to a close. Our bodies will go to dust and our spirit will return to God, for judgement or for salvation. **V 8: CRY** The Preacher's despairing cry, having viewed things from 'under the sun', is 'vanity of vanities' and 'all is vanity'. Life is confusing and meaningless without God's intervention, written revelation through the Bible, and salvation in the Lord Jesus Christ. **V 9–12: COLLECTION** In drawing the book of Ecclesiastes to a close, Solomon talks about his sources and his search to find the right words. The sayings that really drive home, as well-driven nails, come from one Shepherd. Books and learning may produce weariness, but God's word is alive and relevant. **V 13–14: CONCLUSION** The sum of wisdom on earth leads to an important conclusion. We must 'Fear God and keep His commandments'. In doing that, we must realise that God will judge 'every secret thing', and that there is no escape. The book of Ecclesiastes pleads for a Saviour to bear away our sins, to forgive us, to cleanse us from all our selfish disobedience, and to give us peace and purpose in an empty world.

SONG OF SOLOMON

OVERVIEW

PEOPLE AND PRELIMINARIES

Written by Solomon, probably before 965 BC in Jerusalem, Song of Solomon (eight chapters) is the fifth and last of the poetical books of the Old Testament. See comments on Job.

PLAN AND PURPOSE

This book presents Solomon's best song of over a thousand that he wrote. It presents a moving love story in which a beautiful Shulamite maiden is wooed and won by her shepherd-lover. Some think he is the same person as the king, who seeks her affection, and that he assumes the dress of a shepherd to communicate better with her. Others see the king as the shepherd's competitor. The book does not indicate who says what and there is room for legitimate differences of interpretation. To some, the book is purely allegorical, showing God's love for His people, be they Jews or Christians. It certainly teaches much about love and the response to it. Any true love story faintly reflects God's love for us in the gospel, and this book encourages our devotion to the Lord spiritually. But primarily the book is historical and factual, and endorses God's approval of physical sexual intimacy, but only within the marriage bond of man and woman. We see the rightness of courtship, marriage, high esteem for loved ones and the growing together of man and wife, in the context of God's holiness and personal integrity. Caution is needed about subheadings included in the text or margin of some Bibles, which attribute words spoken to particular characters. These subheadings may help, but they are not authoritative. They represent only the view of the person making them.

PROFILE AND PROGRESSION

The way that this book is outlined depends on one's view of who said what and to whom! A simple outline follows: relationship commenced—courtship (1:2–3:5); relationship consummated—marriage (3:6–5:1); relationship continued—rift and restoration (5:2–8:14).

PRINCIPLES AND PARTICULARS

Legitimate intimacy within marriage is sensitively, cleanly and carefully portrayed. Those opposing God's word have, without any justification, sneered dirtily at some of this book, but reading it could never make anyone dirty-minded. In fact, their criticisms illustrate one of the two famous French maxims written on the British royal coat of arms 'Honi soit qui mal y pense' ('Evil be to those who evil think'). Here are no inappropriate descriptions of sexual activity that characterise today's sensually inappropriate books from

sensational bookshops and bookstalls. This book shows that God neither requires sexual abstinence nor tolerates sexual promiscuity. In His plan, sexual relationships are right and good, but only in marriage between a faithful man and his loyal wife. They form an important part of the blessed and God-given package of marriage.

SONG OF SOLOMON

CHAPTER ONE

V 1: SOLOMON AND SONGS Solomon regarded this as his 'song of songs', presumably his best. **V 2–7: SHULAMITE AND SUPPORTERS** As the maiden awaits her wedding, she expresses her desire for the king. She is supported by the 'daughters of Jerusalem' who wait upon her. She is less convinced of her beauty than he is. Those with lovely Christian character see their faults more strongly than anyone else. **V 8–17: SUPERLATIVES AND SHARING** Expressions of love and admiration pass between the king and his bride-to-be. Christ sees us as His beloved, and we know He is beautiful in His sinless perfection and gracious love.

CHAPTER TWO

V 1–7: ANTICIPATION AROUSED The maiden's anticipation of a legitimate sexual relationship is based on her love for the king, and his words to her. She anticipates intimacy, but insists that it should not be stirred up physically before the right time. The balance is right—sex in marriage is a wonderful thing to look forward to, but should not be physically aroused until marriage. **V 8–14: DEVOTIONAL DESIRE** The mutual desires of the couple go beyond a mere physical relationship, important as that is. They want to be with each other, to see and talk to each other. Marriage is a friendship, and they want to develop that. **V 15: FORAGING FOXES** Foxes spoil vineyards and must be caught in order to stop that happening. Those foxes are like the irritants of sin and selfishness that can spoil the closest of relationships. By God's grace and enabling, they must be caught and dealt with, too. **V 16–17: PERSONAL POSSESSION** The Shulamite maiden rejoices that her husband and she have mutual ownership rights with each other, (just as Christ and the church have). She longs to spend time with him, and appreciate his strength and grace.

CHAPTER THREE

V 1–4: DRAMATIC DREAM It seems (though one cannot be dogmatic) that alone in her bedroom at night, the young woman dreams that she has lost her beloved and goes into the city to seek him. In her dream, she finds him and will not let him go. It is a comforting assurance to Christians to know that, once belonging to Christ, we can never lose the Lover of our souls, and that He will never let us go. **V 5: RENEWED REMINDER** Perhaps because of the natural desire to be with her beloved, as a result of the dream, she reminds the daughters of Jerusalem that it is wrong to stir up sexual love before marriage. **V 6–11: SEEKING SPOUSE** Solomon comes, with pomp and ceremony, to seek his spouse to be and to take her with him for the wedding. The king's heart is glad!

CHAPTER FOUR

V 1–11: BEAUTIFUL BRIDE The king becomes more intimate in his expression of love to his bride, as is appropriate after marriage. He uses the word 'sister', along with others, because, in the culture in which he lives, it is understood to imply closeness, and certainly not incest. **V 12–15: PURE PARTNER** Solomon testifies to the virginity of his wife prior to marriage. She was 'shut up' or 'sealed' before marriage. Her sexual purity appears to increase her attractiveness to the king. **V 16: SANCTIFIED SEX** Since marriage, the Shulamite rejoices in the expression of sexual love that the husband-and-wife relationship encourages. This yields 'pleasant fruits' from their love for each other.

CHAPTER FIVE

V 1: SOLOMON SATISFIED The king expresses his satisfaction with his intimate relationship with his wife. He recommends the sexual union, within marriage, to his friends. **V 1–8: RELATIONSHIP RIFT** The first recorded disagreement arises. The cause seems to be an argument about whether to be intimate or not on a particular occasion. Married Christians should consider the needs of each other selflessly. **V 9–16: ABSENT APPRECIATION** The young wife appreciates her husband even more after he has temporarily (and probably wrongly) withdrawn as a result of their first and silly disagreement. She is so concerned that she asks the daughters of Jerusalem to help her. Perhaps some established Christian married couples would appreciate each other more if they anticipated realistically what it would be like to be single again.

CHAPTER SIX

V 1–3: RELATIONSHIP RESTORED The Shulamite answers the daughters of Jerusalem, who ask her if she knows where the king is. Using symbolic language about entering a garden, she confirms that their relationship is restored and resumed. She again rejoices that they possess each other. **V 4–13: WOOING WORDS** Both the king and his wife engage in renewed intimate conversation, which reveals their real love for each other. Their first dispute is over, and others nearby seem glad to hear of the return to their close relationship.

CHAPTER SEVEN

V 1–9: INCREASED INTIMACY The intimacy that the king expresses to his beloved shows that with a restored relationship, there can be an even closer union and expression of love than before the rift. The Christian backslider experiences that, too, in coming back to a loving and pardoning God who loves His own so much. **V 10–13: LESSON LEARNED** If the Shulamite had been a little abrupt and short with her husband prior to the disagreement, she certainly knows how to respond to him in love and conversation now. She has learned her lesson.

CHAPTER EIGHT

V 1–2: SWEET SAYINGS! She now says that she wishes, in one sense, that he had been like her brother, so she could have shown him a public expression of her love earlier! **V 3–4: SECRETLY SENTIMENTAL** This time, her husband's embrace reminds her of the need for self-control, not because being physically intimate would be premature now, but because it should be kept for the right time and place. Self-control is right in marriage, as well as outside it. **V 5–7: STRONG SEAL** Walking with her beloved husband, the bride asks for her love to seal his heart and states it is as strong as death. It is unquenchable and inestimable. However, the best of human love is as nothing compared with God's love to us in Christ! **V 8–9: SISTER'S STATE** The Shulamite expresses a caring concern for her sister, who is still a young girl. She will do her best to safeguard her sister's purity, especially as she herself experiences the blessing of a union into which she entered as a virgin. **V 10–14: SOLOMON'S SWEETHEART** The young wife ends the Song of Solomon by showing again that she is the king's sweetheart. She is now closer to him than at the start. This is a wonderful pattern for the Christian, who should daily get closer to the Lord. It is also a pattern for established married couples, who should pray to be drawn ever closer together each day, in a world of shabby affairs and sad divorces.

ISAIAH

OVERVIEW

PEOPLE AND PRELIMINARIES

✳ Isaiah is the sole author of this book bearing his name (sixty-six chapters), written between 700 BC and 681 BC, probably in Judah. It is the first of five books called the 'major prophets', the others being Jeremiah, Lamentations, Ezekiel, and Daniel. They are so called because, apart from Lamentations, their prophecies are longer than the other prophets (called the 'minor prophets'). An estimate of the period covered by Isaiah is sixty-three years.

PLAN AND PURPOSE

ⓘ The book records Isaiah's prophetic ministry, mainly concerning the southern kingdom of Judah, during the time of the divided kingdom. He prophesied for sixty-three years, between 739 BC and 686 BC, during the reigns of Uzziah, Jotham, Ahaz and Hezekiah. During the reign of the last of these, Assyria, which had overcome the northern kingdom of Israel, unsuccessfully threatened to conquer Judah. It was the joint spiritual impact of Isaiah and King Hezekiah that God used to avert this disaster at that time. Isaiah was a prophet in both the senses of forth-telling and foretelling. He preached strongly against the superficiality and idolatry of Judah. He foretold the Babylonian captivity to come later. He prophesied about the birth and death of the Lord Jesus Christ long before death by crucifixion was even known, and 700 years before the 'Man of Sorrows' died as the 'Lamb of God'. With an historical

interlude sandwiched between, the book features widespread prophetic condemnation and then proclaims the comfort of salvation that is to be found through God's mercy and grace. Isaiah looks forward to God's glorious answering of His people's prayer.

PROFILE AND PROGRESSION

🥚 Captivity coming, including pronouncements against Judah and 🥚 Jerusalem and judgements against surrounding nations (1:1–13:18); God's dealings with Israel through chastisement and restoration (24:1–27:13); A series of woes and warnings (28:1–35:10); Sennacharib, Hezekiah and Babylon (36:1–39:8); God's saving work, including help for and deliverance of Israel's captives, prophecies of the Suffering Servant; and God's final blessings on His restored people after their oppression (40:1–66:24).

PRINCIPLES AND PARTICULARS

☞ The prophetic scan of nearer and more distant scenes of time seem to blend together like successive mountain ranges. Because the nearer prophecies are fulfilled comprehensively, in this 'prophetic foreshortening', we know the distant ones also will be. God's hatred is revealed against idolatry and superficial religiosity. There are important prophecies about Christ, especially His birth and death in chapters nine and fifty-three respectively. There is a similarity between the layout of Isaiah's chapters and the Bible's books: sixty-six in total, thirty-nine in the first section and twenty-seven in the second. Those two sections, like those of the Old and New Testaments, major on judgement in the first half and on salvation in the second half (though, as with the Testaments, each part contains elements of both judgement and salvation).

ISAIAH

CHAPTER ONE

V 1: WHEN Isaiah means 'The LORD saves'. The names Joshua, Elisha, and Jesus mean the same. He prophesies during the reigns of Uzziah, Jotham, Ahaz, and Hezekiah, kings of the southern kingdom of Judah. **V 2–15: WICKEDNESS** Isaiah concentrates his first thirty-five chapters on judgement. He starts by summarising and condemning the wickedness of the people of Judah, who rebel against their God with idolatry, and a superficial compliance rather than heart obedience. **V 16–20: WASHING** Even in the opening judgement, Isaiah bids them to be washed and cleansed and to have a changed lifestyle marking their repentance. He assures them from the beginning that God can cleanse and wash away their sins, until they are as white as snow. **V 21–23: WAYWARDNESS** He underlines the spiritual and physical harlotry of Jerusalem. This results in social injustices and dishonesty. **V 24–31: WILL** Isaiah makes it clear that God's will is to purify, redeem and restore His people, but to judge their idolatry and sins with vengeance and fire.

CHAPTER TWO

V 1–5: EXALTATION OF JERUSALEM Looking far forward, Isaiah sees the coming exaltation of Jerusalem, pure worship of God, widespread blessing on the nations, and peace between them. He calls His people to 'walk in the light of the LORD' now. **V 6–18: EXECUTION OF JUDGEMENT** At first, he predicts great judgement on the rebellious house of Jacob. Soothsaying, self-reliance, materialism, idolatry and pride will all be crushed under God's judgement on 'the day of the LORD of hosts'. **V 19–21: ESCAPE OF JEWS** In that day, the men of Judah will seek refuge in caves and will throw away their useless idols. They will know God's terror. All will realise that the proud rebel against God is doomed. His attempted escape from God's certain judgement is pathetic and useless.

CHAPTER THREE

V 1: PROVISIONS In God's judgement on Jerusalem and Judah, all necessary provisions of food and drink will be taken away. **V 2–7: PEOPLE** People of worth and reputation will be removed, and inappropriate people will be in authority. Unwilling and incompetent people will rule, resulting in oppression and in the breakdown of their society. **V 8–9: PROVOCATION** The open vileness of immoral sin and ungodly talk against God provokes Him against them. **V 10: PROMISE** But God promises that those who remain righteous will find it is well for them. They will benefit from living righteously for God. **V 11–26: PUNISHMENT** All judgements, punishments and consequences of the sinfulness of the wicked will lead to a great downfall. Their oppression of the poor, haughty sensuality, pleasure-seeking, materialism, and preoccupying pride in outward appearance will turn to lamentation, mourning, desolation, death and judgement. The opulence and luxury that are so much loved when God is forgotten will come to nothing, and poverty will replace affluence.

CHAPTER FOUR

V 1: BEREFT The slaughter will lead to such a shortage of the male population that women will be bereft of men. The women will have to supply their own needs in this chronic shortage of males. **V 2: BRANCH** In all of this, God foresees the Branch of the LORD being beautiful, glorious and blessing those children of Israel who escape. In Scripture, the word 'Branch' is a Messianic title applied to the Lord Jesus Christ. **V 3–6: BLESSING** Even in the midst of such judgement, God sees ahead to blessing in Zion and Jerusalem, when the filth of sin is washed away and God's glory will cover Mount Zion in a tabernacle-like manner. Shelter from shame will be provided by God for His people.

CHAPTER FIVE

V 1–7: DIVINE DISAPPOINTMENT God sees Judah and Israel as a vineyard that He has cared for and planted. But it produces wild grapes and must be broken down and laid waste. Despite the need to judge His people, God is disappointed. **V 8–23: WIDESPREAD WOES** In a series of judgements, God foretells woes to come in a wide variety of activities. These include materialistic living, drunkenness, pleasure-seeking, open and presumptuous evil, perversion of justice, pride and bribery. **V 24–25: ANGER AROUSED** God's anger against these sins will be as a devouring fire. A basis for His anger is the rejection of His law and a despising of His word. A solemn and recurring comfort in the book of Isaiah is that that even when God has performed certain judgements, His anger is not turned away, but His hand is stretched out still. The hand that God would stretch out in mercy to welcome those who repent must be held out in judgement because there is still no repentance. **V 26–30: FRIGHTENING FOES** God will bring hostile and terrifying nations from afar to carry out His judgement on His unrepentant people.

CHAPTER SIX

V 1–4: GOD'S GLORY Before Isaiah is called and commissioned to be a prophet, God gives him a glimpse of His wonderful glory and awesome holiness. **V 5–7: UNWORTHILY UNCLEAN** The response, as always, when one understands something of the holiness of God, is that Isaiah sees himself as undone, unclean, and unworthy. Through a seraph touching his lips with a live coal, God demonstrates that Isaiah's iniquity is taken away and his sin is purged. He knows God's complete cleansing. **V 8: READY RESPONSE** Only then does God ask, 'Who will go for Us?' Recently cleansed and put right by God, Isaiah readily says, 'Here am I! Send me.' **V 9–12: DIFFICULT DUTY** God underlines that the task will be hard. Isaiah will be sent to unresponsive people to give them God's word until the cities are laid waste and the land uninhabited, because the citizens will be taken into captivity. **V 13: RETURNING REMNANT** The encouragement, however, is that there will be a remnant that returns, which God regards as a holy seed or as a stump. This will provide the nucleus of future believers who will walk with God.

CHAPTER SEVEN

V 1–2: FRIGHTENING FOES The ten northern tribes of Israel join with Assyria to invade Judah. Even though unsuccessful, their continued presence makes the people fear. Ahaz is king of Judah at this time. **V 3–9: AHAZ ASSURED**

Isaiah brings God's word to Ahaz, that his enemies will be defeated in the future. Using Ephraim as a representative of the ten northern tribes, God says that within sixty-five years, they will be broken as a people. Ahaz, however, must believe in God to be established. **V 10–16: PANORAMIC PROPHECY** God's prophecy is often like looking at a range of mountains or a series of clouds, some of which are close and some distant. It is sometimes difficult to distinguish one range or series from another. Here there are specific prophecies which God gives to Ahaz as a sign. The widest and furthest sweep of prophecy concerns the coming of the Lord Jesus Christ as Messiah. He will be born of a virgin, and that is a sign of God sending His Son. The observable and accurate fulfilment of the closer prophecies justifiably feeds confidence in the future fulfilment of the more important long-term prophecies. Here the closer prophecies concern the invasion of Judah by other countries. **V 17–25: LOST LIVINGS** When Judah is invaded and taken into captivity, it will be very hard to survive and earn a living. Previously fruitful occupations and places will become wastelands.

CHAPTER EIGHT

V 1–4: WITNESSED WORDS To underline that Isaiah speaks God's word, he is told to record what he says on a scroll in the presence of Uriah, the priest, and Zechariah. They will witness that the prophecies are made before the prophesied Assyrian invasions. Isaiah's wife, a prophetess, has a child whose name signifies that Assyria will take away spoil. The prophecy of the coming invasion is witnessed well in advance. **V 5–10: ASSYRIAN ASSAULT** The assault by the king of Assyria, and the consequent captivity, is pictured as a huge river in flood which shatters and breaks the land. Taking counsel together will not be able to prevent it because God is with the invaders. **V 11–18: CONSECRATED CONDUCT** Isaiah is told to live differently from the people around. His consecrated conduct means that he will see God's hand in the events that happen but he will not be frightened by talk of a conspiracy. He is to fear God alone. God's law will be honoured by him, the disciples of God, and his children. **V 19–20: LUMINATING LAW** While others tell him to go to mediums and wizards, God tells him rather to go to God's law and God's testimony. Darkness comes from the other sources. God's word is a light. **V 21–22: HARMFUL HOPELESSNESS** Despite being hard pressed and hungry, the afflicted people will rage against their king and God, and even curse them. Seeing trouble, darkness, and anguish on every hand, they will be driven into darkness because they refuse to turn to the God of light.

CHAPTER NINE

V 1–7: GODLY GOVERNMENT In all this rebellion and darkness, Isaiah prophesies the great light that God will bring, along with His liberty and peace, in the day of His people's repentance and faith. The reason is the coming of God the Son as a Child to be born. He will have an eternal reign, fulfilling perfectly the covenant made to David. He is the 'Wonderful Counsellor, Mighty God, Everlasting Father, Prince of Peace'. **V 8–12: HOPELESS HOPE** Israel, including Ephraim and Samaria, reckon on rebuilding what has been destroyed in judgement. God says that He will bring other enemies to judge them also. Their hope is hopeless because it is not based upon God. As they have offended Him,

His anger still burns. **V 13–17: REPENTANCE REFUSED** Their real problem is that they refuse to turn to God or seek Him. This goes right through their spiritual leaders and prophets and influences everybody in hypocrisy and evil doing. No wonder God is still angry. **V 18–21: FOREST FIRE** The wickedness of the people burns as a forest fire, and the harm that they do to one another is shocking, quite apart from the separate judgement God sends upon them. That is why God's anger continues.

CHAPTER TEN

V 1–4: SINFUL STATUTES Devious injustice, which robs the poor and afflicts the fatherless, also angers God and brings forth His continuing judgement. **V 5–16: OPPRESSOR OVERCOME** God is using Assyria as the rod of His anger to chastise and judge Israel. However, God notes that Assyria is not doing this to please Him but to fulfil its own sinful and wicked desires. Assyria will be judged, too, by God, and be subject to great calamity. The oppressor of God's people will be overcome for its own sins and suffer the fire of God's judgement. **V 17–23: RETURNING REMNANT** Just as God will remove Assyria, so at that time He will cause a remnant of Israel to return to Israel as the light of Israel. God deals in grace with minorities who repent and trust Him. **V 24–34: FREEDOM FORETOLD** Thus God tells Israel, through Isaiah, not to be afraid. What He did for them regarding Egypt, He will do for them regarding Assyria. He will smite Assyria and liberate the remnant of His people. This will be when they repent and trust Him.

CHAPTER ELEVEN

V 1–5: MIGHTY MESSIAH Although cut down, the stem of Jesse will arise from the stump of the remnant that remains. Jesse was David's father. From that stem, the Branch shall come. He will be the Messiah, who will be completely at one with the Holy Spirit and will demonstrate that it is so in His personal attributes of Deity and in His inherent ability, as God, to rule with justice, righteousness, equity, and faithfulness. **V 6–9: PERFECT PEACE** On the day when Messiah comes again, all the aggressive elements of nature will be reversed. Animals once frightened by predators will lie down and eat with them, and children shall not be hurt by poisonous animals and insects. The whole earth will be filled with the knowledge of God. **V 10: GODLY GENTILES** Not only will Messiah stand as a 'Banner to the people' of God, but Gentiles will seek Him, too. The gospel is for all! **V 11–16: RETURNING REMNANT** Just as Israel returned from Egypt out of captivity, so, in that day, the remnant of Israel will come from all over the world to repossess her land. God will dry up rivers to enable His returning people to come home. The blessing of the LORD on the Gentiles will coincide with the return of Israel to her land.

CHAPTER TWELVE

V 1–3: PRAISE When this happens, God's anger will be turned away, and the nation of Israel, as one person, will praise Him for His salvation. Joyfully Israel will praise the God who has comforted and saved her. **V 4–5: PROCLAMATION** In that day, as she thankfully remembers God and His salvation, she will tell the other nations what God has done, and proclaim His exalted name. The whole world will hear her testimony to her faithful God. Singing will accompany her proclamation of God's word. **V 6: PEOPLE** The people of Zion, both the physical people of God and those Gentiles who have become part of spiritual Israel, will shout and sing for joy because of the greatness of the God who is present with them.

CHAPTER THIRTEEN

V 1: BEGINNING OF BURDENS The first of a series of God's intended judgements, or 'burdens', against nations starts with the burden against Babylon. Those judgements will be against Assyria, Philistia, Moab, Syria and Israel, Ethiopia, Egypt, Edom, Arabia, Jerusalem itself, and Tyre. God places these burdens on His prophet, Isaiah, in order to relay them to the recalcitrant people of God. His task is not easy. **V 2–5: IMMINENCE OF INVASION** He tells Babylon that an invasion will come from a far country to destroy the whole land. Later in the chapter, he reveals this to be an invasion by the Medes. **V 6–10: DAY OF DESTRUCTION** The 'Day of the LORD' will be a day of destruction from God. Hope and strength will be gone, and fear and sorrow will abound. God's use of a godless nation will be underlined by signs in nature itself. This also looks forward to the ultimate Day of the LORD when Christ will return, as foretold in the Gospels. **V 11–16: PUNISHING OF PEOPLE** Through this means, God will punish the rebellious world, exemplified by Babylon. He will lay low the arrogant, proud and haughty. The inhabitants of Babylon will suffer the worst of inhumane crimes against them. **V 17–18: MIGHT OF MEDES** The mighty Medes cannot be bought off because they have no interest in silver or gold. They are cruel and have no pity on men, women, or children. **V 19–22:** **DESOLATION OF DOOM** Babylon will be made as desolate and uninhabitable as Sodom and Gomorrah. It will be a place where wild animals live.

CHAPTER FOURTEEN

V 1–4a: FURTHER PROPHECY Again, combining a nearer and a more distant perspective, Isaiah prophesies the return of Israel to its own land, along with other associates of Israel who trust in God. At the same time, he prophesies against the king of Babylon, even though his past persecution of Israel was as God's unknowing instrument. **V 4b–8: FERVENT PERSECUTION** Babylon, the big persecutor, will itself be persecuted with no one to help it. Rejoicing will break out over its downfall. **V 9–11: FRENZIED PERDITION** Hell (or 'Sheol', the place of the departed dead) will rejoice to meet the king of Babylon as his pomp and arrogance cannot extend beyond the grave. **V 12–23: FALL PICTURED** The fall of the king of Babylon is identified with the fall of Lucifer, the angel of light who rebelled against God and who is the devil. Lucifer is pictured as being cast down to earth. Jesus said his fall was like lightning. Lucifer's fall pictures what will happen to Babylon. It will ultimately become a wasteland occupied by porcupines. **V 24–27: FALLEN PERSECUTOR** Another persecutor of Israel to fall and be utterly broken is Assyria. Although politically powerful, Assyria cannot withstand the LORD of hosts. **V 28–32: FAMISHED PHILISTINES** Isaiah also prophesies, in the year of King Ahaz's death, that Philistia, another persecutor of Israel, will be brought low. Famine will be rife as God slays the remnant of the Philistines.

CHAPTER FIFTEEN

V 1–4: MOAB Chapters fifteen and sixteen deal with the proclamation of judgement against Moab. As God judges Moab, their god is unable to save them, despite their mourning, and their armies are useless. **V 5: MOVED** God has compassion for Moab, nevertheless, and will allow some people to escape as fugitives to Zoar. **V 6–9: MAULED** The green grass will wither, wailing will be throughout the borders, and those who escape to Dimon will be mauled and taken by lions, as will any remnant remaining in their ravaged land.

CHAPTER SIXTEEN

V 1–2: SUBMISSION Moab will be like a wandering bird thrown out of its nest, and is urged to send a lamb to Zion, as a token of submission and tribute. **V 3–5: SHELTER** The mighty Moab will ask for shelter as it flees its land and devastation. God's mercy, meanwhile, will be establishing His throne, David's tabernacle. Justice, judgement, and righteousness will prevail there. **V 6–9: STRICKEN** The great pride and haughtiness of Moab will fall, when stricken for its lies and sins. Wandering in the wilderness, Moab will shed tears over summer fruits and harvests that it will see no more. **V 10–12: SADNESS** Gladness and joy will go. Shouting will cease and wine presses will not be trodden. There will be no prevailing in prayer in the sanctuary, and the gladness of Moab will turn to sadness and despair. Its glory will be despised and its remnant of survivors very small and weak.

CHAPTER SEVENTEEN

V 1–6: COMBINED CRASH Isaiah prophesies against Syria, of which Damascus is the chief city. He also prophesies against Israel, with Ephraim standing for the ten tribes of Israel. Damascus will become a heap of ruins, and Israel become weak, unfruitful and ineffective. **V 7–9: FAITHFUL FEW** Nevertheless, in that day, there will be a few who look to God as Maker and respect God as the 'Holy One of Israel'. Their repentance will cause them to reject the idolatry which has been at the root of so much trouble. **V 10–11: FORGETFULLY FOOLISH** The condemnation is that the people have forgotten God and His salvation and not remembered that He is their Rock and Stronghold. They foolishly feel that by planting their own food, they can manage without God who alone gives the increase and blesses those who repent and trust Him. **V 12–14: NATIONS' NOISE** The mighty noise of many nations will be like the chaff of the mountains before the wind when God rebukes them and drives them away. Millions of men are nothing compared with our great God.

CHAPTER EIGHTEEN

V 1–2: ETHIOPIAN WOE Isaiah pronounces woe on Ethiopia. **V 3–6: EARTH'S WITNESS** All peoples are asked to note what God is doing here. God will intervene at the time which is right for Him. Onlookers will see carcasses eaten by birds of prey. **V 7: EXTENDED WORSHIP** At the same time, tribute will be brought from a mighty Gentile nation to Jerusalem's Mount Zion. Those who will worship Him then will have acquired a fearful reputation as a terrible and powerful nation. This prophecy has a further application through the end times.

CHAPTER NINETEEN

V 1–10: EGYPT'S EMPTINESS God will cause Egypt to fall, the main cause being internal, with Egyptian fighting Egyptian. They will seek idolatrous and occult help, but in vain. They will be ruled by a fierce king. All Egypt's productivity will turn to nothing. Their efforts will be empty. **V 11–15: EGYPT'S ERRING** The wise counsellors and mighty princes will become foolish and will have no positive effect. The perverse spirit sent by God means that they cannot do any work or make any progress. **V 16–17: EGYPT'S ENEMY** Egypt's fear of God's judgement will turn to paranoia and their old enemy, Judah, will be a terror to them. What a reversal! **V 18–25: EGYPT'S ENTRY** However, in that day, God will cause Egypt to enter into blessing through a 'Saviour and Mighty One'. There will be conversions and a turning to Him. Further, Egypt and Assyria will become peaceful neighbours and with Israel will be a blessing to the world. This is because God will use His people, Israel, as a light to lighten the Gentiles and come to regard them also as His own people. This is for the future.

CHAPTER TWENTY

V 1–2: SIGN Isaiah has to remove his sackcloth and sandals and walk uncovered and barefoot as a sign against Egypt and Ethiopia. **V 3–6: STATEMENT** God says, through Isaiah, that just as he has to walk in this way for three years, so the same thing will happen to Egypt and Ethiopia who will be taken captive.

CHAPTER TWENTY-ONE

V 1–10: BABYLONIAN BURDEN Reverting to Babylon, Isaiah prophesies its downfall with all its idolatry. Their fear will be great and Babylon will be treated as grain on a threshing floor. **V 11–12: EDOM'S EXPECTANCY** From Seir (or Edom) comes the cry, 'Watchman, what of the night?' Dumah is an oasis in northern Arabia which will witness the coming of the Assyrian oppressors. There may be a brief morning of relief, but the night of oppression will be resumed. **V 13–17: ARABIAN ASSAULT** The Arabians will flee into the forest but eventually will be overcome by invasion. God says it will happen and so it will.

CHAPTER TWENTY-TWO

V 1–4: VALLEY OF VISION The valley of vision refers to Jerusalem, where God so often has revealed Himself. Her rulers will flee and Jerusalem will be plundered. **V 5–7: DEFEAT OF DOWNTRODDEN** Enemy troops will be all over the area and walls will be broken down. Jerusalem will be downtrodden and defeated. **V 8–11: FAILURE OF FAITH** Jerusalem's inhabitants will not look to God and respect Him. Instead, they will seek their own means of providence and protection. They will fail. **V 12–14: POVERTY OF PENITENCE** When mourning and repentance towards God should be exercised, the Jerusalemites are partying. They are rich in pleasures and poor in penitence. No wonder God does not help them! **V 15–25: REMOVAL OF RULERS** Shebna, effectively the ruler under the king, is a self-seeking man, who Isaiah said will be thrown out and will die. His place will be taken by Eliakim who will act as God's servant and whom God will help. But even he will be relied upon as a mast in a tent (a 'peg') and so he will fall and be cut off in God's judgement on Jerusalem.

CHAPTER TWENTY-THREE

V 1–3: TYRE'S TRIALS The ships that come from Tarshish (probably Spain) are to wail because Tyre, their intended port, is prophesied as being 'laid waste'. They hear of this as they arrive at Cyprus. Nearby Sidon will feel the effect. This 'marketplace for the nations' will be desolate. **V 4–14: CONSEQUENCES CAUSED** All joy, bustling trade, and honour will go from Tyre. One of the strongholds of Canaan, it will be destroyed and brought to ruin. (Alexander the Great fulfilled this prophecy exactly.) **V 15–18: FORLORNLY FORGOTTEN** After seventy years, God promises there will be a small remembrance of Tyre. (This also was fulfilled.)

CHAPTER TWENTY-FOUR

V 1–3: TOTAL DEVASTATION Chapter 24 is the first of four chapters which summarise the previous 'woes' and indicate God's judgements and blessings in His final victory over those who oppose Him. At that time Israel will be finally delivered. A prophecy of emptiness, waste and total devastation commences these prophecies of the day of the LORD. **V 4–13: TOTAL DESOLATION** Mourning and languishing of previously proud people, who have broken God's law and covenant, mark this time of great desolation. They will experience confusion and inability to gain their previous levels of satisfaction from their sinful pleasures. **V 14–16a: TOTAL DEPENDENCE** In comparison with the confessed ruin of those who do not know God, the faithful remnant will be singing and praising God for His majesty and judgements. They are totally dependent on Him in the hostile world. **V 16b–18:**

TOTAL DESPAIR Apart from them, fear and fleeing will mark those who have nowhere to go when God shakes the earth. Even Isaiah is so shocked and overcome by the sense of ruin that he is unable to identify with the faithful remnant emotionally, at this point. **V 19–20: TOTAL DESTRUCTION** God will rock the very earth on its axis. Heavy with the iniquity of sinners, the earth will fall and not rise again. **V 21–23: TOTAL DOMINION** In that day, not only will God punish the guilty, but the 'LORD of hosts will reign on Mount Zion and in Jerusalem'. This will be glorious, when He resumes His total direct dominion.

CHAPTER TWENTY-FIVE

V 1–9: PROPHET'S PRAISE Isaiah invokes and praises God for His faithfulness in all that He has done. He sees Him reducing a rebel city to nothing. Perhaps Babylon is in mind. He sees Him providing a refuge and help for His people. He looks forward to a time of rejoicing at the great banquet God will hold on Mount Zion for those who have remained faithful to Him in the last days. He acknowledges God's power to swallow up death and wipe away tears. **V 10–12: PRE-EMINENT POWER** Moab, a representative of all ungodly and powerful nations in this context, will be trampled, swept aside and brought down by the LORD.

CHAPTER TWENTY-SIX

V 1–6: EVERLASTING STRENGTH In a song of salvation from Judah, God will be praised for His everlasting strength by which He has opened and preserved Jerusalem for His people and brought down her oppressors and those opposing her. Perfect peace is for those whose minds are stayed on their LORD of everlasting strength and who trust in Him. **V 7–11: EARLY SEEKING** The uprightness of those who have a desire for God is demonstrated by their seeking Him early. This is contrasted with the wicked who, although being shown God's grace, abuse it and will be judged. **V 12–15: ESTABLISHING SOVEREIGN** God will establish peace for His people. He alone deals with other nations to liberate His own people. He is the One who expands and increases His people. **V 16–19: EVENTUAL SINGING** The failure of Israel to be God's instrument of deliverance to the earth is compared to a woman in pain who cannot bring forth her child. Yet eventually there will be singing, because God will work and cause those who are dead to live. **V 20–21: ESCAPE SAFELY** The day will come when God will punish the earth for its iniquity. God's people are told to hide themselves in Him from His indignation. This has fulfilment in the history of Israel and Jerusalem, and also in the eternal future of those who refuse to repent and turn to Christ.

CHAPTER TWENTY-SEVEN

V 1: REPTILE An ancient and immensely powerful reptile, possibly a dinosaur, commonly called Leviathan, is symbolically used to portray the nations which are striving against Israel. God will slay that reptile before Israel is restored. **V 2–6: RESTORATION** The restoration of Israel is seen, including its blossoming, budding and fruitfulness, in the future. **V 7–11: RETRIBUTION** However, great retribution will be taken on the nations which were the instruments of judgement on Israel, because of their cruelty to Israel. God does not condone the sin of those whose actions He uses in His sovereign plan. **V 12–13: RETURN** Israel will be gathered and will return from foreign lands to worship the LORD in Jerusalem.

CHAPTER TWENTY-EIGHT

V 1–4: 'WOE' WARNINGS In a chapter pronouncing woe on Ephraim and Jerusalem, a new section of five woes on Israel, and one on Assyria, extends through to the end of chapter thirty-three. This is then followed by a prophecy of judgement in chapter thirty-four and a reminder of the future blessings of God's people in chapter thirty-five. **V 5–6: PRIVILEGED PEOPLE** Amidst the woe warned on Ephraim, Isaiah teaches that the remnant of God's believing people will be blessed in trusting the LORD as a 'crown of glory and a diadem of beauty'. They will receive just judgement and strength from God. **V 7–10: ALCOHOL ABUSE** The people, including the priests and the prophets, have given way to alcohol and thus erred in vision and judgement. Their disgusting behaviour makes them like incoherent children, unable and unwilling to understand. They can only understand a small part of what is said to them at any one time. **V 11–15: REVELATION REFUSED** Because they have refused to accept God's revelation, they will be subjected to an oppressing people whom they cannot understand. (This also will be fulfilled in the historical miracle gift of tongues in the New Testament, which will be a judgement on Israel's rejection of Jesus Christ. They will not understand the Holy Spirit's gift of tongues at Pentecost. Their refusal to accept God's word will lead to falsehood, ignorance and missing out on God's blessings.) **V 16–19: CORNERSTONE CONTRASTED** Their insecurity caused by their sinfulness is contrasted with the calm actions of those who trust in the Chief Cornerstone established by God.

This prophetically looks forward to Jesus Christ. He will deliver us from the covenant of death which will overtake unbelievers. **V 20–22: DESTRUCTION DETERMINED** Just as too small a bed with inadequate coverings deprives the occupant of sleep, so nations will be unable to give rest to those who trust in them instead of in God. Destruction is determined upon the whole earth, and the only shelter can be in God. **V 23–28: PARALLEL PARABLE** Using farming as an illustration, Isaiah shows that there is a time for sowing, reaping and dealing with the soil. The implication is that God has His timing as well. When mercy is offered, it should be accepted with repentance and faith. Judgement is the alternative. **V 29: INFALLIBLE INSTRUCTOR** Isaiah reminds his hearers that this teaching comes from the 'Lord of hosts who is excellent in counsel and wonderful in wisdom'. They will accept His ways in farming, and they should in spiritual matters, too.

CHAPTER TWENTY-NINE

V 1–4: JERUSALEM'S JUDGEMENT Ariel is another name for Jerusalem. The invasion of Jerusalem is depicted by siege. Her speech will be the language of death and hopelessness. **V 5–8: INVADER'S IMPOTENCE** Notwithstanding the fact that Jerusalem will be invaded, in His time God will act in judgement against the invaders. They will find themselves impotent, scattered and stunned when He comprehensively repels them. This was so when the Assyrians invaded Jerusalem, and God will have the last word in the coming final invasion of Jerusalem. **V 9–14: SPIRITUALLY SEALED** Such will be the inability of Israel to understand God's truth, because of the hardness caused by its rejection, that they will be like drunken people or those who cannot

wake up. God's word will be sealed, whether they are literate or illiterate. The wisdom and prudence of their wise men will come to nothing. **V 15–16: POTTER'S POSITION** A further woe is announced, after the woe on Ariel. This is on those who say God does not know them or see what is happening. His position as the Master Potter renders such thinking stupid. **V 17–24: CHILDREN CHANGED** The woe announced on Ariel and on those who hide from God precedes the prediction that, with the downfall of the wicked, Israel will return to honouring God and following Him. God's children will come to understand and learn the doctrine that they once rejected.

CHAPTER THIRTY

V 1–7: HELPLESS HUMILIATION Another woe is pronounced on Israel for seeking help from Egypt. Egypt can do nothing to help. Israel is pictured as a caravan going through the desert, in humiliation forlornly seeking Egypt's aid. **V 8–14: REJECTED REBELS** A lying and rebellious Israel, having rejected God's law and prophets, will be broken like a collapsing wall or smashed piece of pottery. **V 15–17: REJECTED REPENTANCE** Real repentance is the only way to return to and trust God in strength-giving 'quietness and confidence'. But even this repentance is currently rejected in favour of vain self-help, which produces defeat and fear. **V 18–26: GRACIOUS GOD** God, in His graciousness, will still wait for His people to return to Him so He can have mercy upon them. He will teach them again and guide them. He will grant them fruitfulness and blessing. He will bind up their bruises and heal their wounds in the day when they turn to Him. **V 27–28: INDIGNANT INTERVENTION** In wrath, God will, nevertheless, judge Assyria who oppresses His people. **V 29: SALVATION'S SONG** At that time, Israel will sing a song with gladness because of God's salvation, bringing them to His mountain and to Himself. **V 30–33: FLAMING FIRE** The flaming fire of God's punishment will, nevertheless, fall upon Assyria. Long established Tophet will become a large and continually burning rubbish heap, similar to Gehenna in the New Testament. Both remind us of the eternality of God's judgement for those who will not repent and trust Christ.

CHAPTER THIRTY-ONE

V 1–3: FOOLISH FAITH Again, woe is pronounced on those who are foolish enough to put their faith in Egypt rather than looking to God and seeking Him. **V 4–5: PROTECTOR'S POWER** As a roaring lion with its prey is not put off by the voices of men, so God will not be deterred from completely scattering Israel's enemies, with great power. He will fight 'for Mount Zion and its hill'. He will defend Jerusalem, protect and preserve it. The fulfilment of this prophecy is to be both short term and long term. **V 6–7: REBELS RETURN** Isaiah pleads with the children of Israel to leave their rebellion, throw away their idols, and return to Him. **V 8–9: OPPRESSION OVER** The day will come when God will throw out the oppressor, Assyria. Jerusalem will be delivered by the fire of the LORD.

CHAPTER THIRTY-TWO

V 1–4: RIGHTEOUS REIGN The Messianic reign of Jesus Christ is seen in these verses, producing justice, refreshment, increased understanding and sensitivity, and straightforward speaking. **V 5–8: VALUES VINDICATED** During that reign,

false values will be rejected and proper values will be vindicated. **V 9–15: WORLDLY WOMEN** Returning to the present, the prophet speaks to complacent women who are comfortable with the prospect of plenty of provisions and nice homes, and who need stirring in repentance and mourning. One day, their worldliness, and everyone else's, will be transformed when 'the Spirit is poured upon us from on high'. **V 16–20: PEACEFUL PEOPLE** In that day of God's reign, righteousness, quietness, assurance, fruitfulness and peace will be experienced by God's people. Normal work will be resumed.

CHAPTER THIRTY-THREE

V 1: PLUNDERERS PLUNDERED Assyria now, and all nations to come, will be plundered by God as they seek to plunder Israel. **V 2: SALVATION SOUGHT** God's people can say they have waited for God and seek His salvation. **V 3–9: ENCOURAGING EXALTATION** The LORD will exalt Himself at this time. He will cause the fleeing enemy to be scattered. He will establish His reign in godly fear. Conviction of sin and mourning will be deep. **V 10–13: ALMIGHTY ACTIVE** God will be active in mighty judgement as a testimony both to those who trust Him and to those who reject Him. **V 14–16: SINNERS SCARED** Fear seizes the hypocrites and rebels in Zion. They recognise that God's judgement requires real repentance and a changed life. Those who trust in God in this way will be safe and preserved by Him. Sometimes it takes God's hard hand on sinners to bring them to sense and repentance. **V 17–24: MAJESTIC MONARCH** The chapter ends with a Messianic prophecy of 'the King in His beauty' and reminds us of the blessings experienced by those who live under His control as Saviour, Judge, Law-Giver and King.

CHAPTER THIRTY-FOUR

V 1-7: NATIONS God's indignation is pronounced against all the nations, and His fury on all their armies. Amidst great bloodshed, they will be destroyed. **V 8-12: NOTHING** After God's vengeance on Edom, no one shall be there and 'all His princes shall be nothing'. **V 13-17: NETTLES** In accordance with God's command and judgement of the nations, the land will be desolate. Thorns, nettles and brambles will grow there. These are reminders of His curse on sin. The sole inhabitants of the land will be animals and birds.

CHAPTER THIRTY-FIVE

V 1-2: DESERT DELIGHT Zion's future glory will be seen in a blossoming of the desert. The desert will rejoice and God's glory will be seen by all. **V 3-4: STRONG SALVATION** Given the certainty that, with vengeance, God 'will come and save you', Isaiah tells His faithful people not to fear but to be strong hearted. **V 5-7: MARVELLOUS MIRACLES** During this time, spiritual and physical miracles will occur, both to the inhabitants and to the land. God's reign will pervade all. **V 8-9: HOLY HIGHWAY** The safe way to walk is on the Highway of Holiness. The redeemed will walk on it on their return to Zion. **V 10: RANSOMED RETURN** They will return with singing and everlasting joy! Sorrow and sighing 'shall flee away'.

Note on Isaiah chapters 36, 37, 38 and 39 Isaiah chapters 36, 37, 38 and 39 are quoted in 2 Kings 18:13 to 2 Kings 20:19, almost verbatim. Isaiah chapter 38 includes the personal prayer of Hezekiah

which is not included in 2 Kings. Either the compiler of 2 Kings used the same source as Isaiah, or, more likely, quoted from Isaiah as the prophet of the day. Isaiah chapters 36 and 37 show how the predictions of Assyria's downfall, bringing the deliverance of Jerusalem, are fulfilled exactly. Isaiah chapters 38 and 39 set the scene for the rest of Isaiah, which deals with the Babylonian captivity. Because of the very close similarity of these chapters in Isaiah to those in 2 Kings, reference should be made back to the notes on the chapters in 2 Kings.

CHAPTER THIRTY-SIX

V 1-22: See the above **Note on Isaiah chapters 36, 37, 38 and 39** and the notes on 2 Kings 19:1-37.

CHAPTER THIRTY-SEVEN

V 1-38) See the above **on Isaiah chapters 36, 37, 38 and 39** and the notes on 2 Kings 18:13-37.

CHAPTER THIRTY-EIGHT

V 1-8: See the above **on Isaiah chapters 36, 37, 38 and 39** and the notes on 2 Kings 20:1-11. **V 9-20: PERSONAL PRAYER** Not quoted in 2 Kings is Hezekiah's personal prayer to God. It shows his anguish in praying for healing and his gratitude in answer. It also leads to confidence that God will save him in the future. It is a pity that this spiritual attitude did not last long enough to stop him parading all his wealth to Merodach-Baladan in the next chapter. Today's blessing does not guarantee tomorrow's walk with the Lord. That has to be a daily matter of trust and obedience. **V 21-22:** See the above **on Isaiah chapters 36, 37, 38 and 39** and the notes on 2 Kings 20:1-11.

CHAPTER THIRTY-NINE

V 1–8: See the above on Isaiah chapters 36, 37, 38 and 39 and the notes on 2 Kings 20:12–19.

CHAPTER FORTY

V 1–2: COMFORT The word 'comfort' introduces the second half of Isaiah's prophecy. Unlike the first thirty-nine chapters, which deal with Judah at the time Isaiah was prophesying, chapters 40 to 66 see Isaiah prophesying as though the Babylonian captivity has already taken place. (Isaiah finished prophesying around 686 BC and the captivity began at 605 BC, around eighty years later.) Chapters 36 to 39, tabling the downfall of Assyria and warning that Babylon will rise in the future, are the preparation for chapters 40 to 66. Isaiah starts this section by comforting the people of God and telling them that war is over and sin is pardoned. **V 3–8: CRYING** In the role fulfilled by John the Baptist, in the time of the Lord Jesus Christ's ministry here on earth, we hear the voice of one 'crying in the wilderness' to prepare God's way. He is to remind people of their passing lives and of the permanence of God's word. John took this further to point to the 'Lamb of God, who takes away the sin of the world'. **V 9–11: COMING** The prophecy is that God will come to the cities of Judah. He will rule strongly, feed His flock like a shepherd, and care for His lambs. The LORD provides strength and compassionate concern. **V 12–14: COUNSEL** God is the powerful and sovereign Creator who has never taken counsel from any man. **V 15–17: COUNTED** The nations are counted as dust on the scales and the resources of the earth are as nothing to Him when compared to His own greatness. **V 18–26:**

COMPARISON Rhetorically, Isaiah asks how people can possibly compare the great God of creation with some meaningless image made by a craftsman. The rulers of the earth are nothing compared with Him: they are like chaff to be taken away in a whirlwind. He asks who can compare with the One who lights the starry host and who has created the whole universe. **V 27–31: CONFIDENCE** Yet this mighty Creator, the Everlasting God, the One who 'neither faints nor is weary' is close to those who are weak and who trust Him. While others fail, those who 'wait on the LORD shall renew their strength'. They can be confident that He will uphold them, lift them up, and strengthen them. They will then run without being weary and walk without fainting.

CHAPTER FORTY-ONE

V 1–4: GOD'S INVOLVEMENT God will be involved in helping His people when the Babylonian captivity is over. He will remind them that He, the LORD, is the First and the Last. The same truths, in the New Testament, are attributed to the Lord Jesus Christ, our Saviour God. **V 5–7: GRAVEN IMAGES** The response of some is not to turn to God, but to produce graven images which needed to be fastened so that they might stand. **V 8–13: GREAT INSPIRATION** God greatly inspires Israel, His servant. He reminds His people that He has taken them from the ends of the earth, that they are chosen, that they need not fear, and that He is with them to strengthen them, help them, and uphold them. He will hold their right hand against their idolatrous enemies. **V 14–16: GLORIOUS INSTRUMENT** Although Israel is called 'a worm'. God will so forge her into an instrument of judgement on godless nations that rejoicing in Him will be accompanied by great glory accruing to His name. He will make this 'worm' into a glorious instrument of judgement and blessing. **V 17–20: GRACIOUS INTERVENTION** God will take care of the poor, needy, and thirsty. His people will appreciate His intervening hand to help them and bless them. **V 21–29: GODLESS INEFFECTIVENESS** God challenges idolaters to present their case for the value and efficacy of idols. This passage shows their idols are absolutely useless. They can do nothing, say nothing, and hear nothing. They are 'wind and confusion'. We, too, should thank God that He is our living God and forsake idolatry in all the subtle forms it takes today.

CHAPTER FORTY-TWO

V 1–4: SPIRIT AND SERVANT In one of the Bible's 'Servant Songs', the Messiah is foreseen as One chosen and upon Whom the Holy Spirit dwells. He brings justice to the Gentiles. He has compassion, justice, truth, faithfulness and a lasting reign. **V 5–9: LIGHT AND LIBERTY** God's creating power is no less than His concern for righteousness. God the Father addresses the Messiah, God the Son, who will be 'a light to the Gentiles', who will open blind eyes, and free imprisoned people from all nations, bringing them out of their darkness. He alone is glorious and He hates idolatry. **V 10–13: PRAISE AND PREVAILING** When Christ establishes His reign, there will be praise upon praise. Praise will come from the ends of the earth, the sea and coastlands, the wilderness and the cities, and from the villages and mountains. The LORD will respond with His power and strength as He acts to prevail over Israel's enemies. **V 14–20: LORDSHIP AND LABOUR** The time will come when God will bring in a new regime, just as a woman in labour will give birth to a child. At that time, He will deliver judgement on the earth, but He will also lighten the darkness of the blind, make crooked places straight, and convict the hearts of those who stupidly and rebelliously follow idolatry. **V 21–25: LAW AND LAWLESS** The effect of the law on lawless people is dealt with. God rejoices in His law. But those who reject it are robbed, plundered and imprisoned. Yet they will not obey Him or turn back to Him until His judgement falls upon them. Even then their hardness of heart stops them turning to Him. We need God's grace even to repent of sin.

CHAPTER FORTY-THREE

V 1–4: REDEEMER GOD God reminds Israel that He has redeemed them to be His people. He will uphold them through the rivers and the flame and save them because of His enduring love. **V 5–7: REMNANT GATHERED** He tells them not to fear because He will gather the remnant of those called by His name from all over the earth to glorify Him. What an ingathering that will be when the remnant is gathered! **V 8–13: RECOGNISE GODHEAD** God calls that those who are blind and are deaf should recognise that He is the only God and the only Saviour. His people are to witness to that fact, too. Only God can be our Saviour, which is why we rejoice in Emmanuel, 'God with us', the Lord Jesus Christ. **V 14–21: REVERSING GLOOM** God will bring an oppressor on the Babylonians who will make them flee. He will liberate His people. Things will be changed and He will 'make them a road in the wilderness and rivers in the desert'. His people will praise Him. **V 22–28: REPENT GENUINELY** God complains that Israel's failure to give the sacrifices He has prescribed is because they have neither called upon Him nor turned from their sins. He reminds them that He is the One who can blot out their transgressions and put their sins behind Him. He commands them to come and state their case so that they can be acquitted. Unlike man's law, a repentant person pleading guilty is both pardoned and acquitted at the bar of God! What a merciful, gracious and generous God we have!

CHAPTER FORTY-FOUR

V 1–5: BOUNTIFUL BLESSING God's bountiful blessing will fall on Israel as water on a parched ground. His Spirit will come upon Israel and His people will be pleased to own His name. **V 6–8: GREAT GOD** God emphasises again that there is only one God, one Redeemer and one Rock. Israel is to witness to this, just as Christians must witness to the only One who is 'the Way, the Truth and the Life'. **V 9–20: ILLOGICAL DOLATRY** Not only is idolatry evil and rebellious, it is downright stupid. Everyone knows that idols are made from commonly available materials by frail and failing human beings. They cannot see, hear, talk or walk. Having made these detestable objects, man rebels against God by bowing down and worshipping them. Just one word of warning—our houses, cars, money, careers, celebrities, and relationships can be our meaningless idols today and replace or dilute our pure worship of God and obedience to Him. **V 21–23: REDEEMED RETURN** Again, God emphasises that He has done all that is necessary to redeem the children of Israel. He will not forget them and they will return to their land, glorifying Him. God's appeal is always based on what He has done in redeeming us. **V 24–28: POWERFUL PROPHECY** The LORD Redeemer reminds Judah and Jerusalem

that He is the Creator who can frustrate the actions of sinful man at will. He will restore His people to Jerusalem and Judah and make their land useful and fruitful. They will please Him and rebuild the temple to worship Him. This Sovereign God of theirs announces His intention to perform this through Cyrus, king of Persia, 150 years before Cyrus does His bidding. This prophecy was accurately fulfilled as all prophecies of Scripture have been or will be.

CHAPTER FORTY-FIVE

V 1–7: CYRUS CHOSEN God makes it clear that He has chosen Cyrus as His instrument to bless Israel, even though Cyrus does not know God. The accomplishment of this prophecy should make everyone realise that God is who He says He is, and that He does what He says He will do. **V 8: SENDING SALVATION** God, who is the mighty Creator, can send forth righteousness and salvation as if they were torrents of rain, upon His people. **V 9–10: WOEFUL WARNINGS** God warns those who strive with Him. They are like a pot complaining to the potter while being fashioned, or like a child who questions its existence apart from its parents. **V 11–13: CREATOR'S CHOICE** God emphasises His holiness and His creation of the heavens and the earth. He reminds His children, through Isaiah, that He has a perfect right to choose Cyrus to perform His will. **V 14–19: UNDERSTANDING UNIQUENESS** In a passage which applies both to the current situation and to the end of the age, God reminds His people that He is the Creator and Saviour who reveals Himself and that He can be found when people seek Him properly. **V 20–21: INEFFECTIVE IMAGES** God repeats yet again, through Isaiah, how useless idols and images are. Again

God reminds them that 'there is no other God beside me', and underlines that He is 'a just God and a Saviour'. **V 22–25: SAVIOUR'S SOVEREIGNTY** God demonstrates His Lordship by inviting the whole of the earth to look to Him and be saved. Christ's incarnate deity and second coming are foreshadowed in the fact that God says every knee will bow to Him, and every tongue will take an oath before Him. God is in control and will save those who turn to Him.

CHAPTER FORTY-SIX

V 1–2: IMPOTENT IDOLS The idols of Babylon, Bel and Nebo, are a burden to carry. They will be captured when Babylon falls. **V 3–4: CONTINUAL CARE** Compare this with the God who upholds His people from birth to the grave. He carries and delivers them. **V 5–7: MEANINGLESS MATERIALS** Idols are nothing more than raw materials fashioned by sinful men. They can neither answer nor save those who cry to them. **V 8–11: PROPHETIC PURPOSE** God calls Israel to remember their sins and that their God is the only God. His divinity is seen in His prophetic purpose. He declares the end from the beginning and it comes to pass. Not only does He use prophets to make His will known, but He always accomplishes His will after He has made it known. How different! **V 12–13: SAVING SOVEREIGN** God alone can call unrighteous, stubborn people to righteousness through His salvation. His salvation will not linger in coming to Israel in Zion.

CHAPTER FORTY-SEVEN

V 1–3: DOOM Babylon will be doomed. God will take vengeance on Babylon for what has happened to Israel. **V 4: DIFFERENT** At that time, Israel will be rejoicing in the LORD as their Redeemer. **V 5–9: DISASTER** Having used Babylon to judge Israel, God will cause her to know defeat at the hand of Cyrus and the Persian army. (This happened suddenly and they were unexpectedly bereft of their position and their children.) **V 10–11: DESOLATION** Because Babylon trusts in sin and wickedness, sudden desolation will come upon her. She will literally not know what has hit her. **V 12–15: DESTINY** All Babylon's enchantments, sorceries, astrology, and ungodly counsel will not be able to save her. They will all perish with Babylon, and nobody will be there to save Babylon.

CHAPTER FORTY-EIGHT

V 1–5: REVELATION'S RECORD To show the Israelites that God has been speaking to them, He made predictions in advance which come true. They cannot therefore say that their idols have caused it to happen. **V 6–8: TOPICAL TRUTH** From now on, God is going to tell them new things. This signals both Israel's return from the Babylonian captivity (although the captivity has not yet happened as this prophecy is made), and the longer-term prophecies concerning Israel and the end of the world. **V 9–11: GOD'S GLORY** What God does for His children is for His glory and for His name's sake. Christians should live with those thoughts in mind, also. **V 12–19: CONSIDER CAREFULLY** God commands Israel to listen and remember that He is the First and the Last, who created the whole universe. He reminds them of His prophecies well in advance of their fulfilment, and that He is the Redeemer. Had they walked with Him and trusted Him from the start, their lot would have been very different and they would now be experiencing far greater blessings. Our Sovereign God is not a fatalist! **V 20–22: DIVINE DELIVERANCE** Even before the captivity takes place, God declares His ultimate divine deliverance from it and His redemption from it. As in their initial redemption from Egypt, He will look after His people when they return from Babylon. He will also redeem all Israel, physically and spiritually, when His worldwide timetable dictates. But there will be 'no peace' for the wicked.

CHAPTER FORTY-NINE

V 1–13: SERVANT The second Servant song deals with how Messiah will come from God to redeem Israel and to make Israel a light to the Gentiles. True worship of God will be restored. He will help and deliver His people, and feed and protect them. Rejoicing will come forth because of His mercy. **V 14: SADNESS** Despite God's assurance of His coming as the Servant in the form of Messiah, sadness reigns! This is very depressing. Zion insists that God has forsaken and forgotten her. Her feelings mean more to her than God's unshakeable word! **V 15–23: SOLACE** God assures His people that they are wrong! He is far more concerned for them than a loving nursing mother is for her child. He will restore them and their children. Nations will do obeisance before Israel. They will know the reality of the LORD in their lives. **V 24–26: SAVIOUR** His people ask how is it possible that they should be taken from their captors to whom they are but prey. God says that He will deal drastically with their captors and He will be the Saviour and Redeemer as the 'Mighty One of Jacob'.

CHAPTER FIFTY

V 1–3: SURE God assures Judah that He has not given a certificate of divorce or put her out of the way like a defaulting creditor. His power to save is sure and He can (and will) redeem Judah. **V 4–11: SUBMISSIVE** In the third Servant song, we learn how Messiah has a learned tongue and an open ear to His Father. His suffering and submission are foretold. He knows that He will be upheld. He warns that torment will come upon those who reject God's light and urges them to 'trust in the name of the LORD and rely upon His God'. Because He is submissive to the will of God, others can be blessed.

CHAPTER FIFTY-ONE

V 1–3: HOPE God comforts Zion with the knowledge that the wilderness will become as fruitful as Eden was. His people will know joy, gladness and thanksgiving. The basis of this comfort is history. Here is a God who has hewn His people from the rock, and blessed Abraham and Sarah through faith in Him. Abraham was but one man when called by God, but now is a father of multitudes of people who trusted and trust in God. **V 4–8: HEAR** Twice God gives the command to listen, first to His people who are His nation, and then to those who know righteousness and God's law in their hearts. God will make justice, righteousness and salvation real to them and they will trust in Him. He will preside over the destruction of the present creation before replacing it with new heavens and a new earth. His salvation and righteousness will last for ever. His people are to honour His law and fear no one else. Those opposing His people will be consumed. **V 9–11: HASTEN** Prayer is made for God to hasten to awake and to act for His people. God acted before, in slaying their 'monsters', and took them over dry land in the midst of the river. So

He can act again to bring them to Zion with singing and everlasting joy. **V 12–16: HISTORY** God reminds them that, in comforting them, He does so as their Maker and Creator of the world. He has delivered them in the past and protected them. Furthermore, He tells Zion, 'You are my people.' He will not abandon them. **V 17–23: HUMBLE** God reminds His people in Jerusalem that He has humbled them in the past because of their disobedience. He will deliver them in the future. He will punish those nations who have been the agent of humbling for Israel, because of what they have done to His people.

CHAPTER FIFTY-TWO

V 1–2: AWAKENING God calls Jerusalem to awake, to be liberated, and to rediscover her status as His daughter. **V 3–6: AUTHORITY** The authority of God will be known in the day He liberates His people from captivity. Israel has already been captive in Egypt and Assyria and will be delivered from the prophesied Babylonian captivity. When that happens, they will recognise the fulfilment of Isaiah's prophecy. **V 7–10: ACCLAIM** News of Israel's liberation will be proclaimed on the mountains around Jerusalem. With peace and gladness, they will realise that 'Your God reigns'. This is also Messianic and is true for Christians who are liberated from their sin. One day, 'all the ends of the earth shall see the salvation of our God.' **V 11–12: ACTION** Knowing this, Israel is bidden to depart and to touch nothing unclean. As they so repent and trust God, He will fight for them and protect them. **V 13–15: ASTONISHMENT** This will be accomplished through the suffering Servant, the Lord Jesus Christ. In the fourth Servant song, which goes into chapter fifty-three, Isaiah tells us that people will be astonished at His appearance. He who is exalted and extolled will be marred more than any man as He bears the punishment of the sins of men. But by this means, many nations and individuals will be sprinkled clean from their sins by His grace and by His mercy.

CHAPTER FIFTY-THREE

V 1–3: SORROWS Carrying on the thought of chapter fifty-two, Jesus, the Servant, is portrayed as a 'Man of Sorrows and acquainted with grief'. He is 'despised and rejected by men'. There is nothing in Jesus which the heart of a sinful rebel finds attractive, until he turns from his sin and trusts Him. **V 4–6: SMITTEN** We are told that He was smitten by God in our place for our transgressions. His stripes heal us from our waywardness and sinfulness as we repent from going our own way and trust Him. The LORD and Father God has laid the sins of us all on His Servant and Son, Jesus. **V 7–8: SHEEP** He is submissive and willing to accept this judgement as a sheep before shearers or as a lamb being led to the slaughter. He is to be cut off because of human sin. **V 9: SINLESS** The prophecy of His having 'His grave with the wicked—but with the rich in His death' was fulfilled perfectly. **V 10–11: SIN OFFERING** 'It pleased the Lord to bruise Him' means that it was the will of God, the Father, that Christ should be punished for us. It was also the will of the Son 'who loved me and gave Himself for me'. Because He has died, individuals can enter into the benefit of that sin-offering on their behalf, knowing that Jesus has borne their iniquities. The Servant Saviour is satisfied to see those trusting Him in this way. **V 12: SUPPLICATION**

Jesus will benefit from the blessings of His work, both from the hand of God the Father and from the hearts of grateful sinners. Because He is the sole sin-bearer, and having risen and ascended He makes supplication for sinners, many will be saved.

CHAPTER FIFTY-FOUR

V 1–3: EXPANDING God's final kingdom will be far greater than at any time through Israel or Judah. It will be worldwide and immense and include all those who turned to Him through Christ the suffering Servant. **V 4–10: EVERLASTING** The blessings of God for His people, both for believing Israel and for all those who trust Him, are everlasting. Never shall His covenant of peace be removed, and His great mercies will apply to all who repent and trust Him. **V 11–17: EXALTED** His people, who have been afflicted and rejected, will be exalted in the nations. Nobody will be able to have the victory over them, because God is for them. They will be established in God's righteousness.

CHAPTER FIFTY-FIVE

V1–5: COME All who thirst are bidden to come and drink of the waters of God's mercy and grace. Spiritual and physical food and drink are freely available to all who will 'trust in the sure mercies of David' and follow God. Because of their relationship with God, they will attract other nations. His people will be blessed as a nation and as a people. **V 6–7: CALL** Isaiah commands people to call upon God 'while He is near' and to repent from unrighteousness. Abundant pardon is on offer through the mercy of God for those who 'return to the LORD'. **V 8–9: COMPARISON** God makes it clear,

through Isaiah, that His thoughts and ways are very different from those of sinful men. Just as the heavens are higher than the earth, so His ways and thoughts are higher than ours. **V 10–11: CONFIDENCE** God's people can have the confidence that just as water coming down as rain or snow achieves its aim in watering the earth and bringing forth fruit, so His word will have the same effect and will prosper to that end. God intends His word to be life producing, refreshing, and to accomplish what He has purposed. **V 12–13: CHANGE** When Israel comes back from exile, there will be a tremendous change as God rules in His kingdom. Joy, peace and singing will be the environment in which thorns and briers will give way to cypress trees and myrtle trees. This is an everlasting sign that the LORD will fulfil His word and that they will not be cut off again.

CHAPTER FIFTY-SIX

V 1–2: SALVATION AND SABBATH God's salvation, bringing His righteousness, enables people to do righteousness and keep justice. It also provides a heart obedience that means that His Sabbath is kept and that evil is resisted. **V 3–8: SONS AND SABBATH** Eunuchs whose love for the Lord is such that they are keen to keep His Sabbath and honour His covenant will receive God's everlasting name. They will be treated as better than sons and daughters. Sons of foreigners who do the same also will be blessed both in the return from Babylon and in the last days. **V 9–12: SLEEPING AND SLUMBERING** This is contrasted with Israel's leaders who are like sleeping or slumbering dogs. They are more concerned with drink and self-interest than with the nation which God has committed to them.

CHAPTER FIFTY-SEVEN

V 1–2: DIVINE DELIVERANCE All believers who die, whether through persecution or natural causes, are at peace. They are 'taken away from evil'. **V 3–10: IDOLATROUS IMMORALITY** The idolatrous children of Israel are called sorcerers and adulterers. Not only is idolatry spiritual immorality but it also often leads to immoral practices and to other sins. **V 11–13: COMPELLING COMPARISON** Such idolaters will be removed and their idols will not help them when they cry out. What a compelling comparison we find between them and those who trust in God. The latter 'shall posses the land, and shall inherit My holy mountain.' **V 14–21: PENITENTIAL PEACE** However, although there is no peace for the wicked, God offers peace to those who are far off, who will turn from their sin and trust Him. God's dwelling is not only on high and in the holy place, but also 'with him who has a contrite and humble spirit'. He restores those who turn from their sin and come to him in such a spirit.

CHAPTER FIFTY-EIGHT

V 1–5: FALSE FASTING Isaiah is bidden to tell Israel of the hypocrisy of their sin. He starts by criticising them for their fasting. This is not accompanied by repentance for sin which causes them to seek the well-being of others and the glory of God. Rather, their fasts parade their shallow and false signs of repentance. Repentance is a true sorrow for sin, and the forsaking of it before God. True repentance makes a real difference. It is not a wallowing in apparent misery over failure to seek to give the impression of being holy. **V 6–12: FRUITFUL FASTING** Real heart-fasting demands being a blessing to others and to sacrifice one's privileges, time and pleasures, to see others blessed. This concerns undoing heavy burdens, loosening bonds of wickedness and sharing with the needy. Then prayer will be answered, darkness will be turned into light, and fruitfulness will be experienced along with God's restoration. True fasting means replacing time spent in personal interests with time invested specifically for the glory of God, be it in prayer or in other ways. **V 13–14: FAITHFUL FOOTSTEPS** Isaiah passes from fasting to resume his teaching on the Sabbath. Blessing on the Sabbath comes when a person turns his or her foot from doing his or her own pleasure on this holy day of God. Selfish ways, pleasures, and words are forsaken so that God is made the delight of the day. He will respond by adding spiritual elevation and feeding to the delight that He gives. This Sabbath principle is even more meaningful to the Christian since the Lord's Day underlines the wonder of the resurrection of the Lord Jesus Christ.

CHAPTER FIFTY-NINE

V 1: SHORTENED 'The LORD's hand is not shortened that it cannot save.' Isaiah tells Israel that God can redeem her. The same principle is true for any sinner who will turn to Him. **V 2–8: SEPARATED** Israel's problem is that her sins have separated her from God. Sin always does that, which is why everyone needs a Saviour from sin. Isaiah reveals some of Israel's sins which cause this separation from God. **V 9–15a: SINFULNESS** On behalf of the Israelites, Isaiah confesses their sinfulness before God. They are in darkness, they are blind not seeing, they are lacking justice, rejecting salvation, multiplying transgressions, lying against God, departing from Him, oppressing and rebelling, and ignoring justice and truth.

Those who would depart from evil are attacked as prey by others. **V 15b–21: SALVATION** God is displeased at the lack of justice and wonders that there is no intercession. He takes the initiative Himself in righteousness, salvation, and vengeance. He will redeem Israel and deal with her enemies. He will establish His covenant with His people and confirm it by His Spirit.

CHAPTER SIXTY

V 1–2: GLORY The glory of God will rise upon Israel, and upon the world, as a great light. **V 3–9: GENTILES** As Israel is 'a light to lighten the Gentiles', so the Gentiles will come to Israel and seek God's glory and wonder. They will praise God and bring their tribute from afar to Him in Israel. **V 10–18: GOLDEN** A golden age will be experienced by Israel. Jerusalem will be called 'the city of the LORD, Zion of the Holy One of Israel' with continually open gates. Kingdoms and nations which oppose Israel will be ruined. Not only will there be great material prosperity, but the knowledge of the Lord, Saviour, Redeemer, 'the Mighty One of Judah' will prevail. Righteousness and peace will reign and violence, wasting, and destruction will be banished. Salvation and Praise will be the names of Jerusalem's walls and gates. **V 19–22: GOD** This will all be because God Himself will be an everlasting light to them and their glory. God will bring this to pass and will hasten it. He will be the glory of His people, Israel, whom He shall make righteous. God will give His people immense strength and influence.

CHAPTER SIXTY-ONE

V 1–3: MISSION OF MESSIAH Jesus, the Servant, applied this passage to Himself, to show He was Messiah. He says that 'the Spirit of the Lord God is upon Me', and that 'the LORD has anointed Me to preach glad tidings to the poor'. This will result in the benefits of salvation for Israel and also for all who will trust in our Saviour and Lord. Those benefits include healing for the broken-hearted, liberty for captives and prisoners, seeing God's timing in His salvation and judgement, comfort for mourners, and God's giving joyful praise and righteousness. **V 4–7: REJOICING OF RESTORED** There will be restoration and repair of both buildings and people. The children of Israel will rule over the Gentiles, possessing double and experiencing everlasting life. They will resume their offices of priesthood and serve God again. 'Instead of confusion they shall rejoice in their portion.' **V 8–9: LORD OF LOVE** Not only does the Lord love justice, which directs His righteous actions, but He also loves His people and will make an everlasting covenant with them. Gentiles will recognise that these are people blessed by the LORD. **V 10–11: ROBE OF RIGHTEOUSNESS** Every person counted righteous before God through the death and merits of the Lord Jesus Christ, is foreseen in these verses. Security in God will not be because of our own poor efforts at righteousness but because the righteousness of Christ adorns every Christian as a robe. This is the garment of salvation which is worn by those cleansed from sin. All nations will praise God and rejoice in His wonderful provision in Christ.

CHAPTER SIXTY-TWO

V 1–5: LIGHT AND LOVE God's will for His people is that they should shine forth as a bright light to the Gentiles. Their relationship with God will be such that the Gentiles will see the love that God has for His people, and how He delights in them and rejoices over them. **V 6–9: PRAISE AND PROTECTION** God will continue to send prophets, as watchmen, to bring God's word to Jerusalem, until it is praised in all the earth. He will protect His holy city so the inhabitants can eat and drink the products for which they have laboured, rather than have them taken by invaders. **V 10–12: BUILD AND BEHOLD** A highway is to be built. Stones that would hinder people are to be taken out of the way and a banner is to be lifted for people. That is to facilitate the proclamation to 'the end of the world' concerning God's coming salvation and the reward that He brings with Him for His holy people. God's redeemed people shall be known as those whom God has sought out and not forsaken.

CHAPTER SIXTY-THREE

V 1–6: DAMNATION AND DELIVERANCE God is pictured as One who treads down in wrath those who have disobeyed Him, such as Edom, but who comes to bring salvation for His people. Though awesome in judgement, He is 'mighty to save'. Damnation and deliverance are always twin themes showing God's compassion and love at the same time as His justice and judgement. **V 7–14: REDEMPTION AND REBELLION** Similar twin themes are God's redemption and man's rebellion. He has redeemed His people and dealt with them in love, mercy and pity. Their history is one of intermittent periods of rebellion and grieving Him, causing God to chastise them often through enemies coming in, punctuated by brief periods of seeking Him and obeying Him. God often takes them up again and blesses them with His protection and care. One day, restoration

will be consummated both for Israel as a nation and for every child of God in heaven. **V 15–19: PRAYER AND PINING** His people pray to God, reminding Him that He is their Father and Redeemer. They pine for Him to make them return to Him with a soft heart and so that they can be reclaimed as His people. God is always pleased to hear prayer like that, but it calls for repentance, too. That will be seen in the next chapter.

CHAPTER SIXTY-FOUR

V 1–5: REND Israel's desire to know God reaches a crescendo where He is asked to 'rend the heavens' and 'come down'. His people ask for almighty tokens of His presence as in the past. They recognise that 'we have sinned' and that, without God, they will continue in their sinful ways. They confess that 'we need to be saved'. Christian assurance today does not need such a dramatic manifestation. We can rely in repentant trust on His promises in the Bible, accept His gracious forgiveness, and return to Him in quiet confidence. **V 6–7: ROTTEN** The Israelites see that their problem is that they are rotten and unclean. Even their righteousnesses are like filthy rags. They admit that they are powerless, and that they are suffering because of their sin. They do not pray and do not know God intimately. **V 8–12: REMEMBER** They now ask God to remember that He is their Father and their Potter. They ask for His fury to be turned away and that He will not remember their iniquity. They remind God of the consequence of their sin, in calling to Him to forgive them and to change them and their lot.

CHAPTER SIXTY-FIVE

V 1–7: SEEKING Whereas Gentile nations,

which had previously not looked for God, can now seek Him and find Him, God's own people are sought by Him and abuse His mercy and grace by perverted sacrifice and rebelliousness in their hearts. It is with these reminders that God replies to the prayers of His people. **V 8–10: SERVANTS** God will bless and preserve the remnant of His people who serve Him. **V 11–12: SINFULNESS** God declares that He will punish those who sinfully forget and neglect Him and pervert His offerings. They did not reply to His call to repentance but continued to do evil before Him. **V 13–16: SEPARATION** God goes on to show how He will deal separately with His seeking servants as opposed to those who shamefully abuse His sacrifice and neglect Him and His truth. He will bless His servants in many ways, but those blessings will be denied to those who are wicked and do not repent. **V 17–25: SERENITY** But God will create new heavens and a new earth in which Jerusalem will become a new centre of rejoicing. There will be no weeping, and life will be extended. Prayer will be answered and communion will be sweet. Animals will be at peace with one another, even the predator with its former prey. Isaiah deliberately blends the blessings of the last times with those of the new heavens and the new earth wherein dwells righteousness.

CHAPTER SIXTY-SIX

V 1–2: HOLY HABITATION God makes it clear that there are two places where He dwells. One is in heaven itself, and the other is in the contrite heart of a person who trembles at His word. **V 3–4: SINFUL SACRIFICES** God is greatly displeased with those who go through the motions of sacrifice as if they were in combat, or killing a dog. He will cause them to be deluded and fearful, because they do not respond to Him but carry on in their evil. **V 5–6: SUSTAINING SOVEREIGN** However, those who honour His word, and are therefore opposed by sinful rebels, are told by God that He will repay her enemies, who have made themselves His enemies too. **V 7–11: PRODUCTIVE PAINS** The remnant of Israel faces much trouble and will do so, as she is opposed by others. As labour pains give way to childbirth, so God will bring them into the blessing of His kingdom and closeness, after those troubles and opposition. **V 12–13: COMING COMFORT** In that day, God will extend peace and comfort to His faithful people and the Gentiles will come to them and glory in the LORD in Jerusalem. **V 14–17: DIVINE DEALINGS** God will deal with those who trust Him as His servants, and cause them to rejoice. He will rebuke and take vengeance on those who reject Him. Those who set themselves apart for evil sacrifice will be judged. **V 18–21: GOD'S GLORY** In that day, all nations will see God's glory. The faithful remnant of Israel who escaped persecution will testify to them of God's glory. Those nations will come to worship Him in Jerusalem. God will have an acceptable priesthood of those who trust Him. **V 22–24: EVERLASTING EFFECTS** In the future there will be new heavens and a new earth which will remain. All flesh will come to worship before God. Tragically, the worshippers will see the eternal fate of those who have transgressed against God and refused to repent. Heaven and hell are twin realities.

JEREMIAH

PEOPLE AND PRELIMINARIES

✳ Jeremiah (fifty-two chapters) is the second of five books called the 'major prophets'. See comments on Isaiah. It was written by Jeremiah, between 586 BC and 570 BC, in Jerusalem and Judah. The estimated period covering this book is forty-one years.

PLAN AND PURPOSE

ⓘ Jeremiah, a prophet and a priest, lives and prophesies at the same time as Zephaniah, Habakkuk, Daniel and Ezekiel. He prophesies mainly to Judah but also to a wider international audience, between 627 BC and 586 BC, when unrepentant Jerusalem fell to Babylon and the captivity he prophesied took place. He pronounces God's judgement on the sins of His idolatrous and increasingly wicked people during the reigns of the last five Judean kings, Josiah, Jehoahaz, Jehioakim, Jehoiachin, and Zedekiah. Jeremiah is regarded groundlessly as a traitor for telling his people to surrender to Babylon. He wants to avoid Jerusalem's destruction, knowing that the Jews will return to Jerusalem in God's time. The book reveals the great personal hardships of Jeremiah, including imprisonments and opposition from all quarters. His compassionate heart for his sinning people earns him the title of 'the weeping prophet'. His obedience to God, and rugged determination to do what he has to do, despite much opposition and difficulties, make him a unique servant of God, at a time when false religion advance and the word of God is vilified and attacked.

PROFILE AND PROGRESSION

🐚 Jeremiah's preparation (1:19); Jeremiah's prophesying to Judah (2:1–45:5); Jeremiah's pronouncements on the surrounding nations (46:1–51:64); Jerusalem's fall (52:1–34).

PRINCIPLES AND PARTICULARS

☛ The book of Jeremiah shows how God can take a man with no confidence, for a task beyond the ability of the strongest of men, to go through physical and mental suffering that would break most men, and yet give him an amazing and persevering compassion and faithfulness. However, a faithful servant does not always get what he longs for, but learns that God is in control. This book is not presented chronologically or by themes, but simply to emphasise the spiritual issues that needed to be raised at the time. Thus there is no order of events or specific scheme of subjects.

JEREMIAH

CHAPTER ONE

V 1–3: CONTEXT The context of Jeremiah's prophecy is set in the opening three verses. He prophesies from the thirteenth year of King Josiah of Judah to the last year of King Zedekiah, between 627 BC and 586 BC. In the last year of Zedekiah, Judah is taken into Babylonian captivity in the fifth month. Jeremiah is a priest and a prophet. **V 4–5: CALL** God's word comes to Jeremiah and tells him that God ordained him a prophet before his conception took place. **V 6: 'CANNOT'** Jeremiah replies that he cannot prophesy because he is 'a youth'. **V 7–10: COMMISSION** God commissions him, nevertheless, and tells him not to be afraid of men. He touches his mouth, gives him His words, and assigns to him the hard task to root out and pull down, destroy and throw down, and to build and plant. **V 11–16: COMMUNICATION** God reveals to Jeremiah an almond tree branch which blossomed early—speaking of God's early judgement. He also reveals a boiling pot from the north—picturing the Babylonian invasion of Judah. God thereby communicates to Jeremiah the solemnity of the task ahead. **V 17–19: COMMANDED** God commands Jeremiah to prepare himself and speak as he is told, and not to be dismayed by the faces of the people to whom he goes. God will fortify and strengthen Jeremiah. The task will be very hard but God will enable him, strengthen him and deliver him.

CHAPTER TWO

V 1–3: PAST PARTNERSHIP Jeremiah is to remind Israel of the past partnership, as a happy marriage, between God and Israel. All went well at the start. **V 4–8: PRESENT PERVERSENESS** Israel has become a race of idolaters and sinful rebels. Her priests, prophets and rulers lead the people astray. **V 9–19: POINTED PUNISHMENT** Desolation will follow Israel's abandoning her love for God to worship worthless gods. Israel has forsaken God and made her own gods. Israel will be laid waste, without inhabitant, plundered, and burned. In time her own wickedness and backsliding will rebuke Israel, because God is forsaken and Israel has no reverential fear of Him. **V 20–28: POLLUTED PROSTITUTION** Israel's idolatry is like spiritual prostitution.

Polluted with Baalism and other forms of idolatry and immorality, Israel passionately seeks wickedness like an escaping runaway camel or like a wild donkey in heat that seeks a mate. Israel's predisposition to such evil will be of no avail to them when they need to be saved from invaders. **V 29–37: POINTLESS PLEADING** God's people are wasting their time asking for God's deliverance when there is no repentance from sin. They have chosen to forget and abandon God and have indulged in sin. They do not even admit that they are sinful and claim that they are innocent. God tells them not to waste their time pleading with Him. Because they continue with their sin, and refuse to repent and trust, neither Egypt nor Assyria can rescue them from their captivity to come.

CHAPTER THREE

V 1–5: HARDENED HARLOTRY Although a divorced and remarried man is forbidden to return to his first wife, because that union would be considered to be adulterous, happily, the position is different for the backslidden people of God in their relationship with Him. His amazing grace will allow Him to take them back where there is real repentance and faith. In Israel's case, however, she is hardened in the harlotry of her sin. **V 6–11: REPENTANCE REFUSED** Israel has not simply gone off with one other partner, but has played the harlot with many, in the spiritual wickedness of idolatry. Judah's sin is even worse because Judah saw what her sister, Israel, did and, despite that, deliberately repeated her sister's spiritual adultery. Worse still, she pretended to be repentant. **V 12–22a: COMPASSIONATE COMMAND** Jeremiah is commanded by God to go to the people of Israel, whom He regards as an unfaithful wife or as rebellious children, and tell them to avoid His anger by returning to Him. He will bless them and acknowledge them if only they will turn from their sins and return to Him. They will know Him as their Father again. God's compassionate command is, 'Return, you backsliding children, and I will heal your backsliding.' The backsliding Christian also needs to obey that compassionate command. **V 22b–25: SINFUL SHAME** They acknowledge their sinful shame and realise the emptiness of the hope given by the idolatry they have practised in the mountains. Only God can save. They are covered by their reproach, having sinned against God. They admit that their fathers and they have sinned and not obeyed God's voice.

CHAPTER FOUR

V 1–4: REAL REPENTANCE It is not enough simply to admit one's sinfulness and need. God demands a return to Him with real repentance that shows itself turning them from their idolatry and embracing God's truth. There must be a breaking up of the fallow ground, in confession. Sin must be removed from the heart, by God's grace, in the same way that the foreskin is cut away in circumcision. God's final fury is the alternative to proper preparation leading to repentance. **V 5–13: IMMINENT INVASION** The imminent invasion from Babylon is foreseen as something terrible. After God's assurance of long-term spiritual restoration where there is true repentance, Jeremiah is horrified as he tells the people of the impending disaster that their current impenitence will bring. What lamentation and mourning will follow! Even Jeremiah errs in accusing God of having deceived the people. This emotional reaction, rather than biblical truth, is because he confuses the short-term and long-term plans of God for His rebel people. Great judgement will come as a mighty wind. **V 14–18: WICKEDNESS WASHED** Still God pleads with His people and urges them to wash away their wickedness from their hearts so they can be saved. It is their wickedness and their rebellion which causes the suffering to come. Inevitably poised for judgement, God always offers repentance and return. **V 19–31: DESOLATE DESTRUCTION** It seems that Jeremiah's heart beats again in time with God's as he expresses tremendous sorrow about the desolation and destruction that will come upon Israel. God describes the people as foolish and silly children, without understanding. They know more about evil than good. The whole passage is a picture of desolation, destruction, darkness, plunder and pain. True repentance and faith in God could avoid all this, by God's grace.

CHAPTER FIVE

V 1–2: NO RIGHTEOUSNESS Despite their spiritual talk, not one righteous person seeking truth can be found in Jerusalem. If God had been able to find one such person, He would have pardoned Jerusalem. This is a very low point. **V 3–5: NO REPENTANCE** Despite God's chastisement and correction, the leaders refuse to repent. They have become hardened in their sins, even though they have known God's way. **V 6–11: NO RESCUE** Therefore, there is no rescue for Israel, either from the ravages of wild animals or from the effects of their own idolatry and immorality. Neither is there rescue from God's avenging punishment. He will not completely destroy them, but there is no rescue because there is no repentance. **V 12–13: NO REVERENCE**

They lie about God, His presence and His activity. They deny that judgement will ever come. They see God's prophets, like Jeremiah, as empty wind with no substance in what they say or prophesy. **V 14–17: NO RESPITE** The frightening invasion from the mighty nation (Babylon) will give them no respite from famine, slaughter, desolation, and fear. **V 18–31: NO RECOGNITION** God warns them that they will be carried away captives, rather than be completely destroyed. Yet, they have no understanding, eyes to see, or ears to hear. They do not fear God. They have rebelled. They recognise neither their sins, even now, nor the need to turn. Their wickedness is endemic, and they seek to snare others in it. Although God will avenge and judge them, they still prefer to follow false prophets and live their profligate lifestyle. The last words of the chapter are very sad, 'And my people love to have it so, but what will you do in the end?'

CHAPTER SIX

V 1–9: DISASTER AND DESTRUCTION Disaster and destruction will come from Babylon in the north. The commanders will be like shepherds with their soldiers as numerous as flocks. They will pitch around Jerusalem to destroy it. Wickedness, violence and plundering will be directed against Jerusalem. There will be no 'pickings' left from the hostile gleaning from Babylon. **V 10–15: PROPHETS AND PEACE** God's people will not listen to His word and so will not heed His warning. This is because they are intent on sinning and listening to false prophets who are prophesying, 'Peace, peace.' Widespread punishment, not peace, will follow. **V 16–20: REST AND REJECTION** God offers rest in repentance and a return to the old paths of trust and obedience. While the people reject His law and His teaching, they continue the hypocrisy of outward religious ceremony and observances. **V 21–26: STUMBLING AND SACKCLOTH** God will cause His own people to stumble, to show them their need for forgiveness and help from Him, when the cruel invader comes upon them. He then bids them to dress in sackcloth and to mourn in sorrow for their sin. **V 27–30: TASK AND TEST** Jeremiah's task is to stand against God's rebel people and test them. He finds that they are not properly refined, but, rather, polluted. They will be rejected, just as they have rejected God.

CHAPTER SEVEN

V 1–7: PENITENCE PROCLAIMED In the gate of the temple, Jeremiah proclaims the need for repentance from the heart, and for a change of conduct. Trust must not be placed in lying words. Injustice, oppression, bloodshed, afflicting the innocent and idolatry must all go. God offers a safe and blessed dwelling in the land for generations to come if only His people will repent. **V 8–11: POLLUTED PATHS** Jeremiah goes on to detail the terrible sins of God's people, which, even in these few verses, leave very few of the Ten Commandments intact. **V 12–15: PEOPLE PUNISHED** As a result of their sin, Jerusalem will fall, just as Shiloh fell before the Philistines. God will preside over the destruction of the temple. **V 16–20: PRAYER PROHIBITED** God prohibits Jeremiah to pray for this rebellious people. This is to draw their attention to the awfulness of their idolatrous rebellion and wickedness, and their need for repentance, rather than parading outward tokens of what should be an inward spiritual life. Until there is repentance, God will not bless them. **V 21–27: POTENTIAL POSSESSION** God underlines, again, that it is not the outward sacrifices that count but an inward obedience from the heart. That produces a different walk with Him. Through the prophets, God has called His people back to Himself so that He can become their God again, but they have refused in the past and still do. They are even worse, now, than their sinful fathers, because they fail to learn the lessons that their fathers' evil should have taught them. **V 28–34: PARALYSING POLLUTION** Because of the pollution of lies, child sacrifice, and general wickedness, Judah and Jerusalem will be paralysed. Mirth, gladness, and weddings will be absent. Both the consequences of their sin and God's resulting chastisement will paralyse them into joyless existence, rather than into joyful living for Him.

CHAPTER EIGHT

V 1–3: DESECRATION Such will be the desecration in the judgement to come on Jerusalem, that bones of kings, princes, priests, prophets, and people will be scattered like refuse and ignored. **V 4–7: DEGRADATION** Jerusalem's degradation causes their backsliding to continue, with deceit and wickedness going hand in hand with ignorance of God's coming judgement. **V 8–12: DEVIATION** They will be misled by false scribes, shameful 'wise men', covetousness, falsehood, and shameless abomination. They will expect peace, but only receive punishment. They will not be able to blush over the foulness of their sin. **V 13: DAMNATION** God will consume them and take away all their means of livelihood, pictured here by the failure to grow grapes, figs and leaves. **V 14–22: DOMINATION** As Babylon invades from the north via Dan, a

realisation dawns that peace is not for Israel. The conquering invaders will be as serpents and vipers, and bitter will be the state of those who sin against the LORD. Sorrow and faintness are in the heart of Jeremiah, as he mourns his people's idolatry and hurt. There is no balm or physician to relieve their sin-sickness, and they are not saved.

CHAPTER NINE

V 1: WEEPING Jeremiah, 'the weeping prophet', expresses his overwhelming desire to weep for his people. **V 2: WILDERNESS** But he also wishes that he could go to a place in the wilderness to separate himself from all the wickedness of Israel. **V 3–6: WAYWARDNESS** He describes the Israelites' wayward habits as going 'from evil to evil'. God says they do not know Him. This is evident in their dealings with others and one another, characterised by lack of trust, slander, deceit, lying, and a passion for sin. **V 7–11: WRATH** God's refining wrath and punishment will be upon them. Thus Jeremiah weeps. God says He will make Jerusalem a 'heap of ruins'. It will be desolate and without human inhabitant. **V 12–16: WORMWOOD** Wormwood, a bitter tasting plant, pictures the bitterness that God will send to Israel for her forsaking of His law, her idolatry and her rebellion. The water she will drink will be as poisonous and vile as gall, a plant growing in that region. They will be scattered among the Gentiles and consumed by the sword. **V 17–21: WAILING** Wailing women will lead the mourning, lamentation and grief. Children and young people will be killed. **V 22–25: WORDS** God commands Jeremiah to 'speak' His words about the grim future. Bodies will be lying in the open fields. Man's former glorying in his wisdom, might and riches will disappear. The only subject of glory will be in knowing God and understanding Him. The uncircumcised nations involved will be punished, as will the Israelites with uncircumcised hearts.

CHAPTER TEN

V 1–5: GENTILE NATIONS God tells Israel not to follow the godless Gentiles in their idolatry. Idolatry is powerless to help them, and is futile. **V 6–16: GOD'S NAME** A comparison follows between God and idols. God is the eternal Creator who acts in history and deals with His people. Nobody can endure His wrath. Jeremiah reiterates that idols are useless, false, made in error, and will perish. He compares this with 'the Maker of all things' who has Israel as 'the tribe of His inheritance'. He ends by reminding them of God's great name—'the LORD of hosts'. **V 17–22: GREAT NOISE** In the coming pain and distress of Judah, when Babylon takes her captive, there will be a great noise and commotion as the invaders come from the north to make Judah's cities desolate. **V 23–25: GRACE NEEDED** Jeremiah pleads with God to deal with the Gentiles who will oppose Israel. But first he asks personally for God to correct him so that he may walk in justice with Him. He cannot do this unaided and would incur God's anger if left to himself. His request reminds us all that we need God's grace to come to Him and walk with Him.

CHAPTER ELEVEN

V 1–8: COVENANT, COMMAND AND CURSE Jeremiah tells Israel that God's gracious covenant, which He commands them to follow, has been broken. Thus, not only do they forgo the blessings, but they suffer the curses that God threatened, too. Anyone continuing to disobey that covenant remains cursed, and will therefore not know God's blessings. **V 9–17: CONSPIRACY, CALAMITY AND CRY** Judah's idolatrous rebellion has been the result of conspiracy against God and His word. When God brings calamity to them, they will cry to Him but He will not listen because there has been no real repentance and faith. Because of their rebellion, God tells Jeremiah not even to pray for this wayward people. That is very grave indeed. His anger is provoked by their hypocritical offerings to Baal. **V 18–23: CONTINUATION, COMMITMENT AND CATASTROPHE** There is another conspiracy, this time against the life of Jeremiah by the men of Anathoth. They plan to kill him if he continues to prophesy in God's name. Jeremiah commits his course to the 'LORD of hosts'. God tells Jeremiah that He will punish them and bring a catastrophe on them that leaves no remnant. Jeremiah's task is hard, but God is on his side.

CHAPTER TWELVE

V 1–2: PROSPERITY—WICKED Jeremiah is concerned about the prosperity of the wicked. He cannot understand why his righteous God allows them to do so well. **V 3–4: PRAYER—WHEN?** He then prays to God and asks Him to remove those wicked people. He asks how long this captivity will last. 'When?' is perhaps the second most frequent question asked of God. Only 'Why?' seems to be asked more often. **V 5–6: PATIENCE—WEARIED?** The LORD tells Jeremiah that the battle has only just begun and implies that his future trials will be far greater. He is now only running with the footmen; he has not yet run with the horses. He is walking in a land of peace, but he has huge floods to go through in the future. He must not be wearied. He must be unmoved when even his family turn against him. **V 7–13: PUNISHMENT—WARRANTED** God has temporarily forsaken His people because of their idolatry and abandoned them to their enemies. **V 14–17: PROMISE—WAYWARD** But God promises not only to bless Israel, but also other nations who will learn from repentant Israel's blessings. On the other hand, those disobedient to Him will be plucked out of the land, whether they are in Judah or in foreign nations. God is concerned with real repentance from the heart that causes rebel sinners to turn from sin and idolatry, and trust and obey Him.

CHAPTER THIRTEEN

V 1–11: SIGN OF THE SASH At God's instruction, Jeremiah hides a linen waist sash in a hole near a rock. When he later returns to claim it, it is spoiled. God says He will ruin the pride of Judah and Jerusalem in the same way. He also says that He has chosen them as His people to be close to Him, like the sash, but they have rejected that relationship. God's glory and their blessings have suffered. Their sin has dirtied them, weakened them, and made them useless, just like that sash. **V 12–14: INTOXICATION OF THE INHABITANTS** Just as bottles are filled with wine, so all in Jerusalem will be filled with drunkenness, including the political and religious leaders. They will be dashed against one another in their stupor and not be spared. **V 15–27: PUNISHMENT OF THE PROUD** Jeremiah passionately pleads again for his people's repentance. Because the people, along with the king and queen mother, are filled with pride against God, captivity will come from the north. They will be in pain

and be greatly shamed, just as captive women and prostitutes are shamed. They have chosen to be dirty and will reap the consequences of such a walk, which means they cannot be close to God.

CHAPTER FOURTEEN

V 1–6: PARCHED PASTURE As drought hits the land, the pasture becomes parched and the animals begin to perish. The people cry for water, but there is none. **V 7–9: PROPHET'S PETITION** Jeremiah acknowledges sin in Israel, but asks why is it that God seems unable to save them. He acknowledges that God is in the midst, and reminds Him that the people are called by His name. **V 10–12: PRAYER PROHIBITED** God sees His people's obdurate and proud intent to continue in sin. He tells Jeremiah not to pray for them. He will not hear their prayer or fasting and not heed their sacrifices. He will judge them. Without repentance, there can never be blessing. **V 13–18: PERILOUS PROPHETS** Jeremiah reminds God that their prophets are prophesying a false peace to the people. God replies that these lying prophets are neither authorised nor commissioned by Him, that they do not honour His word, and that they will themselves be consumed. But those who listen to them and heed them will also suffer for their own wickedness. The sword and famine will afflict the people, the prophets and the priests, who also go astray. God weeps for them but nevertheless will judge them. **V 19–22: PEOPLE'S PLEA** God's people ask if He has rejected them. They remind Him of the history of His dealings and of His covenant. They have the audacity to tell Him that He can do what the idols which they worship cannot do! But there is no hint of repentance and trust in Him.

CHAPTER FIFTEEN

V 1–9: REBELLION AND REPERCUSSIONS
God replies to the people's plea. Even prayer warriors such as Moses and Samuel would not be effective in their prayers to have these people dealt with favourably. Death, sword, famine and captivity will come. They will become prey to beasts as well as to the sword. God remembers the idolatrous wickedness of Judah, of which Manasseh is the named evil example. That wickedness continues, despite God's warning and history of grace. His forsaking people continue to reject His gracious overtures of mercy. **V 10–14: PATHOS AND PROMISE** At this stage, Jeremiah is overcome and makes a pathetic prophet. He wishes he had not been born. He reminds God of his selfless faithfulness which causes him to be cursed by everybody. God promises to him that it will be well with the remnant of Israel, and that He will look after him in the events that follow the captivity. **V 15–21: DESPAIR AND DELIVERANCE** Still, Jeremiah seems racked with self-pity and worry. He is separate from the mockers, and yet sees himself as afflicted by the God whom he is seeking to represent. His joy and rejoicing have gone. God reassures Jeremiah that He will look after him as His mouthpiece, the prophet, and strengthen him in the trials that he encounters in that work. He will deliver him and redeem him. Sometimes God's servant must depend solely on the promise of His word, even when there is no obvious evidence of fulfilment at the time of his trust in it.

CHAPTER SIXTEEN

V 1–4: NO MARRIAGE To emphasise the problems coming to Israel, and to deliver Jeremiah from them, he is told not to marry and raise a family at this time, because of the terrible suffering that would come to his dependants. This provides a solemn warning to rebellious Israel. **V 5–7: NO MOURNING** Jeremiah must not engage in mourning, as a sign to the people that God has withdrawn His peace, mercy and lovingkindness from them. **V 8–9: NO MIRTH** At the other extreme, Jeremiah is also told not to feast with them, so that they know that there is no cause for rejoicing. God tells Jeremiah that all mirth, rejoicing, gladness, and normally happy events like marriage will be non-existent. This will be a very lonely path, indeed, for God's prophet. **V 10–13: NO MERCY** The lack of marriage, mourning, and mirth will cause the Israelites to ask what God has done to them. He tells Jeremiah to tell them that there is no mercy because they have forsaken Him, rejected Him, and refused to repent. They follow their own ways and ignore His voice, and thus are rejected by Him. In the judgement soon to come upon them, in the absence of repentant faith, there will be no mercy for them. **V 14–15: NO MISTAKE** Yet God assures Jeremiah that He will restore His people to their land, as He has promised. The day will come when He brings back Israel from the Babylonian captivity in the north, just as He brought them out of Egypt in times past. Israel will be more taken with that deliverance than with the Egyptian one, possibly because they will suffer even more in Babylon. But the immediate cloud of God's inevitable shorter-term judgement carries God's merciful silver lining of His assurance of their future restoration. **V 16–18: NO MISSING** However, in the immediate context of God's impending judgement, He will send the invading soldiers, as hunters and fishermen, to capture the Israelites from every mountain, hill and hole in the rocks. He will overlook none of the iniquities committed by His rebellious people. He will repay their sins doubly. No offender will avoid that judgement on rebel idolaters, and no sin will be missed by God. If that is so for Israel, how much more will it be so for those who do not repent and turn to Christ as Saviour? **V 19–21: NO MISUNDERSTANDING** The Gentiles will see Israel's sin and idolatry and God's judgement upon them. They will then clearly understand that God is in control. There can be no misunderstanding when God works either in judgement or deliverance.

CHAPTER SEVENTEEN

V 1–4: SUCH SIN! Just as idolatrous Israel writes the name of her idols on the altar with an iron pen with a diamond tip, so God tells her, through Jeremiah, that sin is etched in the very centre of her heart as well as on her worship of idols and her idolatrous practices. She chose to leave her privileged godly heritage and God will allow her enemies to take her much farther down that route than she will want. God's anger will burn for ever against such sin. **V 5–6: CURSED CONFIDENCE** When a man departs from God, he trusts in man rather than God. But such confidence is cursed, and he will be dried and parched, like a shrub in the desert or a place in the salty wilderness. **V 7–8: FRUITFUL FAITH** In comparison, the man who trusts in God will be like a growing tree, fruitful and without anxiety, as he trusts the LORD. **V 9–10: HUMAN HEART** A key principle about the sinfulness of human nature is that the 'heart is deceitful above all things and desperately wicked'. No one can fully know it except God who searches it, tests the mind, and sees the actions it produces. **V 11: PASSING PROSPERITY** After God's

analysis of the human heart, He immediately goes on to talk about the folly and emptiness of acquiring riches through sinful means. They will not last. Trust in God is still rivalled by man's desire to trust in materialism today. **V 12–13: FORSAKEN FOUNTAIN** God's glorious sanctuary throne, from which living waters flow to those who trust Him, provides no relief to those who forsake Him. Those who forsake the fountain deny themselves its offered cleansing and the quenching of soul thirst. **V 14–18: SEEKING SALVATION** Jeremiah prays for God to save him and keep him as he seeks to live a godly life amidst great opposition. He asks that God will deal with his enemies. **V 19–27: SANCTIFIED SABBATH** Keeping the Sabbath day free from the normal work of the week is a timeless principle of God's moral law. The breaking of it produces pride and hardness against God, accompanied by an increase in idolatry. The Sabbath is given not only as a day of rest, but also as a day dedicated to God's worship. Thus, the determination to keep the Sabbath indicates a desire to turn from idols and worship the LORD God. Breaking the Sabbath shows a rebellious and idolatrous spirit. Israel's repentance would bring revival made evident by a desire to worship God and to keep His Sabbath. Her continued rejection of it will bring about God's judgement. Christians today should remember seriously and obey joyfully these principles about God's Sabbath day, the Lord's Day.

CHAPTER EIGHTEEN

V 1–11: REPENT AND RELENT Jeremiah tells Israel that God is the Potter who can do what He likes with the clay and with the pot. If Israel will repent from her sins,

He is willing to relent from His judgement; if she persists with evil, He will persist with judgement and a plan against them. They must repent and return to Him. **V 12–17: REJECTION AND RESPONSE** The immediate rejection of God's message by the people is deliberate and plain. They prefer to follow their own plans and their own evil hearts. God's response is that they are leaving clean waters which could refresh and cleanse them. He will scatter them because of their idolatry and sin so that even He will turn His back on them in a calamity. **V 18–23: REACTION AND RECOURSE** The reaction is to persecute Jeremiah. They initially will speak against him and not listen to anything he says. Jeremiah's recourse is to bring the whole matter before the LORD, to ask for His support and help. He prays that God will deal severely with those who oppose Him, His word and His prophet.

CHAPTER NINETEEN

V 1–9: WITNESS AND WORDS At God's command, Jeremiah gets a potter's flask and takes some of the elders, priests and prophets to witness God's message. They are words of judgement and catastrophe caused by the sinfulness, idolatry, and refusal of Israel to repent. They will fall to the sword of their enemies, and their corpses will be scattered and eaten by beasts and birds. Cannibalism will take place. They will be in despair. **V 10–13: FRAGMENTED FLASK** To illustrate the point, Jeremiah is told to break the potter's flask as a sign that Jerusalem and its people will be broken because of all their idolatry. **V 14–15: POINTED PROPHECY** Jeremiah then comes from Tophet, where he made the last prophecy, and stands in the temple court, telling the people plainly that God will bring doom

upon Jerusalem because they are stiff-necked in their rejection of God's word. God holds us accountable for how we respond to His word.

CHAPTER TWENTY

V 1–2: PERSECUTION THROUGH PASHHUR Pashhur is the chief governor of the temple. He objects strongly to Jeremiah's prophecy, strikes him, and puts him in the stocks near the temple. **V 3–6: JUDGEMENT THROUGH JEREMIAH** When he is released the next day, Jeremiah tells Passhur of a change of his name to Magor-Missabib, which means that terror will come on every hand. He reiterates the prophecy of Babylon's captivity, great slaughter and impoverishment. Pashhur will go to Babylon and will die there, along with his friends to whom he prophesies lies. **V 7–18: OSCILLATION THROUGH OPPOSITION** In a moving passage, Jeremiah first reveals how close he is to quitting because of the mockery that he suffers as he faithfully proclaims God's word. He wants to be silent but God's word burns in his heart. He then pleads his cause before God and reflects on the awe and might of God. His persecutors will fail. He reaches a high point of praising God as he foresees God's deliverance of the poor of Israel from the evildoers. Perhaps he foresees the return from Babylon in this moment. But then a tide of dejection comes over him and, Job-like, he wishes that he had never been born, and ends up in abject desolation. It is never easy to represent a holy God in a sinful, rebellious world, and Jeremiah does this without the hope and direct knowledge of the cross, resurrection and ascension of the Lord Jesus Christ.

CHAPTER TWENTY-ONE

V 1-7: RESPONSE TO REQUEST How tempting could be the request from King Zedekiah, through Pashhur and Zedekiah, to Jeremiah! He is asked to enquire of the LORD if God will give His people wonderful deliverance against Nebuchadnezzar, king of Babylon. Jeremiah's response is to tell them immediately that God Himself will fight against them. They will be besieged and overcome. Amidst great slaughter, captivity will take place. Zedekiah is told that he and his sinful people staying in Jerusalem will be killed and shown no mercy. Despite Jeremiah's inner fears, he remains faithful to the commission God gives him. This is a lesson for us all. **V 8-10: PEOPLE TO PART** Jeremiah adds that the people should go with the Chaldeans into captivity, otherwise they will perish. Jerusalem will be burned with fire by the king of Babylon. This is not what Zedekiah wants to hear! **V 11-14: JUDGEMENT TO JUDAH** Jeremiah adds that the people of Judah must listen to God's word. He tells them to regulate their life justly in such a way that God will withhold His fury which will come on them because of their evil doings. Jeremiah tells them again that God says He is against them and will punish them, as a forest fire devours things around it.

CHAPTER TWENTY-TWO

V 1-10: JUDGEMENT ON JUDAH STATED Jeremiah announces God's judgement on the house of the king of Judah, if repentance does not produce righteous conduct. Judah will be made like a wilderness and destroyed by invaders. Her forsaking of God's covenant and her practice of idolatry will become a topic of conversation between the nations. Instead of mourning the dead, sorrow will be expressed for the king who is taken captive who will not return. **V 11-30: JUDGEMENT ON JOSIAH'S SONS** Josiah is a king who performs godly reforms, but his sons are evil, and rebel against God. The rest of this chapter gives reasons for their downfall and captivity. These are the result of their failure to follow God, and their idolatry and rebellion against Him. Those to be afflicted are Shallum (or Jehoahaz), Jehoiakim, and Jehoiakim's son named Coniah (or Jehoiachin). Their judgements respectively are recorded in verses 11, 18 and 24.

CHAPTER TWENTY-THREE

V 1-6: SCATTERING SHEPHERDS The false religious leaders of Israel are like shepherds who scatter the sheep. God says he will set up faithful shepherds who will feed and care for the sheep. In some small measure, this will be fulfilled in God's faithful prophets, but the ultimate fulfilment will be in the Good Shepherd Himself, who is 'THE LORD OUR RIGHTEOUSNESS'. **V 7-8: FREEDOM FORETOLD** The day will come when Israel will return to her own land, not only from captivity in Babylon, but also from around the world where she is scattered. **V 9-22: PROFANE PROPHECIES** Prophets and priests falsely and profanely prophesy peace and well-being for Israel at the same time that they are following Baal, idolatry and wickedness. Their adultery is both spiritual against God and physical. God regards them like Sodom and Gomorrah. His whirlwind of anger will fall upon them. Claiming to speak in His name, they have added false prophecies to their sins of rebellion and idolatry. **V 23-24: GREAT GOD** God reminds His people that He is near, knows everything, and is so great that He fills the heavens and the earth. We need to remember this when iniquity and godlessness increase. God is still in control. **V 25–40: ARDENT ANGER** Having heard the lies of the wicked and idolatrous prophets, and their claim to revelation in their visions and their words, God compares their puny utterances with the fire and hammer of His powerful word. He reiterates His anger against these people, whom He has not sent, and to whom He has not given His words. Judgement will fall upon Jerusalem and upon the people. Great reproach and shame will come with that fall.

CHAPTER TWENTY-FOUR

V 1–3: FIGS God chooses two baskets of figs for Jeremiah. In one basket are good figs, but the figs in the other basket are poor and completely inedible. **V 4–7: FAVOUR** God tells Jeremiah that the exiles from Judah in Babylon are like the good figs and will be brought back. **V 8–10: FALL** Those who remain with Zedekiah in Jerusalem will fall. They are like the bad figs. They will be ridiculed, cursed, reproached, and subject to the sword, famine and plague; they will be destroyed.

CHAPTER TWENTY-FIVE

V 1–11: SEVENTY The scene here returns to several years before the Babylonian captivity which begins in chapter 24. Under King Nebuchadnezzar of Babylon, God reveals to Jeremiah that the captivity will last for seventy years. This is because, despite constant pleading by God's true prophets, His people have refused to repent and turn to God. They have continued to provoke Him with idolatry and sin. **V 12–33: SWORD** After the seventy years of captivity in Babylon are finished, God will punish

Nebuchadnezzar, make his land desolate, and make his people servants to many nations. All nations who have persecuted and afflicted God's people will also be put to the sword. Although God will use them as instruments to discipline His people, He holds them accountable for the wrong they have done to them. **V 34–38: SHEPHERDS** The shepherds of those nations, the leaders themselves, are told to weep and wail because of God's anger to be released on them.

CHAPTER TWENTY-SIX

V 1–6: PREACH! At the start of Jehoiakim's reign, Jeremiah is commanded to preach every single word that God gives him in the temple courts. He is to preach that refusal to repent means that Jerusalem will be cursed and become a desolation. **V 7–11: PERSECUTION** The priests, prophets and people seize Jeremiah, intending to put him to death. In effect, they accuse him of treason. They take him to the princes and tell them that Jeremiah deserves to die. **V 12–15: PERSISTENCE** Jeremiah seizes the opportunity to preach to the princes as well as his previous audience. He tells them that this is God's word and they must repent. He is ready to die, but they will be guilty before God if they kill him. **V 16–24: PROTECTED** The princes and the people tell the religious leaders that Jeremiah does not deserve to die. This is supported by elders who cite Micah's similar message in the time of Hezekiah. But Jehoiakim's killing of Urijah is also cited. Jeremiah is in peril. However, God's earlier promise to protect him is realised under Ahikam, and Jeremiah survives.

CHAPTER TWENTY-SEVEN

V 1–11: YOKE SYMBOL Jeremiah puts

bonds and yokes on his neck as a symbol of captivity and then sends them to six neighbouring kings, to tell them that they, too, will come under the power of Babylon. Despite the lies about liberty proclaimed by false prophets, Nebuchadnezzar will rule over these nations and over Judah, and those who submit to him will remain in their own land. **V 12–18: YOU SERVE!** Jeremiah then speaks first to Zedekiah, King of Judah, and then to the priests and people, telling them not to follow the false words of their prophets. They say that Nebuchadnezzar will not prevail over God's people. Jeremiah assures them that Nebuchadnezzar will prevail, and that the only way to stay in the land is to bow the neck to Nebuchadnezzar in service, otherwise they will perish. Contrary to the false prophecies, the captured temple vessels held in Babylon will not be returned soon. **V 19–22: YOUR SANCTUARY** Jeremiah also prophesies that the remaining furniture in the temple, God's sanctuary, will be taken to Babylon. But one day there will be a return, and all those holy things will be restored to the temple. Amidst the correct prophecies of doom, he indicates God's long-term plan for His people. This is a repeated principle of Scripture.

CHAPTER TWENTY-EIGHT

V 1–4: DECEIT The false prophet, Hananiah, deceitfully prophesies in God's name that the yoke of the king of Babylon will be broken and that the king of Judah, the exiles and the treasures of the sanctuary will be returned within two years. **V 5–9: DIRECTNESS** Jeremiah confronts Hananiah, confirming that the objects will, one day, come back to the sanctuary, but speaking against false prophecy and saying that the prophecy

will only be recognised if it comes true. **V 10–11: DEMONSTRATION** Hananiah then takes the yoke off the neck of Jeremiah and breaks it. He says that the yoke of Nebuchadnezzar on the neck of other nations will be broken within two years. Jeremiah leaves. **V 12–14: DIRECTION** God directs Jeremiah to tell Hananiah that an iron yoke will replace the wooden yoke from Nebuchadnezzar, and that God will enable Nebuchadnezzar to control everything. **V 15–17: DEATH** Faithful Jeremiah then confronts Hananiah again and tells him that he is a false prophet. He prophesies the death of Hananiah. Two months later, Hananiah dies in accordance with Jeremiah's prophecy.

CHAPTER TWENTY-NINE

V 1–4: COMMUNICATION TO CAPTIVES Jeremiah sends a letter to all the captives in Babylon giving them God's instructions as to how they must behave in captivity. **V 5–9: BUILD IN BABYLON** The captives are to get established in Babylon as peace-loving inhabitants. Normal work and family life are to continue and they are to seek Babylon's peace in prayer and in the way they live. They are to reject false prophets who give them other advice. **V 10–14: REALITY OF RETURN** Jeremiah underlines that, after seventy years, they will return to their own land. God will accomplish this as they seek Him wholeheartedly. He will also bring back His people from other nations. This is one of those prophecies with fulfilment to come both in the long-term and in the short-term. **V 15–20: PUNISHMENT ON PROPHETS** They are told that God will punish those prophets who lead them astray and who have rejected true prophets and God's word. **V 21–32: DEALING WITH DECEIVERS** Specific judgements are announced against Ahab, Zedekiah, and Shemaiah. These are people who prophesied against the truths that God told Jeremiah to take to His people. God's concern for His word, His people and His prophet are seen in these prophecies.

CHAPTER THIRTY

V 1–7: TROUBLED TIMES Despite the terrible troubles that Israel must go through, God promises Jeremiah that He will restore His children. **V 8–11: REBELS' RETURN** In the day when God brings back His rebellious children to the promised land, He will also bring back descendants from lands afar. Again, this prophecy has both an immediate and a far-reaching application. **V 12–17: CAPTORS COMPARED** Although God will do the 'impossible' in healing the incurable wounds of Israel, He will send their captors into exile, and plunder and spoil them. **V 18–22: PROMISED POSSESSION** God will greatly bless the descendants of Jacob in every way. He will show positively that they are His people and that He is their God. **V 23–24: FIERCE FURY** God will send the furious whirlwind of His anger on the wicked.

CHAPTER THIRTY-ONE

V 1–6: GOD'S DECLARATION God again declares His intended future blessing on His people. His love for them is everlasting and He has called them to Himself. He will rebuild them. Joy will be theirs again and others will want to go to worship in Zion. **V 7–14: GOD'S DETERMINATION** The LORD repeats through Jeremiah that they should sing and praise Him for His determination to bring them from all over the earth to their own land. He will ransom Jacob.

Restoration, renewal, satisfaction and joy will mark their restored relationship with their God. **V 15–20: GOD'S DELIGHT** Despite the weeping and the moaning that God's discipline causes, His children—typified here by Ephraim—are His delight. He has only disciplined them to act in compassion. **V 21–22: GOD'S DESIRE** God urges His unfaithful and backsliding daughter, Israel, to heed His signposts and come back to Him. **V 23–34: GOD'S DOING** Before Jeremiah wakes from his dream, God stresses again that He will bring back Israel from captivity. He will refresh and bless them. When Jeremiah is awake, God speaks to him directly and underlines again what He will do to bring His people back and bless them. He will make a new covenant to replace the old covenant. That covenant will extend beyond Israel now to all who turn from their sin and trust Christ in the future and will involve a new law in the hearts and minds of those who come to know God. This can only be God's doing. **V 35–40: GOD'S DECREE** God declares that the whole land again will be holy and that the city of Jerusalem will be His permanently. The certainty of this happening in the future is no less than the certainty that He currently and continuously sustains His creation and universe. Just as the sun, moon, stars, and sea, continue in the mode that God set in creation, so His instructions about the return and blessing of His people will never change.

CHAPTER THIRTY-TWO

V 1–5: CONFINED BUT CONSTANT Jeremiah, imprisoned by King Zedekiah of Judah in the prison fort, remains constant to his message. Babylon will take God's people captive, and no resistance will be successful. This constancy annoys and worries King Zedekiah. **V 6–15: PURCHASE A PLOT!** Jeremiah reveals that God has told him to purchase a plot of land, which he does. This is God's way of telling Judah that there will be a return to the promised land. Jeremiah's investment is not in vain. **V 16–25: SUBMISSION TO SOVEREIGN** Jeremiah clearly does not fully understand the significance of the investment at that time. But he lays the whole position out before God. Nebuchadnezzar is about to invade and take Jerusalem very soon, yet God has told His prophet to purchase some land there. Out of obedience to God, he does so. Prayer and obedience go hand in hand. **V 26–35: 'IMPOSSIBILITY' AND IDOLATRY** It seems highly unlikely that Israel will be back in her own land as the pressure from Babylon mounts. But God reminds Jeremiah that nothing is impossible with Him. Despite persistent idolatry and rebellion which has severely provoked God and caused Israel's downfall and captivity, God will restore her in His time. God is sovereign and will always perform His will. **V 36–44: CALAMITY THEN COVENANT** God explains again that the calamity upon His people is because of their sin, idolatry, and refusal to repent. However, He has now instigated an everlasting covenant which will turn His people's hearts to Him and will continue to be fulfilled long after the promised return of Israel to the promised land.

CHAPTER THIRTY-THREE

V 1–3: GOD'S WORD: PRAYER FROM PRISON Jeremiah's faithfulness to God causes him to be in stocks, dungeons and prisons. Still in prison, Jeremiah is told by God to pray to Him and that He will answer with completely unexpected and 'great and mighty things'. **V 4–9: GOD'S WORD: CONFIDENCE DESPITE CAPTIVITY** God repeats that He will deal with Judah and Jerusalem and restore them to a place of real blessing. Jeremiah never fails to repeat God's continued judgement on sin and blessing for repentance, coupled with His eternal purpose. **V 10–13: GOD'S WORD: WORSHIP FROM WILDERNESS** Judah and Jerusalem will be made into a desolate wilderness, but God will bring praise and joy in those very places and bring back the captives. Normal life will return. **V 14–16: GOD'S WORD: PERFORMANCE AND PROMISE** God has not forgotten His promises, to Israel and Judah, of His Messiah to come (the 'Branch of Righteousness'). So great will the change be, then, that Jerusalem will be called 'THE LORD OUR RIGHTEOUSNESS'. **V 17–18: GOD'S WORD: DELIVERING ON DAVID** This is because God will remember His Davidic covenant with Israel about His king. Neither will they lack a priest; Jesus Christ will ultimately fulfil that prophecy as both King and Priest, when not only God's physical people are restored, but when those who have turned in repentance and faith to Christ will be saved. **V 19–22: GOD'S WORD: COVENANT LIKE CREATION** Just as sure as night follows day, we can be sure that God's covenant will never be broken. The physical and spiritual descendants of David, through faith in God, will be more than the stars in heaven and the sand on the seashore. **V 23–24: GOD'S WORD: JACOB AND JUDAH** Often the chastisement and blessings pronounced on Jacob, Judah, Israel, or Ephraim stand for God's dealing with the whole of His physical people, and in principle with the way He deals with His spiritual people. **V 25–26: GOD'S WORD: RECKON ON RETURN!** God says that His people will definitely be caused by Him to return; He will deal with them mercifully. They are the children of the patriarchs, Abraham, Isaac, and Jacob, and of King David. God has made promises to them and will fulfil them. God always keeps His promises.

CHAPTER THIRTY-FOUR

V 1–7: WARNING OF REPERCUSSIONS Jeremiah repeats his warning to Zedekiah, king of Judah, that Jerusalem will go into captivity. Zedekiah will go with them but He will not die by the sword. Jeremiah's faithfulness to his commission to tell Zedekiah the truth causes him to be imprisoned. (Remember that Jeremiah is not written chronologically but topically.) **V 8–16: WAYWARDNESS OF RENEGADES** Zedekiah apparently repents of the abuse of slaves, who, under the law, should be set free every seventh year. Perhaps he is hoping for God's mercy if he covenants with God. He instructs the people to release the slaves. But, after initial compliance, his subjects change their minds and reverse the release, without intervention from Zedekiah. The covenant is broken and God's name is profaned thereby, bringing more suffering to the slaves. **V 17–22: WRATH ON REBELLION** God proclaims His wrath on this transgression and breaking of the covenant, which has been ratified by the correct procedure of walking between parts of a divided animal sacrifice. The rebels will be killed, Zedekiah and the princes will be taken, and Judah will be made desolate.

CHAPTER THIRTY-FIVE

V 1–5: SETTING THE SCENE God tells Jeremiah to invite the Rechabites into the temple to offer them wine to drink. Jeremiah does this. **V 6–11: FAITHFUL TO FOREFATHER** The Rechabites refuse the drink because Jonadab, the son of Rechab the founder father, had told them to abstain from wine in order to help them to protect their holiness. (Such a precaution may repay careful thought today.) The Rechabites will not go back on the promise given—they will remain faithful. **V 12–16: LEARN THE LESSON** God draws the parallel through Jeremiah. Why should the Rechabites be so faithful to a human relation, when God's people take no notice of God their Father? **V 17: APPLICATION OF ALMIGHTY** God says that because of such unfaithfulness, which compares so badly with the loyal example of the Rechabites, doom will fall on Judah and Jerusalem. **V 18–19: COMMENDATION OF COMPLIANCE** However, Jeremiah tells the Rechabites that God commends them for their faithfulness in keeping Jonadab's wise requirement, and that He will preserve their posterity.

CHAPTER THIRTY-SIX

V 1–3: INSPIRATION AND INTIMATION Jehoiakim is in his fourth year of reign. God tells Jeremiah to write what He reveals to him on a scroll. This is the inspiration of God's word through man. God's sovereignty is balanced between His great desire to see people repent and their responsibility to do so. He says that it 'may be' that Judah will repent and turn so that He can forgive them. He clearly intimates His purpose to forgive repentant sinners. **V 4–10: INSTRUCTION AND IMPLEMENTATION** Jeremiah is confined and cannot go to the temple. So he instructs the faithful scribe, Baruch, to write down the words that God gives him to dictate. Baruch is to read them to all the men of Judah who come into Jerusalem for the day of fasting. Baruch performs his task and, in the fifth year of Jehoikim's reign, reads the scroll so all the people can hear. **V 11–19: IMPACT AND INSIGHT** Micaiah hears this and arranges for scribes and princes to hear the word. Baruch reads it to them and it makes its impact: fear hits them. They decide to tell the king about God's word, no doubt hoping that this will produce repentance and blessing. With wise insight, they tell Baruch and Jeremiah to hide, in case the king reacts unfavourably. **V 20–26: INIQUITY AND IMPLORING** The king and those with him are arrogant in their rebellion against God. The king cuts the scroll, bit by bit, and burns it, despite three men imploring him not to do so. The king commands that Jeremiah and Baruch be seized, but God hides them. **V 27–32: INITIATIVE AND INDIGNATION** God again takes the initiative and gives Jeremiah the words to tell Baruch to write down again, and, in addition, a message to the king indicating God's indignation. God will punish him, his family and Judah. For good measure, God reveals added words to Jeremiah for Baruch to record.

CHAPTER THIRTY-SEVEN

V 1–15: PRISON—PERSONAL PERSECUTION (The context is that after the death of Jehoiakim and the brief succession of his son, who was deported to Babylon, King Nebuchadnezzar of Babylon puts Zedekiah on the throne of Judah in 597 BC.) When Pharaoh's army comes up from Egypt, the Babylonians need to take action against them and leave. Perhaps Zedekiah's men then think that the captivity is over, and that they will be free to deal with Jeremiah in their own way. But this is only a lull, and the Chaldeans come back under Nebuchadnezzar. Because Jeremiah tells the truth that Judah will be taken into captivity by Babylon, he is persecuted and prevented from leaving the city on the false charge that he is absconding to Babylon. He is beaten and is placed in prison. **V 16–20: PRIVATELY—PRIVATE PETITION** King Zedekiah asks Jeremiah privately what will happen. Jeremiah tells the king that He will be delivered into the hand of the king of Babylon. He then makes a personal petition to the king to be brought out of prison or he will die. **V 21: PLACED—PERSONAL PROVISION** The king places him in the prison court and orders that food be made available to Jeremiah for as long as the food lasts. God has His hand on His servant, even through a wicked king.

CHAPTER THIRTY-EIGHT

V 1–6: CRUEL CAPTIVITY This time, Jeremiah's faithfulness to his message causes him to be put into a dungeon which, in effect, is a cistern previously used for storing water, but from which it is impossible to escape. The bottom of the dungeon will be miry clay if there is any water remaining. **V 7–13: CONCERNED COMPASSION** However, Ebed-Melech, an Ethiopian, is concerned for Jeremiah and he arranges with the king for thirty men to lift him out with the use of ropes. Old clothes and rags pad the ropes so they can be put under Jeremiah's arms. He is thus rescued through a non-Israelite. Jeremiah is again to be located in the prison court. Once more, God's sovereign hand is at work on his behalf. **V 14–28: CONFIDENTIAL CONSULTATION** Escaped from the cistern, Jeremiah is approached, in confidence, by Zedekiah. Zedekiah guarantees his safety if he will answer his questions about the captivity. Again, Jeremiah tells the king that if he yields to Babylon and goes into captivity, he will survive. Any resistance will result in disaster. Zedekiah tells Jeremiah not to tell anyone of the private consultation or he will die. Jeremiah agrees that he will tell the inquirers that he asked not to be put in prison again, which, of course, is true. He is under no obligation to reveal the whole confidential conversation to someone just because that person asks. Jeremiah will remain in the prison court until the downfall of Jerusalem.

CHAPTER THIRTY-NINE

V 1–4: FALL After two-and-a-half years of siege, Jerusalem is penetrated and Nebuchadnezzar takes the city in Zedekiah's eleventh year. Zedekiah and his soldiers flee from the city. **V 5–7: FULFILMENT** Amidst bloodshed and suffering, Zedekiah's sons are killed, and he is blinded and taken into captivity, just as Jeremiah prophesied. God's word is again fulfilled. **V 8–10: FIRE** Jerusalem is set on fire and Nebuzaradan, Nebuchadnezzar's chief military officer, takes away captive all except the poor who are left there. They are given the vineyards and the fields. **V 11–14: FAVOUR** Nebuchadnezzar shows favour to Jeremiah. He gives instructions that Jeremiah must not be harmed, but that his wishes must be respected. Jeremiah is taken out of prison and put under Gedaliah, the governor under Nebuchadnezzar. Thus Jeremiah is among his people. **V 15–18: FAITH** Ebed-Melech, the Ethiopian, whose compassion earlier caused Jeremiah to escape from the cistern and dungeon, is told by Jeremiah that God will spare him because his trust is in God. In judgement, God always spares those whose faith is in Him.

CHAPTER FORTY

V 1–3: PERCEPTION OF PAGAN Nebuzaradan tells captive Jeremiah the reason why Israel has gone into captivity. He has it exactly right and repeats what Jeremiah has been telling God's people over a long period. Sometimes a perceptive pagan understands God's word and purposes better than His rebellious people do. **V 4–6: GOING TO GEDALIAH** Jeremiah is given a degree of freedom under Nebuzaradan that Zedekiah gives to him. But Nebuzaradan recommends Jeremiah to go to Gedaliah, the governor of the captives. Jeremiah does so. **V 7–12: RETURN TO REGULARITY** As Jeremiah prophesied under Gedaliah, regularity returns. Jews, who would live quietly under the king of Babylon, gather wine, summer fruit and oil in abundance. Jews from further afield are returning because they have heard of the good deal available under Gedaliah. **V 13–16: WASTE OF WARNING** However, Johanan hears of a plot by Ishmael to murder Gedaliah and warns him accordingly. Gedaliah does not believe the warning, even when Johanan offers to kill Ishmael to save him. Gedaliah tells Johnanan that he is not telling the truth about Ishmael. This unheeded warning is the trigger point for much suffering to come.

CHAPTER FORTY-ONE

V 1–9: MURDER AND MASSACRE Ishmael murders Gedaliah. He also massacres all the Jews with him. He then kills seventy out of eighty men from Shechem who come mourning the downfall of Jerusalem and bringing offerings and incense to the temple. Ten of those men are spared because they have food and provisions hidden in a field, and Ishmael knows that those can be useful to him. The dead bodies fill a pit. **V 10: CONTROL AND CAPTIVITY** So much is Ishmael in control that he carries away all the rest of the people in Mizpah, the king's daughter, and those whom Nebuchadnezzar committed to restrain Gedaliah. He now purposes to take them in captivity to the Ammonites. **V 11–18: RESCUED AND RUNNING** Johanan, whose warning is unheeded by Gedaliah, goes in pursuit of Ishmael and rescues the captives from him. Ishmael and eight men escape and run to Ammon. Johanan and his military forces, along with the rescued captives, also run towards Egypt. They fear the wrath of Babylon, even though Johanan tried to prevent the murders and massacres perpetrated by Ishmael.

CHAPTER FORTY-TWO

V 1–3: APPROACH TO JEREMIAH Commendably, Johanan and the military leaders come to Jeremiah to ask him to approach God for divine guidance about what they should do. So far, so good. **V 4: AGREEMENT OF JEREMIAH** Jeremiah agrees to consult God and give a verbatim response to those who consult him. **V 5–6: ASSURANCE TO JEREMIAH** Johanan and his men assure Jeremiah that whatever God says they will do. Later developments will reveal the insincerity of this assurance. **V 7–18: AFFIRMATION THROUGH JEREMIAH** They receive the same message which Jeremiah passed on to the children of Israel: if they stay in the land and obey the king, they will be safe; if they seek to get out of submission to the king of Babylon, in this case by fleeing to Egypt, they will be destroyed and there will be calamity. Jeremiah faithfully relays God's message. **V 19–22: APPLICATION BY JEREMIAH** Good preachers not only present truth; they apply it to their hearers. Johanan is urged not to go to

Egypt but to stay in the land, trusting God's promise. Jeremiah admonishes him for his hypocritical request for God's directing when he remains unwilling to obey God's word. Johanan and his supporters will die.

CHAPTER FORTY-THREE

V 1–3: REJECTION The insincerity of Johanan, Azariah and 'all the proud men' is exposed. They reject Jeremiah's counsel from God and tell him that he is speaking falsely. **V 4–7: REBELLION** Johanan, the military personnel, and all the people disobediently take the remnant from Judah, and all whom Nebuzaradan left there, on the instructions of Nebuchadnezzar, and lead them out to Egypt. Jeremiah and Baruch are included. **V 8–13: RESPONSE** In response, God directs Jeremiah to place stones in mortar in the brick courtyard at the entrance of Pharaoh's house. He places them in clay in full view of the public. Jeremiah tells the rebels that it is here that God will enable Nebuchadnezzar to establish his throne, and that devastation, disaster and death will come upon them. Egypt will be conquered by Babylon. God says that Nebuchadnezzar will act as 'My servant' in this matter.

CHAPTER FORTY-FOUR

V 1–6: REMINDER Jeremiah reminds the Jews living in Egypt that their conduct repeats the pattern of Israel's previous unfaithfulness. They had provoked God and rejected His prophets. God's fury and anger burned then, and it will burn again. **V 7–10: REMEMBER** God asks them if they have forgotten the wickedness of their forefathers and kings, and their own wickedness. He stresses their obligation to obey him and walk in His statutes. They are to remember their sins. **V 11–14: RESOLVE** God's resolve is to punish those who remain in Egypt against His word. This will be by the sword and famine. Only a very small remnant will escape. **V 15–19: REACTIONS.** The women burn incense to other gods, including the 'queen of heaven'. Their men support them in this, and tell Jeremiah that they will carry on burning such idolatrous sacrifices and making such evil offerings. They claim that things were better when sacrificing in this way than when following God. The women claim that they act with the men's permission. Their reactions are self-justifying, evil, and dishonest. **V 20–23: REASON** Jeremiah argues from God's word, history, and reason. Why are the Jews in such a mess? It is because they sinfully followed idolatry. Now, they are in the same position again. **V 24–30: REMNANT** Jeremiah declares that just as they are resolute in their idolatry, so God will consume them by sword and by famine. A very small number will escape from Egypt to return to Judah. The majority will be punished, and their adversity will underline the truth of God's word. King Nebuchadnezzar will overcome Pharaoh Hophra, king of Egypt, and the safe haven of the rebellious Jews will be no more.

CHAPTER FORTY-FIVE

V 1–3: SORROW In King Jehoiakim's fourth year of reign, Jeremiah speaks to Baruch, his faithful scribe. He says that grief is added to his sorrow. He is fainting, sighing and restless. **V 4: SEVERITY** God tells Jeremiah to tell Baruch that things will become a lot worse yet. The whole land will be broken down and plucked up. **V 5: SEEKING** Jeremiah tells Baruch not to 'seek great things' for himself. Adversity

will come on everyone, but God will preserve his life.

CHAPTER FORTY-SIX

V 1: JEREMIAH'S JUDGEMENTS God gives Jeremiah a series of prophecies proclaiming judgement against nations. (These are not in chronological order but are gathered together to deal with the topic of judgement against nations.) **V 2–26: EGYPT ENGULFED** Prophecies of Egypt's downfall at the hands of Nebuchadnezzar are graphically told. **V 27–28: PEOPLE PRESERVED** Nevertheless, God will preserve Israel, even though He will punish them for their unfaithfulness.

CHAPTER FORTY-SEVEN

V 1a: JEREMIAH'S JUDGEMENTS The word of the LORD continues to come to Jeremiah, proclaiming judgement against the nations. **V 1b–7: PHILISTIA PLUNDERED** The downfall of the Philistines is prophesied in this section. This appears to refer to the Babylonians coming from the north, before Philistia is attacked at Gaza by Pharaoh.

CHAPTER FORTY-EIGHT

V 1a: JEREMIAH'S JUDGEMENTS God's judgement on the nations, foretold through Jeremiah's prophecies, continues with Moab. **V 1b–46: MOAB MOURNED** Moab, which is descended from Lot and which often fought against Israel, will be overcome and devastated. Babylon appears to be the main destroyer, according to history. There will be lamentation over a nation that once was a military force but exalted itself against God and becomes an object of derision. Even God will mourn and wail over devastated Moab. **V 47: REMNANT RESTORED** Yet God promises that 'in the latter days' He will bring back a remnant of captives of Moab to their land.

CHAPTER FORTY-NINE

V 1a: JEREMIAH'S JUDGEMENTS Jeremiah continues to prophesy of God's judgement on nations. The first judgement is against Ammon. This is followed by judgements on Edom, Damascus, Kedar and Hazor, and Elam. **V 1b–6: AMMON ATTACKED** Ammon, like Moab, is a descendant of Lot. Ammon will be attacked and go into captivity. But again, like Moab, a remnant of the captives will return to their land. **V 7–22: EDOM'S EXTINCTION** The prophecy against Edom, the descendants of Esau, offers complete desolation with no future restoration. Edom will cease to exist as a political nation. **V 23–27: DAMASCUS'S DOWNFALL** Damascus will grow feeble and flee. Fear and anguish will precede the burning of the city. **V 28–33: JOINT JUDGEMENTS** Joint judgements are prophesied against Kedar and Hazor. Nebuchadnezzar will strike and devastate these desert areas. **V 34–39: ELAM EXILED** Elam will be exiled among many nations as if blown by four winds. Nevertheless, God will restore Elam's fortunes in the future.

CHAPTER FIFTY

V 1a: JEREMIAH'S JUDGEMENTS Again, the LORD continues His judgements against the nations through the mouth of His prophet, Jeremiah. This time, the prophecy is against Babylon and Babylonia, 'the land of the Chaldeans'. Such is the extent of this judgement that two chapters concentrate on it. **V 1b–46: BEHOLD BABYLON** Although Babylon was used to invade and take Israel captive, Babylon itself will be totally devastated from the north. God will take revenge on the way that Babylon has lifted itself up against Him and the fact that it has maltreated His people. He will bring about its total devastation and humiliation. It will become like a desert place. The repeated use of the word 'Behold' emphasises the amazing change to come to this once proud nation.

CHAPTER FIFTY-ONE

V 1a: JEREMIAH'S JUDGEMENTS Jeremiah continues to herald judgements to come as 'Thus says the LORD'. **V 1b–58: BEHOLD BABYLON** 'Behold' and 'Babylon' continue the detailed emphasis in this chapter on Babylon's coming judgement. Once the main aggressor against God's people, Babylon will be completely devastated and flooded with God's judgement. The aggressor is identified as the Medes. God will judge the Babylonians for their idolatry, comparing its uselessness with His might in creation. Such is the fall of mighty Babylon, predicted in these chapters, that one is led to consider what the final state of this once proud nation will yet be. **V 59–64: EXTRA EMPHASIS** Jeremiah emphasises Babylon's coming fate by commanding Seraiah to read the book of prophecies against Babylon. The book is then to be tied to a stone and to be thrown into the River Euphrates. Babylon will sink, just as the book will.

CHAPTER FIFTY-TWO

V 1–7: FALL The fall of Jerusalem is catalogued again, one of several accounts in the Bible, to emphasise how God's word comes to pass. **V 8–11: FULFILMENT** The fulfilment of prophecy is again underlined as Zedekiah is captured and blinded and the princes of Judah killed. Zedekiah spends the rest of his days in a Babylonian prison. **V 12–13: FIRE** Nebuzaradan, captain of the guard under Nebuchadnezzar, burns the temple, the kings' house and the houses of Jerusalem. **V 14–16: FARMERS** Although some of the poor people are to be taken away captive, some of them will remain as vine-dressers and farmers. **V 17–23: FRAGMENTED**

Valuable contents and furniture of the temple are taken to Babylon. Its bronze pillars, carts and Sea are broken up, and the fragments are taken as well. **V 24–30: FORLORN** How forlorn Jerusalem is! The leading people are put to death and others are taken away captive. **V 31–34: FAVOUR** Jehoiachin, king of Judah, is brought out of prison and treated kindly by Evil-Merodach, king of Babylon. He gives him provisions each day for the rest of his life.

LAMENTATIONS

OVERVIEW

PEOPLE AND PRELIMINARIES

✳Lamentations (five chapters) is the third of five books called the 'major prophets'. See comments on Isaiah. However, this short book of Lamentations is included here because it was written by Jeremiah, though not named after him. It follows the book of Jeremiah. It was probably written in Jerusalem soon after its fall to Babylon in 586 BC and just before Jeremiah was taken to Egypt, probably two or three years later.

PLAN AND PURPOSE

ⓘThe book of Lamentations consists of four chapters of twenty-two verses each, which follow the sequence of the Hebrew alphabet in the original, to aid memory. The third chapter, however, has sixty-six verses, tripling the content under each letter of the alphabet. The theme is the devastation of Jerusalem and God's people for their sin, and the mercy and grace of God which is yet to come.

Jeremiah, having prophesied Jerusalem's fall to Babylon, weeps as he surveys the results of the onslaught on Jerusalem which leads to the city being destroyed and its temple being burned, in two separate attacks. Although Jeremiah knows, and constantly emphasises, that it is the sins and failure to repent on the part of God's people that cause God's judgement on Jerusalem, he nevertheless demonstrates great compassion and sorrow of heart over the catastrophe, which he examines in detail. This causes him to pray for the restoration of God's people, who are also his people.

PROFILE AND PROGRESSION

Lamentation one—the sorrow of Jeremiah and of Jerusalem (1:1–22); Lamentation two—God's anger and Jeremiah's prayer (2:1–22); Lamentation three—Jeremiah's mourning, hope and spiritual aspiration (3:1–66); Lamentation four—God's wrath against Jerusalem and Edom (4:1–22); Lamentation five—the requests, remembrance and restoration of the remnant (5:1–22).

PRINCIPLES AND PARTICULARS

Jeremiah is sorry that his prophecies are proved right, because the suffering of others is involved. For him, acceptance of God's righteous judgement does not remove compassion for the judged, but rather leads to prayer for them. This book unveils the heartfelt love and acute sadness of God for a people whose failure to repent means that He has to chasten them. God's sorrow is transferred to Jeremiah by the Holy Spirit.

LAMENTATIONS

CHAPTER ONE

V 1–15: LAMENTATION ONE: JERUSALEM AND JUDAH The first portion deals with Jerusalem's affliction, Judah's captivity in Babylon, and the utter and complete devastation suffered. The tapestry of this chapter and of the book are woven from the threads of Israel's unrepentant sinfulness and rebellion, cruel oppression from enemies, God's harsh and co-ordinating hand of judgement on that oppression, and the tragic and pathetic desolation which follows. **V 16–22: LAMENTATION ONE: JEREMIAH AND JUSTICE** Jeremiah weeps over the situation, yet sees the righteousness and justice of God against Jerusalem which had become unclean. He knows that God must deal with His people's sin.

CHAPTER TWO

V 1–9: LAMENTATION TWO: DIVINE PUNISHMENT Even though Israel's downfall is through Babylon, God makes it clear that He is the one bringing punishment upon His people 'like an enemy' in the horrific ways described. **V 10–18: LAMENTATION TWO: DEVASTATED PEOPLE** Elders, daughters, virgins, mothers, prophets, and all who sin are helpless and hopeless in this situation. They have found that deliverance from sin has not resulted from the messages of their false prophets. Enemies ridicule and pronounce their aggression against the hated Jerusalem. Jeremiah not only weeps, but is physically sick because of his fallen people. **V 19–22: LAMENTATION TWO: DESPERATE PRAYER** Jeremiah urges them to cry out in the night and pour out their hearts to God for the hopeless and desperate state in which Jerusalem and God's people find themselves. He pleads with God for his wayward but severely stricken people. Hardships and trials are often the things God uses to draw His people back to Himself, but it is very hard.

CHAPTER THREE

V 1–20: LAMENTATION THREE: PERSONAL GRIEF The fact that this central chapter is three times longer than the other four emphasises its vital message. Jeremiah relates the affliction, anguish, and desperate state that he is in. He feels as if he has been opposed by God, even though he has been trusting in Him. He has that 'sinking feeling' within his soul. **V 21–36: LAMENTATION THREE: PROMISED GRACE** In all of this, he fixes his mind on God's mercies and compassions. He reminds himself of God's daily faithfulness, and he hopes in Him. He knows that grace is both promised and available now for those who walk with God, even in the hard times. In the pit of despair, he looks to the LORD for that grace. He hopes in Him, and quietly waits for Him to act. **V 37–66: LAMENTATION THREE: PETITIONING**

GOD Starting from the basis that God is just in His punishment of men, Jeremiah urges himself and others to search within and then turn back to God. He starts with confession of sin and an acknowledgement of God's righteousness. This requires true sorrow and seeking God continually. Jeremiah knows that God has drawn close to him and has redeemed him. He commits his enemies to God for Him to deal with them.

CHAPTER FOUR

V 1–16: LAMENTATION FOUR: CATASTROPHIC CONTRASTS Jerusalem is so devastated and brought low that it is a city of contrasts. The old blessings are replaced by the current desolations. Gold and valuable jewels are worthless. Compassion and the ability to nurse babies have gone. The finer things of life, such as delicacies and scarlet, have been reduced to desolation and to the ash heap. The radiant Nazirite people now look like pitiable skeletons. Cannibalism is practised by those who loved their children before. Because of Jerusalem's sins, God decrees its overthrow, and it is now hopeless in its misery. Kings of other nations would not believe that all this was possible. The sins of the prophets and priests, in shedding innocent blood, are cited as a reason for this catastrophe. **V 17: LAMENTATION FOUR: CAPRICIOUS CONFIDENCE** Even in this, the citizens of Jerusalem are looking to be saved by another nation that cannot deliver them. **V 18–20: LAMENTATION FOUR: CRUEL CONQUEST** Instead, their invaders—the Babylonian army under Nebuchadnezzar—pursue them cruelly and lay them low. **V 21–22: LAMENTATION FOUR: CONTINUING CUP** Nearby Edom has no cause to rejoice in Jerusalem's downfall. Jerusalem's punishment will spread to Edom, and the cup of suffering will continue because of Edom's sins.

CHAPTER FIVE

V 1a: LAMENTATION FIVE: REMEMBER Jeremiah asks God to remember what has come upon His people. **V 1b–15: LAMENTATION FIVE: REPROACH** He lists the reproaches and terrible suffering which the inhabitants of Zion have suffered: loss of inheritance and home; death of parents and spouses; no free water; economic need and oppression; failure of support from expected allies; unworthy people ruling over them; insufficient food to eat and danger in seeking to get it; fever; rape; murder; elders not respected; forced labour; and mourning instead of music and joy. All these followed the downfall of Jerusalem. **V 16–18: LAMENTATION FIVE: RECOGNITION** There is no king humanly to follow David because of the sin of Israel against God. (Jesus Christ Himself will be the next and last King in the line of David.) **V 19–22: LAMENTATION FIVE: RESTORATION** In all of this, Jeremiah looks to the ongoing sovereignty of God and pleads with Him to remember them, to turn them back to Him, to restore them, and renew them. Without stating it specifically, Jeremiah's prayer clearly acknowledges God's promises in the past not to reject His people utterly.

EZEKIEL

OVERVIEW

PEOPLE AND PRELIMINARIES

✳ Ezekiel wrote this book (forty-eight chapters) that bears his name, which is the fourth of five books called the 'major prophets'. See comments on Isaiah. It was written between 590 BC and 570 BC from Babylon, where Ezekiel was in exile. Thus the period covered by Ezekiel is estimated at twenty-one years.

PLAN AND PURPOSE

ⓘ Ezekiel, also a priest, begins to prophesy to Israel and Judah in captivity in Babylon, during the days of Jeremiah and Daniel. Ezekiel starts his prophetic ministry when he is thirty years old, having been taken captive at the age of twenty-five years. The book of Ezekiel starts with a vision of the glory of God, goes on to comment on Jerusalem's judgement, and prophesies judgement to seven neighbouring nations. It stresses both the need to repent of sins and the need to warn sinners to repent. It concludes with aspects of Israel's restoration. Ezekiel contains varied forms of prophecy, including visions, enacted parables, signs, and illustrations. It reveals the suffering of Ezekiel through speechlessness, lying inactive for periods of time, denial of normal food, and the death of his wife at the same time that Jerusalem fell. Ezekiel prophesies not predominantly either to Judah or to the remaining tribes, like the pre-exilic prophets, but to 'the whole house of Israel'.

PROFILE AND PROGRESSION

🌊 Prophecies—the downfall of Jerusalem (1:1–24:27); Prophecies—🐚 wrath on the surrounding nations, with parenthetical note on Israel's restoration (25:1–32:32); Prophecies—Israel's re-gathering, restoration, revival of worship, and re-occupation of the land by tribes (33:1–48:35).

PRINCIPLES AND PARTICULARS

👉 The faithfulness of God's prophet is observed on foreign soil. God is referred to over 350 times, and frequent emphasis is placed on the authority of God's word. The visions are similar to others found elsewhere in the Bible. Conviction of sin, repentance and trust in God through His word are prerequisites of revival and restoration. The emphasis is that God's glory and blessing will finally prevail. God's desire is to bless all His people who repent and turn to Him.

EZEKIEL

CHAPTER ONE

V 1–3: SCENE SET We learn elsewhere that Ezekiel, a prophet/priest, is in Babylon as one of ten thousand Jewish captives. The date is 593 BC, being the fifth year of King Jehoiachin's captivity. God's hand is on Ezekiel, and He gives him direct visions to prepare him for his work of prophesying to God's exiled people. **V 4–28: VARIOUS VISIONS** The visions which Ezekiel receives are a direct revelation from God, and God's hand is upon him. A whirlwind, with a raging fire, speaks of judgement to come. The four living creatures with wings and different faces symbolise God's holiness, mobility, and sovereignty over each part of His creation, represented by the different faces of creation. The fire and lightning emphasise God's holiness. The wheels full of eyes underline God's mobility and omniscience. But above all is the vision of the throne of God, where the Godhead appears as a man of glory and splendour. This is a picture of the Lord Jesus Christ. This prepares Ezekiel for submission, worship, and listening to what God has to say to him. He falls on His face before God in the awesomeness of His revealed glory.

CHAPTER TWO

V 1–2: STANDING AND SPIRIT God tells Ezekiel, the 'Son of man', to stand up. As he does so, God's Spirit enters him and God speaks to him. **V 3–5: STUBBORNNESS AND SENDING** Prepared by the visions and God's communing with him, Ezekiel is told that he must go to a stubborn people to whom God is sending him. God's people will resist God's message in their sin and backsliding, but they will know that God has spoken through His prophet. **V 6–8: SCORPIONS AND SPEAKING** It will be as though Ezekiel will be among scorpions, briars, and thorns, but he must, nevertheless, speak God's words faithfully to these rebellious people. Ezekiel himself must not rebel against God, who tells him to eat what He gives him. An unusual 'meal' will be put before him soon! **V 9–10: SCROLL AND SPREADING** God presents Ezekiel with a scroll which He spreads before him. Lamentations, mourning and woe, are written on both sides of the scroll.

CHAPTER THREE

V 1–3: CONSUMED As commanded by God, Ezekiel eats the scroll; it is as sweet as honey in his mouth. He must take in God's message personally before he shares it with others. **V 4–11: COMMISSION** Ezekiel is then again commissioned to go to the rebellious house of Israel, who will understand him but not respond. God will make him hard-headed for this task. He must tell them God's message, whether they will hear or not. He is not to fear them. He must take to heart all God's words to him. **V 12–15: COMPELLED** With a thunderous voice proclaiming God's glory, and the noise of the wings of the living creatures above the wheels, God's Spirit compels Ezekiel to go to the captives at Tel Abib. He is bitter and heated in spirit but God's hand is strong upon him. He sits, for seven days, astonished among the captives. **V 16–21: CONCERN** God then spells out to Ezekiel what his main concern must be. He is a watchman. It is vital that he must warn the people to turn from their wickedness, and for the righteous to continue in their righteousness. Ezekiel is to be a stumbling block to their backsliding. His ministry of warning is urgent and crucial. **V 22: COMFORT** Ezekiel has the comfort of knowing that God's hand is upon him, again, as he is told to go into the plain where God will speak with him. **V 23–27: COMMUNION** God again reveals His glory to Ezekiel and he falls on his face. Once more, God's Spirit enters him and puts him on his feet before speaking to him. God tells him that he will be bound and unable to speak until God opens his mouth. He is preparing Ezekiel for the fact that his task of preaching God's word to 'a rebellious house' will be hard. He cannot do it without God's Spirit and help, but he can do it with that gracious help. This is a lesson for us all!

CHAPTER FOUR

V 1–6: SIEGE PORTRAYED Ezekiel is told to enact a siege against Jerusalem by taking a soft clay tablet and modelling a siege. He then has to lie 390 days on his left side and 40 days on his right side, signifying the punishment that will come first to Israel and then to Judah. A day signifies a year's punishment. **V 7–8: SPECIFIC PROPHECY** Ezekiel then has to prophesy against Jerusalem. His arm is to be bare, as a sign of God's readiness to afflict Jerusalem. **V 9–15: SUPPLY PROVISIONS** As a sign of the resultant siege, Ezekiel has to supply reduced provisions during his enacted siege. For the acting out of the siege, God allows him to use cow dung as fuel, which will not be available during the siege of Jerusalem. **V 16–17: STARVATION PREDICTED** God tells Ezekiel that Jerusalem will lack food and water. The people will be dismayed and waste away. The reason for all this is their iniquity against God.

CHAPTER FIVE

V 1–4: BARBER'S SWORD Ezekiel is to shave his head with a sharp sword acting as a barber's razor, and to divide his hair into thirds. One third is to be burnt in the midst of the city; one third is to be struck with a sword; the rest shall be scattered in the wind, but some of the hairs are to be put in his garment and some of those are to be burnt. **V 5–12: BITTER SUFFERING** Dealing with the hair signifies bitter suffering. Because of Israel's wickedness in rebelling against His judgements and statutes and following detestable idolatry, God's severe punishment will come upon her. This will include cannibalism within Jerusalem. A third will die because of pestilence and famine; a third will be

killed by the sword of enemies; and a third will be scattered, with a small remnant being saved, but even some of the remnant will suffer. **V 13–17: BLOOD SHED** Only then will God's anger be spent against His people's hardness and rebellion. God's sword of judgement will bring famine, savage attacks by wild beasts, pestilence, and bloodshed. Jerusalem will become a reproach to all the nations around.

CHAPTER SIX

V 1–7: RETRIBUTION God announces His intention to smash idolatry in the mountains, hills and valleys. He will devastate and lay waste the area. The people will be slain. In all this, God's sovereignty will be recognised. **V 8–10: REMNANT** A remnant will be saved. Escapees will remember the evil nature of their adulterous hearts and their idolatry, and know that God has carried out His threat. **V 11–14: REALISATION** Ezekiel is to demonstrate his emotional involvement in the coming tragedy by stamping his feet, clapping his hands and crying out 'Alas'. This will mark God's hatred of the people's evil abominations. Death and devastation will come, through famine, pestilence, and the sword. Then they will know that God has done it and realise, too late, that He is LORD.

CHAPTER SEVEN

V 1–2: LORD'S JUDGEMENT REVEALED— AUTHORITY Ezekiel's LORD again reveals Himself by His word of authority and power and tells the prophet to announce to Israel that the end has come upon the whole of the land. In this chapter of great solemnity and concern, there are obvious overlaps in the three sections, each of which ends by repeating again that Israel will know that God is the LORD. **V 3–4: LORD'S JUDGEMENT RECOGNISED— ABOMINATION** Israel's detestable practices are an abomination to God and it is this idolatry and rebellion against His clearly revealed will, which stirs God to wrath in judging them so that they will know that He is the LORD. **V 5–9: LORD'S JUDGEMENT RECOGNISED—ANGER** God's anger and wrath will be poured out in an unprecedented disaster which will produce abject panic. As the anger of God's wrath strikes Israel, they will recognise that it is the LORD. **V 10–27: LORD'S JUDGEMENT RECOGNISED— ABSOLUTE** The judgement will not only be far reaching geographically, but will reach every area of life. Commerce will be pointless, wealth valueless, and hunger rife. Desecration of the Holiest Place by foreigners and looters will go hand in hand with terror, calamity and despair. Bloodshed will abound. There will be no spiritual input or guidance through the prophets, the priests or the elders. Overwhelmed by the invaders, and judged by God, the people will mourn and know that God is the LORD.

CHAPTER EIGHT

V 1–4: INSPIRATION God is about to take Ezekiel in a vision into the temple area to see just how deep and wicked the idolatry is. But before that, God inspires him with a vision of Himself and lifts him up by His Spirit. As he sees the idol in the Inner Court of the temple, he also sees the glory of God, as he had seen before. **V 5–6: IDOL** The idol is at the entrance of the north Gate near the altar. It provokes God to jealousy. It is the springboard for all the other idolatrous practices in the temple. **V 7–12: IDOLATRY** Ezekiel is then shown seventy elders of Israel worshipping their individual idols, with incense, in

darkness. The walls are covered with animal cult figures. **V 13–15: IMMORALITY** Then he is shown women sitting and mourning for Tammuz, the Babylonian fertility god. Worship of this god involves great immorality, as well as idolatry. **V 16: INSULT** He is then shown a further insult to God where twenty-five men are worshipping the created sun, in direct idolatrous disobedience to the Creator of it. **V 17–18: INDIGNATION** God expresses His indignation to Ezekiel. These idolatrous abominations also lead to violence. He will deal with these people in anger and without pity. He will not listen to their cries which will result.

CHAPTER NINE

V 1–2: GUARDS INSTRUCTED Six armed guards, probably angels, are instructed to draw near. One of them has a writer's ink horn, and they all stand by the bronze altar. **V 3: GOD'S INTENTION** God's intention to destroy the city and the temple is marked by the departure of His glory from the cherubim. This departure is noted in stages, and this is the first stage. **V 4: GOSPEL INITIATIVE** In the midst of the impending doom and judgement, God graciously instructs the holder of the ink horn to go to Jerusalem and mark the forehead of each person who sighs and cries over all the abominations of idolatry and rebellion against God. In judgement, God is remembering with mercy those who repent—a precursor of the wonderful gospel of our Lord Jesus Christ. **V 5–8: GOD'S INDIGNATION** The other angel guards are told to go into the city and slay everyone who does not bear the mark. As this is being done, Ezekiel falls on his face, cries out to God, and asks Him if He is going to destroy all the remnant of Israel as He pours out His fury on Jerusalem.

V 9–10: GREAT INIQUITY God repeats His earlier emphasis that the iniquity of Israel and Judah is so great that He will neither spare nor have pity, but will judge those unrepentant people in the city. **V 11: GRACIOUS INTERVENTION** As a reminder of God's forgiveness to the repentant, His gracious intervention is underlined to Ezekiel, as the holder of the ink horn reports that he has marked all the repentant on the head. God never judges truly repentant people who trust Him.

CHAPTER TEN

V 1–8: DIVINE PREPARATION God prepares to move His glory from the temple. With a throne, the wheels, the cherubim, and the man clothed in linen all ready, His cloud fills the inner court and He passes over the threshold of the temple. The wings of the cherubim sound like the voice of God Himself. The man in linen is given coals to spread on the earth, signifying judgement. **V 9–17: DETAILED PARTICULARS** The details of the cherubim, the wheels, and the faces of the cherubim are given, and are very similar to the details given before. The symbolism seems to refer to God's mobility, control over timing, ability to see everything at all times, sovereignty over all aspects of nature, and holiness. **V 18–22: DEPARTING PRESENCE** At this stage, God's glory departs from the threshold of the temple and stands over the cherubim. Always in unison, God's party moves straight forward.

CHAPTER ELEVEN

V 1–4: CROOKED COUNSEL The Spirit now takes Ezekiel to see the leaders of the city who have been guilty of ignoring God's word and giving their own counsel to direct the citizens. They have rejected Ezekiel's message. **V 5–13: POINTED PROPHECY** God tells them that they will be removed from the city, slain and judged. These particular men will be judged at the borders of Israel. (This prophecy will be fulfilled at Riblah.) The seriousness of this is all underlined as Pelatiah dies during Ezekiel's prophecy. Ezekiel then asks God again if He is going to bring an end to Israel. **V 14–21: GOD'S GRACE** God again assures Ezekiel of His grace and of His future plan for His people. The Jews will return, and a new covenant will be instituted to give them a new heart, a new spirit, and a knowledge of God that causes them to know Him and obey Him. He will judge sin, however. **V 22–23: GOD'S GLORY** The cherubim and seraphim fly high with the wheels beside them, and God's glory is transferred to the mountain on the east side of Jerusalem, the Mount of Olives. **V 24–25: STRAIGHT SPEAKING** Taken up by God's Spirit to those in captivity, Ezekiel immediately shares with them everything that God has told him. After a time of spiritual intake and understanding, God expects us to get back to the job of telling His word to others.

CHAPTER TWELVE

V 1–5: EXILE ENACTED Ezekiel is in the midst of a rebellious people in exile. God now speaks to them through him to tell them that they will not return quickly to Jerusalem. Their captivity is confirmed. God then tells Ezekiel to enact the exile by bringing out his belongings, digging through the wall with his hands, and carrying his things away on his shoulder in their sight. He is to explain this action to his fellow captives and tell them that the prince (Zedekiah) will thus be taken into exile. Even Zedekiah's coming blindness, at the hands of his captors, is foreseen. God again declares that His people will know who He is when the scattering happens. **V 16: REMNANT'S REALISATION** Despite the scattering of Israel throughout the nations some will be saved as a remnant. They will tell the Gentiles about their abominations. They will know that God is the LORD when all this happens. **V 17–20: WASTED WILDERNESS** Jerusalem will become a wasted wilderness of anxiety, terror, and need. **V 21–28: PRESENT PERFORMANCE** In answer to those who say that other prophecies have not been fulfilled, and that neither will this one be, God tells Ezekiel to instruct the rebellious house of Israel that it will be performed within their lifetime. God will do it. On the other hand, false and flattering visions will cease.

CHAPTER THIRTEEN

V 1–7: PLAUSIBLE PROPHETS Ezekiel is told to prophesy against the seductive and false prophets of Israel who foolishly pervert God's word and give their own words. Woe will come upon them because of their falseness and futility. **V 8–9: DIVINE DISPLEASURE** God confirms that He is against them, and that His hand will be against them, excluding them from His people and their future blessing. Then they will know that He is the LORD God. **V 10–16: WHITED WALL** God tells the false prophets that their false prophecies of peace, when there will be no peace, are like a flimsy wall that has been covered in whitewash to give it a good appearance. God will destroy that wall, and people will know that the white veneer of religion that the false prophets put upon it is only skin deep. When God's wrath is revealed in this way, the people will know that He is the LORD. **V 17–21: MAGIC MINISTRY** Ezekiel is told to prophesy against women who use magic in their ministry, and thus lie to the people. When God releases His people from their evil sorcery and seductive teachings, they will know that He is the LORD. **V 22–23: SEDUCTION STOPPED** God confirms that He will deliver His people from the seductive efforts of such false prophets and divination, and at that time people will know that He is the LORD.

CHAPTER FOURTEEN

V 1–3: ELDERS The elders, the leaders of the people, have gone astray with idolatry in their hearts. God will not let them approach Ezekiel to inquire of the LORD. **V 4–5: ESTRANGED** All who have idolatrous hearts are estranged from God, who hates idolatry. No comforting answer will come from God or from His prophet. **V 6: EXHORTATION** Even in the midst of a passage which deals with judgement, God urges Israel to repent and turn from her sins. He will always pardon truly repentant people who turn to Him. **V 7–20: EXECUTION** God's face is set against the rebel idolaters. He will make an example of them; He will execute His judgement by cutting them off. Those making false prophecies will be destroyed, as will those who act on them. The land will not escape from famine, desolation by incursion of wild beasts, being put to the sword, or pestilence. Even if the most righteous people of the Old Testament, Noah, Daniel, and Job, could be there to pray and plead for them, no one could be saved by those prayers and pleadings. God would still have to punish Israel for its intense and immense wickedness. Noah was saved by God from His judgement. Daniel was kept by God during man's opposition and persecution. Job was upheld by God through intense personal suffering and trials initiated by Satan. (Jesus bore God's judgement at Calvary, man's opposition and persecution, and intense personal suffering and trials caused by Satan. Unlike Noah, Daniel and Job, He is alive and saves all who come to Him in repentance and faith.) **V 21–23: ESCAPE** However, there are a few, 'the remnant', who will escape by God's grace. Today there are few on the narrow way that lead to life, but the invitation is to all.

CHAPTER FIFTEEN

V 1–6: FIRE Unlike other wood when it has stopped bearing fruit, the vine is no good for anything except fuel. Israel is often pictured as a vine, and when it stops bearing the fruit of righteousness, it is only good to be burnt. So Jerusalem will be burnt, Ezekiel tells the people. (This happened.) **V 7–8: FACE** Because of the unrepentant wickedness and idolatry of the people, God's face will be set against them. How solemn this is. The reason for God's judgement is the complete lack of faithfulness among His people.

CHAPTER SIXTEEN

V 1–7: LEFT God commands Ezekiel to show Jerusalem her abominations. He gives him a running illustration of His relationship with Israel and Judah. Jerusalem came from the same root as the rest of Canaan, and was occupied by the Amorites and the Hittites. At that stage, Israel was like a newly-born child which is abandoned without pity. Left ravaged by sin and with no hope outside of God, God rescued the baby that no one else wanted. **V 8–14: LOVED** The illustration changes to one of marriage: God enters into a marriage covenant with Israel and treats her as a bride whom He loves and on

whom He lavishes wonderful gifts. Israel's history can be seen in this illustration, and possibly this points to the time of David and Solomon. **V 13–34: LUST** But Jerusalem, Judah and Israel practised spiritual harlotry against God, through their detestable practices of idolatry and profanity. Child sacrifice and great immorality follow. The surrounding nations' abominable practices, idolatry, immorality, and worship of other gods are accepted by Israel. 'How degenerate is your heart!' is God's summary. Even worse than this, unlike a prostitute who is paid for her immoral services, God's special city, Jerusalem, pays others to commit immorality with her. She is like a prostitute who pays her clients. **V 35–43: LOATHED** In line with a common practice at the time of Ezekiel, whereby immoral women would be stripped publicly, Ezekiel says that this will happen to Jerusalem. Stripped of all splendour and privileges, she will be reduced to nothing and loathed by those with whom she had previously indulged in lewdness and abomination. **V 44–59: LOWEST** Judah has become the lowest of the low. Her sins are more numerous and deeper than those of Samaria and Sodom. When God's people backslide from His grace, sometimes they enter depths of wickedness that even non-Christians do not practise. **V 60–63: LORD** The LORD's faithfulness and love is shown by firm determination to remember His covenant with His people and to provide an atonement for them.

CHAPTER SEVENTEEN

V 1–10: MYSTERIOUS PARABLE God gives Ezekiel a parable which is by way of a riddle or allegory. It concerns two eagles. One crops off the top of a cedar tree and plants it in a fertile field. The other has a vine growing towards it. This vine cannot grow deeply and firmly in the soil and will wither. **V 11–21: MEANING PLAIN** God's word gives Ezekiel the meaning of the parable. The Bible does not provide the names, but, looking at the history of Israel, the interpretation seems to be that Babylon takes captives and weakens Judah, making Zedekiah a puppet of Babylon. Zedekiah breaks the agreement to submit to Babylon and asks for Egypt to help (the second eagle). Egypt fails to do this and Judah has no roots for its own prosperity or survival. **V 22–24: MOUNTAIN PROMINENCE** One of the highest branches from the highest cedar will provide a twig that will be planted on a prominent mountain. It will grow mightily and provide blessing and protection for birds of every sort. All that God does will be acknowledged. This seems to be a picture of the pre-eminence of Messiah, the Lord Jesus Christ, who will come and reign. He will attract all sorts of sinners to Himself.

CHAPTER EIGHTEEN

V 1–3: PROVERB PROHIBITED The proverb that the children's teeth are set on edge, because their fathers have eaten sour grapes, is wrong and God prohibits it. **V 4–9: PRIME PRINCIPLE** Instead, God's prime principle is that everybody will be punished according to his or her own sin. Those with righteous lives, which throughout this chapter must mean those who manifest repentance and faith in God leading to a changed life of righteousness, will be delivered. **V 10–18: PERSONAL PUNISHMENT** The logic follows that if a righteous father has a sinful son, the son will be punished, and not the father. Conversely, if an unrighteous father has a righteous son (his righteousness being evidence of his faith and repentance) it is

the father and not the son who will be punished and die for his iniquity. The son will neither be protected nor punished because of his father's sin; he has his own walk and accountability before God. **V 19–29 PENITENTS PROTECTED** The principle is discussed in the next verses and God declares that it is perfectly fair that those who turn from sin to righteousness will be saved. Those who turn from righteousness to sin, thus manifesting no saving faith, will be punished. God has no pleasure in the death of the wicked. His ways are fair. **V 30–32: PASSIONATE PLEA** God is not a disinterested bystander, shown in the fact that He says, 'I have no pleasure in the death of one who dies.' Thus, He passionately pleads with people to repent and turn from their sin so that they may live. God wants sinners to turn and be saved.

CHAPTER NINETEEN

V 1–9: LAMENTATION ABOUT A LIONESS Israel is pictured as a lioness producing cubs who are its princes. Successive cubs mature but are trapped and unable to fight. This underlines the captivity in Babylon of some of its kings. **V 10–14: VIEWED AS A VINE** In a second illustration, Israel is viewed as a vine that was initially fruitful, but has been plucked up and consumed. This tells the same sad story as the lioness illustration.

CHAPTER TWENTY

V 1–4: REBUKE Ezekiel rebukes the hypocrisy of the elders who come to enquire of the LORD through him, but continue in their abominations. **V 5–32: REVIEW** God then, through Ezekiel, reviews Israel's history. He has delivered His people, taken them as His own, given them His word and law, and blessed them in so many ways. In response, their walk with Him has been inconsistent and intermittent in their obedience. Rebellion, idolatry and immorality prevent them knowing and honouring God. He deals with them in anger to bring them back to repentance and faith, but they keep on straying. The thermometer of their idolatry is their negative response to the Sabbath. When idolatry is high, God's Sabbath, a day of worship, is neglected. When God is honoured, His Sabbath is also honoured. God gave up His people because of their refusal to obey Him and repent. He says His people are now repeating the same sinful pattern. This review of Israel's history makes very sad reading, especially when one considers the blessed and privileged position of God's people. Christians, today, also need to be aware of the dangers of such intermittent faith and varying obedience. **V 33–44: RESTORATION** Although God will chastise and punish His people, He will restore them and bring them into the land He has promised to give them. They will then know that He is the LORD and they will walk with Him. Idolatry will go. **V 45–48: RETRIBUTION** But Ezekiel reminds the elders that God has yet to punish the land and He will do it as a forest fire. All flesh will know that God is the LORD. **V 49: REJECTION** The elders are so tied to their idols and rebellion that they have no spiritual understanding of what Ezekiel says. They dismiss Ezekiel's word from God as speaking in 'parables'.

CHAPTER TWENTY-ONE

V 1–17: SWORD, SCEPTRE AND SLAUGHTER Jerusalem and its inhabitants will be decimated by God's sword, in this case Babylon. The sceptre, speaking of the kings of Judah, is treated with spite and is unable to save Jerusalem from downfall and slaughter. **V 18–27: DIVINATION, DEVASTATION AND DOWNFALL** The invading king of Babylon uses divination to determine where to go. This leads to the devastating overthrow of Jerusalem and its inhabitants. **V 20–32: AMMONITES, ATTACK AND ANGER** The Babylonians will also attack the Ammonites. God's anger on Ammon is let loose because of the great pleasure they take in the downfall of Jerusalem.

CHAPTER TWENTY-TWO

V 1–5: JERUSALEM JUDGED Bloodshed and idolatry ensure God's judgement of Jerusalem. Israel will become a reproach to all kingdoms and a mockery to all countries. **V 6–13: WIDESPREAD WICKEDNESS** This passage specifies many wicked sins, from despising God's holy things and the Sabbath, through to immorality, idolatry, oppression, extortion and bloodshed. **V 14–16: DEFILING DISPERSION** God's people, who have defiled themselves while in their land, will be defiled further still, as they are scattered among the nations and dispersed because of God's judgement upon them. Then they will know that God is the LORD. **V 17–22: FIERY FURNACE** Jerusalem will become as a great smelting pot. God will blow the refining fire of 'His wrath' upon them and in His fury they will know that He is the LORD. **V 23–34: MISSING MAN** Despite the faithful prophecy of God's men such as Jeremiah and Ezekiel, there is no man who can stand in the gap to save Israel. God's holy things and Sabbaths have been profaned, robbery has been rife, blood has been wrongly shed, people have been oppressed, false prophecies have been made, and ungodliness has prevailed. God says that He 'sought for a man' to stand in the gap so that God need not destroy Jerusalem. He found nobody. Judgement must fall.

CHAPTER TWENTY-THREE

V 1–4: OHOLAH AND OHOLIBAH Samaria, called here Oholah, and Jerusalem, called here Oholibah, are presented as two harlot daughters. **V 5–10: SAMARIA AND SIN** Oholah (Samaria) is put forward as a worldly and sensual sinner. The illustration of immorality is that she prostitutes herself to nations who do not love God or keep His word. **V 11–21: WICKED AND WORSE** Oholibah (Jerusalem) is presented as being worse than her immoral sister. She is more corrupt than Samaria and her immoral idolatry goes further, despite her knowledge of her sister's immorality, and despite her heritage. **V 22–35: JERUSALEM AND JUDGEMENT** God is so angry at Judah's sin that He says He will bring Babylon and other ungodly nations to scourge her and bring her down. **V 36–49: SISTERS AND SINNING** Both the sinful sisters will be judged for their sin. Child sacrifice for idolatry was one of the defilements that angered God and followed the profanity associated with the breaking of Sabbaths. In the judgement that God brings upon them, they will know that He is the LORD. All such unfaithfulness and idolatry will cease.

CHAPTER TWENTY-FOUR

V 1–14: BURNING POT Ezekiel uses the symbol of a cooking pot to portray Jerusalem. All the meat will be taken out, but the empty pot will be burned. This speaks of the devastation and wrath on Israel and Jerusalem and its inhabitants.

Judgement is to come. **V 15–27: BEREAVED PROPHET** Ezekiel is told that his wife will die but that he must not mourn for her. In the morning, he speaks to the people, and in the evening, his wife dies. He follows God's commands. He explains to the house of Israel that in the same way that he must not mourn the death of his wife, so they must not mourn the death of their families and the absolute downfall of Israel and its holy places. The Babylonians will take lives and capture Jerusalem. Ezekiel is told to keep silent when he hears about the destruction of Jerusalem, as judgement will have fallen then. When the captives come to him, he can then speak about Judah again.

CHAPTER TWENTY-FIVE

V 1–7: PROPHECIES AGAINST AMMON God instructs Ezekiel to prophesy judgement against the nations which have oppressed and hindered Israel. The first of these is against Ammon. **V 8–11: PROPHECIES AGAINST MOAB** Ezekiel then prophesies against Moab. **V 12–14: PROPHECIES AGAINST EDOM** Edom is the third nation against which Ezekiel prophesies. **V 15–17: PROPHECIES AGAINST PHILISTIA** God's wrath in punishing the Philistines is prophesied by Ezekiel.

CHAPTER TWENTY-SIX

V 1–14: PROPHECIES AGAINST TYRE: PARTICULAR PROPHECY The prophecies against the nations continue, and a lot of space is given to the proclamation against Tyre. Tyre's downfall will be at the hands of Nebuchadnezzar, king of Babylon. It will be scraped to the ground, and thrown into the sea. (This will be fulfilled later in exact detail.) Before this point, Tyre is a mighty city of commerce and power. **V 15–18: PROPHECIES AGAINST TYRE: PETRIFIED PRINCES** When the princes around the area hear of what happens to Tyre, they will be petrified and tremble. No one can foresee that such devastation will hit Tyre. God does, and foretells it long before it happens. **V 19–21: PROPHECIES AGAINST TYRE: PERISHING PIT** Tyre will descend 'into the Pit', and its glory and people will perish. God always accomplishes His word.

CHAPTER TWENTY-SEVEN

V 1–26: PROPHECIES AGAINST TYRE: SPLENDID SHIP Tyre is represented as a wonderful sailing ship made of the best of materials, having the best of crews, and engaging in quality and profitable trade. The world deals with Tyre. **V 27: PROPHECIES AGAINST TYRE: SUNKEN SHIP** However, the ship of Tyre will sink to the seabed with loss of life, riches, and acclaim. **V 28–34: PROPHECIES AGAINST TYRE: SHOCKED SPECTATORS** All the neighbours, seafaring people, traders, and nations will be shocked by the sudden sinking of so mighty a ship as Tyre. **V 35–36: PROPHECIES AGAINST TYRE: SALUTARY SIGN** What God will do to Tyre, through invading forces, will make inhabitants astonished, kings frightened, and merchants scorn their one-time leading competitor. The horror that Tyre will become will be a sign to all of what happens when God shows His wrath.

CHAPTER TWENTY-EIGHT

V 1–5: PROPHECIES AGAINST THE KING OF TYRE: HAUGHTY HEART The king of Tyre is a man with a proud heart. He thinks he is wise and that his wealth makes him important. He sees himself as a god. **V 6–10: PROPHECIES AGAINST THE**

KING OF TYRE: DREADFUL DOWNFALL God describes his downfall at the hands of strangers and terrible nations. He will be thrown into the pit and die in the midst of the seas. He will be shown that he is not a god, but a sinful, mortal man. **V 11–19: PROPHECIES AGAINST THE KING OF TYRE: SATANIC SCENARIO** Ezekiel is told to lament the king of Tyre, and, in so doing, he reveals the satanic inspiration behind this wicked man. This is also a description of Satan himself, his rebellion against God, and his being cast out of heaven by God. The king of Tyre will 'be no more for ever'. **V 20–24: PROPHECIES AGAINST SIDON: SPREADING SIN** Sidon, Tyre's neighbouring sister trader, also receives a prophecy of judgement for her neglect and rejection of God. Then she will know that God is the LORD. Sin spreads but will always be judged by God unless there is repentance. **V 25–26: PROPHECY ABOUT ISRAEL: PEACEFUL PROSPERITY** Israel will be gathered in peace to her own land. There she will dwell safely, and be blessed by God materially as well as spiritually. God will judge the surrounding nations. They will all then know that He is Israel's God.

CHAPTER TWENTY-NINE

V 1–12: PROPHECIES AGAINST EGYPT: MUTED MONSTER Ezekiel now gives prophecies about Egypt that will take up the next four chapters. A continual and repeated principle in all God's dealings is that people will know that He is the LORD. Egypt is portrayed as a powerful sea monster. However, in God's judgement, Egypt will be caught and trapped, and her influence muted. She will no longer have the international power once enjoyed. Her cities will be desolated and her people scattered. **V 13–16: PROPHECIES AGAINST EGYPT:**

RELATIVE RESTORATION God promises to bring the Egyptians back to their land after forty years, but never again will they have their former influence and strength or merit 'the confidence of the house of Israel'. Israel will be reminded thereby that God is the LORD. Egypt will never be an exalted nation. **V 17–21: PROPHECIES AGAINST EGYPT: COMPENSATED CONQUEROR** The Babylonians, under Nebuchadnezzar, are God's agent for bringing about the judgement of Tyre, but they gain very little from it, because Tyre is cast into the sea. God will compensate them by giving them the spoils of Egypt, when Nebuchadnezzar overthrows Egypt. Israel's power will return and she will know that God is the LORD.

CHAPTER THIRTY

V 1–9: PROPHECIES AGAINST EGYPT: AILING ALLIES In the day that God judges Egypt, He will also judge all the nations that support Egypt as allies. They will all be brought down and be made desolate. Thus they will know that God is the LORD, who has 'set a fire in Egypt'. **V 10–19: PROPHECIES AGAINST EGYPT: EGYPT'S EXECUTION** The slaughter by Nebuchadnezzar and the drought caused by the Nile and its tributaries running dry are foretold. Egypt will be in great fear and distress, especially as God destroys her idols and images. Those previously under bondage to Egypt will be set free. This execution of judgement on Egypt is God's doing, although through third parties. Then Egypt will know that God is the LORD. **V 20–26: PROPHECIES AGAINST EGYPT: POWERLESS PHARAOH** The ruler of Egypt, Pharaoh, is depicted as a man with two broken arms. This seems to refer to successive defeats of Pharaoh, leaving Egypt powerless. In their powerlessness, they will know that God is the LORD.

CHAPTER THIRTY-ONE

V 1–9: PROPHECIES AGAINST EGYPT: TALL TREE Egypt is compared to a tall tree and reminded that mighty Assyria, brought down by God, was once higher still. **V 10–17: PROPHECIES AGAINST EGYPT: FRIGHTFUL FALL** Egypt will come crashing down as Assyria did. No more support and shelter will be available from Egypt. She will lie smashed. **V 18: PROPHECIES AGAINST EGYPT: EGYPT'S END** God reminds Egypt that she will be brought down low and slain by the sword. This is God's word.

CHAPTER THIRTY-TWO

V 1–10: PROPHECIES AGAINST EGYPT: EGYPT EXTINGUISHED Ezekiel goes on to lament for Pharaoh and to explain that Egypt will be extinguished like a light being put out and overcome like a lion, or like a sea monster which has been netted and then slain. Nations will be astounded at Egypt's downfall. **V 11–16: PROPHECIES AGAINST EGYPT: EGYPT'S EXECUTIONERS** God will use the Babylonians to destroy Egypt and He will also intervene by nature to devastate Egypt. **V 17–30: PROPHECIES AGAINST EGYPT: EGYPT'S ETERNITY** The multitudes of unrepentant Egyptians, along with those from nations who supported Egypt and rebelled against God, will be in 'the Pit'. They will be there from Egypt, Assyria, Elam, Mishek and Tubal, and Edom. All men will die and face God's judgement for sin. **V 31–32: PROPHECIES AGAINST EGYPT: EGYPT'S 'ENCOURAGEMENT'** In the light of the terror caused by God and His wrath on those who do not repent, the only comfort to encourage Pharaoh, king of Egypt, is that Egypt will not be alone in facing God's judgement. This is faint encouragement indeed!

CHAPTER THIRTY-THREE

V 1–6: WATCHMAN A watchman's task is to warn a city of impending invasion and danger so that individuals can move to save themselves and their loved ones. It is significant that this chapter on a watchman's warning follows the prophesied judgements both on God's people and on surrounding nations, and precedes the teaching of God through Ezekiel on the future blessings of Israel and Judah. Before God's blessing is on an individual's life, there has to be repentance. This 'warning' chapter reminds us of the need to repent and turn to God to have judgement averted and blessings to come. The responsibility of being a watchman is laid squarely on Ezekiel's shoulders. Each Christian has the same responsibility today to share the Christian message with a lost world. **V 7–11: WARNING** Ezekiel is to warn Israel to turn from her sins and to repent. God repeats that He has no pleasure when the wicked die because He wants them to turn and live. **V 12–20: WICKEDNESS** The basis for judgement will be the wickedness of the people. Those whose conduct demonstrates repentance and faith, by producing a righteous life, will live. Those who are not characterised by righteousness will die. Turning from wickedness to God, in a way that makes a real difference, is the way to acceptance by God. God's judgements are always fair. **V 21–23: WORD** Ezekiel resumes his prophetic word to God's people. This is after an escapee from Jerusalem has confirmed the downfall of the city, and after God has prepared Ezekiel for this

news. Having received this worst of news, the following chapters will be taken up with the good news of Israel's future restoration. **V 24–29: WICKED** But now Ezekiel addresses those forming the remnant of Israel living in the ruins of Jerusalem. They think that they will possess the land because of their numerical strength. Their dubious logic is based on the fact that Abraham was only one person, but he inherited the land! Ezekiel tells them that they will be judged by God for their wickedness towards God shown in their evil conduct and idolatry. They will be made desolate and will know that God is the LORD. **V 30–33: WANTING** Here are people who even enjoy listening to the prophecy and want to hear it, but do not intend to repent and take it to heart. It is dangerous to like listening to God's word without responding to it. They will recognise Ezekiel as God's true prophet when the judgement from God that he prophesies takes place.

CHAPTER THIRTY-FOUR

V 1–10: SELFISH SHEPHERDS Ezekiel prophesies against the shepherds of Israel who have no compassion or concern for the sheep. They fail to perform each duty of care expected of a shepherd. It is possible to have a position of authority and influence and to forget that God intends us to be a blessing to individual people. We, too, can be selfish shepherds. **V 11–24: SOVEREIGN SHEPHERD** God, who is against those selfish shepherds, will Himself act as a personal shepherd towards those who trust Him. He will seek, gather, feed, protect and save His sheep. But He will also judge wickedness and act in judgement against those who are not His sheep. The reference to David as a shepherd points to Christ, from David's line, as the 'good Shepherd'.

V 25–31: SAVIOUR SHEPHERD When God is shepherd, 'the covenant of peace' will prevail, and blessing, safety, protection and a sense of belonging to God will follow. His people are His flock. His sheep are people who know God as their Saviour and Shepherd.

CHAPTER THIRTY-FIVE

V 1–4: MOUNT SEIR Mount Seir represents the whole of Edom, which has long been one of Israel's most bitter enemies. God tells the inhabitants, through Ezekiel, that He will lay Edom waste and that they will know that He is God. **V 5–9: MANY SLAIN** In the same way as many Israelites have been slain by Edomites, so God will fill the land of Edom with blood and slaughter. Their cities will be perpetually desolate and uninhabited. **V 10–13: MOUTH SINFUL** Edom's sin in its speech against God offends Him. Edom's desire to possess Israel and Judah offends God, who is their possessor. God has heard the many blasphemies made against Him. He will judge them. **V 14–15: MADE SOLITARY** Ezekiel says that Mount Seir and the whole of Edom will be made desolate. As God acts, they will know that He is the LORD. God is on the side of His people.

CHAPTER THIRTY-SIX

V 1–7: GOD'S PROVOCATION God is provoked by nations, such as Edom, who take delight in afflicting and mocking His people. When God blesses His people, He will deal with their oppressors, even though He uses them to discipline His people. **V 8–15: GOD'S PROMISES** God promises that the very mountains, which are the subject of mockery and plunder, will be blessed by Him for Israel. Fruitful agriculture, increased cooperation, and

increase of towns will demonstrate that God will bless His people in the future. Israel is special to God. **V 16–21: GOD PROFANED** Israel was scattered by God in judgement for her rebellion against Him. Israel profaned God's name among the nations where they were scattered. God has not forgotten that her profanity against Him has been immense and caused much suffering and punishment. His people's profanity brought disgrace to His holy name. **V 22–32: GOD'S PURPOSE** Nevertheless, God's purpose is to save Israel. He will save them from the nations around, and make them a testimony to them. He will also save them from their sin. He will give them a new heart, a new spirit, and cause them to be guided by His Spirit and to walk in His statutes. Restored spiritually, Israel will also know God's great material and physical provision and blessing. God has purposed to bless His physical people spiritually and finally. **V 33–38: GOD'S PROSPERITY** On the day of Israel's cleansing and turning back to God, the cities will be rebuilt, the land will become fruitful, and the population will increase. Then they will know that He is the LORD.

CHAPTER THIRTY-SEVEN

V 1–14: DRY BONES, DYNAMIC BODIES God's people are portrayed, in a vision to Ezekiel, as dry bones in a valley. Death and hopelessness are characterised. Then, as Ezekiel prophesies God's word, the bones become living bodies that stand on their feet and become an exceedingly great army as the breath of God enters into them. Israel, which is hopeless and cut off, will be revived and brought to life by God's Spirit. Israel will go back to its own land and know that God has spoken, and that He has done what He said He would do. There is also a wider principle that God can take a situation that is without human hope and, through His word and Spirit, fill it with life, purpose and hope. Christian conversion is also pictured in this vision of life from the dead. **V 15–28: UNITED KINGDOM, UNENDING KING** Just as Ezekiel is asked to join two sticks together, so Israel and Judah will be joined together as one nation when God brings His people back. When God brings back all His scattered people, idolatry will be purged from both Judah and Israel. They will be God's people and He will be their God in practice as well as by His right of possession. They will know His cleansing and deliverance. There will also be one King for ever. Here, that King, Jesus Christ the Messiah, is referred to as 'David' because He is of the Davidic line, fulfilling the Davidic covenant. With one kingdom and one King, God's presence will be evident among His people.

CHAPTER THIRTY-EIGHT

V 1–17: INVASION BY GOG An alliance of northern nations, headed by Gog, will attack Israel in hordes. Their evil intent will be to plunder her and carry away all that Israel possesses. There are different views as to what this represents in detail, but it seems that it could refer prophetically to a time when a world alliance will gather against Israel in the end times. Human history will pivot around Israel. **V 18–23: INTERVENTION BY GOD** God's fury and fire of wrath will be demonstrated. An unprecedented mammoth earthquake will precede self-destruction of the forces rallied against Israel. God will send huge rain showers, hailstones, fire, and brimstone. As God magnifies Himself in that day, in the defence of His people, the world nations will know that truly He is God when the alliance against Israel is defeated, and the ruler of those forces (who can only be the Antichrist) is utterly deposed and smashed.

CHAPTER THIRTY-NINE

V 1–8: DEFEAT AND DESTRUCTION The destruction of the forces, allied against God's people and led by Gog, is detailed in this chapter. Their weapons will be useless, they will fall on the mountains of Israel, they will be devoured by birds and animals, and the land of Magog in surrounding coastlands will be subject to God's fire. The nations will know that God is the LORD, 'the Holy One in Israel'. This will surely happen. **V 9–10: FUEL FOR FIRE** The weapons of the would-be invaders are so numerous that it will take seven years to burn them as fuel for fire. Israel will plunder those who came to plunder them. The best army is far too strong for Israel, but no match for our Sovereign God. **V 11–16: BURIAL OF BODIES** So many invading troops will be killed that it will take seven months to bury the remains and cleanse the land. **V 17–20: FEEDING ON FALLEN** Because of the great carnage, wild animals and birds are summoned to the 'sacrificial meal' where they gorge themselves on the bodies of those who dared to lift themselves up against God and His people. **V 21–29: PERFORMANCE OF PROMISE** God's glory will be set 'among the nations'. Israel will be prospered and blessed by God from that day onwards. Her unfaithfulness, idolatry, and chastisement for her uncleanness will be over. The whole house of Israel will experience God's mercy and be made holy. Brought back from captivity, she will be possessed by God, who will pour out His Spirit on His people. God will perform His promise for Israel. With equal certainty, the Christian can know that God will perform His promise of blessing to each individual sinner who turns to Christ.

CHAPTER FORTY

V 1–3: CONDUCTED TOUR God takes Ezekiel through a vision to the next stage of Israel's blessing, the restoration of worship. He receives a conducted tour of the new temple, being guided by a 'man' who appears to be an angel. As he goes, the temple is measured. Opinions of commentators vary as to whether the visionary temple is symbolic or whether it actually will be built. We must bear in mind that Ezekiel learns all about it in a vision. In either case, it teaches important principles and the sacrifices in the vision will look back to Calvary, as a memorial of what Jesus fulfilled, rather than looking forward to Christ's sacrifice as previously in the Old Testament. **V 4–5: CONSIDERED TEACHING** Ezekiel is told to absorb everything in great detail so that he can declare to Israel everything that he witnesses. His teaching must be factual and considered. The measurements are thus important to show the beauty and accuracy that God uses both in revelation and in worship. **V 6–37: COMING TEMPLE** The gateways, outer court and inner court of the new temple are then visited, and Ezekiel reports upon them in detail. **V 38–46: CONSECRATED TASKS** Rooms are set aside for preparation of sacrifices, and priests are set aside to make them. The sacrifices obviously look back to what Christ has done on Calvary. The consecrated tasks of the priests are to focus on what those sacrifices mean. **V 47–49: CUBITS TAKEN** The dimensions of the inner court and the vestibule are taken and recorded.

CHAPTER FORTY-ONE

V 1–17: DIVINE DIMENSIONS The whole of the temple is measured. God's work always reflects His order and beauty. The temple of Ezekiel's vision is no exception. **V 18–26: DIVINE DÉCOR** The furnishings and decoration of the outer sanctuary and inner sanctuary are given. Each item has its significance and symbolism dealing with the worship of God.

CHAPTER FORTY-TWO

V 1–14: ROOMS There are rooms built into the temple in Ezekiel's vision. Their structure and size diminish as they go upwards. These rooms are for the priests to use. There they will eat the offerings and leave their priestly garments before leaving the temple. **V 15–20: RODS** The outside of the temple is measured in rods. Ezekiel's visionary temple is smaller than that of Solomon, but it is to be more glorious because of God's presence. Size is not always the most important thing!

CHAPTER FORTY-THREE

V 1–5: GLORY RETURNS God's glory returns from the east to the temple. In Ezekiel's vision, he is lifted up by the Spirit into the inner court to behold God's glory. **V 6–9: GOD'S REVIEW** God reveals to Ezekiel that it is here that He will dwell with the house of Israel for ever and that His people will completely forsake their sin and idolatry. God's anger will be turned away. They will put away their evil doings and enjoy the dwelling of God for ever. **V 10–12: GODLY REQUIREMENT** So that Israel can maintain a sense of shame for her iniquities, she is to understand the reason and the design of the temple, which shows how sinful people should approach God. Thus Ezekiel is to describe the details of the temple and its laws to them. The area surrounding the temple is holy. **V 13–17: GRACIOUS RETROSPECT** The dimensions of the altar in this vision are given. It is a bigger altar than that built before and is ascended by steps, which are made by each platform being smaller than the one underneath it. In Ezekiel's vision, this altar will help worshippers look back to God's grace to sinners at Calvary, where the last sacrifice for sins was offered by the last Priest. It will focus the attention of God's people on their redemption achieved through Christ crucified. **V 18–27: GREAT REDEMPTION** Similarly, the offerings and sacrifices detailed here are to underline Jesus Christ's great redemptive work done on the cross. As the Mosaic sacrificial system looked forward to the cross, so the sacrifices in this vision look back to it. The Lord Jesus Christ is both their fulfilment and their focus.

CHAPTER FORTY-FOUR

V 1–5: PRINCE In the vision, there is a prince who is the only one who can eat bread before God in the east gate to the temple. That east gate is to be closed because of the LORD's prophesied entry by that way to restore the glory of the temple. **V 4–5: PRIORITY** Ezekiel sees God's glory again in his vision and falls on his face. He is told to mark well what he sees and hears, and to take in all the laws. Especially he is to mark well those who can enter the temple and use the sanctuary. **V 6–14: PROHIBITIONS** God will exclude all rebels and their abominations. He forbids entry into His sanctuary by those who are uncircumcised in heart or in flesh. These are foreigners and include foreigners staying with the Israelites. He will not have His sanctuary defiled again. He also prohibits the Levites from acting as priests or coming near to Him with any holy thing for the Most Holy Place. This is because of their past idolatry and sin. They will act as temple caretakers. **V 15–31: PRIESTS** But the Levites who are the sons of Zadok are to minister as priests because Zadok took charge of the sanctuary when Israel was straying from God. The details of their morality, dress, appearance, and duties are given. They are all to be holy to God in their priesthood and not to fail as priests have failed in the past. God will be their possession and inheritance, and they shall be fed from the firstfruits and from the sacrifices.

CHAPTER FORTY-FIVE

V 1–3: LORD'S LAND The first division of the land is to be made to the LORD, who will keep it for His faithful priests. It is their provision. **V 6–8: ISRAEL'S INHERITANCE** The rest of the city shall belong to the 'whole house of Israel'. The prince's section is defined. The princes are to oppress the people no more. **V 9–12: CONSECRATED CONDUCT** The prince is to behave honestly in matters of justice, righteousness, and relationship with the people. His measurements are to be honest and he must not be violent or plunder. His conduct is to be consecrated. **V 13–17: OFFERINGS OBSERVED** The offerings that both the people and the prince are to observe are prescribed. These are to apply on the feast days, New Moons (marking the start of each month for God), and the Sabbaths. **V 18–25: FESTIVAL FEASTS** The feasts to be kept are also prescribed as a time for worship and sacrifice.

CHAPTER FORTY-SIX

V 1–3: SABBATH PRINCIPLE The priest shall enter by the east gate on the monthly new moon and each day on the Sabbath. That gate is to be shut on the six working days. The people also are commanded to worship on the Sabbaths and on the New Moons. **V 4–15: SACRIFICES PRESCRIBED** The sacrifices to be made and the way in which they are to be made are prescribed for the prince and for the people. **V 16–18: SOVEREIGN'S POSSESSIONS** Rules are laid down about the inheritance laws applying to the land possessed by the prince. He must not take the people's property but can give his own as an inheritance to his sons. **V 19–24: SANCTIFIED PREPARATION** The preparation of the offerings and where they are to be made are prescribed. Details of the priests' kitchens are given.

CHAPTER FORTY-SEVEN

V 1–12: LIVING RIVER In Ezekiel's vision, he is brought back to the door of the temple where he sees a vision of a river of water flowing from under the threshold of the temple towards the east. It is a living and a deepening river, and it has a miraculous effect of turning salt water into fresh water and producing life in terms of fish, and trees and lush vegetation growing on its banks. **V 13–23: LAND REDISTRIBUTED** The redistribution of the land of Israel, after her restoration, is detailed. Then land will be restored to the tribes and to strangers who dwell among them.

CHAPTER FORTY-EIGHT

V 1–8: PARTIAL PARTITION The division of the land between the first six tribes is detailed in the vision. **V 9–22: PRIESTS' PROPERTY** The property allocated to the priests, who are the sons of Zadok and faithful to God, is also described again. Their land is holy to the LORD. Also described again is the land allocated to the Levites, the city and the prince. **V 23–29: PARTIAL PARTITION** The second six tribes will receive the land according to the details given. **V 30–34: PRESCRIBED PORTALS** The gates of the city are named after the twelve tribes of Israel. Levi is included and so Joseph represents both Ephraim and Manasseh. **V 35: PROPHESIED PRESENCE** The name of the city fulfils the prophecy and the promise that the LORD has given to restore Israel, namely, 'THE LORD IS THERE'. Ezekiel's vision closes with that assurance. God will restore repentant Israel and its worship, and will mightily bless His people.

DANIEL

OVERVIEW

PEOPLE AND PRELIMINARIES

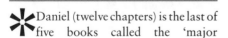Daniel (twelve chapters) is the last of five books called the 'major prophets'. See comments on Isaiah. It was written by Daniel between 536 BC and 530 BC, probably in Persia, though he could have started writing it in Babylon where his exile began. It is estimated that Daniel covers a period of seventy-three years.

PLAN AND PURPOSE

(i) Daniel is a Jewish youth taken into captivity in Babylon by King Nebuchadnezzar from Jerusalem. His close colleagues are the three young Jews who miraculously brave and survive the fiery furnace. Daniel's spirituality and principled prayerfulness, under God, make him a godly influence in high positions of respect and authority. He remains faithful to God, whatever the circumstances or environment. The first half of the book is mainly historic and the second part is mainly prophetic. God honours his servant who confesses his own sins and those of his nation. This book is a panorama, of past history and future prophecy (tomorrow's history) through which Daniel's interpretations of Nebuchadnezzar's dreams, and the receiving of dreams from God, are a major channel of prophecy. The end of world history is prophesied here. The church's apostasy, the appearance of the man of sin, the inevitability of the great tribulation, the return of the Lord Jesus Christ, the theme of judgement, and Israel's restoration are all in this remarkable book. Much of the interpretation is clear because it is given in the book itself. The fulfilment of some of the prophecy is obvious (for example, only Alexander the Great meets the Greek criteria), while other parts must be handled humbly and more cautiously!

PROFILE AND PROGRESSION

Daniel, the faithful witness, from the conquest of Jerusalem to King Nebuchadnezzar's second year (1:1–2:1); Daniel, the inspired and promoted prophet with his three faithful companions, dealing with the visions of King Nebuchadnezzar (2:1–4:37); Daniel, the protected prophet testifying to God

under the godless rulers, Belshazzar and Darius (5:1–6:28); Daniel's dreams and visions, including those regarding the beast, the Ancient of Days, the ram and goat, the seventy weeks, God's glory, the man of sin, Israel's humiliation and restoration (6:1–12:13).

PRINCIPLES AND PARTICULARS

The book challenges each reader to apply spiritual principles of living an uncompromised holy life, to be counted as a disciple and follower of God, and to pray regularly, daily and also in crises. In marvelling at God's amazing prophecies, we should avoid purely intellectual interest that can occupy disproportionate time and attention and leave us still wondering, without promoting the desire to be godly people. See how God protects those who trust Him, when it is in His will and for His glory to do so. Remember that even Daniel was at a complete loss to understand some of the prophecy in the book of his name—so do not despair if you get a little lost, too! The big lesson is that our Sovereign God is in control and will have His way in future history, with His people and with the whole world. We must submit to His will, His ways, and Himself now!

DANIEL

CHAPTER ONE

V 1–2: CAPTIVITY Nebuchadnezzar, king of Babylon, takes captive Jehoiakim, king of Judah, with articles from the temple in Jerusalem. **V 3–7: CONSCRIPTS** Ashpenaz, the master of the king's eunuchs, is instructed to bring young conscripts to Babylon to be educated. They are to be trained to serve Nebuchadnezzar. These young men must be of good appearance, wise, knowledgeable, and teachable. They are young men of ability. Such are Daniel, Hananiah, Mishael, and Azariah. As part of their induction into Babylonian culture, their names are changed into the Babylonian names of Belteshazzar, Shadrach, Mesach, and Abednego. **V 8–14: CHARACTER** The character of the young men, especially Daniel, who is the spokesman and leader, is such that they will not defile themselves with the king's delicacies or wine. (This would have involved consuming things offered to idols and foods prohibited for Israelites.) Daniel persuades Ashpenaz's steward to let them consume vegetables and water, and invites him to examine them after a period of time to see if they really look in worse shape than those who feed on the richer fare. The steward is worried that the king will notice the deterioration in their appearance. **V 15–16: COMPARISON** The comparison, made after ten days, reveals that they are much better and fatter than those who have 'eaten the king's delicacies'. Accordingly, they are allowed to continue to eat their chosen food. **V 17–21: COMPREHENSIVE** God comprehensively gifts these young men with knowledge, literature skill, wisdom, and understanding. Daniel, in particular, is gifted by God in understanding visions and dreams. Their service to the king is ten times better than the magicians and sorcerers of Babylon. Daniel continues until the first year of King Cyrus.

CHAPTER TWO

V 1–3: TROUBLED TYRANT Nebuchadnezzar, the tyrant king of Babylon, is troubled by a dream. He calls his astrologers, magicians, and sorcerers together to tell him what it means. **V 4–11: ADVISERS AGHAST** His advisers ask the king to tell them the dream so that they can interpret it. Nebuchadnezzar insists that they tell him the dream as well as the interpretation, because he knows they will lie about an interpretation once they have the facts. They are aghast when he insists on this. They say that no man on earth is able to do it, knowing that the king has promised great reward or threatened the death penalty, dependent on whether or not the dream is revealed and interpreted. **V 12–13: ROYAL REACTION** The king is irate at their response, and orders that all the wise men are to be put to death. This is to include Daniel and his three companions. **V 14–16: CALM COURAGE** Daniel, through the captain of the King's Guard, Arioch, gets an audience with the king to ask for time to interpret the dream. **V 17–18: PRAYERFUL PLEADING** The four young Israelites then have a prayer meeting to ask God to be merciful to them by revealing the king's secret. **V 19–23: GODLY GRATITUDE** In a night vision, God reveals the dream and its interpretation to Daniel, who thanks Him, giving Him all the glory for His power and His wisdom. **V 24: SAGES SAVED** Before revealing God's response to the king, Daniel pleads with Arioch that the wise men of Babylon should not be destroyed because he is going to make known the interpretation to the king. Daniel's concern goes far wider than himself, his companions, and his Israelite background. He has an impact on ungodly people where he works. **V 25–30: HUMBLY HONOURING** Daniel starts his presentation to the king by emphasising humbly that it is only 'God in heaven who reveals secrets'. Right from the start, God gets all the glory from Daniel for what he is about to say.

V 31–35: DREAM DESCRIBED Daniel tells the king about his dream about the great image. The image has a golden head, a chest and arms of silver, body and thighs of bronze, legs of iron, and feet of mixed iron and clay. A stone, not cut by human hands, strikes the image on its feet, and the image is smashed and blown away as chaff by the wind. **V 36–45: INSPIRED INTERPRETATION** Daniel tells the king that he is the head of gold and the other parts of the image are the kingdoms to follow his kingdom. Finally, God will bring down the kingdoms. The stone that breaks the image will stand for ever. This symbolises God's sovereign control over the kingdoms of men, and could be Messianic. **V 46–49: EXPECTATIONS EXCEEDED** Not only are Daniel and his three companions saved, as well as the advisers to the king, but Nebuchadnezzar acknowledges that Daniel's God is 'the God of gods, the Lord of kings and a revealer of secrets'. With extravagant generosity, Daniel is promoted to be ruler over the whole province of Babylon and chief administrator of all Babylon's wise men. At Daniel's petition, his three colleagues are put over the affairs of Babylon. Daniel sits in the gate of the king. How God honours those who honour Him, and at times exalts them for His own glory!

CHAPTER THREE

V 1–3: INIQUITOUS IMAGE Nebuchadnezzar's respect for God is short lived. He commands that a huge gold image he has commissioned must be worshipped. **V 4–7: COMPLIANCE COMPELLED** At the dedication of the image, the people are told that they must fall down at the playing of prescribed music. Those who do not obey will immediately be cast into a burning fiery furnace. Understandably, everyone complies! **V 8–15: THREE TAKEN** But there are exceptions! Three men—Shadrach, Mesach and Abednego—are reported because they will not bow down. Nebuchadnezzar has them brought in to him, and reiterates the threat of the fiery furnace, asking, 'Who is the god who will deliver you from my hands?' **V 16–18: SOLID STAND** The three Israelites tell him that God is able to deliver them, but even if He does not, they will not bow down to the golden image. Through grace, their stand for God is solid. **V 19–23: FIERY FURNACE** Nebuchadnezzar commands that the furnace be heated to seven times its normal heat, so much so that the soldiers taking the three men into the furnace are burnt to death at the entrance to it. The three bound men are thrown into the furnace. **V 24–26: RULER'S REACTION** Immediately, King Nebuchadnezzar sees four people in the flames. He sees they are not hurt and declares that 'the fourth is like the Son of God'. He calls the three men out of the fire and they oblige. **V 27: MIGHTY MIRACLE** All the king's party witness that the men are unhurt, unburnt, unsinged, and that their garments do not even smell of fire. God has performed a mighty miracle for His glory! **V 28–29: GOD GLORIFIED** Nebuchadnezzar is again so taken up with the power of God in delivering His servants, that he forbids any speaking against them and declares that there is 'no other God who can deliver like this'. **V 30: PERSECUTED PROMOTED** The king promotes the three men in the province of Babylon.

CHAPTER FOUR

V 1–3: TELLING TESTIMONY Nebuchadnezzar is about to relate how, in Old Testament terms, he is converted to

God. He wishes everyone to know of the change in his life. **V 4–18: TALL TREE** He had a dream about a tall tree that was stripped and broken and fell to the ground, depicting his own downfall. This is witnessed by a holy 'watcher', probably an angel. The stump of the tree and its roots were bound with iron and bronze and remained in the ground. He was told that the tree would be wet with the dew of heaven and would be left in the grass with the beasts. His heart would be changed from that of a man to that of a beast and 'seven times' would pass over him. **V 19–27: TRUTH TOLD** Daniel, astonished and troubled for a time, told Nebuchadnezzar that the tree represented him and that the dream referred to the king's downfall through pride. Although his kingdom would be restored, signified by the iron and bronze binding the stump and the roots, the king would fall and be wet with the dew of heaven and eat grass like oxen. This would happen for 'seven times', perhaps meaning seven years. The king would come to know that 'heaven rules' and Daniel pressed him to urgent repentance and righteousness by showing mercy to others. **V 28–33: THRONE TOPPLED** Nebuchadnezzar goes on to say that the prophecy was fulfilled accurately and completely. While he was in the act of proudly boasting about his building of Babylon, God dealt with him and humiliated him. He was driven away from men, and ate grass like oxen. His body was wet with dew and his hair grew like eagles' feathers and his nails grew like birds' claws. God humbled this proud king. **V 34–37: TOTAL TRUST** But Nebuchadnezzar can now say that his faith and confidence are in this omnipotent God who humbled him. As he lifted his eyes to God, his understanding and sanity returned. He now wishes to praise and extol the King of

heaven who is truthful and just and who can put down the proud.

CHAPTER FIVE

V 1–4: WICKED ADORATION King Belshazzar, son of Nebuchadnezzar, wickedly praises the gods of gold, silver, iron, bronze, wood and stone, as his debauched and drunken party takes its wine from the gold vessels that had been consecrated for the temple in Jerusalem. **V 5–6: WRITING APPEARS** At that very hour, a man's hand appears and the fingers of that hand write words in the plaster of the walls of the king's palace. The king becomes a nervous wreck as this unwanted and solemn judgement miraculously invades his debauchery. **V 7–9: WONDERING ANXIETY** Despite the offer of promotion to the third ruler of the kingdom, none of the king's wise men or advisers can read the writing or make known to the king the interpretation of it. Belshazzar is 'greatly troubled'. Everyone is astonished. **V 10–12: WOMAN'S ADVICE** The queen steps in to remind Belshazzar what Daniel did for his father Nebuchadnezzar. She advises him to call in Daniel to interpret the writing. **V 13–16: WISDOM ACKNOWLEDGED** Daniel is summoned by the king, who acknowledges the wisdom and ability which Daniel has had in the past because the Spirit of God is in him. He repeats his offer of making Daniel third in the kingdom if he can interpret the writing. **V 17–24: WILLING ANSWER** Daniel brushes the offer of a reward aside, and then interprets the writing for Belshazzar. He tells him that, unlike Nebuchadnezzar, who repented of his pride when God spoke to him, Belshazzar is guilty of great pride against God and rebellion against the 'Lord of heaven'. **V 25–28: WORDS APPLIED** He then reads the words and interprets them. Belshazzar's kingdom has been numbered and is finished. He has been found wanting, as God has weighed him in the balances. His kingdom will be given to the Medes and Persians. **V 29: WIDE ACCLAIM** Belshazzar seems more concerned to carry out his promise to make Daniel the third ruler in the kingdom than to repent of his sin and turn to God. The wide acclaim that Daniel will receive, as a result of Belshazzar's promoting him, will not save the unrepentant and sinful king. **V 30–31: WHIRLWIND ACCOMPLISHMENT** That very night, Belshazzar is slain. Darius, the Mede, becomes king at the age of sixty-two. (One extra-biblical account reveals that the invaders came into Babylon through a dried-up watercourse.)

CHAPTER SIX

V 1–3: PROMOTION EXPERIENCED As in the reigns of Nebuchadnezzar and Belshazzar, Daniel is promoted to a position of high influence under King Darius. His lack of corruption means that he is trustworthy, and his exceptional qualities set him above others whom the king could have put in high positions. **V 4–9: POLITICAL EXPLOITATION** Those over whom Daniel was preferred waste no time in exploiting the situation politically to have Daniel deposed. They know that they have to find some fault with him in connection with his relationship with God. This must appeal to Darius so that Daniel can be overthrown. First, they get the vain king to sign a decree that anyone praying to any god or man in the next thirty days, except to Darius, shall be thrown into the den of lions. **V 10: PRAYING EARNESTLY** Daniel hears that the decree has been published but continues his practice of praying three

times a day towards Jerusalem, with the windows open, whatever the situation. **V 11–18: PLOT EFFECTIVE** This, however, gives his observing opponents an opportunity to harm Daniel. They report him to King Darius who, having passed the law which according to the Medes and Persians cannot be changed, feels obliged to have Daniel thrown into the lions' den. But even the king seems reluctant to carry out his changeless decree, and he expresses the wish to Daniel that his God might rescue him. The king even fasts. He has a sleepless night. **V 19–23: PROTECTED EFFECTIVELY** As soon as dawn breaks, the king cannot wait to see how Daniel has fared in the lions' den. Daniel assures him that God has preserved him by His angel and that he did the king no wrong, anyhow. The king is overjoyed to bring Daniel out of the den unharmed. Daniel trusted in his God, who protected him. **V 24: PUNISHMENT EXECUTED** The king has the false accusers of Daniel punished by being thrown into the lions' den, sadly with their wives and children, where they are killed by the lions. **V 25–27: PROCLAMATION EVERYWHERE** King Darius writes to everyone, everywhere, proclaiming the living God who delivers and rescues and works signs and wonders. Yet another king acknowledges the greatness of God through Daniel's faithfulness and trust. **V 28: PROSPERITY EARNED** Through God's grace and mercy, Daniel again prospers in the reign of Darius and in the reign of Cyrus the Persian. God honours his servant who honours Him.

CHAPTER SEVEN

V 1: VIVID VISION The book of Daniel is not in chronological order and this vision, in the first year of Belshazzar's reign, forms the basis of much prophecy concerning the end times. **V 2–8: ANIMALS' APPEARANCE** Four different animals appear in Daniel's vision, coming up from the Great Sea, (thought by most to be the Mediterranean). The first animal is a lion with an eagle's wings. The wings are plucked from the lion and the animal stands on two feet to receive a man's heart. The second animal is like a bear with one side raised up and three ribs in its mouth. The third animal is a leopard with four birds' wings on its back and with four heads. The fourth beast is different from the others. It is dreadful and very strong with giant teeth and powerful feet that trample. It has ten horns but a small eleventh horn arises that plucks out three of the horns. This small horn has eyes like a man and a mouth that speaks pompous words. **V 9–10: GOD'S GLORY** In Daniel's vision, the thrones are put in their place and the Ancient of Days (God the Father) appears in holiness and glory, and is ministered to by millions of saints with even more millions standing before Him. As the court is seated, the books are opened. **V 11–12: BEAST BURNED** The fourth beast with the pompous speaking horn is killed and burned. The other beasts survive but with no power. **V 13–14: SON SERVED** 'One like the Son of Man' comes to the Ancient of Days and receives dominion, glory, and a kingdom. All peoples and nations and languages serve Him. His power is everlasting. His kingdom will remain for ever. This clearly speaks of the Lord Jesus Christ. **V 15–27: INSPIRED INTERPRETATION** We can be sure of the interpretation of this vision because the Bible itself gives the interpretation that Daniel received. The four beasts are four kings, but God's saints will finally receive the kingdom and possess it. The pompous speaking horn appears to be Antichrist because it makes war against the saints,

and prevails against them until the Ancient of Days steps in to judge, on behalf of the saints. The fourth beast is a kingdom that will devour the whole earth, and the ten horns are the ten kings. The eleventh king will arise and subdue three kings, speak pompously against God, persecute the saints, and seek to change times and law. They will prevail against the saints 'for a time, times and half a time.' (The 'time, times, and half a time' are interpreted by some to represent the last three-and-a-half years of the seven-year reign of Antichrist. Some other interpreters do not take this to represent a specific period of time but merely the shortening of times because God intervenes.) God will have the last word, and the dominion of the pompous speaking horn will be taken away, and greatness and power will be given to the saints of God whose kingdom is everlasting. All dominions will serve and obey Him. **V 28: CHANGED COUNTENANCE** Despite the final outcome, Daniel's thoughts trouble him, and his countenance is changed, but he keeps the matter to himself.

CHAPTER EIGHT

V 1–4: RAMPANT RAM In another vision in Belshazzar's third year as king, Daniel sees a ram with two horns, one coming up later and growing bigger than the other one. The ram pushes to the west, to the north and to the south, and is irresistible in its power. **V 5–8a: GREAT GOAT** Then from the west, a fast running and powerful goat with a single large horn between its eyes runs to attack the ram, breaks its horns, and tramples it. No one can deliver the ram. The goat grows 'very great'. **V 8b–12: HAUGHTY HORN** The goat's large horn is broken and replaced by four others. From one of these, a little horn grows that becomes great towards the south, the east, and the Glorious Land (Israel). It casts down some stars and exalts itself as high as the Prince of the Host of heaven. The daily sacrifices of the temple are removed and the sanctuary is cast down. An army supports the horn in opposing the daily sacrifices. He casts truth down to the ground and prospers. **V 13–14: DESOLATION'S DURATION** One angel asks another what the time span is regarding the daily sacrifices, the desolation of the temple, and the trampling of the host of heaven. The reply comes back, 'for two thousand three hundred days, then the sanctuary shall be cleansed'. **V 15–26: ANGEL'S APPLICATION** The angel Gabriel is bidden to explain the vision to Daniel, who fears and falls on his face, but is put back on his feet by Gabriel. The vision is to be fulfilled geographically in history, but also applies to the end times. The ram stands for the Medo-Persian empire, crushed by the great goat of Greece, for whom its first king is the large horn. (Historically, there is near-universal agreement that the only realistic candidate is Alexander the Great.) Four kingdoms take over when the large horn is broken, and the little horn of evil and sinister design will cause deceit, destruction and blasphemous rebellion against the Prince of princes (God). (The 'little horn' is seen by most to have been fulfilled historically by Antiochus IV Epiphanes. He replaced the four rulers of Greece succeeding Alexander, after his death at the age of thirty-three. Antiochus died without being killed in battle or murdered, and therefore was 'broken without human means'.) Gabriel confirms that the visions of the evenings and mornings—the previously stated two thousand three hundred days—is true, and commands Daniel to seal up the vision, because it applies to many days in the future. **V 27: UNDERSTANDING UNATTAINABLE** After the vision, Daniel faints and is sick for days, then goes about serving the king. The vision astonishes him and no one is able to understand it. Sometimes it is a good thing to admit that we do not really understand some of the visions of God's Word. There is room for humility and teachability.

CHAPTER NINE

V 1–4: SCRIPTURAL SUPPLICATION In the first year of the reign of Darius, God reveals to Daniel, from Jeremiah's prophecy, what is meant by the seventy years of desolations in Jerusalem. Daniel then mourns, prays, confesses, and makes supplication to his 'great and awesome God' of covenant mercy. **V 5–19: PENITENT PRAYER** Daniel's prayer of penitence which follows is a model for all who know the Lord. He confesses the sin of his people and includes himself in it. They have rebelled against God's word and ignored God's prophets. He acknowledges that God is quite right and just to judge His people for their rebellion and sin. He recognises that the disasters that God has brought and allowed upon Israel are because of her sin. He then prays, simply on the basis of God's great mercies, for God to hear, forgive, listen, and act. He asks God to do it without delay, and reminds Him that Jerusalem and Israel are called by God's name. In confessing his sin, he prays because God's honour, glory, and name are at stake. In the midst of prophetic looking forward, we must remember the reality and priority of penitent prayer. **V 20–24: SEVENTY 'SEVENS'** Gabriel flies to Daniel to tell him that 'seventy weeks' being the seventy weeks of years, or four hundred and ninety years, are prescribed to finish the transgression against God, to have sins put away, and for reconciliation to be made which will bring in everlasting righteousness and will complete God's revelation. **V 25–27: TIMING TOLD** Seventy weeks is best understood as seventy sets of seven years (490 years). The period of seventy weeks (490 years) is then divided into seven weeks (forty-nine years), then sixty-two weeks (434 years) and later one week (seven years). There are different interpretations as to whether anything happens between the prescribed lots of seven years, but the restoration of Jerusalem is foretold and the fact that Messiah will be killed after the stated period of sixty-two weeks of years (434 years). Then the city and the sanctuary will be finally destroyed by a flood. Until the end of war, desolations will continue. Then a covenant will be confirmed with many for the remaining one week (seven years) but in the middle of that week (taken by many to mean three-and-a-half years) the little horn of Antichrist will end sacrifice and offering and cause abomination in the temple. (There is much room for humility in respecting other people's varying interpretations about the timing of these climactic events. All these things will come to pass according to God's timetable.)

CHAPTER TEN

V 1–3: MOURNING AND MESSAGE God reveals His message to Daniel in the third year of Cyrus, king of Persia, while he was mourning and fasting for three weeks. Probably it is the state of Jerusalem which causes him to mourn. **V 4–9: VISION AND VIGOUR** Daniel sees a vision of a glorious man in dazzling appearance. Terror falls on others who see the vision, and they flee. As Daniel remains, he is without strength and his vigour turns to frailty. Yet

he hears the words of the glorious man while his face is to the ground in a deep sleep. **V 10–21: STRENGTHLESS AND STRENGTHENED** Strengthless, Daniel is strengthened as a hand touches him and tells him that his prayers have been heard by God and that the humbling of his heart before God has led to this response. The one who touches him tells him that he has been resisted by the prince of the kingdom of Persia, possibly a reference to Satan's activity in the heavenly places. Michael, the chief angel, helps the one who now speaks to Daniel to overcome the twenty-one day opposition of this opponent. Daniel is lost for words and without strength. He is again touched on his lips and told not to fear but to be strong, and peace will be his. Thus strengthened, he can take in the message which his messenger must deliver before going back to fight with the prince of Persia. The prince of Greece will come. The messenger confirms his source of authority is the 'Scriptures of Truth', and that Michael, the chief angel, supported him.

CHAPTER ELEVEN

V 1: MESSENGER AND MICHAEL Daniel's messenger reveals to Daniel he also supported the chief angel, Michael. **V 2–35: HISTORY AND HARMONY** The detailed prophecies of the kings mentioned in this passage are many. Much of this deals with the conflict between the Egyptian kings from the south and the Syrian kings from the north. Historians tell us that the pinpoint accuracy of this chapter is such that it is easy to identify the specific kings who have been involved in history. From verse 21 onwards, the references seem to fit Antiochus IV Epiphanes, the most cruel king from the north. Those denying the

Bible give a strange testimony to the accuracy of the record of God's inspiration, by suggesting that this chapter could only have been written after the events prophesied! This is an unintended compliment to the accuracy of God's Word! **V 36–46: ANTIOCHUS AND ANTICHRIST** Unlike the earlier verses in the chapter which can easily be seen to refer to Antiochus Epiphanes, it is accepted by most commentators that verses 36 to 45 cover events to come that were not fulfilled in his life. Antiochus Epiphanes is thus not only the subject of near-time prophecy, but also a type of Antichrist for the end times. The seventieth week of years is nowhere spelled out in the Bible, but many think that verses 36 to 45 deal with what will happen in those last seven years, on the assumption that this speaks of the arrival of Antichrist. After all his evil, power, and influence, it is good to note that under the hand of the Sovereign God 'he shall come to his end and no one shall help him'. God has all power.

CHAPTER TWELVE

V 1: TERRIBLE TRIBULATION 'A time of trouble' which is unprecedented in history will be experienced at the end. (This seems to be a clear reference to the final tribulation.) But there will be deliverance for God's people through the intervention of the chief angel, Michael. **V 2–3: ENJOYING ETERNITY** The dead will awaken from the sleep of death either to everlasting life, or to shame and everlasting contempt. Those whose spiritual life is made evident by wisdom

and righteousness will be as the brightness of the firmament and everlasting stars in God's eternal purposes and plans. Those who know God will enjoy eternity. **V 4: SEAL SHUT** Daniel is told to 'shut up the words and seal the book until the time of the end'. There will be frantic activity to look for knowledge but it will only be available through God's revelation. **V 5–12: FINAL FULFILMENT** One angel asks another how long will it be until these wonderful things will be fulfilled. The glorious man swears before God that it will be for 'a time, times and half a time'. (This is thought by many to be three-and-a-half years, thus completing the second half of Daniel's seventieth week of years.) The end times will come after the shattering of God's holy people, and God's glorious restoration. Daniel does not understand but is told that the words are sealed. However, many will be 'purified, made white, and refined', so that the wicked will continue in their wickedness until they are dealt with. The period of 1,290 days (three-and-a-half years plus thirty days) will occupy the time from the start of the desolation of abomination until the end. Blessedness comes to those who wait until the accomplishment of 1,335 days, which is forty-five more days than the 1,290 days. (There are different interpretations put on these two figures and different reasons given for the variation between them.) **V 13: DANIEL'S DESTINY** Daniel will soon die but he will be raised in the resurrection and receive the inheritance that God has for this trusted and trusting servant of God.

HOSEA

OVERVIEW

PEOPLE AND PRELIMINARIES

✳Hosea (fourteen chapters) is the first book of the twelve 'minor prophets'. Hosea wrote it between 750 and 710 BC. Perhaps it was written in exile in Judea after the northern kingdom of Israel had been taken captive by the Assyrians prior to its dispersal among other nations. The other minor prophets are Joel, Amos, Obadiah, Jonah, Micah, Nahum, Habakkuk, Zephaniah, Haggai, Zechariah, and Malachi. Hosea has two more chapters than the 'major' book of Daniel but occupies less space and uses fewer words. Also, Hosea is longer than Lamentations of Jeremiah which is in the 'major' section because it attaches to the book of Jeremiah. Why is Hosea—or for that matter Zechariah, which also has fourteen chapters—classed as a 'minor prophet'? Simply because 'major' or 'minor' refers to the length of the prophecies within each prophetical book, and not even to the length of each book. In practice, however, the longest books do also contain the longest individual prophecies. The 'minor prophets' are in no sense inferior to, less important than, or less inspired than the 'major prophets'. Every section of the Bible, in both Old and New Testaments, is equally inspired by the Holy Spirit as God's Word. An estimate of the period covered by the events in Hosea is sixty years.

PLAN AND PURPOSE

ⓘHosea's prophecies to the ten tribes in Israel, in the north, are similar in principle to Jeremiah's prophecies in the south to Judah. He is a tender prophet who, nevertheless, has to preach against the adultery of Israel's idolatry and consequent other sins, foreseeing and describing the Assyrian invasion. This came about in accordance with his inspired prophecies. It is written for a backsliding nation of backsliding individuals, and is still an appropriate and much-used book to help backsliders return to Christ. The first three chapters are based on Hosea's relationship with his unfaithful wife and the rest of the book covers the prophetic rebukes and calls to repentance of his unfaithful nation. The book closes with Israel's restoration to a merciful and forgiving God who loves to heal backsliding and restore backsliders.

PROFILE AND PROGRESSION

🐚 God's word through Hosea (1:1); a loving husband living with an unfaithful wife—Hosea and Gomer as a picture of God and Israel—reconciliation, restoration and redemption (1:2–3:5); Hosea's message to spiritually adulterous Israel—including the idolatry and guilt of princes, priests and people, and the command to repent (4:1–6:3); Israel's covenant-breaking, godless living, judgement and punishment, tempered with God's constant love for them (6:4–11:11); Israel's sinful deceit and judgement incurring God's wrath (11:2–13:16); the restoration, renewal, blessing and future of hope for Israel by God's free love (14:1–9).

PRINCIPLES AND PARTICULARS

👉 The book of Hosea can seem 'heavy' and forbidding because of its insistent and continual denunciation of Israel's many sins coming from the people's idolatrous refusal to submit to God. But it deals with the actual situation, namely ongoing sinfulness and rebellion. Sin has to be addressed and forsaken if God is to bless. There can never be any blessing of God's people, communally or individually, without repentance from sin. Hosea's compassion and commitment are amazing, as he lives out the message he preaches by obeying the command to take an immoral and unfaithful wife and show her real love. This mirrors God's redemptive and unconditional love to any backsliding nation, people or individual coming to Him through Christ.

HOSEA

CHAPTER ONE

V 1: PROPHET Apart from Jonah, Hosea is the only prophet in the Bible who comes from the northern kingdom of Israel. God's word comes to him to prophesy against both Israel and Judah during a period spanning the reigns of the kings who are detailed in verse 1. **V 2: PROSTITUTION** As an object lesson in prophecy, Hosea is told to marry a wife who will be unfaithful to him. She will be a harlot, or prostitute. (One view is that she was pure when married to Hosea, but that she became unfaithful during the relationship and this unfaithfulness is prophesied from the start by calling her 'a wife of harlotry'.) God is pictured as the faithful husband. Israel's idolatry is spiritual immorality and Israel is seen as God's unfaithful wife, who follows wicked Canaanite practices. **V 3–8: PROPHETIC** His wife, Gomer, bears him three children. Each of their names is prophetic, reflecting the dealings that

God will have with His people, Israel and Judah. Their names and meanings follow: Jezreel means 'God will scatter' and predicts judgements; Lo-Ruhamah means 'not pitied' and predicts God judging Israel without mercy because of her failure to repent; Lo-Ammi means 'not My people' and signifies God's rejection of Israel. **V 10–11: PROMISE** God's rejection of Israel, however, will be reversed at her restoration. Even in the midst of the predicted judgement, God promises that Israel will be restored and be called 'sons of the living God'. God's earthly people will be immeasurably great 'as the sand of the sea'.

CHAPTER TWO

V 1: REMINDER A great day of God's bestowal of mercy and grace on Israel is yet to come when He will call them 'My people'. **V 2–3: REPENTANCE** However, repentance is always required before God's blessing. Just as Gomer has broken the marriage relationship through her prostitution, so Israel has with her spiritual idolatries. Wrong must be put away, lest judgement follow. **V 4–7: RESTRAINTS** In view of the waywardness of Gomer towards Hosea, and Israel towards God, restraints are required to limit wickedness. God will take Israel into hard times so that she will crave for the better times she once had with God, and come back to Him. **V 8–13: RETRIBUTION** As part of this process of retribution leading to restoration, God will withdraw some of the provisions of grain, wine, oil, silver and gold. He has given these to His people, but they have been misused in Baal worship. To come into the richness of spiritual blessing, often we have to be stripped of sin, as well as things that replace God in our priority and worship. **V 14–23: RESTORATION** However, just as

Gomer will return to Hosea, so Israel will return to God. He will provide for her, keep her safe, be loving and kind in righteousness and justice, and she will know the LORD. Prayer will be answered and blessing will flow materially as well as spiritually. The chapter ends on the note on which it started, that as mercy from God reaches His people, they will be declared 'My people' and they will say, 'You are my God.' But there is a hard road of repentance to walk before that blessing becomes Israel's. The same principle applies to any sinner turning to God.

CHAPTER THREE

V 1: LORD'S LOVE Hosea is told to go back to Gomer, although she is committing adultery. This is just like the LORD seeking idolatrous Israel. **V 2: BOUGHT BACK** The theme appears to be the slave market. They are paying fifteen shekels of silver and one-and-a-half homers of barley (the offering for one accused of adultery). Hosea buys Gomer back from the slavery into which she has been sold. Speculation is that the total value of the ransom price would equal thirty pieces of silver, which is the price paid for a slave. The Christian sees himself or herself in the slave market, ransomed by the blood of Christ. **V 3: CHANGED CONDUCT** Faithfulness and purity are to follow the ransom price for Gomer. The same requirement is on Israel and on the Christian today. **V 4–5: PARDON PREVIEWED** The whole incident previews the pardon of God for Israel and the pardon of God for sinners. The result will be a return and seeking God, producing reverential fear and a sense of His goodness.

CHAPTER FOUR

V 1–3: LORD'S CHARGE The LORD's basic charge against Israel is that she has left truth and mercy and that there is no knowledge of God in the land. This leads to swearing, lying, bloodshed, and theft. In fact, leaving God leads to breaking 'all restraint'. When we ignore Him, others suffer. **V 4–6: LAW CONTRAVENED** God's law is contravened, not only by the people, but by the prophets and the priests. Because of this, they have no knowledge imparted to them about God, who rejects His priests. **V 7–10: LICENTIOUS CONDUCT** As they grow more affluent, God's priests sin more and more against God and against people. Their hearts are set on iniquity. God will punish their licentious conduct. Their immorality stems from their idolatry. **V 11–14: LEWD COUNSEL** Because the people turn to wooden idols for counsel, they justify their lewd conduct. This involves harlotry, drunkenness, and idolatrous sacrifice in the context of immorality involving their daughters and their daughters-in-law. Everyone is involved in this immorality so that God cannot distinguish between the unfaithful brides committing adultery, the daughters who commit harlotry, and the men whose idolatry leads them into immorality. Ignorant people will be trampled under this pressure. **V 15–19: LIMITING CONSEQUENCES** God, through Hosea, pleads with Judah not to follow the terrible example of Israel. Israel is stubborn and (identified as Ephraim, the largest of the ten tribes) is bent on idolatry and immorality.

CHAPTER FIVE

V 1–5: JUST JUDGEMENT Israel, and especially Ephraim as the largest tribe representing Israel, will be judged by God along with Judah, because of 'the spirit of harlotry', both spiritual and physical. **V 6–7: GOD GONE** God will not answer them when they pray, but has 'withdrawn Himself from them'. He will not countenance their immorality and idolatry which produces 'pagan children'. **V 8–9: DESOLATION DEFINITE** The watchman's trumpet in Ramah and Beth Aven will herald the attack from outside that will make God's rebellious people desolate. **V 10–12: WAITING WRATH** God's wrath is waiting to be poured out on the princes of Judah, in their oppression and dishonesty, on Ephraim, who has preferred human precept to God's word, and on Judah, who has followed wicked Israel despite God's warning. **V 13–15: HELP HOPELESS** Ephraim and Judah have asked for help from an outside king. God says this is hopeless because such a king cannot help them. God will be violently against them until they repent of their sin. He must afflict them to make them earnestly seek Him.

CHAPTER SIX

V 1–3: REAL REPENTANCE? The words 'Come, let us return to the LORD' seem to signify a change of heart but, on closer reading, there is no mention of turning from sin, only relief from the consequences of it. While it is true that God will come to Israel (and to the repentant sinner) 'like the rain', He requires repentance from sin first. **V 4–6: MORNING MIST** God's response is to tell Ephraim (again standing for Israel) and Judah that their repentance is like a cloud of morning mist, a light dew that goes away so quickly. This superficial repentance has long averted His judgement before, but will not do so

again. God desires mercy to be given and received, and their knowledge of Him to be more than a mere external observance of sacrifice. **V 7–11: SIN'S SATURATION** Transgression of God's covenant, such as bloodshed and robbery, murderous priests, and lewd idolatry, all underlines the need for repentance. A harvest of judgement is reserved for Judah as well as for Israel.

CHAPTER SEVEN

V 1–2: INTERVENING INIQUITY Here, again, Ephraim represents Israel. Samaria is the capital city of the northern kingdom. Just when God would have healed Israel, Israel moves away from any place of repentance. Fraud, theft, robbery, hard hearts and wicked deeds put them out of reach of mercy and spiritual healing. **V 3–7: ROTTEN RULERS** Their rulers appease wickedness and lies. Their adultery, drunkenness, scoffing, and rejection of God lead a rebellious people even further away from God. Despite that, He remains willing to pardon them if they repent. But they refuse to call upon Him. **V 8–10: SIMPLE SOLUTION** Israel will neither recognise her failures, nor confess her compromised and half-baked spiritual life that is marked by pride. All God asks is that they return to God from sin and seek Him. **V 11–16: SUBSTITUTE SAVIOURS** Rather than calling out to God for forgiveness and help, Israel turns vainly to other nations which will ultimately betray her. Like Israel, many today vainly seek inadequate and powerless saviours rather than the only Lord and true Saviour.

CHAPTER EIGHT

V 1–3: IMPENDING DOOM God, through Hosea, tells Israel to sound the trumpet alarm as the invading nation (Syria) will come upon God's rebellious people who have rejected His covenant, law and goodness. Their cry to Him will be ineffective because there is no repentance. **V 4–6: IDOLATROUS DEVOTION** God repeats that the kings and idols of silver and gold have been worshipped by His people. They have followed calf-worship, imported from idolatrous neighbours. The calf of Samaria will be smashed. **V 7–9: INEVITABLE DEFEAT** Israel has sown the wind of rebellion and will reap the whirlwind of devastation. Aliens will overcome Israel completely. **V 10: INGATHERING DELIVERANCE** Yet even in this judgement, God again prophesies that one day He will gather in His people to Himself. **V 11–14: INSTRUCTION DESPISED** In all the idolatry and false sacrifices, Ephraim has sinned and rejected God's law. Israel has chosen to forget God and Judah has built up mere human defences which will not protect against God's impending judgement. With all the blessings that God showers upon His people, they have despised His instructions and will reap accordingly.

CHAPTER NINE

V 1–2: REJOICING TO EVAPORATE When ungodly nations rejoice, Israel has no cause to rejoice. Her spiritual harlotry against God, often manifested in physical immorality, will mean that she will benefit from neither the food nor the drink that they have produced. **V 3–4: RETURN TO EGYPT** Egypt stands for captivity in the minds of the Israelites. The 'return to Egypt' signifies the return to captivity under Assyria. Because of their uncleanness and rebellion, their offerings will be like mourning in captivity. **V 5–17: RESPONSE TO EVIL** God will respond to the evil of His people by

captivity, destruction of their land, loss of valuables, absence of faithful prophets, remembrance of their wickedness and sins, departed glory, loss of fruitfulness and of children, miscarriages, famine, exclusion from God's house, suspension of the experience of God's love, and being cast away by God. God's severe response is because His people will not obey Him. They will wander among hostile and ungodly nations.

CHAPTER TEN

V 1–2: SELF-SUFFICIENCY One of Israel's problems is self-sufficiency. The very bounty of God has led them to neglect Him in self-sufficiency and to rely on their idolatrous practices. **V 3–4: REJECTED RULER** God is rejected as their King, and many of their previous kings were useless to them because of their dishonesty and failure to respect God and His laws. They could not lead the people into godliness. **V 5–8: IDOLATORS' IMPOTENCE** Calf-worship in Beth Aven is a passion of the priests and the people. The meaningless idol will be carried to Assyria as a present for its king. It is useless to deliver Israel, who will realise that its counsel of idolatry is worthless. Idolatrous idols will lie barren and overgrown as God's people ask the mountains to fall on them to save them from the rigours of captivity. **V 9–11: CHILDREN'S CHASTENING** God will use ungodly Gentiles to chasten His ungodly children. They will all be put to hard labour. Previously, His children were like a trained heifer, unfettered and free to thresh the corn and eat what she wanted. Now, the previously trained heifer will be put to pull a plough, under close control of the captors. **V 12: RAINING RIGHTEOUSNESS** But still God says that He will come and 'rain righteousness on you'. (He will sow in righteousness, and reap in mercy.) God requires their repentance, and the breaking up of their fallow ground, in order to deal with them in such mercy and grace. **V 13–15: HORRIFIC HARVEST** But for now, God's people have ploughed the seeds of wickedness into their lives, and iniquity is being reaped. The fruit of this is lies and self-trust. Thus Israel will be plundered, smashed and cut off.

CHAPTER ELEVEN

V 1–4: LEAVING LOVE God has rescued His people of Israel and taught them how to walk properly and uprightly. Yet they have left His love and followed Baal worship and idolatry. They continue to go further away from Him. **V 5–7: REPENTANCE REFUSED** Despite the fact that cruel captivity is foretold, God's people are determined to backslide. Their empty prayer means nothing. **V 8–11: GOD'S GATHERING** Yet God cannot give up Israel, and one day will gather them from all over the world and establish them in their land, in their houses. They shall walk with Him in that day. **V 12: DISHONESTY DEMONSTRATED** Ephraim and Israel are filled with lies and deceit. (At this stage Judah is the exception, according to some translations, but is also at fault according to others.)

CHAPTER TWELVE

V 1: COMPROMISED COVENANT Ephraim's empty life involves increased lying and desolation and making a covenant with the Assyrians. Additionally, Ephraim seeks to gain the favour of the king of Egypt. **V 2–6: CONTINUANCE COMMANDED** God cites the father of the nation, Jacob (also called 'Israel'), as an example of perseverance. Not only did he demonstrate this in the

hour of his birth, but also in his persevering prayer when he wrestled with the angel of God. Israel is commanded to observe mercy and justice and wait continually on the God of their fathers. **V 7–8: COMING CANAANITES** The word 'Canaanite' is so linked with trading that it came to mean 'merchant'. Israel has become as deceitful and dishonest as a fraudulent trader and is so taken up with wealth that she does not recognise her own sin. **V 9: CAPTIVITY COMING** Just as the Feast of Tabernacles signifies Israel's living in tents or booths in the past, so in the coming captivity, Israel will again live in such low circumstances. **V 10: CLEAR COUNSEL** Her sin is compounded by the fact that God has clearly spoken to her by prophets and by visions. He has shown them His word and she has rejected it—and still does. **V 11–13: CONTINUING CONESEQUENCES** The idol altars of God's rebellious children will become heaps in the fields. God's reproach for their sin will remain upon them. They have not learned the lessons from Israel's history of the need to turn from wandering and to trust in God. The consequences of their evil will continue until they repent.

CHAPTER THIRTEEN

V 1: POWER AND PRIDE Ephraim, the largest and most powerful tribe of Israel, was exalted in Israel when he 'spoke, trembling'. Yet Israel 'died' as a powerful witness to God when pride led to Baal worship. **V 2–3: TRANSGRESSION AND TRANSIENCE** Now, sin is increasing and idolatry with it. Any goodness of Ephraim, and Israel, is like a morning cloud of mist that passes away, and like chaff or smoke that is blown around. **V 4–6: FAITHFULNESS AND FEARLESSNESS** God has always been faithful to Israel. He redeemed them from Egypt, looked after them in the wilderness, and is unique as their Saviour and their God. Yet despite this faithfulness, their pride exalted them when they prospered, and they forgot God. They are still in that position, now, as Hosea addresses them. **V 7–11: DESTRUCTION AND DELIVERANCE** God will destroy them because of their sinfulness. Yet finally, He will help them as their King. He will not be like the transient and unfaithful kings that they have had in the past. **V 12–13: SIN AND SORROW** Because of Ephraim's store of sin, great sorrow and pain will come upon them. **V 14–16: RANSOM AND REBELLION** Hosea contrasts the future blessing of Israel in their ransom and deliverance from death and the grave with their present dryness, rebellion and guilt. They face impending judgement for their sins because of their refusal to repent.

CHAPTER FOURTEEN

V 1–3: WORDS TO TAKE The last chapter in Hosea is powerful, comforting and full of hope. It shows the way back to God and reiterates God's promise of restoration. What is good for Israel as a nation is good, in principle, for anyone who is now away from God. God even gives words to take in prayer, provided there is a truly repentant heart and a looking to Him alone as the Saviour. **V 4–8: WAYWARDNESS TO TERMINATE** 'I will heal their backsliding' is one of the sweetest messages of Scripture. Finally, God will turn His anger away and receive His beloved people and bless them spiritually and materially. This will produce spiritual freshness like the dew, growth like a lily taking root downwards and progressing upwards, beauty like an olive tree, and fragrance like Lebanon. The same principles apply to the sinner responding to the gospel, or the backsliding Christian coming back to the Lordship of Christ. The result of this blessing is that idolatry and sin will be forsaken, and God's fruit will be evident in His repentant people. **V 9: WISDOM TO TRUST** God's right ways are to be trusted and walked in by the righteous. This is how wisdom and prudence are imparted to those who come to know Him and walk with Him.

JOEL

OVERVIEW

PEOPLE AND PRELIMINARIES

✳ Joel (three chapters) is the second of the twelve 'minor prophets'. See comments on Hosea. It was written by Joel between 835 BC and 796 BC, probably in or near Jerusalem. Joel was a contemporary of Elisha.

PLAN AND PURPOSE

ⓘ Joel prophesies 'long term' concerning the coming judgement on 'the Day of the Lord', and uses a catastrophic local plague of locusts to illustrate this. He arouses those to whom he ministers in Judea, in or near Jerusalem, to consider their ways, and to repent, fast and pray. Judgement on Gentile nations will come. Israel will be blessed after suffering God's chastening. The book ends on the note of restoration.

The plague of locusts (1:1–20); the Day of the Lord to come (2:1–2:32); the restoration of Israel (3:1–21).

PRINCIPLES AND PARTICULARS

The vivid descriptive language of an invasion by an army of locusts demonstrates Hosea's God-given ability to take such a major event from current affairs, apply it searchingly, and use it to pass on God's message concerning a far more severe judgement to come.

JOEL

CHAPTER ONE

V 1–4: LOCUSTS Joel is a prophet of God. He is only referred to in one other place in the Bible, in the book of Acts. Locusts have devastated the land, and he uses this as a basis for the start of his prophecy. **V 5–14: LAMENTATION** He bids the country lament like a young widow. This wake-up call comes through the tremendous consequences of the devastating stripping of the land by locusts. Drunkards, priests, farmers, and vineyard dressers are his immediate points of reference. Mourning and prayer are called for as the priests are to summon the nation to a sacred assembly with the elders present. They are to 'cry out to the LORD'. God can use natural disasters to heighten a sense of need for Him. **V 15–20: LORD** The prophet then uses the terrible physical situation to underline that the 'day of the LORD is at hand'. God's judgement will come like locusts on Israel. Joy, gladness, fruitfulness and success will dry up as that day comes.

CHAPTER TWO

V 1–9: DESTRUCTION OF THE LAND A vivid picture is given of destruction of the land by an army of locusts. **V 10–11: DAY OF THE LORD** This 'great and very terrible' day of the LORD, in which judgement will be poured out upon sin, is prefigured by the horror of the locust invasion. **V 12–14: DIRECTIONS OF THE LORD** Through Joel, God commands His people to repent, telling them to turn to Him wholeheartedly and to mourn. He is looking at their hearts and not at the externals. He is 'gracious and merciful, slow to anger and of great kindness'. Blessing and access is always possible where people are prepared to listen to God's message and turn to Him. **V 15–17: DEPTH OF THE LAMENTATION** Such repentance must be marked by real heart sorrow demonstrated by outward action. Thus Israel is to fast, gather together to pray, include the whole of the population, and be led by repentant, weeping priests who are to plead for God's mercy and for the honour of His name to be realised among the nations around. The lamentation is to be deep, heartfelt and real. **V 18–32: DELIVERANCE FROM THE LORD** In response to such repentance, God will bless the land and make it fruitful. He will pour down His rain and blessing, restore the years that the locusts have eaten, and meet all the physical needs of His people. But more than that, their repentance will be met by a pouring out of His Holy Spirit with signs that demonstrate it. There will also be signs in heaven and on the earth and 'whoever calls upon the name of the Lord shall be saved'. This passage has a threefold application: it refers in principle to Israel in their current situation; it addresses the end times; and it reveals the principle of blessing that God always uses to restore sinners who will turn to God through Christ. It has partial fulfilment in the day of Pentecost but is yet to be fulfilled in all its wonder. Meanwhile, God's offer of salvation is open to 'whoever calls on the name of the LORD' in repentance and faith.

CHAPTER THREE

V 1–2a: THE VALLEY The final judgement of the nations in the end times will include their being brought to the 'Valley of Jehoshaphat' (also called 'The valley of decision' later in this chapter). This name means that God judges, and reminds us that King Jehoshaphat saw one of God's amazing victories over nations in 2 Chronicles 20. **V 2b–6: THE VIOLATION** Although God has used nations to chastise and punish His rebellious people, He still holds those nations guilty and accountable for the wicked things they have done to His beloved Israel. This includes taking His people into captivity, buying up God's land, harlotry and child

slavery, desecration of God's temple and worship, and slavery. God will judge them for all of this. **V 7–8: THE VINDICATION** God will raise up His people and make them retaliate against the oppressing nations, who will suffer in similar ways to Israel. **V 9–17: THE VICTORY** In the Valley of Jehoshaphat, the nations will gather against Israel. They will be reaped in God's judgement as the 'Day of the LORD' comes. God will 'roar from Zion and utter His voice from Jerusalem'. Amidst amazing and exceptional natural signs, the nations will be judged and Israel will be re-established. God will have the victory in history. **V 18–21: THE VISION** In those days, while the enemies of Israel become desolate because of their violence against God's people, Israel and Judah will be established for ever. They will be greatly blessed by God in His wonderful provision and His acquitting them from all their sin, in His mercy and grace. All will know the vision is fulfilled when 'the LORD dwells in Zion'.

AMOS

OVERVIEW

PEOPLE AND PRELIMINARIES

Amos (nine chapters) is the third of the twelve 'minor prophets'. See comments on Hosea. It was written probably by Amos about 750 BC. Amos was a 'layman' from Tekoa, near to Bethlehem in the south. He prophesied during the time of King Jeroboam II, in the northern kingdom of Israel at Bethel, the religious capital of the backslidden idolatrous nation. It is probable he wrote this book there.

PLAN AND PURPOSE

(i) Amos denounces the superficial and ritualistic worship of a people whose heart is not for God, and the injustice that follows their bad treatment of their neighbours. Amos announces God's coming judgement on other nations before focusing on His coming dealings with Israel. But God's covenant faithfulness will mean a remnant of His people will be saved and restored. To present His prophetic truth, God gives Amos a series of visions concerning locusts, fire, a plumb line, a basket of fruit, and the altar.

PROFILE AND PROGRESSION

Judgements against surrounding nations (1:1–2:3); judgements against Judah and Israel (2:4–16); God's condemnation of His own people (3:1–6:14); a series of visions given to Amos underlining both God's coming judgements and restoration (7:1–9:15).

PRINCIPLES AND PARTICULARS

Amos is a herdsman. This rustic 'layman' moves from Judah in the south to Israel in the north. His new environment is more sophisticated but it is sinfully compromised and spiritually dark. He faithfully represents his Lord with an unpopular but necessary message. His warnings may seem improbable, but nevertheless the kingdom will be destroyed within fifty years. God has His own reason for choosing 'the weak things of the world' to declare and show His strength and power. He will perform His sovereign will, however improbable that may seem to those who do not heed Him.

AMOS

CHAPTER ONE

V 1: PROPHET'S PARTICULARS Amos is a sheep-breeder from Tekoa who prophesies against Israel and Judah during the reigns of Jeroboam in Israel and Uzziah in Judah. **V 2: RULER ROARS** The LORD is depicted as roaring from Zion and Jerusalem, as when a lion attacks the flock. Mourning follows and fertile Carmel withers. **V 3–5: DAMASCUS DAMNED** Before pronouncing judgement on Israel and on Judah, Amos carries the message of

judgement on the nations which have oppressed them. Damascus will suffer because of Syria's cruel attacks on Israel. They themselves will also be taken captive. **V 6–8: GAZA'S GRIEF** Because Gaza took captive the whole of the population, it will be devoured by the fire that God will send. He is against the Philistines. **V 9–10: TYRE'S TYRANNY** In delivering Israel to their enemy Edom, Tyre reneged on the covenant of brotherhood that they had enjoyed with Israel since the days of David. God will send fire upon them. **V 11–12: EDOM'S END** The continuous anger and the compassionless pursuit of Israel by Edom, and its continuous anger against her, mean that God will send fire upon Edom. **V 13–15: AMMON AXED** Ammon, too, will suffer from fire from God which will devour its palaces. Its king and princes will go into captivity as the axe of God's judgement falls upon Ammon. They have cruelly ripped open pregnant women in Gilead.

CHAPTER TWO

V 1–3: MOAB'S MISERY Moab will also be punished by fire from God, and its palaces will be burned. Moab will die as judges and princes will be cut off. Moab took vengeance too far by burning 'the bones of the king of Edom to lime', something not mentioned anywhere else in the Bible. **V 4–5: JUDAH'S JUDGEMENT** Having pronounced judgement on six of the enemies of Israel and Judah, God now pronounces judgement on Judah and then on Israel. Judah has despised God's law, disobeyed His commands, and followed lies which led her astray. Again, God will send fire and devour its palaces. **V 6–16: ISRAEL'S INIQUITY** The main burden of Amos is to pronounce judgement on Israel. Her wicked lifestyle shows her spiritual departure from God. Israel is guilty of slave-trading, exploitation of the poor, perversion of justice, gross immorality, sacrilege, wantonness, self-sufficiency, backsliding from God's standards and blessings, leading godly people astray, and forbidding God's word to be faithfully spoken. Amos reminds Israel that she cannot deliver herself in the day when God judges. God is 'weighed down' by all the iniquities of His chosen people.

CHAPTER THREE

V 1-2: RECIPIENTS Amos' message is against God's 'whole family' which includes Judah as well as Israel. God takes special responsibility for His earthly people, including punishing them for their iniquities. How grateful is the Christian that he looks back to see that his punishment for sin has been taken fully by Christ. **V 3-6: REASON** Amos uses various illustrations to show that there is always a reason that triggers a consequence. In this case, calamity for Israel is a consequence of God's punishing them. **V 7-8: ROARING** God never acts in judgement without warning His people through His prophets. They should fear His word as one should fear a roaring lion. Amos must prophesy because God has 'roared'. **V 9-10: RHETORIC** Amos rhetorically invites Israel's enemies—the Philistines and the Egyptians—to witness how wicked, violent, and dishonest Israel has become. **V 11: RUIN** Because of all this, God will send an adversary to weaken and plunder Israel. (This was fulfilled when the Assyrians took Israel captive.) **V 12: REMNANT** A remnant of Israel will be saved, just as a shepherd snatches the remnant of a stray lamb from the mouth of a lion he has killed. **V 13-15:**

RETRIBUTION When God punishes the people of Israel for their transgressions, He will destroy both the altars which are being used for idolatrous sacrifice, and all their houses.

CHAPTER FOUR

V 1: BASHAN'S COWS The luxury-loving, wine-bibbing, oppressive wives of Samaria are referred to as 'cows of Bashan'. God has a word of judgement through Amos for them, too. **V 2-3: 'BEHOLD'—CAPTIVITY** When these wanton women are taken captive, they will be led away through breaches in the walls. They will be part of the miserable captivity and their living in luxury will be at an end. **V 4-5: BETHEL'S CONDEMNATION** Jacob, the father of Israel, met God in a dream at Bethel and was circumcised at Gilgal. Now Israel's children love to offer idolatrous sacrifices at these landmark places of spirituality and blessing. **V 6-10: BLESSINGS CURTAILED** God has curtailed His blessings of food, rain, drink, and fruitfulness. Israel was plagued, as Egypt was, and the stench of death was in its cities, as even young men died. Despite all those judgements, Israel did not return to God. **V 11: BRASH CONTINUATION** Although God has already judged His people on numerous occasions and saved some from His judgement, like a 'firebrand plucked from the burning', yet He repeats for the fifth time in this chapter, 'Yet you have not returned to Me.' God's withholding of blessings and allowing afflictions are intended to produce repentance and turning to Him. His hardened rebellious people have brashly failed to repent. **V 12-13: BITTER CONSEQUENCES** God tells Israel to be prepared to meet Him, when He will act against them because they have failed to repent. He reminds them of the awe due to Him because of His great power and authority.

CHAPTER FIVE

V 1–3: LAMENT Amos takes up a lament for Israel as if she is a young woman who has died. Israel's military strength is decimated, with only a small proportion returning of those who left their cities to fight. **V 4–7: LIVE!** Amos calls Israel to repentance and to seek God in order that the nation may live. Such life will be found in God alone and not in the reputation of the past. God, who can give life, will bring judgement if there is no repentance or seeking Him. **V 8–9: LORD** God is revealed, again, as the great Creator with power to judge as He deems fit in His righteousness and sovereign strength. **V 10–13: LOSS** Israel's sins will cause great loss to be sustained. All her efforts will be unproductive and futile because God's rebuke is despised, the poor are trodden down, justice is denied, bribes are taken, and wise people keep their mouths closed. Israel's 'mighty sins' are the cause for the loss of blessing and judgement to come. **V 14–15: LOVE** Israel's repentance must be shown by hating evil and loving good. If the people love to do good, they will seek it instead of evil. Only then will they know the presence of God, and the possibility of the return of His gracious dealing with Israel. **V 16–20: LIGHT?** When the 'Day of the LORD' arrives, it will not be a time of light, but a time of darkness and fear, as God judges His sinful people. There will be wailing in the streets and at the workplace. Irrational optimism that 'all will be well' will soon evaporate. In fact, things will get far worse, not better. **V 21–27: LOATHING** God expresses His loathing of mere outward observances, of sacrifices and

singing that seek to cover up idolatry and an unjust and unrighteous heart. It was so in Israel's past, when God sent them into captivity. It will be so again. God wants justice and righteousness to be expressed by hearts that turn from sin and trust Him.

CHAPTER SIX

V 1–2: COMPLACENCY Those at ease and with false confidence, in Zion and Samaria, are told to consider the foreign cities which have fallen to judgement. How, then, can they escape? **V 3–8: CAPTIVITY** In all the leisure, laxity and self-indulgence of Israel's ease, there is no grief for the state of the people spiritually, and thus no repentance. For this reason, the nation will go into captivity and the banqueting will be finished. Pride against God is the root cause. **V 9–11: COMPREHENSIVENESS** That captivity will involve dead bodies being taken out of houses to be burned. There will be few survivors. As a result of God's judgement, His name will not be mentioned. **V 12–13: CONFUSED** Israel's thinking has been confused by her sinfulness and pride. She claims justice and strength that she does not have. The so-called justice practised by Israel is as out of place as horses running or oxen ploughing on rock. She proudly thinks that her own strength, rather than God, has enabled her to make her past conquests. **V 14: CONQUEST** God will correct her twisted and proud thinking about her justice and strength by raising up a nation (which turned out to be Assyria) to conquer her.

CHAPTER SEVEN

V 1–3: REVEALED VISION 1:—POWERFUL LOCUSTS God shows Amos powerful swarms of locusts which will devour the late crop. Understanding this to indicate the downfall of Israel, Amos pleads for God's people. God grants his request that He will not fulfil this vision. **V 4–6: REVEALED VISION 2:—PARCHED LAND** God reveals that the land will be consumed by fire which causes a drought so severe that even the water supply dries up. Again Amos pleads, and God promises not to accomplish the vision. **V 7–9: REVEALED VISION 3:—PLUMBLINE** God again reveals a vision to Amos in which He measures wicked and idolatrous Israel with a plumb line. Their perverted centres of worship will be thrown down and a sword will come against Israel. Amos accepts that this oppression and following captivity is God's will for His rebellious people. **V 10–13: RESISTED VISIONS—PRIEST'S LAXITY** Amaziah, Bethel's priest, reports Amos to Jeroboam, king of Israel, as a conspirator, and then tells Amos to flee from the city. The religious and political centre at Bethel does not want to hear such messages! **V 14–17: REINFORCED VISIONS—PROPHET'S LOYALTY** Amos tells him that God has taken him from an ordinary occupation to prophesy to Israel. Dismissing the words of unfaithful Amaziah, he then prophesies against him personally, and against his family, as well as prophesying that Israel will be taken captive. Such loyalty to God in the face of opposition can only come from a close walk with Him.

CHAPTER EIGHT

V 1–4: GRIEF IMMINENT A fourth vision of a basket of summer fruit is given to Amos. Just as a basket of summer fruit is ripe for eating, so Israel is ripe for God's judgement. There will be great grief as worship is stopped. Wailing will be heard, and death will be everywhere. Those who have persecuted the poor will themselves be in great grief in that day. **V 5–6: GREEDY IMPATIENCE** Israel cannot wait for the New Moon Feast or the Sabbath to finish so they can embark again upon their dishonest trade and money-making. In so doing, the poor will be exploited mercilessly. **V 7–14: GOD'S INTERVENTION** God will not forget any of Israel's evil works. He will make the land 'tremble for this'. In the day of the LORD there will be darkness, mourning, lamentation, famine of God's word, aimless wandering, fleeing, and the downfall of the idolatrous rebel people of God.

CHAPTER NINE

V 1–10: RUIN The destruction and ruin of Israel is foretold in the fifth vision of Amos. In it, the LORD is standing by the altar. Judgement and death will fall upon His people and there will be no hiding place for them. Even in captivity, God will judge them. God reveals Himself, again, as a powerful Creator who is willing and able to bring about His judgement by destroying the house of Jacob. He will sift them and make sure that calamity falls upon the unrepentant rebels. **V 11–15: RESTORATION** Yet this chapter, and the whole of the book, ends on a note that shows God's heart for His people. He will finally repair the damage, raise up the ruins, and rebuild His people and His land. He will also bless Gentiles who trust in Him. Hope, blessing and fruitfulness will follow in the land which God has given them. God longs to bless those who repent and turn to Him, whether the nation of Israel or individual sinners.

OBADIAH

OBADIAH

OVERVIEW

PEOPLE AND PRELIMINARIES

✳Obadiah (one chapter) is the fourth and shortest of the twelve 'minor prophets'. See comments on Hosea. It was written by Obadiah in Judah between 850 BC and 840 BC.

PLAN AND PURPOSE

ⓘThe book pronounces God's judgement on the Edomites, descendants of Esau, in terms of its punishment for its proud wrongdoing. Specifically, God saw Edom's failure to support Israel, or seek to rescue her when she was attacked, as violence against her. Judgement upon all nations is also pronounced and the final restoration of Israel is predicted.

PROFILE AND PROGRESSION

🐚 God's judgement on Edom for her evil (1:1–14); God's judgement on heathen nations (1:15,16); God's deliverance and restoration of Israel ((1:17–21).

PRINCIPLES AND PARTICULARS

👉Failure to help one's own brothers is condemned by God and will carry consequences. Pride is shown to be at the heart of sins. There is a constant link in this book, as in the wider context of Scripture, between judgement for sins and restoration of the repentant sinner.

CHAPTER ONE

V 1: EDOM Obadiah's vision concerns Edom. Edom will be opposed by other nations and cut off in battle. Edom is the nation that came from Esau and is therefore related to the Israelites, because Esau and Jacob (Israel) were the twin sons of Isaac and Rebekah. Despite that relationship, Edom is one of Israel's fiercest enemies throughout their history. **V 2–4: EXTRACTION** Edom is well installed in mountain fortresses and thinks no one can cause her to come down in any sense. God says that He will extract her from her mountain fortress. **V 5–9: EXECUTION** God will use an internal confederacy inside Edom to topple her. So great will be her downfall that she will be 'cut off by slaughter'. The nation will be executed. **V 10–14: ENMITY** This is because of Edom's enmity against Israel and the fact that she rejoiced at Israel's captivity, plundered Jerusalem, and prevented escapees from making a full escape. **V 15–16: EXAMPLE** On the 'day of the LORD', God will judge all nations and His judgement on Edom will prefigure this. In effect, Edom will be an example to the nations of how God will judge those who oppose Him and His children. **V 17–21: ELEVATION** By contrast, deliverance will come to Israel. As Esau perishes, Israel will prosper materially and spiritually with holiness. Israel will again possess the land, including that currently possessed by Edom. On that day, after judgement of the nations on the 'day of the LORD', Obadiah proclaims that 'the kingdom shall be the LORD's'.

JONAH

OVERVIEW

PEOPLE AND PRELIMINARIES

✱ Written by the reluctant prophet of the same name, in about 775 BC, Jonah (four chapters) is the fifth of the twelve 'minor prophets'. See comments on Hosea. The book could have been written in the northern kingdom of Israel or in Nineveh, the capital of Assyria.

PLAN AND PURPOSE

ⓘ The book shows how God will forgive anyone who repents. This is as true for a disobedient servant of His as it is for the threatening enemies of His people, in this case the Assyrians at Nineveh. Jonah's reluctance and rebellion over going to preach repentance in the Assyrian capital of Nineveh is because he knows that God will have mercy on the Assyrians if they repent, and he sees them, quite correctly, as a great threat to Israel's safety. This book underlines the need for those who know God to obey Him unconditionally. It also reminds us that God is sovereign in His timing and in the way He arranges circumstances.

PROFILE AND PROGRESSION

🐚 Jonah's original commission, disobedience and three-day incarceration in the great fish (1:1–17); Jonah's prayer and proving that 'salvation is of the LORD' (2:1–9); Jonah's renewed commission, obedience, the Ninevites' radical repentance and God's working in mercy (3:1–10); Jonah displeased and God displeased: the contrast between Jonah wanting his own way and God's compassionate desire to save (4:1–11).

PRINCIPLES AND PARTICULARS

☞ God prepares four things in order to have His way with His prophet, including the 'great fish' (believed by some to be a whale). God will have His way with His servants eventually. We must put obedience to God even before national loyalty. Rebellion against God, for whatever reason, is illogical and stupid, as well as sinful. God will always forgive repentant sinners, whether we like them or not! Jonah sets the biblical groundwork for Jesus' prophecy of His death and resurrection—a much greater miracle than the prophet's survival after being swallowed by the fish.

JONAH

CHAPTER ONE

V 1–3: FOOLISH FLEEING God tells His prophet, Jonah, to go and preach to wicked Nineveh. Instead, he runs away from the LORD to go to Tarshish in a ship that he takes from Joppa. He thinks he can escape the presence of the LORD by changing his geographical position. How foolish! **V 4–5: STORMY SEAS** God sends a storm on the sea, so severe that the sailors fear that the ship will be broken up. Cargo is thrown out to lighten the load, but Jonah is below deck, fast asleep. **V 6–9: CONFESSION COMPELLED** The captain knows that Jonah acknowledges God and asks him to call on God. There is no hint that Jonah does that. By casting lots, the sailors find out, either by chance or by divine providence, that Jonah is the cause of the trouble at sea. He then has to confess that he is a Hebrew, and that he 'fears the LORD, the God of heaven, who made the sea and the dry land'. **V 10–16: JONAH JETTISONED** The men know that Jonah is fleeing from God because he tells them so. He tells them to throw him into the sea, and the sea will become calm. The men, nevertheless, try to row to land but fail to do so and reluctantly throw Jonah overboard. The sea becomes calm. The men fear God and offer a sacrifice to Him. **V 17: PREPARED PATH** Jonah's future path is prepared. A great fish, sent by God, swallows Jonah, and he is in its belly for three days and three nights.

CHAPTER TWO

V 1–7: PROPHET'S PRAYER Sometimes God puts His rebellious people in a place where they have to pray to Him to be set free and to get to know Him better. So it is that Jonah prays to God from the belly of the fish. His prayer acknowledges God's dealings with him, the fact that he cannot help himself, his own despair, his remembering God, and God's promise to answer prayer prayed towards His temple. He also recalls, in his prayer, 'You heard my voice.' **V 8–9: PENITENT'S PRIORITIES** Jonah shows that he knows he cannot trust idols, but that his sacrifice must be directed to God alone and with thanksgiving. Also, there must be a sincerity to pay what has been vowed and an acknowledgement to 'pay what has been offered to the Lord'. These are the priorities of a penitent man or woman. Jonah acknowledges that only God can bring about salvation. **V 10: PUZZLING PROVISION** God answers Jonah's prayer by the provision of dry land, in the right place and at the right time, when the fish vomits him out. No doubt Jonah is more than a little puzzled to find himself there! Although he is still at least 600 miles from

Nineveh, God has put him back en route. God is sovereign in circumstances and in timing, all of which He can plan and co-ordinate so easily.

CHAPTER THREE

V 1–4: GRACIOUS RE-COMMISSIONING The restored rebel prophet is re-commissioned to go to Nineveh and preach God's message. He goes and tells that large and wicked city to repent because, in forty days, it shall be overthrown. **V 5–9: GREAT REPENTANCE** So repentant are the people, from the greatest to the least, that they mourn, wear sackcloth, and sit in ashes. The king issues a decree telling all the people to turn from their wickedness and violence and to seek God's ways, in the hope that He will turn from His anger and save them. **V 10: GOD RELENTS** God sees from their works that they have turned from their sin. He relents of the judgement He had planned. Under His sovereign will, His threats of judgement are always conditional. Repentance and faith always meet with His mercy and grace. In answering prayers of confession from broken people, God achieves His plan and purpose.

CHAPTER FOUR

V 1–4: ANGER ADDRESSED Jonah knew that if Nineveh, an avowed enemy of the Israelites, repented, she might rise to beat Israel in the future. This is probably why he is angry at Nineveh's restoration by his 'gracious and merciful God'. He asks God to take his life, which God does not do. Rather, God challenges him about his anger. **V 5–8: PROVIDENTIAL PREPARATIONS** Jonah continues to hope that Nineveh will be destroyed, and he goes to the east side to make a shelter to observe. God prepares a plant to shade Jonah from the sun, and Jonah is grateful. God then prepares a worm to destroy the plant. Without the shelter, and being battered by a vehement wind, Jonah again wishes to die. (However, he does not attempt the sin of suicide.) **V 9–11: PERISHING PITIED** God challenges Jonah about his anger concerning the destroyed plant, and comments that Jonah has more pity for the plant than he has for a great and wicked city in which 120,000 ignorant people would have perished if they had failed to repent. The book leaves us with the implied open question as to whether our own priorities are for the souls of men and women, or for our own preferences, prejudices and comforts.

MICAH

OVERVIEW

PEOPLE AND PRELIMINARIES

Micah wrote this book that bears his name (seven chapters) between 735 BC and 710 BC in Judah. It is the sixth of the twelve 'minor prophets'. See comments on Hosea. He prophesied against Samaria and Judah in the time of Isaiah during the reigns in Judah of Jotham, Ahaz and Hezekiah and the reigns in Israel of Pekaniah, Pekah and Hoshea. An estimate of the period covered by the events in this book is forty years.

PLAN AND PURPOSE

(i) Micah's prophecies against Samaria and Judah are detailed in this book. He deals with the sins of the people, their political leaders and their religious leaders, whom he targets for the sins of exploitation, pride, false religion and false prophecies. The book's divisions are marked by three commands to 'hear', as if in a court of law, with each case heard dealing with accountability for sins and hope of forgiveness and restoration. The predicted judgements came about through Assyria on Samaria and through Sennacherib on Judah. After the judgement, there is hope for the remnant from a covenant-keeping God who blesses those who repent.

PROFILE AND PROGRESSION

The first hearing concerning Samaria, Judah, oppression, false prophets, judgement, punishment and deliverance (1:1–2:13); the second hearing concerning Israel's unjust and evil rulers and deceitful prophets—their guilt, and the coming of the Lord to lead and to deliver (3:1–5:15); the third hearing concerning God's complaints against His people, His punishment for their sins, Israel's confession, forgiveness and restoration (6:1–7:20).

PRINCIPLES AND PARTICULARS

The constant prophetic theme of sin, judgement, repentance and forgiveness is maintained. The birth of Jesus at Bethlehem is prophesied. In the last chapter, God says exactly what He seeks in and from every follower of His, then and now—justice, mercy, and humility. These are the tracks upon which the gospel train runs.

MICAH

CHAPTER ONE

V 1: MICAH This prophet comes from Moresheth and prophesies during the reigns of Jotham, Ahaz and Hezekiah, who are kings of Judah. Although his burden is mainly against the southern kingdom of Judah and Jerusalem, he also prophesies against Israel, which has Samaria as its capital. **V 2–7: MESSAGE** His message is that the sovereign, all-powerful God will judge both Israel and Judah, and smite their capitals, Jerusalem and Samaria, bringing about captivity. Idolatry, rebellion and spiritual harlotry are the reasons. **V 8–16: MOURNING** Such will be the downfall of Israel and Judah that the prophet is in personal mourning for them. The references to foreign towns underline that this will be a matter of shame when the enemies of God's people know that God's people will be carried away to them in a disastrous captivity, because of their sins.

CHAPTER TWO

V 1–5: WOE ON WICKEDNESS Through Micah, God pronounces woe on the wickedness of His people. Their land will be taken from them in a disastrous and evil destruction from a foreign nation. This is because the evil scheming of Israel and Judah causes the people to steal fields and property by violence from poor people whom they oppress. **V 6–11: PRATTLING OF PROPHETS** The wicked rebels against God's truth and Spirit tell God's prophets not to prophesy, and accuse them of prattling. They act as God's enemy, rather than as His children. They themselves promote false prophets who tell sinful people things they want to hear, rather than things God says they

need to hear. **V 12–13: RESTORATION OF REMNANT** Overshadowed by the dark cloud of the prophesied coming judgement, Micah points out the silver lining of the restoration of the remnant of Israel. They will be gathered to God as sheep to their Shepherd, and will be led out by their King 'With the LORD at their head'.

CHAPTER THREE

V 1–4: RUTHLESS RULERS The cruel rulers who ruthlessly afflict the people are told that God will not hear them. He will hide His face from them because of their evil deeds. **V 5–7: 'PEACE' PROPHETS** The false prophets tailor their message according to whether people feed them or not. Those who give them food are told there will be 'peace' and those who do not are told there will be war. God will take away their vision and their light. He will be silent to all who lead the people astray. **V 8: SPIRIT'S SUPPORT** By contrast, in his task of prophesying God's truth, Micah's power, justice and might come from 'the Spirit of the LORD'. His power is specifically 'to declare to Jacob his transgression and to Israel his sin'. **V 9–12: FAITHFUL FORTHRIGHTNESS** This is why Micah is faithful and forthright to tell the rulers, prophets and priests of Jacob and Israel of their wickedness, injustice, perversion, bloodshed, bribery and materialism. All this is so while, at the same time, they claim God's presence with them. They will be churned up, ruined, and put in heaps when God judges them.

CHAPTER FOUR

V 1–5: 'LATTER DAYS' In the 'latter days' nations from all over will come to worship God in Zion. International peace will reign and individuals will have peace to enjoy the prosperity of the land. Just as nations are following their own gods now, Israel will follow the true God then. **V 6–8: LAME DOMINANT** The sins and afflictions of God's people make them 'outcast' and 'lame'. But 'in that day', the former dominion given to the children of Israel will be restored. **V 9–13: LORD'S DELIVERANCE** The labour pains caused by sin and Babylonian captivity will all be over when God delivers and redeems His people from their enemies. Then their presumptuous creditors will be gathered by God as sheaves to a threshing floor. Israel will finally be victorious by God's deliverance, strengthening and help.

CHAPTER FIVE

V 1: BESIEGED CONQUERED In the siege of Jerusalem, Israel and Judah will be beaten and the judge will be struck. **V 2–5a: BETHLEHEM'S CHRIST** A Messianic prophecy arises like a light in a dark place. The everlasting ruler, the Lord Jesus Christ, will come out of 'little' Bethlehem Ephrathah (where King David, Israel's second most revered ruler, was also born). According to His timetable, He will stand and feed His people, and His greatness will be seen all over the earth. True peace will come with Him. This prophecy covers the whole sweep of history from Bethlehem to the end days. **V 5b–9: BEATEN CONQUERORS** Assyria and Babylon, referred to here as 'Nimrod', will take God's people captive. They themselves will be comprehensively defeated by the princes of Israel after God has restored and blessed His people. **V 10–15: BLESSED CONSEQUENCES** In that day, there will be no more need for instruments of war as God helps Israel. Sorcery, soothsaying, idolatry, and the cities associated with them will be

destroyed. Those opposing Israel will be dealt with in anger and fury.

CHAPTER SIX

V 1–2: COURT CASE God, as the Judge, asks Israel to answer the charges. He has a complaint and says, 'I will contend with Israel'. He calls the hills and mountains to be witnesses. **V 3–5: HEED HISTORY** God draws out the historical lessons of Israel's intermittent failure, His holiness and His faithfulness. They know He has delivered them and He is righteous. **V 6–8: REAL REQUIREMENT** Micah declares that it is neither Israel's prescribed external sacrifices, nor the perverted and cruel sacrifices of the idolaters that please God. The one thing He requires is 'to do justly, to love mercy, and to walk humbly with your God'. This requirement is neglected and rejected by Israel. **V 9–16: CONDEMNATION'S CONSEQUENCES** Because of God's people's wickedness, dishonesty, injustice, deceit, violence, and lying, God is not only judging them by the sword, but they will also suffer hunger, thirst, and failure to reap what they have sown. The wickedness of their most evil rulers of the past, Omri and Ahab, is still with them, and they continue to walk in their ungodly and wicked counsels. God will make them desolate and a reproach. Having shown them the bright future, He then shows them the present and prior need for repentance.

CHAPTER SEVEN

V 1–6: MICAH'S MISERY Micah is filled with woe and misery at the abject spiritual bankruptcy and dishonest conduct of the rebel people to whom he prophesies. They should be producing fruit for God but bring forth wickedness instead. There is no trust in the land, loyalties are divided, and punishment and perplexity must come. **V 7: MICAH'S MASTER** In all of this, however, he says, 'Therefore, I will look to the LORD; I will look to the God of my salvation; my God will hear me.' In the most godless generation, each individual can have a relationship with God like that. We need such a relationship in order to reach our godless generation with the Word of God. We have the same Master as Micah. **V 8–10: MERCY'S MESSAGE** As Israel confesses that 'I have sinned against Him', there is, nevertheless, the confidence that the enemy will not rejoice but will be trampled down. Light, righteousness, and the knowledge of God will be experienced in the future. The principle governing Israel's future history also governs a Christian's daily walk with God. **V 11–13: MASSIVE MIGRATION** The day is coming when there will be a massive migration from the whole of the world to come to Israel to worship God. Desolation will await those who refuse to surrender and worship God in this way.

V 14–17: MICAH'S MOTIVATION Micah pleads with his God to shepherd His people as before, when He led them and blessed them, so that the nations' ridicule of God's people will be stopped. Like serpents, those nations will crawl back into their holes, fearing the 'LORD our God'. Micah's motivation is not only the blessing of those who trust God, but also the glory of the God in whom they trust. **V 18–20: MARVELLOUS MERCY** Micah's messages alternate between judgement on unrepentant sin and God's blessing in the future on His repentant and trusting people. It is fitting that the last part of the book ends with a description of God's marvellous mercy. There is no one who can pardon sin like God. His anger will not be 'for ever'. The reason is that 'He delights in mercy' which brings His compassion and His 'casting away of all our sins' into the sea of His forgiveness. All His promises of mercy down the years will be fulfilled when this marvellous mercy is finally experienced.

NAHUM

OVERVIEW

PEOPLE AND PRELIMINARIES

Nahum wrote this book (three chapters) about 650 BC, possibly in Nineveh. It is the seventh of the twelve 'minor prophets'. See comments on Hosea. He prophesied against Nineveh about 150 years after Jonah, in the reign of King Hezekiah.

PLAN AND PURPOSE

When Jonah prophesied to pagan Nineveh, the people repented from their sins, and God forgave them. Over a hundred years later, the same people again enter into sin. Their pride and wickedness will be judged. Their latter wickedness is even worse because they rebel despite having been forgiven and spared by God through their earlier repentance under Jonah's preaching. Nahum's sole message now is that they will be judged and destroyed. This will be fulfilled soon after by the Babylonian invasion and destruction of the city. God's holiness in judging sin is Nahum's theme.

The burden of Nineveh (1:1); the God who will judge sin but who promises to come with good tidings (1:2–15); Nineveh ruined in judgement (2:1–13); God's charges against Nineveh (3:1–19).

God is not only a forgiving God who pardons those who are truly repentant, whatever their sins, as Nineveh found under Jonah's preaching but He is also a holy Judge who will judge those who do not repent. Nahum's prophecy, set alongside and balancing Jonah's, is a solemn reminder of this. We need to remember both these emphases on mercy and judgement. God's Word teaches that there is eternal blessing in heaven for those who repent and believe, but eternal condemnation in hell for those who do not.

NAHUM

CHAPTER ONE

V 1: NAHUM ON NINEVEH Nahum prophesies against Nineveh, the capital of the cruel and mighty Assyria. **V 2–6: AWESOMENESS OF ALMIGHTY** He starts by describing God's jealousy, vengeance, fury and wrath towards His enemies. Although He is 'slow to anger and great in power', He will punish the wicked. Just as nature cannot resist His power, man cannot resist His judgement. **V 7–14: DELIVERANCE OR DARKNESS** Whereas deliverance will come to His trusting people, to whom He is a stronghold, the darkness of death and destruction will be poured out on His enemies, including Nineveh. **V 15: PROCLAMATION OF**

PEACE As Assyria faces judgement, God is working out His redemptive purpose for Judah. Peace will come to His people. In safety from invasion, they will perform their vows and keep God's appointed feasts.

CHAPTER TWO

V 1: WATCHMEN WARNED The watchmen are warned about coming invasion and told to get their forces ready. **V 2: RUINED RESTORED** Ruined Israel will be restored by God. **V 3–4: SCARLET SOLDIERS** Battle is prepared with scarlet-clad soldiers and chariots at the ready. **V 5–12: DEVASTATING DOWNFALL** The enemy comes in like a flood, and, amidst fear, the city of Nineveh is plundered and left empty. The lion's den has been flattened. (Possibly the destruction of the walls by a flood was a fulfilment of this prophecy.) **V 13: OMNIPOTENT OPPOSITION** God is against Nineveh, and will burn their very chariots of war in the way that Nineveh used to burn other cities. Nineveh will be cut off.

CHAPTER THREE

V 1–3: WOE 'Countless corpses' of the previously cruel aggressor lie in its streets. Woe is pronounced against 'the bloody city'. **V 4: WITCHCRAFT** Witchcraft, idolatry, and immorality are the reasons why God has brought down Nineveh, the Assyrian capital. **V 5–7: WITNESS** The public shame of Nineveh will be exposed and witnessed by other nations when God deals with it in His anger. **V 8–13: WOMEN** Just as other strongholds and seemingly impregnable towns have been brought down by God, so Nineveh will fall. Such will be the slaughter of the army and the men that only women will be left, and the city will be left open for its enemies to enter at will. **V 14–18:**

WEAKENED God invites Nineveh to strengthen itself and muster its many people, and then prophesies, through Nahum, that they will all be weakened and run away through defeat and scattering. Their time is up. Their shepherds and nobles are powerless. **V 19:**

WELCOMED The fatal wound inflicted by God through the invading army, that brings about the death of Nineveh, will bring rejoicing from all those who have been oppressed by this wicked nation in the past.

HABAKKUK

OVERVIEW

PEOPLE AND PRELIMINARIES

✳Habakkuk is the author of this book (three chapters) which is the eighth of the twelve 'minor prophets'. See comments on Hosea. He wrote it in Judah between 615 BC and 605 BC. Habakkuk probably conducted his prophetic ministry towards the end of the reign of Josiah, and just before the captivity.

PLAN AND PURPOSE

ⓘHabakkuk prophesies as the sun is about to set on the Assyrian empire and about to rise on the Babylonian empire. The book presents Habakkuk's problem, namely that he cannot understand why sin, violence and injustice can proliferate. Then, when he is told that God will judge His people by oppression from the even more heathen and extremely cruel Chaldeans, he cannot grasp how God, who is holy, can use such evil people as His instrument of judgement on His own people. (This was probably during the time that God had stayed His hand of judgement because of the repentance of Josiah.) Without a perfect understanding, Habakkuk

humbly prays for God's mercy, and praises Him for His mighty power. He finds his comfort in God who is His strength and who remains faithful in all circumstances, even adverse ones.

PROFILE AND PROGRESSION

Habakkuk's frustration—the character of God, the waywardness of His people and God's purpose to use the Chaldeans (1:1–17); Habakkuk's fear—seeking God and getting His answer (2:1–20); Habakkuk's faith—God's glory and Habakkuk's unconditional faith in Him even when nothing seems to go right for him (3:1–19).

PRINCIPLES AND PARTICULARS

Habakkuk's open approach to God causes him to voice everything to Him, even his inability to understand what is happening and how God seems to act against His own character. In turn, this leads to his being content to accept God's way and God's word. God controls the affairs of men, even bringing good out of evil circumstances and through enemies. God is so sovereign that He can take and use those who sin against His standards and His word, to produce His own perfect pre-planned will, without ever being the author of their sin. The cross of Calvary is all about that, too.

HABAKKUK

CHAPTER ONE

V 1–4: WICKEDNESS The prophet, Habakkuk, enters into a dialogue with God. Habakkuk's first question is to enquire how long he must cry out in prophecy without an apparent answer. Wickedness of all kinds seems to proliferate in Israel. **V 5–11: WATCH!** God tells him to watch and see the amazing thing that He will do. He will bring up the 'terrible and dreadful' Chaldeans (the Babylonians) and judge Israel through them. Israel will be taken captive. **V 12–17: WHY?** Habakkuk knows that God is eternal, and he does not think that Israel will die. He then asks why God proposes to use someone as wicked as the Babylonians to judge a nation which, though rebellious and sinful, is less wicked than the coming oppressors. Surely God is too pure to use someone so wicked and cruel?

CHAPTER TWO

V 1–4: WAIT! As Habakkuk sets himself as a watchman to see how God will work, God tells him to write down a vision and wait for its fulfilment. He assures him that 'the just shall live by his faith' no matter what the fate of the wicked. **V 5–19: WOES** God then reveals that although He will judge Israel through the Babylonian invasion and captivity, He will also act in judgement against the wickedness of the Babylonians. He pronounces five woes against them covering their exploitation of others, their coveting evil gain, their sinful shedding of blood, their drunken immorality and violence, and their idolatry. **V 20: WONDER** Habakkuk is reminded that 'the LORD is in His holy temple'. The whole earth should keep a worshipful silence before Him.

CHAPTER THREE

V 1–2: WORK! Having heard God's answer, Habakkuk prays that God will work in revival 'in the midst of the years'. While working in wrath against the Babylonians, he asks God to remember mercy towards His people. **V 3–16: WONDER** Habakkuk then looks back in wonder at all God's powerful and awesome dealings on behalf of His people. It makes him tremble as he realises again the authority and might of God. He now accepts that God will invade Israel through her cruel enemies. **V 17–18: WILLING** He faces the fact that nothing may turn out the way he would choose, yet he declares that he 'will rejoice in the LORD' and will 'joy in the God of [his] salvation.' In accepting God's will, he himself is made willing. **V 19: WALK** He is now confident in God who is 'my strength'. He knows that God will enable him to walk on a higher level of trust and obedience. After talking to God, he is a different person.

ZEPHANIAH

OVERVIEW

PEOPLE AND PRELIMINARIES

Zephaniah (three chapters) is the ninth of the twelve 'minor prophets'. See comments on Hosea. The book was written by Zephaniah between 635 BC and 625 BC in Judah. He prophesied at the same time as Jeremiah, during the reign of King Josiah and during a time of revival which preceded the captivity.

PLAN AND PURPOSE

This book traces the ministry of Zephaniah as he prophesies about the judgement of the world by God on 'the Day of the LORD'. He also prophesies imminent judgement on Judah and its surrounding nations for their prevailing sins, with the purpose of bringing about repentance. The book concludes with the expectation of God's future blessing on repentant people from all the nations of the world, and especially from His people.

PROFILE AND PROGRESSION

The invasion to come, pointing to the Day of the LORD (1:1–2:3); the judgement to come on the world, on Judah, and on surrounding nations (2:4–15); Jerusalem's moral and spiritual decadence (3:1–7); judgement on nations (3:8); restoration blessings for the nations and for Israel (3:9–20).

PRINCIPLES AND PARTICULARS

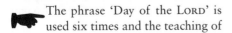
The phrase 'Day of the LORD' is used six times and the teaching of

the book of Zephaniah centres on it. Though immediate judgement would be through invasion by Nebuchadnezzar, who would prefigure the coming great Day of the LORD, God still offers mercy to those who repent and seek Him. There will be a saved remnant of believers.

ZEPHANIAH

CHAPTER ONE

V 1–3: 'THE WORD OF THE LORD' Zephaniah is to relay 'the word of the LORD' to Judah. He is the only prophet of royal descent, with King Hezekiah being one of his ancestors. He starts by announcing to Judah that the land will be consumed and man will be cut off, as well as the animal kingdom, because of Judah's wickedness. **V 4–6: THE JUDGEMENT OF THE LORD** He tells God's people in Judah, and especially the inhabitants of Jerusalem, of His judgement to come because of their idolatrous priests, the worship of the stars, the backsliding of God's people, and the failure to seek God or enquire of Him. **V 8: 'THE PRESENCE OF THE LORD'** Judah is told to be silent 'in the presence of the LORD God'. There is no defence to be made. **V 7b–18: 'THE DAY OF THE LORD'** God's punishment on His people and on the land will result in crying, wailing, desolation, trouble, distress, devastation, darkness, gloom, alarm, and hopelessness. There will be no defence against God's wrath.

CHAPTER TWO

V 1–3: JUDGEMENT—JUDAH The judgement of God's fierce anger is due to fall upon Judah. The meek and just among them are called upon to seek righteousness and humility so that they may 'be hidden in the day of the LORD's anger'. **V 4–7:**

JUDGEMENT—PHILISTIA The land of the Philistines will be forsaken, desolate and judged. The faithful remnant of Judah will live there after their judgement. **V 8–11: JUDGEMENT—MOAB AND AMON** Moab and Amon will be judged for their insulting opposition to God's people. They will be a place where weeds and salt pits proliferate and will be perpetually desolate. They will be plundered by God's faithful remnant. Idolatry will be wiped out as God will be worshipped. **V 12: JUDGEMENT—ETHIOPIA** God will slay Ethiopia by His sword. **V 13–15: JUDGEMENT—ASSYRIA** Nineveh will be desolated when Assyria is judged. The self-confident nation will be a place where animals lie down and will be dealt with contemptuously by those passing by.

CHAPTER THREE

V 1–5: JERUSALEM'S JUDGEMENT Zephaniah then pronounces woe on rebellious and polluted Jerusalem. Her disobedience, intransigence, and her failure to trust and draw near to God are why she will be judged. The sins of her violent people, wicked prophets and polluted priests have led this once privileged city away from God. **V 6–7: PEOPLE'S PERVERSITY** Despite the fact that God's people have seen how God has overthrown ungodly nations, they refuse to turn to Him. Indeed, they increase their corruption and evil deeds. **V 8: ANGER AWAITED** Judah is told that she must wait for God, until His day of wrath and anger has been poured out upon the nations. Judah is not the only nation who will know Him, but there will be a remnant saved to see Him judge the other nations. **V 9–20: REMNANT RESTORED** Such a work will be done by God in that day that the pure language of repentance and worship will be given to Israel, who will be gathered to her own land. Meekness, humility, trust, righteousness, truth, peace, rejoicing, strength, love, salvation, and praise will show God's great work in, for and through His people. God's captive people will finally return from afar.

HAGGAI

OVERVIEW

PEOPLE AND PRELIMINARIES

✳ Haggai (two chapters) is the tenth of the twelve 'minor prophets'. See comments on Hosea. He wrote this book about 520 BC, probably in or near Jerusalem. All the final three 'minor prophets', Haggai, Zechariah and Malachi, prophesied after the remnant of the Jews came back to Jerusalem and its surrounding country from the seventy years of Babylonian captivity. Hence, these three are known as 'post-exilic' prophets. Haggai and Zechariah prophesied together after the return under Zerubbabel led to the rebuilding of the temple, while Haggai encouraged the renewed rebuilding of the temple. The books of Ezra and Nehemiah provide the background detail.

PLAN AND PURPOSE

ⓘ Haggai gives five messages exhorting and encouraging the people to renew their work to rebuild the temple and reminds them that drought and food shortages, through poor crops, are caused by their failure to put God first. He sees the temple as representing God's presence with His people. He ends the book by looking forward to the coming Messianic temple, and the times of blessing, peace and prosperity to come.

The challenge to Haggai—motivate a disheartened people to work on God's temple (1:1,2); the rebuke through Haggai—get your priorities right (1:3–11); the response of the remnant—obedience, building and leadership (1:12–15); God's assuring, presence, promise of glory in His temple and peace (2:1–9); God's chastening because of uncleanness and His promised blessing (2:10–19); God's mighty reign over the nations (2:20–23).

PRINCIPLES AND PARTICULARS

The balance of the book is struck between perseverance in God's work and temple rebuilding and the glory of God's presence in the immediate and long-term future. The link between judgement and hope is clear. There is a need to admonish, exhort and rebuke in the work of the LORD. The value of being in a team of like-minded people, with a heart for God, is demonstrated. God's sovereignty again shines out. The presentation of Zerubbabel as a 'signet ring' in the last chapter is a key to the fulfilment of Messianic prophecy.

HAGGAI

CHAPTER ONE

V 1–2: COMPLACENCY It is not so much enemy action as the complacency of God's people that causes the ruined temple not to be rebuilt. So God gives Haggai, the prophet, the burden to command God's people to build the temple. As an encouragement to today's senior citizens who belong to the LORD, Haggai is probably in his seventies, and achieves this great service over a period of four months! His commitment is a stark contrast to the complacency which necessitates his mission. **V 3–4: CHALLENGE** Knowing that the people claim that it is not the right time to rebuild the temple, Haggai challenges them about the time they spend on their own houses, while God's house lies in ruins. Effectively, he is asking where their priorities are. **V 5–7: CONSIDER** He tells them twice, from 'the LORD of hosts', to consider their ways. Little that they do is effective or satisfying, and they have not realised that God is withholding His hand of blessing from them. **V 8: CONSTRUCT** Haggai passes on God's command to go and bring wood from the mountains to build the temple, so that God may be pleased and glorified. **V 9–11: CONSEQUENCES** God reveals that His withholding of fruitfulness and success is because they have not honoured Him and rebuilt His temple. **V 12: COMPLIANCE** Led by Zerubbabel (the governor) and Joshua (the priest), the people comply with God's wishes and obey Him. They now have a holy fear at the presence of God. **V 13–14: CONFIRMATION** God confirms His presence with them. He stirs up everybody from the leaders downward to work on the temple.

CHAPTER TWO

V 1–9: ENCOURAGEMENT—GREATER GLORY God encourages the workers, through His prophet, with the further confirmation of His presence. Although the temple they build may seem less glorious than the previous one, God has other plans. He reminds them of His covenant with Israel, and His Spirit with them. They are not to fear. The 'desire of all nations' (the Lord Jesus Christ) will come. The final glory will be greater than the former, and God will give peace. **V 10–19: ENCOURAGEMENT—BIG BLESSING** The people of God have contaminated everything by their sinfulness and sharp practice in the past. Previous judgements by God did not turn them from sin to Him. But they will be blessed by God in the future, as they repent and obey Him. **V 20–23: ENCOURAGEMENT—**

SOVEREIGN'S SIGNET Haggai is told to speak to Zerubbabel, Judah's governor. He is to remind him that God will shake heaven and earth and overthrow all Gentile kingdoms in the end times. God has chosen Zerubbabel as a 'signet ring', the sign of authority of the King of kings. Zerubbabel, whose place in genealogy is in both the lines of Joseph and Mary, effectively re-establishes the Davidic line (and thus benefits from the Davidic covenant), as King Jehoiachin was disqualified by sin and removed by God. To and through Zerubbabel come God's authority and sealing stamp of prophecy and confirmation that the Messiah will come.

ZECHARIAH

OVERVIEW

PEOPLE AND PRELIMINARIES

✳Zechariah (fourteen chapters) is the eleventh of the twelve 'minor prophets'. See comments on Hosea and Haggai. Zechariah was written between 480 BC and 470 BC, probably in or near Jerusalem.

PLAN AND PURPOSE

ⓘ Zechariah joins Haggai in urging the rebuilding of the temple, but concentrates more than Haggai on repentance, the assurance that God will bless in the future, and that the Messiah will come to live in the temple. Thus, in dealing with the present, he concentrates on the future and reminds the people of God's faithfulness to keep His covenant with His people. The book of Zechariah

has an apocalyptic style with much use of symbols. It starts with a call to repent, then goes through the prophet's eight visions of the night, four messages, and two burdens. The two comings of Christ are clearly prophesied here.

PROFILE AND PROGRESSION

Zechariah commands repentance (1:1–6); eight visions of the night— the man who rides among the myrtle trees, the four horns and the four craftsmen, the man holding a measuring line, Joshua the high priest being cleansed, the gold lamp-stand and the two olive trees, the flying roll, the woman in the basket, and the four chariots— followed by the symbolic crowning of Joshua (1:7–6:15); Zechariah's four messages in response to a question put to the priests about fasting—a rebuke for shallow formalism, unanswered prayer because of no practical repentance, God's purpose to restore and bless Israel, and a new cheerfulness in their fasts to come from a love for truth and peace (7:1–8:23);

Zechariah's two burdens—the rejection of Messiah at His first coming, and the victory of and blessing from the second coming of Messiah (9:1–14:21).

PRINCIPLES AND PARTICULARS

☞ The apocalyptic approach distinguishes the book of Zechariah from the other 'minor prophets'. Some think that this book is to the Old Testament what the book of Revelation is to the New Testament. Some prophecies of the Messiah have been fulfilled clearly, already, in the first humble redemptive coming to earth of the Lord Jesus Christ. Some are yet to be fulfilled, in His glorious second climactic coming. The mighty power of God is emphasised by the use of the phrase 'LORD of hosts' on over fifty occasions, constituting nearly one fifth of the use of the phrase in the rest of the Old Testament.

ZECHARIAH

CHAPTER ONE

V 1–3: REPENTANCE COMMANDED Zechariah prophesies to Judah, in order to join Haggai's efforts to hasten the rebuilding of the temple. He starts with the spiritual problem, and declares that God commands repentance, and a turning to Him, from His rebellious people. That command carries a promise that God will return to those who return to Him. **V 4–6: REPENTANT CONTRITION** Zechariah faces the people with the fact that their forefathers would not repent or heed God's words and asks, 'Where are they?' This reminder produces repentance from them as they return to God, owning up that God is completely justified in doing with them as He sees fit because of their evil works. **V 7–17: REVELATION— COMFORT** On one night, Zechariah has eight visions (not dreams) from God. The detail of each vision is not always easy to work out, but the meaning behind it is stated or more obvious. The first vision, concerning a man on a red horse standing among myrtle trees in the presence of three other horses, is to do with God's comfort towards Judah. God declares His anger with the oppressing nations and the fact that He will return to Jerusalem with mercy and prosper His people. **V 18–20: REVELATION—CONFRONTATION** This vision of four horns, which are cast out by craftsmen, is to teach that God will cast out the nations which have cast out and scattered Judah. When God confronts His enemies, there is only one result: victory for Him and punishment for them.

CHAPTER TWO

V 1–12: REVELATION—COME This vision concerns a man who is measuring Jerusalem and is told that Jerusalem will need no walls because God will protect it and God will be the glory within it. He bids His people escape and come into Jerusalem, into His land which He will re-establish. He will deal with their enemies and His people will rejoice. Such will be the blessing, other nations will also come to Him there.

CHAPTER THREE

V 1–10: REVELATION—CLEANSING The next vision concerns Joshua, the priest, opposed by Satan, whom God rebukes. Joshua's filthy clothes are removed and replaced by clean and rich robes and a turban. This underlines the need for holiness in God's people and priesthood.

God gives him a sign that one day 'My Servant the BRANCH' will be brought forth. This will be fulfilled in the Messiah, the Lord Jesus Christ. 'Jesus' is the same Greek word as 'Joshua' is in Hebrew, and means 'God saves'. In that day, iniquity will be removed and there will be fruitful fellowship among God's people. God will give peace.

CHAPTER FOUR

V 1–14: REVELATION—COMPLETION This vision concerns Zerubbabel, who is the governor. He is to the political life of Judah what Joshua, the priest, is to its spiritual life. The vision encourages him to continue building the temple, which will be completed as a testimony to God's wonder and grace. God's Spirit will accomplish this. In this vision of the lamp-stand and two olive trees, the two olive trees represent 'two anointed ones who stand before the Lord of the whole earth'. It is likely that this refers to Joshua and to Zerubbabel, and confirms the earlier vision as well as this particular one about Zerubbabel. What God starts, God completes.

CHAPTER FIVE

V 1–4: REVELATION—CURSE The huge flying scroll in this vision stands for the greatness of God's word. God's word pronounces a curse upon all sin, including theft and lying, which are specifically mentioned. God's word will ultimately have free course in convicting sinners of their sin. **V 5–11: REVELATION— CONSECRATION** In this vision, the woman in the basket is wicked. God confines her to the basket and covers it with a lead cover before two winged women take that basket out of Judah, to be housed in Shinar (another name for Babylon). This speaks not only of the cleansing, but also of the consecration of Judah. Evil will be cleared from her boundaries in the end times.

CHAPTER SIX

V 1–8: REVELATION—COMMUNICATION The final vision concerns red, black, white and dappled horses pulling four chariots and going to the north and the south of the country. (The sea and the desert were to the east and the west, and opposition came from the Babylonians in the north and from the Egyptians in the south.) The chariots represent four 'spirits of heaven', or angels, who communicate God's judgement throughout the country and underline His sovereignty. After conquest in the north, rest is given there. **V 9–15: REBUILDER CROWNED** Joshua, prefiguring the 'BRANCH' (the Messiah—the Lord Jesus Christ) is to be crowned, thus combining the priesthood with kingship. As such, he is a picture of what will happen in the last days when Jesus Christ, the last High Priest and the King of kings, will reign supreme. God's temple will be rebuilt.

CHAPTER SEVEN

V 1–3: REQUESTING CLARIFICATION The people send Sherezer and Regem-Melech to pray and to ask the priests and the prophets if their habitual weeping and fasting must continue in the fifth month. **V 4–7: RESPONDING CHALLENGE** Through Zechariah, God's word challenges them to ask whether they are really fasting for God (meaning in repentance of sin and seeking Him with a whole heart), or if they are using this as an excuse for feasting rather than fasting. They are asked whether they do not think that obedience is more important. **V 8–10: RIGHTEOUS CONDUCT** Zechariah then tells them that God wants them to show true justice, mercy and compassion to everyone, and no oppression of the under-privileged or evil planning against family members. Repentance manifests itself in action and not merely in outward observances. Righteous conduct is required. **V 11–14: REFUSAL'S CONSEQUENCES** God's wrath against the refusal of His people to repent and live the righteous life that He has detailed is the reason why His people are scattered and in captivity. That is why their land is desolate.

CHAPTER EIGHT

V 1–23: REVELATION CONFIRMED As God's word comes to Zechariah, eight times he says, 'For thus says the LORD,' and contrasts the desolation and punishment of the unrepentant with the blessings of restoration of the repentant remnant and its consequent blessings on others. They will return and live in Jerusalem. Jerusalem will be populated with both old and young. God's people will be gathered as His possession 'in truth and righteousness'. He will bless His remnant, make them prosperous, and turn them into a blessing to other nations. His punishment on them will be turned to good and blessing. Fear will give way to peace. Their fasts will become meaningful because of their new love for truth and peace. The spiritual exercise of prayer will be an example to all who approach God through His people. Such will be the reputation of the restored Jews that the nations will want to go with them because they know that 'God is with you'. (What a joy for the Christian to know that the Lord Jesus Christ is Emmanuel, which means 'God with us'.)

CHAPTER NINE

V 1–8: OPPRESSORS OVERCOME In the second half of Zechariah's prophetic ministry, recorded in chapter nine and beyond, he makes specific prophecies which will come true. Zechariah announces that God is against the enemies of Israel and lists some of them. The self-sufficiency of Tyre and Sidon will be overcome and other nations will fear when they see it. God will deal with the Philistines and camp around His people to save them from future oppressors. **V 9–10: MEEK MONARCH** Thus, the coming of the Messiah is seen as a King who is 'Just and having salvation, lowly and riding on a donkey'. Peace will follow and dominion will be His. (Prophecies often merge the first and the second comings of Christ.) **V 11–17: DEFENDING DELIVERER** God's people will be taken from their imprisonment and will benefit from God's restoration and protection. God's might and splendour will be seen as His restored people thrive.

CHAPTER TEN

V 1: SPIRITUAL SHOWERS Judah and Israel are told to ask God for the blessing of His spiritual rain in the time of the latter rain (springtime). As rain makes vegetation flourish, so the rain of His mercy and grace will make them flourish. **V 2–3a: SINFUL SHEPHERDS** As idolatry, divination, lies, and falseness proliferate, false shepherds (the religious leaders of Judah and Israel) cause God's sheep to err. There is no true shepherd. God is angry with His false shepherds. **V 3b–8: SHEEP STRENGTHENED** In the absence of the guiding shepherds, God will so strengthen His sheep that they will become a mighty force against their enemies. It will be as if they were never cast off and they will prevail because of God's redemption and ownership of them. **V 9–12: SCATTERED SAVED** Just as God's people will be scattered like seed among the nations, the day will come when God will save them and bring them back. At that time, their enemies will fail and God will strengthen them in Him, and in their walk with Him.

CHAPTER ELEVEN

V 1–3: DEVOURED AND DESOLATE Fire devouring the trees in Lebanon is symbolic of God's dealing with Israel, making her desolate because of her sin. This chapter goes back to emphasising God's judgement. **V 4–14: 'BEAUTY' AND 'BONDS'** During this period of judgement, God will no longer pity those sheep. They will be attacked and devoured. God dismisses their 'three shepherds' in one month. (This may refer to prophets, priests, and rulers then, or alternatively to later priests, scribes and Pharisees.) The two staffs that a shepherd uses, one as a baton against wild animals and the other as a crook to gather straying sheep to bring them into the fold, are both cut in two by Zechariah at God's direction. They symbolise the breaking of the covenant between God and His people, consequent judgement, and the breaking of relationships between Judah and Israel which follows. Zechariah acts out the role of the rejected shepherd, whose value is only put at thirty pieces of silver. This is the price of a common slave and the price that the priests later will pay Judas for his betrayal of the Lord Jesus Christ. **V 15–17: WORTHLESS AND WOEFUL** Zechariah then acts out the part of a foolish shepherd who not only fails to care for the sheep or their needs but also treats them selfishly and cruelly. He will be an object of woe at God's judgement.

Great suffering will come upon him. Because he has used neither his eye nor his arm to fulfil a true shepherd's duty, both will be smitten by God. Some see the false shepherd as a picture of the Antichrist to come.

CHAPTER TWELVE

V 1–9: DELIVERANCE FOR DOMINATION Again, Zechariah turns to the deliverance of Israel and Judah and, under Almighty God's strengthening and blessing, their domination against all the nations. God will make Jerusalem unassailable under the coming attack of the opposing nations. He will strike them with confusion and destroy them all. As Jerusalem is turned into a victor, the weakest inhabitants will be made as strong as King David, and God's people will be seen by the enemy as having the strength of the Angel of the LORD. God will have the last word in human history. **V 10–14: MOURNING FOR MESSIAH** When Christ comes again, the repentant house of David and those in Jerusalem will be given a 'spirit of grace and supplication'. As God opens their eyes, they will look on God the Son whom they pierced, and mourn for Him because of their sin and rebellion that put Him on the cross. This mourning will start at Jerusalem, go through the whole land, and include every family. The deity of Christ is underlined in this whole passage. Through Zechariah, God says, 'They will look on Me whom they pierced.'

CHAPTER THIRTEEN

V 1–6: FOUNTAIN FLOWING— FAITHFULNESS FOLLOWS Israel's sin will be cleansed away in that day when a fountain will be flowing 'for sin and uncleanness'. Separation from sin will become such a priority among the people that a desire to live holy lives will be more important even than family ties. Idolatry and false prophets will be dealt with, and God's true word will be honoured. **V 7: SHEPHERD STRUCK—SHEEP SCATTERED** Intermingled with the wonderful prophecy of the end times is the rejection and death of the Lord Jesus Christ, as the Shepherd who will be struck causing the sheep to be scattered. In Matthew's Gospel, Jesus applies this prophecy to Himself and to His fleeing disciples at His arrest. **V 8–9: REMNANT REFINED— REDEEMED RESTORED** Two thirds of the people will be cut off and one third saved. This is God's remnant of repentant, refined and redeemed people who will be restored and enter into prayerful communion with God. God will acknowledge them as His people; they will acknowledge Him as their God.

CHAPTER FOURTEEN

V 1–2: REMNANT REASSURED When the day of the LORD comes, Jerusalem will be attacked and taken. Houses will be rifled, women ravished, and half of the people taken captive, but the remnant of the people 'shall not be cut off from the city'. **V 3–5: FAITHFUL FLEE** With Christ's return to the Mount of Olives, God will fight against the nations and the Mount of Olives will split, leaving a large valley

through which the faithful remnant will escape. The LORD God will come, and 'all the saints' with Him. **V 6–7: LORD'S LIGHT** Despite the disappearance of normal lighting, God will provide light even at evening time. **V 8–11: SAFETY SECURED** The whole land will be watered from the east to the west in that day. God's ruling, as King, will raise up Jerusalem which will be safely inhabited without any further destruction. **V 12–15: PUNISHING PLAGUE** Those who fight against Jerusalem will be punished with an horrific plague which dissolves their flesh and destroys their eyes and tongues. The panic so caused will cause them to fight against one another. Judah will also fight at Jerusalem and great spoil will belong to the children of God. However, even the livestock of their enemies will be killed by the plague. **V 16–21: WIDESPREAD WORSHIP** Widespread worship of God, not only from Israel but from other nations, will follow and the message that rings out from the bells of the horses will be 'holiness to the Lord'. The Canaanites (the symbolic term for anything that was unclean or dirty, morally or ceremonially) will never again be in God's temple. Holiness will mark the final restoration in peace and prosperity. Holiness should also mark Christians today in their spiritual peace and spiritual prosperity.

MALACHI

PEOPLE AND PRELIMINARIES

✳Malachi (four chapters) is the twelfth and last of the twelve 'minor prophets', therefore being the last prophetical book, and the last book in the Old Testament. See comments on Hosea and Haggai. Malachi, whose name means 'my messenger', wrote this between 433 BC and 424 BC, probably in or near Jerusalem.

PLAN AND PURPOSE

ⓘ Malachi prophesies far later than Haggai and Zechariah, during the time of Nehemiah's initial leadership in Jerusalem which produced the completion of the rebuilding of its walls and spiritual renewal of the people. He also probably prophesied after Nehemiah's return from a period of absence. By the time Malachi prophesies, the Jews have strayed again into disobedience, compromise, formalism, corruption, hypocrisy, mixed marriages, withholding tithes and offerings, and half-heartedness. Malachi faithfully addresses this with comprehensive condemnations of priests, people and leaders, calling them to repentance and renewal. He speaks in clear unmistakeable language from the heart, from the shoulder, and from God, though with excellent use of illustration to make his point. Nevertheless, the forgiving love of God illuminates his condemnations. The book closes with the second coming of the Lord Jesus Christ firmly in focus.

PROFILE AND PROGRESSION

🐚 God's love for Israel (1:1–5); God's hatred for Israel's sins both of the profane and polluted priests and of the unfaithful, unrighteous and immoral people (1:6–2:18); God's coming messenger to prepare the way for the LORD, the need for repentance, and God's record of Israel's self-pitying and sinful words (3:6–15); God's remembrance of those who fear Him (3:16–18); the coming 'great and dreadful day of the LORD' will be preceded by the burning of stubble, the rising of the Sun of Righteousness, and the prophet who will turn hearts to God. (4:1–6).

PRINCIPLES AND PARTICULARS

👉 But for the extremely challenging nature of this book, its question-and-answer style would make it easy to read. The vivid and relevant imagery used to make spiritual and practical points repays careful consideration. The need for the man of God boldly to withstand and rebuke the errant people and the errant leadership, both religious and political, is clearly established here. The last book of the Old Testament reaches across to the New Testament with prophecies about the first and second comings of Christ. God's sovereignty, justice and mercy in tying up world affairs is comfortingly obvious from His control of the last things, including the coming of 'the great and dreadful day of the LORD'.

MALACHI

CHAPTER ONE

V 1–5: CONTRAST Malachi (meaning 'My messenger') contrasts the love that God has shown for Jacob and the Israelites with the relative hate that He has shown in His dealings with Esau and the Edomites. In the Bible, the word 'hate' sometimes refers to hatred by comparison with a greater love for something else or someone else. The great love that God has for Israel makes any other love seem like hatred in comparison. This is not 'hate' in the normally understood sense of the word. Esau has been thrown down and will not be rebuilt successfully. **V 6–8: CONTEMPTIBLE** Yet despite God's love for Israel, her offerings are polluted and there is no reverence or fear of God, even from the priests. The sacrifices offered make the altar 'contemptible'. God is greatly displeased. **V 9–12: COMMAND** Israel is commanded to call on God now by entreating His favour and seeking His grace. Only He can put right the failure to want to worship Him properly in presenting polluted sacrifices and offerings. Even Gentiles make acceptable offerings to God, but His own people profane His name. Sick, stolen and lame animals—all sub-standard for sacrifice— are being offered in a deceitful façade for worship. **V 14: CURSED** Malachi confirms that such deceivers will be cursed. God is a 'great King' and must be honoured and feared. His name is to be feared among the nations.

CHAPTER TWO

V 1–3: CURSED PRIESTS The priests have already had their blessings turned into curses because they refuse to turn to God and listen to Him. The same will happen again if they do not listen. Their descendants will be rebuked, and the refuse of their 'solemn feasts' will be spread on their faces. **V 4–6: COVENANT PERPETUATED** God will do this to bring them to repentance, so that the covenant

He made with Levi will be perpetuated. He holds up the original Levitical covenant, its blessings, and Levi's honouring of it as an example to these wicked priests. **V 7–9: CONTAMINATING PEOPLE** Whereas the priest should set an example by word and by deed, he has caused many people to stumble and depart from God in his corrupt ways. Thus, the people see the priests as contemptible and base. **V 10–12: COMPROMISED PARTNERSHIPS** The first complaint against the priests is that they seek to justify taking foreign wives from pagan nations, against God's specific commands by saying that 'God is the Father of all' and that He has created everybody. God will cut off His people for transgressing this command. **V 13–16: CULPABLE PRETENCE** The second complaint against God's priests is that they weep 'crocodile tears', supposedly because of broken communion with God. At the same time, they completely ignore that they are sanctioning the breaking of the marriage covenant and treating wives with spite and lack of respect. God is against this treacherous dealing and He hates divorce. Even violence is involved. **V 17: CONTEMPTUOUS PRIDE** These priests have not ceased to use words towards God, yet they never have connected with Him because of their sin. They deliberately confuse evil with good, and say that God is pleased with the evildoers. Their pride and contempt is even greater when they ask, 'Where is the God of justice?' They even deny God's existence and character.

CHAPTER THREE

V 1: 'MY MESSENGER' God says that He will send His messenger to prepare God's way before His coming to His temple. ('My messenger' is a play on the name

Malachi.) This has implications for both first and second advents of Jesus Christ. **V 2–3: AWESOME APPEARANCE** When Christ does appear the second time, He will come as a refiner's fire and as the soap of a launderer. He will come to refine, purge and cleanse. Repentance and forgiveness are prerequisite to God's final blessing, just as they are to our personal blessing. **V 4: PLEASING PRESENTATION** Only then will the offerings made by God's people be pleasing to Him as in the days of faithfulness in the past. **V 5–7: JUST JUDGEMENT** At the second coming of Christ, not only will His people be purified but all the sins listed will be dealt with. Those who sinned in the ways mentioned do not now fear God, but they will then, and it will be too late. God, who never changes, has abstained from consuming Judah, and bids them return to Him so that He will return to them. It is always the sinner's responsibility to turn to God. If he does this with a pure heart, God will always return to him. **V 8–12: BOUNDLESS BLESSING** Despite the fact that His people have robbed God by not giving Him all the tithes that the law required, if their repentant hearts will now cause them to reverse this and 'bring all the tithes into the storehouse', the blessings of God will be boundless and generous. Not only will His people receive blessing upon blessing but He will defend them and make them fruitful, so that other nations will call them blessed and the land will become 'a delightful land'. **V 13–15: WANTON WORDS** Yet God tells His people of the harsh and wanton words that they have used against God. They say that to serve God is useless, to obey Him is pointless, mourning over sin has no effect, and therefore they pronounce proud people blessed, and they honour wicked people. Their whole attitude is one of tempting God by going as far into sin as they can. **V 16–17: SERVANTS SPARED** Yet God remembers and records in His 'book of remembrance' those who fear Him and meditate on His name. In the day when God makes up His jewels, He says that they will be His and that He will spare them 'as a man spares his own son who serves him'. God's serving children will be spared by Him and counted as very valuable. **V 18: DISTINCTION DISCERNED** When that happens, their blurred distinction between righteousness and wickedness and between serving Him and not serving Him will be restored. Discernment will be given to those who walk with Him.

CHAPTER FOUR

V 1: EXECUTION The day of the LORD will be like a furnace in which the arrogant and adulterers will be subject to God's executing His holy fire of judgement. **V 2–4: ELEVATION** In that day, those who fear God will know the rising of the 'Sun of righteousness' who will have 'healing in His wings'. They will be elevated with Him and greatly blessed, with total victory over the wicked. The lasting value of the law of Moses is recorded in that these people are commanded to keep his statutes and judgements, which God gave them through him. **V 5–6: ELIJAH** But before this 'great and dreadful day of the LORD', a prophet will come to 'turn the hearts of the fathers to the children and the hearts of the children to their fathers'. They will thus be given repentance and faith from God which will prevent Him striking the earth with a curse. This prophecy was fulfilled by John the Baptist at Jesus' first coming. Malachi prepares the way for the coming of the Lord Jesus Christ, Messiah, Saviour and Lord.

THE BIBLE
PANORAMA

Surveying the scenery of Scripture
Each chapter of each book of the Bible plainly
summarised and explained

NEW TESTAMENT

MATTHEW

PEOPLE AND PRELIMINARIES

✳Matthew (twenty-eight chapters) was written by Matthew between AD50 and AD70 probably in Antioch in Syria. It is the first and longest of twenty-seven New Testament books, the first of the four Gospels, and the first of the three 'synoptic Gospels'. The other three Gospels are Mark, Luke and John, of which John is the non-synoptic one. 'Gospel' means 'good news'. 'Synoptic' implies that a synopsis (meaning a summary, outline or brief general survey) is taken. Put together, a synoptic Gospel is one that gives a summary, outline or brief general survey of the good news concerning the birth, life, ministry, death, resurrection, ascension, and imminent return of the Lord Jesus Christ. Each Gospel is a reliable, Holy Spirit inspired part of God's Word but each one has a different emphasis. Matthew, Mark and Luke have much material in common and are more similar to each other than to John's Gospel. Distinctively, the non-synoptic Gospel of John focuses, even more than the synoptic Gospels, on the actual person, character, attributes and mission of the Lord Jesus Christ. The matters recorded in Matthew occurred in a period estimated to be thirty-eight years.

PLAN AND PURPOSE

ⓘMatthew's Gospel summarises the good news of the Lord Jesus Christ, from before His birth up to and including His resurrection and commission to His disciples to make other disciples.

Matthew has a Jewish ring to it and starts by tracing the royal line of King Jesus to Abraham. It portrays Jesus, the King of the Jews, specifically as the King who has come to deliver. King and kingdom are themes that recur, therefore. Matthew, a converted tax collector, is also one of the twelve apostles. As with Mark and Luke, his Gospel traces Jesus' footsteps through history in His birth, baptism, temptation by Satan, public ministry, sermons, miracles, choosing and commissioning of the twelve disciples, teachings on various subjects, parables (especially in Matthew about the kingdom of God), opposition and rejection, prophecies of His death and resurrection, His second coming, the Lord's supper, passion, betrayal, crucifixion, resurrection, and commissioning of His disciples. The great theme in Matthew is the authority of Christ. He assumes authority when He speaks. The whole Gospel shows that He has authority over sickness, circumstances, Satan, and sin, as well as over man, his deliverance, and his destiny.

PROFILE AND PROGRESSION

🐚Jesus' birth and infancy (1:1–2:23); the Son of God identified in His baptism and tested in temptation (3:1–4:11); the Teacher begins His ministry—the sermon on the mount (4:12–7:29); early miracles of the Master (8:1–9:38); disciples called and discipleship described (10:1–42); Jesus confirms He is the Messiah and teaches on repentance and rest (11:1–30); the Lord of the Sabbath heals, faces blasphemous religious opposition, and teaches about His death, resurrection and the need for a new relationship (12:1–50); the King tells the kingdom parables (13:1–53); the growing and unjust rejection of Jesus by the religious authorities despite His continuing demonstration of His divine kingship through His sign miracles, authoritative teaching on many things, holy living and foretelling of His death and resurrection (13:1–23:39); Christ's predictive teaching through parables about the end times (24:1–28:15); the way to Calvary—the King crucified and buried (26:1–27:66); the risen Lord (28:1–15); the great commission (28:16–20).

PRINCIPLES AND PARTICULARS

To highlight briefly anything in the Gospels of Matthew, Mark, Luke or John is like telling someone to explore Africa in a day! There is so much, that it is inappropriate to emphasise any point at the expense of others. Remember, however, that the emphasis of Matthew is that Jesus is King. Accordingly, look for references to His kingship and kingdoms and see His dignity and authority. Note that sinners (especially religious sinners) rebel against the King of righteousness. Apply Matthew's teaching to test your own loyalty, as a Christian, to the King who was crucified for you. Remember the King will return in great glory! See what Jesus says is the real meaning of being 'blessed'.

MATTHEW

CHAPTER ONE

V 1–17: HISTORICAL FACT The New Testament starts with real people who live in history, forming the ancestry of the Lord Jesus Christ on earth. **V 18–23: HEAVENLY FULFILMENT** God's prophecy of His Son, JESUS, the Saviour from sins, coming to earth through virgin birth is about to be fulfilled through Mary, who has conceived through the Holy Spirit. God's angel reveals this to her godly and faithful husband, Joseph. **V 24–25: HUSBAND'S FAITHFULNESS** Joseph is obedient, faithfully looks after Mary, and abstains from sexual union with her until Jesus is born. Joseph obediently names his Son 'JESUS'.

CHAPTER TWO

V 1–2: WISE After Jesus' birth, wise men from the east arrive, following a star to search for Jesus, so they can worship Him. **V 3–8: WILY** Wily King Herod seeks to manipulate their visit to find out where Jesus is born, so that he can destroy the young Child. **V 9–11: WORSHIP** Guided by the star, with rejoicing, the wise men come to the house where Jesus and his mother Mary are staying. They worship Him with their gifts of gold, frankincense, and myrrh. **V 12–15: WARNINGS** God warns the wise men not to return to Herod and they depart for their own country by another way. Through an angel appearing to Joseph in a dream, God warns the stepfather of Jesus to take the young child and Mary, and flee to Egypt to escape Herod. (In verse 22, God will warn Joseph again.) **V 16–18: WICKEDNESS** In an endeavour to kill Jesus, Herod orders the destruction of all male children of two years and under. He chooses that age group to ensure that Jesus will be among them based on the timing he deduced from what the wise men had said. **V 19–21: WORD** Through a dream, God gets word to Joseph after the death of Herod, to return to Israel. As always, Joseph obeys. **V 22–23: WARNED** God continues to guide Joseph, again warning him in a dream, as a result of which, Joseph, Mary, and Jesus settle in Nazareth.

CHAPTER THREE

V 1–3: 'REPENT' John the Baptist preaches repentance, in preparing the way for his Master, the Lord Jesus Christ. **V 4–6: REGION** The whole surrounding area is attracted to hear this rustic man as he preaches and as he baptises in the Jordan. **V 7–12: RESULTS** John insists that true repentance will result in the fruit of changed lives. He confronts the religious hypocrites, and magnifies the coming Saviour and His convicting work through the Holy Spirit. Christ will also exercise final judgement. **V 13–15: RIGHTEOUSNESS** Despite John's protest, Jesus is baptised by John, so that Christ can set the right example by being baptised. His baptism in water prefigures His being engulfed by a world's sin on the cross, although sinlessly righteous Himself. He has no sin of His own that calls for His repentance. **V 16–17: REVELATION** The Trinity of God the Father, God the Son, and God the Holy Spirit is seen in action, as the Spirit makes a dove-like descent upon Jesus, and as the Father speaks His words of complete commendation of His Son, Jesus.

CHAPTER FOUR

V 1–11: DEVIL RESISTED Jesus fasts in the wilderness, having been led there by the Spirit. Despite Satan's best efforts to urge Jesus to indulge His physical appetite, to work an unnecessary miracle, and to claim His kingdom too soon, Jesus resists these temptations and is ministered to by angels. He uses the Bible to resist Satan's temptations in this combat. **V 12–17: DARKNESS REPELLED** The great Light of the world shines through Jesus' presence and through His preaching of repentance in Capernaum. **V 18–22: DISCIPLES RECRUITED** Jesus calls Simon and Andrew to follow Him and 'fish for men'. James and John leave their father and their work and, like the other two, immediately answer Christ's call. **V 23–25: DIVINE RESULTS** Widespread teaching, preaching, and healing by Jesus cause Him to be widely followed by great multitudes.

CHAPTER FIVE

V 1–12: DESCRIPTION The progressive blessings of a heart in fellowship with God are reflected in the inner qualities shown in Jesus' Sermon on the Mount. These 'blessed' sayings are known as the Beatitudes. **V 13–16: DIFFERENCE** The Christian should be to the world what salt is to food and what light is to darkness— much needed and distinctively different. **V 17–20: DESTRUCTION** The whole of God's Word, in the smallest detail, will endure after the destruction of the heavens and the earth as we know them. God's law is our guide to entering the kingdom of heaven. The righteousness of mere religious observance, like that of the Pharisees, cannot give entry to it. **V 21–26: DANGER** Those whose sinful and unrepentant hearts reveal their anger and hatred for others, even for those who are close enough to be brothers, are in grave danger of judgement and hell. Bringing a gift to God is no substitute. Repentance will produce a desire to be reconciled to the person offended. Judgement is the only alternative to repentance. **V 27–30: DRASTIC** In our personal fight against sin, drastic action is called for, emphasised here through striking illustrations. This involves self-denial, reconciliation with offended people, and recognising that, in the eyes of God, hatred and anger in the heart count as murder, and lust counts as adultery. **V 31–32: DIVORCE** Jesus teaches the permanence of the marriage bond, which He teaches can only be broken in the case of marital unfaithfulness. **V 33–37: DIRECTNESS** Our language and conduct must be such that we need not invoke oaths to make people believe we are telling the truth. **V 38–48: DOING** A Christian must always do good to others, even when he can insist on an enforceable legal right and even when enemies oppose him. His generosity will evidence his desire to follow God's directions, as far as possible. His perfect heavenly Father is his standard.

CHAPTER SIX

V 1–18: SECRECY Secrecy in giving (verses 1 to 4), praying (verses 5 to 8), and fasting (verses 16 to 18) is taught by Jesus. It is in this context that the pattern of the Lord's Prayer (verses 9 to 15) is given. This contrasts with the hypocrisy of men, which is encountered in this chapter. **V 19–23: SIMPLICITY** Our attitude to wealth should be such that we are not seeking to live to gain money. Our heart is where our treasure is, and that should be in spiritual things. We also need simplicity to look honestly at the darkness inside us and have it dealt with by the Light of the world. **V 24: SINGULARITY** The Christian must be single-minded in serving God and not 'mammon'. Mammon stands for being dominated by money and materialistic considerations. **V 25–34: SERENITY** Nature tells us that God cares even for birds and flowers. Those with a special relationship with God should not worry, therefore, about provision of needs, now or in the future, but seek to please God first by seeking as a priority His kingdom and His righteousness. (This is not to encourage laziness but to underline the need for faith and trust.)

CHAPTER SEVEN

V 1–5: 'FIRST' Before criticising or judging others, especially on relatively small things, we should 'first' examine ourselves to see and correct our own faults. Perhaps we are far more culpable than those we criticise or judge. **V 6: FOOLISHNESS** Jesus warns against giving holy things to dogs and 'casting pearls before swine' as the pearls may be trampled and the person casting them may be hurt. Both illustrations apply to the sharing of God's holy Word with ignorant, reckless and aggressive people who will refuse to listen. **V 7–11: FAITH** Faith consists of asking, seeking, and knocking, with the sure promise that God will answer even more than any earthly father will answer the needs of his own children. **V 12: FULFILMENT** The working out of keeping God's law and the teachings of the prophets will be such that I will treat others as I want them to treat me. **V 13–14: FINDING** Only a few people find the narrow way that leads to life compared with the many who go to destruction. Jesus nevertheless urges His hearers to enter by the narrow gate to find life. **V 15–20: FRUITS** False prophets can be detected by the fruits of their lives and activities. Their fruits will show that they are not what they pretend to be. **V 21–27: FOUNDATION** The people whom Jesus will accept to be with Him in eternity will not necessarily be those who call Him 'Lord' and who have done great exploits in His name. Only those who know Him will be safe eternally. We must build our lives on the rock of Scripture rather than on the sand of anything else. **V 28–29: FLABERGASTED!** The crowds are astonished when they compare the authoritative and powerful teaching of Jesus with the weak words of the scribes.

CHAPTER EIGHT

V 1–17: COMPREHENSIVENESS Jesus heals the unclean leper (verses 1 to 4), the centurion's servant (verses 5 to 13), Peter's mother-in-law (verses 14 and 15) and demon-possessed people (verses 16 and 17). He meets the needs of many different types of people, irrespective of their background, social standing, gender, or age. **V 18–22: COST** Jesus' responses to a scribe and then to a disciple reveal that following Him must come before where we prefer to live and what our family wants us to do. (There is no suggestion that the disciple's father is actually dying at the time when his son wants to delay following Christ until after his burial.) **V 23–34: CALM** The Lord Jesus Christ stills the storm, showing His power over nature, and casts out demons from demon-possessed people, showing His power over Satan. He can deal with the storms and domination of Satan in men and women. That is why the whole city comes out to meet Him.

CHAPTER NINE

V 1–8: FRIENDS The concern, faithfulness, and faith of the friends of the paralytic cause him to be in a position where Christ heals him and is glorified. The scribes are hostile but the people marvel. **V 9–13: FOLLOWING** The call to the corrupt Levi was simply 'Follow me'. In eating at Levi's house with his friends, Jesus reveals that He touches the hearts of sin-sick sinners and needs no outward religious show. He is unimpressed with religious self-righteousness. **V 14–17: FASTING** Jesus teaches that there will be a time to fast, but there is also a time not to fast. Fasting is not intended to parade to others our devotion to God. **V 18–33: FAITH** Jesus meets the needs of very different people always through their putting their faith in Him. He restores to life the dead daughter of a ruler (verses 18 to 19 and 23 to 26), heals a woman who had been haemorrhaging for twelve years (verses 20 to 22), gives sight to two blind men (verses 27 to 31), and releases a mute demon-possessed man (verses 32 to 33). Jesus shows that He can meet the needs of all types of people who will come to Him. **V 34: FALSEHOOD** The Pharisees falsely accuse Jesus of driving out demons by the prince of demons. **V 35–38: FEW** Jesus has compassion on the helpless crowds during His teaching, preaching and healing in the villages, cities and synagogues. He teaches that the harvest of need is plentiful but the workers in it are few. He tells His own to pray that the Lord of the harvest will send out other workers into His harvest field.

CHAPTER TEN

V 1–4: TWELVE Jesus calls and equips the twelve apostles, who are named here. **V 5–16: TASK** The twelve are given specific instructions for their specific apostolic mission. **V 17–26: TRIALS** The apostles are to expect to suffer before religious leaders, rulers, political leaders, and before their own families. Nevertheless, aided by God's Spirit, they are to witness and not to be frightened. **V 27–31: TRUST** God knows and will reveal everything one day. The apostles are to fear Him who alone has power that lasts into eternity. This almighty and all-seeing God cares for them and they can trust Him. **V 32–39: TROUBLES** Armed by God's promise to acknowledge His own servants in heaven, they are to face the troubles and opposition that lie ahead—even from within their own families—and live a 'death to self' life of carrying their cross. **V 40–42: TEST** They will know who is on

God's side by the generosity and kindness shown to them by fellow disciples when they are being oppressed in the way described in this chapter.

CHAPTER ELEVEN

V 1–19: JOHN Jesus teaches His disciples, goes to preach and teach in Galilee, and is approached by disciples of the imprisoned John the Baptist, who want to find out who Jesus really is. Jesus factually reports what He has been doing, in order to encourage John, who knows that these signs are cited in the Bible as precursors of the Messiah. Jesus then commends John's whole-heartedness, sacrificial living and faithfulness as the special prophet who prepares the way for Him. But John, like Jesus, faces opposition and slander from those around. **V 20–24: JUDGEMENT** Comparing the cities with Tyre and Sidon, Jesus tells Chorazin and Bethsaida that they can expect judgement for failing to recognise His miracles. He tells Capernaum that it would be easier to have spared Sodom, already judged by God, than to overlook the pride of Capernaum. **V 25–30: JESUS** Jesus praises His Father for revealing His truth to childlike believers. He reveals the special relationship in the Godhead that the Son has with the Father. Jesus then invites all who are weary and burdened to come to Him, take His yoke, learn from Him, and to find the rest that He can give, in walking with Him and asking Him to bear our burdens.

CHAPTER TWELVE

V 1–14: SABBATH Jesus is very concerned to make sure that the Sabbath, the fourth of God's permanent moral commands of the Ten Commandments, is observed properly. He declares Himself to be the Lord even over the Sabbath. Jesus wants to clear the Sabbath of legalism. Here He teaches that preparing and eating food, healing, ministry, and works of emergency or kindness are all permitted on the Sabbath day. Because Jesus points to the spirit of Sabbath-keeping, rather than to the man-made, non-biblical legalistic details observed and promoted by the Pharisees, they seek to kill Him after He heals a man with a withered hand. **V 15–21: SERVANT** Despite the intent to kill Him, Jesus continues healing people and applies to Himself, as the Servant, the prophecies of the Messiah, taken from Isaiah 42:1–4. **V 22–32: SATAN** Jesus makes a blind and mute demon-possessed man see and speak, and causes the crowd to ask whether Jesus is the Messiah, the son of David. The Pharisees accuse him of casting out the demons by Beelzebub, the ruler of the demons. (Beelzebub was a Philistine god but Jesus understands that they mean that Satan is working through Him.) By their saying that He casts out demons through the spirit of an evil god, He identifies their sin as blasphemy against the Holy Spirit— the unforgivable sin. This means that because they have become too hardened to respond in repentance to God, they are unable to call to Him for His mercy. **V 33–37: SPEECH** Jesus points out that what we say reveals the true state of our hearts and that every word we speak will one day be subject to God's judgement. **V 38–42: SIGNS** The scribes and Pharisees wickedly ask for special signs and yet reject Jesus Christ, who quite clearly manifests God on earth. Jesus is greater than Jonah and greater than Solomon, and He says that they will be given no further sign than that given by Jonah. He was three days and nights in the belly of the great fish. Jesus, foretelling His resurrection from the dead, says that He, too, will be buried for three days and three nights. **V 43–45: SPIRITS** Jesus teaches that self-reformation is no answer to being possessed by evil spirits. Things will get worse without the operation of God's grace in our hearts through His Holy Spirit. **V 46–50: SURPRISED?** Jesus reveals to his disciples, in the presence of His biologically related family, that His real family are those who trust in and live for Him, and seek to do the will of His heavenly Father.

CHAPTER THIRTEEN

V 1–3a: PREACHING AND PARABLES: 1: MASTER AND MULTITUDES Multitudes come to hear Jesus, the Master teacher, by the seaside. He takes a boat to preach through parables to them. His first parable is foundational to all teaching of truth and the other parables concern the kingdom of heaven. **V 3b–23: PREACHING AND PARABLES: 2: SOWER AND SEED** Jesus tells a parable about a sower who sows seed. The seed falls on different kinds of ground, and only some falls on good ground, and yields fruit. After the parable the disciples ask why Jesus uses parables, and Jesus explains His method to them. Only those who belong to the kingdom of heaven, namely those who have Jesus as their King and whose citizenship is in heaven, will be able fully to appreciate the value of God's word. Jesus then interprets the parable and explains what the different grounds signify. The devil snatches some seed. Superficiality, tested by persecution and tribulation, causes other seed not to produce lasting fruit. Yet other seed is choked by this world's cares and the deceitfulness of riches. The good ground is the person who hears, understands, and produces fruit. Even good ground can vary according to the fruit it produces. **V 24–30: PREACHING AND PARABLES: 3: TARES AND TIMING** Having stated that only disciples can understand kingdom truth, Jesus tells them about a man's enemy who sowed tares among his wheat. Later, the disciples ask Jesus to explain this parable. He tells them that the tares and wheat must grow till harvest and that the tares must first be gathered up and burned before the wheat can be gathered into the barn. His explanation comes later. **V 31–32: PREACHING AND PARABLES: 4: MUSTARD SEED AND MIGHTY STRENGTH** Jesus compares the kingdom of heaven to a Palestinian mustard seed. (When full grown, it can be fifteen feet tall.) The kingdom of heaven starts small but becomes big. **V 33: PREACHING AND PARABLES: 5: UNSEEN AND UNSTOPPABLE** Leaven (or yeast) is the subject of the next parable that Jesus teaches. A woman hides it in three measures of meal until it is all leavened. The kingdom of heaven is at times unseen but its effect permeates all. **V 34–35: PREACHING AND PARABLES: 6: POLICY AND PROPHECY** Jesus uses parables all the time, and this policy is in line with the prophecy of the psalmist in Psalm 78:2. **V 36–43: PREACHING AND PARABLES: 7: TARES AND TRUTH** Jesus, now on His own with His disciples, is asked to explain the parable of the tares in the field. He explains that He is talking about the end of the age and that all unrepentant sinners will be cast into the furnace of fire. They will be gathered out first, and then those who, through faith in Him, are counted as 'righteous' will shine forth in that kingdom. **V 44: PREACHING AND PARABLES: 8: INVALUABLE TREASURE AND INVESTING TOTALLY** Jesus says that the kingdom of heaven is like a man who finds treasure and is so overjoyed that he hides it in the field and sells everything he has to buy the field. To have Christ's salvation, and to follow Him totally, is to possess everything. **V 45–46: PREACHING AND PARABLES: 9: PRECIOUS PEARL AND PURCHASE PRICE** A similar truth is told about a merchant who finds one pearl of great price and sells everything he has to buy it. **V 47–50: PREACHING AND PARABLES: 10: DRAGNET AND DAMNATION** The next kingdom parable concerns the separation of the wicked from the justified at the end of the age. It teaches the same message as the parable of the tares, which Jesus has explained. Jesus uses the picture of a dragnet. Only the good fish are retained after anything bad is thrown away. **V 51–53: PREACHING AND PARABLES: 11: DISCIPLES AND DEBRIEFING** Jesus confirms that the disciples understand what He has said. He uses an illustration about treasure to tell them that His new teaching is based upon old truth. He finishes the parables and leaves. **V 54–58: PROPHET AND POPULARITY—ASTONISHMENT AND ANTAGONISM** Jesus, now in Nazareth, amazes His countrymen by both His wisdom in His synagogue teaching and by His mighty works. They are offended because of Him, and familiarity with His family leads to contempt. The innuendo is that Jesus is illegitimate, as there is no mention of Joseph. He teaches that a prophet can expect greater unpopularity and opposition nearest to his own roots. Jesus does relatively few mighty works there because of the unbelief of His own people. This is a pointed truth for all His blood-bought people to bear in mind.

CHAPTER FOURTEEN

V 1–5: BAPTIST'S BOLDNESS John the Baptist not only honours God in his own life, but tells King Herod that his immoral relationship with Herodias, the wife of Herod's brother, Philip, is wrong. **V 6–12: HEROD'S HARDNESS** Herodias' daughter dances before Herod at his birthday party. She pleases the sensual king so much that he makes her a promise that she can have whatever she wants. It seems that he may be offering the young woman her own mother's place as queen, being half the kingdom, out of lust aroused by the dancing. If that is so, he is outwitted. Herodias causes her daughter to ask for the head of John the Baptist, and Herod obliges. He is sorry about it, but is bound by his own proud promise. John's disciples take his body and bury it, and tell Jesus what has happened. **V 13: SON'S SOLITARINESS** Upon hearing this news about John's death, Jesus withdraws to a solitary place by boat. However, the crowd hear where He is and follow Him on foot from the towns. **V 14–21: MASTER'S MIRACLE** Jesus has compassion for the great crowd that come to Him. He heals the sick. It is late and they are hungry. From five loaves and two fish, Jesus feeds over five thousand men, besides women and children. Twelve basketsful of fragments are left over and collected. **V 22–33: SAVIOUR'S SALVATION** In adverse weather conditions, the boat returns to the other side of the sea without Jesus. Jesus walks on the water towards the boat and Peter leaves it to come towards Jesus. His initial faith enables him to walk on the water but then he falters and begins to sink. Jesus hears his cry and saves him. The storm subsides as Jesus, with Peter, gets into the boat. Peter's confession, that Jesus really is the Son of God, follows. **V 34–36: HELPLESS HEALED** Having landed in Gennesaret, sick people come to Jesus from all over. Even touching the edge of His garment is sufficient to heal those who exercise faith in Him.

CHAPTER FIFTEEN

V 1–9: HYPOCRISY Jesus criticises the Pharisees and teachers of the law for keeping outward rules but not having a heart compliant with the reason for those rules. For example, they do not support needy parents because they say that their finance has to go to God. Their words are not consistent with the state of their hypocritical hearts. **V 10–20: HEART** Jesus shows in detail that all sins committed by men and women are because of sinful hearts that produce those sins. The uncleanness is within. This offends the Pharisees, but Jesus explains the sinfulness of the human heart to His disciples. **V 21–28: HELP** Jesus seems to ignore the cry of a Canaanite woman asking Him to deal with her demon-possessed daughter. In fact, He is simply intensifying the earnestness of her prayer. He grants her request in answer to the faith she puts in Him and heals her daughter. **V 29–31: HEALING** Great multitudes in Galilee bring the lame, the blind, the mute, the maimed and many others to Jesus, who heals them. **V 32–39: HUNGER** Jesus' compassion for the large and hungry crowd—which has been with Him for three days—means that, again, He feeds the people (this time four thousand men besides women and children) with a small amount of food (this time seven loaves and a few small fish). Seven large baskets full of fragments are gathered. After sending the crowd away, Jesus goes by boat into the vicinity of Magdala.

CHAPTER SIXTEEN

V 1–4: CONDEMNED The Pharisees and Sadducees ask Jesus for a sign from heaven. Jesus tells them to look at what is happening around them and points them to Scripture. He focuses specifically to the sign of Jonah. Thirsting for miraculous signs reveals their spiritual adultery and wickedness. **V 5–12: CAUTION** Jesus cautions his disciples against the false teachings of the Pharisees and the Sadducees. He uses leaven as an illustration. Initially, they cannot understand what He means and Jesus again explains His words to them. **V 13–20: CONFESSION** Jesus confirms that God has revealed to Peter that Jesus is 'the Christ, the Son of the Living God'. Before commanding that this truth should not yet be spread abroad, Jesus declares that He is the rock on which the church will be built, and that the exercise of the authority given to His gospel messengers to proclaim liberty will have eternal consequences. **V 21–23: COST** Jesus then begins to tell His disciples of the sufferings, death, and resurrection that await Him. He rebukes Peter seriously when he tells Jesus there will be no suffering or cross. **V 24–26: CROSS** Jesus uses this as a teaching opportunity to point out that discipleship involves bearing the cross of death to self, by following Him. This is to be more important than any worldly gain, but will be rewarded by God finally. No matter what their worldly gain, those who refuse to die to self to follow Christ will lose their souls—a tragic and bad bargain. **V 27–28: COMING** Jesus will come again in glory with His angels to deal with all people according to their works. Some of His disciples will see Him in His kingdom before they die. (This is immediately fulfilled in the next chapter as Peter, James and John will see Jesus transfigured.)

CHAPTER SEVENTEEN

V 1–8: TRANSFIGURATION With Peter,

James, and John, Jesus goes to a high mountain. He is transfigured before them with a face like the sun and clothes as white as light. Moses and Elijah appear. As Peter proposes making tabernacles for Jesus, Moses and Elijah, God the Father tells the disciples to hear Jesus, His well pleasing and beloved Son. Jesus reassures them in their fear, and then they see only Him. **V 9: TIMING** Jesus tells them not to reveal the transfiguration to anyone until after His resurrection. **V 10–13: TEACHING** Jesus reinforces the unique revelation they have had by teaching God's truth to them, while discussing Elijah. He links the events with the ministry of John the Baptist. **V 14–23: TESTED** The disciples are unable to heal an epileptic boy whose epilepsy is caused by demon-possession. Jesus heals him and tells them that faith in Him and more concentration on prayer and fasting would have enabled them to see him healed. He then underlines His coming sufferings, death, and resurrection, and they are very sorrowful. **V 24–27: TAX** Jesus teaches the disciples through Peter, that they should pay taxes due from them (here the temple tax). He then provides the money miraculously through a fish.

CHAPTER EIGHTEEN

V 1–5: COME Jesus uses a little child to teach that whoever comes to God must come with childlike faith and simplicity. **V 6–9: CONDEMNATION** Jesus underlines the grave consequences that will fall on those who cause any little one to sin who trusts in Him. He then develops the thought of condemnation further, through an illustration of drowning the offender. By striking illustrations, he teaches very strict self-control as a necessity. Anyone choosing sin, instead of Christ's word, is, in fact, choosing hell.

V 10–14: CARING Jesus teaches God's care over every little one (even one in a hundred who strays greatly concerns Him), and that guardian angels watch over them. **V 15–20: CONFRONTATION** A person offended should address the matter with the offender. The aim is to gain him as a brother. Refusal to listen should be met by addressing the matter before other witnesses, and, if necessary, putting church discipline into operation. The aim is to bring the person to repentance and blessing, and the prevailing environment should be that Christians are praying together in the name of the Lord Jesus Christ. **V 21–35: COUNTING** Just as God has forgiven us all our many sins, we should forgive others who sin against us. Their sins against us are minute compared with the immensity and amount of sin that we have committed against God and others. Forgiven people forgive others.

CHAPTER NINETEEN

V 1–2: LARGE MULTITUDES Many people follow Jesus from Galilee to Judea beyond the Jordan. Jesus heals there. **V 3–12: LASTING MARRIAGES** The main thrust of Jesus' teaching, in answer to the trick question of the Pharisees, is to ask them if they have not read the Old Testament and to emphasise that marriage is intended to be between one man and one woman on earth for life. God has joined them together and man must not separate them. In answer to their false statement that Moses commanded divorce, Jesus teaches that divorce is permitted, though not commanded or obligatory, in the case of sexual immorality. Marriage, however, is not for everyone. Some have physical defects, some have received injuries, and some are of a disposition where they can commit themselves wholly to God's work and do not need to be married. **V 13–15: LOVING MASTER** The disciples rebuke those who bring little children to Jesus so that He can put His hands on them and pray. The Master remonstrates with His disciples, showing His love for little children and emphasising that even they can come to Him. In doing this, Jesus teaches us a lesson about the kingdom of heaven. Jesus blesses the children and goes. **V 16–26: LOVING MONEY** A rich young man asks Jesus what good thing he can do to inherit eternal life. Jesus points him to five of the last six commands (all of which deal with man's relationship towards man). He does not cite the last commandment about coveting. Jesus summarises those commandments, that he should love his neighbour as himself. Jesus tells him that if he is able to keep those commandments perfectly, he will have eternal life. (Jesus knows that no-one can keep the commandments perfectly!) The man glibly replies that he has done this all his life, and asks what he still lacks. Jesus then tests him practically about coveting, by telling him to get rid of his possessions and give them away. Does eternal salvation mean more to this man than current gain? Sadly, he goes away sorrowful, and Jesus teaches that it is well nigh impossible for a man attached to his riches to have eternal life. He then adds that 'with God all things are possible'. **V 27–30: LORD'S MAXIMUM** Peter asks Jesus what those who have left all to follow Him will receive. He learns that he has the Lord's maximum blessings! Such people will feature in a restored heaven and earth, have a position of authority and influence, receive a new Christian family, a hundredfold blessing, and inherit eternal life. There will be many reversals of earth's wealth in that day, when some poor people will find themselves incredibly and eternally rich. The reverse will also be true.

CHAPTER TWENTY

V 1–16: FAIR DEALING Jesus illustrates that God's sovereign dealings with men are always just and fair. Those who come to Him late in the day will be just as saved and blessed as those who come earlier. The promise of God is open to all and any who trust it, during any time of their lives. They will know Him and His blessing even though they may be one of the last to come. Sadly, not many of those who are called will come, but those who do come will find that they are chosen. **V 17–19: FORETELLING DEATH** Jesus tells his twelve disciples, before they get into Jerusalem, that there He will be betrayed, condemned, delivered up, mocked, scourged, and crucified. He also tells them that on 'the third day He will rise again.' **V 20–28: FOOLISH DEMAND** The mother of James and John, sons of Zebedee, makes a foolish demand of Jesus in requesting that her sons sit on His right and left hand in the kingdom. Jesus reminds her that suffering precedes blessing and privilege for the Christian. He then reveals that this is part of His authority that He has left entirely to the Father to decide. Rather He emphasises to the ten, who are upset by the request, that the greatest Christians are the greatest servants, and that He Himself, the Son of Man, came to serve not to be served and 'to give His life a ransom for many'. If Christ had not been servant-hearted, He could not be the suffering Servant of Calvary. When Jesus foretells His death, He focuses on the cross while the disciples are fighting over a crown. He talks about suffering, and they squabble about ruling and leading. **V 29–34: FAITH DEMONSTRATED** The crowd want to ignore two blind men calling out to Jesus as the 'Son of David' to have mercy on them. Told to be quiet, they cry louder for mercy. Jesus answers their request, touches their eyes, and immediately they receive sight and follow Him. Faith is demonstrated in an urgent insistence for the need of mercy, a looking to Jesus, the receiving of a new understanding, and following Him.

CHAPTER TWENTY-ONE

V 1–11: PROPHECY Now near to Jerusalem, Old Testament prophecy is about to be fulfilled as Jesus the King enters the city riding on a donkey. He sends His disciples to find the donkey and colt and to bring them to Him. He is greeted with an enthusiastic welcome and the homage of clothes and branches being spread before Him as He enters the city as King and 'Son of David'. People want to know who Jesus is. **V 12–13: PROFANITY** Jesus then goes to God's temple and purges it by driving out those who are using it for financial gain when it should be a house of prayer. **V 14–17: PRAISE** The religious leaders are indignant, as the blind and the lame come to Him in the recently purged temple and are healed and as children cry out 'Hosanna to the Son of David!' (Hosanna literally means 'Save now' and that is why Jesus has come.) Jesus refers them to yet another fulfilment of Scripture and leaves for Bethany. **V 18–22: PUZZLED** Jesus' next miracle puzzles the disciples (and still puzzles some today). He curses an unfruitful fig tree, which withers away immediately. This has deep biblical, Jewish and symbolic significance but Jesus' immediate lesson is that Christians exercising faith (which can only ever be validly exercised in accordance with a desire to see God glorified and His will

done) will see greater things done. Mountains can be removed and cast into the sea. Many have found that their gracious and faithful God answers prayer and has removed mountains in their lives. **V 23–27: PRIESTS** Jesus is confronted by the chief priests and elders, who question His authority to do these things. He replies with a question as to whether the baptism of John is from heaven (namely from God) or from men. If they reply 'from heaven', their unbelief is exposed. If they reply 'from men', the crowd will be against them. They lie, saying that they do not know, and Jesus says, in that case, He will not answer them either. It is quite clear where the authority of Jesus comes from! **V 28–32: PENITENCE** Jesus then teaches by a parable about two sons that penitence is vital in knowing and serving God. It is not only what we say that is important. It is more important to repent of our sins and do what God demands. Still speaking to the chief priests and elders, He tells them that repentant tax collectors and harlots will be received, whereas they, by their rejection, will not. He underlines the rightness of the teaching of John the Baptist on righteousness and repentance. **V 33–41: PUNISHMENT** He then tells His religious opponents a parable about a landowner who sent servants to receive fruit from his vineyard. The servants are killed and so he then sends his son, who is also killed. Those wicked men will be punished for their wrongdoing. The strong implication, that the religious Jews have rejected the prophets and now reject God's Son, is clear to see. **V 42–44: PRE-EMINENT** The Lord will take the rejected stone and make it into the chief cornerstone. That stone will break those who do not bring forth the fruits of repentance and faith. This is clearly a reference to the pre-eminence of the Lord

Jesus Christ, His rejection, death, resurrection and ascension, as well as a reminder to His religious hearers of their desperate position before Him. **V 45–46: PERCEPTION** The chief priests and Pharisees perceive that the parables are about them. They are the sinful rebels who need to repent and turn to Christ. They dare not lay hands on Jesus because the multitudes revere Him as a prophet.

CHAPTER TWENTY-TWO

V 1–14: INVITATION Jesus then tells the religious leaders that the kingdom of heaven is like a king who arranges a marriage feast. Not only do his invitees not come, but some abuse and murder his servants who give the invitation. The king destroys the murderers and their city and sends his servants into the highways and byways to gather for the wedding those whom they can find. Yet one man comes in without a wedding garment and is excluded and cast out into outer darkness. The invitation to come into the kingdom is for all, but we must come properly clothed, in the righteousness of Christ. There are few who will be there, though many are called. **V 15–22: INTUITION** The Herodians, a party following Herod and seeking to blend the sinful lifestyle of ungodly people with certain observances of God's people, mix with the Pharisees to plot Jesus' downfall. They ask Him if taxes should be paid to Caesar. Taking a coin, Jesus asks them whose head it is on the coin and they reply 'Caesar's'. He tells them to pay to Caesar what is his and to God what is His. The divine intuitive perception of Jesus in discerning their wicked trap and His reply causes them to marvel and leave. **V 23–33: INSPIRATION** The Sadducees do not believe in the resurrection, unlike the Pharisees. The same day, they test Jesus about the resurrection by putting a hypothetical case of a woman who married seven brothers on the preceding death of each one. They want to know after this life whose wife she will be. Jesus tells them that they err because they know neither the Scriptures nor the power of God. In heaven there is no marriage, and God has already proclaimed to His people that He is the God of Abraham, Isaac, and Jacob. As God is not the God of the dead, they must still be living, as Jesus speaks. Clearly, death has not annihilated them. These words also refute the doctrine of conditional immortality, namely that people cannot exist after death outside their body. Jesus' teaching astonishes the crowds. His words demonstrate that those who believe in the resurrection believe in the inspiration of infallible Scripture. **V 34–40: INSTRUCTION** The Pharisees return to the fray, having heard that the Sadducees have been beaten! They are competing with one another to ensnare Jesus in an argument. One asks Jesus what the greatest commandment in the law is. Jesus summarises the Ten Commandments in two halves; the first four commandments tell us to love God with all our heart, soul, and mind, and that is the greatest commandment; the second, summarising the remaining six commandments, is to love our neighbour as ourselves. All the law and all the prophets hang on these two commandments. **V 41–46: INCARNATION** Jesus takes the initiative in the questioning and asks the Pharisees what they think about Christ and whose Son He is. They reply that He is the 'Son of David'. Jesus proves to them from the Scripture that therefore Christ is also the Lord. The Bible, always inspired by the Holy Spirit, says He is David's Lord as well as in the line of David's descendants. The religious leaders know that they have met their match and ask Him no further questions. They cannot catch Him out. Rather, Jesus has shown them to be sinful and in error.

CHAPTER TWENTY-THREE

V 1–12: WARNING—NO OTHER Jesus warns the multitudes and the disciples not to follow the hypocritical example of the Pharisees, but to follow that part of their teaching which is in accord with Moses' teaching. Jesus teaches that He, the Christ, is the only Teacher to whom they should listen, and that all who trust Him are brothers in His family with only God as their Father. They should listen to no other. Servanthood is more important than self-exaltation. God's exaltation will come with self-humbling. **V 13: WOE—NUMBER ONE** Jesus then starts a series of 'woes' to the scribes and Pharisees who are wicked and hypocritical religious leaders. The first one is that they exclude people from salvation by their legalistic hypocrisy which prevents both themselves and others from being saved. **V 14: WOE—NUMBER TWO** They exploit others and will receive a greater condemnation because of their exhibitionism. **V 15: WOE—NUMBER THREE** They are a bad example. Through their perverted teaching, they try to make proselytes from far and wide of those who seek to turn to God. They will make their converts twice as bad as they are. **V 16–22: WOE—NUMBER FOUR** Their religious and superstitious legalism demonstrates their ignorance and that they have completely wrong priorities. As with the way they consider gold in the temple, they look only on the externals and thus defy logic, common sense and justice, as well as God's word. **V 23–24: WOE—NUMBER FIVE** In pursuing their ritualistic and exhibitionist external religion, they

completely ignore justice, mercy and faith, and are blind guides to others. Their tithing is a self-centred monument to their own legalism, rather than giving to God from the heart to please Him. **V 25–26: WOE—NUMBER SIX** They are filthy inside and have not been cleansed, but seek to present a hypocritically clean outward appearance to others. **V 27–28: WOE—NUMBER SEVEN** They concentrate on their pretended outward religious beauty. That supposed beauty is like the whitewash on a tomb full of bones. It merely hides their spiritual deadness, hypocrisy and sin. **V 29–36: WOE—NUMBER EIGHT** Although they give outward acclaim to past prophets of God and build monuments to them, they reject the very teaching that those prophets gave. In fact, they are following the example of those who persecuted and killed those prophets. They will carry on that persecution and killing now and cannot escape the condemnation of hell because they will not recognise their sin and turn from it to God for mercy. **V 37–39: WINGS—NO REPENTANCE** Jesus laments over Jerusalem, where so much opposition to God and persecution of His messengers has happened. Jerusalem will be desolated. Jesus wants to gather the people of Jerusalem under His wings, as a hen gathers her chickens, but they are not willing to come to Him. His compassionate concern and offer is open to all sinners, even though many will reject Him and not come to Him to be saved.

CHAPTER TWENTY-FOUR

V 1–2: STONES The disciples are struck by the beauty of the temple building. Jesus tells them that the temple will be destroyed. Its stones will fall. Christianity is more than buildings! **V 3: SIGN** Jesus' disciples privately ask Him about the sign of His coming at the end of the age. **V 4–8: START** Jesus warns them not to allow anyone to deceive them. He teaches the start of the process leading to His coming will include the arrival of false christs, wars and rumours of wars, famines, pestilence, and earthquakes. These things are only the start. **V 9–14: SAVED** These things will be followed by tribulation, international hatred against Christ's disciples, betrayal and hatred by some of their own Christian brethren, false prophecy, growing lawlessness, and increasing coldness of love for God. The confidence is that those who endure to the end shall be saved, because their salvation is eternal. They must concentrate on preaching the gospel to all nations. This commission is still ours today as we see these days approaching and perhaps arriving. **V 15–26: SACRILEGE** Jesus teaches that Daniel's prophecy that the abomination of desolation will stand 'in the holy place' is a signal to those who live in Jerusalem to flee immediately. They must pray that their flight will not be in winter or on a Sabbath day, which, interestingly, will still be observed then. Unprecedented tribulation will follow, which will be shortened so that the elect will be saved. Strong deception will cause many to believe in false christs and false prophets. But the elect need not be deceived and must not follow the popular and sensational fads of the time. Jesus tells this to His disciples, then and now, so that when it happens all will be reminded that His Word is true and thus all will be encouraged to stand. Discernment is needed so that Christians do not stampede to follow those who claim Christ has come. All will know when He comes again. **V 27–31: SIGN** Christ's coming will be visible to all just as lightning which flashes across the heavens is visible. After the darkening of the heavenly light, which follows the tribulation, the sign of Christ's coming will appear in heaven. All tribes of the earth will mourn Him and He will be seen 'on the clouds of heaven with power and great glory'. His angels, accompanied by a great trumpet sound, will gather His elect who will be borne by the four winds into heaven for that gathering, at the second coming. **V 32–35: SCRIPTURE** Just as the arrival of tender branches and new leaves on a fig tree proclaims the coming of summer, so the escalation of the things that Jesus teaches will proclaim the coming of the Son of Man. Jesus reminds His disciples of the permanence of Scripture by saying that heaven and earth will pass away, but His words never will. **V 36–44: SUDDENLY!** Jesus teaches that only God the Father knows the exact hour of His coming. This is an aspect of Christ's divine knowledge that He has chosen to lay aside in His humility to become our Saviour. But, just as the world ignored the righteous preaching of Noah and would not prepare to escape the judgement of the flood, so a failure to prepare in repentance and faith for Christ's second coming will lead to judgement then. Despite the warnings to repent and turn to God, and despite the prophecies of His coming, it will be upon them unexpectedly, suddenly, and too late. Christians, however, should confidently expect His coming and remain ready. **V 45–53: SERVANTS** Those belonging to Christ are compared to a wise and faithful servant who does God's will and is ready for his Master's return, which will be a great blessing to him. Those who do not trust Christ, but remain in their sin, will, with the hypocrites, face 'weeping and gnashing of teeth'.

CHAPTER TWENTY-FIVE

V 1–13: THE TEN Jesus continues to tell parables concerning the second coming and His kingdom. At a wedding, ten bridesmaids are to await the coming of the bridegroom and to be ready for it. Five have their lamps trimmed and are ready. Five are foolish and are not ready. As the bridegroom delays, the foolish ones sleep and are found out when the bridegroom comes at midnight. In the same way, Jesus tells His disciples to watch because no one knows the day or the hour when He will be coming again. **V 14–30: THE TALENTS** Jesus then tells the parable about a man with three servants. In his absence abroad, he gives them respectively five, two and one talent to use on his behalf to make money for him. He comes back and finds that the first two have doubled their talents but the last one has buried it so that he does not lose it. He commends the first two telling them to 'Enter into the joy of your lord', but censures the third servant for being wicked and lazy. He reminds him that his master expected a return. The third servant's talent is given to the servant with the most talents, but the master's commendation is equally shared between the two faithful servants. The unfaithful servant is cast into the outer darkness where there is 'weeping and gnashing of teeth'. Those using what God gives them, spiritually and practically, will know God's fruitful and multiplying blessing as they work for Him. Those who are not prepared to work for Him show that they have not received His work of grace and mercy in their hearts. **V 31–46: THE TEST** Jesus goes on to say that when He comes again in His glory with His angels, He will reign, and the nations will gather before Him to be separated by Him. Those belonging to Him will inherit His kingdom and blessing. Those who do not belong to Him will be cast into the everlasting fire reserved for Satan and his angels. (This is also taught in the book of Revelation.) The test is whether they belong to Him as His sheep or whether they are the goats, signifying the unbelievers. The test of true faith is whether the works of a changed lifestyle follow, and this involves a loving, compassionate, concerned attitude to others which Christ takes as if the deeds were done for Him. Jesus emphasises that the two choices are 'everlasting punishment' or 'eternal life'. We can only be counted righteous through receiving His righteousness when we turn to Him.

CHAPTER TWENTY-SIX

V 1–5: PLOT Having completed His teaching about the second coming and the kingdom, Jesus tells the disciples that He will be delivered up to be crucified at the Passover in two days' time. The chief priests, scribes and elders assemble at the palace of Caiaphas, the high priest, to plot to take Him and kill Him. They will use trickery. They will not take Him during the feast, in case the people riot. **V 6–13: PREPARATION** A woman (elsewhere identified as Mary) pours out fragrant oil on Jesus as He is at the table. Facing the disciples' criticism that the oil could have been sold and the money distributed to the poor, Jesus tells them that He will not be long with them, and that she has done this act in advance for His burial. The fulfilment of His prediction, that her act will be remembered wherever the gospel is preached, is evidenced by the very fact that this incident is contained in the Bible itself. **V 14–16: PRICE** Meanwhile Judas promises to the chief priests to betray Jesus and is paid the price of a slave, thirty pieces of silver. Judas looks for his opportunity to betray Jesus. **V 17–19: PROVISION** As the disciples seek to prepare a place for the Passover memorial, Jesus tells them to go into the city. They must tell a certain man that 'His time is at hand'. Jesus and His disciples will use the man's house. They follow His directions and prepare for Passover in accordance with this provision. **V 20–25: PREDICTION** Before taking the Passover, which becomes the Lord's Supper, Jesus predicts that someone, for whom it would have been better if he had never been born, will betray him. Judas asks Him if he is the one, and Jesus confirms that he is. **V 26–30: PASSOVER** The significance of the Passover is fulfilled in the Lord Jesus Christ. He takes and adapts the form of the Passover and likens the broken bread to His body which will be broken, and the poured out wine to the shedding of His blood which He is giving in order that sins may be remitted. Even in this, He again implies His resurrection and His ascension because He tells His disciples that He will drink with them again in His Father's kingdom. Many think that the hymn they sing is probably Psalm 118. They go to the Mount of Olives. Christ's eternal purpose and destiny is soon to find fulfilment at Calvary. **V 31–35: PRESUMPTUOUS** Jesus tells the disciples that they will stumble and be scattered that night because of Him, but that He will rise again and go before them to Galilee. Facing the solemnity of Christ's coming cross, and the wonder of His resurrection, Peter says that he will never stumble, even though all the others do. Jesus tells him that before the rooster crows, he will deny Him three times. Peter protests that he will die rather than deny Christ. The other disciples say the same thing. Humble trust is always better than presumptuous bravado, whatever the emotional state of Christ's

disciples. **V 36–46: PRAYER** Jesus goes to Gethsemane. In deep distress and sorrow, He asks His disciples to stay with Him to pray. On three occasions His disciples sleep rather than pray as their Master requests. Jesus shows both His true humanity and His perfect obedience in asking, three times, if it is possible that His Father should let this cup of suffering and punishment pass from Him, and yet in the same sentence declares that He will do His Father's will by going to the cross. Unsupported by His disciples, He wakes them up and goes to meet His betrayer and his sinister band. **V 47–50: PREDATORS** At that very moment Judas, with a great crowd bearing swords and clubs, comes with the religious leaders to take Jesus. They come as predators to attack the Lamb of God. The sign is that Judas will kiss Jesus to ensure, in those dark hours, his correct identification. This he does, greeting Him at the same time. The composure and quiet control of Jesus is evident as He calls him 'Friend' and asks him why he has come, knowing full well the answer. The crowd descend on Jesus and take Him. **V 51–56: PURPOSE** One of Jesus' disciples, identified elsewhere as the impetuous Peter, strikes the ear of a servant of the high priest and cuts it off. Jesus rebukes and restrains him. (We learn elsewhere that Jesus healed that man at this time.) Jesus confirms that if He asked for twelve legions of angels to deliver Him, they would be sent to His aid. He says that His sufferings 'must happen thus' in order to fulfil the Scriptures and so He can achieve His grand purpose to redeem lost sinners by His death on the cross. As He allows the rabble to take Him, all His disciples forsake Him and flee. **V 57–63a: PERJURY** As Jesus is taken away to the high priest's palace, followed afar off by Peter, His wicked religious accusers unsuccessfully seek perjurers who will substantiate their claim that Christ has blasphemed. Eventually they find two such false witnesses whose miserable testimonies are accepted by the high priest, while Jesus remains silent. **V 63b–68: PROPHECY** Under oath, the high priest asks Jesus to confirm whether He is 'the Christ of God'. Jesus confirms this and states that He will be at God's right hand in heaven and that He will come 'on the clouds of heaven'. The prejudiced judge becomes the jury and the prosecutor. He finds Christ guilty of blasphemy, to the delight of the religious leaders, who declare Him worthy of death. (This is an unconstitutional nonsense, since the Jewish court should not put anyone to death for blasphemy in the Roman judicial system.) Jesus is abused and subjected to spitting, beating and insults. **V 69–75: PETER** Peter sits outside in the court and makes the first of his three denials of his Lord. He repeats three times, with increasing emphasis, that he does not know Jesus Christ. His third denial is made to seem more authentic and sad by his cursing and swearing. 'Immediately a rooster crowed.' Peter remembers the words of his suffering Lord, and goes out to weep bitterly.

CHAPTER TWENTY-SEVEN

V 1–2: BOUND The religious leaders' plot to kill Jesus moves nears its ultimate and evil climax as morning breaks, and they plot further together. He is bound and taken to Pontius Pilate, the Roman governor. (They know that the Jews have no power of death penalty because they are under Roman law.) **V 3–10: BETRAYER** Judas, seeing what happens to Jesus, is remorseful, but not repentant. He throws down the thirty pieces of silver before the chief priest and elders, who cannot put it into their treasury because it is the price of blood. They buy a potter's field in which to bury strangers, now called 'the field of blood'. Even this fulfilled the prophecy of Zechariah (which, being in the prophetic division of the canon of Scripture started by the book of Jeremiah, is here called 'Jeremiah'). Those who betray Jesus never have peace. **V 11–14: BEWILDERED** Jesus bewilders and amazes Pilate, when accused before him by the chief priest and elders. He answers nothing. Pilate asks if He has heard what has been said against Him. This is an unconstitutional and unwarranted 'kangaroo court' despite its appearance of authority. **V 15–26: BARABBAS** Despite a strong warning from his wife to have nothing to do with the unjust trial of Jesus, Pilate sees a way out of this predicament by offering to set Jesus free as the one prisoner released each year at the feast. He knows that envy, not justice, has motivated the hunters of Jesus. The crowds have cried for Christ's blood, having been manipulated by the religious leaders. Pilate offers to release Jesus as an alternative to Barabbas, a notorious criminal. But, whipped up by their religious leaders (as we see elsewhere), the crowd shout for Barabbas to be released and for Jesus to take the punishment that Barabbas would have taken, namely crucifixion. Pilate, seeing that his scheme has backfired, washes his hands publicly to show that he is innocent of the blood of 'this just person'. Of course he is not innocent, because he has unjustly agreed to be influential in a judicial matter which should not concern him. The people's cry is, 'His blood be upon us and on our children,' which is later to be fulfilled in two entirely different ways. Barabbas is released and Jesus is scourged prior to crucifixion. **V 27–31: BULLIES** The mocking soldiers of the whole garrison in the Praetorium strip Jesus, clothe Him in a scarlet robe, put a twisted crown of thorns on His head, and a reed in His hand. The bullies then give Him mock praise, spit on Him, take the reed, and hit Him on the head. They then put back His own clothes and take Him to be crucified. All this is suffered by the spotless Son of God, who humbly accepts this ignominy and shame, though He has the inherent power to destroy His oppressors at a word. **V 32–34: BRAVERY** The bravery of the Son of Man is further shown as, after Simon of Cyrene has been forced to carry His cross to Golgotha, the 'Place of the Skull', He refuses the sour wine mingled with gall which would have dulled His pain. **V 35–37: BIBLE** So many prophecies of the Bible are being fulfilled at this point. He is crucified as predicted in Psalm 22 and Isaiah 53, though this Roman form of execution was unknown when the prophets penned those words hundreds of years before. His crucifiers fulfil another prophecy of Psalm 22 by dividing His garments between them and casting lots for His clothing. Watching Him die, they put the accusation over the cross 'THIS IS JESUS THE KING OF THE JEWS'. Unknowingly, they get that right. **V 38–44: BLASPHEMY** Jesus is crucified in the centre of two robbers. Even they join in the blasphemy and insults that are hurled upon Him by the mocking crowd, chief priest, scribes, and elders. His ability to save, His trust in God the Father, and His claim to be the Son of God are all now thrown in His face. He can only answer those accusations by staying on the cross and accomplishing His work. **V 45–50: BLACKNESS** At the brightest part of the day, the sixth hour (which is our midday), darkness covers the whole land until the ninth hour when Jesus calls out, 'My God, My God, why have You forsaken Me?' Some misunderstand this

as a call for Elijah, and others offer Him sour wine to drink on a sponge attached to a reed. Jesus, still in control, cries out again in a loud voice, (which we know was, 'It is finished!') and then yields up His spirit, knowing that His work on the cross has been accomplished and completed. **V 51–56: BEHOLD** Matthew is so amazed by what follows that he precedes it with 'Behold!' God sends amazing signs to indicate that His eternal, incarnate Son has died, and that the way is open to Him through that death for sinners to approach Him. The veil of the temple (dividing the Most Holy Place from the holy place) is torn from the top to the bottom, rocks are split in an earthquake, graves are opened, and there is an exceptional appearance of resurrected bodies of saints for a limited period. These signs are to convince people of the person and authority of Jesus, and are effective in so doing, for even the centurion who guards Him, on seeing these things, says, 'Truly this was the Son of God.' Many Galilean women, supporting Jesus, look from afar, including Mary Magdalene, Mary the mother of James and Joseph, and the mother of Zebedee's sons. **V 57–61: BURIAL** Joseph of Arimathea, a rich disciple of Jesus, begs for Jesus' body to be buried in his own new tomb. Pilate concurs and commands that the body be given to him. Joseph wraps it in clean linen, lays it in the tomb, and rolls a large stone against the door of the tomb before departing. The two Marys sit opposite that tomb. They have a good long look at its location. **V 62–65: BLOCKED** The religious leaders remember Jesus' words that 'After three days I will rise', so they approach Pilate to make sure that the tomb is made secure until the third day in case His disciples come to steal Him and claim the resurrection of Christ. Pilate tells them to take a guard of Roman soldiers and make the tomb as secure 'as you know how'. They secure the tomb, sealing the stone and setting the guard. The way for fraud and deceit is blocked, and the way in to and out of the tomb is blocked. (That is unless its Inhabitant will rise from the dead and have a resurrection body!)

CHAPTER TWENTY-EIGHT

v 1–4: STONE REMOVED The two Marys come to see the tomb early on the first day of the week (the first of the 'Lord's days'). There is an earthquake and an angel of the Lord descends, rolls back the stone from the door of the tomb and sits on it. The guards shake through fear and become as dead. (The stone is rolled back to let outsiders in, not to let the Insider out—that has already happened.) **v 5–7: SAVIOUR RISEN** The angel tells the women not to be afraid, but that the crucified Jesus has risen. They are to relay this news to the disciples and tell them that Jesus will meet them again in Galilee. **v 8–10: SUDDEN REUNION** Emotionally mixed between fear and great joy, they run to tell the disciples and are met by Jesus, whose opening comment is 'Rejoice!' They hold Him and worship Him. He repeats the angels' instructions not to fear, to go to the disciples, and to tell them that He will meet them in Galilee. **v 11–15: SOLDIERS' RUMOUR** Some of the soldiers come to the city to report to the religious rulers what has happened. They consult together and pay them a large bribe that they will dishonestly say that while they were asleep the disciples came and stole the body away. (It was a poor excuse: if they were asleep, how could they know that it was the disciples who stole the body?) The soldiers are to be safeguarded before Pilate if he hears that they were supposed to have been asleep. The soldiers' false rumour circulates and is still believed by Jews, as Matthew writes in this Gospel. **v 16–17: SPECIAL REVELATION** Jesus has promised that He will meet His eleven disciples in Galilee and He appoints a mountain as the meeting place. As He reveals Himself to them as the risen Lord, they worship Him. It seems from elsewhere in Scripture that others were there too. However, some people doubt. (The Bible is so faithful in relaying the faults of Christ's disciples, while portraying the righteous perfection of the Saviour.) **V 18–20: SPECIFIC REASON** The once-crucified, now risen Jesus confirms His authority in heaven and on earth and says, 'Go therefore.' Because of that authority, His disciples are to make disciples of all nations, baptising them in the name of the triune God, and teaching obedience to His word. He confirms that He is with His own always, 'Even to the end of the age.' No wonder the Gospel concludes with a most appropriate 'Amen!'

MARK

OVERVIEW

PEOPLE AND PRELIMINARIES

✳ Mark (sixteen chapters) was written by Mark between AD50 and AD70 probably in Galilee. It is the second and shortest Gospel. **See comments on Matthew.** The estimated period covering the events in Mark is under ten years, probably only seven.

PLAN AND PURPOSE

ⓘ Like Matthew and Luke, but with valid variety, Mark's Gospel focuses on the Lord Jesus Christ. **See comments on Matthew.** He presents the life and ministry of the Lord Jesus Christ, from His baptism by John the Baptist in the River Jordan up to and including His resurrection, commission to His disciples and His ascension. Mark was not one of the twelve apostles, but was a very close associate of the apostle Peter and no doubt drew from Peter's experience of Christ. His Gospel is written largely for Gentiles, especially Romans, using Latin expressions and translating Aramaic terms as it goes along. It underlines Jesus as a servant, and thus carries no genealogy, for who is concerned about the family tree of a servant? It is the shortest and simplest of the Gospels. Servants have less to say than kings! In the focus on Christ's service, immediacy is readily apparent. The teaching ministry of Jesus is, of course, authoritatively portrayed here, but it is the deeds of Christ, rather than His words, which are accentuated. The word 'immediately' or its equivalent expression comes over forty times. A servant appreciates quick response! This servant, who is also the Master, sees nature and the forces of evil respond immediately to His command. Although He is a servant, He is also God in the flesh.

PROFILE AND PROGRESSION

🔡 John the Baptist prepares the way for Jesus and baptises Him, and Satan tempts Him in the wilderness (1:1–13); Jesus starts to serve in and around Galilee—including disciples' commissioning, disputes with scribes and Pharisees, teaching parables, and doing mighty miracles (1:14–7:23); Jesus continues to serve with the Gentiles—including more miracles, Peter's confession of Him as Christ, Jesus foretelling His death and resurrection, and teaching (7:24–9:50); Jesus continues to serve with Jerusalem in view—including teaching on divorce, children, discipleship—and enters Jerusalem where He curses the fig tree and purifies the temple and concentrates on teaching (10:1–13:37); climax of Jesus' service through the Lord's supper, betrayal, Gethsemane, illegal trials, crucifixion, and burial (14:1–15:47); highly exalted Servant—Jesus risen again from the dead (16:1–8); added note about His servants' task and Jesus' ascension (16:1–20).

PRINCIPLES AND PARTICULARS

👉 **See comments on Matthew.** Because of Mark's portrayal of Jesus as a servant, we should note carefully how the King of kings humbled Himself to serve, even to His death on the cross. Those who serve Him today should seek, by God's help, to follow His example. Thus the teaching about, and role model for, dedicated discipleship should be especially heeded. We must not lose sight of the power of the Lord Jesus who humbled Himself to do all this for sinful rebels.

MARK

CHAPTER ONE

V 1–11: BEGINNING AND BAPTISM There is no introductory genealogy in Mark. The Gospel has the flavour of Christ's servanthood throughout, and no one is interested in the ancestry of a servant. The beginning of the Gospel is marked by John the Baptist's preparation of the way for the Lord Jesus Christ, the Son of God. He baptises to underline repentance. Jesus needs no repentance but is baptised by John. Immediately the three Persons of the Trinity are evident, the Holy Spirit descending as a dove, and the Father confirming that he is well pleased with His 'beloved Son'. **V 12–20: TEMPTATION AND TEAM** Immediately after this blessing, the Holy Spirit drives Jesus into the wilderness for forty days, where he is tempted by Satan, accompanied by wild animals, and served by angels. This marks the start of his ministry commanding people to 'Repent and believe in the gospel'. He then calls those who will become fishers of men in His discipleship team: Simon, Andrew, James and John, all of whom are fishermen. Both sets of brothers immediately leave all to follow Him. **V 21–34: MASTER AND MIRACLES** Jesus shows his mastery by authoritative teaching that astonishes those who note the difference between Him and the scribes. He demonstrates the power of the Son of God by casting an unclean spirit out of a man in the synagogue, healing Simon Peter's mother-in-law from a fever so that she serves immediately, and healing many who are sick with all kinds of diseases and who are demon-possessed. **V 35–39: PRAYER AND PREACHING** Jesus departs to pray on His own and is found by His searching disciples. From there, Jesus goes to preach to the crowds who are looking for Him. Preaching is His priority, but He also casts out demons. **V 40–45: OUTCAST AND OUTSIDE** Jesus has compassion for the unclean leper, a social and religious outcast, and heals him by touching him. Instead of going to the priest as the law requires to validate his healing, the leper cannot keep quiet about what Christ has done for him. He tells everyone he meets! Jesus can no longer openly enter the city, but has to go outside to deserted places. Even there, the crowds come to Him.

CHAPTER TWO

V 1–12: OPPOSITION—SCRIBES AND FAITH In Capernaum, Jesus preaches God's word. He answers the faith of four men, who lower a paralytic man through the roof into a crowded house, by forgiving the man's sins. The scribes hold Him guilty of blasphemy because they say that only God can forgive sins. Jesus knows their thoughts, answers them, and endorses His power by telling the paralytic to rise, take up his bed, and go. He does so, and the amazed people glorify God. **V 13–17: OPPOSITION—SINNERS AND FORGIVENESS** Jesus then calls the unpopular tax collector, Levi, to follow Him. He dines with Levi in the company of other tax collectors and 'sinners'. The Pharisees make criticisms to the disciples about the company Jesus keeps. Jesus points out that He has come to call sinners to repentance. **V 18–22: OPPOSITION—SUSPICION AND FASTING** Some people notice the difference between John's disciples and the Pharisees' disciples, on the one hand, and

Jesus' disciples, on the other hand. The first two groups are fasting, but the last group is not. In answering their question, Jesus points out that the time to fast will be when He is no longer with them. He goes on to demonstrate the difference that He makes, by making reference to putting new cloth on old cloth, and new wine into old bottles. The new life available in Christ cannot be contained in the old system. **V 23–27: OPPOSITION— SABBATH AND FOOD** Jesus justifies His disciples' eating of ears of corn on the Sabbath, after the Pharisees complain to Him about them. He points to the example of David. He confirms that the Sabbath is still current as a blessing to mankind, but that He is the Lord of the Sabbath.

CHAPTER THREE

V 1–6: SABBATH Jesus heals a man with a withered hand and incurs great opposition because He does it on the Sabbath. Again, confirming the Sabbath's continued existence, He shows that it is in the spirit of Sabbath to be a blessing to people and to do them good. His concern is for a Sabbath that will honour God in spirit as well as in the letter. The Pharisees and Herodians plot to kill Him as a result. **V 7–12: SON** Following His preaching to huge crowds drawn from all quarters, which necessitates speaking from a boat to the shore, Jesus heals many. Evil spirits are cast out and publicly acclaim Jesus as the Son of God. Jesus warns them not to make Him known. **V 13–19: SENT** Jesus selects twelve named disciples, first of all to be with Him, and then to be sent out by Him to do His work of preaching, healing and casting out demons. **V 20–30: SERIOUS** Starting with aggressive opposition from His family and closest friends, serious rebellion against Jesus is expressed by the hardened scribes, who accuse Him of working through Satan. Jesus answers this malicious accusation and reveals that they have committed the sin against the Holy Spirit which can never be forgiven. They have never known forgiveness and never will. The detail of their unpardonable sin is the deliberate, wicked, irreverent and malicious attributing of the work of the Son of God to Satan, claiming that Jesus is possessed by an unclean spirit. **V 31–34: SPIRITUAL** Jesus teaches that His closest family are not biological, but consist of those who are trusting and obedient to God's will.

CHAPTER FOUR

V 1–20: PARABLE OF SOILS Jesus tells and then explains the parable of the four different soils in which seed was sown. The soils depict four different states of mind and heart in which the Word of God can be received and responded to. Jesus speaks about Satan's snatching of the seed sown on the wayside, the shallowness of some early growth revealed and destroyed by persecution, the choking of some growing seed by a spirit of worry and worldliness, and seed on the good ground. Lasting fruit is only produced from good ground, and the yield from it will vary. **V 21–23: PARABLE OF SHINING** Jesus explains the need to shine publicly for God, just as a lamp is put on a stand to give light. **V 24–25: PRODUCTIVITY OF SOWER** Jesus teaches that the level of blessing that we receive from God is governed by our attitude and by the degree of effort we put into our relationship with Him. If we sow liberally, we will produce liberally, and vice versa. **V 26–32: PARABLES OF SEEDS** Jesus tells two parables about seed. One of them, concerning a germinating seed, teaches that the growth of the kingdom of God is gradual but definite. The second, about a mustard seed, demonstrates the ultimate vastness of the kingdom of God, from a very small start. **V 33–34: PARABLES OF SAVIOUR** In teaching the disciples, Jesus uses many other parables. He uses them continually and afterwards explains their meaning in private to His disciples. It is only those today who have become His disciples, by being born again through the Holy Spirit, who really understand the Bible's spiritual teaching. **V 35–41: POWER OF STORM** By stopping the power of the storm, Jesus shows His divine power and His ability to create peace in nature, or in the human heart. Even His disciples are amazed at His authority.

CHAPTER FIVE

V 1–20: DEMONS DISPLACED Jesus delivers an uncontrollable, self-harming, demon-possessed man by sending the evil spirits who possess him into a herd of pigs, which rush into a lake and are drowned. The man becomes self-composed, dressed and sane, and tells the amazed people what Jesus has done for him. Sadly, the people ask Jesus to leave the area of Decapolis, rather than trust and follow Him. Jesus refuses to allow the delivered man to go with Him. He obeys the Lord in going home to tell his friends in Decapolis what the Lord has done for him. The people there marvel. **V 21–24: DAUGHTER DYING** On the other side of the lake, a synagogue ruler, Jairus, asks Jesus to go with him to heal his dying daughter. Jesus starts out with him and is followed and thronged by many people. **V 24–34: DISEASED DELIVERED** Jairus must have felt frustrated by the intervention of a woman who had been losing blood for twelve years and found no cure or relief for her disease. Jesus knows the touch of her deliberate

individual faith in Him, in contrast to those who merely brushed by Him. To His disciples' amazement, Jesus asks who touched Him and causes her to make a public confession of her faith. He assures her that she is healed and sends her off with His peace and assurance. **V 35–43: DEATH DEFEATED** After a discouraging start, when the death of Jairus' daughter is confirmed, his patience is rewarded. Jesus accompanies him, with Peter, James and John. The Lord asserts that his daughter's death is but sleep to Him, and is ridiculed by the assembled mourners for making that statement. Jesus, takes Jairus' dead daughter by the hand, and awakens the twelve-year-old from the sleep of death to life. Practical and caring as ever, He instructs them to give her some food!

CHAPTER SIX

V 1–6: TEACHING Jesus, as usual, teaches on the Sabbath. He is rejected by those who live nearest to His physical home. Because of this, He works comparatively few miracles there. Saddened by their unbelief, He travels and teaches around the villages. **V 7–13: TWELVE** Jesus calls, sends out and instructs the twelve apostles. They go and preach repentance, demonstrating their authority from Him by doing appropriate miracles. **V 14–29: TRIBUTE** When people guess who Jesus is, King Herod, (obviously greatly impressed by John the Baptist, whom he murdered), wrongly states that Jesus is John the Baptist risen from the dead. After John had resolutely stood against Herod's immoral, illicit and incestuous relationship with Herodias, his brother's wife, she conspired to have John beheaded by Herod after her daughter had gratified the king's sensuality by dancing for him. **V 30–44: THOUSANDS**

The return of the apostles causes Jesus to tell them to come to a deserted place to rest for a while with Him. Multitudes hear and come, and the day passes, leaving them hungry. Jesus, full of compassion, feeds five thousand men (as well as women and children) with five loaves and two fishes. There is far more left over than ever there was to start with! In performing His miracle, He is both organised and keen to involve His disciples in the task. **V 45–52: TROUBLED** Jesus directs his disciples to go by boat to Bethsaida, while He stays on to pray on a mountain. They struggle to row against the strong wind, and Jesus walks on the water over to them. They are troubled because they think He is a ghost. He stills their troubles and calms the storm. Although amazed, their hardened hearts still fail to understand the lesson of His sovereign control and care seen in the earlier miracle of feeding the five thousand men with the fish and loaves. **V 53–56: TOUCHING** Arriving in Gennesaret, crowds come to Him so that many sick people can be healed. Even those who merely touch the hem of His garment are healed. Had they heard about the woman with the flow of blood who did the same when Jesus was on the way to raise Jairus' daughter?

CHAPTER SEVEN

V 1–8: RELIGION The Pharisees, with some scribes, criticise the disciples of Jesus for not complying with the external ritual of their ceremonial washing. Quoting from Isaiah, Jesus exposes that all the external religious observances of the Pharisees and Jews count for nothing because their hearts are far from God. **V 9–13: RESPONSIBILITY** Jesus illustrates this by showing that their responsibility to honour and care for needy parents is

being avoided wrongly in the name of religious observance. **V 14–23: REALITY** Jesus shows that all human wickedness comes from a sinful heart and defiles. It is the heart that needs to be put right. **V 24–30: RESPONSE** Illustrating that God deals with any person of any nation (male or female, Jew or Gentile), Jesus commends the faith of a Syro-Phoenician woman. She demonstrates her faith by responding correctly to His illustration about food being offered to little dogs. Her daughter, with an unclean spirit, is made whole accordingly. **V 31–37: RELEASE** Jesus, back in Decapolis, opens the ears and loosens the tongue of a deaf and mute man. Despite the Lord's command to tell no one, those witnessing this miracle cannot keep silent and comment that Jesus 'has done all things well'.

CHAPTER EIGHT

V 1–10: COMPASSION Having previously fed five thousand people from five loaves and two fishes, Jesus now feeds four thousand from seven loaves and a few small fish. The miracle not only shows His power, but His compassion to feed people who have been with Him a long time, and who are hungry. Jesus departs with His disciples by boat to Dalmanutha. **V 11–13: CONFRONTATION** Back in the region of Dalmanutha, the Pharisees test Jesus by asking Him for a sign from heaven. He reiterates that no further sign will be given. (They have the Old Testament Scriptures.) Jesus crosses in a boat to the other side. **V 14–15: CAREFUL** Jesus warns the disciples to take care against the influence of the Pharisees (by their wrong teaching) and Herod (by his hostile opposition). He uses 'yeast' to illustrate these evil influences. **V 16–21: CONFUSION** Amazingly, the use of the word 'yeast' makes the disciples think that Jesus is talking about bread. He reminds them from His earlier miracles of feeding thousands of people from virtually nothing, that lack of bread is not a problem for Him! He challenges their culpable lack of understanding. **V 22–26: CLARITY** A blind man is able to see clearly after Jesus gives him his sight. Although there is no time lag or failure, this is the only miracle that Jesus chooses to perform in two parts. Jesus tells him to go home and tell no one. **V 27–30: CONFESSION** Peter confesses, on being asked by Jesus, that he knows that Jesus is the Christ. Others have guessed that Jesus is John the Baptist, or Elijah, or a prophet. Once again, Jesus warns that at this time this must not be told to anyone. This is because His hour for final opposition and death has not yet come, as the next verse shows. **V 31–33: CROSS** Jesus immediately teaches that He will suffer, be rejected, be killed and rise again. Peter rebukes Him and is himself rebuked strongly by Jesus, reminding him that truth comes from God and not from man. Peter was so wrong about the cross, having just been so right about the Christ! **V 34–38: COMMITMENT** Having talked about His cross, Jesus tells each disciple to deny himself and take up his own cross and follow Him. Those who are prepared to lose themselves in this way show that their soul is saved and that one day they will be owned by Jesus in glory. If it were possible to gain the whole world, anyone doing so at the cost of losing his own soul would be an eternal loser.

CHAPTER NINE

V 1–13: TRANSFIGURATION Six days after Jesus teaches that His disciples will see a powerful presentation of God's kingdom before they die, He is transformed before Peter, James and John in an amazing and glorious way on the mountain. The Father's voice underlines the supremacy of His Son over Moses (speaking of the law) and Elijah (speaking of prophecy). In the conversation that takes place afterwards, they do not understand what 'rising from the dead' means, and also are confused about Elijah. Jesus, although apparently not understood by them, refers to John the Baptist as 'Elijah who has already come'. **V 14–29: TRUST** Having descended from the mountain of transfiguration, Jesus is confronted by the scene where the other disciples have been unable to cast out an evil spirit from the son of a concerned father. The scribes dispute with His powerless disciples before the crowds. Jesus rebukes His disciples and talks to the father. The honest faith of the father is shown in his prayer: 'Lord, I believe; help my unbelief!' Jesus casts out the spirit, and lifts the boy up by the hand. The trust of the father has been met, but Jesus tells His disciples that such miracles can be performed only in the context of really serious prayer and fasting. **V 30–32: TEACHING** Jesus avoids the crowds at Galilee to teach His disciples about His death and resurrection. They still do not understand about the resurrection and dare not ask Him about it. **V 33–37: TWELVE** Ironically, the disciples then dispute among themselves who will be the greatest. Jesus challenges them and teaches them a basic lesson about child-like humility, by setting a child among them. **V 38–50: TRUTHS** The chapter closes with Christ teaching on the need to recognise others in His work, the need to meet the needs of others, the danger of causing little ones to stumble, the importance of serious self-discipline (which He teaches in figures of speech about cutting off limbs and plucking out one's eye) and the eternal reality of hell (underlined three times). If someone really belongs to Christ, then he or she will, like salt, have a flavour and function different from those around.

CHAPTER TEN

V 1–12: PRIORITY OF MARRIAGE Two things emerge as most important. First, marriage is intended to be permanent, and thus the first response to a marriage difficulty must be to try to save the marriage. This is so, even though divorce is permitted because of the hardness of people's hearts. Second, to divorce wrongly and to marry after such a wrong 'divorce' is to commit adultery. (The context of the New Testament, as Matthew 19:19, obviously refers here to a divorce on non-biblical grounds.) **V 13–16: PRINCIPLE OF MEEKNESS** In willingly accepting and blessing children, despite His disciples' reluctance, Jesus teaches that grown-up people must come to God as little children in order to be accepted by Him. **V 17–31: PERIL OF MONEY** Jesus' dealings with the rich young man reveal that coveting possessions and money can be a great hindrance to a willingness to repent and surrender daily to Christ. Thus having great possessions can be a real barrier to entering the kingdom of God. But everything is possible with God, and those who have sacrificed for Christ are the final winners. **V 32–34: PREDICTION OF MASTER** Jesus again underlines to His disciples the facts of His coming betrayal, condemnation, suffering, death, and resurrection. **V 35–45: POSITIONS OF MIGHT** Jesus rebukes James and John for wanting positions of authority for selfish reasons, and points out to them the cost of discipleship and to the other ten critical disciples the requirement of being servants. He again underlines that He Himself has come as a servant to 'give His

life as a ransom for many'. **V 46–52: PROVISION OF MERCY** Jesus gives sight to blind Bartimaeus in answer to his plea for mercy. He cries to Jesus, despite being told by some to be quiet. Having received his sight, he follows Jesus along the road.

CHAPTER ELEVEN

V 1–6: READY A colt is waiting, ready to be released to two of Christ's disciples in order that the Lord may ride it into Jerusalem. **V 7–10: RESPONSE** The crowds, who do not understand the true meaning of Christ's ministry yet, acclaim Him as the coming Messiah with 'Hosanna'. Sadly, their cry will change shortly. **V 11: REVIEW** As a prelude to its later purging, Jesus goes to the temple and surveys it. He leaves for Bethany with the disciples. **V 12–14: REBUKE** Jesus rebukes a fig tree with a curse and, in the hearing of the disciples, says that no one will eat fruit from it again. **V 15–19: RIGHTEOUSNESS** Having reviewed the temple earlier, Jesus goes to it and turns out all those who are abusing it for the sake of commerce. The scribes and the chief priests fear Him and discuss how they can have Him killed. He leaves the city in the evening. **V 20–26: RESULT** The next day the disciples notice that the cursed fig tree is already withered from the roots. Jesus tells them that if they have faith, God can answer their faith in the same amazing way. He then emphasises that they must forgive people before their prayers can be heard. **V 27–33: REASON** When questioned about His authority, Jesus reasons by drawing a parallel from John the Baptist. The chief priests, scribes and elders attempt to embarrass him, but find that by His questioning them, the tables are turned. They will not reply whether John's baptism was from God or from man. Jesus also refuses to answer their question on authority, knowing that they already know the answer and reject it.

CHAPTER TWELVE

V 1–12: TENANTS Jesus uses a parable about tenants who kill the landlord's servants and finally his son. The religious leaders know that He has spoken against them. God's prophets and servants have been rejected. God's Son is also rejected and will be killed. They will soon cause His crucifixion. Their sinful action will fulfil prophecy. They seek to arrest Him, but are afraid of the crowd and so go away. **V 13–17: TAXES** Jesus answers the Pharisees and Herodians, who seek to trip Him up with a question about paying tax to Caesar. He teaches that we must pay taxes that are required by authorities, but also give God what He demands. Even his opponents marvel at Him. **V 18–27: TRUTHS** The Sadducees, who do not believe in the resurrection, put a trick question to Him about a woman who was married seven times. They ask who will be her husband in heaven. He uses the occasion to teach something about the nature of heaven and to tell them that they have got the two major truths wrong. First, they do not know the Scriptures. Second, they do not know the power of God, because they reject the resurrection. **V 28–34: TWO** A sincere teacher of the law is told by Jesus that two commandments are most important. The first commandment is to love God completely, and the second one, linked to it, is to love your neighbour as yourself. His sincere response leads Jesus to tell the man that he is not far from the kingdom of God. His answer makes others afraid to question Him further. **V 35–40: TEACHING** Jesus shows from the Old Testament that the Messiah is the Son of David and then warns people about the hypocritical and haughty falseness and pride of the religious teachers of His day. **V 41–44: TOTAL** Jesus commends a poor widow woman who gives all that she has. This gift is much more in God's eyes than those of many rich people whose amounts far exceed the mere financial worth of the widow's gift.

CHAPTER THIRTEEN

V 1–2: TEMPLE The disciples are admiring the temple. Jesus says that one day all the stones will be thrown down. **V 3–4: TIMING** Peter, James, John and Andrew ask Him later, on the Mount of Olives, when the temple will be destroyed, and what will happen first. **V 5–31: TRUTHS** Jesus gives important truths about what will happen first and how the things to come will precede His coming in the clouds with power and great glory. Jesus will come in great power and glory in the clouds, and His angels will gather the elect. His second coming will be preceded by the following: deception, wars and rumours of war, international conflict, widespread earthquakes, famines, persecution of Christians, the spread of the gospel, opposition to Christians both from their families and generally, the fulfilment of Daniel's prophecy, great tribulation, false claims that Christ has come again, a darkening of the sun and moon, failure of the stars, and a shaking of heavenly powers. Every Christian should be aware of what Jesus said and also that His words will never pass away. **V 32–37: TEST** Jesus makes it clear that nobody knows when the day of His return will be. This is a great test of a heresy: only heretics say they know when He will return. Men who have predicted the timing of the second coming have always been wrong. It is our responsibility to keep watch and be ready. Submit to this test those who claim to know when Christ will come.

CHAPTER FOURTEEN

V 1–2: LEADERS SLY The religious leaders, the chief priests and scribes, slyly plan how they can take Jesus by trickery and have Him put to death. They are frightened of the people, however. **V 3–9: LASTING SYMBOL** Pointing to the death and burial of Jesus, a woman breaks an alabaster flask of very costly oil and pours it on His head. Jesus answers criticism of her that she has wasted something that could have been sold, thus releasing money for the poor. He confirms that, throughout the world, her loving and sacrificial deed will be remembered. **V 10–11: LOYALTY SURRENDERED** Following this, Judas (interestingly, the treasurer for the twelve disciples!) goes to the chief priests to arrange to betray Jesus at a convenient time and for personal financial gain. Later he will lead a great crowd of Jesus' enemies against Him when not many 'ordinary citizens' are around. **V 12–16: LAMB'S SACRIFICE** This is the time when the Passover lamb will be sacrificed. Jesus sends His disciples to meet an unknown contact in order to make ready a large upper room which has been furnished and prepared. They will eat their Lord's Supper there later. **V 17–21: LOOMING SORROW** That evening, Jesus tells His disciples that He will be betrayed by one of them. This is the beginning of their sorrow, which will become far worse. Jesus tells them that it would be better for the betrayer if he had never been born. **V 22–26: LORD'S SUPPER** The Lord's Supper is instituted. Jesus transfers the format of the Passover supper to this new Christian feast. His body will be broken and His blood will be shed in order that sinners may be forgiven and come to know and love God. They sing a hymn and go out to the Mount of Olives. **V 27–31: LEFT SCATTERED** Not only Peter, but all the disciples contradict Jesus when He says that they will stumble because of Him that night. Impetuous Peter, however, is told that before the rooster crows twice, he will deny Him three times. The sheep will be scattered when the Shepherd is struck. **V 32–42: LONELY SUPPLICATIONS** Despite the disciples' claims that they will stay with Christ, they cannot even watch with Him in the Garden of Gethsemane, where Jesus prays that He will do the Father's will. Three times, Jesus finds them sleeping while He is praying. He goes to meet His betrayer. **V 43–52: LOVELESS SALUTATION** Judas comes with the armed mob to take Jesus. He identifies Him with a cynical kiss—a loveless salutation. Jesus is taken, despite violent opposition from a disciple elsewhere identified as Peter. A young man (probably Mark himself) flees from the scene. **V 53–65: LORDSHIP STATED** Trailed by Peter, Jesus goes to the Sanhedrin where false and inconsistent testimonies fail to produce a case to be answered. Eventually flawed and perjured witnesses are found. Jesus maintains His right to silence until He is asked by the high priest if He is 'the Christ, the Son of the Blessed'. Jesus not only replies 'I am' (which may be linked with the Old Testament name for God), but also tells the high priest that He will come again in power in the clouds of heaven. Based on this supposed 'blasphemy', He is condemned to death and is verbally and physically abused. **V 66–72: LAMENTING SIN** Peter denies Jesus three times, just as Jesus predicted. As the rooster crows for the second time, he thinks about the words of Jesus and weeps.

CHAPTER FIFTEEN

V 1–15: CONSPIRACY The elders, scribes and council conspire against Jesus and deliver Him to Pilate with one thing in mind: His death. Here is a man about to be condemned in a Roman court for a supposed offence against Jewish law! What a travesty of justice! Jesus confirms that He is the King of the Jews, but refuses to answer the charges placed against Him. Judge Pilate, knowing of the envy of the chief priests, proposes that Jesus should be the prisoner released in accordance with the annual amnesty custom. The chief priests manipulate the mob to put pressure on Pilate to release Barabbas and crucify Jesus. Pilate gives way and has Jesus scourged before crucifixion. **V 16–20: CRUELTY** The cowardly soldiers then cruelly and blasphemously abuse the innocent and spotless King. **V 21–22: COMPULSION** Simon of Cyrene is compelled to carry Christ's cross to Golgotha. **V 23–28: CRUCIFIED** Jesus refuses the pain-dulling wine mixed with myrrh, and is crucified. His garments are divided, with lots being cast, and 'The King of the Jews' is put over His cross. He is placed in the middle of two crucified robbers, thus fulfilling Isaiah's prophecy. **V 29–32: CROWD** Blasphemy, insults, error, confusion, and the malicious stirring of the mocking religious leaders are to accompany the death of the Prince of life. Even the crucified criminals revile Him. **V 33–37: CONQUEST** The misunderstood cry of Jesus at the end of three hours of darkness over the whole land, 'My God, My God, why have You forsaken Me?' shows that as He bears our sins, He is separated from His eternal Father for the first and last time. But, always in control, Jesus cries out in triumph and then breathes His last breath. He has paid for our sins. **V 38–39:**
CONFESSION As the temple veil is torn from top to bottom, signifying that the way is now open to God, the centurion on duty witnesses the last cry of Jesus. This gentile soldier confesses that Jesus is the Son of God. **V 40–41: CONCERNED** Amidst the cruelty, one sees a faithful band of concerned women, looking on from afar. No men. No disciples. **V 42–47: CONFIRMATION** As Joseph of Arimathea, a prominent council member, courageously asks and receives permission from Pilate to take the body of Jesus, in order to treat it and put in his own tomb, we see two matters of important confirmation: first, Pilate ensures through the centurion that Jesus really is dead; secondly, Mary Magdalene and Mary, the mother of Joses, note carefully where His tomb is.

CHAPTER SIXTEEN

V 1–5: WOMEN Mary Magdalene, Mary the mother of James, and Salome come to the tomb to anoint Jesus with spices. This is early on the very first Lord's Day, namely Sunday. Worried about how they will be able to roll away the very large stone, they see that it has already been rolled away. They are alarmed by the presence of a young man in a long white robe, identified elsewhere as an angel. **V 6–7: WELCOMED!** What a welcome they get! The angel confirms that Jesus, once crucified, is risen. He is not in the tomb where He was laid, and they are to tell the disciples, including Peter, that He will meet them in Galilee. The angel reminds them that Jesus said that He would rise again from the dead. **V 8: WORRIED** Amazed and trembling, this is too much for the women, who flee from the tomb and keep silent at that time because they are afraid. **V 9–20: WORK** (*Even some convinced Bible-believing teachers feel* *that there is legitimate doubt whether verses 9 to 20 were actually in Mark's Gospel originally or whether they were added later. Most of what is taught is found elsewhere in Scripture and what is contained here neither contradicts nor is crucial to any teaching of the rest of the Bible. However, as even sincere Christians can be wrong, a comment on the verses is in order, in case they are mistaken. There is every reason to hold that, even if the verses have been added, they nevertheless reveal accurate historical fact in accord*

with Scripture and historical records.) Mary testifies to having met the risen Christ, who also continues to appear to men and women. The work of preaching the gospel of the risen Christ must carry on to the whole world. God will give signs to attest the validity of the authority of those working for Him at this immediate post-resurrection time. Jesus ascends to heaven and His disciples continue the work of preaching the gospel, attested by God.

LUKE

OVERVIEW

PEOPLE AND PRELIMINARIES

✳Luke (twenty-four chapters) was written by Luke between AD60 and AD70, probably in Galilee or possibly from Rome (along with his writing the book of Acts) during the imprisonment of Paul there. It is the third Gospel. **See comments on Matthew.** Luke was a doctor with an eye for fact and for detail, as is seen both here and in Acts. The estimated period covering the events in Luke is thirty-nine years.

PLAN AND PURPOSE

ⓘ Like the other synoptic Gospels of Matthew and Mark and the non-synoptic Gospel of John, Luke's Gospel centres on the person and work of the Lord Jesus Christ. **See comments on Matthew.** Luke presents this from before the miraculous conception of Jesus by the Holy Spirit, on through His virgin birth, His baptism in the Jordan by John the

Baptist, and His public ministry, to His death, resurrection, commissioning of His disciples, and ascension. Luke, a Gentile non-apostle, was closely associated and identified with the apostle Paul and wrote, under the influence of God's Holy Spirit, mainly for other Gentiles. To do this, he coordinated and collated reliable reports to write this book. His Gospel harmonises perfectly with the other Gospels, yet with authentic variety. This third Gospel portrays Jesus as a man, and thus traces his genealogy to the first man (Adam) through Mary's line. The key-phrase is 'the Son of Man'. Jesus' humanity is underlined by the inclusion in this Gospel of the ten prayers that He prays. But Jesus is both fully man and fully God, and His deity shines forth from this Gospel as from the other three. This Gospel is unique in emphasising the work of the Spirit in Jesus, indicating that we should look for clues to see how this Gospel focuses on Christ as Messiah in His office as the prophet.

PROFILE AND PROGRESSION

Preamble, the birth, the infancy and the baptism of Jesus (1:1–4:13); Jesus ministering in Galilee—including miracles done, disciples called, authoritative teaching, prediction of His death, His transfiguration, His time with the disciples (4:14–9:50); Jesus' journey from Galilee to Jerusalem—including rejection, sending out the seventy, hospitality at Bethany, denunciation of religious leaders, varied and key teaching both directly and by parables, and His predicting His death and resurrection again (9:51–19:27); the week leading to Jesus' death on the cross—including His entering Jerusalem in triumph, His weeping over it, purging the temple, teaching, disputes with Pharisees and Sadducees, teaching about the end times, the Passover plot against Him and Judas' part, Passover, the Lord's Supper, Gethsemane's agony, His arrest, Peter's denial, scourging and unlawful trials, Pilate's uncharacteristic indecision, the death of the cross, the tomb, and the Sabbath (19:28–23:56); Jesus' resurrection, the Emmaus Road and the amazed disciples, and Jesus' ascension (24:1–53).

PRINCIPLES AND PARTICULARS

See comments on Matthew. The focus of Luke is on Jesus as a man. Thus we see the emotions and agonies of the man, Christ Jesus, as He performs His Father's will on earth. What a tightrope to tread! If Jesus had been seen to fail for a second in the smallest point, He would have lost all right to be regarded as a perfect and sinless man, and as God incarnate. Had He not demonstrated that blend of perfect righteousness and divine nature, He could never have been our spotless sin-bearer and sacrifice on Calvary's cross. As the Son of Man, Jesus came to seek what was lost. The seeking Triune Saviour-God is portrayed (in chapter 15) as a shepherd seeking a straying sheep (picture of Christ, the good Shepherd, seeking), as a woman looking for a lost coin (picture of the illuminating Spirit seeking), or as a father yearning for and welcoming his prodigal son who repents and returns (picture of the forgiveness of God the Father). Note that Luke concentrates on reliable sources and on the accuracy of his book, and the word 'certain' (or words to mean the equivalent) occur very regularly. See also the compassionate care of Jesus, the Man, for His fellow men.

LUKE

CHAPTER ONE

V 1–4: ACCURATE ACCOUNT Not only is the Bible trustworthy as the infallible Word of God, but Luke's Gospel itself is well marshalled and presented from eyewitnesses. Luke writes it to Theophilus, to whom Acts is also addressed. We have confidence both in the Bible generally and in Luke's Gospel specifically. **V 5–17: ANGEL'S ANNOUNCEMENT** Zacharias is a priest ministering in the temple. His wife, Elizabeth, is barren and they are both old. While on temple duty, the angel of God appears to him to tell him that God will give them a child who will be great, holy, and Spirit filled. His task will be to turn people to God, to mend human relationships and to prepare them for the Lord. Zacharias is troubled and frightened. **V 18–22: SILENT SIGN** Instead of taking God at His word, Zacharias asks for a sign. God tells him, through the angel Gabriel, that he will not be able to speak until his son is born. From that moment onward, he is literally speechless. **V 23–25: CHILD CONCEIVED** His wife Elizabeth conceives and goes into confinement for five months. She is thankful to God for acting to give her a personal answer to her prayer. **V 26–33: SAVIOUR SON** When Elizabeth is six months pregnant, the angel Gabriel appears in Nazareth to troubled Mary. He tells her that she will have a child whose name will be JESUS, which means 'God saves'. He will be the Son of God with an everlasting kingdom. Her Son will thus be the Saviour of sinners and the everlasting King. **V 34–38: MIRACULOUS MOTHERHOOD** God tells Mary that she will conceive in her womb through the direct operation of the Holy Spirit, who will overshadow her. This is in answer to her asking how her birth will come about since she is a virgin and therefore has never had a sexual relationship with a man. God reminds her that nothing is impossible for Him, and tells her of Elizabeth's conception. Mary commits herself to God and to His word. **V 39–45: COMFORTING CONFIRMATION** When Mary greets Elizabeth, Elizabeth's baby leaps in her womb and she is filled with the Holy Spirit. She responds with a prophetic blessing, stating clearly that Mary's baby is God incarnate and that Mary herself is blessed through faith in her God. **V 46–56: MARY'S MAGNIFICAT** The Magnificat, as this song of Mary is sometimes called, is Mary's response to God in which she thanks and praises God for who He is, rejoices that God is her Saviour, and is grateful for the way that He has dealt with her in her lowly estate. She remembers God's promises to Abraham as well as His powerful intervention for His people in the past. After three months, Mary returns home

from Elizabeth. **V 57–60: BAPTIST'S BIRTH** The baby of Elizabeth and Zacharias is born. Those coming to circumcise him want to call him by his father's name. Elizabeth insists that his name is 'John'. **V 61–66: LORD'S LOOSENING** The speech of Zacharias, the baby's father, is returned to him by God as soon as he writes down, 'His name is John.' Fear and amazement follow. **V 67–79: FATHER'S FORETELLING** Zacharias uses his rediscovered faculty of speech, under the influence of the Holy Spirit, to prophesy about his son's ministry. His main task as God's prophet will be to prepare the way of the Lord of salvation and light. **V 80: STRONG SPIRIT** John grows physically and becomes strong in spirit. He stays in the deserts until the time when God will show him to Israel.

CHAPTER TWO

V 1–7: SON In Bethlehem, where Joseph and Mary go to register in response to Caesar Augustus' census, Jesus is born and laid in a manger. There is no room for them in the adjoining inn. **V 8–20: SHEPHERDS** The first announcement of the birth of the Lord Jesus Christ is by an angel to shepherds working in the fields at night. The angel is joined by a heavenly throng who glorify God and declare the coming of peace on earth. The shepherds go to Bethlehem and find the Child with His mother and Joseph. They spread the news, and return, glorifying and praising God. Mary retains and reflects on what God has told them. **V 21: SAVIOUR** Mary's Son is circumcised after eight days and given the name indicated by the angel, 'JESUS'. The name means 'God saves' and underlines that Mary's son is to be the Saviour of the world. **V 22–24: SACRIFICE** After the legal requirement of days spent in ceremonial purification, the sacrifice of two appropriate birds, required upon birth of the firstborn, is made. **V 25–35: SIMEON** By the Holy Spirit, the prophet Simeon confirms that Jesus is the awaited Saviour of both Gentiles and Israel. Having seen Jesus, Simeon is ready now to die. He declares that Jesus will be the cause of the fall and rising of many and that Mary will be pierced through in her own soul. **V 36–38: SERVANT** An aged and godly servant and prophetess, Anna, confirms the truth of Simeon's prophecy independently. **V 39–40: STRENGTH** Returning to Galilee, Jesus grows and becomes strong in spirit. He manifests the abundance of God's wisdom and grace. **V 41–50: SPEECH** The first recorded words of Jesus in the New Testament underline that He has come to do His Father's business. Unwittingly, he is left behind at Jerusalem at the Feast of the Passover, at the age of twelve years. His parents miss him, ask him why he stayed there, and receive the answer that He must be about His Father's business. **V 51–52: SUBJECT** Nevertheless, in His journey to manhood, Jesus remains subject to Joseph and Mary. At all times He is increasing in wisdom and stature, growing in favour with God and men, and His words are kept closely by His mother in her heart.

CHAPTER THREE

V 1–14: PREPARE! The historical arrival of John the Baptist is identified, by naming the rulers and high priests of his day. John is there to prepare the way for the coming of the Lord Jesus Christ, which he does by preaching and baptising for repentance, in accordance with Isaiah's prophecy. He is practical and uncompromising in his preaching. He addresses the Jews and people generally.

He also identifies specific groups, underlining that repentance is not merely in words, but in actions demonstrating a changed heart. As people are aware of their sin, so they are more likely to turn to the Saviour. The same principle applies today. **V 15–17: PURPOSE** John is quick to counteract the rumour that he himself is the Christ. In proclaiming the purpose for which Christ comes, he declares his own unworthiness. Only Christ can gather His own as wheat into the barn of heaven, and judge the unrepentant as chaff for unquenchable fire. John can baptise with water, but only Jesus can baptise with the Holy Spirit and with fire. **V 18–20: PRISON** As John continues preaching, with practical exhortation, Herod's conscience is touched as John rebukes him at having taken his brother's wife. King Herod puts John in prison. **V 21–22: PLEASED** Prior to going to prison, John baptised Jesus. Heaven opened and the Holy Spirit descended on Jesus in bodily form. The other Person in the Trinity, God the Father, proclaimed Jesus as His beloved Son in whom He was 'well pleased'. The sinless and righteous life of the Man, Christ Jesus, completely pleased the Father. **V 23–38: PROOF** The proof of the historicity of the Man Christ Jesus is underlined by the genealogy given in Luke. Whereas the genealogy in Matthew presents the line of Joseph, the stepfather of Jesus, showing the legal and royal descent of Jesus, the genealogy in Luke shows the natural and physical descent of Jesus from David through Mary's line. That is why they differ. There is no contradiction.

CHAPTER FOUR

V 1–13: TEMPTED During forty days in the wilderness, Satan tempts Jesus in three different ways. The temptations focus on physical appetite, powerful authority, and public acclaim. Each time Satan is repelled by quotations from the Word of God by the incarnate Lord of glory. **V 14–21: TEACHING** Returning in the Spirit's power to Galilee, Jesus is concerned to teach throughout the whole countryside, including in the synagogues. All who hear Him teach, glorify Him. He applies the prophecies of God's Messiah to Himself. **V 22–30: TAKEN** Jesus is the object of both marvelling and opposition. Using Elijah and Elisha as examples, Jesus explains that a prophet is not honoured in his own country. This makes Him unpopular with the religious leaders. They take Him in order to throw Him down a cliff. But Jesus walks right through the crowd and goes on His way. His time has not yet come. **V 31–37: TELLING** The teaching of Jesus on the Sabbaths and His striking authority and power which enables Him to cast out demons has great effect on the amazed crowds. As they engage in telling of His miraculous works, news of Him spreads throughout the region. **V 38–39: TENDER** Jesus now heals Simon's mother-in-law from a high fever after being asked to help. His tenderness towards one sick woman is seen as He stands over her, rebukes the fever, and it leaves her. She begins to serve Him and those with Him. **V 40–41: TOTAL** In healing many people of sicknesses and in the casting out of many demons, we see the total authority of Jesus Christ. He never has a failure. This is very different from some who claim the power of healing today. **V 42–44: TASK** The people try to keep Jesus from leaving them when they find Him in a solitary place. He will not be kept there, because His main concern is to preach the good news throughout Judea. He has other towns and other synagogues to visit in order to preach.

CHAPTER FIVE

V 1–11: FISHING DISCIPLES Jesus sees some fishermen by the Lake of Gennesaret. He enters into Simon's boat and teaches the crowds from there. Then He tells him how to catch more fish. Peter answers that that they have toiled all night and failed, but he is staggered when they obey His command and have a bumper catch. Jesus then directs them to fish for men rather than for fish. They leave everything and follow Him. **V 12–15: FAITH DEMONSTRATED** The 'untouchable' outcast, the leper, demonstrates faith in Jesus by asking if He is willing to make him clean. Jesus heals him and sends him not to tell anyone but to go first to the priest to have his cleansing ratified ceremonially according to the law of Moses. However, crowds hear of this and come to hear Jesus and to be healed by Him. **V 16: FAITHFUL DEVOTIONS** As more and more people come to hear Jesus and to be healed, He often goes to lonely places to pray on His own. This is a prime example to us all. **V 17–26: FORGIVING DEITY** Jesus teaches the crowds, in the presence of Pharisees and Jewish teachers. A paralytic let down through the roof to Jesus is healed after Jesus tells him he is forgiven. The Pharisees and religious teachers object that only God can forgive sins. Jesus demonstrates that He is God by reading and answering their thoughts and by healing the man. He amazes the witnesses. **V 27–32: FRIENDS DINE** The despised tax collector, Levi, immediately responds to Jesus' command to him, 'Follow Me.' Despite the opposition of the scribes and the Pharisees, he opens his house to other needy people he knows so they can come to a feast to meet the Saviour. Jesus declares that He has come to bring sinners to repentance. **V 33–39:**

FASTING DISTINGUISHED Answering a question about why His disciples are not fasting like others, Jesus teaches that there is a valid reason and the right time to fast. An occasion for joy is not the time to fast. He takes the opportunity to point out the difference between the old legalism of the Pharisees and the new life that there is in Christ, by using illustrations from new patches on old garments and new wine in old wineskins.

CHAPTER SIX

V 1–11: SENSIBLE SABBATHS The desire of Jesus is to rid legitimate Sabbath observance from the hypocrisy of the Pharisees, and make it the special God-honouring day it should be. This is shown on another Sabbath when He walks through the grain fields with His disciples, who rub in their hands the heads of grain just picked and eat them. He appeals to Old Testament examples showing that a sensible observance of the Sabbath does not preclude preparing or eating necessary food. He reminds people that He is still the 'Lord of the Sabbath'. He then proceeds to heal a man with a withered hand on the Sabbath day, reminding His hearers that it is a good use of God's special day to do good and to save life, despite the opposition and rage of the scribes and Pharisees. **V 12–16: DRAWING DISCIPLES** Jesus prays all night on a mountain before calling His disciples by name to Himself so that He may choose twelve of them as apostles. **V 17–19: COMING CROWD** Crowds of people from all over come to see Him, to hear Him, and to be healed by Him. His healing them all and His teaching are evidence of the power that He possesses as the Son of God. **V 20–26: PRIORITY PRINCIPLES** Jesus underlines, through beatitudes and warnings, the principles that bless His disciples and the woes that come to those who are self-sufficient and who seek satisfaction from the world. There is a progression of blessing from being poor in spirit and hungering for God, through to suffering persecution for God's sake. **V 27–36: LEARNING LOVE** Jesus teaches that love includes caring for enemies and those who are hateful, being graciously generous, doing good to others, and being merciful as the Father in heaven is merciful. A Christian's love should be far greater than that of others. **V 37–42: JUDGING JUSTLY** Jesus warns against an over-critical spirit and tells His disciples that those who are generous will be treated generously. He warns them about the stupidity of seeking to lead other people, when they themselves are so blinded by their own faults that they cannot see properly. He also tells them to put right the obvious wrong in their own lives before looking at details that displease them in the lives of others. The planks in their own eyes must be removed before they attend to the specks in other people's eyes. **V 43–45: FRUIT FOLLOWS** Just as trees and vines are known by their fruit, so a man's heart is known by what he says and does. Evil conduct comes from an evil heart. **V 46–49: CATASTROPHIC CONTRAST** Jesus talks about foundations. A house with solid foundations built on a rock will stand in the storm, and one without foundations that is not built on the rock will fall and be ruined. So it is with those who either trust or mistrust the words of Christ. Eternal blessing or eternal ruin is at stake. Only those built securely on Christ, the Rock, will survive God's storm of eternal judgement on sin.

CHAPTER SEVEN

V 1–10: SOLDIER'S SERVANT Jesus

commends and marvels at the unique faith of a Gentile Roman centurion who is a kind and generous friend of the Jewish nation. He sends friends to Jesus on his behalf, because he feels personally unworthy to approach the Lord. They ask Christ to heal his sick servant by giving the word from a distance. The centurion knows that just as he commands troops who do what he tells them, Jesus' immeasurably greater power and authority is immediate and absolute and not geographically limited. Jesus heals his sick servant in response to the centurion's faith. Jesus has not encountered such great faith even in Israel. **V 11–16: DEATH DEFEATED** Jesus raises from the dead the son of a widow at Nain. The people fear and glorify God. They proclaim Jesus as a 'great prophet', and note that 'God has visited His people'. **V 17–23: CONFIRMING COMMUNICATION** The report of Jesus' miracles spreads. John the Baptist sends two of his disciples to find out if the One he has heard about really is Jesus Christ, the Messiah. Jesus tells his disciples to go back and tell John what they have seen and heard, knowing full well that John will know that His miraculous, compassionate and gospel works fulfil the Old Testament predictions about Him. **V 24–30: MESSIAH'S MESSENGER** Jesus goes on to commend the frugal and faithful lifestyle of John the Baptist who has gone before to prepare the way for Him. In preparation for Jesus, he baptises for repentance. Those thus baptised show their sincerity by accepting Jesus' word. Great as John is, the least member of the kingdom of God is greater than him. The worst of sinners today can know God through the new birth into His spiritual family, that none of the prophets could then have known in the same way. **V 31–35: CHILDISH CHATTER** Jesus says that those who oppose God are like children who sulkily refuse to dance when the flute is played and refuse to weep when there is mourning. They reject John the Baptist for his frugal lifestyle, and reject Jesus because He dines with tax collectors and sinners. Either way, they will reject God's will and word. God's wisdom will justify itself in His children. **V 36–50: FORGIVENESS' FRAGRANCE** Jesus forgives a wicked woman, who, from other Scriptures, we know was one of the women named Mary. She washes Jesus' feet with her tears, wipes them with her hair, and anoints them with expensive fragrant oil in an alabaster flask. Jesus is wrongly criticised for either seemingly not knowing that she is a sinful woman, or knowing it and allowing her to touch Him. Jesus then tells a parable, about two debtors released from their debts, to illustrate the fact that those who have been forgiven much will love much, and those who have not been forgiven will not show that same love. He tells one of the Pharisees, Simon, that her forgiven love for Him is far greater than anything the religious people have shown. He confirms to the woman that her sins are forgiven and tells her to 'Go in peace'.

CHAPTER EIGHT

V 1–3: DISCIPLES AND DEVOTEES Jesus preaches in every city and village with the twelve disciples and some named women, who provide for Him from their own possessions. **V 4–15: SEED AND SOILS** Jesus tells the parable of the sower who sows seed in different kinds of soil. Each soil produces a different response to the seed, and illustrates how men and women can hear God's Word and behave differently as a result. Only the good ground produces lasting fruit. Devilish intervention, temptation, and materialism are the reasons why fruit does not come from the other soils in which the seed of God's Word is sown. **V 16–18: ILLUMINATION AND INFLUENCE** A light has to be displayed to be of any use. When a light shines, it will illumine things previously hidden in the darkness. A Christian should listen to God's Word in such a way that the light shines into his life. Those who listen like that will be given more light, and those who refuse to listen will have the light taken away. **V 19–21: FAMILY AND FAITHFULNESS** Jesus teaches that those who hear and do God's word have a closer link with Him than even His earthly, natural family. **V 22–25: STORM AND STILLNESS** Jesus makes the disciples marvel when He stills the storm that fills their boat with water and puts them in danger. He uses the occasion to ask them where their faith is. They marvel at His authority and power. **V 26–40: PIGS AND PROCLAMATION** Jesus, correctly recognised as the 'son of the Most High God', liberates a tomb-dwelling savage man who is naked and out of control as a long-term victim of demon possession. Jesus casts the demons into a herd of pigs which consequently rush down the hill into the water and are drowned. The inhabitants of the region urge Jesus to leave. They are afraid when they see God at work. The newly liberated man now sits quietly, properly clothed, and in his right mind. Jesus tells him to go home and tell his folks what God has done for him. En route, he shares his great news with the whole city! Jesus returns from the Gadarenes to be welcomed by the waiting crowds. **V 41–48: INVITATION AND INTERRUPTION** A pressing request to Jesus comes from Jairus, a ruler of the synagogue. His twelve-year-old daughter is dying, and he begs Jesus to come to his house and heal her. On the way, a woman, suffering with a flow of blood for twelve years, is healed as she puts her faith in Him. To the astonishment of Peter and the others, Jesus clearly distinguishes between her touch of faith and the physical brushing by of the multitude. He assures the woman of His healing work and tells her to go in peace. **V 49–56: FAITH AND FOOD** The news then reaches Jesus that the daughter of Jairus is dead. Jairus is told not to 'trouble the Teacher'. Jesus, however, comes, and is ridiculed by the crowd when he equates the girl's undoubted death to sleep. Accompanied by Peter, James and John, He raises her from the dead, as easily as one may wake up someone asleep. He tells them to give her some food. Her astonished parents are told to keep the matter to themselves. Jesus never seeks public applause. He simply seeks to do God's will.

CHAPTER NINE

V 1–6: SENT The twelve disciples are empowered and sent by Jesus to preach the kingdom of God and to heal the sick. They obey His commission to go to the villages throughout the region. They travel light and leave if people reject the message. **V 7–9: SEE** Herod wants to see Jesus. He is perplexed because someone says that Jesus is John, risen from the dead, whereas others have told him that He is Elijah or a prophet. Sadly Herod's seeking does not result from spiritual conviction of his sin. **V 10–11: SELFLESS** Jesus takes the returning disciples aside near Bethsaida, to be with them. However, when crowds come, He gives Himself selflessly and unstintingly to speaking to them and healing them. **V 12–17: SUSTENANCE** The amazing miracle follows of feeding 5,000 people from five loaves of bread and two fish. It blends Christ's compassion and divine power with good organisation and use of the disciples in the Lord's work. There is a lot more left over than there was to start with! We must never doubt Christ's power to sustain us in any situation where we trust Him. **V 18–22: SUFFERING** Peter correctly answers that Jesus is 'The Christ of God', in stark contrast to the other speculation that Jesus is John the Baptist, Elijah or a prophet risen from the dead. Jesus immediately warns His disciples that He must suffer, be put to death, and rise from the dead. **V 23–26: SHAME** Jesus goes on and teaches His disciples that they, too, must take up their cross to follow Him daily, as must any disciple of Christ. The Christian must crucify self, refuse sin and the overtures of the world, and live for Christ. Those who are ashamed of Jesus and His words will find that He will be ashamed of them at His second coming. **V 27–36: SUPREME** Jesus tells His disciples that some who are standing with Him will not taste death before they see the kingdom of God. About eight days later, He is transfigured in front of them and immediately focuses on His death to come. The sleepy disciples wake up to see His glory, in which He is shown to be supreme over Moses and Elijah (standing for the Old Testament law and prophets). God the Father declares from a cloud that His Son pleases Him and that all must hear Him. Jesus then remains as Moses and Elijah disappear. The disciples keep this amazing experience to themselves. **V 37–43a: SPIRIT** Jesus casts out an evil spirit from a man's son, after His disciples are unable to do so. The people are amazed at God's greatness and Jesus returns the renewed boy to his father. **V 43b–45: SPECIFIC** While everyone marvels, Jesus repeats to His disciples that He will be betrayed. They do not understand and dare not ask about it. **V 46–48: SIMPLICITY** An argument starts among the disciples about who will be the greatest. Jesus shows them the need for simplicity of spirit by placing a child in front of them to show them how a child reacts. Humility and childlikeness are required. **V 49–50: SUPPORT** Jesus warns against party spirit in His work and cause. Those who are not against Him and His disciples are with them. **V 51–56: SAMARIA** En route to Jerusalem, when a Samaritan village refuses to listen, James and John want to emulate Elijah in calling down fire on its inhabitants. Jesus turns, rebukes them, emphasises that He has come to save, and passes on to another village to teach. **V 57–62: SACRIFICE** Two people express a superficial desire to follow Jesus but 'first' have other matters to attend to. Jesus teaches that His disciples must sacrifice to follow the Lord. This must take priority over all our desire for comfort and over all our family ties. The follower of Christ must look ahead, not dwell on the past.

CHAPTER TEN

V 1–7: MISSIONARY MIND Jesus sends out His larger band of seventy disciples, two by two, and they are told that the harvest is plentiful but the workers are few. He commands them to pray that God will send workers into the harvest field. They are to go, following His instructions as His disciples, and to lodge with those sympathetic to the message. **V 8–16: REPENTANCE REQUIRED** If a town will not receive the message and repent, they are to move to the next town, shaking the dust off their feet. Jesus teaches that the punishment on the towns of Chorazin, Bethsaida and Capernaum—which now see Him at work, but reject Him—will be greater than that suffered in the past by the towns of Sodom, Tyre and Sidon. Those towns offended God but had not seen Him working in the same way that Chorazin, Bethsaida and Capernaum witnessed. To reject the message and messengers of Jesus is to reject Him. **V 17–20: REAL REJOICING** The band of seventy return full of joy because they have been able to cast out demons. Jesus tells them to rejoice rather because their names are written in heaven. Success may evade them tomorrow, but their salvation is still secure! **V 21–24: SPIRITUAL SENSE** Jesus thanks His Father that His blessing is on those who come to Him as children rather than those who are learned in this world's sense. He stresses the oneness between Father and Son and underlines how blessed people are who have come to trust Him. Many kings and prophets in history longed to have the privilege of knowing God that those enjoy who trust Him now. **V 25–28: CONCISE COMMANDS** Jesus summarises the Ten Commandments into two: first, love God; second, love your neighbour as yourself. This is His response to a question as to what must be done to inherit eternal life. Clearly none of us has loved God or our neighbours like that. **V 29–37: NEIGHBOUR'S NEEDS** Jesus tells about the caring Samaritan, who goes to the help of a needy and injured victim of robbers, after two religious Jewish men fail to help him. The Samaritan also provides for the man's future care. Jesus teaches that anyone in need is our neighbour, and that we should all do 'likewise'. **V 38–42: PRIORITY PRACTISED** Jesus commends Mary to overburdened and distracted Martha, and tells her that the most necessary thing is to sit at His feet and listen to what He says. Martha does much that is right but misses the 'one thing' that is 'needed'.

CHAPTER ELEVEN

V 1–4: PATTERN FOR PRAYER When asked to teach His disciples to pray, in view of the fact that John had so taught his disciples, Jesus teaches the famous 'Lord's Prayer' as a pattern. God's holiness, kingdom, and willingness to meet our daily needs are balanced with our need to receive forgiveness, to forgive others, and not to be led into temptation. **V 5–13: ANSWERED WHEN ASKING** Jesus goes on to teach that just as a true friend will answer his friend who needs and requests help, and just as a father will look after the needs of a child whom he loves, so God, our heavenly Father, will answer those who ask, seek, or knock at His door. God will never give a sincere and trusting seeker anything that harms him. Specifically, He will give the Holy Spirit to those who come to Him in this way. **V 14–26: DRIVING OUT DEMONS** Some maliciously accuse Jesus of driving out demons by Beelzebub, the prince of demons. Jesus shows how illogical this is, and warns against the worthlessness of self-reformation, which can lead to a worse state than at the beginning. He claims that He drives out demons by the 'finger of God'. **V 27–28: BASIS FOR BLESSING** Jesus teaches that those who hear His word and obey it are more blessed even than Mary, His godly mother. That is despite her unique relationship with Him, including the fact that she gave birth to Him and cared for Him. **V 29–32: SIGNS FROM SCRIPTURE** Jesus underlines that the only miraculous signs concerning Him are in the Scriptures. Jonah is one such sign, and so, too, is Solomon. The resurrection of Jesus is foretold in the escape from the fish by Jonah after three days, and Solomon's wisdom was as nothing compared to that of the Lord Jesus Christ. **V 33–36:**

DEALING WITH DARKNESS Jesus teaches that the eye is the lamp of the body and that we should use it to see that there is no darkness within us. Through the Light of the world, shining in our hearts and lives, we can know His light. **V 37–54: WASHING AND WOES** Jesus dines with a Pharisee and ignores their practice of ceremonial washing of the hands. Other Pharisees make much of the external activity of washing without being concerned about the inward man being cleansed. Jesus says they are like crockery which is spotless on the outside but filthy on the inside. Their desire for the outward recognition of the scribes and Pharisees hides the deadness of a tomb within. He pronounces six woes against the lawyers, all of which emphasise the danger of being externally compliant, yet without a heart that is right with God. Those woes cover pride in tithing, desire for public recognition, hypocrisy, uncompassionate injustice, opposing of God's revealed word, and denying others the key of knowledge. The response of the scribes and Pharisees is not to repent, but to seek to find fault with Jesus.

CHAPTER TWELVE

V 1–3: HIDDEN HYPOCRISY Jesus warns against the hypocrisy of the Pharisees and says that nothing at all can be hidden from God. What is said in darkness will be manifested in light, and what is whispered in secret will one day be proclaimed from the rooftops. **V 4–5: FOUNDED FEAR** Those who plan to kill the body ought not to cause us any fear. Real fear should be towards the Lord who has the power to cast into hell after death. **V 6–7: FEARLESS FAITH** The Christian, however, should know that God sees everything and will supply all his needs, more than He does for His created creatures in nature. He knows the number of our hairs and cares for us more than for the sparrows! So Jesus tells His followers not to be afraid. **V 8–10: BLESSING'S BASIS** Those who know God and acknowledge Him before men will be acknowledged by Jesus, even in front of the angels of God. Those who are unable to confess Him, because they do not know Him, will be disowned before God. The blasphemy against the Holy Spirit can never be forgiven. **V 11–12: HOLY HELP** In cases of pressure, through persecution, a Christian should not worry about what to say before authorities, but rely on the Holy Spirit, who will teach His followers what to say at the right time. **V 13–21: GODLESS GREED** Triggered off by a man who asks Jesus to work out an inheritance problem so that he can get what he wants from a will, Jesus tells a parable that warns against coveting by looking for riches in this world. This world is empty of the knowledge of God, with disastrous eternal consequences for those who do not consider eternity. He talks about a foolish man who has big barns and much grain, and who mistakes his body for his soul, and earthly life for eternity. He will die very soon and have nothing. He will answer to God then. **V 22–34: SEEKING SOUNDLY** Jesus tells His disciples not to worry about provision of their needs. God, who provides for nature, can provide for them. Instead, His followers should seek His kingdom as a priority, and all their needs will be met by God. This means living sacrificially and giving to others. Where our treasure is, there our hearts will be also. **V 35–48: EAGER EXPECTANCY** Jesus uses illustrations of servants, constantly waiting for, ready for, and expecting the coming of the groom at a wedding banquet, and of a manager coming back to find his workers lazy and misbehaving. From these illustrations,

Jesus counsels watchfulness and eager expectancy, especially with His second coming in mind. **V 49–53: FRACTURED FAMILIES** Families will be divided against one another based on the presence or absence of their trust in, right attitude to, and relationship with the Lord Jesus Christ. **V 54–56: SEEING SIGNS** Just as men look at the signs of nature to predict a coming storm, so we should be careful to look at the events of history which indicate that the coming of the Lord Jesus is getting nearer. **V 57–59: SETTLE SOON** Jesus counsels the urgent settling of differences instead of going to court. This will avoid much cost, time, trouble and damage.

CHAPTER THIRTEEN

V 1–5: REPENT Jesus uses both Pilate's harsh persecution of the Galileans and the tragic death of eighteen people, killed when a tower collapsed at Siloam, to point out that the victims were no worse sinners than anyone else. We must recognise the shortness and uncertainty of life and repent now to avoid perishing later. **V 6–9: REVIEW** Just as it is wise to cut down a tree that bears no fruit, so a principle is established that things which are fruitless are to be destroyed unless they can be changed. God works on this principle. We see in Scripture that it applies to the nation of Israel. It also applies to individuals who fail to bring forth the fruits of repentance, and to apostate and rebellious churches. **V 10–17: RECTIFICATION** Jesus heals a bent-up woman who has suffered for eighteen years. He does this on the Sabbath and thereby incurs the wrath of the synagogue ruler. Jesus points out that if a mere animal is lost or thirsty, its needs are rightly met by men on the Sabbath day. How much more should a suffering woman be healed on God's special day. Jesus seeks to rectify the legalistic abuse of the Sabbath day by teaching that it is a day on which to do people good. His adversaries are shamed, but the people rejoice. **V 18–21: REMARKABLE** The remarkable growth of a mustard seed into a tree, or leaven in a measure of meal, is compared to the growth of the kingdom of God. From small, almost unnoticed beginnings, it grows strong and big. **V 22–30: REJECTION** While teaching itinerantly, Jesus answers the question 'Are there few who are saved?' He simply urges people to strive to enter the kingdom of God through the narrow gate, because those who do not enter will be rejected. Punishment and immense sorrow will result. Simply knowing who Jesus is and what He has done will save no one. However people from all over who do come to God will be accepted by Him. **V 31–33: RESOLUTE** Some Pharisees want to silence Jesus by making Him flee from the scene of spiritual battle. They say, cynically, that Herod wants to kill Him. Jesus is resolute in carrying on God's work. He also knows that His death will be at Jerusalem. He tells them to relay His words to Herod, the 'fox'. **V 34–35: REFUSAL** Jesus laments over Jerusalem, where prophets have been killed before. He now invites its inhabitants to come to Him as a hen gathers her chickens. However they are not willing, and He predicts desolation to come. He also prophesies His later return when His people will say, 'Blessed is He who comes in the name of the LORD!'

CHAPTER FOURTEEN

V 1–6: SENSIBLE SABBATH Jesus is challenged at a leading Pharisee's house, in the presence of a man with dropsy, as to whether healing on the Sabbath is lawful.

He responds by healing the man! Then, using the analogy that an ox in the ditch will be pulled out on the Sabbath day, Jesus shows how ridiculous it is for the Pharisees and lawyers to oppose healing on the Sabbath. Jesus, eager to reclaim the Sabbath day from the legalistic distortion of the Pharisees, underlines that a sensible Sabbath includes glorifying God by doing good to others. Clearly, He has future plans for the Sabbath and for blessing people on it! **V 7–11: HUMBLE HONOURED** Using a parable about a wedding feast, Jesus teaches that His disciples should seek the lowliest place, not the highest. Self-exalters will be humbled and humble people will be exalted. **V 12–14: GENUINE GENEROSITY** Hospitality and kindness should be shown without any thought of reciprocation. In offering these to the really needy and underprivileged, there can be no thought of being repaid for that generous kindness and no opportunity for it to happen. God will repay such love at the 'resurrection of the just'. **V 15–24: REPLACEMENTS RECRUITED** Jesus tells of a man who invites many to a banquet. All make excuses for not coming based on preoccupation with property, work requirements and marriage. The host of the banquet instructs his servants to bring in the poor, crippled, blind, and lame from wherever they can find them. They will occupy the places of those initially invited who rejected the invitation. The parable applies to the Jews, but also in principle to any who turn down God's invitation to repent and trust Him. **V 25–27: CRUCIAL 'CANNOTS'** A person's love for God must exceed that of all family ties. By comparison only with love for God, the best human love should be seen as hatred. Without a love that puts God first like that, an individual cannot be God's disciple. Neither can he be a disciple if he puts his own life first and does not crucify his own preferences and follow Jesus. **V 28–33: COST COUNTING** However, before trusting and following Christ in discipleship, one must count the cost and be willing to meet it. This is similar to a builder who checks his costs before embarking on a building project, or a king who ensures he has the resources he needs before going into battle. They both ensure that they are able to finish what they start. **V 34: SAVOURLESS SALT** Flavourless salt is useless and unusable. Any Christian who loses his trust in and obedience to God also loses his distinctive flavour. He is then of no use to the kingdom of God. We should all heed this message.

CHAPTER FIFTEEN

V 1–7: LOSTNESS: THE SEEKING SHEPHERD The Pharisees and the scribes criticise Jesus because of His association with tax collectors and sinners. Jesus responds in parables by giving three illustrations of how important it is to seek what is lost. The first concerns the sheep that has strayed and the shepherd who goes to seek it. Jesus says that in heaven, one sinner will produce more rejoicing than the ninety-nine who have already come to repentance. Jesus Himself is the seeking Shepherd giving His life for the sheep. **V 8–10: LOSTNESS: THE SWEEPING SEEKER** Similarly, a woman with ten coins will go to great lengths to find just one of the ten that is lost, lighting her lamp and sweeping around her house to find it. She, too, rejoices with her neighbours when the coin is found. The sweeping seeker is seen by some as a picture of the Holy Spirit, who enlightens and reaches us when we are unable to reach out to Him. **V 11–32: LOSTNESS: THE FORGIVING FATHER** The third illustration is of a son who follows a selfish and sinful lifestyle, who takes all the money he can from his father. At the end of the period in which he has wasted everything in a profligate lifestyle, he comes back to his father for forgiveness. He finds ready restoration and joy in the heart of his father who runs to welcome him and treats him with great love and generosity. God the Father is like this to sinners who repent and come to Him. The son's father seeks to bring his older son into the blessing of forgiving his wayward brother. The older son is obviously jealous at his brother's return and undeserved welcome. This second son, in some ways, seems harder to win than the first! May churches and Christians beware!

CHAPTER SIXTEEN

V 1–12: LEARNING FROM LIFE Jesus illustrates from the dishonest actions of a poor and self-seeking steward, not in order to counsel dishonesty, of course, but to point out that Christians should deal as shrewdly in God-honouring ways, as ungodly people deal selfishly for their own ends. The man discounts the debts of his master's debtors, in order to have their support, in case he is dismissed and without money. His actions increase his master's cash flow, by getting the money in. His master commends his shrewdness, but not his integrity! **V 13: SERVING WITH SINGLENESS** The option is clear: we either serve God or we serve Mammon. (Mammon stands for money and materialism.) **V 14–15: CONDEMNED BY COMPARISON** Jesus applies the teaching to the Pharisees who love money and deride Christ. He reminds them that God knows and sees the abominable state of their hearts. **V 16–18: LASTING THROUGH LIFE** Jesus teaches that not the smallest part of the law of God will ever fail. It will outlast creation itself. Taking the principle of permanence, He goes on to remind them of the permanence of marriage. Marriage, like all of God's moral law, is for the whole of life. **V 19–31: EXAMPLES FOR ETERNITY** Jesus describes the great gulf fixed between the man who is separate from God after death and the man who is with God after death. He refers to two men with different eternities to experience. Lazarus is the saved beggar and the other is the lost rich man. The lost man's fervency for warning others not to neglect their salvation is only greater in the case of Jesus, Himself, and of Paul. Jesus teaches that even if someone rises from the dead, people will not be convinced if they refuse to accept the Scriptures. How true that is today!

CHAPTER SEVENTEEN

V 1–2: OFFENDING OTHERS Jesus warns those who cause others to offend. Specifically those who cause little ones to sin would be better off dead. We must be watchful. **V 3–6: FORGIVING FAITH** Jesus teaches both the need to rebuke and continually to forgive a repentant brother. Outfaced by this, the apostles ask the Lord to increase their faith. Jesus illustrates what faith can do by reference to a mustard seed. **V 7–10: SINFUL SERVANTS** He then uses an illustration of a servant working for his master, to remind His disciples that at their best, they are unworthy. We can never outdo our duty as unworthy, grateful and saved sinners. **V 11–19: NEGLECTFUL NINE** Ten lepers are healed and sent by Jesus to the priests who declare them cleansed. Only one of the ten, a Samaritan, comes back to thank Jesus and glorify God. The neglectful nine miss the words of commission and assurance that Jesus gives to this grateful Samaritan. **V 20–37:**

KINGDOM'S KING Jesus teaches the Pharisees that the kingdom of God is already within the believer. He talks to the disciples about the fact that the King will come again. His second coming will be observed as obviously and easily as lightning. He describes some aspects of His coming. As in the cases of Noah and Lot, God's judgement will fall on a world of people who go about their normal ungodly lives seeking for pleasure. Jesus' second coming will reveal a great division between those who know and are ready for Him and those who are lost.

CHAPTER EIGHTEEN

V 1–8: PERSISTENT PRAYER Jesus teaches by a parable how a persistent widow gets the results she wants from an unjust judge by going to him repeatedly. Our heavenly Father is more willing to answer prayer than that, and we must never give up. Jesus asks a question which reveals that true faith will be hard to find when He returns. God's people have always been in a minority. **V 9–14: CONTRITE CONTRAST** A self-righteous Pharisee, the doer of many good religious things, fails to impress God. A self-effacing and contrite tax collector, hardly daring to ask for mercy, is justified. By this parable, Jesus teaches that the way up is down. God answers honest humility shown by a repentant search for mercy. He rejects any attempt to parade one's religious activities and status as a means of salvation or acceptance. **V 15–17: CALLING CHILDREN** Jesus teaches that unless our hearts are childlike in our response to God, we will never enter the kingdom of God. **V 18–27: RICH RULER** A rich, self-righteous, ruler approaches Jesus. Almost in passing, Jesus demonstrates His deity by probing the meaning of the word 'good'. The man

goes away with great sadness after Jesus asks him if he is willing to sell everything to give to the poor, in order to follow Jesus. Despite his earlier claim to keep five of the last six commandments, the spirit of covetousness is very evident. In itself, this shows He does not love God. Jesus teaches that it is hard for a rich man to enter the kingdom of God, but never impossible with a God of impossibilities. **V 28–30: INFINITE INVESTMENT** Peter claims that the disciples have left all to follow Jesus. Jesus' assurance is that those whose lives are so invested receive an amazing return on that investment both now and in eternity. **V 31–34: TIMELY TRUTHS** On the way to Jerusalem, where He will be crucified, Jesus again emphasises to the disciples that, in accordance with the prophecy in God's Word, He will suffer, die and then be resurrected. The disciples still do not understand. **V 35–43: BLIND BEGGAR** Although a blind beggar is told to shut up when he cries out, 'Jesus, Son of David, have mercy on me,' Jesus stops, asks the man what he wants, and gives him his sight back in answer to his faith. The man follows Jesus, praising God. The crowd also praise God.

CHAPTER NINETEEN

V 1–10: SON SEEKING AND SAVING Jesus' mission 'to seek and to save' includes blessing Zacchaeus, a tax collector. He comes to Christ, gives half of his goods to the poor, and makes generous restitution to those from whom he has wrongly extracted money. **V 11–27: SERVANTS SERVING AND SCARED** As Jerusalem looms ahead and the disciples think that His kingdom will suddenly appear, Jesus teaches the need to be faithful while waiting. He shows, by a parable of three servants, that His disciples should use what He gives them responsibly and obediently while awaiting His coming kingdom. Two servants serve Him very faithfully and well and invest what is left with them by their departing master. They make a financial return, for which they are rewarded on his return as king. The other servant is scared of potential failure incurring his master's displeasure and so he is disobedient. He does not invest his master's money as commanded. His master is displeased and directs that his share should be given to the most fruitful of the faithful servants. A worse fate still, however, will await the enemies of the new king. **V 28–44: SAVIOUR SALUTED AND SADDENED** About to enter Jerusalem, Jesus details two disciples to acquire a colt prepared for Him. His entry into Jerusalem on it is met by loud and joyful praise from the crowd because of the miracles they have seen. Jesus refuses to heed the Pharisees' request to quieten His disciples. He then weeps over Jerusalem, because He knows its citizens will reject Him and that the city will suffer greatly in the days to come. There will be cruel oppression and destruction. **V 45–48: SACRILEGIOUS SELLING AND SCOURGING** Jesus drives out dishonest sellers who are defiling the temple. Elsewhere we read that He did this with a whip. He teaches daily in the purged temple. The desire of the religious leaders to kill Him intensifies, while the people listen to Him with growing attention.

CHAPTER TWENTY

V 1–8: QUESTIONERS QUESTIONED The chief priest, scribes, and elders question the authority that Jesus uses while teaching in the temple and preaching the gospel. He turns the tables on them by asking where John's baptism came from:

was it from heaven or from men? They cannot answer for fear of what the crowd will say, and Jesus replies that neither will He answer their question. They and He know that His authority and John's baptism came from the same place, namely from God in heaven. **V 9–19: REJECTERS REJECTED** Jesus tells the parable of three servants and the son of a vineyard owner who are sent to and killed by evil tenants. The owner will destroy them and give their vineyard to others. Jesus teaches that 'the stone which the builders have rejected has become the chief cornerstone'. They recognise themselves as the rejecters, and Jesus says that one day such people will be broken to pieces or crushed. Their antagonism against Him is again intensified. **V 20–26: SCHEMERS SILENCED** Again, the religious people scheme against Jesus to trap Him into saying something which is politically incorrect. They send undercover spies to observe Him. His religious adversaries ask if it is right to pay taxes to Caesar or not. Jesus tells them to give God what is due to God, and to give to Caesar what is due to Caesar. They are silenced by this answer before the people. **V 27–40: RESURRECTION REALITIES** The Sadducees deny the resurrection and try to trick Jesus by asking a question about one woman who, over a period of time, married each of seven brothers after the successive childless deaths of each previous husband. To whom will she be married in heaven? Jesus teaches that marriage does not exist in heaven. He goes on to say that, even in the Old Testament, the resurrection is foreseen because Moses refers to 'the God of Abraham, Isaac, and Jacob'. They are physically dead, of course, but God knows that they live on in their own spirits, in an intermediate state, awaiting the resurrection. 'All live to

Him,' in that sense: no one is annihilated. Some scribes appreciate His answer. After it there are no more questions! **V 41–44: LORD'S LORDSHIP** Quoting from the Psalms about David, Jesus clearly shows that He is not only David's Son, but also David's Lord. **V 45–47: TAINTED TEACHERS** Jesus warns against the scribes who love to have the acclaim of men and increase their self-esteem and status. They are self-seeking materialistic men who will be punished very severely.

CHAPTER TWENTY-ONE

V 1–4: SACRIFICIAL GIVING Jesus teaches that a poor woman, putting into the treasury two very small coins, puts in more than all the wealthy people give from their reservoirs of wealth. In effect, she is giving all. **V 5–36: SIGNS GIVEN** After Jesus announces that the temple will be destroyed one day, He is asked what signs will show that this will take place. Extending this to the signs of His coming, He teaches the need to be aware of false claims. He then gives more detailed teaching of many signs that will indicate His coming is near. It seems these signs are like bubbles rising from a boiling cauldron, that will come vigorously to the boil before Christ comes again. A brief summary of the signs follows: false christs; wars and commotions; international strife; various earthquakes; signs in the heavens; witness by Christ's persecuted followers; betrayal, even to death, by family members; universal hatred of Christians; Jerusalem besieged and cruelly subjugated; more signs in the heavens; further international distress; the sea turning angry; and widespread hopelessness and fear. Christ will then come in power and great glory. His disciples should read the signs in the same way as one looks at the fruit growing and

maturing on a tree. God's Word will come to pass. Personal faith, holiness and watchfulness are essential for all Christ's followers. **V 37–38: SPIRITUAL GOALS** Significantly, and as a good example for Christians, Jesus gets on with His daily spiritual goals of teaching in the temple, and praying at night on Mount Olivet. We, too, should be involved in the spiritual goals of getting close to God ourselves and making His word known to others, as His coming draws nearer.

CHAPTER TWENTY-TWO

V 1–6: PASSOVER PLOT When the religious leaders look for a way to kill Jesus, Satan influences Judas Iscariot, one of the twelve. Judas agrees to betray Jesus in return for monetary payment. He will lead them to Jesus at a time when there is no crowd to be antagonised by or to witness their taking Jesus into custody. **V 7–23: SPECIAL SUPPER** Peter and John prepare the Passover in a room designated by Jesus for the Lord's Supper and divinely preserved for Him. Jesus, with His disciples, takes the form of words of the Passover and applies them to Himself. His body and His blood will be given for them and God's covenant will be ratified in the shed blood of His Son. But He knows that one will go out to betray Him. The disciples question who the betrayer will be. **V 24–30: DISTURBING DISCORD** Amazingly, at such a sacred time, the disciples then dispute which of them will be the greatest. Jesus teaches that the greatest is the one who serves. He bestows kingdom rights and privileges on His disciples who have continued with Him in various trials. **V 31–34: PETER'S PRESUMPTION** Jesus prophesies about Peter, that he will fall but will be restored to strengthen his brothers. Peter then proclaims, with impulsive presumption, that he is ready to be imprisoned or to die. Jesus responds that before the rooster crows, he will deny Jesus three times. **V 35–38: COMING CLIMAX** Jesus gives other instructions to the disciples to meet the changing circumstances. God tells Him that the climax is coming when He will be 'numbered with the transgressors', (in accordance with the prophecy of Isaiah chapter 53), and that the Scriptures will be fulfilled about Him. He faces the cross. The disciples tell Jesus that they have two swords. Jesus tells them he has heard enough about that. **V 39–46: PAINFUL PRAYER** Jesus continues His habit of praying on the Mount of Olives. His disciples follow Him. He tells them to pray that they will not enter into temptation, and then goes a short distance away and prays that the will of the Father will be done by Him, even if it means His taking the cup of suffering and sacrificial death on the cross. In agony and in earnest prayer His sweat becomes 'like great drops of blood falling down to the ground'. Christ returns from prayer to find His heavily sorrowful disciples not praying, but asleep. He wakes them to rise and pray in order to resist temptation. **V 47–53: DIVINE DIGNITY** Judas leads the crowd of people to arrest Jesus and approaches to kiss Him. Jesus quietly rebukes Judas by asking if he will betray Him with a kiss. He restores the right ear of one of the servants of the high priest, severed with a sword wielded by one of Jesus' disciples (identified elsewhere as Peter). Jesus, calmly and rhetorically, asks the religious rulers and the captains of the temple why they did not try to seize Him when He was with them in the temple every day. Then He quietly concedes that this is their hour of darkness, and He does not resist. What dignity we see in Christ. **V 54–62: DISTANT DISCIPLE** Peter, following afar off, three times denies that

he knows Jesus. As His Master prophesied, the rooster crows. Jesus turns and looks at Peter, who remembers. He goes outside to weep bitterly. **V 63–65: MASTER MOCKED** The guards mock and beat Jesus. They play a game with Him. They blindfold Him and ask Him to prophesy who hit Him. They insult Him in many ways. There is no response from Jesus. **V 66–71: TRUTHFUL TESTIMONY** After an all-night ordeal, Jesus is led to the council (the Sanhedrin) of the elders, chief priest and scribes. Jesus tells the Sanhedrin that in the future, the Son of Man (a title used to refer to Himself) 'will sit on the right hand of the power of God'. He then confirms, in answer to their question, that He is the Son of God. Jesus never shrinks from telling the truth about Himself, or about others. They take this as a confession of blasphemy and move on to the next unconstitutional stage in their perverted judicial process, intent to do to death the Son of God.

CHAPTER TWENTY-THREE

V 1–7: FAULTLESS FINDING Jesus is taken to Pilate. The cynical accusations against Him are that He perverts the nation, encourages non-payment of taxes to Caesar, and holds Himself out to be a king. Pilate ignores the first two false accusations and then ascertains that Jesus confirms that He is King of the Jews. Pilate says that he finds no fault in Him. That is not a matter for Roman jurisdiction. No doubt with some relief, he sends Jesus of Galilee to Herod in Jerusalem. **V 8–12: CRUEL CONTEMPT** Herod is disappointed that Jesus does not do a miracle for him, and questions Him. Jesus does not answer. Jesus is vehemently accused by the religious leaders, and Herod and his soldiers treat Him with contempt, mock Him, and put Him in a robe to send Him back to Pilate. The enmity that existed between Pilate and Herod is bridged on that day. But Herod does not find Jesus guilty of anything. **V 13–25: INEXCUSABLE INJUSTICE** Pilate knows that this matter is outside his jurisdiction, that Jesus has done no crime deserving of any punishment, and that Herod also found no fault in Him. Yet, despite initial protests and after his failed suggested compromise to have Jesus chastised and released, he bows to the pressure of the crowd. Jesus will be crucified and Barabbas, a convicted rebel and murderer, released in His place. Such injustice is inexcusable but inevitable if Christ is to die for sinners. **V 26–38: CHRIST CRUCIFIED** Simon of Cyrene is made to carry the cross for Jesus. As a great multitude follows Jesus on the way to Calvary, He turns to console the weeping women of Jerusalem, and to warn of trouble to come. He is crucified, flanked by criminals. While soldiers divide His garments and cast lots, rulers sneer and revile Him, and other soldiers mock Him. He prays for forgiveness for His oppressors. He shows Himself to be what the inscription on the cross says: 'The King of the Jews.' **V 39–43: PENITENT'S PARADISE** One of the criminals crucified with Him blasphemes Jesus, but the other rebukes him and turns to Jesus, admitting that while he, personally, has done wrong, Jesus has done nothing wrong. He asks Jesus to remember him when He comes into His kingdom. Jesus assures him that he will be with Him in Paradise on that very day. **V 44–49: CENTURION CERTAIN** Sunless darkness veils the cross for three hours from the sixth to the ninth hour, corresponding with twelve noon until three in the afternoon. The veil dividing the Most Holy Place in the temple from the holy place is torn from top to bottom, signifying that the way to God is now open. Jesus commits His spirit to God the Father. His work is done and He breathes His last breath. The centurion looking on glorifies God, knowing that Jesus is completely righteous. The crowd is grief stricken and convicted and people beat their breasts. Those who know Jesus watch from a distance. **V 50–56: BODY BURIED** Joseph of Arimathea, a dissenting council member, begs and gets the body of Jesus from Pilate. He has it placed in his own new tomb. The women observe where the body is, return and prepare the spices and fragrant oils that they will use on the body. But they rest on the Sabbath, according to God's law.

CHAPTER TWENTY-FOUR

V 1–8: RISEN! REMEMBER? On the first day of the week, the women find that the stone is rolled away and that the tomb is empty. Two angels appear as men in shining clothes to tell them that 'He is risen!' They remind the women of the prophecy that He will be 'delivered into the hands of sinful men, and be crucified, and the third day rise again'. Only then do they remember His words. **V 9–12: DOUBTING DISCIPLES** Mary Magdalene, Joanna, Mary (James' mother), and others tell all this to the disciples. Their doubts are such that they do disbelieve what they hear as 'idle tales'. Peter, however, goes to investigate, sees the grave clothes lying by themselves, and marvels at what has happened. **V 13–35: BROKEN BREAD** The risen Jesus appears to two disciples, walking seven miles from Jerusalem to Emmaus. They are very depressed at what they regard to be the final defeat of their precious Master. By astute use of questions, and pointing them to Himself from the Scriptures, Jesus redirects their minds and causes their hearts to burn within them. When He breaks bread and gives thanks, their eyes are opened, they recognise Him, and He disappears. They thrill that Jesus has opened the Scriptures to them. They rush back to the eleven to hear that Jesus has also appeared to Simon. **V 36–49: PROMISED POWER** While they are there, Jesus appears with the words 'Peace to you.' He assures them, shows them His hands and His feet, and asks for something to eat. He then reminds them that they must have an unshakeable trust in the Scriptures which had to be fulfilled concerning Him. He then opens their minds to understand God's Word about His death, resurrection, repentance, forgiveness of sins, and the need to be His

witnesses to all nations. He tells them that He is going to the Father, and then promised power will come from on high. They later understand that Jesus is referring to the Holy Spirit. **V 50–53: AMAZING ASCENSION** He then leads them out to Bethany. He lifts His hands and blesses them. The blessing is an unfinished one, as during it, He is carried up into heaven through His ascension. In heaven, that blessing will continue! Worshipful and rejoicing, they return to Jerusalem, completely new and different people. They now continually visit the temple to praise and bless God. What a difference a crucified, resurrected, ascended Saviour and Lord makes to those who trust Him and His Word!

JOHN

OVERVIEW

PEOPLE AND PRELIMINARIES

✳ John (twenty-one chapters) was written by the apostle John between AD60 and AD70 probably in Galilee but just possibly while in exile on the Isle of Patmos (where he also wrote Revelation). John also wrote three letters—1 John, 2 John and 3 John. John's Gospel is the fourth and only non-synoptic Gospel. **See comments on Matthew.** Like Mark, the estimated period covered by the events in this Gospel is under ten years, probably only seven.

PLAN AND PURPOSE

ⓘ John is written partly to complement the synoptic Gospels of Matthew, Mark and Luke, but mainly to show and prove that the Lord Jesus Christ is the everlasting Son of God and, at the same time, God the Son. He is also the King, servant and perfect man, as the focuses of the first three Gospels show. Because He is God, there is no genealogy. He always has been, always is, and always will be! There are no genealogies in eternity! Thus John stresses the Lord Jesus Christ's eternality, creator-hood, incarnation and deity. He is God, despite being despised and rejected by some of those He came to save. Signs are given in His miracles to help the humble observer see who Jesus is. Salvation by faith in Him is clearly portrayed. The Gospel constantly underlines His special relationship and entity with God the Father, the signs validating His eternal Sonship, the need to 'believe', the person of Jesus (seven times He says 'I am', clearly claiming Godhood), and the emphasis on new, spiritual and eternal life that He alone can give. John is written to the 'whomever' of any generation and any national, religious or ethnic background.

PROFILE AND PROGRESSION

Jesus as the eternal Word made flesh and His acclaim and baptism by John the Baptist—including His eternal nature, creating work, life-giving and illuminating power, witness to Him by John the Baptist, rejection, acceptance, incarnate deity, and Spirit endorsed baptism (1:1–34); the public ministry of the incarnate Son of God—including calling the disciples, first miracle at Cana, the temple cleansed, new birth teaching to Nicodemus, the Samaritan detour, healings and other sign miracles leading to applied teaching in Cana and Jerusalem, opposition encountered and teaching opportunities taken, public entry into Jerusalem acclaimed and further teaching about trust and rejection (1:35–12:50); the Son of God's preparatory time with His disciples—including servant-hood demonstrated in washing His disciples' feet, His betrayal foretold, His farewell talk, and His interceding in prayer (13:1–17:26); the Son of God rejected, crucified and buried—including Gethsemane, illegal trials, denials by Peter, the crucifixion of Jesus and His burial and embalmment in the tomb of Joseph of Arimathea (18:1–19:42); the glorious resurrection of the Son of God and some of His witnessed appearances—including the Lord's day discovery of the empty tomb, and His appearances to Mary Magdalene and the disciples (without, and then with, Thomas), the disciples again and Peter (20:1–23); the many wonderful deeds done by the Son of God (20:24,25).

PRINCIPLES AND PARTICULARS

See comments on Matthew. The emphasis of John is on the divine nature of Jesus, the co-Creator and eternal Son of God. He is unique, and there is (and can be) no other Saviour. The 'I am's of Jesus display both His Godhead and His relationship to sinners. His miracles are presented as signposts to His identity. Eternal life, as a current possession and as an everlasting state, is featured as the sinner's immediate birthright when he becomes born again. The true nature of saving personal belief and the eternal security of the believer are clearly seen here. Christ's loving and co-equal relationship with the Father and the Spirit demands the doctrine of the Trinity. In all of this, the loving compassion and care of the man Christ Jesus is manifested in the way He deals with sinners. In emphasising that He is the eternal God in flesh, we must never forget the flesh of His perfect manhood and the warmth of His loving humanity. He is truly man as well as truly God.

JOHN

CHAPTER ONE

V 1–10: DEITY DEMONSTRATED The teaching that Jesus is God is tasted throughout the whole of John's Gospel in the same way as sugar is tasted in sweetened tea. We start by seeing that Jesus is eternal, the Creator, and the Light of men, as John the Baptist clearly witnessed. We also see His rejection. **V 11–13: RIGHT RECEIVED** Despite being rejected by His own, those who receive Him also received the right to become children of God. That right is received through faith in Christ, and not through family considerations, human will, or the design of man. It is God's work. **V 14: GLORIOUS GRACE** Jesus is the 'Word'. When the Word takes on human flesh, His glory is seen in His human life as being 'full of grace and truth'. **V 15: PRE-EXISTENT PREFERRED** John's testimony is that Jesus, though born on earth after him, is preferred before him as the pre-existent God. **V 16–18: CHRIST'S COMPLETENESS** So complete is the eternal Son of God on earth, that John testifies that all have received His fullness and His grace. Moses could only bring the law, but Jesus brings grace and truth and, as God the Son, declares His heavenly Father. **V 19–28: TELLING TESTIMONY** As he baptises, John's witness to the priests and Levites, sent by the Jews, is clear. He is not the Christ, but merely a preparer and forerunner for Him. This witness is to Jesus, of whom he is unworthy. **V 29–34: SPIRIT SEEN** When John sees Jesus, he declares Him to be the 'Lamb of God who takes away the sins of the world'. He confirms the identity of Jesus. Referring to His baptism, John confirms that he has seen the Spirit descending on Jesus, in the form of a dove. Jesus is the Son of God, who will baptise with the Holy Spirit. **V 35–42: FIRST FOLLOWERS** The next day John declares, again, 'Behold the Lamb of God!' His testimony causes Andrew, the brother of Simon Peter, to follow Jesus. He soon finds his brother, who follows Jesus, too. Jesus tells Peter that his name will signify a 'stone'. **V 43–51: CONVINCING CALL** Philip is the next to follow Jesus and he finds Nathanael. Nathanael is sceptical at first, but becomes convinced and follows Jesus after Jesus reveals that He saw him under a fig tree before ever he came to Jesus. Nathanael declares Jesus to be the Son of God and the King of Israel. Jesus tells him that he will see greater things as he follows Him.

CHAPTER TWO

V 1–11: MIRACULOUS MANIFESTATION
Jesus performs the first miraculous sign, showing that He is the Son of God. When the wine runs out, He turns water into wine at a wedding feast. This manifestation of His glory encourages His disciples to believe in Him. **V 12: SHORT STAY** Jesus goes to Capernaum for a few days, with His mother, brothers, and disciples. **V 13–17: TABLES TURNED** He then goes to Jerusalem and turns over the tables of those who are abusing the temple. He drives the abusers out of the temple because they are irreverently using it as a place of commerce and not as a place of worship towards God. The disciples note that His zeal is in accordance with the Scriptures. **V 18–22: RESURRECTION REMEMBERED** The Jews ask Him to show a sign to establish His authority to deal with the temple, in the way He has. Jesus dramatically predicts His resurrection by telling them that the temple (of His body) will be destroyed and raised up in three days. Much later, His disciples are to remember this prediction and believe what Jesus said. **V 23–25: CHRIST'S COMMITMENT** Jesus performs some signs to authenticate His authority as Son of God. This attracts many who believe only on the basis of the signs alone. Jesus knows how superficial this can be and does not commit Himself to them. Their belief in signs alone is not true faith. He wants to see hearts that are really close to Him and that follow Him. He knows what is in the hearts of men and women.

CHAPTER THREE

V 1–12: LOST LEADER Jesus tells Nicodemus, a Pharisee and ruler of the Jews, that he must be born again to understand and enter the kingdom of God. This is the work of God's Holy Spirit. Nicodemus confesses his ignorance. **V 13–18: GOD'S GOSPEL** Jesus reveals that Moses' lifting up of the bronze serpent on a pole in the wilderness is a picture of how He Himself will be lifted up on the cross to take the punishment for the sins of all those who will turn from their sin and believe in Him. The only alternatives are condemnation or eternal life. The deciding factor is whether there is deliberate personal belief in Christ. Verse 16 is probably the best known verse in the Bible, and has been called 'the gospel in a nutshell'. **V 19–21: CONDEMNATION'S CAUSE** People will be judged according to the light they have received. Through our evil deeds we have rejected the light and the truth of God. Only repentance and faith in Christ's death on the cross can restore this. Those knowing the truth of the Light of the world, the Lord Jesus Christ, can have no cause for complaint if they fail to turn to Him. **V 22–24: JOINING JOHN** Jesus and His disciples identify with the work of John the Baptist, later to be imprisoned and beheaded. By being with John as he baptises, Jesus identifies with and ratifies the Baptist's calls to repent. Through His disciples' involvement in baptism, Jesus is said to baptise, though He personally baptises no one, as the next chapter reveals. **V 25–36: SON'S SUPREMACY** Some of John's disciples resent the fact that people are flocking to Jesus, where He, through His disciples, is baptising. John is quick to show that his role is only as the 'best man' at the wedding, and that the bridegroom must be centre stage. That bridegroom is Christ. John says, 'He must increase, but I must decrease,' and focuses on Jesus, who has come from heaven as the co-equal Son. Jesus alone can give everlasting life to those who believe in Him. He alone can turn people from the wrath of God, which abides on those who will not trust in

Christ. The Son is the supreme and unique Saviour.

CHAPTER FOUR

V 1–6: WEARY AT THE WELL Jesus leaves Judea for Galilee, having seen the pressure from the Pharisees upon Him because His disciples baptised more people than John. He goes through Samaria. Wearied, He sits by Jacob's well around midday. **V 7–18: WATER FOR THE WOMAN** A Samaritan woman is asked by Jesus to give Him a drink, but she remonstrates on the basis that Samaritans have no dealings with Jews, and in any case she is a woman. Jesus reveals Himself as the well of living water, which quenches thirst forever. His water springs to eternal life. The woman asks for the water and Jesus points out her sin by outlining both her past and her present immorality. Eternal life is only available to those who are willing to turn from their sin, and for that to occur, a person has to be conscious of his or her sins. **V 19–26: WAY TO TRUE WORSHIP** The woman compares Samaritan worship with Jewish worship. Jesus reveals that true worshippers worship God, who is Spirit, in spirit and truth through the work of God the Holy Spirit. He also reveals Himself as the Messiah. **V 27–38: WHITENESS OF THE WHEAT** The disciples come back from having found food and are surprised to see Jesus talking with the woman. She goes into the city with the water pot and tells what has happened. Because of this, many come out from the city, probably mainly dressed in white, and Jesus tells His disciples that the fields are white for harvest. He encourages sowing and reaping. **V 39–42: WITNESS OF THE WOMAN** Many Samaritans who hear her testimony come to believe in Christ. Later, their trust is confirmed through the word of Jesus. A true testimony will often lead someone to receive God's word and accept Christ as Saviour. **V 43–54: WONDERS OR THE WORD?** Jesus returns to Galilee, where He teaches that a prophet is not honoured by his own people, and goes to Cana where the first miracle had been performed by Him. The second one follows, as, from a distance, He heals the dying son of a nobleman. Some come to seek signs, but the nobleman believes the word of God, through Jesus.

CHAPTER FIVE

V 1–9a: PARALYTIC A man, paralysed for thirty-eight years, is healed by Jesus at the pool in Jerusalem called Bethesda where sick people congregate each day to hope for a miraculous healing. His healing is immediate and effective. He later takes up his bed and walks. **V 9b–14: PERSECUTION** Because Jesus heals on the Sabbath day, the Jews seek to persecute and kill Him. They criticise the man for carrying his bed on the Sabbath day and interrogate him about Jesus. Their own legalistic rules replace the true spirit of the Sabbath, which God gave to be a blessing to mankind. Jesus assures the man that he is healed and tells him to sin no more. **V 15–18: PRESUMPTION** The man tells the Jews that Jesus has healed him. Their wicked desire to kill Jesus, because He heals on the Sabbath, intensifies because He identifies with God the Father, making Himself equal with God. **V 19–30: POWER** Jesus claims absolute identification and oneness with the Father in the works that He does, including raising the dead, exercising judgement and giving everlasting life. His power is the power of God, because that is who He is. **V 31–35: PREPARER** Jesus then refers to John the Baptist's witness to His identity. He was a lamp who prepared the way for Christ. **V 36–40: PROCLAMATION** Jesus goes on to reveal three witnesses proclaiming who He is. His works, His Father and the body of Scripture all witness to His identity. Jesus is quick to point out that searching the Scriptures will not save you, unless you are willing to come to Him personally to receive eternal life. **V 41–47: PURPOSE** Jesus exposes the inconsistency of the people. They will not honour Him, although He comes from God, but highly esteem self-seeking people. Jesus reveals the purpose of the law through Moses, who writes about Jesus. Those who really believe his words will come to Christ. The law is indeed a schoolmaster to bring us to Christ.

CHAPTER SIX

V 1–3: SIGNS AND SITTING Jesus crosses the Sea of Galilee and many follow Him because of His signs in healing diseased people. After that, He goes to a mountain and takes time to sit down with His disciples. Jesus is as interested in personal time with His disciples as He is in working in the lives of others. **V 4–14: POWER TO PROVIDE** A huge crowd, including 5,000 men, are fed by the miraculous multiplying by Jesus of five loaves and two fish. All are filled. The disciples are involved in the distribution of the food and in the collection of what is left over. This sign convinces the men that Jesus is the Prophet who is to come into the world. **V 15–21: WALKING ON WATER** Jesus resists the popular acclaim and goes to a mountain to be alone. His disciples start rowing to the other side of the lake, towards Capernaum. It is night and a storm arises while they are three or four miles out. Jesus walks to them on the water and assures them of who He is. When Jesus enters the boat, it immediately reaches its destination.

V 22–42: GIVEN FROM GLORY The people, still impressed by the feeding of the huge multitude from a few loaves and fish, come to find Jesus. He warns them about seeking Him just because of signs, and tells them that the important thing is to believe in Him. He declares Himself as coming from heaven in just the same way as manna was given from heaven in the wilderness. He is the Bread of Life. He gives eternal life and fulfilment to those who come to Him. The Jews complain, because they recognise that He is talking about His heavenly origin and they know that He is the 'son of Joseph', probably remembering that Joseph was not the natural father of Jesus. They dispute that Jesus is given from glory. **V 43–66: DIFFICULT DOCTRINE** Jesus teaches that those who come to Him are drawn by the Father and then develops the thought of Himself as the Bread of Life. He says no one may have everlasting life without eating His flesh and drinking His blood. The disciples are offended by this difficult saying and do not understand it. Jesus then explains that He is speaking spiritually. This is merely an illustrative parallel, and not a literal cannibalistic requirement! He is talking about spiritual faith in Christ, and stresses that it is belief that saves. (Over the years, some people have sought to support a wrong view of the meaning of holy communion from these verses, but Jesus is clearly teaching a spiritual belief in Him through a dramatic illustration. Nowhere in the Bible is it taught that the bread and the wine actually become His body and His blood. If that were a requirement for everlasting life, then all of His physical disciples would be lost because at the time they ate communion with Him, He had not even died upon the cross, and clearly His body and blood were intact.) Some go back and walk with Jesus no more when He tells them that He knows those who believe in Him, and who will betray Him. **V 67–71: DIFFERENT DISCIPLES** Simon Peter confesses that Jesus has the words of eternal life, and that He is 'the Christ, the Son of the Living God'. Jesus reveals that one of the twelve is against Him but He does not reveal that his name is Judas Iscariot.

CHAPTER SEVEN

V 1–5: REJECTION BY RELATIONS Jesus stays in Galilee, rather than going to Judea. His half-brothers advise Him to go from Galilee to Judea for the Feast of Tabernacles. They challenge Him to do His miracles openly. They do not believe in Him yet, though later they will. **V 6–13: SENSITIVITY ABOUT SECRECY** Jesus knows that if He goes publicly to Judea now, He will unnecessarily speed up the opposition against Him, and He knows that this is not yet the right time for Him to die. He remains in a world that hates Him, because of His testimony about the evil within it. Many want to kill Him. So He goes in secrecy and indeed there is a lot of complaining and mixed opinion about Him. Misunderstanding and murmuring is rife. Fear of the Jews silences those who would like to commend Him. **V 14–24: TEACHING IN TEMPLE** At the middle of the feast, Jesus goes public by teaching in the temple. The Jews cannot understand the source of His teaching. He declares that His doctrine is from God. He asks why they want to kill Him. They respond that this is not so and that He is demon-possessed. He shows the inconsistent hypocrisy of their agreeing to circumcise on the Sabbath, while at the same time as judging Him for making someone well on the Sabbath. He accuses them of not judging righteously and only with regard to external appearance. **V 25–31:**

DIRECTNESS ABOUT DEITY Debate is on every hand about who Jesus is. Some conclude from the rulers' public silence that they agree that He is the Christ. Jesus makes His claim to Deity clear by saying that He comes from God and has been sent by God. Some seek to kill Him but are unable to do so, because His time has not yet come. Many believe on Him, reasoning that Christ would not do more signs than Jesus has done. **V 32–36: MURMURING AND MISUNDERSTANDING** The Pharisees hear the murmuring of the crowd and, with the chief priest, send officers to take Him. He tells them that He is going to go to God. Although they will seek Him, they will be unable to find Him or to follow Him. The Jews misunderstand His statement and wonder if He is going to go to the Greeks. **V 37–39: GIFT AFTER GLORIFICATION** Jesus promises the gift of the Holy Spirit, as rivers of living water, to those who will believe in Him. The Holy Spirit will be given to believers after Jesus has been glorified. **V 40–44: IGNORANT OF IDENTITY** Opinions are divided as to the identity of Jesus Christ. Many ignorantly say that if Jesus really is the Christ, He would have come from Bethlehem! They seem ignorant of the fact that Bethlehem is the birthplace of Jesus! Yet again, those wanting to take Him are unable to do so. **V 45–53: CONFUSION ABOUT CHRIST** The confusion continues about the identity of Jesus Christ. The officers tell the chief priest and the Pharisees that no one ever spoke like Jesus. The Pharisees criticise them and the crowd. Nicodemus, who earlier came to Jesus by night, tells them that a man should be heard and the facts looked at before he is judged. At this stage their opposition is rationalised because they say that Jesus came from Galilee. They argue that therefore Jesus cannot be a true prophet. They do not realise that Jesus came from Bethlehem, not Galilee, and in any case prophets did come from Galilee, including Jonah and Nahum! Biased opposition seldom stops to look at the facts!

(Note: there is debate whether chapter 7, verse 53 to chapter 8 verse 11 is in the best original manuscripts. As with the very few other occasions where differences of opinion arise concerning the content of the original manuscripts, no doctrine is taken away or added to by the inclusion or exclusion of the particular passage, because God's Word stands as a whole. It is also true that, after further research, some previously doubted passages are now again given greater credibility than formerly, and we have to be careful not to jump to wrong conclusions. These notes continue as if the passage is in the original.)

CHAPTER EIGHT

V 1–11: HYPOCRISY HIT The scribes and Pharisees bring Jesus a woman caught in the act of adultery and say that she should be stoned. Jesus simply advises that the person without sin should cast the first stone. The crowd melt away. Jesus then tells the woman to stop sinning. **V 12–18: TELLING TESTIMONY** Jesus claims to be the Light of the world. Those following Him shall walk in 'the light of life'. He is told that He cannot testify of Himself. Jesus replies that He knows His origin and destiny and that, as His Father testifies of Him also, His witness is corroborated. **V 19–59: CRUCIAL COMPREHENSION** This statement produces various discussions about the relationship between Jesus as God the Son, who is the Son of Man on earth, and the first Person of the Trinity, God the Father. Jesus says He is going away to His Father after He has been killed. The innuendo from the opponents is that Jesus is illegitimate. Jesus says all His teaching comes from the Father, and that the Father is with Him. He always pleases the Father. This causes many to believe in Him. He encourages them, as His disciples, to continue in God's word and truth. The scribes and Pharisees take up Christ's claim to give freedom and claim that, as Abraham's descendants, they are not in bondage. Jesus teaches that anyone who sins is a slave of sin, but He, the Son, can set them free. Their sinful works testify that God is not their Father. The devil is their father spiritually. That is why they want to murder Him. Jesus refutes that He is possessed by a demon. He always follows His Father and seeks His glory. Those who keep His word have eternal life. To show that His external existence predated Abraham's life He says, 'Before Abraham was, I AM.' ('I AM' is an Old Testament title of God.) Jesus passes through the midst of them, unharmed, despite their attempt to stone Him to death for blasphemy. Jesus is not just a prophet but the eternal Son of God.

CHAPTER NINE

V 1–5: BLAME AND BLINDNESS Jesus' disciples ask Him who is to blame for a blind man's blindness from birth. Is it himself or his parents? Jesus replies no one is to blame, but He, the Light of the world, will use this to reveal God's working in this man. **V 6–10: SALIVA AND SIGHT** Jesus makes clay with His own saliva and anoints the man's eyes. He sends him to the nearby pool of Siloam and the man comes back washed and seeing. Such is the change that people find it is hard to believe it is the same man, and ask him how his eyes were opened. **V 11–27: ENQUIRY AND EVALUATION** The man tells what has happened, but he does not know where Jesus now is. The Pharisees interrogate him and tell him that Jesus is not from God, and this is shown because He does not keep the Sabbath! Others ask how a sinful person can do such signs. The man himself declares Jesus to be a prophet. His frightened parents refer the Pharisees' question to them back to their son. Their son simply states that 'Though I was blind, now I see.' The Pharisees again ask how it happened. He asks them if they want to know so they can become disciples of Jesus! **V 28–34: OPENNESS AND OPPOSITION** They revile him and tell him that Jesus cannot be from God. Because he tells them that he believes Jesus must be from God, he is accordingly cast out. His fresh and open stand for Christ leads to opposition to him and to his banishment. **V 35–38: FINDING AND FAITH** Now Jesus finds the man, and asks him if he believes in the Son of God, revealing Himself to be that Person. The man confesses and worships Jesus. Christ has found him and now he has received saving faith as well as physical sight. **V 39–41: BLINDNESS AND BLAME** Whereas the man's blindness is not the result of anyone's blame, Jesus reveals that the Pharisees choose to be blind to the truth and are to be blamed. Their sin remains. They will be judged unless they repent and believe in the Lord Jesus Christ.

CHAPTER TEN

V 1–16: SHEPHERD Jesus reveals Himself both as the Good Shepherd who gives His life to save His sheep, and as the door to salvation for any who enter by Him. He not only seeks the lost sheep of Israel, but other lost sheep, too. All saved people will be one under their Shepherd. **V 17–18: SACRIFICE** Jesus reveals that His life is to be laid down to save His sheep. He also makes it clear that He has the power to take His life back again, foreshadowing His resurrection. **V 19–21: SAYINGS** His sayings cause division. Some accuse Him of demon possession and badness, but others recognise that this cannot be so. **V 22–24: SURROUNDED** The Jews surround Him at the Feast of Dedication in Jerusalem and demand to know if He is the Christ. **V 25–30: SHEEP** Jesus replies that He has told them, but they will not believe. Those who believe in Him become His sheep, know Him and follow Him. They receive eternal life, will never perish, and will never be snatched out of the hand of Jesus or the hand of His Father. He declares complete oneness between the Son and the Father. **V 31–33: STONING** The Jews then again wish to stone Him for blasphemy because they know that He declares Himself to be God through what He said. **V 34–39: SHOWN** Jesus shows through biblical logic and Scripture that He is the Son of God. He tells them that if they do not believe it, then they should believe Him because of the works He has done. They try to seize Him again but Jesus escapes. His hour has still not yet come. **V 40–42: STAY** Jesus then stays in the initial place where John was baptising. People there can see that though John did no signs, he was a true prophet and what he said about Jesus is true. John's work is still productive, because many believe in Jesus there.

CHAPTER ELEVEN

V 1–10: FAMILY FRIEND Jesus is the family friend of Mary and Martha and their brother, Lazarus. Mary will soon anoint Jesus in a truly memorable way. Hearing that Lazarus is sick, Jesus delays for four days before going to see him, after He knows he has died. He says that God will be glorified by this sickness which is not 'unto death'. Then, in spite of the fact that the Jews are seeking to stone Him, He determines to go to Bethany and tells His disciples it is time to wake Lazarus from his sleep. **V 11–15: PARTICULAR PURPOSE** The purpose in waiting is so that the disciples will see Jesus wake him from the dead, and believe in Him. **V 16: DETERMINED DISCIPLE** Thomas, knowing that death will await Jesus in Jerusalem, encourages the other disciples to go and die with Jesus. **V 17–27: RESURRECTON REALITY** Martha tells Jesus that Lazarus would not have died, if Jesus had been there. Nevertheless she believes that Jesus can act now, even though Lazarus has been in the tomb for four days. When Jesus says that Lazarus will rise again, she thinks Jesus is talking about the resurrection in the last days, but Jesus reveals that anyone believing in Him now receives a new resurrection life and will never suffer eternal death. Martha confirms her belief in Jesus as Christ and the Son of God. **V 28–32: DISAPPOINTED DESPAIR** Martha secretly calls Mary and tells her that Jesus is calling for her. Followed by the Jews she comes to Jesus and repeats Martha's earlier comment that if Jesus had been there, Lazarus would not have died. There is no conversation about resurrection with Mary, however. **V 33–39: SADDENED SAVIOUR** Jesus weeps when He sees Mary and the Jews weeping. As well as sympathy, this is probably caused by the lost-ness of the unbelievers around Him. Groaning in Himself, Jesus comes to the cave and commands the sealing stone to be moved. Mary protests that, after four days, there will be a stench from her brother's corpse. **V 40–44: MIGHTY MIRACLE** Jesus says God will be glorified and prays to His Father. He commands Lazarus to come out, and Lazarus is raised from the dead. His disciples are told to unwrap the grave clothes. **V 45–53: POLITICAL PLOTTING** Many Jews believe in Jesus, but some report Him to the Pharisees. They worry that a wave of public belief in Christ will weaken their religious power and influence in the eyes of the occupying Romans. The chief priests and Pharisees hold a council to decide how to put Him to death. Caiphas, the high priest, unwittingly prophesies that Jesus will be put to death for the nation, and for sinners elsewhere who will become the children of God. **V 54–57: SECRET STAY** Jesus retreats in secret to Ephraim with His disciples. Passover is near, when Jerusalem will be full. Meanwhile the religious rulers command that anyone knowing where Jesus is should report it so they can seize Him.

CHAPTER TWELVE

V 1–8: DEVOTION AND DEVIATION Mary is so devoted to Jesus that she anoints Him by pouring costly perfume on Him and wipes His feet with her hair. Jesus says this is to signify His burial. Judas complains that this is a wrong use of the money, however, because he seeks dishonest personal gain from the common purse. While one person shows her godly devotion, the other shows his greedy deviation. **V 9–11: LORD AND LAZARUS** Not only are Christ's enemies seeking to put Him to death, but they also want to kill resurrected Lazarus, because people believe in Christ through His testimony. **V 12–19: PRAISE AND PROPHECY** As Jesus comes into Jerusalem, riding on a young donkey, the people praise Him and acknowledge Him as King of Israel. This fulfils the prophecy of Zechariah. Only after His death, resurrection and ascension will the disciples understand why Jesus came on a donkey. The Pharisees realise from the people's praise of Christ that their attempts to stop them following Him have been in vain. **V 20–36: DEATH AND DARKNESS** As Greeks come to see Jesus, He prophesies His death as a grain of wheat producing a great harvest, once it has died. As His Father testifies of His Son from heaven, Jesus reveals the significance of His death on the cross through which many will be drawn to Him. He tells people to walk in His light while He is with them, rather than in the darkness of ignorance. **V 37–43: REJECTION AND REFUSAL** Despite the signs, there are those who refuse to believe in Him, because their eyes are blinded and their hearts hardened, as prophesied by Isaiah. Some of those who believed in Him refuse to testify to Christ in case they are put out of the synagogue and incur the opposition of men. They prefer man's praise to pleasing God. **V 44–50: ILLUMINATION AND IDENTIFICATION** Jesus teaches that to believe in Him is to believe in the Father. He confirms that He is the Light of the world and that He is one with God the Father. He speaks according to the Father's word and commands eternal life. Judgement is sure for those who reject Him and His works.

CHAPTER THIRTEEN

V 1–17: LESSON FROM LOVE Facing betrayal by Judas after the Lord's Supper, Jesus washes the disciples' feet and shows them that this is what love will do. The Master serves the servants, as He loves them 'to the end'. He explains to Peter what it means to be made clean. He urges His disciples to follow His example by serving others. **V 18–30: BREAD FOR BETRAYER** Jesus announces that He will be betrayed by one of His disciples. He knows that it is Judas Iscariot and passes him the piece of bread, as a sign that he must go and do his evil deed quickly. Satan takes over Judas. He goes out into the night on his evil mission, which is not yet apparent to the disciples. **V 31–32: GLORIFYING OF GOD** The glorifying of God is, and will be, achieved in the glorifying of the Son of Man, the Lord Jesus Christ. **V 33–35: DEMONSTRATION OF DISCIPLESHIP** Jesus emphasises that the demonstration of true discipleship is shown in Christians really loving one another, with the same holy and self-sacrificing love that He has shown to them. **V 36–38: FORETELLING OF FAILURE** Despite Peter's spontaneous and extravagant claim that he will lay down his life for Jesus, Jesus tells him that He knows that Peter will deny Him three times very soon.

CHAPTER FOURTEEN

V 1–4: PREPARED PLACE Jesus balances the current solemnity with the great comfort that He is going to prepare a place for those who trust in Him. **V 5–7: SOLE SAVIOUR** Thomas asks, 'How can we know the way?' Jesus answers by making it clear that He is the only way to God, as well as the truth and the life. To know Him is to know the Father. **V 8–14: ESSENTIAL ENTITY** Philip asks Jesus to show them the Father. Jesus' reply teaches quite clearly the divine entity and oneness between the Father and the Son in the Trinity. The believer in Him will do important work that glorifies the Father and have his, or her, prayer answered. **V 15–28: TRINITY TRUTHS** Jesus expands on the wonder of God being three separate Persons in the Godhead by talking about the Holy Spirit. The Christian is to obey Christ. Jesus will pray to the Father so that the Holy Spirit will help and abide for ever with those who

know Him. After Jesus has died, risen again and ascended to heaven, the Spirit will come to help and to reveal God's truth to those who trust Christ. Jesus says that those who love Him and keep His word will be indwelled by the Father and by the Son. The Spirit will teach God's Word to the believer and bring to mind the words of Jesus. **V 29–31: FUTURE FORETOLD** Jesus tells His disciples about His impending death and resurrection so that they may believe. He declares His love and obedience on earth to God the Father.

CHAPTER FIFTEEN

V 1–8: FRUIT AND FIRE Jesus reveals Himself as the true Vine, His Father as the vine-dresser, and His disciples as branches abiding in Him. The mark of discipleship is fruit-bearing. Fruitless branches are to be burnt, because they are not linked to Him in faith and discipleship. His disciples bear fruit, and even much fruit, in glorifying the Father. **V 9–11: COMMUNION AND COMMANDMENTS** Christians are to abide in Christ's love in close communion. In so doing, they will keep His commandments and experience His joy. **V 12–17: PRIORITY AND PRODUCTIVITY** Sacrificial, self-giving love is a priority for the disciples of Christ. Another mark of close friendship with Christ is loving obedience to Him, which produces a spiritual fruitfulness. The command to love one another is repeated. **V 18–25: WORLD AND WORD** The world which is against the Master is also against His servants who will keep His word. People at large ignore the works that Jesus has done. God's word will be fulfilled when it states that they hate Him without cause. They therefore hate the Father also. Opposed by the world, the Christian must keep close to the word of God. The world is culpable because it ignores or rejects what Jesus has done. **V 26–27: TRINITY AND TESTIMONY** Jesus says that God the Holy Spirit will come as the Helper, whom He will send from the Father. He is the Spirit of truth coming from the Father and testifying of Jesus. Jesus' disciples will also witness of Him, aided by the triune God, because they have been with Jesus from the beginning of His ministry.

CHAPTER SIXTEEN

V 1–4: PERSECUTION Jesus predicts a time when His disciples will face death from those who imagine they are doing God's service by killing them. **V 5–15: PROMISE** He promises them that, when He goes away, the Holy Spirit will come to them. He will convict the world of sin, righteousness, and judgement. He will guide them into all truth and glorify Jesus. **V 16–22: PREDICTION** Jesus tells them that soon they will not see Him and later they will see Him again, as He goes to His Father. He predicts His death, resurrection, and ascension and that their sorrow will be turned to joy, much as a woman rejoices when a child is born. **V 23–24: PRAYER** When He is ascended into heaven, they will be able to pray in His name and receive what they ask for, having their joy full. **V 25–30: PLAIN** In plain language Jesus tells them that the Father loves them because they love His Son and because they believe that Jesus came from the Father. Therefore He will grant their requests in His name and in accordance with His will. He confirms that He came from the Father and will return to Him. His disciples believe in Him. **V 31–33: PEACE** Despite all the troubles surging around, Jesus tells them that in Him they will have peace and that He has overcome the world.

CHAPTER SEVENTEEN

V 1–5: GLORIFY Jesus asks His Father to glorify Him as He will glorify His Father, recalling that the authority He exercises leads to the giving of eternal life. This is a particular prayer as the hour of His betrayal, trial, and crucifixion draws near. **V 6–19: GIVEN** Having prayed for Himself He then prays for His disciples. He has given them God's word. He sees them as gifts from the Father to Him! He prays that they will be kept, sanctified, and be sent into the world without conforming to it. That is still His desire for Christians today. **V 20–23: GAINED** He then prays for those who will come to know Him through His disciples and their witness. We are included in this prayer! He prays for them that they will be one in Him, with one another, and with those already being saved. They, too, are to be a testimony to Jesus and His love to a lost world. **V 24–26: GLORY** Specifically, Jesus looks forward to the lost souls given to Him by the Father, saved by His grace, to be with Him in glory. Meanwhile He wants us all to be filled with His love and presence while living for Him on earth.

CHAPTER EIGHTEEN

V 1–5: JESUS AND JUDAS Jesus crosses the brook Kidron with His disciples, and enters the Garden of Gethsemane. Judas arrives at the Garden with troops, officers and religious leaders to take Jesus. In answer to His question 'Whom are you seeking?' they state they are seeking Him. Jesus replies, 'I am He' to the arresting party which includes Judas. ('I AM' is an Old Testament name for God.) **V 6–9: DEITY AND DISCIPLES** At this, they all are compelled to move back and fall to the ground. Jesus asks them again whom they seek, and they tell Him again that they seek Him. He ensures that His disciples are free to leave before surrendering Himself, with dignity, grace and authority. **V 10–11: STRIKING AND SUBMISSION** Impetuous Peter uses a sword to strike the right ear of Malchus, the servant of the high priest. Jesus tells him to sheathe his sword, because this experience is the cup that He must drink. (We know from another account that Jesus also healed Malchus' ear.) **V 12–18: TRIAL AND TEMPTATION** He is led to influential Annas, the father-in-law of the current high priest, Caiaphas. Annas is also known by the title 'high priest', having held that office before Caiaphas. Peter fails his first temptation and denies Christ to a servant girl, while warming himself with the servants and officers. **V 19–24: UNFAIR AND UNCONSTITUTIONAL** Jesus is illegally hit on the face by a soldier for a factual answer to a question from Annas. The unconstitutional and unfair first trial has begun. Things will get worse. Annas sends Jesus bound to Caiaphas for His second Jewish trial. **V 25–27: DISCIPLESHIP AND DENIALS** Twice more Peter denies that he is a disciple of Jesus. As Jesus predicted, the rooster crows. **V 28–40: PASSOVER AND PILATE** The prejudice and the mockery of the legal process cause the Jews to lead Jesus from Caiaphas to the Praetorium, where He appears before Pilate. Pilate consults with the Jews and interrogates Jesus. The Lord tells him that He is a King, but not the sort of king for whom His followers will fight physically. Pilate knows full well that there is no fault in Him and that He has broken no aspect of the Roman law. Furthermore, he knows that the Jews have not got the power to sentence to death under Jewish law. So he suggests that the custom of releasing someone at Passover should be applied, to enable Jesus to go free. This solution would avoid both the illegal and judicial complications and also the risk of displeasing the Jews. But the opponents of Jesus are out for blood and they insist that Barabbas, a convicted criminal, should be released rather than Jesus, whom Pilate openly calls 'the King of the Jews'.

CHAPTER NINETEEN

V 1–3: FLOGGED Even though Pilate is convinced of the innocence of Jesus and knows that He has no valid jurisdiction in these circumstances, he has Jesus flogged and arrayed as King. Jesus is then mocked and abused by the soldiers. They crown Him with thorns, give Him a purple robe, and call Him 'King of the Jews'. **V 4–6: FAULTLESS** Twice Pilate declares Jesus to be without fault. Meanwhile, the chief priest and officers call for Him to be crucified, which is not available as a Jewish punishment, but only under Roman law for a breach of Roman law. **V 7–11: FEAR** Pilate is now frightened that Jesus will be crucified under him, and he is also frightened of the opposition of the Jews. Jesus tells him that he has no inherent power to crucify Him. Any power he has comes from above. **V 12–16: FEEBLE** Pilate, known to be a hard and cruel man, acts feebly under the threat that it will be reported to Rome that he is no friend of Caesar's. He sways to the pressure to have Jesus crucified under the chief priest's cynical cry 'We have no king but Caesar'. Jesus is led away to be slaughtered as God's Passover lamb. **V 17–22: FOCUS** The focus of this chapter, the New Testament, the Bible, and history, is on the cross of Christ. Here Jesus is nailed between two convicted criminals and proclaimed to be 'King of the Jews'. Pilate confirms that this is correct. The righteous King of kings is dying on the cross for the sins of rebellious people. **V 23–24: FULFILMENT** More prophecies of Scripture are fulfilled including the fact that His garments are divided, but that lots are cast for the tunic. **V 25–27: FAMILY** From the cross, Jesus asks John and His mother to regard and care for each other as mother and son. He shows loving concern for others even while He is dying in agony on the cross. **V 28–30: FINISHED** Knowing that He has fulfilled Scripture, Jesus proclaims, 'It is finished.' These words are the triumphant cry of a victorious gladiator in the arena. He then bows His head and gives up His spirit. His suffering on the cross, to take the punishment for our sins, is complete. **V 31–37: FAITHFUL** John testifies to faithful eye-witnessing of what happens. To hasten death by suffocation, caused by increased pressure on the lungs, the legs of the crucified thieves are broken. Jesus, however, is already dead, and a soldier's spear pierces His side, resulting in the outflow of blood and water. (This is held by some medical doctors to be a description of the separation of blood and serum through the piercing by the spear of the pericardial sack after acute heart failure.) The death of Jesus is well attested. The Bible is also faithfully fulfilled in that none of His bones are broken and those who pierced Him look on Him. **V 38–42: FRIENDS** The former secret disciple, Joseph of Arimathea, joins with Nicodemus, who first came to Jesus at night before putting his trust in Him. They ask for Christ's body from Pilate and lay it in the tomb. The body is bound tightly and one hundred pounds of spices are placed on it. Two intelligent men know that they are dealing with a body that really is dead. They put it in a safe tomb.

CHAPTER TWENTY

V 1–2: LORD'S DAY Here is the first Lord's day, the day of resurrection! Early in the morning, Mary Magdalene finds the tomb empty and runs to find Peter and John telling them that Jesus has been taken out of the tomb and she does not know where He is. **V 3–10: LOOKING DISCIPLES** John and Peter run to the tomb. Peter goes in and sees the grave clothes neatly folded. John confirms this. Not yet believing the resurrection, the mystified disciples go back home. **V 11–18: LOVING DIRECTNESS** Mary stays outside the tomb and sees two angels. She weeps because she does not know where Jesus is. Jesus appears, initially mistaken by Mary to be the gardener. When he lovingly directs His words to her using her name, 'Mary,' she recognises Him. Jesus, not yet ascended, prevents her from embracing Him. Her faith in Him must be a spiritual trust rather than a physical dependence. She goes to report these events to the disciples. **V 19–23: LIVING DEMONSTRATION** That Lord's day night, with doors shut, Jesus appears to His disciples and wishes them 'Peace'. He shows them His hands and side. He tells them to receive the Holy Spirit and to spread the message of forgiveness. Both of these requirements and promises will be fulfilled later. **V 24–29: LEADING DOUBTER** Thomas, absent at Jesus' first resurrection appearance, will not believe unless he has physical evidence. A day later, Jesus returns when Thomas is there. Thomas believes, declaring Jesus to be 'My Lord and my God!' Jesus tells him that those who believe without seeing are more blessed than those who believe because they have seen. That makes Christians today more blessed than Thomas! **V 30–31: LIFE DISPENSING** Many other unrecorded signs of Jesus are witnessed by His disciples. The recorded signs are to assist belief in Jesus as the Christ, the Son of God, and so lead to life in Him.

CHAPTER TWENTY-ONE

V 1–11: FRUITFUL FISHING Peter meets the other disciples in a fishing trip on Lake Tiberius. They catch nothing all night. Unrecognised, Jesus appears on the shore in the morning and tells them to cast their nets on the right side of the boat. When so many fish are caught that they cannot pull the net in, Peter recognises Jesus and plunges into the sea to meet Him. The rest drag the net ashore and see that Jesus is there, with fish cooked on a fire He has prepared, along with some bread. Peter then drags the 153 large fish to shore in the unbroken net. **V 12–14: BLESSED BREAKFAST** They accept Jesus' invitation to have breakfast with Him, knowing that the Man on the shore is their Lord Jesus Christ. This is the third time that Jesus appears to them since His resurrection. **V 15–17: LIMITLESS LOVE** Three times Jesus asks Peter if he loves Him. The Greek word used for 'love' indicates a love without limit. Three times Peter's reply implies that he only has a strong love for Jesus. This time Peter is careful to make no claim about the depth or fervour of his love, still being conscious of his earlier failure. Jesus tells Peter to shepherd and feed His sheep. For this he will need an unreserved love for the Shepherd. **V 8–19: DISCIPLE'S DEATH** He also indicates to Peter that one day he will die for his faith, but tells Peter, 'Follow Me.' **V 20–23: PETER'S PRIORITIES** Peter asks what will happen to John. Jesus tells him that that is no concern of his. If Jesus so chooses, He can arrange that John will never die. He does not say that that is what He has chosen. **V 24–25: TRUE TESTIMONY** John ends his Gospel by declaring again the truth of the testimony within it. He reminds us that all the libraries of the world cannot even contain the wonder of the works that the Lord Jesus Christ has done!

ACTS

OVERVIEW

PEOPLE AND PRELIMINARIES

The book of the Acts of the Apostles (twenty-eight chapters) bridges the gap between the four Gospels and the first of the letters teaching Christian doctrine, namely the book of Romans. Luke, a close associate and faithful supporter of Paul wrote it probably between AD60 and AD65. It was possibly written from Rome, along with Luke's Gospel, during the time of Paul's imprisonment. The period covered by the happenings in the book of Acts is estimated as thirty-two years.

PLAN AND PURPOSE

The Acts of the Apostles is the history book about the early church. It makes clear that Jesus' resurrection is well testified before His ascension into heaven, when His second coming is promised. Then it records the church's formation, through faithful and boldly sacrificial evangelism led and empowered by God's Holy Spirit, involving the preaching of the gospel of Christ crucified and risen again. Repentance from sin and personal faith in Christ is the apostles' message. This book reveals the growth, persecution and missionary efforts of the early church. It records the coming of the Holy Spirit to it in different regional areas as new ground is broken. The expansion of the gospel from Jerusalem, through Judea and

Samaria, into the worldwide mission field is catalogued excitingly. The three-point mission statement to witness to Christ in Jerusalem, in Judea and Samaria, and throughout the world provides a good framework for the book, which deals with the gospel's advance in those three sections. Paul's three missionary journeys are integral in this and are recorded. This book makes compulsive reading, as well as being divinely inspired history.

PROFILE AND PROGRESSION

The solid background for the book (1:1–7); the mission statement—go to Jerusalem, Judea and Samaria, and worldwide (1:8); Christ's ascension, waiting for the Holy Spirit to come, and replacing Judas with Matthias (1:9–26); witnessing in Jerusalem—including the foundation, growth, activities, persecution and martyrdom, and organisation of the church (2:1–8:3); witnessing in Judea and Samaria— including conversions following the preaching of the good news and further persecution (8:4—12:25); witnessing worldwide—including Paul's three missionary journeys and witness in Rome as follows: first mission to Cyprus and Asia Minor, second mission (following the council at Jerusalem) to Europe after revisiting Asia Minor, third mission to Asia Minor, Macedonia and Greece, and then his voyage to Rome as a prisoner and two-year ministry there after his earlier arrest and trials (13:1–28:31).

PRINCIPLES AND PARTICULARS

Holy boldness characterises the gospel witness of these New Testament Christians, despite persecution and martyrdom. The emphasis is on the church as a caring but outgoing family and body of believers, not as a construction of bricks and mortar or their equivalent. Foundational to the preaching of the gospel and the founding of the church are the Old Testament Scriptures and New Testament revelation of the Holy Spirit, blended together by the God of the Bible and of the Spirit. See how many sermons you can find. God validates the authority of His servants, the apostles and their immediate colleagues, by sign miracles from time to time. This is seen especially where previously uncharted territory opens up to the good news of Jesus. God gives conversions after the clear preaching of the gospel message of repentance from sins and trust in the risen Christ. Persecution is the usual environment in which the early Christians live, grow and witness.

ACTS

CHAPTER ONE

V 1–3: PROLOGUE Luke, the author both of Luke's Gospel and also of the book of Acts, directs his historical account to Theophilus. He stresses the reliability of the facts upon which the gospel message is based. Especially he underlines the well witnessed resurrection of the Lord Jesus Christ up to the time of His ascension. **V 4–8: POWER** Jesus promises that His praying and waiting disciples will receive power when the Holy Spirit comes upon them. They are to concentrate on Him, not in speculating on the details of the last days. The power of the Holy Spirit will enable them to be witnesses where they are, as well as further away from home, and even to the very ends of the earth. His power is available for us to witness for

Christ also. **V 9–11: PROMISE** Luke records the ascension of the risen Christ into heaven itself. With His ascension comes the promise of His coming again from heaven to the earth. The promise of Christ's second coming is a major factor in Christian living and doctrine. **V 12–14: PRAYER** The remaining eleven disciples, along with the women, Christ's mother Mary, and His physical brothers, return to Jerusalem to pray together. **V 15–22: PETER** Peter takes the initiative in encouraging his brothers in Christ to find a replacement for the traitor, Judas, who is dead. (The account in this chapter of Judas' death by his falling headlong and bursting open is fully consistent with the fact that he hanged himself. The branch on which he hanged himself could have broken, or the rope could have slipped or he could even have been cut down and allowed to fall. He could have been torn open on a branch or by the way in which he hit the ground.) Peter details the minimum qualifications for the replacement apostle. **V 23–26: PROPOSAL** Peter's exhortation is acted upon. Two viable candidates, Barsabas and Matthias, are proposed and prayed over and lots are cast. Matthias is selected. Careful selection and prayer precedes the casting of lots, and it seems the casting of lots is a good way to decide whom to appoint when there is nothing to choose between the candidates, as far as the disciples can tell.

CHAPTER TWO

V 1–4: SPIRIT The Day of Pentecost comes fifty days after the Sabbath in Passover week. When this historical Lord's day arrives, God sends His Holy Spirit in a remarkable way as the followers of Jesus are praying together. He appears as 'divided tongues, as a fire'. Each person is filled with the Holy Spirit and begins to speak with other tongues, as enabled by the Spirit. **V 5–13: STAGGERED** The multinational population of Jerusalem is staggered as they hear in their own language the wonderful message of God. The 'tongues' given to the disciples are many other discernible languages which the disciples did not normally speak and had not learned. Some ignorantly suggest that the disciples are drunk! **V 14–21: SCRIPTURE** Peter takes the opportunity to show that they are not drunk but that this amazing occurrence is a fulfilment of Old Testament Scripture. Any valid spiritual experience must be based upon God's Word. **V 22–36: SOVEREIGN** Peter goes on to show that the Christ whom they have rejected and crucified has been raised by God the Father and that He is the Sovereign Lord. The testimony and prophecy of David in the Psalms underlines this, and Peter concludes that the crucified Jesus has become 'both Lord and Christ'. **V 37: SMITTEN** The message of the Lord Jesus Christ cuts the hearers to the heart and they ask Peter and the apostles what they must do. **V 38–40: SALVATION** Peter urges them to be saved, to take advantage of God's promise, and to repent of their sins. This repentance and faith in Christ will be manifest in baptism in the name of Christ. This will underline the remission of sins, which is given to all who trust in Him. Those who are saved receive the gift of the Holy Spirit as their birthright. Peter earnestly urges his hearers to be saved. **V 41–45: STEADFASTNESS** Approximately three thousand people come to God and are baptised. The evidence of their conversion is a steadfast continuing in the apostles' doctrine, fellowship, breaking of bread, and prayers. God-honouring fear and open-hearted oneness in sharing demonstrate that God has changed their hearts in saving them through Christ. **V 46–47: SIMPLICITY** Their lifestyle includes daily fellowship and breaking of bread, and praising God. This manifests the simplicity of heart that has become theirs since coming to know Christ. At this stage, their wonderfully changed lives gain favour with the people. Each day God saves people and adds them to the church.

CHAPTER THREE

V 1–8: LAMENESS AND LEAPING A lame beggar at a gate of the temple is blessed through Peter and John using their apostolic authority, in the name of Christ, to heal him. From lameness, he leaps and praises God. **V 9–16: ONLOOKERS AND OPPORTUNITY** All the people see this and are amazed. They recognise the man who leaps as being the formerly lame beggar. Peter takes the opportunity to proclaim to them that it is God who has done this. This God is the Old Testament God of their forefathers who has glorified Jesus after He has been crucified through the sinfulness of men. Only faith in Christ has produced this miracle from the risen Lord. They take the opportunity to expose the guilt of the people and to proclaim Christ. We should do the same whenever possible! **V 17–21: REPENTANCE AND REFRESHING** Peter goes on to urge repentance from sin, and conversion to Christ. He proclaims that this leads to times of refreshing from God Himself. **V 22–26: BASIS AND BLESSING** The basis of this blessing is underlined as coming from the Scriptures. The essence of the blessing is through faith in Christ. God blesses us by turning every one of us from our iniquities. Separation from sin and trust in Christ is always a double blessing from God's own hand.

CHAPTER FOUR

V 1–4: ARREST Peter and John are arrested and placed in custody because the Sadducees, who do not believe in the resurrection, are grieved by their preaching the resurrection of the Lord Jesus Christ. God blesses their testimony and about 5,000 men come to believe. **V 5–12: ADDRESS** Taken the next day before the officials of the Sanhedrin, with Annas and Caiaphas among those who are present, Peter is filled with the Holy Spirit to preach God's word to them. He proclaims Christ crucified and risen again from the dead. He shows them that Jesus' resurrection was always foreseen as 'the stone which was rejected by you builders, which has become the chief cornerstone'. He underlines that salvation is only in Christ, the One who has been crucified and raised again on that first resurrection Lord's day. **V 13–18: ATTEMPT** The Sanhedrin is concerned about the boldness of Peter and John, and threatens them not to say anything else in case this should spread like wild fire. **V 19–22: ANSWER** The apostles answer that they have to do what pleases God. After further threatening they are released. No one can deny the miracle on the previously lame beggar of forty years of age. **V 23–31: ASSEMBLY** Peter and John immediately go to the assembled Christians and praise God with them wholeheartedly for His power in creation and in the person and work of the Lord Jesus Christ. They ask God to bless and use them in demonstration of the truth of their message to others through signs and wonders. Again the Holy Spirit shakes the place where they are and fills them. Their prayer is that they will 'speak God's word with boldness'. The blessings of the Holy Spirit in a believer's life should always lead to boldness to speak God's word.

V 32–36: ACCORD The outworking of God's salvation and filling of the believers with the Spirit is a manifestation of oneness in so many ways. Possessions are shared, powerful witness is given to the risen Jesus, needy people are looked after, 'great grace [is] upon them all' and sacrificial giving marks their love for the Lord. Barnabas is introduced as an encourager and as a generously kind sacrificial giver.

CHAPTER FIVE

V 1–2: DECEIT Ananias and Sapphira purport to give to the Lord all the proceeds from a property they sell. In fact, they keep some back. Their sin is best understood in the context of this passage and is not immediately evident without it. It is not that they fail to give all, but that they seek to deceive others about how much they are giving and pretend to give all. **V 3–4: DIRECTNESS** Peter plainly tells Ananias that Satan is behind their actions, and they have lied to the Holy Spirit. He points out that it was up to them how they dealt with the money but they should not have pretended to have given more than they really had. **V 5–10: DEATH** Ananias dies immediately. Three hours later, his wife also dies when she is confronted with their sin. The Bible does not say that they lost their salvation, only that they lost their lives. **V 11: DREAD** As the account of their deaths spread among the people, great fear seizes the church and all who hear. **V 12–16: DYNAMIC** God is working dynamically in this situation through His Holy Spirit and through the apostles. Many miraculous signs and wonders are done to authenticate their authority and to show the reality of God. Such is the different level of holiness experienced by the believers that only those who trust Christ will join with them. How different from the emphasis of many today that a church must appeal to people by being like them, in order to see them saved! Yet the Christians have a high reputation with the people. Many people are saved and God vindicates the authority of His apostles by miraculous signs done through them. **V 17–18: DANGER** But the high priest and the Sadducees, who reject the resurrection, are indignant. They have the apostles put in jail. They are in danger. How will they deal with it? **V 19–20: DELIVERANCE** God's angel delivers them from jail. He also delivers them from fear, because he tells them to go and witness in the temple courts about the gospel. **V 21–24: DAYBREAK** At daybreak, the apostles go into the temple and share God's word. Meanwhile their absence at the jail is detected and everyone is confused. The doors are locked but while the guards are still on duty, the prisoners have gone! The authorities remain confused! **V 25–32: DETERMINATION** The apostles are found preaching in the temple. This time, they are brought quietly to be questioned by the Council by the high priest. Peter tells him that they have to obey God in preaching the gospel, and that Christ's death, over which the high priest presided, was murder. Jesus has been raised from the dead! Repentance and forgiveness are available. The apostles and the Holy Spirit are witnesses to these things and the Holy Spirit is given to those who obey God. Peter's determination to present Christ does not end because he is before the authorities! **V 33–40: DIRECTION** As the threat of death looms, a teaching Pharisee, called Gamaliel, tells the oppressors that they need to be careful in case they find themselves fighting against God. (The Pharisees do believe in the resurrection and in angels.) He says that the apostles' message will come to nothing if it is not from God. His pragmatic speech persuades them. Nevertheless, the disciples are flogged and told to keep quiet. **V 41–42: DAILY** Rejoicing because their suffering has been for Christ, they leave the council and daily continue to teach and preach the gospel, based in the temple courts and in individual houses. Surely God the Holy Spirit is at work when His people trust Him and preach His word, even under threat.

CHAPTER SIX

V 1–6: SENSIBLE SEPARATION Inevitably, even in a spiritually-minded church, sin arises and cause disputes. Here it is concerning the care of widows. The apostles tell the church to seek out seven men with a good reputation who are full of the Holy Spirit and wisdom. These men will be over the business affairs of the church. They will be the first deacons. The apostles themselves will separate themselves to continual prayer, preaching, and teaching God's word. The Christians choose seven such people, notably Stephen who is 'full of faith and the Holy Spirit'. The apostles authenticate their choice by laying hands on them after they have considered the matter and prayed. **V 7: SPIRITUAL SUCCESS** After this, God's word spreads. Many disciples are multiplied in Jerusalem and even large numbers of priests are converted. **V 8–10: STEPHEN'S SPEECH** Stephen is a 'deacon', meaning 'servant', and not one of the apostles. God, nevertheless, uses him in a mighty way. Those opposed to him dispute with him but are unable to resist his wisdom, because the Holy Spirit enables him to speak the right things. **V 11–14: SECRET STIRRING** The opponents of Stephen secretly induce false witnesses to say that

he is guilty of blasphemy, and they stir up malicious opposition against him at every level. False witnesses are produced to say that he is against the Jewish faith. **V 15: STEADFAST SURVEILLANCE** All the council members look steadfastly at Stephen. His face is like that of an angel. God is with him.

CHAPTER SEVEN

V 1–50: HISTORICAL ACCOUNT When the high priest asks Stephen if it is true that he has blasphemed against Moses and God, he responds by giving a historical account of Israel and God's dealing with His people. He traces the forefathers of Israel's faith through Moses and Joshua to David. His account shows accurately God's faithfulness and His people's intermittent trust and obedience, underlying their rebellion and hard-heartedness. **V 51–53: HOLY ACCUSATION** With great boldness and truth, Stephen accuses the council of being stiff-necked and having uncircumcised hearts and ears. They resist the Holy Spirit just as their forefathers did. The prophets who foretold the coming of Jesus were also treated in the same way that he is now being treated. **V 54–58: HATEFUL ATTACK** His accusers are cut to the heart by his words. They respond not by repenting but by a frenzied attack upon him. Meanwhile God is enabling Stephen to see Jesus in heaven, as the Holy Spirit fills him. Preoccupied with his entry into heaven through the Saviour, he is taken by the mob out of the city and stoned, while Saul keeps the clothes of the murderers. **V 59–60: HEAVENLY ACCESS** With great grace and dignity Stephen kneels down among the stones that are thrown at him, and asks God not to charge his murderers with this sin. He then falls asleep on earth, and wakes up in the presence of His Saviour in heaven. The first Christian martyr has come home.

CHAPTER EIGHT

V 1–3: PERSECUTION The martyrdom of Stephen triggers the martyrdom of the church. Saul is in the forefront of the havoc wrought upon the people of God. Christians scatter widely, but the apostles remain in Jerusalem. **V 4–13: PHILIP** The scattering of the disciples is the seedbed of evangelism; as they scatter, they preach. Philip goes to Samaria to preach Christ. God attests to the authority of his work in this new area by signs and wonders. God's power is more striking than the perverted power of sorcery, and people turn from that to the gospel. One of the sorcerers, Simon, also believes and is baptised. But is his belief a saving belief or only a head belief? **V 14–17: PETER** Peter is sent with John from the apostles to Samaria to identify with the work that God is doing through Philip. As the apostles lay hands on those who have repented and been baptised, the Holy Spirit comes upon those people. This is God's way of validating the gospel that Philip has preached in the presence of those who are there. **V 18–24: POWER** The power of the Holy Spirit is evident, and Simon, the former sorcerer, asks if he can buy that power with his money. He is rebuked by Peter and urged to repent. Was his earlier confession genuine? **V 25: PREACHING** Then the apostles and Philip testify and preach about Jesus in the Samaritan villages. New territory is being opened for the gospel. **V 26–34: PREPARED** Philip is led by God's angel to the desert road between Jerusalem and Gaza. There he comes across an Ethiopian eunuch of high authority in the government. He is a prepared man,

actually reading the part of Isaiah talking about the death of Christ to come (Isaiah 53 in our Bible). The eunuch wants to know more and asks Philip to explain the passage to him. **V 35: PROCLAMATION** From the selfsame passage, Philip proclaims Jesus to him. **V 36–39: PROFESSION** Having put his trust in Jesus Christ the Son of God as his Saviour, the Ethiopian eunuch goes down into the water where Philip baptises him. Coming up from the water, God's Spirit takes Philip away and there is rejoicing over God's salvation for the eunuch. **V 40: PASSING** God places Philip at Azotus, twenty miles away. As he passes through the land, he preaches in all the cities till he comes to Caesarea.

CHAPTER NINE

V 1–2: CRUELLY COMMITTED Murderous Saul gets the consent of the high priest to carry on his cruel persecution of the Christians, whom he plans to take bound to Jerusalem. **V 3–9: SAUL STOPPED** On the Damascus Road, he is stopped by a bright light from heaven. Jesus reveals Himself to Saul and tells him to go into the city. He takes away his sight for three days. Saul, no doubt in shock as well as under conviction, neither eats nor drinks for three days. God has stopped the worst of the persecutors and spoken to his heart. **V 10–16: GUIDE GUIDED** The Lord prepares Ananias, despite his fearful reservations, to go and guide Saul into receiving his sight, spiritually as well as physically. He will begin a life for God that will bring him much suffering. **V 17–18: BLINDNESS BANISHED** When Ananias greets Saul, his sight is restored and he is filled with the Holy Spirit. He arises and is baptised. Clearly, Saul's early conviction has led to conversion and faith. **V 19: DAMASCUS DISCIPLES** Saul eats with and is cared for by the Damascus disciples. It is good to put a young convert in the family of Christ's disciples. **V 20–22: EVANGELSITIC ENDEAVOUR** He wastes no time in proclaiming Christ in the synagogues. People are amazed at seeing this recent persecutor sharing the good news of his Saviour with others. His deep theological foundation enables him to prove that Jesus is the Son of God and Christ, the Messiah. **V 23–25: PERNICIOUS PLOT** The Jews plan to kill Saul. He escapes by being let down in a basket through the wall by the disciples. **V 26–30: FAITHFUL FRIGHTENED** Saul arrives at Jerusalem, but the disciples are frightened and do not believe that he is a Christian. Barnabas reassures them by telling what has happened. In Jerusalem, he joins with them in faithful witness to Christ and he disputes with the Hellenists, who are Greek-speaking Jews who had earlier opposed Stephen. When another death threat occurs, the Christians bring him to Caesarea and send him to Tarsus. Their fear has been changed into fellowship. **V 31: MIGHTY MULTIPLICATION** A period of peace and building up spiritually follows for the churches in Judea and Samaria. They walk with the fear of God and are comforted by the Holy Spirit. God multiplies their numbers. **V 32–43: TELLING TESTIMONIES** Peter continues the work of evangelism himself. God heals a paralytic, Aeneas, and raises from the dead a faithful caring woman disciple, Tabitha (or 'Dorcas'), through Peter. God's vindication of this miraculous work through His apostles is such that many people believe in the Lord. Peter stays with Simon, a tanner.

CHAPTER TEN

V 1–2: CORNELIUS Cornelius is a Roman centurion. He is devout, fearing God, influencing his household towards God, generous in almsgiving, respected by the people, and he prays. **V 3–6: COMMUNICATION** God communicates with this Gentile by a vision in which He says that Cornelius' prayers have been heard, and He gives directions for Cornelius to send men to go to Joppa to fetch Simon Peter, the apostle. **V 7–8: COMMAND** Cornelius calls two household servants and a devout soldier to send them to Joppa to meet with Peter. **V 9–16: COMMON?** God gives Peter a vision three times of all kinds of unclean animals and birds in a sheet being let down from heaven. In the vision, Peter is told to kill and eat and he refuses because he says that they are common or unclean. God tells him not to call common the things which God has cleansed. Three times this happens, with each revelation of the sheet of animals. **V 17–20: CONFIRMATION** Peter wonders what this means when Cornelius' party arrives to meet him. God's timing is always right! God tells Peter to go with them. **V 21–27: CONTACT** Peter goes to meet the men who tell him about Cornelius and the next day he goes with them to meet Cornelius. Cornelius falls down before Peter, who lifts him up and corrects him, telling him that he is only a man. Many people are with Cornelius. **V 28–33a: CONTEXT** Peter explains that although it is unlawful for a Jew to meet with Gentiles, God has told him that he must meet with Cornelius. Cornelius tells him of the vision of an angel and that he has been commanded to send for Peter. He expects Peter to speak to them. **V 33b: CONGREGATION** Cornelius brings many people to hear what Peter has to say about God! This is a meeting prepared by God. **V 34–35: COMPREHENSION** Peter tells them that he now understands that God is impartial and willing to accept anybody anywhere who is willing to come to Him. **V 36–43: CHRIST** He then preaches Jesus as 'Lord of all', detailing His crucifixion, resurrection, and the fact that He will be Judge. He explains the prophets' witness to Jesus. He then tells them that anybody believing in Christ 'will receive remission of sins'. **V 44–48: CONVERSIONS** The Holy Spirit attends the preaching of the gospel by Peter. God again gives the miraculous sign of the apostles' authority and of these Gentiles' conversion, by enabling them to speak in tongues and magnify God. The believers are baptised in the name of Christ. Peter stays a few days.

CHAPTER ELEVEN

V 1–18: EXPLANATION The apostles and Christians in Judea wonder why Peter associates with uncircumcised Gentiles and dines with them. Peter explains the vision from God of the sheet of animals and its outworking, as detailed in Acts chapter 10. They are silenced by the argument, glorify God, and rejoice that the Gentiles are 'granted repentance to life'. **V 19–21: EVANGELISM** The scattering of the disciples, by persecution, leads to the spreading of the gospel through evangelism. This is widespread, God's hand is on them, and many believe and turn to the Lord. **V 22–24: ENCOURAGEMENT** Faithful and Spirit-filled Barnabas is sent from Jerusalem to observe what is happening. He encourages the new believers to continue with the Lord. Many others are added to Christ. **V 25–26: EDIFICATION** Barnabas brings Saul from Tarsus to Antioch, where for a whole year they meet with the church and teach people. The church is edified. The name 'Christians' is first applied here to the disciples. **V 27–30:**

EXERCISE Agabus exercises the New Testament prophetic gift of predicting a great famine. His prediction comes to pass. Relief is sent to Judean brethren through Barnabas and Saul.

CHAPTER TWELVE

V 1–3: PERSECUTION Herod Agrippa persecutes the church. James, John's brother, is killed by the sword and Peter is seized. **V 4–5: PRISON** Peter is securely guarded in prison after his arrest, with the intention to present him to the people at Passover. But while Peter is in prison, constant prayer to God is made by the church for him. **V 6–11: PETER** Peter is miraculously delivered from his chains, from his guards, and from prison by an angel, just before Herod intends to send for him. Peter is on the outside before he grasps what is happening, but then realises that God has delivered him. **V 12–17: PRAYER** He goes to the house of Mary, John Mark's mother, where the Christians are praying. He is kept waiting, knocking at the door. Rhoda, the servant girl, recognises him at the door and reports it to the people gathered there. She is not believed. Some say it is Peter's angel who has come! When he is finally let in, he tells them to go and tell James and the rest of the Christian brethren about his miraculous release. He goes elsewhere, having found it is harder to get into the prayer meeting than to get out of prison! **V 18–19: PERPLEXED** The soldiers are perplexed about the absence of Peter when day breaks. Herod has the guards examined and commands that they be put to death. Peter goes to Caesarea. **V 20–23: PRIDE** The people of Tyre and Sidon, who need to curry favour with Herod for his continued support, flatter him after he has given a speech. They say that he is a god. Herod is struck immediately by an angel of the Lord, because he does not give the glory to God. He dies. Pride against God is a very dangerous sin. **V 24: POWERFUL** The power of God's word on the other hand is manifest, as it grows and multiplies. **V 25: PARTNERS** Barnabas and Saul return from Jerusalem and take, as their junior partner, John Mark. No doubt the prayer meeting at his mother's house will be praying for him, too!

CHAPTER THIRTEEN

V 1–3: SPIRIT'S SEPARATION The Holy Spirit separates Barnabas and Saul from the team of teachers for special missionary work. The church fasts, prays, and lays hands on Barnabas and Saul as a means of identification with their work. **V 4–5: MISSIONARY MOBILITY** Barnabas and Saul, assisted by John Mark, journey to Cyprus, where they preach in the synagogues of the Jews. This is the start of Paul's first missionary journey. **V 6–12: APOSTOLIC AUTHORITY** Saul, who from this point on is called Paul, exercises his apostolic authority in resisting a sorcerer, Elymas, who stands against the gospel. True to Paul's prophecy, Elymas is struck blind. The proconsul, Sergius Paulus, is converted. **V 13–41: SCRIPTURAL SALVATION** Paul and Barnabas carry on to Perga in Pamphylia, but John Mark returns to Jerusalem. Paul and Barnabas go onto Antioch in Pisidia. There in the synagogue Paul spends the Sabbath teaching the facts about the Lord Jesus Christ from a background review of Jewish history. He emphasises that Jesus fulfils Old Testament prophecy as Son of God and Saviour. He has died on the cross and been raised. Only through Him is forgiveness available, and that comes by faith. He warns of the danger of not trusting Christ. **V 42–44: EARNEST ENQUIRERS** After the synagogue meeting,

the Gentiles beg Paul to preach to them on the next Sabbath. There are believers among the many Jews and Jewish proselytes. Paul and Barnabas urge them to continue in the grace of God. The earnestness of their enquiry spreads to the city. Nearly everyone comes to hear God's word on the next Sabbath. This, of course, means that many Gentiles are there as well as enquiring Jews. **V 45: OPEN OPPOSITION** Envious Jews contradict and blaspheme in opposing Paul. **V 46–49: GENTILES' GOSPEL** Paul and Barnabas boldly tell the Jews that, if they reject God's word, from now on they will concentrate on preaching to the Gentiles, in fulfilment of the Scripture. The Gentiles are glad and glorify God as a result. Many believe and God's word spreads through the region. God demonstrates that enquiring Jews and repentant Gentiles are all blessed through the same gospel. **V 50–51: PLANNED PERSECUTION** The leading men and women are stirred up by the Jews to persecute and expel Paul and Barnabas, who continue on their missionary journey to Iconium. **V 52: FILLED FULL!** The disciples of the Lord Jesus are filled with joy and with the Holy Spirit. Those dedicated to Christ and to His message will always know His joy, presence, and power.

CHAPTER FOURTEEN

V 1–7: SCATTERED SEED Paul and Barnabas witness in the Iconium synagogue. Both Jews and Gentiles are saved. Despite opposition, they continue to preach boldly. God attests their work though miraculous signs. The people of the city are divided and some seek to stone them. They flee to Lystra and Derbe where they carry on preaching the gospel. **V 8–18: AVERTING ADORATION** After

Paul is enabled to work a miracle on a lame man, the people there want to deify Paul and Barnabas. The two men insist that they are only men who are bringing God's good news. They stress that God is the Creator and provider. Even then, they only just manage to stop the crowd from making sacrifices to them. **V 19–20: MULTITUDE MANIPULATED** Human fickleness is seen as Jews from Antioch manipulate the crowd so that now Paul is stoned and dragged outside the city. He is left for dead. The disciples gather around him. (Is this a prayer meeting?) He rises up and goes back with them into the city and travels with Barnabas the next day to Derbe. **V 21–25: FIRM FOUNDATIONS** Returning to Lystra, Iconium and Antioch, they strengthen the disciples, urge them to carry on through hardships, and appoint elders. They pray and fast with them and commit them to God. They travel to Perga, preach the word there, and go on to Attalia. **V 26–28: GOD'S GRACE** Arriving back at Antioch from Attalia, they report back to the church on what God has done in opening up the word to the Gentiles. It is here that they were committed earlier to God's grace. It is fitting to report back now on how God has given His grace upon their efforts. They stay there a long time with the disciples.

CHAPTER FIFTEEN

V 1–5: CIRCUMCISION Christians are taught wrongly by some that circumcision is necessary for salvation. Paul and Barnabas dissent and dispute with the false teachers. They then go to Jerusalem to discuss this with the leaders and the elders. On the way there, through Phoenicia and Samaria, they relate the wonder of the conversion of the Gentiles, to the great joy of their Christian hearers. In Jerusalem they again encounter the erroneous teaching that circumcision is necessary for salvation, this time coming from believing Pharisees. **V 6–21: CONSIDERATION** The apostles and elders discuss the matter and consider the conversion of the Gentiles. After the participation of Peter, Barnabas and Paul, James confirms that only believing in Christ is necessary for salvation. Nevertheless, to avoid offending the Jews, the Gentiles are to abstain from certain idolatrous practices which also break the law of Moses. They will write to them to explain. **V 22–29: CONFIRMATION** The discussion is confirmed in a decree, from the apostles and elders and the whole church, to Gentiles in Anticoch, Syria and Cilicia. Judas and Silas, from Jerusalem, are to accompany Paul and Barnabas to make this agreed position known. **V 30–35: CHURCH** The church in Antioch rejoices in receiving the letter. Judas and Silas minister to the church and return. Paul and Barnabas remain there teaching and preaching, with many others. **V 36–41: CONTENTION** Later, after a sharp disagreement between Paul and Barnabas, as to whether John Mark should accompany them, Barnabas and Mark go to Cyprus while Paul and Silas go to Syria and Cilicia. All are still involved in the Lord's work.

CHAPTER SIXTEEN

V 1–5: DECREE DELIVERED Timothy joins Paul and Silas at Derbe and Lystra, having been commended by the Christians there. His father is Greek and his mother is Jewish. Paul has him circumcised to identify with the Jews because they know he has a Greek father. The apostles' decree is delivered and the churches are strengthened and increased numerically. **V 6–12: MACEDONIAN MISSION** God prevents the missionaries going to Asia or Bythinia and appears to Paul during the night in a vision of a man from Macedonia asking for help. This is taken as God's call to God's servants to preach the gospel to the Macedonians. They sail from Troas to Philippi, the main city and a colony. **V 13–15: SABBATH SERVICE** The Lord opens the heart of Lydia, a woman trader, who is at a women's riverside prayer meeting. The party stay with her after she and her household are baptised. **V 16–18: FORTUNETELLER FREE** A spirit-possessed slave girl is liberated in the name of Jesus Christ, after she trails Paul and his companions for many days, proclaiming them to be servants of 'the Most High God' who have come to 'proclaim to us the way of salvation'. **V 19–24: PERSECUTION, PRISON** Her masters drag Paul and Silas before the authorities in the market place, because they face financial loss through her liberty. They accuse Paul and Silas of stirring up trouble and cause the crowds to rise against them. Then the magistrates tear off their clothes and have them beaten with many stripes then thrown into prison. The jailer is charged to keep them secure and puts them in the inner prison in the stocks. **V 25–34: SONGS, SALVATION!** In an amazing sequence, Paul and Silas pray and sing hymns to God at midnight after which a great earthquake shakes the foundations of the prison, opening all the doors and loosening all the chains. The jailer is about to commit suicide when Paul and Silas intervene and preach the gospel to him. He and all his family believe and are baptised. They take care of Paul and Silas. No prisoners are lost physically, but he and his family are saved spiritually! **V 35–40: ROMANS RELEASED** After day

breaks, the magistrates command that Paul and Silas be set free. No doubt aware of the need to support the local Christians, Paul insists that they be given official clearance by the magistrates as Roman citizens, it being illegal to beat a Roman citizen without trial. They authorities come and plead with them to leave. Paul and Silas go to the house of Lydia again, see their fellow Christians and encourage them before departing.

CHAPTER SEVENTEEN

V 1–9: RESISTING REVELATION Passing through Amphipolis and Appollonia, Paul preaches Christ to the Jews in the synagogue at Thessalonica. Converts to the crucified and risen Christ include many devout Greeks and some leading women, who all join Paul and Silas. However, God's revelation is resisted by envious Jews who stir up a mob to attack the house of Jason, where Paul and Silas are thought to be staying. Paul and Silas are not found, and Jason is dragged before the city rulers where he has to give security. The rebel-rousers accuse the Christians of rivalling Caesar politically. Jason gives security and is freed. **V 10–12: SEARCHING SCRIPTURES** Paul and Silas are sent by night to Berea. There the Jews in the synagogue are fair-minded and search the Scriptures daily to check what they are taught. Consequently, many believe, as do a number of Greeks and prominent women. **V 13–15: PAUL PROTECTED** The Thessalonian Jews pursue Paul to stir up the mob. The brethren there send Paul away, and he goes to Athens, later to be joined by Silas and Timothy. God protects him from the Jews through this Christian intervention. **V 16–31: ATHENS AREOPAGUS** As Paul waits for his co-workers in Athens, he is provoked by idolatry to go and preach the gospel in the market place each day. This causes people to take him to the Areopagus, an Athenian public speaking area, where people share their thoughts and philosophies. Beginning with their own slogan, Paul develops his message by teaching that God is Creator and Judge, and by declaring the truth about Jesus Christ and His resurrection from the dead. **V 32–34: PRODUCTIVE PREACHING** The people listen to his message. On hearing about the resurrection, some mock, others determine to return to hear the gospel again, and some believers join him, including Dionysius and Damaris. Preaching that makes people listen, brings enquirers back, and produces new converts is truly from God!

CHAPTER EIGHTEEN

V 1–4: EVANGELISM Paul moves to Corinth and stays with Aquila and Priscilla, Christian tent-makers. From that base, he reasons every Sabbath in the synagogue and persuades both Jews and Greeks to turn to Christ. Evangelism is his lifestyle. **V 5–8: EMPHASIS** Up to now, Paul's first evangelistic emphasis has been his witness to the Jews. Now he declares a change in emphasis. He will concentrate on the Gentiles, after blaspheming Jews oppose him. Working from a house next to the synagogue, Paul sees Crispus, the synagogue ruler, and his entire household believe on Christ. Many Corinthians believe and are baptised. The effectiveness of the gospel is evident. Paul's new missionary strategy, concentrating on the Gentiles, in no way excludes the salvation of seeking Jews! **V 9–18a: EXTENSION** Despite aggressive opposition, in a dream God assures him of His protection and Paul extends his stay to over eighteen months, teaching the word of God and preaching. God's promise is fulfilled in

the way that Gallio, a senior official, protects him. Paul still remains 'a good while' testifying to Christ. **V 18b–23: ENTHUSIASTIC** Paul's enthusiasm for the gospel and for the Lord is seen in his travels for the gospel and his witness wherever he goes. It encompasses Cenchrea, Ephesus, Caesarea, and Antioch. Leaving Priscilla and Aquila at Ephesus, Paul witnesses there in the synagogue. He then journeys to Galatia and Phrygia, strengthening all the disciples. **V 24–26: EXPLANATION** An Alexandrian-born Jew, Apollos, who will become a mighty proponent of the gospel, has the gospel explained to him in Ephesus by Priscilla and Aquila. Up to now, he has only understood the baptism of John. The husband and wife team thus contribute much to his blessing and to the spread of the gospel. **V 27–28: ENCOURAGED** The Christians write to the Achaian believers, recommending Apollos as the one who encourages them there, vigorously refuting the Jews publicly, and demonstrating from the Scriptures that Jesus is the Christ.

CHAPTER NINETEEN

V 1–7: HOLY SPIRIT Paul builds on the teaching of John the Baptist when he is at Ephesus. The people there have only been baptised with John's baptism. Paul emphasises the need to believe on Jesus Christ and to be baptised. As they believe, the Holy Spirit comes on them and the twelve men speak in tongues and prophesy. God again vindicates his apostles' authority in a new arena. **V 8–10: HARDENED SINNERS** After preaching for three months in the synagogue, hardened Jewish sinners defame Christianity before the multitude. Paul moves to the school of Tyrannus for two years to continue teaching in Asia to both Jews and Greeks about the Lord Jesus Christ. **V 11–20: HISTORIC SIGNS** As a further authentication of Paul's authority as an apostle, God works unusual miracles through him. These historic signs cause Jewish exorcists to try to use the name of Jesus to overcome evil spirits. One such man is himself overcome by a man possessed by evil spirits, who say that although they recognise Jesus and Paul, they do not recognise him. The fear of God falls on many people as a result, and many who practise magic burn their books. God's word grows and prevails. **V 21–41: HOSTILE SUPERSTITION** Paul stays in Asia, while colleagues go to Macedonia, Achaia and finally Jerusalem. Many turn to Christ. The maker of the silver shrines of the goddess, Diana, is financially disadvantaged and stirs up opposition from the crowd against Paul. The opposition is in the name of 'Diana of the Ephesians'. Paul's travelling companions are seized. The Christians prevail upon Paul not to get involved with the volatile crowd, whose hostility has been aroused by the manipulation of their superstitious worship of Diana. The city clerk quietens the crowd by insisting that differences should be solved in the law courts and not in a riot. God even controls non-Christian men in authority to effect His purposes.

CHAPTER TWENTY

V 1–6: TRAVELS TO TROAS After going to Macedonia and Greece, where his travel plans are changed because of Jewish opposition, Paul and his party travel to Troas. They meet other Christians there who have gone ahead of them. **V 7–12: PREACHING TO PEOPLE** Paul speaks on the Lord's day, until midnight, to the people who are there. He has to depart early the next day. He restores to life a young man, Eutychus, who falls asleep during Paul's preaching and drops from the third storey to his death. After that, Paul continues preaching to the people until daybreak. His passion is preaching the word to people, notwithstanding personal tiredness and effort. **V 13–16: JOURNEYING TO JERUSALEM** Paul's extensive travel plans are based on his desire to be at Jerusalem for Pentecost. He meets up with the rest of his party who went ahead of him to Assos. **V 17–35: FAREWELL TO FAITHFUL** Paul exhorts the Ephesian elders who come to him at Miletus. He reminds them how his life has been completely focused on the need to testify to Jews and Greeks about repentance towards God and faith towards Christ. Everything has been put into that priority task. He knows that opposition awaits him, and he is willing to die for the gospel. They will see him no more. He has declared to them 'the whole counsel of God'. He warns them about error from outside and being drawn away by false disciples from within. He commends them to God's grace and reminds them that the important thing is to give to the Lord and to others, and not to seek personal gain. He shares the words of the Lord Jesus that 'It is more blessed to give than to receive'. **V 36–38: GRIEVED TO GO** They pray together, weep, and embrace Paul. They are grieving most of all because he will go and they will see him no more. They then go with him to the ship.

CHAPTER TWENTY-ONE

V 1–14: CONCERN Paul travels towards Jerusalem. The disciples at Tyre and a prophet named Agabus at Ptolemais, warn him about going to Jerusalem. Agabus tells him that he will be bound and delivered to the Gentiles. The concern of his fellow believers causes them to plead with Paul not to go, but Paul tells them that he is willing not only to go, but also to die for Christ. They then commit the whole matter to God's will. **V 15–25: COUNSEL** Paul meets with and debriefs James, the elders and the brethren at Jerusalem. Certain disciples go with him. He is counselled to go to the temple with devout Jews who have taken a vow. This is for Paul to identify with Judaism as a man with a Jewish heritage, in order to negate the accusation that he is against the law of Moses. The apostles' previous directions to the Gentiles, however, are confirmed. **V 26–29: CONTENTION** Paul acts on the counsel of James and the elders and goes with the men to the temple. However, Asian Jews stir up the crowd against him, falsely stating that he has brought an uncircumcised Greek into the temple. **V 30–36: CROWD** The crowd in the city run at Paul and drag him from the temple. He is rescued by Roman soldiers, who have to carry him away because of the mob. **V 37–40: COMPOSURE** Paul persuades the commander to let him talk to the crowd, by underlining that he is a Roman citizen. Paul then begins to address the crowd in Hebrew. This is God-given composure in a situation of great crisis and danger.

CHAPTER TWENTY-TWO

V 1–21: TESTIMONY Paul speaks to the Jews in Hebrew, underlining his Jewish background, and begins to relay his testimony to them. He describes how God met him, and how previously he was leading the persecution of the church. The crowd listens until he comes to the word 'Gentiles'. **V 22–23: TURNING** At the mention of 'Gentiles', the turning point comes and the crowd erupts and demands Paul's death. **V 24–30: TIED** The commander has Paul tied up in the barracks away from the crowd, as a preliminary to examining him by a scourging. Paul protests that he is a Roman citizen and uncondemned. It is against Roman law to bind and scourge a Roman citizen who has not had a trial. His examiners withdraw from him. The commander has Paul taken to the Jewish council the next day to find out for sure why Paul is accused.

CHAPTER TWENTY-THREE

V 1–5: STRUCK As Paul tells the council that he has lived in good conscience before God, he is struck by Ananias, the high priest. Paul calls him a 'whitewashed wall'. He is corrected by those around, and admits that he did not know that this man is God's high priest. Is this because of Paul's absence from Jerusalem, or because of his failing eyesight, or for some other reason? **V 6–9: SADDUCEES** Unlike the Pharisees, the Sadducees do not believe in the resurrection of the dead, angels or spirits. Paul sees that Sadducees are present in the council with Pharisees, and divides the council by proclaiming that this whole issue is a question of believing in the resurrection of the dead. **V 10: SOLDIERS** The dissention is so great that the commander feels that Paul will be physically harmed, and orders the soldiers to take him to safe custody in the barracks. **V 11: SUSTAINED** God personally sustains Paul, confirming to him that he will testify both at Jerusalem and at Rome. **V 12–22: SHAMEFUL** Over forty shamefully zealous Jews bind themselves to an oath to fast until they kill Paul. They collude with the chief priest and elders who are to ask for Paul to come back to them so they can make further enquiries, when their real intent is to ambush and kill him en route. However,

Paul's nephew, on hearing of the plot, tells the commander, who instructs him to say nothing to anyone else. **V 23–30: SAFEGUARDS** The commander sends for two centurions to take soldiers, horsemen and spearmen to ensure that Paul gets safely to Felix, the governor. He also relays the situation to Felix in a letter, which they take. **V 31–35: SECURE** The military party, Paul, and the letter arrive safely at Caesarea and Felix determines to hear the case later when Paul's accusers arrive.

CHAPTER TWENTY-FOUR

V 1–9: PROFESSIONAL LEGAL REPRESENTATION The Jews hire Tertullus, an orator, to represent their case before the governor, Felix. Ananias is present also. Tertullus repeats false accusations against Paul. **V 10–21: PAUL'S LOGICAL REPLY** Paul responds with great composure, politeness, procedural correctness, and logic. He indicates his background and his belief in the resurrection, factually states what happened, underlining that there is no evidence against him. His 'courtroom style' seems at least equal to that of Tertullus. Paul restates that he is being judged concerning the resurrection of the dead. **V 22–23: PARTIAL LIBERTY RESTORED** Felix adjourns the proceedings, stating that he will make his decision when Lysias, the commander, arrives. Paul has some degree of liberty restored to him and his friends are free to provide for and visit him. **V 24–26: PROUD LEADER RESISTING** Felix and his wife send for Paul. Paul reasons with them about righteousness, self-control and judgement. Felix is afraid and retreats 'until a convenient time'. He hopes he might get a bribe from Paul and speaks with him often. He is resisting God's

standards and message in his own life. **V 27: PRISONER LEFT RETAINED** Two years elapse and Festus succeeds Felix. Felix, currying favour with the Jews, leaves Paul bound.

CHAPTER TWENTY-FIVE

V 1–8: HEARING ARRANGED Festus insists that he will hear Paul's case at Caesarea and not at Jerusalem, as the Jews request. They hope to ambush and kill Paul as he travels to Jerusalem. Jews come down to Caesarea and spend at least ten days with Festus. Paul answers their complaints before Festus, saying that he has not offended Jewish law, temple law, or Caesar's authority. **V 9–12: HIGHER AUTHORITY** Festus then asks Paul if he will go to Jerusalem to stand trial before him there. Festus wants to please Paul's accusers. Paul appeals to Caesar, and Festus confirms that the appeal will be heard before Caesar, as is Paul's legal right. This also means that Paul will not go to Jerusalem and risk murder by the Jews. **V 13–22: HELP ASKED** King Agrippa (his full name is Herod Agrippa) and Bernice, his sister with whom he has an incestuous relationship, come to Caesarea to see Festus. Festus tells Agrippa of the background regarding Paul's arrest and detention. He confesses that no valid accusation has been brought and wonders what to say to Caesar. Agrippa, who is well-versed in Jewish law, says that he wants to hear Paul. Festus readily agrees that this will occur the next day. **V 23–27: HEROD AGRIPPA** The next day, Paul is brought before Agrippa and Bernice. Festus introduces the matter before Agrippa, again stating that Paul has done nothing that deserves the death penalty, but that he has appealed to Caesar. Not knowing what charges to specify against Paul, he looks to this unconstitutional hearing before Agrippa to help him to formulate the indictment!

CHAPTER TWENTY-SIX

V 1: PERMISSION Agrippa gives Paul permission to speak, and Paul begins his speech. **V 2–3: COMMUNICATION** Paul communicates on Agrippa's level, telling him that he knows that Agrippa is conversant with Jewish law and expert in its customs and questions. **V 4–8: RESURRECTION** Paul tells of his background, and of his certain hope in the resurrection of the Lord Jesus Christ. (Agrippa evidently would take the Sadducees' view on the resurrection, and so would find the resurrection incredible.) **V 9–18: CONVERSION** Paul relates how he persecuted the church, how he travelled to Damascus with authority to do so from the chief priest. He describes how Jesus appeared to him on that road through a light brighter than the sun and through God's speaking to him personally in Hebrew. He relates Christ's promise to make him a witness and to deliver him so that he can proclaim forgiveness and an inheritance to those who have faith in Him. **V 19–23: PROCLAMATION** Paul goes on to say that he obeyed this vision, and proclaimed the gospel to Jews and then to Gentiles, telling them to repent and turn to God. In facing persecution, he affirms his trust in Christ crucified and risen from the dead, and that this message must be proclaimed both to Jews and Gentiles. **V 24: REACTION** At this stage, Festus reacts and tells Paul that he has been made mad by too much learning. **V 25–29: APPLICATION** Paul proclaims that he is not mad, nor is he unreasonable or untruthful. He states to Herod Agrippa that the resurrection has happened and that 'this thing was not done in a corner'. He tells Agrippa that he knows he believes the prophets. He then applies the message to Herod Agrippa. In answer to Agrippa's comment that Paul is almost persuading him to become a Christian, he volunteers that he wants King Agrippa and each person who hears him to become a Christian, as he now is. Presentation of truth always requires application of truth. **V 30–32: CONCLUSION** Agrippa, Bernice and Festus are all of the opinion that Paul has done nothing wrong. Agrippa concludes that Paul might be free if he had not appealed to Caesar.

CHAPTER TWENTY-SEVEN

V 1–8: SAILING SLOWLY With fellow prisoners and soldiers under the control of Julius, a Roman centurion, Paul sets off to sail in stages to Italy. They make a slow start because of the sailing conditions. **V 9–12: SUGGESTION SIDELINED** Paul expresses his opinion that there will be danger and disaster for the ship, the cargo, and the lives of the travellers. But the centurion takes the advice of the navigator and the ship owner, supported by majority opinion, and carries on regardless. **V 13–20: SAVAGE STORM** After a gentle start, a savage storm arises which drives the ship a long way for a long time in perilous conditions. All hope of survival is lost. **V 21–26: SERVANT'S SERENITY** Paul tells the men that they should have listened to him. But he encourages them and declares that he serves God. An angel has told him that he will arrive at Rome where he has to stand trial. They will all be saved with him but they must run aground on an island. God's man is the man for the crisis and should be serene when others around are panicking. **V 27–32: SHIPMATES SAVED** After the fourteenth night had come, the sailors know they are getting close to land and make an attempt to commandeer the skiff, which is, in effect, their lifeboat. Paul draws this to the centurion's attention and the lifeboat is cut off and released. This action will ultimately lead to all Paul's shipmates being saved. **V 33–38: SENSIBLE SPIRITUALITY** Not having eaten for fourteen days, Paul encourages the people on board to eat, and then he gives thanks to God for the food. The 276 people eat and then throw away the surplus grain to lighten the ship. Paul's mix of spiritual faith and commonsense is an example to all. **V 39–41: SHIPWRECK SUFFERED** Inevitably the ship runs aground, is stuck fast, and broken up by violent waves. **V 42–44: SECURELY SAFE** Despite the soldiers' plan to kill the prisoners, to avoid allowing them to escape, the centurion wants to save Paul and lets swimmers swim ashore and everybody else holds on to boards or parts of the broken ship that will take them aboard in the surf. They all land secure and safe.

CHAPTER TWENTY-EIGHT

V 1–10: FRIENDLY The island on which the ship is wrecked is Malta. The kind and friendly inhabitants welcome the shipwrecked party, then think that Paul is an escaped murderer because a viper attaches itself to his hand. When he does not die, they then think he is a god. Then Paul is used to heal from dysentery the father of Publius, the leading citizen. Others come and are healed through Paul. The inhabitants honour Paul in many ways with warm hospitality and provision

of necessities. **V 11–15: FELLOWSHIP** During the travels on the way to Rome, Paul enjoys fellowship with some Christian brothers at Puteoli. The seven-day stay with them is an encouragement and blessing to Paul. **V 16: FREEDOM** Arriving at Rome, Paul and the other prisoners are delivered to the captain of the guard. Paul is allowed to dwell on his own, with a guarding soldier. This degree of freedom will be used for the gospel! **V 17–22: FOCUSED** Paul draws the Jews together and explains the situation and the charges against him. They have not heard of anything evil about him but have heard about the 'sect' of Christianity, which is spoken about everywhere. They want to hear Paul. His policy is to begin by witnessing to the Jews, despite his new concentration on reaching the Gentiles. **V 23: FERVENT** They come back to his lodgings and he spends all day persuading them about Jesus from the Old Testament. **V 24: FRUITFUL** Although some disbelieve, others are persuaded. Paul's gospel is fruitful! **V 25–29: FEARLESS** To those who do not believe, Paul tells them that they are hardened in their sin as Isaiah prophesied. He will pursue his policy of concentrating on taking the gospel to the Gentiles. The departing Jews dispute much between themselves. **V 30–31: FAITHFUL** For two whole years, Paul lives in his own rented house and receives all comers, preaching God's kingdom and teaching everything about the Lord Jesus Christ. He does this with confidence and freedom from restrictions.

ROMANS

OVERVIEW

PEOPLE AND PRELIMINARIES

✳There are twenty-one New Testament letters, of which the first nine presented in the Bible are all to churches. Paul wrote all the church letters and certainly four of the others. Some think he also wrote the letter to the Hebrews. These letters were written from different places at various times, with four of them (Galatians, Ephesians, Philippians, Colossians and Philemon) written during Paul's first imprisonment in Rome and 2 Timothy during his second imprisonment there. Romans (sixteen chapters), dated probably between AD55 and AD60 and possibly written from Corinth, was not the first letter he wrote but it comes first in the New Testament, immediately after Acts.

PLAN AND PURPOSE

ⓘThe theme of this book is the gospel itself, as applying not only to Jews but to lost sinners everywhere. Romans is basically about justification by faith based on the righteousness of God in Christ and on the promises of God. It has been called 'the gospel of Paul' but is entirely consistent with the unified teaching of the whole of the Bible on salvation. It shows how all people are sinners under God's righteous condemnation and how the answer is in Christ whose righteousness is credited to the repentant sinner trusting Him, just as that sinner's sin is debited to Jesus' substitutionary death on the cross. This produces a practical application and outworking of God's righteousness in the sanctification of the believer through God's Spirit. Christian conduct will always flow from the correct application of biblical doctrine. Romans is generally considered to provide both the foundation and the seedbed of New Testament theology.

PROFILE AND PROGRESSION

Introduction and theme—God's righteousness is by faith for Jews and Gentiles (1:1–17); guilt and condemnation of Gentiles, Jews and all humanity (1:18–3:20); acceptance and acquittal only through God's righteousness, as described, appropriated and imputed through the gospel (3:21–5:21); sanctification following and showing salvation and underlining Christian liberty, assurance and the Spirit's work (6:1–8:39); Israel is not forgotten by God because the Gentiles are included in God's plan of salvation (9:1–11:36); Christian life and service reflecting salvation, sanctification and separation (12:1–15:13); Paul's plans and hopes (15:14–33); greetings, warning, and closing prayer (16:1–27).

PRINCIPLES AND PARTICULARS

☞The use of the words 'righteous,' 'righteousness' and concepts or words meaning the same are significant. There is a balance between the convicting of God's Spirit through the insistence of God's law having been broken, and the liberation of His Spirit in the life of the believer. The book is liberally seasoned with Old Testament examples to illustrate evergreen principles of God's working. The proclamation of God's changeless moral law is essential if the gospel is to be applied to sinners, who need first to be convicted of breaking it.

Only then can liberty in Christ be obtained through repentance and faith. The three Persons of the Trinity are interchangeably depicted in the life of the believer, in chapter eight, thereby demonstrating that God is one in three and three in one. The same chapter also provides a classical statement of God's sovereignty and work in salvation.

ROMANS

CHAPTER ONE

V 1–7: CREDENTIALS Paul describes himself as 'bond servant [a slave] of Christ' who is 'separated to the gospel'. He extols the Holy Scriptures and proclaims Jesus Christ as the Son of God. He says that it is through God's grace that he has become an apostle, with the aim of bringing obedient faith to all the nations. He brings his greetings, as an apostle, to the Christians in Rome. **V 8–15: COMING** Paul wants to come to be a spiritual blessing to them. He has tried before but has been hindered. His concern is to discharge his debt in the gospel to those who are not Jews, including those in Rome. He is thankful and encouraged because the faith of the church in Rome is spoken of 'throughout the whole world'. He is already praying ceaselessly for them. **V 16–17: CONVICTION** Paul's bedrock and springboard conviction is that the gospel is the 'power of God to salvation' to everyone who believes. This is true for Jews and Greeks (standing for Gentiles). The gospel is to do with Christ's righteousness and faith in Him that enables a Christian to live spiritually and eternally. **V 18–20: CONDEMNATION** Sinful man is under God's condemnation and God has revealed that He is wrathful

towards this. Man everywhere is without excuse, because even without knowledge of the gospel, God is discernible in the wonderful things He has made in nature. No one can say from a sincere heart that there is no God. **V 21–32: CORRUPTION** Man has rejected the God he knows to be there and to be good, and this has led to perverted worship and an increasing moral slide into corruption. This manifests itself in sexual immorality, idolatry, and the worship of corruptible created things instead of the incorruptible Creator. In turn, the sinfulness of man's heart has led him further astray into homosexuality, debased minds, and a whole catalogue of evil doings that reads like an index to a criminal law textbook, or to a chapter in a sociology textbook about today's social decay. When man rejects God, his worsening sinfulness becomes increasingly apparent as time goes on. When a person is determined to rebel against God and His righteous standards, God gives him up to his sins and gives him over to a debased mind.

CHAPTER TWO

V 1–4: INEXCUSABLE Because one man judges another, and finds him to be culpable, he shows that he is inexcusable himself. He acknowledges that there is a standard, and the truth is that he has fallen from the standard of God, who is the Judge. He cannot escape the judgement of God. How stupid to despise God's goodness, gracious forbearance and longsuffering which are intended to lead sinful man to repentance from sin and to forgiveness through faith in Christ. **V 5–12: INEVITABLE** There is an inevitable and eternal consequence of our response to God. God is equal-handed in applying a simple but vital test. Those whose lives manifest their faith in Christ, by patient continuance in doing good and seeking God's glory and honour, will for ever know His eternal life. Those who, with hard and impenitent hearts, continue in their self-seeking and sinfulness as they disobey God's truth, must expect God's wrath as a result of His righteous judgement. God impartially looks in judgement at both Jews, who have received His law externally, and at Gentiles, who have not. **V 13–16: INBRED** The truth is that there is a natural law written in the hearts of men which includes some knowledge of right and wrong instinctively, even though that is not as finely tuned or as well detailed as God's written law. Thus Jews, with the law, or Gentiles, only having the law which is written in the hearts of all men, are equally to be judged by God who knows their secrets. Jesus Christ will, one day, judge those secrets in the case of those who have not taken Him as their Saviour. **V 17–24: INSINCERITY** The sad thing is that the Jews think that because they have God's law, they are accepted by Him. The truth is that because of their sinful insincerity, in both knowing and teaching God's law while breaking it with blatant disregard, they will be judged. The Gentiles blaspheme God because of the insincerity and poor witness of the unbelieving and rebellious Jews, who, paradoxically, boast that they have God's law. **V 25–29: INWARDLY** A true Jew is one 'who is one inwardly'. Those who rely on outward circumcision, yet still live sinful lives of unbelief and rebellion, are not really Jews at all! The inward circumcision that counts is not like the putting away of the flesh outwardly, but is the cutting of sin from the human heart by God's Spirit in the new birth produced by the gospel. It is spiritual and can be known by Jew or Gentile who trusts in Christ.

CHAPTER THREE

V 1–8: ADVANTAGED? This chapter asks a lot of questions. First, if acceptance with God is a circumcision of the heart, and not an outward circumcision, what advantage does a Jew have in being a member of the circumcision? Paul confirms the great privileges of being a physical Jew. Of course, he knows this as a Jew himself. They have the Scriptures as the 'oracles of God'. The sinful unbelief of some of the Jews does not negate God's faithfulness in giving them these privileges. The very sinfulness of the Jews demonstrates the wonder of those Scriptures and the righteous and holy standards of God by which they are judged. That is not to say that Jews must sin more to make God's standards of holiness appear greater. God loves holiness and will judge the world for being unholy. **V 9–20: BETTER?** Paul asks if Jews are better than Gentiles, and concludes, 'Not at all.' Everyone is unrighteous, self-seeking not God-seeking, practising evil in word and deed, and living without the conscious fear of God. As the whole world is guilty, then there is no one in the world who can be justified by anything he or she does. **V 21–26: CHRIST** Only Jesus Christ can justify a sinner, be he Gentile or Jew. Given that 'all have sinned and fall short of the glory of God', it is the righteousness of God, put to our account when we put our faith in Christ, that is seen by God as ours and justifies us because we have no righteousness of our own. Not only that, but Christ shed His blood as a 'propitiation'. That means that, when Christ died on the cross for our sins, our wicked rebellion that offended our holy God was punished by His wrath falling on Christ in our place. Thus cleansed by His precious blood and with

His righteousness put to our account, we find that, as we put our faith in Him, we are justified by Him who is both just and the Justifier. **V 27–31: DIFFERENCE?** The five questions put in this short section basically ask a more fundamental question: what difference does this make? It excludes boasting because we are justified by faith, not by our own deeds. He is the God of the Gentiles as well as of the Jews because all can come to Him by faith. God's law is not annulled by faith in Christ, but rather it is fulfilled, because His just sacrifice fulfils the law for us. We have a desire to walk in that law through Christ, not in order to be justified, but to obey Him.

CHAPTER FOUR

V 1–8: RIGHTEOUSNESS COUNTED Neither Abraham, who Jews and Christians can rightly claim is 'our father' in the faith, not David, from whose line Jesus came, were justified by works. Their faith was counted to them as righteousness, and their sins were therefore not imputed to them. **V 9–15: REGARDING CIRCUMCISION** Paul then deals with circumcision in the light of being justified by faith alone. He points out that Abraham was justified before he was circumcised and thus circumcision cannot save anyone. For Abraham, circumcision was only 'a seal of the righteousness of the faith which he had while still uncircumcised, that he might be the father of all those who believe'. They can either be uncircumcised (Gentiles) or circumcised (Jews) but neither will be justified without personal faith from the heart in Christ. The promise of God would be meaningless if one could only be saved if circumcised. The law brings about wrath, but faith brings about justification in Christ. **V 16–25:**

RESURRECTED CHRIST Thus the promise is to all who exercise the same faith in God's word and promise that Abraham did which made him the 'father of many nations'. In his case it meant that, as a man of about a hundred years of age with a wife whose womb was 'dead', he did not waver at the promise of God but believed Him. This was counted to him as righteousness. Paul teaches that this Old Testament lesson was also written for those of us in the New Testament era as a type of shadow of the resurrection of the Lord Jesus Christ. We believe in the God of the greater miracle of raising up Christ from the dead for our justification after He had been delivered to the cross for our sins. Our faith is not simply in a crucified Saviour who bore our sin, but in a living Saviour whose resurrection was God the Father's seal on the sufficiency of His Son's sacrifice for us.

CHAPTER FIVE

V 1–5: RESULTS The immediate results of being justified by faith are peace with God through Christ, access by faith into His grace, and rejoicing in the hope of God's glory. But even tribulations bring their character-shaping blessings for those who are justified. This is especially so because of God's pouring His love into our hearts through the Holy Spirit. **V 6–8: REMARKABLE!** The demonstration of God's own love for us, in dying for us 'while we were still sinners', is remarkable. Very occasionally someone will give his life for a good man, but Christ gave His life for us while we were hopeless and weak rebel sinners. **V 9–11: RECONCILED** There is a double reconciliation to God. Because of our justification through His blood we shall be saved from wrath through Him: His death has reconciled us. But now, having been justified through that blood, we find that we are reconciled through His saving life in that, each day, we seek to live reconciled lives through His strength, presence and power. This causes us to rejoice because we have received this reconciliation. **V 12–17: REIGN** Death reigned over humanity since man's fall in sin. But now the gift of righteousness reigns through God's abundance of grace to those who are justified through Christ and freed from the condemnation deserved. Thus the sin that spread and led to death need no longer reign in the life of those who are justified and who have received His righteousness. **V 18–21: RIGHTEOUSNESS** The law shows sin abounding, but God's grace has abounded much more producing eternal life through Christ our Lord. Through one man, Adam, sin and judgement came upon all. Through another Man, Jesus Christ, and His righteous act in dying on the cross for us, many are 'made righteous', which is what justification means.

CHAPTER SIX

V 1–4: CONTINUE SINNING? Paul picks on the objections of some by asking if we are already justified, shall we sin more to show how great that justification is? He exclaims dogmatically, 'Certainly not!' Spiritually we were buried into Christ in His death. His resurrection life has become ours. If we are truly born again, we will want to walk in newness of life. Baptism echoes that meaning. **V 5–7: CRUCIFIED SELF** Just as we share in Christ's resurrection, we share in His crucifixion. Our position, as those risen with Christ, is therefore that our 'old man' (our unsaved self) is crucified with Christ. I cannot claim the one without the other. **V 8–14: CALCULATED SEQUENCE**

We are to reckon ourselves to be 'dead indeed to sin, but alive to God in Christ Jesus our Lord'. That reckoning is based upon the knowledge that we are both crucified with Christ and also risen with Him in our status before God. God never asks us to make false calculations! This reckoning results in the sequence of logic and holiness that if we are dead to sin and alive to Christ we must not let sin reign in our bodies, but we must present our bodies as alive from the dead for instruments of righteousness to God. We are no longer under the dominion of sin and death caused by the law, but we are under God's grace. **V 15–19: CONSECRATED SLAVES** We are not now the slaves of the broken law, fearing judgement and death, but we present ourselves as slaves of 'righteousness for holiness' having been set free from one tyrannical master, and become the willing slaves of another Master who is gracious. **V 20–23: CHRIST'S SALVATION** Previously, we faced death and produced fruit of which we were ashamed. Now we have God's gift of 'eternal life in Christ Jesus our Lord' and, as joyfully consecrated slaves, seek to produce holy fruit for our loving Master who has saved us.

CHAPTER SEVEN

V 1–6: FREEDOM FROM THE LAW Just as a woman is no longer bound to a dead husband, so we are no longer bound to the law, in the sense of being punished for breaking it. We have a new 'husband', Christ. We share in His risen life 'in the newness of the Spirit', being already recipients of eternal life. **V 7–12: FORCE OF THE LAW** The law is neither evil nor sinful. It simply is powerless to save a sinner who is condemned under it. The force of the law is to show me my sin, my guilt, and the judgement I merit. It is 'holy and just and good' because it points out to me my need of salvation, which it cannot provide. **V 13–24: FAILURE UNDER THE LAW** Paul develops the preceding principle and applies it to himself. He says that the law shows him that he is doing wrong, that he cannot do good. Even when he wants to do good, he cannot do it. He feels wretched because of his inability to conquer indwelling sin, and asks who can deliver him from this 'body of death' which he cannot control as he would like. **V 25: FAITH IN THE LORD** He answers the question of who can deliver him, thanking God that it is 'through Jesus Christ our Lord'. Even with this knowledge of Christ's deliverance through faith, eternally and daily, he is still aware of the twofold contrary pull in his life: God's law pulls him towards righteousness, and the law of the flesh towards sin.

CHAPTER EIGHT

V 1–7: CONDEMNATION Although every sinner deserves condemnation for his sin, there is 'therefore now no condemnation for those who are in Christ Jesus'. The evidence of being in Christ is a new walk according to the Spirit, which also produces liberty and freedom from the law. This means that spiritual-mindedness replaces a carnal following of 'the things of the flesh'. Such a carnal mindset reveals enmity with God, whereas a spiritually renewed mind shows reconciliation with and justification by God. Without this mindset we cannot please God. **V 9–11: CHRIST** Because Christ lives within the believer, he is possessed by Christ and possesses the 'Spirit of Christ', also identified as the 'Spirit of God'. No person can rightly claim to belong to Christ unless He has

the Spirit of Christ. The benefits springing from this relationship are spiritual righteousness through Christ, and sharing His resurrection life. The wonderful and indivisible union in the Trinity is seen here as the Holy Spirit is interchangeably described as the 'Spirit of God', the 'Spirit of Christ', the 'Spirit of Him who raised Jesus from the dead', and 'His Spirit who dwells in you'. **V 12–17: CO-HEIRS** Because of this new relationship, liberty, and indwelling Spirit, we are the Spirit-led children of God and therefore His heirs, and co-heirs with Christ. If we suffer with Him here below, we need to remember that we will be glorified with Him one day! **V 18–25: CREATED** Until that final state of affairs in glory, we are not the only ones who groan because of our sufferings, which are light in comparison with the glory to come. The whole creation groans to be delivered from the 'bondage of corruption'. One day there will be a new heaven and a new earth, as well as completely renewed believers to enjoy them, in worshipping and having fellowship with their justifying God. Believers eagerly and patiently wait for that. **V 26–27: COMFORT** In our groanings and problems within, we have the help of God's Spirit in our weakness, who intercedes for us 'according to the will of God'. **V 28–30: CALLED** Those whom God has called can be absolutely certain that, in God's sovereign purpose, everything will work together for their good. Their salvation is not an accident. God planned it in eternity, performed it in time, works it out in time, and will eventually perfect it in eternity. Our standing in Christ is absolutely watertight because of who He is and because He has chosen us and planned our way. **V 31–39: CONQUERORS** A whole range of problems, trials, disappointments, and suffering will come against the child of God. In all this he is to remember that God 'did not spare His own Son' but freely gave Him for us, and freely gives us all other things that we need. With God on our side as our Justifier, our Intercessor, our Lover, and our Keeper, we are more than conquerors 'through Him who loved us'. Once saved by Christ, nothing at all in the past, present or future, and nothing on this earth or anywhere else is able to 'separate us from the love of God which is in Christ Jesus our Lord'. We conquer because we have the Conqueror living within and working for us.

CHAPTER NINE

V 1–5: SORROW Paul explains his great sorrow for the lostness of his fellow Israelites. They have had all the privileges of God, and His revelation, including the promise of Christ's coming in the flesh as the 'eternally blessed God'. Such is Paul's sorrow and grief that he could wish himself accursed if they could be saved. **V 6–9: SCRIPTURE** But God's Word, His holy Scripture, is thereby fulfilled. Israel is not simply a physical nation of those descended biologically from Jacob. The promise was not only to the seed of Abraham but to the seed of Isaac, Jacob's father. Those who are their children are children of the promise. Today, those who come to faith in God through Christ are the spiritual children of the promise. **V 10–21: SOVEREIGNTY** God is sovereign in all matters, including salvation. In God's sovereignty, it is His mercy and compassion that saves. He is in control. He is the potter fashioning the clay; the clay does not have the right to protest about the vessel which the potter makes from it. **V 22–29: SUPPOSE** Paul then enters a hypothetical argument which underlines that, if God wanted to make

vessels for destruction, it would be His right so to do. This supposition is not put forward as a fact, but to demonstrate that God's sovereign right negates the questioning objection of anyone who wishes to argue with what God does or plans. His sovereignty, in fact, causes Him to call non-generic Israelites to be His people—those who are not Israelites after the flesh—who nevertheless shall be called 'sons of the living God'. His sovereignty also decrees that though Israel as a nation rejects Him, a remnant will be saved. Otherwise they would all have been destroyed like Sodom and Gomorrah. The basic supposition is that God can do what He chooses, though in practice He will respond in compassion and mercy to those who, by His grace, call upon Him for that mercy. **V 30–33: STUMBLED** Paul's conclusion is that the ignorant Gentiles, with no knowledge of God, have now come to that knowledge through the 'righteousness of faith', which is the righteousness that God imparts to those who put their faith in Him and His promise. Israel, however, in seeking righteousness by doing the law, has stumbled over Christ, the stone and rock, because salvation is not by works of the law but by believing on Him. They neglect or refuse to come to Him by faith.

CHAPTER TEN

V 1–4: CONCERN Paul's 'heart's desire and prayer to God for Israel is that they may be saved'. Their zeal in trying to establish their own righteousness, which they can never do, shows their ignorance of God's righteousness. That can only be found in the Lord Jesus Christ, who is 'the end of the law to righteousness to everyone who believes'. In other words they must come to faith in Christ to be saved. **V 5–13: CONFESSION** Paul shows from the

Scriptures the principles of salvation which now apply to faith alone in the Lord Jesus Christ alone. That principle is that when one's faith in the living Christ is personal and real, that believer will confess this openly and by mouth to others. This will form part of a changed lifestyle. The challenge is whether one's faith is real enough to produce the willingness to stand out and confess personal faith in Christ. The encouragement given is that anyone trusting in Him, whether Jew or Gentile, will never be put to shame, but will be saved. God's richness of mercy more than compensates for the poverty caused by our sin. **V 14–16: CALL** Given that whoever calls on Him will know His salvation, the logical question is asked as to how unbelievers are going to hear of Christ in order to call upon Him. The answer is that preachers of the gospel must be sent to tell them, always bearing in mind that even then there will be many who do not obey the gospel and turn to Christ, though the offer is open to them. **V 17: CONCLUSION** The simple conclusion is that saving faith is produced by hearing God's Word. **V 18–21: COMPARISON** Using the Old Testament Scriptures, the comparison is made between Gentiles, who have believed and come to know God's blessing, and the Israelites, who are thus provoked to jealousy by seeing outsiders come to know the God who longs that they should turn to Him. Although God will judge sin, He confirms to Israel that 'All day long I have stretched out my hands to a disobedient and contrary people'. God is always willing to welcome returning sinners, be they Jews or Gentiles.

CHAPTER ELEVEN

V 1–2a: REJECTION? Paul asks if God has cast away Israel, His people, and responds, 'Certainly not!' He himself is an Israelite who is saved and God has foreknown His people from eternity. **V 2b–6: REMNANT** Even when Elijah pleaded against Israel with God because of her rebellious conduct, God told him that there was a remnant of faithful men. Paul reminds us that this is still true. By grace, not by works, a remnant of Israel will be saved. **V 7–10: REMAINDER** The remainder of Israel, apart from the remnant, are blinded, have a spirit of stupor, cannot hear, and are snared and stumbled. But this is not true of God's elect in Israel who are saved and enlightened. **V 11–12: RICHES** But not only will a remnant be saved from God's physical people, Israel, but the downfall of the majority of Israel has led to God's spiritual riches being granted to the Gentiles. God accepts believing Gentiles as His spiritual people and thus, in a sense, the fall of Israel has led to their enrichment. If their fall has led to this, how much more will the future restoration of Israel underline the richness of salvation that the Gentiles experience. **V 13–15: RECONCILIATION** The casting away of the majority of Israel has led therefore to the reconciling of the world of Gentiles. A final repentance of Israel as a whole will seem like resurrection! God is working out His sovereign purposes in the salvation both of the Gentiles (through the rejection of the Jews), and also one day of the Jews (through their final acceptance following their repentance). **V 16–24: ROOT** Israel is like a plant. Because Israel has been rooted in God and His covenant, it is a holy people and, through holy branches it should produce holy fruit. The branches are the Jews, some of whom have sinned and been broken off, enabling believing Gentiles to be grafted into that plant through the gospel. The fruit of salvation borne through the Gentile branches is based on the same root of faith in the promise of God. Paul warns that if unbelieving Israel was cut off, then Gentiles 'should not continue in unbelief' but show repentant faith in Christ in order to also experience the fruit of salvation in their own lives. Either one has spiritual life that produces fruit, or one is cut off and rejected. **V 25-32: RESTORATION** Although a large majority of Israel opposes the gospel and is blind spiritually, the time will come, after all the Gentiles have been saved that will be saved, that physical Israel will be saved as a nation. This will be only because they have become God's people spiritually through God's mercy and repentant faith in Christ. God's eternal calling of His people will be completed, but en route many Gentiles will be saved, too. **V 33-36: REJOICING** Paul breaks into rejoicing concerning 'the depth of the riches of the wisdom and knowledge of God'. His ways and thoughts are indeed higher than ours, and He must be and will be glorified for ever.

CHAPTER TWELVE

V 1-2: LIVING SACRIFICES Because of all God's mercies, Paul pleads with the Gentile believers in Rome to respond to God's gracious salvation by presenting their bodies as 'a living sacrifice'. This alone is holy, acceptable and reasonable. It will mean that instead of following the world, they will prove experientially God's good, acceptable and perfect will through a consecrated body and through a renewed mind which He will give them. **V 3-8: LOOK SPIRITUALLY** The grace that brings salvation, and enables personal sacrifice in following Christ, also produces a humble and spiritual mindset.

This enables the Christian to consider things from a spiritual point of view. Thus self should not be exalted, and one should recognise that whatever God has given is a gift from Him and not a matter for personal pride. Those gifts, given liberally, should be exercised graciously and faithfully within the body of Christ. The gifts mentioned are to glorify God and help other Christians. **V 9-21: LOVE SINCERELY** Sincere love abhors hypocrisy and extols and exemplifies all the spiritual characteristics in dealings between Christians. The following things result from a spiritual love for Christ: kindly affection, preferring others, diligence, fervent service, rejoicing, hope, patience, continuing prayer, generosity towards the needs of others, rejoicing under persecution, sympathy, single-mindedness, humility, refusal to fight back, peace, compassion, seeking good, and overcoming evil with good. This love will be displayed both to Christian brethren and to the world at large. This can only be done by God's gracious enabling through bodies presented as living sacrifices and through minds renewed by God's grace and Spirit.

CHAPTER THIRTEEN

V 1-7: SUBMISSION A Christian must submit to governmental authorities. This is not just because he will suffer the wrath of authority if he fails to do so, but because of his Christian conscience and the need for government and judicial control in a civilised world. Obligations must be met which are rightfully due to civil authorities. Thus taxes are to be paid and honour is to be given. **V 8-10: SUMMARY** A Christian should not have outstanding financial debts. This means that any money borrowed should be repaid by the agreed due date. The

Christian's debt is to show the love of Christ to others and to obey God's commandments. Five of the six commandments relating to relationships with men are then mentioned. The only one not referred to is the fifth commandment to honour parents. This is because the passage deals primarily with relationships outside the family. All those commandments quoted are summarised under loving one's neighbour. The practical application of love fulfils the law. But love is not just a warm feeling; it is doing what God requires, and He requires that we keep His commandments. **V 11–13: SLUMBER** Paul bids his readers to wake out of their spiritual sleep and realise that time is short. That awakening should mean casting off 'the works of darkness' and putting on 'the armour of light'. They are to walk as children of the day, rejecting their former worldly and lustful lifestyle of strife and envy. **V 14: SANCTIFIED** A sanctified walk involves both a positive and negative intent. They must 'put on the Lord Jesus Christ', which means experiencing His cleansing and living under His righteousness. But also they must make 'no provision for the flesh, to fulfil its lusts'. They must reject not only sin, but the situations that will lead them into sin. Temptation is to be avoided, as well as resisted.

CHAPTER FOURTEEN

V 1–4: WATCH OUT FOR THE WEAK A Christian is not to judge someone whose weakness of faith is translated by him into scruples and foibles that the Scripture does not require. Thus someone who is a vegetarian by conviction should be left to eat vegetables, and is not to be judged for that conviction. God is able to make that person stand. He or she is responsible to God. **V 5–6: MAKE UP YOUR OWN MIND**

The principle is that we live to the Lord and we die to the Lord, and thus we are accountable to God. Thus in peripheral things, like keeping extra days as holy days, or in deciding what to eat, we should not be divisive, but simply walk in our own conscience before God. 'The day' cannot refer to the weekly Sabbath, which is a creation principle of God enshrined in His moral law of the unchanging Ten Commandments. It refers to added holy days and New Moons. Today, it could include days like saints' days, Good Friday or Christmas Day. If a Christian wants to keep those as additional holy days, he should be allowed to do so, though he has no mandate from the Bible to seek to impose them on others. **V 7–12: LIVE UNDER JESUS CHRIST'S LORDSHIP** Jesus Christ died and rose again to be our Lord, and one day He will judge us as to how we have stewarded our lives before Him. We need to live under His Lordship, accountable to Him for how we live our own Christian lives, rather than judging others. **V 13–18: STOP YOUR BROTHER BEING FROM STUMBLING** Another cardinal principle of Christian living is not to do anything that will cause a Christian brother to stumble or fall. Thus, for example, eating certain food that he may regard as unclean may cause him to fall even though another Christian feels he can eat that food. It is best if that other Christian does not eat that food for the sake of that weaker brother. Other people's consciences and welfare are to come before our preferences, bearing in mind that the kingdom of God is to do with peace and joy in the Holy Spirit and in serving Christ. It is not a matter of what we eat or drink. **V 19–21: PURSUE PEACE AS A PRIORITY** With the aim of edifying one another in the Lord, and giving no unnecessary offence to a weaker brother, we should pursue things that make for peace. **V 22–23: DO NOT DO ANYTHING DOUBTFUL** It is good to have a clear conscience ourselves before God, but if what we are about to do is something about which we have any doubt, either for ourselves or about making another stumble, we would be better not to do it. 'If in doubt, don't!' is a good guide for conduct in non-essential matters and in matters that can cause others to stumble.

CHAPTER FIFTEEN

V 1–6: PLEASING AND PATIENT A Christian who is strong ought to support the weaker brother and not please himself. Even Jesus did not please Himself, and nor should we. This calls for patience, but the 'God of patience' can give us a like-mindedness and a desire to glorify God which will make us want to please others, rather than follow our own preferences. **V 7–13: PRAISING AND PEACEFUL** Having been received by Christ, along with others, to glorify God, we must receive others with the same servant-like attitude of Jesus, who accepts both Jews and Gentiles. There is much reason to praise Him and rejoice in Him. Such joyful believing will produce peace and hope, by the power of the Holy Spirit. These things are far more important than petty secondary matters. **V 14–21: PROCLAIMING AND POWER** Confident that the Roman Christians are able to help and encourage one another, Paul now seeks to remind them of his calling to reach the Gentiles with the gospel. He does not boast of his accomplishments, but gives glory to God for the power of the Holy Spirit, which enables him to preach the gospel fully to unreached Gentiles. God has attested Paul's apostolic authority and work by signs, wonders and the power of the Holy Spirit. Paul's aim is to preach the gospel where Christ is

unknown. **V 22–29: PLAN AND PURPOSE** Paul shares with the Roman Christians his great desire to come and see them, both to be helped by them and to help them as he comes 'in the fullness of the blessing of the gospel of Christ'. He shares his plans with them, mentioning that he is taking a gift from Christians in Macedonia and Achaia to the poverty-stricken believers in Jerusalem. This Spirit-guided apostle seeks to optimise his use of journeys, time and resources: this is an excellent pattern for every Christian involved in itinerant gospel work. **V 30–33: PRAYING AND PRESENCE** Paul begs the church to strive together with him in prayer. He knows that opposition awaits him in Judea and he wants them to pray for his deliverance, for acceptable service in Jerusalem, and for a joyful and refreshing return to them. He commits them to the 'God of peace'.

CHAPTER SIXTEEN

V 1–16: GRACIOUS GREETINGS Paul enthusiastically recognises and greets the individuals, with whom he has enjoyed spiritual fellowship and laboured in Christian service. Some have been in prison with him. This is another reminder to us that the church, however large or small, consists of individuals, and is not a mere organisation. No servant of Christ is ever too important or gifted to ignore the fellowship of all believers. Paul also encouraged them by relaying greetings from other churches. **V 17–19: DANGEROUS DECEIVERS** Paul knows of the obedience of the Roman Christians, but he wants them 'to be wise in what is good, and simple concerning evil'. Thus he warns them to mark dangerous, self-seeking, deceivers. Using false doctrine and smooth, flattering speech, they seek to deceive the hearts of simple Christians. Every church should keep a similar watch for those peddling error, in order to expose them and protect Christians and God's honour. To avoid the dangers of false teaching, Paul refers the Christians 'to the doctrine which you learned'. **V 20: PEACEFUL POWER** Paul encourages the saints that 'the God of peace' is the One who will crush Satan under their feet shortly. God's peace is powerful against evil and is linked very closely to the grace of the Lord Jesus Christ toward them all. **V 21–23: FRIENDLY FELLOWSHIP** Paul then relates greetings from his Christian friends to the church in Rome. This includes greetings from his secretary, Tertius. **V 25–27: MYSTERY MANIFESTED** Paul commits the church to God, who is able to establish them through the gospel and the preaching of Jesus Christ. He proclaims that the eternal mystery of Christ has been made manifest, and, by the prophetic Scriptures, has been made known to all nations to bring them to obedient faith in Him. This will bring glory to God through Christ, eternally. A mystery in the Bible is something that would be hidden but for the fact that God has revealed it through His Word. Even when it is so revealed, it contains a huge element outside our natural understanding, or it looks forward to a future event to complete our understanding of the mystery. The mystery referred to here is that Christ has been manifest in the flesh, and is the Saviour of those who trust Him.

1 CORINTHIANS

OVERVIEW

PEOPLE AND PRELIMINARIES

Paul wrote 1 Corinthians (fifteen chapters) from Ephesus between AD53 and AD57, probably in AD55. It is his first of two letters to the church at Corinth and the second letter presented in the New Testament. **See comments on Romans.**

PLAN AND PURPOSE

Corinth is such a morally decadent place that a new word for living immorally is coined, namely 'to Corinthianise'. In the first half of the book, Paul tackles matters that have been reported to him personally, and in the second half he answers issues the Corinthian Christians have raised in their letter to him. Paul's response to these situations produces a letter that deals with the problems of division through party spirit, the priority of preaching and honouring the message of the cross, lawsuits before a watching and hostile world, rampant immorality in the church, marriage and divorce, identification with idolatry and carefulness not to make others stumble, the Lord's Supper, spiritual gifts, the factuality and centrality of the resurrection of the Lord Jesus Christ, and stewardship. In answering these issues, 1 Corinthians underlines the importance of sanctification, what it means to be baptised by the Spirit, the cross, judgement of believers (not in the eternal sense), wisdom, consideration, love and consecration. It stands testimony to the solemn and challenging fact that a New Testament church can experience God's spiritual gifts and yet dishonour Him in its profligate and worldly lifestyle. It is a very spiritual and practical book.

Introduction, grace, godliness and gifts (1:1–9); dealing with factions, need for recognising team-work, stewardship and parental care (1:10–4:21); dealing with immorality and solving disputes (5:1–6:20); the marriage bond and problems arising (7:1–40); the place of others' conscience in Christian liberty (8:1–13); self-denial and preaching the gospel (9:1–27); cautious living, idolatry and glorifying God (10:1–11:1); order and worship in the church—including the relationship of the sexes, the Lord's Supper, use of spiritual gifts, the higher demand of love, tongues, and running the meetings (11:2–14:40); the resurrection of Christ and of Christians (12:1–58); closing directions and greetings (16:1–24).

PRINCIPLES AND PARTICULARS

All church life is here, and many issues are raised, both theological and practical. The teaching on the resurrection of the Lord Jesus Christ is key, logical and essential for all Christians and especially for those who are concerned to preach the message of the cross. The connection between orderly discipline and Holy Spirit sanctification is shown, not only in controlling sexual activity and limiting it to within marriage, but also in regulating the worship of the church. The Christian needs to be and to live what he is already in Christ, through His power and grace. Faithfulness to our giving God is far more important than being gifted.

1 CORINTHIANS

CHAPTER ONE

V 1–3: CORINTH Paul writes to the saints in Christ at Corinth, but what he says is of universal application to all those 'who in every place call on the name of Jesus Christ our Lord, both theirs and ours'. The very word 'Corinth' is synonymous in Paul's time with living an immoral, and even a perverted, lifestyle. It is from that background that these Christians are urged to benefit from the grace and peace from God the Father and God the Son.

V 4–9: CHRIST Paul is going to address some cardinal practical issues of behaviour and so starts by emphasising God's grace to them in Christ Jesus. He has enriched them, and will confirm them to the end. They are in fellowship with their faithful God through the gospel.

V 10–17: CONTENTION Paul is concerned that the party factions in the church claim to follow him, or Apollos, or Cephas (Peter). In this debate Christ is seen by some as simply being the leader of another faction instead of the Head of the church. Paul relates that he did not baptise many people, and that he is not seeking a following for himself, but to preach the gospel, emphasising the message of the cross of Christ which alone can be effective in saving sinners.

V 18–25: CROSS Paul expands the theme. Our attitude towards the message of the cross is the touchstone to whether we are saved or not. It is foolishness to the lost, but wisdom to those who know Christ and are being saved. The cross causes the Jews to stumble, because they look for a sign, and the Greeks, because they seek out philosophical wisdom. Neither Jew nor Greek can see that fulfilled in a crude and cruel form of Roman criminal execution. The saved person knows God's wisdom and power in knowing Christ crucified. **V 26–31: CALLING** Not many mighty or noble people are called. Rather, those who come in their foolishness, weakness and shame, bringing nothing in which they can glory, are saved by Christ, who becomes for them God's wisdom, righteousness, sanctification and redemption. Thus their salvation promotes a glorification of God who has saved them, rather than pride in their own efforts, which they know could never save them.

CHAPTER TWO

V 1–5: RESOLVE Paul's determined resolve in preaching to the Corinthians is never to parade his excellent vocabulary or wisdom, but to concentrate solely on 'Jesus Christ and Him crucified'. He admits that he feels his great weakness, fear, and trembling and that it is not human wisdom or persuasion that gives power to the message, but the Holy Spirit, as he concentrates on the message of the cross, the true preaching of which always is accompanied by God's power to save. **V 6–10: REVELATION** God's revealed wisdom is shared with those who are spiritually mature. The world has rejected this wisdom and this is why 'the Lord of glory', the Lord Jesus Christ, was crucified. But, through His Spirit, God has revealed the truths of His word and the blessings He has prepared for His redeemed people. The same Holy Spirit, who reveals the word of God, is at work in the hearts of men to reveal to them their sin and need for this gospel of Christ crucified. **V 11–15: RECEPTION** The Christian has received 'the Spirit who is from God' who teaches him both the truth about God and the truth about himself, underlines his need, and intensifies his desire for God's revelation through His

word. The unconverted man (the 'natural man') cannot understand these things, because they are spiritually discerned and only become real to a person who has turned from sin and received the Holy Spirit by faith in Christ. God's enlightenment follows the receiving of the Holy Spirit in conversion. **V 16: RÉSUMÉ** No one can have God's mind unless he or she has been converted. The simplest person who trusts Christ, through grace, receives 'the mind of Christ' within through the indwelling of the Holy Spirit.

CHAPTER THREE

V 1–4: CARNAL The childishness and carnality of the Christians, in following anyone other than Christ, is condemned by Paul. Envy, strife, and divisions are always caused by following a man rather than Christ, impede the spiritual appetite and Christian development, and demonstrate the sinfulness of human nature within. **V 5–15: CHRIST** Paul stresses that neither he nor Apollos do anything other than plant the seed or water it, but that the increase comes from God alone. God is the life-giver to the Christian who, like a growing plant, shows he is alive spiritually by growing in grace. God is the master builder, building up each Christian and church. But the foundation is Christ, and no one else. There is no salvation unless we are built on Him, and build on Him we must with gold, silver or precious stones of trusting obedience. The searching fire of God's judgement on the works of Christians will consume those works just as fire will devour wood, hay or stubble. However, anyone built on Christ will be saved, even though fire takes away his or her unworthy works. Whenever God is at work, Christ and His sacrifice will be central to growth and foundation.

V 16–17: CONSECRATED A Christian is indwelt by God's Spirit as the 'temple of God'. His life must be dedicated to the service of God, surrendered to God, and given to the worship of God as a consecrated human temple. God takes infringement of that consecration very seriously. **V 18–23: CONCENTRATE** Worldly wisdom is foolishness with God, and promotes men when God alone should be elevated. Thus Paul tells the Corinthians not to concentrate on Paul, Apollos, or Cephas or anything else, except the fact that they belong to Christ.

CHAPTER FOUR

V 1–5: FAITHFULNESS Paul stresses that, in the light of the fact that the Lord will shed His light on the dark deeds of Christians when He judges their works, we must be faithful stewards. Faithfulness is more important than anything else to a Christian. **V 6–7: FAVOUR** Neither Paul, nor Apollos, (nor anyone else) should puff themselves up in pride. Anything that a Christian has is a result of God's gracious and generous favour, and something received from Him, not the result of self-achievement or self-effort. **V 8–13: FOOLS** Paul sarcastically criticises the fact that some Christians in Corinth think they are already full, rich, and ruling as kings. By comparison, he says that he is among those who are despised and facing death. Using the picture of a procession of condemned prisoners being led away to fight and die in the Romans' bloodthirsty arena, he compares himself with their boasts and self-exalting claims. Those with him are 'fools for Christ's sake' in the eyes of the world, and are weak, dishonoured, hungry, thirsty, poorly clothed, beaten, homeless, reviled, persecuted and defamed. Despite being treated as the world's filth and off-scouring, they respond as faithful servants, in grace and love to those who treat them so brutally and unfairly. **V 14–21: FATHERLY** Paul is acting as a father in criticising the Corinthian Christians so that they can imitate him insofar as he walks with Christ, as a child imitates its father. He, through grace, is responsible for their coming to new life in Christ through the gospel he has shared, and takes a fatherly interest in them. So he sends another spiritual son, Timothy, to remind them and help them regarding how they should walk with their father's Lord. But he warns those puffed up in pride that he will come again with a father's rod of chastisement, though he would prefer to come in loving gentleness to obedient children.

CHAPTER FIVE

V 1–5: DISCIPLINE Continuing in fatherly mode, Paul expresses his great concern over immorality that even the unsaved Gentiles would abhor, namely, incest between a man and his stepmother. Paul judges this as if he was there, and tells the church to exercise discipline and put that offending person out of their fellowship so that repentance can bring him back to God. This is the meaning of being delivered 'to Satan for the destruction of the flesh, so that his spirit may be saved in the day of the Lord Jesus'. Discipline is not negated by love; rather, it is demanded by it. **V 6–8: DRASTIC** Their proud glorying means that they have completely overlooked this wickedness that spoils and taints the whole church, as yeast permeates the whole of something baked with it. Thus this sin must be completely purged away, so that the life of the Christians is as free from sin as unleavened bread is free from yeast. This drastic action must be taken for the common good and for the glory of God. The sacrificial death of 'Christ, our Passover' demands holiness in the lives of those who benefit from it. **V 9–11: DISTINGUISH** Paul says that he has already told them not to keep company with sexually immoral people. He now amplifies that and points out that he is excluding identification with compromised Christians engaging in obvious forms of wickedness, whether it be related to sex, coveting, idolatry, riotous living, drunkenness, or extortion. They must not even eat with such unrepentant Christians who openly practise sin. On the other hand, they need to have appropriate contact with unconverted people who practise the same sins, in order to influence them with the gospel. **V 12–13: DO!** Paul repeats that they must do the difficult thing and 'put away from yourselves the evil person'. Grasping the nettle is, at times, part of obeying our holy God.

CHAPTER SIX

V 1–8: CHURCH AND LAW Where Christian brothers have a contentious matter between them, they should not go to the law courts to decide it. Our position, in Christ, will be even higher than that of angels in heaven. Just as the fallen angels have been judged by Christ, it seems that we will have seniority to angels there. Why, then, cannot those in authority in our churches down here decide matters of dispute between Christians? It is better to suffer harm from another Christian than to take him to law before an unregenerate world. **V 9–10: CHARGE OF LEWDNESS** People living unrighteous and lewd lifestyles 'will not inherit the kingdom of God'. But it is not only those who have offended sexually by excess, immorality or perversion who will

be excluded. So will other sinners whose lifestyle reveals that they are not under God's kingship. They, too, are guilty as charged. **V 11: CHANGE IN LIVES** What a testimony to the power of God through the gospel that some of the Corinthians, who were crawling in that filthy bog of sin, have been washed and set apart for God. This is because they have been counted as righteous through the name of the Lord Jesus and changed by the operation of the Holy Spirit. **V 12–20: CHALLENGE OF LOGIC** Expanding the principle that a changed life marks faith in Christ, Paul goes on to say that he will now deny certain things that are lawful for him but that do not help him. He then homes in on sexual immorality, and quite logically argues that the body is for the Lord and not for sinful disobedience. The God of resurrection can help us live for Him. It is absolutely inconsistent, illogical and wrong for a Christian to be involved in sexual immorality which, not only is a sin against God, but is also harmful to his own body. If his body is 'the temple of the Holy Spirit' indwelt by Him and bought by Him, then the Christian does not have the right to use it as if God is not the owner or occupant. God must be glorified in both the Christian's body and spirit, as they are His by purchase as well as by possession.

CHAPTER SEVEN

V 1–9: SEX AND SANCTIFICATION Paul turns to the question of marriage, singleness and abstention from sexual relationships. The summary of the teaching is that those who are gifted to remain single should so remain, and must not be involved in sexual relationships. Those who are married should regard marriage as sanctified by God, and conduct their sexual relationships together with due regard for the other partner. Those who find themselves burning with sexual desire, and are single, should not see themselves as gifted for singleness. It is best for them to marry. God has gifted some people with the ability not to burn and they should pursue singleness. **V 10–16: STAYING AND SALVATION** Paul deals with Christians who, for whatever reason, are married to non-Christians. (This is not a state that a Christian should enter into but may be one in which he or she finds himself or herself after conversion or backsliding.) The apostle uses his authority to say that there should be no divorce, provided that the non-Christian partner is willing to live with the Christian partner. They are regarded as being set apart for each other, and any issue from that marriage is completely legitimate and clean. However, if the unbeliever leaves the believer (possibly the believer's Christian testimony and lifestyle is something he or she cannot accept), the deserted spouse is not bound to the deserter but is free to remarry. If the unbeliever is willing to stay, Paul argues that the faithful witness of the Christian to the non-Christian spouse may lead to the other one's conversion. **V 17–28: STATE AND STABILITY** The principle applied by Paul is that one should seek to serve and follow God, after conversion, in the state in which one is called, be it circumcised or uncircumcised, slave or free, unmarried or married. This teaching is not to bind a Christian in a rut, but to assure him or her that God is at work in the circumstances in which he or she is converted. Thus he makes quite clear that if an unmarried person does marry, he or she has not sinned, but that there is a down-side to marriage as well as an up-side. It really depends upon individual circumstances and whether God has gifted such a person

for singleness without burning, as taught in verse nine. **V 29–35: SENSIBLE AND SACRIFICIAL** Paul points out some of the problems that marriage can bring in a world where Christians are to live for the Lord under pressure of persecution. This emphasises again that, if singleness is the gift that God has given, it has definite advantages in these circumstances. Even those who are married should live sacrificially for God, not denying conjugal rights and the normality of a married life, but stewarding their time and their relationship sacrificially for the sake of the gospel and for the glory of God. **V 36–38: SENSITIVITY AND SUPPORT** A father with an unmarried daughter might have determined to keep her unmarried for the sake of Christian service. If he then decides to let her marry, presumably because she has opinions on the subject or because of a change in circumstances, he is quite right to let her marry. If, however, she carries on with him so that he supports her, he does well. Again this will revolve around the issue of what is that daughter's disposition and circumstances. **V 39–40: SPOUSES AND SPIRITUALITY** An overriding spirituality is to govern marriage. A wife is to be bound as long as her husband lives, and by implication vice versa. If he dies, she is free to be married to the Christian man of her choice, as God guides; the spiritual stipulation is that the marriage must be 'in the Lord'. Paul expresses a serious opinion that women may be happier to be unmarried, but he does not state this as a command to be followed. He does remind the Corinthians, however, that he too has the Holy Spirit. They, too, have the Holy Spirit to guide them into the right decisions, based on biblical principles.

CHAPTER EIGHT

V 1–3: SUPREMACY Love must reign supreme over knowledge, especially in dealing with areas difficult for others to work out, such as things offered to idols, and in facing up to the fact that we do not know as much as we may think we do. **V 4–8: SENSITIVITY** The mature Christian knows that an idol is a mere inanimate object with no intrinsic power. Human-made 'gods' are nothing, and we know God the Father and the Lord Jesus Christ, the source of life and all good things. However, some in Corinth feel that they are defiled by eating food offered to idols, possibly because they think the idol is stronger than it is. The mature Christian, while knowing that the food is the same whether offered to idols or not, must be sensitive of the conscience of the weak Christian in this matter. **V 9–13: STUMBLING** A lack of love and sensitivity can lead to a stronger Christian causing a weaker one to stumble, by ignoring his problem with his conscience in these matters. It will be better for the stronger Christian to abstain from the food that offends, rather than wounding the weak conscience of the less-established child of God. Otherwise, the liberty of the mature Christian can make the weaker Christian stumble, and, in that, he 'would sin against Christ'.

CHAPTER NINE

V 1–2: SEAL Paul defends his apostleship and his liberty in Christ. The seal of his apostleship to the Corinthians is that God started the church through him and through his gospel witness. They know he is their apostle. **V 3–14: SUPPORT** He argues from illustrations taken from warfare, husbandry, and farming, as well as from Scripture, that, as an apostle, he

has a right to be supported by them financially. **V 15–18: SURRENDERED** Paul then declares that he has surrendered the right, in their case, to be paid. He wants his passionate concern to be recognised as that of preaching the gospel for which 'necessity is laid upon' him. He regards it as woeful if he does not do it. If he preaches the gospel willingly, he is rewarded; but if not, he has a stewardship to discharge. So he presents the gospel without charge so that no one can accuse him of abuse of his authority as an apostle. **V 19–23: SOUL-WINNER** Paul makes himself a servant (or slave) to everyone, in order to be a soul-winner. He fashions his lifestyle to identify with the lost he seeks to win, without participating in their sins, and sinks his personal preferences. His priority is the preaching the gospel to those who are Jews, to those who are not Jews, to the weak, and, in fact, to all men. For the sake of the gospel and for the sake of the Corinthians, he declares that 'I have become all things to all men, that I might by all means save some'. **V 24–27: STRIVING** As a runner in a race, or a boxer in a fight, Paul strives to conquer for Christ. To do this he exercises self-discipline so that his own faith is not shipwrecked and that his example will be clear and consistent to those to whom he has preached.

CHAPTER TEN

V 1–12: EXAMPLES Paul carries on with the theme of self-discipline under God's enabling to live a holy life. He uses telling examples from Israel's history to show that no one should be complacent in following God, and ends with, 'Let him who thinks he stands take heed lest he falls.' **V 13: ENCOURAGEMENT** He then encourages the Christians by reminding them that temptation is a common factor for all men, but God is faithful who will not allow them to be tempted beyond their ability to resist and will also make a way of escape so that they can bear the temptation. **V 14–22: EVALUATE** In the light of all of this, he calls upon the Corinthians to evaluate carefully exactly what they participate in when taking the Lord's Supper. Their communion is in Christ, whose body was broken and blood was shed. Such evaluation should cause them to reject out of hand anything to do with idolatry, demon worship, immorality, paganism, or that which provokes God to jealousy. We are too weak to resist, and should claim His strength to resist the devil. **V 23–30: EDIFICATION** In order to edify both himself and others, Paul rejects things which do not help his spiritual life, and embraces those which do. He urges the Corinthians to do the same, bearing in mind the conscience of other Christians. So as not to offend their consciences, some things must be rejected which are not a question of conscience to the rejecter personally. **V 31–33: EXALTATION** Whatever a Christian does in Corinth and in our world today should be to glorify God and for the profit of others, in order that they should be saved and blessed. I should not live simply to please myself.

CHAPTER ELEVEN

V 1: CHRIST Christ is the example to follow, as seen in His faithful servant Paul. **V 2–16: COVERING** The principle of authority in the Corinthian church is being worked out behind this instruction that women's heads should be covered. The men should lead. **V 17–22: CONDUCT** Conduct unbecoming to Christians in coming to the Lord's Table is deplored. **V 23–26: COMMUNION** The purpose of the communion together at the Lord's

Supper is to remember the broken body and shed blood of the Lord Jesus Christ and to look forward to His second coming. **V 27–32: COMMAND** The command to examine ourselves to make sure we know and walk with the Lord, before taking communion, is urged. Judging ourselves can prevent serious disciplinary sanctions from God. **V 33–34: CONCLUSION** The church must regulate its poor conduct, which tolerates selfishness and gluttony rather than promoting a reverent remembrance of Christ crucified.

CHAPTER TWELVE

V 1–6: SPIRITUAL GIFTS The Spirit of God will always exalt Jesus. When He is at work, idolatry will give way for the true worship of God. He gives the spiritual gifts to the church at Corinth. Although members of that church possess different spiritual gifts, they all come from the same Lord. **V 7–11: SPECIFICALLY GIVEN** The gifts are given to the Corinthians on a varied and specific individual basis, as God wills, to benefit the whole church. **V 12–14: SAME GROUNDS** Blessings for all Christians are found in Christ. All Christians are baptised into Christ's body by the Spirit and so drink in His Spirit as a result. **V 15–26: SENSIBLE GRACE** Sensible grace is needed to recognise that all parts of the body are vital to each other, whether they are seen or not. A healthy body benefits all its component parts. **V 27–30: SAVIOUR'S GIFT** The Saviour's gifts to this church are people divinely enabled to perform various ministries planned by God, starting with apostles, prophets, and teachers. **V 31: SUPERIOR GOAL** A reminder is given of the superior goal to seek among all the gifts, namely love. This is dealt with more fully in chapter 13.

CHAPTER THIRTEEN

V 1–3: EMPTY WITHOUT LOVE No matter what gifts, abilities, generosity or level of commitment any Christians may possess, these things mean nothing unless God's love fills and controls the person concerned. Attitudes as well as actions have to be right. **V 4–7: EVIDENCE OF LOVE** Love is to be worked out in the attitude which governs practical living and relationships with others. Note that the word 'Christ' could be put where the word 'love' occurs throughout this chapter. Could you honestly substitute your name there? **V 8–13: EVERLASTINGNESS OF LOVE** Love is the most important thing because it will outlast even faith and hope. It will continue in heaven.

CHAPTER FOURTEEN

V 1a: OBLIGATION Their first obligation is to follow God's love, and then to seek gifts which are spiritual. **V 1b–25: OBVIOUS** The Corinthian church needs to know that prophecy is superior to speaking in tongues because people can more easily understand prophetic messages and so be edified. In using their gift of tongues, interpretation must be given. Paul emphasises the need to be clearly understood by one's hearers. Tongues are given as a sign for unbelievers. **V 26–40: ORDER** The conduct of church worship is to be controlled, not chaotic. Also women must exercise quiet submission to their own husbands. When the Holy Spirit is at work, Paul insists that 'all things be done decently and in order'. The idea that a Spirit-led meeting means chaos and lack of control is not a biblical notion.

CHAPTER FIFTEEN

V 1–2: BEWARE A belief 'in vain' comes from mere mental assent. Real faith causes adherence to God's word and this demonstrates salvation. **V 3–4: BIBLICAL** The death of Christ on the cross and His resurrection are foretold in the Scriptures. Paul insists on the priority of preaching the cross and the resurrection. There is no gospel without that twin emphasis. **V 5–10: BASIS** Christian confidence in the resurrection of Christ is based on ample, reliable, first-hand, corroborated evidence from credible witnesses of good character. Paul himself became such a witness, fulfilling one of the main qualifications to be an apostle. Although an apostle, he sees his own insignificance and sinfulness, but rejoices in God's grace working in him and through him. **V 11: BELIEF** The Corinthians came to trust in God through the teaching of Christ crucified and risen again. **V 12–19: BARREN** Christianity would be barren, dishonest, empty and fruitless if Christ had remained dead. **V 20–28: BATTLE** Through the victory of His death and resurrection, Christ will ultimately triumph over all enemies, including death itself. Christians who have died physically will live eternally through their risen Lord. He has won the battle for them! **V 29–32: BOASTING** Paul boasts of what the risen Jesus has done for him and for others. The resurrection has led to the conversion and baptism of sinners, who were drawn to faith in Christ through observing the way that real Christians died. Boldness in martyrdom and Paul's changed lifestyle also result from the knowledge of the risen Christ. **V 33–34: BADNESS** Bad habits can be caught from association with evil companions. Those following the risen Christ will show their salvation by seeking righteousness, rather than settling for sin. **V 35–57: BODY** A completely different, new resurrection body will clothe every saved soul, and be the ultimate possession of every convert to Christ. That resurrection body will be permanent, glorious, powerful and spiritual. It will reflect Christ's likeness. It will be given to each believer in an instant at Christ's second coming. Victory over death and the grave is for those who know Christ. **V 58: BRETHREN** In view of this awaited and wonderful future through Christ's resurrection, Paul's urges his 'beloved brethren' to stand firm and to keep labouring abundantly for the Lord. A good understanding of our salvation encourages us to work for it in others.

CHAPTER SIXTEEN

V 1–4: COLLECTIONS Collections of money at Corinth are to be avoided when Paul visits the church. Instead, tithes and offerings, already designated for Jerusalem, are to be set aside weekly on each Lord's day. **V 5–9: COMING** Paul plans to come to them when his gospel work allows him the time. Currently he experiences both a wide open door for the gospel at Ephesus and opposition from 'many'. **V 10–12: COMPANIONS** Paul commends Timothy to them. Despite pressure from Paul to go to Corinth, Apollos will come later at a convenient time. The apostle allows his co-labourer to make up his own mind. **V 13–14: COURAGE** Courage is urged on the believers to stand firm and to act in love. **V 15–18: COMMENDATION** Paul also urges the church to support those Christians who work for the Lord and commends, with gratitude, Christians who provided personally what was lacking in the work. This probably includes financial giving. **V 19–24: CONCLUSION** The letter is concluded with greetings from churches in Asia, a serious warning to those who do not love Christ, and personal greetings from Paul.

2 CORINTHIANS

OVERVIEW

PEOPLE AND PRELIMINARIES

Paul wrote 2 Corinthians (thirteen chapters), en route between Ephesus and Corinth, probably in AD55 or AD56. It is his second of two letters to the church at Corinth and the third letter presented in the New Testament. **See comments on Romans and 1 Corinthians.**

PLAN AND PURPOSE

Paul builds on and follows up his first letter to the Corinthian church in three main divisions, namely, Paul's ministry seen in action, his appeal to give to others through Christian concern, and his defence of his God-given apostleship. As well as relating to the situation he addressed in his first letter, he also covers new ground. Whereas the first letter largely reveals Paul's message, the second letter reveals even more of Paul's character. Although written to a church, it is personal, giving his biographical details. Vital teachings and emphases are viewed from all angles, such as: forgiveness towards penitent believers; what Christian service really is; some attributes of the triune God the Father, Son and Holy Spirit; the meaning of the substitutionary death of Christ on the cross; the need for separation; teaching on God's comfort in affliction; knowing His strength in weakness; the reason and outworking of Paul's evangelistic zeal; Christian giving; an insight into Paul's desire to major on God rather than on his own unusual personal experience; loving care for God's church; and the need to stand firm for God when facing opposition.

PROFILE AND PROGRESSION

Paul's introduction, change of plans, forgiveness for a restored backslider, nature and outworking of his ministry, the need to separate from evil, the need for reconciliation, the Corinthians' repentance caused by the first letter (1:1–7:16); Christian giving to those in need in light of the example of the Macedonians and of Jesus Himself (8:1–9:15); Paul defends and vindicates his apostolic authority, citing his manifested signs of an apostle, and his preference to come to them gently next time (10:1–13:14).

PRINCIPLES AND PARTICULARS

The use of 'comfort', 'comforted' and similar words and phrases teaches how God comforts His people. Closely related is the encouragement coming from the knowledge that God's strength is evident in our weakness, not excluded by it. The moving example of a major Christian leader impresses as we see his humility and bearing of hardship, rather than desiring affluence or seeking status. Accordingly, he delights to forgive a repentant Christian, and has a generous spirit regarding supporting other Christians. Yet, he is strong in advocating separation from evil and he marshals his arguments powerfully to vindicate his apostleship, because the glory of God and the gospel is at stake in both of those matters. A big heart for the gospel, for God and for people beats in this most effective preacher of the gospel and caring teacher of God's word.

2 CORINTHIANS

CHAPTER ONE

V 1-2: SAINTS Paul's introduction to this letter is written to 'all the saints who are in all Achaia', as well as to the church at Corinth. **V 3-7: SUFFERING** God can comfort us in all our suffering and sorrows. We should pass on the comfort we receive to others who need it. **V 8-11: SALVATION** Despairing even of life at one time, Paul finds that God's deliverance is past, present, and future for those who trust Him. It also results from the prayers of many people. **V 12-14: SINCERITY** Holiness with simple sincerity from God, according to His grace, is the basis of Paul's dealing with the Corinthian church. **V 15-22: SEALED** Paul's attitude is positive when he says he will come to the Corinthians; he wishes to help and be helped. This reminds him that God is positive in His words and actions. That is why the Christian's position is certain in Christ, who has sealed us by putting the Holy Spirit into our hearts. This 'deposit payment' of salvation guarantees that there is more to come. **V 23-24: SPARING** Paul says that he has stayed away from Corinth because, if he had come, he would have needed to deal with them firmly. He has spared them that. He does not seek to domineer but to work for their joy, faith and standing in Christ.

CHAPTER TWO

V 1–4: DISCIPLINE AND DISTRESS
Although both the Corinthian letters
show that Paul is in agreement with
disciplining an errant Christian, he is in
sorrow and distress over any offender.
V 5–11: PUNISHMENT AND PARDON
Since the church's disciplinary action
against the offending Christian has led to
his repentance, now is the time to forgive
him and restore him into the fellowship.
Failure to do this will play into Satan's
hands. **V 12–17: TITUS AND TRIUMPH**
Paul's former uneasiness, because he
could not find out where Titus was,
caused him to seek him in Macedonia,
despite having an open door for the gospel
at Troas. He really does care for his co-
workers. He interrupts his narrative to
thank God for the triumph God gives
which enables him, though feeling his
inadequacy, to share God's word sincerely.

CHAPTER THREE

V 1–3: SELF-COMMENDATION Paul refers
to letters of introduction, often used to
assure new churches that those coming to
them are authentic Christians. Initially,
the false apostles commended themselves.
Paul says he needs no letter of
commendation when coming to the
Corinthian church, because they
themselves are his letter of
commendation. They are saved because
he has been there with the gospel. **V 4–6:
SPIRIT'S CONFIDENCE** He quickly adds
that his confidence is not based on self-
effort, but on what the Holy Spirit has
done. His confidence comes because of
God's action through Christ. **V 7–11:
STRIKING COMPARISON** He then
compares the fading glory on Moses' face
after the Ten Commandments were given,
with the surpassing lasting glory through

the gospel. The Ten Commandments
condemned men, but the gospel saves
them. **V 12–18: SUPERIOR COVENANT**
The Old Testament covenant can never
unveil a person's spiritual blindness. That
only happens through God the Holy
Spirit, when He gives understanding,
transforming power, and glory through
faith in Christ.

CHAPTER FOUR

V 1: ENCOURAGED God's mercy and
commissioning for service encourage
Paul not to lose heart. **V 2–6:
ENLIGHTENED** Unlike unbelievers,
Christians renounce the hidden and dark
paths of shame because gospel light has
shined in their hearts to give them a
personal knowledge of God through
Jesus Christ. Accordingly, they preach the
Lordship of Jesus Christ to blind and lost
sinners. **V 7–12: ENABLED** Despite
crushing pressures from every side and
persecution, Paul's willingness to die to
self and to live for Christ means that
God's resurrection life is at work in Paul
to the glory of God. All Christians know
the same truth when they trust the risen
Christ. **V 13–15: EMBOLDENED** The
Christian, knowing that Jesus has risen
from the dead and will cause them one
day to rise and be accepted in God's
presence, has his faith encouraged and he
is emboldened to speak for Christ.
V 16–18: ENERGISED Despite the
temptation to be discouraged within, and
the physical weakness of their bodies,
God's servants know God's daily renewal
and are motivated by the prospect of
glory to come. They do not lose heart.
Their current trials are light in
comparison with the weight of that glory
that will be theirs.

CHAPTER FIVE

V 1–5: RESERVED! Our bodies, the earthly dwelling place for our souls, are deteriorating. But Christians in Corinth then, or anywhere now, own the title deeds to an eternal home to come! Furthermore, there will be a new resurrection body to clothe us, in which we will enjoy our glorious privileges for ever. We have been given the Holy Spirit now as a guarantee of this glorious future blessing. **V 6–10: REWARDS** Notwithstanding the certainty of salvation in Christ through grace alone, and the fact of one day being present with the Lord in heaven, Paul reminds the Corinthians that they must appear before the 'judgement seat of Christ' where good or bad stewardship will receive its just and appropriate rewards. **V 11–15: RATIONALE** With that accountability in mind, Paul persuades men to turn to Christ. Christ's love compels him to do this, knowing that Christ 'died for all' and 'rose again'. **V 16–21: RECONCILIATION** Those reconciled to God, through Christ, have become completely new people. Furthermore, they urge others to be reconciled to God. The basis of that reconciliation is that the sinless and righteous Christ was made sin for sinful and unrighteous sinners, who trust Him, so that they are counted as sinless and righteous in Him.

CHAPTER SIX

V 1–2: PLEADING PREACHERS Paul's pleads with people to accept God's grace immediately and be saved. **V 3–10: TRANSPARENT TESTIMONY** The lifestyle of those serving God is to be transparent and spiritually minded. Their testimony should reflect God-enabled blamelessness, patience, perseverance, purity, knowledge, longsuffering, sacrifice, kindness, love, power, consistency, rejoicing, self-giving, generosity and contentment. **V 11–16: SCRIPTURAL SEPARATION** It is illogical, inconsistent and unscriptural to compromise with worldliness and ungodliness. Christians are to walk with God, who indwells them, and this calls for clear separation from unbelievers in things that are doubtful or inconsistent. In this way they will have a clean walk with God. **V 17–18: FATHER'S FAMILY** As His children come out from uncleanness to separation, their Father calls them all to experience the blessings of being sons and daughters of 'the LORD Almighty'. Their separation is in two parts—from sin and to God. Only in that way can the family likeness be noticed!

CHAPTER SEVEN

V 1: RESPONSE In response to God's promise of indwelling and the assurance of His fatherhood, Paul calls for cleansing and holiness to be sought and applied. **V 2–5: RESTLESSNESS** Paul appeals for an open attitude towards his team and himself. He describes his restlessness on his last visit, when he had battles outside and fears inside. He was totally positive in his attitude, aspirations and dealings with them, but was obviously uneasy because he had to confront sin in the church at Corinth. **V 6–9: REJOICING** He rejoices that the hurtful things he had to say have brought them to repentance. God used the coming of Titus to Paul as an encouragement at that time. His arrival with good news of the offender's repentance, and the church's zeal for Paul, comforted him. **V 10–12: REPENTANCE** Paul underlines that truly godly sorrow leads to life-changing repentance, in contrast to worldly sorrow—perhaps he has mere emotional remorse and self-pity in mind here—which leads to spiritual death. Paul's faithful dealing with the open sin shows his care for the church. **V 13–16: REFRESHMENT** Comfort, rejoicing, growing together and reverent obedience to God flow from the repentance. Titus is also refreshed in his spirit because of what God's grace has done in that church, and how they received him.

CHAPTER EIGHT

V 1–7: SACRIFICIAL GIVING Paul gratefully holds up as an example to the Corinthians the generous and sacrificial attitude and giving of the Macedonian church. They gave willingly, urgently, specifically and compassionately for needy brothers in Christ elsewhere. (We know from the first Corinthian letter that they gave to the poor Christians in Jerusalem.) But first they gave themselves. Then they were keen to give to others. Paul's concern is to urge the Corinthians to do the same, both through the encouragement of Titus and now through his own words. **V 8–9: SAVIOUR'S GRACE** The giving of Jesus is their, and our, example. He became poor through giving Himself for others, though no one had been richer than He. **V 10–15: SENSIBLE GUIDELINES** Paul urges that their year-long stated intention to give should now be accomplished. As long as a heart-willingness to give exists, the amount given is of secondary importance. Christians giving from their plenty should meet the needs of others who are poor and needy. **V 16–24: SENDING GIFT** Accountability, care and fellowship mean that Titus is chosen to carry the financial gift from Corinth to those poor saints in need in Jerusalem. He is accompanied by two members of the church, thus strengthening the accountability, care and fellowship.

CHAPTER NINE

V 1–9: GENEROUS GIFT Previously the Corinthians told Paul that they were ready to give generously to the Macedonians. Now Paul urges them to put that good desire into practice, and helps them by sending Christians to them to help them to prepare the gift! He seeks generous, not grudging, giving. As with sowing seed and reaping a harvest, giving meanly produces a mean harvest and giving generously produces a generous one. God's grace not only helps people to give willingly, but is also a means by which God blesses them incidentally when they give to please Him. **V 10–15: GLORIFYING GIVING** Their giving meets the needs of poor Christians, causing the recipients to glorify God. It produces thanksgiving, prayer and praise, as the benefits both from the gospel and from their giving cause others to thank God wholeheartedly. Paul reminds them of God's 'indescribable gift' to them. He gave His own Son.

CHAPTER TEN

V 1–2: BOLDNESS Paul says that if he has to come to deal with the sin of the church face to face, he will be as bold in his presence as he is in his letters. **V 3–6: BATTLE** Dealing with sin is part of spiritual warfare to be fought with God's help. It is not a physical war. The aim of this war is to pull down everything that opposes obedience to Christ in the life of the believer and to turn disobedience into obedience. **V 7–11: BUILDING** Paul's allegiance to Christ means that he must be hard on disobedient Christians at times, but he wants to build them up rather than tear them down. Whether by letter or in person, he will pursue this aim. **V 12–18: BOASTING** Paul's boasting has only been to distinguish himself from false apostles. No Christian should boast about self and self-achievement, but should 'glory in the LORD'. Only God's commendation counts.

CHAPTER ELEVEN

V 1–3: CONCERNED Paul does not want Satan to entice away or spoil the bride of Christ, His church. He shows his belief in the book of Genesis, when illustrating from Eve's temptation, by citing it as historical fact. **V 4–6: COUNTERFEITS** The false teachers and preachers present 'another Jesus', different from the Lord Jesus Christ, a 'different spirit', different from the Holy Spirit of God, and a 'different gospel', different from the gospel of God's grace and forgiveness through faith alone in Christ alone. Paul reminds them that he has proved his apostleship to them. **V 7–12: COMPLIMENTARY** Out of love for the church, he labours for them in the gospel for no payment, so as not to be burdensome to them, and will continue to do so. This is not for his personal gain but for their welfare. **V 13–15: CORRUPT** The false apostles appear as true apostles of Christ and as 'ministers of righteousness', just as Satan himself appears as an angel of light. They are corrupt but their 'end will be according to their works'. **V 16–33: CREDENTIALS** Paul is finally forced to show the church why he is a genuine apostle. He is made to enter into the foolishness of boasting, simply to reveal his apostolic pedigree, his God-given gifts, and his amazing sacrificial suffering as Christ's servant. They need to realise that he is God's genuine and authoritative apostle and they must heed

his teaching. The sufferings Paul has experienced for Christ and His gospel have taken him to the boundary of life and death, and challenge every Christian to live and witness for the Lord, at personal cost.

CHAPTER TWELVE

V 1–6: COMPARISON Paul continues in his assumed boasting just to make the comparison clear between him, a true apostle, and the false 'super-apostles'. He prefers to boast about his weaknesses, however, which reveal God's strength. He does not detail or boast about his own remarkable spiritual experience that has taken him fourteen years even to mention. **V 7–10: CONCEIT** Paul has a God-given affliction, a 'thorn in the flesh', to prevent him from becoming conceited. On three occasions, he unsuccessfully requested its removal, but was told by God that His grace was sufficient for him. Instead, he would experience God's strength being perfected in his weakness. **V 11–13: CLEAR** The distinctive and authenticating 'signs, wonders and mighty deeds' of a true apostle have been worked through Paul, clearly differentiating him from false apostles. The church witnessed those things. The only difference between the Corinthian church and other churches was that Paul did not rely on them for support. He asks them to forgive him for that! **V 14–21: CONCERN** Paul's desire to sacrifice himself for the good of the church is obvious. He seeks to come to edify them, and again not to be supported financially by them. He is prepared to risk unpopularity and personal sadness, if necessary, in confronting unrepentant Corinthian Christians with the need to turn from their offending sins. He fears, in case various sins are tolerated and no repentance is shown. That would humble him and make him mourn.

CHAPTER THIRTEEN

V 1–6: EXAMINATION Paul again states that he is willing to come and deal harshly with sin that has not been dealt with. That will prove that Christ speaks though him. However, he prefers that the Christians examine themselves before God to check their relationship with Christ. **V 7–10: EDIFICATION** In exhorting them to righteousness, he restates that he wants to build them up and not tear them down. **V 11–14: EXHORTATION** His closing greetings include exhortations to maturity, oneness with other Christians, experiencing God's grace, and knowing God's Holy Spirit among them.

GALATIANS

OVERVIEW

PEOPLE AND PRELIMINARIES

✻Paul wrote Galatians (six chapters), either in AD49 or AD50 (if written to the Celts in the north of Galatia), or possibly 54 AD to 55 AD (if written to southern Galatia). It is his fourth letter presented in the New Testament. **See comments on Romans.**

PLAN AND PURPOSE

ⓘLegalistic Judaisers are men who seek to undermine the gospel of God's grace in Christ by insisting on a mere external keeping of the law and its ordinances, majoring on their false belief that no one can be accepted by God unless he is circumcised. Thus they oppose Paul's apostolic insistence that salvation is by faith alone, in Christ alone, by His death alone, as revealed by God alone. They seek to discredit Paul, claiming he is inferior to other apostles, in order to annul his teaching. Galatians is written, therefore, both to vindicate Paul's authority as an historic apostle, through whom God reveals His word, and also clearly to restate and demonstrate that redemption can only be through the Lord Jesus Christ and His all-sufficient redemption purchased by His death on the cross. Paul's defence is not conducted for his own self-aggrandisement, but to contend for the divine origin and inspiration of his message.

PROFILE AND PROGRESSION

Paul's introduction, criticism of the Galatians' slide from grace, reminder of his credentials and proof of apostleship, and his equal standing with the apostle Peter in correcting him about legalism and contending for justification by faith alone (1:1–2:21); justification by faith—including the Spirit's presence and working, Abraham's pattern and covenant, the law and the curse, the principle of promise, Paul's appeal, the two covenants, Christian liberty and the fruit of the Spirit (3:1–5:25); responsibility to restore others, spiritual sowing, the cross rather than circumcision, and final greeting (6:1–18).

Under God's Holy Spirit, Paul blends personal, doctrinal and practical inputs. His emphases are: God has given him this authoritative message; Christ crucified is all the repentant sinner needs; and this must be worked out and made evident by sanctification in the practical arena of daily Christian living.

GALATIANS

CHAPTER ONE

V 1–2: GREETING In his greeting to the churches of Galatia, Paul stresses that his apostleship is God-given, and reminds them immediately of Christ's resurrection from the dead. One of the characteristics of an apostle is that he has seen the risen Lord personally. **V 3–5: GRACE** Paul wishes them God's grace and peace. He reminds them that the basis of blessing is that Christ has died for our sins to 'deliver us from this present evil age'. This was in God's will and for His glory. **V 6–10: GOSPEL** Paul is concerned about those who pervert the gospel of grace and turn others from it. Twice he states that anyone who perverts the gospel of Christ should be cursed. His concern is to please God and so fulfil his role as Christ's servant. **V 11–24: GOD** In authenticating his apostleship, Paul makes it quite clear that his call as an apostle has come from God. He refers back to God's work of grace in his life, marked by an immediate desire to preach the gospel to Gentiles. God revealed to him the same gospel that he revealed collectively to the apostles, as he found out three years later when he went to Jerusalem to see Peter and James, the Lord's brother. God underlines his status as an apostle by the blessing that

He gave to Paul's ministry among the churches. No wonder God has been glorified in Paul.

CHAPTER TWO

V 1–5: CONFIRMATION Fourteen years later, Paul, along with Barnabas and Titus, went to Jerusalem to meet the other apostles. He confirmed that the truth that he preached was given to him directly by God. It was the same truth that God had given to the other apostles. There was, right from the start, a real concern that no falseness, especially legalism, should creep into the doctrine and spoil the truth 'even for an hour'. Titus, a Greek, was not compelled to undergo circumcision. That Jewish rite could never bestow salvation. **V 6–10: COMMISSION** God confirmed to Peter, James and John that Paul was His apostle. Accordingly they commissioned him, along with Barnabas, to take the gospel to the Gentiles. They also were asked to remember the poor. **V 11–15: CONFRONTATION** Later, when Peter came to Antioch, Paul confronted him openly because Peter's correct practice of eating with the Gentiles was suspended when Jews came along. Paul saw this as a hypocritical undermining of the gospel, which adversely affected the Jews and even his companion Barnabas. **V 16–21: CORRECTION** Paul insisted to them that it was only by grace in Christ that anyone could be saved, and that salvation could only come by personal faith in Him. In dying to justification by the works of the law, and living by faith in the Son of God, Paul taught that Christians should reflect the fact that salvation is by grace and not by the works of the law. The death of Christ and His risen life are fundamental to this. The false teaching of salvation by works empties the cross of Christ of its real meaning and purpose.

CHAPTER THREE

V 1–9: FOOLISHNESS AND FAITH Paul now tells the Galatians that it is foolish to seek to be perfected in Christ by keeping Jewish legal observances. We are saved by faith and indwelt by the Holy Spirit because, like Abraham, we believe and trust in the promise of God. **V 10–14: CHRIST WAS CURSED** To attempt to be saved by keeping God's law and then to fail would mean that coming under the curse of God's judgement on sin. But Christ has taken our sin and our curse when He died on the cross in our place. When we trust Him, we are forgiven, cleansed, and counted as righteous because He has been cursed in our place. God gives us His Spirit to confirm this. The principle is the same as that through which Abraham was blessed, namely receiving God's promise through faith. **V 15–18: PERMANENCE OF PROMISE** Paul stresses that there is only one spiritual seed of Abraham. It is not to do with Jewish nationality or race, but with trusting God's promise. In that sense, Abraham is the father of all who are justified by faith in God's promise, whether Jew or Gentile. The arrival of the law, 430 years after the promise to Abraham, cannot annul that fact. In Christ we are saved through trusting God's promise. **V 19–25: LAW IS LEGITIMATE** The law is not intended to make us righteous before God and cannot do so. It is not against the promises of God, but shows us our sin, so that it leads us to faith in Christ alone. Righteousness and salvation become ours only in Christ, as we trust Him, realising that we can do nothing to save ourselves. Just as a tutor would lead an infant to school for education, the law leads us to Christ for salvation. He is our mediator. **V 26–29: SONS IN SALVATION** Faith in Christ makes us sons of God and, as those who have believed Him, also Abraham's spiritual seed. We inherit that ancient promise in our crucified and living Saviour. So does every other Christian, irrespective of background, social status or gender.

CHAPTER FOUR

V 1–5: ADOPTION Paul states that Christians are adopted by God as His sons. An adopted child is brought from one family into another. We have been brought from the 'family' of condemnation to the 'family' of salvation in Christ. As such we are heirs who inherit His eternal blessings. **V 6–7: ABBA** Paul is quick to point out that this is not only a legal position, but that God's Spirit works in our hearts so that we know Him as 'Abba Father'. 'Abba' literally means 'daddy'. We are not slaves, but sons and heirs. **V 8–16: ASTRAY** Paul applies this truth and tells them of his concern, because having been saved by faith in Christ according to God's promise, they are now putting themselves into bondage by observing days, months, and seasons. They seek to fulfil unnecessary legalistic requirements either of a past and extinct ceremonial law, or of man-made laws. Paul observes the difference that this has made to their former conduct towards him. Previously he had been encouraged by their love and their warmth. Now he feels treated as an enemy because he insists on God's truth about salvation. **V 17–20: APOSTATE** The comparison between the false apostles, who seek to exclude the Galatian Christians from the grace of God, and Paul's fatherly concern is obvious. Nevertheless, he is prepared to act as a good father and reprimand them if necessary. **V 21–31: ABRAHAM** Paul refers to scriptural history. Abraham and

Hagar had a son, Ishmael. Abraham and Sarah, his wife, had the son God promised, namely Isaac. Paul illustrates two distinct and opposing covenants of law and of freedom, represented by the two different relationships, which underline what he teaches the Galatians in this chapter. As Isaac inherited God's promises to Abraham, so we inherit God's promises magnified to repentant sinners in Christ. Thus we are the free 'children of promise' and are born of the Spirit of God. We do not become God's children of promise through the law or our works.

CHAPTER FIVE

V 1–10: CIRCUMCISION Paul develops the principle and applies it to circumcision. Circumcision is the putting away of the flesh as a mark of entering the covenant of Israel. Paul says that this is now outdated and to continue to observe it would logically mean that the circumcised person needs to keep the whole law in order to be accepted. The Christian is counted righteous through faith in Christ. Sadly, the pernicious teaching of being saved by circumcision has hindered obedience to God's word and has grown like yeast in bread. **V 11–12: CROSS** Paul's insistence on preaching the cross has led to his persecution because it is an offence to those who wish to justify themselves rather than relying solely on what Jesus has done for them. So grave is this error that troubles the church, that Paul could wish them cut off. **V 13–15: CALLING** The gospel has called the Galatians to liberty. That liberty should be used lovingly to be a blessing to others and not in destructive in-fighting that evidently characterises their lives, and flows from the false teaching, as Paul writes. **V 16–18: COMMAND** The Galatians are commanded to 'walk in the Spirit'. Only

in so doing can they conquer the lust of the flesh, because it is the Spirit, given through faith's response to God's promise, who gives liberty. Such a Spirit-led life cannot be achieved by seeking salvation by keeping the law. **V 19–23: CONTRAST** The evil of the works of the flesh are contrasted in detail with the goodness of the fruit of the Spirit borne by those who, turning from sin, trust Christ. There is no law against the fruit of the Spirit. **V 24–26: CRUCIFIED** Paradoxically those who have freedom in the Spirit are those who count themselves as crucified with Christ and follow Him. This alone deals with conceit, strife, and envy.

CHAPTER SIX

V 1–5: BEARING BURDENS The outworking of the previous teaching to the Galatians means that the Christian bears the burdens of others. This means a genuine desire to restore those who have gone astray, in a humble and gentle spirit, and a realistic assessment of one's own 'nothingness' apart from Christ. Self-examination is called for. **V 6–10: SOWING SEED** Generosity is a hallmark of a spiritually alive person. He will constantly support those in Christian work, sow generously God's word in his own life and in others' lives, and do good to others. He will reap a bountiful harvest and not lose heart. Christians are to be His special target of good works. **V 11–15: CHRIST'S CROSS** Paul adds a note in this letter in his own handwriting. Although those who insist on circumcision will continue to persecute Paul, he is determined that his only boasting will be in the cross of the Lord Jesus Christ. That cross not only deals with his sin: it deals with his heart. It crucifies Paul to the world, and the world to Paul. It has become the instrument making him into a new person. Circumcision can never do that. **V 16–18: WISE WALK** God's peace and mercy rest on those who walk with God. The apostle, seeing himself as

crucified with Christ, prays for the grace of the Lord Jesus Christ to be with the spirit of those who have received his crucial letter.

EPHESIANS

OVERVIEW

PEOPLE AND PRELIMINARIES

✳ Paul wrote Ephesians (six chapters), between AD60 and AD62, from Rome, during Paul's two years of custody. It is his fifth letter presented in the New Testament. **See comments on Romans.**

PLAN AND PURPOSE

ⓘ The Ephesian church suffers from misguided teachers who insist on unscriptural and legalistic rules, such as forbidding marriage and abstinence from certain foods, and concentrating on fables and genealogies which go on and on. (Paul later writes to Timothy to instruct him to seek to rectify those errors in their false teaching.) The first half of the letter is doctrinal and is written to the Christians to correct the errors and teach sound doctrine by emphasising all that they have in the glorious Head of the church, the Lord Jesus Christ. The second half is practical and encourages the outworking of God-honouring teaching in practical living. In so doing, important themes and issues are dealt with, including God's purpose and plans for His church. Key teaching is given on election, predestination, redemption through shed blood, the resurrection, the church as the body of Christ, salvation by God's grace

through faith in Christ, working out what God works in, Christ as the cornerstone, God's plans to save Gentiles, true Christian oneness, the ascension, God's gifting to the church, sanctification and not grieving the Spirit, conduct in special relationships including marriage, and the Christian armour. It is a letter of great encouragement and doctrinal depth.

PROFILE AND PROGRESSION

🐚 Paul's introductory greeting (1:1–2); the Christian's glorious standing in Christ through God's grace and will—including our position in glory, in predestination, in His riches, in His life, in His power, and in Christian oneness (1:3–3:21); the Christian's walk, worship and warfare, worked out in life— including church life, daily life, Spirit-filled life, life lived with others, life in spiritual conflict, and prayer life (4:1–6:20); Paul's final greeting (6:21–24).

PRINCIPLES AND PARTICULARS

☞ The theme of 'in Christ' predominates, touching the Christian's heavenly status, predestination, redemption, spiritual riches, power, life, and oneness. Christ is put forth as our Head, our peace and our cornerstone. The results of being continually filled with the Holy Spirit, in Ephesians, compare with the injunction, in Galatians, to let God's Word dwell richly within. Sadly, the doctrinal truths and the practical exhortations did not have lasting effects. This is the church that the apostle John later revealed left its first love, despite the careful attention of the apostle Paul and all God's available resources in Christ for them. This is a warning to us all.

EPHESIANS

CHAPTER ONE

V 1–2: GODLY GREETING Paul, as an apostle of Jesus Christ, greets the Ephesian Christians. His apostleship comes from God the Father and the Lord Jesus Christ. So does his greeting of grace and peace. **V 3–12: GLORIOUS GRACE** Paul recounts God's blessing already received by those whom God has chosen before the foundation of the world. His grace is the means through which Christians have been redeemed through the blood of Christ and have received forgiveness of sins. God's grace is full of riches, accomplishes His will in the believer's predestination, and causes those who trust Him to glorify Him through their praise. **V 13–14: GOSPEL'S GUARANTEE** When a person trusts the Lord Jesus Christ through the gospel of salvation, he or she is sealed through God's Holy Spirit. He enters that believer's life as a guarantee of completed redemption to come, which will result in praise to God's glory. **V 15–21: GREAT GIFT** In thanking God for the Ephesian Christians, Paul asks that they will have the most important gift of the spirit of wisdom and revelation in knowing Him. With this gift they will understand something of the hope of their calling, the riches which are theirs, and the resurrection power available to them as Christians. They will see the pre-

eminence and wonder of the Lord Jesus Christ. **V 22–23: GOVERNING GOD** God the Father has put all things under the feet of God the Son, the Lord Jesus Christ. Jesus is the head of the church. His fullness fills it and everything else.

CHAPTER TWO

V 1–3: SIN Now alive in Christ, the Ephesian Christians were formerly spiritually dead, led by Satan, and following their sinful lusts. Like others, their sins would have resulted in God's wrath, but for His salvation. **V 4–10: SAVED** God, rich in mercy and great in love, has saved them by His grace through Christ. They have been raised spiritually and have heavenly standing in Christ. They have not worked to earn their salvation, but they are saved to work for Him. **V 11–13: STANDING** Before this, they had no standing before God. They were not God's Old Testament people, Israel, who had special covenants with God. However, now in Christ they, as uncircumcised Gentiles, are brought near to God through Christ's blood, which was shed for sinners. **V 14–18: SAME** As both Jews and Gentiles are only made right with God through the reconciling death of Christ upon the cross, those who trust Christ are now one through Him. They have the same access through the Spirit to the Father. Jews and Gentiles come the same way to God. They are now reconciled to each other as well as to God because the wall between them has been broken down. **V 19–22: SPIRIT** As fellow citizens with saved Jews, based on Jesus Christ the chief cornerstone, the Ephesians know the dwelling of God the Holy Spirit in their lives, just as converted Jews do. Together, founded on the apostles and the prophets, they are built up by God into a spiritual temple, and indwelt by Him.

CHAPTER THREE

V 1–7: REVELATION The fact of the oneness of all believers in Christ leads Paul to pray the prayer that comes later in verse 14. But first, writing from prison, he digresses to disclose his apostolic authority which enables him to deal with some important things. God revealed to Paul individually what, through the Spirit, He revealed to His prophets and apostles collectively, that believing Gentiles would be part of the same body as believing Jews. Thus his message is not a subjective 'bright idea' of Paul's own making, but one that can be seen objectively as having come from the Holy Spirit. **V 8–13: RICHES** His task is to make the 'unsearchable riches of Christ' known to the Gentiles and to make all see the wonderful things that God has done in Christ. He expects to suffer tribulation in doing this and tells them so. His tribulation will lead to their glory. **V 14–19: REQUEST** He prays, in submission to the Lord Jesus Christ, that these Gentile believers will be strengthened by the Spirit inwardly, and know Christ's indwelling in their hearts. He asks for stability in their Christian life and an understanding, with all of the Christians, of the immensity of the will of God. **V 20–21: REMINDER** Paul reminds them that God is able to answer their prayers 'exceedingly abundantly' above their expectations. God acts with the power of the resurrection and the power of the Holy Spirit, which power is also experienced within each Christian. Both are limitless. Paul wants God to be glorified for ever in the church.

CHAPTER FOUR

V 1–6: UNITY Paul urges the Ephesians to a worthy walk which reflects the oneness of the body of Christ in spiritual unity. In so doing, he clearly emphasises that there is only 'one Lord, and one faith, one baptism; one God and Father of all'. Unity for him does not mean sacrificing truth. It is because of his stand for God's truth that he writes as 'the prisoner of the Lord'. **V 7–10: INDIVIDUALITY** This unity does not detract from the fact that grace is individually given to each person who trusts Christ, and that God gives enabling gifts to individual believers. He is the universe's highly ascended Lord, and can do that easily! **V 11–16: COMMUNITY** God has given certain gifted people to His church. They are apostles, prophets, evangelists, pastors and teachers. His aim, through them, is to equip and edify His people so, together, they know Christ, stand firm on biblical doctrine against those who would deceive, and recognise how they all fit into the body of Christ together. **V 17–19: FUTILITY** The Christian Gentile is to be contrasted with the other Gentiles who, as unbelievers, walk ignorantly, blindly, and in sin and greediness. **V 20–24: IDENTITY** In coming to know Christ, their old ways are dispensed with and the 'new man' is put on, in righteousness and holiness. There is a spiritual renewal of the mind and a radical change of identity for the born-again Christian. **V 25–32: QUALITY** There is a new quality of life of the Christian which reflects the fact that he does not 'grieve the Holy Spirit of God'. He rejects former sinful ways, and applies himself to replacing them with positive good. He gives the devil no place in his life and rejects his former negative behaviour and sin. His new quality of life is shown by tender-heartedness, showing forgiveness to others, and avoiding grieving the Spirit. The springboard for this is that 'God in Christ forgave you'.

CHAPTER FIVE

V 1–7: IMITATION In imitating God and walking in love as Christ did, the Ephesian Christians must reject fornication, uncleanness, covetousness, filthiness, foolish and coarse talking, and idolatry. They must reject empty words of false teachers that do not come from God's word. **V 8–14: ILLUMINATION** All those things to reject belong to the darkness of the past life. The Christian is now filled with God's light and shows forth the fruit of the Holy Spirit. This demands separation from sin and leads to personal revival and illumination. **V 15–21: INTOXICATION** Christians are to be filled with the Holy Spirit, not with intoxicating wine. They will know God's harmony in their hearts. They must walk wisely, redeeming the time, and honouring God in their conversation, worship, thanksgiving and praise. Submission to each other will result from a proper fear of God. **V 22–33: INSTRUCTION** The theme of submission to each other is focused on husband and wife. The relationship between them must glorify God. It parallels the relationship between Christ and His bride, the church. The husband is to take the lead and love his wife. She is to be subject to his authority, which he will exercise in a God-honouring way. Marriage is between one man and one wife as long as life shall last. It is to be marked by love and respect.

CHAPTER SIX

V 1–4: FAMILY EXHORTATIONS The outworking of oneness with Christ and unity with Christians is to be reflected in the relationship between children and parents. Children must obey and honour their parents, who must give fair, non-provocative and faithful training and spiritual admonition to their children. **V 5–9: FAITHFUL EMPLOYMENT** Similarly, those under authority in their place of work are to honour and give good service to those responsible for them, as to the Lord. They are not to work well only when observed; they are always to work well 'as to Christ'. Those responsible for employing others must also act responsibly before the Master, and renounce threatening. That is how Christ would act in their place. **V 10–20: FIGHTING EFFECTIVELY** Strengthened by God and His mighty power, all Christians must put on each piece of their spiritual armour prayerfully. Thus fully equipped and strengthened by the all-prevailing weapon of prayer, the Christian soldier should do what Paul aspires to do, namely to proclaim the gospel boldly, even if it means imprisonment. **V 21–23: FINAL ENCOURAGEMENTS** Paul wants the Ephesians to know his situation. He tells them that Tychicus will fill in gaps in their knowledge and encourage them. Paul closes the letter by wishing them peace, love, faith, and grace, all from God through Christ.

PHILIPPIANS

OVERVIEW

PEOPLE AND PRELIMINARIES

Paul wrote Philippians (four chapters) almost certainly from Rome, during Paul's two years of custody. It was written probably between AD60 and AD62, though other estimates vary between AD51 and AD64. It is his sixth letter presented in the New Testament. **See comments on Romans.**

PLAN AND PURPOSE

This 'letter of rejoicing' is written from prison to encourage the Philippian Christians to live in single-minded oneness close to Christ, rejoice in Him, and to stay faithful to God's task for them as witnesses to His gospel. Paul describes the gospel in a nutshell in chapter 3. It shows Paul's priority to honour His Saviour and to defend and promote the gospel while in prison, where he endures opposition from misguided Christians, and faces the prospect of death. It majors on Christ, whose example of a truly humble mind, as the divine Son of God, should be put into practice by them all, and especially in view of a personality clash between two established Christian lady workers. The letter has a glorious passage about Christ's self-humbling and His exaltation that followed. It also teaches the all sufficiency of knowing God's presence even in suffering and deprivation. It challenges Christians to give financially to the Lord and His work. It portrays what true Christian ambition should be, and gives valuable teaching on prayer. A key thought is the nearness of Christ,

whether seen as His presence now with believers, or the expectation of His coming, or both!

PROFILE AND PROGRESSION

Opening and prayer for all saints, Paul imprisoned but gospel free, the dilemma to live or die, and being worthy of the gospel (1:1–30); being one-minded, Christ's example of humble mindedness, His self-humbling and mighty exaltation, conversion worked out, shining and being poured out included, and the examples of Timothy and Epaphroditus (2:1–30); description of a Christian as the 'circumcision', what the Christian should know, from the past to the future through the present, and living with eternity in view (3:1–21); the challenge and comfort of the nearness of Christ, satisfaction and strength, sharing and supply, and greetings and grace (4:1–23).

PRINCIPLES AND PARTICULARS

The frequent use of 'joy' and 'rejoice'—or connected words and thoughts—encourage Christians in adverse circumstances to look to Christ and experience His strength in weakness. The emphasis is on 'all' Christians and the need for oneness of mind and spirit in Christ. The wonder of the person and work of Jesus shines through His sevenfold humbling and resultant glorious exaltation. Christ is all-sufficient to meet all our needs in His salvation, sanctification, strengthening, and satisfying us: this encourages us to press on for Him with glory in mind. The godly and selfless examples of Timothy and Epaphroditus in their support of Paul illustrate in practice what the book teaches as spiritual principle. The overriding need to preach the gospel and magnify Christ shines through this letter.

PHILIPPIANS

CHAPTER ONE

V 1–2: PEOPLE Paul gives a brief but all-embracing description of the church to which he and Timothy write. 'All the saints' (which means every Christian) and 'the bishops and deacons' are the recipients of the letter. Paul prays that they will all receive God's grace and peace. **V 3–11: PRAYER** Paul thankfully prays for the Christians. He is grateful for gospel fellowship with them and is confident of their salvation. He specifically prays that their love will abound in a knowledge and discernment that will help them to live holy lives. **V 12–18: PREACHING** Paul's witness for Christ is as a prisoner in chains. Paradoxically, this helps some to preach more boldly. Although some preach from wrong motivation, Paul rejoices that Jesus Christ is proclaimed. **V 19–26: PRIORITY** With his Christian confidence that Paul will gain greatly when he dies, his priority is to live for Christ now. If the choice were his, he would find it hard to decide whether to be 'with Christ, which is far better' or whether to serve Him and His people on earth. **V 27–30: PURPOSE** He urges them to live lives worthy of the gospel and to strive together, taking persecution without fear by God's grace.

CHAPTER TWO

V 1–4: LOVING LOWLINESS Selfishness and strife is to be rejected as, through the fellowship of the Spirit, God's love in Christ makes Christians humble, like-minded, and causes them to care for others. **V 5–11: LIFTED LORD** This likeminded humility to be sought was exemplified by Jesus in His incarnation and death for us. Although He was God by nature, He humbled Himself, through becoming a man and a bondservant, to the very lowest point of death on the cross. This resulted in His exaltation to the very highest place in heaven. Humility produces elevation, by God's grace. **V 12–18: LIVING LIGHTS** God's working in the lives of the Christians produces a reverent outworking of His salvation, irrespective of whether the apostle Paul is with them or not. The Philippian Christians are urged to live in such a way that their blamelessness and shining example will be obvious to all, in contrast with the wicked world around. They will proclaim God's word so that Paul, who is imprisoned and facing death, knows that his labour has not been in vain. **V 19–30: LOYAL LABOURERS** Paul now commends Timothy for his son-like service in the gospel. He esteems Epaphroditus highly for his courage, sacrifice and selfless love for Christ and for Christians, including for Paul himself. Epaphroditus was near to death as a result of his sacrificial service for the Lord. It is good to see how God's grace is lived out in the lives of those who are 'sold out' for Christ.

CHAPTER THREE

V 1–2: REJOICE In this 'letter of rejoicing', rejoicing and joy feature strongly. Here, that is so even though Paul has to address the false teaching that salvation is not possible without circumcision. **V 3–8: RUBBISH** Real Christians worship God in the Spirit, rejoice in Christ, and put no confidence in themselves, in anything else or in anyone else for salvation. Paul even counts his immaculate Pharisee's pedigree and religious zeal as rubbish, now, compared with the joy of knowing Jesus Christ. **V 9: RIGHTEOUS** Paul rejoices that his acceptance by God is because, having trusted Jesus Christ, his account is credited with the righteousness of his Saviour. He is now counted righteous through Jesus. **V 10–11: RESURRECTION** Paul is determined to know Jesus Christ closer, and even the fellowship of His sufferings. This can only be because he is also determined to know the power of the resurrection of Jesus in his daily life. **V 12–14: REACHING** Paul honestly admits he has a long way to go, but has learned to leave the past with God, press on with the present, and reach on into the future. He wants to lay hold of that which God has for him, and for which Christ has laid hold of him. His concern is to answer the 'upward call of God in Christ Jesus'. Only when the past is dealt with, and Christ is known in the present, can Paul have confidence and determination like this. **V 15–16: REVEALED** With this mindset, Paul tells the Philippians to build on what they have already learned in the knowledge that God will reveal to them other lessons which they need to learn. **V 17–21: REALITY** Contrasting the walk of the Christians with lost people who despise the cross and live sinfully for this passing world, Paul reveals the reality of a Christian's invisible and spiritual home in heaven. He looks forward to the future reality of the second coming of Christ and to the transformed resurrection body which will be given to each person who trusts Him.

CHAPTER FOUR

V 1: FIRMNESS In the light of Christ's second coming and the present personal knowledge of the risen Christ, Christians are to stand fast in the Lord. **V 2–3: FELLOWSHIP** This is expressed in fellowship with each other, both in solving our differences and in working together with others. The Philippian Christians are urged to do both of these things in the aftermath of a dispute between two women in the church. **V 4: FERVOUR** Again, Paul urges the Christians to always rejoice in the Lord and repeats this exhortation again immediately. **V 5: FUNDAMENTAL** 'The Lord is at hand' is fundamental to this verse, this chapter, the whole of the book of Philippians, and the whole of the Christian life. The knowledge of Christ's presence with us now, and the certainty of His glorious coming again soon, should shape the Christian's life in every facet. This should be true individually, with other believers, and in the world in which every Christian lives. **V 6–7: FAITH** Prayer, supplication, and thanksgiving are the expressions of faith to be made known to God in everything. Thus anxiety is dealt with and is replaced with the surpassing peace of God through Christ. **V 8–9: FINALLY** Paul's final exhortation is to concentrate on things that are noble, just, lovely, of good report, virtuous, and praiseworthy. Christians should concentrate and meditate on these things, rather than on the things of the world. This is the example Paul set at Philippi. In following it, the church knows the presence of the God of peace with them. **V 10–13: FORTIFIED** Paul rejoices in the material support of Christians. Nevertheless, in all circumstances, adverse and favourable, Paul finds that he 'can do all things through Christ who strengthens [him]'. This brings contentment to him even when he is in physical need. **V 14–16: FAITHFULNESS** Notwithstanding this confidence in God, the repeated and continual faithfulness of the church is gratefully commended by him. They sent money to Paul when he was in distress and continually when he was in Thessalonica, **V 17–20: FULNESS** Paul is grateful that, currently through their giving, God is fully supplying everything that he needs. Selflessly, he is grateful for the fruit that will come to the giver, knowing that God will also supply all their needs 'according to His riches in glory by Christ Jesus'. Their gift rises to God like a pleasing and sweet-smelling sacrifice. **V 21–23: FRUIT** The fruit of the gospel is not only in Philippi, where people have trusted Christ, but also among his captors in Rome. Some may have been Christians before Paul went there, but doubtless some have been the fruit of his witness, even in chains. God's grace, which he wishes for them all, is certainly upon him.

COLOSSIANS

OVERVIEW

PEOPLE AND PRELIMINARIES

Paul wrote Colossians (four chapters), between AD60 and AD62, from Rome, during Paul's two years of custody. It is his seventh letter presented in the New Testament. **See comments on Romans.**

PLAN AND PURPOSE

The fullness of the Godhead in Christ, and the fullness of the believer in Christ, are twin themes of this book which emphasise the person and deity of the Lord Jesus Christ. The believer's completeness in Christ is linked closely to His death for the believer on the cross. This is emphasised to combat the Gnostic heresy. Gnosticism teaches that, although God alone is good, all matter must be evil, including physical flesh itself, and thus Jesus could not be God come in the flesh. The same heresy concludes that it does not matter if someone sins, since flesh can only be sinful. Therefore, Jesus is held to be less than God. A system of legalism follows this evil and erroneous teaching. The rules being kept are seen to be more important than the need to be pardoned and liberated from sin. Dietary regulations and observing miscellaneous obscure sabbaths or past seventh day Sabbaths and holy days become the criteria for judging a person's standing with God. (These sabbaths do not include the weekly Sabbath of the fourth commandment, which is the Lord's day commemorating Christ's resurrection.) Nebulous mystical experience and angel worship fills the lamentable gap in the false teachers' low view of Jesus, and in many ways they are the forerunners of the (so-called) 'New Age' movement. The letter not only underlines the person and work of Jesus, but calls all Christians to live holy lives, because what they do matters to God who loves (and requires) holiness from His people.

PROFILE AND PROGRESSION

Introduction, thanksgiving and prayer (1:1–14); Christ's headship and reconciliation (1:1–23); Paul's ministry and concern for the church at Colosse (1:24–2:7); the errors of philosophy, man's traditions, legalism and carnality—but seek things above, put off the spiritually undesirable and put on Christ (2:8–3:17); Christian living at home and work (3:18–4:1); Christian walk and talk (4:2–6); Greetings and Christian family (4:7–18).

PRINCIPLES AND PARTICULARS

See the many direct references to Christ: the letter is full of Him, and the ultimate answer to any heresy is the person of Jesus Himself. See what happens when someone lets God's Word dwell richly in him, or her, and compare that with what the contemporaneous letter to the Ephesians teaches about being continually filled with the Holy Spirit. Note the teaching on wisdom, and what the difference will be if we 'put off' sinful ways and 'put on' Christ. Avoid keeping man-made religious rules or outdated rules from a past order. But do not confuse legalism based on man-made rules with obedience to God's moral law in the Ten Commandments. His moral law is unchanging and should be followed obediently, not to give salvation, but to please God and show the converted person's love for Christ.

COLOSSIANS

CHAPTER ONE

V 1–2: FAITHFUL Paul, with Timothy, desires God's grace and peace for the 'faithful' Christians at Colosse. **V 3–8: FAITH** Paul gives thanks for their faith which produces love for all the saints. That faith gives them a home in heaven and makes the gospel become real to them. It has produced fruit among them. It is through faithful Epaphras that the church was founded. He came to Christ through Paul. He informs Paul of the Colossian church's state. **V 9–14: FRUITFUL** Paul and his fellow Christians pray continually for the church members at Colosse, that they will please God and be fruitful in everything they do. Knowing His enabling strength, they will experience patience, longsuffering and joy, too. They are delivered from darkness, belong to the kingdom of Jesus Christ, and are redeemed through His shed blood. **V 15–18: FIRSTBORN** Jesus Christ is the Creator, and therefore was never created. But He is the firstborn of the creation in the sense that He has the right of the firstborn to inherit everything from the Father. Paul emphasises the deity of Christ with this truth. He is the One who holds all things together, the Head of the church, and the first Person to rise from the dead never to die again. Jesus Christ must have the pre-eminence as God. **V 19–23: FULLNESS** All the fullness of the deity dwells in Christ, and not only has He reconciled sinners to Himself, but ultimately He will reconcile the whole of creation to Himself. Our reconciliation brings us peace with God through the blood of His cross. The evidence of reconciliation is ongoing holy living for Him and being grounded steadfastly in Him. **V 24–29: FLESH** Paul suffers physically in the flesh because he is a minister of the gospel and a representative of Christ. His focus all the time is on Jesus Christ. The previously hidden 'mystery' is now revealed as 'Christ in you, the hope of glory'. Gentiles can now know the indwelling Christ. While in the flesh, he is determined to preach Christ and to warn sinners to turn to Him. He labours to strive to do this according to God's strength within him which so enables him.

CHAPTER TWO

V 1–5: ENCOURAGED Paul wants to encourage the hearts both of the Colossians and the Laodiceans so that each fellowship of Christians will increase in love to one another, with assurance and understanding of God's message. That assurance concerns what God has done in Christ, and is the basis of all our wisdom and knowledge. His 'great conflict' is his concern that they should not be deceived by anybody. He encourages them by rejoicing at their good order and their steadfast faith in the Lord Jesus. **V 6–7: ESTABLISHED** His desire is to see them established like a well-rooted tree or a building with good foundations. As they have received Christ, so they must walk in Him with faith and thanksgiving. **V 8–10: EMPTINESS** People seeking to persuade them through worldly philosophy and deceit are empty and have nothing to offer from this world. It is only in Jesus Christ that all Godhead dwells bodily and therefore it is only in Him that each Christian is complete. Jesus is over all and more powerful than all. **V 11–19: EMANCIPATED** Christ has put off the sins of those who trust in Him, by spiritual circumcision. Baptism reminds them of a new life through death to the old sinful life and benefiting from the eternal life given by the resurrected Christ. There is no power in claiming that they must now keep to man-made ordinances. They have been emancipated from that by the risen Christ. Thus man-made laws are not to enslave them, whether in the form of dietary laws, man-made festivals, or additional sabbath days. Any man-made system of worship, including angel worship, comes from false humility and a proud mind. Our freedom depends upon being under the headship of Christ, over the body of the church.

Each Christian is part of that body and takes his directions from Christ. **V 20–23: EXHORTED** Paul now exhorts the Colossians to avoid legalistic man-made rules which will perish along with every other man-made commandment and teaching. They may have an attraction of organised religion, false humility, and abstaining from things, but can do nothing to forgive sins or combat the inward pull of the old nature. Only Christ can do that.

CHAPTER THREE

V 1–4: PRINCIPLE OCCUPATION In contrast to earthbound legalistic observance of man-made rules and procedures, the principle occupation of the Colossian Christians must be to realise that Christ is risen and is ascended. He now resides above, at the right hand of God. Accordingly, the Christian must focus his mind on heavenly and eternal things, bearing in mind that he is to reckon himself crucified with Christ and risen with Him. Jesus Christ will come again and take the believer with Him to glory. **V 5–9: PUT OFF** Doctrine leads to conduct. The Christian's body is to be dead to sin. Paul stipulates the evil attitudes and specific sins which have to be put off. The world will be condemned for those sins from which the Christian has been cleansed. They include sins of attitude and word, as well as the more obvious high profile sins of action. **V 10–17: PUT ON** Whatever the background, the Christian is renewed in Christ. He has 'put on the new man', reflecting this in increasing likeness to his Saviour. This produces great oneness with other Christians and a sense of Christ's presence and sovereignty. Paul then tells the Colossians specifically what to 'put on' as Christians. It includes attitudes, motives and relationships with one another as fellow forgiven Christians. Love must cover everything and God's peace will arbitrate in the hearts of those who follow Christ. Only by letting the word of Christ have its place in the life of a believer can a Christian be reprogrammed from his sinful life to a life of praise, singing, wisdom and concern for other believers. All must be done for Christ and with thanksgiving to God through Him. **V 18–25: PRACTICAL OBEDIENCE** Obedience to God will be shown in the way others are treated in practice. This includes spouses, children and parents, and the place of employment (covered under 'bond servants' in the passage). The principle is to do something for Christ from a full heart, and not just to seek the acclaim of men, while concentrating on the individual's selfless duty to do the right and best thing for others. Reward and retribution are both in the hand of God, dependent upon attitude and action.

CHAPTER FOUR

V 1–6: GRACE Having given masters and slaves mirror image obligations (see chapter 3), and having asked for continuation in prayer in order that the gospel may do its work, through doors open for Paul and his companions, the apostle urges wisdom and redemption of time in dealing with outsiders. Grace must always characterise speech. If so, it will enable the right answer to be given when needed. **V 7–15: GREETINGS** Greetings are sent from those with Paul, including Tychicus (his faithful messenger), Onesimus (the runaway slave of whom we read in Philemon), Aristarchus (a fellow prisoner), Mark (Barnabas' cousin), Jesus called Justus, Epaphras (the founder of the church and a zealous fellow worker and prisoner with Paul), Luke (the doctor), and Demas (who later chooses the world and deserts Paul). He asks them to pass on these greetings to those in Laodicea and the church in the house of Nymphas. **V 16–17: GRASP** Paul asks for the letter to be read elsewhere and urges Archippus to grasp his responsibility and his gifting for the ministry of the Lord. **V 18: GRACE** In signing off and asking them to remember his chains, Paul again reverts to the question of 'grace.' He knows that they need God's grace just as much as he needs it in prison.

---

1 THESSALONIANS

OVERVIEW

PEOPLE AND PRELIMINARIES

Paul wrote 1 Thessalonians (five chapters), in AD50 or AD51, probably from Corinth. It is the first of two letters written to the church at Thessalonica and is his eighth letter presented in the New Testament. **See comments on Romans.**

PLAN AND PURPOSE

The main theme of both letters to the Thessalonians is the coming again of the Lord Jesus Christ. In 1 Thessalonians the emphasis is on the unexpectedness of the timing of His coming which is compared to that of a burglar. But the Thessalonian letters are also written to help and edify young disciples, to encourage them to live in purity and brotherly love, and to encourage the church to grow. There are over 100 references to God or Christ. 1 Thessalonians has a pastoral theme, especially comforting worried Christians about the saved state of their brothers and sisters who had died. It contains a firm emphasis on the gospel, the work of evangelism, missions and follow-up of converts.

PROFILE AND PROGRESSION

The church of God—including Paul's thanksgiving for their election, fruitfulness, exemplary evangelistic zeal and work, reception of God's word, and prayer for them (1:1–3:13); the children of God—including the need for sanctification and sexual purity, the increase in brotherly love, and the comfort and challenge of the second coming (4:1–5:28).

PRINCIPLES AND PARTICULARS

The second coming of Christ triggers off so much wonderful and needed teaching to a young church where Paul had spent only a few weeks, but where he preached the gospel and taught deep Christian truths simply. The second coming is a springboard for personal assurance, comfort and discipleship and for the urgent need to share the gospel with those lost sinners needing Christ. The letter reminds us to focus on God, revealed to us in Christ.

1 THESSALONIANS

CHAPTER ONE

V 1: GRACE Paul, along with Silvanus and Timothy, greets the Thessalonian church. Again, he wishes them God's grace and peace. **V 2–3: GRATITUDE** Paul always gives thanks to God for them and prays for them. It is the outworking of the gospel through their faith, and through their love and patience, which causes him to thank God. Not only do they have faith, but they have a certain hope for the future in Christ. **V 4–6: GOSPEL** The fact that they are elect is shown by the way the gospel came in power to them through the Holy Spirit. Contributing, under God's grace, to the conversion of the Thessalonians was the clear testimony of Paul and his companions. Now they follow their example, having received God's word in difficult circumstances though with joy given by the Holy Spirit. **V 7–10: GODLINESS** The evidence of their conversion is that they have heralded the gospel by godly life and by sharing the message. Their idols have gone. They have turned from them to God. This is widely known, as is their confidence in Christ's second coming, the resurrection, and deliverance from eternal wrath. Here are people whose repentance is shown through their rejection of idolatry, evangelistic zeal and their understanding of good doctrine.

CHAPTER TWO

V 1–3: PROBLEMS Paul reminds them of the problems he suffered at Philippi, which involved cruel and spiteful treatment by others. That, however, has not stopped his boldness in the gospel. **V 4–5: PLEASING** Paul reiterates that his aim is not to please men but rather, by taking seriously the gospel entrusted to him, to please God who tests the heart. At no time does he flatter men or misuse his position as a preacher of the gospel. **V 6–9: PREACHING** Paul's preaching is characterised by seeking glory for God, gentleness with his hearers, concern for those who hear in the church, labour and toil, and being on duty twenty-four hours a day for the gospel. He earns his own living so as not to be financially burdensome to them. **V 10–12: PARENTAL** His attitude is parental to the children of God in Thessalonica. He longs to see his children walking with God and can point to his devout, just, and blameless witness to encourage them in this. **V 13–14a: POWERFUL** It is the gospel of God working in their hearts that causes the Thessalonians to imitate the churches of God that follow Christ. There is power in the truth of God. **V 14b–16: PERSECUTED** They, too, have suffered persecution by those who want to forbid them to share the gospel with Gentiles, in case they should be saved. God's wrath is upon such people, who not only sin, but try to prevent the spread of the gospel. **V 17–20: PASSIONATE** Paul has a passion to see them again, but has been hindered by Satan. They are his 'glory and joy' through the gospel and he looks forward to the day when he will be with them in the presence of Christ.

CHAPTER THREE

V 1–5: TRIBULATION The Thessalonians have gone through tribulation and afflictions. Paul sent Timothy to them to encourage them, edify them, and let them know that such trials are normal for the Christian church. Paul is concerned that Satan may tempt them to compromise or abandon their faith because of their tribulations. **V 6–8: TIMOTHY** Timothy

returned to Paul with good news of their progress, especially in faith and love. They remember Paul, and want to see him and his fellow workers. Paul is also going through afflictions, and this news comforts him. He lives for the joy of seeing his converts stand and glorify Christ. **V 9–11: THANKS** He describes the joy and rejoicing which lead him to thank God for the Thessalonians. His round-the-clock prayer emphasis is that he may see them and help them in their faith in Christ. He continues to pray that God will direct his way to them. **V 12–13: TIES** Meanwhile Paul prays that their love will strengthen towards one another and that they will be established in holiness. He reminds them that Christ is coming again with His saints.

CHAPTER FOUR

V 1–2: INCREASE AND INSTRUCTION Their spiritual lives should increase continually and abundantly. They should remember Christ's commandments received through Paul and his Christian colleagues. **V 3–8: SANCTIFICATION AND SEX** God's will is to have a holy people in contrast to the unregenerate Gentiles. This means that sexual immorality has no place whatsoever in the life of any believer. Adultery and lustful passion is out. To reject this clean and holy teaching is to reject God and His Holy Spirit. **V 9–12: LOVE AND LIVING** Heavenly love towards each other must predominate. As it increases, it will produce a quiet, industrious, ordered life. This will ensure that they have a good testimony to those outside and that their needs are met by their daily work. **V 13–18: COMFORT AND COMING** Some suggested to the Thessalonians that Christians who had died had missed the blessing of Christ's second coming. Paul teaches them that, when Christ comes, those who have died physically will be raised with a resurrection body first and reunited with Christ in the air. Christ will bring their redeemed souls with Him, so there will also be another reunion—that of the body and soul of the believer. Then those who are alive physically will join that blessed reunion with their returned Lord of glory. This is, of course, a great comfort. The Christian who has died and the Christian who is alive both have their future gloriously secured in Jesus Christ. Those who died trusting Christ only fell 'asleep' in death, and awoke immediately in His eternal presence. Now they will be given a resurrection body also when Christ brings them back with Him.

CHAPTER FIVE

V 1–3: SUDDEN SURPRISE When the world least expects Christ, and when it is said that peace and safety has come, Jesus will return 'as a thief in the night'. This is as sure to happen as the labour of a pregnant woman will bring forth birth. **V 4–11: WAKEFUL WATCH** The world is not prepared for that. Christians should be ready and waiting for the coming of the Lord. Preparation for this event involves living a sober life characterised by faith, love, assurance of salvation, comforting one another, and building one another up in the faith. Christians, whether sleeping the sleep of death or awake at Christ's coming, rejoice that He died for them and that they will be together with Him. Salvation, not wrath, awaits them. This knowledge comforts those worried about the salvation of Christians who have died. **V 12–22: WISE WORDS** Paul then exhorts the Thessalonians in different practical matters. We see in these that true spirituality is always translated into practical living, working on good relationships with others, turning from evil, rejoicing, prayer, honouring God's Spirit, Christian discernment, and submitting to God with thankfulness for who He is and what He has done. **V 23–24: COMPLETE CONSECRATION** Paul prays that God will sanctify the Christians completely in spirit, soul and body, so that they are ready for the coming of the Lord Jesus who is faithful to them. **V 25–28: GRACIOUS GREETINGS** Paul's greetings include a request for prayer, a holy kiss for them all, an instruction to read the letter to everyone, and the desire that they will know the grace of the Lord Jesus Christ with them.

2 THESSALONIANS

OVERVIEW

PEOPLE AND PRELIMINARIES

As with his first letter to the church at Thessalonica, Paul wrote 2 Thessalonians (three chapters), in AD50 or AD51, probably from Corinth. It is the ninth and last church letter presented in the New Testament. **See comments on Romans.**

PLAN AND PURPOSE

The main theme of both letters to the Thessalonians is the coming again of the Lord Jesus Christ. See also comments on 1 Thessalonians. 2 Thessalonians builds on the teaching in the first letter and emphasises that it has not yet happened. It gives milestones that need to be passed before Christ will return, including the apostasy to come and revelation of the man of sin, who will be destroyed by the breath and brightness of the all powerful coming Lord! But the second coming of Christ, that comforts the believer in his Sovereign God, should strike terror in the heart of those who are lost and facing God's condemnation. 2 Thessalonians also has a pastoral theme centred on the need to live a Christian life, which includes working hard and not using the eagerly expected coming of Christ as a rationale or excuse for laziness.

PROFILE AND PROGRESSION

Encouraging opening greetings (1:1–4); stark contrast at Christ's coming (1:1–12); correcting error and comforting the saints (2:1–17); priority for prayer, and confronting laziness (3:1–15); encouraging closing greetings (3:16–18).

PRINCIPLES AND PARTICULARS

The fact of the second coming is prey to false teaching, whether propagated deliberately or in ignorance. The balance needs to be struck between eagerly expecting His coming and realising that God has His timetable. Thus, in waiting for the Lord from heaven, the Christian must expect certain things to happen and, meanwhile, work diligently and live wholehearted and responsible lives. The link between practical holiness and Christ's second coming is again underlined. The two Thessalonian letters should be read together, as they form two sides of the same coin.

2 THESSALONIANS

CHAPTER ONE

V 1–2: THESSALONIANS Paul, along with Sylvanus and Timothy, again writes to the church of the Thessalonians. He uses an identical greeting to the one in the first letter. **V 3: THANKSGIVING** Paul again thanks God for them because of their growing faith and love which abounds towards each person in the church. **V 4–7: TRIBULATIONS** The growth of their faith and love is in the context of the tribulations that they are enduring along with persecution. This is producing patience in them that causes Paul to hold them up as an example to other churches, and he reminds them that God will repay those who are troubling them at Christ's second coming. **V 8–10: THEN** This takes Paul on to his focus on the second coming of the Lord Jesus Christ. This will be a day of vengeance for those who do not obey His gospel and who will be punished with 'everlasting destruction from the presence of the Lord'. 'In that day', He will come to be 'glorified in His saints'. **V 11–12: THEREFORE** This causes Paul and his party to pray for the Thessalonian church, that they will glorify God and the name of the Lord Jesus Christ, and receive divine grace.

CHAPTER TWO

V 1–4: DON'T BE DECEIVED Continuing teaching on the second coming of Christ, Paul deals with those who have been deceived into thinking that 'the day of Christ' has already come, because of the tribulations they are facing. He tells them to stay firm: that day will not come without a falling away, and the revelation of the man of sin (the Antichrist), who will oppose everything to do with God, and exalt himself. He will even sit in the temple of God claiming to be God. **V 5–12: REMEMBER MY REMINDERS** Paul reminds them that he had often told them what would happen before the second coming of Christ. (The verb for 'told' is in the imperfect tense, indicating he kept on doing it.) As God withdraws His restraining influence (thought by some to mean that the Holy Spirit will withdraw), the lawless one (the man of sin, or Antichrist) will be revealed. God will consume him with the breath of His mouth and 'destroy him with the brightness of His coming'. The lawless one will perform satanic works and lying wonders with great powers and signs. Those who are perishing will be deceived. Having rejected God's truth, He will send them a delusion that they will believe. Condemnation awaits them. **V 13–15: SALVATION AND SANCTIFICATION** Paul thanks God that the Thessalonian Christians have been chosen for salvation to be sanctified through God's Holy Spirit and a belief in the truth of His word and His gospel. This glorifies the Lord Jesus Christ, and he urges them to stand fast in these godly traditions. **V 16–17: GRACE OF GOD** Grace from the Father and Son will give those Christians consolation and comfort, establishing them in 'every good work and word'. Paul prays for this for them.

CHAPTER THREE

V 1–2: IMPORTANT INTERCESSION Paul asks for prayer regarding two matters. He asks that God's word may 'run swiftly and be glorified'. He seeks deliverance for his companions and himself from unreasonable, wicked and faithless men. **V 3–4: CONFIDENT COMMAND** He underlines his confidence that his faithful Lord will establish and guard them from the evil one, and that they will obey God's commands given through him to them. **V 5: GOD'S GUIDANCE** He prays that God will direct their hearts into love and patience from the Lord Himself. **V 6–12: WISE WITHDRAWAL** Paul commands that the church withdraw from disorderly brethren and from those who are too lazy to work. Those who can work should do, so that they are self-supporting and not burdensome. He himself has set an example in this. **V 13–15: DISCIPLINE'S DESIGN** While Christians continue to do good, they should withdraw from anyone who is disobedient to God's word, so that the offender may be ashamed, and, by implication, repent and be restored. He is not to be counted as an enemy to fight, but as a brother to admonish. **V 16: PERPETUAL PEACE** Paul prays for perpetual peace from God for the church. **V 17–18: SPECIAL SIGN** In leaving the Christians to the grace of the Lord Jesus Christ, Paul authenticates the letter by the special sign of his own signature.

1 TIMOTHY

OVERVIEW

PEOPLE AND PRELIMINARIES

✱There are twenty-one New Testament letters. The last twelve, not written to local churches, are pastoral letters. Each of those is to a designated individual person or, in the case of Hebrews, a scattered audience of individuals. We have noted **(see comments on Romans)** that Paul wrote all nine church letters and certainly four of the twelve pastoral letters, namely, two letters to Timothy, one to Titus and one to Philemon. The other pastoral letters are written by James, Peter (two letters), John (three letters), and Jude. Between the church and the individual pastoral letters comes Hebrews, a communication to scattered Jews. **See comments on Hebrews.** 1 Timothy (six chapters) is thus the tenth of Paul's letters and the first pastoral one. He wrote it between AD62 and AD64 from Macedonia to his spiritual protégé and fellow labourer, Timothy.

PLAN AND PURPOSE

ⓘ Both the letters to Timothy and the letter to Titus were written for leaders and pastors of all ages. Not only do they remind Christians in authority of their need to live close to Christ and His Word, but they instruct them in the discharge of their responsibilities in leading the church and helping various groupings of Christians. 1 Timothy covers the importance of sound biblical teaching and dealing with false teaching, prayer, the role of women in the church, what qualifies a man for responsibility and leadership in a church and the discharge of those responsibilities, the inspiration of the Scriptures by God, and how to view wealth and use it.

PROFILE AND PROGRESSION

Opening greetings (1:1–2); false doctrine, the purpose of the law, and the task for Timothy (1:3–20); church life—including praying, the role of women, qualification for bishops, qualifications for deacons, and conduct in the light of the doctrine of Christ (2:1–3:16); the contrast between false and true teachers, and advice to Timothy (4:1–16); how to pastor a church—including relating to different age groups, widows, elders—discernment about sinning members, slaves, false and greedy teachers, personal vigilance, and the wealthy (5:1–6:19); closing exhortation (6:20–21).

PRINCIPLES AND PARTICULARS

Spiritual leadership of the church must be married to personal, practical and holy living. The man of God must watch his own spiritual life and also guard the church from error. Paul's method of teaching the teacher is a good example to mature Christians to help younger men in leadership and to use God's Word as the primary source of teaching. Christians need to avoid not only false teaching, but also a false valuation of their passing material wealth, which should be used for God's glory. This letter gives us a cameo of the identity of Paul as well as insights of how to relate to a junior team member.

I TIMOTHY

CHAPTER ONE

V 1–2: SPIRITUAL SON Paul writes, as an apostle, to his spiritual son, Timothy, and reminds him of the need for grace, mercy and peace from their common Father and Saviour. **V 3–7: FAITHLESS FABLES** Timothy is urged to stay in Ephesus in order to correct the teaching of fables which produces no faith. Edification, love, good conscience, and sincere faith are the results of good doctrine being taken in the right spirit by the hearers. Timothy is to resist those who pervert the truth. **V 8–11: LEGITIMATE LAW** The correct use of law is to show sinful people their need for a Saviour. Sinners of all types need sound teaching in a gospel context. The law gives the foundation to enable the recognition of the need for forgiveness. **V 12–14: GOD'S GRACE** Paul records his thankfulness for God's grace which has saved him from his former life of blasphemy, persecution and insolence, and has put him into Christian service. **V 15–16: 'ALL ACCEPTANCE'** Paul recommends to Timothy a saying which is 'worthy of all acceptance'. It is simply that 'Christ Jesus came into the world to save sinners'. Although Paul sees himself as the chief of sinners, he recognises that, through his conversion, God is showing His longsuffering to other sinners. If God's longsuffering can bring to salvation such a rebel as Paul, this is an encouraging pattern for other sinners, who come to believe on Christ. **V 17: MARVELLOUS MONARCH** The thought of God's grace to Paul leads him to praise Jesus Christ as King, whose attributes belong to God alone. **V 18–20: WAGING WARFARE** Paul urges Timothy to fight the good fight of faith and keep his conscience and his faith as priorities. Others who have rejected

this counsel have shipwrecked their faith. They have been put out of fellowship (the meaning of 'delivered to Satan') so that the sin of blasphemy, resulting from their ignoring of conscience and faith, may be terminated ultimately when the discipline of being put out leads them to repentance and faith.

CHAPTER TWO

V 1–2: ACCESS Paul's first exhortation to Timothy is in the realm of prayer. Nothing is more important than to use this means of grace which gives us access to God. The Christian should pray especially for kings and those in authority, in order that a life that is quiet, peaceful, godly and reverent may be lived. **V 3–7: ALL** In urging Timothy to pray, Paul reminds him that God 'desires all men to be saved and to come to the knowledge of the truth'. Christ 'gave himself a ransom for all', and this involves not only preaching, but praying, which should be done peacefully and faithfully everywhere. The message to preach and to support in prayer is of 'one God, and one Mediator between God and men, the Man Christ Jesus'. **V 8–10: APPROPRIATENESS** While Paul uses the 'lifting up holy hands' as a picture of prayer, he reminds the women that they should be dressed appropriately and that godliness and good works are more important than the outward show of riches and fashion. **V 11–15: AUTHORITY** Paul emphasises the authority of men in leading the church, so that women do not have the role of leaders or teachers in the church. This has been so since creation and was evidenced by Eve's seeking to lead Adam, which led him into his own sin in following her weakness to Satan's temptation. Paul corrects the wrong conclusion of some, however, that because a woman was involved in that, there is now something wrong about childbearing. He confirms that, like anyone else, a mother can know God's salvation. It is demonstrated by resultant 'faith, love, and holiness with self-control'.

CHAPTER THREE

V 1–7: SUPERVISORS The word 'bishop' means overseer or supervisor. Such a man in the church must have well-defined spiritual and practical qualities about which Paul reminds Timothy. No one should be the leader in a church unless God has worked in his heart to give him a mature Christian character. **V 8–13: SERVANTS** The word 'deacon' literally means servant. In the church, they are given specific areas of responsibility which they are to exercise as spiritual service. They, too, must be people of proven spiritual character, and perhaps some of them, with blossoming teaching gifts, will eventually become bishops. **V 14–15: SOON** Paul intends to see Timothy soon, but writes to him now so that he will know how to conduct himself in church matters. **V 16: SAVIOUR** Paul quotes part of an early church hymn, as a testimony to his Saviour, who he confirms is God 'manifested in the flesh'.

CHAPTER FOUR

V 1–5: DECEIT AND DOCTRINE Deceit by satanic forces will lead false teachers to follow false doctrine. They themselves will have seared consciences as a result, causing the promotion of legalistic teaching, opposition to marriage, and eating certain foods, rather than the encouragement and demonstration of real faith in God. **V 6–11: GOOD AND GODLY** A good servant of Christ will teach and be sustained by the good doctrine of God's Word, and reject falsehood and profanity. The spiritual input of God's Word is more important than bodily exercise, because it lasts into eternity. Christ's servants both labour and suffer for their trust in the Saviour, who is to be declared to 'all men'. Paul tells Timothy to preach and teach what is now shared with him. **V 12–16: DEVOTION AND DILIGENCE** As Timothy shows devotion to God's teaching and spiritual inputs, and diligence in discharging the commission given to him, he will be an example to the Christians. How he lives and the attitudes he displays will glorify Christ. Older Christians will not then have any cause to despise his younger years, and he will experience God's salvation on a daily basis as well as helping others to trust the Lord.

CHAPTER FIVE

V 1–2: APPROPRIATENESS OF ATTITUDES Paul tells the younger man, Timothy, to treat older Christians with great respect, as parents, and younger women as sisters, demonstrating purity. **V 3–16: WISDOM ABOUT WIDOWS** Godly widows of sixty years or over, who have proved their faithfulness to God in their lives, should be cared for if there are no children or grandchildren to care for them. However, younger capable widows should be encouraged to work, as this aid is not to be used as an excuse for irresponsible women to be free to waste their time and their energy in trivial pursuits. Believers should look after the widows in their families. **V 17–20: ESTEEMING THE ELDERS** Elders who rule well should be doubly honoured, especially those who 'labour in the word and doctrine'. They should be supported materially and no accusation should be heard unless there are two or three witnesses prepared to testify properly. Open sin should be rebuked openly. **V 21–22: PREJUDICE AND PURITY** Prejudice and partiality should not affect the objective dealing with people who need to be disciplined or challenged. But Timothy needs to be careful to keep himself pure and not to be tainted by the sins of others. **V 23: SENSE ABOUT SICKNESS** Timothy's frequent stomach troubles could have been caused by impure water. Paul sanctions the use of 'a little wine' medicinally. **V 24–25: CAREFUL ABOUT CANDIDATES** Timothy needs to be aware that both those who sin publicly and those later known to have sinned privately are accountable. This is probably written in the context of Timothy's quest to appoint spiritual men as elders in the church. Whether such candidates are gifted or not is clearly secondary. If they fall at the first and most important hurdles of obedience and spirituality, they cannot be considered.

CHAPTER SIX

V 1–2: SLAVES The word 'bond servants' means 'slaves'. They are told to honour their masters so that God will be glorified. They must not take unfair advantage of Christian masters who bestow great benefits coming from their Christian character. Timothy is to insist on this. (Some slaves became more privileged and better supported than many free people.) **V 3–5: SEPARATION** Timothy is to separate himself from those who have selfish, corrupt and ungodly attitudes and lifestyles which cause them to seek gain rather than godliness. **V 6–10: STRAYING** Carrying on with the thought of gain, Paul tells Timothy that some have strayed from the faith, and injured themselves, because of a love of money. Godliness brings its own contentment. Paul advocates a simple lifestyle with gratitude for needs being met, and a desire to glorify God. **V 11–16: SPOTLESS** Timothy, as a man of God, is to flee all spiritually harmful influences and seek the qualities and characteristics which are consistent with the 'good fight of faith'. He is to seek to be kept spotless and blameless in the view of Christ's appearing. He is to remember the coming appearing, the holiness and the greatness of his 'King of kings and Lord of lords'. **V 17–19: SHARING** Timothy is to tell the rich Christians, for whom all their riches have come from God, that they should be willing to share with others and invest in eternal life. **V 20–21: STEWARD** That which has been committed to the stewardship trust of Timothy is to be protected from any teaching that would pollute it. Some have strayed through those polluted teachings and Paul prays for God's grace for his protégé.

2 TIMOTHY

OVERVIEW

PEOPLE AND PRELIMINARIES

✸ 2 Timothy (6 chapters) is the eleventh of Paul's letters, the second of his pastoral letters and the second one to Timothy. **See comments on 1 Timothy.** He wrote it between AD64 and AD68 from Rome, where he was in prison for the second time.

PLAN AND PURPOSE

(i) Both the letters to Timothy and the letter to Titus are written for leaders and pastors of all ages. Not only do they remind Christians in authority of their need to live close to Christ and His Word, but they instruct them in the discharge of their responsibilities in leading the church and helping Christians. 2 Timothy continues some of the themes of 1 Timothy and majors on the need to be bold and faithful, and to serve and teach faithfully, as false teachers extend their ungodly influence. Paul's close relationship with Timothy is evident as he stresses the need to study God's Word, to stay faithful, and be aware that 'the last days' will usher in increased spiritual and moral wickedness and darkness. Paul faces the prospect of his imminent death and gives his closing instructions and testimony to his younger protégé. See also comments on 1 Timothy.

PROFILE AND PROGRESSION

Opening greetings and thanksgiving (1:1–5); encouragement towards boldness and faithfulness encouraged by Onesiphorus's example (1:6–18); what a Christian leader should be—including a good soldier, a competitive athlete, an industrious farmer, faithfully tenacious, an approved worker, an analyser of Scripture, an honourable vessel, a fugitive from temptation, and a gentle servant (2:1–26); things to beware of, and how to continue (3:1–17); what and how to preach in the light of Paul's expected departure (4:1–8); Paul's personal needs and concerns, and his faithful Lord (4:9–18); final greetings (4:19–22).

PRINCIPLES AND PARTICULARS

Paul's concerns, as he expects to die soon, are focused on the continuance of his younger Christian brother with the Lord and in the work of God. This is like a father's deathbed speech to his son, urging on him the things that matter most, while rejoicing in his faithful God and his crown of righteousness which he will receive from the Lord. So the need as a Christian leader to uphold truth, teach against error, and show the pattern for living are priorities. Paul has only a few humble personal requests, and nowhere else in the Bible does he ask for anything for himself, thus showing the intimacy he shared spiritually with his son in the faith. Even in this, he spends more space on other people, showing his fatherly heart for the church and for others.

2 TIMOTHY

CHAPTER ONE

V 1–2: BELOVED Although writing with apostolic authority, Paul salutes Timothy with his usual, heartfelt greeting, calling him 'a beloved son'. Paul takes a fatherly interest in Timothy, notwithstanding his existing spiritual maturity and leadership ability. **V 3–7: BACKGROUND** He prays daily for Timothy, greatly desiring to see him. He is joyful in recalling the godly example of Timothy's mother and grandmother that brought him to faith in Christ. Paul's spiritual fatherhood role encourages him through discipleship to maturing leadership. He urges him to serve by stirring up God's gift in service with a fearless, powerful and loving mind from God. **V 8–12: BEATEN!** Jesus Christ has beaten death, and through the gospel has brought 'life and immortality to light'. Paul is neither ashamed of the gospel nor of his Saviour, who will keep him through life and eternity, despite his own imprisonment in Rome. He urges Timothy not to be ashamed of him either, but to share in his sufferings. **V 13–14: BASIS** Timothy must hold the pattern of sound teaching given him by Paul through faith and love in Christ. Timothy's gift of ministry and service, and his commission to serve Christ, is to be kept through the Holy Spirit who dwells in them both. **V 15: BEREFT** Paul relates to Timothy that all those in Asia turned away from him, including Phygellus and Hermogenes. Sometimes it is a lonely task to be a Christian leader and gospel preacher. **V 16–18: BOLSTERED** But Paul has been bolstered by the refreshment gained from the household of Onesiphorus, who 'zealously' sought Paul out in Rome to minister to him as he had done at Ephesus. Paul commends to God his unashamed, supportive and faithful co-worker in the gospel.

CHAPTER TWO

V 1: GRACIOUS STRENGTH Paul encourages his son in the faith to be 'strong in the grace that is in Christ Jesus'. **V 2: GENERATE SUCCESSORS** Just as Timothy has heard God's truth from Paul, he is to commit the same message to faithful men in order that they may teach others. He is to seek to generate leadership successors, by God's grace. **V 3–7: GODLY SIMILARITIES** Timothy must endure hardship as Christ's good soldier and not get entangled with the affairs of this life, but please his commanding officer, God. A Christian is like a competitive athlete who will not get his crown unless he keeps the rules in competing. He is also like a hard-working

farmer whose effort will be rewarded by benefiting from the harvest. He prays that God will give him understanding to apply these truths. **V 8–10: GOSPEL SUFFERING** Paul's imprisonment is because of his proclamation that Jesus Christ has risen from the dead. He is prepared to endure suffering for the sake of others who will come to know salvation in Christ. **V 11–13: GREAT SAVIOUR** Paul then quotes a saying emphasising the Christian's death-to-self life, risen life, endurance, reign to come, and the need to remain faithful to Him and not to deny Him. All this is based on a wonderful and great Saviour who 'remains faithful'. **V 14–18: GRASP SCRIPTURE** Rather than following fruitless and unprofitable works, Timothy is urged to work at rightly dividing God's truth so that he will not be ashamed. This will help him to reject false teaching, such as that of two named men who claim that the final resurrection has already passed. **V 19: GOD'S SEAL** God's seal of truth on a Christian is based on the fact that God knows those who belong to Him and that personal conversion is made evident by turning from iniquity. Assurance of salvation is based on God's faithfulness and demonstrated by a changed life. **V 20–23: GOD'S SERVICE** Christians are like vessels in God's house and must be clean in order to be used for God's honour, and be ready for Him to use. Righteousness, faith, love and peace must be pursued along with other people in fellowship, but youthful lusts and divisive discussion must be rejected and keenly avoided. **V 24–26: GENTLE SERVANT** God's servant must not be quarrelsome, but gentle and patiently humble while teaching others, even if they oppose him. In this way, they may come to know God's truth, wake up to reality, and be liberated from the devil through God's salvation.

CHAPTER THREE

V 1-5: TUMULTUOUS TIMES The last days will be perilous and tumultuous, with all kinds of evil and sin prevailing. Pleasure will be regarded as more important than godliness by many. Timothy is to turn away from those espousing such values and practices. **V 6-9: CREEPING CAPTORS** Those who teach false doctrine always learn yet never understand the truth. They are marked by sexual immorality with gullible women. As Moses resisted Pharaoh's magicians, so these men must be resisted. Like those magicians, their lack of progress towards God will be seen by all. **V 10-12: DIVINE DELIVERER** In living an exemplary Christian life, Paul has been persecuted and yet has been conscious of the Lord's deliverance for him. All who have a desire to live a godly life in Christ will also be persecuted. **V 13-15: OBVIOUS OPPOSITES** As evil men and impostors get worse and worse, both in their deception and in their self-deception, the Christian must continue in the Word of God and in Christ, demonstrating an obvious opposite lifestyle to those men. **V 16-17: INFALLIBLE INSPIRATION** All Scripture is breathed out by God and is profitable for teaching, reproof, correction, and righteous instruction, so that God's man might be completely equipped to work for his Master.

CHAPTER FOUR

V 1-5: PREACHING PRIORITY Bearing in mind that Jesus will come as judge, Timothy is told to 'Preach the word!' This he must do all the time with different approaches but always 'with all long-suffering and teaching'. Men will prefer made up fables and things they want to hear rather than the sound doctrine of God's Word. Timothy must be watchful, persevering, working as an evangelist, and fulfilling his ministry. **V 6-8: FACING FUTURE** Paul knows that death is near, but, looking back upon the fight that he has fought and the race that he has run, he concentrates on the crown that God has promised to him and to all who love His appearing. His eye is on the tape! **V 9-16: ABANDONED APOSTLE** Paul is abandoned with only Luke at his side. Of those who have left him, a few—Crescens, Titus and Tychicus—have moved on in the Lord's service elsewhere. Demas, however, has finally backslidden into the world and abandoned Paul. Mark is now a useful support to Paul in his service to God, and Timothy is to bring him. Paul also asks for a cloak and some books and parchments. In the face of earlier strong opposition from Alexander and others, Paul records that he stood alone, forsaken by all. **V 17-18: PRESERVED PREACHER** God preserved His preacher even when he was alone, so that he might fully preach the Gospel to all the Gentiles. Just as he was delivered from the lion's mouth of cruel and evil opposition, he is confident that he will be delivered eternally as well by the God he seeks to glorify. **V 19-22: FAITHFUL FRIENDS** He sends greetings to and presents greetings from his Christian family members. Timothy is included in his greetings as Paul prays for Christ's presence and grace to be his.

TITUS

PEOPLE AND PRELIMINARIES

✳ Titus (three chapters) is the twelfth of Paul's letters and the third of his pastoral letters. **See comments on 1 Timothy.** He wrote it between AD62 and AD64 from Macedonia.

PLAN AND PURPOSE

ⓘ Titus concentrates on the church order to be established and Titus' commission to do that, the qualifications for spiritual leadership in the church, dealing with erroneous teachers, and pastoral work. In it we see Christian living and responsibility, sound doctrine, the need for salvation to be shown by good works, and church discipline. See also comments on 1 Timothy.

PROFILE AND PROGRESSION

Greetings emphasising the need to preach God's Word (1:1–4); Titus in Crete to organise the church and appoint elders and resist false teachers (1:5–16); Titus to instruct regarding practical Christian living and sound teaching in the church, looking to God's grace, Christ's coming, living under authority in a sinful world, and dealing with contentious people (2:1–3:12); final requests and farewell (3:12–15).

PRINCIPLES AND PARTICULARS

☛ The need for godly leadership in the church of Christ is the pivot in this letter. The basis for personal and communal spirituality is submission to God's Word, linking salvation and service, saving faith and works, God's working and pastoral activity, church purity and witness in the world. In this short book is teaching on God's election, saving grace, provision of substitutionary atonement, regeneration and renewing, the deity and second coming of Christ.

TITUS

CHAPTER ONE

V 1–4: INTRODUCTORY REMARKS Paul, bond servant and apostle, writes to his spiritual son Titus, and sends him Christian greetings having emphasised the importance of faith, truth, godliness, eternal life, God's faithfulness, preaching His Word, and his own commission to obey his Saviour. **V 5–9: IMPORTANT RESPONSIBILITIES** Titus had been left in Crete to help organise the churches in each city and appoint elders. Elders (the same as bishops) are to be spiritually mature and godly men whose essential characteristics and abilities are spelled out to Titus by Paul. Theirs is an important responsibility in the churches, and so is that of Titus in appointing them on Paul's behalf. They must be able to hold, teach and defend the truth of God's Word. **V 10–16: INTERNAL REBELS** Insubordinate, idle, deceiving, self-seeking, false teachers—many of whom are Jewish legalists—are to be opposed and rebuked, so that the Christians acquire a soundness in the faith of God. Jewish fables and man-made commands are to be opposed. The false teachers' wicked, self-seeking, materialistic and disobedient lifestyles disqualify them from any good work, obviously including eldership, as they profess to know God but show by the way they live that they do not.

CHAPTER TWO

V 1: TEACH TRUTH Titus must speak things which are appropriate to sound teaching from God's truth. **V 2–8: ALL AGES** In a wide-ranging panorama of the church, each age range of people is to be taught and exhorted to follow God's work and to honour Him in what they think and say. **V 9–10: SUBMISSIVE SLAVES** Slaves are to obey their masters, without answering back, and show faithfulness that adorns God's Word. **V 11–14: GOD'S GRACE** God's grace has caused His salvation to be offered to all men. The evidence of acceptance of God's offer is a sober, holy, and righteous lifestyle, a looking for the appearing of the Lord Jesus Christ, an appreciation of His redemptive death on the cross, and a purity and zeal that mark His people out as different. **V 15: CONSISTENT CONDUCT** In speaking, exhorting and rebuking with God's authority, Titus is to live in such a way that no one will despise him because of any lack of correlation between his lifestyle and his teaching and preaching.

CHAPTER THREE

V 1–2: ACCEPT AUTHORITY Church members are to be told to accept lawful authority and to be ready to do good works. They must live peaceably and gently, speaking no evil and showing humility to all men. **V 3–8: CONVERSION CONDUCT** Paul reminds Titus of the shameful and wicked ways that he and they lived before coming to know Christ. But God's kindness and love in Christ have changed that, through His mercy, His cleansing and the work of His Holy Spirit in response to faith in Jesus Christ. Because of God's grace, which has justified repentant sinners, they should now maintain good works, and Titus must teach this because it is good and profitable for them all. **V 9–11: DAMAGING DIVISIONS** Foolish disputes and unprofitable discussions which are going nowhere, and lead to strife, are to be avoided. A person causing division is to be warned twice only. If he still continues in his selfishness and sin, he is then to be rejected. The implication is that church discipline should then exclude him until repentance and faith are manifested. **V 12–14: SUPPORTING SAINTS** Paul looks forward to a visit from Titus soon, and briefs him on the itineraries of some of his co-labourers in the gospel. He urges Titus to make sure that God's saints are supported in their needs, lacking nothing. The church people must also maintain good works to meet their needs, and thus be fruitful. **V 15: GRACIOUS GREETINGS** Again, Paul ends one of his letters by sending the greetings of all with him and asking Titus to greet all who love him in the faith. They need what he wants for them, namely God's grace.

PHILEMON

OVERVIEW

PEOPLE AND PRELIMINARIES

✳ Philemon (one chapter) is the thirteenth of Paul's letters and the fourth and last of his pastoral letters. **See comments on 1 Timothy.** He wrote it between AD60 and AD62 from prison in Rome.

PLAN AND PURPOSE

ⓘ A runaway slave, Onesimus, became a Christian in Rome when he met Paul. His deprived master, Philemon, had also been saved under Paul's earlier ministry. This is a letter from Paul asking the master to take back the converted slave, who has been 'profitable' to Paul in his imprisonment in Rome, not as a slave, now, but as a brother. Paul does not write from the lofty heights of apostolic authority, but as one caring brother in Christ to another, pleading for another member of God's family. He graciously uses a powerful argument, but does hint that he could demand obedience, without actually demanding it!

PROFILE AND PROGRESSION

🐚 Gracious greetings (1:1–3); appreciation of Philemon (1:4–7); plea for Onesimus (1:8–16); Paul's personal concern and touch (1:17–22); final greetings (1:23–25).

PRINCIPLES AND PARTICULARS

👉 The courtesy, grace, logic and care taken by Paul to plead for the slave

with the master give an excellent example of how someone in authority can appeal for co-operation rather than seek to impose his authority autocratically. The reflection of the gospel illustrated incidentally by this action is unmistakable, as the humble apostle asks Philemon to transfer any debt of Onesimus to Paul's own account. The need of respected leaders to care for those of low profile and the fact that all Christians are brothers on level ground before their Saviour are lovely emphases. May we follow Paul's example of always being involved in personal witness in all circumstances to all people, high and low. It seems that every individual was important to him, spiritually and personally.

PHILEMON

V 1–3: PEOPLE Paul, the prisoner, and Timothy, his brother in Christ, write to Philemon, Apphia, Archippus, and to the church in Philemon's house. He desires God's grace and peace for the beloved recipients who have laboured and fought along with him in the gospel. **V 4–7: PRAYERS** Paul always thanks God for them in his prayers because of the effect of Jesus on them, causing them to share their faith effectively. Philemon also has given great joy because of his refreshing of the Christians. **V 8–16: PLEA** Paul now pleads with Philemon about a runaway slave, Onesimus, who has come to faith in Christ through Paul, and whom Paul regards as a spiritual son. He explains how profitable to him Onesimus has become. (His name means 'profitable'.) He urges Philemon to accept him back as a brother in Christ, and not as a slave. **V 17–20: PARTNER** Paul speaks not from high ground as an apostle, but from level ground as a partner in Christ. He offers to pay anything to Philemon that is owing to him from Onesimus. He reminds Philemon that he, too, has come to blessing through Paul. **V 21–22: PREPARE** Paul's letter is not instead of personal contact, but to make that contact more meaningful. He asks for hospitality and for prayer that he will be able to visit Philemon soon. **V 23–25: PRISONERS** He and Epaphras are prisoners for Christ. They greet Philemon along with other named fellow labourers, praying that God's grace will be with Philemon.

HEBREWS

OVERVIEW

PEOPLE AND PRELIMINARIES

✳The author of Hebrews (thirteen chapters) is not named or directly identified. If Paul wrote it, and opinion is divided upon this point, Hebrews would be his fourteenth letter. **See comments on 1 Timothy.** The divine authorship of this instructive letter is never in doubt. God the Holy Spirit inspired the writer to send God's Word to scattered Jewish recipients who had received the gospel before the persecution that dispersed them from Palestine. It was possibly written between AD67 and AD69 from Italy, and perhaps from Rome.

PLAN AND PURPOSE

ⓘHebrews is written to scattered and persecuted Jews, probably mainly in Italy, to encourage them about the rock solid nature of faith in Christ, which is firmly based on God's revelation and His fulfilling the promises of the Old Testament. Before their dispersion from Palestine, they received the gospel. The book of Hebrews warns and urges any lingering on the borders of salvation to enter by faith in Christ, or face God's judgement. Those who have entered into forgiveness are assured of their salvation and encouraged to persevere. Hebrews provides an amazing and inspiring analysis of salvation through Christ, and illustrates vividly the need and comforts of faith in Him and in God's promises. This book is truly Christ-centred in all its teaching. The key thought is 'better'. The word itself is used twelve times and demonstrated many times more. Salvation in Christ is so much better than everything in Judaism, all of which was intended to prepare for and point to Christ. Jesus has a better name, is better than the angels, is better than Moses, gives a better rest, is better than the Aaronic priesthood, provides a better covenant, enters a better sanctuary through the better blood of a better sacrifice which gives better hope and security. Other 'better' things are the results of salvation, hope, promises, possessions in Christ, heavenly country, resurrection and provision for the Christian. The key to all this is faith in Christ, which is illustrated in principle by the men and women of faith who are listed in the gallery of faith in chapter 11.

PROFILE AND PROGRESSION

Christ has a better name (1:1–3); Christ is better than the angels (1:4–2:18); Christ is better than Moses (3:1–19); Christ gives a better rest (4:1–13); Christ is a better priest (4:14–7:28); Christ provides a better covenant (8:1–13); Christ entered a better sanctuary (9:1–10); Christ provides a better sacrifice with better blood (9:11–10:18); Christ gives better assurance through faith, and the need to proceed through to appropriate that faith (10:19–39); the nature of faith, the gallery of faith, the cost of faith, the race of faith, and Jesus as the object of faith (11:1–12:3); chastening as an evidence of true faith, perseverance and godly reverence (12:4–13:25).

PRINCIPLES AND PARTICULARS

Hebrews is the best commentary ever written on the Old Testament sacrifices, priesthood, covenant and promises. It clearly shows the Lord Jesus Christ as fulfilling all these, and much more. The finished work of Christ is striking, as the final High Priest offering the final sacrifice on the final altar at Calvary. So much more of the eternal nature and deity of God the Son and the true nature of faith are included in this book of doctrine which inspires the Christian reader to leave sin and weights behind to follow his Saviour and Lord. This is the book to recommend to any searching person from the Jewish faith. Open minded non-Jews also will be amazed at its contents if they study them honestly.

HEBREWS

CHAPTER ONE

V 1–4: RADIANT REVELATION God has revealed Himself by prophets in the past. Now He has revealed Himself by His eternal Son, Jesus Christ, who, being God, radiates deity just as the sun's rays radiate the sun. The key word in Hebrews is 'better', and here Jesus is seen as better than the angels. **V 5: SUPERNATURAL SON** From eternity, Jesus is the supernatural, begotten Son of God. Thus He is both the Son of God and God the Son. **V 6–7: WILLING WORSHIP** Only God can be worshipped, according to the Bible. As the very angels of heaven are told to worship Jesus, clearly He is God. **V 8–9: GREAT GOD** The Father addresses Him as 'O God', and yet Jesus has an eternal filial relationship within the Trinity with God the Father. This mystery is unfathomable by the mere human mind without the illuminating teaching of God's revelation in Scripture. **V 10–12: CREATION'S CLOAK** Jesus, within the Trinity, created the world, and one day will fold it up like a cloak. **V 13–14: MIGHTY MONARCH** The Father's will is that the Son should reign from the right of the throne. Compare this with the angels who are simply there to minister to those who will become saved.

CHAPTER TWO

V 1–4: SALVATION The Hebrew readers are told that they must give careful consideration to what they hear lest they 'neglect so great a salvation'. God has confirmed that great salvation historically with signs and wonders through the Holy Spirit. The danger of neglecting His salvation and facing judgement applies to all. **V 5–9: SON** The quotation from Psalm 8 refers to mankind being made 'a little lower than the angels'. The eternal Son of God, in appearing in flesh as the Son of Man, also was made lower than the angels for the task He had to do on earth. Having died on the cross for our sins and risen again, He is now crowned with glory and honour. By God's grace, He did this that

He 'might taste death for everyone'. **V 10–16: SONS** Because Jesus completed His work through the suffering of the cross, He can bring 'many sons to glory'. This includes all who trust in Him and become children of God. Because Jesus came to take on flesh to save us and to die for us, He has defeated the devil and takes away the fear of death from those who put their trust in the living Saviour. **V 17–18: SACRIFICE** Jesus is the 'faithful High Priest' who offered Himself as a sacrifice on the cross. Despite being tempted, He suffered there, taking the punishment of our sins to make propitiation for them. Today He is not only able to save, but also able to help those who are tempted.

CHAPTER THREE

V 1–6: BETTER BUILDER Jesus is better than Moses through whom the law came. Moses was part of the house of Israel, but Jesus is the builder of it as the Son of God. Moses was a servant, but Jesus is a Son, as well as a faithful High Priest. The builder is greater than the house He builds. **V 7–15: EXHORTATION ESSENTIAL** Because in the past Israel has sinned, been hardened, and been rejected by God, it is essential for the scattered Jews to exhort one another to make sure that they are not being deceived by sin, but that they really are turning from it and trusting Christ. The principle of exhortation for blessing applies even to Christians who lovingly look out for one another and are prepared to be truthful with one another. Christian exhortation is one of God's antidotes to evil, unbelieving hearts and it can spur the person exhorted to immediate repentance. **V 16–18: HEARTS HARDENED** We are reminded that those who came out of Egypt hardened their hearts, disobeyed, and were unable to enter into

the promised land. Hard hearts and unbelief always prevent God's gracious blessings in our lives.

CHAPTER FOUR

V 1–11: REST REMAINING There is no personal rest without responding to the gospel message by faith in Christ. There is a weekly rest, in remembering the Sabbath day, now the Lord's day. There was a Canaan rest for the children of Israel when Joshua led them into the promised land. There is rest from the guilt of sin for anyone who trusts Christ. But there is a rest remaining in heaven for those who renounce trust in their own work and trust in the work of God in redemption. It is vitally and eternally important to enter into that rest by faith. **V 12–13: REVEALING REVELATION** The written revelation of God, the Word of God, is alive and judges even the thoughts and attitudes of the hearts of men and women. The Bible reveals what our hearts are really like when we let its searchlight focus on our lives. God sees everything, and all must give account to Him. **V 14–16: REASSURING RELATIONSHIP** Converted Jew and converted Gentile have a great High Priest who is in heaven now. He sympathises with weak sinners and gives us mercy and grace to help in our need. Although we come humbly to His throne of grace, we are to come 'boldly' because He has commanded it.

CHAPTER FIVE

V 1–4: COMPASSION OF HIGH PRIEST A high priest needed to be identified with sinners so that he could have compassion for them. A high priest had to be called by God, as Aaron was. **V 5–11: COMPLIANCE OF HIGH PRIEST** Jesus, as the Son, was called by God according to the order of

Melchizedek. This meant that He had neither start nor finish to His life, and that He continues forever. He learned obedience by experience, especially when He suffered on the cross, so that He could perfect those who trust Him. At no stage was He ever disobedient. He was compliant, in every sense, with the will of His Father. **V 12–14: CONCERN OVER HESITANT PROGRESS** Despite all this, the spiritual immaturity of some of the Hebrew Christians concerns the writer. They should be growing in grace and moving from a baby diet of milk on to more solid meat. However, they are hesitant in their progress, and still lack discernment and maturity. A person can be a Christian for a long time, without ever becoming a mature Christian. Spiritual maturity is to do with faith and commitment, not with longevity!

CHAPTER SIX

V 1–3: PROGRESS The readers are urged to progress from the foundational truths of the gospel in order to get to know God better. They are not told to abandon those truths, but to go on from them, as a boat would leave the harbour. It still needs that harbour! **V 4–6: PARTAKERS** There are those who come to the very edge of faith in Christ and even partake of some of the Holy Spirit's blessings (partake literally means 'to go along with') without ever having turned to Christ. Their hearts have become hardened by tasting God's Word without taking it in, and by skirmishing around the border instead of entering into the blessing. **V 7–8: PARABLE** The parable used here, of thorns and brambles coming up from the ground, reminds us that our fruit will show whether we are truly saved or not. **V 9–12: PERSUADED** The writer, however, tells his readers that he is confident that they are saved and that

there are things that accompany their salvation that he has noticed. This includes labouring in love for other Christians. He urges them to be diligent to walk with God day by day, through faith and patience, inheriting God's promises. **V 13–18: PURPOSE** Just as God confirmed His word and intentions through Abraham, He has confirmed it through His promise and His oath, fulfilled in Jesus Christ. **V 19–20: PRESENCE** The Christian's sure hope is anchored, as is his soul, in the presence of Jesus Christ in heaven. Like an anchor securing a boat, Jesus is there to ensure that those who trust in Him will be there with Him.

CHAPTER SEVEN

V 1–10: PICTURED PRIEST Melchizedek is a type of Christ. Many believe that he was an Old Testament appearance of the Lord Jesus Christ (known as a theophany). He was the king of righteousness and peace. His being started without his having any human father or mother. Thus he had no antecedents, nor end of life. He was made 'like the Son of God' and 'remains a priest continually'. Abraham, the father of those who are saved through faith, gave him tithes, indicating the greatness of Melchizedek. Jesus is pictured in all this typology, even if Melchizedek is not a theophany. **V 11–19: PERFECTED PRIEST** The Levitical system could not produce a perfect priest. Jesus is a better priest than Aaron. His power comes not from the line of descent, but from the 'power of an endless life' as he rose again from the dead and ascended into heaven. Because He is perfect, He enables us to 'draw near to God'. **V 20–25: PERMANENT PRIEST** God has sworn an oath to confirm the priesthood of Jesus Christ who has become the surety of a better covenant.

He lives for ever and is unchangeable. He always intercedes for us. He is our permanent Priest. **V 26–28: PRE-EMINENT PRIEST** Unlike all the other priests, Jesus is sinlessly perfect and higher than the heavens. With no sins of His own to necessitate a sacrifice, He could offer Himself as a spotless sacrifice for all sinners who would come to Him.

CHAPTER EIGHT

V 1–2: MAJESTY Our High Priest is 'at the right hand of the throne of the Majesty' above. That sanctuary is not man-made. **V 3–6: MEDIATOR** Jesus is a mediator of a better covenant than the other priests. Their gifts and sacrifices were only shadows of things to come. His covenant is established on better promises, since He promised Himself to bear our sins and to be our High Priest. **V 7–13: MERCY** The first covenant was limited in its application. By the second covenant, God will deal with the hearts of men and women and they will know Him and the ultimate mercy of God. He will remember no longer their sins and lawless deeds. Mercy, both objectively and shown in the heart of the believer, marks the covenant established by Christ, who takes over from the Old Testament covenants.

CHAPTER NINE

V 1–5: SETTING The setting for the first covenant to be performed was a tabernacle containing the furniture designated by God. Inside were the two veils, the second of which hid from sight the Holy of holies and, among other things, the ark of the covenant containing the manna, Aaron's rod that budded, and the Ten Commandments. The mercy seat was above that. **V 6–10: SERVICE** The service of the priesthood was conducted

in the setting described above. Once a year, the high priest would go and offer a sacrifice for sins at the mercy seat in the Holy of holies. This was symbolic of forgiveness of sins, but could never really remove them. **V 11–15: SUPERIOR** The superiority of Christ as High Priest is that He shed His own blood and offered it through the eternal Spirit without spot to God. Because of this, consciences can be cleansed and saved people can serve the living God. This new covenant redemption, with Jesus as the Mediator, brings eternal life, and is obviously better than anything under the old covenant. **V 16–23: SHEDDING** Death was needed under the old regime, just as the death of a testator is needed to validate a will. But the old covenant could only give a picture of what forgiveness and access was like, through the sprinkling of the shed blood of the animals. **V 23–28: SACRIFICE** However, Jesus Christ Himself, the great High Priest who now lives in heaven for us, offered His own life and His own blood when He died once on the cross to take our judgement. Having borne our sins once, the day is coming when He will return again without sin. The final act in salvation is yet to occur, notwithstanding that every Christian can know now that he is saved, having already escaped judgement.

CHAPTER TEN

V 1–4: REGULAR REMINDER The regular sacrifice and entry by the high priest was an annual reminder that sins had to be forsaken and forgiven. The need to repeat the sacrifice often shows that those sacrifices could never remove sin. **V 5–10: BIBLICAL BASIS** When God came to earth in a human body which would become a sacrifice for sins, prophecies of Scripture were fulfilled. **V 11–18: SINGLE**

SACRIFICE The Old Testament priests made many sacrifices. But Jesus has made 'one sacrifice for sins for ever and sat down at the right hand of God'. Thus 'there is no longer any offering for sin'. Either a sinner is saved through Christ, or he is not saved at all. Evidence of salvation includes God's laws being written in his heart. **V 19–23: COME CONFIDENTLY** Because of the 'new and living way' which Jesus has made for us through His flesh, into heaven, we can come with boldness, knowing that we are cleansed and accepted by our faithful God. Boldness is not the same as presumption! **V 24—25: ENCOURAGING EXHORTATIONS** It is important to encourage one another to live for Christ, and to have regular fellowship and worship together. Time is short. **V 26–38: ENDURANCE EVIDENT** Because 'there no longer remains a sacrifice for sins' other than the finished work of Christ on the cross, Jews or Gentiles will be lost if they trample that sacrifice underfoot. As in this passage, people can go to the very edge of conversion and even experience the influence of the Holy Spirit, without getting saved. One can experience all those overtures of God's love and yet still trample on the shed blood of Christ, incurring God's judgement. The test of conversion is endurance in Christ, which shows that a real work has been done. The ground of conversion is the death of Christ on the cross for us. **V 29: SOULS SAVED** Notwithstanding the solemn warning of the preceding verses, we can know that 'we are not of those that draw back to perdition, but of those who believe to the saving of the soul'. Blessed assurance!

CHAPTER ELEVEN

V   1–2:   FAITH—UNDENIABLE

CONSTITUENTS Faith is based on substance and evidence. These things, which gave Israel's elders a good testimony, were no less true because they were eternal and invisible. They were from God. **V 3: FAITH—UNDERSTANDING CREATION** God's creation of the world from nothing is based on faith in the word of Almighty God, who, by definition, could do what He chose to do. **V 4–12: FAITH—UNFORGETABLE CHARACTERS** Abel, Enoch, Noah, Abraham, and Sarah, are all taken as evidences of God's blessing on even weak people who put their trust in Him. Faith is always rewarded when it is put in God. **V 13–16: FAITH—UNCOMPLICATED CONFESSION** The Old Testament saints, mentioned above, received none of the promises that we have in the New Testament, but saw them afar off, through the principles of God at work, confidently took them and embraced them personally, and confessed by mouth and by their lifestyle, that they were following God as strangers and pilgrims on this earth. Simple faith makes an uncomplicated confession of trust in, and following of the Lord. Their eyes are on heaven. God is not ashamed of them and has prepared heaven for them! **V 17–22: FAITH—UNDERLYING CONTEXT** The whole context of faith is based on Israel's Patriarchs, Abraham, Isaac, and Jacob. It is further demonstrated by Israel's first human saviour, Joseph. God had promised that He would count the faith of Abraham as righteousness. Abraham even believed that God could raise Isaac from the dead when, in obedience, he was willing to sacrifice him if God required it. God did not require it, but, figuratively, did raise him from the dead by providing a ram as a sacrifice in his place. In faith, Isaac's blessing of Jacob and Esau extended into the future, as did Jacob's later blessing of Joseph's sons. Joseph, too, followed the steps of faith of the Patriarchs in his dying instructions. **V 23–29: FAITH— UNCOMPROMISING CHOICES** Moses is the next person featured in this catalogue of faith. He made uncompromising choices because his faith looked to his invisible God and caused him to follow Him. Thus he had a great effect on the children of Israel, leading them out of Egypt through the Red Sea, also keeping the Passover by faith. **V 30–38: FAITH— UNFLINCHING COMMITMENT** Many other believers are commended for their faith which enabled them to stay faithful to God in the face of cruel opposition and persecution. Seven are named, but most of them are anonymous. Some were delivered from their ordeal, while others, through faith, accepted sickening torture and cruel martyrdom in a way that glorified God and witnessed to others. Although God blessed them and helped them all, we are told that 'the world was not worthy' of them. Under God, these people should be our real heroes, not today's celebrities of stage, screen, music, sport and politics. **V 39–40: FAITH— UNBEATABLE CLIMAX** Although the testimony of these faithful followers was good, we are privileged to have received 'something better', namely the clear gospel promise that was unavailable to them in such clarity. For this reason, one day we will be perfected with these people whose faith was in God.

CHAPTER TWELVE

V 1–2: ENCOURAGING ENDURANCE Before the encouraging and watching cloud of witnesses encountered in chapter eleven, every Christian should refuse sin and anything that hinders progress, to look to Jesus in the race of endurance. Through the shame and the cross, Christ

has gone before to the right hand of the throne. We look to Him there. **V 3–13: DIVINE DISCIPLINE** Jesus was weary and suffered much in coming to earth to be our Saviour and Lord. Christians should have confidence in suffering while experiencing God's overruling and sovereign chastening, which is for our good now and produces peace and righteous fruit in the days ahead. Although not a joyful experience at the time, divine discipline is a sign of our sonship from on high. First we should strengthen ourselves in Christ, and then keep on going straight ahead. **V 14–29: HEEDING HOLINESS** In pursuing peace with others and avoiding bitterness, holiness is essential. We need to be holy to resist a sinful attitude and lifestyle and to know and commune with God. Esau's unholy failure, and the need for awesome reverence in approaching the mountain when God communed with Moses, are Old Testament examples which illustrate these principles. There was fear on the mountain when Moses received the Ten Commandments because God is holy and to be reverentially feared. We have a Mediator who shed His blood to bring us close to God, the Judge. Through Him, we are 'registered in heaven' and will be there with the angels and all who are saved. We should ask for grace, to show reverence, to listen to His voice, and to serve Him with reverence and godly fear. He is a 'consuming fire'.

CHAPTER THIRTEEN

V 1–7: IMPORTANT ISSUES After so much good doctrine centred on the 'better' things mentioned in this book, Christians are urged to better living by practising brotherly love, showing hospitality, remembering those in prison, honouring marriage and marital purity, avoiding covetousness, and remembering those in authority. God's ever present help will enable them. **V 8–16: CHRISTIAN CONSISTENCY** Given that 'Jesus Christ is the same yesterday, today and forever', they are told also to be consistent in their doctrine of God's grace and in their conduct. They are to refuse 'various and strange' legalistic teachings about foods. They must focus on Christ's self-giving sacrifice on the altar of Calvary. Jesus suffered and died 'outside the gate'. Christians following Him, therefore, are to bear His reproach willingly. Continual thanksgiving, doing good to others, and sharing are 'sacrifices' that please God. **V 17: ACCEPT AUTHORITY** They are reminded that those in authority in the church are accountable for the well-being of the flock. The submissiveness and obedience of Christians should cause their leaders joy, not grief, in watching for their souls. **V 18–19: PLEASE PRAY** They are asked to pray for the writer and his companions, who have two desires: the first is to live honourably; the second is to see the Hebrew Christians soon. **V 20–25: GODLY GREETINGS** Coming back to the death and resurrection of the Lord Jesus Christ, 'that great Shepherd of the sheep', he wants them to be complete in Him and to please Him. He asks them to bear with the exhortations made. He informs them that Timothy has been set free. They are to greet the rulers of the church and receive the greetings from others in Italy. God's 'grace' closes this wonderful book of grace.

JAMES

OVERVIEW

PEOPLE AND PRELIMINARIES

✳ James (five chapters) is the fifteenth of the twenty-one letters of the New Testament and the sixth of the twelve non-church letter section of those letters. It is the only letter written by James, the half-brother of Christ and brother of Jude. He wrote it probably between AD44 and AD49 and probably from Jerusalem. **See comments on 1 Timothy.**

PLAN AND PURPOSE

ⓘ James writes to scattered Jewish Christian brethren who are being tried by persecution and tempted by Satan. Its message is that either works will follow saving faith, or the so-called faith is not true saving faith. This teaching complements and is founded on the teaching of the whole of the Bible that a person is saved by faith alone. The letter challenges the reader on a number of practical points, the attitude to which demonstrates whether a person is under new management or not. These include the use of the tongue, the nature and obtaining of real wisdom, attitudes to riches, strife with others, patient and persevering prayer, and the desire to see others converted and restored.

PROFILE AND PROGRESSION

🗢 Trials, temptation, testing, deeds not words, the tongue, and true religion (1:1–27); the relationship between faith and law, and faith and works (2:1–26); the taming of the tongue (3:1–12); what wisdom is not and what it is (3:13–18); the flesh, the world and the devil (4:1–7); drawing near to God, humility, brotherly love, dependence on

God, and the nature of sin (4:8–17); the rich warned, patience and endurance, simple speech, prayer and persistence, the rescue mission (5:1–20).

PRINCIPLES AND PARTICULARS

James is basically a book urging that faith must be made evident in practice to demonstrate that it really is faith. This involves standing firm in testing, living a changed life, guarding the tongue, demonstrating God's wisdom in practice by showing a non-worldly approach to life, keeping relationships good, being generous with riches, and looking out for others with a reliance on God in prayer. Saving faith will lead to this, and the challenge of the book is to see if it is so leading in practice on a personal basis.

JAMES

CHAPTER ONE

V 1: TWELVE TRIBES James, Jesus' half-brother, writes to the dispersed twelve tribes of Israel. **V 2–8: TESTING TRIALS** In dealing with trials, our attitude should be one of joyfulness, knowing that God is at work in us through them. Our faith and patience from God is fed by wisdom which He gives to all who ask Him. Single-mindedness, applying that wisdom, and exercising that faith, is the answer, by God's grace, to our trials. **V 9–11: TEMPORARY TREASURE** A materially poor Christian should rejoice in his exaltation in Christ. The rich man should rejoice in the fact that his wealth is nothing, and that only what he is in Christ lasts. His treasured wealth is temporary, like a fading flower. **V 12–15:**

TEMPTATION TRUTH Blessing comes to those who endure temptation. God does not tempt anyone. Our evil desires cause us to be tempted and give birth to sin. Sin produces death. **V 16–18: TOTALLY TRUSTWORTHY** God is referred to as the 'Father of lights'. He is totally trustworthy. He will neither change direction, nor cast a shadow over the truth He has already given. It is by that truth that we come into blessing. He is a God who gives good and perfect gifts from above. **V 19–25: TOTAL TRANSPARENCY** Because God is the God of light, we are to behave in a transparent way. This affects our attitudes and our words. We should be good hearers as well as careful speakers. Filth must be left on one side and we should look at ourselves in the Word of God as in a mirror, and deal with what we see there with God's help. **V 26–27: TAMED TONGUE** Only someone walking with God can have his tongue tamed. That person will also practise concern for orphans and widows and be careful not to be soiled by worldliness.

CHAPTER TWO

V 1–7: FAVOURITISM FORBIDDEN Christian brothers should not treat people with different wealth in a different way. Poor people are as precious as rich people. Poor people are oppressed in a world which bows to riches. The Christian church must not adopt the same discriminatory approach. **V 8–13: JUST JUDGEMENT** Showing favouritism breaks the command that summarises the last six commandments, namely, to love our neighbours as ourselves. That should be seen in the same light as adultery or murder or any other breaking of the commandments. If we have not received God's mercy to the extent that we demonstrate it to less privileged people, we ourselves are under judgement. **V 14–20: PRACTICAL PROOF** James develops the thought. If I say that I have faith and show no evidence of it by a changed lifestyle that produces good works towards others, then I do not have saving faith. I am lost. Faith is more than a mental assent, sometimes called 'belief'. Even demons have that type of 'belief', and tremble! Personal trust in God for salvation changes the true believer's entire life. **V 21–26: BIBLICAL BASIS** James quotes two examples from the Bible to demonstrate this. Although Abraham was justified before God by faith, making him the 'Father of the faithful', his justification before men was by his works. His preparedness to obey God in the question of offering his son, Isaac, showed that he had that saving faith in God. (We know that God always had other plans for Isaac!) Rahab's faith, too, was demonstrated by the fact that she received the spies and helped them to escape. Her faith in the God of Israel conditioned her action. A dead body has no spirit. Dead, so-called faith has no works.

CHAPTER THREE

V 1–7: TONGUE'S WONDER Like a horse's bit or a ship's rudder, the tongue is a small member of the body with a gigantic and disproportional influence on the direction to be taken. It can be like a spark that ignites a forest fire. It is the hardest part of the body to tame, and may be influenced by hell itself. For this reason, those who use words in teaching other people will be judged more strictly about their own use of words. **V 8–12: TONGUE'S WICKEDNESS** The tongue is untameable by man. Its poisonous use reveals evil within, hypocrisy and double standards that make our conversation so inconsistent and dishonouring. **V 13–18: TRUE WISDOM** How we need God's wisdom! It is available from on high and is pure, leading to a holy and open lifestyle of gentleness and graciousness. Envy and bitter self-seeking come from worldly wisdom influenced by the devil. As God works in us, to make us wise and understanding, our conversation will reflect that.

CHAPTER FOUR

V 1–3: WARS All wars and fighting come from wilful and wayward human hearts. How different is submission to God which seeks for what pleases Him, rather than what pleases us. **V 4–5: WORLDLINESS** Those who are friends of the world and its standards, pastimes and entertainments show that they are enemies of God. This is equivalent to spiritual adultery, and God yearns jealously for His people, as a husband would for an unfaithful wife. **V 6–10: WEEP** Benefiting from God's grace enables us to resist the devil, to draw near to God, and to weep over our sins and double-mindedness. God thus enables us to cleanse our hands and purify our hearts and minds. As we humble ourselves, God will exalt us. **V 11–12: WRONG** It is always wrong to speak evil of Christian brothers. Christians should obey God's law, not use it to judge other Christians. Who am I to make myself the judge? **V 13–17: WILL** We should live in dependence on God's will. We should not boastfully count the future as ours, but realise that God can take away the vapour of our lives instantly. To think otherwise is sin. In fact, whenever we fail to do what we know to be good, we sin.

CHAPTER FIVE

V 1–6: SINFUL STORING Those who

sinfully store riches, especially where they have been gained by taking advantage of others, and concentrate on pleasure and luxury, will be judged. This shares, with murder, the evil root of trampling on the welfare of others. **V 7–11: PATIENT PERSEVERANCE** God's people should patiently wait for the Lord to come, just as the farmer waits for the seed to germinate and be harvested. Such patience is an antidote to grumbling and an encouragement to perseverance, knowing that the Lord is compassionate and merciful. **V 12: STRAIGHT SPEAKING** The Christian does not have to dress up his everyday language with oaths and assurances. He should tell it as it is, and have a reputation for telling the truth. **V 13–18: PRUDENT PRAYING** Prayer should be made with and for people in all states of life and emotion. Those suffering and sick should be prayed for and church leaders should be ready to respond to a call to go and pray with someone who is suffering. Confession of sin is a prerequisite for restoration spiritually and may even affect the way we feel physically. The pattern of Elijah's patient endurance in prayer is an encouragement to all who feel that their prayers are ineffective. **V 19: SINNER SAVED** James tells the twelve scattered tribes that if someone among them wanders from the truth and is turned back from sin, the person responsible for that turning will save a soul from death and cover over a multitude of sins. God, who is sovereign in salvation, expects us to be actively involved in the privilege of seeing lost sinners being saved, including those who keep company with Christians.

1 PETER

OVERVIEW

PEOPLE AND PRELIMINARIES

 1 Peter (six chapters) is the sixteenth of the twenty-one letters of the New Testament and the seventh of the twelve non-church letter section of those letters. **See comments on 1 Timothy.** It is the first of two letters written by Peter, between AD60 and AD68, probably from Rome, symbolically referred to as 'Babylon' in chapter 5 verse 13.

PLAN AND PURPOSE

Both the letters of Peter deal with opposition. 1 Peter deals with opposition coming from outside the church, via persecution, and 2 Peter deals with opposition attacking the inside of the church, via false teaching. 1 Peter urges these bewildered saints to stand firm in Christ. It counterbalances the physical and time-bound afflictions they experience against the spiritual and eternal blessings which belong to them through Jesus. It is a 'how to live in trying times' letter. It thus deals with holy and consistent living in the church and in society, practical living of husband and wife together, the issue of suffering, and living a death-to-self life through Christ. Throughout the letter is the strong flavour of salvation through Christ's suffering in the place of sinners. The letter anticipates His glorious second coming. With this in mind, Christian service must continue.

PROFILE AND PROGRESSION

Greetings (1:1,2); salvation and trials (1:3–12); holiness, fear, redemption, and the gospel (1:13–25); the church as a family, a building and a priesthood (2:1–11); submission to authority and masters, with Christ's substitutionary death on the cross as our example of submission (2:12–2:25); family submission (3:1–7); one-mindedness, suffering and sanctified hearts (3:8–17); Christ's suffering, resurrection and authority (3:18–22); living now, understanding personal suffering and the Christian's attitude to it (4:1–19); leadership, humility, grace to stand in suffering, and desire for God's glory (5:1–11); closing greetings (6:12–14).

PRINCIPLES AND PARTICULARS

God is in control of suffering and of those who trust Him. The Christian's main goal in suffering should be the same as when he is not suffering, namely the glory of God in his life and in his witness. The letter thus seeks to set the focus right and to encourage the church to honour Christ, who has died and who will help and strengthen those who trust Him.

I PETER

CHAPTER ONE

V 1–2: PILGRIMS Peter, the apostle, writes to the Christian pilgrims who have been dispersed throughout what we know as modern Turkey. He wishes them multiplied grace and peace. Although geographically scattered, their position as the elect is focused in God. The Father's foreknowledge, the Spirit's sanctifying, and the shed blood of Jesus Christ are all highlighted in the greeting. Sanctification and obedience are to be priorities for them. **V 3–9: PRECIOUS** Starting with God's mercy and their hope, through the resurrected Christ, Peter reminds them of an incorruptible and undefiled inheritance that awaits them in heaven, and of the preciousness of their faith which is being tried through grievous trials. This will lead to great rejoicing and the certainty of their eternal salvation. **V 10–12: PRIVILEGE** Prophets, and even angels, would love to know what these Christians now know about the sufferings and glory of Christ, made real to them through His gospel. They are privileged people! **V 13–16: PRIORITY** They are to reject former sins and lusts. They are to be holy because God is holy. Holiness is the hallmark of real conversion, and must be the priority of each Christian. **V 17–21: PRAYER** Those who call on the Father in prayer should have a consistent conduct that honours Him. The precious blood of Christ, shed in God's economy before the world was founded, has redeemed them. Their faith and hope are in God, knowing that the once crucified Christ is risen from the dead. **V 22: PURITY** The Holy Spirit has given them purity through obeying the truth. Their love for one another is to blend purity with fervency. **V 23–25: PERMANENT** Just as God lives forever, so His Word endures forever. They have been born again spiritually through incorruptible and unchangeable seed. Their gospel blessings will also last for ever.

CHAPTER TWO

V 1–3: BABES Just as babies desire milk, so they should desire the Word of God. This implies laying aside everything that is evil, deceitful and hypocritical in order to taste God's graciousness personally. **V 4–8: BUILDING** Jesus is a living stone to us and a cornerstone. Based upon that certainty, Christians are living stones themselves, and are built up into God's building, the church. Trusting in Christ means that we are built on Him. Those who reject Him will stumble in their disobedience because of Him. **V 9–10: BELONGING** As Christians, they now belong to God, who has called them into light and praise, as a priesthood to Him. Previously they were not His people but are now His special people because they have obtained mercy from Him. They are chosen, royal, holy and special. **V 11–12: BATTLE** To win the battle for holiness, the Christians are told to abstain from fleshly lusts and, rather, glorify God by their good works. What they are will contradict the false accusations spoken against them by their enemies. **V 13–23: BEHAVIOUR** Because of this, their behaviour should be distinctive, and include keeping the law, obeying authorities, doing good, honouring and fearing God. Servants should obey masters to be a good testimony to them, even if they are made to suffer. Christ is the supreme example of this, by life and by lip. He never reacted to the wicked behaviour against Him. **V 24–25: BODY** Peter reminds them that Jesus was much more than a good example. In His body on the cross, He actually bore their sins so that they should die to sin and live righteously for Him. They have returned from their sinful straying to the Shepherd who takes care of their souls.

CHAPTER THREE

V 1–7: SPIRITUAL SPOUSES The same high degree of conduct and consideration should apply both to wives and to their husbands. Submissiveness to their husbands and cultivating an inner life of beauty should be the wives' concern. That is more important than wearing fashionable clothes and jewellery and having a nice hairstyle. Their godliness should be such a powerful testimony that it will win unsaved husbands for Christ. Christian husbands should treat their wives with great understanding and consideration as the weaker vessel. The test for husbands is whether they can pray openly with their wives after the way they have treated them. **V 8–12: HUMBLE HARMONY** One-mindedness, compassion, tender-hearted love, courtesy, giving way to others, and controlled speech are all tokens of the harmony that comes from a humble lifestyle marked by repentance and actively seeking what God wants. **V 13–17: CLEAR CONSCIENCE** It is important that believers sanctify God in their hearts so that they can always give a response to anyone who asks why they hope in Christ. With good conscience, their testimony will be strong, and they will be upheld by God even if they suffer wrongly. **V 18: EXCELLENT EXAMPLE** The excellent example of Christ is quoted. He 'suffered once for sins, the just for the unjust, that He might bring us to God'. No suffering we endure for Him, or for His cause or teaching, can compare with His suffering for us. **V 19–22: SALVATION'S SYMBOL** In between Christ's death and resurrection, He proclaimed His victory to departed spirits. Linking this with those who were disobedient in the days of Noah, Peter makes the connection between water and salvation and passes on to the picture of baptism as a mere symbol of salvation. Baptism can never cleanse the soul or conscience. The crucified and risen Christ does this for those who trust in Him.

CHAPTER FOUR

V 1–6: DEFINITE DIFFERENCE Christians are urged to have the same mind as Christ, who was willing to suffer. Those given to crude pleasures and sin think it strange that newly converted people no longer join in with them. This will cause gossip and evil speaking about them. Peter reminds them that the Judge knows the real position and all must answer to Him. **V 7–11: PRODUCE PRAISE** Vigilance, prayerfulness, Christian love, hospitality, lack of grumbling, faithful stewardship of what God has given, and faithful use of God's gifts in serving Him will cause God to be glorified and praised through Jesus Christ. This praise will last for ever, but should also be the current aim of every Christian. **V 12–19: SUBMISSIVE SUFFERING** Peter tells them not to be surprised at the suffering which will come upon them. If this is for the sake of Christ, they can even experience His joy as He is glorified. However, suffering should not be because of any evil that Christians are doing. The final suffering of those who reject the Saviour will be far worse in length and intensity. Christians should accept God's will and commit themselves to God in their suffering.

CHAPTER FIVE

V 1–5: ALL AGES Elders and younger people are all urged to honour God in the way they behave. Elders should act as willing shepherds, knowing that they have a Chief Shepherd. Younger people should be submissive to elders, and there should be a spirit of submission and humility that clothes all. God resists proud people. He gives humble people His grace. **V 6–7: LORD'S LIFTING** When Christians humble themselves under God's mighty hand, they experience His uplifting as they cast all their care on Him, knowing that He cares for them. **V 8–9: RESOLUTE RESISTANCE** By trusting God, we should soberly, vigilantly and steadfastly resist the lion-like devil. Christians who suffer should remember that, worldwide, other believers also suffer. **V 10–11: GRACIOUS GOD** God is the 'God of all grace' who will 'perfect, establish, strengthen and settle' those who trust Him, after their suffering. They will share in His eternal glory and dominion. **V 12–14: CLOSING CONCERN** Peter shows his concern for individuals in highlighting Sylvanus and Mark along with 'the church in Babylon' (perhaps a code word for Rome). He urges them all to greet one another 'with a kiss of love' and wishes them Christ's peace.

2 PETER

OVERVIEW

PEOPLE AND PRELIMINARIES

✳ 2 Peter (three chapters) is the seventeenth of the twenty-one letters of the New Testament and the eighth of the twelve non-church letter section of those letters. **See comments on** 1 Timothy. It is the second of two letters written by Peter, between AD65 and AD68, probably from Rome.

PLAN AND PURPOSE

ⓘ Both the letters of Peter deal with opposition. See 1 Peter. 2 Peter deals with opposition attacking the inside of the church, via false teaching. It seeks to meet, rebut and repel these false teachers who deny Christ and seek to exploit the church through covetousness.

2 Peter underlines the facts supporting the truth of the Christian gospel and how this truth should be worked out in a growing lifestyle of purity, integrity and loyalty. This is altogether different from the corrupt and immoral example of the false teachers, whose lifestyle reflects their erroneous teaching. It concludes with teaching on the end times and on the second coming of Christ, which has been derided by them. The Gnostic heresy is leading its followers into unfettered immorality or into legalistic asceticism. This letter promotes the reverse, namely godly conduct by God's grace in salvation. The work of the Holy Spirit is emphasised.

PROFILE AND PROGRESSION

Godliness is demonstrated in Christians through the promises and working of God (1:1–14); the inspiration, reliability and sovereignty of Scripture (1:15–21); warning against and marks of false teachers on doctrinal and moral issues (2:1–22); the coming return of the Lord will be derided, disbelieved, but definite—God's longsuffering, Christian care and caution, and grace from and glory to the Lord Jesus Christ (3:1–18).

PRINCIPLES AND PARTICULARS

The fight against error demands that Christians be doctrinally and morally pure. Both doctrine and living must accord with the Bible. Peter stresses that God-inspired written Scripture is even more sure than the eye-witnessed revelation of the glorious transfiguration of Jesus. God will do what He promises and Christ will come again according to the divine timetable. God holds back now, through longsuffering, to allow sinners

time to repent. God wants us to know this. 'Knowledge' (or variations of the word) features sixteen times. In repelling error from within, the Christian church must get to know its Bible and its God more and more.

2 PETER

CHAPTER ONE

V 1–4: PRECIOUSNESS Starting his second letter, Peter reverts to the thought of preciousness. Here, he extols the precious faith obtained by the righteousness of our Saviour God, Jesus Christ. He also recommends the 'exceedingly great and precious promises' which enable Christians to partake of God's divine life and blessings in a world of corruption. **V 5–11: PURPOSE** Pleased to escape the corruption in the world, the Christian should add certain things to the salvation he has in Christ. These things are virtue, knowledge, self-control, perseverance, godliness, brotherly kindness and love. Fruitfulness follows. So does an awareness of sin and gratitude at having been cleansed from it. The Christian's purpose should be to live a fruitful life, sensitive to his Saviour. This is the evidence of a true call of God and will keep a Christian from stumbling. It is saving faith that produces a life like this, giving us assurance of an abundant entry into everlasting life through Jesus Christ. **V 12–15: PASSING** Peter believes his life will soon pass away. He is determined to establish the Christians in God's truth and leave behind him a reminder of the importance of living for Christ. **V 16–21: PROPHECY** The Christian did not follow man-made fables, but God's Word attesting the fact that He was 'well pleased' with His Beloved Son. That voice came from heaven, but there is a surer prophetic Word, the Bible, which guides us into God's truth. Someone may mistakenly think he has heard a voice from heaven, but the Word of God can readily be seen and examined. God revealed His Word in the Bible by moving holy men, by His Holy Spirit, to record His infallible truth.

CHAPTER TWO

V 1–3: HARMFUL HERESIES The first letter of Peter deals mainly with opposition from outside the church by way of persecution that brings suffering. This second letter deals mainly with opposition from within from those who bring false doctrine and harmful heresies. Such heresies will cause people who follow them to deny Christ, to cause the truth to be blasphemed, to produce covetous exploitation, and to use deceptive words. God will judge people who pervert His truth in this way. **V 4–11: DIVINE DELIVERANCE** God judged the fallen angels, the wicked in Noah's day, and Sodom and Gomorrah. He will judge sinners on the day of judgement. But He will deliver from temptations those who seek to be godly, including the temptation to believe error, even though He will punish those who lead others astray through their heresies. God is well experienced in delivering people, such as Noah and Lot, from the worst of situations. He can deliver those who look to Him in the midst of error and sinfulness surrounding them. **V 12–17: INIQUITOUS INSTRUCTERS** A description of these false teachers follows. Brute-like, lacking understanding, covetous, sexually promiscuous and sensual, their vileness leads unstable souls astray. Their godless self-interest is like that of Balaam. Like

dry wells, they offer much but deliver nothing, and have eternal darkness awaiting them. **V 18–22: LEWD LUSTS** They vainly promise liberty from sin at the same time as they practise the lewdest of lusts. The head-knowledge that the Saviour can save them and lead them to righteousness does not deliver them; rather it makes their rebellion and their condemnation worse. Their returning to their sins is like dogs eating their vomit, and sows wallowing in the mire of their own filth. God's commandments are not just for information, but to turn us from our sins to Christ.

CHAPTER THREE

V 1–9: CHRIST'S COMING Peter assures his readers that Christ is coming. The mocking taunts, that everything continues as it did before, is similar to what happened before when God judged the earth by a flood in the days of Noah. He will judge the earth by fire, but according to His timetable. Meanwhile, time is available for those, who will do so, to repent. **V 10–13: COMFORTING CHALLENGE** The coming of Christ will come as unexpectedly for the unprepared as a thief comes to a house in the night. When He comes, He will judge the world and burn it up. Christians should be holy and godly, looking for that coming day. That is the challenge. The comfort is that God will replace the burnt up heavens and earth with 'new heavens and a new earth in which righteousness dwells'. **V 14–18: CONTINUING CONSECRATION** Christians should diligently seek peace and live spotless and blameless lives. God's longsuffering causes Him to postpone judgement in order to extend the day of grace during which sinners may repent and turn to Him. He is giving them more time to see their lostness and come to

Him. Our confidence must be in all the Scriptures, including those 'hard to understand'! Growing in grace and in the knowledge of Christ will stop us from falling into wickedness. Our desire should be to see our Lord and Saviour glorified, 'both now and for ever'.

---

1 JOHN

OVERVIEW

PEOPLE AND PRELIMINARIES

✳ 1 John (five chapters) is the eighteenth of the twenty-one letters of the New Testament and the ninth of the twelve non-church letter section of those letters. **See comments on 1 Timothy.** It is the first of three letters written by John, the apostle, who also wrote his Gospel and the book of Revelation. It was written from Ephesus before AD110, probably between AD90 and AD95 or even earlier.

PLAN AND PURPOSE

ⓘ In common with some other New Testament letters, 1 John is written to combat false teaching, especially that of the Gnostic heresy. This leads to immorality and, paradoxically, legalistic asceticism, and a denial that God had come in the flesh in the person of Jesus Christ. Going back to fundamentals, 1 John combats this. It stresses the historicity of Jesus Christ, that, as a fact, He has come in the flesh, and that His coming was seen by eyewitnesses. It then goes on to show how the gospel, when believed, also becomes real in spiritual experience and in its outworking at all points of living. Thus, the answer to the attacks is both objective and subjective. It is found in the objective truths of Jesus Christ and the gospel message. It is manifested, too, in the genuine personal experience of Christ that enables the Christian convert to know he has been raised from death to life. The evidence of this new spiritual life is his experiential discovery of fellowship, joy, desire for holiness, victory over sin, and assurance of salvation. Thus blessed, he will walk in the light with his Lord and with fellow Christians. How does a person know that he knows Christ? By obeying God, loving Christian brethren, resisting worldliness, practising righteousness, living a pure life, and not living for sin. These are tests given in the letter. The truth that, once a person is saved, he (or she) will always be saved is put in the context of testing oneself to see if the evidence of salvation is there. This gives deep assurance, without shallow presumption, to the one trusting Christ.

PROFILE AND PROGRESSION

🐚 The fact of Christ's coming in flesh (1:1–4); light, darkness, sin, cleansing, holiness and an Advocate (1:5–2:2); obedience, love for others, and not being worldly show that we know Christ (2:3–17); antichrists and truth (2:18–27); God's children and Christ's return (2:28–3:3); righteousness, love and obedience as evidence that we are God's (3:4–4:6); God's loving nature manifested in sending Christ to be our propitiation, and God's requirement to replicate His love in us (4:7–5:1); keeping God's commandments shows that we love God (5:2–5); the witness of God and the certainty of eternal life now (5:6–13); prayer, knowing Christ, and separation (5:14–21).

PRINCIPLES AND PARTICULARS

👉 Teaching about Jesus forms the factual basis for spiritual experience: In the letter we see His eternality, nativity, advocacy for sinners who trust Him, Godhead, humanity, atonement, and second coming. There is much importance attached to the things a Christian can 'know': thirty-nine times that verb is used in the five chapters of this letter. Christianity deals with certainty, not speculation! But there must be certain evidences and tests of having been born again spiritually so that assurance of salvation is not lightly claimed by someone with no spiritual life in Christ. Note that although God forgives and cleanses sin through the blood of Christ, God's desire is that the Christian should not sin. It matters to God how we live.

I JOHN

CHAPTER ONE

V 1–4: FLESH, FATHER AND FELLOWSHIP Jesus, God the Son, really came to earth in a human body. All the evidence of eyewitnesses and those who knew Him underline not only His true Godhood, but also His true Manhood. Eternal life, shared between the Father and Son, was manifest to mankind when Christ took on flesh. Because of that, those who turn from sin and trust Him have fellowship not only with other Christians, but with the Father and Son as well. This produces joy! **V 5–7: LIGHT, LIES AND LIFESTYLE** Because God is light, Christians should adopt the lifestyle of walking in the light and rejecting the darkness of sin and selfishness. A Christian who says he has fellowship with God, but habitually walks in the darkness of sin, is a liar. In the light, we see and confess our sin, knowing that Christ's blood cleanses us from it and facilitates fellowship with other blood-cleansed sinners. **V 8–9: CONTRADICTION, CONFESSION AND CLEANSING** It is a self-deceiving contradiction to claim that we are without sin. Confession of our sin to God from a repentant heart leads to a total cleansing from all that is wrong, and His faithful and just forgiveness.

CHAPTER TWO

V 1–2: STOP SINNING Although all Christians do fail and sin, a mark of the new birth is the desire and determination not to settle for sin. Our habitual lifestyle is to please Christ. If we do sin, Christ is our righteous Advocate and propitiation, having borne the wrath of God for our sin. This message must be shared with the whole world. **V 3–8: COMPELLING COMMANDMENT** This letter contains various tests of conversion. One of them is that the Christian is constrained to keep the commandments of God, through the mercy and grace of God. He wants to walk as Jesus walked, but can only do so with His grace and strength. **V 9–11: LOVE'S LIGHT** The Christian who walks in the light will love his fellow Christian. If he does not, he is not in the light, but is still in the darkness of unforgiven sin. **V 12–14: FAMILY FOCUS** Stages of Christian growth as little children, as young men, and as fathers are dealt with. Forgiveness of sin, indwelling of Christ, certainty of knowing God, the blessing of God's word abiding within, and overcoming evil, are the themes simply stated. **V 15–17: WORLDLY WAYWARDNESS** The person pursuing a lifestyle of loving the world does not know God or the Father's love. The trinity of evil—the lust of the flesh, the lust of the eyes, and the pride of life—are the basis of this passing world. They are to be contrasted with God's will which lasts for ever and blesses the Christian who seeks to do it now. The world and its things are to be rejected. Love for and obedience to God are to be embraced. **V 18–23: DECEPTIVE DENIAL** John combats the Gnostic heresy that Jesus never took on a human body. Having dealt with the fact that Antichrist and many antichrists have come, John underlines that, through the Holy Spirit and the truth of the Word of God, we know that Jesus Christ has come in the flesh. Anyone denying the Son does not have the Father. We need to keep these simple truths in mind, even today. **V 24–27: TRUE TEACHING** Our Christian privilege and duty is to abide in God and enjoy the promise of eternal life now and in the future. This results from ensuring that the truth of God's Word, blessed through His Holy Spirit, abides in our hearts and minds each day. We need constantly to seek the Holy Spirit's help to understand His Word. **V 28–29: CONFIDENT CHILDREN** God's children who abide in Him will avoid being ashamed at Christ's coming. They will face it with confidence. The righteousness of Christ will be reflected in their righteous lifestyles that confirm and demonstrate their new birth.

CHAPTER THREE

V 1–3: PRIVILEGE AND PURITY The child of God already has the Father's love bestowed on him or her. The Christian will see Christ and ultimately be like Him. This hope causes a desire for purity and a life which reflects purity. **V 4–9: SIN AND SEED** A person who plans to sin habitually has not been converted. The new birth produces an attitude of seeking righteousness. The seed of God's word and eternal life have taken root in that person's life. **V 10–15: MANIFESTATION AND MESSAGE** There is a manifest difference between children of God (Christians) and children of the devil (those who have not yet become Christians). The former seek to practise righteousness because of a changed life, and the latter live for self, thus producing sin. Loving one's fellow Christians shows that a person has passed from death to life. God's desire for people to love one another can only be realised by those who have turned away from sin and trusted Christ. Otherwise, they have the same murderous heart towards others, even if it shows itself in subtle hatred rather than murder, such as Cain inflicted on Abel. **V 16–18: LIVING AND LOVING** We should live by laying down our lives for others just as Christ lay down His life for us. We should also support others in need. With God's love and grace in our hearts, we can love like that. But this love must be demonstrated in practice, and not be merely a question of empty words. **V 19–23: CONDEMNATION AND CONFIDENCE** Often our hearts condemn us because of the sin within and the failures in our lives. Our confidence, however, is that God knows all about that and is 'greater than our hearts'. In believing on Jesus Christ, our sin has been cleansed, and we have received God's love in our hearts. An evidence of this is a desire to keep His commandments. **V 24: SPIRIT AND SURE** God gives us His Holy Spirit when we turn to Christ, and it is by His Holy Spirit that He abides in us. The Christian has the assurance of the Holy Spirit within, and this is shown by keeping God's commands.

CHAPTER FOUR

V 1–3: TEST OF TRUTH False prophets give false teaching by spirits other than the Holy Spirit. There is one main test of truth to apply to expose them. What do they make of the Lord Jesus Christ? The spirit of Antichrist is that the Lord Jesus Christ is not God who has come in the flesh. The deity of Christ is the crucial first test of truth. It is not the only one. **V 4–6: GREATNESS OF GOD** Even when opposed by persuasive false prophets and wrong teaching, the simplest Christian knows that he is a child of God because he is indwelt by God Himself through His Spirit. God, who indwells the Christian, is greater than the devil who is in the world. The Christian is in communion with God. Based on the objective truth of the Lord Jesus Christ and the subjective experience of being born again and trusting Him, the Christian knows that he is walking in truth. **V 7–11: LORD OF LOVE** 'God is love.' He is the source of all love in a Christian's life. True self-effacing love that puts others first is thus produced by faith in Christ that makes God's love real to the repentant sinner. This new love underlines that he knows God. God's love was made known through sending His Son so that we might 'live through Him'. That is why Jesus died to take the punishment for our sins. Consequently we should love others. **V 12–16: APPRECIATION OF ABIDING** The outside world sees God's love through God's abiding in the Christian. We know that He abides in us because we have received His Spirit, and joyfully confess the truth about the person and work of the Lord Jesus Christ. By grace, we seek to abide in God's love. **V 17–19: FLIGHT OF FEAR** God's love in Christ takes away the fear of judgement and underlines that 'We love Him because He first loved us'. **V 20–21:**

CONSISTENCY OF COMMAND No one claiming to love God can hate his brother. That would be an inconsistent lie. God commands the Christian to love both God and his brother.

CHAPTER FIVE

V 1–5: BORN-AGAIN BELIEVERS Someone whose heart belief is in the Lord Jesus Christ as Saviour is 'born of God'. Evidence of this is a love for other Christians, a desire to keep God's commandment, and a new life which overcomes areas which could never be overcome in one's own strength. **V 6–9: WITNESS TO WORD** The witness of history is that Jesus came. The Holy Spirit witnesses to Him still when the gospel is preached. Jesus' coming 'by water and by blood' could refer either to natural human birth or to the fact that He was baptised in the Jordan by John and shed His blood upon the cross. Both are true. Man witnesses to Christ's historicity and so does God! (It is possible that the words in verses 7 and 8 between 'in heaven' and 'on earth' were marginal notes that were wrongly put into the text. However, they do accurately reflect biblical teaching.) **V 10–13: CONFIDENCE IN CHRIST** The believer's confidence in Christ depends on God's promise of eternal life in trusting Him, and the God-given witness of a new life within after he has come to know Christ as Saviour. Eternal life is his present possession, here and now, as well as in eternity. **V 14–17: PREVAILING THROUGH PRAYER** A Christian praying for God's glory and God's will to be done will have his prayers answered. He should pray for wayward Christian brothers and sisters as well. If God disciplines a continually errant Christian by taking his physical life from him (though not his spiritual life), there is obviously no point in praying about that sin. **V 18–21: TRUTHS TO TREASURE** There are three truths that Peter says Christians know as a sign of being born of God: first, our attitude is changed towards habitual sin against God and we do not settle for sinning; second, a Christian is under God's sway and the world is under the devil's sway; third, our faith in Christ has given us spiritual understanding, including the certainty of having received eternal life. These truths will strengthen Christians to fight against all forms of idolatry.

2 JOHN

OVERVIEW

PEOPLE AND PRELIMINARIES

2 John (one chapter) is the nineteenth of the twenty-one letters of the New Testament and the tenth of the twelve non-church letter section of those letters. **See comments on 1 Timothy.** It is the second of three letters written by John, the apostle, who also wrote his Gospel and the book of Revelation. Like 1 John, it was written from Ephesus before AD110, probably between AD90 and AD95 or even earlier.

PLAN AND PURPOSE

2 John mirrors, in briefer treatment and addressed to a family, the question of false teaching in 1 John, Gnosticism, and how to deal with it and its many false teachers, from the problems. This involves the question of Christian hospitality. Should a Christian give hospitality to someone who comes specifically to peddle error and specifically to deny the person of the Lord Jesus Christ as God who has come in the flesh? The answer is 'no', and the reasons are given. Clear Christian teaching and holiness are the bases for true fellowship of believers in Christ.

Thus truth is the touchstone. Real love discerns against identification with error that will eternally condemn the lost.

PROFILE AND PROGRESSION

Greetings to the family, rejoicing in converted children walking in truth, and requirement for love and obedience (1:1–6); the dangers of deceiving teachers who belittle the person of Christ (1:7–9); the command not to offer hospitality or associate with such people (1:10,11); concluding greetings (1:12,13).

PRINCIPLES AND PARTICULARS

The emphases are on truth and love. John's loving concern and priority for this family is that they will continue in God's truth, despite there being many deceivers. The briefly stated test to detect deceivers and antichrists is to ask what they make of Jesus Christ. All heresies make less of Christ than His being God the Son, as the second Person in the Trinity. We should use that same test today, and also beware of any teaching that seeks to dilute or distort that Jesus is both fully God and fully man. Like the recipients of John's letter, we should not identify with those whose task it is to corrupt the doctrine of Christ.

2 JOHN

V 1–3: RECIPIENTS John's spiritual greeting at the start of this letter is addressed to a family, namely 'to the elect lady and her children'. It seems reasonable to accept that he writes to an actual Christian family, headed possibly by a widowed Christian lady. Some, however, take it to signify that John wrote to a church, called 'the elect lady'. His introduction introduces the subjects of the truth and the Godhead. **V 4–6: REJOICING** John rejoices in children walking in truth. This is true for physical children or for people who have become children of God through faith in Christ. They are to love one another and keep God's commandments. **V 7–11: REJECTION** Deceivers abound who deny that the Lord Jesus Christ has come in the flesh. They have the spirit of antichrist.

They should be rejected and not be welcomed into the house. The test of true Christian conversion is whether someone abides in the teaching of the Lord Jesus Christ as fully God and fully man. Such a person, having turned to God for salvation, possesses both the Father and the Son through God's indwelling his life. John warns his readers to be vigilant. **V 12–13: REUNION** John says that this letter is short, but he hopes soon to have a reunion with them. There will be fullness of joy as they speak face to face. He passes on greetings from another. The 'elect sister' to whom John refers could be the real sister, spiritually and probably biologically, of the elect lady to whom he writes. Some hold that it is another church which passes on its greetings through John to the church to whom he writes.

3 JOHN

OVERVIEW

PEOPLE AND PRELIMINARIES

�֍ 3 John (one chapter) is the twentieth of the twenty-one letters of the New Testament and the eleventh of the twelve non-church letter section of those letters. **See comments on 1 Timothy.** It is the third and last of three letters written by John, the apostle, who also wrote his Gospel and the book of Revelation. Like his other letters, it was written from Ephesus before AD110, probably between AD90 and AD95, or even earlier.

PLAN AND PURPOSE

(i) 3 John deals with hospitality from a different angle than 2 John. Here, we see faithful workers for Christ commended to the hospitality of John's friend, Gaius, the recipient of the letter. Unlike Gaius himself and the faithful Demetrius, there is in the church an arrogant man, Diotrephes, who likes to be centre stage. Not only does he refuse to receive Paul and his colleagues hospitably in Christian love, but he maliciously speaks against them. This man, probably influenced by the Gnostic heresy that John deals with in his other letters, has put out of the church those faithful Christians who would have welcomed the Lord's true heralds. John has him in mind, on any future visit there, as someone to confront.

PROFILE AND PROGRESSION

Greetings, appreciation and joy that Paul's spiritual children walk in truth (1:1–4); encouraging hospitality for God's faithful servants and strangers (1:5–8); condemnation of actions of Diotrephes and warning to support good and not evil (1:9–11); commendation of Demetrius (1:12); farewell greetings (1:13–14).

PRINCIPLES AND PARTICULARS

Open hospitality is both a privilege and a duty as part of the Christian fellowship 'package'. Beware of the grave danger of admitting an unspiritual man into a position of authority and allowing him to carry on unchecked. Beware also of the more subtle and pleasing danger of desiring status and influence in the work of God and of wanting to be seen by others.

3 JOHN

V 1: PERSONAL Like Paul's letter to Philemon, this is a letter written by an apostle to an individual Christian, Gaius. John, the writer, expresses his Christian love for Gaius. **V 2–4: PRAYER** John prays that the physical health of Gaius will be as good as his spiritual health. The apostle rejoices to hear that his children in Christ walk in truth. In fact he has 'no greater joy' than this. **V 5–8: PLEASED** John expresses his pleasure at the way that Gaius shows hospitality to Christian brothers and to strangers. This is a witness to both groups, and helps Christian servants to work for the Lord without having to take money from unbelievers. Such workers should be received so that the one giving hospitality can have fellowship in that work. **V 9–10: PRE-EMINENCE** By contrast, Diotrephes is a proud man seeking personal pre-eminence in the church. He acts in arrogant authoritarianism. Visiting Christians are refused fellowship, and those who would open their homes to them are put out of the church by Diotrephes. **V 11–12: PATTERN** Gaius is told not to imitate the evil works of people like Diotrephes, but to do good. Those who know God do good. Demetrius is cited as a good example. All testify of his honourable Christian life, including John himself. His is a good pattern to follow. **V 13–14: PEACE** As in his second letter, John has no time to put everything down in writing. He wants to see Gaius soon, and prays for God's peace upon him. He sends a greeting from his friends to the friends of Gaius.

JUDE

OVERVIEW

PEOPLE AND PRELIMINARIES

Jude (one chapter) is the last of the twenty-one letters of the New Testament and the last of the twelve non-church letter section of those letters. **See comments on 1 Timothy.** Jude wrote it between AD65 and AD70 from an unknown location.

PLAN AND PURPOSE

Jude warns against apostasy and declares God's judgement upon it, drawing illustrative Old Testament authority from the fallen angels, the rebellious Israelites, the sexually perverted Sodomites, Cain's wickedness, Balaam's avarice, and Korah's presumption. God will have the last word as Judge, but meanwhile the Christians are to contend earnestly for their historic and God-given faith, with full confidence in God's Word. It concludes with Jude encouraging his readers to advance spiritually, to show Christian compassion and to snatch needy people from the fire, and reaches a worshipful and climactic description of 'God our Saviour'.

PROFILE AND PROGRESSION

Greeting (1:1–2); contend for the faith under attack (1:3–4); apostasy is not new, as Old Testament examples illustrate (1:5–11); apostates and their destiny described (1:12–16); apostasy should not take Bible believers by surprise (1:17–19); Christians should concentrate on their own godliness and on reaching out to others (1:20–22); our keeping, glorious, saving, wise, majestic, powerful and eternal God! (1:24–25).

PRINCIPLES AND PARTICULARS

The sum total of God's revealed Word is referred to as 'the faith which was once for all delivered to the saints'. Faith not only refers to the exercise of personal trust, therefore, but also to God's revealed body of truth. Both are under constant attack. The saturation of this very brief book with Old Testament truth demonstrates the relevance of the whole of the Bible in addressing apostasy and encouraging spiritual and holy living in the Christian churches. Jude shows that it is right to take a firm stand against error and ungodliness, and for Christians to pursue truth and godliness in their lives. Note

that God is referred to as 'our Saviour'. Jesus is 'our Saviour'. Jesus is God.

JUDE

V 1–2: CHRISTIAN In Jude's opening greeting, we see a wonderful profile of a Christian. Like Jude, he is a 'bond servant' of Jesus Christ, and receives from God multiplied 'mercy, peace, and love'. This is because God has called and set him apart to be preserved in Jesus Christ, the only Saviour. **V 3–4: CONTEND** Because of stealthy and ungodly perverters of truth and morality, who deny the person of the Lord Jesus Christ, John urges Jude to 'contend earnestly for the faith'. That faith, 'delivered' by God 'once', is neither negotiable nor changeable. **V 5–7: CONDEMNATION** God's condemnation of sin is seen as a continuing principle throughout Scripture. We see this in the judgement of unbelievers as Israel exited from Egypt, in the everlasting punishment of angels who rebelled against God, and in the destruction of Sodom and Gomorrah and surrounding cities because of sexual immorality and sexual perversion. The 'vengeance of eternal fire' is a reality. **V 8–11: CORRUPTION** A mark of these false and immoral teachers is their lack of respect for authorities. Unlike Michael the archangel, these wicked people show their corruption not only in what they do, but also in what they say. Like Cain, Balaam, and Korah, they will be punished. **V 12–15: CONVICTED** They are ugly spots, waterless clouds, fruitless trees, frothing waves, and wandering stars. They will be in 'the blackness of darkness for ever' when they are convicted of their sins at the coming of 10,000 of His saints. They will answer for their profligate lifestyle and harsh words. They will be convicted and sentenced.

V 16–21: CONTRAST In contrast to the sensual, wicked, perverted conduct of these non-spiritual people, Christians should build themselves up in their faith, through the Holy Spirit, and through looking to Jesus Christ. **V 22–23: COMPASSION** While hating the sin that these people commit and spread, the Christian should have compassion on them as individuals, seeking to 'pull them out of the fire' of judgement. **V 24–25: CONFIDENCE** Only 'God our Saviour', the Lord Jesus Christ, can prevent us from stumbling, and present us faultless in glory. The Christian has confidence in this wise, majestic, glorious, sovereign and powerful God of eternity.

REVELATION

OVERVIEW

PEOPLE AND PRELIMINARIES

Revelation (twenty-two chapters) is the twenty-seventh and last book of the New Testament and the sixty-sixth and last book of the Bible. This unique book was written, probably between AD94 and AD96, by the apostle John, who was also the author of John's Gospel and three letters. He wrote Revelation while in exile on the Isle of Patmos in the Aegean Sea, to the south west of Ephesus.

PLAN AND PURPOSE

Some of Revelation's vivid imagery is difficult to understand. Views vary on some aspects of the book's overall plan and contents. Blessing is promised to those who hear and heed its message. Which parts are literal or illustrative is a question of context and judgement. Revelation 1:19 sets John's three-point plan for recording his vision into 'things which you have seen', then 'things which are', and then 'things which must shortly take place'. From a glorious vision of the Lord Jesus Christ as the Son of Man, John relates a series of messages to seven churches, only two of which are without censure. We then observe heaven's throne room and the centrality of the Lamb. Future chapters deal with: the seven seals of judgement on the book being opened; the sealing of the remnant; the seven trumpets of judgement coming from opening the seventh seal; the angel and the eating of the bitter-sweet book; the two heavenly witnesses and the seventh trumpet of judgement; the sun-clothed woman, the dragon's attack and the defence of the Man child; the archangel's fight with Satan and the great tribulation; the sea beast and the earth beast; the Lamb on Mount Zion with His 144,000 sealed followers, the proclamation by the three angels and the fall of Babylon, and the reaping of the earth's harvest and grapes of wrath; the vision about the seven angels with the last seven remaining plagues and golden bowls of God's wrath; the pouring out of those bowls; the fall of Babylon and warning to the people of God and the mourning of the world about Babylon; heaven's rejoicing over Babylon's downfall; the marriage of the Lamb; the 'Word of God' on the white horse; Satan bound in the bottomless pit for 1,000 years, the saints reigning with Christ for 1,000 years and the first resurrection; Satan's release after 1,000 years and his final doom in the Lake of Fire, and the judgement of the great white throne; the new heavens, new earth and

New Jerusalem with the Lamb as its light, and those excluded from it; the river of life, the tree of life, the throne of God and of the Lamb, fellowship between the saints and Him, the self-identification of the Lord Jesus Christ, and His commands to be ready for His second coming; and the warning never to add to or subtract from the Word of God.

PROFILE AND PROGRESSION

Part One—'The things which you have seen'—including the prologue, greetings and eulogy, vision of the glory of Christ, three-point commission to record the vision, and the key to Part Two (1:1–20); Part Two—'The things which are'—being the state of the seven churches in Asia Minor (Turkey) at Ephesus, Smyrna, Pergamos, Thaytira, Sardis, Philadelphia, and Laodicea (2:1–3:22); Part Three—'The things that will take place after this'—including the items covered in **'Plan and Purpose'**, above, in seven phases as follows: Phase One—the seven sealed scroll (4:1–8:1); Phase Two—the seven angels with seven trumpets (8:2–11:19); Phase Three—the woman's child delivered from the Dragon (12:1–6), Satan ejected from heaven (12:7–12); the woman (12:13–17); the sea beast (13:1–10), the earth beast and the mark of the beast (13:11–18); the 144,000 (14:1–5); three angels with messages (14:6–13); reaping in wrath (14:14–20); Phase Four—the seven bowls of God's wrath ((15:1–16:21); Phase Five— Babylon judged, heaven praising, and the marriage supper of the Lamb (17:1–19:10); Phase Six—the King of kings defeats the Beast and his armies (19:11–21); Phase Seven—the thousand years when Satan is bound and the saints reign with Christ, followed by the Lake of Fire and the judgement of the great white

throne, and the New Jerusalem (20:1–22:5); Christ's reminder of His coming soon, warning not to tamper with Scripture, and final reminder that the Lord Jesus will come 'quickly'.

PRINCIPLES AND PARTICULARS

Some Bible students interpret some parts of Revelation differently from others who study God's Word. Our understanding of this part of God's Word and our humility in accepting that others may have a different view can be testing! It is dangerous to assign meanings where none is given in Scripture, though some are obvious from the context of the passage concerned, from the plain statements in that passage, and from the general context of Scripture. Because it focuses on the triumph of the Lord Jesus Christ and the sovereignty of God over the consummation of history, this is a book filled with judgements on the wicked and hope for believers. Especially does it provide comfort in persecution and affliction. It reminds us of the supreme position in the Godhead occupied by our Saviour and Friend, the Lord Jesus Christ. Much of the book of Revelation is interpreted by different commentators in different ways, and it is dangerous to be too dogmatic. Because of its figurative speech and explanation of things to come beyond our experience or knowledge, it is a favourite fishing ground for cults and sects. That should not prevent us imbibing its principles, comparing Scripture with Scripture, and acting upon its many clear lessons. We should approach the rest with humble and cautious confidence that we are dealing with the Word of our God who will have the last word in history and who rules in eternity. The three main views about the Millennium, held equally sincerely by different Christians, are (alphabetically): amillennialism, which takes the millennium as symbolic only; post-millennialism, which believes the millennium will be brought in by a golden age of gospel teaching and its fruitful results; and pre-millennialism, which sees the millennium as a literal 1,000 year period. While some points are common to more than one view, different opinions exist on certain points even within the three main views. Additionally, speculation is rife about the significance of 666 as the number of the sea beast. Being 'the number of a man', and noting that 7 is often God's number of perfection in the Bible, '666' may imply an imperfect man in a trinity of evil. It is unwise to be too dogmatic.

REVELATION

CHAPTER ONE

V 1–3: REVELATION'S REVELATION The final book of the Bible is 'The Revelation of Jesus Christ'. It is centred upon Him and is written for 'His servants'. It comes to us via John, the apostle, through whom God speaks both by an angel and directly. He bears witness to God's word and to the 'testimony of Jesus Christ'. Blessing is in store for those who heed this book of prophecy, even though there are many things in it which are not always easy to understand or to interpret. **V 4–8: GRACIOUS GREETINGS** John starts by greeting the seven churches in Asia, wishing them grace and peace from his eternally consistent and unchanging God. Jesus is pictured as crucified, risen again and ruling in the earth. This majestic Jesus has loved us, washed us from sin in His blood, and made us kings and priests.

He will come again and be seen by all. God in Christ is the Beginning and the End. He is Almighty. **V 9–11: COMMUNICATOR'S COMMISSION** John describes himself as a brother and is experiencing tribulation and Christ's patience while exiled on Patmos, because of his stand for God's word and for Christ's testimony. God appears to him on 'the Lord's day' and tells him to write the book and send it to the seven churches in Asia—Ephesus, Smyrna, Pergamos, Thyatira, Sardis, Philadelphia and Laodicea. **V 12–18: AWESOME APPEARANCE** Jesus Christ appears to him as the 'Son of Man'. His dazzling glory, unrivalled holiness, perfect purity, absolute authority, eternal character, resurrection from the dead, and control over death shine out of the wonderful description given of Him. God gives John a sense of the wonder of his Saviour before he starts his special assignment from God. This is a lesson for us all. **V 19: DIVINE DIRECTIONS** Christ's directions to John, about what he must write, form a good outline of the Book of Revelation. They concern things which John has seen (the awesome vision of the Lord Jesus Christ), things which currently are (the next two chapters dealing with the state of the seven churches in Asia), and things which will take place after this (the rest of the book). **V 20: INTRODUCTORY ILLUMINATION** Jesus reveals to John that the seven stars in the vision are the angels (or 'messengers') of the seven churches and that the seven lamp stands are the seven churches.

CHAPTERS TWO AND THREE: THE SEVEN CHURCHES AS EVALUATED BY JESUS

The messages from the Lord Jesus Christ, through John, to the seven churches in Asia all follow a similar pattern, though with slight variations in the order. They all involve a greeting, an emphasis on some aspect of the character of Christ, a comment on the state of the church, a criticism of shortfall and/or commendation of aspects of faithfulness, a command to follow to remedy anything that is wrong or to continue in what is right, a plea to continue to listen to the Holy Spirit, and an encouragement. The table below summarises the Lord's evaluation of the seven churches. **Smyrna** and **Philadelphia** are emphasised in the box at the foot of page 561 as the only two churches that do not come under His censure.

CHAPTER TWO

V 1–7: CHURCH AT EPHESUS—LEFT FIRST LOVE Here is a church that is discerning about doctrine and faithful since its founding, but has left its first love. **V 8–11: CHURCH AT SMYRNA—PERSECUTED BUT PURE** Smyrna is one of the only two churches which Jesus does not criticise adversely. The church is persecuted greatly but shows by its works and spiritual richness that it has remained pure and loyal to its heavenly Bridegroom. **V 12–17: CHURCH AT PERGAMOS—CONFESSING YET COMPROMISING** This church is holding fast to the name of Christ and refusing to deny its Christian faith, even though martyrs have died because of opposition. Yet, sadly, this church that is confessing Christ is also compromising with worldliness, idolatry and sexual immorality. It has not taken a clear stand and is positively identified with those whose lifestyle and doctrine is contrary to the Christ they confess. **V 18–29: CHURCH AT THYATIRA—SERVING BUT SEDUCED** There is much to commend in the Thyatira church in terms of 'love, works,

service, faith, and your patience'. In fact, the works are increasing. But this serving church is seduced because a wicked and immoral woman, calling herself a prophetess, is advocating sexual immorality and idolatry. Significantly, the longest letter to the churches is written to address and redress this staggering and alarming problem. A church or Christian, even though serving, can lose spiritual health through compromise with immorality and idolatry. This church is serving, but is being seduced.

CHAPTER THREE

V 1–6: CHURCH AT SARDIS—DEAD BUT DISCIPLES Despite its reputation for being alive, the church at Sardis is dead. Yet even in this dead church there are some disciples of Christ who have not been soiled in its filth. They will walk with the Lord in eternity. **V 7–13: CHURCH AT PHILADELPHIA—GODLY AND GUARDED** Philadelphia is the second of two churches not to be censured by Jesus for any sin. Though in great weakness, the church has kept God's word and not denied His name in the face of great opposition. When the hour of trial comes, this church will be kept by Christ. It is godly and guarded. **V 14–22: CHURCH AT LAODICEA—TEPID AND TOTTERING** The Laodicean church is in some ways the saddest of them all. This church thinks it is rich and that it needs nothing. Its works are so lukewarm that Jesus will spit it out unless there is repentance. Repentance is available for anybody in that church who will hear His voice and open the door to Him as Lord and Saviour. But this church is tepid and tottering, like many today.

CHAPTER FOUR

V 1: TESTING TRUTH In chapter 1, John

has introduced us to what he has seen. The current state of things is featured in chapters 2 and 3. Chapter 4 commences the complex and larger section of Revelation, dealing with things which are yet to be. While much teaching is clear, other points are difficult to understand. **V 2–5: GOD'S GLORY** The dazzling glory of God is shown to John who is 'in the Spirit'. God is on a throne, being worshipped by twenty-four elders. Thunder and lightning surround Him, and seven burning lamps of fire, 'seven Spirits of God', give the picture of the illuminating and perfect work of the Holy Spirit. **V 6–8: CURIOUS CREATURES** A sea of glass, like crystal, surrounds the throne. Around the throne are four curious six-winged creatures. They have faces like different created beings—a lion, a calf, a man, and an eagle. They are similar, but not identical, to Ezekiel's four creatures, and they proclaim God's holiness and 'the Lord God Almighty, Who was, and is, and is to come!' **V 9–11: WORTHY WORSHIP** The creatures, possibly signifying all created life, and the twenty-four elders, possibly signifying Israel and the universal church,

worship God as the great and worthy Creator.

CHAPTER FIVE

V 1–5: ONLY ONE The One on the throne (God the Father) holds the scroll sealed with seven seals. John weeps because he learns that no one is worthy to take the scroll and open the seals. At that stage, an elder tells him that 'The Lion of the tribe of Judah, the Root of David has prevailed to open the scroll and loose its seven seals'. This is clearly a picture of Christ, who has conquered through His death, resurrection and ascension, and who alone can save. **V 6–7: LIVING LAMB** Right in the midst of the throne, sharing the glory with God the Father, is a Lamb that had been slain. The Lamb (the Lord Jesus Christ) takes the scroll from the Father. He will open the scroll later. Then the significance of each seal will be revealed. **V 8–10: REDEMPTION'S REFRAIN** As the Lamb takes the scroll, worship breaks out from the living creatures and the twenty-four elders. They proclaim the Lamb as worthy because He can open the scroll. He has redeemed them to God by His

EPHESUS	SMYRNA	PERGAMOS	THYATIRA	SARDIS	PHILADELPHIA	LAODICEA
1. He names the recipient—He is personal and specific.						
2:1	**2:8**	2:12	2:18	3:1	**3:7**	3:14
2. He reminds the recipient of Who He is—He starts with HIM, not with the church.						
2:1	**2:8**	2:12	2:18,23	3:1	**3:7**	3:14
3. He commends whenever He can—He applauds their appropriating His enabling grace.						
2:2–3,6	**2:9**	2:13	2:19,24	3:2,4	**3:8,10**	None
4. He exposes their sins and weaknesses—He loves them too much to keep silent.						
2:4	**None**	2:14–15	2:20–22	3:1–2	**None**	3:15–17
5. He always gives them His solution—He encourages them to go on with Him.						
2:5	**2:10**	2:16	2:22,25	3:2–3	**3:10,11**	3:18–20
6. He reminds them of the need to listen carefully—today we listen through His Word.						
2:7	**2:11**	2:17	2:29	3:6	**3:13**	3:22
7. He gives them His promise to encourage them to overcome—He only seeks their good.						
2:7	**2:10–11**	2:17	2:26–28	3:4–5	**3:10–12**	3:20–21

blood from 'every tribe and tongue and people and nation'. He has set up a spiritual kingdom and priesthood. Through Him, they shall reign on the earth. **V 11–14: WIDENING WORSHIP** The angels, who number millions, join in the refrain with a loud voice and praise the worthy Lamb. All the creatures in heaven, on the earth, and under the earth then pick up the crescendo of praise. At this the four living creatures say 'Amen!' and the twenty-four elders fall down and worship 'Him who lives for ever and ever'. All the key principles for true worship of God are found in this passage.

CHAPTER SIX

V 1: SEVEN SEALS—'COME AND SEE' The Lamb opens the first seal and John is bidden by one of the four living creatures to 'Come and see'. The seven seals have been likened to the title deeds of the universe which reveal God's judgements. The first six seals are dealt with in chapters 6 and 7, and we are introduced to the seventh seal in chapter 8. This seventh seal contains the seven trumpets, the first six of which are encountered in chapters 8 and 9. The seventh of those trumpets, which sounds in chapter 11, contains the seven bowls of final judgements poured out in chapter 16. All these 'sevens' speak of God's perfect judgement. The number seven in the Bible often indicates perfection. **V 2: SEVEN SEALS—THE FIRST SEAL OPENED** The seal reveals a man sitting on a white horse. He has a bow and is given a crown to signify that he is conquering. **V 3–4: SEVEN SEALS—THE SECOND SEAL OPENED** This time, the rider is on a fiery red horse. A time of no peace, massacre and conflict is signified by his great sword. **V 5–6: SEVEN SEALS— THE THIRD SEAL OPENED** Here the rider is on a black horse with scales in his hand.

A time of great scarcity and need is foreshadowed in this judgement. **V 7–8: SEVEN SEALS—THE FOURTH SEAL OPENED** The fourth horse is a pale horse and the rider is called Death, and is followed by Hades. A quarter of the earth's inhabitants will be killed by the sword, hunger, natural death, and beasts. **V 9–11: SEVEN SEALS—THE FIFTH SEAL OPENED** The opening of the fifth seal reveals an altar. Under the altar are the souls of those who have been slain because of God's word and their testimony. They ask God how long it will be before their blood is avenged. They are told that other servants and brothers will also be martyred before God acts in vengeance. **V 12–16: SEVEN SEALS—THE SIXTH SEAL OPENED** The opening of the sixth seal heralds a great earthquake, the blackening of the sun, and the moon becoming like blood. Stars fall to the earth, the sky recedes, and the mountains and islands move. Such is the fear of everyone that they seek to hide in caves and under mountain rocks. They are aware of God's face being set in vengeance against them, and of the 'wrath of the Lord'. None of God's enemies will be able to stand in this 'day of His great wrath'.

CHAPTER SEVEN

V 1–3: ANGELIC ACTION Chapter 7 affords a pause between the end of the sixth seal of judgement and the opening of the seventh seal. Here, we see four angels at work holding back the winds of the earth that could harm the earth, the sea and the trees. Another angel, specifically sealed by God, tells them not to cause this harm 'till we have sealed the servants of God on the forehead'. **V 4–8: SERVANTS SEALED** John then records that 12,000 of each of the tribes of Israel are sealed, making 144,000 in total. These are 'the servants of our God' to whom He has just referred. **V 9–10: COUNTLESS CROWDS** It is impossible to number the people included from the nations, tribes, peoples, and tongues of the earth who stand before the Lamb, clothed in white, holding palm branches, and crying out loudly, 'Salvation belongs to our God who sits on the throne and to the Lamb!' If the 144,000 refers to the children of Israel, the great multitude cited here must refer to the Gentiles who have been saved. **V 11–12: PROSTRATE PRAISE** The angels, elders and four living creatures continue their worship and praise, prostrate before God, at this sight of His salvation accomplished among Jews and Gentiles. **V 13–17: IDENTITY IDENTIFIED** An elder informs John of the identity of 'the great multitude that no one could number'. They have come out of 'the great tribulation' and their robes have been washed white in the blood of the Lamb. They serve God continually in His temple. God will dwell among them and they shall never suffer in any way again. The Lamb will be their Shepherd and lead them to living water. They will never know tears again.

CHAPTER EIGHT

V 1–6: SEVEN TRUMPETS—SEAL'S THEME Initially, there is silence for about half an hour after the Lamb opens the seventh seal. Then seven angels of God prepare to sound seven trumpets given to them after another angel, who offers incense along with the prayers of the saints, throws the censer and the incense to the earth, causing 'noises, thunderings, lightnings, and an earthquake'. The theme of the seventh seal is thus contained in the judgement of the seven trumpets which follow. **V 7: SEVEN TRUMPETS—FIRST TRUMPET** A third of

the trees and grass burn as hail and fire, mingled with blood, hit the earth after the first trumpet is sounded. **V 8–9: SEVEN TRUMPETS—SECOND TRUMPET** A third of all living creatures in the sea die, and a third of the ships are destroyed as, at the second trumpet, a great mountain-like mass burning with fire is thrown into the sea, causing a third of the sea to become blood. **V 10–11: SEVEN TRUMPETS— THIRD TRUMPET** Wormwood, the name of a great burning star that falls from heaven on to a third of the rivers and springs of water, makes those waters into poisonous and bitter wormwood, causing many to die. **V 12: SEVEN TRUMPETS— FOURTH TRUMPET** At the fourth trumpet, a third of the sun, a third of the moon, and a third of the stars are struck with ensuing darkness for a third of the day and a third of the night. **V 13: SEVEN TRUMPETS—SOLEMN TASK** John then hears a flying angel proclaiming a triple woe to the inhabitants of the earth because of the judgements which are to come, represented by the three trumpet blasts yet to sound.

CHAPTER NINE

V 1–12: SEVEN TRUMPETS—FIFTH TRUMPET The fifth trumpet fulfils the first of the three woes that the flying angel has just announced. Here we see 'a star fallen from heaven' (Satan) who opens the bottomless pit from which smoke rises from its great furnace and darkens the air. Horrible locusts appear from that smoke but are commanded not to harm the vegetation, but only those whom God has not sealed on their foreheads. They are permitted to torment, but not to kill, for five months. The tormented will wish to die but cannot. The locusts, for whom a graphic and horrific description is given, have as king the 'angel of the bottomless pit' named Abbadon, in Hebrew, or Apollyon, in Greek. Here is direct satanic activity on earth. Two more woes are to come. **V 13–21: SEVEN TRUMPETS— SIXTH TRUMPET** The sixth angel is told to release the four angels at the River Euphrates who then kill one third of mankind. This is done through two hundred million horsemen, whose frightening appearance is described vividly. Fire, smoke and brimstone, as plagues, lead them to kill the third of mankind. This they do by their mouths and by their serpent-like tails. The remaining two thirds of mankind, however, neither repent of their demon worship, idolatry and materialism, nor of their murders, witchcraft, sexual immorality or thefts. So hardened are they against God that even His horrific judgements do not move them to repentance. This is an alarmingly sad and tragic state to be in.

CHAPTER TEN

V 1–7: SEVEN TRUMPETS—DELAY A delay between the sounding of the sixth and seventh trumpets sees another mighty and glorious angel descend, with a book in his hand and crying with a loud voice, like a roaring lion. Seven thunders speak to John as he is told from heaven to seal their message up and not to write it down. The angel takes an oath before God, and confirms there will be no delay in the judgement after the sounding of the seventh trumpet. **V 8–11: SEVEN TRUMPETS—DEVOUR** God tells John to take the angel's book and eat it, which he does. He finds, as he is told will be the case, that it is as sweet as honey in his mouth but bitter in his stomach. He is then told that he 'must prophesy again about many peoples, nations, tongues and kings'. (Could the sweet taste of the book that was eaten imply that salvation is sweet to those who belong to God? Perhaps the bitterness in the stomach may mean that it is not pleasant to announce to unrepentant, lost sinners that eternal judgement awaits them?)

CHAPTER ELEVEN

V 1–6: SEVEN TRUMPETS—TWO WITNESSES EXPLAINED As the sounding of the seventh trumpet draws nearer, John is told to measure the temple of God, its altar, and the worshippers there. At the same time, he is told that the outer court will be trodden down by Gentiles for forty-two months. He is then told about God's power being given to two witnesses who will prophesy for 1,260 days, clothed in sackcloth (signifying a message of repentance and mourning for sin). They are described as olive trees and lamp stands, and during this period will be invulnerable. They will devour their enemies with God's fire from their mouths. They will have amazing powers of judgement which God will give to them for this period of time. **V 7–10: SEVEN TRUMPETS—TWO WITNESSES EXECUTED** When they have finished testifying, the beast will come out of the bottomless pit and make war against them, overcome them and kill them. Their dead bodies will lie in the street of Jerusalem, 'where our Lord was crucified', here identified with Sodom and Egypt because of its sin. For three and a half days, the world will see them and rejoice about their death, because they tormented the earth. **V 11–12: SEVEN TRUMPETS—TWO WITNESSES EXALTED** After three and a half days, 'the breath of life from God' will enter and raise the witnesses and great fear will come upon those who observe them. God calls them to heaven and they ascend in a cloud, in front of their enemies. **V 13–14: SEVEN TRUMPETS—TWO WOES EXPERIENCED** As the once martyred, now resurrected and ascended, witnesses of God are taken into heaven, the seventh woe, which precedes the seventh trumpet, is experienced. In a great earthquake, a tenth of the city falls. Seven thousand people are killed and the rest are afraid and give glory to God. The second woe (the sixth trumpet) is now over and the third woe will come quickly. **V 15–19: SEVEN TRUMPETS—TRUE WORSHIP ESTABLISHED** The seventh angel sounds the seventh trumpet, which, by implication, brings in the third woe. This trumpet will cover all events until Christ's kingdom is established for ever and ever. In the book of Revelation this will take us through to the end of chapter 19. The twenty-four elders again prostrate themselves in worship and give thanks for 'the One who was and who is and who is to come', for God's power and righteous judgements, and for His gracious rewards for those who love Him and serve Him. God's heavenly temple is opened, the ark of His covenant is seen, and there are 'lightnings, noises, thunderings, an earthquake and great hail'. The next chapters unroll the events that will lead to Christ's kingdom being established, and will include the judgement of the seven bowls.

CHAPTER TWELVE

V 1–6: THE WOMAN, THE CHILD AND THE DRAGON A sign in heaven is given of a woman clothed with the sun, with the moon under her feet, and wearing a garland of twelve stars. She is giving birth to a baby. Another sign reveals a great fiery dragon with seven diademed heads and ten horns. His tail sweeps a third of heaven's stars to earth and he seeks to devour the male Child, who is the ruler to come. The male Child is caught up to the throne of God. The woman flees to the wilderness prepared by God. She will be there for 1,260 days. (Scripture shows that the woman is Israel, the Child is Christ, and the dragon is Satan in his attempt to destroy Israel and then the Messiah. A third of the angels were cast down to earth in that rebellion caused by Satan.) **V 7–12: THE WAR, THE CONQUEST AND THE DRAGON** The archangel Michael, with his angels, fights and prevails over Satan, in a war in heaven. Satan and his angels are cast out. The conquest is acknowledged by a loud voice from heaven proclaiming that the power of Christ has come in the casting out of Satan. Accused and persecuted Christian brethren have overcome by Christ's blood, by their testimony, and by not loving their lives even to death. Heaven rejoices but earth will suffer as Satan, knowing his time is short, will increase his activity and his wrath on earth. **V 13–17: THE WINGS, THE CHASM AND THE DRAGON** On earth, the dragon seeks to destroy the woman who gave birth to the Child, but God causes her to fly away on two great wings from the serpent, another form taken by Satan in Scripture. She is hidden and nourished in the wilderness for 'a time, times and half a time'. The serpent spews out a flood to engulf the woman but a chasm appears in the earth into which the river goes and the woman is delivered. Now all who are God's offspring, identified because they keep God's commandments and have Christ's testimony, are the objects of the dragon's diabolical wrath. The dragon declares war on them.

CHAPTER THIRTEEN

V 1–10: THE SEA BEAST John sees a beast

coming up out of the sea. It is a mixture of leopard, bear and lion, and has seven heads and ten crowned horns. A blasphemous name is on the heads. The dragon (Satan) delegates his evil power, throne and authority to this sea beast. The world marvels that one of his heads, which looked as though it was mortally wounded, is healed. The dragon and the beast are therefore worshipped. The beast is thought to be invulnerable in war. For forty-two months, the beast speaks arrogantly and blasphemously against everything to do with God. He and His followers go to war with the saints and overcome them. Only those whose names are written in the 'Book of Life of the Lamb slain from the foundation of the world' will refuse to worship him or bow to his evil authority. The saints need patience and faith in the face of the vast captivity and carnage that this sea beast will bring. He is the Antichrist, controlled by Satan in a way that no one else in history has been, is, or will be. **V 11–17: THE SECOND BEAST** 'Coming up out of the earth', probably from the abyss, is a second beast with two lamb-like horns. He speaks like a dragon and is also known as 'the false prophet'. Exercising the sea beast's authority, he uses great signs and wonders to spread propaganda about the sea beast, and makes people worship not only the sea beast, but also an animated image of the sea beast to which he is enabled to give breath. Commercial activity and normal life are only available to those whom he can compel to bear the mark of the sea beast or 'the number of his name' on their right hands and foreheads. **V 18: 'THREE SIXES' BEAST** The number assigned to the beast (meaning the sea beast) is 666, and John tells us that 'it is the number of a man'. However temporarily powerful and

damaging that man may be, God is sovereign over him.

CHAPTER FOURTEEN

V 1–5: REFRAIN OF REDEEMED The new song, which can only be sung by 144,000 redeemed undefiled followers of the Lamb, and who live without deceit and faultlessly by God's grace, is now sung on Mount Zion. The Lamb is standing there with the 144,000. It may be that the reference to being 'not defiled with women, for they are virgins' speaks symbolically of their refusal to be involved in the spiritual adultery of Babylon, as well as being sexually pure and free from immorality. **V 6–11: ANNOUNCEMENTS OF ANGELS** Three angels now make announcements. The first, who has the 'everlasting gospel to preach' to everyone, says loudly that God must be feared and glorified because His hour of judgement is coming. God must be worshipped. The second angel declares that Babylon is fallen because all the nations have drunk 'of the wine of the wrath of her fornication'. The third angel proclaims that those bearing the mark of the beast will be the subject of God's eternal wrath. The 'smoke of their torment' is never ending. **V 12–13: SECURITY OF SAINTS** The saints, marked by their steadfast and patient keeping of God's commandments and having faith in Jesus, are confirmed as blessed after death because of the rest that God will give them in Him. **V 14–19a: REAPING OF REAPERS** The earth is now reaped by 'One like the Son of Man' at the prompting of an angel. A second angel reaps also after a third angel declares that the grapes of the earth's vine are 'fully ripe'. The grapes are gathered. **V 19b–20: WINEPRESS OF WRATH** God's wrath is depicted as a great winepress into which the grapes are placed and trampled outside the city. The juice of the grapes, like blood, is so plentiful that it comes up to the horses' bridles for a distance of 1,600 furlongs. (This approximates to 180 miles or 290 kilometres).

CHAPTER FIFTEEN

V 1: SEVEN PLAGUES John sees another 'great and marvellous' sign in heaven. Seven angels have the seven final plagues that will complete the wrath of God and, by implication, the third woe. These seven plagues, contained in seven golden bowls full of God's wrath, will thus complete the judgement announced by the seventh trumpet, which itself is the last judgement under the seventh seal. **V 2–4: SINGING PRAISE** But first, there is a prelude and a victory song of praise for those enabled by God to overcome the beast, his image, his mark, and the number of his name. They sing the song of Moses and the song of the Lamb. It is a song of worship acknowledging the justice and truth of God's judgements. **V 5–8: SOLEMN PREPARATION** After this, the seven angels having the seven plagues are given seven golden bowls full of God's wrath by one of the four living creatures. The temple is filled with smoke from God's glory and power, so that no one can enter it until the completion of the seven plagues from the seven bowls of the seven angels.

CHAPTER SIXTEEN

V 1: SEVEN BOWLS—ALL BOWLS— SENDING John hears the seven angels being sent out to pour out all the seven bowls of God's wrath on the earth. **V 2: SEVEN BOWLS—BOWL 1—SORES** The pouring out of the first bowl causes terrible sores upon those bearing the mark of the beast and worshipping his image. **V 3: SEVEN BOWLS—BOWL 2— SEA** The world's seas are turned into congealed blood by the second bowl, causing every living sea creature to die. **V 4–7: SEVEN BOWLS—BOWL 3— SOURCES** The sources of water, namely rivers and springs, become blood as a result of the third bowl being poured out. The angel of the waters bursts into praise to God, because of the avenging of the blood of saints and prophets. From the altar, the location of the slaughtered martyrs, comes a confirming echo of that praise. **V 8–9: SEVEN BOWLS—BOWL 4— SCORCHING** The sun itself has the fourth bowl poured on it, causing scorching with great heat from the fire. Suffering men blaspheme God's name but do not repent or give Him the glory. **V 10–11: SEVEN BOWLS—BOWL 5—SATAN'S** The very throne of the beast is the recipient of God's wrath from the fifth bowl. As the beast's entire kingdom becomes 'full of darkness', great pain causes the gnawing of tongues. Again, the response is not repentance, but blasphemy. **V 12–16: SEVEN BOWLS—BOWL 6—STRATEGIC** The sixth bowl is poured out 'on the great River Euphrates' to prepare a highway from the east. Frog-like spirits come from the mouths of the dragon, the beast and the false prophet (who is the earth beast). They will gather the nations' kings at the end of the world to the battle of Armageddon, where their final defeat will be complete. One of the last sayings by Jesus in the Bible is made at this time when He says He will come as unexpectedly and suddenly as a thief. He urges His people to be ready for His second coming. Armageddon follows that. **V 17–21: SEVEN BOWLS—BOWL 7— SHAKE** This seventh and last bowl of wrath is poured into the air and the voice of God from the throne in the temple cries, 'It is done!' Huge cosmic interactions follow this, including the greatest earthquake that the world has ever known. This shakes the earth and, while the cities of the nations fall and Babylon especially receives the wrath of God, Jerusalem is divinely reorganised into three parts. Islands and mountains disappear as huge hailstones from heaven fall upon men. Again, the response of the sufferers is blasphemy, rather than the repentance which would have brought blessing.

CHAPTER SEVENTEEN

V 1–3a: INSTRUCTION—WILDERNESS IN SPIRIT To concentrate on some of the detailed results of pouring out the seven bowls of wrath, the angel invites John to come with him to learn of the judgement of 'the great harlot who sits on many waters' and who led astray the political rulers of the world. John is carried away in the Spirit into the wilderness, in order to focus on this revelation. **V 3b–6: INTRODUCTION—WOMAN IN SCARLET** There he sees a woman dressed in purple and scarlet, sitting on the beast whose description matches the sea beast, the Antichrist. At John's introduction to this vision, he notices that the beast is also scarlet and that the woman is arrayed in splendour and glory. She holds a golden cup which is full of abominations and the filth of her fornication. Like other prostitutes in that region, her name is written on her head. She is called 'Babylon'. She is drunk with the blood of the saints and martyrs of Jesus. John is amazed at his introduction to this terrible truth. **V 7–18: INTERPRETATION— WICKEDNESS IN SYMBOLS** The angel reveals the general meaning of this vision to John. Here are symbols of great wickedness, and, as often applies in the Bible, immorality can indicate idolatry

and a general rejection of God, as well as sexual sin. The beast (Antichrist) will ascend from the bottomless pit and finally go to perdition. Non-Christians will marvel at his false resurrection in coming up out of the abyss. Biblical symbolism has inbuilt flexibility, and the angel says that the seven heads are seven mountains on which the woman sits to exercise her power. They also stand for seven kings, of whom five have fallen, one is in existence and one is to come. The beast, who supports the woman's exercise of her false religion on the world, is both the seventh and the eighth king. His eighth kingship will be after he has risen from the abyss and before he goes to eternal perdition. The ten horns are ten unidentified kings who will make war with the Lamb, who will prove His absolute sovereignty in overcoming them. The waters signify all the people of the world over whom the harlot will reign, in her false religion. This will end when the ten kings, of one mind and orchestrated by Antichrist, will destroy this false religion. They will give their kingdom to Antichrist, who will then take up absolute and evil power himself. God will allow this within His own timetable. He will permit Babylon, which may symbolise a world centre of wickedness, to reign over the political leaders of the world. But God is sovereign and is allowing all this to happen for His eternal purposes.

CHAPTER EIGHTEEN

V 1–3: BABYLON—FALLEN While the earth is illuminated with the glory of an angel coming down with great authority, John hears a mighty and great cry that Babylon is fallen and is now a prison for foul spirits and unclean and hated birds. The reason for her fall is the spiritual fornication of the political leaders and the materialism that she has produced. This symbol of false religion is destroyed by the very world system that supported it, but there is no return to God. **V 4–8: BABYLON—FIRE** From heaven, God's people are told to get out of Babylon to avoid the influence of her many sins and plagues. She is to be resisted and opposed vigorously by God's saints. God will burn her with fire. **V 9–20: BABYLON—FEAR** 'The kings of the earth' (the political leaders), along with the merchants whose profit has gone, will mourn and weep for Babylon. However, as the kings see the smoke of God's fiery judgement rising, the fear of her torment keeps them away from her. This judgement has come 'in one hour'. By contrast, heaven, the apostles and the prophets are commanded to rejoice over the destruction of such an evil system and influence. **V 21–24: BABYLON—FINALITY** Every trace of Babylon, symbolic of the world's evil religious system, will go, just as the great millstone disappears without trace when the mighty angel throws it into the sea. This is because of her trading in evil, her spiritual trading in sorcery, and the fact that she caused the death of the 'prophets and saints and all who were slain on the earth'. There is a finality about the fall of Babylon which again underlines the sovereignty and ultimate plan of God.

CHAPTER NINETEEN

V 1–8: WORSHIP AND HALLELUJAH! At the downfall of Babylon and God's vengeance against her evil system, a great multitude in heaven praise God and sing their own 'Hallelujah Chorus'. God has avenged the martyrdom of his servants and they repeat the chorus again! The twenty-four elders and the four living creatures again prostrate themselves to worship God, as the echoes of the 'Hallelujah Chorus' spread. God then bids His servants, 'both small and great', to join in the refrain. The 'great number' of worshippers focus their praise on God's omnipotent reign. They gladly and joyfully give Him glory for 'the marriage of the Lamb has come and His wife has made herself ready'. Christ will reign finally with His saints, His bride. **V 9–10: WRONG AND HELPED** John is told to write of the blessings of those who are called to the Lamb's marriage supper. He is informed that these are 'the true sayings of God'. But even an apostle can get things wrong, even when God is blessing him! He falls at the angel's feet to worship him, but is instantly rebuked and told that the angel is but a fellow servant. He is told to 'Worship God! For the testimony of Jesus is the Spirit of prophecy.' Our Triune God alone is worthy of worship. **V 11–16: WORD AND HOLINESS** The Lord Jesus Christ now makes an appearance in flaming holiness. He is 'faithful and true'. His robe is dipped in blood and His name is 'The Word of God'. He appears on a white horse and is followed by the armies of heaven, 'white and clean', also on white horses. The nations will be destroyed by the sword coming out of His mouth and He will be the ruler and tread 'the winepress of the fear and wrath of Almighty God'. He is 'KING OF KINGS AND LORD OF LORDS'. **V 17–21: WAR AND HELL** The angel tells John of the coming battle of Armageddon, where the defeat of the enemies of God will be so comprehensive that it will be referred to as 'a supper' in which their dead bodies will be devoured by birds. Antichrist (the sea beast), the kings of the world (the world's political rulers) with their amassed armies, and the false prophet (the land beast) gather together to war against the Lord Jesus

Christ and His people. All except the beast and the false prophet are killed with the sword coming from Christ, 'the Word of God', and the birds are filled with their flesh. The beast and the false prophet are captured and are cast alive into the lake of fire burning with brimstone. This is later identified as eternal, continuous and conscious punishment. This is the hell of eternal damnation. At this stage, Satan himself is not confined there, but the next chapter shows that he soon will be.

CHAPTER TWENTY

V 1–3: MILLENNIUM—SATAN SEALED We now come to the first mention of 1,000 years, otherwise known as the millennium. Here we read that for 1,000 years, Satan will be cast into the bottomless pit, shut up and sealed by Him, so that he is unable to deceive the nations. He will be released after 1,000 years. **V 4–6: MILLENNIUM—SAINTS' SOULS** While judgement is committed to those on the thrones, the souls of martyred saints who had resisted the beast and not received his mark live and reign with Christ for 1,000 years. The rest of the dead do not come to life until after the millennium. This is a blessed and first resurrection and is untouchable by death. Those reigning with Christ are known as 'Priests of God and of Christ'. **V 7–16: MILLENNIUM—SATAN SMASHED** The first of two major events, which will happen at the end of the millennium, is described. Satan will be released, symbolised by Gog and Magog, to battle against God's saints and the beloved city, Jerusalem. Fire from God's mouth devours them. Satan is sent to the lake of fire and brimstone for ever to accompany the beast and the false prophet and to experience eternal torment there. **V 11–15: MILLENNIUM—SOVEREIGN'S**

SENTENCING The second great event after the end of the millennium is called the judgement of 'the great white throne'. Here, God the Son judges sinners according to their works. Those dead people whose names are not written in the 'Book of Life' are thrown into the lake of fire. At this stage, everyone who has died will be judged. The Sovereign's sentencing to the lake of fire of all unrepentant, unbelieving sinners is called 'the second death'. The Book of Life contains the names of those who have come to eternal life in Christ.

CHAPTER TWENTY-ONE

V 1–5: NEW CREATION Just as sin and sinners have been dealt with and confined to the lake of fire, so a newly created heaven and earth replace the old world, which passes away. The new Jerusalem, the capital of heaven which signifies the presence of God, comes to this new heaven and earth where God will dwell with His people for ever. Tears, death, sorrow, crying and pain will be no more. **V 6–8: NEW COMPARISON** Jesus is confirmed as the 'Alpha and Omega, the Beginning and the End'. He gives the water of life, an overcoming life, and a godly inheritance to all who will trust Him and have become His children by grace. But He immediately makes the new comparison that those guilty of sin, and not reconciled to God, will be in the eternally burning and consciously experienced lake of fire, the second death. There is no middle way and no annihilation. **V 9–21: NEW CITY** A glorious explanation of new Jerusalem is given by all the angels who had the seven bowls filled with the seven last plagues. New Jerusalem is depicted as the Bride of the Lamb, the Lord Jesus Christ. Glory, splendour, symmetry, beauty and inestimable value mark this city which, by the twelve tribes of Israel, represents the redeemed from Old Testament times and, by the apostles, represents those who have been redeemed since Jesus came on earth to save sinners. **V 22–26: NEW CONCENTRATON** In the eternal presence of the Lord God Almighty and the Lamb, no temple building is needed in heaven. Neither will there be any concentration on a physical sun or moon in the new creation, but God's continual illumination by the Lamb is central. All saved people will walk honourably for ever in that light and glory. Night will cease to exist and the redeemed from all the nations will walk in its light. **V 27: NEW CONFIRMATION** John confirms anew, however, that nothing with a shadow of sin will enter there. Only those will be found in heaven whose names are written in 'the Lamb's Book of Life', and who thus have had their sin cleansed away through the blood of Christ.

CHAPTER TWENTY-TWO

V 1–5: CHRIST'S SALVATION Flowing from the throne, shared by God the Father and the Lamb, is a pure, crystal clear river. It waters the tree of life which produces its twelve fruits every month. Its leaves heal the nations. Guilt has been removed. God's servants shall see His face and bear His name on their foreheads. They will reign for ever and ever in this land where there is no night because God gives them light. **V 6–7: COMING SOON** The truth of God's word and accuracy of God's inspired prophets are restated. In the first of the last four sayings by Jesus in the Bible, He declares that He is coming soon. Those who keep 'the words of the prophecy of this book' are blessed. **V 8–9: CORRECTED SERVANT** Despite all this truth and spirituality, John repeats his

earlier error of worshipping the angel! The angel corrects him constructively, again, and reminds him that he is only a fellow servant and that he, John, must worship God. **V 10–11: CONTINUOUS STATE** John must herald the words of this prophecy because 'the time is at hand'. When the deadline is passed, the saints will be saved and the lost will be lost, and there will be no reopening of the case. The state that each person is in, then, will continue eternally. **V 12–13: COMING SOON** The second of Jesus' four final sayings again proclaims that He is coming soon to reward and to deal with people according to the deeds they have done. Jesus reminds us of His divine and eternal nature. **V 14–15: CONTRAST SHOWN** The blessing of those whose conversion to Christ has led them to obey His law, look forward to the tree of life, and have access to the heavenly city is contrasted with those people who sinful lifestyles show that they remain outside His forgiveness. **V 16: CONFIRMED SOURCE** Jesus confirms that He commissioned and authorised the angel to testify to God's truth to the churches. He reminds them again of His own divine character and authority as 'the Root and Offspring of David, the Bright and Morning Star'. **V 17: COME SIMPLY** God's pressing invitation by His Spirit is clear: 'Come!' Three times in one verse is that word used, and the Christ's bride, the church, endorses it. Anyone who hears, thirsts, or desires is bidden to take the water of life freely. This is as true for a lost sinner coming for salvation as it is of a Christian needing renewal. Simply, 'Come!' **V 18–19: COMPLETED SCRIPTURE** In the Bible's last warning to its readers, God solemnly consolidates the principles found elsewhere, that no one must add to or take away from His Word. The book of Revelation is the last book of Scripture to be written, and anyone adding to or subtracting from it will be plagued by God. To say that God has not spoken enough, or that He has said too much, is a blasphemous insult to Him, His wisdom, and His sovereignty. God-breathed Scripture is completed with this last chapter of Revelation. **V 20: COMING SOON** Jesus underlines the importance of His second coming. The last recorded words of the Lord Jesus Christ in Scripture are 'Surely I am coming quickly', repeating what He has already said twice in this chapter. Clearly the Christian is to take the second coming of Christ as factual, imminent, and important. The enthusiastic response should be that which John gives, namely, 'Amen. Even so, come, Lord Jesus!' **V 21: CLOSING SALUTATION** The last words of the Bible are 'The grace of our Lord Jesus Christ be with you all. Amen.' Until the day when Christ comes again, those who have put their trust in Him for salvation and remain on the earth will be given His grace. There are no exceptions. His grace is with all who trust Him and honour Him. The book of Revelation, the New Testament, and the Bible end with the word 'Amen', which literally means 'May it be so.' May our hearts always rejoice with a willing trust and obedience, in response to what God has done, is doing, and one day gloriously will do.

THE BIBLE
PANORAMA

Enjoying the whole Bible with a
chapter-by-chapter guide

PART TWO

Enjoying the unhindered
view with confidence

Practical topics about the Bible to help you trust and read it

What is the Bible?

An overview

As shown in *Appendix 1*, as well as being a unique and single God-breathed book, the Bible is an amazing library of sixty-six books, divided into two Testaments, the Old and the New. The Old Testament traces the effect of sin on mankind from creation, follows Israel's formation and development as God's earthly people through its wanderings and entry into the promised land and its subsequent history, and looks forward to the coming to earth of the Lord Jesus Christ to redeem lost mankind. The New Testament starts with the miraculous conception and virgin birth of Jesus, chronicles His life, ministry, death, resurrection and ascension into heaven, and looks forward to His glorious second coming and to the events by which God will usher in an everlasting new heaven and a new earth. It records the birth, growth and missionary activity of the early church and contains vital teaching and instruction on practical living for Christians.

The constituent parts of the Bible

Although elements of law, history, poetry, prophecy, gospel truth and Christian teaching are liberally scattered throughout this infallible and inspired revelation of God, the books of the Bible are broadly divisible as follows:

Old Testament (39)

Law of Moses (5)—these first five books are collectively known as the 'Pentateuch';

Israel's history (12)—from Jacob's call through the moves to and from Egypt, including their wilderness wanderings, being taken in successive captivities, and returning in stages to their land;

Poetical books (5)—which are nevertheless factually and spiritually accurate and profitable;

Major prophets (5)—dealing with God's forth-telling of His truth and foretelling of His plans to His people ('major' describes only the length of prophecies made);

Minor prophets (12)—exactly the same as the major prophets except that they are 'minor' only in the length of the prophecies made within them: their message is just as important and divinely inspired as the major prophets.

New Testament (27)

Four Gospels (4)—the birth, life, ministry, death, resurrection and ascension of the Lord Jesus Christ;

Acts of the Apostles (1)—the historical account of the birth, growth, evangelism and ministry of the early church;

Church letters (9)—teaching about Christian truth, daily living, right behaviour and church leadership, contained in Holy Spirit-inspired apostolic letters to the churches;

Other letters (12)—cover the same principles and much similar ground in common with the church letters regarding Christian doctrine and living, but in both a pastoral context and to Jewish Christians scattered abroad;

Revelation (1)—God's teaching of things that were, are now and are to come: tomorrow's history in advance, shown to be under God's glorious and sovereign control.

Too wonderful to pigeonhole!

The helpful division of the books into categories (such as law, history, poetry and prophecy) is an observed division by men rather than a directive of God. Thus you will find that there are elements of those categories in the other divisions. For example, the first five books of the law are all historically accurate (as is the whole Bible) and contain some prophecy and poetry. Psalms, the historically accurate poetic book, contains prophecy and also statements which emphasise the truth of God's law and our obligation to keep it. The divisions reflect general observations to help the Bible reader, and not exclusive categories to bind him or her. God's word is far too wonderful to pigeonhole!

Different

Just as the Lord Jesus Christ is different from all other leaders, religious or otherwise, so the Bible is different from all other books. Those leaders and those books are of earthly origin. The religious leaders are men (or women) with all the weaknesses and failures of sinful humanity, and all the other books, even religious ones, are written merely from a human point of view. Just as Jesus is the living Word of God, whose origin is from heaven (John 3:13; 1 Corinthians 15:47), so the Bible is the written Word of God, also of heavenly origin (2 Peter 1:18–19). Jesus came to earth from heaven, and took on the form of sinless manhood even though he was the offspring of a woman who was godly but nevertheless sinful. In the same way, the Bible was sent from heaven, put together on earth, and is infallible and God-breathed despite coming through the instrumentality of godly writers who were, nevertheless, sinners (2 Peter 1:21). In each case, God the Holy Spirit worked to produce God's infallible word—the Lord Jesus as the living Word, and the Bible as the written word.

The Bible is ...

Learned men have written large and profound books on what the Bible is! Here we are taking just a few paragraphs to focus on God's marvellous word. We will see below that it is:

A book/a library

God-breathed/man-made

Miraculous/practical

Unified/diversified
Loved/hated
Eternal/temporary
Judging/saving
Read/unread
In briefly considering those, remember that we are only scratching the surface!

The Bible is ... *a book/a library*

You can hold in your hand a single volume, in one of many languages and often in different translations and versions, of the whole of God's revealed will to men and women. That is exciting! Almighty God has given us a book to own, to read, to learn, to consult and to live by. It is an amazing book! And yet it is more than a book—it is a library! Those thirty-nine Old Testament and twenty-seven New Testament books, which make up the written Word of God, can be regarded as comprising various sections of God's library. As we have seen, that library is divided into sections dealing with subject matter as diverse as law and poetry, or history and prophecy. Just as there is a huge difference between this book of God and any other book, so there is an enormous difference between His library and all other libraries. There is no library in the world where all the books, being so different and written by different authors at different times, are in perfect harmony and accord with each other. This library, the Bible, has a perfect and infallible oneness without contradicting itself elsewhere, because it is God's library.

The Bible is ... *God-breathed/man-made*

The Bible claims to be breathed out by God (2 Timothy 3:16). That is what the word 'inspired' conveys. God wrote it. He inspired every original word that made up the Bible, in the original languages of Hebrew, Greek and Aramaic. That is why it is infallible: because God is infallible, and He is its author. Yet the Bible came to us through men. Like us, they were sinful and fallible. They could make mistakes and their knowledge and intelligence were limited, just as ours is today. Yet, because God the Holy Spirit came upon them and inspired them to write His word, God protected them and His written word from any errors in the words He gave them originally. (Obviously, in making translations it is not always possible to convey the depth of meaning that God gave in those original infallible words. However, careful translations by scholars of integrity from the oldest manuscripts give us the written Word of God today which is very close to the original meaning, at the least, and is usually completely on target.) The same Holy Spirit who caused the miraculous conception of the incarnate and perfect Son of God in the womb of Mary produced a miraculously infallible written word, the Bible, when the Holy Spirit came upon the thoughts and minds of those who penned Scripture. Did Jesus reflect some of the physical features of His biological mother? Perhaps. Certainly the books of the Bible reflect different characteristics of their authors. Yet the Bible demonstrates the same faultlessness and infallibility as did the Word of God made man (Proverbs 30:5–6).

The Bible is ... *miraculous / practical*

Sometimes we use the word 'miraculous' too lightly. We usually mean that something has happened which was wonderful, unlikely and unexpected. But wonderful, unlikely and unexpected things can happen which are by no means 'miraculous'. A miracle is when God personally steps into a situation to do something that otherwise just could not be done. That is why, for example, the creation of the world was miraculous, as was the incarnation and the resurrection of Jesus. Genuine Christian conversion is miraculous, also. By definition, no one could write 'the word of God' because it is 'of God' (Hebrews 4:12). By very nature, it is a miracle. God did what no one else could do. Only He had the power, the authority, the knowledge and the wisdom to write it. Yet the Bible is practical, too. Jesus lived among us as a practical man, despite also being 'Immanuel' or 'God with us' (Matthew 1:23). He worked with His hands, ate our food, walked our roads, talked our words—His miraculous nature and origin blended with His practical and sinless humanity. Similarly, the teaching of the written word from heaven, the Bible, is profitable in every possible practical situation in human life and equips the Christian to do good in every circumstance of life (2 Timothy 3:16–17). Thus it speaks to us in the home and in the workplace, in sorrow and in joy, in sickness and in health, in society or in solitude, in richness or in poverty, in youth or in old age, in life or in death, in success or in failure, and in the church or in the world. God speaks to us in every situation through His Self-revelation in the Bible.

The Bible is ... *unified / diversified*

The Bible is a running unity of God's written revelation. Not only has it no contradictions, but all its separate themes are interconnected and in perfect harmony. Its themes dovetail perfectly together and run through the whole of its contents. No single theme takes away from or contradicts another one, though each theme is different. The balance held between them is perfect. All the major themes can be found in the very first book of the Bible, yet they are still being echoed and expanded in the last one, having been clearly demonstrated throughout the Old and the New Testaments. But despite this unity and harmony, the amazingly vast range of topics, historical accounts, principles, disciplines, teachings, problems, blessings, societies and people gives us the world's most comprehensive and authoritative encyclopaedia which is never out of date. Unified diversity and diversified unity run together throughout God's word. The infallible oneness of the Bible is seen supremely in the way it testifies to the centrality, person and work of the Lord Jesus Christ. He is the key. This theme will be developed more fully in Chapter 7.

The Bible is ... *loved / hated*

There has never been a book that is so loved by some, yet so hated by many others. You can understand why when you heed its message. God is love, and He wants His message of love in Christ to conquer our sinful hearts. We have rebelled against that love and, by nature, we love darkness rather than light because of our wickedness (John 3:19). There is a totally evil being, Satan, who manipulates an anti-God world system with the support of sinful human hearts. He hates the thought that the message of redeeming love and the cleansing blood of Christ should ransom lost sinners from the tyranny of sin. Thus whenever the Bible is preached and taught, there is a potential life and death struggle of a spiritual nature (Ephesians 6:12). That is why so many in the world, though giving much lip-service to the Bible, hate it and its message, and ridicule and oppose the preaching of the cross and resurrection of Christ. They hatefully rebel, no matter how refined or religious they may seem to be, against the biblical insistence that the Lord Jesus Christ is the only Saviour of sinful, lost and dying men and women. Satan will even use religion, including nominal Christianity, to give his evil designs some respectability and acceptance among those he wishes to see and keep on the broad road to destruction (Matthew 7:13). The testimony of history is that religious people can be the fiercest and cruellest in their attacks on the Bible and on those who uphold its truths. On the other hand, those whose belief in the Bible's message has led them to forgiveness and new life in Christ so love the book from God that they will live and die to proclaim and follow it (Psalm 119:97–101). Among their number are many who, like the apostle Paul, once hated its message, but now have come to love the Bible because they have come to love its Author, God Himself. Do not be surprised at opposition if you take the Bible seriously—it is a much-hated as well as a much-loved book.

The Bible is ... *eternal / temporary*

God's word came from heaven and is settled in heaven (Psalm 119:89). Like an old building that was fashioned elsewhere and later reassembled at a given place after being transported there, the Bible fits together perfectly on earth because it was fashioned in heaven and brought down stone by stone, as God the Holy Spirit inspired the very words of the men who wrote it down. It is thus both eternal and temporary. How? Its truths are timeless and unchanging, because they come from and describe God, who is eternal and eternally consistent and changeless. Obviously, the *physical* books of paper, print, and cloth, board or leather that contain God's written word will one day decay or be destroyed. Although the Bibles we have in our homes and in our hands contain God's only, complete and final revelation of Himself to us on this side of eternity, that revelation contains only a whisper of the immeasurable depth, height, length, width and magnitude of the whole truth about God. Eternity will be needed to grasp that! It is rather like sending a birthday card to someone you love dearly. That card is true and right, but it only reveals the tip of the iceberg of the real love you have for that person. How much more is that true of God! The Bible is His wonderful earthly 'birthday card'. It is nothing, however, in comparison with the limitless love, mercy, grace and truth that He will show in eternity to those who have believed its message, repented from sin and trusted Christ.

The Bible is … *judging / saving*

There is another parallel between Jesus, the living Word, and the Bible, the written word. Jesus will come again to judge those who do not trust Him as Saviour (2 Timothy 4:1). Lost mankind has only two alternatives: *either* become saved, *or* continue in condemnation (John 3:18). The difference between those two states is either knowing the Lord Jesus Christ as one's personal Saviour, or facing Him as a personal Judge. So it is with the Bible. It is a signpost to salvation, actually able to make us wise to the extent that we trust its message of salvation and turn to Christ from our sins (2 Timothy 3:15). But it is also a signpost to judgement, revealing quite clearly that eternal judgement will follow the death of those refusing or neglecting to turn from their sins (Hebrews 9:27; Romans 1:18). Thus the Bible stands at the crossroads of unbelief and belief, of sinful pride and repentant trust, of continuing in sin and coming to forgiveness, of hell and heaven, of eternal death and eternal life, and of the broad way and the narrow way. When one has come to know Christ, the Bible continues to offer to the Christian the daily salvation from sin's power that is open to those who trust its message and follow it. But it warns of personal shipwreck to those who will waste their lives through rebellion or neglect. The judgement seat of Christ will be the place where we Christians will know God's assessment of how we stewarded God's gifts of grace and how we responded to the wonderful truths of His word (Romans 14:10; 2 Corinthians 5:10). Once we have trusted Christ, we can never be lost eternally (John 10:27–29). However, we can bring much dishonour to God's name and lose the blessing He wants for us and through us if we do not choose the ways of daily salvation by being filled with His word and revering it in our lives.

The Bible is … *read / unread*

Unconverted people rarely read the Bible thirstily, seriously and continuously—if they did they would probably not remain unconverted for long! They prefer the movies, TV, soap operas, leisure pursuits, and other books to the Bible. They may occasionally be worried or frightened enough, or stung, or aroused to read God's word, but generally non-Christians would rather tell you what is wrong with the Bible than read it! Christians understand that, because many of them were once also like that! Before Christ takes over in a person's heart and life, any desire within for God is stunted and spoiled by our sin. There are, of course, some wonderful exceptions: some men, women and children do set their hearts to seek God, and read the Bible in their search for its Author. Such people will always be rewarded because God says that those who seek Him wholeheartedly really will find Him (Jeremiah 29:13) and thus be found by Him.

If you are not yet converted to Christ, consider the potential investment from the time you could set aside to read the Bible. Depending on your reading speed, you could read the whole Bible in a year if you spend about twenty minutes a day! If that is too much, why not consider devoting ten minutes a day to reading the New Testament? You will read it at least once in a year with time to spare! If the whole of your eternal future—in heaven with Christ, knowing God's everlasting blessings, or in hell without Him, experiencing God's everlasting judgement on your sin—depends on your response to the message of the Bible, then can you afford *not* to read it?

And what could possibly be more important to a Christian than knowing God better? How can you ever get to know Him better if you do not read, learn and apply His word to your life? You ought to study the Bible (2 Timothy 2:15) and plan to read it all through regularly and often. But how much time do we, who belong to Christ, spend in unnecessary and secondary things, which if not necessarily wrong will never bring blessing? Compare that with the time each week we spend reading God's word, the Bible. Can we justify our conduct before the judgement seat of Christ when we give an account of the stewardship of our time, gifts and opportunities since we trusted the Christ of the Bible? Never has there been a book about which so much has been said, but which so few have read all the way through! May you join the blessed ranks of those, if you are not in those ranks already, who determine by God's grace to read and know the *whole* of the Word of God!

My Bible in verse

Roy Mohon's cleverly written poem *My Bible* gives a helpful summary of the contents of God's word. As with all brief summaries of the books of the Bible, including those in *The Bible Panorama*, the summary is not definitive and exhaustive but it is helpful. Sometimes readers of the Bible justifiably differ in how they summarise a book of the Bible. Each could be right. It is rather like describing a sparkling diamond, or trying to relay to another a beautiful sunset or breathtaking scenery: there are many different ways of doing it that are all equally valid! Roy Mohon's poem follows:

My Bible

In Genesis the world was made by God's almighty hand.

In Exodus the Hebrews marched to gain the Promised Land.

Leviticus contains the Law: holy and just and good.

Numbers records the tribes enrolled, all sons of Abraham's blood.

Moses in Deuteronomy records God's mighty deeds,

Brave Joshua into Canaan's land, the host of Israel leads.

In Judges their rebellion oft provokes the Lord to smite,
But Ruth records the faith of one well pleasing in his sight.
In 1st and 2nd Samuel of Jesse's sons we read,
Ten tribes in 1st and 2nd Kings revolted from His seed.
The 1st and 2nd Chronicles see Judah captive made,
But Ezra leads a remnant back by Princely Cyrus' aid.
The city walls of Zion, Nehemiah built again,
While Esther saves her people from the plot of wicked men.
In Job we read how faith will live beneath affliction's rod,
And David's Psalms are precious songs for every child of God.
The Proverbs like a godly string of choicest pearls appear,
Ecclesiastes teaches how vain all things are here.
The mystic Song of Solomon exalts sweet Sharon's Rose,
While Christ the Saviour and the King the rapt Isaiah shows.
The warning Jeremiah apostate Israel scorns,
His plaintive Lamentations, then their awful downfall mourns.
Ezekiel tells in wondrous words of dazzling mysteries,
While Kings and Empires yet to come Daniel in vision sees.
Of judgement and of mercy Hosea loves to tell,
Joel describes the blessed days when God with man shall dwell.
Among Tekoa's herdsmen Amos receives his call,
While Obadiah prophesies of Edom's final fall.
Jonah becomes a type of Christ now risen from the dead
Who warns us that our judgement lies a few short days ahead.
Micah pronounces Israel lost—lost, but again restored.
Nahum declares on Nineveh just judgement shall be poured.
A view of Chaldea's coming doom Habakkuk's visions give,
Next Zephaniah warns the Jews to turn, repent and live.
Haggai wrote to those who saw the temple built again,
And Zechariah prophesied of Christ's triumphant reign.
Malachi was the last who touched the high prophetic chord,
Its final notes sublimely show the coming of the Lord.

Matthew and Mark and Luke and John the holy Gospel wrote

Describing how the Saviour died, His life and all He taught.

Acts proves how God the apostles owned with signs in every place,

While Paul in Romans teaches us how man is saved by grace.

The Apostle in Corinthians instructs, exhorts, reproves,

Galatians shows that faith in Christ alone the Father loves.

Ephesians and Philippians tell what Christians ought to be,

Colossians bids us live to God and for eternity.

In Thessalonians we're taught the Lord will come from Heaven,

In Timothy and Titus a Pastor's rule is given.

Philemon marks a Christian's love which only Christians know,

Hebrews reveals the gospel was prefigured by the Law.

James teaches without holiness faith is vain and dead,

And Peter points a narrow way in which the saints are led.

John in his three epistles, on love delights to dwell,

But Jude gives awful warning of judgement, wrath and hell.

The Revelation prophesies of that tremendous day,

When Christ—and Christ alone—shall be the trembling sinner's stay.

Overviews and study helps

The Holy Spirit and the purpose of this chapter

T he best way to learn God's word is through the Holy Spirit leading us as, with yielded hearts and minds, we read the Bible itself and rely on God to speak to us. John chapters 14, 15 and 16 contain the key teaching of Jesus on the person and work of God the Holy Spirit. Our Lord and Saviour makes it quite clear that the Holy Spirit is 'the Spirit of truth' (John 14:17), that He will teach Christ's disciples all things they need to know and remind them of those things (John 14:26), that He comes from the Father and testifies about the Son (John 15:26), that He will guide His followers 'into all truth' which includes 'things to come' (John 16:13), and that He will declare to Christians the things of Christ (John 16:15). In learning God's word there is no substitute for the Holy Spirit of truth teaching committed disciples through God's word of truth.

Yet the same God also placed teachers of His word among His people in both Old Testament and New Testament times. So today, the Christian who wants to get the most out of his, or her, Bible should join a Bible-believing, Bible-teaching and Bible-honouring church where the ministry will be from and about the Word of God. But God has also given teaching talents to many who write good Christian books. We would do well to benefit from their ministry by supplementing our own reading and studying of the Bible with their books.

This brief chapter is simply intended to explain the place of the overviews in this book, and to suggest just a few reference books and study Bibles that might help someone needing initial guidance on that subject. More established Christians reading this book will probably have their own list, and this will be reflected on their bookshelves.

Sixty-six *overviews*

In *The Bible Panorama*, sixty-six brief *overviews* are given—one for each book of the Bible. Each *overview* precedes the chapter-by-chapter explanation of the book of the Bible concerned in Part I of this book. But please remember that, while understanding an *overview* of each book is important and helpful, there is no substitute for reading the Bible itself! It is the Word of God! Let Him speak through His word to you.

Only signposts!

It is outside the scope of this panoramic approach to each chapter of the Bible to provide a detailed background explanation of each of the sixty-six books, but rather to concentrate on the teaching itself in each chapter in the Bible. The *overviews* included in this book are very brief and intended to help you to 'see the next page of the map' on your privileged and exciting journey of reading through the Bible. Hopefully the explanations of the Bible's chapters will act as signposts to blessing. In some chapters, as you follow your route through the Bible, you may well want to stop and examine some of the places in more detail, and engage in some in-depth study before proceeding. Hopefully the headings, covering all the verses, will help you to do that too. The aim of each *overview* is not to limit you or to be over dogmatic, but simply to act as a guide to provide some background context. If you do not think you need or want that, or already have material that provides that for you, please skip the *overviews* and get straight to the chapter-by-chapter summaries. Even more important, get to the Scripture itself!

Area covered in the *overview* of each book

Each preceding *overview* is in four parts and addresses the subject matter shown below:

People and preliminaries: number of chapters; where the book fits into the Bible as a whole and relates to other books in the Bible; who wrote it, when and where; estimate of period of time covered by the book.

Plan and purpose: whom it was written for and why; the main purpose of the book; the ground it covers generally.

Profile and progression: the main profile of the book is analysed broadly by showing which subjects are dealt with in its consecutive teaching—almost like a brief running general index of the book; thus the progression in its contents and teaching is shown and enables you to know what to look for and where.

Principles and particulars: this part highlights some specific, distinctive points in the book. It is not intended to be all embracing, but just to point out a few landmarks in the panoramic scene.

Helps on background

There are some excellent publications and reference Bibles that give very helpful background detail on the Bible and on all or parts of each of its sixty-six books. They are far more detailed and scholarly than *The Bible Panorama* and have a different aim. You may never find a reference book with which you agree completely on every point made, and some writers adopt a particular doctrinal stance or emphasis that others might not hold. But many books and reference Bibles represent the work of godly Bible-believing writers and give excellent background information and thought-provoking general analyses of the Bible's books, even if you choose to differ on some points. It is very helpful to get good Bible background aids to put each book in the overall context. If you have no such works in mind that trusted Christian leaders or friends have recommended, try one of the reference Bibles or one of the books recommended below. They provide very useful background information, though it must be underlined that they are only a very small part of a very big selection. Inclusion in this list does not mean that most Christians would consider these books as the best study aids. The fact that other books are excluded does not imply that they are less helpful.

All the books mentioned here are written by Christians who believe that the Bible is God's inspired, infallible and complete written Word of God.

Some recommended reference Bibles

John MacArthur, ed., *The MacArthur Study Bible—NKJV* (Nashville: Thomas Nelson). (Book-by-book analysis and background at start of each book. Most helpful in dealing with anticipated problem areas and their solutions.)

The Open Bible—NKJV (Nashville: Thomas Nelson). (Book-by-book analysis and background at start of each book.)

R.C. Sproul, ed., *The Reformation Study Bible—NKJV* (Nashville: Thomas Nelson). (Book-by-book analysis and background at start of each book. Again, helpful flagging of possible problem areas and their solutions.)

Kenneth Barker, ed., *The NIV Study Bible* (Grand Rapids: Zondervan). (Book-by-book analysis and background at start of each book.)

Some Bible reference books

F.B. Meyer, *Bible Commentary* (Tyndale House Publishers). (Focuses on some important events or topics in each chapter. Spiritually inspiring and helpful. This is not really a traditional commentary as it does not cover all sections of each chapter.)

J. Vernon McGee, *Briefing the Bible* (Thru the Bible Books). (Describes and outlines each Bible book. Clear, concise and helpful. Comprehensive bibliography on each Bible book. Came from the author's radio broadcasts of the Bible.)

J. Sidlow Baxter, *Explore the Book* (Grand Rapids: Zondervan). (Large, detailed, spiritual and readable overview on each book for a serious reader. This makes no attempt to be a commentary on each verse or to cover each chapter in the Bible.)

Trevor F. Knight, *God's Wonderful Word* (Young Life). (Encouraging, quickly readable, concise, clear and simple introductory guide to each book of the Bible. Spiritual, informative and devotional. Signals key points to look for.)

Keith L. Brooks, *The Bible Summarised Handbook* (World Bible Publishers). (Very short pen-sketches of each book. Extremely brief chapter summaries, helpful conclusions and one-word guides. Does not try to explain each chapter fully. A helpful menu rather than a recipe.)

John MacArthur, *The MacArthur Bible Handbook,* (Nashville: Thomas Nelson). (Thorough, clear and large book-by-book survey of the Bible, complete with charts, graphs and illustrations. Deals head on with difficulties.)

Verse by verse commentaries—many commentaries (whether on the whole Bible or on an individual book) provide background of each book. They are too numerous to list. It is important to take advice and recommendations from trusted Christian friends and mature and faithful Christian leaders.

Can I trust the Bible?

The anvil that outlasts and breaks the hammers

The Bible is like an anvil. Many hostile hammers have crashed down upon it. Those hammer blows have been, and still are, struck by those whose opposition to the truth of the Bible is religious, political, moral, personal, philosophical, theological or supposedly 'scientific'. Some opponents combine a number of those approaches. For hundreds of years, their hammers have been slammed down on that anvil. Yet the anvil remains intact and unharmed, and one by one the hammers have been worn and broken, while those wielding them pass on life's short and uncertain road in spiritual blindness, through death, into eternity. But new antagonists, blind and biased against the saving message of God's word, arise to continue to pick up old broken hammers and attack the Bible. The Christian has nothing to fear. God's word is eternal and durable and we can safely put our full confidence in it. There is no known *fact*, as opposed to theories or models, that has ever contradicted the Bible. There never will be, because it is *God's* infallible word (2 Timothy 3:16). Meanwhile, despite the attacks, many intelligent, learned and converted men and women from all the places where rebel sinners pick up their petty hammers join with millions of 'ordinary people' to confirm their confidence in the reliability and infallibility of Scripture and its message of forgiveness, hope, peace and new life. History is well flavoured with the testimony of people who knew that the biggest discovery that anyone could make is that he or she is a guilty sinner, and that Jesus Christ is the repentant sinner's friend.

Defending the Bible's integrity

C.H. Spurgeon, when asked how he would defend the Bible, told his questioner that he would rather defend a lion. The Bible must simply be let off its chain to defend itself! We need to remember that. We do not need the permission of some intellectual philosopher, or sin-hardened and arrogant university professor, in order to preach the gospel of the cross and resurrection of Jesus, or to know God's peace through His word. Neither the most qualified, unbelieving academic opposing the Bible, nor any scientist who refuses to pursue an objectively fair scientific method and approach to arrive at a fair conclusion, has anything to teach us except about sinful and rebellious human nature. That self-loving nature has always had a propensity to hate and oppose God's truth, and will continue to have, unless and until God's mercy and grace change the individual concerned. We need no mandate from any pleasant and well-meaning, but spiritually dead, TV celebrity to believe that our great God made the world in six days of twenty-four hours each, or that mankind is a separate creation who differs basically from animals, whatever biological similarities the great Creator may have given us! We do not abandon the truth that the all-knowing Son of God believed about Adam—that he was a separate and specific creation by God—because of some ridiculous and contrived attempt to reconstruct cavemen to look like apes, when the purported evidence motivating people to do so would be laughed out of court. (If that were not so tragically misleading to the general public, it really would be laughable. The arguments on which such conclusions are based are invalid and ludicrous.) Trust, read, study, learn, teach, preach and share the Bible's saving and sanctifying message, and it will become increasingly evident to you and to others that this *is* the Word of God! God has never sought the applause or approval of sinful rebels—even clever or well-known ones—to declare His word and His will authoritatively. That very word leads us to expect that the Bible, like the Lord Jesus Christ, will be rejected and opposed. In fact, the very opposition of man confirms the Bible's accuracy and integrity in foretelling the inevitability of that opposition! Pray that those who oppose God's word will come into the blessing of believing its saving message as did Christianity's greatest and most qualified antagonist of all, Saul of Tarsus, whose name was changed to Paul and whose nature was changed by God's power and forgiveness after God spoke to him (Acts 26:12–18).

The Bible on trial—look externally, internally and at opposing arguments

We now turn to look at some of the evidences for the truth of God's word. Sceptics, atheists and many religious people accuse the Bible of being fraudulent and deceptive. They dismiss, often superficially and with contempt, strong examinable evidence to support the claim that the Bible is God's revealed and reliable written word. We will consider some *external* evidence first, to see if the Bible, viewed from outside its pages, can substantiate its claim to be God's entirely trustworthy word. Then we will look within it to decide if the *internal* evidence points to that conclusion. Finally, we will touch upon the *weakness* of some of the often glibly accepted arguments against the Bible. But you must come to your own conclusion. Your conclusion will not change the truth of the Bible, but it could change your life. These are only signposts, which I hope will help your further thinking and enquiries.

External evidence—call in the witnesses!

FIRST WITNESS—WHAT WE KNOW *NOW* THAT MAN COULD NOT KNOW *THEN*

The argument here is that there are a number of assumptions, statements, events and situations in the world and the universe that could not have been known by man when they were written about, so accurately, in the Bible. Their technological knowledge then could not compare with ours today. There were no microscopes, scanners, telescopes, computers, DNA analyses, worldwide communications and travel, or chemical engineering, for example.

How could man then know that there were as many stars in the heavens as there were grains of sand on the earth when only comparatively few were visible to the naked eye (Genesis 22:17)? Today we know that is so because we have powerful telescopes, not available to the writer of Genesis.

Have you heard people ridicule the Bible by saying that, if they believed like Christians believe, they would think the world was flat? They are unaware that the Bible taught from the beginning that the earth's horizons are circular (Job 26:10; Isaiah 40:22) and that God hangs the world 'on nothing' (Job 26:7). Other alternative 'solutions' which were seriously believed then, were that the earth rested physically on an elephant, or some strong man's shoulders! But the Bible never promoted fanciful fairy stories or unscientific nonsense.

The Bible's description of God's created world always assumed a round world and Columbus could have known that before he explored the world, had he trusted his Bible!

In the realm of geography, some have asked why the earth's sulphur content is so high around the ancient city of Sodom. The explanation is simple: God rained fire and brimstone (sulphur) on it when He judged it for its wickedness (Genesis 19:24).

And are we 'fearfully and wonderfully made' (Psalm 139:14) or did we come from an amoebic blob? Before you answer, consider DNA and look at the scan of a growing baby in its mother's womb. An amazingly complex and designed human being in miniature exists within. (Babies killed by abortion are sometimes tragically dismissed and disposed of by pro-abortionists as 'p.o.c' or 'product of conception', but the Bible reflects God's truth that they are 'infants who never saw light' (Job 3:16).)

These few examples demonstrate that the Bible had the truth first, when its writers had no technical or scientific access to arrive at that knowledge. People who seek honestly will eventually discover the veracity of established biblical truths as they advance, though it may take time as we are so small and limited, even with our growing technology.

SECOND WITNESS—CHRISTIANITY IN THE MULTI-FAITH MAZE

To avoid any misunderstanding, it is right to clarify the role of Christians in an increasingly multi-faith world, at least in the West. Then we can consider in detail the reason why the comparison between all other systems of faith and biblical faith underlines, and is entirely consistent with, the Bible's claim to be the only written revelation of God.

The argument developed below is basically that all non-Christian faiths or religions have three essential principles in common, but that the Bible alone teaches that there is one certain way, and only one, by which men and women can come to know God, and that this unique and distinctively different way claims absolute exclusivity for itself. That different way is biblical Christianity. If God were to reveal Himself, as Christians claim, would we not expect His revelation of

Himself to be entirely different from the imaginations and suggestions of mere men, however sincere they were (which is often the case) and whatever their cultural, racial or geographical origins (Isaiah 55:8–9)?

But first, how should the Christian see 'multi-faithism'? No Bible-believing Christian can, or should, seek to impose genuine Christianity upon others by statute, and much less by force. The much-hated Crusades had very little to do with the saving gospel of Jesus Christ and a lot to do with politics and with hypocritical and superficial religion which all should condemn. So Bible believers should argue for the right for followers of other religions to follow their consciences in western countries or anywhere else in the world. (How I wish that members of all other faiths would also allow Christians that same freedom to worship and follow Christ in their own countries. Is it too much to ask that those who argue for freedom of religion for their own adherents outside their own countries should campaign for the same freedom for members of other faiths within the borders of their own countries?)

In willingly conceding religious freedom to others, Christians also have the right and duty to present the Bible's unique message openly, unapologetically and boldly. That message is that faith in the Lord Jesus Christ is the only way to God, and that Jesus alone can save sinners from eternal judgement and present them faultless in heaven, through His shed blood and risen life (Matthew 28:18–20; Acts 4:12; Jude 24–25).

That is not blind dogmatism. It is right, logical, objective, loving and, above all, biblical. Every real Christian should graciously but firmly insist on the exclusiveness of Christ as the Son of God, whatever the personal consequences. Why? Because Jesus claimed and demonstrated that He was different from all religious leaders (John 11:25–27; Acts 1:3). Other religious leaders are basically the same in three ways, as we shall see, but with many peripheral variations, of course. Biblical Christianity differs from all religions, which in fact are all man-made if the Bible is true. If God has inspired the Bible as His sole revelation of Himself, is it not logical to expect that revelation to be different? And surely the One who is the focus of that revelation will be completely different from leaders of all the other faiths, notwithstanding the sincerity of some of those leaders and their followers? Let us see if He was.

Which religious leader could ever be said to have created the world (John 1:1–3), to have been born of a virgin (Matthew 1:18–25), or to be God in the amazing triune Godhead of Father, Son and Holy Spirit (John 14,15,16)? All of this marks out Jesus as very different from the rest! Which prophet or sage lived a completely sinless and righteous life (Hebrews 7:26), bore the sins and eternal punishment for sinners in His death (Mark 10:45; 1 Peter 2:24), and rose bodily from the grave (1 Corinthians 15:3–4)? That is all very different, too! Which chief of faith ascended into heaven, to be seated in glory there (Acts 1:9–11; Hebrews 1:13), and promised to return publicly and gloriously one day to the earth as King of kings and Lord of lords to terminate this world as we know it, and usher in a new one (Matthew 24:29–31)? This Man, who is also God, is truly different (John 14:6; Acts 4:12). He is not a religious leader among others: He is the Lord of glory among men (Philippians 2:9–10), and He came to save the lost (Luke 19:10). Not only that, but we can know His indwelling our lives now, in the Person of the Holy Spirit (John 1:12; Colossians 2:6; Romans 8:9). No other leader could claim that!

Compare the Bible's message of faith in Christ with any and all religions in the multi-faith maze, especially the three things they have in common. What do they say? First, however they dress it up, they all tell us that we can save ourselves (whatever 'saved' may mean to them). Second, they can give no assurance that we are saved because they can never tell us if we have 'arrived' or done enough to be sure we are accepted. Third, they all fail to deal with the basic personal problem of our guilt, our sinfulness and our many sins, and offer no pardon or cleansing that gives peace of heart now and knowledge of God that lasts through all eternity. They teach that we can come to know 'God' (whoever or whatever they think 'God' is) either by what we do, or a ceremony we go through, or a philosophy we adopt, or through experiencing or achieving a state of consciousness (or unconsciousness!). They all have their basis in trying to reach their 'God' through human religious self-help.

The Christian message claims to be, and is, entirely different. It concerns God's having come down to man. He came down in His teaching through the Bible, His word (2 Peter 1:21). He came down in humanity through the Person of Jesus Christ, both to show us His truth and to save us (Matthew 1:21, 23; John 1:1–14). He still comes down into the hearts of repentant sinners through His Holy Spirit, who enters every Christian when personal faith is put in Jesus (John 1:12; Ephesians 3:16–17; 1 John 4:13).

If the Bible is true at all, it is entirely true, because of its claims of absolute exclusivity (Proverbs 30:5–6). There is no other way to God. The multi-faith maze asks us to look at the intersection of many roads at one point, and see a huge and confusing signpost indicating hundreds of different directions. Yet it claims that all 'believers', irrespective of the faith they espouse, have something in common. Yes they *do* have something in common—they are all hopelessly lost! Worse, they are dying and under judgement for their sins (Hebrews 9:27) as were Christians before they came to Christ. Why should God clearly state in the Bible that there is only one way to know Him, through Christ, and then ask us to consider the other confused, confusing and contradictory direction indicators? They all lead to a lost eternity.

Does not the multi-faith confusion underline the distinctiveness and clarity of the authority of the Bible? Grace given to the unworthy repentant sinner! Personal assurance now of sins forgiven! The certainty of eternal life now and for ever! A settled and experienced relationship with God by faith alone in Christ! And none of this can be worked for or earned by us: we receive it as a gift, or we will not receive it at all (Romans 6:23).

No wonder the Bible is powerful, in any language, to bring to God any man or woman who is honest about personal sin and turns to Christ. Some religious followers insist that their faith means nothing when translated into other languages. Not so the Bible! 'God so loved the *world* that He gave His only begotten Son, that whoever believes in Him should not perish but have everlasting life' (John 3:16). God is unique. So is His salvation. So is His word, the Bible.

THIRD WITNESS—THE WORLDWIDE IMPACT OF THE BIBLE'S MESSAGE

We could fill libraries to demonstrate the impact that the Word of God has had on individuals, localities, nations and the world. Space only allows me to mention a few examples, below, of some of the areas where embracing the Bible and its message has caused dramatic change.

The abolition of slavery; the freeing of women and children from cruel service in factories, down mines, and up chimneys; the elevation of the status and role of women from being considered as mere chattels to being valued as individuals who are precious to God; the establishment of hospitals; pioneering the care and aftercare of prisoners; the transformation of vastly different communities through Bible-based influence, such as the rough Welsh miners, or the feared head-hunting Auca Indians of South America; the revivals in Britain, under Whitefield and Wesley, that some say averted a repeat of the French Revolution on British soil; the New England revivals and its effects on many in the USA; the establishment of judicial systems which, for all their weaknesses and inconsistencies, were so much more righteous and compassionate than countries where the Bible did not go; the care for the poor; the furtherance of education; the establishment of homes for orphans and abandoned children, still going on today in parts of the world previously starved of Bible light; the unpopular fight in today's immoral and uncaring world, to save unborn children from being killed, before they see the light of day, by abortion as a means of belated birth control.

Wherever the open Bible has gone, its effects have been marked. It has worked, and continues to do so, in all cultures, in all ages, in all countries, in all races, in all conditions of poverty and riches, and in all situations. No human philosophy or man-made religion has ever had such a worldwide impact as the Bible. No wonder that some of the fruits of its teaching have been, and are still, copied by non-Christians for the good of society around the world. Christians should pray that the same people would embrace the book from which all this good came— the Bible—and trust Jesus Christ, who is the central message of that book.

FOURTH WITNESS—THE OBJECTIVITY OF SUBJECTIVE EXPERIENCE

The argument here is that the message of the Bible has an amazing and life-changing effect on each individual who trusts it, irrespective of that person's background or character, and that the commonality of this experience is for everyone who truly comes to Christ and confides in God's word. There is an objectivity of biblical truth that is demonstrated in each person's subjective experience. In short, millions can say individually: 'My life has been changed, and is being changed, by reading and trusting the message of the Bible.'

Subjective experience alone could not be a valid basis for establishing evidence without observable objectivity. 'What on earth does that mean?' you may well ask. Let me demonstrate the point by reference to drunkenness!

Assume that alcoholic drink had never been invented. No one has ever tasted alcohol, and thus drunkenness and its chaotic consequences have never been experienced. Then a lady tells you that she has heard of a man who drank a few glasses of something called 'alcoholic drink' (you do not know what that is— remember it has not been invented yet!) and she understands he started singing loudly, shouting, laughing uncontrollably and then pouring out vulgar abuse. Also she learned he was swaggering all over the place, fell into a hedge and vomited there. Then she says that this man was normally the quietest, sweetest, gentlest and most reasonable person in his town, and lots of people had gone to him for help before.

Now do remember that you have never heard about alcohol before. This is a first, and it is hearsay, three or four times removed. You are a little sceptical, especially because you know the lady has got things wrong before! Then the next day, your very reliable neighbour tells you that he saw similar results when his friend drank some bottles of what he called 'alcoholic drink', previously unknown to him.

In successive days, you meet others who have witnessed similar experiences. You then meet a man who says he drank a lot of it, and then describes that same experience of drunkenness. Finally, and with some reluctance, you try it yourself, and you drink too much. You begin to feel dizzy, lose control of your balance, are unable to concentrate, lose coherent speech, and cease to care about what others think.

You do believe in 'alcoholic drink' now. You probably did before you drank it yourself because it was so well witnessed to you by others. But now you have experienced it, you know it is a fact, whether you like it or not!

In each of the cases of drunkenness you heard of or witnessed, the person got drunk personally and *subjectively* experienced it. Yet, as time went on, there was an *objectivity* about the different personal testimonies you heard that led you to believe that each subjective testimony really was based on fact: in this case, the fact of intoxication through alcohol. The objectivity of their subjective experiences produced strong evidence that 'alcoholic drink' had an effect. But when you experienced drunkenness yourself, you knew personally and *subjectively*, as well as from *objectively* considering what other witnesses had said, that alcoholic drink was a reality and had certain effects.

I cannot think of much in common between getting drunk and getting converted! Unlike drunkenness, Christian conversion puts people back in control of their lives because they are now controlled by God. It makes the convert more considerate towards others, less selfish and produces a genuine love for others.

But, nevertheless, there is a parallel between the two. In each case the onlooker could see the effects on others before personally experiencing those effects.

So it is in personally experiencing the message of the Bible. The first time I heard it, I dismissed it. When I heard of a few other people's conversions, I did not take it too seriously because they were remote from me, and I had other things to do. Then my sister started reading her Bible and telling me about it, and about how she had asked Christ to be her Saviour. I ridiculed her faith and the 'irrelevant' and 'contradictory' Bible she now read each day. Then I was introduced to others who also shared their subjective experiences of coming to know the Saviour, and how God spoke to them and blessed them through their daily Bible reading. The evidence was mounting. Could they *all* be wrong? Here were people of different backgrounds, gender, age, education, intelligence, colour and race. They had all found this new love for God's word. I even started going to a church where the people listened avidly, and with great appreciation, to nothing more than an explanation of the Bible twice on a Sunday and at a mid-week Bible study. My sister bought me a Bible. I tried to read it through from Genesis and gave up before I got to the end of that first book! Yet all the time people were telling me how they were being helped and blessed by the God they now knew through the Bible.

It was not until the night I received Christ that I had the same experience as they had. I turned from sin to Christ for forgiveness, and found my life began to change. And at the heart of that change was a new habit of reading the Bible, which now became alive to me. I was not 'drunk'—I was 'saved', and one of the evidences was a desire to read God's word and be blessed through it. My life began to change both in the way I had seen in others, and also in ways I had never imagined. I was under new management and God led me through His word, the Bible.

But, sadly, I later proved the truth of the Bible in the wrong way, too. Despite having come to Christ and having experienced enlightenment through His word, I came to a point where I refused to let God have his way in my life. I preferred my own way, which I knew was selfish and wrong. I lost the sense of blessing and stopped reading my Bible. The vicious circle turned quickly. Neglect of my Bible reading led to more sin. More sin led to no appetite for reading the Bible. Someone said that either God's word will keep you from sin, or sin will keep you from God's word. I knew that the Bible was God's word, but I was not willing to yield to Him according to its teachings. I knew I was an unhappy hypocrite.

Then I came across a group of young adult Christians in Leeds Young Life ('YL'), led by the late Professor Verna Wright. Drawn from different churches, they had trusted Christ and were encouraged and helped to study the Bible personally each day, as well as at the Lord's Day services and mid-week Bible studies at their churches, and on Saturdays at YL. The counter-attraction of a lively youth Bible study instead of my usual Saturday night activities, and the love and respect that those young folks had for God's word, along with the ever-caring and watchful eye of an involved older Christian, brought me back into blessing by God's grace. And with it, guess what? That's right—a new love and determination to read the Bible became mine! I now started reading it all the way through every year, as well as having a separate daily quiet time based on a smaller selected passage. How God blesses me still through the Bible, many years later! He promises to bless everyone through it who yields to Christ's Lordship, under its teaching.

Millions across the world and down the ages have said, do say and will say the same thing: 'The entrance of your words gives light' (Psalm 119:130) and 'Revive me, O LORD, according to Your word' (Psalm 119:107).

It is an objective fact that God speaks, in blessing and life-changing grace, through His word to those who surrender to Him. Every Bible-believing Christian can know more of God's help, blessing and word on a daily basis, through reading the Bible.

Internal evidence—the Bible speaks for itself!

FIRST CLAIM—FULFILLED PROPHECY

We have seen that things existed when the Bible was written that could not have been known by its writers unless God had revealed those things. But there is even more striking internal evidence, namely fulfilled prophecy. The Bible predicted in great detail many events that would occur centuries later and, concerning which, history attests that they did happen. These were not obvious matters that could have been foreseen, or guesses with a fifty per cent chance of success. This is all in line with God's claim recorded in the Bible, that in His uniqueness,

'I am God, and there is no other;
I am God, and there is none like Me,
Declaring the end from the beginning,
And from ancient times things which are not yet done,
Saying "My counsel shall stand,
And I will do My pleasure".' (Isaiah 46: 9–10)

Archaeology and other types of discovery have spotlighted some of these events. Consider, for example, the 'impossible' but prophesied decline and fall of the kingdom of Edom, of which Petra was the principal city. This landmass of 6,600 square miles (compare New Jersey at 7,500 square miles) and the city of Petra saw amazing prophecies fulfilled with pinpoint accuracy (Isaiah 34:6–15; Jeremiah 49:17–18; Ezekiel 25:13–14; 35:5–7). Professor Peter Stoner in his book, *Science Speaks* (Moody Press), looks at the likelihood of fulfilled prophecies based on his statistical analysis in the light of the theory of probability. He points out that the fulfilment of just three of the prophecies would be against odds of 10 to the power 4, or 10,000 to 1. But there were at least nine highly unlikely prophecies which were fulfilled, and Professor Josh McDowell in his Campus Crusade book *Evidence that Demands a Verdict* (which provides many evidences where the Bible can be seen to be God's fully reliable word), brings the position to life when he says: 'Many probably realise that [Stoner's] estimate of prophecy is difficult to grasp; the best course of action is to bring it closer home ... Consider a prediction. 1. New Jersey will become desolate. 2. It will never be re-inhabited after it is conquered. 3. It will be invaded by men of the East, across the sea. 4. It will also be conquered by men of the North. 5. It will have an even bloodier and more corrupt future than any other nation in the United Kingdom of America. 6. It will be totally destroyed up to Philadelphia. 7. The site of the old kingdom will be infested with wild animals and beasts.' The point is that the Petra prophecies all happened, just as prophesied, and a thriving metropolis became a ghost town, forgotten and lost for hundreds of years. Presumably the odds against that would be 10 to the power 9, or 1 in 1,000,000,000! Take a few noughts away, and the point is still made!

Then consider the amazing fulfilment of the prophecy regarding the demise of Tyre, fully according with Ezekiel's detailed, six-point prophecy in chapters 26–28. Or how Babylon's unimaginable downfall, prophesied in Isaiah 13:1–14:23 and in Jeremiah 50:1–51:58, was carried out to the letter much later. John MacArthur's excellent book, *Nothing But The Truth* (Crossway Books), gives the detail of these amazing facts. We certainly can trust the Bible, which abounds in prophecies that have been fulfilled.

Some critics used to say that the walls of Jericho could not have fallen in accordance with Joshua 6:1–20. It took later excavation to establish that this occurred just as the Bible had said it would and then reported it did. The Bible was vindicated again.

These are only a few of the many examples that could have been taken. But, more amazing still are the many detailed, fulfilled prophecies concerning the birth, life, death on the cross and resurrection of the Lord Jesus Christ. Chapter 9 of McDowell's *Evidence that Demands a Verdict* concentrates on a good number of these, and is most convincing. For now, look at Micah 5:2; Isaiah 9:6–7; 52:13–53:12; Psalm 22.

Taking fulfilled prophecy as a whole, if the Bible got it all exactly right, then surely we can trust the Bible now and have full confidence in its teachings on things beyond our area of knowledge, apart from God's revelation? No wonder that Gallup, the well-known statistician to whom we owe the Gallup polls, said he had proved God mathematically! He applied the laws of probability to fulfilled prophecy in order to reach that conclusion.

SECOND CLAIM—THE 'IMPOSSIBLE' UNITY OF THE BIBLE
Many sceptics have said that the Bible is a mere collection of stories passed down from one person to another and so is 'full of contradictions'. Their argument is that as stories are passed down they get distorted and result in something very

different from the starting story. Even a story passed around a campfire from one person to another suffers when just twenty people are involved over a ten-minute period! My response to people who oppose the Bible on those grounds is twofold: first, I ask them to show me some of those contradictions that the Bible is supposed to be 'full of'; and second, I tell them that I agree it would take a miracle for stories to survive without a single contradiction after being passed down for over 1,600 years, in three different languages and using all forms of speech (poetry, prose, narrative, songs and story format) by over forty people of different cultures and ethnic origins and having vastly varied intellectual and academic abilities. Only a miracle could do that, but that is exactly what happened. The Bible is a miraculous book! God intervened to give us His perfect revelation while using imperfect writers. In context, the Bible as originally given is without contradiction. Under the inspiration of God the Holy Spirit, the greatly diversified human authorship has produced a miraculously infallible and reliable book that never contradicts itself in any way. It is the Word of God—and God is not 'the author of confusion' but the One who prescribes that all things should be done 'decently and in order' (1 Corinthians 14:33, 40).

THIRD CLAIM—THE INTERNAL WITNESS OF THE BIBLE IN ITS TEACHINGS

Christians of a bygone age used to refer to the *Testimonium spiritus internum*, a Latin phrase meaning the 'internal witness of the spirit' in the Bible. This is something that cannot be appreciated by someone who does not read the Bible, and is best understood by those who read the whole Bible and read it through systematically and regularly. For example, the book of Hebrews is a wonderful book dealing with how much 'better' is Jesus and His salvation than anything else that went before. 'Better' is the key word, occurring thirteen times. Jesus is portrayed as a better sacrifice and as a better Priest than those of the Old Testament, having established a better covenant (Hebrews 7:20–8:6). It thus majors on the shed blood of Christ (Hebrews 9:14) to cleanse sinners from their sin, to bring them nearer to God, and to open up the way to know and worship God personally. But those themes of sacrifice, priesthood and shed blood run throughout the Bible from Genesis to Revelation. God had those themes in mind when He planned His word, the Bible, and inspired vastly different writers at different times to take up the themes, so that their inputs dovetail perfectly together. Someone has said, 'Wherever you cut the Bible, it bleeds!' But there are many separate, yet wonderfully related, crucial themes that also go all the way through the Bible. The running unity of these themes is testimony to its sole Author, God Himself. How else can this harmonised running unity be explained throughout this library of God? If you look at an artificial flower closely, you will soon see that it has no life or detailed structure. But an examination of a living flower under a microscope reveals it as a living entity, wonderfully put together. The more you examine it, the more you see that. The Bible is to all other literature, religious or secular, what a natural flower is to a false flower. It has been intricately created and assembled, is perfectly harmonised, and manifests itself as a living creation of God. The more you study its themes, the more you see it is the Word of God.

FOURTH CLAIM—WHO IS THE 'MASTER PSYCHOLOGIST' OF ALL TIME?

How could human nature have been so well and so incisively analysed hundreds of years ago by all the varied men who wrote the Bible and who made no claim to have special insight into the machinations of the human psyche? How is it that its analysis of human nature is entirely consistent and never self-contradictory throughout the sixty-six books of the Bible? Why are Christians never surprised at what happens in the world as the downgrade in human behaviour seems inversely proportional to our technological knowledge and achievements? Why does no other book in the world accurately diagnose and prescribe a remedy for the problems of human nature? How do you explain that its diagnosis and remedy have always been relevant, accurate and consistent through all times and circumstances, underlining that neither basic human nature, nor God Himself, changes?

The answer has to be that the Bible was masterminded by the Master Psychologist of all time. For Him, in analysing human nature, centuries of time were no more a barrier than the billions of people of completely diverse ethnic and cultural backgrounds. This Master Psychologist is able to identify the malady and prescribe the remedy. There is obviously only one 'candidate'—God Himself! The Bible is seen again to be God's word in its analysis, diagnosis and treatment of human nature centuries before psychologists and philosophers unsuccessfully tried to come up with their different solutions. Though often well meaning and sometimes correct in part, all non-biblical solutions are limited and fallible, being only man-made.

The Bible's analysis is that the basic root problem of human nature is sinful rebellion against God. This has led to man's estrangement from God, to his inability to live harmoniously with man, and to a lack of settled personal peace, joy and fulfilment—a lack that is often triggered by the ups and downs of life. We see the undeniable evidence of this in so many ways: in worsening and unstable international relations; in the frightening rise of terrorism; in mushrooming national scandals and shame of all types, but especially in moral decline and an obsession with out-of-control sex and sexual perversion; in the breakdown of marriages; in the slaughter of unborn babies; in frightening behaviour, dishonesty and unrest in our streets and stores necessitating a universal 'big brother' approach to video surveillance; in the need for neighbourhood watch schemes and burglar alarms to protect our property and ourselves in and near our homes; in the torrents of filth and anti-God standards coming out of TVs and videos, like an open sewer in the nations' homes; in the lack of harmony and domestic breakdown in our families; and in the sense of personal guilt, failure and powerlessness to help ourselves. Only in the Lord Jesus Christ, and in trusting and applying the Bible's counsel about coming to know God (and consequently developing our relationships with God and each other) can we find the remedy which not only settles our eternal destiny, but also gives us on earth 'the peace of God, which surpasses all understanding' (Philippians 4:6–7) and 'joy inexpressible and full of glory' (1 Peter 1:8).

The book of the all-time Master Psychologist, the Bible, tells us that the problem is that we all have deceitful and desperately wicked hearts (Jeremiah 17:9), and that when left to our sins and obnoxious practices we become worse. We deny God rather than repenting and knowing His loving forgiveness and restorative cleansing (Romans 1–3). We are like errant sheep following one another in our rebellious and lost ways (Isaiah 53:5–6). But the Bible tells us that God alone can create a clean heart and restore a right spirit within the worst of sinners (Psalm 51:10). Our sin-hardened hearts can be so softened and changed, and our behaviour so radically altered by Christ's indwelling life that we become a 'new creation', with the old passed away, as 'all things become new' (2 Corinthians 5:17). Jesus is the Good Shepherd who gave His life for lost sheep (John 10:11). He will become the personal Shepherd, Saviour, Lord and Friend of any who will trust Him and follow Him so that, by God's grace, they can say and know, 'The LORD is my Shepherd' (Psalm 23:1). The whole of the Bible helps us to build on and enjoy that relationship and to develop the new nature He gives to those who trust Him.

The weakness of opposing arguments

We have considered some of the external and internal evidences supporting the claim that the Bible is God's unique written word. We now will look at some of the common arguments against the unique status and nature of the Bible.

ARGUMENT NUMBER 1: 'YOU CAN'T PROVE IT'

How often have I heard passers-by at open-air meetings shout, 'You can't prove it!' and then hurry away before you can even discuss with them the evidence for the truth of the Bible! Some more polite opponents will say the same thing without walking away, but remain as closed in attitude as those who will not support their words with their physical presence. They have no intention of seriously considering the evidence. Their minds are like concrete—all mixed up and permanently set!

But in fact these people are right as well as wrong. 'You can't prove it' has to be true if the 'jury' will not listen to the evidence. No case can be proved in front of a jury if the jury is absent, asleep or has made up its mind in advance. The failure to prove the case is not, however, because of any paucity of evidence, but because the facts to be presented are not given serious consideration.

But these folks are also wrong as well as right! To prove a case in most courts in the western world, there are two alternative burdens of proof. One is known as 'the balance of probability' burden of proof. It is used in civil cases and means that the case is regarded as proved if it is deemed that it is more likely than not that the facts presented in evidence happened. The other burden of proof requires that, to establish the case, the evidence has to be proved 'beyond reasonable doubt'. This higher burden of proof is required in criminal cases in the UK, for example. Taking the higher burden of proof, can we say that the Bible has been proved 'beyond reasonable doubt'? As a former criminal advocate, I would say an unhesitating and emphatic 'Yes!'

Take, for example, the biggest miracle of all, the bodily resurrection of the Lord Jesus Christ. If that greatest of all miracles can be shown to have happened, then anything less 'demanding' than that is easily in range. I have presented a summary of that evidence in the first chapter of the book *The Resurrection: the unopened gift* (Day One) and I would argue that the case is proved beyond any doubt in the mind of any fair-minded, objective person. Lord Justice Darling has said that there is more evidence for the resurrection than for any other fact in ancient history. Professor Norman Anderson has commented that the evidence for the resurrection is greater than for the existence of Julius Caesar. Who would seriously deny Caesar's existence? If the jury will listen to the case, it can be proved. If the jury will listen to the same case for the truth of the Bible, it also can be proved. Can it be proved to your satisfaction? The question is, not so much 'How strong is the evidence?' but rather 'How open are you to considering it seriously?' And remember that Jesus stated, 'Seek and you will find' (Matthew 7:7). That is a promise and a challenge that anyone can put to the test.

ARGUMENT NUMBER 2: 'I AM AGAINST ANYTHING FUNDAMENTALIST'

The rise in extremist fundamentalist factions, which has included terrorism and suicide bombing, has given some people a fear of the term 'fundamentalist'. This phobia is illogical. We believe many 'fundamentals' upon which life depends, without attacking or murdering people. A belief in free speech, for example, is a fundamental of our society, but it does not make believers in it terrorists. Often, Bible-believing Christians are ridiculed as being 'fundamentalist', without an appreciation of what that means in the context of believing the Bible. 'Fundamentalism', in the Christian context, simply means that one takes the Bible as being true in every aspect. It does not mean that every obvious figure of speech is taken in a naïve, literal way. For example, when Jesus said He was the 'Good Shepherd', we do not look for a flock of literal sheep around Him, and when He described Himself as the 'Way' we do not look for a road or path! Similarly, when we read of mountains skipping like rams, and smaller hills as lambs (Psalm 114:6), we are simply considering a graphic description of an earthquake. When Psalm 75 talks about the 'pillars' of the earth, it is speaking just as poetically and figuratively as when it talks about the boastful having a 'stiff neck' or where Galatians 2:9 cites leading men in Christian work as those who 'seemed to be pillars'. These figures of speech are as easily identified in the Bible as in any other literary work. No one who criticises the Bible on these grounds would reject an account in another book because the author wrote, 'she lost her head', 'his jaw dropped' or 'he blew his top'!

However, when the Bible speaks factually, on any subject at all, it speaks with complete accuracy and with the authority of its Author, God. So we can believe what it says about creation, or the virgin birth of Christ, or the miracles performed by Jesus, or His resurrection and ascension, without having to explain any part of them away, 'spiritualise' any of them as mere illustrations of truth, or accommodate any of them into some human theory to give the Bible credibility in the eyes of an unbelieving and rebellious world. We take the whole of the Bible as God's word, and argue for it as such. But Christians who take a fundamentalist view of the Bible are commanded to show love, not violence, towards any who do not agree with them!

ARGUMENT NUMBER 3: THE COMMON UNTHINKING RELIANCE ON OTHERS' OBJECTIONS TO THE BIBLE

It is not my purpose here to answer many of the oft-quoted detailed objections to the Bible, but to throw out the challenge as to how many of those who repeat those objections have ever looked seriously into the supposed objections before trotting them out. A few examples of common objections follow:

ISN'T THE BIBLE FULL OF CONTRADICTIONS?

Really? How many have you found, looked into, and politely asked a believer in the Bible to explain? Usually, those who say that cannot produce a single weighty 'contradiction' to discuss! (See Chapter 4 for a fuller discussion of this topic.)

HOW CAN A GOD OF LOVE ALLOW SUFFERING?

The Bible alone explains the origin, growth and effects of suffering, how long it will be allowed to continue, and what the final answer is to it. It also gives some good guidelines about why God allows it. But to know all that, you need to get to know the Bible, and you will find out more and more as you advance in your love for and understanding of God's word. And remember that Jesus was innocent when He suffered on the cross for people like you, to bring you to God (Luke 24:46–47). (The question of suffering is beyond the scope of this book, but carefully read the book of Job and see the comments on it.)

I WILL NOT BELIEVE THE BIBLE UNLESS YOU CAN TELL ME WHERE CAIN GOT HIS WIFE

Read Genesis 5:4. If that was a real objection and problem for you, now that you have read the answer in the Bible, will you now trust the Bible and its message that tells you to repent and put your faith in Jesus Christ?

I CAN'T BELIEVE THE BIBLE WHEN SOME MINISTERS ARE IMMORAL OR MOLEST CHILDREN

It is a sad fact that some influential people in the church have done some shameful things. But the Bible condemns, more than any other book, those who claim to be

Christians but whose lives show a life of wickedness, hypocrisy and rebellion. There are many Christian ministers who live exemplary lives, but that is not always the case. But because we thoughtlessly call some unregenerate men 'Reverend', God is not fooled. A person can have his collar turned round without having his heart turned round! All sinners, whether religious or otherwise, must turn from their sins and come to Christ for mercy and pardon, or they will be condemned and judged by God. Some well-known people, like John Wesley, were church ministers *before* they became Christians! Christ's death on the cross can be the means of their finding forgiveness and new life, too, if they really repent and trust Christ. And by the way, you also need to repent and trust Christ to have your sins forgiven! The only person who is smaller than a hypocrite is one who tries to hide behind one. Those sinful religious people you mention will have to account to God for their actions: but so will you. I will, too. We all need a Saviour, and only the Bible tells us about Him.

ARGUMENT NUMBER 4: HASN'T SCIENCE DISPROVED THE BIBLE?
Scientists are as divided in their attitude towards the Bible, God and Jesus Christ as are jewellers, lawyers, beauticians, milkmen, postmen, teachers, football players, housewives, farmers—or any other group of people! Throughout history, there have been notable scientists on both sides of the argument. Many genuine scientists and qualified engineers, with a whole-hearted belief in the whole of the Bible including the book of Genesis, are involved in or support organisations like The American Scientific Affiliation, Answers in Genesis, Biblical Creation Society, Creation Science Foundation, Creation Science Movement, and Creation Resources Trust. The width of the bibliography of *Genesis for today*, a balanced and helpful book by Professor Andy McIntosh on the creation/evolution debate (Day One Publications), demonstrates the point, as does his list of the books that helped him to compile much of his appendix material. Honest scientists know that there has never been a scientific reason or fact why the Bible should not be believed. There never will be!

So much of that which is deemed 'scientific' is not scientific, and so much of that which has been assumed to be factual is not factual. For example, the evolutionary account of the origin of life and the development of diverse life forms is neither factual nor even a real scientific theory. A theory can be tested by experiment to see if it is true, but the evolutionary scenario of origins is unobservable, unrepeatable and untestable. Evolution is a model, not a genuine scientific theory. As a model, it was an imaginative and ingenious attempt to explain origins without reference to an intelligent Creator as revealed in the Bible. However, many genuine scientists, Christians and non-Christians, who may respect but strongly reject the Darwinian model of evolution as unscientific and unproved, do not regard it as credible.

Although some scientists are sincere, we need to remember that some are dishonest, just as some non-scientists are dishonest. Some come with a mindset that makes their opposition to God and the Bible almost a statement of personal faith. So, for example, the Piltdown Man was a hoax that, for years, duped evolutionists into thinking they had found the answer to the infamous 'missing link'. When it was found to be a hoax, did that cause most of the supporters of evolution to rethink their position honestly? Were references to Piltdown Man scrupulously and promptly removed from school textbooks on evolution? Guess what the answer is! 'A man convinced against his will is of the same opinion still'—especially regarding the neo-religious belief in evolution.

Popular television wildlife series often present wild guesses about periods of millions of years during which the earth is supposed to have existed, without any justification or explanation. Because the programmes are well produced and presented, and the photography is often stunning, the evolutionary untruths receive reflected glory and appear more credible. But we need to remember that neither biblical revelation nor established scientific *facts* can justify an earth that is older than a few thousand years. The earth was created by God, just as the Bible says it was.

If there is a devil, as the Bible insists is the case, and if, through sin, humankind has a darkened and rebellious mind that rejects the very existence of God and His word, it is not surprising that there are attacks from non-Christian sceptics on the truthfulness of the Bible. That is sad enough. It is even sadder when professed Bible-believing Christians seek to adjust, interpret and manipulate Scripture to accommodate the erroneous theories of others who have never tasted the blessings of faith in Christ or in believing in God's word. The Bible does not need to be changed to accommodate them. It really is *God's* word.

ARGUMENT NUMBER 5: THE ATTACK FROM FALSE AND UNINFORMED LOGIC

Some people attack the Bible's authority and truthfulness, and encourage others to do so, by using false and uninformed logic based on premises which either they know are false, or negligently do not bother to verify. Such people reject the Bible and launch false and empty accusations of biblical inconsistency and unreliability, like specially tailored 'clay pigeons' which they feel they can shoot down easily. We will demonstrate this by looking briefly at three such 'clay pigeons'.

First, some say, quite wrongly, that the Bible cannot be taken seriously because the Old Testament contradicts what Jesus said about responding to evil. Second, others affirm that the teachings of Paul and James differ on whether salvation comes by faith or by works. Third, yet others contend that the Bible's teaching on God's character is inconsistent, in that God is shown as the God of love and yet He condemns some people to hell. Like most criticisms of the Bible, the accusations are superficially made. This type of attack is often presented without any reference to context, which always underlines, rather than undermines, the consistency of the biblical truth taught. We will now briefly examine these three attacks on the Bible.

Firstly, from a reading and comparison of Exodus 21:24 and Matthew 5:38–39, we can see that Jesus explained that, although the law indicated that the abuse of the legal right of anyone aggrieved could be remedied by 'an eye for an eye and a tooth for a tooth', His disciples should not insist on exercising their undoubted personal rights, but should turn the other cheek. (It is worth noting that the 'eye for an eye' teaching was given to limit the response to nothing greater than the damage suffered.) Those opposing the Bible on these grounds should know the reason for Jesus' summary of the law and why He asks His followers to waive their rights at times. When I was given a black and cut eye by a drunken man at a late-night open-air meeting, I could have reported him to the police and pressed for criminal charges to be brought. I would have been justified had I done so. I could also have sued him under the law of tort for damages. Also, had I so decided (and recovered from the first unexpected blow in time!), I could have struck back by using reasonable force in self-defence. I chose none of these options, not because it was wrong to do so, but because I applied a higher principle. There was no contradiction: just a choosing to turn the other cheek for the sake of Christ and the gospel. (In other circumstances, of course, someone so assaulted may not be wrong to exercise one or more of those options.)

Secondly, the apostle Paul stresses that a sinner can only be saved by faith in Christ and that good works can save no one (Ephesians 2:8–9). James stresses that if a person really exercises faith that saves him or her, a completely changed lifestyle of good works will result; otherwise their so-called 'faith' is 'dead' (James 2:17–20). Christians are justified before God by faith alone, but their testimony and credibility is justified before their fellow human beings by the works that demonstrate a changed life. Thus, in James 2:20–24, we read of Abraham's faith which justified him before God, and of his actions which justified him before an enquiring world, which could see that his faith in God was real. This is completely logical and consistent, and yet prejudiced opponents continue to trot out this supposed contradiction as if they were unaware of the clear explanation. The same unerring and inspired influence of the Holy Spirit caused both Paul and James to write Scripture. Perhaps those opposing the twin truths so produced do so because they do not want their lifestyles to be changed by personal repentance and saving faith in the Lord Jesus Christ.

Thirdly, many who oppose the Bible know the biblical logic and rationale that God's holiness and justice are no less than His love and compassion. We see this throughout the Bible. Of course, God must punish sin or He is seen to condone it, just as an anarchic society would not be expected to apply the rule of law. But God loves sinners and longs to pardon them. Is this a contradiction? Clearly not! Jesus bore the just punishment of our sins on the cross (1 Peter 2:24), so that those who truly repent and put their faith in God's promise of pardon and restoration will know His forgiveness and cleansing. His holy justice and His loving compassion meet at the cross (1 Peter 3:18), where those claiming God's promise can prove that if they confess their sins through Jesus, God 'is faithful and just to forgive us our sins and to cleanse us from all unrighteousness' (1 John 1:9). Why do biased people say there is a contradiction here? Could it be that the real ongoing problem is an unwillingness to repent and come to God?

ARGUMENT NUMBER 6: IF THE BIBLE IS GOD'S WORD, WHY HAVE SO MANY CONTRADICTORY VERSIONS?

Some object that there are too many versions of the Bible, many of which contradict each other, so how can we know what God's word really is? The basis of biblical infallibility is that the Bible is God's word as given in its original languages. In any translation in any field of communication, there is always some loss of clarity from the original. That is as true of Agatha Christie being translated from English to French, as it is of a translation of *Mein Kampf* from German into Spanish. It must also necessarily be true of any translation of the Bible into any language from Hebrew, Greek and Aramaic. No medical or legal textbook is rejected because of inevitable difficulties in translation. Neither should the Bible be rejected on that basis.

As language is not static but dynamically changing, certain aspects of versions of past translations will inevitably not be as accurate as when they were first made. A small number of words change their meaning. But there is no inherent contradiction or unreliability of biblical revelation involved, and genuine translations (distinguished from paraphrases, which can be more or less helpful) have a very high level of consistency and agreement. I personally read through a different translation each year, including (but not limited to) the Amplified Version, the Authorised Version, the New American Standard Version, the New International Version, the New King James Version, and the Revised Standard Version. It is good to reach a reasoned preference for normally using a particular Bible translation, but reading through other versions can widen your understanding of the Bible, and help you to learn from the nuances of each. Paraphrases are also interesting to read, but should never be treated with the same weight as a translation by well-qualified believers in the Bible.

ARGUMENT NUMBER 7: BUT DOESN'T THE BIBLE PROMOTE IMMORALITY?

Incredibly, some claim to dismiss the Bible because they charge it with referring to and focusing on immorality. This objection is hard to take seriously. You might just as well condemn a medical textbook on gynaecology or a criminal law report of a sexual assault case! The Bible faithfully reports immorality when it occurs, and also boldly states God's condemnation of it, demonstrating the sad results of it. Immorality in the Bible is never glamorised, justified or recommended. The Bible never communicates the harmful sensual detail that today pollutes our television screens and provides an unsavoury role model for viewers, including adolescents and young adults. No one ever became foul minded by reading the Bible: in fact, just the reverse is true. Holiness becomes a lifestyle for those who come to know the Christ of the Bible and follow biblical teachings from the heart.

Jesus demonstrated the need for purity both in His teaching and in His lifestyle, and He calls us to follow Him. Those who see the Bible as immoral are looking into it as a mirror in which they see themselves as they really are.

ARGUMENT NUMBER 8: BELIEVING THE BIBLE DEMANDS AN UNREALISTIC BELIEF IN ABSOLUTE TRUTH

We live in an age of relativism, where we are told that there is no such thing as absolute truth (which itself is an attempt to establish an 'absolute truth' that absolute truth does not exist!). We are now told to be so open-minded that it seems that the only offence is to be sure of anything and close your mind on it! So, especially in Western multi-faith and inter-faith societies, it is offensive to some that Christians say that there is absolute truth and that truth is the Bible. It seems strange that many who seem to be offended by the insistence of Christians on biblical authority live in countries that are supposed to embrace freedom of religion. The last official UK Government Census revealed that 72% of the population claimed to be 'Christian' (whatever they meant by that word). It is noticeable that the same degree of religious freedom allowed in the UK is often missing from other countries, whose religions are freely practised here. Sadly, however, recent trends in applying so-called 'political correctness' to unwarranted and unreasonable levels may mean that religious freedom will be restricted in the UK. 'Political correctness' seems to have burst its originally well-justified banks and now floods areas which should have been protected from that flood. Like all floods, it causes destruction and brings dirt in with it.

Surely, if there really is a self-revealing God who loves sinners and wants to see them blessed on earth and then in heaven eternally, He is going to make it crystal clear how a person can come to know Him and experience His blessings. That is why we can know with certainty what God has revealed, and that is why we can trust the whole of the Bible. God wants to make it clear, and wants us to believe what He says. So we have His sure and certain written word, the Bible. Why not look up a few things it says about being sure? Read, for example, Romans 8:1, 1 John 5:10–13, and John 10:25–30.

Does the Bible contradict itself?

Are there contradictions in the Bible?

The question 'What about all the contradictions?' is a challenge often thrown at the Bible. Yet many of the challengers have rarely read the Bible seriously in a mature way and only a few seem to have read all of it. Whether there are contradictions or not, most of those accusing the Bible of being contradictory use second-hand arguments and have little or no knowledge of the background and context of the part they criticise. The Christian position is that the Bible, as originally given in its original languages and taken in context, nowhere contradicts itself or any established fact. There are some occasional minor problems in translation, or where a manuscript might have been damaged or was not copied correctly. These occurrences are relatively very few when you consider the huge size of the Bible. An occasional detail may have suffered in the translation or in copying variant readings in the manuscripts available to us. These are rare and virtually none of them affects our understanding of the truth expressed. In any case, these are not contradictions in the truth that God the Holy Spirit produced through the holy men of God whom He used to record His original revelation in the Bible.

Principles

It is beyond the scope of this chapter to look at all the Bible's alleged discrepancies and supposed contradictions, and those wishing to look at this subject in more detail will find John W. Haley's book *Alleged Discrepancies* (Whitaker House) both interesting and helpful. But there are *principles* that govern the way a Christian should approach supposed contradictions. As those principles are applied, a growing confidence in God's word justifiably results. We will look at some of those principles now.

Starting premise

As seen in Chapter 3 of *The Bible Panorama*, the Bible can be shown to be God's word both by internal and external examination. So that is how we should approach it, namely taking it to be the word of the all-wise, all-knowing, all-powerful, eternal God, whose thoughts, ways and character are infinitely higher than ours. We have a mind that is both biased and closed, and we should admit that. Would it surprise you if I said that a Christian's mind should be both biased and closed about the Bible? It should be about other issues too! For example, we should be closed to driving on the wrong side of the road, or drinking poison! If we are married, we should be unerringly and faithfully biased towards our spouse and be closed about the possibility of an intimate relationship with anyone else. That is the nature of love and loyalty where a commitment has been made. So it is with the Bible. With good reason, we should love the book that God has used to give us the only message that can save, bless, guide and keep us. We should remain loyal to its teachings, however unfashionable that may be in a selfish and rebellious world, and declare that we espouse no other revelation and will not enter into unfaithfulness to God, or doubt or deny what He has said through the Bible. Do not apologise for such a stance—it is a sure sign that God has wrought His work in your heart and produced a love for the things of God, including the Bible. Our starting premise is not that we have an open mind that may change, but that we have closed our mind around the words of our faithful and unchanging God. This stance is strengthened by the fact that all the evidence underlines that the Bible is God's word. We are, of course, open to be taught new things from God's word and to respond to those truths, provided they are in line with the context of the whole Bible.

God is not the author of confusion

A statement urging discipline and order in the church, 1 Corinthians 14:33, reveals an important principle about God. That principle is demonstrated throughout His creation and His dealings with mankind. It is that 'God is not the author of confusion'. In 1 Corinthians 14:40 the application of that principle to the Christian church shows how God's mind works: 'Let all things be done decently and in order'.

Because God is the God of order and not of confusion, it follows that He who made a fully harmonised world, who created the human body that perfectly fits together and works without any 'contradictory parts', and who revealed Himself in the faultless perfection of His living Word, the Lord Jesus Christ, would produce a faultless, harmonised, integrated, ordered, perfectly working and non-contradictory written word. He has! It is the Bible.

No contradictions

Because of the constant attacks on the truth of the Bible as the Word of God, it is worth repeating often that there is no contradiction of any kind in it. This is despite the fact that God caused it to be written through fallible men. God, the Holy Spirit, infallibly inspired it. The very fact that its writers or compilers have not sanitised the Bible, in order to remove parts which could be thought to be contradictory by those viewing it superficially, is in fact a further evidence of its divine origin. If man wanted to persuade others of the perfect harmony of a man-made book, he would carefully check and eliminate anything that could even raise the question of the book's contents.

An apparent contradiction therefore cannot be a real contradiction

But apparent contradictions will confront Bible readers, whether introduced by friend or foe of the Bible, or encountered in their personal reading. How should the Christian deal with these apparent contradictions? Ten simple, but non-exhaustive, guidelines are suggested. In applying them, remember a two-sided rule: doubt your doubts and believe your beliefs, as long as those beliefs come in context from the Bible.

Guideline 1—The biblical order is not always the chronological order

Generally speaking, the events recorded in the Bible are related to each other in a progressive time span, but there are many exceptions, sometimes to emphasise a point made, or because the chronology is not an important issue. Thus the biblical order is not always the chronological order and the Bible may 'replay' a past event or 'fast track' to a future one. These instances do not, however, constitute contradictions.

Guideline 2—A different point of view of the same event may be presented

The supposed contradiction may concern the reporting of a single event, or a certain aspect of a single event, from different points of view. As is normal in any reporting, different reporters can observe the same thing from various, though not necessarily contradictory, stances. For example, one sportswriter may focus on one player and present him as the match winner. Another may emphasise the fitness of the whole team and the good job the manager has done in pulling them together. These are not contradictions. Similarly, a violent offence may be reported by concentrating on the aggrieved, while another will focus on the ringleaders, and yet another will present the main culprit's criminality. No contradiction is involved just because a different viewpoint is taken. Law courts recognise that a different emphasis in an eye-witnessed testimony does not thereby contradict other witnesses. In fact, it is often regarded as a healthy indication of truthfulness, because the witnesses have not got together to concoct a story. So, regarding the Bible, men of intelligence, integrity and judgement have had no problem in producing a harmonised view of different Bible events. To illustrate this point, consider the harmonised summary of all the events in the four Gospels in a study Bible, such as *The MacArthur Study Bible* (Nelson).

Guideline 3—Do not confuse similar events with identical events

A number of happenings in the Bible are very similar to others, but are not the same events. As today, some basically similar events could occur in different circumstances. Sometimes the Bible makes clear reference to the difference between events, and sometimes it is implied. Be careful not to draw a contradiction from a genuinely different, but similar, occasion. A superficial and unthinking reading of the Bible can lead to that, when in fact closer study always emphasises the Bible's reliability. Certainly no contradictions are involved.

Guideline 4—An event may concern different elements and people

There are occasions when only one aspect of an event, or only one of the characters involved, is the focus of attention in one account, whereas another account of the same event may take a broader brush approach or focus on another aspect or individual involved. Such different elements or personalities can always be harmonised. Again, no contradiction is involved. At a time when textbooks and tape recorders were unknown, similar truths would be taught on many different occasions, though not necessarily in identical words.

Guideline 5—Reported mistakes do not contradict the Bible's truthfulness

There are a number of times in the Bible when someone says something that is wrong. That may be through malice, ignorance or a failure to understand fully. When the Bible accurately records the giving of an inaccurate account or opinion by someone, that is not a contradiction. It is a truthful report of a misguided or dishonest person's wrong account. When Teriq Aziz, the then Defence Minister of Iraq, commented that the invading allied forces had been routed near Baghdad, it became apparent that what he said was not true. But CNN did not contradict itself when it simply reported what he said. Similarly, the Bible does not contradict itself by reporting information wrongly given by others.

Guideline 6—Remember the context!

One of the cardinal rules in understanding the Bible is always to look at what you read in context. There is never a supposed contradiction that remains when the searchlight of context is shone upon it. Almost like concentric circles of light, the context of the whole Bible, then the context of the book of the Bible concerned, then the context of the chapter and verse(s) concerned in that book, then the context of the prevailing circumstances, will always show the truthfulness of God's word. If you come across two or more allegedly contradictory passages, simply look at the context of each and then compare them together. They are always able to be reconciled. The more a fraud or a fake is closely examined the more obvious are its faults. In stark comparison, the more closely the Bible is examined, the more it is seen to be entirely trustworthy.

Guideline 7—Do not be in a hurry

When using these guidelines, or any others, it may not always be immediately clear what the answer is to an apparent contradiction. Do not worry about that— rather take your time sorting it out. God's word will not 'unbecome' God's word because some Christian does not fully understand something for a time! As a young Christian, someone told me to read the Bible like I eat fish: consume, enjoy and digest the pieces I can easily get, and leave the rest on the side! Obviously, the illustration is limited. There are no indigestible bones or skin in the Bible! But the underlying principle is good. If you do not immediately understand something, especially something that seems to be contradictory, keep trusting the Bible as God's word and ask God to show you the answer in His time. But do not be lazy, either! As well as praying, thinking it through and reading around the various contexts dealt with by 'Guideline 6', consult a mature Bible-believing Christian, or leader. And use a good evangelical Bible commentary and study Bible. But, above all, keep reading through the Bible. It is amazing how a completely different part of the Bible can shed light on, and resolve difficulties found in, difficult passages elsewhere. C.H. Spurgeon's humorous comment about one Bible commentary was that it was surprising how much light the Bible shed on that particular commentary! In a more serious vein, it really is amazing how much light the Bible sheds on itself.

Guideline 8—Pray!

The study of the Bible, including the resolution of parts wrongly said to be contradictory, must always be undertaken carefully and with prayer. Remember that the Bible is a spiritual book and so should be approached spiritually, and with an attitude of prayer. Bathe the alleged contradiction in prayer, and God the Holy Spirit will lead you into all truth, as Jesus promised He would (John 16:13).

Guideline 9—Do not confuse the words 'inspired' and 'inspiring'

All parts of the Bible are equally inspired by God the Holy Spirit and therefore equally infallible and non-contradictory. But not all parts are equally inspiring to the reader. For example, few readers buzz with delight when they read a genealogy. But such parts of the Bible are foundational to its historicity and accuracy. The details of the foundations of a house for sale never get the same exposure to a potential buyer as the size and number of the rooms, the location of the house, or the wonderful views from the windows. But without the foundations the exciting parts of the house could not exist. In the same way, do not fall into the trap of thinking that parts of the Bible are less inspired, and therefore potentially more likely to be contradictory, than other parts. Whether you find a particular part inspiring or not, the whole of the Bible is inspired as God's word. It is all profitable and given for our instruction and blessing, and none of it is contradictory.

Guideline 10—Take courage: you are not alone!

Satan's first tactic in the Garden of Eden was to try to instil doubts in the minds of Eve and Adam. He still asks the malicious question 'Has God indeed said?' (Genesis 3:1) to seek to undermine faith in, and obedience to, God's word. Often the devil poses that question through others. But take courage! Every Christian who ever lived has been tested at some stage in the fires of doubting God's word. God has brought, is bringing, and will bring every born-again, blood-bought child of His through that temptation to confidence in His word and eternal blessing. Like the heroes of faith in Hebrews 11, those who run that race of faith now can be encouraged by countless witnesses who have run it before them and found God is true to His inspired, infallible and complete word, the Bible. They could find no justifiable contradictions in it, and neither will you!

CHAPTER 5

Getting the most out of my Bible

Ten guidelines—and how *not* to do it!

This chapter does not seek to give comprehensive advice that will exhaust all there is to say about getting the most out of the Bible. It provides ten guidelines that may help those considering becoming serious about getting to know God through His word. Those who are already involved in serious reading and study of the Bible will know the truth of the practical counsel given below, which is gleaned from conversations over the years with many Christians, as well as from the author's own experience. The guidelines are in no order of priority and are both individually independent and mutually interdependent.

But first, let us emphasise the point by ten *negative* guidelines, given tongue in cheek by Trevor F. Knight, in his excellent and thoroughly readable book *God's Wonderful Word* (Young Life):

1. Always read at night when you are tired.
2. Open at random: your chances of striking a genealogy are pretty good.
3. Never read more than five verses at a time: you might get the idea of the story.
4. Tackle the most difficult passages first: they will encourage you to give up more quickly.
5. Don't have a system: you might know where to start.
6. Fill your bookshelves with translations: they prove it's too hard to understand.
7. Never make notes: you might learn something.
8. Never share what you have read with others: speech often brings thoughts into focus.
9. Never attend a group Bible study: confusion might disappear.
10. Whatever you do, never become a regular daily reader: it might affect the way you live.

Hopefully, you will prefer some more constructive guidelines! Here are another ten:

1. READ THE BIBLE *PRAYERFULLY*

The Bible is a spiritual book because its Author is Spirit and He deals with spiritual truths, whatever the context of the part of the Bible you are reading. So the approach needs to be genuinely spiritual. That means we should approach God's word not only carefully and reverently but *prayerfully*, too. Before, during and after reading God's word, we should ask God to make our reading of the Bible real and personal to us through His Holy Spirit and use it to produce a renewed spiritual life that is of increasing honour to God and more like Christ each day. This means we need to open our hearts to God whenever we open His book. We should be looking for His truth that we need, not just intellectual discovery or greater information (though we will often get both of those as well). Here we read not only truth about God, but how God sees us. Our response to His truth about us cannot be applied without serious prayer and seeking His will and way in our lives.

2. READ THE BIBLE *THOUGHTFULLY*
The Bible is the expression of the mind of God to the mind of people. God used His mind in giving us the Bible and we must use our minds to understand it and apply it. There is much of Christian experience that rightly affects our emotions, such as peace, joy and compassion, but God never bypasses our minds in understanding His truth, and any emotional appreciation or outworking of God's character and dealings must be based on objective truth as revealed in His word. So we are to love God with all our minds (Deuteronomy 6:5) and we are to display the mind that was in Christ Jesus in pursuing harmonious relationships with fellow Christians (Philippians 2:5). We cannot do that without using our minds in reading and thinking through God's word and then applying its truths to our situation. Although human reason is never to be regarded as a substitute for God's revelation through the Bible, we should thoughtfully build on the clear authority of the teachings of God's word, and then reason from those biblical bases to reach conclusions about the teaching of God's word in any given situation. The practice of making daily notes of your reading and study, however brief, will help you to retain and think through what you are reading. It will also provide a platform to review yesterday's reading before you continue with today's portion. *The Bible Panorama* was born out of many years of making daily notes, while reading through the Bible, using a page to a day diary that always forms part of my 'Christmas stocking' from my wife. When I started making notes, I had no idea where the practice would lead me!

3. READ THE BIBLE *SENSIBLY*
Common sense is not really very common! The best common sense is achieved by humbly asking for God's wisdom which, according to James 1:5, He is always willing to give liberally. Having asked for wisdom, then use a basis of thoughtful prayer to apply it to any situation needing either understanding or action. This means that, in reading the Bible, we will not rush to interpret the Bible according to some whim or supposed individual insight or vision, but we will sensibly consider the context of what we are reading, and its primary meaning. We should look at the context of the Bible as a whole, then of the book concerned, then of the passage we are reading, then of anything we know about the situation existing where and when the part of the Bible concerned was first expressed. If we come to an understanding of a verse that contradicts the context, as described above, we need to jettison that understanding and start again, perhaps helped by

a good commentary or study Bible. After being clear that we know what the Bible is saying (and after a while the approach will become as much second nature as changing gear when driving), we apply the teaching to ourselves practically and sensibly. In so doing, we must take the primary meaning first. That means understanding the obvious, main and natural meaning and lesson of the passage before thinking about relatively minor matters. To 'major on the majors and minor on the minors' is a principle to be applied not only to our Christian lives, but also to our reading and study of the Bible.

4. READ THE BIBLE *REGULARLY*

Regular Bible reading means two things. First, I should read it regularly each day, and set apart prime time to do so. Most Christians feel it is most helpful to dedicate disciplined time first thing in the morning after waking up and freshening up, though that should not prevent a 'nightcap' of reading before sleeping, or a short 'snack' at lunchtime for those able to do so. But some people find their personal lifestyles and inclinations indicate that the best time to spend quality time with God's word is in the evening or at midday, with 'nibbles' at other times. There is no point in legalistically insisting on a certain time to read. Each Christian is on trust to find meaningful, regular, unhurried time each day to read God's word and pray, knowing that we all answer to God personally, and that He longs to bless us.

But regular reading not only means the regularity of daily reading. Second, it also involves the regularity of reading the whole of God's word. Again, there are no set rules for this, but surely the aims must be to get to know the whole of God's word, involving reading through all the Bible regularly and repeatedly, and spending time on given books and passages, involving more detailed digging into smaller passages to go deeper with God in those areas. That is why some Christians rejoice that they were raised spiritually on a diet of reading enough of the Bible to enable them to read through the whole of it in a year, and were taught then to spend further time each day concentrating on far smaller bite-sized portions of individual books. Some regard reading through the Bible not as a normal 'quiet time' of Bible reading and prayer but as extra time redeemed from valid but less worthy use of time; they pursue a more detailed study of the Bible in their daily 'quiet time'. Some have been helped by the slogan 'Less TV—more Bible!'

5. READ THE BIBLE *SYSTEMATICALLY*

Enough is said about systematic reading through of the Bible elsewhere in *The Bible Panorama,* especially in Appendix 3. Suffice it to say that we plan our holidays, our weddings, our examination revision, our careers, our finances and our Christian meetings. Why should we not carefully plan our Bible reading, both to ensure that we keep reading it through, and also to study parts in greater depth? To do this we need to read the Bible systematically. We should adopt and follow closely a system of reading which suits us. That does not prevent us from reading through a book one night, or taking a pocket-sized Bible with us for extra unplanned reading when we are on the train, or on holiday, or in the dentist's waiting room. But we need a basic system, too, or we will always gravitate to those 'easier' passages or to our favourites. Some of the harder and less favourite passages will become easier and more favourite as we get to grips with them, because we will meet God there. Some have used these unscheduled reading opportunities to learn verses, chapters and even books off by heart. When you do that, you really find you turn over the verse in your mind!

6. READ THE BIBLE *TRUSTINGLY*

When we come to the Bible, we are not coming to a mere literary masterpiece, though it certainly is that. Neither are we taking up a story of great adventure and intrigue with many mysteries, sub-plots and absorbing situations, though the Bible is full of such elements in telling the greatest story ever told. Nor is this just an authoritative history book, though no history book ever written could be more accurate, unbiased or relevant. Through the Bible, we see the will of an entirely trustworthy, unchanging, faithful, caring God. He is the Maker of promises and blessings and is lovingly involved with His people. So we read it as wonderful literature, as an amazing adventure story containing hundreds of other amazing adventures, and as history. But more than that, we read it with absolute trust in what it says because the One who said it is God Himself. This book is not like a scientific textbook, which changes with new findings and shifts of opinion, or like a law book, which is out of date even before it is published. It is truthful, fixed, certain, settled and sure. And it will never change. Yet it is dynamic, too, because as we trust its principles and promises, obey its commands, heed its warnings, and follow its examples and advice, the Holy Spirit, who caused it to be written infallibly, illuminates it to us unmistakably. Here is the book of God that we can completely trust. We thus must read it trustingly, and so trust God to change and mould our lives continuously through it. And remember to look for the centrality, person and work of the Lord Jesus Christ throughout the Bible's pages, whether as foreseen in the Old Testament as the One to come to save and rule, or in the New Testament as the One who has come as our incarnate Saviour God, or as in both Testaments as the One who will come again and who will reign as King of kings and Lord of lords. In trusting the Bible as God's written word, may our trust grow in Jesus as the living Word of God.

7. READ THE BIBLE *ENTHUSIASTICALLY*

A treasure seeker rejoices when he gets on the island and finds the hidden map. Then when he finds the treasure chest packed with sparkling and precious jewels, he is euphoric. The Bible is both the map to God's will and the chest with many priceless treasures to bless us. But our treasures are spiritual and eternal: they will last for ever though we can begin to enjoy them now!

A hungry person rejoices to be taken to a restaurant where the best food, and plenty of it, comes to him or her course by course. The Bible is that feast: we feed spiritually, taking as much as our spiritual appetites can manage (yet never getting indigestion or becoming overweight!). Should we rejoice less in our gourmet spiritual provisions than we would if we were treated to a meal at a five-star restaurant?

When I was away from home but engaged to be married, I could not wait for the next letter from my fiancée to arrive. When it came, I would open it to read it as soon as I could. I re-read those letters (especially the endings!) because I loved her, she loved me, and she wanted to share something with me that I wanted to have shared. Should I be less keen to read the letter from the One who 'loved me and gave Himself for me'? Of course not!

The treasure seeker, the hungry person, and the man absent from his loved one show, above all, one characteristic: enthusiasm! May we cultivate that same enthusiasm to meet God in His word, both in our own private daily readings, and also in fellowship with other Christians throughout the services and meetings on the Lord's Day and at weekday Bible studies and prayer meetings. But I will never be enthusiastic for God's word in fellowship with others if I am not enthusiastic for it in my daily personal and private fellowship with God. Let us pray that God will give us constant, holy enthusiasm!

8. READ THE BIBLE *FAITHFULLY*

One of the biggest enemies confronting the daily reading of the Bible is reliance on our feelings. We may respond emotionally to a stirring message, a challenging book, or a devoted Christian whose example motivates us. Being with others at a large conference can also excite emotions. With feelings on our side, we can promise to maintain our quiet times, to read through the Bible, and to spend quality time in studying it. Then we forget the message, stop reading good Christian literature (or get used to it), forget the example of the Christian, or lose the kindred feeling of being with like-minded people at a conference. What happens? Our devotions begin to wane and our Bible reading becomes a chore, if we carry on with it. Perhaps we begin to watch, or resume watching, unhelpful programmes on the television or compromised videos, and the vicious circle spirals downwards. Remember the comment that 'God's word will keep you from sin or sin will keep you from God's word'.

So, what is the answer? We must walk with God from day to day, where feelings are welcomed when they help us to read the Bible, to pray, to worship, to have fellowship and to witness to Christ's saving grace, but where, when they are not helpful, we leave them behind and walk on with the Captain of our salvation. Feelings should follow our faith in Christ and our faithfulness to him and never lead to it or replace it. So make that commitment to God now, and every day, that by His enabling grace and strength, you will remain faithful to a daily prayer life that is fed from the spiritual input of the Bible. Faithfulness is everything in Bible reading, and eventually your feelings will catch you up again and may even help for a while. But never trust them, as they are fickle. Rather, trust God through His word.

9. READ THE BIBLE *PRACTICALLY*

God did not give the Bible merely to inform us, but to change us to be more glorifying to Him. Just as 'faith without works is dead' (James 2:26), so Bible reading without applying its teachings in our lives will become dead too. You cannot be a man, or woman, of God without being a man, or woman, of the Bible. But you can be a man, or woman, of the Bible without being a man, or woman, of God. Why is that? Because to know is not enough, and we must be willing to see the answer to our own prayers for God's blessing by being willing to be changed ourselves from day to day. That can only happen when we read the Bible *practically,* with a trusting and obedient heart to apply practically what we read and learn. A challenging question to ask ourselves is this: in how many ways, positive and negative, have I changed my life today, this week, this month or this last year because of what God has shown me in the Bible? Unless we were perfect when we started reading it, surely there should often be changes. Some of those changes will be to return to standards, principles and practices we once had but have wandered from. Other changes will concern new issues not understood or realised before. Some changes will be to do certain things, or to stop doing things that do not honour God. Some will be changes in attitude, to be carefully guarded in prayer. Some will be a grasp of teaching never understood before, or an abandonment of views previously believed to be correct but now shown by the Bible not to be so. Relationships, ambitions, service, personal evangelism, use of time and money, giving and possessions, entertainment and leisure, work and home-life: all these are in the arena of potential change for good when we ask God to give us a heart and mind to immediately apply the principles of His word that we read each day.

10. READ THE BIBLE *SUBMISSIVELY*

It follows from all that has gone before in this chapter that when we read the Bible, we must do so *submissively* with a humble, teachable and devoted spirit. The Bible is the Word of God. Jesus challenged some: 'Why do you call me Lord and do not do the things that I say?' (Luke 6:46). When we read the Bible, we hear the things the Lord says, and, if He is Lord, we should take them as our loving but firm orders from the One who deserves to be our Lord. It is for that reason that He died and rose again (Romans 14:9). So let us come to His word, the Bible, saying and meaning, 'Lord, what do you want me to do?' (Acts 9:6). God blesses those who come to Him like that (Hebrews 11:6)!

CHAPTER 6

How were the contents of the Bible decided?

The canon of Scripture and the Apocrypha

Afully detailed discussion of the canon of Scripture and the Apocrypha is beyond the scope of both this chapter and *The Bible Panorama*. If you wish to look further into this subject, you should consult one of the many reliable Bible-based books available. Two recommended chapters are chapter 3 of Professor Wayne Grudem's very readable *Systematic Theology* (IVP) and chapter 3 of the apologetic classic *Evidence that demands a verdict*, by Josh McDowell (Campus Crusade for Christ). Much of this chapter has been shaped and influenced by the clarity of those books on this subject, but there are many other good authors who also deal well with this topic, and both Grudem and McDowell generously give them credit where it is due.

The word 'canon' has graduated from its original meaning of 'reed' or 'cane', through its associated meanings of 'standard' and then 'rule of faith', via 'list' or 'index', to its usage in connection with the Bible as 'an officially accepted list of books'. Thus it consists of the list of books of the Bible that exclusively constitute the Bible—no more and no less. To hold that the Bible has fewer books than those included in the canon is to take away from God's word. To seek to include others (such as the books of both the Old Testament and New Testament Apocryphas) is to add to God's word. Both those errors and sins are taught against in the Bible (Deuteronomy 4:2; Proverbs 30:6; Revelation 22:18). The question of what is included in the canon of Scripture, and why, is dealt with later in this chapter.

The word 'apocrypha' literally means 'things that are hidden' and it seems that scholars are unsure why the books in the Apocrypha, included in Roman Catholic and some other Bibles, have been given that name. The books of the Apocrypha are still best kept 'hidden' as they form no part of the Word of God, confuse the enquirer, and should have no place in our Bible! The Roman Catholic inclusion of the Apocrypha, after the Council of Trent in AD 1546, was largely to seek to combat the biblical teachings of grace expounded by Martin Luther. Those apocryphal books are erroneous in a number of areas, including the assertion that God hears the prayers of the dead, or that a sinner can be saved by good works, or the justification of falsehood and deception. The books included in the Old Testament Apocrypha are: 1 and 2 Esdras; Tobit; Judith; the Rest of Esther (no relation to the Bible's book of Esther); the Wisdom of Solomon (no relation to the Bible's books of Proverbs and Song of Solomon); Ecclesiasticus (no relation to the Bible's book of Ecclesiates); Baruch (including the Epistle of

Jeremiah which is not related to the Bible's books of Jeremiah or Lamentations of Jeremiah); the Song of the three Holy Children; Susanna; Bel and the Dragon; the Prayer of Manasseh; and 1 and 2 Maccabees. The New Testament Apocrypha includes, but is not limited to, the following books, with a note of McDowell's approximation of the dates when they were written: Epistle of Pseudo-Barnabas (AD 70–79); Epistle to the Corinthians (AD 96—no relation to the Bible's 1 Corinthians or 2 Corinthians); Ancient Homily (AD 120–140—also known as Second Epistle of Clement); Shepherd of Hermas (AD 115–140); Didache, Teaching of the Twelve (AD 100–120); Apocalypse of Peter (AD 150—no relation to the Bible's 1 Peter or 2 Peter or to Revelation); The Acts of Paul and Thecla (AD 170—no relation to the Bible's Acts of the Apostles or to any of its writings by Paul); Epistle to Laodiceans (4th century?); The Gospel According to the Hebrews (AD 65–100—no relation to the Bible's book of Hebrews); Epistle of Polycarp to the Philippians (AD 108—no relation to the Bible's book of Philippians); and The Seven Epistles of Ignatius (AD 100).

Why is the Apocrypha not part of the Bible?

The Old Testament Apocrypha was not found in the Hebrew Bible, but was placed with the translation of the Hebrew Old Testament into Greek (the Septuagint version), and used by Greek-speaking Jews when Jesus walked this earth. So Jesus knew about it, but never used it, and neither did any of the apostles. That is an interesting contrast to the fact that the Old Testament we possess is quoted, as Grudem points out, 295 times in the New Testament! In answering why the Apocrypha is not part of the Bible, some pointers will be given as to the criteria used in accepting or rejecting books in the canon of Scripture. The same principles apply to the New Testament Apocrypha as to the Old Testament Apocrypha, but with the seal of apostolic approval being added to the test for New Testament canonicity. The criticisms of apocryphal books run parallel to their failure to qualify as canonical, as they fail the tests which determine true biblical canonicity.

The question is asked, in Romans 3:1, as to the advantage that the Jews enjoyed over the Gentiles. The answer given in the next verse is: 'Much in every way! Chiefly because to them were committed the oracles of God.' This means they were given the Holy Scriptures—'the oracles of God'. But what were these Holy Scriptures?

1. The Jews themselves recognised only those books which are now the thirty-nine books of the Old Testament, though they were grouped differently then, as is explained later in this chapter.

2. The Lord Jesus Christ, when commenting on His persecution by the Jews, said, '... on you may come all the righteous blood shed on the earth, from the blood of righteous Abel to the blood of Zechariah, son of Berechiah, whom you murdered between the temple and the altar' (Matthew 23:35. See also Luke 11:51; Genesis 4:8; Hebrews 11:4; 2 Chronicles 24:20–21). Why did Jesus say that? The

answer to us may seem obscure, until we take note that our complete Old Testament is now placed in the order of Genesis to Malachi, but the Jewish Bible began with Genesis, containing the story of Cain and Abel, but ended with the second book of Chronicles, relating the murder of Zechariah. (The different order of the Jewish Bible is detailed below.)

So Jesus was saying that all the hostility against the godly recorded from Genesis to 2 Chronicles, namely in the whole of the Old Testament Scriptures, would come upon this generation. Thus we see that Jesus held that the Old Testament canon of Scripture is the same as we hold it to be, and we note that it did not contain any of the Old Testament apocryphal writings.

3. As mentioned above, Jesus quoted extensively from the Old Testament itself, and established authority from its teachings. He never quoted from the Apocrypha. Even if He had done so, that would not have implied it formed part of God's word, since there are times when the Bible quotes illustratively (though never to establish authority) from extra-biblical sources. But the fact that Jesus never considered any of the Apocrypha of sufficient relevance to quote, even to illustrate a point, is a further indication that it did not match the influence or authority of Scripture. He stayed within 'Moses and all the Prophets' (Luke 24:27)—that was Jewish shorthand for 'Moses (or the Law), the Prophets, and the Writings' or alternatively put as 'the Law of Moses and the Prophets and the Psalms' (Luke 24:44). Each expression meant the same and encompassed the books that comprised all the Old Testament. Luke 24:27 is evidence of this by the fact that, on the road to Emmaus, that same verse 27 makes it clear that Christ's teaching from 'Moses and all the Prophets' is synonymous with His expounding to the two travellers 'in all the Scriptures the things concerning Himself'. The Old Testament clearly always comprised exactly the same material as is in the thirty-nine books that are still in our Bibles today.

WHY WERE THE BOOKS OF THE OLD TESTAMENT APOCRYPHA REJECTED AS NOT BEING CANONICAL?

McDowell quotes Unger (in his *Bible Dictionary*) as to why the books of the Apocrypha were not in the canon:

1. They contain many historical and geographical inaccuracies and anachronisms.

2. Their teaching, unlike the books in the canon of Scripture, are at variance with the books in the canon. McDowell helpfully gives a pen-sketch of some of the contents of each apocryphal book of the Old Testament, which illustrates the truth of this assertion. The books of the Apocrypha demonstrably disqualify themselves.

3. They 'resort to literary types' and show artificiality in subject matter and styling, which distinguishes them from real God-breathed Scripture.

4. They do not have the distinctive features of Scripture that mark it out as God's word. Thus prophetic power, and poetic and religious feeling is missing. Spiritual reality is absent. Although it may be hard to explain in writing the difference in taste between a pebble from the beach and a mint, it is undeniable that there is a huge difference between them. Those who 'taste and see that the LORD is good' and who know that 'Blessed is the man who trusts in Him' (Psalm 34:8) know the difference between the flavour of God's word, the Bible, and any other man-made book, religious or otherwise. The objective truth that God's word is different is experienced subjectively by those with spiritual life in Christ.

Grudem reminds us that the apocryphal books do not even 'claim for themselves the same kind of authority as the Old Testament writings'. In short, the apocryphal books are nowhere near to being in 'the same league' as the canonical books. They are as different from the Bible as a false flower is from a beautiful rose or daffodil. That difference is self-evident.

HAS THE CANON OF SCRIPTURE CHANGED TO GIVE US OUR CURRENT SIXTY-SIX BOOKS?
The canon of Scripture consists of sixty-six books comprising thirty-nine in the Old Testament and twenty-seven in the New Testament. The New Testament books are exactly the same twenty-seven books now as they always have been, but the thirty-nine Old Testament books were formerly constituted differently in twenty-four Hebrew Old Testament books, though they contained exactly the same material. There is no change in content. The books in our Old Testament are arranged topically. The order of the twenty-four books of the Hebrew Old Testament was in an official order, as follows:

Law (Torah):
   Genesis, Exodus, Leviticus, Numbers, Deuteronomy
Prophets (Nebhim):
   (A) Former Prophets:
      Joshua, Judges, Samuel (1 & 2), Kings (1 & 2)
   (B) Latter Prophets:
      Isaiah, Jeremiah, Ezekiel, The Twelve (Minor Prophets)
Writings (Kethubhin or Hagiographa):
   (A) Poetical Books:
      Psalms, Proverbs, Job
   (B) Five Rolls (Megilloth):
      Song of Solomon, Ruth, Lamentations, Ecclesiastes, Esther
   (C) Historical Books:
      Daniel, Ezra-Nehemiah (originally one book), Chronicles (1&2)

How do we know that our Old Testament canon is correct?
Although much modernistic comment and so-called 'higher criticism' are directed against the Old Testament, it is very clear and simple to establish its

canonical authority. See the paragraph above, headed *Why is the Apocrypha not part of the Old Testament?*, concerning the arguments why the constituent parts of the canon are exactly the same as our current thirty-nine books. They are the 'flip side' of the argument as to why the Apocrypha is not included in the canon. Other factors include the following:

1. Jesus disputed and disagreed with some of the oral traditions of the Pharisees but never questioned their well-known concept of the Hebrew canon. He accepted the Old Testament canon they used as the divine Scriptures.

2. The threefold division of the Old Testament canon into Law (or Moses), Prophets and Writings is testified to in the Apocrypha in Ecclesiasticus.

3. Josephus (first century), the celebrated historian of the Jews, recorded that the books were in place and that no one was allowed to meddle with them or even speak against them under pain of torture or death, or both.

4. There are various other extra-biblical sources, including the Jewish Talmud, that confirm the fact that the canon of the Old Testament was in existence.

5. The New Testament abounds with references demonstrating that the Old Testament canon, as we now know it, was authoritative as the written Word of God. The apostles accepted it and appealed to it for doctrine and practice. More important still, so did God incarnate, our Immanuel, the Lord Jesus. If the Lord of eternity accepts it, who can refuse it? To see how the New Testament testifies to the Old Testament as God-breathed Scripture, simply keep your eyes open as you read through it. McDowell cites a helpful list as: Matthew 21:42; 22:29; 26:54,56; Luke 24; John 5:39; 10:35; Acts 17:2, 11; 18:28; Romans 1:2; 4:3; 9:17; 10:11; 11:2; 15:4; 16:26; 1 Corinthians 15:3–4; Galatians 3:8; 3:22; 4:30; 1 Timothy 5:18; 2 Timothy 3:16; 2 Peter 1:20–21; 3:16. Time taken to check out that list will be well spent.

We need to remember that the Old Testament canon, under God, 'chose itself'. Whereas it is true, as Grudem indicates, that the Council of Trent *chose* to include the Apocrypha (apart from 1 and 2 Esdras and the Prayer of Manasseh) in the Scriptures unjustifiably and for wrong reasons, much earlier the Council of Jamnia *recognised the already accepted books* in the Old Testament canon that corresponded to our thirty-nine books. (The gathering at Jamnia was probably less formal than an official 'Council' and took place after the fall of Jerusalem in AD70 under the presidency of Rabbi Yochanan ben Zakkai, who received permission from the Romans to call the Sanhedrin together for spiritual reasons rather than for political reasons.) The reason for the Old Testament canon having been *recognised*, rather than having been *chosen* at Jamnia, was because its constituent books had already *'chosen themselves'* in practice and were already in use. The books specifically discussed and recognised were (per Professor F.F. Bruce, quoted by McDowell) Proverbs, Ecclesiastes, the Song of Solomon, and Esther. The canonicity of the other Old Testament books was not even questioned and the discussion on the few books involved ended in 'the firm acknowledgement of all these books as Holy Scripture'.

How do we know that our *New Testament* canon is correct?

McDowell very helpfully summarises the five tests or principles for acceptance of a book in the *New Testament* canon, which he takes from Geisler and Nix, and which form the basis of the discussion below. They concern the need for each book to be authoritative, prophetic, authentic, dynamic, and consensual (my word).

1. Is a book *authoritative*? Does it come with God's stamp of authority on it? The main issue in this regard for New Testament books is whether it came with apostolic approval. Obviously, the witnessed and quoted words of Jesus did, but signs and wonders were given to the apostles to mark them out as God's authoritative men both to write, to recognise and to approve the written Word of God. So when Paul's claim that 'Truly the signs of an apostle were accomplished among you with all perseverance, in signs and wonders and mighty deeds' (2 Corinthians 12:12), he was building on a fact well known, demonstrated and accepted in the church. Just as the Old Testament canon of Scripture came through holy men of God being inspired by the Holy Spirit (2 Peter 1:21), so God continued that principle in the New Testament through demonstrably Spirit-led and authoritative apostles. That fact was completely in line with the following statements: the church was 'built on the foundation of the apostles and prophets, Jesus Christ Himself being the chief cornerstone' (Ephesians 2:20); 'the Spirit of truth ... will guide [these men] into all truth; for He will not speak on His own authority, but whatever He hears He will speak; and He will tell [them] things to come' (John 16:13); and that the early Christians 'continued steadfastly in the apostles' doctrine' (Acts 2:42). It was apostolic *approval*, rather than apostolic *authorship*, that was the acid test of New Testament canonicity. That canon consists mainly of books written by the apostles, but also includes some written by those with whom they had close links and influences and whose works would have been known to them before inclusion in the canon.

2. Is a book *prophetic*? This does not deal so much with its 'foretelling' (though that is sometimes included, as in the book of Revelation), but rather with its 'forth-telling'. In other words, was it written by a man of God, commissioned by God to be God's agent of revelation? Did he write with the same authority that was noted when the apostles spoke? (See, for example, Acts 1:8; 4:13; 4:33; Colossians 1:27–29.)

3. Is the book *authentic*? The early church fathers followed the policy of rejecting anything about which they were not completely sure. The unique quality of books which were truly from God stood out then, just as the Bible stands out now from mere religious books written by men alone. Thus, just as the Council of Jamnia *recognised*—rather than *chose*—the Old Testament canon, so, too, the Council of Hippo and the ratifying Third Synod of Carthage *recognised*—rather than *chose*—the New Testament canon.

4. Is the book *dynamic*? Does it manifest God's life-transforming power? A whole book could be written to demonstrate that this is so for each of the New

Testament books. Suffice it to say that new life in Christ, truly spiritual life, shines out from every chapter and reflects that here are the words of eternal life concerning, and from, the One who came 'that they may have life, and that they may have it more abundantly' (John 10:10). It is a happy accident of the English language that the initials of The New Testament are 'TNT': here is truly spiritual *dynamite*!

5. Is the book *consensual*? In other words was it already received by Christian leaders and people, and collected, read and used by them? Did God's people accept it? In a very real sense the canon chose itself and all man had to do was to recognise it. Of course, there were those who would dispute the canon and promote their own ideas, as you would expect in a fallen world with no spiritual light except from God. Indeed, it was the influence and wrong activity of such heretics as Marcion (AD 140) in this arena that made the definition of the canon important. Additionally, the use of some non-canonical books by churches in the East made clarity on this issue important. Those who might soon become martyrs also needed to be sure that, if they were soon to be put to death when their Christian Scriptures were to be destroyed under the Edict of Diocletan (AD 303), they would die for the sake of God's truth and not for mere writings of men. So, in AD 367, Athanasius' letter to churches confirmed that the same books of the New Testament canon were in existence then as we have today. His confirmation was ratified by other church fathers and the New Testament ranked with the established canon of the Old Testament as God's inspired Scripture. It is worth repeating MacDowell's quote from Professor Bruce, summarising the confirmed position in AD 393 at The Synod of Hippo. He says that 'when at last a Church Council—The Synod of Hippo in AD 393—listed the twenty-seven books of the New Testament, it did not confer upon them any authority which they did not already possess, but simply recorded their previously established canonicity. (The ruling of the Synod of Hippo was re-promulgated four years later by the Third Synod of Carthage.)'

Grudem similarly concludes, concerning the established canon comprising the sixty-six books of our Bible today, that 'Christians today should have no worry that anything needed has been left out or that anything that is not God's word has been included'.

A final word of warning

The late pastor, Bible teacher, author and evangelist, Leith Samuel, would make a very valid point whenever he spoke about the inspiration of the Bible as God's Spirit-breathed written word. I am quoting him from memory when I say: 'The battle used to be for the inspiration and infallibility of Scripture. Today it is for its sufficiency and completeness.' What did he mean by that? Simply that the devil has subtle ways of undermining the absolute authority of the Bible. Whatever our valid differences in opinions might be about the gifts of the Spirit and the role of the Holy Spirit in the life of each believer, each church, and the church at large, we must never allow any perceived utterance, vision or insight to rival the authority of Scripture or to be counted in any way as equal to it. The Bible is the whole of God's revealed word to man. We need no other revelation and should seek none other. We should seek in our lives that soul-refreshing influence of God's timeless word applied, always in context, with new force and effect. We must constantly seek to turn from sins, and to make the Lord Jesus Christ of the Bible the centre of our walk, worship and witness. Only then will we know personally the continuation of those promised 'times of refreshing [which] come from the presence of the Lord' (Acts 3:19). We seek no new truth, just a new appreciation of old truth that will change our lives.

The Bible's central message

The New is in the Old concealed; the Old is in the New revealed

The central message of the New Testament is contained in the seed corn of the Old Testament. The Old Testament's prophecies, pictures and glimpses of the future come to fruition in the New Testament. Together, the Old and New Testaments comprise the total written Word of God, the Bible.

The pivot of history and truth

The Lord Jesus Christ is the pivot of history and truth. God's message is totally contained in a Person, God the Son. God's earlier revelation looked forward to Him, in the Old Testament. God's later and final revelation looked back to Him, from the New Testament.

In His post-resurrection walk from Jerusalem to Emmaus with two very disillusioned and downcast disciples, Jesus could have simply overwhelmed them with His resurrection glory. Instead of that, He chose to relate to them all the then available truths of Scripture about Himself. Those truths were from the same Old Testament that we have today. Jesus believed the whole of the Old Testament—which is authority enough for us to follow suit! Luke 24 records that the risen, omniscient Lord of glory told them they should have believed 'all that the prophets have spoken' (verse 25) and 'beginning at Moses and all the Prophets, He expounded to them in all the Scriptures the things concerning Himself' (verse 27). He dealt with fulfilled prophecy simply as history that had been waiting to occur, because He believed in the infallibility and reliability of God's written word. Verse 32 reveals that their testimony after His departure from them was clear, spontaneous and enthusiastic. It can be the experience of all who know Him as Saviour and read His word today! They asked rhetorically: 'Did not our hearts burn within us while He talked with us on the road, and while He opened the Scriptures to us?' They had found that confidence in His word went hand in hand with confidence in His resurrection. It is the same today. Belief in the Bible and belief in the risen Lord are inextricably linked. That is why it is so often true that those who deny the Bible as God's word are the same people who refuse to accept the overwhelming evidence that Jesus rose again.

But the point here is that Christ saw the whole of the Old Testament as witnessing to Him. He is God's message, foretold in the Old Testament and revealed in the New Testament. Why is Jesus Christ the central message of the Bible?

Christ in all the Scriptures

The title of an inspiring classic based on that Emmaus Road walk of Jesus with those two disciples is *Christ in all the Scriptures* by A.M. Hodgkin (Pickering & Inglis). It demonstrates graphically how Jesus fulfils some key Old Testament prophecies, pictures and typology. It is well worth purchasing and reading. The title of that book is now the theme of this chapter, albeit in outline only. The message of all the Scriptures is the message of a divine Saviour who came to reconcile sinful people to God, and to exercise His lordship and presence in the lives of those who repent and trust Him. This crucial biblical message reveals the only way that sinful people can approach a holy and eternally sovereign God to be accepted by Him. This requires forgiveness, cleansing and being brought into fellowship with God through turning from sin and yielding to Christ, whose blood was shed to bring sinners to God (Ephesians 2:13).

To demonstrate that message of Christ in all the Scriptures, two separate approaches are taken below. The first approach, headed 'Jesus in the books of the Bible', consists of a list of the books of the Bible with some key aspects of the Person, office, work and accomplishments of the Lord Jesus Christ which are foreseen, implied, revealed or indicated in each book. The list below cannot be more than a sample index. There is far more revealed in each book about Christ than is suggested below, of course, but the list does display some aspects of the centrality of the Lord Jesus shown in each book of the Bible and the pre-eminence which the Bible insists must be accorded to Him (Colossians 1:16–18). Each aspect connects with the Bible's central message of forgiveness, restoration and fellowship with God through personal repentance and faith in Christ as Saviour, Lord and King. Different writers could easily and justifiably emphasise different key words than those selected here. The second approach, headed 'A schematic survey of Jesus throughout the Bible', is far more scholarly and thought provoking. I am obliged to David Harding, pastor of Milnrow Evangelical Church, for permission to reproduce, with minor amendments, from notes he prepared for a pastors' conference in Nigeria.

Jesus in the books of the Bible

The Book	Some (but not all) aspects of the Lord Jesus Christ, foreseen or revealed
Genesis	Beginning. Creator. Prophesied redeemer. Seed of Abraham. Promised Son.
Exodus	Deliverer. Lamb of God. Tabernacle. Law keeper. Covenant maker.
Leviticus	Fulfilled sacrifices. Priest. Atonement.
Numbers	Rock. Water. Brazen serpent. City of refuge.
Deuteronomy	Prophet. Guide. Mediator. City of refuge.
Joshua	Commander of the LORD's army. Conqueror. Faithful. Scarlet thread.
Judges	Judge. Deliverer. Spirit-filled.
Ruth	Kinsman redeemer.
1 Samuel	King. Great David's greater Son.
2 Samuel	King. Great David's greater Son.

1 Kings	King. Wisdom. Temple. Ark.
2 Kings	King. Purifier.
1 Chronicles	King. Temple.
2 Chronicles	King. Temple. Glorious.
Ezra	Sovereign Lord. Restorer. Temple.
Nehemiah	Leader. Co-labourer. Accomplisher.
Esther	Merciful. Sovereign. People's representative.
Job	Living redeemer. Intercessor. Innocent sufferer. Resurrected.
Psalms	Messiah. Shepherd. King. Judge. Saviour. Praiseworthy. Son.
Proverbs	Wisdom. Omniscient.
Ecclesiastes	Reality. Eternal.
Song of Solomon	Fairest of all. Lover of souls.
Isaiah	Messiah. Prophesied mighty God. Judge. Suffering servant. Prophet.
Jeremiah	Prophet. Judge. Compassionate.
Lamentations	Man of sorrows.
Ezekiel	Priest. Prophet. Restorer.
Daniel	Righteous. Coming King. Prophet. Judge.
Hosea	Redeemer. Love. Judge.
Joel	Outpourer of Holy Spirit. Judge. Coming again.
Amos	God. Coming again. Judge. Restorer.
Obadiah	King. Judge. Deliverer.
Jonah	Prophet. Resurrected. Merciful.
Micah	Judge. Prophesied. God on earth. Prophet.
Nahum	Judge. Comforter.
Habakkuk	Judge. Sovereign. Deliverer.
Zephaniah	Judge. Saviour. Prayer answerer.
Haggai	Judge. Coming. Desire of nations.
Zechariah	Prophet. Priest. King.
Malachi	Prophet. Judge. Sun of righteousness.
Matthew	King. Saviour.
Mark	Servant.
Luke	Son of man. Perfect.
John	Son of God. Eternal. I AM.
Acts	Risen Saviour. Ascended Lord.
Romans	Justifier.
1 Corinthians	Crucified and risen Lord. Firstfruits.
2 Corinthians	Reconciler. Powerful enabler. Comforter.
Galatians	Cursed. Liberator.
Ephesians	Supreme Sovereign. Head of church.
Philippians	Exalted Lord. Ever-present Saviour. Coming Lord.

Colossians	Incarnate God. Firstborn over all creation. Head of church. Reconciler.
1 Thessalonians	Coming Lord. Saviour.
2 Thessalonians	Coming Lord. Judge.
1 Timothy	Eternal King. Saviour. Ransom. Mediator. Man Christ Jesus.
2 Timothy	Seed of David. Reigning. Pure. Deliverer.
Titus	Saviour. Great God. Coming soon.
Philemon	Debt payer. Faultless representative.
Hebrews	Better. High Priest. Sacrifice. Creator. Terminator of universe.
James	To be trusted. Patient.
1 Peter	Cornerstone. Lamb. Sin bearer. Intermediary. Precious.
2 Peter	Righteous. Everlasting King. Beloved Son. Coming again.
1 John	Son of God. Righteous. Propitiation. Coming again.
2 John	Son of God. Son of man.
3 John	Truth.
Jude	Preserver. Merciful. Saviour.
Revelation	Alpha. Omega. Lamb. Holy. Judge. Saviour. Coming Lord.

A schematic survey of Jesus throughout the Bible

This summarises Campbell Morgan's *The Unfolding Message of The Bible* as expanded independently from various sources, mainly from Sidlow Baxter, Trevor Knight, Stuart Olyott and David Harding, who produced the summary below (with minor changes).

(A) Before the Lord Jesus Christ came to earth, the Old Testament promised, pictured and prefigured Him as the Anointed One, the Messiah, the Christ. There were three officers anointed before Christ: Priest, King and Prophet. The very shape of the Old Testament reinforces that hope of the coming of the Messiah, based on the promises given in it.

	Genesis–Deuteronomy	Joshua–Esther	Job–Malachi
	LAW	**HISTORY**	**PROPHECY**
Man's problem	Sin	Anarchy	Ignorance
God's remedy	Sacrifice	Authority	Instruction
Anointed 'messiahs' who mediated that remedy.	A priest	A king	A prophet
The failure	All these priests 'failed'. They had to offer for themselves first, and they died!	All these kings 'failed'. They could not control their own anarchy.	All these prophets 'failed'. There was always something more to say, and they did not fully understand what they prophesied.

	Genesis–Deuteronomy LAW	Joshua–Esther HISTORY	Job–Malachi PROPHECY
God promised … to dismiss the three 'shepherds' (Zechariah 11:8), but also …	'I will raise up a faithful priest' (1 Samuel 2:35).	'When your days are fulfilled and you rest with your fathers, I will set up your seed after you, who will come from your body, and I will establish his kingdom. He shall build a house for My name, and I will establish the throne of his kingdom for ever. I will be his Father, and he shall be My son' (2 Samuel 7:12–14).	'The LORD your God will raise up for you a Prophet like me from your midst, from your brethren. Him you shall hear' (Deuteronomy 18:15).
When Christ came …	Mark displayed Him as priest, even sitting down after the resurrection.	Matthew displayed Him as King—almost all references to king and kingdom are in Matthew.	Luke displayed Him as prophet, showing exclusively the work of the Holy Spirit in Him.
Why four Gospels then? Why not just three?	John tells us Who He is.	The Messiah is the Son of God.	

(B) Consider the promised Messiah and *faith* in Him: faith first anticipated, and then reflected upon, the Lord Jesus Christ of prophecy and then of history.

Faith in Christ the promised Saviour anticipated:

1. An anointed Priest to save sinners from sin by a Sacrifice, *and*

2. An anointed King to save sinners from anarchy by Authority, *and*

3. An anointed Prophet to save sinners from ignorance through Instruction.

Consider faith's anticipation of Christ in those three offices: first as:

1. The anointed Priest to save sinners from sin by a Sacrifice.

Those believers needed salvation.

FROM RUIN—GENESIS

Begins with the eternal God putting a living man in a garden in Eden, and ends with dying men putting a dead man in a coffin in Egypt.

Outline:

Creation

Curse

Covenant

Catastrophe

Call

THROUGH REDEMPTION—EXODUS

The elect are:

1. Called 1–19
   Persecutions 1–6
   Plagues 7–12
   Passover
   Pilgrimage 13–19.

2. Consecrated 20–40
   Covenant established 20–23
   Tabernacle designed 24–31
   Covenant reviewed 32–34
   Tabernacle erected 35–40.

LEADING TO REGULAR FELLOWSHIP—LEVITICUS

1. Attaining fellowship with God.
   Oblation 1–7
   Mediation 8–10
   Separation 11–15
   Expiation 16 (Day of atonement).

2. Maintaining fellowship with God.
   Sanctification 17–22
   Celebration 23–25
   Ratification 26–27 (Promises and threats).

FACING RETARDED PROGRESS—NUMBERS

1. Preparing for the journey 1–9.
2. Progress on the journey 10–21.
3. Progress in Moab 23–36.
   Two lists! More set out than got in! 1:2; 26:2.
   No one who apostatised got in.

BY A RENEWED COMMITMENT—DEUTERONOMY

Remembering
and Renewing the covenant.
1–4 Remembering God's gracious dealings.
5–26 Regarding God's holy commandments.
27–28 Promising! God's promises and threats.
29–30 Renewing—The covenant in Moab.
31–34 Parting—Farewell and death of Moses.

But it also anticipated:
2. The anointed King to save sinners from anarchy by Authority
Those believers needed

Jesus—The leader who takes us in and gives us victory,
Joshua
Jesus causes His people to enter 1–5.
Jesus causes His people to conquer 6–12.
Jesus causes His people to inherit 13–22.
without whom everyone does what is right in their own eyes,
Judges
A regular routine of:
Sin, Suffering, Supplication, Salvation
or Rebellion, Retribution, Repentance, Restoration, Rest.

YET GOD RULES TO BRING CHRIST OUT OF CONFUSION, BLESSING OUT OF BACKSLIDING—RUTH

This is a tract written to show that the Gentiles lay the Saviour in the lap of the Jews! It is an amazing book. See Romans 9.
Giving up! Going out. Grieving.
Going back.
Gaining everything.

THOUGH GOD IS REJECTED FROM RULING OVER MEN—1 SAMUEL

Man rejects God's rule.
God rejects the alternative!

HE SETS HIS KING ON THE THRONE—2 SAMUEL

David's triumphs.
David's troubles.

DWELLING AMONG HIS PEOPLE—1 KINGS

Days of blessing.
Days of backsliding.

TO MAKE THEM SAINTS,—2 KINGS

A life of loving discipline.

SERVANTS AND SOLDIERS—1 CHRONICLES

The Lord knows us by name.

WHO SORROW FOR THEIR SINS—2 CHRONICLES

The failure of the kings.
The final downfall of the kings.

As they repent:

HE RESTORES THEIR WORSHIP (THE TEMPLE)—EZRA
Return and rebuild 1–6.
Return and reform 7–10.

HE REBUILDS THEIR DEFENCES—NEHEMIAH
A man of prayer.

HE PROTECTS THEM FROM THEIR ENEMIES—ESTHER
Haman's 'luck' runs out.

but it also anticipated:
3. The anointed Prophet to save sinners from ignorance through Instruction.
So believers experience:

LUXURIES WORTH LOSING—JOB
1:1–5. Job before the trial.
1:6–2:10. Satan and suffering.
2:11–3. The end of Job's patience.
4–37. Heated and fruitless philosophy.
38–41. Jehovah and suffering.
42 Job and the purpose of the Lord.

SONGS WORTH SINGING—PSALMS
Five books of songs corresponding to the five books of Moses. The fear of the Lord is the beginning of wisdom.

LESSONS WORTH LEARNING—PROVERBS
What think ye of Christ is the test, to try both your state and your scheme, you cannot be right in the rest, unless you think rightly of Him.

A LIFE WORTH LIVING AND—ECCLESIASTES
A summary, four sermons and a conclusion.
Fear God and keep His commandments, for this is the whole duty of man.

A LORD WORTH LOVING—SONG OF SOLOMON
A love song of a girl who longs for friendship, but is aware of failure.
She pursues, praises and longs to please her fiancé.

As Christ is portrayed as:

JEHOVAH OUR SUBSTITUTE—CARRYING OUR SINS—ISAIAH
A bible within the Bible. Thirty-nine chapters of history; twenty-seven chapters of prophecy in three groups of nine, each ending with 'no peace to the wicked'.

The central thought of the central chapter of the central nine is Isaiah 53: 'He was led as a lamb to the slaughter.'

JEHOVAH OUR RIGHTEOUSNESS—COVERING OUR SINS—JEREMIAH

God appeals, 'What evil have your fathers found in me?'

This is Jeremiah's sermon folder. Some dated, some undated. Some introduced, some giving a result.

'COME AND SEE IF THERE EVER WAS SORROW LIKE HIS.'—LAMENTATIONS

Lamenting over the death of Josiah, Jeremiah writes this poetic book about a people in such a sad condition because they set no value upon their God (1:12).

HE IS THE SHEPHERD WHO WILL FEED HIS PEOPLE.—EZEKIEL

The priest cannot begin a ministry in the Temple so he is made a prophet in captivity to speak to the destitute people of God. He shows that God works His purposes out, even in discipline.

The watchman (33).

The shepherd (34).

HE IS THE SOVEREIGN WHO WILL RULE HIS PEOPLE—DANIEL

The God of:

History 1–6.

Prophecy 7–12.

Daniel maintained personal principle while others accommodated cultural pressures.

He makes four lone stands:

Practical living

Public worship

Personal witness

Private devotion.

He lovingly promises His people:

I WILL RANSOM THEM—HOSEA 13:14

I WILL RESTORE THE WASTED YEARS—JOEL 2:25

I WILL RAISE UP THE TABERNACLE OF DAVID THAT HAS FALLEN—AMOS 9:11

I WILL BRING THEIR ENEMIES DOWN—OBADIAH 1:4

'SALVATION IS OF THE LORD'—JONAH 2:9

I WILL GATHER THE OUTCASTS—MICAH 4:6

BUT I WILL DIG THEIR ENEMY'S GRAVE—NAHUM 1:14

'O REVIVE YOUR WORK'—HABBAKUK 3:2

I WILL RETURN YOUR CAPTIVES—ZEPHANIAH 3:20

I WILL COME AND FILL THIS PLACE WITH GLORY—HAGGAI 2:7

BUT I WILL DISMISS MY THREE SHEPHERDS IN ONE MONTH—ZECHARIAH 11:8

AND WILL SEND MY MESSENGER BEFORE MY FACE—MALACHI 3:1

So faith in the Old Testament looked forward to the One who was to come.

The *Priesthood* failed. Those priests could not continue by reason of death. They offered sacrifices for themselves because they sinned like everyone else. They were only a picture of the *Priest* we need, and the faith of the Old Testament looked through them and beyond them to the promise that God would raise up a faithful *Priest*—the Anointed One, Christ (1 Samuel 2:35).

The *Kingdom* failed because the kings could not even control themselves, so how could they control the people under their authority? But they were a provision and a picture of the *King* we need.

The faith of the Old Testament looked through them to the promise that God would set a Son of David upon the throne, David's Lord as *King*—the Anointed One, Christ (Psalm 89:3–4; 110:1).

Even the *Prophets* failed because they too were fallible, lacked understanding even of what they prophesied, and none had complete vision of the future. They spoke in various ways and at different times, but were a preparation for the *Prophet* we need. The faith of the Old Testament looked through them to the promise that God would send a *Prophet,* one like Moses—the Anointed One, Christ (Deuteronomy 18:18).

Four hundred years of silence followed that last revelation of the Old Testament, and the eye of faith kept looking forward into that silent void. It was kept alive by the Word of God. There was a certain conviction that God, who ordained the three shepherds of Israel as prophet, priest and king, would dismiss them on one day, and He would send a messenger before the appearing of His anointed Messiah. As we know, 'in the fullness of time', God sent His Son to perfect His will and plan (Galatians 4:4–7).

(C) A summary of the New Testament
Faith in the Lord Jesus Christ:

AS KING—MATTHEW

Almost exclusively refers to Him as King, more than any other Gospel. The Gospel divides into the Coming, Campaign and Conquest of the King. See references Matthew 27:11, 29, 37, 42.

AS PRIEST—MARK

Always active, with a focus on the word 'immediately' and distinguishing what was unclean. Also He sat down (!), His priestly task finished. This is only recorded in this Gospel. It divides into his service in the Outer court, the Holy Place and the Holy of Holies (see 16:19).

AS PROPHET—LUKE

This Gospel focuses on Christ the man filled by the Spirit. He quotes that the Spirit is upon Him. He is led by the Spirit, in the power of the Spirit, etc. (see 4:1, 14, 18).

AS THE SON OF GOD—JOHN

This Gospel is written in simple Greek and conveys the most profound doctrine of Christ as Son of God and God the Son. It divides as a thesis would. The proposition, the proof, the purpose, the appendices (see 3:18; 5:25; 9:35; 11:27; 19:7; 20:30–31).

AND AS THE SAVIOUR OF THE WORLD—ACTS

Luke part 2! But Christ as Lord of history and Saviour of the world is the theme (see 8:37; 15:7, 11; 16:31).

JUSTIFIES—ROMANS

Sin, salvation, sanctification, sovereignty and service. That is the outline. (See 3:22; 5:1 for the remarks on justification.)

SANCTIFIES—1 CORINTHIANS

A muddled church needed to be what it was made of— 'saints' (see 1:30).

COMFORTS—2 CORINTHIANS

Opening with the focus on comfort, despite all the pleas for further opening of their hearts to Paul (see 1:3–11, and also verse 9—learn not to trust yourself in a trial!).

AND LIBERATES—GALATIANS

The problem of re-entanglement is faced and addressed (see 5:1; 3:2).

IT ASSEMBLES THE SAINTS INTO CHURCHES—EPHESIANS

Jew and Gentile come together into churches through faith (see 2:1–10; 3:14–21).

The outline is that every believer has every reason to: praise God, pray to God, walk worthily of God, and put on the armour of God.

IT UNITES THE SAINTS IN THE CHURCHES—PHILIPPIANS
A letter defying clear outlines! Yet it presses the need for unity between believers (see 1:27; 4:2).

AND MOTIVATES THE SAINTS TO HOLY LIVING—COLOSSIANS
After showing the pre-eminence of Christ and our union with Him, this epistle emphasises that union by faith is the motive for holy living (see 2:6–9,11–12 and then 3:1, etc.).

IT SUFFERS—1 THESSALONIANS
See 1:3; 2:13; 3:5; 5:14. This church was born to trouble, but Paul longs to know that they have not yielded.

BUT IT GROWS—2 THESSALONIANS
The second letter confirms that suffering was like a greenhouse to them (see 1:3).

IT IS COMMITTED TO ITS CHARGE—1 TIMOTHY
See 1:2–3; 6:20–21. Timothy was to work to Get it Right. How? By his public ministry: establishing the spiritual life and leadership. By his personal example, and by private counselling.

ACCOMPLISHES ITS TASKS—2 TIMOTHY
A leader's last letter urging to do as he has done and finish the course, keeping the faith (see 1:13; 4:7).

AND BUILDS LIVING CHURCHES—TITUS
Timothy had one church, but Crete was an island of 100 cities (see 1:1,5; 2:1).

IT WILL GO BACK TO SERVE—PHILEMON
Saving faith made Onesimus respond by returning to serve his former master.

BUT IT WILL NEVER GO BACK TO SIN—HEBREWS
Don't go back! See 10:39. Faith keeps before us that Christ is better than angels, Moses, Joshua, and Aaron. He offers a better sacrifice in a better sanctuary. And the life of faith, hope and love is a better life.

FAITH ALWAYS WORKS—JAMES
See 2:14–26.

FAITH ALWAYS STANDS FIRM—1 PETER
See 1:5.

FAITH ALWAYS MAKES SURE—2 PETER
See 1:5–10. Faith is not daunted by doubt, but presses on, diligent to add to faith and to make sure of calling and election.

FAITH ALWAYS PASSES THE TEST—1 JOHN
Many tests of true faith are presented. If you fail them, your faith is not real. But true faith passes the tests (4:1, 5:1–4).

IT LOVES—2 JOHN
See verses 6–7. Love discerns and acts to exclude error.

IT BLOSSOMS—3 JOHN
See verse 2.

IT FIGHTS—JUDE
We do not belong to the 'peace at any price' brigade. Faith fights errors and sins, even when it wishes it didn't have to. See verse 3.

AND IT WINS—REVELATION
See 2:13 and all of chapter 14, especially verse 12. Faith will never find itself in the torment, but will endure to discover it has won.

(D) So a summary of the whole Bible in relation to faith in Christ says:

FAITH IN THE LORD JESUS CHRIST AS KING, PRIEST, PROPHET, SON OF GOD AND SAVIOUR OF THE WORLD:
•justifies, sanctifies, comforts and liberates;
•assembles and unites the saints into churches and motivates them to holy living;
•suffers, but it grows exceedingly;
•is committed to its charge, accomplishes its tasks and builds living churches.

•Faith will always go back to serve but it will never go back to sin;
•faith always works, always stands firm, always makes sure, faith always passes the tests;
•it loves, it blossoms, it fights, and it wins!

Why read through the whole of the Bible?

Many 'experts'—few readers—few knowledgeable!

What would you think of a TV commentator on football who did not have a good grasp of the game? Or a political analyst who did not understand how his country's political system worked? How about a professor of Shakespearian literature who had only read two or three of the famous bard's plays? Experts have to know about their subjects. Yet when it comes to the Bible, there is no shortage of 'experts' and commentators who have not even read the whole book through! Those who claim 'The Bible is full of contradictions!' are often the ones who read only parts of it and who could not show you even one of their supposed 'contradictions' if you asked them to be specific. But, to be fair, Christians are sometimes inconsistent, too, and claim to believe the Bible as God's word without making any attempt to read it all through regularly.

Sympathy

Bible-believing Christians are right to suggest that those who criticise the Bible should know it and, at least, have read it through once. For example, we urge young men and women, who often have been put off because of their lessons at school, to give the Bible adult consideration and start reading it systematically (perhaps starting with one of the Gospels) with as open a mind as possible. Some of these 'victims' have been taught by some unfortunate teacher who was pushed into teaching Religious Education with no passion for (or grasp of) biblical Christianity, or of anything else to do with the Bible. Similarly, we sympathise with some dear folks who have faithfully attended church for years but have only encountered a dead, formal or shallow approach to the Bible and its message of personal repentance, faith in Christ, and growth in the Christian life through daily prayer and searching the Scriptures. We urge them to read God's word regularly for themselves, with a seeking, humble, reverent and expectant spirit.

Christians must be consistent

But how consistent are many Christians? Of course, some who have only recently come to faith in Christ, or returned to Him from backsliding, cannot be expected to have read through the whole Bible in a short space of time. Bible reading is a marathon, not a sprint! When I was first introduced to reading through the Bible by Young Life, the annual challenging venture to read through the Bible was named 'The Bible *Marathon*'! (See Appendix 3 for the Young Life scheme to accomplish this.) I am reminded of the child who, when urged to read the Bible each day, replied, 'But I can't read *all* the Bible each day—there's too much!' We only mean a *part* of it each day, of course! But surely, should not those who confess and maintain their faith in the Bible apply the same standards to themselves as they do to those who criticise and question it? They should read the *whole* of the Bible in a planned and systematic way. What is more, they should plan to read it through again and again. Reading the Bible through is like travelling regularly down a motorway or freeway. The more you travel, the more you see the lie of the land and understand the background context. Each time you go down that route, if you are observant, something new will take your attention. Of course, there is also a place for stopping and having a good look around at a specific spot, and maybe picnic there! So it is with the Bible. We should keep travelling through it to get an increasingly wide knowledge of it, but we need to stop at particular books, chapters, verses, topics, characters, teachings and challenges, and explore them more fully. I have often found it very helpful to expand my daily reading through the Bible at one time of the day, and then 'picnic' at something specific at another part. Perhaps I could carefully go through a little of Romans, or Acts, or Genesis, or Psalms in my 'picnic' quiet time, and leave twenty minutes or so to read through my set chapters at another time. The investment of time and discipline is demanding, but the return on capital employed is (literally!) 'out of this world'. If we Christians urge others to read the Bible, then we should follow our own advice and read it through, too.

Why read it *all*?

Quite apart from the need for consistency from people who urge those ignorant or critical of the Word of God to read the entire Bible, there are some very good and logical reasons why you should read it *all*, and read it *all* again and again. Some of those reasons are given below: Note the emphasis on the word '*all*'. (Compare, in Appendix 3, Robert Murray McCheyne's observations on the dangers and advantages of reading through the Bible that precede the excellent scheme he devised to achieve this.)

1. THE BIBLE CLAIMS THAT *ALL* OF IT IS GOD'S WORD

Every word, as originally given, was inspired by the Holy Spirit working through the instrumentality of men. The Bible also declares that God loves people like you and wants to tell you things that will be of benefit to you. It is like a love letter from God to you, though not sloppy and sentimental as are some love letters. Those who receive a love letter from a far-off loved one do not just read parts of it, though there may be special or personal sections that they particularly cherish. They will read it *all*. Their loved one wrote it *all*, for them to read it *all*, and so they will willingly read it *all*. Should we do less with God's letter from heaven to us?

2. NOT ONLY IS *ALL* THE BIBLE GOD'S WRITTEN WORD, BUT THE BIBLE IS *ALL* OF GOD'S WRITTEN WORD

There is nothing else that He has revealed to us on earth. Everything that God wants us to know about Himself and His truth on this side of heaven is in the Bible. There is obviously a lot more to learn about God in eternity, and we could not possibly assimilate or appreciate it here, limited as we are in our earthly thinking. But everything we need to live a godly, useful, joyful, helped and blessed life comes to us from His written word, as the Holy Spirit makes it real to those who approach it spiritually and with trusting obedience. How wonderful that you can read and know *all* the truths that God wants you to know until you meet Him in heaven!

3. *ALL* THE BIBLE IS PROFITABLE FOR US

2 Timothy 3:16 tells us why 'All scripture', having been 'given by inspiration of God' is 'profitable'. It is 'profitable' 'for doctrine, for reproof, for correction, for instruction in righteousness, that the man of God may be complete, thoroughly equipped for every good work.' Do we need good clear 'teaching'? (That is what 'doctrine' means.) Read the Bible! Are there times when we are sinfully wrong, or in error, and need to be informed of our wrong by the 'reproof' of a faithful God, who loves us too much to refrain from telling us what we need to hear? Go to the Bible! Having been reproved, do we need to be put back on the right path, personally or theologically? Let us seek our 'correction' by studying the Bible. Do we need constant and ongoing 'instruction' to advance in a Christ-centred 'righteousness'? Again, read the Bible. The more we read it, and the more times we read *all* of it, the more will we profit spiritually in these ways. We thus neglect reading through it *all*, to our loss. Specifically, we read throughout the Bible of how it can keep us from sin, increase our faith, help us to have God's wisdom, make God's guidance clear, revive us spiritually, feed us in our faith, and make us approved to God. So much more could be said about the way that every part of the Bible profits those who read and follow it.

4. *ALL* THE BIBLE IS RELEVANT

The Bible has been planned by God to be His revelation and thus no part is wasted or superfluous. Just as *all* the Bible is God-breathed (the meaning of the word 'inspired'), so all His inspired Scriptures are there for a reason. But note the comments in Chapter 5 that while *all* the Bible is equally 'inspired' it is not *all* equally 'inspiring', nor intended to be.

5. READING *ALL* THE BIBLE HELPS YOU TO UNDERSTAND EACH PART OF IT

No verse or truth of Scripture stands alone. It is best understood in the widest context of the Bible, the wide context of the Old or New Testament where it is found, the context of the book of the Bible in which it is found, and then in the far narrower context of the chapter (or chapters) and verse (or verses) where it is located. Only then can its context in history and its context to you personally be seen with any meaning. Putting it another way, it is amazing how many of your unanswered questions, arising from the first few times you read through the Bible, begin to be answered as your familiarity with the Bible grows as you keep reading through it. The entire Bible is integrated, and you will realise that increasingly as you keep reading it through, time after time.

6. READING THROUGH *THE ENTIRE* BIBLE WITH OTHERS HELPS FELLOWSHIP WITH THEM

Fellowship is enhanced with other individual Christians, or within churches and fellowships, or groups of churches and fellowships, when Christians agree to read *the entire* Bible by using the same scheme and time frame. As well as helping the resolve and discipline of one another, this communal (yet individual) reading through enables you to have helpful fellowship in God's word with others, as you discuss the passages you are all reading, consider how to resolve any problems that arise, and together apply God's word to your daily lives. The truths you have all seen as you read through *the entire* Bible together go deeper as you discuss them with one another.

7. *ALL* THE VERSES IN THE BIBLE LIVE AND CAN SPEAK TO YOU

The Bible is alive. *All* its verses, chapters and books can speak to you, day by day, as you read them, trusting that God will teach you through them. It is like daily bread that needs to be fresh each day. It is like the manna from heaven that fed the children of Israel in the desert: it needs to be gathered and consumed every day, and to be continually gathered and consumed. So reading through *the entire* Bible *must* continue time after time. Bread goes stale if it is not consumed. Manna is to be gathered daily. So keep reading through, feeding, gathering, consuming and benefiting from this living, written Word of God.

8. *ALL* THE BIBLE NEEDS TO BE READ ALL THE WAY THROUGH, BECAUSE IT CAN NEVER BE 'FINISHED'

I remember seeing a cartoon in which a reverend gentleman had laid down his Bible and was reading another book in its place. His wife was asking him why he had stopped reading the Bible. He replied, 'I have finished it, my dear!' The very thought of 'finishing' the Bible brings a wry smile to your face. You may read it again, but you can never 'finish' it. The deepest Bible scholar is but paddling in the waves that lap the shore. There are depths to plumb that most of us will never appreciate. You cannot 'finish' the Bible—you must go on reading it *all*.

9. READING *THE ENTIRE* BIBLE HELPS GODLY DISCIPLINE

Some will object that reading *the entire* Bible regularly can be hard. That is true. But we do need discipline in the Christian life, and one of the side blessings of reading it through, quite apart from its unsurpassed literary merits and its challenge to our intellects, is that God can teach us godly discipline in developing a godly habit—namely, reading it *all* through successively. Which plan and timescale you use is a matter of choice, but to choose none may seriously undermine your resolve to read it *all*.

10. JESUS READ AND KNEW *ALL* THE SCRIPTURES AVAILABLE TO HIM DURING HIS LIFE ON EARTH

After His resurrection, on the road to Emmaus where he met and encouraged two discouraged disciples, Luke 24 testifies to Jesus' belief in *all* the Scriptures, and of their testifying of Him from historical Old Testament incidents and events. We now have the completed Word of God, since the life, death, resurrection and ascension of Jesus, the coming of the Holy Spirit on the church in Acts of the Apostles, and the unique revelation that God gave through the apostles and a few closely identified with them. We too must believe *the entire* Bible, as Jesus did in His earthly life, and see Christ in it *all*, seeking to live for Him with the help of the Holy Spirit and of the Bible. No doubt Mary and Joseph encouraged Jesus, as a child, to read and understand the Old Testament. At the age of twelve, He discussed it meaningfully in the Temple with the teachers (Luke 2:41–50). Parents who cultivate reading through the Bible are best qualified to pass on that godly habit to their children. Single, married, or to be married in the future, we must read the Bible through regularly as the best way to encourage others to be blessed by so doing themselves. In this way we can encourage future generations to know and love God's word.

The Bible

'The New is in the Old concealed—The Old is in the New revealed'
(The numbers in square brackets indicate the number of chapters.)
THE OLD TESTAMENT [929] THE NEW TESTAMENT [260]
Note: The Bible consists of 2 Testaments in 66 Books in 1,189 chapters.

LAW OF MOSES	ISRAEL'S HISTORY	POETICAL BOOKS	MAJOR PROPHETS	MINOR PROPHETS
[187]	[249]	[243]	[183]	[67]
Genesis	Joshua	Job	Isaiah	Hosea
[50]	[24]	[42]	[66]	[14]
Exodus	Judges	Psalms	Jeremiah	Joel
[40]	[21]	[150]	[52]	[3]
Leviticus	Ruth	Proverbs	Lamentations	Amos
[27]	[4]	[31]	[5]	[9]
Numbers	1 Samuel	Ecclesiastes	Ezekiel	Obadiah
[36]	[31]	[12]	[48]	[1]
Deuteronomy	2 Samuel	Song of Solomon	Daniel	Jonah
[34]	[24]	[8]	[12]	[4]
	1 Kings			Micah
	[22]			[7]
	2 Kings			Nahum
	[25]			[3]
	1 Chronicles			Habakkuk
	[29]			[3]
	2 Chronicles			Zephaniah
	[36]			[3]
	Ezra			Haggai
	[10]			[2]
	Nehemiah			Zechariah
	[13]			[14]
	Esther			Malachi
	[10]			[4]

THE BIBLE PANORAMA

FOUR GOSPELS	ACTS OF APOSTLES	CHURCH LETTERS	OTHER LETTERS	BOOK OF REVELATION
[89]	[28]	[73]	[48]	[22]
Matthew	Acts	Romans	1 Timothy	Revelation
[28]	[28]	[16]	[6]	[22]
Mark		1 Corinthians	2Timothy	
[16]		[16]	[4]	
Luke		2 Corinthians	Titus	
[24]		[13]	[3]	
John		Galatians	Philemon	
[21]		[6]	[1]	
		Ephesians	Hebrews	
		[6]	[13]	
		Philippians	James	
		[4]	[5]	
		Colossians	1 Peter	
		[4]	[5]	
		1 Thessalonians	2 Peter	
		[5]	[3]	
		2 Thessalonians	1 John	
		[3]	[5]	
			2 John	
			[1]	
			3 John	
			[1]	
			Jude	
			[1]	

The Bible's chapters (1,189)

Old Testament chapters [929]

Genesis (50) 1 2 3 4 5 6 7 8 9 10 11 12 13 14 15 16 17 18 19 20 21 22 23 24 25 26 27 28 29 30 31 32 33 34 35 36 37 38 39 40 41 42 43 44 45 46 47 48 49 50 Exodus (40) 1 2 3 4 5 6 7 8 9 10 11 12 13 14 15 16 17 18 19 20 21 22 23 24 25 26 27 28 29 30 31 32 33 34 35 36 37 38 39 40 Leviticus (27) 1 2 3 4 5 6 7 8 9 10 11 12 13 14 15 16 17 18 19 20 21 22 23 24 25 26 27 Numbers (36) 1 2 3 4 5 6 7 8 9 10 11 12 13 14 15 16 17 18 19 20 21 22 23 24 25 26 27 28 29 30 31 32 33 34 35 36 Deuteronomy (34) 1 2 3 4 5 6 7 8 9 10 11 12 13 14 15 16 17 18 19 20 21 22 23 24 25 26 27 28 29 30 31 32 33 34 Joshua (24) 1 2 3 4 5 6 7 8 9 10 11 12 13 14 15 16 17 18 19 20 21 22 23 24 Judges (21) 1 2 3 4 5 6 7 8 9 10 11 12 13 14 15 16 17 18 19 20 21 Ruth (4) 1 2 3 4 1 Samuel (31) 1 2 3 4 5 6 7 8 9 10 11 12 13 14 15 16 17 18 19 20 21 22 23 24 25 26 27 28 29 30 31 2 Samuel (24) 1 2 3 4 5 6 7 8 9 10 11 12 13 14 15 16 17 18 19 20 21 22 23 24 1 Kings (22) 1 2 3 4 5 6 7 8 9 10 11 12 13 14 15 16 17 18 19 20 21 22 2 Kings (25) 1 2 3 4 5 6 7 8 9 10 11 12 13 14 15 16 17 18 19 20 21 22 23 24 25 1 Chronicles (29) 1 2 3 4 5 6 7 8 9 10 11 12 13 14 15 16 17 18 19 20 21 22 23 24 25 26 27 28 29 2 Chronicles (36) 1 2 3 4 5 6 7 8 9 10 11 12 13 14 15 16 17 18 19 20 21 22 23 24 25 26 27 28 29 30 31 32 33 34 35 36 Ezra (10) 1 2 3 4 5 6 7 8 9 10 Nehemiah (13) 1 2 3 4 5 6 7 8 9 10 11 12 13 Esther (10) 1 2 3 4 5 6 7 8 9 10 Job (42) 1 2 3 4 5 6 7 8 9 10 11 12 13 14 15 16 17 18 19 20 21 22 23 24 25 26 27 28 29 30 31 32 33 34 35 36 37 38 39 40 41 42 Psalms (150) 1 2 3 4 5 6 7 8 9 10 11 12 13 14 15 16 17 18 19 20 21 22 23 24 25 26 27 28 29 30 31 32 33 34 35 36 37 38 39 40 41 42 43 44 45 46 47 48 49 50 51 52 53 54 55 56 57 58 59 60 61 62 63 64 65 66 67 68 69 70 71 72 73 74 75 76 77 78 79 80 81 82 83 84 85 86 87 88 89 90 91 92 93 94 95 96 97 98 99 100 101 102 103 104 105 106 107 108 109 110 111 112 113 114 115 116 117 118 119 120 121 122 123 124 125 126 127 128 129 130 131 132 133 134 135 136 137 138 139 140 141 142 143 144 145 146 147 148 149 150 Proverbs (31) 1 2 3 4 5 6 7 8 9 10 11 12 13 14 15 16 17 18 19 20 21 22 23 24 25 26 27 28 29 30 31 Ecclesiastes (12) 1 2 3 4 5 6 7 8 9 10 11 12 Song of Solomon (8) 1 2 3 4 5 6 7 8 Isaiah (66) 1 2 3 4 5 6 7 8 9 10 11 12 13 14 15 16 17 18 19 20 21 22 23 24 25 26 27 28 29 30 31 32 33 34 35 36 37 38 39 40 41 42 43 44 45 46 47 48 49 50 51 52 53 54 55 56 57 58 59 60 61 62 63 64 65 66 Jeremiah (52) 1 2 3 4 5 6 7 8 9 10 11 12 13 14 15 16 17 18 19 20 21 22 23 24 25 26 27 28 29 30 31 32 33 34 35 36 37 38 39 40 41 42 43 44 45 46 47 48 49 50 51 52 Lamentations (5) 1 2 3 4 5 Ezekiel (48) 1 2 3 4 5 6

7 8 9 10 11 12 13 14 15 16 17 18 19 20 21 22 23 24 25 26 27 28 29 30 31 32 33 34 35 36 37 38 39 40 41 42 43 44 45 46 47 48 Daniel (12) 1 2 3 4 5 6 7 8 9 10 11 12 Hosea (14) 1 2 3 4 5 6 7 8 9 10 11 12 13 14 Joel (3) 1 2 3 Amos (9) 1 2 3 4 5 6 7 8 9 Obadiah (1) 1 Jonah (4) 1 2 3 4 Micah (7) 1 2 3 4 5 6 7 Nahum (3) 1 2 3 Habakkuk (3) 1 2 3 Zephaniah (3) 1 2 3 Haggai (2) 1 2 Zechariah (14) 1 2 3 4 5 6 7 8 9 10 11 12 13 14 Malachi (4) 1 2 3 4

New Testament chapters [260]

Matthew (28) 1 2 3 4 5 6 7 8 9 10 11 12 13 14 15 16 17 18 19 20 21 22 23 24 25 26 27 28 Mark (16) 1 2 3 4 5 6 7 8 9 10 11 12 13 14 15 16 Luke (24) 1 2 3 4 5 6 7 8 9 10 11 12 13 14 15 16 17 18 19 20 21 22 23 24 John (21) 1 2 3 4 5 6 7 8 9 10 11 12 13 14 15 16 17 18 19 20 21 Acts (28) 1 2 3 4 5 6 7 8 9 10 11 12 13 14 15 16 17 18 19 20 21 22 23 24 25 26 27 28 Romans (16) 1 2 3 4 5 6 7 8 9 10 11 12 13 14 15 16 1 Corinthians (16) 1 2 3 4 5 6 7 8 9 10 11 12 13 14 15 16 2 Corinthians (13) 1 2 3 4 5 6 7 8 9 10 11 12 13 Galatians (6) 1 2 3 4 5 6 Ephesians (6) 1 2 3 4 5 6 Philippians (4) 1 2 3 4 Colossians (4) 1 2 3 4 1 Thessalonians (5) 1 2 3 4 5 2 Thessalonians (3) 1 2 3 1 Timothy (6) 1 2 3 4 5 6 2 Timothy (4) 1 2 3 4 Titus (3) 1 2 3 Philemon (1) 1 Hebrews (13) 1 2 3 4 5 6 7 8 9 10 11 12 13 James (5) 1 2 3 4 5 1 Peter (5) 1 2 3 4 5 2 Peter (3) 1 2 3 1 John (5) 1 2 3 4 5 2 John (1) 1 3 John (1) 1 Jude (1) 1 Revelation (22) 1 2 3 4 5 6 7 8 9 10 11 12 13 14 15 16 17 18 19 20 21 22

Bible Reading Schemes (BRS) and The Flexible Bible Reading Scheme (FBRS)

(1) Bible Reading Schemes (BRS)

A Bible reading scheme (BRS) is simply an organised way of helping you to read through the whole of the Bible in a disciplined way. Many Christians have seen the enormous benefit of following a BRS every year, and thus they read the entire Bible at least once every year. There is no BRS which is the 'right one'. Each one simply presents a good alternative way of helping people to pursue and achieve the valuable goal of reading through the whole Bible. Some schemes go through the Old Testament consecutively and then through the New Testament consecutively: in other words, you literally read through the Bible in the order of the books as listed in the Bible index. Some schemes 'mix and match' by designating a combination of Old Testament and New Testament books for you to read on the same day. Some go though the Old Testament once and the much shorter New Testament twice. Some go through a combination of Old Testament and New Testament books once and Psalms and Proverbs twice. They are all excellent! What they have in common is that they stipulate where you must be in your reading through on a certain day of the reading year, so you know what you will cover if you follow the scheme in a disciplined way. Some schemes are dated so that day 1 starts on January 1. Others can be started on any day of the year.

Most good study Bibles contain their own BRS. Some excellent examples of existing BRS follow below. One is from YL/UBM and two were devised by Robert Murray McCheyne, one of which is now attractively presented by IFES and IVCF.

Daily Bible Readings—In a Year! by YL/UBM (see below)

This printed, easy-to-follow Bible Reading Scheme is reproduced below. A double-sided, folded and dated A4 Bible reading schedule fits easily into your Bible. The scheme goes through the two Testaments simultaneously each day. The whole Bible can be read in a year, or you can take a year on the Old Testament and a year on the New Testament. It is offered free of charge in the UK by Young Life / United Beach Missions at office@younglife.org.uk or office@ubm.org.uk

Daily Bread—being a calendar for reading through the Word of God in a year by Robert Murray McCheyne (see below)

McCheyne's basic original calendarised plan is reproduced on pages 657 and 660 is preceded by his inspiring summary of the dangers and advantages of using his scheme to read through the whole of the Bible. The scheme is available from the

Internet on the following website:
http://www.wholesomewords.org/biography/bmcheyne5.html

More Precious Than Gold—read the Bible in one or two years: a printed presentation of Robert Murray McCheyne's schedule

This is a most attractive and helpful presentation of Robert Murray McCheyne's calendarised reading plan to read the New Testament and Psalms twice and the rest of the Old Testament once in either one year, or two years, at your choice. It is in a glossy cover with a page a month dedicated to the scheme. It is available free of charge in the UK from IFES (info@fesworld.org) and in the USA from IVCF (info@IVCF.org).

(2) What is the FBRS and how does it work?

(A) WHAT IS THE FBRS?

Like all BRS, the FBRS seeks to promote the same aim of helping you to read through the whole Bible. However, 'F' signifies 'flexible'. FBRS does not prescribe your chapters for you but leaves you to choose the rate of your progress and the order you read in a way that suits you. You can read right through the whole Bible following the scheme in *Appendix 2—The Bible's Chapters*, or mix and match however you choose, and yet maintain your organisation and discipline. You can select how many chapters per day you wish to read and know how long, at that rate, it will take you to read the whole Bible. Or you can vary your rate of reading by deciding how long you want to take to read through the entire Word of God. (For example, at ten chapters a day you can cover the Bible in a little under four months, whereas by reading two chapters every three days you can proceed more slowly and take five years.)

(B) HOW DOES THE FBRS OPERATE?

Here are the steps to make FBRS work for you:

1. Photocopy the numbered list of Bible chapters given in *Appendix 2—The Bible's Chapters*.

2. Decide either to read the Bible in a given period of time (see 3 below), or to read a set number of chapters each day (see 4 below).

3. Decide either to read through the whole Bible consecutively, in accordance with *Appendix 2—The Bible's Chapters*, or to 'mix and match'. If the latter, read the rest of this Appendix and then write down how you plan to 'mix and match' books and the order of the books you intend to read in your plan.

4. If this is the first time you plan to read through the Bible, it may be best to start at Genesis 1 and go through the books in the order of *Appendix 2—The Bible's Chapters*. That is the author's preference, but some Bible readers may disagree. There are no absolute rules!

5. As there are 929 Old Testament chapters and 260 New Testament chapters

in the Bible's 1,189 chapters, you can see that if you decide to read the Old Testament and the New Testament once each, the proportion of chapters is approximately 3 OT to 1 NT. If you decide to read through the New Testament twice, then that proportion would be 3 OT to 2 NT.

6. If you wish to read any book more than once in the period of reading through, you can see from *Appendix 2—The Bible's Chapters* how many chapters are involved. Psalms and Proverbs, combined together, cover 181 chapters, so those books can be covered twice a year if desired (with a little extra time for Psalm 119). Alternatively, they can be read once, and then the Major Prophets (183 chapters) can fill in the other six months in the year. Or other combinations can be worked out according to your preference.

7. Remember that some chapters are short, whereas others are very long indeed! So, for example, you may decide to increase the daily number of Psalms to read on certain days to make room for the giant Psalm 119!

8. Simply put a line through each chapter number noted on your photocopy of *Appendix 2—The Bible Chapters* as you read the chapter. Thus, for example, if you choose the 3/5 Combination detailed below (which takes you through the Bible in almost exactly a year) you would put a line through the three chapters you read each day, except on the Lord's Day when you would put the line through five chapters. If you decide to read any book twice in the period, put another line through the first line, making a cross.

9. Why not invest in a notebook, or in a page-to-a-day diary, and jot down one thought (or more) each day from each chapter you read? If you read through the Bible each year, your page-to-a-day diaries can begin to build your own informal commentary on the Bible. (That is how *The Bible Panorama* came into being!)

10. How about getting other Christian friends to commit to the same scheme of reading as yourself, and then encourage each other by sharing thoughts with each other that you have gleaned from reading the same chapters? Some churches and fellowships start this together each New Year. Others agree a starting point and scheme with a few others. It has the added advantage of challenging each participant to keep to the agreed scheme—a sort of 'weight watchers' approach to Bible reading!

If you prefer to follow an established scheme, one of those reproduced below would be an excellent starting place. It is the author's hope that *The Bible Panorama's* brief explanation of each chapter will help you to get to know each chapter better and appreciate its shape and context before you read it. That is the main reason for this book.

ASSUMPTIONS MADE IN CALCULATING FBRS ALTERNATIVES

Assumptions made for calculations on which these figures are based are:

1,200 chapters in Bible (in fact 1,189); 360 days in year (in fact, 365 or 366 in leap years); 180 days in six months (in fact, 182.5 or 183 in leap years); average of 30 days in a month (in fact, 30.41); each of twelve months is same length (in fact, not so.) The effect of working on these assumptions is that it will take a little less time to read through the scheme than is indicated.

FBRS TO READ THE WHOLE BIBLE THROUGH IN A CHOSEN TIME PERIOD

This scheme enables you to choose how long you want to take to read through the whole Bible and then indicates how many chapters you must read to accomplish that.

Time chosen to read the Bible	Daily chapters to read in time chosen	Daily chapters rounded up or down rounded rate	Time to read at chosen rate
6 months	6.6	6 or 7	200d (0y 6m 20d) or 172d (0y 5m 22d)
1 year	3.3	3 or 4	400d (1y 1m 10d) or 300d (0y 10m 0d)
2 years	1.6	1 or 2	1,200d (3y 4m 0d) or 600d (1y 8m 0d)
3 years	1.1	1 or 2	1,200d (3y 4m 0d) or 600d (1y 8m 0d)
4 years	0.833	0.84* or 1	1,429d (3y 11m 9d) or 1,200d (3y 4m 0d)
5 years	0.667	0.67** or 1	1,792d (4y 11m 22d) or 1,200d (3y 4m 0d)

* 0.84 chapters per day approximates to reading 4 chapters every five days.

** 0.67 chapters per day means reading 2 chapters every three days

FBRS TO READ THE WHOLE BIBLE THROUGH IN A CHOSEN NUMBER OF DAILY CHAPTERS

This scheme enables you to choose how many chapters you want to read each day and then indicates how long it will take you to read through the Bible on that basis.

Reading rate of chapters per day	Total days needed to read Bible through	Total days needed in years/months/days
1	1,189	3y 3m 19d
2	595	1y 7m 25d
3	396	1y 1m 5d
4	297	0y 9m 27d
5	238	0y 7m 28d
6	198	0y 6m 18d
7	170	0y 5m 20d
8	148	0y 4m 28d
9	132	0y 4m 12d
10	118	0y 3m 28d
3/5 Combination: (3 for six days but 5 on the Lord's Day)	360	Just under a year (308 on ordinary days + 52 on Lord's Days)

Read the whole Bible through using YL / UBM's *Daily Bible Readings—In a Year!* Scheme

YL / UBM's Daily Bible Readings—In a Year! Scheme

JANUARY

1 Matt. 1	**1** Gen. 1,2,3	**2** Matt. 2	**2** Gen. 4,5,6
3 Matt. 3	**3** Gen. 7,8,9	**4** Matt. 4	**4** Gen. 10,11,12
5 Matt. 5:1–26	**5** Gen. 13,14,15	**6** Matt. 5:27–48	**6** Gen. 16,17
7 Matt. 6:1–18	**7** Gen. 18,19	**8** Matt. 6:19–34	**8** Gen. 20,21,22
9 Matt. 7	**9** Gen. 23,24	**10** Matt. 8:1–17	**10** Gen. 25,26
11 Matt. 8:18–34	**11** Gen. 27,28	**12** Matt. 9:1–17	**12** Gen. 29,30
13 Matt. 9:18–38	**13** Gen. 31,32	**14** Matt. 10:1–20	**14** Gen. 33,34,35
15 Matt. 10:21–42	**15** Gen. 36,37,38	**16** Matt. 11	**16** Gen. 39,40
17 Matt. 12:1–23	**17** Gen. 41,42	**18** Matt. 12:24–50	**18** Gen. 43,44,45
19 Matt. 13:1–30	**19** Gen. 46,47,48	**20** Matt. 13:31–58	**20** Gen. 49,50
21 Matt. 14:1–21	**21** Exod. 1,2,3	**22** Matt. 14:22–36	**22** Exod. 4,5,6
23 Matt. 15:1–20	**23** Exod. 7,8	**24** Matt. 15:21–39	**24** Exod. 9,10,11
25 Matt. 16	**25** Exod. 12,13	**26** Matt. 17	**26** Exod. 14,15
27 Matt. 18:1–20	**27** Exod. 16,17,18	**28** Matt. 18:21–35	**28** Exod. 19,20
29 Matt. 19	**29** Exod. 21,22	**30** Matt. 20:1–16	**30** Exod. 23,24
31 Matt. 20:17–34	**31** Exod. 25,26		

FEBRUARY

1 Matt. 21:1–22	**1** Exod. 27,28	**2** Matt. 21:23–46	**2** Exod. 29,30
3 Matt. 22:1–22	**3** Exod. 31,32,33	**4** Matt. 22:23–46	**4** Exod. 34,35
5 Matt. 23:1–22	**5** Exod. 36, 37,38	**6** Matt. 23:23–39	**6** Exod. 39,40
7 Matt. 24:1–28	**7** Lev. 1,2,3	**8** Matt. 24:29–51	**8** Lev. 4,5
9 Matt. 25:1–30	**9** Lev. 6,7	**10** Matt. 25:31–46	**10** Lev. 8,9,10
11 Matt. 26:1–25	**11** Lev. 11,12	**12** Matt. 26:26–50	**12** Lev. 13
13 Matt. 26:51–75	**13** Lev. 14	**14** Matt. 27:1–26	**14** Lev. 15,16
15 Matt. 27:27–50	**15** Lev. 17,18	**16** Matt. 27:51–66	**16** Lev. 19,20
17 Matt. 28	**17** Lev. 21,22	**18** Mark 1:1–22	**18** Lev. 23,24
19 Mark 1:23–45	**19** Lev. 25	**20** Mark 2	**20** Lev. 26,27
21 Mark 3	**21** Num. 1,2	**22** Mark 4:1–20	**22** Num. 3,4,5
23 Mark 4:21–41	**23** Num. 6,7,8	**24** Mark 5:1–20	**24** Num. 9,10,11
25 Mark 5:21–43	**25** Num. 12,13,14	**26** Mark 6:1–29	**26** Num. 15,16
27 Mark 6:30–56	**27** Num. 17,18,19	**28** Mark 7:1–13	**28** Num. 20,21,22

MARCH

1 Mark 7:14–37	**1** Num. 23,24,25	**2** Mark 8:1–21	**2** Num. 26,27
3 Mark 8:22–38	**3** Num. 28,29,30	**4** Mark 9:1–29	**4** Num. 31,32,33
5 Mark 9:30–50	**5** Num. 34,35,36	**6** Mark 10:1–31	**6** Deut. 1,2
7 Mark 10:32–52	**7** Deut. 3,4	**8** Mark 11:1–18	**8** Deut. 5,6,7
9 Mark 11:19–33	**9** Deut. 8,9,10	**10** Mark 12:1–27	**10** Deut. 11,12,13
11 Mark 12:28–44	**11** Deut. 14,15,16	**12** Mark 13:1–20	**12** Deut. 17,18,19
13 Mark 13:21–37	**13** Deut. 20,21,22	**14** Mark 14:1–26	**14** Deut. 23,24,25
15 Mark 14:27–53	**15** Deut. 26,27	**16** Mark 14:54–72	**16** Deut. 28,29
17 Mark 15:1–25	**17** Deut. 30,31	**18** Mark 15:26–47	**18** Deut. 32,33,34
19 Mark 16	**19** Josh.1,2,3	**20** Luke 1:1–20	**20** Josh. 4,5,6
21 Luke 1:21–38	**21** Josh. 7,8,9	**22** Luke 1:39–56	**22** Josh. 10,11,12
23 Luke 1:57–80	**23** Josh. 13,14,15	**24** Luke 2:1–24	**24** Josh. 16,17,18
25 Luke 2:25–52	**25** Josh. 19,20,21	**26** Luke 3	**26** Josh. 22,23,24
27 Luke 4:1–30	**27** Judg. 1,2,3	**28** Luke 4:31–44	**28** Judg. 4,5,6
29 Luke 5:1–16	**29** Judg. 7,8	**30** Like 5:17–39	**30** Judg 9,10
31 Luke 6:1–26	**31** Judg 11,12		

APRIL

1 Luke 6:27–49	**1** Judg. 13,14,15	**2** Luke 7:1–30	**2** Judg. 16,17,18
3 Luke 7:31–50	**3** Judg. 19,20,21	**4** Luke 8:1–25	**4** Ruth 1,2,3,4
5 Luke 8:26–56	**5** 1 Sam. 1,2,3	**6** Luke 9:1–17	**6** 1 Sam. 4,5,6
7 Luke 9:18–36	**7** 1 Sam. 7,8,9	**8** Luke 9:37–62	**8** 1 Sam. 10,11,12
9 Luke 10:1–24	**9** 1 Sam. 13,14	**10** Luke 10:25–42	**10** 1 Sam. 15,16
11 Luke 11:1–28	**11** 1 Sam. 17,18	**12** Luke 11:29–54	**12** 1 Sam. 19,20,21
13 Luke 12:1–31	**13** 1 Sam. 22,23,24	**14** Luke 12:32–59	**14** 1 Sam. 25,26
15 Luke 13:1–22	**15** 1 Sam. 27,28,29	**16** Luke 13:23–35	**16** 1 Sam. 30,31
17 Luke 14:1–24	**17** 2 Sam. 1,2	**18** Luke 14:25–35	**18** 2 Sam. 3,4,5
19 Luke 15:1–10	**19** 2 Sam. 6,7,8	**20** Luke 15:11–32	**20** 2 Sam. 9,10,11
21 Luke 16	**21** 2 Sam. 12,13	**22** Luke 17:1–19	**22** 2 Sam. 14,15
23 Luke 17:20–37	**23** 2 Sam. 16,17,18	**24** Luke 18:1–23	**24** 2 Sam. 19,20
25 Luke 18:24–43	**25** 2 Sam. 21,22	**26** Luke 19:1–27	**26** 2 Sam 23,24
27 Luke 19:28–48	**27** 1 Kings 1,2	**28** Luke 20:1–26	**28** 1 Kings 3,4,5
29 Luke 20:27–47	**29** 1 Kings 6,7	**30** Luke 21:1–19	**30** 1 Kings 8,9

MAY

1 Luke 21:20–38	**1** 1 Kings 10,11	**2** Luke 22:1–20	**2** 1 Kings 12,13
3 Luke 22:21–46	**3** 1 Kings 14,15	**4** Luke 22:47–71	**4** 1 Kings 16,17,18
5 Luke 23:1–25	**5** 1 Kings 19,20	**6** Luke 23:26–56	**6** 1 Kings 21,22
7 Luke 24:1–35	**7** 2 Kings 1,2,3	**8** Luke 24:36–53	**8** 2 Kings 4,5,6

9 John 1:1–28
11 John 2
13 John 3:19–38
15 John 4:31–54
17 John 5:25–47
19 John 6:22–44
21 John 7:1–27
23 John 8:1–27
25 John 9:1–23
27 John 10:1–23
29 John 11:1–29
31 John 12:1–26

9 2 Kings 7,8,9
11 2 Kings 13,14
13 2 Kings 17,18
15 2 Kings 22,23
17 1 Chr. 1,2,3
19 1 Chr. 7,8,9
21 1 Chr. 13,14,15
23 1 Chr. 19,20,21
25 1 Chr. 25,26,27
27 2 Chr. 1,2,3
29 2 Chr. 7,8,9
31 2 Chr. 13,14

10 John 1:29–51
12 John 3:1–18
14 John 4:1–30
16 John 5:1–24
18 John 6:1–21
20 John 6:45–71
22 John 7:28–53
24 John 8:28–59
26 John 9:24–41
28 John 10:24–42
30 John 11:30–57

10 2 Kings 10,11,12
12 2 Kings 15,16
14 2 Kings 19,20,21
16 2 Kings 24,25
18 1 Chr. 4,5,6
20 1 Chr. 10,11,12
22 1 Chr. 16,17,18
24 1 Chr. 22,23,24
26 1 Chr. 28,29
28 2 Chr. 4,5,6
30 2 Chr. 10,11,12

JUNE

1 John 12:27–50
3 John 13:21–38
5 John 15
7 John 17
9 John 18:19–40
11 John 19:23–42
13 John 21
15 Acts 2:1–21
17 Acts 3
19 Acts 4:23–37
21 Acts 5:22–42
23 Acts 7:1–21
25 Acts 7:44–60
27 Acts 8:26–40
29 Acts 9:22–43

1 2 Chr. 15,16
3 2 Chr. 19,20
5 2 Chr. 23,24
7 2 Chr. 28,29
9 2 Chr. 32,33
11 Ezra 1,2
13 Ezra 6,7,8
15 Neh. 1,2,3
17 Neh. 7,8,9
19 Neh. 12,13
21 Esth. 3,4,5
23 Esth. 9,10
25 Job 3,4
27 Job 8,9,10
29 Job 14,15,16

2 John 13:1–20
4 John 14
6 John 16
8 John 18:1–18
10 John 19:1–22
12 John 20
14 Acts 1
16 Acts 1:22–47
18 Acts 4:1–22
20 Acts 5:1–21
22 Acts 6
24 Acts 7:22–43
26 Acts 8:1–25
28 Acts 9:1–21
30 Acts 10:1–23

2 2 Chr. 17,18
4 2 Chr. 21,22
6 2 Chr. 25,26,27
8 2 Chr. 30,31
10 2 Chr. 34,35,36
12 Ezra 3,4,5
14 Ezra 9,10
16 Neh. 4,5,6
18 Neh. 10,11
20 Esth. 1,2
22 Esth. 6,7,8
24 Job 1,2
26 Job 5,6,7
28 Job 11,12,13
30 Job 17,18,19

JULY

1 Acts 10:24–48
3 Acts 12
5 Acts 13:26–52
7 Acts 15:1–21
9 Acts 16:1–21
11 Acts 17:1–15
13 Acts 18
15 Acts 19:21–41
17 Acts 20:17–38
19 Acts 21:18–40

1 Job 20,21
3 Job 25,26,27
5 Job 30,31
7 Job 34,35
9 Job 38,39,40
11 Ps. 1,2,3
13 Ps. 7,8,9
15 Ps. 13,14,15
17 Ps. 18,19
19 Ps. 23,24,25

2 Acts 11
4 Acts 13:1–25
6 Acts 14
8 Acts 15:22–41
10 Acts 16:22–40
12 Acts 17:16–34
14 Acts 19:1–20
16 Acts 20:1–16
18 Acts 21:1–17
20 Acts 22

2 Job 22,23,24
4 Job 28,29
6 Job 32,33
8 Job 36,37
10 Job 41,42
12 Ps. 4,5,6
14 Ps. 10,11,12
16 Ps. 16,17
18 Ps. 20,21,22
20 Ps. 26,27,28

21 Acts 23:1–15	**21** Ps. 29,30	**22** Acts 23:16–35	**22** Ps. 31,32
23 Acts 24	**23** Ps. 33,34	**24** Acts 25	**24** Ps. 35,36
25 Acts 26	**25** Ps. 37,38,39	**26** Acts 27:1–26	**26** Ps. 40,41,42
27 Acts 27:27–44	**27** Ps. 43,44,45	**28** Acts 28	**28** Ps. 46,47,48
29 Rom. 1	**29** Ps. 49,50	**30** Rom. 2	**30** Ps. 51,52,53
31 Rom. 3	**31** Ps. 54,55,56		

AUGUST

1 Rom. 4	**1** Ps. 57,58,59	**2** Rom. 5	**2** Ps. 60,61,62
3 Rom. 6	**3** Ps. 63,64,65	**4** Rom. 7	**4** Ps. 66,67
5 Rom. 8:1–21	**5** Ps. 68,69	**6** Rom. 8:22–39	**6** Ps. 70,71
7 Rom. 9:1–15	**7** Ps. 72,73	**8** Rom. 9:16–33	**8** Ps. 74,75,76
9 Rom. 10	**9** Ps. 77,78	**10** Rom. 11:1–18	**10** Ps. 79,80
11 Rom. 11:19–36	**11** Ps. 81,82,83	**12** Rom. 12	**12** Ps. 84,85,86
13 Rom. 13	**13** Ps. 87,88	**14** Rom. 14	**14** Ps. 89,90
15 Rom. 15:1–13	**15** Ps. 91,92,93	**16** Rom. 15:14–33	**16** Ps. 94,95,96
17 Rom. 16	**17** Ps. 97,98.99	**18** 1 Cor. 1	**18** Ps. 100,101,102
19 1 Cor. 2	**19** Ps. 103,104	**20** 1 Cor. 3	**20** Ps. 105,106
21 1 Cor. 4	**21** Ps. 107,108,109	**22** 1 Cor. 5	**22** Ps. 110,111,112
23 1 Cor. 6	**23** Ps. 113,114,115	**24** 1 Cor. 7:1–19	**24** Ps. 116,117,118
25 1 Cor. 7:20–40	**25** Ps. 119:1–88	**26** 1 Cor. 8	**26** Ps. 119:89–176
27 1 Cor. 9	**27** Ps. 120,121,122	**28** 1 Cor. 10:1–18	**28** Ps. 123,124,125
29 1 Cor. 10:19–33	**29** Ps. 126,127,128	**30** 1 Cor. 11:1–16	**30** Ps. 129,130,131
31 1 Cor. 11:17–34	**31** Ps. 132,133,134		

SEPTEMBER

1 1 Cor. 12	**1** Ps. 135,136	**2** 1 Cor. 13	**2** Ps. 137,138,139
3 1 Cor. 14:1–20	**3** Ps. 140,141,142	**4** 1 Cor. 14:21–40	**4** Ps. 143,144,145
5 1 Cor. 15:1–28	**5** Ps. 146,147	**6** 1 Cor. 15:29–58	**6** Ps. 148,149,150
7 1 Cor. 16	**7** Prov. 1,2	**8** 2 Cor. 1	**8** Prov. 3,4,5
9 2 Cor. 2	**9** Prov. 6,7	**10** 2 Cor. 3	**10** Prov. 8,9
11 2 Cor. 4	**11** Prov. 10,11,12	**12** 2 Cor. 5	**12** Prov. 13,14,15
13 2 Cor. 6	**13** Prov. 16,17,18	**14** 2 Cor. 7	**14** Prov. 19,20,21
15 2 Cor. 8	**15** Prov. 22,23,24	**16** 2 Cor. 9	**16** Prov. 25,26
17 2 Cor. 10	**17** Prov. 27,28,29	**18** 2 Cor. 11:1–15	**18** Prov. 30,31
19 2 Cor. 11:16–33	**19** Eccl. 1,2,3	**20** 2 Cor. 12	**20** Eccl. 4,5,6
21 2 Cor 13	**21** Eccl. 7,8,9	**22** Gal. 1	**22** Eccl. 10,11,12
23 Gal. 2	**23** Song. 1,2,3	**24** Gal. 3	**24** Song. 4,5
25 Gal. 4	**25** Song. 6,7,8	**26** Gal. 5	**26** Isa. 1,2
27 Gal. 6	**27** Isa. 3,4	**28** Eph. 1	**28** Isa. 5,6
29 Eph. 2	**29** Isa. 7,8	**30** Eph. 3	**30** Isa. 9,10

OCTOBER

1 Eph. 4	**1** Isa. 11,12,13	**2** Eph. 5:1–16	**2** Isa. 14,15,16
3 Eph. 5:17–33	**3** Isa. 17,18,19	**4** Eph. 6	**4** Isa. 20,21,22
5 Phil. 1	**5** Isa. 23,24,25	**6** Phil. 2	**6** Isa. 26,27
7 Phil. 3	**7** Isa. 28,29	**8** Phil. 4	**8** Isa. 30,31
9 Col. 1	**9** Isa. 32,33	**10** Col. 2	**10** Isa. 34,35,36
11 Col. 3	**11** Isa. 37,38	**12** Col. 4	**12** Isa. 39,40
13 1 Thes. 1	**13** Isa. 41,42	**14** 1 Thes. 2	**14** Isa. 43,44
15 1 Thes. 3	**15** Isa. 45,46	**16** 1 Thes. 4	**16** Isa. 47,48,49
17 1 Thes. 5	**17** Isa. 50,51,52	**18** 2 Thes. 1	**18** Isa. 53,54,55
19 2 Thes. 2	**19** Isa. 56,57,58	**20** 2 Thes. 3	**20** Isa. 59,60,61
21 1 Tim. 1	**21** Isa. 62,63,64	**22** 1 Tim. 2	**22** Isa. 65,66
23 1 Tim. 3	**23** Jer. 1,2	**24** 1 Tim. 4	**24** Jer. 3,4,5
25 1 Tim. 5	**25** Jer. 6,7,8	**26** 1 Tim. 6	**26** Jer. 9,10,11
27 2 Tim. 1	**27** Jer. 12,13,14	**28** 2 Tim. 2	**28** Jer. 15.16.17
29 2 Tim. 3	**29** Jer. 18,19	**30** 2 Tim. 4	**30** Jer. 20,21
31 Titus 1	**31** Jer. 22,23		

NOVEMBER

1 Titus 2	**1** Jer. 24,25,26	**2** Titus 3	**2** Jer. 27,28,29
3 Philem.	**3** Jer. 30,31	**4** Heb. 1	**4** Jer. 32,33
5 Heb. 2	**5** Jer. 34,35,36	**6** Heb. 3	**6** Jer. 37,38,39
7 Heb. 4	**7** Jer. 40,41,42	**8** Heb. 5	**8** Jer. 43,44,45
9 Heb. 6	**9** Jer. 46,47	**10** Heb. 7	**10** Jer. 48,49
11 Heb. 8	**11** Jer. 50	**12** Heb. 9	**12** Jer. 51,52
13 Heb. 10:1–18	**13** Lam. 1,2	**14** Heb. 10:19–39	**14** Lam. 3,4
15 Heb. 11:1–19	**15** Ezek. 1,2	**16** Heb. 11:20–40	**16** Ezek. 3,4
17 Heb. 12	**17** Ezek. 5,6,7	**18** Heb. 13	**18** Ezek. 8,9,10
19 James 1	**19** Ezek. 11,12,13	**20** James 2	**20** Ezek. 14,15
21 James 3	**21** Ezek. 16,17	**22** James 4	**22** Ezek. 18,19
23 James 5	**23** Ezek. 20,21	**24** 1 Peter 1	**24** Ezek. 22,23
25 1 Peter 2	**25** Ezek. 24,25,26	**26** 1 Peter 3	**26** Ezek. 27,28,29
27 1 Peter 4	**27** Ezek. 30,31,32	**28** 1 Peter 5	**28** Ezek. 33,34
29 2 Peter 1	**29** Ezek. 35,36	**30** 2 Peter 2	**30** Ezek. 37,38,39

DECEMBER

1 2 Peter 3	**1** Ezek. 40,41	**2** 1 John 1	**2** Ezek. 42,43,44
3 1 John 2	**3** Ezek. 45,46	**4** 1 John 3	**4** Ezek. 47,48,49
5 1 John 4	**5** Dan. 1,2	**6** 1 John 5	**6** Dan. 3,4
7 2 John	**7** Dan. 5,6,7	**8** 3 John	**8** Dan. 8,9,10

9 Jude	**9** Dan. 11,12	**10** Rev. 1	**10** Hos. 1,2,3,4
11 Rev. 2	**11** Hos. 5,6,7,8	**12** Rev. 3	**12** Hos. 9,10,11
13 Rev. 4	**13** Hos. 12,13,14	**14** Rev. 5	**14** Joel
15 Rev. 6	**15** Amos 1,2,3	**16** Rev. 7	**16** Amos 4,5,6
17 Rev. 8	**17** Amos 7,8,9	**18** Rev. 9	**18** Obadiah
19 Rev. 10	**19** Jonah	**20** Rev. 11	**20** Micah 1,2,3
21 Rev. 12	**21** Micah 4,5	**22** Rev. 13	**22** Micah 6,7
23 Rev. 14	**23** Nahum	**24** Rev. 15	**24** Habakkuk
25 Rev. 16	**25** Zeph.	**26** Rev. 17	**26** Hag.
27 Rev. 18	**27** Zech. 1,2,3,4	**28** Rev. 19	**28** Zech. 5,6,7,8
29 Rev. 20	**29** Zech. 9,10,11,12	**30** Rev. 21	**30** Zech. 13,14
31 Rev. 22	**31** Mal.		

(From: http://www.wholesomewords.org/biography/bmcheyne5.html)

Daily Bread, being a calendar for reading through the Word of God in a year

by Robert Murray McCheyne

'Thy Word is very pure; therefore thy servant loveth it.'

MY DEAR FLOCK,—The approach of another year stirs up within me new desires for your salvation, and for the growth of those of you who are saved. 'God is my record how greatly I long after you all in the bowels of Jesus Christ.' What the coming year is to bring forth, who can tell? There is plainly a weight lying on the spirits of all good men, and a looking for some strange work of judgement coming upon this land. There is need now to ask that solemn question—'If in the land of peace wherein thou trustedst, they wearied thee, then how wilt thou do in the swelling of Jordan?'

Those believers will stand firmest who have no dependence upon self or upon creatures, but upon Jehovah our Righteousness. We must be driven more to our Bibles, and to the mercy-seat, if we are to stand in the evil day. Then we shall be able to say like David—, 'The proud have had me greatly in derision, yet have I not declined from thy law.' 'Princes have persecuted me without a cause, but my heart standeth in awe of thy Word.'

It has long been in my mind to prepare a scheme of Scripture reading, in which as many as were made willing by God might agree, so that the whole Bible might be read once by you in the year, and all might be feeding in the same portion of the green pasture at the same time.

I am quite aware that such a plan is accompanied with many

Dangers

1. *Formality*. We are such weak creatures that any regularly returning duty is apt to degenerate into a lifeless form. The tendency of reading the Word by a fixed rule may, in some minds, be to create this skeleton religion. This is to be the peculiar sin of the last days— 'Having the form of godliness, but denying the power thereof.' Guard against this. Let the calendar perish rather than this rust eat up your souls.

2. *Self-righteousness*. Some, when they have devoted their set time to reading the Word, and accomplished their prescribed portion, may be tempted to look at themselves with self-complacency. Many, I am persuaded, are living without any Divine work on their soul—unpardoned, and unsanctified, and ready to perish—who spend their appointed times in secret and family devotion. This is going to hell with a lie in the right hand.

3. *Careless reading*. Few tremble at the Word of God. Few, in reading it, hear the voice of Jehovah, which is full of majesty. Some, by having so large a portion, may be tempted to weary of it, as Israel did of the daily manna, saying 'Our soul loatheth this light bread;' and to read it in a slight and careless manner. This would be fearfully provoking to God. Take heed lest that word be true of you— 'Ye said, also, Behold, what a weariness is it! and ye have snuffed at it, saith the Lord of Hosts.'

4. *A yoke too heavy to bear*. Some may engage in reading with alacrity for a time, and afterwards feel it a burden grievous to be borne. They may find conscience dragging them through the appointed task without any relish of the heavenly food. If this be the case with any, throw aside the fetter and feed at liberty in the sweet garden of God. My desire is not to cast a snare upon you, but to be a helper of your joy.

If there be so many dangers, why propose such a scheme at all? To this I answer, that the best things are accompanied with danger, as the fairest flowers are often gathered in the clefts of some dangerous precipice. Let us weigh

The advantages

1. *The whole Bible will be read through in an orderly manner in the course of a year*. The Old Testament once, the New Testament and Psalms twice. I fear many of you never read the whole Bible; and yet it is all equally divine. 'All Scripture is given by inspiration of God, and is profitable for doctrine, for reproof, for correction, and instruction in righteousness, that the man of God may be perfect.' If we pass over some parts of Scripture, we shall be incomplete Christians.

2. *Time will not be wasted in choosing what portions to read*. Often believers are at a loss to determine towards which part of the mountains of spices they should bend their steps. Here the question will be solved at once in a very simple manner.

3. *Parents will have a regular subject upon which to examine their children and*

servants. It is much to be desired that family worship were made more instructive than it generally is. The mere reading of the chapter is often too like water spilt on the ground. Let it be read by every member of the family beforehand, and then the meaning and application drawn out by simple question and answer. The calendar will be helpful in this. Friends, also, when they meet, will have a subject for profitable conversation in the portions read that day. The meaning of difficult passages may be inquired from the more judicious and ripe Christians, and the fragrance of simpler Scriptures spread abroad.

4. *The pastor will know in what part of the pasture the flock are feeding.* He will thus be enabled to speak more suitably to them on the Sabbath; and both pastor and elders will be able to drop a word of light and comfort in visiting from house to house, which will be more readily responded to.

5. *The sweet bond of Christian love and unity will be strengthened.* We shall be often led to think of those dear brothers and sisters in the Lord, here and elsewhere, who agree to join with us in reading these portions. We shall oftener be led to agree on earth, touching something we shall ask of God. We shall pray over the same promises, mourn over the same confessions, praise God in the same songs, and be nourished by the same words of eternal life.

JANUARY BIBLE READING

Date	Family		Secret		Date	Family		Secret	
1	Gen. 1	Matt. 1	Ezra 1	Acts 1	2	Gen. 2	Matt. 2	Ezra 2	Acts 2
3	Gen. 3	Matt. 3	Ezra 3	Acts 3	4	Gen. 4	Matt. 4	Ezra 4	Acts 4
5	Gen. 5	Matt. 5	Ezra 5	Acts 5	6	Gen. 6	Matt. 6	Ezra 6	Acts 6
7	Gen. 7	Matt. 7	Ezra 7	Acts 7	8	Gen. 8	Matt. 8	Ezra 8	Acts 8
9	Gen. 9,10	Matt. 9	Ezra 9	Acts 9	10	Gen. 11	Matt. 10	Ezra 10	Acts 10
11	Gen. 12	Matt. 11	Neh. 1	Acts 11	12	Gen. 13	Matt. 12	Neh. 2	Acts 12
13	Gen. 14	Matt. 13	Neh. 3	Acts 13	14	Gen. 15	Matt. 14	Neh. 4	Acts 14
15	Gen. 16	Matt. 15	Neh. 5	Acts 15	16	Gen. 17	Matt. 16	Neh. 6	Acts 16
17	Gen. 18	Matt. 17	Neh. 7	Acts 17	18	Gen. 19	Matt. 18	Neh. 8	Acts 18
19	Gen. 20	Matt. 19	Neh. 9	Acts 19	20	Gen. 21	Matt. 20	Neh. 10	Acts 20
21	Gen. 22	Matt. 21	Neh. 11	Acts 21	22	Gen. 23	Matt. 22	Neh. 12	Acts 22
23	Gen. 24	Matt. 23	Neh. 13	Acts 23	24	Gen. 25	Matt. 24	Esther 1	Acts 24
25	Gen. 26	Matt. 25	Esther 2	Acts 25	26	Gen. 27	Matt. 26	Esther 3	Acts 26
27	Gen. 28	Matt. 27	Esther 4	Acts 27	28	Gen. 29	Matt. 28	Esther 5	Acts 28
29	Gen. 30	Mark 1	Esther 6	Rom. 1	30	Gen. 31	Mark 2	Esther 7	Rom. 2
31	Gen. 32	Mark 3	Esther 8	Rom. 3					

FEBRUARY BIBLE READING

Date	Family		Secret		Date	Family		Secret	
1	Gen. 33	Mark 4	Est. 9,10	Rom. 4	2	Gen. 34	Mark 5	Job 1	Rom. 5
3	Gen. 35,36	Mark 6	Job 2	Rom. 6	4	Gen. 37	Mark 7	Job 3	Rom. 7
5	Gen. 38	Mark 8	Job 4	Rom. 8	6	Gen. 39	Mark 9	Job 5	Rom. 9
7	Gen. 40	Mark 10	Job 6	Rom. 10	8	Gen. 41	Mark 11	Job 7	Rom. 11
9	Gen. 42	Mark 12	Job 8	Rom. 12	10	Gen. 43	Mark 13	Job 9	Rom. 13
11	Gen. 44	Mark 14	Job 10	Rom. 14	12	Gen. 45	Mark 15	Job 11	Rom. 15
13	Gen. 46	Mark 16	Job 12	Rom. 16	14	Gen. 47	Lk. 1:1–38	Job 13	I Cor. 1
15	Gen. 48	Lk. 1:39–80	Job 14	1 Cor. 2	16	Gen. 49	Lk. 2	Job 15	1 Cor. 3
17	Gen. 50	Lk. 3	Job 16,17	1 Cor. 4	18	Ex. 1	Lk. 4	Job 18	1 Cor. 5
19	Ex. 2	Lk. 5	Job 19	1 Cor. 6	20	Ex. 3	Lk. 6	Job 20	1 Cor. 7
21	Ex. 4	Lk. 7	Job 21	1 Cor. 8	22	Ex. 5	Lk. 8	Job 22	1 Cor. 9
23	Ex. 6	Lk. 9	Job 23	1 Cor. 10	24	Ex. 7	Lk. 10	Job 24	1 Cor. 11
25	Ex. 8	Lk. 11	Job 25,26	1 Cor. 12	26	Ex. 9	Lk. 12	Job 27	1 Cor. 13
27	Ex.10	Lk. 13	Job 28	1 Cor. 14	28	Ex.11–12:21	Lk. 14	Job 29	1 Cor. 15

MARCH BIBLE READING

Date	Family		Secret		Date	Family		Secret	
1	Ex.12:22–51	Luke 15	Job 30	I Cor. 16	2	Ex. 13	Luke 16	Job 31	2 Cor. 1
3	Ex. 14	Luke 17	Job 32	2 Cor. 2	4	Ex. 15	Luke 18	Job 33	2 Cor. 3

5	Ex. 16	Luke 19	Job 34	2 Cor. 4	6	Ex. 17	Luke 20	Job 35	2 Cor. 5
7	Ex. 18	Luke 21	Job 36	2 Cor. 6	8	Ex. 19	Luke 22	Job 37	2 Cor. 7
9	Ex. 20	Luke 23	Job 38	2 Cor. 8	10	Ex. 21	Luke 24	Job 39	2 Cor. 9
11	Ex. 22	John 1	Job 40	2 Cor. 10	12	Ex. 23	John 2	Job 41	2 Cor. 11
13	Ex. 24	John 3	Job 42	2 Cor. 12	14	Ex. 25	John 4	Prov. 1	2 Cor. 13
15	Ex. 26	John 5	Prov. 2	Gal. 1	16	Ex. 27	John 6	Prov. 3	Gal. 2
17	Ex. 28	John 7	Prov. 4	Gal. 3	18	Ex. 29	John 8	Prov. 5	Gal. 4
19	Ex. 30	John 9	Prov. 6	Gal. 5	20	Ex. 31	John 10	Prov. 7	Gal. 6
21	Ex. 32	John 11	Prov. 8	Eph. 1	22	Ex. 33	John 12	Prov. 9	Eph. 2
23	Ex. 34	John 13	Prov. 10	Eph. 3	24	Ex. 35	John 14	Prov. 11	Eph. 4
25	Ex. 36	John 15	Prov. 12	Eph. 5	26	Ex. 37	John 16	Prov. 13	Eph. 6
27	Ex. 38	John 17	Prov. 14	Phil. 1	28	Ex. 39	John 18	Prov. 15	Phil. 2
29	Ex. 40	John 19	Prov. 16	Phil. 3	30	Lev. 1	John 20	Prov. 17	Phil. 4
31	Lev. 2–3	John 21	Prov. 18	Col. 1					

APRIL BIBLE READING

Date	Family		Secret		Date	Family		Secret	
1	Lev. 4	Ps. 1,2	Prov. 19	Col. 2	2	Lev. 5	Ps. 3,4	Prov. 20	Col. 3
3	Lev. 6	Ps. 5,6	Prov. 21	Col. 4	4	Lev. 7	Ps. 7,8	Prov. 22	1 Thess.1
5	Lev. 8	Ps. 9	Prov. 23	1 Thess.2	6	Lev. 9	Ps. 10	Prov. 24	1 Thess.3
7	Lev. 10	Ps. 11–2	Prov. 25	1 Thess.4	8	Lev. 11,12	Ps. 13–4	Prov. 26	1 Thess.5
9	Lev. 13	Ps. 15–6	Prov. 27	2 Thess.1	10	Lev. 14	Ps. 17	Prov. 28	2 Thess.2
11	Lev. 15	Ps. 18	Prov. 29	2 Thess.3	12	Lev. 16	Ps. 19	Prov. 30	1 Tim. 1
13	Lev. 17	Ps. 20–1	Prov. 31	1 Tim. 2	14	Lev. 18	Ps. 22	Eccles. 1	1 Tim. 3
15	Lev. 19	Ps. 23–4	Eccles. 2	1 Tim. 4	16	Lev. 20	Ps. 25	Eccles. 3	1 Tim. 5
17	Lev. 21	Ps. 26–7	Eccles. 4	1 Tim. 6	18	Lev. 22	Ps. 28–9	Eccles. 5	2 Tim. 1
19	Lev. 23	Ps. 30	Eccles. 6	2 Tim. 2	20	Lev. 24	Ps. 31	Eccles. 7	2 Tim. 3
21	Lev. 25	Ps. 32	Eccles. 8	2 Tim. 4	22	Lev. 26	Ps. 33	Eccles. 9	Titus 1
23	Lev. 27	Ps. 34	Eccles. 10	Titus 2	24	Num. 1	Ps. 35	Eccles. 11	Titus 3
25	Num. 2	Ps. 36	Eccles. 12	Philem. 1	26	Num. 3	Ps. 37	Song 1	Heb. 1
27	Num. 4	Ps. 38	Song 2	Heb. 2	28	Num. 5	Ps. 39	Song 3	Heb. 3
29	Num. 6	Ps. 40,41	Song 4	Heb. 4	30	Num. 7	Ps. 42,43	Song 5	Heb. 5

MAY BIBLE READING

Date	Family		Secret		Date	Family		Secret	
1	Num. 8	Ps. 44	Song 6	Heb. 6	2	Num. 9	Ps. 45	Song 7	Heb. 7
3	Num.10	Ps. 46–7	Song 8	Heb. 8	4	Num.11	Ps. 48	Isa. 1	Heb. 9
5	Num.12,13	Ps. 49	Isa. 2	Heb. 10	6	Num.14	Ps. 50	Isa. 3–4	Heb. 11
7	Num.15	Ps. 51	Isa. 5	Heb. 12	8	Num.16	Ps. 52–4	Isa. 6	Heb. 13
9	Num.17–8	Ps. 55	Isa. 7	James 1	10	Num. 19	Ps. 56–7	Isa. 8–9:7	James 2
11	Num. 20	Ps. 58–9	Isa.9:8–10:4	James 3	12	Num. 21	Ps. 60–1	Isa.10:5–34	James 4

	Family		Secret			Family		Secret	
13	Num. 22	Ps. 62–3	Isa. 11–2	James 5	14	Num. 23	Ps. 64–5	Isa. 13	1 Pet. 1
15	Num. 24	Ps. 66–7	Isa. 14	1 Pet. 2	16	Num. 25	Ps. 68	Isa. 15	1 Pet. 3
17	Num. 26	Ps. 69	Isa. 16	1 Pet. 4	18	Num. 27	Ps. 70–1	Isa. 17–8	1 Pet. 5
19	Num. 28	Ps. 72	Isa. 19–20	2 Pet. 1	20	Num. 29	Ps. 73	Isa. 21	2 Pet. 2
21	Num. 30	Ps. 74	Isa. 22	2 Pet. 3	22	Num. 31	Ps. 75,76	Isa. 23	1 John 1
23	Num. 32	Ps. 77	Isa. 24	1 John 2	24	Num. 33	Ps.78:1–37	Isa. 25	1 John 3
25	Num. 34	Ps.78:38–72	Isa. 26	1 John 4	26	Num. 35	Ps. 79	Isa. 27	1 John 5
27	Num. 36	Ps. 80	Isa. 28	2 John 1	28	Deut. 1	Ps. 81–2	Isa. 29	3 John 1
29	Deut. 2	Ps. 83–4	Isa. 30	Jude 1	30	Deut. 3	Ps. 85	Isa. 31	Rev. 1
31	Deut. 4	Ps. 86–7	Isa. 32	Rev. 2					

JUNE BIBLE READING

Date	Family		Secret		Date	Family		Secret	
1	Deut. 5	Ps.88	Isa. 33	Rev. 3	2	Deut. 6	Ps.89	Isa. 34	Rev. 4
3	Deut. 7	Ps.90	Isa. 35	Rev. 5	4	Deut. 8	Ps.91	Isa. 36	Rev. 6
5	Deut. 9	Ps.92–3	Isa. 37	Rev. 7	6	Deut. 10	Ps.94	Isa. 38	Rev. 8
7	Deut. 11	Ps.95–6	Isa. 39	Rev. 9	8	Deut. 12	Ps.97–8	Isa. 40	Rev. 10
9	Deut. 13,14	Ps.99–101	Isa. 41	Rev. 11	10	Deut. 15	Ps.102	Isa. 42	Rev. 12
11	Deut. 16	Ps.103	Isa. 43	Rev. 13	12	Deut. 17	Ps.104	Isa. 44	Rev. 14
13	Deut. 18	Ps.105	Isa. 45	Rev. 15	14	Deut. 19	Ps.106	Isa. 46	Rev. 16
15	Deut. 20	Ps.107	Isa. 47	Rev. 17	16	Deut. 21	Ps.108–9	Isa. 48	Rev. 18
17	Deut. 22	Ps.110–1	Isa. 49	Rev. 19	18	Deut. 23	Ps.112–3	Isa. 50	Rev. 20
19	Deut. 24	Ps.114–5	Isa. 51	Rev. 21	20	Deut. 25	Ps.116	Isa. 52	Rev. 22
21	Deut. 26	Ps.117–8	Isa. 53	Matt. 1	22	Deut.27–28:19	Ps.119:1–24	Isa. 54	Matt. 2
23	Deut.28:20–68	Ps.119:25–48	Isa. 55	Matt. 3	24	Deut. 29	Ps.119:49–72	Isa. 56	Matt. 4
25	Deut. 30	Ps.119:73–96	Isa. 57	Matt. 5	26	Deut. 31	Ps.119:97–120	Isa. 58	Matt. 6
27	Deut. 32	Ps.119:121–144	Isa. 59	Matt. 7	28	Deut. 33,34	Ps.119:145–76	Isa. 60	Matt. 8
29	Josh. 1	Ps.120–122	Isa. 61	Matt. 9	30	Josh. 2	Ps.123–5	Isa. 62	Matt.10

JULY BIBLE READING

Date	Family		Secret		Date	Family		Secret	
1	Josh. 3	Ps.126–8	Isa. 63	Matt. 11	2	Josh. 4	Ps.129–131	Isa. 64	Matt. 12
3	Josh. 5–6:5	Ps.132–4	Isa. 65	Matt. 13	4	Josh. 6:6–27	Ps.135–6	Isa. 66	Matt. 14
5	Josh. 7	Ps.137–8	Jer. 1	Matt. 15	6	Josh. 8	Ps.139	Jer. 2	Matt. 16
7	Josh. 9	Ps.140–1	Jer. 3	Matt. 17	8	Josh. 10	Ps.142–3	Jer. 4	Matt. 18
9	Josh. 11	Ps.144	Jer. 5	Matt. 19	10	Josh. 12–3	Ps.145	Jer. 6	Matt. 20
11	Josh. 14–5	Ps.146–7	Jer. 7	Matt. 21	12	Josh. 16–7	Ps.148	Jer. 8	Matt. 22
13	Josh. 18–9	Ps.149–50	Jer. 9	Matt. 23	14	Josh. 20–1	Acts 1	Jer. 10	Matt. 24
15	Josh. 22	Acts 2	Jer. 11	Matt. 25	16	Josh. 23	Acts 3	Jer. 12	Matt. 26
17	Josh. 24	Acts 4	Jer. 13	Matt. 27	18	Judg. 1	Acts 5	Jer. 14	Matt. 28
19	Judg. 2	Acts 6	Jer. 15	Mark 1	20	Judg. 3	Acts 7	Jer. 16	Mark 2

21	Judg. 4	Acts 8	Jer. 17	Mark 3	22	Judg. 5	Acts 9	Jer. 18	Mark 4
23	Judg. 6	Acts 10	Jer. 19	Mark 5	24	Judg. 7	Acts 11	Jer. 20	Mark 6
25	Judg. 8	Acts 12	Jer. 21	Mark 7	26	Judg. 9	Acts 13	Jer. 22	Mark 8
27	Judg.10–1:11	Acts 14	Jer. 23	Mark 9	28	Judg.11:12–40	Acts 15	Jer. 24	Mark 10
29	Judg.12	Acts 16	Jer. 25	Mark 11	30	Judg.13	Acts 17	Jer. 26	Mark 12
31	Judg.14	Acts 18	Jer. 27	Mark 13					

AUGUST BIBLE READING

Date	Family		Secret		Date	Family		Secret	
1	Judg. 15	Acts 19	Jer. 28	Mark 14	2	Judg. 16	Acts 20	Jer. 29	Mark 15
3	Judg. 17	Acts 21	Jer. 30–1	Mark 16	4	Judg. 18	Acts 22	Jer. 32	Ps. 1–2
5	Judg. 19	Acts 23	Jer. 33	Ps. 3–4	6	Judg. 20	Acts 24	Jer. 34	Ps. 5–6
7	Judg. 21	Acts 25	Jer. 35	Ps. 7–8	8	Ruth 1	Acts 26	Jer. 36,45	Ps. 9
9	Ruth 2	Acts 27	Jer. 37	Ps. 10	10	Ruth 3,4	Acts 28	Jer. 38	Ps. 11–2
11	1 Sam. 1	Rom. 1	Jer. 39	Ps. 13–4	12	1 Sam. 2	Rom. 2	Jer. 40	Ps. 15–6
13	1 Sam. 3	Rom. 3	Jer. 41	Ps. 17	14	1 Sam. 4	Rom. 4	Jer. 42	Ps. 18
15	1 Sam. 5,6	Rom. 5	Jer. 43	Ps. 19	16	1 Sam. 7–8	Rom. 6	Jer. 44	Ps. 20–1
17	1 Sam. 9	Rom. 7	Jer. 46	Ps. 22	18	1 Sam. 10	Rom. 8	Jer. 47	Ps. 23–4
19	1 Sam. 11	Rom. 9	Jer. 48	Ps. 25	20	1 Sam. 12	Rom. 10	Jer. 49	Ps. 26–7
21	1 Sam. 13	Rom. 11	Jer. 50	Ps. 28–9	22	1 Sam. 14	Rom. 12	Jer. 51	Ps. 30
23	1 Sam. 15	Rom. 13	Jer. 52	Ps. 31	24	1 Sam. 16	Rom. 14	Lam. 1	Ps. 32
25	1 Sam. 17	Rom. 15	Lam. 2	Ps. 33	26	1 Sam. 18	Rom. 16	Lam. 3	Ps. 34
27	1 Sam. 19	1 Cor. 1	Lam. 4	Ps. 35	28	1 Sam. 20	1 Cor. 2	Lam. 5	Ps. 36
29	1 Sam. 21–2	1 Cor. 3	Ezek. 1	Ps. 37	30	1 Sam. 23	1 Cor. 4	Ezek. 2	Ps. 38
31	1 Sam. 24	1 Cor. 5	Ezek. 3	Ps. 39					

SEPTEMBER BIBLE READING

Date	Family		Secret		Date	Family		Secret	
1	1 Sam. 25	1 Cor. 6	Ezek. 4	Ps.40–41	2	1 Sam. 26	1 Cor. 7	Ezek. 5	Ps.42–43
3	1 Sam. 27	1 Cor. 8	Ezek. 6	Ps.44	4	1 Sam. 28	1 Cor. 9	Ezek. 7	Ps.45
5	1 Sam.29–30	1 Cor.10	Ezek. 8	Ps.46–47	6	1 Sam. 31	1 Cor.11	Ezek. 9	Ps.48
7	2 Sam. 1	1 Cor.12	Ezek.10	Ps.49	8	2 Sam. 2	1 Cor.13	Ezek.11	Ps.50
9	2 Sam. 3	1 Cor.14	Ezek.12	Ps.51	10	2 Sam. 4–5	1 Cor.15	Ezek.13	Ps.52–54
11	2 Sam. 6	1 Cor.16	Ezek.14	Ps.55	12	2 Sam. 7	2 Cor. 1	Ezek.15	Ps.56–57
13	2 Sam.8–9	2 Cor. 2	Ezek.16	Ps.58–59	14	2 Sam. 10	2 Cor. 3	Ezek.17	Ps.60–61
15	2 Sam. 11	2 Cor. 4	Ezek.18	Ps.62–63	16	2 Sam. 12	2 Cor. 5	Ezek.19	Ps.64–65
17	2 Sam. 13	2 Cor. 6	Ezek.20	Ps.66–67	18	2 Sam. 14	2 Cor. 7	Ezek.21	Ps.68
19	2 Sam. 15	2 Cor. 8	Ezek.22	Ps.69	20	2 Sam. 16	2 Cor. 9	Ezek.23	Ps.70–71
21	2 Sam. 17	2 Cor.10	Ezek.24	Ps.72	22	2 Sam. 18	2 Cor.11	Ezek.25	Ps.73
23	2 Sam. 19	2 Cor.12	Ezek.26	Ps.74	24	2 Sam. 20	2 Cor.13	Ezek.27	Ps.75–76
25	2 Sam. 21	Gal. 1	Ezek.28	Ps.77	26	2 Sam. 22	Gal. 2	Ezek.29	Ps.78:1–37

27	2 Sam. 23	Gal. 3	Ezek.30	Ps.78:38–72	28	2 Sam. 24	Gal. 4	Ezek.31	Ps.79
29	1 Ki. 1	Gal. 5	Ezek.32	Ps.80	30	1 Ki. 2	Gal. 6	Ezek.33	Ps.81–82

OCTOBER BIBLE READING

Date	Family		Secret		Date	Family		Secret	
1	1 Ki. 3	Eph. 1	Ezek.34	Ps.83–84	2	1 Ki. 4,5	Eph. 2	Ezek.35	Ps.85
3	1 Ki. 6	Eph. 3	Ezek.36	Ps.86	4	1 Ki. 7	Eph. 4	Ezek.37	Ps.87–8
5	1 Ki. 8	Eph. 5	Ezek.38	Ps.89	6	1 Ki. 9	Eph. 6	Ezek.39	Ps.90
7	1 Ki. 10	Phil. 1	Ezek.40	Ps.91	8	1 Ki. 11	Phil. 2	Ezek.41	Ps.92–3
9	1 Ki. 12	Phil. 3	Ezek.42	Ps.94	10	1 Ki. 13	Phil. 4	Ezek.43	Ps.95–6
11	1 Ki. 14	Col. 1	Ezek.44	Ps.97–98	12	1 Ki. 15	Col. 2	Ezek.45	Ps.99–101
13	1 Ki. 16	Col. 3	Ezek.46	Ps.102	14	1 Ki. 17	Col. 4	Ezek.47	Ps.103
15	1 Ki. 18	1 Thess.1	Ezek.48	Ps.104	16	1 Ki. 19	1 Thess.2	Dan. 1	Ps.105
17	1 Ki. 20	1 Thess.3	Dan. 2	Ps.106	18	1 Ki. 21	1 Thess.4	Dan. 3	Ps.107
19	1 Ki. 22	1 Thess.5	Dan. 4	Ps.108–9	20	2 Ki. 1	2 Thess.1	Dan. 5	Ps.110–1
21	2 Ki. 2	2 Thess.2	Dan. 6	Ps.112–3	22	2 Ki 3	2 Thess.3	Dan. 7	Ps.114–5
23	2 Ki 4	1 Tim. 1	Dan. 8	Ps.116	24	2 Ki 5	1 Tim. 2	Dan. 9	Ps.117–8
25	2 Ki 6	1 Tim. 3	Dan. 10	Ps.119:1–24	26	2 Ki 7	1 Tim. 4	Dan. 11	Ps.119:25–48
27	2 Ki 8	1 Tim. 5	Dan. 12	Ps.119:49–72	28	2 Ki 9	1 Tim. 6	Hos. 1	Ps.119:73–96
29	2 Ki. 10–1	2 Tim. 1	Hos. 2	Ps.119:97–120	30	2 Ki. 12	2 Tim. 2	Hos. 3–4	Ps.119:121–44
31	2 Ki. 13	2 Tim. 3	Hos. 5–6	Ps.119:145–176					

NOVEMBER BIBLE READING

Date	Family		Secret		Date	Family		Secret	
1	2 Ki. 14	2 Tim. 4	Hos. 7	Ps.120–2	2	2 Ki. 15	Titus 1	Hos. 8	Ps.123–5
3	2 Ki. 16	Titus 2	Hos. 9	Ps.126–8	4	2 Ki. 17	Titus 3	Hos. 10	Ps.129–31
5	2 Ki. 18	Philem.	Hos. 11	Ps.132–4	6	2 Ki. 19	Heb. 1	Hos. 12	Ps.135–36
7	2 Ki. 20	Heb. 2	Hos. 13	Ps.137–8	8	2 Ki. 21	Heb. 3	Hos. 14	Ps.139
9	2 Ki. 22	Heb. 4	Joel 1	Ps.140–1	10	2 Ki. 23	Heb. 5	Joel 2	Ps.142
11	2 Ki. 24	Heb. 6	Joel 3	Ps.143	12	2 Ki. 25	Heb. 7	Amos 1	Ps.144
13	1 Chr.1,2	Heb. 8	Amos 2	Ps.145	14	1 Chr.3,4	Heb. 9	Amos 3	Ps.146–7
15	1 Chr.5,6	Heb. 10	Amos 4	Ps.148–150	16	1 Chr.7,8	Heb. 11	Amos 5	Lk. 1:1–38
17	1 Chr.9,10	Heb. 12	Amos 6	Lk. 1:39–80	18	1 Chr.11–12	Heb. 13	Amos 7	Lk. 2
19	1 Chr.13–14	James 1	Amos 8	Lk. 3	20	1 Chr.15	James 2	Amos 9	Lk. 4
21	1 Chr.16	James 3	Obad. 1	Lk. 5	22	1 Chr.17	James 4	Jonah 1	Lk. 6
23	1 Chr.18	James 5	Jonah 2	Lk 7	24	1 Chr.19–20	1 Pet. 1	Jonah 3	Lk. 8
25	1 Chr.21	1 Pet. 2	Jonah 4	Lk 9	26	1 Chr.22	1 Pet. 3	Micah 1	Lk. 10
27	1 Chr.23	1 Pet. 4	Micah 2	Lk. 11	28	1 Chr.24–25	1 Pet. 5	Micah 3	Lk. 12
29	1 Chr.26–27	2 Pet. 1	Micah 4	Lk. 13	30	1 Chr.28	2 Pet. 2	Micah 5	Lk. 14

THE BIBLE PANORAMA

DECEMBER BIBLE READING

Date	Family		Secret		Date	Family		Secret	
1	1 Chron.29	2 Pet. 3	Micah 6	Luke 15	2	2 Chr.1	1 John 1	Micah 7	Luke 16
3	2 Chr.2	1 John 2	Nahum 1	Luke 17	4	2 Chr.3–4	1 John 3	Nahum 2	Luke 18
5	2 Chr.5–6:11	1 John 4	Nahum 3	Luke 19	6	2 Chr.6:12–42	1 John 5	Hab. 1	Luke 20
7	2 Chr.7	2 John 1	Hab. 2	Luke 21	8	2 Chr.8	3 John 1	Hab. 3	Luke 22
9	2 Chr.9	Jude 1	Zeph. 1	Luke 23	10	2 Chr.10	Rev. 1	Zeph. 2	Luke 24
11	2 Chr.11–12	Rev. 2	Zeph. 3	John 1	12	2 Chr.13	Rev. 3	Haggai 1	John 2
13	2 Chr.14–15	Rev. 4	Haggai 2	John 3	14	2 Chr.16	Rev. 5	Zech. 1	John 4
15	2 Chr.17	Rev. 6	Zech. 2	John 5	16	2 Chr.18	Rev. 7	Zech. 3	John 6
17	2 Chr.19–20	Rev. 8	Zech. 4	John 7	18	2 Chr.21	Rev. 9	Zech. 5	John 8
19	2 Chr.22–23	Rev. 10	Zech. 6	John 9	20	2 Chr.24	Rev. 11	Zech. 7	John 10
21	2 Chr.25	Rev. 12	Zech. 8	John 11	22	2 Chr.26	Rev. 13	Zech. 9	John 12
23	2 Chr.27–28	Rev. 14	Zech. 10	John 13	24	2 Chr.29	Rev. 15	Zech. 11	John 14
25	2 Chr.30	Rev. 16	Zech.12–13:1	John 15	26	2 Chron.31	Rev. 17	Zech.13:2–9	John 16
27	2 Chr.32	Rev. 18	Zech.14	John 17	28	2 Chr.33	Rev. 19	Malachi 1	John 18
29	2 Chr.34	Rev. 20	Malachi 2	John 19	30	2 Chr.35	Rev. 21	Malachi 3	John 20
31	2 Chr.36	Rev. 22	Malachi 4	John 21					